Russia and Denmark 1856-1864
A Chapter of Russian Policy towards the Scandinavian Countries

Københavns Universitet
Institut for Slavisk
og Øststatsforskning

Studier 14

University of Copenhagen
Institute of Slavonic and
East European Studies

Emanuel Halicz

Russia and Denmark 1856-1864

A Chapter of Russian Policy towards the Scandinavian Countries

Translated from the Polish by Roger A. Clarke

C. A. Reitzel's Forlag · Copenhagen

This book has been published with the support of the Danish Research Council for the Humanities, the Faculty of Arts of the University of Copenhagen and the Giese Foundation.
© 1990 by the authors.
Typesetting: ih-fotosats ApS. Printed in Denmark by B. Stougaard Jensen
This book is copyright under the Berne Convention. All rights are reserved. Apart from any fair dealing for the purpose of private study, research, criticism or review, as permitted under the Copyright Act 1956, no part of this publication may be reproduced, stored in a retrieval system, or transmitted, in any form or by any means, electronic, electrical, chemical, mechanical, optical, photocopying, recording or otherwise, without the prior permission of the copyright owner. Enquiries should be adressed to the publishers.
ISBN 87-7421-661-9
ISSN 0107-3273

'L'histoire a ses fatalités, celle des faits accomplis. Malheur au prince qui ne veut pas s'y soumettre'.
A. Custine, *La Russie en 1839,* vol. II. Bruxelles, 1843, p. 295

'Was die Erfahrung aber und die Geschichte lehren, ist dieses das Völker und Regierungen niemals etwas aus der Geschichte gelernt'.
G.W. Hegel, *Grundlinien der Philosophie des Rechts oder Naturrecht und Staatswissenshaft im Grundrisse.*

For ANNA

Contents

Acknowledgments
Preface

Part 1:
Introduction, Sources, State of Research 13
  1. Russian Foreign Policy after the Crimean War, Change of Strategy
     or merely Change of Tactics? 52
  2. Denmark's Place in Russian Policy after the Paris Peace Treaty.
     Russia and the Problem of Scandinavianism 84
  3. Russia, the Danish Sound Dues and Command of the Baltic 145
  4. Russia and the Growing Conflict between Denmark and Germany
     in 1859-1862 157
  5. The January Insurrection in the Kingdom of Poland. The Scandinavian
     Countries and Russia 219

Part 2:
  6. The Federal Execution and the Ewers Mission 295
  7. Gorchakov and the Outbreak of the Danish-German War 326
  8. From the London Conference to the Treaty of Vienna,
     April-October 1864 380
  9. The Semi-Official *Le Nord – Journal International* and the Danish-
     Russian Conflict 473
 10. Russian Public Opinion and the Danish-German Conflict 502

Conclusion 545

Appendices:
A. The London Treaty of 8 May 1852 575
B. The Vienna Treaty of 30 October 1864 578
C. Table of the Staff of the Russian Ministry of Foreign Affairs 587
D. Table of the Staff of the Danish Ministry of Foreign Affairs 589
E. Table of Ministries of the Great Powers and of Sweden-Norway 590
F. Foreign Representatives in Copenhagen 591
G. The Danish Representatives 592
Bibliography. Archives 593
Newspapers and periodicals (1856-1864) 598
Printed Sources 599

List of Abbrevations

A.M.I.D.	Arkhiv Ministerstva Innostrannykh Del, Moscow
A.V.P.R.	Arkhiv Vnyeshnyei Politiki Rossii, C.A. Moscow
A.P.P.	Die auswärtige Politik Preussens
G.W.	Die gesammelten Werke
H.H.S.A.	Haus-, Hof- u. Staatsarchiv, Vienna
P.A.	Polititisches Archiv
H.H.A.	Haupstaatsarchiv Stuttgart
A.M.A.E.	Archives du Ministère des Affaires Étrangères, Paris
P.R.O.	Public Record Office, London
F.O.	Foreign Office
R.A.	Rigsarkivet (Public Record Office), Copenhagen
R.A.St.	Riksarkivet, Stockholm
A.S.-D.	Archivio Storico-Diplomatico del Ministero degli Affari Esteri, Rome
Z.d.G.f.S.H.G.	Zeitschrift der Gesellschaft für Schleswig-Holsteinische Geschichte

Acknowledgments

My work has been made possible by kindness of many, and I should like briefly to express, however inadequality, my gratitude at least to whose who helped me most.

In the preparation of this work, I have received advice and assistance from many people. To Professors P. Bagge, T. Kaarsted and B. Nørretranders I am indebted for their suggestion to undertake this study.

In writing this book I benefited greatly from my association with the Institute of Slavonic and East European Studies of Copenhagen University, which provided me with a setting in which there were opportunities to engage in a serious dialogue on many problems close to the subject of my interest.

My warmest thanks are due to the Directors of the Institute, Kristine Heltberg and Per Jacobsen for their lively interest in my work. More specifically, I also wish to acknowledge the help of several individuals who made substantial contributions to this work. I have received valuable assistance from Dr. John Barnie whose work in correcting has removed many errors of copying and of style. Dr. Barnie was relentless in offering substantive criticism and refinements. My special thanks are due to Roger A. Clarke, Editor of *Soviet Studies,* for translating this work from the Polish and proof-reading.

I have used archives and libraries in many countries but owe special thanks to two of them because I tried the patience of their staff more than all the others. My debt of gratitude to the staff of the Public Record Office (Rigsarkivet) Copenhagen, and of the Royal and University Libraries in Copenhagen is enormous.

I also acknowledge with gratitude the assistance of the staffs of the archives, libraries, and research institutions whose holdings have provided the raw materials for this study – especially the Rigsarkivet (Stockholm), Archives du Ministère des Affaires Étrangères (Paris), Hof-, Haus- u. Staatsarchiv (Wien), the Public Record Office (London), Arkivio Storico-Diplomatico (Roma), Haupstaatsarchiv (Stuttgart), and the Slavonic Library (Helsinki).

My warmest thanks are due to the Ministers of Education Mrs. Dorte Bennedsen and Mr. Bertel Haarder, and the Danish Research Council for the Humanities for the scholarships I have been given. I should also thank the Danish Research Council for the Humanities, the Faculty of Arts of the University of Copenhagen and the Giese Foundation for their grants to cover the cost of translation and printing.

Some of my research and visits to other countries were made possible by a grant awarded by the Provinsbanken in Odense, to which I should like to express my thanks.

Finally, the book would not have appeared without the help of my most devoted encourager, my wife, Anna. At all the stages my wife has encouraged my efforts and shared my troubles, for which I am eternally grateful.

June 1990 *Emanuel Halicz*

Preface

This is an analytical work dealing with diplomacy and politics. I have also attempted to answer the question of what role public opinion in Russia played in the unfolding of events in the years 1856-64.

The subject is of fundamental importance for the history of Europe in what was a period of transition. The birth of Bismarck's Germany, Russia's loss of hegemony in the Baltic, Denmark's escape from the high politics in which she had been entrammelled since 1848 on account of the Elbe duchies, the political collapse of Scandinavianism and Sweden's adoption of a policy of neutrality, are just the major events which occurred in northern Europe in the period, from 1856 to 1864, and particularly as a result of the military defeat of Denmark in the war with Germany in 1864.

In an otherwise rich historical literature there is a striking lack of monograph studies on Russian policy towards the Scandinavian countries in these years so pregnant with consequences. Both Western and Soviet historians have noted this. The difficulty of access to Soviet archives, both in the nineteenth century and at present, was certainly no encouragement to historians to tackle the subject. But in my view there was also a more fundamental reason, namely that historians underestimated the importance of Scandinavia in Russian policy and strategy in those years.

The special role of Scandinavia in Russian policy was recently pointed out by Z. Brzezinski,[1] who stressed the importance for Russia, a largely land-locked country, of strategic choke points, such as the Kattegat and Skagerrak, 'narrows linking the Baltic Sea to the North Sea'.

Basing myself mainly on the archival sources to be found in the Danish, Swedish, German, Austrian, French, Italian and British archives, and on the microfilms obtained by the Copenhagen and Stockholm archives before the Second World War and recently from the Archives of Russian Foreign Policy (AVPR) in Moscow,[2] as well as the literature and the press, I have tried to portray both Rus-

---

1. Z. Brzezinski, *Game Plan: How to Conduct the U.S.-Soviet Contest,* (Boston and New York, 1986) p. 31.
2. In presenting Russian documents a special problem arises from the persistence of use of the Julian calender (Old Style) in Russia until 1918. The dates of the Russian (or Julian) calender in the nineteenth century were twelve days behind those of the European (or Gregorian) calender. But in many diplomatic documents from St. Petersburg the Old Style (O.S.) date as it appeared on the documents has been followed with the New Style (N.S.) equivalent.

    Many of the people mentioned in this book have been called by several different versions of their names. But only the Russian names are transliterated according to the Library of Congress system

sia's position and the attitude of Russian public opinion to the central problems of Scandinavia, and particularly Denmark, during the period from the Treaty of Paris in 1856 to the Treaty of Vienna in 1864.

(except for those dealing with linguistics which should adhere to the standard international system of transliteration).
 Place names are rendered according to the official language of the country in which they are located. Exceptions are made in the cases of cities, whose English names differ significantly from their native-language forms.

Part 1

Introduction, Sources and the State of Research

I

The present work is a continuation of my monograph *Danish Neutrality during the Crimean War (1853-56). Denmark between the Hammer and the Anvil*, published in 1977, and deals with Russia's policy towards the Scandinavian countries, and in particular Denmark, in the years from the end of the Crimean War to the turning-point in the history of the Scandinavian countries caused by the Danish–German war of 1864. It is the product of my reflections over many years on the history of Europe at the turn of the 1850's and 1860's, the period which in my view forms the threshold of modern Europe.

The revolutionary years of 1848-49 only weakened the system established at the Congress of Vienna in 1815. The Crimean War and the defeat of the "Gendarme of Europe" created the preconditions for the victory of the idea of nationality in Europe and the rise of the national states. The German question occupied a special place in this historical process. The turning-point in the struggle for the unification of Germany came when Bismarck took the matter in hand, and the conflict with Denmark over the Schleswig–Holstein problem made the task easier for him.

The position of Russia was of special importance for the history of Scandinavia, and particularly for the course of the German–Danish conflict, in the period 1856-64. It is the key to understanding the reasons for the political and hence the military defeat of Denmark and the reasons for the emergence of Prussia in the struggle for the unification of Germany under its aegis. Prussia's victory against Denmark was a giant step in the execution of Bismarck's plans.[1]

In this work I trace the attitude of Russia towards Scandinavia, and in particular Denmark, from the Treaty of Paris in 1856 to the Treaty of Vienna of 30 October 1864, which set the seal on the defeat of Denmark in the war with Germany. I try to explain what features connected with the internal situation in Russia after her defeat in the Crimean War decisively influenced her moves in the international arena, how the strategy and tactics adopted by the St. Petersburg cabinet were coordinated, and why there was a reorientation of Russian policy towards the Scandinavian countries, particularly Denmark, in 1863-64. I also analyse the reason why Russia abandoned Denmark in 1864, what part was played by factors such as Russia's age-old anti-Scandinavian and anti-Polish complex, and finally, what

---

1. E. Engelberg, *Bismarck, Urpreusse und Reichsbegründer*, (Berlin, 1985), pp. 756-7; E. Franz, *Der Entscheidungskampf um die wirtschaftspolitische Führung Deutschlands (1856-1867)*, (München, 1933, reprint Aalen, 1973); N. Amstrup, De tyske staters udenrigspolitik 1859-1864 og Slesvig-Holsten, En fodnote til »Helstatens Fald«, *Historie*, 17.2.1988 pp. 202-27.

part was played by fear of being cut off from the civilised world should a united Scandinavia close the Baltic sea to Russian passage.

I have also sought to demonstrate the methods used by Russia to attain her foreign policy goals, with particular attention to the wide range of propaganda employed by Russia. The years 1856-64 provide a great deal of instructive material in this field. It also seemed to me desirable to present not only the official policy of the St. Petersburg cabinet but also Russian public opinion on the central problems.

The work consists essentially of two parts. The first covers the period 1856-63 and discusses the attitude of Russia to such central problems as Scandinavianism, the Danish-German conflict over Schleswig-Holstein, the problem of the Sound, and the influence of the January Uprising in the Kingdom of Poland on Russia's attitude to the Scandinavian states. The second part covers the chronologically shorter period from the end of 1863 to the end of October 1864 and deals mainly with the attitude of the Russian government and society towards Denmark and the latter's conflict with the German states, as well as discussing Russian policy during the Danish-German war up to the conclusion of the Treaty of Vienna.

In order to understand the essence of Russian-Danish relations after the Crimean War we must analyse both the domestic and foreign policies of Russia following her defeat, and consider how far such factors as the quest for economic and social change, together with social unrest in the 'spring' following Sebastopol[2] influenced Russian moves in the international arena and changed Russian policy towards Scandinavia, especially Denmark. This work is thus a fragment of the larger problem of 'Russia and the Baltic', which has not yet been fully treated by historians.[3]

There is no question that there were changes in Russian policy after the Treaty of Paris and that these were fundamental compared with the period before the Crimean War. But did the change in political orientation resulting from the collapse of the Holy Alliance and the defeat in the Crimea lead to a change in strategy, or only a change in tactics; and what part was played by Alexander II and what part by his minister, Gorchakov, in drawing up this new policy? This is the topic discussed in the first chapter of the present work.

The answer to these questions may be facilitated by examination of Russia's Scandinavian policy during the years 1856-64. Why did Russia intensify her criticism of every manifestation of Scandinavianism, why did her distrust of Sweden increase, why did she incline more and more to the side of the German states in their conflict with Denmark, even though from a global political point of view she had an interest in maintaining the integrity of Denmark? The place of Denmark and Sweden in Russian policy, Russia's attitude to Scandinavianism and to the problem of the Sound form the subject of discussion in the second and third chapters.

2. Post-Sebastopol thaw. (Po Sevastopolskaya vesna).
3. R.M. Hatton, 'Russia and the Baltic', in T. Hunczak ed. *Russian Imperialism from Ivan the Great to the Revolution,* (New Brunswick, New Jersey, 1974), p. 334.

The fourth chapter examines the attitude of Russia to Denmark in the years 1859-62, with particular reference to the Schleswig–Holstein question and the growing conflict between Denmark and Germany. I examine the reasons why Russia, the 'prison of nations', spoke up for the rights of the Germans in Holstein and Schleswig as well as the role of the question of the Elbe duchies in Russo–French and Russo–British relations.

The year 1863 marked the turning-point in Russo–Danish relations, or more precisely, in Russian policy towards Prussia and Denmark. This cannot be satisfactorily explained without reference to the role of the Polish uprising of 1863 in both Russian policy and that of all other European powers. The collapse of the Franco–Russian entente dating from 1856, the collapse of the system established during the Crimean War based on Franco–British cooperation, Russo–Prussian co-operation against the Polish uprising, and finally the rapprochement between Prussia and Austria were factors which exerted a far-reaching influence on the policy of the powers, and particularly Russia, towards Denmark. The effect of the January Uprising on the constellation of political forces within Denmark, as well as on Russo–Danish relations and Russia's Scandinavian policy, is the theme of the chapter 'The January Insurrection in the Kingdom of Poland, the Scandinavian Countries and Russia'. From an historical perspective it is clear how the fates of Denmark and Poland were connected, how immensely important the collapse of the Polish uprising was for Denmark, and what an adverse effect the new political line-up in Europe following the Polish events had on Russian policy towards Denmark at a crucial moment in her history.

Chapters 6-8 are concerned with the attitude of Russia towards the Scandinavian countries, and particularly Denmark, from the second half of 1863 to the end of the military engagement between Denmark and the German states in 1864. I have devoted a separate chapter to the Ewers mission, the only real diplomatic initiative undertaken by Gorchakov during the 1863-64 conflict. Chapter 7 is principally concerned with a consideration of the tactics and strategy of Gorchakov in relation to the situation which arose in Europe as a result of the January Uprising and the repercussions of the new situation on Russian policy. An interesting question here is how the general policy which Gorchakov advocated at this time, namely to preserve peace at any price and not to allow the Danish–German conflict to spread, affected his attitude to, in particular, the conservative German states, and above all to Prussia. What were the crucial factors in the pro-Prussian position of the St. Petersburg cabinet; what was its real attitude to Bismarck's actions, particularly in 1864; and what was the nature of Russia's neutrality?

In connection with the London Conference we need to analyse Russian policy in detail and to consider what essentially was the role of Russia at the conference. We must also consider whether there were any differences of opinion on tactics between Gorchakov and P. Brunnow, the official representative of Russia at the conference, who enjoyed the name of 'Amicus Daniae'. We also need to go into greater detail concerning the attitude of Alexander II to the Danish–German conflict and try to decide whether there were any differences of opinion on this matter between the Tsar and his minister of foreign affairs and, if so, what they were, and whether they exerted a fundamental influence on Russia's decisions and behaviour.

In my view, the whole problem of 'Russia and Denmark' should not be confined exclusively to analysis of the position of the St. Petersburg cabinet. For this reason I have also analysed the contents of the semi-official organ of the Russian ministry of foreign affairs, *Le Nord,* and showed how Gorchakov's propaganda mouthpiece, which aimed to acquaint European opinion with the position and policy of Russia on the central problems of the time, reacted to the Danish-German conflict. This seemed appropriate also because the articles in *Le Nord* enable us to cast more light on many questions which the Russian diplomatic correspondence scarcely mentions or even passes over in complete silence. (Chapter 9).

In addition I have also analysed the opinions of various individuals and of Russian military circles which sometimes took a different position from the official one on certain matters, and I have presented the views expressed in the pages of the various sections of the Russian press, starting with the press under direct influence of the ruling circles and of the conservatives, Slavophiles, liberals and, finally, democrats operating both in Russia and in exile. I have sought as far as possible to present a broad range of Russian views on Denmark, Scandinavianism and the conflict and war between Denmark and Germany in 1863-64. (Chapter 10).

Although the book deals with relations between Russia and Denmark, if we are to understand all aspects of this question we cannot restrict ourselves to a narrow definition of this theme. The field of study must be broadened to include consideration of the problems with which the Danish government was wrestling in the period 1856-64 – Copenhagen's policy on the question of the Elbe duchies and, in this connection, towards Germany; as well as the attitude of the Danish government towards Scandinavianism – matters which had repercussions on Russo-Danish relations.

Nor can we ignore the problem of the peculiar duality of opinion in Danish policy, by which I mean the different conceptions of the central problems and the varying attitudes towards Russia of, on the one hand, the conservative camp, which enjoyed the support of King Christian IX and many of the diplomats representing Denmark in the most important diplomatic posts, and, on the other hand, the government of Hall and Monrad, which was connected with the national-liberal party and received much popular support, especially in the capital. The St. Petersburg cabinet was aware of this duality and backed the conservative camp, trying on every occasion to bring about a change in the make-up of the government in Copenhagen by a variety of methods, and using its ambassadors accredited to the King to intervene cautiously in the contest for power in Copenhagen. Gorchakov also tried to make use of the Danish ambassador in St. Petersburg, O. Plessen, who was well-known for his conservative views and well-regarded by Nesselrode, Gorchakov, Nicholas I and Alexander II. For this reason I have devoted a relatively large amount of space to the activities of Plessen in 1864 since, in a critical period for Denmark, he played a distinctive role as intermediary between the court of the Tsar and the court in Copenhagen. This is illustrated by hitherto unused documents in the Central Archive of Russian Foreign Policy in Moscow, which I have studied. On the basis of a suggestion by Gorchakov, Plessen sought to bring about a fundamental change in Danish policy. I have tried to indicate Russia's methods of operating – both those of the St. Petersburg cabinet and those of her ambassadors in Copenhagen and Stockholm, and the methods employed by Russian diplomacy to try to achieve its aims in relation to the Scandinavian countries, and especially Denmark, as far as possible on the basis of archival sources, especially those in Moscow.

Elucidation of these mechanisms is all the more important in the light of the thesis, which I am inclined to accept, of historical continuity in Russian foreign policy dating back to the period of the Grand Duchy of Moscow, a continuity both of content and of form, though in each period this continuity had to be fitted into the context of the changes which were occurring both in Russia herself and beyond her borders.

In my conclusion I also try to reflect on the attitude of the great powers, and particularly Russia, towards Denmark as a small state, and on how far this was an important factor in St. Petersburg's policy towards Denmark.

The work ends with a list of the archival sources used and a select bibliography of works cited in the book.

To assist the reader in following 'who's who' I have prepared lists of Russian and Danish diplomats, the composition of the Danish cabinets and the ambassadors accredited to Copenhagen in the period 1856-64. Finally I have appended the texts of the Treaty of London of 8 May 1852 and the peace treaty concluded by Austria, Prussia and Denmark on 30 October 1864.

The problem I have tackled is certainly difficult and complicated, particularly as the question of the Danish-German conflict became a central political question for the powers of Europe and involved the most varied interests. The rich literature on the subject, especially in Germany and Denmark, is tendentious, since, as the German historian. J.H. Voigt quite rightly observed a hundred years after the events,[4] it is 'unter dem Einfluss der durch das Ergebnis des Konflikts ausgelösten Gefühle: des Stolzes und des Schmerzes. Beide brachten Verzerrungen – in deutschen Darstellungen wird der erfolgreiche Ausgang fast ausschliesslich der Diplomatie Bismarcks zugeschrieben, während man in dänischen geneigt ist, die Niederlage in ausserdänischen Umständen zu suchen. Beide aus nationaler Eitelkeit und Empfindlichkeit geborenen Geschichtsbilder sind korrekturbedürftig'.[5] In the same spirit G. Ritter said 'der dänische und der deutsche Nationalismus in ihren blinden Leidenschaft sich gegenseitig ins Unrecht setzten'.[6] An equally critical attitude to the way the problem had been presented was taken by the distinguished Danish historian Troels Fink,[7] who recognised that the presentation of the Schleswig-

---

4. J.H. Voigt, 'Englands Aussenpolitik während des deutsch-dänischen Konflikts, 1862-1864', in *Zeitschrift der Gesellschaft für Schleswig-Holsteinische Geschichte,* (Z.d.G.f.S.H.G.) vol. 89, 1964.
5. *Ibid.* pp. 61-2.
6. G. Ritter, *Europa und die deutsche Frage,* (Munich, 1948), p. 90.
7. Troels Fink, *Geschichte des schleswigschen Grenzlandes,* (Copenhagen, 1958). See the preface.

Holstein conflict had been lacking in objectivity on both the German and the Danish sides; in his opinion this applied not only to earlier studies but also to the most recent works, Danish as well as German, which had been published after the Second World War – almost a hundred years after the events.

These comments also apply to studies of the policy of the great powers, including Russia, towards the Danish-German conflict. But where Russian policy is concerned there is an additional obstacle to objective examination of the matter in the form of the difficulty in gaining access to archival sources. This applies both to the tsarist and the Soviet periods. An example of the difficulty is provided by the paradoxical fact that the well-known Russian historian S.S. Tatishchev, an apologist for Nicholas I and Alexander II, when writing about Russian foreign policy in the 1850s and 1860s, did not have access to Russian sources and had to rely on German material and the works of H. Sybel.

On the subject of Russian sources Halvdan Koht said: 'Nur russischerseits sind noch keine dergleichen Quellenschriften erschienen, was sich in jeder Darstellung dieser Begebenheiten merkbar empfinden lässt ... Nur die russische Politik liegt noch heute vielfach im Dunkeln'.[8] Although many years have passed since these words were written, there has been little improvement in the matter of access to Russian archival sources. For the same reason L.D. Steefel's classic work, *The Schleswig-Holstein Question,* published in 1932, devotes scant space to Russian policy, and Keith A.P. Sandford, without going into the reasons for this, criticised Steefel, saying 'his treatment of Russian diplomacy was somewhat cavalier'.[9]

In the period between the first and second World Wars the only Russian sources to appear in the field were some letters from Bismarck to Gorchakov[10] and a selection of diplomatic documents from the years 1863-64.[11] The situation did not improve after the second World War. Only the difficulty of access to sources can explain the fact that in her book on the Schleswig-Holstein question and the policy of the European powers in 1863-64, published in Tallin in 1957, L. Roots did not use any new archival material and relied exclusively on sources already published. Nor is our knowledge of the period really enriched by L.I. Narochnitskaya's *Rossiya i voiny Prussii v 60-ykh godakh XIX v. za ob"edinenie Germanii 'sverkh',* published in Moscow in 1960, which made minimal use of Gorchakov's correspondence for the years 1863-66, to be found in the Arkhiv Akt Davnykh in Moscow, and of fragments from the papers of D.A. Milyutin, the Minister for War, in the manuscripts section of the Lenin Library in Moscow. The same applies to N.S. Kinyapina's work *Vneshnyaya politika Rossii vtoroi poloviny XIX veka,* published

---

8. Halvdan Koht, *Die Stellung Norwegens und Schwedens im Deutsch-Dänischen Konflikt, zumal während der Jahre 1863 und 1864,* (Christiania, 1908). Preface, pp. viii, ix.
9. Keith A.P. Sandiford, *Great Britain and the Schleswig-Holstein Question, 1848-64,* (Toronto and Buffalo, 1975), p. 4.
10. A.S. Eruzalimsky ed. 'Pisma O. Bismarka A.M. Gorchakovu', *Krasnyi Arkhiv,* 1933, vol. 61, documents 1-8, pp. 1-15.
11. S. Lesnik ed. 'Rossiya i Prussiya v Schlesvig-Golshtinskom Voprose', *Krasnyi Arkhiv,* 1939, vol. 2 (93).

in Moscow in 1974; the contents and references show that the author did indeed have the good fortune to work in the Archives of the Ministry of Foreign Affairs, but out of the entire Archives of the Foreign Policy of Russia she used only fragments from Gorchakov's annual reports.

For this reason one of the most important tasks I faced early on in my work was to reconstruct the Russian archival base, using the collections of diplomatic and personal documents to be found in European archives.[12] I studied all the available documents in the Rigsarkivet in Copenhagen and also Danica-Films, which has among other things microfilms taken by Danish historians in the 1930s in the Archives of the Ministry of Foreign Affairs in Moscow, as well as the full set of reports from the Russian ambassadors in Copenhagen between 1848 and 1864, Ungern-Sternberg and Nicolay, of which there are copies in the Rigsarkivet in Copenhagen. Thanks to the efforts of the Chief Directorate of Archives in Copenhagen, and my own efforts, we also succeeded in obtaining from Moscow microfilms of diplomatic documents on Russo-Danish relations in the years 1863-64 and of the correspondence between Gorchakov and Brunnow during the London Conference. In the Riksarkivet in Stockholm I studied microfilms and photocopies of documents made during the 1930s in Moscow and, in particular, the correspondence between Gorchakov and the Russian ambassador in Stockholm, Dashkov, for the years 1856-64, as well as official Swedish diplomatic documents from those years. In the Hauptstaatsarchiv in Stuttgart I read the letters of Gorchakov to Olga Nikolaevna, the daughter of Nicholas I and later Queen of Würtemburg, some of which are valuable sources of information on the views of the Russian Minister on the Danish-German conflict, especially in 1863-64. I have also made a detailed search of the documents concerning Russian policy towards the Scandinavian countries in the diplomatic and personal papers in the Haus-, Hof- und Staatsarchiv in Vienna, the Archives du Ministère des Affaires Etrangères in Paris, the Public Record Office in London, the Archivio-Storico-Diplomatico in Rome, and in the central, university and institute libraries in Copenhagen, Stockholm, Lund, Helsinki, Frankfurt, Marburg, Mainz, Paris, Vienna and London.

I should also mention the use of published collections of documents from many West European and Scandinavian countries concerning the history of the years 1856-64,[13] and also the use of the Russian press, mainly on the basis of the collections in the Royal and university libraries in Copenhagen, the Slavonic library of the University in Helsinki, the British Museum and the Bibliothèque Nationale in Paris. Although my ambition was to base myself primarily on archival sources I

---

12. I totally agree with V.H. Galbraith's point of view concerning the value of the Archival documents and expressed in his book *"An Introduction to the Study of History"*. "What really matters in the long run is not so much what we write about history now, or what others have written, as the original sources themselves ... The power of unlimited inspiration to successive generations lies in the original sources". (C. Watts, 1964, p. 80).
13. Cf. the list of these documents on pp. 599 ff of the present work. In the case of *Les origines diplomatiques de la guerre de 1870-1871* I would like to point out that in this publication a number of valuable documents held in the A.M.A.E. in Paris are omitted and others are printed only in an abbreviated form.

could not ignore the existing literature on the subject, especially as some works contain valuable theses and in some cases working hypotheses which, although not based on careful research, turned out to be partially confirmed by thorough study of the sources.

II

We shall begin our review with the French historiography since it was the first to discuss the essence of the Danish-German conflict and the aims underlying Prussia's actions and to assess critically the policies of the great powers, particularly Russia, towards the Scandinavian states. French historians began this even while the conflict was going on, and the tone was set by two leading writers in *Revue des Deux Mondes,* A. Geffroy and E. Forcade, who were soon joined by the prominent pamphleteer J. Klaczko. *Chronique de la Quinzaine* presented their view of the problem of the Danish-German crisis, Scandinavianism, and the attitudes of the great powers, particularly Russia.

La question brûlante du moment, la crise dano-allemande ... A prendre cette question par le point de vue des grandes puissances, il s'agit là de l'équilibre du Nord. En quelques mains reseteront ou vont se trouver les passages de la Mer du Nord et de la Baltique? Celle des grandes puissances que cette question intéresse le plus directement est celle justement qui fait le moins de bruit à cette heure, c'est la Russie. Si l'Allemagne s'empare de la rade de Kiel, et si par une réaction contraire les peuples scandinaves se fusionnent, la débouché maritime de la Russie au nord va se trouver à la merci de puissances capables d'en ouvrir ou d'en fermer à volonté issue. L'intérêt russe veut manifestement que les choses restent comme elles ont été jusqu'à présent, et que l'intégrité de la monarchie danoise soit respectée ...[14] Le gouvernement prussien a contracté envers le gouvernement moscovite une telle solidarité [the author is referring to Prussia's attitude during the January Uprising] qu'il ne lui est guère possible de contrarier la Rusie dans un intérêt vital de son existence, ...
  ... Que la Suède prête son concours militaire au Danemark, la Russie ne pourra pas souffrir que le gouvernement de Stockholm porte la main sur les clés de la Baltique ...
  L'union du Danemark et de la Suède rencontrerait de la part de la Russie et peut-être de l'Angleterre une résistance insurmontable; mais, sans insister sur les obstacles extérieurs qui s'opposeraient à cette union, comment ne voit-on pas que la fusion des Scandinaves, au lieu de pacifier le différend actuel, ne ferait qu'envenimer et prolonger une lutte de races? ..[15]

Revue des Deux Mondes anxiously follows the development of events on the Danish-German front and then the course of the London Conference with its unhappy outcome for Denmark. After the provisions of the Treaty of London of 1852 were overthrown and Russia opposed the candidature of Prince Augustenburg, putting forward instead Prince Oldenburg as the next ruler of the duchies taken from Denmark, A. Geffroy saw the possibility of Holstein falling into the hands

---

14. *Revue des Deux Mondes,* 31 January 1864 (vol. 49, p. 762), by E. Forcade.
15. *Revue des Deux Mondes,* 31 December 1863, 14 February 1864, vol. 49, pp. 252, 763, 1018.

of the Russian government.[16] This said little for the perceptiveness of the author.

Revue soon saw, however, that it was not Russia but Prussia that was taking over the Baltic:

'Un démembrement du Danemark qui donnerait les clés de la Baltique à l'Allemagne serait bien plus menaçant pour la Russie que pour l'Angleterre. La Russie n'a pas d'autre issue maritime que le Sund, et qu'est-ce que la petite Baltique auprès des mers où domine le pavillon anglais?'[17] And when various plans for the future of Denmark appeared in the summer of 1864, *Revue* stated firmly that just as France could not agree to the incorporation of Denmark into the German Confederation, nor would Russia permit the union of Scandinavia.[18]

And on June 14, 1864 *Revue des Deux Mondes* wrote:

"Si Kiel ou un outre port enlévé au Danemark est transformé en forteresse maritime allemande, que deviennent devant un tel voisinage l'indépendance et la securité du Danemark du côté de la mer? Le Danemark ainsi diminué et affaibli, que devient l'équilibre du Nord".

The fullest presentation of views on the role of Russia in the Danish-German conflict, however, was by J. Klaczko, in a series of articles in *Revue des Deux Mondes,* published from 15 September 1864 to 15 August 1865, and issued in book form under the title *Études de diplomatie contemporaine. Les cabinets de l'Europe en 1863-64* (Paris, 1866). Klaczko's essays appeared in 1865 in Danish translation[19] and in 1903 in Polish, with a foreword by S. Tarnowski. This work, like Klaczko's later volume, *Deux Chanceliers, Le Prince Gortchakof et le Prince de Bismarck* (Paris, 1876), exercised a great influence, particularly on French historiography, and was really the first attempt, not only in France, at a broader examination of Gorchakov's policy in 1863-64.

A feature of Klaczko's views was his emphasis on the role played in European, and especially Russian, policy by the January Uprising and the close connection between events on the Vistula and the Eider. Grateful for the position taken by Prussia during the Polish uprising, Gorchakov favoured Bismarck throughout the Danish-German conflict in ways which were all the more effective, wrote Klaczko, as he did it under the cover of neutrality. The vice-chancellor defended Bismarck's actions to Russell and Napier and recommended Denmark to make concessions and to accept without a fight the fact of the occupation of Schleswig by German troops. This was how the tsar behaved in 'defence' of his 'friend' Denmark and despite Russia's interest in maintaining the freedom of the Baltic and preventing Kiel from becoming a German port. From the time of Peter the Great and Catherine II Russia had fought for supremacy over the German states. As the price for the support and co-operation of the two conservative courts in the imprisonment

---

16. "La Conférence de Londres et les intérêts européens dans la question Dano-Allemande". *Revue des Deux Mondes,* 31 May 1864, vol. 51, p. 764.
17. *Revue des Deux Mondes,* 30 June, vol. 52, p. 254.
18. Chronique de la Quinzaine, *Revue des Deux Mondes,* 14 June 1864, vol. 51, pp. 1017-20.
19. On 22 January 1866 the Danish government decorated Klaczko with the honour of the Danebrog cross, third class. See *Kongelig Dansk Hof og Staatskalender for aaret 1867,* p. 97.

of Poland (and ultimately, though this could not be foreseen in 1864, the abolition of the clauses in the 1856 Treaty of Paris [article 2] which were harmful to Russia's interests), Gorchakov – wrote Klaczko – agreed to the loss of Kiel and the strengthening of Prussia's position in the Baltic. He also concurred in the dismemberment of Denmark and the subjugation of the second rank German states, including Würtemburg, the country of Olga Nikolaevna, daughter of Nicholas I, and countries close and loyal to Russia.[20] As Klaczko put it, even at the time of the events,

... la peur causée par la réapparition du nom de la Pologne dans les conseils de l'Europe avait été si grande et avait laissé un souvenir si amer, l'exaspération nationale du peuple moscovite avait été poussée si loin, que le cabinet de Saint-Pétersbourg était prêt à sacrifier à ce sentiment plus d'une considération politique comme il y avait déjà sacrifié le port de Kiel.[21]

Another French historian, A. Sorel, described Russian policy towards Prussia as follows:

En 1863-65, la Russie laissa la Prusse démembrer le Danemark; la Prusse força l'Autriche, ouvertement favorable à l'insurrection de Pologne, à abandonner la neutralité bienveillante et à fermer les Polonais insurgés la frontière de Gallicie. La Russie – wrote Sorel elsewhere – ne demandait qu'une action commune en Pologne et des concessions en Orient; la Prusse avait tout intérêt à s'accommoder avec la Russie.[22]

Later this problem was discussed by A. Debidour.[23] In his opinion Bismarck appreciated that no attack on Denmark would be possible without the agreement of the Tsar.[24] Until then St. Petersburg had indeed supported Denmark in its struggle against Germany, but in the situation in which tsarist Russia found itself in 1863-64 because of the Polish uprising, it was not hard for Prussia to gain concessions from Russia. Furthermore, the Polish question caused the Tsar to be inclined to betray the King of Denmark even in 1863. The reason for this, in Debidour's opinion, was Russia's fear of the nationality policy of Napoleon III and the possibility of an explosion of national movements in the Spring of 1864. The Tsar was grateful to Bismarck because he had succeeded in persuading Austria to adopt a firmly anti-Polish position, which was reflected in the decree of 29 February 1864 declaring a state of emergency in Galicia.[25] This decree was a mortal blow to the uprising.

It follows from Debidour's view that by actively seconding Russia during the Polish uprising, Berlin insured itself *(s'était prémunie)* against any Russian opposition over the Danish question and that in these years Russia was dependent on Prussia.[26] With a confidential agreement with Russia in his pocket. Bismarck could manipulate the claimants to Schleswig-Holstein and the Grand Duchy of Oldenburg.

20. J. Klaczko, *Deux Chanceliers* ..., Paris, 1876, pp. 324, 400-402.
21. J. Klaczko, *Études de Diplomatie Contemporaine* ..., Paris, 1866, p. 442.
22. A. Sorel, *Histoire diplomatique de la guerre franco-allemande,* vol. 1 (Paris, 1875), pp. 46, 28.
23. A. Debidour, *Histoire diplomatique de l'Europe 1814-1878,* vol. II, (Paris, 1891).
24. *Ibid.* p. 252.
25. *Ibid.* p. 270.
26. *Ibid.* p. 274.

A similar position, ascribing a special role in Russian policy to the Polish question, was taken by Pierre de la Gorce:

M. de Bismarck fut le vrai, le seul bénéficiaire des affaires polonaises. Sans l'insurrection, rien de lui eût éte possible, surveillé qu'il eût été entre ses deux voisins de l'Orient et de Occident ... L'affaire polonaise a bouleversé toutes les alliances; la longue et énervante question du Danemark va peu à peu affaiblir dans les consciences la nation du droit, en sorte que l'Europe s'offrira sans défence à qui aura l'audace d'y établir un ordre noveau.[27]

Discussing the November crisis after the proclamation of the constitution of 18 November in Copenhagen, de la Gorce commented on the Evers mission, which he described as of little help (*peu secourable*) though no more vague (*mais pas plus vague*) than the British Wodehouse mission:

On ne pouvait espérer que la Russie, encore embarrasée dans les affaires polonaises, liée d'ailleurs au cabinet de Berlin, fût très empressée à s'engager à fond dans la question danoise.[28]

Summing up the course of events in 1864 the author once again stresses Russia's dependence on Prussia: 'il [Bismarck] tient la Russie par les souvenirs de la Pologne'.[29]

Emile Ollivier emphasises two features in his discussion of Gorchakov's policy: Russia supported Prussia without reservation and never for a moment had any intention of opposing Prussia, but warned Bismarck of the possibility that France, Britain and Sweden might support Denmark, and in view of this urged him to observe the London 'protocole' (this should be 'treaty'), but, on the other hand, if Russia insisted on the preservation of the integrity of Denmark, it did so out of fear of the idea of Scandinavianism.[30]

The well known diplomatic historian E. Driault emphasises two factors in his discussion of Russian policy which might seem to be fundamental: he attributes considerable significance to the visit of Alexander II to Potsdam on 9-11 June, followed by visits to Munich and a meeting with both German monarchs in Kissingen from 16-21 June and, in Karlsbad, on 22-23 June. However, he gives no details in support of this statement. The same applies to his assertion that Denmark should join the German Confederation in the summer of 1864.[31] He also adds:

Il était étrange que la Russie prit l'initiative d'une proposition qui pouvait aboutir à lui fermer la mer Baltique, en livrant le passage des détroits à l'Allemagne; mais elle avait bien elle-même en 1841 demandé la fermeture des détroits du Bosphore et des Dardanelles.[32]

27. Pierre de la Gorce, *Histoire du second Empire,* vol. IV, (Paris, 1911), pp. 466, 469.
28. *Ibid.* p. 486.
29. *Ibid.* pp. 519-20. Pierre de la Gorce was wrong in arguing that the treaty of 8 May 1852 had ensured Denmark a guarantee from Europe and placed Denmark in the same situation as Belgium had been in for twenty years. Vol. 4, pp. 472-3.
30. Emile Ollivier, *L'Empire Libéral,* Vol. III, (Paris, 1911), pp. 57-58, 70.
31. E. Driault, 'La diplomatie Française pendant la guerre de Danemark', (d'après les Origines diplomatiques de la guerre de 1870-71), *Revue Historique,* vol. CVII, 1911.
32. *Ibid.* p. 92. Cf. S. Goriainov, *Le Bosphore et les Dardanelles,* (Paris, 1910).

The fullest picture of Russian policy during the reign of Alexander II to appear before the first World War is to be found in François Charles-Roux' work *Alexandre II, Gortchakoff et Napoléon III,* which was published in Paris in 1913. The author argues that Russia's pro-Prussian policy during the conflict between Denmark and Germany was in a historical tradition dating back to 1813 and was based on dynastic connections. Even during the period of rapprochement between Russia and France after the Crimean War, the connections with Prussia were the most important for Alexander II. It was out of regard for Prussia that in 1857 Gorchakov induced Walewski to agree to treat the question of the duchies as an internal German rather than an international affair, as the French minister initially proposed. During the Polish uprising, when there was a split between Russia and France, the links between Russia and Prussia became closer and Prussia became the one country on which Russia could count.

La Russie de ce temps avait un champ d'activité et un point faible. Son champ d'activité était l'Orient et son point faible la Pologne. La Pruse ne menaçait pas la Russie dans son champ d'activité, où elle n'avait pas alors d'intérêts propres, et elle la couvrait du côté de son point faible, où elle avait des intérêts concordants avec ceux de la Russie. Mieux qu'une tradition, une longue habitude avait accoutumé la Russie à considérer la Prusse comme inoffensive pour ses intérêts et utile à sa sécurité.[33]

This is how Charles-Roux explains the pro-Prussian attitude of Gorchakov, particularly during the war of 1864.

La conduite que Gortchakoff recommandait au Danemark touchait en effect au ridicule: il lui conseillait de considérer l'invasion des troupes austro-prussiennes dans les duchés comme une simple occupation, afin de sauvegarder jusqu'au bout les apparences de la paix. Tant que le Danemark et les duchés de l'Elbe furent seuls en cause, la Russie n'eut aucune violence à se faire pour que sa partialité en faveur de la Prusse ne se démentît pas. La cause était, depuis longtemps, jugée à Pétersbourg. La seule concession que Gortchakoff fit à la pudeur fut de s'efforcer, sans succès d'ailleurs, à rendre son parti pris le moins apparent possible.[34]

The unchanging line of French historiography since that time is shown by two works published after the second world war, *Histoire de la France pour tous les Français,* Vol. II, by G. Lefebvre, Ch.H. Pouthas and M. Baumont, and Pierre Renouvin's *Histoire des relations internationales,* Vol. V. I. De 1815 à 1871, (Paris, 1954).[35] The author of this latter work stresses the special role of the Polish question in Franco-Russian relations.[36] In his view 'l'abstention de la Russie dans la question des duchés danois'[37] was connected with this rapprochement as well as with fear of the spread 'des passions révolutionnaires' in Europe.[38]

33. François Charles-Roux, *Alexandre II, Gortchakoff et Napoléon III,* (Paris, 1913), p. 540.
34. *Ibid.* p. 371.
35. See also: L. Girard, *Napoléon III,* (Paris, 1986), IV,2, Les années incertaines: Rome, Pologne, Danemark.
36. Pierre Renouvin, *Histoire des relations internationales,* vol. 5. (Paris, 1954), p. 362.
37. *Ibid.*
38. *Ibid.* pp. 365, see Ch. XVIII.

The work of British and American historians does not devote a great deal of attention to Russian policy towards Denmark in the years 1856-64, with the exception of W.E. Mosse.[39] Even the classic work by Lawrence D. Steefel, *The Schleswig-Holstein Question,* devotes only a few of its almost 400 pages to Russian policy. The reader of the book could get the impression that Russia played an insignificant part in this affair. Occasionally a few casual remarks about Russia's policy towards Denmark in connection with the crisis of 1863-64 are thrown in. Russian policy after 1856 is said to have been 'cautious and unassertive'.[40] In Steefel's opinion Russia had no desire to see a German fleet in the Baltic, based in Kiel, nor to see Denmark so weakened by the loss of the duchies that it would join with Sweden and Norway in a Scandinavian union and thus place the entrance to the Baltic in the hands of a single fairly strong power.[41] Steefel also considers that during the crisis towards the end of 1863 Gorchakov 'was more reserved with the Prussian minister' than in his conversations with the Danish ambassadors, but finally decided to address a sharp note to the Danish government.[42]

Unlike many French historians, Steefel pays much less attention to the place of the Polish uprising in Russian policy. On the other hand he says that 'Danish participation in the representations to Russia in favor of Poland, and the acceptance of the throne of Greece by Prince William of Denmark were regarded as having added to the Danish credit account with the two 'Western Powers'.[43] Russia's attitude to Prussia and Denmark underwent a change, particularly in 1863, and Bismarck 'had earned the gratitude of Russia and especially of Tsar Alexander by his vigorous and ostentatious action in the Polish crisis. Denmark however had joined with the 'Western Powers' in protesting to Russia in favor of the Poles'.[44] Danish support of Western demands during the Polish uprising had aroused considerable resentment in St. Petersburg. He also stressed such points as that 'Russia did not understand, nor had she sympathy with the national ambitions of the Eider Danes', and says that 'although it sympathised with King Christian personally, the Russian government disapproved of the democratic tendencies of Denmark'.[45]

Russia's attitude towards Denmark is assessed in many British works in a superficial manner and on the basis of British material alone.[46] The authors of these works are agreed that 'the Treaty of London in some consequences was beyond

---

39. W.E. Mosse, *The European Powers and the German Question 1848-71. With Special Reference to England and Russia,* (Cambridge, 1958).
40. Lawrence D. Steefel, *The Schleswig-Holstein Question,* (London, 1932), p. 129.
41. *Ibid.* pp. 39, 130.
42. *Ibid.* pp. 131, 132.
43. *Ibid.* p. 61.
44. *Ibid.* p. 130.
45. *Ibid.*
46. Examples are: *The Cambridge History of British Foreign Policy, 1783-1919,* Vol. II, 1815-66, ed. A.W. Ward and P.G. Gooch, (Cambridge, 1923), A.W. Ward and S. Wilkinson, *Germany,* Vol. II 1852-71, (Cambridge, 1917), H. Temperley and L.M. Penson, *Foundations of British Foreign Policy from Pitt (1782) to Salisbury (1902),* (Cambridge, 1938), R.W. Seton Watson, *Britain in Europe, 1789-1914, A Survey of Foreign Policy,* (Cambridge, 1937).

all doubts one of the most unfortunate of the achievements of European diplomacy',[47] as is clear from their assessment of Gorchakov's policy. The latter, we know, attributed particular importance to that treaty and based his position on the Danish-German crisis on the expectation that the provisions of the treaty would be executed by both parties. The provisions of the treaty also formed the starting point of the instructions sent to Brunnow in connection with the convening of the London Conference in the spring of 1864. In assessing Russian policy, British historians are inclined to accept the view formulated by Russell on 5 May 1864 'that Russia is divided between her wish to save Denmark and her unwillingness to break with the conservative Monarchies of Austria and Prussia'.[48]

Among works published after the second world war the fullest treatment of Russian policy is undoubtedly to be found in Mosse's book. In his opinion Russian policy in 1864 was determined by the following factors: the Polish question, mistrust of Napoleon III and fear of the revolutionary movement in Europe.[49] Because of this, Gorchakov sought to strengthen ties with Bismarck, to create an entente embracing Prussia, Austria, Great Britain and Russia and to keep the 1852 Treaty of London in force. In Mosse's view it was impossible simultaneously to strengthen the position of Bismarck and maintain the integrity of Denmark. Gorchakov attained these initial objectives, for there was no outburst of revolution, Napoleon III did not have the opportunity to carry out any *coup d'état,* Russia strengthened its friendship with Bismarck and achieved an entente between the four powers (though in reality this understanding was no more than wishful thinking on the part of Gorchakov), – but this was done at the expense of Denmark. Russia, Mosse argues, emphasised from the very beginning that it would not take up arms in defence of Denmark, called on Berlin, Vienna and Copenhagen to exercise restraint and, almost to the end, adhered to the Treaty of London. Russian diplomacy, he considers, was not subservient to Bismarck, the Tsar and his minister restrained Bismarck's aspirations, and if they agreed to his plans, they did so in order to prevent the dismissal and fall of Bismarck or, alternatively, an alliance between him and France. Conservatism and dislike of Napoleon III were the reasons why Russia accepted 'faits accomplis' which she was unable to change by peaceful means. These feelings were shared by H.J.T. Palmerston too. 'Peace at almost any price became Russia's basic need'.

The Polish question demonstrated the coincidence of interests between Russia and Prussia. 'Russian diplomacy, in fact, was torn between a clear recognition of military and political realities and the longing for a conservative, legitimate solution. In the end internal weakness, Poland, distrust of Napoleon and fear of a Ger-

---

47. *The Cambridge History,* p. 538.
48. 'The Compromise Scheme of John Russell', in *Foundations,* pp. 273-5. Both the authors of *Foundation,* (p. 260) and Medlicott and Coveney, *Bismarck and Europe,* (London, 1971), (p. 27), wrongly interpret the provisions of the constitution of 18 November 1863 relating to Schleswig as meaning the incorporation of Schleswig into Denmark. They also lay the blame for the eruption of the crisis on Denmark. It is symptomatic that they use terms such as 'German nationalism' but 'violent chauvinism in Denmark', *(Foundations,* p. 260).
49. Mosse, *The European Powers and the German Question,* (Cambridge, 1958), p. 210.

man revolution led Russia to acquiesce – albeit reluctantly – in the dismembering of the Danish monarchy'.[50] Finally, he says, 'Prussia was herself disinterested in the Eastern question, her position enabled her to hold the balance between England, Russia and Austria'. These last theses are very close to the formulations used by Palmerston in his letter to Russell on 13 September 1865:

... It was dishonest and unjust to deprive Denmark of Schleswig and Holstein. It is another question how those two duchies, when separated from Denmark, can be disposed of best for the interests of Europe. I should say that, with that view, it is better that they should go to increase the power of Prussia than that they should form another little state to be added to the cluster of small bodies politic which encumber Germany, and render it of less force than it ought to be in the general balance of power in the world. Prussia – Palmerston continued – is too weak as she now is, ever to be honest or independent in her action, and, with a view to the future, it is desirable that Germany, in the aggregate, should be strong, in order to control those two ambitious and aggressive powers, France and Russia, that press upon her west and east ... [51]

There is no question that Mosse treats too many questions as having equal importance. Gorchakov's short-sighted policy is considered a success for Russia and Gorchakov himself is regarded as a great statesman.

Other British works dealing with this problem, which appeared after the second World War, like Lewis Napier, *Vanished Supremacies. Essays on European History 1812-1918,* (London, 1962) and E.M. Almedingen, *The Emperor Alexander II. A. Study,* (London, 1962) do not contribute anything new, nor does A.J.P. Taylor in *Bismarck* and *The Struggle for Mastery in Europe 1848-1918,* (London, Oxford, New York, 1974). As far as the latter is concerned it may be worth mentioning that Taylor considers that the Polish uprising exhausted Russia to such an extent that it was incapable of any large-scale action. 'It would be a mistake' – warns Taylor – 'to exaggerate the importance of Russia's favourable disposition towards Prussia'. But he continues, 'As it was there came from St. Petersburg much sympathy with Prussia, and no murmur of condemnation. This was, no doubt, a minor factor. Both Russia and Great Britain had virtually eliminated themselves from the European balance; this gave the years between 1864 and 1866 a character unique in recent history'.[52]

It is worth noting here two works by American historians. Chester Wells Clark, *Franz Joseph and Bismarck. The Diplomacy of Austria before the War of 1866,* (Cambridge, Harvard U.P., 1934) argues that Alexander II was firmly opposed to rapprochement with Austria in 1864 and that Gorchakov in 1863-64 'was a mortal enemy of Austria'.[53] B. Jelavich, 'Russland und die Einigung Deutschlands unter preussischer Führung', *Geschichte in Wissenschaft und Unterricht,* Vol. 9, (1968), detects differences between the attitude of the Tsar and his minister towards Prus-

---

50. *Ibid.* p. 364.
51. *Foundations,* pp. 279-80.
52. A.J.P. Taylor, *Bismarck,* (London, 1955). Chs 4 and 5, and *The Struggle for Mastery in Europe, 1848-1918,* (Oxford, 1974), p. 156.
53. C.W. Clark, *Franz Joseph and Bismarck. The Diplomacy of Austria before the War of 1866,* (Cambridge, MASS, 1934), p. 34.

sia in 1864; in contrast to Alexander II, Gorchakov, she says, was 'zurückhaltender' and more critical of Prussia, even though he relied on co-operation with her, whilst in Jelavich's opinion documents show that Alexander II was consistently in favour of a Prussian victory over Denmark.[54] Returning to Clark's work, I would like to stress that he maintains that dislike of Austria was an essential feature of Russian policy in 1863-64 and that, in his opinion, this was one of the reasons for the lack of co-operation between them at the London Conference – although there was a certain rapprochement between the two powers from March 1864 and a meeting took place between Alexander II and Franz Josef at Kissingen in June 1864. Despite the differences between Russia and Austria, however, – the cause, in Clark's opinion, being their relations with Turkey – their interests coincided as fas as the Polish question was concerned. Both powers pursued conservative policies. In addition, Russia was in favour of a Prussian-Austrian alliance, an alliance directed against revolutionary forces in Europe, though this was 'purely a cabinet combination', 'against the wishes of the majority of both Austrians and Prussians'.[55]

German historiography of the Danish-German dispute took a tendentious position and from the start laid the blame for the outbreak of the conflict exclusively on the Danish government. The tone was set by H. Sybel in his fundamental multi-volume work *Die Begründung des Deutschen Reiches durch Wilhelm I*. Although connected with liberal circles, Sybel approved of Bismarck's policy of the unification of Germany. In Narochnitskaya's opinion he created the legend that the neutrality of Russia in 1864 was the result of Alexander's subjective feelings towards the Prussian King and of 'gratitude on the part of Russia to Prussia for the latter's disinterested attitude and support in 1863'. The dynastic links between the Russian and Prussian courts were also a basis for the rapprochement, in Sybel's view. He stressed that Alexander II favoured the maintenance of peace in Europe, and of united action by Russia and Prussia, as a necessary condition for counteracting Napoleon's plans for the annexation of the Rhineland and to avoid irritating Britain, which might lead to closer relations between Britain and France. In Sybel's opinion there was a connection between the Copenhagen government's issue of the decree of 30 March 1863, which, it should be noted, like all German historians, he wrongly regards as 'die definitive Inkorporation Schleswigs in das Königreich',[56] and the new political constellation in Europe as a result of the January Uprising. Moreover, he maintains, the fact that the Eider party sided with the anti-Russian forces and spoke out in the cause of the liberation of Poland contributed to the freeze in Russian-Danish relations and to the growth of pro-Danish sympathy in Britain. Brunnow, as in all German historiography, is disliked by Sybel since he

---

54. B. Jelavich, 'Russland und die Einigung', pp. 523, 532. Cf. von Schweinitz, *Denkwürdigkeiten*, (Berlin, 1927), vol. I, p. 235.
55. C.W. Clark, *Franz Joseph*, pp. 53-54.
56. H. Sybel, *Die Begründung des Deutschen Reiches durch Wilhelm I*, (Berlin u. Leipzig, 1890), vol. III, p. 113.

sees him as a friend of Denmark and criticises the part he played in the London Conference. He calls Brunnow's speech on 28 May, announcing Alexander's granting of his rights to some possessions in Holstein to Prince Oldenburg, a Russian comedy.[57]

Sybel's views were adopted by other German historians such as M. Lenz, E. Marks and, subsequently, E. Brandenburg. Earlier, too, Karl Jansen and Karl Samwer had written in the same spirit.[58] The last two were closely connected with Prince Augustenburg, initially the main claimant to Schleswig and Holstein, and Samwer was minister of foreign affairs to Prince Friedrich Augustenburg from 23 November 1863. They stressed that the friendly relations between Alexander II and Wilhelm I, and the position adopted by Prussia during the Crimean War and the Polish uprising, had generated a special regard in Russia for their western neighbour. 'Es war von vornherein nicht denkbar, dass Russland die dänische Frage als wichtig genug ansehen werde, um darüber mit Preussen zu zerfallen'. Nor, in their opinion, was Alexander blind to the illegality of the Danes' behaviour towards Germany. They emphasise that Russia warned Denmark against the adoption of the new constitution and that after the conclusion of the agreement between Austria and Prussia Gorchakov had no wish to see them split again on account of the Danish question. They dismiss Gorchakov's statement in January 1864 proposing a conference to discuss the question of the duchies as of little significance, since at the time Gorchakov declared himself in favour of the occupation of Schleswig by the allies.[59] Jansen and Samwer place special emphasis on the publication of the text of the Warsaw protocol of 5th June 1851[60] in the *Journal de St. Pétersbourg* on 9 January 1864, by which Russia wished to demonstrate its entitlement to grant its rights to the Gottorp line, the Oldenburg line, in order to oppose the candidature of Prince Friedrich Augustenburg.

For familiar reasons they take a hostile attitude towards Brunnow and criticise his conduct at the London Conference. They stress the discrepancy between the attitude of the ambassador and that of the St. Petersburg cabinet:

Brunnow empfand natürlich Schmerz darüber, dass sein und Palmerston's Werk vernichtet werden sollte, aber Kaiser Alexander II und Gortchakoff wollten nichts gegen Preussen unternehmen, dessen Haltung während des Krimkrieges und der polnischen Wirren von 1863 dem Zarenreiche genüsst hatte.[61]

Returning to Russia's proposal of Prince Oldenburg at the conference, they quote the words of Nicholas I to the Grand Duke of Oldenburg in 1851, that with him the Tsar could do whatever he wanted. They see his candidature as an attempt by Rus-

---

57. *Ibid.* p. 333.
58. Karl Jansen and Karl Samwer, *Schleswig-Holsteins Befreiung,* (Wiesbaden, 1897), M. Lenz, *Geschichte Bismarcks,* (München, Leipzig, 1913), E. Marks, *Kaiser Wilhelm I,* (Leipzig, 1910), E. Brandenburg, *Die Reichsgründung,* (Leipzig, 1922).
59. *Schleswig-Holsteins Befreiung,* pp. 135, 192-3.
60. For the text see N. Neergaard, *Under Junigrundloven,* vol. 1, (Copenhagen, 1892), pp. 729-31.
61. Jansen and Samwer, *Schleswig-Holsteins Befreiung,* p. 297.

sia to strengthen its influence in the duchies.[62]

At his meeting with Bismarck on the way to Kissingen on 9 June, Alexander II approved Bismarck's view that the Prussian government's main task was the fight against revolution, and commended Bismarck's sympathetic acceptance of Prince Oldenburg's candidature, but warned against annexation of the duchies by Prussia, as that might evoke a reaction on the part of Britain and lead to a general outbreak of war – 'er warnte davor, England zu sehr zu reizen und einen allgemeinen Krieg zu entzünden'.[63]

The duality of Russian policy, and the differences between the positions of Gorchakov and Brunnow, particularly during the London Conference, were discussed by F. Cierpinski.[64] Brunnow, he says, ... sehr deutschfeindlich war. Die ganze folgende Politik Russlands in der schleswig-holsteinischen Frage war nicht kriegerisch; es ist darum höchst wahrscheinlich, dass Baron Brunnow in London mehr gesagt hat, als man in Petersburg für gut hielt'. So in Cierpinski's view, the ambassador's anti-German statements did not reflect St. Petersburg's intentions.[65]

Cierpinski emphasises that the roots of Russia's pro-Danish policy lay in the fact that Russia, and all the northern states, had a special interest in the fate of Denmark because of its geographical position. Denmark occupied such an important economic and strategic place in Europe that it could be said to owe its existence not so much to its own efforts as to the envy and rivalry of the great powers. Furthermore, Cierpinski continues, Russia was afraid of any change in this region, and especially of a Scandinavian Union which included Denmark. On the other hand, she was afraid of the growth of liberal tendencies in Germany. She therefore saw the best solution as defence of the provisions of the Treaty of London, thereby confirming the integrity of Denmark. Britain, too, saw an advantage in this, even though Russia derived additional benefit from it. In essence, Russia lost in the dispute about the succession to the Danish throne. Wanting to preserve the situation created in 1852, Russia disapproved of a Danish policy towards Germany and the issue of new legal documents, particularly the constitution of 18 November 1863, which were contrary to the provisions of the Treaty of London.[66]

In the volume 45 of *Zeitschrift* Graef[67] put forward the notion that Gorchakov probably lay behind O. Plessen's proposal in June 1864 that Denmark should join the German Confederation, since in this way he sought to prevent the effective development of a close link between Denmark and Sweden.[68]

---

62. *Ibid.* pp. 357-8 and 733.
63. *Ibid.* p. 355.
64. F. Cierpinski, 'Die Politik Englands in der Schleswig-Holsteinische Frage von 1861 bis Anfang Januar 1864', *Zeitschrift der Gesellschaft für Schleswig-Holsteinische Geschichte,* vol. 44, (Leipzig, 1914), pp. 220-97 and vol. 45, 1915, pp. 105 ff.
65. *Ibid.* p. 265.
66. *Ibid.* pp. 263-4.
67. Prof. dr. Graef, '1864, Schleswig-Holstein und das Ausland', *Zeitschrift der Gesellschaft für Schleswig-Holsteinische Geschichte,* vol. 45, 1915, pp. 310-28.
68. *Ibid.* pp. 324-5.

According to F. Frahm's paper 'Die Bismarcksche Lösung der schleswig-holsteinischen Frage' published in *Zeitschrift der Gesellschaft für Schleswig-Holsteinische Geschichte* (vol. 59, 1930) anti-Scandinavianism was the essential factor which determined Russian policy towards Denmark and Prussia in 1864. In his paper he basically followed the theses put forward by the Norwegian scholar H. Koht in his fundamental work *Norwegen und Schweden im deutsch-dänischen Konflikt*.

Another aspect of the problem is raised by Veit Valentin.[69] He argues that:

> Der neue dänische Nationalismus, der ein Stück der modernen skandinavischen Bewegung war, und eine Wiedergeburt des nordischen Volkstums bedeutete, machte die dänische Sache dem legitimistisch und, trotz liberaler Anwandlungen, autokratisch gesinnten Russland sehr unsympatisch. Sowohl für Dänemark wie für Deutschland war Schleswig-Holstein ein nationales Problem, die Mehrzahl seiner Einwohner war zweifellos deutsch, aber nicht nur eine Minderheit war dänisch, sondern auch die Verbindung mit den Herzogtümern war für Dänemark eine Angelegenheit des nationalen Ehrengefühls.[70]

A much more detailed discussion of Russia's attitude to Denmark and Germany than in the works mentioned so far is provided by G. Heinze.[71] This was possible thanks to the publication of documents from the German and Austrian archives during the 1930s, and these sources influenced his understanding of the problem. An apologist for Bismarck, Heinze argues that Bismarck's merit was that he caused Russia to behave in 1863 as she herself wished. Bismarck, he argues, conducted his campaign extremely skillfully, particularly in relation to Russia. Initially he agreed to Russia's demand that Austria and Prussia should declare themselves in favour of the integrity of Denmark, if the lattter carried out the obligations undertaken in 1852. After the outbreak of war, however, he induced Russia to begin to act in accordance with his plan. Quoting the report by Bismarck's ambassador Pirch on his conversations in St. Petersburg on 20 April 1864, Heinze says:

> Also ein erneuter Beweis, wie weit es Bismarck gelungen war, Russland auf seine Politik einzuspielen. Freilich darf man nicht vergessen, dass die Haltung Gortchakows immer durch die Rücksichtnahme auf die Mentalität des Zaren bestimmt war: Gortchakow selbst hätte Preussen gern ebenfalls zur Nachgiebigkeit gebracht und Dänemark durch Dankbarkeit an die russische Allianz gefesselt.[72]

In Heinze's opinion Gorchakov was not fundamentally on Prussia's side, as he liked to present himself. But he did this out of fear that France and Britain might reach an understanding, and he used the threat of this possibility to urge Bismarck to make concessions. The latter, however, relying on the Tsar's friendship, was not

---

69. Veit Valentin, *Bismarcks Reichsgründung im Urteil englischer Diplomaten*, (Amsterdam, 1937).
70. *Ibid.* p. 205.
71. G. Heinze, *Bismarck und Russland bis zum Reichsgründung*, (Würzburg, 1939). Among other sources he drew on the results of research by Ch. Friese, *Russland und Preussen vom Krimkrieg bis zum polnischen Aufstand*, (Berlin and Königsberg, 1931).
72. *Ibid.* p. 58.

intimidated. Bismarck, on the one hand, was aware of Russian plans in the east and was able to exploit this to bind Russia to Prussia while, on the other hand, knowing the views of Alexander II, he manipulated, among other things, the latter's fear of revolution and the threat of abdication of the King, as had occured at Kissingen.

Der dänische Konflikt – eine Episode im Kampf des monarchischen Prinzips gegen die europäische Revolution: so machte Bismarck den Zaren gefügig. Kommt man den berechtigten nationalen Bedürfnissen entgegen, so werden der Revolution die Vorwände genommen, aus denen sie ihre Kraft erhält![73]

While the Tsar, who seemed disinclined to agree that Denmark should lose too much territory, succumbed to the arguments of Bismarck, who, knowing the Tsar, played on his fear of Napoleon III and the possibility of a war in which Germany would stand beside France, and in which Russia would have to participate on account of Poland.

In supporting the candidature of Prince Oldenburg (Heinze follows K. Jansen[74] and H. Oncken[75] in tending to view this question from the standpoint of Russia's fear of a Scandinavian union), Bismarck wanted to render the Tsar a service, but he was concerned that in return the Tsar should agree not only to the division of Schleswig but to the transfer of both Holstein and Schleswig to Prince Oldenburg. Heinze concludes:

Dank der wohlwollenden Haltung Russlands ... konnte Bismarck allem Widerstand Dänemarks und allen englischen Einmischungsversuchen Trotz bieten und die schleswig-holsteinische Frage zu einem dem preussischen Interesse gemässen Abschluss bringen .... Bismarck konnte ruhig seinem Ziele näherschreiten. Der russischen Freundschaft gewiss, blieb diese die aussenpolitische Vorbedingung seiner Erfolge.[76]

Thus Heinze considers that only the Tsar favoured absolute support for Prussia, while Gorchakov was of a more pro-Danish persuasion and acted with reservation; during the war, however, public opinion in Russia 'war aber vollkommen gegen Preussen eingestellt'.[77]

In Ritter von Srbik's opinion[78] these was no doubt about Russia's friendly attitude towards Prussia. The fact that, while the Tsar was pro-Russian, Gorchakov was more pro-Danish, did not affect Russia's attitude to Denmark during the crisis, During the crisis Russia strove to avoid complications between the great powers.[79]

'Die vielgeschmächte Politik der Alvenslebenschen Konvention trug jetzt [towards the end of 1863] ihre Früchte,' was another German historian, A.O.

---

73. *Ibid.* p. 59.
74. K. Jansen, 'Grossherzog Peter von Oldenburg und die Schles.Holst. Frage', *Deutsche Revue,* vol. 27, no. 4.
75. H. Oncken, 'Grossherzog Peter von Oldenburg', *Preussisches Jahrbuch,* vol. 102.
76. Heinze, *Bismarck,* pp. 60-61.
77. *Ibid.* p. 101.
78. H. Ritter von Srbik, *Deutsche Einheit. Idee und Wirklichkeit vom Heiligen Reich bis Königsgrätz,* Munich, 1942.
79. *Ibid.* vol. 4, p. 163.

Meyer's, assessment of the reasons for the Tsar's pro-German policy.[80] The same opinion was shared by E. Eyck, who also considered that the Polish uprising and its political consequences, and fear of European revolution, led the Tsar and Gorchakov to take a passive, pro-Bismarck position in 1864.[81]

Yet different opinions are to be found in German historiography of Russian policy during the war of 1864. It was true, wrote Gustav Roloff, that Russia was grateful to Prussia for her attitude during the Crimean War and the Polish uprising, and supported Prussia as a result, but this support was not unqualified [rückhaltlos] and Russia viewed the war itself with disapproval. During the London Conference Russia, along with Britain, tried to save Schleswig-Holstein and keep the duchies as part of Denmark.[82]

In works published in Germany in the course of the last twenty years, historians are inclined to stress the role of the Polish question in the Russian-Prussian rapprochement of 1863-64 and to explain Russian passivity in 1864 by her absorption with it. This view is expressed by, among others, Eberhard Kolb,[83] Alexander Scharff,[84] Andreas Hillgruber[85] and Eckart Fleischhauer.[86] Contemporary German historians are also agreed that there were indeed differences between Alexander II and Gorchakov, but that they did not influence Russia's attitude to Denmark during the war of 1864.[87]

Fleischhauer considers that, in contrast to the years 1848-49, when her thinking on Prussia was negative, Russia's attitude to the Prussian government changed after the Crimean War as a result of her military and diplomatic weakening, the international difficulties she was experiencing, and because of her concentration on domestic reforms and growing interest in central Asia.

Since 1860 Russia had made Bismarck aware that she did not want a European war on account of Denmark and during his years as ambassador in St. Petersburg Bismarck became convinced that he could secure the understanding both of Gorchakov and of the pro-Prussian Tsar for Prussia's policy towards Denmark. Fleischhauer is struck by the fact that, in contrast to the lively correspondence between Bismarck and Gorchakov during the Polish uprising, their contacts were

---

80. A.O. Meyer, *Bismarck, Der Mensch und der Staatsmann,* (Stuttgart, 1949), p. 219.
81. E. Eyck, *Bismarck. Leben und Werk,* (Zurich, 1941), vol. 1, p. 627.
82. Gustav Roloff, *Deutschland und Russland im Widerstreit seit 200 Jahren,* (Stuttgart and Berlin, 1914), pp. 24-25.
83. Eberhard Kolb, 'Russland und die Gründung des Norddeutschen Bundes', in *Europa und der Norddeutsche Bund,* ed. Richard Dietrich, (Berlin, 1968), pp. 190-91.
84. Alexander Scharff, 'Vom übernationalen zum nationalen Staat. Ursachen und Bedeutung des deutsch-dänischen Konflikts von 1864', in *Schleswig-Holstein in der deutschen und nordeuropäischen Geschichte,* (Suttgart, 1969), p. 232.
85. Andreas Hillgruber, *Bismarcks Aussenpolitik,* (Freiburg, 1972), pp. 57-8.
86. Eckart Fleischhauer, *Bismarcks Russlandpolitik im Jahrzehnt vor der Reichsgründung und ihre Darstellung in der sowjetischen Historiographie,* (Cologne and Vienna, 1976). L. Gall, *Bismarck, Der weisse Revolutionär,* (Frankfurt, Berlin, Vienna, 1983).
87. Steen Martenson, *Württemberg und Russland im Zeitalter der deutschen Einigung 1856-70. Die Diplomatischen und dynastischen Beziehungen eines deutschen Mittelstaates,* (Göppingen, 1970).

much less intensive during the Danish-German conflict. Gorchakov, fearing exorbitant Prussian demands, stood for the integrity of Denmark and adopted a position of 'benevolent neutrality' during the dispute and the war. He did not protest against the entry of German troops into Schleswig and did not want Britain to lodge a protest either. He supported Bismarck, but both he and the Tsar rejected the proposal for an alliance between Russia and Prussia as that would have led to the division of Europe into two hostile camps. Unlike the Tsar, his minister did not regard relations with Prussia as intimate and did not have a clear picture of what policy should be pursued towards Bismarck. He did not want a Scandinavian union, nor, says Fleischhauer, German control of the Baltic, but neither did he believe that this could come about overnight. The objective of putting forward Oldenburg as a candidate was not only to block Augustenburg, but to torpedo plans for the inclusion of the duchies in the major German power, and to please Denmark, Britain and France. Finally, he regards the conversations in Berlin and Kissingen as a political success for Bismarck, rather than Russia, because they did not produce the results which Russia hoped for and did not contribute to progress at the London Conference. In the last phase of the war, Russia aimed to localise the conflict. Unlike many other German historians, Fleischhauer thinks that, during the crisis, Russia approved less and less of Prussian policy and tried to influence it, but the desire to maintain good relations with Prussia predominated. The years 1863-64 showed that, despite differences, Russo-Prussian relations were closer than Russian relations with other states.

As far as the Danish political aims in 1863 are concerned, it may be worth mentioning that some of the German historians are entirely mistaken. That is why they repeat indiscriminately the German nationalistic interpretation of the reason for the outbreak of the 1864 war. For instance, one expert in 19th century German history, H. Böhme, wrote in his book *The Foundation of the German Empire:* 'At the end of 1863 Denmark received a new constitution, whereby the Duchies of Schleswig, Holstein, and Lauenburg were to be incorporated into the Kingdom. Thus, in Germany's view, Denmark broke the London Protocol of 1852 which had linked the continuation of Danish rule with a guarantee of the *status quo* leaving the Duchies with their rights of autonomy intact'.[88]

Finally, it is worth citing the opinion of the East German historian E. Engelberg who, reflecting on how and why Bismarck was able to implement in 1864 the plans he had drawn up towards the end of the 1850s, argues:

Es war ihm in der Tat gelungen, die Entente mit Russland zu festigen und in der schleswig-holsteinischen Frage eine solche diabolische Kombination zustande zubringen, die den strategischen Gegner Österreich vorübergehend zum taktischen Verbündeten machte.[89]

The foundations of the rapprochement between Russia and Prussia, which had

---

88. (Oxford University Press, 1971), p. 62. See also H. Böhme, *Die Reichsgründung,* (München, 1967), pp. 67-68. Cf. S. Haffner, *Preussen ohne Legende,* (Hamburg, 1980), p. 369. 'Dänemark setzte sich über das Londoner Protokol hinweg und annektierte Schleswig'.
89. E. Engelberg, *Bismarck. Urpreusse und Reichsbegründer,* p. 553.

deep historical roots, were strengthened, in Engelberg's view, during Bismarck's period in St. Petersburg (1859-62) and, as far as Bismarck's policy was concerned, at the time of the Polish uprising.[90] Engelberg ascribes great significance to the convention of Alvensleben since, thanks to it,

> ... so hatte Preussen mit der Konvention Alvensleben, ob sie nun in Kraft gesetzt wurde oder nicht, Petersburgs moralisch-politische Isolierung durchbrochen. Überdies hatte Russland ja bei allen Verstimmungen, die es dann und wann gab, keine ernsthaften Gegensätze zu Preussen, das stärker denn je an Russlands Seite rücken konnte, so dass auch offiziell manchmal von einer Entente gesprochen wurde.[91]

Thus, in Engelberg's opinion, the key to the situation lay in Russia's hands and Bismarck managed to persuade Russia to take a positive view of his plans and to strengthen the ties linking Russia and Prussia during the conflict with Denmark, particularly during the war of 1864.

In Danish historiography of Russian policy towards Denmark, among the older works those by A. Thorsøe and N. Neergaard and, of the newer writers, E. Møller and T. Fink, deserve attention. Most recently, there is the article by P. von Linstow, 'Bismarck, Europa og Sleswig-Holstein 1862-1866', which appeared in *Historisk Tidsskrift,* Vol. 78, No. 2 (1978). Thorsøe's undoubted merit was that he was the first to use printed and archival sources, predominantly Danish, to portray Russia's attitude to Denmark in 1856-63, up to the death of Frederick VII. He was also the first[92] to depict the attitude of the Danish government and society to the January Uprising, emphasising the attitude of the national-liberal party to the Polish national liberation movement. In view of the narrow range of sources at his disposal, however, he confined himself to a general presentation of Russian policy towards Denmark and did not analyse the reasons why, even in 1856, Russia took a different position towards Denmark than previously.

A much fuller presentation of Russia's position *vis-à-vis* Denmark, with special consideration of her attitude to the Danish-German conflict in 1856-64 and to Scandinavianism, is given by Neergaard in his fundamental multi-volume work *Under Junigrundloven.*[93] Even though he did not have access to many Russian sources, he presented a generally faithful picture of the outlines of Russian policy and indicated the reasons why, after 1856, Russia became more and more firmly pro-German and from 1858 specifically pro-Prussian. During the Polish uprising the Danish government hoped to derive a certain advantage from the new European political constellation and the fact that the Western states and Austria were opposed to Prussia and Russia, but it failed to see the dangers of opposing Russia when Prussia had spoken out in her support. The Copenhagen government only hesitantly took this dangerous step, sending its note of 8 May concerning the Polish question through Plessen.

90. *Ibid.* pp. 459 ff and 542-5.
91. *Ibid.* p. 545.
92. A. Thorsøe, *Kong Frederik den Syvendes Regering,* Vols. I and II, (Copenhagen 1884 and 1889).
93. See the review by A. Friis in *Historisk Tidsskrift,* IX, Series I, (1918), pp. 89-128.

The St. Petersburg government received the note without any noticable irritation. A much more unfriendly impression was created in Russia by Denmark's attitude to Col. Lapinski's expedition, and her suspicion was exacerbated by the demonstrations in favour of Poland in Copenhagen in the spring and summer of 1863, which showed the pro-Western mood of Danish society.[94]

In Neergaard's opinion, Russia's gratitude for Prussia's attitude during events in Poland in 1863 had momentous consequences and led Gorchakov to support Bismarck to such an extent that he, incomprehensibly, lost his sense of reality and failed to see the danger to Russia if the duchies and Kiel should fall into Prussian hands. Fear of the plans of Napoleon III created a nervous atmosphere in Russia and Gorchakov saw the best guarantee of torpedoing the French emperor's designs in a rapprochement between Russia, Austria and Prussia and in avoiding a break between Britain and Prussia.[95]

In 1864 the Russian government very cautiously exerted pressure on Copenhagen, first to offer concessions to the German states and then to agree to a conference and, at the same time, not to protest against or to resist the entry of German troops first in Schleswig and then in Jutland, arguing that Austria and Prussia were acting on the Treaty of London and intended to observe it. Gorchakov acted in this way from fear that the war might spread to other European countries. But in fact, Neergaard argues, no power had as great an interest in maintaining the integrity of the Danish monarchy as Russia, which also had an interest in delaying the build-up of German power in the Baltic, although in 1864 these efforts seems to have weakened.

In spite of everything, Gorchakov sought to preserve friendly relations with Prussia, thinking that this would enable him to prevent the spread of the war and to maintain Denmark as an independent State. At the same time he pressed Copenhagen to make concessions. Alexander II acted in the same spirit, and Neergaard, not without reason, sees Russian inspiration in Plessen's behaviour in the spring of 1864 too.[96]

Finally, he came to the conclusion that Russia's attitude towards Denmark in 1864 was unfriendly. Nicholas I behaved differently in 1848 when Prussian forces entered Jutland than did Alexander II when German troops entered that some Jutland in 1864. This change in Russian policy was symbolised by two awards of decorations – to Danish officers who fought in the battle of Isted in 1850 and to Prussian officers after their capture of Dybbøl in 1864.[97] The truth is that Russia adhered longest to the Treaty of London and was in favour of the duchies and Kiel remaining under the Danish King, linked to the monarchy by a personal union; but this was because Russia did not want Denmark to fall into the hands of Sweden as part of a Scandinavian union nor Kiel to join Prussia or the German Confederation. The

---

94. N. Neergaard, *Under Junigrundloven,* vol. II, 1, pp. 658-64.
95. *Ibid.* vol. II, pt. 2, p. 922.
96. *Ibid.* p. 1299.
97. *Ibid.* p. 1159.

fact that the idea of a personal union between the Danish monarchy and the duchies was the most unpopular one in Denmark did not concern Russia at all.[98]

Many of Neergaard's theses have stood the test of time. His general outline of Russian policy was correct. But because of the inaccessibility, then, of both Russian and other west European sources, it was not possible to examine many questions concerning the policy of the St. Petersburg cabinet towards Denmark in late 1863 and during the 1864 war, nor the differences in Russia over what attitude to adopt to the warring parties. His picture of Brunnow as 'Amicus Daniae' seems too one-sided and, through lack of the documents, he was unable to reach a true estimate of the Russian ambassador's behaviour during the London Conference.

Some new material concerning our subject was contributed by the works of E. Møller.[99] In particular, Møller was the first to use copies of the reports by the Russian ambassadors in Copenhagen, E. Ungern-Sternberg and N.P. Nicolay, and of J.A. Dashkov, the Russian ambassador in Stockholm. Thanks to these he was able to give a fuller picture than his predecessors of the position taken not only by St. Petersburg, but also by Russian diplomats, – in particular the ambassadors in the Scandinavian capitals – who undoubtedly influenced Gorchakov's decisions and the opinions of his closest advisers.

In Møller's opinion Gorchakov minimised the importance of the Danish-German dispute from the start, as he did not want to incur German displeasure, and considered the dispute a purely German problem. One has to ask whether this interpretation is sufficient. Møller goes on to argue that Gorchakov took this position until the succession to the Danish throne came into question and was endangered. As far as German demands in Schleswig were concerned, he says, Gorchakov took a one-sided position from the beginning and urged Denmark to make concessions.

In Møller's view, the Polish question in 1863 placed the Danish government between Scylla and Charybdis, although at the time it did not lead to a deterioration in the relations between Copenhagen and St. Petersburg.[100] But a few months later the Polish question again affected Denmark's position, this time to a much greater extent, in connection with Napoleon III's plan to convene a European congress.[101] It is true that Russia expressed herself in favour of the integrity of Denmark and the observance of the provisions of the Treaty of London. But she did so out of fear, and Gorchakov's view that the link between German conservative states and Russia was essential because of what he saw as the imminent wave of revolution threatening Europe. Russia confined herself, as a result, to moral support for Denmark while in practice backing the actions of Austria and Prussia.[102] In the spring

---

98. *Ibid.* pp. 1159-60.
99. E. Møller, *Skandinavisk stræben og svensk politik omkring 1860*, (Copenhagen, 1948), and *Helstatens Fald*, (Copenhagen, 1958). The latter is reviewed by P. Bagge, *Historisk Tidsskrift*, vol. 12, No. 1 (1963) pp. 136-40.
100. Møller, *Helstatens Fald*, vol. I, pp. 514-15.
101. *Ibid.*
102. *Ibid.* vol II, p. 52.

of 1864 she abandoned any pretence of preserving the integrity of Denmark, a policy which had been unswervingly adhered to since the reign of Nicholas I. She approved Bismarck's actions, thinking that in this way she could strike a blow at the revolutionary movement in Europe and the liberal movement in Denmark.[103]

In his work on Scandinavianism, Møller pointed out that Russia regarded this movement as one of the least desirable results of the Danish-German conflict and foughit in every way. In this, she enjoyed the support of Britain. If forced to choose whether Denmark should join the German Confederation or a Scandinavian Union, Russia would unhesitatingly have opted for the first alternative. Reflecting on political solutions to the crisis, Møller doubts whether a constitutional Helstat on the basis of the conditions of 1851-52 was possible and could have been put into effect. It required mutual trust between the Germans and the Danes, and this was lacking.

Møller's thesis that Russia abandoned Denmark in 1863-64 is opposed by P. von Linstow, who writes: '... current criticism of Russia for deserting Denmark must be repudiated'. He is also indignant at Møller for claiming that Russia bears the main responsibility for Bismarck's success. Linstow also criticises Møller for treating British and French policy much more leniently than Russian. In Linstow's opinion, 'the risk of French war resulting in the creation of a new Poland made an anti-French coalition the most exacting goal of the weakened Russia and of England as well'. But this thesis is unconvincing and is based on a very limited perusal of the sources, mainly official Prussian documents,[104] without reference to other basic sources, and completely ignoring any Russian sources. Linstow's sharp attack on Møller's work, in the form of categorical demands and complaints that, instead of attacking France, Møller attacked Russia, have little to do with scholarly debate.[105]

The well-known historian Troels Fink argues[106] that Russia, like France, behaved cautiously during the conflict in order to avoid a European war. Russia and Prussia were linked by common interests (the Polish question). Russia, like Austria, sincerely wanted Helstat to exist and Denmark to satisfy German demands within this framework. Russian passivity at the London Conference was due to the fact that Scandinavian tendencies underlay Danish policy. Russia did not want the North united under the aegis of Sweden. She remembered the attitude Sweden had taken during the Crimean War.

J. Vogt, in a work written during the Second World War to counter Hitlerite propaganda that Russia was the main threat to the existence of the Scandinavian countries,[107] treats the problem of Denmark and Russia in 1863-64 in an over-

---

103. *Ibid.* p. 153.
104. *Die Auswärtige Politik Preussens,* (APP) vols III and IV.
105. P. von Linstow, 'Bismarck. Europa og Slesvig-Holstein 1862-1866', *Historisk Tidsskrift,* vol. 78, no. 2 (1978) pp. 40-44.
106. Troels Fink, *Otte foredrag om Danmarks Krise 1863-64,* (Aarhus, 1964).
107. J. Vogt, *Rusland og Norden,* (Copenhagen, 1947).

simplified manner and ignores some of the facts. He claims that in 1863-64 Denmark renounced Russian help and instead associated herself with the Scandinavianism proclaimed by the Swedish King.[108] Russia had no interest in seeing Denmark become a vassal of Prussia, but Scandinavianism, in Vogt's view, was aimed at creating a block of northern states directed against Russia. Denmark was thus to blame for the consequences of her Scandinavian policy.

And finally there is John Nielsen's *1864 – Da Europa gik af lave,* which came out in 1987. The author has not paid sufficient attention to Russian policy towards the Danish-German conflict and has made no use at all of either primary or secondary Russian sources. The evaluation of Russian policy which he offers in this work in based on the books or articles by Neergaard, Linstow and Mosse.[109]

Turning to the first Swedish and Norwegian historians to deal with the problem of Russo-Scandinavian relations in 1856-64, mention should be made of Cecilia Bååth-Holmberg and H. Koht.[110] The former describes the attitude of the King (Charles XV) and society to the Polish question in 1862-63 and points out Russia's two-faced attitude to Denmark and the double game played by the Russian cabinet, which co-operated confidentially with Prussia under a cloak of neutrality. Cecilia Bååth-Holmberg argues that if Sweden-Norway had stood by Denmark she would have risked war with three powers – Austria, Prussia and Russia. The latter would have sent her forces into Finland. At the same time Russia claimed that she was interested in the integrity of Denmark and showed her dislike of a Scandinavian union. The Russian government's double game, with a pro-Danish official policy but *de facto* covert support for Germany, especially Prussia, was intended to compel Sweden-Norway to adopt a passive attitude to the Danish-German conflict. Thus, in her opinion, Russia's position in 1864 had a decisive influence on Stockholm's policy.[111]

Koht's valuable work does not tell us much about Russian policy. The author himself was conscious of this, writing in his introduction: 'Nur die russische Politik liegt noch heute vielfach im Dunkeln'.[112]

The studies by C. Hallendorff, *Illusioner och verklighet,* (1914) and E. Hedin, *Sveriges ställning i förhållande til Ryssland och västmakterna år 1863,* (1922) initiated research into Russo-Scandinavian relations in the middle of the nineteenth century. It was continued by C.P. Palmstierna, *Sverige, Ryssland och England 1833-55,* (1932), S. Eriksson, *Svensk diplomati och tidningspress under Krimkriget,* (1939) and *Carl XV,* (1954), A. Holmberg, *Skandinavismen i Sverige vid 1800-talets mitt (1843-1863),* (1946), and, to some extent, E. Gullberg, *Tyskland i svensk*

---

108. *Ibid.* p. 64.
109. A Review by E. Halicz, *Historisk Tidsskrift,* (1988), vol. 88, I. pp. 202-4.
110. Cecilia Bååth-Holmberg, *Carl XV,* (Stockholm, 1891), H. Koht, *Die Stellung Norwegens und Schwedens im deutsch-dänischen Konflikt, zumal während der Jahre 1863 und 1864,* (Christiania, 1908).
111. Cecilia Bååth-Holmberg, *Carl XV,* p. 444 and note.
112. H. Koht, *Die Stellung,* p. IX.

opinion 1856-1871, (Lund, 1952).[113] All these works take the same line in their assessment of Russo-Scandinavian relations. The lack of commitment to Denmark on the part of the Western powers, and fear of Russia, which was far stronger than the Scandinavian countries, together with the impossibility of adopting a hostile attitude towards Germany, led Sweden to take a neutral position during the war of 1864. 'Der Krieg 1864', says Gullberg, 'hatte Schweden in Gegensatz zu Deutschland gebracht. Und doch konnte es Schweden sich nicht leisten, Deutschland zum Feind zu haben. Schwedens Wehrwesen befand sich in schlechtem Zustande. Der Ausbau des schwedischen Wirtschaftslebens erforderte Kapital und vermehrte Handelsverbindungen'.[114]

What particularly influenced Manderström was Russia's pro-German policy, the fear that Russia might exact retribution against Sweden for her attitude during the Crimean War, and the pro-Polish policy of the King and the Scandinavinists during the Polish uprising of 1863.[115]

A. Jansson[116] provides a synthesis of Swedish foreign policy, taking account of new material concerning relations between Russia and Sweden, but he adds nothing to previously established conclusions. Swedish historians, namely K. Fellenius, C. Hallendorff, E. Hedin, D. Lundström, and recently L. Postén-Kowalska, are notable for their greater understanding of the connection between the Polish uprising of 1863 and Russo-Scandinavian relations in 1863-64.

The one Danish historian to examine this problem has been A. Olsen, Danmark og den polske opstand 1863, (1946), while in Norway there is only one work by R. Hammering Bang and F. Bull, *Norge og den polske frihetskamp,* (Oslo, 1937).

A much fuller presentation of the problem is given in my book *The 1863 Polish Uprising and Scandinavia. The Year 1863, The Turning-Point in Russo-Scandinavian Relations,* (Copenhagen, 1988).

In the Russian literature the first works concerning Denmark and the conflict with Germany appeared shortly after the end of hostilities in 1864. They were by V. Chudovsky and Akunin, and dealt mainly with the course of operations at the front, though Chudovsky also discussed the reasons for the war. He disapproved strongly of Prussian policy and declared himself on the side of Denmark, attacking German injustice and aggression. Chudovsky was an officer on the Russian general staff and expressed the views of military circles close to the Minister of War, D. Milyutin.

A different position was taken by the *Journal de St. Pétersbourg* in 1883 in an occasional article on 13 (1) March on the death of A. Gorchakov.

---

113. See also Lolo Krusius-Ahrenberg, 'Skandinavismens inställning till den slesvig-holsteinska frågan och Rysslands hållning till bägge vid det dansk-tyska krigets utbrott', *Historisk Tidskrift för Finland,* vol. 27, no. 1-2, (1942), pp. 1-35.
114. E. Gullberg, *Tyskland,* pp. 352-3.
115. See E. Hedin, 'Sveriges ställning till Ryssland och västmakterna år 1863, *Historisk Tidskrift,* vol. 42, no. 1 (1922), and Lolo Krusius-Ahrenberg, 'Skandinavismens inställning'.
116. A. Jansson, *Den Svenska utrikespolitikens historia,* vol. III, (1844-1872), 1961.

La crise polonaise a été le point culminant de la politique européenne et des erreurs de la politique napoléonienne .... Dans ces conjonctures, l'œuvre de l'unité allemande était inévitable. Cette question dix fois séculaire était mûre, aucun obstacle ne pouvait l'entraver. L'œuvre s'accomplirait-elle sous l'hégémonie de l'Autriche ou sous celle de la Prusse? Là était toute la question. Elle était urgente, car déjà en 1863 l'Autriche avait tenté de la résoudre en sa faveur. Le Prince Gortchacow essaya encore plus d'une fois de réunir les tronçons épars du concert européen qui seul pouvait prévenir ces graves complications au fond desquelles se cachait un redoutable inconnu. Il l'essaya pour sauver le Danemark, il l'essaya avant et après la guerre de 1866 pour maintenir la Confédération germanique placée en 1815 sous la garantie de l'Europe. Personne ne répondit à cet appel.

L'issue étant inévitable, la logique conseillait au prince Gortchacow de préférer l'Allemagne dirigée par la Prusse à l'Allemagne conduite par l'Autriche. Les relations de la Russie avec la première de ces deux puissances étaient bassées sur de vieilles traditions d'amitié et de solidarité vis-à-vis de la Pologne. Avec la seconde, elles auraient été entravées par les tendances catholiques, polonaises et orientales de la politique viennoise. D'ailleurs la force effective était du côté de la Prusse, et dans ces sortes de questions c'est un élément qu'un homme d'Etat pratique ne doit pas dédaigner ...

This article become an inspiration for Russian historiography, which did not deny Russia's pro-Prussian position in the years after the January Uprising, and during the 1864 war, but placed the blame for her attitude towards Denmark on Napoleonic France. It was also characteristic of Russian historiography to view the attitude of Russia to Denmark through the prism of the central problem, which was the question of the unification of Germany.

The first serious historical work which touched on the broader question of Russia's attitude to the Scandinavian countries after the Treaty of Paris was S.S. Tatishchev's book on Alexander II, a continuation of his previous study of Nicholas I.[117] In Tatishchev's view, friendly relations with Prussia had played an essential role in Alexander II's foreign policy ever since the meeting in Warsaw in 1859. Prussia was Russia's principal ally.[118] In the Danish-German conflict Gorchakov took Prussia's side to repay Prussian help for Russia in 1863.[119] Gorchakov was convinced, however, that this dismemberment of Denmark would lead to the rise of a greater Scandinavia which was contrary to Russian interests, and he was determined to oppose it with all the power at his disposal.[120]

Tatishchev also touched on other factors which influenced Russian policy, such as the peaceful intentions of Russia; and particularly Alexander II's friendship with the Prince Regent, later Kaiser Wilhelm I; the significance of his contacts with Bismarck; solidarity over the Polish question; and the desire to contain any out-

---

117. S.S. Tatishchev, *Imperator Aleksandr II. Ego zhizn' i tsarstvovanie,* (St. Petersburg, 1911) and *Vneshnyaya politika imperatora Nikolaya I,* (1887).
118. Tatishchev, *Imperator Aleksandr II,* vol. I, pp. 236, 376.
119. *Ibid.* vol. II, p. 48, In a more recent work, *Itogi i zadachi izucheniya vneshnei politiki Rossii,* ed. A.L. Narochnitsky, the view of an older Russian historiography, and that of some Western historians, that Russia 'repaid' Prussia for its attitude to the Polish uprising is criticised, as is their 'exaggeration' of the role of the Polish question in Russo-Prussian relations in 1864 and 1866 (p. 253).
120. *Ibid.* p. 49.

break of revolution in Germany and Europe generally. In connection with the last point, Alexander advised Bismarck to co-operate closely with Austria, to avoid misunderstandings, especially with France, and to act so as to prevent an alliance between Britain and France.[121] As we can see, Tatishchev was an apologist for Alexander II and atttributed to the Tsar a special role in the conduct of Russian policy. Yet Tatishchev, who justified Russian policy and neutrality in the Danish-German conflict, was convinced that this neutrality benefitted Prussia and that the break-up of Denmark was done without the least opposition from Russia:

> Thus, after the signing of the treaty of Vienna on 30 (18) October 1864, the Danish monarchy, whose integrity had been guaranteed by the great powers twelve years before, was broken up without the slightest opposition or protest from any direction.

And finally Tatishchev argued that the process of the unification of Germany by Prussia had been possible only thanks to Russia's consent and with her help.[122]

This point of view had been disproved by the Russian Ministry of Foreign Affairs.

According to a history of the Russian Ministry of Foreign Affairs for the period 1802-1902,[123] published by the Ministry of Foreign Affairs in 1902, as a result of the defeat of 1863, the great powers were not in a position to prevent the Prussian government, under Bismarck, from carying out its far-reaching plans. Russian international policy at this time was concentrating on central European affairs.

When relations between Denmark and the German states became aggravated at the end of 1863, Russia made efforts to persuade Denmark to make concessions, and this was the purpose of the mission led by O.I. Ewers. When these differences led to war, and when at the London Conference convened to make peace between the warring parties, Prussia and Austria declared that, as a result of the war, they were no longer bound by the peace treaties previously concluded with Denmark, the Russian emperor, who had thereby regained his original rights to part of Holstein, decided to transfer them to the Grand Duke of Oldenburg. During the conference, attempts were made to bring about an agreement between the two parties. At this troubled time, when Germany was in the grip of social disturbance, when there were fears in Russia of a renewal of the Polish uprising and of unpredictable moves by Napoleon III, meetings were held between Alexander II and the King of Prussia in Berlin, with the Emperor of Austria in Kissingen, and with the King of Prussia and the Emperor of Austria jointly in Karlsbad, all of which were evidence of a rapprochement between the three monarchs aimed at preventing general turmoil.[124]

As we can see in the light of this official account, even when Russian relations with the larger German states had deteriorated, it was not possible to conceal the

---

121. *Ibid.* p. 51.
122. *Ibid.* pp. 53, 376.
123. *Ocherki istorii Ministerstva Inostrannykh Del 1802-1902*, (St. Petersburg, 1902).
124. *Ibid.* pp. 143-44.

facts demonstrating Russia's pro-German position in 1864; but in the years of rapprochement with France, and the building of the Entente, Napoleon's France was no longer blamed for the events of the 1860s, as Gorchakov, for example, had done in his memoranda to the Tsar in 1864 and 1865.[125]

Lobanov-Rostovsky took a similar position to Tatishchev, emphasising the special importance of the Polish question and the 1863 uprising in the rapprochement between Russia and Prussia. He argues that even before the uprising, on the occasion of the Gotha Telegram of 24 September 1862, it transpired that Russia stood firmly beside Prussia:

Russia acquiesced to this proposal, thereby disappointing those Danes who had been hoping for Russia's support. They could not know that from now on in the Danish question Russia was going to take a stand with Prussia.

Now [after the outbreak of the Danish-German war] that the war was on, Gorchakov had no further interest in the matter beyond the desire to be agreeable to Bismarck and to repay to Prussia the debt contracted at the time of the Polish rebellion.[126]

As far as the matter of putting forward Prince Oldenburg was concerned, this, as he puts is, 'was not displeasing to Bismarck, who, wishing to annex the Duchies to Prussia, was opposed to the Augustenburg venture ... The situation was now so completely dominated by the Iron Chancellor that the other powers were forced to become mere onlookers'.[127]

Another Russian historian, B.E. Nolde, maintains that as early as 1860 Gorchakov, in contrast to previous governments which had been guided by legitimacy, showed no interest in the question of the duchies in his conversations with Bismarck, and that the latter felt even then that the St. Petersburg cabinet would take 'an attitude of polite indifference to his plans concerning the Danish duchies'.[128]

Among Soviet historians, only three have really dealt closely with our subject, S. Lesnik, L. Roots and L.I. Narochnitskaya.[129] A characteristic feature of Soviet historiography is frequent use of the pronouncements of Marx and Engels, especially on nineteenth century history. Following Marx, Soviet historians judge all problems associated with the history of Germany in the 1860s from the viewpoint of what they call the progressive process of the unification of Germany, and, as a result, critical evaluation of Bismarck, the creator of that unified Germany, has generally been lessened, even though, as they say, he did it by undemocratic methods. This also affects their assessment of the Danish-German conflict and the role of Russia.

Soviet historians following Engels quote his statement that Denmark's encroachments upon the Holstein constitution and the attempts at a forcible Danification of Schleswig made the German bourgeois indignant ... The Russian Tsar had been won over to Bismarcks's side by the service the latter had rendered in 1863

---

125. For the texts see *Krasnyi Arkhiv,* 1939, no. 2, pp. 105-11.
126. A. Lobanov-Rostovsky, *Russia and Europe 1825-1878,* (Ann Arbor, 1954), pp. 233, 235.
127. *Ibid.* p. 235.
128. B.E. Nolde, *Petersburgskaya missiya Bismarka 1859-1862,* (Prague, 1925), p. 266.
129. See Conclusion p. 545ff.

as executioner of Poland ... Since it was a Prussian political tradition to use a favourable situation 'ruthlessly to the extreme' in Herr von Sybel's words, it was self-evident that under the pretext of freeing the Germans from Danish oppression about 200,000 Danes of North Schleswig were annexed to Germany ... In 1864 the Duchy was wrested from Denmark with tsarist permission.[130]

But they are not inclined to quote other statesments by Marx about the close connection between the Polish question in 1863 and Russia's policy towards Prussia in 1864, nor about the perfidious role which Russia played in the Schleswig-Holstein question in 1864 or even before that at the time of the signing of the 1851 protocol and the 1852 Treaty of London.[131] It was only really A. Kan who called the 1852 treaty essentially reactionary, which in Soviet terminology indicates disapproval.[132]

The omission of these particular pronouncements by Marx is not accidental and is associated with the Kremlin's official political line, imposed by Stalin in 1934-41 and maintained even today, which seeks to justify and whitewash the actions of tsarism in the field of foreign policy.[133]

Lesnik was the first Soviet historian to attempt to show what Russian policy in 1863-64 really was in the introduction to the selection of Russian diplomatic documents from the Russian Foreign Policy archives which he edited.[134] He argues that without Russia's help, Bismarck could not have carried out his plans and that from the start of the conflict Alexander II was on Prussia's side. The Tsar gave his agreement to the entry of Prussian and Austrian troops into the duchies and persuaded Britain to accept the situation. In acting in this way he was guided by the desire to block the plans and activities of Prince Augustenburg and the German revolutionary party. Throughout the conflict, Russia's principal consideration was the maintenance of peace in Europe. Gorchakov, says Lesnik, did everything he could to be helpful to Bismarck in the implementation of the latter's plans, and did much to reassure Britain about Prussian actions. As events unfolded, Russian policy became more and more pro-Prussian and cleared the way for Bismarck. But as Bismarck went from success to success he changed his tune, became more and more arrogant, and resorted to blackmail, continually frightening Russia with the possibility that he might conclude an alliance between Prussia and France. Russian policy, Lesnik concludes, led to the seizure of the duchies by the German states.

---

130. F. Engels, The Role of Force in History, Marx and Engels, *Selected Works,* vol. III, (Moscow, 1973), pp. 396-7. *The Foreign Policy of Russian Czarism,* (1890), p. 48.
131. Marx and Engels, *Werke,* vol. 30, (Berlin, 1964), pp. 374, 408, 414, 666-7.
132. A.S. Kan, *Istoriya Skandinavskikh stran,* (Moscow, 1980), p. 121.
133. See Stalin's letter to the members of the Politbureau on 19 July 1934, published in *Bol'shevik,* vol. XVIII, no. 9, (May, 1941), pp. 1-5. In this letter Stalin criticised Engels' theses about the foreign policy of tsarism. Engels first published his article on 'The Foreign Policy of Russian Tsarism' in *Die Neue Zeit,* vol. VIII, (1890), pp. 145-54 and 193-203. In English see Marx and Engels, *The Russian Menace to Europe,* ed. by Paul W. Blackstock and Bert F. Hoselitz, (Glencoe, Ill, 1952), pp. 25-55.
134. *Krasnyi Arkhiv,* 2 (93), 1939. That is when the negotiations for a Soviet-German agreement were carried on.

This point of view, however, which in my opinion was more or less objective,[135] was revised after the second world war by L. Roots in her work on the European powers' policy towards the Schleswig-Holstein question, which is really the only study published in the USSR devoted entirely to this matter. The work was based predominantly on sources published in the West and did not introduce any new Russian material. Nor did the authoress make use of any of the Scandinavian literature, not even Danish, although the problem is after all a part of the history of Denmark. Her presentation is comprehensive but it is far from original. The authoress draws unstintingly on the works of other historians such as Steefel, when she discusses the problem of the London Conference, but does not indicate her debt to the American historian. From beginning to end the work is a defence of the policy of Gorchakov and Russia, in accordance with the foundations of official Soviet policy after the second World War. Roots does not deny that Russian policy favoured Prussia, but she links this pro-Prussianness with the person of Alexander II and his gratitude for Prussia's attitude to Russia during the Polish events of 1863 and, earlier, to the Treaty of Paris (an obvious error, as when Prussia was finally invited to the Paris Conference in 1856 she played no part in it). She defends Gorchakov's policy, however, maintaining that he was under pressure from the Tsar, that he personally did not trust Bismarck, and that he appreciated the threat from Prussia as Russia's western neighbour. (Note that here she wrongly claims that Gorchakov spoke of the western frontier, when what Gorchakov wrote was that a naval power is not born quickly.) Roots emphasises that Russia's policy was determined by her internal and international situation after the defeat in the Crimean war. The consequences of the Treaty of Paris, the Polish question, and British antagonism in Asia caused Russia to be cautious. Neutrality and support for Prussia had their limits, in Roots' opinion, and Bismarck did not succeed with his provocative tricks designed to draw Russia into the war with Denmark.

Russia wanted to avoid war with the Western states, so as not to find herself in the same situation in the Baltic as she had been in the Black Sea after the Crimean War. For the same reason, too, she tried hard to secure co-operation between all four powers and to obtain Britain's agreement to this. She was similarly ready to agree to a British proposal for a demonstration of naval strength in the Baltic, argues Roots, though without giving any sources to support this claim. In the light of the documents with which I am familiar the position was quite the opposite. Gorchakov did everything he could to prevent such an anti-Prussian demonstration taking place and never for one moment had any intention of participating in it.

Roots also discusses the question of Scandinavianism and stresses that Russia took a negative attitude towards it. Scandinavianism, according to her, was purely an aspiration to hegemony on the part of Sweden, a chauvinistic political trend, and 'pan-Scandinavianism' or 'ultra-Scandinavianism' – she uses both these terms – were not only anti-Russian but anti-German too.

---

135. See *Itogi i zadachi*, pp. 253-4.

A notable feature of the whole of the Soviet historiography is an extremely critical attitude to Scandinavianism, which is treated in a very one-sided manner as a nationalistic and expansionist political trend. Soviet historians see it as a movement which arose in bourgeois circles in Denmark in the 1820s and 1830s in reaction to the backwardness of Scandinavia and Scandinavian isolationism, and aimed at creating a single Scandinavian market for the purposes of countering competition from Britian and Germany. This is the picture given by, among others, V.V. Pokhlebkin.[136]

Scandinavianism is also criticised by A.S. Kan, who sees it as a cultural and above all political movement, the aim of which was the unification of Scandinavia, and which, despite its liberal tinge, served to justify the annexation by Denmark of Schleswig and thus stood in the way of German national unification. The objective of Scandinavianism was the merger of Sweden and Norway in a union, which meant the imprisonment of Norway by Sweden and the recovery of Finland by Sweden. In Kan's opinion the desire to recover Finland was contrary to the national aspirations and interests of the latter, and it is only in the field of cultural life that he sees any positive contribution from Scandinavianism. Kan also blamed Sweden for the deterioration of her relationship with Russia in the period from the Crimean War to the 1860s.[137]

Roots linked the deterioration in Danish-Russian relations with the policy of the Eider party and the signs of anti-Russian activity – the meeting of 20 March 1863 and Denmark's participation in the diplomatic campaign in the defence of Poland in May 1863.[138] There are many oversimplifications and factual mistakes in his work. The Eider party, in his opinion, sought the incorporation of Schleswig into Denmark, wishing to free itself of competition from Holstein industry,[139] and as early as 1858 the government, when changing the constitution in respect of Holstein and Lauenburg, included Schleswig in Denmark (sic! E.H.).[140] She treats the decree of 30 March 1863 as subsequent proof of the final incorporation of Schleswig.[141] Nor is it at all objective to argue that the British government and press, particularly *The Times,* sought to provoke Denmark and push her into war against Germany,[142] and encouraged Prussia to conquer her. The principal aim of the British cabinet in proposing action in defence of Denmark to Russia was to bring about a deterioration in relations between Russia and Prussia.[143]

Gorchakov's policy in 1863-64 is defended even more zealously by Narochnitskaya, who attacked German and French historians, (Sybel, Brandenburg, Sorel,

---

136. V.V. Pokhlebkin, 'Skandinavskii region. Mezhdunarodnoe polozhenie v proshlom i nastoyashchim', *Voprosy istorii,* 1980, No. 2.
137. A. Kan, *Istoriya,* pp. 119-20, *Istoriya Shvetsii,* ed. Kan, (Moscow, 1974), pp. 396-98.
138. Roots, *Slesvig-Golshtinskii vopros,* (Tallin, 1957), pp. 97-98.
139. *Ibid.* p. 25.
140. *Ibid.* p. 27.
141. *Ibid.* p. 50. Many historians have made the same mistake, including M. Florinsky, *Russia. A History and Interpretation,* (New York, 1953), vol. II. p. 962.
142. *Ibid.* p. 109.
143. *Ibid.* p. 219.

Charles-Roux, Debidour) for their thesis[144] that the tsarist government from the start wanted Prussia to succeed and did what Bismarck wished.[145] She argues that Gorchakov did not want the conflict to be extended because he was aware that Russia would not be in a state to counteract the complications to which this could give rise, the consequences of which would be the disturbance of the existing order in Europe. The tsarist government, in her opinion, realised that the detachment of the duchies from Denmark and their merger with Prussia would alter the balance of forces and change the situation in the Baltic to Russia's disadvantage. Narochnitskaya's view is that Gorchakov did not trust Bismarck but could not oppose him lest he endanger the co-operation between Russia, Austria and Prussia, which he wanted Britain to join as well. The claim that Russian diplomacy saw through Bismarck's game was put forward by E. Tarle and F. Rotshtein.[146]

Narochnitskaya rejects what she calls the bourgeois theory about the decisive importance of personal relations between the Tsar and King Wilhelm of Prussia in strengthening Russo-Prussian co-operation, that is to say, she rejects the role of the so-called subjective factor in her assessment of Russian policy. Russia's policy, in her view, followed from the interests of Russian landowners and capitalists and was a product of the country's domestic and international situation after the Crimean War. Russia had an interest in co-operation with Prussia because of the difficulties in Poland, such co-operation being essential for her in view of the rapacious plans of Napoleon III and the revolutionary movement in Europe.

Narochnitskaya maintains there was no preliminary or secret alliance between Russia and Prussia in 1863 and 1864. Russia did not want to get involved in a war, urged Prussia not to do anything which might lead to an Anglo-French rapprochement, and herself avoided everything which might complicate her relations with the large German states. It is wrong, she argues, – and here she is attacking the French historians – to claim that Prussia owed its success solely to Russian neutrality, since in her opinion the neutrality of France and Britain was even more crucial to Prussia's success. Britain, in her view, was interested in strengthening Prussia as a bulwark against the democratic movement.[147] Narochnitskaya clearly underestimates the significance of the Polish question in international relations in 1863-64, presents an oversimplified picture of Russo-French relations, attacks French historiography for its allegedly oversimplified view of relations between Russia and Denmark and the German states in 1863-64, and, finally, defends the policy of Gorchakov.

The positive feature of Narochnitskaya's work, which I would like to mention, is that it includes an analysis of the various political trends in Russia, based on the Russian press. This analysis shows that although there was general support for the

---

144. Narochnitskaya, *Rossiya i voiny Prussii,* (Moscow, 1960), pp. 276-77.
145. *Ibid.* pp. 37-8, 47, 276-7.
146. E. Tarle, *Istoriya diplomatii,* Vol. I. (Moscow, 1941), p. 490; F. Rotshtein, *Iz istorii prussko-germanskoi imperii,* (Moscow, 1948), p. 72.
147. *Itogi i zadachi,* p. 254.

government's peace efforts, part of the press took a different position from Gorchakov on foreign policy questions and that virtually all (apart from the extreme conservative faction, which we may call the 'German party'), had numerous reservations about the policy of supporting Prussia and Bismarck in the way Gorchakov did and showed understanding and sympathy for Denmark in her struggle. During the war, in fact there were growing expressions of sympathy for Denmark from broad circles of public opinion.[148]

Similar views to Narochnitskaya's are put forward by V.G. Revunienkov and N.S. Kinyapina.[149] Revunienkov argued that in 1864 Russia was not guided by Prussian interests but acted in accordance with the interests of Russian landowners and capitalists, and that her policy was the product of the economic, financial and military situation, internal difficulties and the need to carry out reforms. He maintains that the rapprochement with Prussia was partly brought about by differences between Russia and Britain, and Russia and France. Because of these powers' anti-Russian attitude Gorchakov could not actively oppose Bismarck, although he condemned his aggressive policy. Revunienkov also criticises the view expressed in the nineteenth century by B.N. Chicherin[150] that Gorchakov had no definite policy line in 1864, did not understand Prussian policy, and, repaying Prussia for her attitude in 1863, permitted the dismemberment of Denmark. Revunienkov regards this criticism as one-sided and places the main blame for the pro-Prussian policy on the Tsar. Gorchakov, on the other hand, distrusted Prussia completely, was inclined to seek an understanding with France, and gave evidence of his anti-Prussian attitude in 1863 when he caused the *de facto* annulment of the Convention of Alvensleben (this was actually done mainly by Bismarck – E.H.), although owing to the attitude of the Tsar he could not torpedo it or prevent its signature.

Kinyapina's enumeration of the reasons for Russia's neutral policy in 1864, beside the desire to localise the war, fear of international isolation and attachment to conservative principles, also includes the point that Gorchakov entertained hopes of Prussian help in his efforts to cancel the clauses in the Treaty of Paris concerning the neutralisation of the Black Sea. Only Prussia supported Russia's eastern policy, because she needed Russian assistance for her policy of unification of Germany. This support, like the links at the time of the Polish uprising, were of real value to Russia.[151]

Some of these arguments were not new. They were put forward by A.S. Eruzalimsky in the introduction to the edition of Bismarck's letters to Gorchakov which he published in 1933,[152] where he argued that the Russo-Prussian alliance

---

148. In 1958, in *Istoriya SSSR*, vol. II, pp. 735-56, Narochnitskaya described the position of Russia towards the Danish-German war as neutrality favouring Prussia, and the reason for this war, among other things, the belief that Prussia could help Russia in her efforts to secure changes in the provisions of the Treaty of Paris. She wrongly gives the place of signing of the treaty of 30 October 1864 as Prague.
149. V.G. Revunienkov, *Pol'skoe vosstan'e 1863 g., i evropeiskaya diplomatiya*, (Leningrad, 1957), I.S. Kinyapina, *Vneshnyaya politika Rossii vtoroi poloviny XIX veka*, (Moscow, 1974).
150. B.N. Chicherin, *Moskovskii universitet*, (Moscow, 1929), p. 130.
151. Kinyapina, *Vneshnyaya politika*, p. 42.
152. Pisma O. Bismarka A.M. Gorchakovu. *Krasnyi Arkhiv*, vol. 61, 1933.

concluded in 1863 had even greater strategic than it had diplomatic significance and that, furthermore, Prussian help with the cancellation of the clauses in the Treaty of Paris could only be secured by the enormous political advance which Russia's friendly neutrality represented at the time of her three battles with Denmark, Austria and France.[153]

The works of Roots, Narochnitskaya, Kinyapina and Revunienkov defend Gorchakov's policy and attack the views of other Soviet historians who do not act as apologists for the Russian minister's policy, such as Tarle, Rotshtein and Eruzalimsky. Tarle stressed the importance of Polish events for the development of friendly relations between Alexander II and Wilhelm, and argues that they were the reason why Bismarck, despite Gorchakov's suspiciousness of him, did not have to worry about Russia's reaction in the Schleswig-Holstein affair. Rotshtein concluded that Bismarck had achieved the subordination of Russian diplomacy to himself; both the Tsar and his government yielded to Bismarck in order to avoid extreme measures.[154] Eruzalimsky argued that in return for his help in 1863 Bismarck demanded a reward from St. Petersburg in the form of Russian neutrality in Prussia's war against Denmark. The key to this war lay in Russia's hands, and Bismarck himself recognised this in his letter of 5 July 1864 to Gorchakov: 'from the European point of view', wrote Bismarck at the moment when the future fate of Schleswig and Holstein was in the balance, 'everything depends on whether Russia throws her weight behind the Grand Duke [Oldenburg - E.H.] or confines herself to withdrawing from the dispute'.[155] In his 1968 work, Eruzalimsky[156] said that in 1864 Russia decided, after some hesitation, to withdraw from the dispute between Prussia and Denmark. Russia adopted a neutral position. Dynastic considerations were reinforced by strategic ones. Russia reckoned that a strong Prussia would be able to oppose Austria and that, with a secure western frontier, thanks to Prussia, she would be able to continue her policy of conquest in Asia.

Soviet historiography is thus, in principle, in no doubt that Russia's neutrality in 1864 aided Prussia considerably in the defeat of Denmark. There is dispute about whether Russian policy was the consequence of her own internal situation (mainly the bad state of her finances and her military weakness) and the unfavourable constellation of European forces, or whether Russian policy was mainly influenced by dynastic considerations. There is discussion of the real objective of Gorchakov's policy. To what extent did he influence the final decisions of Alexander II? Was Russian diplomacy already aware then of the aims of Bismarck's policy, and if

---

153. 'The political rapprochement between Prussia under Bismarck and tsarist Russia,' wrote Eruzalimsky, 'went so far that on some matters, particularly the common fight against the Polish national liberation movement, the relations established between the two countries did not differ greatly from those which normally exist between two sections of one and the same department,' *Ibid.,* p. 5. Cf. *Iz zapisnoi knizhki arkhivista. Bismark o polozhenii v Evrope v 1868 g.* ed. A.S. Eruzalimsky, *Krasnyi Arkhiv,* (1936), vol. 74, p. 193.
154. Rotshtein, *Iz istorii,* pp. 71, 72, 74.
155. *Krasnyi Arkhiv,* vol. 61, p. 14.
156. A.S. Eruzalimsky, *Bismarka diplomatiya i militarizm,* (Moscow, 1968).

so why did it assist him, even though in the long run his policy could threaten Russia's interests in the Baltic?

During the last thirty years there has been a clear tendency in Soviet historiography to justify Gorchakov's policy and to lay the blame for mistakes on the Tsar, who imposed his decisions on his minister. Gorchakov, according to S.K. Bushuev,[157] could not act in any other way, as he did not want to run the risk of making more enemies.[158] S. Semanov[159] holds a similar opinion, claiming that there were fundamental differences between the Tsar's position and his minister's policy and that Gorchakov, in contrast to Alexander II, was decidedly hostile to the Prussian attack on Denmark, doing everything he could to persuade Prussia to agree to a compromise settlement of the dispute. In this, however, he encountered resistance from Berlin and could not press Bismarck more strongly lest the latter should conclude an alliance with France.[160] Bushuev also argued that Gorchakov's difficulty was the result of the fact that he was caught in the crossfire between Britain and France.[161] Both historians lay the blame for the course of events and the desertion of Denmark on the western states, especially France.

On one issue there is no difference at all between the old Russian and the modern Soviet historiography. This is the attitude to Scandinavianism. Faced with the dilemma of Scandinavianism or Germanism, the choice falls on the latter. Russian and Soviet historians both consider that Russian policy was dominated by a fear that Denmark might join a Scandinavian union, placing the Sound and the Belt in the hands of a single state, and that this factor had a decisive influence on Gorchakov's policy in 1863-64.

As our review of the literature shows, debate continues about the assessment of Russia's policy towards the fundamental problems which Scandinavia, and particularly Denmark, faced in the years 1856-64. In both the Western and the Russian literature there are basic differences of view involving ideological, methodological, political and scholarly aspects. I have in mind here the insufficient familiarity with the sources, especially the Russian ones.

Historians try in various ways to answer the questions, what was the key to Russia's decidedly pro-German policy, why did she abandon her old ally Denmark in a moment of crisis for the latter, to what extent was Russia's position influenced by 'obligations' to Prussia because of the latter's attitude since 1853, and was Russia, at a time of major reforms, in a position to intervene militarily and in this way influence the course of events? They also consider whether Russia merely supported Prussian policy uncritically – as F. Rotshtein argued – or whether she was pursuing an independent policy in conformity with her own opportunities and interest and gave her approval *nolens volens* to Bismarck's policy for fear of the

---

157. S.K. Bushuev, *A.M. Gorchakov*, (Moscow, 1961).
158. *Ibid.* p. 92.
159. S. Semanov, *A.M. Gorchakov, Russkii diplomat XIX veka*, (Moscow, 1962).
160. *Ibid.* pp. 78-82.
161. Bushuev, *A.M. Gorchakov*, p. 92.

spread of the conflict and revolutionary war in Europe, (Narochnitskaya). The discussion also deals with the question of when the change in Russia's policy on relations with Berlin really took place – in 1859 or not until 1863 – or was there an unchanging policy towards Prussia from 1856 to 1864, with variations in nuance in individual years but not in essence?

There is dispute on the role of the Tsar and his influence on Russia's foreign policy, and on whether there were really fundamental differences between him and Gorchakov. There is also a diversity of views on the role of Brunnow in 1863-64; were there differences of opinion between him and the minister, particularly during the London Conference, and if there were, then of what kind? This question is the topic of vigourous discussion in the German literature.

Clarification is required on the major problem of whether Gorchakov realised the consequences of a Prussian victory in 1864 – including the consequences of the growth of Prussian influence in the Baltic for Russia; and whether he believed what he declared officially, that such dangers did not exist for many years since naval power was not built up overnight.[162] Clarification is also needed on whether French or Russian historians are right in placing the main blame for the desertion of Denmark and its consequences not on their own government. On this last question there is also a diversity of view in Danish historiography, which is typified by P. von Linstow's criticism of the position taken by Møller.[163] Møller placed the main responsibility for the collapse of Denmark on Russia, while Linstow justified Russia's behaviour, explaining it by the argument that her internal situation made it impossible for Russia actively to assist Denmark. There are also differences among Danish historians about whether Denmark's participation in the diplomatic campaign in support of Poland affected Russia's attitude towards her, and, if so, to what extent. (Compare the differences between Thorsøe and Neergaard, on the one hand, and Møller on the other.)

Finally, there is dispute about whether Gorchakov gave his support to Prussia in 1864 because he saw a stronger Prussia as a force which, in the near future, would enable him to repudiate the clause in the Treaty of Paris restricting Russia's rights in the Black Sea.

While these are all genuine academic problems which deserve elucidation, it is certainly also necessary to reject the claims of some American historians that Gorchakov should bear the responsibility both for his short-sighted policy and for the development of events in Europe up to the outbreak of the First World War. This thesis, of course, was thought up not by historians but by certain British diplomats, notably Lord Redesdale.

---

162. Memorandum to Tsar Alexander II of 3 September (old style) 1865, *Krasnyi Arkhiv,* (1939), no. 2, pp. 105-11.
163. E. Møller, *Helstatens Fald,* vol. II, pp. 152-3.

1. Russian Foreign Policy after the Crimean War: Change of Strategy or merely Change of Tactics?

> "Es ist eine alte Geschichte
> Doch bleibt sie immer neu."
> H. Heine, Lyrisches Intermezzo

I

The Crimean War, and the military and diplomatic reverse which it brought for Russia, were undoubtedly a turning point in the country's history. Military defeat, on a scale unprecedented in Russia's history since the beginning of the seventeenth century, caused a deep convulsion inside Russia and had a substantial effect on the international constellation of forces. The gendarme of Europe, the mainstay of the Holy Alliance, had proved to be a colossus with feet of clay.

M. Reutern, a subsequent minister of finance, described Russia's image on the morrow of the defeat in the following terms:

Russland ging aus dem gewaltigen Ringen um die Krim ermüdet, mit enkräfteten Finanzen und einer Valuta hervor, deren Grundlage durch die Emission von 400 Millionen Kreditbilets zerrüttet war. Die moralische Autorität der Regierung war erschüttert, der Krieg hatte viele Mängel unserer Militär – und Zivilverwaltung aufgedeckt und auch jene dominierende Stellung erschüttert, die Russland seit der Zeit des Wiener Kongresses in Europa einnahm. Die Folge davon war im Ausland das Sinken unserer Autorität, im Innern der Reiches Misstrauen gegen die Kraft und Fähigkeit der Regierung.[1]

Almost all strata of Russian society were in agreement really in their assessment of the reasons for the defeat. On hearing the news of the fall of Sebastopol the Slavophile Ivan Aksakov wrote that the collapse was the result of the rottenness of tsarism. Another Slavophile, Yuri Samarin, considered that Russia had succumbed, not to foreign forces, but primarily because of the internal weakness of the country.[2]

The convulsion caused by the defeat, the bitterness, the blow to national pride and, above all, reflection on the reasons for the humiliation led to an upsurge of theorizing in Russia. Not only revolutionary democrats and liberals, but even conservative circles close to the court and the Tsar himself, realised that the introduction of reforms in virtually all areas of life was a necessity and that they had to be carried out as quickly as possible in order to save Russia from violent social upheavals if her strength and especially her military power were to be rebuilt.

---

1. Ed. and with a biographical sketch by W. Graf Reutern, Baron Nolcken, (Berlin, 1914), p. 17: Cf. Ch. Friese, *Russland und Preussen vom Krimkrieg bis zum polnischen Aufstand*, (Berlin and Königsberg, 1931), p. 10; Cf. also P.A. Khromov, *Ekonomicheskoe razvitie Rossii v XIX i XX vekakh, 1800-1917,* (Moscow, 1950) p. 214 and *Revolyutsionnaya situatsiya v Rossii v seredine XIX veka,* Collective monograph ed. by M.N. Nechkina (Moscow, 1962), (new edition 1978).
2. Cf. E. Halicz, *Rosyjski ruch rewolucyjny a sprawa polska w latach 1856-62* (Cracow, 1947).

'The Crimean War', A. Herzen wrote in his article 'War is a Pirate', 'was intended to damage Russia but in reality it benefitted her. The fetters which bound our feet were loosened and frayed during the war. The siege of Sebastopol was at the same time the beginning of the liberation of the peasants, a signal for thinking and fighting, and from this time on Russia will advance strongly along a broad road.' Pisarev expressed his feelings as follows: 'we felt pain from the blow, followed by the desire to put it behind us'.[3] M. Chernyshevsky was more sceptical, putting these words into the mouth of his hero, Volgin, in his story 'What is to be done?': 'If the allies took Kronstadt, little would happen; if they took Kronstadt and St. Petersburg, still little would happen; if they took Kronstadt, St. Petersburg and Moscow, then social and political reforms worth talking about would be introduced'.

'Society', wrote A. Kornilov,[4] 'has awoken from its long sleep, not only in the two capital cities but in the provinces too. People who hitherto did not read newspapers have begun to subscribe to papers and journals, articles on social and political problems and statistics illustrating the state of Russia have been appearing in the press. The previously sleepy provincial committees have come to life, discussion clubs and agricultural economic societies have sprung up, young people, especially in the universities, have moved to tackle the task of rebuilding Russia.' In St. Petersburg, wrote the historian K.D. Kavelin, social thought was developing and expanding in ever widening circles. 'Zemlya i Volya' (Land and Freedom), land to the peasants, abolition of serfdom, political rights for all strata of society, became the general slogans and targets, although the meaning and form of these ideas varied.

A new period began in the political life of Russia. The weakness of the liberals, the absence of a modern middle class, the demoralisation of the majority of the clergy, who had no prestige among the lower strata of society on the one hand, and a lack of civil freedoms on the other, favoured the development of the radical movement. This faction demanded that all the land be handed over to the peasants, immediately and without redemption payments, and called the whole of Russia 'to battle'.

This situation explains Alexander II's call for change in the serfdom law, by way of reform from above rather than waiting until the changes were carried out by the peasants themselves 'from below'. 'It is better to begin to abolish serfdom from above than to wait for it begin to abolish itself from below', declared the Tsar to the gentry of Moscow on 18 (30) March 1856.[5] This was followed by his appointment of a committee under the chairmanship of A.F. Orlov to examine the peasant question and work out a programme of reforms. Many years of struggle for peasant reform between the opponents of any reform and its advocates, between different groups of landowners, accompanied by bitter political battles, and

3. L. Plotkin, *D.I. Pisarev,* (Leningrad and Moscow, 1945), p. 20.
4. A. Kornilov, *Krest'yanskaya reforma,* p. 22.
5. Hugh Seton-Watson, *The Russian Empire, 1801-1917,* (Oxford, 1967), p. 335; S. Tatishchev, *Imperator Alexandr II,* (St. Petersburg, 1911), vol. I, p. 205.

pressure from the radical camp, as well as the peasants' unwavering fight for land, finally culminated in the Tsar's manifesto on the abolition of serfdom, issued on 19 February 1861.[6]

The peasant reform, by granting the peasants personal rights, was of great importance for the future economic development of Russia. The unlimited reservoir of free labour which resulted from the reform was one of the most fundamental preconditions of the economic development of Russia in the late nineteenth and early twentieth centuries.[7]

The abolition of personal serfdom in 1861 ushered in many other reforms. They were put into operation either by a single act of legislation, as in the case of the rural and urban local government reform, the judicial and military reforms, or by the issue of numerous statutes or decrees, as occurred with the reform of the school system, censorship and banking.

These reforms, which went on from 1856 until 1874, occupied the apparatus of government for almost twenty years, compelled it to concentrate on matters of domestic policy and placed enormous financial demands on the resources of the state, at a time when the state's finances were in dire straits.[8]

Although these reforms embraced practically all areas of life in Russia, they were limited in character, were carried out in an inconsistent and incomplete manner, and were based on a static view of affairs which frustrated the full modernisation of the country. As a result, the nature of the regime was not really affected. The principle of the absolute power of the Tsar, for example, was not infringed in any way, for no changes limiting the power of the autocrat were introduced. Nor was any basis for a representative or parliamentary system established, nor were changes made to the central executive. In fact, no institution resembling a government, in the modern sense of the word, was created, nor were any principles or statutes regulating the functioning of the central apparatus of power introduced.

All the reforms had one great common shortcoming, which could not be eliminated under the autocratic system prevailing in Russia: the reforms were introduced 'by the grace of the Tsar'. Paradoxically, they also really strengthened the power of the autocrat. Thus both domestic and foreign policy remained in the hands of an absolute ruler.[9]

---

6. *Polnoe sobranie zakonov Rossiiskoi Imperii,* Sobranie vtoroe, vol. 36, pt 1 (St. Petersburg, 1863), no. 36650, pp. 126-134.
7. M. Raeff, *Comprendre l'ancien régime russe. Etat et societé en Russie impériale,* (Paris, 1982), pp. 175-6.
8. Cf. I.S. Bloch, *Finansy Rossii XIX stoletiya,* (St. Petersburg, 1882); Khromov, *Ekonomicheskoe razvitie ...; Dietrich Geyer, Der russische Imperialismus. Studien über den Zusammenhang von innerer und auswärtiger Politik 1860-1914,* (Göttingen, 1977), J.F. Gindin, *Gosudarstvennyi bank i ekonomicheskaya politika tsarskogo pravitel'stva, 1861-1892* (Moscow, 1960).
9. Raeff, *Comprendre ...* pp. 175-6.

II

What shape did Russian foreign policy take following the Treaty of Paris? Even during the final phase of the Crimean War, particularly after the death of Nicholas I, the necessity for changes in the field of foreign policy was recognised. The moment Austria declared herself on the side of the coalition of Western countries, although militarily she remained neutral, the Holy Alliance collapsed. From the arbiter of Europe, Russia now became a country to which the victors dictated peace terms.[10] These terms were comparable to the conditions imposed on Prussia by Napoleon in 1807.

A change in the post of minister of foreign affairs was now the slogan of the day. Even circles close to the court thought that Nicholas I and his minister, Chancellor Ch. Nesselrode, had pursued an unsuitable policy which was contrary to Russia's interests. 'The Emperor Nicholas I', wrote A.F. Tyutcheva,

> played the role of police chief of Europe for twenty years, saw his mission as the guardian of law and order in the civilised world and sacrificed the interests of his country to this end. Russia paid dearly for wanting to play the part of police chief of Europe. We are hated, just as the police are hated everywhere. Nicholas I [in her opinion] misconceived Russia's historical mission, which is the unification of the Slavs. Russia's task is to fight, not for material, worldly interest, but for eternal ideals.[11]

> Governments betrayed us, nations hated us, and the order we established was disrupted, is being disrupted and will be disrupted, so our policy was not only harmful but generally unsuccessful too,

wrote the famous publicist M.P. Pogodin. He concluded that it was not possible to fight against the spirit of the times and there should be a fundamental review of Russian policy.[12]

This mood was recognised perfectly well by the ageing chancellor, who submitted his resignation after the fall of Sebastopol in November 1855. For the moment it was not accepted.[13] From the late autumn there was much thought in St. Petersburg about who should be the next minister. One thing seemed certain; that Nesselrode's place would be taken by a diplomat of Russian origin. This was a reaction to the policy of the previous period, when German names were predominant.[14]

Thus P. Brunnow, E. Stackelberg, A.F. Budberg and P. Meyendorff were out of the running. Among the diplomats of Russian origin Orlov seemed unacceptable to the Tsar because of his indecisive character. Panin was not liked by the Tsar and in addition was too conservative ('eine Art russischer Kreuzzeitungsmann'), Kiselev seemed to be too old, and A. Lobanov and V. Balabin, going by contemporary

---

10. E.A. Adamov, ed. *Sbornik dogovorov Rosii s drugimi gosudarstvami, 1856-1917,* (Moscow, 1952).
11. A.F. Tyutcheva, *Pri dvore dvukh imperatorov, Vospominaniya dnevnik 1855-1882,* (Moscow, 1928), pp. 35, 38, 112, 124. Cf. also A.V. Nikitenko, *Dnevnik,* vol. I, 1826-1857, (Moscow, 1955), p. 418.
12. The quotation is drawn from M.N. Pokrovsky, *Diplomatiya i voiny tsarskoi Rossii v XIX stoletii. Sbornik statei.* (Moscow, 1923), p. 177.
13. W.E. Mosse, *European Powers ...,* p. 70.
14. Cf. Constantin de Grunwald, *Trois siècles de diplomatie Russe,* (Paris, 1945), p. 200.

age criteria, were too young. From January onward the name of A.M. Gorchakov began to be heard more and more frequently as the most probable new minister.[15] In the opinion of some diplomats accredited to the Russian court the Grand Duchess Olga, daughter of Nicholas I and the then wife of Prince Carl, heir to the throne of the Kingdom of Württemberg, who had been friendly with Gorchakov for many years when he served in Stuttgart, drew the attention of her brother Alexander II to him.[16]

The recall of Prince Gorchakov from Vienna, or more accurately his summoning from Vienna, where he was performing the duties of ambassador, was interpreted in St. Petersburg as an important event and he was expected to assume a very high position. 'Everybody was glad at this news, although it was unofficial', wrote A.F. Tyutcheva, the daughter of the poet and diplomat, a lady of the imperial court well attuned to the moods prevailing there, in her diary for 25 March 1856, in connection with the mass celebrated on the occasion of the conclusion of the Treaty of Paris and rumours of the departure of Nesselrode and the arrival of Gorchakov.

If we now finally succeeded in renouncing our old mistakes and openly and joyfully allying ourselves with France, abandoning Germany, directing all our sympathies towards the Slav countries, and giving up the role of policeman to other states, we could still make up for everything,

she continued.[17]

I would like to draw attention to the passage about rapprochement between Russia and France. It shows that this idea was not foreign to circles close to the court even before Gorchakov arrived in the capital.

In diplomatic circles too the recall of Gorchakov was thought to be connected with forthcoming promotion.[18] Gorchakov himself, in a letter to Olga Nikolaevna sent to her from Vienna on 21 February (4 March), expressed satisfaction with the fact that the emperor wanted to see him in St. Petersburg, but it does not follow from the contents of the letter that he already knew that such a high appointment awaited him.[19] On 18 April Alexander accepted the resignation submitted by Nesselrode (the first resignation, submitted in November, had been temporarily refused[20]) and the next day it was known definitely that Gorchakov would take his place. The appointment was to be announced officially during the Easter holiday, as was the

15. Seymour to Clarendon, Private, 15 January 1856; Mosse, *The European Powers* ... p. 70; B.E. Nolde, *Rossiya i Evropa v nachale tsarstvovaniya Aleksandra II*, (Prague, 1925), pp. 39-50.
16. O. Plessen, in telegram no. 33, 1 May (19 April) 1856, in Depecher, Rusland, Rigsark., Copenhagen. A similar opinion was expressed by N.V. Meshchersky, *Moi vospominaniya*, vol. 1. (St. Petersburg, 1897), p. 296.
17. Tyutcheva, *Pri Dvore* ... p. 112; S. Semanov, *A.M. Gorchakov. Russkii diplomat XIX v.* (Moscow, 1962), p. 112.
18. O. Plessen, Rusland Depecher 1854-56, no. 27, 2 April (21 March) 1856, Rigsark. Copenhagen. W. Esterhazy to Buol-Schauenstein, 15 (3) April 1856, H.H.S. Archiv, Vienna, P.A. X, Rusland, Karton 43, 1856, Berichte, Weisungen, Varia, N. 24B.
19. H.S.A., Stuttgart, G. 314 Bü 1851-1871.
20. Mosse, *The European Powers* ... p. 70.

nomination of Prince Ivan Tolstoy, who was to take the place of L.G. Senyavin, as deputy minister.[21]

The Tsar's edict of 17 April (old style) indicated Gorchakov's previous service, his abilities and the experience he had gained during his diplomatic service, and in particular his role during the Vienna negotiation in 1855. The Tsar emphasised that he saw him as a diplomat who would contribute to the strengthening of peace and the establishment of friendly relations between Russia and all states.[22]

The appointment of Gorchakov, descended from an old aristocratic family which could trace its genealogical roots back to the time of Rurik, educated at the lycée in Tsarskoe Selo, once a friend of Pushkin and many others who later took part in the Decembrist movement, regarded by Nesselrode and A.K. Benckendorff[23] as a liberal and consequently for many years holding only second-rank positions in the diplomatic service, was received with mixed feelings in Russia despite his intellectual qualities.

Liberal circles and some Slavophiles placed new hopes in him. They saw him as a Russian diplomat, a continuation of the Russian diplomatic tradition going back to the time of Peter the Great. Gorchakov's view that Austria was Russia's political opponent suited them; they supported Gorchakov's argument about the need for rapprochement with France; and were pleased with his view that the Treaty of Paris was an onerous and shameful document and that every effort should be made to change it, particularly in the points concerning the restrictions imposed on Russian control of the Black Sea and the Balkan peninsula. The responsibility for signing the treaty was placed on Nesselrode. Gorchakov, on the other hand, was seen by this camp and the reform camp as a person who would be capable of recovering Russia's lost authority in the international arena.[24]

Conservative circles, on the other hand, received the appointment of Gorchakov unfavourably and in the ministry of foreign affairs itself only really A. Jomini and F. Tyutchev, who was close to Gorchakov, welcomed the appointment of the new minister, regarding it as an important event. 'More than at any time', said Tyutchev, 'he was a man who was necessary and irreplaceable for the country.[25]

Diplomats of the Nesselrode school expressed decidedly negative views of him, mindful of the opinion of the former chancellor, who thought that he should not hold any important position. Budberg expressed his dislike of Gorchakov in a letter

---

21. H.H.S.A., P.A. X, Rusland, Karton 43, 1856, Berichte, Weisungen, Varia, 1856, I. Teil 3059/2886, Raport télégraphique, 19 Avril 1856, Chiffre, and no. 26 A, B, 22 (10) April.
22. Cf. O.K. Bushuev, *A.M. Gorchakov*, (Moscow, 1961), pp. 73-4.
23. The head of the Third Department, which was established on 3 July 1826.
24. Cf. P.V. Dolgorukov, *Peterburgskie ocherki. Pamflety emigranta 1860-1864* (Moscow, 1934), p. 148 ff; J. Klaczko, *Deux Chanceliers. Le Prince Gortchakof et le Prince de Bismarck*, (Paris, 1876), p. 105; E. Tarle, *Krymskaya voina*, vol. II (Moscow, 1950), p. 302; *Istoriya diplomatii*, vol. I, (Moscow, 1941), pp. 455-6; *Sbornik dogovorov Rossii s drugimi gosudarstvami, 1856-1917*, (Moscow, 1952), pp. 23-39; S. Goriainov, *Le Bosphore et les Dardanelles*, (Paris, 1910), p. 143; Semyanov, *A.M. Gorchakov*, pp. 45-61; W. Baumgart, *Der Friede von Paris 1856*, (Munich and Vienna, 1972), p. 98 ff; E. Schüle, *Russland and Frankreich 1856-1859*, p. 4 ff.
25. Bushuev, *A.M. Gorchakov*, p. 74, *Russkii Arkhiv*, 1905, vol. 7, p. 482.

to the chancellor's son. 'C'est nous autres qui paierons les pots cassés. Cette nomination va produire une impression détestable à l'étranger', he wrote.[26]

To some extent he was right, particularly where the attitude of British diplomats was concerned. 'Every Russian complains of Gortchakoff's appointment', wrote Cowley to Clarendon from Paris on 29 April 1856. Evidently he too had heard the opinions of Russian conservative circles.[27] In Britain Gorchakov's appointment was indeed ill-received, partly because of the negative picture of him given by some British diplomats.[28]

According to G.H. Seymour, who observed him at his post in Vienna, Gorchakov was unsuitable for the position of minister.

> It is, indeed, well known that Gortschakoff's approach was emotional, dramatic, 'feminine' and inspired by an almost pathological vanity ... As a companion Prince Gortschakoff has all the necessary qualifications, – as a minister he will involve himself in constant difficulties. He talks profusely and very well, – but it is not in his power to keep silent – a talent possessed in so eminent a degree by his predecessor Count Nesselrode,

Seymour reported to Clarendon on 11 June 1856.[29]

'Causeur brillant, mais plus brillant que fécond', E. Delessert, a French tutor to Gorchakov's sons, who knew him very well', wrote in 1856.[30]

Among the diplomats accredited to St. Petersburg the predominant view initially was either favourable or to reserve judgement. Count Ch. Morny, who was appointed ambassador to St. Petersburg in the summer and was close to Napoleon III, and with whom Gorchakov had held discussions on his own initiative in Vienna in 1855 – discussions broken off, incidentally, as a result of the intervention of Nesselrode – expressed the most positive opinion of Gorchakov, although even he noted the minister during conversations 's'animant par degrés et disant quelque fois des choses plus vives qu'il n'a l'intention de les dire'.[31]

Morny was particularly satisfied with the atmosphere he found at the court and with Gorchakov's assurance that he would seek to establish good relations with France and cherished 'une grande admiration et un goût personnel' for the Emperor of the French.[32] Morny also assured A. Walewski that 'notre position ici est excellente avec tout le monde et qu'il dépend de l'Empereur de déterminer l'usage qu'il en va faire'.[33]

A positive impression of Gorchakov, and particularly of his political ideas, was

---

26. *Lettres et papiers du Chancelier Comte de Nesselrode.* (Paris), vol. XI, p. 132, letter of 20 April 1856.
27. Mosse. *The European Powers* ... p. 72.
28. *Russkii arkhiv,* 1905, vol. 7, p. 482.
29. Mosse, *The European Powers* ... pp. 72-3.
30. *Le Prince Gortchakoff Ambassadeur Russe à Vienne. Souvenirs intimes (1853-54).* (Paris, 1856), p. 21.
31. A.M.A.E, Paris, Corresp. polit. Russie, 1856, vol. 212, St. Petersburg, 15 August 1856, Direction Politique, no. 2 Morny to Walewski, k. 119.
32. *Ibid.*
33. *Ibid.* Cf. also Semanov, *A.M. Gorchakov,* pp. 45-61; *Istorya diplomatii,* vol. 1, p. 455; Friese, *Russland und Preussen* ... pp. 13-22; Schüle, *Russland und Frankreich* ..., pp. 4-16.

also reported by Charles Baudin, the French chargé d'affaires in St. Petersburg, Baudin had met Gorchakov by chance in the course of his journey from Szczecin to St. Petersburg when Gorchakov was returning from a short visit to Vienna, and for the three days on the way had had the opportunity to listen to the minister's arguments on the topic of Russian foreign policy.[34]

Gorchakov's appointment was very warmly welcomed by the Danish ambassador, O. Plessen.[35] The Piedmont chargé d'affaires, Filipo Oldoini, wrote about him positively, considering him one of the most distinguished Russian statesmen, a man of liberal convictions, whose anti-Austrian inclination (a result of the difficulties in which he had been involved during his mission in Vienna), made him a natural friend of Italy. He was that always, Oldoini stressed, even at critical moments.[36] Even the Austrian ambassador cherished hopes of an improvement in relations with Russia, since not only was Gorchakov's language in dealings with Austria more moderate, but he himself expressed a wish to come to Vienna and establish better relations with the Viennese court.[37] W. Esterhazy also perceived a similar inclination to renew good relations with Vienna in Alexander II.[38]

From the start of his ministerial career Gorchakov was a controversial figure, both in Russia and abroad. As the years passed, however, negative opinions of him began to predominate. 'Zwei Seelen wohnen in Gortchakoffs Brust', on the one hand *homo liberalis,* as schoolfellow of A. Pushkin and V. Zhukovsky, discussing philosophical problems with N. Gogol, discoursing on matters of humanity and civilisation, and as such not acceptable to the conservatives, in Nikolaus Kreuzzüge's view. On the other hand he was the politician, who, despite a hatred for Austria, was opposed to her being submerged in Slav radicalism, favoured the maintenance of the German Confederation exclusively as a defensive structure, and also wanted to localise the war in 1859. That was how he was described by Leopold von Schlözer, secretary at the Prussian embassy in St. Petersburg, in his diary for 24 (12) May 1859.[39]

No one questioned that Gorchakov, who had entered the diplomatic service in 1820, taken part in many international congresses and fulfilled various diplomatic functions over a period of more than thirty years in Britain, Prussia, Italy, Würtemburg, Frankfurt and Austria, possessed great experience and complete familiarity with the international situation. 'His wit and oratorial gifts made him known as a brilliant diplomat'. But from the beginning the attitude towards him and his policy was critical. It is understandable that Russian conservative circles

---

34. A.M.A.E., *ibid.* Baudin to Walewski, 10 July 1856. Excerpts from the report are quoted by Schüle, *Russland und Frankreich ..,* p. 153.
35. Depecher Rusland, No. 33, 1 May (19 April) 1856.
36. Trois missions en Russie, 1856-57, 1859-60, 1862-63, pp. 29-30. Rapporti Della Legazione in Pietroburgo. Pacco 204. Archivio Storico-Diplomatico. Min. Degli Affari Esteri. Rome. Cf. Giuseppe Berti, *Russia e stati italiani nel Risorgimento,* (Moscow, 1959), pp. 706-7.
37. Esterhazy to Buol. 1 May (19 April) 1856, H.H.S.A. as above, no. 27, A-F.
38. *Ibid.* no. 26, in code, 18 May.
39. Kurd von Schlözer, ed. Leopold von Schlözer, *Petersburger Briefe ...* (Stuttgart, Berlin and Leipzig, 1923), pp. 133-4.

and the so-called 'Deutsche Strömmungen', in which Tyutchev numbered, among others, P. Meyendorff and his wife, the sister of the Austrian minister F. Buol, and minister N. Sukhozanet, K. Chevkin, V. Panin and V. Dolgorukii, should take a negative attitude to the pro-French course set by Gorchakov. All those mentioned above were pro-Austrian and thought that the rulers of Poland should not support the national aspiration of other nations. This problem arose in especially acute form on the eve of the war in 1859, in which Russia was bound by treaties with France and took a neutral, but essentially pro-French, position, thereby contributing to the victory of France and Piedmont over Austria.[40]

Gorchakov was also to encounter criticism from these circles in connection with his policy on the Polish question in 1861-62.[41] Government circles, especially the minister of internal affairs, P. Valuev, would criticise him for his lack of interest in the domestic problems of Russia; the military, and particularly the war minister, D. Milyutin, for his negative attitude to the programme of reforms in the military field, and for what they were to regard as his excessive caution concerning the war ministry's policy of seeking to extend Russia's possessions in Central Asia. In the ministry of foreign affairs itself some of the staff would criticise their minister for, as M. Katkov put it, transforming the ministry of foreign affairs into 'inostrannoe ministerstvo russkikh del' (the foreign ministry of Russian affairs) and, as a 'grand seigneur', giving it an aristocratic character, leading to a situation where French became the language of discussion in the ministry and, when a telegram had to be translated into Russian, nobody in the ministry apart from E. Feoktistov was able to do it.[42] Finally, according to N. Barsukov, there was dissatisfaction originating from court circles, since Gorchakov 'did not bow to them and made no attempt to please various highly placed and prominent boors'.[43]

The main reasons for the critical attitude, however, even of those close to Gorchakov, were his character and his attitude to people. He was a talented, experienced diplomat, a master of words, especially adept at composing telegrams and documents, but he was not, according to B. Nolde's account, a great statesman who would move boldly towards the aim he had defined, and he was hampered by his personal character traits.[44] 'He was quick, lively, approachable ... But I did not find much substance beneath this outward friendliness ... His tenuous liberalism was essentially caused by his lack of any firm views', said the prominent liberal B. Chicherin, a professor at Moscow University, who remained in regular contact with him.[45] Chicherin criticised Gorchakov because 'guided by chance moods,

---

40. Tyutcheva, *Pri dvore ...*, p. 193; F.I. Pigarev, Tyutchev i problemy vneshnei politiki tsarskoi Rossii', *Literaturnoe nasledstvo*, 19/21 1935 (Moscow), p. 221.
41. Tyutcheva, *Pri dvore ...*, p. 16.
42. E.M. Feoktistov, *Za kulisami politiki i literatury, 1848-96*, (Leningrad, 1929), p. 62; Dietrich Beyrau, *Russische Orientpolitik und die Entstehung des Deutschen Kaiserreiches 1866-1870/71*, (Wiesbaden, 1974), p. 23; Pigarev, 'Tyutchev i problemy ...', p. 203; Meshchersky, *Moi vospominaniya*, vol. I, p. 303.
43. N. Barsukov, *Zhizn' i trudy M.P. Pogodina*, vol. XV, (St. Petersburg, 1901), p. 104.
44. B.E. Nolde, *Vneshnyaya politika. Istoricheskii ocherk.* (Petrograd, 1915), pp. 91-2.
45. B.N. Chicherin, *Vospominaniya, Moskovskii universitet*, vol. I, (Moscow, 1929), p. 73.

superficial amicability and, in particular, resentful ambition, he was capable of sacrificing the most essential interests of our fatherland. He demonstrated this by co-operating in vastly strengthening Germany, which was contrary to the elementary demands of politics, which forbid allowing any excessive increase in the strength of neighbours'.[46] 'Egoism, delusions of greatness, thirst for publicity, avarice, lust – these were the minister's principal characteristics'.[47] He also had an unceremonious attitude towards his subordinates.[48]

In A. Polovtsev's opinion Gorchakov's chief features were his extraordinary and unlimited boastfulness, his surrounding himself with worthless creatures (originating predominantly from his own family) and his rapacious accumulation of money, so that, although when he began his ministerial career he had nothing beside his salary, he was able to leave his son a fortune estimated at 8 million rubles. Polovtsev added that he knew of no other example of a Russian official behaving in this way and not being accused of corruption.[49]

Tyutcheva called Gorchakov 'le narcisse de l'écritoire' and V. Meshchersky emphasised that behind the flow of verbal fireworks, as he described them, there was no depth of thought.[50] 'Sotte vanité et puérilité' was Tyutcheva's comment on Gorchakov's behaviour when he ostentatiously expressed his disappointment because the congress for which he had prepared at the beginning of 1860 did not take place, and she added that Gorchakov had behaved 'like a dog whose tail had been cut off' ('Gorchakov pokhoze na sobaku kotoroi otrubili khvost').[51]

Although there was not even transparent flattery, which he could mistakenly have thought sincere, a peak was reached in 1863 during the Polish uprising, when he boasted even to the Tsarina Maria Alexandrovna: 'Je suis l'homme le plus populaire en Russie', and immediately controlled himself and added: 'après l'Empereur'.[52] When he had guests at his house, he ordered the waiter to bring a handkerchief from the market at Nizhny Novgorod with his likeness on it, and boasted: 'Vot moya luchshaya nagroda' and 'narod menya znaet i lyubit menya'.[53,54]

There was indeed a moment when he became popular, when he unceremoniously rejected the note from the three Western powers concerning the Polish question (26 June).[55] But as Polovtsev said, there would not have been such a note (the one on 1 (13) July) but for the assurance of Brunnow that Britian would never move. Up to that moment Gorchakov was in consternation, and after receiving the note 'sbilsya s tolku'.[56,57]

---

46. *Ibid.*
47. J.S. Kartsev, 'Za kulisami diplomatii', *Russkaya starina,* (1908), no. 1, p. 90.
48. *Ibid.*
49. A.A. Polovtsev, *Dnevnik gosudarstvennogo sekretarya,* (Moscow, 1966), vol. I, p. 87, vol. II, p. 175.
50. Meshchersky, *Moi vospominaniya,* vol. I, p. 279.
51. Tyutcheva, *Pri dvore ...,* pp. 21-22.
52. Feoktistov, *Za kulisami ...,* pp. 63-64.
53. That is my best reward. The nation knows and loves me.
54. *Ibid.* p. 64.
55. Thun to Rechberg, 30 (18) September 1863, no. 37 B. Reservé. H.H.S.A. Vienna, Karton, 54.
56. Went out of his mind.
57. K. Pigarev, 'Tyutchev i problemy ...', p. 203; Polovtsev, *Dnevnik ...,* p. 87.

The main contributor to the popularisation of Gorchakov in 1863 was the editor of *Moskovskie vedomosti*, M. Katkov, a well known enemy of the Poles. Gorchakov himself continually spoke about national policy, the legal rights and national interests of Russia, but frequently these were only fine phrases. He presented himself as an ardent supporter of the freedom of the press but was very sensitive to even the slightest remarks which appeared there concerning him personally.[58]

His vanity, combined with envy, was particularly evident in relation to O. Bismarck, whom Gorchakov liked to regard as his disciple. 'J'espère que mon cher Raphael n'oubliera pas son Peruggino', he was reputed to have said when bidding Bismarck farewell.[59] These traits in Gorchakov's character are perhaps best illustrated by his own words to Bismarck: 'Si je me retire, je ne veux pas m'éteindre comme une lampe, qui file, je veux me coucher, comme un astre'.[60] His greatest dream was to be the chairman at a European congress, which he partially achieved as a member of the Russian delegation to the Congress of Berlin in 1878. After much manipulation and effort he succeeded in convincing the Tsar that his participation was essential, as Milyutin ironically noted in his diary.[61] Really only his confessor left behind an apologetic view of Gorchakov.[62] As the years passed the diplomatic corps, especially in St. Petersburg, formed a more and more critical opinion of Gorchakov, who suffered increasingly from delusions of grandeur and continually sought to become the arbiter of Europe, so much so that he became an object of ridicule. 'Le Prince Gortchakoff est vain comme un paon', was the impression he made on the Bavarian ambassador, M. Perglas.[63] The British diplomat Lord Redesdale also could not fail to note these conspicuous characteristics.[64] '... Vaniteur a l'excès, au plaisir de briller son esprit' was the description found in the otherwise friendly picture of Gorchakov painted by an unknown person to Baudin, which the latter passed on to Walewski.[65]

A more and more negative impression was produced by the Russian minister on Austrian diplomats accredited to the court of the Tsar.

Le Prince Gortchakoff est de nouveau entré dans un de ces paroxismes d'ébullition, qui le privent complètement de ce sang froid raisonné, de se calme réfléchi, sans lesquels la passion a beau jeu se rendre maîtresse de la nature de l'homme.

58. Feoktistov, *Za kulisami* ..., pp. 67-68. Pigarev: *Ibid*. p. 203.
59. *Dnevnik D.M. Milyutina*, vol. I, (Moscow, 1947), p. 226, 27 November 1874; Cf. also Bülow, *Denkwürdigkeiten*, vol. III, based on E.H. Sumner, *Russia and the Balkans, 1870-1880*, p. 22.
60. Pigarev, 'Tyutchev i problemy ...', p. 200.
61. *Dnevnik* ... vol. III, (Moscow, 1950), p. 60.
62. A.I. Bazarov, in *Russkii arkhiv*, (1896), no. 1, pp. 328-350.
63. Perglas to Maximilian II, no. 143, 5 August (24 July) 1863, in *Russland 1852-1871. Aus den Berichten der Bayerischen Gesandtschaft in St. Petersburg*, ed. by B. Jelavich (Wiesbaden, 1963), p. 113.
64. Lord Redesdale, *Further Memories*, (London, 1917), pp. 289, 292, 296.
65. 15 July 1858. A.M.A.E. Paris. Mémoires et documents. Russie 1858-1862, Vol. 45, 'Notes confidentielles sur les principaux personnages de l'Empire de Russie 1858' contains descriptions on ninety-nine persons occupying key positions in Russia. Quoting this document, Baudin added that the person who produced the document was perfectly familiar with the matters concerned although he did not belong to the offical hierarchy and his views were independent of the influence of ministerial or bureaucratic coteries.

wrote Szechenyi in connection with Gorchakov's reaction to the events in Montenegro in 1859.[66] We can also find this ironical remark:

La célèbre phrase du Prince Gortchakoff 'La Russie se recueille' [taken from the note sent by Gorchakov to Russian representatives abroad after he assumed office as minister] n'a jamais charactérisé la situation d'une manière plus frappante, qu'elle ne le fait dans le moment actuel. Malheureusement, qu'elle se recueille en silence et dans la retraite la plus absolue, car le Prince ne donne presque plus signe de vie. Il n'a encore quitté son refuge de Peterhof, que pour se rendre quelques jours a Hapsal [Gorchakov's birthplace - (E.H.)] auprès de l'Empereur.[67]

This was perhaps revenge for Gorchakov's recent aphorism: 'L'Autriche n'est pas un état, ce n'est qu'un gouvernement', which certainly was unfavourably received in Vienna.[68] 'Etant lui-même d'une vanité sans bornes', 'un homme d'une vanité aussi incroyable', lack of polical principles, tendency to rash treatment of serious matters, something which was expressed by Gorchakov's own maxim 'qu'il faut sacrifier les principes pour sauver quelque chose du naufrage' – such are the phrases to be found in the report of the newly appointed Austrian ambassador, F. Thun. 'Il a été flatté par de belles paroles et se voit déjà dans son imagination – grâce au conseils qu'on lui demande de tout côté – l'arbitre du sort de l'Europe', considered Thun.[69]

Revertera expressed the same idea in his report to Rechberg: 'The idea of playing an eminent role in diplomacy and of seeing his name shine beside the most eminent men of his epoch always has a large place in the schemes of the Russian minister'.[70] Austrian diplomats also held Gorchakov mainly responsible for the failure of Russo-Austrian relations to improve.

Comme homme d'état, ne m'inspire aucune confiance – je dirai plus – aucune estime ... Ce ministre - si je ne me trompe – est un homme d'une telle vanité personnelle, d'une telle confiance dans sa superiorité, et dans son infaillibilité, que toute dicussion avec lui devint parfaitement impossible ou au moins complètement inutile, et même dangéreuse. D'après ma conviction – added Thun – c'est un homme d'état très superficiel, avec des opinions très fausses, un imbu du libéralisme moderne ... On ne saurait lui contester un certain esprit qui peut éblouir pour un moment, mais qui n'approfondit jamais rien.[71]

Austrian diplomats were also the first to draw attention to the fact that Gorchakov, 'par sa position personnelle et le prestige de son esprit et de son éloquence exerce une notable influence sur les opinions de l'Empereur, son Maître, et par consé-

66. 22 (10) May 1859, H.H.S.A., Vienna, 526, Nachlass Rechberg, P.A.I. 2 Teil.
67. *Ibid.* 19. (7) August 1859.
68. Eckhardt, vol. I, p. 80, Klaczko, *Deux Chanceliers*, p. 46. A similar view about Austria was previously expressed by Czech intellectuals F. Palacky and K. Havlicek during the 1848 Revolution. On 27 May Havlicek declared: "L'Austriche n'est plus un État, car chaque nation à l'intérieur de cet État s'oppose à une autre ...". (Bernard Michel, *La mémoire de Prague,* (Paris, 1986), p. 67. See also p. 93 about Palacky's point of view.)
69. Reports from Thun and Revertera, 13 (1) February 1860, 17 (9) March 1860, 16 (4) May 1860 and 28 (16) January 1861. H.H.S.A. P.A.X, Rusland Karton 48, 50.
70. H.H.S.A., P.A.X. Varia de Russie. Privatbriefe aus Petersburg, 13 (1) January 1860, and no. 22 B, 16 (4) July 1862, Karton 52.
71. *Ibid.* no. 19. Confidential, 7 April (26 March) 1861, Karton 50.

quent, aussi sur les affaires, et de otêr, de l'autre'.[72]

The British envoy similarly attributed to Gorchakov motives other than a desire to transact meaningful business. Napier wrote that the Russian foreign minister 'delights to make a stir to occupy the public attention and to conceal the real weakness of his country in a flourish of activity.[73]

In this analysis it would be impossible to overlook the opinion of Bismarck, who was in close contact with Gorchakov when the two represented their governments at the All- German Assembly in Frankfurt and afterwards in St. Petersburg, where Bismarck served as ambassador from 1859 to 1862. The first impression which Bismarck reported was undoubtedly negative, expressing himself in a letter to Leopold Gerlach on 21 April 1854 as follows: 'Gortschakoff ist ein feierlicher, ungelenker Hans Narr, ein Fuchs in Holzschuhen, wenn er pfiffig sein will'.[74] In another letter of the same date he spoke of Gorchakov as 'ein eitler und feierlicher Herr'.[75] In his memoirs, written forty years after, the first thing he recalled about Gorchakov was his exaggerated vanity ('seine ihn beherrschende Eitelkeit').[76]

In spite of these reservations co-operation between them worked out well.[77] Bismarck had the opportunity to renew the acquaintance in 1857 during Gorchakov's visit to Germany, but their closer co-operation began in 1859 when Bismarck found himself in St. Petersburg. Then he was able to get to know the personality of the Russian minister better. His daily contact with Gorchakov did result in a heightened appreciation of Gorchakov's abilities as a diplomat. In time he came to consider him a talented and experienced statesman of the highest integrity. Bismarck once even defended Gorchakov's personal integrity in a conversation with the British ambassador.[78]

Bismarck recognised Gorchakov's outstanding intelligence, and admired his unusual capacity for hard work. He discovered that Gorchakov was free of any political dogmatism, and was in fact a man willing to try new ideas. Moreover he felt a strong desire to please public opinion.[79] So, despite reservations concerning Gorchakov's personality, Bismarck regarded him as a capable diplomat. Bismarck's attitude to the Russian minister is perhaps best described by Zechlin:

72. Esterhazy to Vienna, 3 January 1857 (22 December 1856), no. 2 Reservé H.H.S.A., P.A.X. Berichte, 1857, Karton 44. Cf. Thun to Rechberg, nos. 6 A-E 28 (16) January and no. 19, 7 April (26 March) 1861, Karton 50.
73. Napier to Russell, no. 339, 6 July 1862, PRO FO 65/605.
74. *Briefe an General Leopold von Gerlach*, ed. by Kohl, (1896), p. 145 in *Die Gesammelten Werke, (G.W.)*, XIV/I, p. 354.
75. Letter to Manteuffel, *G.W.*, I, p. 441.
76. *G.W.*, XV, pp. 147 and 150.
77. Dieter Hillerbrand, *Bismarck and Gorchakov: A Study in Bismarck's Russian Policy, 1852-1871*, University Microfilms International, (Ann Arbor, Michigan and London, 1969), pp. 71-2.
78. Bismarck's confidential report to Schleinitz, 11 April 1861, *G.W.*, III, p. 216.
79. See Bismarck to Schleinitz, 14 June 1860, *G.W.* III. p. 68, and 11 April 1861 and 28 June 1861, *G.W.* III, pp. 214-5, 264; Bismarck to Bernstorff, 11 December 1861, *G.W.* III, p. 305; Bismarck to the Prince Regent, 27 April 1859, *Die politischen Berichte des Fürstens Bismarck aus Petersburg und Paris, 1859-1862*, ed. by L. Raschdau, vol. I, (Berlin, 1920), pp. 30-31. Cf. also E. Zechlin, *Bismarck und die Grundlegung der deutschen Grossmacht*, (Darmstadt, 1960), p. 77; Hillerbrand, *Bismarck and Gorchakov*, pp. 116-8.

Gortschakow war schon so, wie Bismarck ihn sah, 'der beste Kopf im amtlichen Russland', 'ein glänzend befähigter Künstler', der 'mit Eleganz und Würde' gymnastische Vorstellungen gab, die im Grunde 'Sham-fight' waren, 'zu lebhaft, um weitsichtige und verwickelte Pläne mit steter Erwägung aller einwirkenden Momente festzuhalten', und 'von mannigfachen sich kreuzenden Einflüssen aus den Richtungen gedrängt, die er selbst vielleicht vorziehen möchte.[80]

It is something of a paradox that J. Klaczko, who severely and fervently criticised Russian policy in the 1860s, gave Gorchakov the best testimonial he ever received, not just in the West European but in the Russian literature too. Furthermore, his assessment of Gorchakov influenced the historiography of the subject.[81] For this reason it is worth quoting him *in extenso*.

Phénomène également nouveau en Russie, ce ministre tient non pas seulement à la faveur de son souverain, mais bien aussi à celle de la nation; il ménage l'opinion publique de son pays, il la soigne, il la flatte même parfois, et elle le paye de retour –

wrote Klaczko, almost warmly, of Gorchakov, placing him in the ranks of the greatest diplomats of the nineteenth century.[82]

He continued:

En 1856, après le congrès de Paris, le choix du prince Gortchakof au même poste fut, nous ne dirons pas imposé, mais certainement indiqué à l'empereur Alexandre II par la voix du peuple ou, si l'on aime mieux, par celle voix des salons qui ne laissait pas à ce moment de prendre de plus en plus un accent populaire. Aussi, dès son début a l'hôtel de la place du Palais, l'ancien l'élève de Tsarskoe-Selo, se distinguat-il par des allures libérales et des avances faites à l'esprit public qui durent parfois bien étonner son prédécesseur encore en vie, et en possession du titre honorifique de chancelier. Pour la première fois, un ministre russe eut des ''mots'' non seulement pour les salons, mais pour les salles de lecture et les bureaux des journalistes, de ces mots qui allèrent droit au cœur de la grande dame et du gentilhomme campagnard, de l'humble étudiant et du superbe officier de la garde.

Son aphorisme sur l'Autriche[83] fit le tour de toutes les Russies; un autre aphorisme, emprunté à une circulaire, vint bientôt transporter la nation: la phase célèbre sur ''la Russie qui ne boude pas, mais qui se recueille'', semblait être dictée par l'âme même du peuple et lui arracha un cri d'enthousiasme. C'était alors, on s'en souvient, le réveil de l'esprit russe après une longue période de compression; les journaux, les recueils périodiques inauguraient leurs joyeux ébats; les écrivains, les hommes de lettres, commençaient à prendre une importance auparavant inconnue: Alexandre Mikhaïlovitch, le diplomate qui a de tout temps montré du goût et de la sympathie pour la littérature russe, l'ancien condisciple de Pouchkine, passa pour l'homme d'État patriote aux yeux des Pogodine, des Axakof, des Katkof, etc.[84]

---

80. Zechlin, *Bismarck und die Grundlegung ...*, p. 77.
81. It was accepted by, among others, E. Ollivier, C. Grunwald, and S. Tatishchev and in Soviet historiography that Klaczko's influence can be detected in the works of Yakubovsky, Bushuev, Semanov and Kinyapina. The works of Semanov and Bushuev, especially the latter, have been criticised as superficial. *Itogi i zadachi ...*, p. 260-1.
82. Klaczko, *Deux Chanceliers ...*, p. 105.
83. L'Autriche n'est pas un état, ce n'est qu'un gouvernement.
84. *Ibid.* pp. 106-7.

The reason why I have devoted so much space to the question of the character of Gorchakov is that his personality exerted an essential influence on the policy of his country, and his individuality similarly affected the making of decisions. The opinions I have cited from contemporaries, many of whom had direct contact with Gorchakov, are often contradictory, as we have seen, and it is not easy, though I believe it is possible, to form our own judgement of the helmsman of Russian foreign policy.

The positive features of his personality were to a considerable extent counterbalanced by his character traits and his manner, and his extraordinary egocentricity and unrestrained egoism were frequently the main motive force for his actions, particularly in his latter career. All this had an adverse effect on the style of operation and the effectiveness of the work of his ministry. These traits influenced his decision making and they diminished the standing of his office in the eyes of foreigners. Perhaps the best picture of this tangle of contradictions is given by the Danish journalist J. Hansen on the basis of an account obtained, he says, from a French diplomat who was extremely well versed in the intricacies of Russian policy.

Quelques critiques que l'on puisse adresser au vieux chancelier russe, on ne peut certes lui refuser une grande, une haute intelligence, des opinions libérales et un profond sentiment de la dignité et des intérêts de son pays. Esprit essentiellement généralisateur, il possède, développée à un degré vraiment exceptionnel, la faculté de saisir d'un mot, d'un moindre fait, toutes leurs significations, toutes leurs conséquences les plus lointaines. Il embrasse une situation d'un coup d'œil, et aime, comme il le dit lui-même, les grandes lignes. Par contre, il déteste les détails. Aussi en laisse-t-il le soin à son adjoint. Bon nombre de personnes en Russie, même parmi les intimes du prince, lui ont reproché et lui reprochent encore de s'accrocher au pouvoir, de s'y éterniser, comme ces vieilles chanteuses qui ne peuvent pas vivre loin du feu de la rampe. Selon l'élévation de leur esprit, les uns attribuent cette persistance à un sentiment d'avarice, à la soif d'amasser de très-forts émoluments, dont il ne dépense pas la dixième partie: d'autres, au besoin de jouer un grand rôle: d'autres enfin à une jalousie incroyable qui lui fait prendre en grippe quiconque – hier le général Ignatieff, aujourd'hui le comte Pierre Schouvaloff – se trouve, au moment de ses violents accès de goutte, porté sur les rangs pour le remplacer ... je suis – conclude Hansen – du nombre de ceux qui pensent, qu'il a surtout obéi en cela à un sentiment, beaucoup plus noble, beaucoup plus élevé.[85]

The behaviour and manner of Gorchakov were as far removed as they possibly could be from what Ch.M. Talleyrand considered appropriate for a minister of foreign affairs.

Il faut en effet qu'un ministre des affaires étrangères soit doué d'une sorte d'instinct qui l'avertissant proprement l'empêche avant toute discussion de jamais se compromettre. Il lui faut la faculté de se montrer ouvert en restant impénétrable, d'être réservé dans les formes de l'abandon, d'être habile presque dans le choix de ces distractions, il faut que sa conversation soit simple, variée, inattendue, toujours naturelle et parfois naïve, en un mot, il ne doit pas cesser un moment, dans les 24 heures, d'être ministre des affaires étrangères ...[86]

85. J. Hansen, *Les coulisses de la diplomatie. Quinze ans à l'étranger 1864-1879,* (Paris, 1880), pp. 344-5. (Conversation avec un Russe en décembre 1878).
86. Quoted from: Heinrich Wildner, *Die Technik der Diplomatie. L'art de négocier,* (Vienna, 1959), p. 104.

If we were to use the criteria which, in Max Weber's opinion, distinguish great personalities, namely 'passion, a feeling of responsibility and the sense of proportion', then, although Gorchakov did not lack some measure of these qualities, he did not possess them to a sufficient degree to be classed among the truly great personalities.

His personality denied him the greatness of which he dreamed. For Gorchakov diplomacy was a game and an art, but not a vocation. He lacked that true and complete devotion which was a characteristic of Bismarck, for example. 'He was not a great statesman moving boldly towards the objective he had determined. He was a professional diplomat, who throughout his life was not engaged in real action but in writing notes and preparing for talks with foreign ambassadors', wrote Nolde, perhaps a little too harshly, but correctly.[87] True, he did it *cum amore* and managed to evaluate the political situation in which Russia found herself after 1856 realistically. But his choice of political line and tactics were not original – nor, more importantly, were they consistent. He wanted to be seen as a liberal in Western Europe, while in Russia he won the laurels for pursuing a chauvinistic great power policy reminiscent of the country's traditional policy in the previous period. He was proud of this popularity, which he owed in large measure to M. Katkov and *Moskovskie vedomosti*.

The issue of personal prestige was always the most important one for him and he placed personal interest above everything, 'un ministre ambitieux, jaloux de sa gloire ou de son prestige personnel'.[88] Egoist, intriguer, vain, at times almost a caricature in his behaviour, Gorchakov did not inspire confidence in his subordinates, to say nothing of the diplomatic corps,[89] and his attitude and conduct could not fail to detract from Russia's international authority.[90] He dreamed of becoming the arbiter of Europe without having either any real basis for this in the political situation of his country or in the personal qualities which could have predestined him to occupy such a position.

III

There is no question that a fundamental change occurred in decision making in the field of foreign policy between the reigns of Nicholas I and Alexander II. The very fact that Gorchakov spoke with pride of national policy, that he stressed the identity of 'Gosudar i Rossiya' and used both terms in dispatches, showed that something had changed, and this was not just playing with words.[91] From the start

---

87. Nolde, *Vneshnyaya politika ... and Bosfor i Dardanele ...* (Petrograd, 1915), pp. 91-2.
88. *Journal de St. Pétersbourg*, I (13) March 1883, the day after Gorchakov's death was of a different opinion.
89. Seton-Watson, *Disraeli, Gladstone and the Eastern Question*, (1935), S. Bradford, *Disraeli*, (1982), p. 490.
90. Later B. Disraeli called him 'that old coxcomb'.
91. *Russkaya starina*, vol. 40, p. 168; Friese, *Russland und Preussen ...*, p. 28.

Gorchakov's position in relation to the Tsar was undoubtedly much stronger than Nesselrode's in relation to Nicholas I. This was only partly the result of the fact that the Tsar concentrated mainly on domestic affairs and the process of reform. Chiefly it was because Alexander II had no experience of international affairs and was not the same type of personality as Nicholas I. There was thus a fundamental difference between Nesselrode's conception of his position as a minister who was the executor of the Emperor's will and did not dare to expound his own views, and that of Gorchakov, who was convinced of his own superiority over the Tsar as far as familiarity with international affairs went and who consequently sought to impose his ideas on Alexander II, using appropriate methods. This feature was perhaps best caught by the Austrian ambassador, Thun:

Il est vrai – Thun reported to J.B. Rechberg – que l'Empereur Alexandre n'a pas la même initiative dans les affaires comme son père, mais d'un autre côté l'influence du Prince Gortchakoff est aussi d'une toute autre nature que celle du Comte Nesselrode. Chez ce dernier on pouvait être sûr qu'il rendrait exactement compte à son souverain de tout ce qu'on lui avait dit, et qu'il laisserait à celui-ci de décider, en se bornant à exprimer consciencieusement son opinion, tandis qu'avec le Prince Gortchakoff on peut être tout aussi sûr qu'il n'en profitera qu'à son avantage, et qu'il se gardera bien de faire à son souverain un exposé impartial, si cela ne convient pas à ses intentions, de manière que l'Empereur Alexandre ne voit malheureusement que par les yeux de son Ministre.[92]

In Thun's opinion Gorchakov had removed able and educated people of principle from the Tsar to such an extent that Alexander discussed matters of foreign policy only with him and, as a result, knew only as much as his minister chose to tell him. Furthermore, Gorchakov took care to work at influencing the Tsar's thinking and sent him and the imperial family articles from *Journal de St. Pétersbourg* and *Le Nord* which he regarded as useful in shaping the opinions of Alexander II.[93]

This does not in the least mean that Gorchakov enjoyed complete freedom of initiative in decision making. A group of people took part in working out foreign policy decisions, and both the War Minister and the Minister of Finance had much to say on the subject. As far as Asiatic policy was concerned, the voice of the military, and especially of the War Minister, D. Milyutin, was predominant and the latter frequently agreed his actions directly with the Tsar, over the head of Gorchakov.[94] In this context I would like to quote the opinion expressed in 1864 by the Italian envoy, Marquis Pepoli. 'Le Prince Gortchakow cryez (! – E.H.) – le moi, c'est libéral; il est, selon moi, Ministre par la forme, pour rédiger des notes, pour recevoir des adresses, mais sa pensée politique ne peut pas se dégager des entraves qu'elle trouve sur son chemin. La phrase, qu'il me disait un jour par fausse modestie, est une verité aujourd'hui, il n'est plus que l'encrier de l'Empereur, qui à son tour est inspiré par le parti de la réaction, qu'on appele ici parti Allemand'.[95]

---

92. H.H.S.A., no. 19, 7 April (26 March) 1861, Karton, 50. (P.A. X Russ.)
93. *Ibid.* no. 6, A-E, 28 (16) January 1861.
94. *Dnevnik* ... vol. I. Introduction, p. 47.
95. Pepoli's report to Turin on March 24, 1864. Rapporti ... Pacco 205, A.S.-D, Rome.

Gorchakov often seemed to be worried about his position at the Tsar's right hand during that period. He was aware that many Russian officials of high rank and diplomats (e.g. Brunnow and Budberg) were ready to undercut his position when the opportunity arose. He was afraid that the close involvement of Tsar Alexander II in foreign policymaking could diminish his independent role as Minister of Foreign Affairs. That is why Gorchakov became more and more suspicious and insecure from the 1860s onward.

As far as the mechanism of decision making is concerned we do not have very many sources available, and some of them are tendentious. I am thinking above all here of the diary of Milyutin, who could not stand Gorchakov and gave a distinctly biased picture of his relations with the Tsar, stressing both his obsequiousness and subservience to Alexander II and simultaneously his cunning. It is also worth noting that Bismarck wrote about the relations between the Tsar and his minister of foreign affairs. Initially, on his arrival in St. Petersburg, he too found it hard to understand the position, and consequently he raised the matter in conversation with Gorchakov.

Es giebt in Russland, fuhr'er fort, nur zwei Menschen, welche die Politik des Cabinets kennen, der Kaiser, der sie macht, und mich [Gorchakov], der sie vorbereitet und ausführt; Seine Majestät ist sehr verschwiegen, und ich sage nur, was ich will, und das sage ich Ihnen lieber und offener als einem Andern.[96]

I have the impression that greater weight should be attached to Bismarck's later observation to A. Schleinitz:

Wenn der Kaiser einmal durchfühlt, dass Gortschakow ihn geschickt und unvermerkt, unter stets neuen Vorwänden, von des Kaisers eigenen Zielen abzulenken weiss, so wird er bis zum Eigensinn selbständig dagegen werden; aber Gortschakow weiss die Gerichte, die er mit Montebello kocht, immer wieder mit einen neuen Sauce zu bedecken, die dem Kaiser mundet, und bisher hält er das Steuer selbständig in der Hand, und das kaiserliche Schiff folgt seinem Druck.[97]

It is characteristic that in 1859 and 1862 Bismarck reported that Gorchakov 'sometimes referred to himself as a sponge which soaked up the Tsar's wishes'.[98]

Le Prince Gortchakoff n'est pas homme à nourrir ou à suivre des convictions indépendantes et dépourvues de l'autorité impériale. C'est un esprit actif et brillant, d'une conception prompte et facile, mais doué de cette souplesse nationale qui lui fait refléter les moindres nuances des dispositions de son maître. Lui-même, pour exprimer sa soumission à la volonté de l'Empereur, se compare à une éponge laquelle la pression de la main de l'Empereur fait rendre le liquide, dont elle est penetrée.

---

96. *Bismarcks Briefwechsel mit dem Minister von Schleinitz 1859-1861,* (Berlin, 1905), p. 19. Friese, *Russland und Preussen ...,* p. 21.
97. 2 January 1861. *G.W.* vol. III, pp. 158-9, Hillerbrand. *Bismarck ...,* p. 63.
98. Cf. *Die politischen Berichte des Fürstens Bismarck aus Petersburg und Paris,* vol. I, pp. 30-31, Immediate report to the Prince Regent, 27 April 1859.

Bismarck, however, failed to discern the true motives which led Gorchakov to speak about himself and his dependence on the Tsar in this way. Despite what he said, Gorchakov was not merely the Tsar's subordinate and the passive executor of his decisions, as B. Jelavich has shown.[99]

Nor do the conclusions reached by W. Mosse sound convincing: Mosse takes a simplified view of the problem of the relations between the Tsar and Gorchakov, saying that 'Russian foreign policy in the days of Alexander II remained decisively the policy of the Tsar'.[100] He is right, however, when he continues: 'The presence of Alexander II with his basically conservative instincts and his veneration for the memory of his father guaranteed a measure of continuity and acted as a brake on his impulsive minister'.[101]

It is known that the views of the Tsar and those of Gorchakov did not always coincide. There were tactical differences concerning even such major matters as their attitude to France under Napoleon III and the question of Piedmont, and there were also differences over Russian policy on German affairs, particularly Austria,[102] and the Balkan question.[103] These differences derived from the different basic principles by which the two men were guided. Alexander II possessed a strong inclination to maintain in practice the principle of legitimacy and solidarity between monarchs, which had been instilled in him by Nicholas I. Gorchakov preached liberalism, as he thought this made it easier to defend the *status quo*. Essentially he pursued a policy which could be called *Realpolitik*. He was a pragmatist for whom principles were not of great importance. This was noted, for example, by the British ambassador, F. Napier, after his arrival at his post in St. Petersburg. In a report to Russell he described Gorchakov's policy as follows:

It would be a great mistake to count absolutely on the partiality of the Prince [Gorchakov] for France and on his antipathy to Austria. That partiality and that antipathy are natural and sincere, but I am confident he would divest himself of them with the greatest alacrity, either from a motive of public policy or personal interest. 'Show me', said the Prince yesterday, 'a national motive for an Austrian alliance and that alliance shall be made in twenty-four hours.'[104]

Gorchakov himself seems to have summed up the essence of his policy better than anyone. In a conversation with the Prussian ambassador he described it as follows:

Ich hoffe, dass man in Berlin nicht mehr glaubt, dass mein alter Hass gegen Österreich noch andauert, heute zolle ich der Loyalität des Wiener Hoffes volle Gerechtigkeit und wünsche aufrichtig, mit ihm zu gehen. Ich bin ein gerechter Mann (je suis juste), aber vor allem bin ich Russe. Ich kenne nur die Interessen Russlands. Ich liebe niemand und hasse niemand.

---

99. B. Jelavich, *Russia and the Rumanian National Cause, 1858-59,* (Indiana U.P. 1959).
100. Mosse, *The European Powers* ..., p. 73.
101. *Ibid.*
102. *Ibid.*
103. *Dnevnik* ..., vol. II, p. 261, vol. III, p. 29.
104. No. 290, 6 September 1861, P.R.O. F.O. 65/578.

Wenn die Interessen Russlands es erfordern, schliesse ich auch einen Pakt mit dem Teufel und werfe mich ohne Zögern in seine Arme. Ich hatte sogar einmal die Absicht, mit Napoleon zu gehen. Wenn die Ereignisse das verhindern, so liegt es nicht an mir. Heute bin ich Österreich zu Dank verplichtet und auch England und hoffe, mich in Zukunft mit dem Londoner Kabinett zu verständigen.[105]

There is no question that the final decision always lay with the Tsar. But when differences existed Gorchakov was sensible enough to keep silent for the moment in order not to reveal them and to act flexibly, with the aim of modifying the position taken by the Tsar. This was not hard for him. The Tsar was known to be a weak character[106] who would agree to compromise, even in personal matters, and he usually inclined towards the opinion of his minister.

Alexander II found it convenient to delegate responsibility for the current conduct of that policy to Gortchakov, freeing his own attention for the urgent problem of internal reform and reorganisation which were his chief concern. It was thus Gorchakov rather than the Tsar who manoeuvred Russian foreign policy successfully through the period of profound changes in the European state system which took place in the 1860s, and it was Gorchakov who enjoyed the personal prestige of restoring some measure of the international position that Russia had lost in 1856.[107]

When making the final decisions in the field of international policy the Tsar relied greatly on Gorchakov's opinion, as he did in personnel decisions, chiefly concerning appointment to posts abroad.

As the years passed the influence of Gorchakov on the Tsar tended to increase and even when the ageing chancellor became a handicap the Tsar would not dismiss him but kept him in his ministerial post.[108]

Let us now consider the merits of the policy pursued by Gorchakov. What justification is there for the view, which he himself expressed from the very beginning, that he represented a fundamentally new course in Russian foreign policy? Was his emphatic claim that he was above all a Russian minister of foreign affairs, rather than a general minister of foreign affairs carrying out a 'Russian' programme, sub-

---

105. Report from Redern, 7 April 1863. Geh. St. A. Berlin, in Zechlin, *Bismarck und die Grundlegung* ..., p. 560. This statement by Gorchakov is confirmed by the assessment of Russian policy made by Walewski in the margin of a report on the La Roncière mission to Russia. On 4 January 1859 Walewski added this note: 'the Russians are known for cheating at play; they do not think it dishonorable to do so; they behave in this way in all their transactions. Business is for them a game to be won – by fair means or foul'. Cf. Bernady F. Chalamon, *Un fils de Napoléon: le Comte Walewski, 1810-1869*, (Paris, 1951), p. 833, Thurston Gary Jay, *The Franco-Russian Entente 1856-1863: P. Kiselev's Paris Embassy* (Ann Arbor, 1973), p. 218; cf. also Alexis Krausse, *Russia in Asia 1558-1899*, (London, 1973).
106. Cf. A. Leroy Beaulieu, 'L'Empereur Alexandre II et la mission du nouveau Tsar', *Revue des Deux Mondes*, 1 April 1881; Cf. also *Dnevnik* ..., vol. IV (Moscow, 1950), pp. 90 ff.
107. Robert M. Slusser, 'The Role of the Foreign Ministry', in Ivo J. Lederer ed. *Russian Foreign Policy: Essays in Historical Perspective*, (New Haven and London, 1962), p. 201. See also R.C. Tucker, 'Autocrats and Oligarchs', pp. 176-7 and G.B. Bolsover, *Aspects of Russian Foreign Policy 1815-1914, Essays presented to Sir L. Namier*, (London, 1956), pp. 320 ff.
108. Cf. *Dnevnik* ... vols III and IV; also Hillerbrand, *Bismarck and Gorchakov* ... pp. 62 ff. Polovtsev, *Dnevnik*, vol. 2. p. 185.

stantiated by his actions? Was the appointment of Gorchakov as minister of foreign affairs in place of chancellor Nesselrode a major turning point in Russian foreign policy, as S. Tatishchev argued?[109] Was Gorchakov's policy 'entirely hostile to the whole line of Nesselrode's policy', or was it true, as B. Sumner argued, that 'In fact the cleavage between the attitude of Nesselrode and that of Gorchakov was never so pronounced as the latter had made it appear'?[110] Or was Mosse correct that 'the transition from Nesselrode to Gorchakov produced a change of emphasis and an accentuation of existing trends rather than a reversal of policy ... The policy pursued by Gorchakov, as Mosse argued, differed only in emphasis from the one a new Nesselrode would have followed in his place'?[111]

We shall begin our discussion with personal questions. It is true that the departure of Nesselrode was followed by changes both in the ministry itself and in many key diplomatic posts. I. Tolstoy, who was close to Alexander II, joined the ministry, and the position of director of the Asiatic department was taken by E. Kovalevsky. A. Budberg was sent to Vienna, P. Kiselev to Paris, P. Brunnow to Berlin M. Khreptovich to London and A. Butenev to Constantinople. There were also changes in the diplomatic postings to Brussels, Stuttgart, Madrid, Turin, Hessen-Kassel and Hessen-Darmstadt.[112] But the holders of these posts were not new people. There was more of a reshuffle of the old Nesselrode team, and the cause of the changes was the new situation resulting from the signing of the Treaty of Paris. There was a great deal of clamour for the relegation of Germans from the diplomatic service. 'Gortchakow will keine Deutschen', wrote K. Schlözer in his letters from St. Petersburg on 4 December (22 November) 1857,[113] but this was a great exaggeration. Germans, predominantly Baltic Germans, like R. Osten-Sacken, E. Ungern-Sternberg, P. Meyendorff, Hillebrand, A. Mohrenheim, E. Stackelberg, O. Ewers and P. Brunnow continued to hold high positions both in the ministry and in diplomatic posts. Many of them did not conceal the fact that they felt a connection with their 'Vaterland', which was particularly significant when German questions were involved, or in the Danish-German conflict. Only the Asiatic department was traditionally staffed by Russians.

As far as the ministry itself was concerned, really only cosmetic innovations were made in its organisation. The importance of the archives section was increased and a commission was appointed which proceeded with the publication of some collections of state documents, *Pisma russkikh gosudarei* and *Sobranie traktatov i konventsii, zaklyuchennykh Rossiei s inostrannymi derzhavami*, edited by F.F. Martens.[114] This was associated with the style of operation brought in by Gorchakov, who placed a high value on the role of propaganda in the work of his ministry.

109. S.S. Tatishchev, *Imperator Aleksandr II*, vol. I, p. 210.
110. Sumner, *Russia and the Balkans* ... pp. 20-21. Baumgart wrote: The attitude of Nesselrode and Gortchakov 'deutlich zutage getreten war'. *Der Friede von Paris 1856*, (München, Wien, 1972), p. 98.
111. Mosse, *ibid.*, pp. 73, 76.
112. *Ocherki istorii ministerstva inostrannykh del, 1802-1902*, (St. Petersburg, 1902).
113. *Petersburger Briefe 1857-1862*, p. 85.
114. *Ocherki* ... pp. 165-7.

IV

In order to answer the question whether Gorchakov's policy was fundamentally different from the policy of the Nesselrode cabinet, not just in style but in content, we must first go back to the last years of Nesselrode's term of office, when the defeat of Russia in the Crimean War was sealed. On 11 February 1856 Nesselrode submitted to Alexander II his Mémoire à l'ouverture des négotiations du traité de Paris au moment de quitter le Ministère des Affaires Étrangères'.[115] The principal theme of this document is that, owing to the imminent conclusion of the peace treaty, 'la Russie aura à adopter un system de politique étrangère différent de celui qu'elle a suivi jusqu' à présent. Des circonstances impérieuses lui en font une loi'. The memorandum continued:

> La guerre a imposé au pays des sacrifices dont on ne connaît pas au juste l'étendue et les conséquences. On peut toutefois se dire, dès aujourd'hui, qu'il en résulte pour la Russie une nécessité presque absolue de s'occuper de ses affaires intérieures et du développement de ses forces morales et matérielles. Ce travail intérieur étant le premier besoin du pays, toute activité extérieure qui ferait obstacle, devra être soigneusement exclue ... Pacifique dans sa tendance générale, notre politique n'admettrait l'éventualité de la guerre que lorsque son inévitable nécessité ou son avantage évident pour la Russie aurait été bien constaté.

Was not the well-known passage in Gorchakov's circular of 21 August 1856, 'La Russie boude, dit-on. La Russie ne boude pas. La Russie se recueille', which made him famous throughout Europe, merely a repetition, in a more striking turn of phrase, of an idea which formed the general thesis of the memorandum of 11 February?[116]

Starting from these premises, Nesselrode warned against association with France since Napoleon III, as the expression of revolutionary feelings and nationalist tendencies, should not enjoy material support from Russia, because his policy was based on principles which differed from Russia's. It was in the interest of Russia and the dynasty that her policy should continue to be *'monarchique* et *antipolonaise'.*[117] (Nesselrode's emphasis). It was equally impossible to find common cause with Napoleon III, in the chancellor's opinion, because the aim of his policy was to gain the left bank of the Rhine, while Russia should remember that during the recent crisis Prussia had been the only country which openly declared that it had no hostile intentions towards Russia. Rapprochement with France could not be effective and would only serve as an inspiration to anti-Russian feeling and lead to suspicion on the part of Prussia, hatred from Austria and the possible rise of an anti-Russian coalition.

---

115. See *Lettres et Papiers du Chancelier Comte de Nesselrode 1760-1856,* vol. XI, 1854-1856 (Paris, 1912), pp. 112-116.
116. *Sbornik izdanyi v pamyati' dvadtsatipyatiletiya upravleniya ministerstvom inostranykh del gosudarstvennogo kantslera svyatleishego knyazya Aleksandra Mikhailovicha Gorchakova, 1856-1881,* (St. Petersburg, 1881), Tsirkulyarnaya depesha v Rossiisko-Imperatorskie missii, Moscow, 21 August 1856, p. 5; Semanov, *A.M. Gorchakov,* p. 53.
117. Cf. Mémoire presenté par le Comte de Nesselrode sur les affaires de Pologne (January 1813). *Sbornik Imp. Russ. Istor. Obs.* (1881), vol. 31, pp. 301-303.

'De plus, depuis le partage de la Pologne, il existe entre la Russie, l'Autriche et la Prusse une solidarité d'intérêts, et nous sommes celle de ces trois puissances à laquelle la conservation de cette solidarité est la plus nécessaire. La révolution de Pologne l'a bien prouvé.... Pour nous résumer, nous dirons: Dans l'intérêt bien entendu de la Russie, notre politique ne peut pas cesser d'être *monarchique* et *anti-polonaise*. Notre rapprochement avec la France, comme moyen de dissoudre la coalition contre nous et d'empêcher qu'elle ne survive à la guerre, doit rester subordonné à ces deux principes fondamentaux. Il ne revêtirait le caractère d'une alliance plus étroite que si les conjonctures favorables le prescrivaient.'

No more than two months later, however, under the influence of news from Paris about France's basically friendly attitude towards Russia during the Paris conference, Nesselrode revised his anti-French point of view.[118] Owing to the change in the constellation of forces in Europe after the conclusion of peace, and the collapse of the alliance of northern states, the only protection against the rise of new difficulties, and the factor which would allow Russia the breathing space she so badly needed, was rapprochement with the Emperor Napoleon. All efforts should be concentrated to this end, Nesselrode instructed Alexei Orlov, the chairman of the Russian delegation at the Paris conference, though this should be done without allowing Russia to be drawn into the undertakings which the French monarch was seeking.[119] 'Thanks to you, and the position you took in Paris', we read in this instruction, 'the first foundations of this policy have been laid'.

It is not impossible that Nesselrode changed his attitude at this time because, among other things, France agreed, as a result of a conversation between Orlov and Napoleon III and Walewski, to withdraw the Polish question from the conference agenda, whereas initially she had intended to include it.[120] This tendency for rapprochement between Russia and France did not escape the notice of *The Times* correspondent, who wrote about it on 10 March 1856.

Russia calculates on the gradual loosening of the bonds which unite England and France, if she cannot cut the knot herself. She believes that two countries with a form of government so opposed ... however they may unite for common safety in day of difficulty and peril, must be dissevered when the danger has gone by, and that there were a hundred chances, any one of which may be advantageously made use of to that end.[121]

---

118. A memorandum, 'O politicheskom sostoyanii Rossii posle zaklyucheniya mira' unsigned but with the date March 1856 written in the margin, was submitted to Alexander II and Nesselrode, condemning Russia's policy of solidarity and Austrian treachery, and arguing that in the new situation Russia should not tie herself with alliances but keep her hands free. The author of the note advocated a reorientation of Russian policy. Russia should move from being the policeman of Europe to a system 'd'abstention'. He also drew attention to the need to use propaganda in the interest of Russia, following Catherine II and the predecessors of Alexander II. Nesselrode added in the margin of the document that a state like Russia could not be politically between heaven and earth. Instead of the word 'alliance' he would advise the word 'understanding'. *Krasnyi Arkhiv*, 2 (75), (1936), pp. 45-51; Cf. Baumgart, *Der Friede* ... pp. 96-7.
119. Nesselrode to count A.F. Orlov, 17 (5) April 1856, *Krasnyi Arkhiv* 2 (75), (1936), p. 51; 'K istorii paryskogo mira 1856 g. ed. M.I. Bessmertnaya.
120. Telegram from Orlov, 8 April (27 March), n. 72, *ibid*.
121. *The Times*, 28 March 1856; cf. Schüle, *Russland und Frankreich ...*, p. 19.

In reality, after her defeat in the Crimean War Russia felt humiliated and had to seek alliances in order to regain her place in Europe and to obtain changes in the humiliating provisions of the Treaty. Her previous alliance with Austria had proved useless as Austria turned out to be weak and was, in addition, Russia's chief antagonist in the Balkans. Prussia, although she could be regarded as Russia's one reliable ally, was still not a power of the first rank. Britain remained Russia's enemy number one and her antagonist in both Balkans and Asia. Such were the conclusions Nesselrode reached,[122] and if one took this view of the situation the only solution, *nolens volens,* was to seek a rapprochement with France.

It is true that in this he was preceded by Gorchakov, who, when at his post in Vienna, had already established unofficial contacts with Morny and talked of the need 'd'un entente intime entre la Russie et la France' on 14 (2) December 1855.[123] In letters to Olga Nikolaevna on the subject at the beginning of 1856 he wrote: 'Un rapprochement entre nous et la France est aujourd'hui le clef de la voûte, la seule chance pratique d'une solution rationelle'.[124] Somewhat later he declared that an alliance with France was the 'pierre angulaire pour une bonne assiette de la Russie au dehors'.[125] It should be stressed that Gorchakov had been an advocate of rapprochement with France for many years and had long tried to promote the idea.[126] But it should also be remembered that this idea was not original and had appeared in circles close to Nicholas I during the 1848-49 revolution and on the eve of the Crimean War.

It is true that after the outbreak of revolution in Paris in 1848 Nicholas I proposed intervention in France jointly with the large German states.[127] But the moment there was any danger to Russia from the German Confederation, the Tsar started to think about a link with republican France[128] and Nesselrode wrote, in a compte-rendu, of the special role of France, whether republican or monarchist, in the European balance of power, as a counterweight of the German Confederation.[129] Faced with the possible rise of a united Germany, the interests of France and Russia were the same, said Nesselrode in a letter to P. Kiselev.[130]

Gorchakov's conception of a Franco-Russian rapprochement had the same purpose as Nesselrode envisaged in March 1856: in the first place to end Russia's political isolation. In the longer term, as Gorchakov said to N. Montebello quite openly three years later in April 1859, to abolish the provisions of the Treaty of Paris.

122. *Krasnyi Arkhiv,* (1936), no. 2 (75) p. 14.
123. To Olga Nikolaevna. H.S.A. Stuttgart.
124. H.S.A. Stuttgart, letter of 3 January 1856 (22 December 1855).
125. *Ibid.* Letter of 16 (4) January 1856. Cf. also Schüle, *Russland und Frankreich* ..., pp. 4-16; Hansen, *Les Coulisses* ... p. 141.
126. Schüle, *Russland und Frankreich* ..., pp. 4-7, 27-28, 33-34, 153-5.
127. See letter from Nicholas I to Friedrich Wilhelm IV, 7 March (24 February) 1848, in Schiemann, *Russland unter Nicholaus I,* vol. V, (1919), pp. 138 ff.
128. See the exchange of letters between Nesselrode and Kiselev about relations with Cavaignac. Martens, *Recueil des traités et conventions conclus par la Russie avec les Puissances Etrangères.* Vol. XIV. pp. 235 ff.
129. Martens, *Recueil* ... p. 233.
130. Letter of 30 (18) August 1849, Martens, p. 237; see also Zechlin, *Bismarck* ... *p. 26.* Montebello to Walewski, 20 April 1859, A.M.A.E. Mémoires et documents, Russie 1858-62.

C'est que nous voulons, et je ne m'en cache pas, c'est d'être relevés du traité de 1856. C'est d'effacer du droit public Européen la neutralité de la Mer Noir; nous y parviendrons, parce que nous y viserons toujours, j'espère bien voir ce jour avant de mourir ...

The same words were expressed to Oldoini.

'... toujours la même tendance pour la Russie à s'affranchir des clauses du traité de Paris, surtout de son exclusion de la Mer Noir, et chaque fois qu'il avait sur le tapis des exceptions le Prince Gortchakoff me (Oldoini) disait toujours donnez des coups d'épingles à ce traité, tant que vous voulez, je lui donnerais à mon tour le coup de sobre'.[131]

In Gorchakov's view, of the two major Western powers, only France could come into the reckoning as a possible ally of Russia. 'Britain is implacably opposed to Russia's interest both in the Black Sea and the Baltic and on the shores of the Caspian Sea and the Pacific Ocean, and everywhere displays her hostility to Russia in the most aggressive manner. Austria is an obedient instrument in the hands of Britain'. There remained France, where Russia saw that Napoleon III would like to free himself of his dependence on Britain; for this reason Paris had indicated understanding of Russia's position several times during the Paris Conference.[132] Hence a Russo-French rapprochement must loosen the ties between France and England. It must weaken the precarious friendship of France and Austria'.[133]

Revision of the provisions of the 1856 treaty, especially those concerning the neutralisation and demilitarisation of the Black Sea, the ban on Russian naval vessels there, and the recovery of Bessarabia, became the basic aims of Russian policy right down to 1871. In the opinion of the Tsar and his ministers, military, economic[134] and prestige considerations all demanded this. The restrictions imposed on Russia were compared with those imposed on Prussia by the Treaty of Tilsit. They were a blow to national ambition and the pride of the Russians.

Russia's loss of special privileges in relation to the Orthodox population, previously guaranteed in treaties with the Port, was also felt to be hurtful.[135] Many

---

131. Schüle, *Russland und Frankreich* ... p. 160; cf. E. Birke, *Frankreich und Ostmitteleuropa im 19. Jahrhundert,* (Cologne and Graz 1960) p. 195; N.S. Kinyapina, 'Bor'ba Rossii za otmenu ogranichitel'nykh uslovii parizskogo dogovora 1856 goda', *Voprosy istorii,* 1972, no. 8, pp. 35 ff. A.S.-D. Rome, Trois missions en Russie, pp. 153-154.
132. A.V.P.R., *Otchet za 1856 god;* Cf. Vinogradov, *Rossiya i ob''edinenie rumunskikh knyazhestv.* (Moscow, 1961) p. 89.
133. Mosse, *Ibid.,* p. 7. Baudin, in 'Influence de la Russie sur la France depuis le traité de Paris, 1856', written in November 1857 as an appendix to political telegram No. 62, in *Mémoires et documents 1850-1857,* vol. 44., (A.M.A.E., Paris) mentioned the following motives for rapprochement between St. Petersburg and Paris; a desire to break up the Anglo-French alliance and to extricate Russia from isolation. In this memorandum he also indicated that 'un vif ressentiment contre l'Angleterre' was felt in Russia, together with much sympathy for France. The reason for this was that during the recent war the French press, in contrast to the British, had maintained a moderate tone in relation to Russia, the French fleet had damaged Russian trade less than the British had during the war, and, finally, the French character was better in tune with the Slav peoples.
134. The importance of the Black Sea and the Sea of Azov is shown by the fact that in the years 1856-60 71% of wheat exports went via these seas, and in 1865-70 this figure rose to 85%. *Sbornik statisticheskikh svedenii po istorii i statistiki vneshnei torgovli Rossii,* ed. V.I. Pokrovsky, vol. I (St. Petersburg, 1902), pp. 18, 19, 22; cf. Narochnitskaya, *Rossiya i voiny,* p. 12.
135. Goriainov, *Le Bosphore* ..., p. 143; M.N. Pokrovsky, *Brief History of Russia,* vol. I, (London, 1933), p. 276.

economic advantages were expected from a rapprochement between Russia and France. Russia counted on France for help with the reconstruction of her economic life and the expansion of her railway network and industry. France saw in Russia the possibility of major capital investment, as well as a market for her industrial goods. 'Je vois dans la Russie une mine à exploiter pour la France', Morny reported to Walewski on 8 August 1856.[136]

On the basis of these considerations Russia expressed herself in favour of an alliance with Paris and, despite several crises, this agreement lasted until 1863. From the start the Polish question cast a dark shadow over the agreement, which was demonstrated as early as 1857, at the time of the meeting of Alexander II and Napoleon III in Stuttgart. It was not, however, the only reason for the difficulties and misunderstandings between France and Russia which ensued.

During the years 1856-63 neither France nor Russia obtained the advantages they expected, particularly in the economic sphere, no treaty of friendship between the two countries was signed, nor was France in fact inclined to help to bring about the changes in the clauses of the Treaty of Paris, which concerned Russia most.[137] The possibility of a rapprochement between St. Petersburg and Paris was not great. On the one hand, Alexander II lost confidence in the policy of Napoleon III especially after the annexation of Nice and Savoy. Nor was he pleased by Napoleon's disinclination to break with Britain. On the other, the opposition of Alexander II blocked Napoleon's plan for the conclusion of an alliance embracing Russia, France and Prussia.[138]

From 1861 the discord between Russia and France steadily intensified. Gorchakov was undoubtedly the architect of rapprochement with France. But as Martens said, 'C'est au Congrès de Paris de 1856 que fut posée une base à l'idée d'une alliance permanente entre la France et la Russie'. In other words, he continued what had been started by Nesselrode. Both were guided by the principle of *Realpolitik,* as F. Martens rightly maintained.[139] But from the beginning Prussia, rather than France, was the closest and surest ally of Russia. There was no clash of interests between Prussia and Russia, either in the Balkans or in Asia. During the Crimean War Prussia showed that she was Russia's only proven ally.

La Prusse nous a seule en Europe témoigné tout le bon vouloir que comportait sa situation, seule elle a montré le prix qu'elle attachait par gratitude pour le passé, par prévoyance pour l'avenir, au maintien des relations d'amitié avec la Russie. Elle a eu le mérite du bon vouloir

---

136. Schüle, *Russland und Frankreich ...* p. 43. On this subject see also Rondo E. Cameron, *France and the Economic Development of Europe, 1800-1914* (Princeton, 1961), pp. 275-83; Bertrand Gille, *Histoire de la maison Rotschild,* vol. II, 1848-1870 (Geneva, 1967), pp. 403-8.
137. N.S. Kinyapina, *Vneshnyaya politika Rossii vtoroi poloviny XIX veka* (Moscow, 1974) p. 32; Pokrovsky, *Brief History ...* p. 276.
138. Martens, *Recueil ...,* vol. XV, pp. 295, 299-300. The Russian ambassador in Paris, Kiselev, favoured such an alliance. Cf. A.P. Zablotsky-Desyatovsky, *Graf P.D. Kiselev i jego vremya,* vol. III, (St. Petersburg, 1883), pp. 68-9.
139. Martens, *Recueil ...* vol. XV, *Traités avec la France 1822-1906* (St. Petersburg, 1909). The term *Realpolitik* was used in the 1850s by Ludwig von Rochow. See Gordon A. Craig and Alexander L. George, *Force and Statecraft,* p. 35.

et n'a en que dans une mesure restreinte la responsabilité d'entraînements inhérents à sa position,

wrote A. Jomini, a high-ranking official in the Russian ministry of foreign affairs.[140] The high value which Gorchakov placed on Prussia's attitude is demonstrated by, among other things, the text of his instruction to Budberg of 24 (12) February 1858:

L'Empereur ne saurait oublier qu'au milieu de conjonctures critiques, la Cour de Berlin a résisté aux efforts qui tendaient à l'entraîner à une coalition contre nous. Cette crise d'Orient qui a modifié nos relations avec d'autres Puissances, n'a donc fait que resserer les liens qui nous unissent à la Prusse; notre Auguste Maître apprécie surtout le sentiment de profond respect qu'on y porte aujourd'hui encore à la mémoire de feu L'Empereur, son père bien aimé.[141]

It must also be remembered that during the Crimean War, owing to the situation in the Baltic, the overland trade had increased between Russia and Europe, and this was virtually synonymous with the growth of trade with Prussia.[142]

After Austria switched to the side of the Western powers, Russia abandoned the policy inaugurated at Olomuntz in 1850 and Austria's place in her German policy became firmly occupied by Prussia. The Alliance with Prussia was a constant element, which continued without interruption from the Crimean War and independently of whether the conservative O. Manteuffel or the representative of the 'new era', A. Schleinitz, was in power in Berlin.

It is impossible to agree with the view advanced by some American historians, such as J.K. Lively, who considered that Gorchakov used 'alliance' with France and Prussia interchangeably.[143]

'The cooperation between the courts of St. Petersburg and Berlin was based on a human affinity between them, on a common autocratic ideology, and on the common anti-Polish interest', said L. Namier,[144] In addition, there were the family bonds linking the Romanovs and the Hohenzollerns. 'J'ai l'intime conviction', wrote Alexander II, in reply to a letter from Friedrich Wilhelm IV after the death of Nicholas I, 'que tant que nos deux pays resteront amis, l'Europe entière pourra encore être sauvée d'un bouleversement général, sinon, malheur à elle, car c'est le dernier frein de l'hydre révolutionnaire'.

And on 19 (7) January 1856, referring to the content of his previous letter, the Tsar wrote:

Puissions-nous rester toujours amis et appelons la bénédiction céleste sur notre *double alliance*. Soyez persuadé, cher oncle, que je vous serai éternellement reconnaisant pour la posi-

---

140. *Etudes diplomatiques sur la guerre de Crimée 1852 à 1856,* vol. II. p. 204; see also Friese, *Russland und Preussen* ... p. 94.
141. Central archives Moscow, in Friese, *Russland und Preussen* ..., p. 110.
142. S.A. Pokrovsky, *Vneshnyaya torgovlya i vneshnyaya torgovaya politika Rossii,* (Moscow, 1947), pp. 247-52, 262-71; Khromov, *Ekonomicheskoe razvitie* ..., p. 99.
143. J.K. Lively, *Life and Career of Prince A.M. Gortchakov: a Political Biography* (Georgetown University Press, 1956).
144. L. Namier, *Vanished Supremacies* ..., (London, 1962), p. 211.

tion si belle, que Vous avez su faire garder à la Prusse pendant toute cette crise et qui nous a été si utile.[145]

The close relations between the Tsar and the King of Prussia were strengthened by frequent meetings of the two monarchs (in May 1856, 1857, 1858 and 1859).[146] The meetings in Wroclaw in 1859 and Warsaw in 1860 are certainly not evidence of a change in Russian policy from a pro-French to a pro-Prussian line, as Tatishchev,[147] and, following him, Kinyapina[148] maintained, and it would be hard to agree with their argument that France's place in Russian policy had already been taken by Prussia at this time. Friendship with Prussia did not become the foundation of Russian policy until 1863, when, during the Polish uprising, the link with France was broken and Bismarck succeeded in making Russian policy dependent on Prussia.

Throughout the whole period since he took office, however, Gorchakov nursed the friendship with Prussia. 'Si la nouvelle Prusse nous reste fidèle, notre assiette politique se raffermera et se développera toujours d'avantage', he wrote to Olga Nikolaevna on 12 October 1858.[149] His view of relations with the states of Europe at this time was as follows: 'Nos relations sont excellentes avec la Prusse, très intimes avec la France, convenables mais froides avec l'Autriche, incertaines avec l'Angleterre'.[150] This exceptionally warm attitude towards Prussia was a substantial factor in the deterioration of Russo-Danish relations.

An instance of Gorchakov's *Realpolitik* was his attitude to Austria. It is impossible to deny that both Gorchakov and Alexander II felt contempt and dislike for Austria because of her behaviour during the Crimean War and the ingratitude she showed after the way Russia had behaved towards Austria during the revolution of 1848-49 and the meeting at Olomuntz.[151] But those historians who attribute Gorchakov's anti-Austrian policy to his personal animosities from the time he was ambassador in Vienna are wrong. Gorchakov rejected the idea of rapprochement with Austria mainly because she could not help with the achievement of the principal objective which he had set himself: 'I am looking for a man who will annul the clauses of the Treaty of Paris, concerning the Black Sea question and the Bessarabian frontier. I am looking for him and I shall find him', wrote Gorchakov to Kiselev in Paris after assuming his ministerial post.[152] Austria could not meet this requirement, and in any case was not in the least interested in annulling provisions of a treaty which limited the role of Russia in south-eastern- Europe. On the other

---

145. Martens, vol. VIII *Traités avec l'Allemagne* (St. Petersburg 1888), pp. 456, 458-9.
146. *Ocherki istorii* ... p. 135.
147. Tatishchev, *Imperator* ..., vol. I, p. 255.
148. Kinyapina, *Vneshnyaya politika* ..., p. 40.
149. H.S.A. Stuttgart.
150. *Ibid.*
151. 'Unter dem vereinten Druck Österreichs und Russlands ... kapitulierte Preussen in Olmütz am 29 November 1850, bedingunglos und vollständig.' 'Das Jena von 1850 hiess Olmütz.' S. Haffen, *Preussen ohne Legende*, (Hamburg, 1980), pp. 326, 332. Cf. *Russkoe Slovo*, I, 1864, pp. 6-7.
152. Zablotsky-Desyatovsky, *Graf P.D. Kiselev* ..., vol. III. p. 37; cf. A.J.P. Taylor, *The Struggle for Mastery in Europe 1848-1918*, p. 91. Austria was regarded as 'une puissance vermoulue', Thun reported on 28 (16) January 1861.

hand, an Austro-Russian rapprochement would not have suited Napoleon III on account of his Italian policy.

The fact that after 1856 Russia gave priority to putting her internal affairs in order does not in the least mean that she became passive or uninterested in what was happening in Europe. Quite the opposite. She followed events in Europe with a vigilant eye and never for one moment abandoned a role in the international arena.

'La Russie ne boude pas, elle se recueille', said Chancellor Gorchakov after the war. He did not know himself how truthfully he spoke. He spoke only for the diplomatic Russia. But the unofficial Russia also drew its forces together. And this gathering of strength ('recueillement') was supported by the government itself.[153]

Engels' description of Russian policy after the Crimean War applied both to Europe and, above all, to Asia. The process of acquiring new territories from the Caucasus to Central Asia, the Amur and the Pacific Ocean continued without a moment's interruption.[154]

The policy of acquisition of new territories cannot be justified solely, or even primarily, by the need for access to sources of raw materials for Russian industry.[155] Nor is it defensible to argue that the tsars in St. Petersburg were not in a position to control the actions of their generals. Firuz Kazemzadeh was right when he argued that, 'in fact the military were tightly controlled from St. Petersburg, all their moves being decided on the highest government level'.[156]

The Russian ministries were involved in Central Asian expansion, and under Alexander II they enjoyed an unusual continuity of leadership under D.A. Milyutin, and the war minister exercised unusual influence in foreign and domestic affairs. While reorganising and modernising the entire military establishment, he sought to enhance Russian prestige while avoiding a major war.[157]

'The principle of militarism is patent throughout Asiatic Russia', argued A. Krausse, a well known expert in the field.[158]

Gorchakov himself was very active in Russian policy towards China, although not he but the director of the Asiatic Department, E.P. Kovalevsky, had the principal responsibility for Asiatic policy', and if Gorchakov initially had reservations about the policy of occupying territories in Asia, they were only caused by fear that the result might be a conflict with Britain. As far as the Minister of Finance,

---

153. F. Engels, 'The Foreign Policy of Russian Czarism', in P.W. Blackstock and B.F. Hoselitz eds., *The Russian Menace to Europe,* (Glencoe, Ill., 1952), p. 47.
154. A. Krausse, Russia in Asia, (London, 1973), pp. 19-20.
155. M.N. Pokrovsky, *Istoriya Rossii v XIX veke,* (St. Petersburg, n.d.) pp. 181-204; S.S. Dmitriev, *Srednyaya Aziya i Kazakhstan v 1860-1880 godakh.* Cf. also 'Zavoevanie Srednei Azii', *Istoriya SSSR* (Moscow 1949).
156. Lederer, *Russian Foreign Policy ...* pp. 391, 493ff.
157. David Mackenzie, 'Expension in Central Asia: St. Petersburg vs. the Turkestan Generals (1863-1866)', *Canadian Slavic Studies,* vol. III. no. 2 (1969), pp. 286 ff.
158. Krausse, *Ibid.* p. 140.

Reutern, was concerned, he was only opposed to excessive expenditure for this purpose, owing to Russia's serious financial situation.[159]

Ultimately Gorchakov too fully approved of Russian aggression in Central Asia, dignifying it with the name of a civilising mission; while motives of security and particularly the protection of Russian trade were presented as the main reason for moving armed forces deep into Central Asia. 'Tel a été le sort de tous les pays qui ont été placés dans les mêmes conditions – les Étas Unis en Amérique, la France en Algérie, la Hollande dans les colonies, l'Angleterre aux Indes ...' we read in a dispatch from Gorchakov to Russian ambassadors.[160] As far as Alexander II was concerned, not only did he not forbid the army to advance in a southerly direction, 'instead he tolerated the refractory attitude of his colonial pro-consuls. This colonial expansion appealed to him'. The Tsar accepted every act of invasion, guided by his father's motto, 'where once the Russian flag has flown, it must not be lowered again'.[161] Martens was correct when he reached the following conclusion from his analysis of Russia's Asiatic policy under Alexander II:

Néanmoins ni l'Empereur Alexandre II, ni son nouveau brilliant Ministre des Affaires Étrangères, le Prince A. Gortchakow, ne songèrent un moment à renoncer à poursuivre dans l'avenir les grandes traditions historiques de la Russie en Orient et en géneral dans le monde entier.

La conscience de la dignité nationale et une foi inébranlable dans le triomphe des vues politiques de la Russie dans l'avenir, – voilà ce qui se trahît dans tous les actes qui émannent de la plume du Prince Gortchacow.[162]

Asiatic policy became an important element in Russia's policy after 1856, and her aim was to transform Asia into an internal Russian colony, a market and a source of raw materials for European Russia, and finally a military and strategic base.

V

Gorchakov's policy is an example of Russia's behaviour in a transitional period when, weakened by military defeat and shaken by internal crisis, she was not strong enough to operate actively on all fronts in the international arena, as she had been earlier. Changes in tactics and methods of conducting policy were made in the

---

159. A.L. Popov, 'Iz istorii zavoevanii Srednei Azii', *Istoricheskie Zapiski,* (1940). no. 9, p. 209; R.K.I. Quested, *The Expansion of Russia in East Asia, 1857-1860,* (University of Malaya Press, Singapore, 1968), pp. 80, 167, 280-1; P.I. Kabanov, *Amurskii vopros,* (Blagoveshchensk, 1959).
160. See Dispatch of 21 (9) November 1864 to Comte de Stackelberg, H.H.S.A., Vienna, P.A. IX, Karton 80, pp. 422-6; British and Foreign State Papers, LVIII, pp. 635-9. Gorchakov's document was his own work, but it suggests a schoolmasters hand rather than a statesman's, wrote Tatishchev, *Imperator* Alexandr II, ... vol. II, pp. 115 ff.
161. Hugh Seton-Watson, *The Russian Empire 1801-1917,* (Oxford, 1967) p. 297.
162. Martens, *Traités avec la France,* vol. XV, p. IV.

light of her changed internal and external situation.[163] This is the crucial difference compared with the period when Nesselrode was responsible for the direction of Russian foreign policy. This difference was reinforced by dissimilarities in the personalities of Nesselrode and Gorchakov. They operated in different historical periods and the policy of the previous period was bound to undergo modification. The strategy, however, remained unchanged. Never for one moment did Gorchakov lose sight of the fact that he was the continuator of a Russian policy of which the chief watchword was the good of the state, which in Russia's case meant an active policy aimed at continued expansion of the empire, both in Europe and in Asia. Not for a moment, despite his liberal phrases, did he cease to be the protector of conservative principles and the defender of the *status quo* – not only with respect to the Polish question but also to the changes occurring in Italy.[164] The case of Russia confirms the definition of politics given by the distinguished Polish scholar and politician Stanislaw Tarnowski:

Politics is an art of unchanging ends and changing means. The means must always be adapted to the time and the situation ... And if the means can and must continually change, the conditions and the general policy directions which stem from them change little and rarely. The geographical position of every country, its frontiers and neighbours, its essential economic needs, the nature of its people and its historical evolution, these contain a certain sum of innate dangers, impulses and ambitions which does not change: which naturally generated the basic logical directions of its actions, or, in other words, the principles of its policy.[165]

Russia's inland position, her inability for centuries to solve her internal difficulties, to modernise her economic and social structure and her despotic system of rule, on the one hand, and her inferiority complex *vis-a-vis* the West and fear of being surprised by the Western states, on the other, caused Russia, with her great military strength, continually to seek to occupy other territories, and this factor became a constant element in Russian policy down the ages. In 1867 Marx summed up his perception of Russian policy in these words:

The policy of Russia is changeless according to the admission of its official historian, the Muscovite Karamsin. Its methods, its tactics, its manoeuvres may change, but the polar star of its policy – world domination – is a fixed star.[166]

Where do all these tend? When will Russia reach her limit? How is she to be restrained? – asks a British diplomat and historian. And he replies – the question has in part been already answered. Russia will continue to advance so long as the exciting forces are at work within, and she meets no insurmountable barrier without. Except in one contingency, Russia

---

163. 'Il faut bien poser la Russie dans l'opinion libérale de l'Europe' – Gorchakov wrote several times in his letters to the Russian envoys in Europe.
164. See Gorchakov to Gagarin, ambassador in Turin, 10 October 1860, for information on incidents in Tuscany, Parma and Modena. C. Grunwald, *Trois siècles de diplomatie russe,* (Paris, 1945), p. 204.
165. St. Tarnowski, 'Kilka pewników politycznych', in *Z doświadczeń i rozmyślań,* (Cracow, 1891), p. 302.
166. K. Marx, 'Poland's Mission', in Blackstock and Hoselitz eds. *The Russian Menace ...,* p. 106. See also Marx 'Traditional Policy of Russia', and *Revue des Deux Mondes,* vol. IX, 1855, pp. 758 ff.

is destined to creep onwards, until she finds herself brought up by a barrier maintained by a power stronger than herself ... She will continue to extend her influence, and to use it for her own benefit, so long as she can do so without disastrous results to herself.[167]

The Polish historian J. Kucharzewski put the problem in the following way: 'The theme of continuity is a deductive one ... Russia is unique among other nations'.[168]

While agreeing with these observations, however, it should also be pointed out that although the similarities are striking, the differences are obvious, too, when we compare different historical periods. P. Geyl was right to conclude that 'history does not repeat itself. Between noticing a parallel and establishing an identity, there is a wide gap'.[169]

---

167. Krausse, *Ibid.*, pp. 318-9, and cf. p. 291.
168. J. Kucharzewski, *From the White to Red Tsardom,* and *The Origin of Modern Russia,* (N.Y., 1948).
169. P. Geyl, *Napoleon: For and Against,* Harmondsworth, 1965), p. 8.

2. Denmark's Place in Russian Policy after the Paris Peace Treaty: Russia and the Problem of Scandinavianism

I

The Russian ambassador to the court of the Tuilleries, the well known diplomat Ch. Pozzo di Borgo, submitted a report on the international situation and the role of Russia to Nicholas I on 21 January (2 February) 1826, a report produced on the instructions of the Tsar immediately after his accession to the throne, in which the place of the Scandinavian countries in Russian policy was assessed as follows:

Le Danemarc est pour nous, pour ainsi dire une partie de nous-mêmes. L'indépendance de sa position nous est nécessaire autant que celle des points les plus essentiels de notre Empire.[1] Cette vérité résulte de l'inspection de la carte. Il nous appartient donc de veiller à sa conservation et à tout ce qui peut le mettre à l'abri des violences et de qui que ce soit et spécialement de l'Angleterre.[2]

On Sweden the memorandum comments:

La Suède, faible par sa position relative avec la Russie, l'est encore par l'origine de la familie qui en occupe le trône. Nous n'avons pas de raison de montrer aucun empressement d'y causer des altérations, mais si nous avions à craindre ou à venger des torts, les points vulnérables de cette monarchie ne seraient pas difficiles à saisir.[3]

Thus we find two distinctly different attitudes, which are the result not only of the

---

1. Cf. Baron Rosen, *Forty Years of Diplomacy,* (London, 1922), vol. II, p. 101.
2. F. de Martens, *Recueil des traités et conventions conclus par la Russie avec lec puissances étrangères,* vol. XV. Traités avec la France, 1822-1906, (St. Petersburg, 1909), p. 49. See also: *Vneshnyaya politika Rossii XIX i nachala XX veka.* Seriya 2. vol. 6, (14), (Moscow, 1985), p. 358.

  'Les relations entre les cours de St. Pétersbourg et de Copenhague ne cessèrent jamais d'être amicales – wrote P.I. Brunnow in 1838 in his note on the Russian foreign policy. Durant tout le règne de l'Impératrice Catherine elles ne furent interrompues par aucun de ces incidents passagers, que la politique toujours variable du 18-ème siècle rendait si fréquens et quelquefois si fâcheux.

  Plusieurs transactions cimentèrent les liens entre les deux Cabinets. Mais leur objet étant plutôt d'un intérêt historique que d'une importance politique, nous croyons devoir nous borner à en indiquer sommairement la substance. Elles ont principalement rapport aux arrangemens de famille qui eurent lieu entre le Roi de Danemarck et la branche cadette de la maison de Holstein-Gottorp.

  Aperçu des principales transactions du Cabinet de Russie sous les règnes de Catherine II, Paul I et Alexandre I, Barona F.I. Brunnova, 1838 god. See *Sbornik Imperatorskogo Russkogo Istoricheskogo Obschestva,* v. 31, (St. Petersburg, 1881) p. 224. 1826-38. Gody uchenyia ego Imperatorskogo Vysochestva Naslednika Tsarevicha Aleksandra Nikolaevicha nyne blagopoluchno tsarstvuyashchego Gosudarya Imperatora. t. II. (St. Petersburg, 1880).
3. F. de Martens, *op.cit.* vol. XV, p. 49.

geopolitical position of the two countries in relation to Russia but also of Russia's past historical experience. Russia's relations with her two Scandinavian neighbours had differed for centuries. Even though in the closing years of the Napoleonic era the situation had been different from what it was in the past, with Denmark in the anti-Russian camp and Sweden in the pro-Russian one, Russia's attitude to the two countries still conformed to the tradition moulded in the course of the preceding centuries, when as a rule Denmark had been on Russia's side in the struggle for *dominium maris Baltici* and Sweden had been the main antagonist, initially of Denmark and later of Russia.[4] The friendly position which Russia took towards Denmark was amply demonstrated in the years 1848-49, during the first Schleswig-Holstein war, when Russia under Nicholas I supported Denmark, without regard to the complications to which this migh have led, especially between St. Petersburg and Berlin. Chancellor Nesselrode expressed his position on Denmark in a letter to the Russian ambassador in Berlin, P. Meyendorff, on 21 April 1848:

La question danoise devient très embarrassante pour nous. Il n'est pas de notre intérêt de laisser détruire la monarchie danoise à nos portes, et si nous prenions des mesures fortes, pour soutenir énergiquement le Danemarc telles qu'apparition de notre flotte sur les côtes de la Prusse, nous risquérions de soulever toute l'Allemagne contre nous et de réveiller à nouveau les sympathies pour la Pologne, qui viennent a peine de s'éteindre.[5]

And a few days later, on 8 May, he again wrote: 'La Russie ne peut pas laisser détruire à sa barbe la monarchie danoise'.[6] Russia regarded the invasion of Jutland by Prussian troops as a threat to her standing in the Baltic and a disturbance of the political balance in northern Europe.

Russia's foremost concern, evidently, was that Jutland should remain under the control of Denmark, a power that would not constitute a threat to Russian shipping, which was paramount to her national interests. This fact is frequently overlooked by a good many historians.

Que l'invasion, étendue au Jutland, porterait une grave atteinte aux intérêts de toutes les Puissances riveraines de la Baltique et tendrait par ses conséquences à rompre dans tout le Nord de L'Europe l'équilibre politique, établi par les traités. La Russie ne saurait admettre une telle éventualité,

wrote Nesselrode to Berlin in May 1848.[7]

No less serious was Russia's fear that a defeated Denmark might be united with Sweden or, alternatively, might be expected to become a republic in the future. This view was expressed by the Russian ambassador in Copenhagen, Ungern-Sternberg,

---

4. B.H. Sumner, *Survey of Russian History*, (London, 1961). Ch. VII, 'The Sea'; R.M. Hilton, 'Russia and the Baltic', in *Russian Imperialism* (New Brunswick, New Jersey, 1974). I. Andersson. *Svenska historia i rysk version* (Stockholm, 1952), pp. 4-5, J. Zutis's Introduction pp. 12-13.
    Despite all that Russia ordered military equipment in Sweden, See: A.S. Kan, Russkie voennye zakazy v Svetsii (1830-50-ye gody). *Eripainos, Turun Historiallinen Arkisto* 28/1973, pp. 240-52.
5. *Lettres et papiers du Chancelier Comte de Nesselrode 1760-1850*, vol. IX, (Paris, n.d., p. 88).
6. *Ibid.* pp. 92-3.
7. Martens, *Recueil* ..., vol. VIII, p. 375. Traités avec Allemagne , (St. Petersburg, 1888).

on 4 (16) June 1848.[8] If this happened, the ambassador argued, *'L'influence salutaire que la Russie est appellée à exercer*[9] sur les destinées du Danemarc serait à jamais perdue'.[10] The navy minister, Menshikov, after returning from a visit to Copenhagen and Stockholm, was greatly disturbed by the development of the Scandinavian idea and used this argument in discussions with the Tsar and Nesselrode to try to persuade them to make concessions to Denmark and thus to influence her course of action.[11]

The interest of Russia and Britain coincided on this point, and the plan of political action designed to settle the Schleswig-Holstein question which was drawn up by Palmerston with the active co-operation of the Russian ambassador in London, P. Brunnow, culminated in the Treaty of London of 8 May 1852. This treaty, signed by Britain, France, Russia, Sweden-Norway, the two large German states, Austria and Prussia, and Denmark, recognised the integrity of the latter as an essential factor in the balance of power in Europe and settled the question of the succession to the Danish throne on the death of the childless Frederick VII. It also recognised the existing links between Holstein and Lauenburg and the German Confederation.[12] The treaty, like the Warsaw protocol between Russia and Denmark signed in 1851 and the London protocol (signed by the signatories of the subsequent Treaty of London,[13] with the exception of Prussia) was favourable to Denmark, but it was really more of a declaration, which no one undertook to defend if it was infringed. 'Il n'a été en réalité qu'un armitrice', was the verdict of the well-known Danish politician Ch. C. Bluhme during a parliamentary discussion on 11 April 1863.[14] It was not a collective act, but, at Russia's suggestion, an agreement concluded between the six states, on the one hand, and Denmark, on the other, and its ratification was therefore done by means of an exchange of documents between the six states and Denmark.

Le traité resta un acte étranger, sans autorité et sans droit ... Un traité oppresif, contraire à la justice, quelques que soient la solemnité de ses formules de perpetuité, n'est qu'un chiffon de papier noirci, à déchirer dès qu'on en a la force - wrote E. Ollivier.[15]

It was a fundamental mistake during the course of the conference not to approach the German Confederation with the suggestion that it should associate itself with the treaty. Of the eleven states in the union which were subsequently approached, six, following the example of Bavaria, refused until the Frankfurt Diet had given its

---

8. Dispatch no. 113 to Nesselrode. Rigsarkiv, Copenhagen, Håndskriftsamlingen XVI. Afskrifter af indberetninger fra det russiske gesandtskab i København til regeringen i St. Petersburg 1848-1864, vol. 40. Cf. also Nesselrode to Meyendorff, 27 April 1848, *Lettres* ... pp. 86 ff.
9. Emphasis in the original.
10. *Ibid.* Cf. also dispatch no. 121, 17 (29) June 1848.
11. Vicomte de Guichen, *Les grandes questions européennes et la diplomatie des puissances sous la seconde république française,* vol. I, (1925), p. 128.
12. L.D. Steefel, *The Schleswig - Holstein Question,* pp. 9-13.
13. See Appendix A.
14. J. Klaczko, *Études* ... p. 245.
15. E. Ollivier, *L'Empire libéral,* vol. VII (Paris, 1903), pp. 9-10, 12.

opinion.[16] The treaty in any case contained so many technical loopholes that it could only encourage both sides to infringe it.[17] It did not introduce any new principles but relied on the old principles of politics and diplomacy, without taking account of the essential aspirations of the population of the duchies, and without asking the opinion of political groupings in Denmark and Germany. The satisfaction of certain politicians, particularly the creators of the document, Palmerston and Brunnow, was not matched by the feelings of the people, particularly the Germans, who felt disappointed and wronged.[18]

The Russian goodwill to the Glücksburg succession sufficed to incline the British Tory cabinet, which was particularly desirous of avoiding renewed friction with Russia, to follow suit in this matter; nor was any opposition to be looked for from France.[19]

The Danes in the Eider party thought the treaty undermined their political ideals and nullified the Danish victories at Fredericia (6 July 1849) and Isted (25 July 1850) and, worse still, it designated Christian of Glücksburg, who was well known for his conservative and pro-German convictions, as heir to the Danish throne. The Germans in the Schleswig-Holstein party were dissatisfied because the treaty shattered the political ideals for which they were fighting. But at the same time as it stifled both these opposing ideas, the treaty could not give any guarantee that calm would ensue or that Schleswig-Holsteinism would be reconciled with this imposed state of affairs.[20]

Some Prussian diplomats opposed it from the beginning, and Chr. Bunsen, the Prussian ambassador in London, preferred to resign his position rather than recognise it.[21] Bunsen remarked that the treaty represented little more than 'a declaration of bankruptcy'. He saw it simply as a triumph of the major powers at Germany's expense, and his only consolation was the possibility that Germany might derive some future advantage from the fact that the Diet had not been consulted.[22] Others again regarded it as useless[23] because the provisions of the treaty led nowhere.[24]

---

16. See *Correspondence between Austria, Prussia and Denmark 1851-52*, (London, 1862). Accessions to the Treaty of London of May 8, 1852, relating to the succession to the Danish Crown. Cf. also *Danske Tractater efter 1800. Første Samling. Politiske tractater. Første Bind, 1800-1865*, (Copenhagen, 1877), pp. 281-5.
17. Klaczko, *Études ...*, pp. 243-4. *The Cambridge History of British Foreign Policy*, vol. II, (1923), pp. 538-41.
18. Ollivier, *L'Empire ...*, p. 10; Z. Grot, *Pruska polityka ...*, pp. 49-50; A. Scharff, *Schleswig-Holstein in der deutschen und nordeuropäischen Geschichte*, (Stuttgart, 1969), pp. 225-227.
19. A.W. Ward and S. Wilkinson, *Germany 1852-1871*, vol. II, (Cambridge, 1917), pp. 119, 122.
20. See the interpretation of Keith A.P. Sandiford, *Great Britain and the Schleswig-Holstein Question. 1848-64.* (Toronto and Buffalo, 1975), pp. 30-31. Cf. Troels Fink, *Geschichte des Schleswigschen Grenzlandes*, (Copenhagen, 1958), p. 146; Grot, *Pruska ...* p. 50.
21. H. Sybel, *Die Begründung ...*, vol. III, pp. 80-89, Klaczko, Études ... pp. 210.
22. Baroness F. Bunsen ed. *Memoires of Baron Bunsen* (London, 1869), vol. II, p. 186. Cf. Sandiford, *Great Britain ...*, p. 30.
23. It was, however, afterwards approved by Electoral Hesse, Hanover, Saxony and Württemberg.
24. Attention was drawn to the absence of guarantees as the main source of weakness of the treaty by

Sind nicht die Londoner Konferenz-Beschlüsse von 1852 eigentlich schon heut obsolet, so das die Nothwendigkeit sie zu modificiren allseiting anerkannt ist? Warum solten solche von 1862 oder später dauerhafter gearbeitet sein?

Das Schicksal des Friedens von Zurich beweist auch, das Verträge nich die Welt beherrschen,

Bismarck wrote to Schleinitz from St. Petersburg on 28 (16) June 1861.[25]

Many Western statesmen recognised its lameness. Some of them, such as the French diplomats, saw its main shortcoming in the fact that it contained no quarantees in case of infringement. This was pointed out by A. Walewski, who proposed to Denmark that she would be given military guarantees if she would join the anti-Russian coalition during the Crimean War. The French ambassador in Copenhagen drew Monrad's attention to this point in the spring of 1864: 'Pour ce qui est du traité de Londres, ce traité n'a fait que proclamer un principe sans attacher aucune garantie à son maintien', replied Dotézac when Monrad complained that despite the existence of the Treaty of London the participants in the London Conference were seeking to break up the Danish monarchy.[26]

The treaty was really imposed on both sides, and this was possible because 1. Britain and Russia were interested in maintaining the *status quo* in northern Europe and co-operated closely on this matter, 2. Austria, seeing Prussia as an antagonist, feared the growth of Prussian power in northern Germany, 3. France, after the accession of Napoleon III to power, was not interested in opposing Britain and Russian and her traditional policy was to aim to maintain the integrity of Denmark.

The treaty, combined with the provision of the Warsaw protocol, regulating the succession to the Danish throne, was essentially a victory for Russian policy. For this reason Russian diplomacy would cling obstinately to the provisions of the treaty. Queen Victoria called the treaty a Russian intrigue in a letter to King Leopold of the Belgians on 19 September 1863.[27] The integrity of the Danish monarchy was upheld, the spectre of Scandinavianism was banished,[28] Russia maintained her dominance in the Baltic and the Danish throne was to pass to her preferred candidate.

Revue des Deux Mondes, 31. December 1863; *Chronique by E. Forcade,* vol. 49, 1864, p. 250; Ollivier, *L'Empire ...,* vol. 3, pp. 12, 93. The predominant view of British historians was that it was 'one of the most unfortunate of the achievements of European diplomacy', A.W. Ward and S. Wilkinson, *Germany,* vol. II, 1852-1871 (Cambridge, 1917), pp. 122ff. A.W. Ward and P.G. Gooch, *The Cambridge History of British Foreign Policy 1783-1919,* vol. II 1815-1866, (Cambridge, 1923), p. 538. *Foundations of British Foreign Policy from Pitt (1792) to Salisbury (1902),* (Cambridge, 1938), p. 260.

25. *Bismarcks Briefwechsel mit dem Minister Freiherrn von Schleinitz, 1858-1861* (Berlin, 1905), p. 184.
26. Dotézac to Drouyn de Lhuys, 21 May 1864, A.M.A.E., Paris, Danemark, vol. 247, Origines, III, p. 69.
27. O. Scheel, *Dannewirk und Düppel,* (Flenburg, 1940), p. 12.
28. H. Becker-Christensen, *Skandinaviske drømme og politiske realiteter, Den politiske skandinavisme i Danmark, 1830-1850,* (Aarhus, 1981).

Aber welch ein Meistercoup der Russen war das Protokolle von 1852!... Dass Preussen und Österreich das Protokol unterschrieben haben, ist eine namenlose Infamie und muss blutig an den Betreffenden gerächt werden.[29]

The intention of British diplomacy, suspicious of Russian plans, was that the London agreements should be a weapon against the whims of Russian power and contribute to the maintenance of equilibrium in this troubled part of Europe. This was to be achieved by means of the integration of Denmark. In reality Russia gained more. It was another matter that future events denied her the opportunity to make use of these trumps.[30]

We can properly agree with the view that the arrangements of 1852 – though perhaps they seemed the best attainable in the circumstances – did not stand the test of time. The system was built on sand, it offered no prospects whatever of a lasting solution of the Danish-German Question.

The Treaty of London was in some of its consequences beyond all doubt one of the most unfortunate of the achievements of European diplomacy.[31]

If I have nevertheless devoted a lot of space to this matter, it is mainly because, during the growing conflict and the war of 1864, Russian diplomacy continually referred to the treaty of 8 May 1852 and strove to build it up as a great event on which agreement between Denmark and Germany should be based, although the experience of the 1850s and the turn of the decade to the 1860s indicated just the opposite.

II

The good relations between Russia and Denmark during the years 1848-52 had already been impaired somewhat at the time of the Crimean war. Russia was not easily reconciled to the fact of Danish neutrality, though she understood that owing to her geographical position and the constellation of political forces in Europe Denmark could not take any other attitude. It was even harder for Russia to reconcile herself to the conduct of the Danish government, which was compelled to provide various services to the Western powers' fleet during the war. But this, too, Russia ultimately recognised was essential from the point of view of Denmark's interests. Of course these grievances against Denmark diminished as Swedish neutrality changed to favouring and, more and more obviously, adhering to the Western camp, culminating in signature of the November treaty with Britain and France (21 November 1855), which would undoubtedly have been the prelude to

---

29. Engels to Marx, 24 November 1863, *Werke,* vol. 30 (Berlin, 1964), p. 374. H. Sybel took a similar view of the treaty: 'ein schlimmeres Armuthszeignis konnte sich die österreichische-deutsche Politik nicht schreiben, als diese Verträge von 1852'. *Die Begründung des Deutschen Reiches durch Wilhelm I,* vol. III, (Munich and Leipzig, 1890), p. 81.
30. T. Cierpinski, Die Politik Englands ... *Z.d.G.f.S.H.* 1914.
31. *The Cambridge History of British Foreign Policy,* vol. II. 1815-1866. (Cambridge, 1923), p. 538.

Sweden's entry into the war if the peace treaty had not soon been signed in Paris. Denmark, on the other hand, remained neutral in accordance with her December 1853 declaration of neutrality.

Another reason for the deterioration in relations between St. Petersburg and Copenhagen in these years was the changes which took place in Denmark, both in the system of government and in the fact that the conservative administration headed by Ch. Bluhme was succeeded by one composed of adherents of the national-liberal party, which the Russian cabinet regarded as being pro-French.[32] But the decisive factor for the new era in Russo-Danish relations was Russia's defeat in the Crimean War and its internal and international remifications.

Copenhagen followed the changes occurring in Russia with interest, especially those in the field of foreign policy. 'Le prince Gortchakoff est arrivé ici de Vienne. Bien des personnes croient – sans le désirer toutefois – qu'il est désigné à de très hautes fonctions', reported Plessen from St. Petersburg.[33]

Le Prince Gortchakoff est un homme, auquel on accorde de grandes capacités et de talents ... C'est Madame la Grande-Duchesse Olga, qui a appelé l'attention de Son Auguste Père sur le Prince Gortchakoff, qui réunis fait alors le poste de représentant de Russie près la Diète de Francfort à celui de ministre à Stoutgard. Le Prince Gortchakoff fut envoyé a la Cour de Vienne, où il devint successeur du Baron de Meyendorff. S'il n'a pas pu changer les dispositions de la Cour d'Autriche envers la Russie, l'Empereur cependant a été très-content de lui. On l'a trouvée brillant dans les négociations qui ont eu lieu, l'année passée, à Vienne, où il avait à discuter avec des adversaires d'une grande habilité. ... Je comprendrais aussi que le nom russe du Prince l'eut recommandé, dans ce moment-ci, après la conclusion de la paix, telle qu'elle est, à l'Empereur pour en faire Son Ministre des affaires étrangères. Le Prince lui-même, n'avait pas l'ambition d'obtenir ce poste, il aurait, à-ce qu'il dit, préféré la place d'ambassadeur à Paris, et ce n'est qu'après d'assez longues hésitations, que le Prince Gortchakoff s'est decidé à accepter la position à laquelle la confiance de son Souverain l'a appellé.[34]

This was Plessen's report of the appointment of Russia's new minister of foreign affairs, the successor to Chancellor Nesselrode, who had held the office since 1822.

The change in this key post was received with satisfaction in Copenhagen and the minister of foreign affairs, Scheele, recalled in a dispatch to Plessen that as ambassador in Vienna, and particularly in Frankfurt, Gorchakov had maintained contact with the Copenhagen cabinet and had used his position to exercise an important influence on the German Diet in a spirit friendly towards Denmark. Scheele believed that relations with him would be as good as they had been with Nesselrode.[35]

By reason of the positions which he had previously occupied, Gorchakov was no stranger to Danish affairs. He had encountered them in Frankfurt as ambassador

---

32. Russo-Danish relations during the Crimean War are treated more fully in E. Halicz, *Danish Neutrality during the Crimean War, (1853-1856)*. (Odense U.P. 1977).
33. Plessen, no. 27, 2. April (21 March) 1856. Rusland. Depecher 1854-1856. R.A. Copenhagen.
34. Plessen, no. 33, 1 May (19 April) 1856.
35. Ordrer, Rusland, no. 15, 14. May 1856.

extraordinary and minister plenipotentiary. In 1851 he had written a memorandum of behalf of his government, the idea of which was to resist the aggressive intentions of Berlin *vis-à-vis* Denmark, and proposed taking diplomatic steps to counter them. He supported the maintenance of the German Confederation in the interests of the security of Russia and as a barrier to the unification of Germany under the aegis of Prussia and the withdrawal of Austria from the Confederation.[36] His actions were regarded in Copenhagen as friendly to Denmark, and on 8 July 1852 he received the high distinction of 'Storkors af Danebrogsordenen'.[37]

Gorchakov frequently went back to this period, which we shall conventionally call the Frankfurt period, emphasising the services which he had rendered Denmark and recalling his pleasant contacts with the Danish ambassador in Frankfurt, B.E. Bülow, whose diplomatic skills he rated highly. He also spoke in a friendly way of his contacts with the Danish ambassador in Vienna, Bille-Brahe.[38]

The first official contact with the Danish ambassador in St. Petersburg occurred on 21 April (3 May), shortly after Gorchakov took over the minister's portfolio. The topic of conversation was the Sund and the recall of the Russian delegate, J. Tegoborski, to St. Petersburg when the Copenhagen conference reached an impasse because of the position adopted by Britain.[39] Plessen reported that the minister referred to Denmark and its government as 'un gouvernement ami' and assured him that if only the work of the conference could be resumed, Tegoborski would return to Copenhagen.[40] A second meeting took place in June.[41] Taking advantage of the first opportunity after Gorchakov's return from abroad, Plessen hastened to express his government's gratitude for Russia's contribution to the Paris declaration of 16 April standardising certain points in maritime law in time of war.[42] The Danish government had acceded to the convention on the invitation of its signatories, and Copenhagen's gratitude was all the greater as the principles of the convention conformed to the spirit of justice and of the principles previously enunciated by the Danish government, and represented 'tel progrès notable dans le droit international'.[43] A fundamental discussion of Russo-Danish relations followed on 30 (18) July 1856.[44]

Gorchakov opened the conversation by voicing his appreciation of the Danish King's personal letter to Nesselrode expressing his gratitude to the former Chancellor and his esteem for Gorchakov personally 'd'une manière fort gracieuse et dans les termes bien aimables, mes faibles services', as Gorchakov called them, alluding

---

36. Martens, *Recueil* ... vol. XIV, pp. 233, 237; Zechlin, *Bismarck,* p. 26; Bushuev, *A. Gortchakov,* p. 49.
37. S.S. Semanov, *A.M. Gorchakov. Russkii diplomat XIX v.* (Moscow, 1962), pp. 35-36, and *Kongelig Dansk Hof- og Staatskalender for aaret 1853,* p. 10 (8 July 1852).
38. Plessen, no. 53, 30 (18) July, and no. 63, 5 September (24 August) 1856.
39. Plessen, no. 36. 3 May (21 April) 1856.
40. *Ibid.*
41. Plessen, no. 47, 7 July (25 June) 1856.
42. Martens, *Recueil* ..., vol. XV, pp. 332-4.
43. Plessen, no. 47.
44. Plessen, no. 53, 30 (18) July 1856.

to his Vienna meetings with Bille-Brahe. Referring to his brief visit to Berlin, where he stopped on the way to Vienna, and to his meeting with the head of the Prussian diplomatic service, Manteuffel, Gorchakov assured Plessen that he had perceived the most sincere intentions of reconciliation with Denmark on the part of Manteuffel. It was very easy, said Gorchakov, for the Russian cabinet to refrain from expressing its opinion on the Danish-German dispute, as the subject of the dispute was a purely German one 'd'un intérêt pûrement germanique', and the German states had not asked him to state his view. The Russian government could give Denmark advice, but would do so only at Denmark's request and if circumstances permitted. 'L'abstention est le mot d'ordre de notre politique', the minister emphasised, and the Emperor took the same position. The minister had informed all Russian ambassadors that this was the position of his government. Referring again to his stay in Frankfurt, Gorchakov mentioned the name of the Danish ambassador, E.B. Bülow, describing him, Plessen reported, as - 'de tous les Plénipotentiaires à Francfort, ... sans contredit, la tête la mieux organisée - comprenant le mieux les affaires, et que notre auguste Maître (the Danish King) avait en lui en serviteur d'une haute capacité - d'un talent remarquable'.

Gorchakov said that the situation in Denmark was a subject of concern to the Emperor. For many years the two courts had been intimately connected. The Russian court took a lively interest in everything that happened in Denmark and valued her attitude during the recent conflict highly - i.e. during the Crimean war. 'C'est - a dit le Prince - un double raison pour l'Empereur d'être affectueusement et très sérieusement préoccupé de l'état de choses chez Vous, qui nous semble être assez grave pour laisser appréhender des dangers pour la Couronne'.

Gorchakov explained that he was talking to Plessen about these matters since he trusted him. On the other hand, he had not put the matter before the Russian ambassador in Copenhagen, nor in Stockholm, since the Emperor had urged him to avoid everything which could cause suspicion of interference in the internal affairs of another state. But he wanted to stress yet again that the Emperor was 'affectueusement préoccupé de la situation des choses dans un pays, auquel Sa Majesté porte, pour plus d'une raison, une sincère et véritable intérêt.

Reporting on his discussion with Gorchakov, Plessen added that this impression of the state of affairs in Denmark was also shared by less official circles in St. Petersburg. 'On trouve, que nous marchons, d'un côté, trop brusquement, - d'un autre côté, avec trop d'insouciance, permettant aux périls de s'amasser et de devenir menaçants pour notre propre sécurité.

Not many weeks had passed when Gorchakov expanded on the topic he had raised, during a meeting with Plessen on 5 September (24 August).[45] Referring to the tribute paid to him by the Danish government in relation to his period as Russian representative at the German Diet in Frankfurt, Gorchakov emphasised that he had to say that it was possible he would not be able to continue to render such services.

45. Plessen, no. 63, 5 September (24 August) 1856.

Le Prince Gortchakoff croît, que nous ne sommes pas exempts de reproches par rapport à l'attitude que le Gouvernement du Roi a prise en face des sujets Allemands de Sa Majesté, l'attitude qui touche de si près nos rapports avec les Cabinets Allemands et la Conféderation Germanique, et qui peut provoquer selon lui les dangers pareils à ceux, que dans sa qualité d'Envoyé de Russie à Francfort il a été appellé à combattre.

According to Gorchakov, the Danish government ought to use Bülow to reach an agreement with the German cabinets, since he possessed immense experience and deep knowledge of German problems.

What was the reason for the changes taking place in Russian policy towards Denmark? It is possible to explain them on the basis of analysis of the situation in which Russia found herself immediately after the ending of the Crimean War, but it is also impossible to overlook other factors accompanying the development of the internal situation in the Scandinavian countries, and particularly Denmark.

As a result of her military defeat Russia's international authority was at a low ebb and the domestic situation forced the government to concentrate on internal problems. The reforms which it proceeded to introduce absorbed the attention of both government and society. Following the conclusion of the peace treaty Russia's principal motto became withdrawal from active foreign policy and avoidance of direct interference in the internal affairs of other nations and states.

Although the quest for an alliance with the premier European power, France, which alone could help Russia to get rid of the restrictions imposed on her in Paris, was one of Gorchakov's basic principles, immediately after the defeat this was no more than an intention for the future, and Russia's only real ally, tested in the difficult years of the war, was Prussia. But from the point of view of Russia's strategic plans this ally could not help her much since Prussia was not yet a power of the first rank, which was demonstrated, among other things, by the fact that it was only at Russia's insistent demand that Manteuffel was invited to Paris, and even then not as an equal partner.

Nevertheless, the Russo-Prussian rapprochement could lead to far-reaching and important changes in Russia's attitude to Denmark, as there was no doubt, especially after the experiences of 1848-50, that Prussia was most interested in securing a positive outcome of events in the Elbe duchies, which were again in dispute with Denmark. Russia, although content with the *status quo* in northern Europe, would not be able to adopt the position which Nicholas I had taken in the event of a conflict between Denmark and Germany.

Another reason for the cooling of relations between Russia and Denmark was the democratic changes taking place in Denmark itself. The transformation of the country from an absolute monarchy into a constitutional state with a democratic system was not to Russia's liking. Another problem disturbing Russia was the conflict between Copenhagen and the duchies of Holstein and Lauenburg,[46] which in St. Petersburg's opinion, at least initially, was not so much a national conflict as

46. Steefel, pp. 17-21.

a question of the defence of conservative circles in the duchies against the Danish government's tendency to impose democratic institutions on them as a means of restraining their dominance in the duchies.

It is true that from an international point of view the problem was not initially regarded as threatening since neither Manteuffel nor Bismarck, who was enjoying greater and greater authority in Prussian diplomatic circles, had yet advanced any demands of a fundamental nature *vis-à-vis* Denmark and at this stage preferred the duchies to remain under Danish rule rather than pass to some liberal German prince.

Finally, Russia was disturbed by the signs of Scandinavianism which appeared in the Scandinavian countries following the Crimean War. Although not as prominent as at the beginning of the 1840s, they were regarded as a threat because France was believed to be behind them.[47]

The Russian ambassador in Copenhagen, Ungern-Sternberg, a diplomat of the Nesselrode school, contributed to the exaggeration of the negative aspects of all these phenomena. He had been at his post in Copenhagen since 1846 and regarded the transformation of Denmark into a democratic country almost as a personal calamity. Consequently he painted an extremely unfavourable picture of Denmark. In Ungern-Sternberg's opinion the situation in the country had changed for the worse ('cette fâcheuse tournure') since the start of the reign of Frederick VII, in spite of his (Ungern-Sternberg's) efforts to maintain the conservative order in Denmark and the rights of the Danish crown. The Ørsted-Bluhme government, with which Ungern-Sternberg had co-operated closely and whose sensible and moderate policy had retarded the development of democracy within the country, the government which had happily settled the question of the succession to the Danish throne, externally maintained good relations with the German Confederation and followed a policy of neutrality, jointly with Sweden-Norway, during the Crimean War and which had won itself esteem both at home and abroad, had, according to the ambassador been shamefully ('ignominieusement') removed by the King. The ministerial portfolios were in the hands of people who professed democratic principles, diametrically opposed to those of the previous government, and who would bring great misfortunes to Denmark. The consequences could already be felt.[48] Inside the country democratic principles were developing with unflagging energy and the ideas of Scandinavianism were running rife, supported by the King.

The conservative party had not only been removed from office but had been paralysed by demagogues and democrats, and the royal authority was dependent on 'les hommes les plus indignes'. 'Les hommes respectables et les vrais patriotes' were inflamed with dissatisfaction.[49]

---

47. K. Döhler considers that Scandinavianism was 'eine Lieblingsgedanke der französischen Politik'. *Napoleon III und die deutsch-dänische Frage,* (Halle, 1913, p. 16.
48. See: Håndskriftsamlingen XVI. Proveniensordnet del Russland Staatsarkiver i Moskva, vol. 48. Afskrifter af indberetninger fra det russiske gesandtskab i København til regeringen i St. Petersburg.
49. Report of 13 (1), February 1856, vol. 48.

The country was governed by a cabal headed by Countess Danner and the minister of foreign affairs was under her influence.[50]

Abroad, the quarrel between Denmark and the German Confederation was becoming dangerous. The duchies were exasperated, and the question of the Sound had been clumsily handled by the government from the very beginning. This government also showed ingratitude to Russia ('envers sa bienfaitrice').[51]

The chief misfortune for Denmark, in Ungern-Sternberg's opinion, was its democratic constitution,[52] which was the source of the conflict, in his interpretation, between the conservative principles held by the leaders of the Holstein opposition and the democratic principles enunciated by the Danish government, acting on the basis of the constitution of 2 October 1855. 'La lutte qui s'est ouverte a principalement pour but de démocratiser les provinces allemandes de la Monarchie'.[53] The conflict broke out with the introduction of the constitution (1855 – E.H.), which was adopted without discussion with the states of the duchies, contrary to the agreements concluded by Denmark with the large German states in 1851-52. When Prussia and Austria joined in the dispute and addressed appropriate notes to Copenhagen on 23 June 1856 Ungern-Sternberg saw great danger or Denmark.

Il y a en outre à remarquer – explained Ungern-Sternberg, que les habitants des Duchés craignant avant tout le régime démocratique que le système actual leur imposerait, se soumettraient bien plutôt au pouvoir du Roi. Tous leurs sentiments de nationalité se révoltent à l'idée d'être subjugués et gouvernés par le *peuple* danois, auquel ils se sentent supérieurs soit en civilisation, soit comme membres de la puissante confédération germanique.

La lutte inégale que cet état de choses fait naître, ne pourra que s'envenimer de part et d'autre par la tenacité que distingue les deux nationalités, et si l'on ne parvient pas à faire adopter à Copenhague une politique plus sage et plus modérée, il me semble inévitable que les Puissances allemandes ne finissent par prendre ouvertement fait et cause pour les Duchés, après avoir epuisé les conseils et les avertissemens.[54]

Ungern-Sternberg had doubts whether Scheele, who did not treat the German states' protests seriously and delayed his reply, thus exacerbating the crisis, was capable of dealing with the increasingly grave situation. This was particularly so after Manteuffel and Buol, dissatisfied with Scheele's reply which had offered minor territorial concessions concerning the domain lands of the Monarchy, but had left the fundamental issue (the question of the constitution) unanswered, adressed much sharper notes to Copenhagen in October 1856, threatening to bring the whole matter before the German Diet.[55]

50. The morganatic wife of Frederick VII. Particulière I (13) February, no. 55, 11 (23) April, 1856. L.N. Scheele was a Holsteiner by birth and a devoted supporter of the Whole-State.
51. See: Report of 1 (13) February 1856, Particulière no. 41, 7 (19) March, no. 55, Réservé, 11 (23) April 1856.
52. Reports of 7 (19) March, 1 (13) November and Particulière, 19 November (1 December) 1856, vols. 48 and 49.
53. Particulière, 28 April (10 May) 1856.
54. No. 113, 5 (17) July 1856, vol. 48.
55. The royal proclamation of January 28, 1852, had included the income from domain lands with the common finances of the Monarchy but had left their administration and control under the heading

Les hommes actuellement au pouvoir, et M. de Scheele en particulier, me parraissent peu disposés à la conciliation, et n'ont pas su gagner, ni en Allemagne, ni dans les Duchés, le degré de confiance nécessaire pour calmer les esprits et les appréhensions. L'élémént danois, dans lequel ils vivent et qui leur sert de point d'appui, ainsi que d'anciennes animosités nationales et personelles contribueront, il faut le craindre, à aggraver la situation.[56]

Towards the end of the year the situation changed, in the ambassador's view, in that the government began to see the danger threatening Denmark.

mais comment redresser maintenant ce vice d'origine et les torts commis, comment surtout donner satisfaction à l'élément germanique sans exciter la jalousie et les susceptibilités danoises? C'est un dilemne dont on ne sortira pas aussi longtemps qu'on voudra maintenir le régime constitutionnel moderne et réunir dans une seule Assemblée législative (Rigsraad) les représentants des deux nationalités parmi lesquelles règne de l'animosité, et dont celle qui ce croit opprimée cherchera et trouvera toujours de l'appui à l'étranger.

The ambassador regretted that the people with conservative views, although very numerous, would not form an organised and disciplined party and that the tone of political life was set by the press, which was under the control of democrats and utopians. He also regretted that the positions of state were in the hands of democratic and destructive elements. 'C'est que l'élément destructif ne fasse pas des progrès plus rapides encore'.

He saw the future of Denmark in sombre colours.

L'apathie du caractère national, des instincts invétérés et une certaine réserve méfiante, jointe à un manque total d'initiative, préservent jusqu'à présent les Danois de ces catastrophes qui précipitent les Etats dans l'abîme des troubles intérieures. Le terrain est cependant miné de telle sorte que le moindre événement révolutionnaire à l'étranger pourrait produire ici un bouleversement funeste, auquel aucun élément conservateur n'opposerait de la résistance.[57]

The same opinion was shared by people whom Ungern-Sternberg called 'les personnes de l'ancien régime', who frequently approached him, asking what should be done. He replied, however, that Russia would not involve herself in their internal affairs and the Danes themselves must find the means to remedy the situation. 'Fidèle au rôle d'observateur', as he himself described his position, he advised them to organise a monarchist and conservative party on the Prussian model 'pour soutenir les principes d'ordre et servir d'appui au trône'. 'On me répond que la tête manque'.[58]

---

of local affairs. This division had been retained in the local constitutions of the duchies but Article 50 of the Common Constitution of 1855 gave the Rigsraad control of the alienation and acquisition of the domains of the Monarchy. The local constitution of Schleswig was modified in this sense by royal ordinance but the Estates of Holstein refused to accept a parallel amendment. See N. Neergaard, *Under Junigrundloven,* vol. II pt. I, Chapter I; also Steefel, *The Schleswig-Holstein Question,* p. 17.

56. No. 173, 1 (13) November 1856, vol. 49.
57. Particulière, 19 November (1 December) 1856.
58. *Ibid.*

In this situation there was no prospect of friendly co-operation between the Russian ambassador and government ministers, particularly Scheele. 'Leurs principes', we read in the embassy's report to St. Petersburg, 'diffèrent trop, et l'Envoyé de Russie ayant vu M. Scheele à l'œuvre, connaissant ses antécédents, ses liasons et son caractère personal, ne saurait lui donner ni son estime, ni sa confiance'.[59] For the same reason Ungern-Sternberg asked Gorchakov to recall him from Copenhagen. He believed that a new ambassador, who had not experienced everything that he had in Copenhagen, would be able to carry out his duties better.[60] Gorchakov, however, was of a different opinion and left Ungern-Sternberg at his post in Copenhagen.

The unfavourable atmosphere prevailing in the Russian embassy did not escape the notice of Scheele, and in his dispatch to Plessen[61] he expressed the fear that the reports which the St. Petersburg cabinet received from Copenhagen did not contain accurate information. In reply Plessen emphasised[62] that he was not in a position to say authoritatively whether this was so as Gorchakov, unlike his predecessor, Nesselrode, did not show him Ungern-Sternberg's dispatches and it would be extremely indelicate on his part to draw Gorchakov's attention to the inaccuracy of the reports he received from his ambassador. 'C'est à mon avis une chose très delicate et de laquelle il faudrait user avec la plus grande circonspection'. Besides, Plessen argued, the Prince's assessments of the situation in Denmark were in part based on facts on which it was impossible to cast doubt. These included that fact that in the duchy of Holstein persons with the reputation of being loyal to the King were dissatisfied and were forming an opposition to the government. This, according to him, was one of the main elements in the unfavourable picture of the internal situation in Denmark which the St. Petersburg cabinet had formed.

III

The second factor which, in Plessen's opinion, influenced the cabinet's unfavourable verdict was the signs of Scandinavianism, and particularly the recent visit of the Viceroy of Norway to Copenhagen. The Tsar, whom Plessen had met in Moscow a short time ago, had not raised the subject, but many people had spoken to him about the fact that these Scandinavianist tendencies were viewed with apprehension and regret in Russia. Gorchakov, although restrained in conversation with Plessen, had expressed regret to others and complained about this visit and the sympathy and the extravagant demonstrations in honour of a foreign prince, which were regarded in St. Petersburg as a blow to the prestige of his royal Majesty the King of Denmark and Danish national pride.

59. E. Halicz, *Danish Neutrality,* pp. 135-136.
60. No. 108 (Reservé), 28 June (10 July) 1856. Halicz, *Ibid.,* p. 136.
61. No. 27.
62. No. 71, 4. October (22. September) 1856.

Towards the end of the Crimean War signs of Scandinavianism began to disturb the ambassador, although they were not as prominent in Denmark as they had been at the beginning of the 1840s. Scandinavianism, the consequence of which might be the rise of a unified state comprising Sweden, Norway and Denmark and controlling the entrance to the Baltic, was unacceptable to Russia. For this reason Russia always sought to break the unity of the Scandinavian nations, and Nicholas I expressed this when he advised Gen. Oxholm in 1848: 'Prenez bien garde que les Danois et les Suédois ne deviennent trop bien amis'.[63] V. Valentin was right when he said that

> Der neue dänische Nationalismus, der ein Stück der modernen skandinawischen Bewegung war, und eine Wiedergeburt des nordischen Volkstums bedeutete, machte die dänische Sache dem legitimisch und trotz liberaler Anwandlungen, autokratisch gesinnten Rusland sehr unsympatisch.[64]

For this reason too Russia had exerted pressure on the government of Christian VIII in the 1840s, encouraging him to suppress all signs of Scandinavianism with the help of police methods, the more so since the movement bore the mark of a liberal, constitutional and national movement.[65] In 1855 the rise of a single Scandinavian state, in Russia's opinion, would have enabled Napoleon's France to establish herself there, and possibly Britain too, and then Russia would be threatened with losing control of the Baltic and being cut off from the sea. The Belts and the Sound in the hands of a single state unfriendly to Russia would make a new Bosphorus and Dardanelles. Russia would be cut off from the sea and, furthermore, the safety of the imperial capital could be endangered. The Russian diplomat Baron R. Rosen put the question of the Baltic straits as follows:

> In reality these Straits of the Bosphorus and the Dardanelles can just as little be considered to represent the key of our house any more than the Straits known as the Sound (Øresund) giving access to the Baltic Sea from the North Sea or German Ocean.[66]

In Rosen's opinion the Sound was more important for the vital interests of Russia than the straits at the entrance to the Black Sea. Ungern-Sternberg had been sensitive about Scandinavianism since 1848, and from the end of 1855 he devoted more and more attention to the problem.

Russia's especial sensitivity to this problem emerged in connection with General Canrobert's mission to Stockholm and Copenhagen and the reorientation of Swedish policy towards the end of 1855. And although Sweden remained neutral to the end of the war and took no steps to provoke Russia or to reclaim Finland, the very fact that she associated herself with, and concluded a treaty with, the Western

---

63. Åke Holmberg, *Skandinavismen i Sverige vid 1800-talets mitt*, (Gothenburg, 1946), p. 255.
64. V. Valentin, *Bismarcks Reichsgründung im Urteil englischer Diplomaten*, (Amsterdam, 1937), p. 205.
65. Becker-Christensen, *Skandinaviske drømme* ... pp. 56 ff, 236 ff. See also A. Thorsøe, *Kong Frederic den Syvendes Regering*, vol. II, p. 441, Nesselrode, *Lettres et papiers*, vol. IX, p. 232.
66. Rosen, *Forty Years of Diplomacy*, vol. II, (London, 1922), p. 101.

powers, and then contributed during the Paris conference to the demilitarisation of the Åland Islands, was sufficient to disturb Russia greatly. There was a conviction in Russia that Sweden wanted to carry out the provisions of the November Treaty and that war had to be expected. Even before this there was great anxiety in Russia on account of Canrobert's arrival in the capitals of the Scandinavian countries in the autumn of 1855. This was expressed, among other, by Gorchakov, who wrote to Olga Nikolaevna on 6 (18) November, when he was at his post in Vienna.

Pour le moment le pivot de la situation est dans la mission Canrobert. Jusqu'ici nous n'avons aucune donnée précise pour ou contre le succès-plutôt des doutes sur la réussite. Si l'on entraîne la Suède, ce qui ne peut avoir lieu que par des promisses qui renfermeraient des acquisitions territoriales, la guerre changerait de physionomie, s'étendrait jusqu'à l'infini, et toute paix serait impossible. Ce serait pour nous un grand embarras du moment, mais finalement la Suède serait infailliblement perdue. C'est de ce côté que j'attends avec l'impatience les premiers avis.[67]

The signing of the November Treaty was a shock for Russian diplomats. When Dashkov, the Russian ambassador in Stockholm, learnt the content of the treaty from the Brussels newspapers he wrote to Nesselrode expressing his regret about this event and added: 'il me serait difficile d'avoir aujourd'hui la même confiance que par le passé dans les assurances de S.M. le Roi et de ses conseillers.'[68] In a conversation with the minister, G.A. Stiernfeld, the ambassador expressed his regret about the pact, which was an unpleasant surprise for Russia.[69] Dashkov, and Nesselrode, regarded both the military preparations and the parade organised by Prince Oscar in memory of Charles XII – who was a figure-head for anti-Russian feeling ('la personification de l'inimitié contre la Russie') – as evidence that Sweden had one foot in the camp of Russia's enemies. The pamphlet by G. Lallerstedt, *'La Scandinavie, ses craintes et ses espérances'*, which caused a sensation in the papers, was also treated as a indication of hostile feelings towards Russia, 'qui y retrouve l'écho fidèle des sentiments qui l'animent à l'égard de la Russie'.[70]

Even so, it was known that the majority of Swedish diplomats, including G. Nordin and L. Manderström, were opposed to Sweden participating in the war against Russia;[71] that at the Paris conference the latter had striven to neutralise the impression which Swedish policy during the final months of the war had made on Russia; and that in Sweden itself there was general discontent with the treaty. 'L'indifférence ou pour mieux dire le désappointement semblerait être l'impression la plus exacte du sentiment qui prédomine ici dans toutes les classes.'[72]

---

67. H.S.A. Stuttgart, G 314 Bü 1851-1871, A.M. Gorchakov to Olga Nikolaevna.
68. Film copy. Centralarkivet Moskva. Handlingar beröranda svensk-ryska förhållande. Rulle 69 (212-215) Stockholm. Rigs. Depecher från Stockholm til St. Petersburg.
69. *Ibid.* no. 12, 27. January (8 February) 1856.
70. Report No. 21, 4 (16) March 1856. Cf. Allan Jansson, *Den Svenske Utrikespolitikens Historia* III:3, 1844-1872, (Stockholm, 1961), p. 109.
71. Dashkov, 3 (15) April 1856; Jansson, *Den Svenske ...* p. 109.
72. No. 25, 24 March (5 April) and No. 31, 19 April (1 May).

Something which could not escape the Russian ambassador's notice, however, was the fact that the King wanted to continue the anti-Russian policy line initiated by the November Treaty, believing that the nation wanted war with Russia in order to recover Finland.[73] The King made this clear in his speech at the opening of parliament, defending the November Treaty as evidence of the renewed strengthening of the old glorious tradition of alliance and friendship linking Sweden with the Queen of England and the Emperor of France.[74] He also recalled 'l'identité d'origine et de souvenirs qui existe entre les nations scandinaves', (Knorring's report to Gorchakov).

Just how negative Russia's attitude to Sweden was after the latter's conclusion of the November Treaty is shown by both Nesselrode's and Gorchakov's comments. Following the publication of the Swedish government's circular of 18 December on the November treaty, Nesselrode wrote to Dashkov on 14 January 1856:

Nous avons de la peine à nous expliquer le motif et le but d'un tel procédé. Aussi nous abstenons-nous encore d'y répondre dans la même voie dont le Ministère Suédois s'est servi; car nous ne voyons aucun motif raisonnable, ni aucune utilité à envenimer une polémique dont la presse devient l'organe, des relations qui ont eu jusqu'à présent à nos yeux au moins le caractère d'une amitié intime et d'une confiance mutuelle. Mon expédition du 11/23 décembre a dû Vous convaincre combien le maintien de ces relations nous était précieux, même en présence des nouveaux engagements la Suède venait de contracter envers les Puissances occidentales, et les ouvertures du Cabinet de Stockholm nous autorisaient croire qu'il était dans les mêmes dispositions.

Je Vous engage Mr. à ne pas laisser ignorer au Baron Stjernfeld la pénible impression que certains passages de sa circulaire a dû produire sur le Cabinet Impérial.[75]

Relations were not improved by the assurances of the new minister of foreign affairs, Lagerheim, who told Dashkov that, despite the dislike the Swedes felt for Russia because of the loss of Finland, 'j'invoque de nouveau la nécessité d'une réconciliation générale'.[76]

Russia felt so resentful of Sweden's behaviour that Gorchakov returned to this subject many times in discussions with the Swedish ambassador, G. Adelswärds. The latter, relating a conversation with Gorchakov, reported:

Je ne dois pas passer sous silence le peu de mots qui ont été dits sur notre politique, lesquels m'ont permis de constater à nouveau que les blessures occasionées au Cabinet Russe par le traité de Novembre ne sont point cicatrisées. Le Prince m'a dit en effet la phrase suivante: il est dans la politique des cabinets les péripéties qui laissent après elles des traces difficiles à effacer et, je Vous le dis franchement, de ce nombre et la dernière de Votre Gouvernement vis-à-vis de nous.[77]

---

73. No. 19, 3 (15) April and no. 26, 12 (24) October 1856, Jansson, *Den Svenske* ... pp. 113, 115.
74. No. 26, 12 (24) October 1856.
75. Film copy. Rigs. Stockholm, Centralarkivet, Moscow.
76. No. 41, 16 (28) October 1856.
77. Report no. 54, 21 (9) November 1857, Depescher från beskickningen i St. Pet. 1857-58. Rigs. Stockholm.

Again, at the end of 1858, during a conversation with the newly appointed Swedish ambassador, F. Wedel-Jarlsberg, Gorchakov returned to the subject of the treaty, though without mentioning it by name. He added:

Je ne puis pas Vous cacher que je pense que Vous avez fait alors un peu *école*. Ceci – the ambassador explained – fut dit sans aigreur aucune et plûtot avec un ton de plaisanterie, mais je n'en cru pas moins devoir réléver le mot d'*école* – et je le fis en répliquant. Sur ce point, mon Prince, nous appréciations diffèrent essentiellement, et Vous comprenez facilement que dans mon position et du point de vue de mon Gouvernement, je ne saurais admettre la Vôtre.

Considerations of independence and national pride demanded this, the ambassador explained. 'Eh bien, ne parlons plus du passé et ne nous occupons que de l'avenir pour vivre en bons voisins et en bonne harmonie', replied Gorchakov.[78]

How deeply the events of the end of 1855 were rooted in the Russians' memories was also demonstrated when, in conversations with Wedel-Jarlsberg in December 1858, Alexander II referred to the Treaty of 21 November 1855, saying 'qu'Il ne connaissait pas et qu'il n'avait jamais compris les griefs et les sujets de mésintelligence, qui avaient déterminé les Royaumes Unis à conclure le traité du 21 November'. Referring to that period, and the question of Lapland, on which Russia and Sweden-Norway were divided, he also explained that Menshikov had been responsible for the closure of the Russian border in Norwegian Lapland and both Nesselrode and Armfelt favoured a conciliatory solution of the dispute with Sweden, but had been overruled by Menshikov, whose point of view was shared by Nicholas I.[79]

If I have gone into this question rather closely, it is because it seems to me that these events had a fundamental influence on Russia's attitude not only to Sweden but also to the problem with which we are concerned here, and directly affected Russia's attitude to Denmark and first of all the Schleswig-Holstein problem.[80] If they had not occurred, and particularly if The Treaty of 21 November 1855 had not been signed, Russia's attitude to signs of Scandinavianism after the Crimean War would undoubtedly have been much more tolerant.[81]

In addition there was the fact that in Denmark itself a growing tendency towards Scandinavianism appeared, and it was enthusiastically advocated by the national-liberal group and its press, especially *Fædrelandet,* edited by C.P. Ploug.

However, there was less than complete unity between Ungern-Sternberg and his

---

78. *Ibid.* No. 101. 13 (1) November 1858.
79. No. 118. Confidential. 15 (3) December 1858. See C.F. Palmstierna, *Sverige, Ryssland och England 1833-1855,* (Stockholm, 1932).
80. Zutis's introduction. In: *Svenska historia i rysk version,* p. 58.
81. The French view of the November treaty was set out in an article by A. Geffroy: 'le traité du 21 novembre et la paix de Paris ont modifié profondément la situation de la Suède en face de ses redoutables voisins, et l'ont en définitive affranchie'). (See note 82).
82. A. Geffroy, 'La Suède avant et après le traité de Paris. (Le Roi Charles-Jean et le Roi Oscar dans leurs rapports avec le Cabinet Russe)', *Revue des Deux Mondes* (Paris, 1856), vol. III, pp. 456-59, The importance of the treaty is also discussed in Jansson, *Den Svenske ...* pp. 116 ff.

deputy, Freytag-Loringshoven, over their assessment of Scandinavianism in 1855-56. The latter, whilst indeed sensitive to signs of Scandinavianism, did not have the tendency to magnify the practical effects of the movement. He distinguished different lines of thought within Scandinavianism. One sought the creation of a federal republic from the three Scandinavian states, a second would like to maintain each of the three states with its constitution and see them linked in a defensive and offensive alliance, others again wanted Scandinavia to be ruled by one monarch, who should be the ambitious King of Sweden. The aims and ambitions of the Swedish court, he reported, did not stop at Finland, whose liking for Sweden seemed to be questionable, but were really directed towards Denmark, which the monarch would like to unite with Sweden in order to possess both shores of the Sound and so move closer to central Europe.

In Freytag-Loringshoven's opinion the Dansh Scandinavianists did not want to join a union unless their liberal constitution was preserved untouched. Moreover, since Denmark represented the highest civilisation in Scandinavia, they hoped that Copenhagen, with its key geographical position, would become the capital of the three Scandinavian states. The Norwegians, on the other hand, while not really claiming primacy in the union, would not give anything up in favour of their neighbours, and clung jealously to their political independence. When one also remembered that there was disagreement among the advocates of Scandinavianism themselves about whether 'le bas peuple' of each country hated each other, one had to conclude that the idea did not seem to be capable of rapid implementation and was no more than a dream. It served only as a pretext for revolutionaries and false liberals.

Referring to an article in *The Times* written by some Norwegian, with its proposal to combine the three states under the sceptre of the Bernadotte dynasty, and to the position of such promoters of Scandinavianism as the editor of *Fædrelandet,* who would be inclined to accept foreign domination as the price of implementing his seditious plans to establish a republic on the ruins of the three monarchies, the Russian diplomat put forward the idea that the then Prince Christian would receive Holstein and Lauenburg as an indemnity. But he would wager that the Danish government would not agree to the Scandinavian idea, which would mean the liquidation of the monarchy and the state.

Pour ce qui concerne le Gouvernement danois, il faudrait qu'il fût bien coupable ou bien aveugle pour ne pas combattre à outrance ces faux scandinavisme, qui anéantirait ou l'existence politique du Danemark, ou ses institutions monarchiques.

La plus grande vigilance à ce sujet est pour les Gouvernans de ce pays un devoir d'autant plus urgent que les relations anormales qui existent à la cour danoise, ont fait tellement accroître le nombre des mécontents, qu'il s'en trouve beaucoup, qui sans être le moins du monde ni libéraux, ni révolutionnaires, accepteraient volontiers tout changement, pourvu qu'il mette fin à l'état de choses actuel.[83]

Scandinavianism was taken much more seriously by Ungern-Sternberg, especially

---

83. No. 210, 26 December 1855 (7 January 1856). Freytag-Loringshoven to Nesselrode.

in the summer of 1856, on account of the visits by Copenhagen students to Stockholm and Uppsala, and meetings generally of students from the three Scandinavian countries, who were feted by the rulers of the Scandinavian countries. In the ambassador's opinion, these extraordinary youth festivities were political in character, and he regarded them as dangerous phenomena.

Les principaux meneurs de cette conspiration – wrote Ungern-Sternberg after the students' return to Copenhagen[84] – à face découverte veulent sans doute une république fédérative, et cette arrière-pensée ne saurait échapper, ce me semble, aux Souverains des pays dont il s'agit. Si malgré cela, on les voit prendre part aux festins et récevoir les émissaires de la propagande avec des démonstrations extraordinaires, on ne saurait se défendre d'une pitié profonde. Jouets de la masse aveuglée et d'une population mensongère, ces Souverains travaillent à leur ruine, en fecondant la germe d'un mouvement qui en tout cas devra coûter la couronne à l'un des deux.

Cet état des choses – he concluded – me paraît de nature à attirer la plus sérieuse attention des puissances du Nord de l'Europe.

In successive reports on 13 (25), 14 (26) and 18 (30) June the central problem is the spectre of Scandinavianism looming over Denmark and the indictment is directed at the leading figures in this movement: C. Houg, C. Ploug, H. Clausen, N. Grundtvig and their press organs *Fædrelandet* and *Dagbladet*. These papers exercised a powerful influence on the King, attacked Princes Ferdinand and Christian, and created a real danger as a result of their activities, especially as

la nation danoise, si facile à mener finirait par s'habituer à l'ordre d'idées qu'on lui enseigne de toute manière et que, moitié par erreur, moitié par apathie, elle laisserait faire et ne mettrait aucun obstacle à se soumettre à une nouvelle dynastie réunissant les trois Royaumes.

They cherished the illusion that Copenhagen would become the capital of Scandinavia and that the combined Scandinavian countries would become a great power. In order to popularise these ideas there was talk of a new Kingdom with the Eider as its southern frontier; in this way they would rid themselves of troubles with Germany. Such a solution, it was thought, would not encounter any opposition from the German Confederation and support for it was expected from London and Paris.

Beneath a mask of hypocritical moderation and observance of laws and existing treaties, minds were being prepared and they were only waiting for a suitable moment to overthrow the dynasty, as once happened in Sweden. In the ambassador's opinion, the courts interested in upholding the treaties of 1852 should intervene, mainly in Denmark, where the core of the revolutionary and republican doctrine of Scandinavianism was to be found. The activities of these elements in Denmark were all the more harmful since the King of that country was weak, there was no direct heir and the King was surrounded by advisers who sought the democratisation of the country and favoured faction. Effective measures were needed, such as freeing the country of the cabal, a radical and complete change in the make-up of

---

84. No. 88, 8 (20) June 1856.

the existing government, restrictions on the press, revision of the common constitution for the Whole – State, a change in the electoral law and a clamp-down on certain journalists.

De telles mesures paraîtraient peut-être dangereuses, mais j'ai la conviction que tout dépend ici de la sagesse et de l'énergie du gouvernement, qu'il y a encore beaucoup d'élemens conservatifs et qu'aucune émeute ni mouvement populaire ne seraient à craindre, si les choses se passaient dans l'ordre-ci dessus indiqué. La masse de la nation est fatiguée et honteuse du régime actuel, et quelques arrestations parmi les journalistes, les plus dangereux et ne jouissant d'aucune considération personelle feraient un excellent effet.

So it was not surprising that *Fædrelandet* compared Ungern-Sternberg's behaviour to that of N. Repnin and O. Stackelberg, the notorious ambassadors of Catherine II in Warsaw in the period of the partitions of Poland.

The ambassador drew succour from the Copenhagen paper *Kjøbenhavnposten,* edited by St. Grune, which attacked what Ungern-Sternberg called the madness of Scandinavianism and relegated the creators of this absurd and dangerous idea to the category of traitors to their country who, like the advocates of Schleswig-Holsteinism, were working for the partition of Denmark. 'Ceux-ci, dit-il, veulent se donner à l'Allemagne, les autres à la Suède, leurs efforts tendent en même but.[85] The ambassador added, referring to the opinion of what he called serious people, that France and Britain, being pro-Swedish, would willingly abrogate the Treaty of 8 May 1852. Fearing the curtailment of Russia's influence if there should be a change in the law of succession depriving Christian of the throne, the ambassador suggested to Gorchakov that the guarantee of the integrity of the Danish monarchy and the right of the dynasty of Prince Christian to the Danish throne given by Europe should be confirmed once again. The ambassador considered this a matter of exceptional importance and assumed that the governments of France and Britain would agree to it, as would Sweden in view of the attitude of the other two, and Prussia and Austria would not be able to renounce the obligations into which they had previously entered.[86]

The Emperor was disturbed by the reports from Copenhagen and Gorchakov issued instructions to the ambassador which indicate that he did not believe it would be possible to influence the Copenhagen cabinet by direct persuasion. He recommended the ambassador to observe the principal agitators in the movement and to investigate their real plans and the resources at their disposal, in order to assess their chances and elucidate on what they were based. It was essential, the minister advised, to listen to the opinions of sensible people and diplomats about the demonstrations which had occurred, since their real purpose was not clearly defined.[87]

In a dispatch to Stockholm on 4 July (old style) Gorchakov emphasised that the

---

85. Reports nos. 94 and 99-100 (Secrète), 13 (25) and 18 (30) June 1856.
86. No. 104, 20 June (2 July) 1856.
87. 2. June 1856. Rus. Film. Rigsarkiv Copenhagen.

ideas of Scandinavianism had come to the notice of the Emperor, who thought that they were a greater danger in Denmark than in Sweden because in Denmark they were combined with democratic tendencies. Alexander II regretted that the government's weakness caused it to indulge and provoke forces which were openly hostile to the system. But the Emperor did not think it would be necessary, as it had been in 1843, to issue a friendly admonition ('une représentation amicale'). Gorchakov recommended the use of the same methods in Stockholm as in Copenhagen, and drew particular attention to the need for observation of the main agitators in the movement and especially to keep track of those manifestations of it which might transmit Scandinavian ideas to Finland.[88]

Ungern-Sternberg's proposal to approach the states which were signatories to the Treaty of London for a renewed guarantee of the treaty's provisions, on the other hand, did not meet with Gorchakov's approval, since he took the position that to put forward such a proposal would mean that even the signatories had doubts about the durability of their creation and would encourage those who were hostile to the agreements concluded in 1852 to take action. If a new guarantee were needed, then the only country which could solicit it would be Denmark herself.[89]

Ungern-Sternberg continued to write about the danger posed by Scandinavianism, and a pretext for this was provided by events such as the ceremonial welcome afforded to the Prince of Sweden and the Viceroy in Norway, in Copenhagen in September 1856;[90] the appearance of a pamphlet by Baron Blixen-Finecke with the title *Skandinavismen praktisk* in January 1857; and the abundance of articles on Scandinavianism in the Copenhagen press.[91]

On the occasion of Prince Oskar's arrival and welcome by the King, which coincided with demonstrations by the party advocating the idea of Scandinavianism, Ungern-Sternberg wrote on 5 (17) September 1856:

Je m'abstiens, mon Prince, de toute réflexion ultérieure sur le triste état des choses que ces faits et ces symptômes dévoilent clairement. En les contemplant d'un œil impartial et en considérant en autre combien les conflicts renaissans avec la Confédération Germanique sont faits pour encourager les tendances dont il s'agit, on se saurait se dissimuler le danger qui menace la Couronne Danoise.

In this context he cited the opinion of *Dagbladet*, which he described as the organ of the goverment party – the organ of Hall and Andrae – about the necessity of a merger of Denmark and Sweden in order, as he put it, to

---

88. Gorchakov to Knorring, 4 July (O.S.) Chiffres. Rigs. Stock. Centralarkiv, Moscow.
    The Austrian ambassador in Stockholm reported contemptuously on the Scandinavian movement: its ideas were a chimera, and its aims utopian. The most dangerous thing was the excitement which it generated. (exaltations dans les agitateurs républicains et socialistes). Langenau to Buol. H.H.S.A., Vienna, 13 P.A. XXVI, Schweden, Berichte, Varia, 1856-58, no. 30, 6 October 1856.
89. Gorchakov to Ungern-Sternberg, 10 July 1856. Rus. Films.
90. No. 137, 5 (17) September 1856. Knorring's dispatch no. 21, 15 (27) September 1856.
91. Cf. J. Clausen, *Skandinavismen* ... pp. 134 ff. Møller, *Skandinavisk* ... pp. 37 ff. Neergard, *Under* ..., vol. II, p. 121.

conjurer le danger dont la Russie menaçerait les trois Royaumes soit à la suite du traité de Novembre, qui aurait envenimé les relations entre les cours de St. Pétersbourg et de Stockholm, soit à la suite de l'affaire de succession, dont l'arrangement est qualifié de 'malheureux'.

As far as Blixen-Finecke's pamphlet is concerned, it evoked a particularly strong response because the author was the brother-in-law of the heir to the throne, Christian, and had been well known hitherto as a supporter of monarchist views.

The author of the pamphlet had no illusions about the difficulties which implementation of his plan would encounter from the great powers, especially Russia and Prussia, who could not agree to the Sound and the Belt coming under the control of a sovereign who would only have to conclude an alliance with Britain and France in order to close the entrance to the Baltic; and who, on his own, would be in a position to make the straits a second Dardanelles; and who possessed a significant fleet with which to defend them. In the ambassador's opinion Britain was behind the project: the court of Queen Victoria appeared to approve the idea of detaching the duchies from the Danish crown, either to transfer them to Prussia or for some other purpose. Knowing the democratic mood of the Danish islands it was thinking about using revolutionary tendencies and Scandinavianist agitation and Great Britain would like to endow the islands with a republican regime under British protection.[92]

A month before, in connection with an article on Scandinavianism which appeared in *Le Pays* under the pseudonym Edmont (behind the pseudonym he saw the Polish exile Bujawski,[93] who was connected with Prince Napoleon Bonaparte) Ungern-Sternberg had argued that France, Canrobert and Prince Napoleon were behind the whole Scandinavianism phenomenon.[94]

The calmest and most objective attitude to the problem of Scandinavianism was taken by the Russian diplomats in Stockholm, Dashkov and Knorring. Dashkov was initially contemptuous about the Uppsala students' invitation of their colleagues from other universities, seeing it as nothing more than a sign of the dreams of Scandinavian youth. He called the published speeches 'ces idées prônées par la presse radicale', and stressed that as they had no support from the governments they could only be treated as 'une excursion de plaisir'.[95] But it was not to be denied that the exchange of students from the four universities contributed to the gradual reduction of the antipathy and prejudices which had divided the neighbouring peoples for so long.[96]

The surprise in the Russian embassy was all the greater, then, when news of the course of the meeting in Uppsala arrived. 'On ne saurait se méprendre sur le véri-

---

92. Nos. 8, 9, 26 January (7 February) 1857. Rus. Flms. R.A. Copenhagen.
93. Edmund Chojecki the author of *Voyage dans les mers du Nord à bord de la corvette La Reine Hortense.*
94. No. 198, 29 December 1856 (10 January 1857), vol. 49.
95. No. 33, 3 (15) May 1856. Depescher från Stockholm til Petersburg. R.A. Stockholm.
96. No. 39, 29 May (10 June) 1856.

table sens de cette démonstration', Knorring wrote to the vice-minister, Tolstoy, Gorchakov's deputy. 'L'union de trois pays du nord – telle est l'idée qui l'a inspirée, tel est le but qu'elle s'est proposé. Cela a été hautement avoué'. He had to recognise that the demonstration had aroused strong sympathy in Sweden, among young people and the lower classes, and what most amazed him was the fact that, although the practical result of Scandinavianism would be the creation of a republican federation of the three northern states – that is to say, it was, in principle, anti-dynastic, representatives of the students were ceremonially received by King Oscar. 'Est-ce désir de popularité, est-ce aveuglement, ou serait-ce calcul?'

The union idea only had a chance of implementation if the democratic element was victorious. The Russian diplomat, however, saw major obstacles in its path, namely, antagonism between the Norwegians and the Swedes, and between the Danes and the Swedes. The Norwegians were already dissatisfied with the existing state of affairs. Nor would the Danes be inclined to accept a similar disadvantageous position in relation to Sweden, and Copenhagen did not want to see its role decrease to that of Christiania (now Oslo). Stockholm would be even less inclined to accept the idea of union. The various interests could only be reconciled on the basis of radicalism and a republican federation, but fortunately conservative forces predominated in Sweden, and even if the bacillus of democracy, which had its source in Norway, won great triumphs in Denmark, it was not ultimately very threatening if it was a matter of banquests and the drinking of toasts to the university of Helsingfors, which General T. Berg, the Imperial Governor in Finland, had certainly reported. In sum, there was no threat and the whole matter deserved little attention from the Ministry of Foreign Affairs.[97]

Nevertheless, it was a fact that the meetings of students had been enthusiastically supported by the King, who stated in his declaration in the palace at Drottningholm on 15 June 1856. 'Qu'à l'avenir une guerre entre les peuples scandinaves sera impossible'. It was also a fact that, whatever Knorring might say about 'les expressions d'enfantillage et de gamins', the king regarded them seriously, not 'en écoliers' but 'en homme politiques'.[98] This compelled Knorring to reflect on the whole problem, since it was spreading wider and beginning to draw in broader circles of society.

He concluded[99] that the period in which Europe treated Sweden as a satellite of Russia (since 1812) belonged to the past, as had the period when Sweden was neutral (1853). The appearance of a British and French fleet and its enthusiastic reception in Stockholm, the warm welcome enjoyed by Canrobert's mission, the reactions to Sebastopol, the November Treaty prepared in secret and its consequences, as well as the preparation for a military operation against Russia, did not balance the fact of dissatisfaction observed in Sweden at the conclusion of the Paris peace treaty. The conclusion of peace showed how useless the preparations and efforts had been. It had frustrated the hopes and calculations of all.

97. Knorring to Tolstoy, no. 2, 15 (27) June 1856. Reservée.
98. Knorring to Tolstoy, no. 5, 5 (17) July 1856.
99. No. 8, 2 (14) August 1856.

A special role in the development of Scandinavianism had been played by Prince Charles, who was admired by the army and by young people, who was popular in republican circles in Norway and who was a liberal of an anti-Russian disposition. 'Il se croit sérieusement appelé à venger Charles XII, à rendre la Finlande à la Suède, et à établir l'Union Scandinave'.[100] The Russian embassy was disturbed by Sweden's international contacts, particularly King Oscar's journey to France and Britain in the summer of 1856, his visit to Copenhagen, and his popularity in Norway.[101] It was also worried by the King's pro-French, pro-British and pro-Scandinavian statements. 'Les plus incrédules commencent à comprendre que l'union scandinave est plus qu'un rêve d'étudiants', concluded Knorring.[102] He saw the spread of these ideas in Sweden as a danger to Russia, which seemed the more threatening since the King, as Prince Hohenhole said to Dashkov, also had thoughts of restoring a real balance in Europe, in the first place by the reconstruction of Poland. The King had to answer for the fact that this would undoubtedly cost much blood, but that was inevitable. Nor did it escape the notice of the Russian embassy that for trade reasons the Western powers were interested in the ports of Slite and Farøsund in Gotland, as *Journal des Débats* described, at the inspiration of Prince Oscar of Sweden.[103]

In fact, however, all these signs taken together were the *pium desiderium* of the King, they were illusions rather than reality. Napoleon III, who had actually moved closer to Russia, could not involve himself in an anti-Russian policy. In Britain a small group of liberals and a part of public opinion were sympathetic to Scandinavianism, while the government's watchword was the maintenance of peace. The Foreign Office warned the British ambassador, M.I.J.R. Crowe, against involvement in matters connected with the Scandinavian movement.[104] In Sweden itself, after the experiences of 1855-56, the conservative opposition started to speak out against the Scandinavian policy and the King's co-operation with radical elements in Copenhagen.[105] The opposition also brought about the restriction of the King's role in foreign policy and the Riddarhuset resolved that the King should not have the right henceforth to sign international treaties without prior consultation with the government.[106]

Although reports on manifestations of the Scandinavian movement did not disappear from the diplomatic correspondence between the Russian embassy in Stockholm and the ministry in St. Petersburg, the tone of the accounts remained calm. The strength of this current and its practical consequences were not overestimated. The numerous difficulties in the way of its implementation, resulting both from the conflicts existing between the Scandinavian countries and from the vary-

---

100. Knorring, 22 September (4 October) 1856.
101. Knorring's reports of 10 (22) August, 14 (26) August and 15 (27) September 1856.
102. 15. (27) September 1856. Reversée.
103. No. 3, 26 June (8 July) 1856.
104. Derry, *A History of Modern Norway,* (Oxford, 1973), p. 85.
105. Jansson, *Den Svenske* ... pp. 141 ff.
106. *Ibid.* pp. 141-4, 147; Holmberg, *Skandinavismen* ... pp. 297-306.

ing interpretations of the essence and aims of the movement in the different countries, were appreciated. For this reason, Knorring argued, rapid implementation of these plans need not be expected.[107]

Gorchakov was more reassured, however, by the news coming from Copenhagen, from October 1856 onward, and in particular by Scheele's explanation that Scandinavianism was a movement lacking a broad social basis and espoused mainly by students, led by Ploug. The army, officials and the bourgeoisie, on the other hand, were thinly represented in its ranks. Although relations between Denmark and Sweden were excellent, and the King was on friendly terms with the Swedish dynasty, Denmark, Scheele argued in his dispatch of 16 October, would never become a province of Sweden.

These explanations were very much to Gorchakov's liking, especially the official statement by Scheele on 20 February 1857 in which he described Scandinavianism as a harmful idea, distancing himself from it as 'l'idée si poétique bien que l'histoire ne l'ait jamais pu qualifié autrement' and calling it an idea which was both impossible to put into practice and a danger to stability and consolidation. The treaty project launched by Oscar I (an alliance with Denmark) fell through.[108]

Dashkov also reported the decline of the Scandinavian tendency, saying among other things, that Scheele's reply to the Swedish proposal 'paraît être peu goûté ici tant dans les régions gouvernementals que dans le public'.[109] The former saw in it 'un certain blâme, ce qu'est du public, elle y produit de pénibles déceptions relativement à l'accomplissement des vœux que plus d'un individu forme en faveur d'une unité scandinave pouvant tenir tête à la Russie'.

In addition, as Dashkov added in later reports, there were the economic difficulties of Sweden, which was experiencing a growing financial crisis in connection with the crisis in the USA and Britain.[110] Sweden and Norway were also feeling a trade crisis.[111] These difficulties meant that no pressure brought to bear on the government by the Scandinavianists to help Denmark would achieve anything in the way of forcing the Swedish government to act.[112] In the face of these facts Gorchakov recommended Ungern-Sternberg not to overestimate the role of Scandinavianism, and simultaneously informed him that the Tsar approved of the Danish government's assessment of it as not being dangerous.[113]

---

107. No. 43, 30 October (11 November) 1856).
108. Møller, *Skandinavisk stræben* ... pp. 56 ff. T.K. Derry, *A History of Scandinavia,* p. 243.
109. No. 18, 15 (27) March 1857 (Rule 216-7). On the subject of Scandinavianism and the reasons why the union of Scandinavian states did not come into effect, see Holmberg, *Scandinavismen* ... Møller, *Skandinavisk stræben* ... and K. Larsen, *A History of Norway, pp. 424ff.*
110. No. 65, 19 November (1 December) 1857.
111. No. 68, 29 November (11 December) 1857.
112. Dashkov to Gorchakov, No. 1, 3 (15) January and No. 2, 14 (26) February 1858, Svensk Rysk Rule 218-20. On the economic stagnation of Sweden in 1857-58 see H.H.S.A. Vienna, P.A. XXVI, 13. Schweden, no, 38, 40, 41, 27. November and 15 and 22 December 1857.
113. 1, 9 and 16 March (old style). Rus. Films. Rigs. Copenhagen.

IV

Gorchakov, who did not have a penetrating mind and never went very deeply into matters, especially when he had to deal with an affair as complicated and deliberately entangled by German lawyers and politicians as the Danish-German dispute was, formulated his opinions in a general and superficial manner. In the autumn of 1856 he set out Russia's position as follows: the Dansh-German dispute was a purely German matter caused by the behaviour of Denmark, and the Copenhagen government should reach an agreement with Germany. Russia would not intervene and did not want to expose herself to the accusation of interference in the internal affairs of other states.

Gorchakov formulated his views of the essence of the Danish-German conflict under the influence of his adviser on German affairs, R.F. Osten-Sacken, who had begun his political studies under the direction of the ageing J. Grüner in the Central Commission in 1814 and was indeed a distinguished expert on the subject but took a position favouring Germany since he himself was of Baltic German origin and did not conceal his friendly feelings towards Germany, his Fatherland.[114]

The Schleswig-Holstein question was *terra incognita* not only to the Tsar but to Gorchakov too, and both relied completely on Sacken's opinion. It was not conceit that Russia was more familiar with the essence of the question than the other powers, said Gorchakov, in order to convince Plessen of the correctness of his behaviour, but he immediately added that this was due not to him but to Sacken. Additional studies were necessary in order to understand these matters.[115]

From the moment the dispute between Copenhagen and the duchies arose, Russia took the German side. In February 1856 Nesselrode had spoken to the Prussian minister to St. Petersburg of his fear that the controversy between the Danish Government and the Estates of Holstein might lead to serious consequences and he expressed his support for the nephew of the late Danish minister to Russia O. Blome, the leader of the Holstein opposition.[116]

In July of the same year Gorchakov warned the Danish government that despite the sympathy felt by Alexander II for Denmark, he would not be able to help her as he had when he represented Russia in Frankfurt. Plessen reported that in Denmark's dispute with the duchies Russia backed the conservative opposition in Holstein.

Gorchakov set out the St. Petersburg cabinet's position more fully in a dispatch to Ungern-Sternberg on 1 March 1857 (old style).[117] The imperial government was anxious to refrain from intervention and recommended moderation to the Copenhagen government. Neither of the two German states wanted to take the matter to

---

114. See Schlözer, *Petersburger Briefe* ... p. 203; also Bismarck to Schleinitz, 28 (16) June 1861, in *Bismarcks Briefwechsel* ... p. 183.
115. Depecher Rusland, no. 15, 27 (15) February 1861. *Istoriya diplomatii,* (Moscow, 1941), vol. II, pp. 489-90.
116. Steefel, *The Schleswig-Holstein* ..., p. 26.
117. Rus. Films. Rigsark. Copenhagen.

extremes, but if the dispute flared up they would not be able to resist the mood in Germany demanding that the matter be passed to the German Diet for deliberation, since this was the only body competent to settle it definitively. On the basis of the facts of 1850 and 1851 the Russian cabinet rejected the Danish government's statement questioning the rights of the German Diet in the matter and reminded it that in 1850 Austria and Prussia had entered into discussions with Denmark as plenipotentiaries of the Diet.[118]

The St. Petersburg cabinet urged the Danish government to take a conciliatory attitude and expressed the opinion that nothing could be achieved by convening the European conference which Denmark sought. The Russian cabinet pointed out that the situation in Europe had changed since 1850 and now Russia could only confirm that she maintained her position on the integrity of the Danish monarchy, without provoking new intervention, the results of which would be hard to foresee. Russia would give no support and had no interest in seeing the dispute grow beyond its present proportions. Denmark's interest required the matter to remain exclusively a federal one and to be settled in an amicable way. This could be achieved by means of an agreement with the two German powers, which was the best way out of the present difficulties for Denmark, or at least by obtaining their support if the matter came before the German Diet.

Gorchakov's views on how the Danish-German dispute should be settled were shared by Brunnow, the joint creator of the Treaty of London and popular in Denmark as *amicus Daniae,* who was now ambassador in Berlin. At the beginning of 1857 he had a meeting in Berlin with Denmark's special emissary, B. Bülow, who was sent by the Danish government to Berlin and Vienna to sound out the opinions of Manteuffel and Buol on the Danish-German dispute. The Danish government was persuaded to undertake this mission by Gorchakov, who saw Bülow as the best negotiator in discussions with the larger German states. Brunnow's dispatches to Gorchakov on 20 February (4 March) and 6 (18) March 1857, and Bülow's reports to Scheele on 5/6 and 16 March 1857, summing up his mission to Berlin and Vienna and setting out the positions of the various interested parties in the dispute, show that Manteuffel and Buol were not ill disposed towards Denmark and wanted to reach agreement. But Scheele was mistrusted in Berlin and the Prussian government did not want to appear 'moins allemand à Berlin qu'on ne le serait à Vienne'. For this reason, wanting to protect itself against the pressure of public opinion and divest itself of responsibility, it preferred to place the dispute with Denmark before the German Diet. In order to avoid possible military action, Bülow thought it would be necessary to enter into negotiations with Berlin and Vienna. It seemed to him, however, that it would be impossible to avoid placing the matter before the German Diet, since the states of Lauenburg, under pressure from the Holstein party, were preparing to present a complaint concerning territory to the Diet. Such action, in Bülow's opinion, was in conformity with the law.

---

118. Resolution of the Diet of the German Confederation, July 29, 1852. *Correspondence between Austria, Prussia and Denmark 1851-52,* pp. 28-9.

In Brunnow's view, Bülow was the first Danish diplomat who wanted to enter into negotiations, understood the matter perfectly and was able to approach it objectively, seeing the mistakes made by the Danish government in the administrative sphere, even though they had been exaggerated by the German press. Bülow's views, Brunow wrote, were not always accepted by the Danish government, among other things because the government did not appreciate the seriousness of the problem. Like Gorchakov, Brunnow considered that there were differences between Russia and Denmark in their assessment of the situation and the nature of the dispute. The Danish government was wrong to regard it as a European matter. Denmark would gain nothing from the involvement of the other states. The situation had changed compared with 1850-52. Then Russia, Britain and France had put pressure on Prussia 'pour neutraliser les vues favorables à la cause des Duchés'. France's attitude, 'embarassé et nulle', in Brunnow's view was the result of the provisions jointly accepted in London.

Today, Brunnow considered, the situation had undergone a radical change. Prussia and Austria were acting jointly and had a common interest. Under pressure from the whole of Germany, they acted in favour of the duchies' cause. Britain, where ultra-liberal tendencies prevailed, would use the situation to cause new troubles for Russia. France, which was no longer passive as she had been in 1852, wanted to exploit the conflict in her own interests. Brunnow was convinced, therefore, that the dispute had to be confined within purely federal limits and agreement reached with the larger German courts. If the matter came before the Diet, it would be necessary to ensure that its resolutions did not threaten the security of Denmark. Copenhagen was making a mistake in failing to understand the differences between 1852 and 1857 and continuing to believe that Russia should bear the burdens resulting from these complications. The whole matter was made more difficult by the personal interest of Scheele, who appeared to have become very involved in the problem in a way which was improper and damaging to the Copenhagen court. This was the impression prevailing in Berlin. Brunnow did not want to condemn this and merely observed the state of affairs. Bülow's efforts had been fruitless, but this did not discourage him and he would redouble his efforts in Vienna.[119]

Bülow's unsuccessful mission to Vienna convinced Brunnow[120] that he was right

---

119. In his report on 18 March Bülow relates the course of his discussion with Brunnow and explains the motives guiding Russia in the Danish-German dispute as follows:
Genug, es wird kein Zweifel darüber seyn können, dass das Petersburger Cabinet dem Hofe von Berlin und den Deutschen Mittelstaaten die in der Orientalischen Krisis bewahrte Stellung zu sehr verdenkt, auf der andern Seite jede Gelegenheit zu Europäischer Verantwortlichkeit zu sorglich von sich abzuweisen wünscht, um für jetzt sein Gewicht für uns die Wagschale zu legen. Ausserdem wird man sich keine Illusion über den Umstand machen dürfen dass Russlands Wort in dieser Frage an Gewicht verloren hat und dass erst dann, wenn es sich vom Bestehen der Monarchie oder Zerreissen der Tractate handeln sollte, das alte Wohlwollen und das Interesse an unserer Existenz sich wieder bethätigen und beleben werden. *Danske Magazin,* 7 Series VI. (Copenhagen, 1954-57), p. 197.
120. Report to Gorchakov, 6 (18) March 1857.

and that the Danish question should not become a European matter; that Austria, in co-operation with Prussia, would like an agreement. The Scandinavian tendencies he was sure were harmful to Denmark, and that their aim was the division of Denmark into two parts, a German and a Scandinavian one, which would mean the end of the integral monarchy.[121]

Brunnow repeated the same thoughts on the subject of Denmark's situation and how to settle the conflict during discussions with the Danish diplomats Brockdorff and Bille-Brahe in Berlin in March and April 1857.[122] He reasoned that the situation in Europe was different from what it had been in 1848-50 and was infavourable to Denmark. 'Vous serez donc entièrement isolé'. In his conversation with Bille-Brahe he used the following words about Russia: 'L'Empereur Nicholas pesait sur la Prusse, l'Empereur Alexandre suit un autre système, il est vrai, à Votre détriment'.

He repeated that transferring the matter to the scrutiny of a European forum could only damage Denmark and he therefore advised her to come to an understanding with the larger German states and make concessions in relation to Holstein and Lauenburg. He advised doing everything possible to prevent the matter going to the German Diet, because if it did, as he put it: 'Votre perte est inévitable tôt ou tard'. He also warned against the consequences of Federal Execution, which would be disastrous. 'Vous ne pourrez pas Vous défendre ... Vous serez battus et non seulement Vous perdrez Vous même, Votre sang et Votre fortune, mais Vous serez forcés de payer tous les frais de l'exécution ... Vos millions pour le Sundzolle y passeront'.[123] Brunnow advised following the example of Russia, which had done everything possible after the fall of Sebastopol to conclude peace.

Je comprends toutes les difficultés de Votre Gouvernement, mais je vois aussi la pente vers laquelle il glisse. Je puis me tromper comme tout le monde mais j'ai beaucoup vu, j'ai de l'expérience en beaucoup de choses, et je suis infiniment convaincu que je ne me trompe pas cette fois'! Cédez! Cédez! Si j'étais à Copenhague – je regrette profondément de ne pas y être aujourd'hui – je dirais franchement et ouvertement mon opinion à Votre Roi ...

The Danish government should take advantage of the fact that a delegation from Holstein was in Copenhagen and reach an agreement with it at any price.

Travaillez-les, gagnez-les, cajolez-les, dites que Vous voulez leur soumettre la question de Constitution, entendez en particulier leurs plaintes, Tâchez d'arriver à un accord sur les points, dont ils se plaignent, ne les repoussez pas.[124]

---

121. See 'Aktstykker og breve m.m. vedrørende kammerherre Bernhard Bülows særlige mission til Berlin og Wien 1856 og 1857 ved Hanna Kobylinski og Erik Møller', *Danske Magazin* (Copenhagen, 1954-57), Brunnow to Gorchakov, 20 February (4 March) and 6 (18) March 1857, pp. 164-7 and 200-2, and Bülow to Scheele, 5/6 and 18 March 1857, pp. 167 ff and 196-9.
122. Brockdorf to Scheele, no. 22, 13 March 1857, Depecher Berlin, P. Bille-Brahe to Scheele, no. 29, 4 April 1857 in *Ibid*.
123. See Chapter 3.
124. Depecher Berlin, no. 29, 4 April 1857, Rigs. Copenhagen.

It is not surprising that Gorchakov showed this report to Plessen with satisfaction, adding 'that is the opinion of *amicus Daniae*'.

The picture of Denmark drawn by Ungern-Sternberg at the end of 1856 and during 1857 was even gloomier than before. The Danish government, in his opinion, faced a difficult dilemma, which it could not resolve. How could the German element be satisfied without evoking envy and suspicion on the part of the Danish population when there was a common constitution which had been in effect for over a year and was contrary to the laws of the duchies and the obligations undertaken by the royal government? How could a modern constitutional system be maintained and combine, in a single Rigsraad, representatives of two peoples between whom there was great animosity, with the section which considered itself oppressed seeking and finding an ally abroad?

The ambassador did not believe that his idea of reconstructing the provincial estates and creating a senate to deal with general matters, appointed by the King rather than chosen by means of universal elections (which would inevitably always guarantee the predominence of the Danish population) could be implemented in circumstances where the King was completely dominated by the constitutional party and would never decide to repeal the constitution. The conservative forces were pro-Russian and not organised, and, to the disgust of Ungern-Sternberg, power rested entirely in the hands of democrats and utopians, while public opinion did not defend the true interest of the country, monarchist principles and property rights. In addition to this, there was the apathy which was an inseparable part of the national character, lack of initiative and a poor state of affairs in the government itself, in which ministers disagreed and were only held together by the German danger: 'l'apathie du caractère nationale, jointe à un manque total d'initiative, preservent jusqu'a présent les Danois de ces catastrophes qui precipitent les États dans l'abîme des troubles intérieures'. The conservative party was without a leader and incapable of effective action.[125] Nor did he believe that the government, and particularly Scheele personally, was capable of averting a crisis with Germany.[126]

Relations between Scheele and the Russian ambassador took a turn for the worse and both were aware of their mutual animosity. This must explain why Scheele approached Kudryavtsev (Koudriaffsky in the dispatches), the Russian representative in Hamburg, rather than Ungern-Sternberg, in December 1856 and asked for his good offices, for mediation by the Russian government and support for Danish policy. To him Scheele lamented the situation prevailing in the government, in which he was the only defender of monarchist principles, while his colleagues were supporters of Scandinavianism and democratic ideas and were working for the partition of the monarchy at the very moment when Prussia and Austria were seeking revision of the Treaty of London.[127]

125. 19 November (1 December) 1856, Particulière.
126. No. 173, 1 (13) November 1856.
127. 2 (14) December 1856, Particulière, and no. 188, 4 (16) December 1856, vol. 49.

Scheele's journey to Hamburg exacerbated the mistrust which had long existed between minister and ambassador. A year before, after all, Ungern-Sternberg had seen Scheele as an exceptionally wily man ('excessivement ruse')[128] in conspiracy with France and Britain. In this judgement he differed from Freytag-Loringshoven, who wrote at the same time: 'quant à moi, je n'ai jusqu'à présent aucune raison de douter de la bonne foi de M. de Scheele'.[129]

Even before Scheele's departure for Hamburg, Ungern-Sternberg criticised him for what he called his demagogic speeches during his journey to Holstein. In them Scheele had criticised the aristocracy there and the provincial Estates, stirring up the lower classes against the aristocracy and promising to introduce democratic reforms which the Russian ambassador thought he would be unable to carry out.[130] Ungern-Sternberg found an ally in his criticism of Scheele during his Holstein journey in *Fædrelandet* and *Dagbladet,* which ironically called Scheele the tribune of the people or simply 'le démagogue Scheele'.[131]

Ungern-Sternberg did not trust Schleele when the latter reported the dispute with Holstein-Lauenburg to him as a new phase of the Schleswig-Holstein revolution and tried to prove that the Prussian government was aiming to exploit the conflict and to separate the duchies from Denmark by occupying them or to bring about a change in the present constitution. He also doubted whether Scheele was really right when he sought to convince him that Scandinavianism and the conflict with Germany were equally dangerous and that there was co-operation between Stockholm and Berlin with the aim of including the Danish monarchy under a single Scandinavian state and absorbing the duchies into Prussia.

Scheele presented Swedish policy towards Denmark as especially dangerous and cunning since, he claimed, just when King Oskar was urging the Danish government not to make any concessions to the German courts and offering 30,000 troops, who would be sent to Zealand in case of war between Denmark and Germany, General Mansbach, the Swedish ambassador in Berlin, was speaking in favour of Schleswig-Holsteinism and inviting Prince Augustenburg to supper, making every effort to incite the Prussian government against Denmark and backing all the duchies' complaints so as to support armed intervention. Later the Swedish government said the initiative for the meeting came from Prince Augustenburg.[132]

In February, however, during the King's illness, and owing to the increasingly complicated domestic and international situation of Denmark, the Russian ambassador began to treat all these facts taken together as a threat to peace and the political existence of Denmark, especially after Scheele acquainted him with a report received from Paris in which J.C. Dirckinck-Holmfeld drew attention to the

---

128. Halicz, *Danish Neutrality* ... pp. 134 ff. Reports of 9 (21) October and 1 (13) November 1856.
129. No. 211, 28 December 1855 (9 January 1856).
130. Ungern-Sternberg, no. 188, 4 (16) December 1856, vol. 49.
131. Ungern-Sternberg, no. 188, vol. 49.
132. No. 198, 29 December 1856 (10 January 1857).

inclination of Napoleon III to divide Denmark between Sweden-Norway and Frederick Augustenburg, who would receive the duchies.[133]

The rapprochement between Scheele and Ungern-Sternberg at the beginning of 1857 was something new and unexpected for the ambassador. Relations with Copenhagen had not been good recently, after all, and in his dispatch to Copenhagen on 21 December (2 January) Gorchakov drew attention to the anti-Russian mood in Denmark and the suspicion which reigned there concerning the Russian cabinet's policy, and to the need to counter the anti-Russian stories being disseminated by the enemies of Russia, who were taking advantage of the ignorance of the masses.[134]

Now, when the Danish government was turning to the Russian cabinet to ask for support in the German courts, it was doing so, the ambassador argued, because Denmark was experiencing a real crisis. In his opinion it was in the interests of Russian policy to maintain the integrity of the Danish monarchy, which was so important for Russia and the freedom of the Baltic. In Ungern-Sternberg's report we read:

En pareille circonstance le cabinet de Copenhague s'adresse toujour de préférence à la Russie, et ce n'est pas la première foi que j'ai été dans le cas d'en faire l'observation. On ne peut malheureusement de dissimuler que mr. Scheele s'est attiré lui-même ces difficultés, et qu'il est la cause première des embarras dont il s'agit, mais cette circonstance, ce me semble, ne saurait nous empêcher de prêter au Danemark toute aide et assistance compatible avec nos intérêts, et de soutenir énergiquement la cause de l'intégrité de la Monarchie danoise, si importante pour la Russie et la liberté de la Baltique.[135]

The crisis in Denmark deepened towards the end of February after the publication of the famous anti-Scandinavian circular on 20 February, following which its author, Scheele, found himself under vehement attack by public opinion. The Eider party and *Fædrelandet* in particular attacked him, saying, as Ungern-Sternberg wrote,

Que cette homme d'Etat ne trouvant de l'appui nulle part, se jette à corps perdu dans le bras de la Russie, et que c'est pour gagner les bonnes grâces du Cabinet Impérial qu'il a lancé la dépêche dont il s'agit.[136]

Scheele fell. In the opinion of *Fædrelandet,* wrote Ungern-Sternberg, he had been 'L'apôtre de la Russie et que c'était là le comble de la honte pour un Ministre danois', and the government offered its resignation. On this occasion the ambassador described his mission in Copenhagen in the following terms:

---

133. This pessimistic view was also a result of conversation between the Russian ambassador and Bülow, who painted reality in dark colours and compared the anti-Danish mood in Germany with the situation in 1848. Nos. 18, 19, 20, (18 February (2 March) 1857), vol 49.
134. Rus. Films. R.A. Copenhagen.
135. Nos. 18, 19, 20, (18 February (2 March) 1857), vol. 49.
136. No. 33, 16 (28) March 1857. See Clausen, *Skandinavismen* ..., pp. 139-42.

Ayant toujours en pour principe de faire abstraction de mes sentiments personnelles quand il s'agit du service, je continuerai à garder vis-à-vis de Mr. Scheele l'attitude qui convient à sa position. Les dangers qui entourent la Monarchie danoise m'en font en autre un devoir comme Représentant d'une puissance qui, en définitive, se trouve toujours appelée à sauver ce pays. La tâche est ingrate et souvent difficile, mais l'histoire et l'intérêt général de l'Europe nous l'indiquent.[137]

Ungern-Sternberg viewed the government crisis with anxiety. He feared that if Scheele's place were taken by Krieger, everything connected with the duchies would be changed and the problem would be exacerbated even further. Krieger, in the ambassador's opinion, was a decisive politician who aimed to incorporate Schleswig into Denmark and was unwilling to make concessions. If, as rumour had it, Andrae became minister of foreign affairs, he would join to the Eider-Danois party.[138]

On the other hand, the return of Bluhme or one of the people from what was called 'l'ancienne école' would be completely impossible and the creation of a new conservative government was unthinkable.[139] During the crisis Scheele became even closer to Ungern-Sternberg, keeping him informed about the situation in the government, relations between the leading politicians and the difficulties in forming a government.

Ce sera peut-être un nouveau plâtrage, et il n'est pas impossible que Mr. Scheele revienne sur l'eau. On manque ici d'énergie, et il n'y a qu'un moyen extrême qui puisse tirer le Danemark de la situation dangereuse où se trouve la Monarchie. Je m'abstiens pour ma part de toute démarche et de tout conseil,

reported Ungern-Sternberg.[140] The ambassador was aware how unpopular he was in the Eider-Danois party, which alone really had a chance to resolve the government crisis. But in spite of that he did not want to remain merely an observer of events, but sought to influence the changes which were taking place. He explained the need to intervene in, or rather to influence, the course of events by the fact that there was no possibility of agreement between the parties without intervention from outside, as the discussions between the representatives of Holstein and the government had been fruitless, neither side having made up its mind or formulated clear and positive proposals. Although Hall and Andreae gave assurances that they were ready to offer major concessions, they encountered opposition from Krieger and in fact made only minor ones. In a situation where Holstein was at the same time criticised for making impossible demands, the negotiations were making no progress.[141]

---

137. Particulière, 19, (31) March 1857. Cf. also report of 16 (28) March, 26 March (7 April) and 28 March (9 April). On Scheele's note see also 13 P.A. XXVI, Schweden, 1856-58, no. 10, 27 March 1857. H.H.S.A. Vienna.
138. Particulière, 28 March (9 April) 1857.
139. *Ibid.* Particulère, 28 March (9 April) 1857.
140. Particulière, 4 (16) April 1857.
141. No. 48. 13 (25) April 1857.

Ungern-Sternberg came to the conclusion that he must talk to Bülow, who was staying in Copenhagen, and persuade him temporarily *(per interim)* to take on the portfolio of the ministry of foreign affairs. He saw this as the only way out of the crisis and of getting agreement with Germany. Ungern-Sternberg appealed to Bülow to agree to this, as he was the only person who could correct the damage, and his entry into the government would be well received by all the courts concerned.[142] During their discussion Bülow did not refuse, and did not raise any serious objections, but wanted to reflect on the offer. In the end he gave no answer.

The Russian ambassador did not trust the Danish government. He saw the hand of the British government behind the government's plan to convene the States of Holstein and present them with a more liberal variant of the statute for the duchy in the sphere of freedom of the press and assembly. He regarded the concession as designed to suit the dominant party in Denmark. But in Holstein, conservative and monarchist principles predominated and there was no desire for democratic concessions which would lead to separation from Schleswig. The representatives of Holstein in the Rigsraad, who were staying in Copenhagen, would not, in the ambassador's opinion, be satisfied with the proposals, especially as there was no question of granting the provincial states the possibility of putting their view on the question of a common constitution for the monarchy, or on their unequal representation in the Rigsraad, which was the German duchies' principal grievance. The absence of an authority which would rise above national rivalries meant that the problem, he feared, could not be settled amicably. On the contrary, its dimensions were becoming more and more alarming[143] and the convening of the States in August did indeed prove pointless.

In the first few months of 1857 Gorchakov, like Brunnow, urged Denmark to do everything in its power to prevent the matter going before the Federal Diet and to reach an agreement with Prussia and Austria in order to stop this. Both Manteuffel and Bismark, Gorchakov indicated, were against extreme measures and inclined towards a sincere reconciliation. But the German countries were dissatisfied, Brunnow argued, with the role they had played in the Neuchatel affair[144] and wanted to get their revenge by playing a greater part on the Holstein question. For this reason, too, Gorchakov, like Brunnow, regarded the possible transfer of the Danish-Holstein dispute to the German Diet as a serious matter. Knowing the mood prevailing in Germany, he anticipated that this would lead to a decision for military intervention.

St. Petersburg turned a deaf ear to Plessen's pleas that the Danish government was encountering great difficulties in conducting discussions with Germany. Gorchakov continually repeated the argument that, owing to the great dangers

---

142. No. 46. (Secrète), 13 (25) April and No. 52, 18 (30) April 1857.
143. Nos. 52, 73, 80, 18 (30) April, 13 (25) July and 4 (16) August 1857.
144. The dispute with Prussia was concluded by the treaty signed in Paris on 26 May 1857 under which Neuchatel was recognised as independent of the King of Prussia. W. Martin, *Switzerland from Roman Times to the Present* (London, 1971), pp. 246-7.

threatening, Denmark should do everything to reach an agreement and that any delay in the matter would only harm Danish interests.[145] During a conversation with the Danish ambassador on 21 February (5 March) he repeated the same line, saying:

Combien il était désirable pour nous de nous entendre avec les Cabinets Allemans – and adding – qu'il était convincu que ceux deux Cabinets n'avaient nullement le désir de nous susciter des embarras et qu'ils étaient selon lui, animés d'un esprit sincère de conciliation, mais, que d'un autre côté, si l'entente ne s'effectuait pas, les Cabinets de Vienne et de Berlin se montraient déterminés à saisir la Diète Germanique de l'affaire holsteinoise – ce que le Prince Gorchakov regardait comme un résultat très fâcheux pour nous.

Gorchakov once again rejected the Danish suggestion to make the dispute a European question by involving the signatories of the Treaty of London.[146]

Gorchakov as usual promised nothing. Plessen telegraphed that his recommendation was limited to the wish that Denmark should use Bülow for talks with Berlin and Vienna and should reach an agreement with Holstein so as to prevent the question coming before the German Diet.[147] When the Danish cabinet presented to Gorchakov the address which it had sent to its ambassadors in Vienna and Berlin, in which it once again set out its position on the matter of the constitution for Holstein and Lauenburg, and asked the Russian government for its support and good offices in relation to these two courts, Gorchakov replied that he did not see any possibility of intervention in Vienna and Berlin.[148]

In a conversation with Plessen on 12 March (28 February) he explained that he had asked Brunnow to give his support to Bülow's mission. As far as a European conference was concerned, however, in the current destabilised situation in Europe the results, in his opinion, could be disadvantageous for Denmark and possible revisions of the London Treaties might have damaging effects.

He blamed the current impasse in discussions exclusively on Denmark, which was not seeking ways to overcome the crisis caused by the proclamation of the 1855 constitution and was taking discriminatory actions against the German population. When Plessen said that the changes in the constitution were made quite openly, in full view of the German powers, and that they did not react and raised no objections, Gorchakov answered that governments do not like to speak out when they are not called upon to do so, in order to avoid the accusation that they are interfering in the internal affairs of others. He understood why the German states did not react until the representatives of the duchies, which belonged to Denmark and were part of the German Confederation, had made it clear that they did not agree with the contents of the constitution.

Differences of opinion existed, Gorchakov argued, in a discussion on 31 March 1857, but Denmark was satisfying neither the demands of the German states nor

145. No. 8, 9 (21) February 1857.
146. No. 9, 5 March 21 (February) 1857.
147. Telegram no. 827, 12 March (28 February) 1857.
148. No. 11, 28 February (12 March) 1857.

the states of Holstein. If, as he assumed, Denmark did not intend to make the question a European matter, as this would involve great risks and dangers, to which Denmark could not close her eyes, the only thing left for her to do was to try to reach agreement directly with the German cabinets, to discover their grievances and acquaint herself with the points on which, in the duchies' opinion, they considered that their guarantees had been infringed, and what they wanted.

The German states' formulations could provide the basis for negotiations. Denmark, Gorchakov went on, possessed provinces which formed part of the German Confederation, and he appreciated the difficulties which stemmed from the fact that the monarchy consisted of heterogeneous parts, but Denmark had to accept this and do everything to extricate itself from these complications and ensure calm in the country. There could only be calm when the government took account, not only of the demands of the Danish element, but also recognised the wishes of the German population and created a situation which excluded the possibility of intervention by Germany in internal Danish affairs.[149]

Come to an agreement with the King's subjects, do not let the German Confederation intervene, was the gist of what Gorchakov said in his next talk with Plessen.[150] For this reason he received with satisfaction the news that the Danish government intended to convene the States of Holstein in August.[151]

Despite his personal animosity towards the Vienna court and the ill feeling caused by the tone of the Austrian press on the one hand and the anti-Austrian mood fanned by the so-called Russian national party on the other, Gorchakov was able to appreciate the spirit of conciliation which marked the Vienna government's attitude to matters connected with the Danish-German dispute,[152] and expressed this during his conversation with Szechenyi.[153] Alexander II also praised the wisdom and caution of the Austrian government and attached great importance to its attitude, believing that, thanks to it, a way would be successfully found to smooth the differences between Denmark and the German states over the matter of the duchies, and he was pleased to learn from Budberg's account of 26 October (7 November) of the moderate position taken by the Austrian minister, Buol.[154]

In his discussions with Plessen and Szechenyi, Gorchakov stressed that Russia respected other sovereigns and did not intend to interfere in their affairs. But taking into consideration the danger threatening Denmark, Russia wished very much that Denmark, in her own interest, would accept the proposals of the two

---

149. No. 17, 19 (31) March 1857.
150. No. 18, 25 March (6 April) 1857).
151. Gorchakov to Ungern-Sternberg, 25 May 1857, Rus. Films. Szechenyi reported that Werther had informed him that the Danish government's message of 13 May had been influenced by advice given to Denmark by St. Petersburg, H.H.S.A. P.A.X. No. 21, Lit. A-E, 5 June (24 May) 1857, Karton 44.
152. Esterhazy's report of 4 April (23 March) 1857.
153. No. 12 A-B, 11 April (30 March); cf. Szechenyi's report no. 54 B of 21 (9) November 1857.
154. Gorchakov's dispatch of 7 (19) November 1857. H.H.S.A. Karton 45.

German countries as a means of eliminating the differences dividing her and them.[155] The Austrian diplomat explained this non-interference by the fact that Russia was preoccupied with internal matters (the peasant question and administrative reforms) and wanted to avoid anything which might make these tasks more difficult.[156]

On 23 (11) June Gorchakov declared that Russia adhered to her statements concerning the rights possessed by the German Confederation in connection with Denmark's dispute with the duchies and would do everything to prevent the affair entering a new phase in which it would become a European matter. Asked by Szechenyi, the Austrian *chargé d'affaires,* whether the differences and reservations in the formulations adopted by the cabinets in Vienna and Berlin in reply to the Danish note did not cause a change in his position, he answered that he had always recognised the rights of the Confederation and considered that the matter should not come under the scrutiny of the whole of Europe, as that could assume dimensions which he described as 'les plus funestes'. The use of coercion against Denmark could cause complications and give France a pretext for intervention,[157] and the question would then become a European one, which seemed to him to be dangerous.[158] If France were joined by Britain and they took a different position from Russia, Russia would not be able to maintain her previous declaration.[159] She would join them, 'en ligue' as Gorchakov put it, contributing an element of restraint (en qualité d'élement modérateur) to the dispute from the start if it came before the tribunal of the great powers.[160]

At the same time he urged Prussia to act cautiously and compromise, owing to the uncertain situation in Europe and doubts about how France might behave in the event of a conflict. 'Man könnte in dieser Zeit der Veranderungen der Karte nie wissen', said Gorchakov to the Prussian ambassador, Werther, who was inclined to ignore the role of France in the Danish-German dispute.[161] Thus Gorchakov received the news that the Danish government intended to convene the States of Holstein in August with satisfaction, seeing it as a step towards settling the problem.[162] The real reason for Gorchakov's satisfaction was that he had succeeded in preventing the dispute from coming before the European aureopagus[163] at a time when Russia could not play a substantial role in its decisions.

---

155. No. 18, 23 (11) May 1857.
156. *Ibid.*
157. Nos 24 Lit B and 25, 19 (7) and 23 (11) June 1857.
158. *Ibid.* See also Gorchakov to Werther, in Szechenyi's report no. 52 A-C of 7 November (26 October) 1857.
159. Report no. 25 of 23 (11) June 1857. Karton 44.
160. H.H.S.A. Vienna, *Ibid,* report no. 54 B of 21 (9) November 1857. Kart. 45.
161. Werthers Berichte, 13 April 1857.
162. Gorchakov to Ungern-Sternberg, 25 May 1857. Rus. Films.
163. The Supreme Tribunal of Europe, i.e. the highest representatives of the European Powers.

V.

The differences between Denmark and the German states had worried the French government for months. When, at the beginning of March, the Danish ambassador in Paris informed Walewski of the contents of dispatches nos. 3 and 4 of 18 and 20 February 1857, which contained an account of Scheele's position *vis-à-vis* the German cabinets in connection with the question of the duchies, and of Denmark's attitude to Scandinavianism, Walewski unexpectedly asked Dirckinck-Holmfeld what was Russia's attitude towards Denmark. The Danish ambassador explained that he was not very fully informed in this, but it seemed to him that the German cabinets had succeeded in making the St. Petersburg cabinet prejudiced and disposed against Denmark.[164] A month later H. Désprez. Sous-directeur Politique in the French ministry of foreign affairs with responsibility for Danish affaits, spoke to the ambassador as follows:

La dépêche Russe à Votre Cabinet[165] a produite ici le plus grand étonnement et Vous pouvez tenir pour sûr quelle eût decidé Vous cause en Votre défaveur, si alors tout en prêchant la modération à Vienne et à Berlin, nous n'y avions pas déjà en même temps insinué que le cas pourrait bien arriver où nous fussions obligés de traiter la question du point de vue Européen et que l'Angleterre, tout en formulant une longue liste de griefs contre Vous, n'eût pourtant accédé à notre manière de voir. Notre but est maintenant à ramener la question sur le terrain qu'elle n'aurait jamais dû quitter, c'est à dire sur le terrain essentiellement danois, afin qu'on la décide chez Vous.

A cela on paraît maintenant vouloir prêter la main à Vienne et à la Berlin et je crois - a ajouté Mr. Désprez - que c'est à la position que nous avons prise dans la question que Vous le devez; nous n'avons pas menacée, mais nous avons fait sentir à quoi la question pourrait entraîner si l'on n'enrayait pas à temps. C'est à Vous maintenant de nous suivre sur le terain, le seul qui paraisse promettre de terminer la question à l'amiable.[166]

Between these two reports there was an important episode, which explains why France took this position towards the Danish-German dispute in April 1857.

Initially France was inclined to accede to Denmark's appeal and to intervene in the dispute with Germany. Before reaching a decision, however, she wanted to learn Russia's position. On 16 March Walewski instructed Morny to inform Gorchakov that the French government was inclined to regard the Danish-German dispute as a European problem and to sound out Gorchakov's opinion on the matter.[167]

---

164. Frankrig, Dep. 1856-60, no. 8, 3 March 1857.
165. The attitude of France, and particularly Napoleon III, to Denmark is shown by the words he addressed to the Danish ambassador when the latter presented his credentials in November 1856: Vous nous êtes restés fidèles dans nos malheurs [an allusion to the Franco-Danish alliance at the time of the First Empire], nous n'oublierons pas dans notre prospérité et vous pourrez toujours compter sur l'appui de la France, quand il pourra vous être utile – Napoleon III assured the ambassador.
'La défense la l'île d'Als par l'armée danoise, en 1864, d'après des lettres du Lieutenant Kilman, engagé voluntaire suédois,' Introduction de P. Desfeuilles, *Revue International d'Histoire Militaire*, (1966), no. 25, p. 567.
166. Frankrig, Dep. 1856-60, no. 15, 5. April 1857.
167. A.Ch. Roux, *Alexandre II, Gortchakoff et Napoléon III*, p. 207.

Gorchakov's reaction was to regret that he had received this information after the Imperial government had already pronounced on the topic and he had presented the position of his government, and could be summed up as follows: Denmark should not spare any effort to reach an understanding with Austria and Prussia, because otherwise the latter, under pressure of public opinion in Germany, would hand the matter over to the Diet in Frankfurt which was competent to examine the dispute – though there was no doubt that it was ill-disposed towards Denmark. The worst thing would be if the matter came before the European aureopagus. To deny this was to assume that the Diet's decision could be a blow to the integrity of the Danish monarchy, whose relations with Europe had been defined in the Treaty of London in 1852. The existence of this treaty was in some measure subject to the guarantee of the great powers.[168]

Walewski decided to accept this Russian point of view, and the Russian ambassador in Paris, Kiselev, was informed of this on 2 April; as a result he rejected the British government's invitation to make a joint approach to Berlin and Vienna.[169] Walewski acted so as not to antagonise Russia, although he was convinced that intervention by the great powers would be more justified than exposing Denmark to the negative consequences which could result from placing the matter before the German Diet. Even Gorchakov did not rule out such negative consequences.[170]

Walewski did not close the door to intervention, however, and, as his dispatch to Morny on 15 April shows, saw this as a possibility in a special case.

La monarchie Danoise est un État mixte dont la conservation importe aux grandes puissances et dont la situation ébranlée par les dernières révolutions a été reconstituée par un traité auquel la France, la Russie et l'Angleterre ont été parties contractantes, comme l'Autriche et la Prusse. Il nous appartient à ce titre de nous intéresser à sa tranquilité et à son existence ... Ce que nous ne pourrions admettre, ce serait que dans le cas où, la question se trouvant portée à Francfort, les partis ne parviendraient pas à s'entendre, la Confédération Germanique s'attribuât le privilège exclusif de la décider et d'imposer sa décision au Danemark, sans tenir compte des intérêts européens de ce pays et des droits des autres puissances.[171]

In other words, if the integrity of the Danish monarchy were in question.[172]

These arguments did not convince Gorchakov, who wrote to Kiselov on 3 (15) April:

Jusqu'au jour où ces conséquences viendraient à se produire, nous demeurons persuadés que la question est et doit rester une question purement fédérale, à résoudre dans les voies d'une entente amiable, entre les parties interessées, et qu'on ne saurait, sans de sérieux inconvénients, la faire sortir de ces limites.

---

168. Morny, 26 March 1857, Roux, *Alexandre II ...*, pp. 207-8.
169. Roux, *Alexandre II ...*, p. 208.
170. *Ibid.*
171. Walewski to Morny, 15 April 1857, in *ibid.* p. 209.
172. Schüle, *Russland und Frankreich*, p. 92.

Walewski was not so naïve as not to understand Gorchakov's intentions. 'Walewski n'était dupe de la propre naïvité – Ch.F. Roux wrote – lorsqu'il s'appliquait, à son tour à atténuer la portée de sa divergence qui séparait les deux gouvernements'. Walewski distrusted Gorchakov.

The Russians – he wrote later (on 4 January 1858) – are known for cheating at play; they do not think it dishonorable to do so. They behave in this way in all their transactions. Business is for them a game to be won ... by fairs means or foul.[173]

But 'que Walewski place l'intérêt de l'entente franco-russe au-dessus de celui de la question danoise et, par suite, qu'il ne passera pas outre à l'abstention de la Russie'.[174] In the face of the planned war with Austria, Russia's support was indispensable for France and far more important than having her own way over the question of the Elbe duchies. Nor did Napoleon III have any intention of falling out with Prussia over such a secondary matter as the Danish-German dispute, the more so since he had seen how close relations were between St. Petersburg and Berlin. The Franco-Russian rapprochement, and particularly the meeting in Stuttgart in September 1857, had a substantial effect on France's policy towards Denmark.

Walewski decided, thought not without resistance, to accept Gorchakov's point of view on the Danish-German conflict, and Gorchakov, not without pride, informed Bismarck of this when, immediately after the conference, the latter questioned the Russian minister about whether the Holstein problem had been a topic of discussion. Gorchakov said that at this 'meeting', as he called it, the problem had taken a secondary place since *'de minimis non curat praetor',*[175] and at the same time informed Bismarck that he, Gorchakov, had given Bülow, who had come to Stuttgart seeking to use the meeting to dispose both France and Russia in a direction friendly to Denmark, the advice one gave 'to quarrelling children', that the stronger (i.e. in his view Denmark – E.H.) should behave more sensibly and give way. He had also told Bülow that both France and Russia thought that the Copenhagen cabinet should solve the problem by means of talks with the leaders of the Holstein party and the German Confederation.[176]

The Stuttgart meeting was in some degree crucial to France's attitude to the question of the duchies. On 17 October, in a conversation with Dirckinck-Holmfeld, Walewski referred to his meeting with Bülow and observed that the time was coming to settle for good the problem of the duchies which, as had been said during the Stuttgart meeting, could not be left in suspense in the long term.

---

173. Bernardy, F. Chalamon de, *Un fils de Napoléon: Le Comte Walewski, 1810-69.* (Paris, unpublished dissertation, 1951, p. 833), in: Thurston, Gary Jay, *The Franco-Russian Entente, 1856-63: P.D. Kiselev's Paris Embassy,* (University Microfilms International, Ann Arbor, Michigan, 1973, p. 218).
174. Ch. Roux, *Alexandre II ...,* p. 210.
175. Praetor is not concerned with trivial matters.
176. Thorsøe, *op.cit.* vol. II, pp. 592-3; Neergaard, *op.cit.* vol. II, pt. I. pp. 160-1; Tatishchev, *Imperator ...* vol. I, pp. 227-8; G. Rothan, Souvenirs diplomatiques', *Revue des Deux Mondes,* (1889), (81), pp. 72-73, 76. On the Stuttgart meeting and the response to it in Germany see Brockdorff's report no. 65 of 30 October 1857, Depecher Preussen, 1856-59, R.A. Copenhagen, and Rothan, p. 77.

Il Vous faut une position nette vis-à-vis de l'Allemagne, mais avant que l'Europe s'en mêle, il vaudrait en tout cas mieux que Vous tâchiez de Vous arranger directement avec le Holstein et l'Allemagne. Il faut que Vous traitîez cette question sous un point de vue plus élevé. ... Vous savez combien nous nous intéressons à Vous, – and to avoid any doubt he added – la Russie marche avec nous, j'en suis bien sûr et l'Angleterre en fera de même. Tâchez donc d'en finir le plûtot possible.[177]

In the course of the conversation, Walewski alluded to the position taken by Luxemburg in relation to Holland, an idea of which, the Danish ambassador assumed, he was not the originator but which had been suggested to him recently in Germany. But the ambassador immediately replied that in the case of Holland and Luxemburg it was a matter of a union between two countries geographically distant from each other who had created a purely personal union. If this principle were to be adopted in relation to Holstein, it would lead sooner or later to the complete separation of Holstein from Denmark, and this would not satisfy Holstein either since its objections went further and the aim of the opposition in Holstein was union with Schleswig. If the principle of personal union of Denmark with Holstein were applied, the opposition would seek to apply this principle in relation to Schleswig too. This would end in the gradual partitioning of Denmark.

Le ministre parassait assez bien comprendre cette manière de voir et s'énoncait en général avec beaucoup de bienveillance pour nous. Mais malgré tout l'intérêt qu'il nous porte, il est encore bien loin d'avoir saisi la question dans toutes les nuances et ses nombreuses occupations ne lui permettent guère de s'y appliquer avec l'attention et la persévérance necéssaires pour des rapports si compliqués.

This conversation with Walewski was supplemented by one which the Danish ambassador had with Kiselev, the Rusian ambassador in Paris, after the latter's return from Stuttgart. In contrast to the reports coming from Gorchakov on the subject of the place the duchies had occupied in the Franco-Russian talks, which had indicated that the question had been a marginal one, Kiselov said, 'on a beaucoup parlé de Vos affaires à Stuttgart et maintenant elles vont être traitées au Congrès'. This astonished the Danish ambassador, who declared that in that case new concessions would be demanded from Denmark. What more were the Holstein party demanding, asked Kiselev. The establishment of Schleswig-Holstein, the ambassador replied, and also that they should have as much connection with Germany as with Denmark. But Kiselev denied this and, referring to the opinion of some German statesman, said that Holstein could expect nothing from Germany.

Kiselev's reaction showed that Russia took a narrow view of the problem, seeing, or wanting to see it, only as a problem of the conservative opposition in Holstein and refusing to appreciate the complexity of the dispute, and that Holstein had become the object of the aspiration of the German people. The Danish ambassador came to the conclusion that in reality the duchies question had been discussed at

---

177. Frankrig, Dep. 1856-60, no. 32, 17 October 1857. Cf. *Kjøbenhavnsposten,* introductory article on this proposal by France, No. 127, 26. October 1858.

Stuttgart in a way 'plus amplement qu'en général' and recommended his government to take the initiative so as to avoid having a decision imposed on it without consideration of Denmark's complicated position ('sans avoir eu assez égard à notre position politique si compliquée').[178]

VI.

On 20 October Lauenburg officially lodged a protest concerning the Danish constitution with the Diet in Frankfurt and on 29 October Austria and Prussia placed the question of Holstein's complaint before the Diet. This created an entirely new situation: the matter had passed out of the competence of the Danish government. In Ungern-Sternberg's opinion the Danish government did not realise the seriousness of the situation. There were disagreements within the government itself. The new Minister of Foreign Affairs, O.V. Michelsen, who was not of 'capacité politique', seemed to be treated by his colleagues 'comme hors d'œuvre plutôt que comme chef et organe officiel de la politique du Cabinet'.

In discussions with the Russian ambassador about the situation Michelsen confined himself to a narrowly Danish approach. He maintained that the duchies were in the wrong, that the government could not make any new concessions, that the duchies' complaints were purely theoretical and had no justification, that the provincial Estates of Holstein consisted of people chosen after the war and no longer represented the opinion of Holstein, and that the cause of the intellectual agitation was the provocative action of the Schleswig-Holstein party in Germany. Like Scheele, he blamed everything on the aristocracy in the duchies and, in Ungern-Sternberg's view, failed to see that this time even people most devoted to monarchist principles were among the leaders of the dissatisfaction, irrespective of their social position. The situation was different with the Prime Minister, C. Ch. Hall, and the Minister of Finance, C.G. Andrae. They understood the problem and

---

178. Frankrig. Dep. 1856-60, no. 32. 17 October 1857. In the Udenrigsmin. Samlede Sager, Den Holstenske Forfatningssag 1856-57, Vol. 221, there is a memorandum dated October 1857 which was attached to the Danish ambassador's dispatch from Paris of 11 October (?), marked 'fortroligt' (confidential); its authorship cannot be established. This memorandum is devoted to Russia's attitude towards Denmark. It says that of all the great powers Russia is the most interested in maintaining the integrity of Denmark. This explains her negative attitude to the idea of the rise of a Scandinavian state, which would be regarded as a hostile act towards Russia, and to the rise, as a consequence of such an act, of a state of Holstein, which would combine with Germany to build a fleet which could occupy a dominant position in the Baltic, something which would be to Russia's disadvantage. In the opinion of the author of the memorandum, Russia probably reckoned that in the event of there being no heir to the throne assigned to Christian of Glücksburg, she would assert rights to a certain part of Holstein and, by guaranteeing the integrity of the Danish monarchy, planned to ensure the throne for a Russian prince. But the Emperor, it had to be assumed, would renounce these rights if it could be the cause of peace in Europe and ensure calm in Denmark. The memorandum ends by saying that Denmark expected salvation from France: 'La France n'a qu'à vouloir et le Danemark sera sauvé'.

were discussing a range of possible variants for the structure and organisation of the Danish monarchy.

Ungern-Sternberg came to the following conclusion:

Dans cet état de choses, m. Prince, il ne reste qu'à attendre que la question soit plus mûre. Les événemens seront plus forts peut-être que les conseils de la prudence, et quand on connait les élémens et les hommes dans ce pays-ci, il n'y a dans la marche des affaires danoises rienne (sic E.H.) que puisse étonner. On laisse flotter le navire sans boussole et sans gouvernail, se fiant au sort, à l'intervention de telle out telle puissance amie, pour sortir heureusement du danger. Cette confidence dans l'étoile du Danemarc, jointe à l'apathie nationale et à une grande présomption, forment un des traits caractéristiques du Gouvernement, et de la population entière.

Vouloir agir sur de tels éléments par des moyens ordinaires serait peine inutile, mon Prince, et quant aux autres circonstances qui rendent les conseils infructueux, je crois devoir les garder sous silence. Elles ne sont que trop connues à V.E.[179]

The reports received from Copenhagen on the delaying policy of the Danish government, the wish to maintain good relations with the German states, especially Prussia, and, finally, the acceptance by the French government of Russia's point of view ruling out transfer of the Danish-German dispute to the European forum and treating it as a German question – all these elements taken together emboldened Gorchakov and he decided to put his point of view on the problem bluntly to the Danish government. He did so in a note to Ungern-Sternberg on 19 November (1 December) 1857,[180] in which he took an unequivocal position on the question of the duchies and the Danish-German dispute. This question, said the introduction to the note, had reached a stage when its seriousness could not be concealed. On the one hand, the German Diet had agreed to examine the complaint lodged by Lauenburg and, on the other hand, Austria and Prussia had taken the question of Holstein into their own hands because they had become convinced that their efforts to settle the dispute by means of direct negotiations with Denmark had proved fruitless. According to article 31 of the final act of Vienna, the Diet had an obligation to pronounce on the matter and it had an indisputable right to do so. The Danish King, as Prince of Holstein and Lauenburg, would have the opportunity to state his position on these regrettable differences and on his intentions concerning fulfillment of the obligations towards the German Confederation undertaken in 1852. This would determine the outcome of the question, which was absorbing all the attention of Germany and keeping Denmark in a state of uncertainty.

The Imperial government wished that the King would make use of the opportunity he had been given to demonstrate that he was inclined towards conciliation and that he would make every effort to adhere to the agreements concluded with the Confederation, especially in respect of Holstein. Russia would refrain from intervention in matters which, in her opinion, lay exclusively in the competence of

---

179. No. 108. 7 (19) November 1857.
180. R.A. Copenhagen, Udenrigsm. Polen, A. 3354.

German public law. But she could not be indifferent to a continuing state of affairs which threatened peace in northern Europe and could not possibly serve the true interests of Denmark.

The Danish government did not realise the extent of the sympathy which the duchies question had aroused among the population of Germany. It should be grateful to the German governments, particularly Austria and Prussia, which hitherto had contained this sympathy within their own borders. But they did not have the right to wait any longer for Denmark to show herself disposed to put out her hand to a just and honourable agreement.

These considerations, we read in the note, would not escape the attention of the King, and the Imperial Cabinet recommended once again that all this should be weighed up very seriously. It was much to be desired that in the explanation he gave to the Confederation the King should not close the door to amicable agreement, which both his own interests and the dignity of the crown demanded.

Asking Ungern-Sternberg to inform the Minister of Foreign Affairs of the contents of the note, Gorchakov expressed the conviction that he (the ambassador), with his deep knowledge of the question of the duchy and of federal legislation, would demonstrate to the royal government what fatal consequences the denial of justice might bring ('et surtout de faire envisager aux Ministres du Roi les fâcheuses conséquences que pourrait entraîner un déni de justice').

That this note was a premeditated step is shown by the fact that during a talk the Danish chargé d'affaires, who was deputising for Plessen while the latter took a long holiday, Gorchakov again criticised the Danish government for not settling the dispute with the German states.

'Il me semble – said Gorchakov – que Votre Gouvernement suit une politique de hazard. Vous avez l'air de compter dans le dernier moment sur l'appui de quelque Puissance, je ne sais pas trop laquelle. Votre Gouvernement devrait s'entendre directement avec les chefs de l'opposition Holsteinoise, qui sont des gens, auxquels Vous accorder pourtant Votre estime, et qui ne sont pas des démocrates ou des révolutionnaires'.

Recounting the course of his talk with Gorchakov, F. Hagemann added that he was making a report 'de relever mot pour mot les expressions assez bizarres dont il s'est servi à cet égard'.[181] In fact they were not very surprising, but they demonstrated Gorchakov's thinking and his unreserved support for the German side.

Gorchakov's note of 19 November (O.S.) led to a lively exchange of opinions between Michelsen and Ungern-Sternberg. Michelsen expressed deep regret that the Imperial government, on whose help and friendly disposition the Danish government had always counted, had now changed its position on the subject of the differences both between Denmark and the duchies and between Denmark and the cabinets of Vienna and Berlin. He argued that responsibility for the failure to resolve the conflict did not lie with Denmark, which had continually made concessions. But the further it went in this direction the more it provoked further de-

---

181. No. 50. 5 December (23. November) 1857.

mands from Austria and Prussia. No one in Denmark, irrespective of which party they belonged to, could agree to adopt the principle that one inhabitant of Holstein had the same right as three Danes.

Ungern-Sternberg rejected Michelsen's reasoning and argued that Gorchakov's dispatch should surprise no one, since, despite repeated pressure from Russia, France and Britain, encouragement and advice had failed to persuade Denmark to take a moderate line and offer concessions, although she had been warned that her attitude, *eo magis*,[182] since the German Confederation's complaints against Denmark had been correct, could lead to regrettable consequences.[183]

The ambassador came to the conclusion that in order to escape from the impasse there had to be an end to mutual accusations and that the governments in Vienna and Berlin, or the Diet in Frankfurt, should present a plan for negotiations based on an objective assessment of the question and the accompanying circumstances. This fruitless discussion, he wrote, should be ended. But he doubted whether, in this state of affairs, the Danish government was capable of proceeding to settle the problem without intervention by the Confederation or the larger German states.

Cette tactique convient aux hommes actuellement au pouvoir et répond également à la tendance générale à se laisser aller qui forme un des traits caractéristique de la nation danoise. Il s'y mêle en outre un certain orgueil governemental qui repousse toute initiative d'accomodement avec des sujets du Roi naguère en révolte ouverte, et vaincus, comme on le croit ici, par les seules forces du Danemarc.[184]

Referring to Ungern-Sternberg's report of 11 (23) December 1857, Gorchakov sent a dispatch to Copenhagen on 28 December in which he maintained his position and at the same time criticised the Copenhagen cabinet's assessment of the situation. In the Russian minister's opinion, his dispatch of 19 November could only be new evidence of Russia's deep concern about a question which was causing Denmark so much trouble and showed how much the Tsar wished the King would put an end to the dispute in a way which befitted the dignity of the crown and served the true interests of the state. What Denmark was doing in the duchies, Gorchakov emphasised yet again, was not consistent with the obligations she had undertaken, nor with the spirit of the rights which the German Confederation was obliged to uphold. He appealed to the King to adopt a positive attitude to these matters, which had been clearly spelt out by Vienna and Berlin and which, in the opinion of those cabinets, required rectification. It seemed to him that the King's present advisers would find fewer obstacles on the road to agreement and justice than had their predecessors.[185]

In a talk with Hagemann Gorchakov defended Russia's position as the only correct one, arguing that Russia was the principal power which had striven most actively to prevent the question of the duchies, a purely German one, from becoming

182. The more.
183. Reports nos. 115 and 119, 1 (13) December and 11 (23) December 1857.
184. Report no. 123, 21 December 1857 (2 January 1858).
185. Rus. Film. R.A. Copenhagen.

a European problem. Russia, as a power friendly to Denmark, had spared no effort to point out the lamentable consequences and dangers to which Denmark could be exposed in the event of political intervention by the great powers. Such intervention would be a blow to the dignity of the country, which would not be the case with intervention by the Federal Diet, which had the right to intervene in the affairs of the German duchies. The Danish government should not draw the wrong conclusions about Russia's motives as they were the motives of a friendly power which wished Denmark nothing but good.

True to his character, Prince Gorchakov boasted that he had personally tried in Stuttgart to persuade France to share his position, but she had then joined up with Britain. The Danish government had to take a decision which it regarded as consistent with its own interests. He regretted that his note of 19 November had evidently been misinterpreted.[186]

The position taken by Gorchakov towards the Danish-German conflict, and particularly his 19 November (1 December) note, were a subject of lively interest to international public opinion. At the turn of the year 1857-58 a number of articles on the topic appeared in the German and the Danish press and the subsequent publication of the full text of Gorchakov's note in the German press in *La Nouvelle Gazette de Prusse* was used by the Danish and the German press for their own political purposes as evidence of Russia's change of course from pro-Danish to pro-German.[187] The publication of Gorchakov's note coincided with a series of articles which appeared in St. Petersburg in the German paper *Petersburger Zeitung,* which argued that Denmark had broken the treaty of 1852, not only in relation to the Elbe duchies but also in relation to the German Confederation, introducing democratic relations in the duchies starting from 1852 and unjust and tyrannical forms of government in Schleswig.

Furthermore, the paper published or reprinted summaries of articles and telegrams from Hamburg, carefully selected for their anti-Danish content and written in the spirit of Schleswig-Holsteinism, which the paper supported. Ungern-Sternberg again drew attention[188] to the reprinting in the semi-official *Berlingske Tidende* in Copenhagen of a letter from St. Petersburg addressed to *'Correspondence Havas'* and dated 18 December which spoke of symptoms of differences between Russia and France over Scandinavianism and the Russians' fear about France's position on this question. On the other hand, it argued, Britain supported the position presented by Gorchakov in his note to Copenhagen.

The tone of the articles in the *Petersburger Zeitung* was so hostile to Denmark that the British ambassador, Lord Wodehouse, *sua sponte,* [189]questioned Gorchakov about the matter. The minister replied that the articles were not inspired by the government and did not express the government's opinion. On his own initia-

---

186. No. 2, 28 (16) January 1858.
187. Ungern-Sternberg's dispatch no. 127 of 26 December 1857 (7 January 1858).
188. Report no. 127, 26 December 1857 (7 January 1858).
189. Of his own accord.

tive the ambassador informed Hagemann about this.[190] A similar answer was given to Hall by Ungern-Sternberg when he was asked about the appearance in the *Petersburger Zeitung* of articles with an anti-Danish content, written in the spirit of Schleswig-Holsteinism, and particularly of an article concerning Schleswig which was subsequently reprinted in the *Gazette d'Augsbourg,* (No. 38, 7 February 1858). This article made a dreadful impression in Denmark. The ambassador did not fail to add that the periodical press in Russia was then enjoying the freedom to express opinions on matters of international policy and articles which appeared in it reflected the views of editors writing for Russian society and not to influence opinion in other countries. It would have been different if the articles had appeared in the *Journal de St. Pétersbourg,* the ambassador added.[191]

Like Gorchakov's previous explanation given to Wodehouse, the ambassador's explanations did not convince Hall. Krieger considered that the Russian ambassador was not in a position to understand Danish difficulties and accepted the ambassador's assurances about the freedom of the press in Russia ironically.[192]

The Danish press, especially the papers connected with the national-liberal group, reacted sharply to the articles mentioned above and to Gorchakov's note of 19 November (O.S.) and *Fædrelandet* (no. 2, 4 January 1858) published a reply ('un des plus haineux', Ungern-Sternberg called it) which the ambassador considered a defamation of Russia as it implied that Russia wanted to claim part of Holstein, which had been mentioned in the Warsaw protocol and in the 31 July 1853 law on the succession. The paper, the ambassador reported, was trying to make out that Russia was an obstacle to the unity of the Scandinavian peoples and was sowing the seeds of animosity between Denmark and Germany so that she could come to the assistance of the Holstein aristocracy when the law on the succession to the throne in Denmark took effect. This, in *Fædrelandet*'s opinion, was the latest evidence of Russia's disinterested friendship. In ancient Rome such behaviour was called *Punica fides.*[193] In the ambassador's view the *Fædrelandet* article demonstrated the existence of an anti-Russian mood in the most influential party of so-called patriots, ultra-Danes or Scandinavianists.[194]

Dagbladet also criticised the articles in the *Petersburger Zeitung.*[195] Although it was known that this was not an official organ of the government, and only represented a fraction of the German party, which Russians hated, the Danish press could not remain silent. The existence of freedom of the press in Russia did

---

190. Dep. Rusland no. 6, 26 (14) February and no. 9, 10 April (29) March 1858. Report no. 15, 2 (14) February 1857. H.H.S.A. Kart. 50.
191. The *Journal de St. Pétersbourg* was the semi-official organ of the Ministry of Foreign Affairs. On this topic Bismarck wrote to Schleinitz on 13 March 1861: 'Ich setze voraus, das *Journal de St. Pétersbourg* im Königl. Ministerium gehalten wird; der Fürst erkennt es selbst als sein persönliches Organ an, und ist nicht ohne Empfindlichkeit, wenn er bemerkt dass man einer Leitartikel nicht gelesen hat'. *Bismarcks Briefwechsel* ... p. 151.
192. A.F. *Kriegers Dagbøger,* vol. I, (Copenhagen and Christiania, 1920), entries for 17 February and 12 May 1858, pp. 255 and 293-4.
193. Punic or Carthaginian faith; treachery.

not mean that the government bore no responsibility at all for what was written in the papers or that Denmark was not entitled to complain about abuse in the German papers in Russia. The law was the same for all countries and there was no reason why small states should remain silent about such a matter, although it was well known that no one would dare to give orders, *Dagbladet* argued, because Denmark's representatives in St. Petersburg – the paper was mainly referring to the ambassador, Plessen, – and in many other European capitals were people of rather conservative views, and too much confidence should not be placed in them. *Dagbladet* wanted to draw to the notice of public opinion the fact that many key positions in the Danish diplomatic service were held by aristocrats from Holstein.

In this situation Gorchakov decided on a propaganda offensive, using *Le Nord-Journal International,* which had been founded in Brussels in 1855 and was subsidised by the St. Petersburg Ministry of Foreign Affairs. Gorchakov intended the paper to help to mould public opinion in the West, particularly in France.[196] The pages of *Le Nord*[197] carried attacks on the articles which appeared in ultra-conservative Prussian papers like *Kreuzzeitung, Nouvelle Gazette de Prusse,* and *Journal de Frankfort,* which (particularly *Kreuzzeitung*) criticised Russian foreign policy, regarded Russia's abandonment of the Holy Alliance policy as a crime, and compared Stuttgart with Tilsit. The articles 'Notre réponse à La Nouvelle Gazette de Prusse' on 18 November 1857 and 'Correspondance politique' on 30 January 1858, based on reports from St. Petersburg dated 10 (22) January, presented an exposition of Russian policy, defending the alliance with France as of great importance for the interests of both Russia and Europe. There was no contradiction between this policy and good neighbourly relations with Germany, the more so since

elle (la Russie) est attachée à la plupart des Etats de la Confédération germanique par des liens de famille, de glorieuses traditions, la continuité de relations intimes et amicales, ou par des rapports de voisinage, source de nombreux contacts et de mutuels avantages: La dernière crise n'a fait que resserer ces liens et en cimenter les mutuelles dispositions.[198]

In both articles *Le Nord* stressed the special role played by Russo-Prussian friendship.

Ces bonnes et cordiales relations ne changeront pas, car elles satisfont à la fois aux souvenirs du passé, aux besoins du présent et aux prévisions de l'avenir.[199]

This last point was made even more prominently in the 30 January 1858 article. Referring to Stuttgart, it said:

---

194. Report no. 127.
195. No. 68. 20. March 1858.
196. See Chapter 9, The Semi-Official *Le Nord-Journal International* and the Danish-German Conflict'.
197. These articles may be found, among other places, in Krieger's archives, No. 5810, R.A. Copenhagen.
198. *Le Nord,* 30 January 1858.
199. *Le Nord,* 18. November 1857.

L'accord de la Russie avec la France n'est point un accident transitoire, mais un fait entré profondément dans la politique du gouvernement russe.

La France et la Russie se sont déjà entendues nommément sur la question des Duchés, et cette entente a été en pleine conformité avec les intérêts et la dignité de l'Allemagne.

Two other articles, 'La Question des Duchés devant la Diète de Frankfort', published on 8 November 1857 and 'La Politique de la Russie, Le démarche de la Russie dans le différent Dano-Allemand', which appeared on 12 January 1858, are closely connected with the first two. These articles are commentaries explaining the current position of Russia in the question of the duchies and the Russian interpretation of the Danish-German dispute from its beginning.

Denmark, the author of the 8 November 1857 article said, on account of its geographical position and its structure, was of exceptional importance for the maintenance of the balance of power in northern Europe and if it ceased to exist that balance would be threatened. In 1848 the Holstein question had appeared as a *Deus ex machina,* and Prince Augustenburg's claims and the nationality principle had made the question of the duchies the banner of democracy in Germany. The weak Danish government had thrown itself into the arms of the democratic and national party and the idea of a frontier on the Eider had become the slogan of the day.

It was a regrettable fact that after 1852 matters on which the future of the Danish monarchy depended had not been settled and the tendency towards a unitary state based on the dominance of the Danish nation had predominated. In the author's view, institutions had been imposed on the duchies which were inconsistent with the obligations undertaken as a result of their different position as part of the German Confederation. The blame for the growth of tension and conflict, and for the fact that a dangerous situation had arisen for Denmark, lay neither with the German parties nor with Germany, but with the Danish government.

In the current phase of the dispute between Denmark and the duchies, the matter unquestionably fell within the competence of the German Confederation. This was a consequence of the fact that the duchies belonged simultaneously both to Denmark and to the Confederation, and of the general and international obligations deriving from the peace treaty with Germany, which included the obligation not to incorporate Schleswig into Denmark. It remained an open question whether the Confederation was strong enough to solve the problem or whether new complications would arise. The matter was important. But the author believed that the commission appointed to examine the question would find a reasonable solution.[200]

The article of 12 January 1858 defended Gorchakov's 19 November 1857 note, published in *Le Nord* on 15 December, and attacked those who argued that in the

---

200. The Danish government's view of the history of Holstein and Schleswig from the 11th century until 1852 was set out by Michelsen in an appendix to his letter of 14 September 1857 to Comte de Reventlow-Criminal, the *chargé d'affaires* in London. London. Ordrer 1857, No. 11, R.A. Copenhagen.

light of that note the only conclusion to be drawn was that Russia had altered her views and had become convinced that because she disagreed with France she must return to her old alliance with the German states and abandon the Danish cause. Russian policy on the duchies had not changed in the least and was exactly the same as it had been six months earlier, that was to say, it remained one of scrupulously balanced impartiality. The St. Petersburg cabinet had never ceased to press the Danish government to seek reconciliation. It had always considered that the German parliament was competent to settle the dispute between the Kind of Denmark and his German subjects. As evidence that this was the policy the Russian government had followed previously, the article quoted Gorchakov's dispatch of 1 March 1857, which, the author claimed, was essentially the same as the 19 November (1 December) note.

The German press, taking their wishes for reality, and encouraged by the fact that the Russian cabinet had given moral support to the Diet's demand, had wrongly concluded that the later note was the first sign of a revision of policy by the St. Petersburg cabinet. The German states were defending an indisputably just cause, aiming to satisfy the rightful demands of the German population in the duchies and maintain order and peace in Europe. There was nothing surprising about the fact that in this they took the same position as Russia. But this was very far from a change in policy and a return to the alliance system before the Eastern War.

The course Russia had followed for almost two years had brought her enormous advantages. Her domestic policy had been exceptionally popular and her external policy had won the approval of the majority of European states. The visit by Alexander II to Germany and the crowds and ovations in his honour were proof of the benefits of this new system. It was essential to refute accusations of the existence of differences between the government in St. Petersburg and the Tuilleries over the question of the duchies. Both in Paris and on the Neva reconciliation, the welfare of the duchies and the integrity of the Danish monarchy were desired. Both powers were agreed on not imposing a solution, but regarded the matter as a purely federal one. They wanted only that the solution should be one which did not infringe the general peace. The essence was the same, though it took different forms. The understanding existing between the two governments did not mean that they gave up all initiative and spontaneity ('à toute spontanéité personnelle'). The article ended with the words:

Deux puissances comme la Russie et la France peuvent voguer de concert, mais elles ne vont jamais à la remorque l'une de l'autre.

VII

On 11 February 1858 the German Diet adopted a resolution, on the basis of article 56 of the final act of Vienna,[201] that the ordinance of 11 April 1854 concerning the

---

201. The Resolution on the Federal Execution of August 3, 1820. E. Huber, *Dokumente zur deutschen Verfassungsgeschichte,* vol. I, (Stuttgart, 1961), p. 103.

constitution for Holstein, the decree of 23 June 1856 and the Danish constitution of 2 October 1855 could not be applied to Holstein and Lauenburg as they had not been presented to the States of Holstein. The Diet in Frankfurt regarded the constitution as null and void in relation to the above-mentioned duchies.

Denmark was called upon to observe the obligations she had undertaken in 1851-52, especially those contained in the royal proclamation of 28 January 1852, and to act in accordance with those obligations and with the constitution of the German Confederation. On 25 February 1858 the Diet adopted a resolution stating:

> The Diet expected that the Danish government would from that time abstain from promulgating in the duchies of Holstein and Lauenburg new enactments calculated to alter the then existing state of things, and founded on those laws which, according to the resolution of February 11th, were without consitutional authority in the duchies.[202]

On 26 March the Danish government responded to the German Diet resolution of 11 February, declaring that it was ready to observe all the Diet's recommendations, if they did not exceed the Diet's authority, and also the obligations undertaken in 1851-52, if they had not been fulfilled by Denmark, although the Danish government denied that such a situation existed in reality.

And finally, [it] observed that in so far as there might be any doubts concerning the nature and scope of these engagements, the Diet could not be allowed the right of enforcing *ex parte* interpretation of the documents concerned.

The government declared its willingness to begin new negotiations with the representatives of the Diet. It decided to give the States of Holstein the opportunity to express their wishes, so that these could be taken into consideration in the new negotiations.

The federal resolution of 20 May regarded this declaration as insufficient and demanded a positive and definitive statement from the Danish government about the way in which it intended to carry out the 11 February resolution. Further Danish declarations, including the announcement of temporary suspension of the constitution in respect of Holstein and Lauenburg, were regarded as insufficient and inadequate by the Diet.

The Diet demanded (12th August) a formal revocation of the impeached laws, and as an opening for negotiations resolved that the Danish plenipotentiary might communicate directly with the Holstein and Lauenburg committee.

The threat of federal action now hung over Denmark.

In this difficult time for Denmark there was little change in the position of either Ungern-Sternberg or Gorchakov. The ambassador condemned the Danish government's delaying policy[203] and came to the conclusion that if even the German Diet resolved that the constitution for Holstein, and the general constitution, were con-

---

202. Charles A. Gosch, *Denmark and Germany since 1815*, (London, 1862), p. 202; Neergaard, Vol. II/I, pp. 170 ff.
203. No. 11, (Particulière) 2 (14) January, no. 47 (249), 8 (20) May, no. 53 (282), 23 May (4 June) 1858.

trary to the obligations undertaken by Denmark, and the Danish government was not displeased with this turn of affairs, this would need to be counteracted since the result of such a resolution would be the separation of these duchies, which had previously been a part *'du Gesamtstaat',*[204] and the establishment *'de l'Eider-Danisme'* (Ungern-Sternberg's emphasis) – the first step towards Scandinavianism. In order to counter this Ungern-Sternberg proposed that, if possible, Gorchakov should arrange that the German parliament would again entrust the matter to the two large German courts, which might then achieve a result which would be impossible if the affair were settled by the Diet.

A new element which became noticeable was a certain *rapprochement* between the ambassador and Hall and greater understanding of the difficult situation in which the government found itself, facing pressure from its own party, the press, the streets of Copenhagen and the Scandinavian movement on the one hand, and the anti-unionist movement on the other.[205]

The ambassador shared Hall's point of view that the increase in the difficulties was caused by the Holstein opposition's rejection of the government's proposals and the Diet's desire to impose demands and that it would jeopardise the internal system and the stability of the Danish monarchy. But he differed from Hall over the way to resolve the conflict. Ungern-Sternberg proposed the creation of a second chamber beside the Rigsraad, in which all parts of the monarchy would be equally represented, but consisting of large landowners and people known for their conservative views. This chamber, in the ambassador's opinion, would form a counterweight to the Rigsraad and a support for the conservative elements which were oppressed by the government and terrorised by the democrats. Apart from this, he urged a rapid agreement with the German Diet and the use of Bülow for the negotiations.[206]

The measure of improvement in the personal relations between Hall and Ungern-Sternberg had no influence on Russian policy. Gorchakov decided to play a waiting game. Asked by the French *chargé d'affaires* in April whether Russia did not intend to abandon her passive attitude to the Danish-German dispute, Gorchakov responded that he did not think the moment for intervention by the great powers had come as the matter remained an internal German problem.[207] To justify his claim that any action would be ineffective Gorchakov used the following argument:

Si nous montrons à Copenhague que nous considérons la communications faite par M. de Bülow comme un pas dans la voie de la conciliation, nous courons grand risque d'arrêter le Danemark dans cette voie. ... Si nous insistons à Vienne, à Berlin et à Francfort pour qu'on accepte tout ou partie des propositions danoises, on nous répondra par une discussion

---

204. I.e. Helstat. The Whole-State.
205. See reports no. 9, (50), 18 (30) January, no. 33 (201), 10 (22) April, no. 38 (210), 18 (30) April, no. 47 (249), 8 (20) May, no. 53 (282), 23 May (4 June), no. 54 (283), 5 June 1858. Cf. Krieger, vol. 1, 17 February 1858, p. 255.
206. *Ibid.* 18 (30) January 1858.
207. Roux, *Alexandre II ...*, p. 227.

approfondie des droits des duchés et de la Diète, discussion dans laquelle je ne me soucie nullement d'entrer, car je dois avouer que la question est à peu près inintelligible pour moi ... J'attendrai les nouvelles résolutions de la Diete et la réponse qu'elle fera à la communication danoise. Pour le moment, je suis résolu à ne pas dire un mot, soit à Copenhague, soit à Francfort.[208]

Appealing to Prussia for restraint, he argued that pressure on Denmark could lead to the strengthening of the Eider party, which neither Prussia nor Russia wanted, or to the intervention of France and Britain in defence of Denmark.[209]

That Denmark heeded the voice of Gorchakov is shown by the sending of Plessen to St. Petersburg after over a year's absence from his Russian post, in the hope that he would be able to accomplish something more than hitherto with Gorchakov.[210] In talks with Plessen, Gorchakov as usual urged agreement with Germany, and particularly acceptance of the point of view of Manteuffel, who advised that Denmark and the Confederation should jointly introduce changes in the general constitution so as to satisfy all the parts making up the Danish monarchy. At the same time Gorchakov emphasised that Prussia did not want to see the duchies detached from Denmark, as it would not be in her interest. It was also easier for her to reach an agreement with the Danish King than with a possible new Prince of Holstein after its separation from Denmark.[211] He warned Denmark that the situation was developing in an infavourable direction for her, as agitation by national-liberal elements in Germany was on the increase.

In conversations with Montebello Gorchakov expressed fear on account of 'la chasse à popularité' on the part of the Prussian Prince-Regent,[212] and Werther detected in him some vague inclination towards mediation. In reality there was no such tendency. When asked by the Danish government to intervene, Gorchakov argued that if the Russian government supported the Danish proposals in Germany the effect would be the opposite, as this would only provoke Germany, which jealously guarded itself against foreign pressure.[213] Gorchakov's caution reached such a level that in a dispatch to Ungern-Sternberg on 23 July he recommended that he should not make use of the letters to Budberg, Oubril and Fonton, the Russian ambassadors in Vienna, Berlin and Frankfurt, which were appended to the dispatch, because if the Danish government saw how keenly the St. Petersburg cabinet was defending its cause (Gorchakov used these words. – E.H.), it might ascribe greater significance to the letters which spoke of what Russia did not want and what must not happen, than they really had. Gorchakov was concerned not to weaken Denmark's efforts to reach an agreement.

---

208. Châteaurenard, 14 april 1858. Roux, *ibid.* p. 227.
209. Werthers Berichte, 20 August 1858; Roux, *ibid,* pp. 227 ff. Friese, *Russland und Preussen,* pp. 152-72.
210. Werthers Berichte, 14 May, 9 and 11 June 1858, Friese, *ibid.* p. 150.
211. Plessen's reports nos. 11 and 15 of 19 (7) and 21 (9) May. See also no. 20, 19 (7) June 1858.
212. Roux, *ibid.* p. 227.
213. Krieger, vol. 11, p. 303. Dep. Rusland, no. 15, 21 (9) May 1858.

In talks with Plessen Gorchakov stressed that it was far from the Tsar's intention to intervene in the internal affairs of Denmark and that Russia was not concerned with the kind of constitution, democratic or semi-democratic, nor with the organisation of power that existed in Denmark. (As we know, these were half-truths. – E.H.). But what Russia was principally anxious about was the maintenance of peace, the prevention of upheaval and the settlement of what was a purely German dispute – one could even say a family dispute – since in relation to the duchies the Danish King was a German ruler.[214] A similar position was taken by Alexander II in a conversation with Plessen.[215] Both Gorchakov and his chief adviser on German affairs, Osten-Sacken, considered that the action with which Denmark was threatened was a legal step and did not necessarily have to bring discredit on Denmark.[216] But Gorchakov preferred that it should not happen as it would cause complications.[217]

The minister was not inclined to answer Plessen's question, whether such action[218] could lead to intervention by the great powers, although he knew from a report received from London that in the event of German intervention Sweden would not fail to send her army to Denmark's assistance and Britain, faced with this situation, would not be able to regard the Danish-German dispute as an internal German matter for long.

This Russia wanted to avoid. For the same reason Gorchakov urged restraint in talks with Szechenyi and asked that Austria in particular should not abandon her moderate line. For otherwise, if it came to the situation mentioned by Clarendon, namely military intervention by Sweden, Russia would have to join forces with France and Britain.[219]

Gorchakov appeared to appreciate that the European horizon could be darkened on account of the duchies. He decided to put even stronger pressure on Denmark and warn her to proceed as soon as possible to settle the whole complex of disputed questions. On 16 (4) June he put the problem of Schleswig to Plessen for the first time, warning him that even after the Holstein question had been settled there would be the problem of Schleswig. His warning took the following terms:

Il me posa la question – Plessen reported "si pour arriver à une solution de la question avec l'Allemagne, Vous consentez à un détachement du Holstein, êtez vous bien persuadé, que la chose en reste là!? La question du Slesvic sommeille, pour le moment – dit le Prince – l'Allemagne n'ose pas y toucher, mais, si cette question est de nouveau soulevé – et elle le sera quand il s'agira de détacher le Holstein – il se peut que vos efforts n'aient pas la même réussite, qu'ils ont eu après l'année 48 pour conserver la Monarchie dans son ensemble." Le Prince paraît croire que dans une éventualité pareille, il n'est pas à prévoir ce qui en arriver-

---

214. Plessen's reports nos. 15 and 18 of 21 (9) May and 16 (4) June 1858.
215. No. 16, 2 June (21 May).
216. 9 June (28 May).
217. 21 (9) May and 16 (4) June.
218. Federal Execution-military action.
219. H.H.S.A., P.A.X. no. 58 A-G, 26 (14) December 1857. Karton 44, and no. 14B, 20 (8) February and no. 25 A-B, 14 (26) April 1858. Karton 45. See also no. 40, 3 July (21 June) 1858. Karton 46.

ait du Slesvic. D'aprés lui, dans un cas pareil, les circonstances peuvent faire surgir des décisions, auxquelles pêut-etre, dans ce moment on ne pense pas.

It was no accident then that just at this time a series of articles appeared in *Le Nord,* on 28-30 July 1858, under the heading 'Le conflit dano-allemand', devoted to the question of Schleswig.

These articles took the German point of view, both in their treatment of the history of Schleswig and in their assessment of the current situation. They accepted as indisputable facts both the so-called Waldemar constitution of 1326 and the resolution of the States in 1460 that Schleswig should never be incorporated into Denmark and that Schleswig and Holstein should be united for all time, arguing that until 1848 this resolution had been confirmed in all public acts and documents concerning relations between the two duchies. They also argued that in 1850-52 Denmark had solemnly promised to renounce the idea of incorporating Schleswig and that as a consequence of this the large German states had renounced the idea of sovereign autonomy for Schleswig, as well as the idea of Schleswig-Holstein, and had agreed to give up their agnate law. Denmark was accused of aiming to merge the German and Danish nationalities forcibly and of conducting a policy of Danicisation. Although Schleswig was not part of the German Confederation and the latter did not have competence in respect of Schleswig, the article claimed that nevertheless, because Denmark had undertaken obligations towards Austria and Prussia in respect of Schleswig, and these had been sanctioned by the German Diet, Denmark should act cautiously and not allow problems to arise in a difficult and entangled situation.[220]

The article on 29 July spoke of the growing Danish-German conflict, intensified after the adoption of the 2 October 1855 constitution. The author attacked the Danish press' arguments on the subject of the legality of the constitution in respect of the duchies and said that in issuing it Denmark had infringed the obligations undertaken towards Austria and Prussia on 6 December 1851 as the provincial States had not been consulted.

Finally, in the last article in the series, *Le Nord* outlined the history of the dispute from the passing of the 11 and 25 February 1858 resolutions by the German Diet. The author expressed the hope that the dispute would be settled in an amicable and peaceful way. 'La guerre ne donne pas raison à celui qui a tort'. He also cited D.G. Monrad's opinion that the constitution should be revised. The revision should put an end to discrepancies and should be done in such a way as to overcome all legal and executive difficulties, thus solving the Danish-German conflict, one of the most complicated problems in European politics.

Russo-Danish relations were influenced to some degree by the personality of the long-serving Danish ambassador in St. Petersburg, Otto Plessen. Immediately after completing his studies in the Law Department of the University of Kiel he was sent to St. Petersburg and from 1841 worked in the Danish embassy, initially as

---

220. *Le Nord,* 28 July 1858.

embassy secretary, then as *chargé d'affaires* and from 1849 to 1867 as ambassador.

Married to a Russian princess, B.S. Gagarina, Plessen occupied an exceptional position among the diplomats at the Tsar's court and enjoyed the complete confidence of Nesselrode.[221]

In a letter to his wife on 14 September 1849, Carl Moltke wrote that Nesselrode's family treated Plessen as their own child.[222]

By reason of his views and his family connections with Holstein, from which he himself came, this conservative politician earned himself the reputation of being 'absolutisk ridderskabelig-russisk.[223],[224] In May 1858 Plessen was in Copenhagen and made the best of impressions on the leading Danish politicians, Hall and Andrae. He did not hide the differences between his views and those which the government represented and for this reason he himself proposed that someone else should be sent to St. Petersburg, but Hall and Andrae concluded that no one would discharge his duties in St. Petersburg better than Plessen.[225]

The differences of opinion between Plessen and the government were fundamental and concerned such matters as the political system of the country, the place of Holstein and the attitude to Germany. Plessen was a keen supporter of Helstat while the government inclined towards the Eider programme. As far as settlement of the conflict with the duchies was concerned Plessen favoured Manteuffel's ideas and also sympathised with the majority of the views expressed by Gorchakov on the subject. Nonetheless, he was loyal to the Copenhagen government and adhered closely to the instructions he received from Copenhagen, although he often carried them out in a formal manner and without conviction.

Influenced both by Manteuffel's ideas and by his talks with Gorchakov, Plessen urged his government to seek an understanding with the German governments and the German Confederation in order to avoid Federal Execution, since the result of this would be to create an unfavourable situation for Denmark. The country would lose the financial resources coming from Holstein and Lauenburg, to say nothing of the moral losses, which would be calamitous for King and state. Plessen was also opposed to the dominant line of thought in the government, which was to submit the dispute with Germany to the judgement of the European powers. The independent character of the state would suffer from this, he maintained, and the lesson of history was that intervention by foreign powers in the internal affairs of another state never brought the latter any benefit. If, he wrote on 9 June (28 May) 1858, the government did not settle the matter, then either Federal Execution or European

---

221. Halicz, *Danish Neutrality* ..., p. 209.
222. H. Hjelholdt, *British Mediation in the Danish-German Conflict, 1848-50*, vol. 1, (Copenhagen, 1965), p. 35.
223. Knightly Russian.
224. Krieger, vol. II, p. 292, Cf. *Dansk Biografisk Leksikon*, Vol. XVIII (Copenhagen, 1940), pp. 402-6; E. Marquard, *Danske gesandter og gesandtskabspersonale indtil 1914* (Copenhagen, 1952), p. 392 and *Berlingske Tidende*, no. 88, 13 April 1897.
225. Krieger, vol. 1, p. 293.

intervention awaited Denmark. Both would be disastrous for the country.[226]

In Plessen's opinion there were only two alternatives and it was necessary to consider what was best for Denmark: to maintain the present state of affairs, which offered no certainty, could not continue in the long run and might cause trouble in relations with Holstein and Schleswig, or to modify the general organisation within the limits of what was currently possible.

De décliner toute influence de l'Allemagne sur notre situation me paraît impossible, et jamais certainement on n'aura accordé une influence plus grande à l'Allemagne qu'en consentant à détacher du Royaume de Danemark une province aussi riche et aussi belle que le Holstein.

En jetant un coup d'œil sur le passé de notre histoire récente, il n'y pas le moindre doute, que nous eussions à nous féliciter, si nous avions accordé à l'Allemagne une influence plus large, si nous l'avions fait, nous n'aurions pas perdu la flotte, et le Roi serait encore souverain de la Norvège.[227]

Plessen thought that Russia had partially revised her position in the middle of 1858 in a direction more favourable to Denmark, and it was therefore absolutely essential to keep the St. Petersburg cabinet informed not only of the decisions of the Copenhagen government but also of its intentions.[228]

Krieger regarded Plessen's epistles as evidence of his pro-German position and saw him, Andrae wrote, as an instrument in the hands of Russia, which wanted to do everything it could to avoid Federal Execution. He also saw him as the ally of his brother, Carl August Scheel-Plessen, one of the leaders of the Holstein opposition, who feared for his Knightly ('ridderskabelig') interests, which conflicted with those of the government. Krieger considered that by his views Plessen was doing great harm to Denmark.[229]

Krieger's judgement seems to have been too sharp, and perhaps damaging to Plessen, who spared no effort in the middle of 1858 to persuade Gorchakov to intervene in Germany, particularly when Michelsen and Andrae, left office and the Danish cabinet, in the person of Hall, made an attempt at reorganisation of the monarchy in the spirit of Gorchakov's advice.

Up till then Plessen appears to have deluded himself that Gorchakov could maintain moderation bordering on impartiality in the Danish-German dispute. His disappointment was consequently all the greater when, after Osten-Sacken had informed him on 12 July that the Russian government would support the Danish proposals and would persuade the British and French governments to do so too, Gorchakov the next day (13 (1) July) denied that the Russian government intended to intervene in the matter and, it later transpired, he did this only because he

---

226. 9 June (28 May) and 7 (19) July, and no. 5522 A I 3, C.C. Hall, pkt. 2, report of 16 (4) June 1858, R.A. Copenhagen.
227. Report of 19 (7) June. Cf. Krieger, *ibid.* pp. 310-313. Reference to the 1814 events.
228. Report of 16 (4) June. Cf. no. 5522 A. I. C.C. Hall, pkt. no. 2. R.A. Copenhagen.
229. Krieger, 21 and 24 June 1858. vol 1, p. 310-11.

had received news that the Danish proposals had encountered difficulties in Germany (27 (15) July).

Gorchakov, however, did not cease to believe, particularly after receiving a report from Brunnow that Lord Malmesbury took a position 'conforme a celles du Cabinet Imperial', that agreement would be reached between Denmark and Germany, since, as Ungern-Sternberg reported,[230] a spirit of conciliation prevailed in the Danish government and Germany was not contesting the principle of the integrity of the Danish monarchy, which was recognised by the powers of Europe. In talks with Plessen Gorchakov confined himself to repeating the same platitudes and only agreed with Plessen when the latter pointed out the great difficulties faced by the Danish government, which recognised the authority of the German Diet in respect of the duchies but at the same time could not agree to the Confederation exercising an influence on the organisation of the remaining part of the monarchy. Gorchakov limited himself to advice such as that it was hard to arrange matters so that the Confederation did not exercise any influence on countries which did not belong to it, if the latter exercised a certain influence on duchies which did belong to it.

C'est la tâche du Gouvernement du Roi d'équilibrer ces deux influences, qui se feront toujours sentir dans l'ensemble de la Monarchie, et de limiter chacun de ces influences à une action, qui soit d'accord avec les intérêts de l'assemble, qui doit former la Monarchie Danoise.[231]

If the Danish government maintained that the basis for its action remained the obligations it had undertaken in 1852, he believed the unity of the monarchy could be upheld, although no one understood better than he, Gorchakov stressed, the difficulties with which the road to agreement was strewn.[232]

Quite a long time elapsed after the Danish government presented its proposals 'de regarder la constitution commune et les lois qui s'y rapportent comme provisoirement suspendues pour les duchés allemands', which Ungern-Sternberg regarded as 'trop vague' and not corresponding to the Federal decisions of 11 February, to the moment when the provisions of the constitution in respect of Holstein and Lauenburg had been *'définitivement revoquées'.*[233] During this time two governments, the French and the Swedish, tried to come to the aid of Denmark in her difficult struggle with Germany and sent appeals to Gorchakov to join them in their efforts. But Gorchakov, who had recently expressed anxiety about the position of the Prussian Prince Regent, rejected the French suggestions and assured France that he had no doubts about Prussia's conciliatory attitude, referring to conversations which he had had with Manteuffel.[234] He also took a negative atti-

---

230. No. 78. 7 August (26 July) and 4 September (23 August).
231. No. 35, 13 (1) October 1858.
232. No. 5522, A.I.3, C.C. Hall, pkt. no. 2.
233. The ambassador's reports nos. 96 and 101 of 1 (13) and 17 (29) October.
234. Châteaurenard, 30 November; Roux, *ibid.* pp. 227-8.

tude to the initiative of the Swedish government, which proposed that the signatories to the Treaty of London should hold talks in connection with the possibility of Federal Execution by Germany, which could have adverse effects on the integrity of Denmark.[235]

When the Prussian ambassador asked what position the Russian cabinet would take on the Swedish initiative, if it were invited, Gorchakov replied that he regarded the move as unjustified, or at least premature, and doubted whether the proposal would be accepted. He rather thought that these were only rumours, because otherwise France, which had very intimate relations with Russia, would have sought Russia's co-operation.[236] He said the same to Wedel-Jarlsberg (who was trying to find out why, when letters were sent to London and Paris, St. Petersburg had been omitted), even adding that such a sudden step by the Swedish government in the current situation would only inflame the matter and would not benefit Denmark's cause.[237] Gorchakov used the same phrases in a letter to Dashkov, informing the ambassador about his talk with Wedel-Jarlsberg.[238]

Thus Gorchakov blocked all initiatives designed to assist Denmark in her conflict with the German states at this early stage. He sought to isolate Denmark in the international arena, and, by depriving her of allies, to minimise her chances in the contest with a Germany consolidated in the struggle over the duchies.

Faced with the threat of Federal Execution, Hall initially intended to confine himself to provisional suspension of the constitution in relation to Holstein and Lauenburg, in order to avoid a conflict with the German Confederation, for he had come to the conclusion that maintenance of the *status quo* was impossible, in the light of the resolutions of the German Diet.[239] But Manteuffel's verdict was that this step was insufficient.[240]

The two larger German powers, on whose decision everything depended in the Diet, moreover declared that, if the impeached laws were cancelled, there would be no further occasion for "execution" in this matter. In consideration of these circumstances, letters patent were issued, dated November 6, 1858, abrogating the first six articles of the special Holstein charter of June 11, 1854, the whole common charters of October 2, 1855, and the decree of June 23, 1856, in so far as these laws applied to Holstein and Lauenburg, but maintaining them in force for Denmark proper and Schleswig. The Holstein Estates were besides convoked for January 3, 1859. These measures were brought to the knowledge of the Federal Diet, in the sitting of November 11th, when the committee had intended to propose that so-called measure of execution. A resolution was passed to the effect: that proceedings of execution should be discontinued, in consequence of the Danish communication, which the

---

235. On Manderström's dispatch to Swedish ambassadors on this matter see Koht, pp. 54-55; H.H.S.A. 13 P.A. XXVI, Schweden, 1856-58, nos. 32, 33, 6 and 25, October 1858. Cf. also Masse to Hall, no. 38, 5 October 1858, Sverige Dep., 1858-61, R.A. Copenhagen.
236. H.H.S.A., P.A. X. Karton 46, no. 54 A-C, 23 (11)) October 1858.
237. *Ibid.* no. 56 B, 13 (1) November.
238. R.A. Stockholm, Rulle 218-20. The letter bears the date 5 November.
239. Ungern-Sternberg's report no. 96 of 1 (13) October 1858.
240. On The Frankfurt Diet's reaction to the first Danish proposal see H.H.S.A., 13. P.A. XXVI. Schweden, no. 31.

Diet declared to have received "only with satisfaction".[241]

Hall did not deceive himself that the problem had been finally settled and therefore prepared a memorandum adressed to friendly governments,[242] in order 1.) to acquaint them with the position of the Danish government, 2.) to set out its efforts hitherto to overcome the conflict, 3.) to correct those who were expecting implementation of the plans of the supporters of Schleswig-Holsteinism, whether separatists or advocates of Scandinavianism.[243]

---

241. Gosch, *Denmark and Germany* ..., p. 203, Cf. Neergaard, *Under* vol. II, pt 1, pp. 191-5.
242. Dépêche circulaire, 8 November 1858, Udenrigsministeriet, A, 3354.
243. Ungern-Sternberg's report no. 101, 17 (29) October 1858.

3. Russia, the Danish Sound Dues and Command of the Baltic

In the last year of the Crimean War and immediately after the conclusion of the Treaty of Paris the problem of the Sound became more and more important in Danish policy. Dues payable for passage through the Sound by vessels entering and leaving the Baltic had been introduced by Eric of Pomerania in 1429 and these dues had been paid to Denmark for no less than 428 years.

The justification for the large sums paid was that Denmark with her 500 sea-washed islands and many shallow channels was obliged to maintain a very complicated service for the benefit of international traffic.[1] At the turn of the eighteenth and nineteenth centuries she undertook to organise a system of lighthouses and after that a coast guard service modelled on the English salvage company in the Shields that had been established in 1789.[2] This system of payments lasted until the middle of the nineteenth century, although there was no lack of friction with other states over it.

During the Crimean War the USA emerged as the leader of the dissatisfaction and became the principal and the most determined advocate of the abolition of the Sound dues, which would have deprived Denmark of financial benefits which constituted a substantial percentage of her state revenue.[3] The income from the dues amounted to 2,250,000 Rdl. in 1853, an appreciable proportion of the total state revenue of 14,000,000 Rdl.[4] However, the importance of the matter was not solely economic; it was also a question of prestige, and the moment when the problem was raised by the USA was a particularly unfortunate one for Denmark since the European powers were engaged in fighting the Crimean War and one of the theatres of war was the Baltic.

The USA's negative attitude to the Sound dues was nothing new, since as early as 1843 the USA Secretary of State, A.A. Upshin, had stated his country's position in the following words:

---

1. The first agreement concerning payment for passage through the Sound was signed by Denmark and the Hanseatic League in 1368.
2. Palle Lauring, *A History of Denmark,* (Copenhagen 1981) pp. 218-21; Charles E. Hill, *The Danish Sound Dues and Command of the Baltic,* (Duke U.P. Durham, N. Carolina, 1926).
3. E. Halicz, *Danish Neutrality during the Crimean War, 1853-1856,* (Odense U.P. 1977) pp. 178-80.
4. Ungern-Sternberg's dispatch, no. 27, 1 (13) April 1855; also A.M.A.E., Paris, Correspondance Consulaire et Commerciale, Copenhagen 1851-1855, vol. 12, no. 157, 15 April 1855.

Le Danemark continue encore, sans aucun titre valuable, à prélever un droit tout-à-fait singulier sur toutes les marchandises qui entrent dans le Sound et sur celles qui en sortent, sans pouvour s'appuyer sur aucun principe naturel ou du droit des gens, et sans aucun raison, que celle de l'ancienne coutume. Il ne peut prétendre à cet impôt, car il ne rend aucun service en échange, et sa prétention est hors de toute proportion avec les forces dont il dispose pour obliger à payer. Le mécontentement qu'éprouvent les nations intéressées au commerce de la Baltique, au sujet de cette contribution inutile et humiliante, est grand et général. Le temps est venu pour les Etats-Unis de faire une démarche décisive, afin de délivrer de cette oppression notre commerce dans cette mer.[5]

'Denmark cannot demand this toll upon any principle of natural or public law nor upon any other ground than ancient usage', was the position of the American government.[6]

The USA questioned the level of the dues which were payable, arguing that

the principle upon which those dues were collected cannot be defended ... It seems clear that no defence can be made in behalf of a principle so flagrantly at variance with the established right of each of the nations of the earth to the *liberum mare*.[7]

They can recognise no 'ancient usage' as obligatory, when it conflicts with natural privileges and international law. These ancient customs have, in many instances, been found to be inconsistent with rights now generally recognized in the more liberal and reasonable practise of commercial nations and have been made to yield to views better suited to improved system of foreign trade.[8]

It is worth stressing that the USA's share of trade in the Baltic was not really very large, since out of 21,588 vessels which passed through the Sound in 1853 only 183 sailed under the American flag.[9] Bluhme did not answer the American note demanding abolition of the Sound dues in respect of American ships.[10] A year later the USA ambassador in Copenhagen received instructions to ask the Danish government whether:

1. s'il voulant ou non, se désister en faveur des navires américains de droits prélevés à leur passage pas le Sund et
2. de dédire, en cas de refus, le traité du commerce qui existe entre les 2 Puissances.

---

5. Quoted from *Précurseur, Journal Belge,* supplément du 18 Février 1855, 'Le Droit du Sund et le Commerce du Monde'. This article was a summary of the pamphlet *Le Droit du Sund et le Commerce du Monde,* which was published in German in Szczecin (Librairie de F. Hessenband, 1854). Cf. F.O. 244, P.R.O. London; R.A. Copenhagen, archive no. 600, film. The aim of this pamphlet was to show that
   La taxe perçue au Sund est contraire au droit des gens, opposée aux usages généraux du monde civilisé, c'est la trangression positive des maximes équitable qui règlent le trafic international, et un danger pour les plus précieux intérêts du commerce. C'est dans cet esprit qu'est écrite la brochure digne d'attention dont nous venons de présenter l'analyse. *(Précurseur).*
6. Hill, *The Danish Sound Dues ...,* p. 275.
7. Legation of the US, Copenhagen, 3 December 1853; Berlin, Ordrer, 1850-56, R.A. Copenhagen.
8. *Ibid.*
9. *Gateshead Observer,* 22 December 1855. *Letters on the Sound Dues Question I-VII,* (.N.Y., 1855). List of Ships of all Nations that passed the Sound in the years 1852 and 1853.
10. R.A. Copenhagen, Handskrif. XVI. Provin. Rusland. Staatsarkiver i Moskva, vol. 47. Report from Ungern-Sternberg to St. Petersburg, no. 27, 1 (13) April 1855.

Bedinger put this matter orally to Scheele on behalf of his government, referring to the note delivered the previous year and giving a year's notice of termination of the General Convention of Friendship, Commerce and Navigation signed in Washington on 26 April 1826.

Scheele, astonished by this action and Bedinger's method of communication, asked for a written note, adding that the USA knew perfectly well that Denmark was not at that moment in a position to satisfy the demands. To this Bedinger said that he was not authorised to lodge such a note.[11]

Scheele reacted to the American action not without bitterness, and in talks with Buchanan and Ungern-Sternberg he also expressed concern about the attitude which Prussia would take in this situation which the USA had created.[12] Although the discussion in the Berlin parliament and Manteuffel's speech did not fill him with fear, he was worried that the USA and Prussia might now reach an agreement concerning the Sound dues.[13] If other states were to follow the example of the USA Denmark would find herself on the edge of a precipice within a year.[14]

The French ambassador, A. Dotézac, reporting on the current situation, said that Scheele recognised that he, the ambassador, was correct in stating that time which could have been used to settle the problem had been wasted.

Il est certain, en effet, que le Danemark est aujourd'hui dans une position moins bonne qu'il ne l'eut été s'il avait lui même les devants, il y a quelques années – the minister recognised. Mais, fidèle à ses habitudes de temporisation, accoutumé à étouffer les difficultés par le silence et fondé dans la politique sur l'espérance de tout obtenir de guerre lasse, le Cabinet de Copenhague a constamment compté sur la Chambre pour reculer d'une maniére indéfinie la solution de ce problème.[15]

In this report Dotézac included a passage concerning Scheele's effusions on the subject of Russia's policy towards the problem of the Sound.

Il – wrote the ambassador – faisait d'ailleurs grands fonds sur l'appui de la Russie, qui beaucoup moins préoccupée de ses intérêts commerciaux que de ses intérêts politiques, trouvait dans la question du Sund un levier naturel pour affermir son influence en Danemark en même temps qu'elle en retirait pour elle même de moyens de police auxquelles elle attachait beaucoup de prix. On m'assure que pressé dans ces dernières temps par les Etats Unis le Cabinet de Pétersbourg avait donné son adhesion formelle à la légitime des droits du Sund.[16]

11. Ungern-Sternberg, *ibid.* and A.M.A.E. Paris, Correspondance Consulaire et Commerciale, vol. 12, no. 157, 158, 15 and 16 April 1855.
12. *Ibid,* A.M.A.E., 15 April 1855.
13. On 21 January and 15 February 1855 Brockdorff reported to Scheele from Berlin that Manteuffel had said that there was no cause why the *status quo* in relation to Denmark had to be changed and that he would respect the treaties which had been concluded. Berlin, Ordrer. R.A. Copenhagen: F. Bajer, *Nordens særlig Danmarks nevtralitet under Krimkrigen,* (Copenhagen, 1914), pp. 486 ff., 495.
14. A.M.A.E., *ibid.* nos. 157, 158, 174, 15 and 16 April and 9 September 1855; Axel Nielsen, *Dänische Wirtschaftsgeschichte,* (Jena 1933) pp. 451ff. Cf. also M. Rubin, 'Sundtoldens Afløsning', *Hist. Tidsskr.* 7R, vol. VI, pp. 172ff; Einar Cohn, *Økonomi og politik i Danmark, 1849-1875,* (Copenhagen, 1967).
15. A.M.A.E., *ibid.* no. 158, 16 April 1855.
16. *Ibid.*

Russia's position was of especial significance, but it must be seen in the context of the general situation in Europe, and in particular of the situation which arose on account of the growing rumours that Sweden would join the anti-Russian coalition of Western states. Russia was especially concerned to keep Denmark neutral, and no move on Russia's part which could have been interpreted as anti-Danish would have been permissible.

The intentions of the Russian politicians, for whom political considerations were superior to all others, were correctly read, as is shown by the report Ungern-Sternberg sent to Nesselrode on 1 (13) April 1855:

Qui qu'il en soit, M-ce le C'te, de cette assertion [that there was a possibility of co-operation between the USA and Prussia] il me paraît de la plus haute importance de laisser cette question, brûlante aussi longtemps que possible, dans son état actuel, car elle pourrait facilement servir à pousser le Danemark dans le bras de l'Angleterre pour y chercher de la protection. Le dernier emprunt anglo-danois étant spécialement garanti par le revenu du droit du Sund, le prétexte pour une intervention de cette nature serait facilement trouvé et accueilli peut-être avec empressement.

Thus as soon as the problem of the Sound emerged, the Russian diplomat saw it as something more than a purely economic problem and considered that it could acquire important political dimensions. There was a fear that the question of the Sound could be exploited by French diplomacy, the helmsman of which, A. Walewski, took an unequivocally anti-American position, condemning the government of the USA for interfering in European affairs, and supporting the Danish cabinet unreservedly. In acting in this way his aim was undoubtedly to draw Denmark onto the side of the Western coalition, 'il a fallû que l'Europe entière se tînt sur ses gardes pour s'opposer à une telle influence, l'objet de la convoitise toujours croissante des Américains du Nord', said Walewski to Moltke.[17] Russian diplomacy, not wanting to lag behind, hastened to address its good offices to Copenhagen.[18]

Nesselrode regretted that it was the USA, which from the trade point of view had relatively little interest in the Baltic in comparison with the other European countries, which had addressed such rigorous demands to Denmark. He emphasised that Russia had good relations with the USA, implying by this that she might be able to undertake talks in Washington with the aim of reaching an agreement between the USA and Denmark. He also suggested that the problem might be dealt with by a special commission, consisting of representatives of the interested European states, and that the meeting could be held in Copenhagen. He doubted, however, whether the USA would be willing to participate. In this he was right, for when the conference on the question of the Sound took place the USA refused to

---

17. Frankrig. Depecher, nos. 68, 70 and 73, 18, 21 and 28 June 1855, and Halicz, *Danish Neutrality* ..., pp. 154-5.
18. Russland, Dep. no. 27, 7 April (26 March) 1855. Also, on Russia's attitude to the capitalisation proposal put forward by Denmark in 1840, see Russland. Dep. no. 67, 11 October (29 September) and no. 39, 5 May (23 April) 1855, and Russland. Ordrer, no. 17, 19 April 1855.

take part.[19] On his own initiative Nesselrode had instructions sent to the ambassador in the USA, Stoeckl, to try to influence the American government towards conciliation, although he had not been authorised to do this by the Danish government.[20] The Danish government was not only opposed to this move but instructed Plessen to reject Russian mediation. Dotézac concurred with this, saying that if Denmark entrusted the matter to the St. Petersburg cabinet it would be interpreted as meaning that Denmark was allied with Russia.

The Russian cabinet had acted on its own account in making this move in Washington, Dotézac reported to Paris, but it would prefer that the settlement of the Sound question was postponed because, owing to this terrible war, it could only play a secondary role in the matter, and hitherto Russia had become accustomed always to playing a primary role. This view was loudly expressed by Ungern-Sternberg.[21] The Russian ambassador also advocated active support of Denmark, for a lack of interest on Russia's part could contribute to the reorientation of Denmark and lead her to seek support from Britain.[22] In order to emphasise his exceptionally friendly attitude towards Denmark, Nesselrode agreed to send to the conference, as Russia's special representative, J. Tegoborski, a former secretary of the embassy in Copenhagen, who would have to sit down at the same conference table as the representatives of states which were currently at war with Russia.[23]

This was of course a gesture of good will on the part of St. Petersburg. But Nesselrode's real concern was well known.[24] Objectively, however, this attitude on the part of Russia had a positive significance for Denmark. We must also bear in mind the fact that Russia came second after Britain in the number of ships passing through the Sound, so the possible financial contribution from Russia towards settlement of the matter, if the dues were to be abolished, would have been very substantial.

Russia's position met a favourable response in Copenhagen and Scheele

---

19. Rus. Dep. no. 39, 5 May (23 April), Handskr. XVI. Prov. Rusland, Freytag-Loringshoven to Nesselrode, no. 180, 15 (27) November 1855, vol. 48. Cf. Scheele to General Oxholm, no. 1, 3 January 1856, Gesand. Berlin. Ordrer 1850-56, R.A. Copenhagen.
20. Rus. Dep. no. 65, 5 October (22 September) and no. 67, 11 October (29 September); also A.M.A.E., Cor. Consulaire et Commer, Copenhague, vol. 13 no. 174, 9. September 1855.
21. A.M.A.E., Corresp. Cons... vol. 13, Cop. 1855 août-1857 mai, Dotézac's report no. 174, 9 September 1855, and no. 884, Danemarc, Corr. polit. vol. 227, 9. September 1855.
22. Ungern-Sternberg's dispatch of I (13) April 1855.
23. Rusl. Dep. nos. 73 and 74. 10 November (29 October) and 20 (8 November 1855). Orme to Clarendon. Disp. no. 15, 6 October 1855, P.R.O. F.O. 22, 244A, R.A. Copenhagen.
24. In a pamphlet which appeared in London in 1856, *'A Few Words on the Sound Dues'*, we find the following comment on Russia's attitude to the matter:
    The Sound Dues give Russia, as well as Prussia, a constant pretext for interference with Denmark. They can, at any moment when it suits them, make the Dues a cause of quarrel, and they give these Powers an opportunity of complaint whether well or ill-founded if they are desirious of embarrassing Denmark.
    See F.O. 22, 244 B, Sound Dues, vol. 2 R.A. Copenhagen film.

expressed his recognition of the St. Petersburg cabinet's attitude.[25] He also assured Ungern-Sternberg that up to then the Danish government had sought advice on the question of the Sound only from the Russian cabinet.[26]

Russia's friendly attitude towards the Danish demands and her willingness to intervene in the USA were all the more significant since Britain, in view of her strained relations with the Washington government, regarded such intervention as inexpedient. Prussia took a similar position. France confined herself to promising her good offices, but, as Freytag-Loringshoven reported, Scheele feared that Denmark would have to pay dearly for these French 'good offices'.[27]

The idea of convening a conference of interested parties was put forward by the Danish King and he also said it would be desirable for it to be held in Copenhagen.[28] The choice of venue was motivated, among other things, by the fact that it would be possible there to provide the participants in the conference with the documents necessary during the negotiations. Initially it was proposed that the conference should open in November, but subsequently this date had to be postponed for procedural reasons.

Beside Russia, France, Britain and Sweden-Norway were all favourable to the idea of convening the conference in Copenhagen. Belgium, Spain and Holland announced their agreement. Among the German states, beside Prussia and Austria, Hannover, Oldenburg, Lübeck and Bremen also agreed to attend.[29] All the states were to be represented by their ambassadors in Copenhagen. Only Russia sent a special representative, J. Tegoborski.[30] Denmark was to be represented by the well-known politician C.C. Bluhme, an expert on treasury affairs, who held the rank of Royal Commissioner.[31]

An essential factor accompanying the opening of the conference was the favourable climate created by the Russian and French governments and the French and London press. The press, especially the London press, which had hitherto been rather critical of Denmark, now almost unanimously supported the position taken by the Danish government. It emphasised that the government of the USA had caused enormous damage to Denmark, quite out of proportion to the minimal advantages which it could obtain if the dues were abolished. It also criticised the USA

---

25. Ungern-Sternberg's dispatches of 23 June (5 July), (Particulière) 24 June (6 July) and no. 118 of 28 August (9 September) 1855. See also Freytag-Loringshoven's dispatch no. 149 of 4 (16) October 1855, vol. 47.
26. *Ibid.* Particulière, 23 June (5 July) 1855.
27. No. 163, 28 October (9 November) 1855, vol. 47.
28. Scheele to Oxholm, no. 18, September 1855, and no. 1, 3 January 1856, London. Gesandtskabet Berlin, Ordrer 1850-56, R.A. Copenhagen.
29. P.A. XXIV. Dän. 18. 1855-56, 4 January and 2 February 1856, H.H.S.A. Vienna.
30. Freytag-Loringshoven's report, no. 172, 4 (16) November 1855, vol. 47.
31. Neergaard, vol. II, p. 63; Rus. dep. no. 73. 10 November (29 October); Sverige, dep. no. 42, 11 December 1855, nos. 3, 8, 13, 15, 20 and 21, 11 January, 12 and 29 February, 18 and 30 March 1856; Holland-Belgien, dep. no. 47 and 48, 15 and 21 November 1855; Dep. Hofrat Juliusz Tegoborski, 30 November (12 December) 1855, MID. Kanc. Rus. Film. R.A. Copenhagen. Buchanan's dispatch of 4 November, F.O. 22, 245, vol. 3. R.A. Copenhagen.

for interference in European affairs and for its intransigent attitude, which was reflected by its refusal to take part in the conference.[32] Many newspapers emphasised that the abolition of the dues was being demanded by a country whose vessels accounted for only 0,81% of passages through the Sound.[33] The *Morning Post,* which was close to Palmerston, took a firm stand in defence of Denmark and, on 24 December 1855, set out the whole history of the Sound dues, explaining the problem in the light of the international treaties since 1386, when Denmark concluded a treaty with the Hanseatic League concerning payment for passage. This privilege was 'against the dangers incident to the navigation of a narrow and intricate strait'. The *Morning Post* condemned the USA's demands and the behaviour of the Secretary of State, Marcy.

According to Freytag-Loringshoven's assessment of their position, none of the governments accepted the Danish plan for buying out the dues ('rachat') without reservation and their representatives came to the conference 'avec une arrière pensée'.[34] Freytag-Loringshoven suspected that Britain and France, supported by Austria, wanted to use the question of buying out the dues to further their political aims, and in this connection there was scope for Russia to act.

L'idée de la capitalisation n'a pas rencontré jusqu'à présent beaucoup d'adhérens,... le Gouvernement Impériale pourrait bien être décisive dans cette question – il faut lui [the Danish government] rendre cette justice (à voir sauvegarder ses droits par une garantie européene).[35]

Sweden had doubts about how the shares should be distributed, Austria reserved her position, Belgium had reservations concerning the principle of capitalisation 'sur la base des marchandises' and preferred 'le principe de la capitalisation sur la base du pavillon', and Holland for a long time did not state its position.[36]

Even during the course of the preparatory work in Copenhagen Russia had expressed her reservations about the sum which she would have to pay, maintaining that to take into account the last three years as the basis of calculation would be wrong since 1853 had been an exceptionally prosperous ('fleurissant') year for Russia. Data for the last ten years should be taken into account, but eliminating 1848-49, when Denmark had been at war with Germany. In the Russian government's opinion Russia should pay not 716,050 Rdl. but only 552,350 Rdl. annually.[37]

Prussia adopted a loyal attitude towards the Danish proposal, as the Danish government recognised. In a letter to Brockdorff on 1 October 1855 Scheele instructed him to thank Manteuffel for the position he had taken and asked him to

32. Frankr. dep. no. 129, 12 November 1855; Preuss, dep. no. 69, 17 October 1855. On Brockdorff's conversation with the USA ambassador Vroom at a reception given by Manteuffel, see *The Times,* no. 5, 1856, *Revue des Deux Mondes,* I, Chronique, 14 January 1856 and vol. III, 31 March 1856, p. 667.
33. *Gateshead Observer,* 22 December 1855.
34. Freytag-Loringshoven, no. 174, 8 (20) November 1855.
35. *Ibid.*
36. Freytag-Loringshoven, no. 165, 29 October (10 November) 1855.
37. Freytag-Loringshoven, no. 149, 4 (16) October 1855, vol. 47.

use his good offices to persuade the government of the USA to take part in the conference on the question of the Sound.[38] At a certain moment, however, difficulties arose because of attempts by Prussia to undermine the legality of Denmark's rights to collect the Sound dues. These were rejected by Denmark on the basis of a copy of a dispatch from the Minister of Foreign Affairs, J.P.F. Ancillon, on 23 July 1835 to the Prussian ambassador in Copenhagen, which was in the possession of the Danish government and in which Berlin begged to inform the Danish government that it had never questioned Denmark's right to collect the Sound dues.[39]

At the first session on 4 January 1856 Bluhme presented his government's proposals, taking as a basis the level of dues paid by individual countries in the years 1851, 1852 and 1853 for vessels entering and leaving the Baltic and the total sum 'which the capitalisation at four per cent of the average yearly returns would yield'. In all this would amount to the sum of 60,913,225 Rigsdalers.[40] He was supported by the Swedish representative, Lagerheim, and the latter was backed up by Tegoborski, who declared

> that his government had no wish to see the Sound dues abolished, but that it was willing to admit the principle of redemption as an act of good will towards Denmark, and the execution would depend upon the moderation in the terms and upon the sacrifices which Russia would have to make.[41]

At the second session of the commission Bluhme demanded as minimum compensation a sum amounting to 32,664,912 Rld.[42] On 12 (24) January 1856 Nesselrode telegraphed the embassy in Copenhagen:

---

38. Gesandtskabet Berlin, Ordrer, 1850-56, no. 7, 1 November 1855 and nos. 8, 9 and 10, and Preussen, Depecher, no. 68, 71 and 72, 11, 23 and 29 October 1855.
39. R.A. Copenhagen. Gesands. Berlin. Ordrer 1850-56, appendix to dispatch no. 2, 4 Januar 1856. A copy of the Prussian government's dispatch of 23 July 1835 is to be found in A.M.A.E, Paris, Corresp. Cons. ... Copenhague, vol. 13, no. 187, 21 February 1856. In this dispatch we read:
    Le droit du Sund est consacré et confirmé par une longue série des traités du vigeur. Nous ne l'avons jamais contesté et il n'entre pas, il ne saurait jamais entrer dans nos intentions de penser à y porter la moindre atteinte. De plus, indépendamment de la sainteté de ce droit, nous savons très bien que les avantages financiers qui en résultant pour le Danemark sont plus que jamais pour lui d'une prise immense et une des principales sources de revenu de l'état. Comment pourrions nous donc avoir en la pensée demander à cet égard des sacrifices qui seraient incompatibles avec la prosperité d'un gouvernement ami et voisin?
    Tout en reconnaissant ainsi le droit incontestable du Danemark sur le péage du Sund, et en faisant la part de sa situation financière, nous ne pouvons cependant nous dissimuler que ce droit met de grandes entraves à notre commerce et qu'il serait désirer d'en rendre la charge moins pénible.
    C'est dans cette vue que avons en 1818 conclu un traité de commerce avec le Danemark par lequel le tarif du Sund a été modifié à notre égard, et les taux diminué sur certain objects. Il y en d'autres qui sont encore imposés outre mesure et même relativement aux premiers le dit traité ne parait pas avoir reçu son entière exécution...
40. Thorsøe, *Kong Frederik den Syvendes regering*, vol. II, (Copenhagen, 1889), p. 564.
41. Hill, *The Danish Sound Dues ...*, p. 243.
42. H.H.S.A. P.A. XXIV. Dänemark. Berichte Weisungen, Varia, 1855-56, no. 7, Cop. 2 February 1856. Some members of the Danish Privy Council proposed the sum of 35 million Rdl. others of 40 million Rdl. *Stats. Forhand. VI*, 26 January 1856, p. 469.

Ditez à Tegoborski: Nous acceptons, mais sous toute réserve quant au montant de l'indemnité, primo le principe du rachat, secundo: que droit prélevé sur navires soit reparti après pavillon, tertio: que droit sur cargaisons soit reparti par moitié sur importations et exportations.

Quant au autres points, il recevra directions quand nous saurons ce que demande Danemarc.[43]

On 2 February Tegoborski lodged the following statement:

Je suis autorisé à déclarer que le Cabinet Impérial accepte, sans toute réserve, quant aux chifres qui pourraient être prise pour base des calculs et quant au montant de l'indemnité, les trois propositions faites par le Gouvernement Danoise dans la première conférence, savoir: 1/ le principe du rachat, 2/ que les droits sur les navires soient réparties selon le pavillon, et 3/ que les droits sur les cargaisons soient répartis par moitié sur les marchandises importées et exportées par le Sund.[44]

Tegoborski's declaration was all the more significant since, according to Bluhme's data concerning use of the Sound by individual states in the years 1842-47 and 1851-53, Russia's share of the total sum demanded by Denmark would be 27,83% or 9,759,993 Rld.[45] Only Britain would have to pay a larger share, 28,93%.[46]

The size of the sum and the method of settlement of the matter were the subject of many months of debate lasting, with breaks, until April 1857. Only Russia and Sweden really accepted Denmark's proposals.[47] France supported her point of view; Belgium was opposed to it. Britain continually put forward reservations and France tried to influence her, while Holland was 'très coulant' and Prussia rather secretive.[48]

The declaration of 9 May was particularly important. In it the representatives of Sweden-Norway, Russia and Oldenburg stated that they accepted the Danish proposal 'tant pour ce qui concerne le principe du rachat qu'en ce qui concerne le mode de répartition proposé par le gouvernement danois'. They stated jointly with Denmark that because of the differences of opinion between Great Britain and Denmark the deliberations of the conference had been suspended, but 'they decided also to leave the protocol open, so that the other powers, which had been represented at the conference, could later accede, if they so decided'.[49]

43. R.A. Copenhagen, Rus. Film. On February 21 Nesselrode telegraphed. "Nous consentons au rachat moyennant 35 millions écus bien entendu que les autres consentent aussi qu'il annonce à Bluhme. Plus tard nos idées sur les mode de payement de notre quote-part.
44. F.O. 22, 249. P.R.O., Sound Dues, vol. 6; R.A. Copenhagen.
45. Hill, *The Danish Sound Dues ...*, p. 347.
46. See Tableau. Montant des quoteparts à payer par les Etats, nommés ci dessous, suivant la distribution des sommes moyennes des droits sur les marchandises, faite selon les procents, calculés d'après les résultats dans le Sund des années 1851-1853, et suivant la distribution des sommes moyennes des droits de fanal dans les 9 années de paix 1842-1847 et 1851-1853, avec une capitalisation moyennant un multiplicateur de 25, y-jointe la quotepart de la somme demandée par le Danemark selon les dites proportions pour les droits sur les marchandises et pour les droits de fanal. *Statistik Tabelværk Ny Række fra 1855 til 1863*.
47. See the Minutes of the Conference for 2 February and 9 May 1856.
48. Sverige. Dep. no. 14, 11 March 1856; Hol-Belg. Dep. no. 21, 13 April 1856; Frankr. Dep. nos. 44, 45 and 50, 4, 10 and 24 April 1856; *Hist. Tidsskr.* 3, Series, I. pp. 489-93.
49. *Hist. Tidsskr.* 3. Series, I, pp. 489-93; Hill, *The Danish Sound Dues ...*, p. 249.

The danger from the USA was partially alleviated on 4 June 1856, the date when the notice given unilaterally by the USA expired, when the Washington government agreed to prolong the contract with Denmark for a further 60 days.[50] The USA government agreed not to use force for a year and to proceed to settle the matter by means of negotiations.[51]

The change of minister of foreign affairs in Russia, and Gorchakov's assumption of the post, had no effect at all on the Russian government's friendly attitude towards Denmark in respect of the Sound problem. In view of the fact that the conference was suspended temporarily owing to the differences of opinion between the British and Danish governments, Gorchakov sent a telegram requesting Tegoborski to return to St. Petersburg[52] and on 10 May the latter proceeded there in order to report personally to the minister on the problems in dispute at the conference. Discussing the question of the Sound with Plessen, Gorchakov assured him that Tegoborski had been only temporarily recalled from Copenhagen and would return there immediately the work of the conference was resumed.[53] Gorchakov spoke of Russia's good intentions and as evidence of this informed him that Stoeckl had been instructed to try to persuade the USA government to prolong the convention after the expiry of its notice on 26 June 1856.[54]

In another talk with the Danish ambassador[55] Gorchakov spoke on the question of the Sound 'avec beaucoup de bienveillance'. He assured him that as soon as the discussions with Britain on the subject of the payments were settled, and if Copenhagen wished it, Tegoborski would go to Copenhagen. The Prince added 'que pour arrangements finals à prendre nous [i.e. Denmark] ne rencontrerions du côté de la Russie aucune difficulté. Il m'a dit positivement: *"notre argent est prêt"* '. [emphasis added – E.H.].[55]

The question of Tegoborski's return to Copenhagen was on the agenda again when the British government decided to rejoin the work of the commission and to send Wodehouse to Copenhagen.[56] This was the topic of the next conversation between Gorchakov and Plessen. Gorchakov showed great interest in the question of settling the payments following abolition of the Sound dues and promised to discuss it with his adviser on Danish affairs, Osten-Sacken.[57] On 15 December [O.S.] he instructed Tegoborski to return to Copenhagen with the task of bringing the negotiations entrusted to him by the Emperor to a conclusion.[58]

Russia remained faithful to the obligations she had undertaken on 9 May 1856

---

50. London, Ordrer. Legation of the USA to Scheele, 12 March 1856.
51. Berlin, Ordrer. 27 June 1856. Ungern-Sternberg's dispatch. nos 62 of 26 April (8 May) and 90 of 8 (20) June 1856.
52. Ungern-Sternberg, no. 64, 27 April (9 May), vol. 48.
53. Udenrigs. Rus. dep. 1856-60, no. 36, 3 May (21 April) 1856.
54. *Ibid.* no. 44, 27 (15) May 1856.
55. *Ibid.* no. 63, 5 September (24 August) 1856).
56. Plessens's dispatch, no. 83 of 24 (12) November 1856.
57. *Ibid.*
58. Ungern-Sternberg no. 190 of 5 (17) December 1856.

and when, at the beginning of 1857, the governments in Berlin and Paris approached St. Petersburg to join them in a draft treaty which the two governments intended should be transformed 'en traité général pour l'abolition des droits du Sund', Russia replied with a note in which Gorchakov informed them that on the question of the Sound Russia had entered into obligations towards Denmark on 9 May which did not allow her to accede to the draft of a general treaty unless Denmark first expressed such a desire.

Votre Excellence – Plessen wrote to Scheele – trouvera sans aucun doute cette réponse du Cabinet de Sa Majesté l'Empereur conforme à l'attitude amicale et bienveillante, dont la Russie nous a donné tant de preuves dans les négociations pour le Sund.[59]

The Russian government, Plessen reported, was awaiting the Danish government's decision and wanted to remain neutral in the matter. Plessen did not rule out the possibility that it was behaving in this way because it might very much wish the question of the Sound to be concluded.

In the last stage of the negotiations there was no lack of differences between the representatives of the various states. They concerned procedural matters, the way in which the plan should be implemented, and the method of payment of the sums due to the Danish government. Tegoborski was very active at the sessions of the conference. He took the initiative in putting forward changes in the proposed treaty, including art. VII, which at his suggestion was to read as follows:

L'exécution des engagemens réciproques contenues dans le présent traité est expressivement subordonnée à l'accomplissement des formalités et règles établies par les lois constitutionelles des Hautes Puissances Contractantes, lesquelles s'obligent à en provoquer l'application dans le plus brief délai possible.[60]

Tegoborski also put forward the proposal, which was favourably received by Bluhme, that 1 April 1857 should be recognised as the date of abolition of the dues.[61] As Buchanan reported to Clarendon, on 17 February the Russian delegate presented Bluhme with a draft of a separate convention concerning Russian payments over a period of twenty years, with interest at the rate of 4%.[62] Under the convention concluded with Russia the latter was to pay 9,739,993 Rdl. in shillings at a rate of 9 Rdl. = 1 pound sterling, that is 1,082,221, in 40 installments payable at six-monthly intervals over twenty years from 1 October (19 September) 1857.[63]

The result of the negotiations was a Treaty dated March 14, 1857, according to the terms of which Denmark gave up her Sound and Belt Dues for ever. The amount of compensation payable for the Sound Dues was fixed at 30,476,325

---

59. No. 5, 14 (2) February 1857.
60. Protocole, séance du 3 Février 1857. F.O. 22, 247, 1857, vol. 5, R.A. Copenhagen.
61. Hill, *The Danish Sound Dues ...*, p. 259.
62. F.O. 248, 1857, vol. 6. Report of 25 February.
63. Conventions spéciales conclues entre Danemark et plusieurs autres Etats en execution de l'art. IV du Traité Général du 14 Marts 1857 concernant le rachat du péage du Sund et des Belts, Copenhague, 1858, Convention avec la Russie, art. I. H.H.S.A., Vienna, 20 Dänemark, P.A. XXIV, 1858-1860.

Rld. Converted at today's rate of exchange this would amount to about £ 20,000,000. The Danish government was to receive this sum over a period of twenty years.[64]

The Danish government, out of gratitude to Russia for the services she had rendered Denmark in this matter, decided to confer the highest Danish honour, 'Son ordre de l'Eléphant', on Gorchakov and 'La Grande Croix du Danebrog' on R. Osten-Sacken and Tolstoy, the vice-minister.[65] As Denmark's new Minister of Foreign Affairs, Michelsen, explained, these honours were conferred as a sign of recognition of 'le service que la Russie, au détriment de ses propres intérêts, s'est prêtée à rendre au Danemark dans l'arrangement de l'affaire du Sund'.[66]

Russia's friendly attitude towards the settlement of the problem of the Sound undoubtedly helped Denmark. The reasons for it were mainly political. Russia was chiefly concerned that the dispute over the dues should not serve the Western powers as a pretext to increase their influence in Copenhagen. A change in the political orientation of Denmark and the abandonment of neutrality would have damaged Russia's interests in the Baltic. For this reason Russia supported Denmark's demands from the start, although it was not easy for her to meet them, as Russia was in an exceptionally difficult financial position.

Russia's conduct showed the supremacy of foreign policy over other problems. This had been an axiom of Russian policy even since the rise of the Russian empire.

---

64. Neergaard, vol. II, 1, p. 64; Thorsøe, p. 564; Dänemark, P.A. XXIV. Berichte. Weis. Varia. 1858-60. Kart. 20. H.H.S.A., Vienna. The Treaty was signed with Austria, Belgium, France, Great Britain, the Netherlands, Prussia and six other German States, Russia and Sweden-Norway.
65. *Kongelig Dansk Hof- og Staatskalender,* 1866, pp. 4 and 11. The Danebrog Cross (Second Class) was confered on J. Tegoborski on August 4, 1857. *Ibid.* p. 18.
66. Ungern-Sternberg's telegram of 5 (17) September and Particulière au Prince Gorchakoff, 16 (28) September 1857, Moscow, vol. 49. See also Plessen, no. 44, 2 October (20 September) 1857 and the dispatch from Copenhagen to Plessen, no. 19.

4. Russia and the Growing Conflict between Denmark and Germany in 1859-1862

I

The years 1859-62 form an important stage in the history of Russia. There were many reasons for this, relating both to the internal situation of Russia and to the international situation. These were the years which saw the greatest reform in Russia's nineteenth-century history – the peasant reform solemnly proclaimed in the Tsar's manifesto of 19 February (3 March) 1861, followed by further reforms which brought a turning point in almost every sphere of life.

In this period, which demanded a concentration of effort on internal affairs, Russia was interested in the maintenance of peace, particularly in Europe. In the Caucasus, Central Asia and the Far East, however – that is to say wherever resistance was not expected from any of the great powers – her expansionist policy continued without interruption and it was in just these years that further conquests were made which led Palmerston to say, in a letter to Russell on 13 September 1865, that the Russian empire would become a power comparable to the Roman empire.

As to Russia, she will, in due Time, become a Power almost as great as the old Roman Empire. She can become Mistress of all Asia, except British India, whenever she chooses to take it, and when enlightened arrangements shall have made her Revenue proportioned to her Territory, and Railways shall have abridged distances, her Command of men will become enormous, her pecuniary means gigantic, and her power of transporting armies over great distances most formidable.[1]

The strategic aim of Russian policy in Europe had not been achieved, however, and Gorchakov had even ceased to believe that with France's support he could succeed in abolishing those clauses in the Treaty of Paris which were so disadvantageous to Russia. He showed this in a talk with Montebello in April 1859, when, among other things, he said:

Ce que nous voulons ... c'est d'être relevés du traité de 1856. C'est d'effacer du droit public Européen la neutralité de la Mer Noire, ... ce que nous voulons ce n'est ni l'Autriche, ni vous qui pouvez nous le donner. La guerre actuelle ne peut pas nous le donner, et c'est pourquoi nous ne nous en mêlerons pas ...[2]

---

1. Harold Temperly and Lillian M. Person, *Foundations of British Foreign Policy from Pitt (1792) to Salisbury (1902)*, (Cambridge, 1938), p. 280. See also Krausse, *Russia in Asia.* Chapters IX-XIII.
2. Montebello's report to Walewski, 20 April 1859, E. Schüle, *Russland und Frankreich ...*, p. 160; Ernst Birke, *Frankreich und Ostmitteleuropa im 19. Jahrhundert* (Köln, Graz, 1960), p. 195.

Gorchakov failed to separate France and Britain and isolate Britain from Europe. The understanding with France, although not broken and even reinforced by a formal act – the treaty of friendly neutrality concluded on the eve of the Franco-Austrian war – did not bring the results which Gorchakov anticipated.[3] Nor did the Franco-Russian rapprochement yield the economic benefits which both sides had initially expected. The plans of French capitalists who expected enormous profits from establishing factories, and particularly railways, in Russia were not fulfilled.[4]

Despite this, the understanding *(entente)* between France and Russia, which went through several crises at the beginning of the 1860s, especially in connection with the situation in the Kingdom of Poland, survived until the outbreak of the January Uprising and the conclusion of the Convention of Alvensleben between Russia and Prussia. The dispute about whether the understanding had outlived its day by 1859 (as Tatishchev maintained) or 1860 (as Nolde argued) or whether this was not the case until 1863, is not very important for our purposes. Personally I would come down in favour of 1863 since the understanding survived till that year, although its honeymoon period was really very brief. It is an indisputable fact, on the other hand, that from 1856 onward the role of Prussia in Russian policy was increasing and the friendship between the two countries was deepening, and that this trend was not disturbed by the departure of the conservative head of government, Manteuffel, and his replacement by Schleinitz, who was close to the liberals and initiated the 'new era'.

Not only for Alexander II, for whom Prussia had always been the nearest and dearest ally, but also for Gorchakov, who had no especial feelings for her and still regarded her then as a second rank power,[5] the policy of rapprochement with Prussia became more and more important, particularly after the Italian war and in connection with the deepening crisis in the Kingdom of Poland, behind which Russia saw the inspiration of the Palais Royal in Paris. Nor can we overlook the fact that Berlin was beginning to play an ever increasing role in the economic life of Russia.[6] After the easing of Russian customs regulations there was a great expansion in trade between Russia and Prussia and both in the import of manufactured goods into Russia and the sale of agricultural products Prussia advanced to become Russia's second trading partner after Britain.

The difference between Russia's treatment of France, on the one hand, and Prussia, on the other, was fundamental. It is no exaggeration to say that the rapproche-

---

3. See Rotshtein, 'K istorii franko-russkogo soglasheniya 1859', *Krasnyi Arkhiv*, vol. 3 (88), 1938.
4. Gille Bertrand, *Histoire de la Maison Rotshchild*, (Geneva 1967); Cameron Rondo, *France and the Economic Development of Europe 1800-1914* (Princeton N.J., 1961), Cameron Rondo, 'Economic Growth and Stagnation in France, 1815-1914', *Journal of Modern History,* 23, pp. 1-13; Kurd von Schlözer, *Petersburger Briefe 1857-1862* (Stuttgart, Berlin, Leipzig, 1923), Schüle, *Russland ...*, pp. 60-61, tables.
5. See the comments on Prussia in A.P. Zablotsky-Desyatovsky, *Graf P.O. Kiselev i ego vremya* (St. Petersburg, 1882), vol. III, pp. 68-69. Kiselev's opinion in 1858.
6. M.N. Pokrovsky, *Izbrannye proizvedeniya,* book 2, (Moscow, 1965), pp. 501-2.

ment with France was to some degree opportunist. Where her relationship with Prussia was concerned, however, the friendship had deep historical and dynastic roots and was based on a real coincidence of interests.[7] The arrival of O. Bismark in the post of Prussian ambassador to St. Petersburg deepened the close relations between the St. Petersburg and Berlin courts. 'Avec la Prusse', Peter von Meyendorff, Russian ambassador first in Berlin and then in Vienna, and then a member of the Council of State, wrote in 1861.

nous sommes dans les meilleurs rapports fondés encore plus sur les relations personnelles des deux Souverains, que sur la solidarité bien entendue des intérêts. Pour le reste de l'Allemagne on ne s'en occupe guère qu'en vue de la question danoise et du concert européen qu'il faudra peut-être opposer au concert allemand. Mais nos sympathies pour le Danemarc n'iront pas aussi loin qu'en 1848.[8]

There was one other element which may have had a certain influence on the attitude of the Russian court towards Denmark, namely the arrival of the new Austrian ambassador, Baron Thun, in St. Petersburg in 1860, after which Russo-Austrian relations began to change somewhat. The gesture by Alexander II on the occasion of Franz Josef's birthday, when he paid no attention to the birthday of Napoleon III which occurred soon afterwards, and the meeting of the three monarchs in Warsaw, although it did not lead to any fundamental changes in Russian policy, could not fail to be of some significance. Relations were also influenced by the Polish question, which was of crucial importance to the three northern courts and had been revived in 1860-61 by a wave of patriotic demonstrations in the Kingdom of Poland and appeared like a phantom threatening the three occupying powers.

II.

The November decisions of the Danish government and the decree of 6 November 1858 created a new situation in relations between Denmark and Holstein. In his dispatch of 28 November 1858 to the Danish ambassadors in London, Paris and St. Petersburg, Hall tried to provide a formal legal justification for the step he had taken,[9] and to present it as a move made by the Danish government under pressure from the German Confederation in order to avoid the threat of execution by the Confederation. But this formal legal point of view, referring to the resolution of the German Diet on 29 July 1852, the royal declaration of 28 January 1851, the talks between Denmark and the German states in 1851-52 and the provisions of the Treaty of London of 8 May 1852, was devoid of historical substance and failed to

---

7. See Mosse, *The European Powers ...*, pp. 92 ff and B.E. Nolde, *Peterburgskaya missiya Bismarka, 1859-1862* (Prague, 1925).
8. Peter von Meyendorff. *Ein russischer Diplomat an den Höfen von Berlin und Wien.* Politischer und Privater Briefwechsel 1826-1863 herausgegeben und eingeleitet von Otto Hoetzsch, vol. III. (Berlin and Leipzig, 1923), p. 236.
9. N. Neergaard, *Under Junigrundloven,* (Copenhagen, 1916), vol. II, pt. I, pp. 305 ff. E. Møller, *Helstatens Fald,* vol. I, (Copenhagen, 1958), pp. 304 ff.

take into account either the new constellation of political forces in Europe after the Crimean War or the changes taking place in Germany as a result of the development of the national movement in Europe, particularly in Italy.

The question arises whether Hall really underestimated the national question or whether he was aware that taking the national point of view and treating it as the key to solving the dispute with Germany would be tantamount to accepting the German demands and capitulating. It would also mean making concessions to Schleswig. Thus he logically preferred to keep to different ground and concentrated on the legal side of the problem, since with a suitable interpretation of the treaties concluded in 1852, it seemed to him he would be able to settle the dispute to Denmark's advantage. In my view, then, this was a tactic chosen with premeditation as most appropriate, in his opinion, to Denmark's interests.

In accordance with the November proclamation, the Estates of Holstein were convened in Itzehoe at the beginning of January 1859. The main topic of debate was the proposed special constitution for Holstein.

The debate began under inauspicious circumstances. The change of minister of foreign affairs in Prussia in the autumn of 1858 and the accession of Schleinitz to power caused the Holstein and Schleswig aristocracy to take an even more uncompromising attitude towards Denmark, as the government in Berlin was in the hands of political circles which were closer to liberal tendencies, and they emphasised their sympathy for Schleswig-Holsteinism even more than the conservatives who had been in power hitherto. This fact, together with the language of the Prussian Regent, his address to the second chamber in Berlin, and the clear tendency to concern themselves with Schleswig and to press Denmark to agree to the union of the two duchies influenced the course of the session in Itzehoe, so the Russian ambassador in Copenhagen thought, as did the increased activity on the part of Prince Augustenburg, his address to the Danish King, and the pamphlet *'Suum cuique'* in which he protested against the law of succession of 31 July 1853. They revived old ideas of Schleswig-Holsteinism and showed that the supporters of Prince Augustenburg in Berlin and other German courts were as active as ever.

In Ungern-Sternberg's opinion these tendencies undoubtedly had to be opposed, but they ought to bring about greater flexibility ('plus souple') on the part of the Danish government and material concessions should be offered by Copenhagen at an opportune time. These should help to bind the duchies to the crown and thus create an obstacle to the whims of the supporters of Scandinavianism. Ungern-Sternberg thus saw a need for action to combat both Schleswig-Holsteinism and Scandinavianism, but he saw no other possibility of achieving the consolidation of the monarchy than by making reasonable concessions to the official, that is, conservative opposition in Holstein.

The demands put forward by the Estates of Holstein aimed to establish definitive relations between Denmark and Holstein on the following principles:

1. that no fundamental law ('aucun loi générale') should have legal force on the territory of the duchy without the agreement of the Estates,

2. that the electoral law of 2 October 1855 should be rescinded as a result of the patent of 6 November 1858, which revoked the common constitution,
3. that the representatives of the four parts of the monarchy (Denmark proper, Schleswig, Holstein and Lauenburg) had inseparable rights in the Rigsraad ('des droits inhérents'), and the fundamental law ('loi générale) could not be passed without their agreement,
4. that the Council of Ministers should consist of members giving a greater guarantee (a pledge) of implementation of these changes.

These principles, the draft of a common constitution and the remarks on a special constitution and on financial matters, which had long been a subject of particular complaint by the duchies, were regarded by Hall and the remaining members of his government as totally unacceptable. They saw them as a symptom of the rebirth of Schleswig-Holsteinism, arrogant provocation or a desire to humiliate the Danish nation, and to accept these points, in their view, could lead either to the restoration of absolutism or to the division of Denmark into a federation of four states.

Ungern-Sternberg interpreted them differently from the Danish government. He shared the opinion of those conservative circles which saw the proposals concerning changes in the constitution, which the Estates in Itzehoe had presented to the government, as elements of conciliation, and he saw nothing impossible or humiliating for Denmark in accepting them. The ambassador came to the conclusion that the government should take note of the main proposals from the Estates of Holstein, reorganise the Rigsraad, which had shown that with its existing structure it could not function normally, make changes in the government, retaining Hall and some ministers but co-opting others who would inspire greater confidence in both nations. The minister for Holstein, for example, could be Baron Plessen, one of the leaders of the Holstein opposition.

Putting these ideas to Gorchakov, Ungern-Sternberg did not conceal the difficulties which would have to be overcome, but he believed that a salutary influence from outside could eliminate them and make a fundamental contribution to a future blessing – the consolidation of the Danish monarchy. If Denmark were forced to come to a reconciliation with the duchies she would be freed of Scandinavianism and would draw closer to her natural ally, Germany, and would enjoy the domestic peace she so badly needed. In the ambassador's opinion the disinterested advice of the Russian cabinet would undoubtedly have the greatest influence on the fate of these countries.[10] He regretted that the Holstein plan had encountered enormous difficulties as a result of the attitude of Hall and his cabinet. He was sorry that there appeared to be no other solution than to place the conflict before the German Diet again. It was also obvious to him that, as always, the question of Schleswig played a fundamental role in the conflict and that the government would willingly agree to any proposals which included a close union of Schleswig and the Kingdom.[11]

10. Particulière, 27 February (11 March) and 15 (27) March 1859.
11. 2(14) and 15 (27) February and 27 March (8 April) 1859.

In Ungern-Sternberg's opinion the Danes were not sufficiently concerned about the danger which could arise as a result of a union between the duchies brought about by a rebirth of Schleswig-Holsteinism, and furthermore, they were still influenced by the outcome of the last war (victory on the battlefield - E.H.). That was ten years ago. Hatred and punishment must have their limits. Prince Augustenburg, the main instigator of the rebellion, had been removed for ever and eliminated, thanks to the 31 July 1853 law of succession. In this state of affairs the Danish government should give an impetus to the sincere rapprochement of the two nations, heal the wounds caused by the civil war, grant Schleswig an administration conforming to the wishes of its inhabitants and end the provocative and unnecessary restrictions on the secular union of the duchies, which would cause no harm ('à l'union séculaire et inoffensive des Duchés'). This was the price which must be paid, the Russian ambassador concluded in a conversation with Hall, for peace with Germany, peace in their own home, and the preservation of the integrity of the monarchy.

While the ambassador was critical of Hall's policy towards the German duchies, where Denmark's policy towards the growing Italian crisis was concerned he expressed recognition and understanding, as the King found himself in a difficult position, being at the same time the Danish monarch, an independent ruler, and a German prince. This latter position gave rise to additional difficulties and the government, wanting to fulfil its obligations to the German Confederation, decided to mobilise the Holstein contingent, which produced objections from France.

If the war spread beyond the borders of Italy Denmark's situation would become exceedingly difficult. The King, who wanted to maintain strict neutrality in this matter, would, as Prince of Holstein, have to take part if the German Confederation were to be drawn into the war. The Copenhagen government did not envisage issuing a joint declaration (of neutrality) with Sweden as it had on the eve of the Crimean War, and intended to follow the actions of the Dutch government, which was in the same position in relation to the Confederation on account of Lineburg as Denmark was on account of Holstein and Lauenburg. This attitude - 'tout correct', as Ungern-Sternberg described it - led to opposition from the Danish ultranationalists, who, counting on French support *(Dagbladet),* would have liked to break with the Confederation or, not believing in the possibility of harmonious coexistence between Danes and Germans, opposed the idea of Helstat - the partial incorporation of Holstein and Lauenburg into Denmark - and recommended abandoning the German duchies and merging with Sweden-Norway. Moderate public opinion took a different position, and the semi-official *Berlingske Tidende* said that the difficulties of the Confederation should not be exploited.

The conservative *Kjøbenhavnsposten* argued that there existed two parallel dangers - Schleswig-Holsteinism and Scandinavianism; and in case of a war Denmark should be neutral.[12]

12. *Kjøbenhavnsposten*, 'Scandinavismen og Slesvigholsteinismen', 18 November 1858, 21 January and 4 February 1859.

Preservation of neutrality in the Italian war, as long as the security of the monarchy was not threatened, and scrupulous fulfilment of its obligations to the Confederation were two tasks which were not easily reconciled, Ungern-Sternberg argued. In the case of war between France and Germany it would be a problem not only for Holstein and Lauenburg, which could be exposed to the effects of the war, but a matter of infringement of the neutrality of the entire monarchy and involvement not only of the duchies but of the whole of Denmark in the orbit of the war.[13] Ungern-Sternberg tried to convince Hall that he should take advantage of the complications brought about by the Italian war, when Germany had become more conciliatory, and try to influence Prussia to exert pressure on the Confederation to reach a compromise.

The main desire of both Alexander II and Gorchakov was to avoid any complications as a result of the Danish-German dispute, and the Tsar said this expressly to Plessen during the Orthodox New Year reception, promising to be helpful to the Danish King. Gorchakov also expressed his disapproval of the proposals Denmark put to the Estates of Holstein, especially as Schleinitz was greatly irritated by them. According to a report from Budberg, Schleinitz was as well disposed towards Denmark as anyone.[14]

Gorchakov was full of complaints about Denmark; he was not interested in the domestic motives which guided the Danish government but only in the possible effects of a negative reaction by the Estates of Holstein.[15] The minister did not think that the Estates had exceeded their authority by raising the question of Schleswig. He did not deny that from a legal point of view the Danish government was right, but the essential point for him was that it was necessary, in Denmark's interests, to avoid anything which could serve as a pretext for broaching the question of Schleswig. In Gorchakov's opinion Schleswig was 'le clef de voûte de la solution' and one day the question would have to be tackled.[16] He did not intend to go into details of the discussions which took place in Itzehoe,[17] but he emphasised that only two things in the resolutions of the Estates of Holstein were of cardinal importance, namely:

1. the Estates' declaration in favour of the unity of the Danish monarchy,
2. the rejection of Schleswig-Holsteinism.

---

13. Cf. Manderström's comments on this subject. H.H.S.A. P.A. XXVI Schweden, Ber. Weis. Varia 1859-1861. K. 14, no. 31, 6 September 1859. Langenau's report. It is worth adding that from 1859 Charles XV was sympathetic to the idea of an alliance with Britain and Prussia, to counterbalance the alliance between Russia and France, and Manderström remained on good terms with Schleinitz. But Charles XV inclined to this on condition that the German Confederation recognised the Eider frontier. He was against the division of Schleswig into a German and a Danish part because it was reminiscent of the partition of Poland.
14. Dep. Rus. nos. 1 and 5, 14 (2) and 20 (8) January 1859.
15. Dep. Rus. no. 5, 20 (8) January 1859.
16. Dep. Rus. no. 9, (Reservée) 23 (11) February 1859.
17. Dep. Rus. no. 14, 11 April (30 March) 1858.

It was the task of the Danish government to find means to eliminate the dispute and the more effective the means to do this and to consolidate the monarchy were, the more the Russian cabinet would applaud them. Gorchakov did not want to involve himself in judging the 1855 constitution, or in the internal affairs of Denmark, and preferred to express his wishes in a general manner.[18]

He considered that advantage should be taken of the outbreak of the Italian war to give the monarchy a form of organisation which would lead to the harmonious coexistence of the two nations.[19] He also stressed that although Germany was busy with the Italian question, neither Germany, the German press, nor the Estates of Holstein would lose sight of the question of the duchies. They regarded the matter as a question of Germany's honour. The passions currently directed against France, Gorchakov warned, would turn against Denmark if the Danish government did not settle the question.[20] Gorchakov advised it to seek an agreement with the Estates of Holstein directly and to make an effort to find a form of organisation which would take in the whole of the monarchy and create conditions under which its two constituent elements, the Danish and the German, could coexist harmoniously.[21]

He considered the main difficulty in the way of an agreement to be the fact that it was not easy to find a method of strengthening the political position of Holstein so as to ensure it a general role which could give it a sufficient guarantee, especially where matters concerning the duchies were concerned.

In Gorchakov's opinion the Danish King had broken the promises to the German Confederation contained in his manifesto of 28 January 1852 by imposing the 1855 constitution on Holstein, because the place he had assigned to Holstein in this constitution did not correspond to his good intentions of three years previously. The series of resolutions adopted after 1855, although their aim was friendly conciliation, could do no more than temporarily heal the damage done by the situation created in 1855. This was the position he presented in a dispatch to Ungern-Sternberg on 24 October 1859.[22]

It also seemed to him – Plessen reported – that the Royal patent[23] of 23 September (old style) of the previous year had postponed rather than advanced the moment when Holstein and the Federal Diet could be satisfied, since it did not give Holstein a decisive say in fundamental matters common to the whole monarchy. This even applied to matters which had previously been in the power of the provincial Estates. If Holstein were represented in the Danish parliament and had the right to speak there, it would be in a false situation, having to accept laws passed by a majority which was not very well disposed, if not actually hostile, to German

---

18. See J. Hansen, *Les Coulisses de la Diplomatie* ..., p. 345.
19. Dep. Rus. no. 20, 5 May (23 April) 1859).
20. Dep. Rus. no. 14, 11 April (30 March) 1859. See also Gorchakov to Ungern-Sternberg, 16 (4) April 1859.
21. Dep. Rus. no. 20, 5 May (23 April) 1859. This was also the wish of Alexander II. Gorchakov to Ungern-Sternberg, 16 (4) April 1859).
22. Udenrigs. Samlede Sager. Den Holstenske Forfatningssag, vol. 213. R.A. Copenhagen.
23. Warrant or decree.

nationality. And to avoid the likelihood of new disputes with the German Confederation, Gorchakov advised the royal government to furnish the German Diet as quickly as possible with explanations of the true content of the 23 September patent, for this would leave no doubt about the conciliatory measures set out in the 1852 manifesto, which had been accepted by the German Diet in its resolution of 29 July 1852. Such action, in Gorchakov's opinion, was not incompatible with the government's sense of dignity.[24]

In a conversation with Plessen[25] Gorchakov supplemented these thoughts with some remarks on the constitution as the source of the conflicts. Preparing to depart for a congress which he anticipated was to begin soon (5 January), Gorchakov mentioned that on the way back he could travel via Berlin and take advantage of the occasion, if the Danish government wished, to talk to Schleinitz. (This congress did not take place). On the other hand, he did not think it would be appropriate for the congress, which was to be convened on account of the Italian question, to have to deal with the Danish question, the more so since in his judgement this would be contrary to Denmark's interests. The difficulties which Denmark was going through should be solved without intervention in internal Danish affairs.[26]

As Plessen reported, the Russian government shared the German cabinets' views on the matter of granting a provisional status for Holstein. As far as this question went, the Russian cabinet pursued exclusively its own interests ('ne poursuit dans notre affaire aucun intérêt que lui soit propre'). It wanted to see a firm foundation for the integrity of the monarchy created on the basis of agreements with the larger German states to protect it from both internal and external upheavals. It believed that this could be successfully achieved.[27]

In the opinion of one interlocutor, whose name Plessen did not mention but whom he called 'un homme qui fait autorité en fait de politique extérieure', nationalist tendencies in Denmark differed fundamentally from such tendencies in other states. In Denmark, in this unnamed Russian's view, nationalist tendencies would, if implemented, lead to a reduction in Danish strength, wealth and resources, whilst everywhere else they sought to expand the national wealth and strength.

Chez nous ces tendances nationales, selon l'opinion de mon interlocuteur, si elles sont realisées, menèraient à une diminution de nos forces, de nos richesses et nos resources, tandis qu'ailleurs les tendances nationales cherchent à s'étendre et à s'arrondir.[28]

This was evidently an allusion to the programme of the Eider party, which sought the complete separation of Holstein from Denmark.

---

24. 3 December (21 November) 1859. Privatarkiver 5810. A.F. Krieger, J.9, R.A. Copenhagen.
25. *Ibid.*
26. Plessen to Hall, 3 December (21 November) 1859, from the portfolio Privatarkiver 5810. A.F. Krieger, J.9, R.A. Copenhagen.
27. Dep. Rus. no. 43, 21 (9) December 1859.
28. *Ibid.*

III.

The brief period of the governments of Rottwitt and Blixen-Finecke (2 December 1859 – 24 February 1860) was decribed in critical terms by Ungern-Sternberg, both from the point of view of internal relations in Denmark and of the government's foreign policy, on account of Blixen-Finecke's inclination to revision of the provisions of the Treaty of London of 8 May 1852 on the succession to the Danish throne. In a letter to Prince Christian, Blixen-Finecke maintained that the coming European congress would deal with the question of revision of the treaty in order to find a way of settling both the conflict with Germany and the succession to the throne. The appearance of the contents of this note in *Dagbladet* was regarded by the Russian ambassador as the height of tactlessness towards the heir to the throne, and to Russia, which had made such a prominent contribution to the treaty accepted by the great powers. Besides, not only Ungern-Sternberg, but the Swedish ambassador, Wachmeister, and the British ambassador, Paget, also asked Blixen-Finecke for an explanation of this matter.

In the Russian ambassador's opinion Schleswig was becoming the dominant question. The Rottwitt government, exasperated by the attitude of the Estates of Schleswig and wanting to court popularity in Denmark, had transgressed all previous norms of behaviour in relation to the actions of the German party in Schleswig. The government's fear of a union of Schleswig and Holstein, in the ambassador's view, had been exploited by the Eider and the Scandinavian parties. They were pushing the government in the direction of the incorporation and Danicisation of Schleswig. Among the means used by the government he listed: persecution of the German language, which was spoken by two-thirds of the inhabitants; the appointment of Danish officials who had done their studies and had their practical experience in Copenhagen; the authorities' rejection of petitions concerning the German language; restrictions on the press, which in Denmark itself was totally free; changing place names into Danish; a ban on the activities of scientific, literary, agronomical and artistic societies which would include residents of both Schleswig and Holstein, when such societies existed in Holstein and the ban did not apply there, and when Danish, Swedish, and other foreign societies were permitted.

One example of such obvious discrimination, in the Russian ambassador's opinion, was the incident in Flensburg when the royal commissioner forbad the Estates to debate an address to the King and possession and distribution of the address were prohibited, on pain of punishment. The persecution connected with this was carried to such an extent that the Dutch consul in Flensburg was arrested and sentenced to three days on bread and water for sending the address to the Dutch embassy in Copenhagen. The intervention of the Dutch ambassador, Du Bois, with the Danish government proved ineffective.[29] Hall, back in power again after the sudden death of Rottwitt, was inflexible, despite the intervention, and although

---

29. Gustav Brieger, Consul for Schleswig, Kongelig Dansk Hof- og Staats-Kalender, 1860, p. XXXIV; his successor was Christian Tramson, *Ibid.* 1861.

he regretted that the incident had taken place, declared that he could not interfere in the matter of the court verdict as the address 'en question était d'une nature déloyale'.

The Danish government, the Russian ambassador thought, was unwilling to see that the situation in Schleswig was abnormal. The government continually explained its measures by the necessity to combat the unionist tendencies which the inhabitants of Schleswig and Holstein nourished, and in doing so it was creating an atmosphere which could lead to war. This fear of a closer union between the two duchies had been skilfully exploited by the Eider party and the Scandinavianists. The people directing the administration of Schleswig, zealous Danicisers like Regenburg, who had been promoted to the post of undersecretary of state and rewarded for his work with the Order of Danebrog, were performing a doubly harmful role by assuring the King in their reports that the complaints of the German population were unjustified and that the state of schooling in mixed-nationality districts was better than in Prussia and Hannover.[30] In Ungern-Sternberg's opinion, Hall and his colleagues were living in a world of illusions. They did not see the difficulties and displayed an incomprehensible blindness where the problem of Schleswig was concerned.

Ungern-Sternberg was more understanding of Hall's policy in relation to the Holstein question. Hall's argument that no government would agree to give Holstein and Lauenburg a decisive voice ('délibératif') in general matters in the constitutional sphere during a two-year transition period could not be completely dismissed – if it was possible to rely on the maintenance of the current state of affairs and the patience of the German Confederation.[31]

The Danish government, which was guided by democratic principles in Denmark itself, failed to carry out a nationality policy which was acceptable to the German population in Schleswig. According to the distinguished expert on the subject Troels Fink, the system of Danish government in Schleswig was bureaucratic, repressive and pernickety. The very fact of failure to grant a general amnesty after 1852 testified to the lack of good will. Signs of discontent multiplied, stemming from intolerance over the question of language in schools and churches, the clumsy behaviour of local and central authorities in seeking to limit the freedoms and rights of the German population in the duchies, right up to attempts at incorporation of Schleswig into Denmark proper.[32] The Treaty of Lon-

---

30. T. Fink, *Geschichte des schleswigschen Grenzlandes,* (Copenhagen, 1958), pp. 147-8, blamed Th.A.J. Regenburg, among others, for the mistakes in nationality policy in Schleswig. See also Holger Hjelholt, *Den Danske Sprogordning og det Danske Sprogstyre i Slesvig mellem Krigene (1850-1864),* and A. Scharff, 'Vom übernationalen zum nationalen Staat', in *Schleswig-Holstein in der deutschen und nordeuropäischen Geschichte* (Stuttgart, 1969), p. 228.
31. 7 (19) March 1860.
32. See Summary List of Complaints by the German Population of Holstein and Schleswig, Memo. on the Schleswig-Holstein Question, F.O. 22. 290, 1861, 26 January. Attachés Manley, Freeman, Seymour, Foreign Various. Domestic Various. Rigsarkivets Danica.fotografering, P.R.O. London, Arkiv nr. 600. See also the memorandum by the consul general Ward, Mr. Ward to the Earl of Clarendon, May 28 1857, in Denmark and Germany. Reports from Mr. Ward and Vice-consul Rainals

don, based on the principles of politics and diplomacy rather than on the wishes of the German population, did not help to settle the matter.[33]

German propaganda was full of exaggeration, with German liberal-democratic circles comparing the situation of the Germans in Schleswig with that of the oppressed national minorities in Russia, Prussia, Austria and Turkey.[34] The situation of the German population in Schleswig was certainly better than that of the Poles in the Prussian sector, nor could the Poles expect help from anywhere, while forty-odd million Germans were speaking out on behalf of the German population in Schleswig. Schleswig enjoyed moral and financial support from them and, military support too when it needed it. And Copenhagen provided pretexts beyond measure for intervention from different quarters.

Influenced by both the Western states and Russia, Hall began to appreciate the complexity of the problem, but he considered that the German Union was putting forward demands which it was impossible to meet, and that Prussia, which could have exercised a decisive influence, did not want to become deeply involved in the matter and was withdrawing. Thus, Hall argued, a vicious circle arose, and owing to the fact that the popularity of every member of the German Confederation depended on its attitude to the question of the duchies there could be dangerous developments.

In spite of this, however, Hall – in the ambassador's judgement – had no intention of making concessions over Schleswig, and considered that Schleswig was going too far in its nationalistic demands. Ungern-Sternberg was also critical of certain plans of Hall's connected with the possible conclusion of an offensive and defensive treaty between Denmark and France if a serious conflict developed between Denmark and the German Confederation. This question emerged after Monrad's return from Paris.

The Russian ambassador confined himself to indicating to Hall that Denmark could gain nothing by becoming involved in a war between larger states and the result could be the direct opposite of what he intended, namely disaster. This episode reminded Ungern-Sternberg of the periode of the Crimean War and the manœuvres by France and Britain to draw Denmark into the coalition against Russia, which under certain circumstances, such as a change of government or intrigue on the part of the court, might have actually happened.[35] He was also sceptical of the so-called Hansen-project – to build a canal through Holstein – which in Hall's opinion could give Denmark important trade and strategic benefits, as the plan included the neutralisation of the canal, and thus of Holstein, to be guaranteed by international agreement. This, Hall argued, was a very important step and

respecting the duchies of Schleswig and Holstein dated respectively 28 May 1857 and 15 February 1861. Presented to the House of Commons by Command of Her Majesty, in pursuance of their address dated 8 March 1864, London. See also Les Duchés danois en 1860. Mémoires et documents, Danemark 1856-1863. Question des Duchés, vol. 13, A.M.A.E., Paris.

33. Fink, *Geschichte ...*, pp. 145-8.
34. H.H.S.A. Vienna, P.A. Nachlass Rechberg. A.I. Teil 4D; Fink, *Geschichte ...*, pp. 145, 151; Steefel, pp. 30-32; *Dagbladet,* Revue, no. 5; no. 24, 29 January 1861.
35. 24 March (5 April) 1860. See Halicz, *Danish Neutrality ...*

rien ne serait plus heureux pour la Monarchie danoise que d'être mise tout entière sous la garantie d'une neutralité reconnue et sanctionnée par toutes les puissances, comme c'est le cas avec la Belgique et la Suisse.

In a report to Gorchakov, Ungern-Sternberg drew attention to the difficult demands which the German Confederation would undoubtedly put forward then on account of the federal levy and the right it had to possible intenvention in the German duchies. The neutralisation of Holstein would be poor compensation for the loss of the duchies from the federal bond. Such a plan and such changes could only be carried out in exceptionally favourable circumstances for Denmark.

The helmsman of Russian policy, Gorchakov, spoke frequently about the Danish-German dispute during the course of 1860. On some matters he took a firm position, on others he remained cautious. He was against the appointment of the Prince of Denmark (Christian) as Governor of Holstein, as he regarded it as a political move which could be interpreted as a step towards the separation of Holstein from the monarchy, and this would not only diminish and significantly weaken the monarchy but would not, he thought, have any effect on German national feelings. Gorchakov also responded negatively to Blixen-Finecke's letter on the subject of revision of the London protocols, since for him they were 'incontesté et incontestable'. He though Denmark should be extremely careful where revision of the Treaty of London was concerned, but he decided not to intervene in this matter, relying on receiving explanations from Copenhagen.[36]

In Gorchakov's opinion the central issue was the question of Schleswig.[37] 'Les affaires du Sleswig ... pourraient prendre des proportions très dangereuses ... amènent des résultats funestes pour la sécurité des états'. Gorchakov considered that means must be found to placate the suspicious and unfriendly Germans, as this was a country in which Denmark did not share power with anyone, as she did in Holstein and Lauenburg. Gorchakov set out his position in a dispatch to Ungern-Sternberg; by this (he said to Plessen), he did not wish in any way to hurt the Danish government and was guided by the best of intentions. He warned, however, that delay in settling the matter could be very dangerous.

As Plessen commented, the view in Russia was that the path the Danish government had followed in connection with the Schleswig problem was not in Denmark's own interests, and attention was drawn to the fact that Copenhagen did not take much notice of what the Estates of Schleswig wanted.

The difficulties between Schleswig and Copenhagen were increasing, especially

---

36. On 20 May 1860 Krieger noted in his diary: 'Gortchakoff kommer stadig tilbage til vor uvillighed til at tage imod raad – navnlig i den slesvigske sag; derfor kan han ikke hjælpe os, siger han, Plessen er naiv nok til at forsikre os, at han ikke ønsker en tysk occupation af Slesvig. (Gorchakov referred incessantly to our unwillingness to accede to his advice concerning the Schleswig problem; that is why he cannot help us. Plessen is naïve enough assuring us that he (Gorchakov – E.H.) does not wish a German occupation of Schleswig). (*Dagbøger*, vol. II, Copenhagen and Kristiania, 1921, p. 173).
37. 'The constant headache was the Schleswig question', says P. Lauring in *A History of Denmark*, (Copenhagen, 1981), p. 222.

after the Estates of Schleswig, which were convened in January 1860, questioned the legality of the Danish warrants of November 1858 and the authority of the Rigsraad in respect of Schleswig. Following this, not only the German press but the parliaments of the German states, and then the Prussian parliament and, in May 1860, the Prussian minister, Schleinitz, joined in the debate about Schleswig, accusing Denmark of infringing rights stemming from the obligations she had undertaken in 1852. In reply to Schleinitz, while not denying the right of parliamentary discussion, Hall accused the Prussian government of interference in the internal affairs of the Danish monarchy, and in a dispatch to the Danish ambassadors in Paris, London, St. Petersburg, Vienna, Berlin and Stockholm on 25 May he emphasised that any discussion concerning a country to which Denmark alone had exclusive rights was impermissible.[38]

Osten-Sacken expressed the view that all the documents and royal warrants concerning the basis of structure and organisation of the monarchy should once again be most scrupulously studied and complied with strictly. If Denmark continued to behave as she had done hitherto, and Germany interpreted this behaviour as a tendency towards incorporation of Schleswig, the Schleswig question would become 'le point cardinal' in the dispute with Germany.

In connection with Schleinitz's speech in the Chamber of Deputies, in which he had said that the German Diet should no longer refrain from examining what rights Germany derived from the agreements of 1851-52, Gorchakov did indeed express his regret that the Danish government had such difficulties, which he understood, but at the same time he added that Denmark did not always act in accordance with the agreements she had concluded. Assuring Denmark of his best intentions, Gorchakov did not fail to point out that little heed had been paid to *his* (emphasis added – E.H.) advice in Copenhagen. The Danish government was asking for support from the Russian cabinet, but sometimes its behaviour and its line of argument did not make it easy for Russia to come to Denmark's defence. As before he urged reaching an agreement with Germany.

In Plessen's opinion, the Russian cabinet believed an agreement with Germany was possible. The Danish government should not fear, Plessen argued, that St. Petersburg was prejudiced against Denmark because of its political freedoms, nor overestimate their influence on Russia's attitude to the whole question. Russia's position, in Plessen's view, was of essential importance also because the Emperor of the French had appeared for a long time to recognise Russia's primacy in the Danish question. That had certainly changed, but France continued to reckon with the position Russia took.

And so, when Schleinitz expressed the wish that France should use her influence

38. See Brockdorff to Blixen-Finecke, 25 and 26 January, and to Hall, 7 March, 1860. Depecher, Berlin, 1857-1861. Schleinitz to Balan, 29 May 1860, Det Tyske Forbund, Depecher, 1860-1862. Privatarkiver 5810, Krieger, J.9. C. Hall's dispatch of 25 May 1860, and of 10 June 1860 to Brockdorff. Det Tyske Forbund, Depecher 1860-1862. See also *Correspondence respecting the Affairs of the Duchies of Schleswig and Holstein 1860-61,* (London, 1861), pp. 30-36; Mémoires et documents. Danemark 1858-1863. Question de Duchés, vol. 13, A.M.A.E., Paris.

in Copenhagen to persuade the Danish government to act in accordance with the 1851-52 agreements, Paris, before taking certain steps, decided to consult St. Petersburg and ask it to state its position on the question of Schleswig.[39]

The document prepared by Osten-Sacken at Gorchakov's request in this connection was the quintessence of Russia's attitude towards the problem. Its conclusions were as follows:

1. Denmark was not discharging her obligations concerning equal treatment of the two nationalities living in Schleswig and the non-incorporation of Schleswig into the Kingdom, for the Danish government was protecting Danes at the expense of Germans and the aim of the government's moves in the administrative sphere was incorporation.
2. Both the German states, acting as plenipotentiaries of the German Confederation, had the right to supervise Denmark's fulfillment of her obligations.
3. The non-German great powers, as they did not participate directly in the negotiations, could not intervene in the Schleswig question, unless the integrity of the monarchy were threatened as a result of the dimensions which the Schleswig question could assume.

Handing this document to Plessen, Gorchakov informed him that in a talk with Budberg's deputy, Mohrenheim, Schleinitz had expressed the wish that the Russian cabinet should put pressure on Copenhagen, but the Russian diplomat thought it would be better if he acquainted the Danish government with his position in the way he had done, through Plessen. Neither Russia nor France, in view of their friendship with Denmark, would press their advice on her and wanted to avoid anything which could be painful ('pénible') for Denmark. In spite of everything, Gorchakov considered that Schleinitz's speech showed moderation. By not fulfilling her obligations, Denmark could expose herself to a new crisis which could be fatal to the country's interests; the Berlin cabinet might feel itself relieved of the obligations it had undertaken towards Denmark and the state of affairs before 1848 could arise again. Denmark should consider what she would gain then.[40]

When O. Bismarck, the Prussian ambassador in St. Petersburg, complained that by announcing a budget without consulting the Estates of Holstein Denmark was infringing the agreements of 1851-52, which could bring her nothing but harm,[41] Gorchakov replied that he had taken appropriate steps in Copenhagen and would do so yet again, and was exclusively in favour of the two sides making conciliatory moves.[42] He warned Plessen, however, on 21 July 1860 that Denmark should not

39. Dep. Rus. no. 17, 18 (6) May 1860.
40. *Ibid.*
41. 15 June 1860.
42. '... da sein Bestreben lediglich sei, beide Seiten zu versöhnlicher Behandling der Dinge zu vermögen'. Gorchakov secretly showed Bismarck a letter he had received from the French embassy in which the French government proposed a joint intervention in the Schleswig-Holstein question in Berlin; after discussion with him Alexander II had rejected this proposal because he did not want to resort to such a joint demonstration. L. Raschdau Ed. *Die Politischen Berichte des Fürstens Bismarck aus Petersburg und Paris (1859-62),* vol. I, 1859-60 (Berlin, 1920), p. 121. (15 June 1860) Bismarck repeated his request on 20 July, but then, too, no action was taken. Nolde, *Missiya Bismarka ...*

create a problem out of minor matters, because it could lead to war or revolution, and urged concessions which would ensure peace and support in Prussia.[43]

Dänemark werde dort besseren Schuss finden und mit anderen minder mächtigen Staaten theilen, als ihm die Kombinationen gewähren könnten, von denen Feindseligkeit gegen Deutschland untrennbar sei.[44]

Alarmed by the situation in Europe, Gorchakov insisted that Denmark should pursue a policy of concessions and not provoke a crisis which could have adverse consequences for her.[45]

He trusted that the Danish government intended to settle the Holstein question on the basis of the provisions of the Treaty of London, but he wished that the question of Schleswig, as well as Holstein, should be finally settled. The general line of Russia was that Holstein could not be placated except by placating Schleswig.[46] Gorchakov stressed that his chief aim was to maintain the principle of the integrity of the monarchy and he trusted that Hall would manage to solve the problem facing Denmark.

Personne aussi ne saurait mieux que Mr. Hall, combiner les moyens que son esprit éclairé et un noble patriotisme lui indiquent pour arriver au but auquel tous les hommes bien pensant en Danmarc, et même les hommes d'Etat en Europe désirent le voir atteindre.[47]

Gorchakov set out his views systematically in two dispatches sent that same day to Ungern-Sternberg.[48] He expressed regret at the nature of the discussion between the Danish and Prussian governments over the debate in the Prussian Chamber of Deputies on Schleswig – 'de cet incident regrettable' – but was critical of the views Hall expressed in dispatch no. 25 and his interpretation of the 1851 negotiations. Hall's explanations, in his opinion, flew in the face of what had been achieved then in connection with the Schleswig question.

In Gorchakov's opinion it would not be possible to placate Holstein, a country socially and culturally linked with Schleswig for centuries, without simultaneously settling such matters as nationality and language, which were common to both duchies. The Russian government had been examining the intentions of the King of Denmark on 28 January 1852, as a consequence of certain binding obligations towards Austria and Prussia, acting in the name of the German Confederation, and for that reason the latter had a right to supervise their fulfilment, even though Schleswig was not a member of the Confederation.

It was true that the decision of 29 July 1852 mentioned only Holstein and Lauenburg, and Gorchakov did not want to dwell on why Schleswig had been omitted. But Hall was wrong to draw the conclusion that the Diet was not entitled to look

---

43. Raschdau, ... *Bismarck* ..., vol. II, pp. 121, 141.
44. *Ibid*. p. 141, (21. July 1860).
45. No. 21, 8 July (26. June).
46. Gorchakov to Ungern-Sternberg, 16 (28) September 1860. Udenrigs. Samlede Sager. Den Holst. Forfatning. Vol. 214. R.A. Copenhagen.
47. *Ibid*.

at the conditions which existed in a country which shared common cultural and material interests with Holstein.

Hall considered that the obligations of the King concerned only three matters connected with Schleswig, namely:

1. not to incorporate it into the Kingdom of Denmark,
2. to recontruct the provincial Estates,
3. to maintain the *nexus socialis* of the knightly state,[49]

but he denied that any guarantees had been given in the negotiations with Austria and Prussia concerning nationality and the German language. Russia did not share this opinion. Russia did not doubt that the data Hall quoted concerning the state of the Danish and German populations were correct, and anyway it would not be possible for Russia to check these data.[50] He did not share his opinion, however, that there were no restrictions on the German language and no restriction or repression of Germans and that not enough had been done to protect the Danish element in Schleswig.

On the contrary, Gorchakov considered that in certain districts where Germans predominated the Danes enjoyed privileges in the use of language, education and religious matters, and German youth received religious instruction in a language it did not understand – something which hurt the feelings of the German population, especially those coming from the lower classes. This behaviour gave rise to feelings of antipathy rather than reconciliation and deepened the differences which already existed. Russia did not deny the government's indisputable rights to maintain Danish nationality and to take measures to frustrate action which could harm the political and constitutional unity of the monarchy. She was aware of the difficulties Denmark was encountering in carrying out these two tasks in the face of opposition, and of the difficulties presented by the existence of territories where it was hard to establish linguistic frontiers, as for example, central Schleswig.

The German nation and the German Diet, however, could not remain indifferent to what was happening in Schleswig. Only by changing the system established by F.F. Tillisch in 1850, which the Imperial Government had criticised already, and by coming to an agreement with the Federal Diet, could the Danish government placate both Schleswig and Holstein. The Russian cabinet, wrote Gorchakov, reiterated its friendly advice, the more so as 'la question des nationalités' threatened to exacerbate and deepen the differences between Denmark and the Confederation.

48. *Ibid.*
49. Connection with the *Ritterschaft*.
50. Data concerning the Danish and German population were biased, as Germany (Biernatzky) exaggerated the number of Germans, and Gosch exaggerated the number of Danes in Schleswig. It was hard to establish in which group the Friisians should be counted; their language, in Gosch's opinion, was closer to Danish then German. There were also difficulties about which language group the population which spoke both languages, German and Danish, should be allocated to. Gosch, *Denmark and Germany since 1815,* (London, 1862), pp. 229, 263, 449-51. See also *Dagbladet,* Revue de la semaine, no. 7, 30 October 1860.

Ce mot de nationalité est de nos jours et dans presque tous les pays de l'Europe un appel aux plus mauvaises passions, et il serait digne de la sagesse du Roi de ne pas laisser prédominer cet élement révolutionnaire dans les discussions avec l'Allemagne.

In 1848 there had existed a fear, as Gorchakov called it,

La crainte affectée ou reéle d'une séparation qui devint pour les Duchés la cause, si non le prétexte du soulèvement.

The German states had intervened militarily, some of them drawn into the action by a general intoxication; others, correctly, by orders received from Frankfurt, and others again by the revolutionary movement. Today, even more than in 1848-49, Germany was divided and the Confederation did not enjoy the support of any of the German powers on this question. Denmark should therefore

se concilier des dispositions de bon vouloir de la part de l'Allemagne comme corps politique, non seulement pour le réglement définitif de l'affaire Schleswig-Holsteinoise, mais plus particulièrement encore pour assurer sa situation vis-à-vis de l'Europe.

Hall had observed that the question of the succession to the throne had been happily decided, but one more essential step remained, namely to ensure the integrity of the Danish monarchy. 'Rien de plus vrai en effet'. Yet Hall should not forget that it was not only thanks to Denmark's efforts that the Treaty of London was achieved. Nor could the question of the succession to the throne have been settled without the co-operation of the great powers. The step which now had to be taken could only be successfully completed through the agreement of 'l'ensemble du Corps Germanique'. By continuing to exclude the German Confederation, the Danish government was postponing this essential agreement indefinitely. Long before the signing of the Treaty of London the signatories, including Austria and Prussia, had appreciated how important the preservation of the Danish monarchy would be for the maintenance of the balance of power in Europe, and they had given an additional pledge of this by settling the question of the succession to Frederick VII. Some second rank German states had acceded to the Treaty of London when invited to do so. Others saw the wisdom of the treaty but preferred to reserve their freedom of action, transferring the matter to the competence of the German Diet. Those who did not respond so favourably said that they could not prejudice the decisions of the assembly. Gorchakov was reminding the Danish government of this in order to point out the facts which indicated the course the government should follow:

Ce n'est point en dehors de la compétence fédérale (Gorchakov's emphasis) qu'il pourra compléter l'œuvre salutaire dont les bases sont établies par le Traité de Londres, et il ne saurait se dispenser de reconnaître cette compétence.

For many years, since 1850, Germany had frequently given evidence of its conciliatory attitude towards Denmark. Austria and Prussia had exercised their special offices ('essentiels') to facilitate the pacification of the duchies and the Treaty of

London had exerted a moderating influence on the decisions of the German Diet concerning Holstein. These two states, thanks to their position as the principal states in the Confederation, could offer help and support in settling the differences over the Schleswig-Holstein question and assist Denmark to make the step which Hall had said was so important.

Mais – et nous ne croyons assez pouvoir insister sur ce point – l'appui et le concours de l'Autriche et de la Prusse ne seront efficaces ni même possibles, tant que le Gouvernement Danois, pour des intérêts minimes en comparaison de ceux qu'il importe à lui-même comme à l'Europe entière de voir sauvegardés avant tout, justifie en quelque sorte le reproche de multiplier les entraves qu'il rencontre dans sa marche et qui peuvent devenir à la longue un obstacle insurmontable à toute entente sérieuse avec l'Allemagne.

J'en dirai autant de l'appui du Cabt. Impl. pour faire accepter le Traité de Londres par l'ensemble du Corps Germanique, si notre intervention était admissible dans une question Européenne, sans aucun doute, mais placée aujourd'hui sur le terrain de la législation fédérale. En résumé, le seul conseil qu'une sincère amitié puisse offrir au Cabt. du Copenhague, est de ne pas empêcher les Cabinets amis de lui être encore utiles.

In talks with Plessen,[51] Gorchakov stressed that he regretted that Denmark had not fulfilled a series of obligations to Germany and Schleswig, and urged rapid agreement with Prussia and Germany while avoiding irritating Germany by recalling its defeat in 1848. He criticised the vacillating position of the Danish government, because he took the view that in the face of the firm position of the whole of Germany, an agreement was essential in order to consolidate the Danish monarchy. Agreement should be reached, he argued, as soon as possible, while the present opposition in Holstein was moderate. For it was well known that behind it lurked people representing Schleswig-Holsteinism, and the Danish government should be wary of an agreement between the present opposition and the supporters of Schleswig-Holsteinism. That banner would be welcomed enthusiastically throughout Germany and would find great support there.

Denmark could not count on real help from the non-German states, nor from Imperial France, whose policy was generating greater dissatisfaction among her allies than her enemies on the field of battle. Nor would help be forthcoming from Britain, which did not want to be at odds with Germany or to oppose a principle as popular in Germany as Schleswig-Holsteinism. As for Russia, could she be expected yet again to alienate the liberal party in order to come to the aid of Denmark? He warned Denmark of the consequences which could await her if she continued on that road.

Plessen attached great importance to possible future talks between Gorchakov and Schleinitz in Warsaw and thought that if Schleinitz would accept Russell's proposals other intervention would not be necessary, but if the Prussian cabinet hesitated about accepting 'le provisoire', then the Russian cabinet could play an important role in overcoming these hesitations, and he urged Hall to make use of this

---

51. 29 (17) September 1860.

opportunity and inform Gorchakov of his wishes before the latter set out for Warsaw.[52]

Gorchakov was displaying growing impatience with the attitude of the Danish government. He thought that everything, taken together, was 'un cercle vicieux', and would not accept Plessen's arguments that the purpose of negotiations was for each side to state its demands and conditions – and as far as Germany was concerned, it was continually stating new demands.

Faitez ces concessions sans les laisser dépendre de telle ou telle outre condition, et si, l'Allemagne élève des demandes qui sont injustes, vous vous trouverez alors placés sur un terrain beaucoup meilleur, que celui, sur lequel vous êtez placés actuellement.

He regarded the decisive voice, which Denmark proposed to give the Estates of Holstein, as useful but not sufficient, since it would be unjust for Holstein to be dependent on the Rigsraad, in which it was not represented. He sharply criticised the half-measures in respect of Schleswig, which were not enough to establish satisfactory relations with Germany.

Les mauvaises passions couvent plus que jamais sous les cendres – warned Gorchakov – c'est la question du Schleswig, qui va les éveiller, si Vous n'y prenez garde.

He thought it was unacceptable that young people in Schleswig should have to give evidence of familiarity with the Danish Language. Nor would he allow any comparison, such as the Danish press and Danish diplomats drew, between the much better situation of the German population in Schleswig and that of the Poles in the province of Poznan.[53] At the same time he assured Plessen that his view, as always, was impartial and motivated only by concern for the fate of Denmark.[54] It should be noted, incidentally, that both French and British politicians had similar reservations about Denmark's policy towards the duchies and the situation in Schleswig, and were concerned about possible international aspects of the problem.[55]

Although Gorchakov did not beat about the bush, Plessen, as Krieger described,[56] was naive if he believed that Gorchakov was impartial, and when he assured his government that Gorchakov did not want a German occupation of Schleswig and that Gorchakov was displaying increasing interest in the attitude of the Danish government.

Just before leaving for Warsaw, Gorchakov was pleased to receive confidential information from Plessen that from July Hall would remain in close contact with Paget and was inclined towards concessions, not only in respect of Holstein but of

---

52. No. 29 c.4. 9 October (27 September) 1860.
53. Dep. Rus. no. 30, c.5. 11 October (29 September) 1860, Plessen. See also Privat arkiv 5810 A.F. Krieger, J.9.C, R.A. Copenhagen. *Dagbladet,* Revue, no. 5, 29 January 1861.
54. No. 38.c.8. 22 (10) November 1860.
55. See Mémoires et documents. Danemark 1858-1863. Question des Duchés. vol. 13, A.M.A.E. Paris; and P.R.O. London, 30/22 vol. 52, k. 1-2, Correspondence respecting the Affairs of the Duchies of Schleswig and Holstein, 1861, no. 12, 1860, no. 45; also *Denmark and Germany* (London, 1864).

Schleswig too. The most important of the concessions for Holstein, in Gorchakov's opinion, was the one which contained

> l'octroi d'un vote délibératif aux Etats provinciaux pour les affaires communes de la Monarchie, de sorte que toute loi, pour devenir exécutoire dans le Duché, pour les personnes et les propriétés, aura besoin de l'approbation des Etats.

He did not have a definite position on the financial concessions, namely the sum of 850,000 Rdl. which Holstein was to pay as a contribution to the common expenditures of the monarchy. He thought that once the sum was fixed it could not be increased except with the agreement of the Estates and on condition that they had a right to supervise the administration of these common funds.

Gorchakov took a positive view of the government's plan to relax the restrictions in the field of public schools, religious education and the law of association in Schleswig; to extend the amnesty for former participants in revolutionary demonstrations; and to include on the roll of those entitled to vote persons who previously had not had that right.

He doubted, however, whether Hall would succeed in gaining agreement from Germany to repudiate Schleswig-Holsteinism openly in exchange for these concessions, or a repudiation of direct intervention in the Schleswig question from the German Diet. But Gorchakov got the impression from Hall's dispatch that the Danish government wanted to obtain just such an assurance. Gorchakov also doubted whether the German Diet was in a position to compel the German press to be silent or to turn it away from the direction in which it had been tending since 1848, or whether it would be sensible to postpone the introduction of appropriate placatory measures – if only because strong feelings still existed in Germany. Ultimately, would it not be necessary to perpetuate the situation which Denmark sincerely aimed to terminate? Gorchakov emphasised that the Imperial government appreciated the trust which the Danish government placed in it and its wish was that it should persevere with its good intentions.[57]

There were other doubts too. They were generated by the dispatch from Budberg on the subject of the talks which had taken place in Baden between Napoleon III and the Prince Regent of Prussia and Schleinitz. Napoleon III, Budberg reported, was supposed to have said to Schleinitz that in his opinion the Danish duchies would sooner or later fall to Prussia. Schleinitz had been rather astonished by this statement because he thought France was encouraging Denmark to resist, but he did not display such absolute 'désintéressement' as Prussia usually demonstrated, arguing that he was more concerned with increasing her influence in Germany. 'Il n'y a pas de fumée sans feu', wrote Budberg, although Schleinitz had not confirmed that such a conversation had taken place, and suggesting rather, that perhaps some conversation had occurred between Napoleon III and the Prince

---

56. 20 May 1860, *Dagbøger,* vol. II, p. 173.
57. Gorchakov to Ungern-Sternberg, 12 (24) November 1860. Copy in Privatarkiv 5810 A.F. Krieger, J.9.C. R.A. Copenhagen, and in Udenrigs. Samlede Sager. Den Holst. Forf.

Regent, and the contents of which had been passed on by the latter to Prince Albert in Koblenz or to Lord Russell.[58] But although the French minister, Thouvenel, denied the rumours which were circulating in London and had reached Copenhagen, Gorchakov was interested in the matter and instructed his ambassadors in Berlin and Paris to report their views on the episode.[59]

Gorchakov personally thought it happened at times that ministers did not know what monarchs were saying, and he may have been right, since the facts of the history of France, Sweden and Russia provided plenty of evidence that monarchs not infrequently pursued their own policy without informing their ministers of their plans.[60]

When Kiselev, replying to Gorchakov's enquiry about the incident in Baden, advanced the suggestion that Napoleon had floated the idea 'comme ballon d'essai', Gorchakov used the episode to warn Copenhagen:

Vous savez ce que est en l'air, nous vous avons indiqué la voie, qui selon nous, est à suivre; – and added reproachfully – Qu'il me semble que Vous vous laissez trop arracher, une à une, les concessions auxquelles vous vous pretêz, ces concessions faite de cette façon, perdent de leur valeur,

and he warned the Danish government: 'moins marchandez', change your behaviour and concentrate on the target.[61] How reminiscent this was of Nesselrode's comment to Plessen in April 1851!

Wir haben Sie nicht fallen lassen wollen, mais à la fin l'Empereur se lassera, machen Sie uns nicht unmöglich Sie zu appuyiren.[62]

Gorchakov returned to the Baden episode in a talk with Plessen in January 1861, arguing that the Emperor of the French would be disposed to substitute the Elbe duchies in exchange for the Rhineland, and he asked Hall to take the matter seriously.[63]

For the time being Russia had not changed the fundamental lines of her policy towards Denmark, although her attitude to the Danish government had changed, for she now saw it as the main culprit in the conflict with Germany because of Denmark's unwillingness to make concessions over the two duchies, despite the fact that, in Gorchakov's opinion, the German side was right in demanding concessions from Denmark.

This is the context in which we should see the sending of Nicholas Nicolay[64] to Copenhagen to replace Ungern-Sternberg. He was the son of Paul Nicolay,

---

58. On this subject see Dep. Rus. nos. 41 and 43, 4 December (22 November) and 10 December (28 November) 1860.
59. 30 November. (O.S).
60. Dep. Rus. no. 44, 22 (10) December.
61. *Ibid.*
62. Plessen to Reedtz, 29 April 1851, in Neergaard, vol. I. p. 541.
63. Dep. Rus. no. 4, 16 (4) Januar 1861.
64. N.P. Nicolay was ambassador in Switzerland from 1858 to 1860.

Russian ambassador from 1816 to 1847, and had spent his childhood in the Danish capital and had been to school there. Moreover, in 1848-49 he had been sent on a mission to Denmark and was personally known to the King.

Il est certain, que le B-on Nicolay arrivera avec les meilleurs dispositions. Il a une femme charmante et distinguée. La societé gagnera qu'au changement,

was how Plessen informed Vedel of the new appointment.[65]

The fact that there had not yet been any fundamental change in Russia's policy towards Denmark is shown by the secret instructions with which the new ambassador was furnished. This document refers to previous documents on the subject prepared and sent to the embassy in Copenhagen and says that the principle of Russian policy was to maintain the integrity of Denmark as sanctioned in a European act – the Treaty of London of 8 May 1852. This act had settled the question of the succession to the throne in the male line. Austria and Prussia had recognised it and German states had acceded to it, but it lacked the formal accession of Germany as a federal body. Denmark should aim to secure recognition of the document by the German Confederation.

Gorchakov argued that the reason for the failure to settle the question of Holstein, which was part of the German Confederation, was the nationality issue and the Schleswig question. Beside this, he instructed the new ambassador to pay attention to the question of Scandinavianism, which had manifested itself for many years, particularly in activities by students in the three Scandinavian Kingdoms, but which also had supporters among the higher social classes and in the administration. Although the significance of the movement in Denmark had diminished at present, he should not lose sight of the problem. Relations with Denmark, in Gorchakov's judgement, were 'd'une matière parfaitement amical', and he instructed the new ambassador to continue them, 'et Vous suivez soin de les maintenir sur le même pied'.

The Danish cabinet, we read in the instructions, remembered the services Russia had performed for Denmark at critical moments, and Alexander II appreciated the position Denmark had taken in the recent (Crimean) War. Finally, the document pointed out that the members of the royal family of Prince Christian of Glücksburg had especial reason to accord the Russian ambassador respect, for the role which Russia had played in securing the Treaty of London.[66]

This document is really only a list of what, in Gorchakov's opinion, were the most important points and a summary of what had been said many times previously by the St. Petersburg cabinet. Perhaps the most essential point was the emphasis on the view that, at the root of the conflict between Denmark and Holstein, lay the nationality issue, and that there was a close link between the question of Holstein and that of Schleswig.

---

65. Letter of 19 (7) November. Vedels papirer, 6498, pk. 12. R.A. Copenhagen.
66. Rus. Films. 9 November (O.S.) 1860.

What was the Danish government's attitude to Gorchakov's instructions? In official talks with the newly appointed Russian ambassador, Hall assured him that his government valued the friendly attitude of the St. Petersburg cabinet very highly, and the disinterested help which that cabinet had frequently rendered Denmark in times of difficulty.[67] In correspondence with Plessen Vedel, Hall's closest colleague and the central figure in the Ministry of Foreign Affairs, said that Hall paid great attention to the Russian cabinet's opinion, but he put forward a series of reservations concerning Gorchakov, and in particular his critical comments on Denmark's policy in Schleswig. He also questioned his opinions about Prussia's good will in the conflict with Denmark, citing, among others, Bülow's views. He feared, moreover, that the moves Gorchakov recommended would actually harm the integrity of Denmark, which Russia so sincerely supported. He also considered that Gorchakov's reservations about Denmark's policy towards Schleswig were groundless. He believed, however, that the Russian government had no intention of departing from its traditional policy of constancy towards Denmark. As for Denmark, the government was not inclined to change its alliances and go in for a peripatetic policy which had no future.[68] Hall was inclined to act in accordance with the Russian cabinet's thinking and go as far as Bülow recommended. Denmark was expecting results from Great Britain's initiative, but she would be more confident if Gorchakov became involved and took the matter in hand. With the support of Russia, Britain and France (of which Vedel had no doubt), an agreement with Germany might be possible. He was convinced that in case of need, Denmark could count on the support of the great powers, and above all Russia.[69]

National liberal circles, on the other hand, were showing an increasing dislike of Russia and her political moves. The personification of this policy for them was the figure of Ungern-Sternberg. Their dislike of the ambassador was expressed when news of his recall reached Copenhagen, of which the government was informed through Plessen. This news was published by *Fædrelandet*,[70] which added that no Dane would express regret on this account. The hostile tone of the article which appeared in *Dagbladet* in connection with the recall of the ambassador forced the Danish government to react. Hall apologised, particularly for the article in *Dagbladet,* and regretted that he had no influence over what was published in the paper. But he expressed his feelings by informing the chief editor how far from the truth the article was, in the government's opinion.

Ungern-Sternberg's departure from Copenhagen and the appointment of Nicolay were the subject of an exchange of correspondence between Plessen, on the one

---

67. Nicolay's dispatch no. 75 of 9 (21) December 1860, vol. 52.
68. In the course of 1860 Plessen warned Vedel that the outbreak of war should be avoided at any price. A successful war for Denmark could give her nothing more than she had, and an unsuccessful one would mean the loss of Holstein and Schleswig. See V. Sjøqvist, *Peter Vedel,* vol. I, 1823-64 (Aarhus, 1957), p. 118. Vedel to Plessen, 5 October 1860.
69. Privatarkiv Vedel, pk. 12, and Afskrift af et privatbrev fra Plessen til Vedel, 16 (4) October 1860, Udenrigsm. Samlede Sager, Den Holst. Forfatnings. vol. 214, R.A. Copenhagen.
70. No. 274, 22 November 1860, p. 1131.

hand, and Vedel and Hall on the other. On 19 (7) November Plessen informed Vedel of the appointment of the new Russian ambassador to Copenhagen, Nicholas Nicolay, on the basis of information received from Gorchakov.[71] On 7 December, in a letter to Hall, Plessen wrote about the articles which had appeared in *Fædrelandet* and *Dagbladet* on the occasion of Ungern-Sternberg's departure, adding that the ambassador felt offended by the way these papers had treated him. For his part, he indicated that Gorchakov had interested himself in the affair, objecting that this was not the way to treat the representative of a government which had done so much for Denmark. Such matters, Plessen observed, did not remain merely an unpleasant impression ('l'impression fâcheuse'), and he advised doing something to erase it. Plessen reminded Hall that Ungern-Sternberg had been in Copenhagen since 1846 and had always been loyal to Denmark when she was going through difficult moments. To remove the bad impression he suggested that the King should present him with the diamond insignia of the Danebrog Cross, which Meyendorff and Brunnow had revieved previously. This suggestion was accepted.

The minister thanked Ungern-Sternberg for the good relations he personally had enjoyed with him and for the way in which he had treated Danish affairs during his long period as ambassador in Copenhagen, since the beginning of the reign of Frederick VII. He congratulated him on his appointment as ambassador in Frankfurt, and at the same time asked him to maintain his impartiality and good will in Danish affairs at his new post. At a specially arranged farewell dinner the King thanked the ambassador for his long years of service in Copenhagen and conferred on him 'les insignes en diaments' of the Cross of Danebrog. This was on 9 (21) December, after the newly appointed ambassador Nicholas Nicolay had arrived in Copenhagen on 5 (17) December.

On 26 December, when the incident had been smoothed over, Vedel reported to Plessen on the farewell arranged by the King.

Le Roi vient de conférer à Mr. de Sternberg la plague de la grande Croix en diamants. Cette faveur qu'il ne partage qu'avec Mr. de Meyendorff et de Brunnow, et un petit article inséré dans le Dagblad le jour même de son audience de congé ont parfaitement effacé chez Mr. de Sternberg la mauvaise impression que le manque de convenance du Fædrelandet avait produite. La veuille du départ du B-on, le Ministre a fait un grand diner où étaient présents les princes (5), les grandes dignitaires des cours, les ministres et le corps diplomatique, et le Mr. de Sternberg occupait la place d'honneur à la droite du Prince Ferdinand, ainsi je ne doute pas que Mr. de Sternberg ne quitte Copenhague dans les meilleures dispositions.[72]

Prompted by Hall, *Dagbladet*[73] published an extensive article on the ambassador's departure and the appointment of Nicolay. This article adopted a friendly tone towards the departing ambassador, mentioning the services he had performed for Denmark, particularly during the long years of conflict with the

---

71. Vedel, Papirer, 6498, pk. 12, R.A. Copenhagen.
72. Ibid. 26 December 1860. The Danebrog Cross (First Class) was confered on Ungern-Sternberg on 6 October 1848. *Kongelig Hof- og Staatskalender for aaret 1866,* p. 7.
73. *Dagbladet,* Revue, no. I, 2 January 1861.

duchies. The article included a description of the ceremonies accompanying the King's conferment of one of the country's highest orders on Ungern-Sternberg as a token of respect. The last part of the article reported that the new ambassador, Nicolay, had presented his credentials and recalled that he had been educated in Copenhagen when his father[74] was ambassador to Denmark,

Il a ainsi le double avantage – de posséder la langue du pays et d'être initié dans nos rapports, de sorte que sa nomination à son poste éminent a été considerée ici comme un signe de la bienveillance avec laquelle le cabinet de S. Pétersbourg continue d'embrasser les intérêts du Danemark.

IV

The year 1861 was pregnant with events for Russia. The emancipation statute entered its decisive stage, and in the Kingdom of Poland the situation was inflamed by the growing national liberation movement in the towns and the peasants' resistance to feudalism in the country.[75] In the international arena new difficulties emerged. There was a chill in Russo-French relations, among other things on account of the Polish cause, which was so popular in Paris. Gorchakov continued to be worried by rumours about France's plans and he did not rule out the possibility that Napoleon III sought to reward Prussia at the expense of the Elbe duchies as the price of obtaining the Rhineland.[76]

He regretted that Russell's action[77] designed to settle the Danish-German conflict had not met with a positive response in Berlin, and that Prussia had dismissed the Danish proposals for Holstein as unsatisfactory and would not agree with Denmark's view that Germany had no say in the problem of Schleswig. He was disturbed by the aggressive tone of the Prussian press, and even more so by the aggressive character of the speech from the throne by Wilhelm I on 14 January 1861, especially its emphasis on Holstein.

The news coming from Copenhagen was not good either. While the newly appointed ambassador had been amicably received, had established contact with Hall and Vedel, and had quickly got the feel of the atmosphere in the Danish capital, he had doubts, because of lack of unity about tactics within the government itself, whether it would succeed in working out a line of action on the Holstein question. These doubts were also connected with the fact that Hall, whilst personally inclined to seek a compromise, doubted whether Prussia, because of its obcession with the principle of nationality and its ambitious and rapacious ideas,

---

74. P.A. Nicolay was ambassador in Copenhagen from 1816 to 1847.
75. Halicz, *Sprawa chlopska w Królestwie Polskim w dobie powstania styczniowego*, (Warsaw, 1955).
76. On 19 March Bille telegraphed from London: '... for the House of Lords yesterday Ellenborough, questioned by Wodehouse about the differences between Denmark and Germany, said that the invasion of Holstein by Prussia would bring a French army on the Rhine ...'. Dep. Rus. no. 15, 27 (15) February and no. 22, 11 April (30 March) 1861.
77. On Russell's attitude towards the Schleswig-Holstein problem see Sandiford, pp. 48-52.

would be satisfied with the concessions the Danish government could offer. This conviction, the ambassador reported, was held not only by the politicians there, but also by the military. The King had reflected it in a speech to a military delegation which came to express its best wishes to him for the New Year.[78]

Nicolay did not support the government's military preparations, but he was aware that they were intended not to provoke conflict but to avoid it and to protect the government against charges of weakness, rather than to frighten Germany.[79] The government, consisting of 'modérés et conciliants', had good intentions but vacillated and, in the ambassador's opinion, would have had much greater freedom of action if it had been certain of the King's support. Ministers were intimidated by the memory of the Bluhme government, which had ended amid condemnation ('condamnation'); the government was hampered by the person of the King, a weak character who disliked the government and, it seemed to Nicolay, would gladly have got rid of it. This government 'de juste milieu' was the only one that was acceptable in the circumstances. For that reason it was in the interests of powers which wanted peace and an impartial solution that there should be no precipitate action or provocation from the German Confederation which would make it impossible for Hall to continue with what the ambassador called 'his good intentions'.

Nicolay was not sparing in his criticisms of the government's policy on 'le noeud gordien Holsteinois – c'est l'affaire du budget'. Nicolay thought it should reach an agreement with the Ritterschaft of Holstein, giving it adequate guarantees. The Ritterschaft was aware of the threat to its privileges posed by the spread of the influence of democratic elements, and the government should take advantage of this and come to an agreement with the Conservative party in Holstein.

Nicolay was very critical of the government's policy in Schleswig. He expressed the opinion that the recently published ordinance on education and religion would do no good if the local authorities responsible for implementing it made it a pretext for chicanery ('un prétexte de chicanes'). The concessions to the German population in Schleswig he called 'assez insignificantes', among other things because there was no mention of the right of assembly (although he understood that meetings of a political nature would naturally arouse suspicions among the Danes). Nor did he support the government's intention to abolish the 'Nationalverein' society in Kiel, which was accused of Schleswig-Holsteinism, while simultaneously creating a Dannewirke society in Schleswig, the members of which supported a constitutional union between Schleswig and Denmark (Blixen, O. Lehman, E. Hagen). Nicolay's reports were not lacking in criticism of the 'Ultradanois', who had great influence on public opinion and opposed the government's conciliatory moves. He also saw that even a stronger and more independent government than the existing one would have difficulty in controlling the situation.

78. Reports nos. 76 and 77 of 16 (28) December 1860 and 23 December (4 January) 1861. Vol. 52.
79. *Ibid.* no. 4 of 16 (28) January 1861. Vol. 52.

Nicolay assured Hall that nothing would please the Russian government more than if he reached an agreement and was finally successful in resolving the question of the duchies.[80] Referring to Gorchakov's dispatch of 15 January, Nicolay indicated what an unfortunate impression the hostile articles which had appeared in the Danish papers had made in St. Petersburg. The government in St. Petersburg wished the Danish government to keep to the path of agreement and not to precipitate events. Denmark, in Nicolay's opinion, attached too much significance to the advantages she might gain through the use of a blockade. Neutral countries, Nicolay warned, would not, in his opinion, allow Denmark to act freely, nor would they allow their trade to suffer because of a blockade of the northern ports.

On the basis of Hall's assurances that the government did not want to provoke war – 'jamais la lutte' – and had only taken military steps when its enemies had made them unavoidable, and because of the opinions expressed by H.I.A. Raasløff, who was close to him because of his moderate views, was a supporter of Helstat and had great understanding for the German demands, Nicolay expected that when the Estates of Holstein were convened by the King they would accept the budget proposals presented by the government.[81]

In fact Nicolay was right when he stressed that the future of relations between Holstein and Copenhagen depended on the settlement of the budget question. The dispute about the budget had been going on for many months and now came to a head. Despite the resolution passed by the Federal Diet on 8 March 1860 that no law was valid on the territory of Holstein and Lauenburg if it was adopted without the agreement of the Estates of the two duchies, Denmark announced a budget for Holstein for the year from 1 April 1860 – 31 March 1861 on 3 July 1860. The reaction to this was a demand from Oldenburg for Federal Execution in Holstein, and the threat of this action caused the Copenhagen government partially to retreat from its previous position, accepting on 10 September 1860 that this was not the budget but only a draft budget. In spite of this, on 7 February 1861 the Federal Diet declared invalid both the budget and Denmark's September statement referring to the decree of 25 September 1859. The Prussian King's speech in the Landtag on 14 January 1861 merely increased the threat of action. Only the ambassadors of Holland and Denmark protested against the federal resolution of 7 February 1861.

All this increased nationalist tendencies on both sides. If federal forces crossed the Eider, war seemed inevitable.[82] There was no lack of readiness on both sides for a violent solution of the dispute. This state of affairs disturbed the neutral states. Britain, France, Russia and Sweden sent a joint demand to Denmark on 1 March 1861 calling for acceptance of the Federal Diet resolution of 8 March 1860 concerning Holstein, which stated that the Holstein question was an internal affair of the Confederation and for this reason the neutral powers could not intervene in the matter.

80. No. 10, 28 January (9 February) 1861.
81. Dispatch (Secrète) of 18 February (2 March) and no. 16 (Très réservée) of 6 March (22 February) 1861.
82. Gosch, *Denmark and Germany* ..., p. 239.

Faced with this situation the St. Petersburg cabinet adopted the following tactics. Above all, it decided to put pressure on the Danish government, and on every occasion urged Denmark to settle the dispute with Germany peacefully. It warned Denmark of the danger to European peace if the dispute were not ended.[83] 'Vous connaissez ma manière de voir. Si je puis être utile au Roi, Vous savez que Je désire de l'être', were the words of Alexander II in a conversation with Plessen at the New Year reception.[84] At the same time Gorchakov decided to use *Le Nord* to reply to the aggressive tone of the speech from the throne by Wilhelm I. *Le Nord* published an article[85] which Bismarck attributed to Budberg, who was then Russian ambassador in Paris, but behind which he saw the hand of Gorchakov. He assumed the article was inspired by the Russian minister and even detected Gorchakov's style in it.[86]

The author of the article sharply criticised the growth of nationalistic feeling in Germany in connection with the Schleswig-Holstein question, and especially the bellicose tone adopted by Wilhelm I. This stemmed, we read, from the traditions of the house of Brandenburg and the German medieval orders. Europe was disturbed at this state of affairs in Germany. The anxiety was evident in Denmark, which was mobilising its army and navy for fear of the measures that might be taken by the Prussian government. In conclusion the author expressed the hope that Wilhelm I would take the road of peace, which would be welcomed in Europe.

The tone of this article was alarmist. The author warned Prussia against the consequences of following a wrong and dangerous course of action. Russia had the least interest of all in such a development. Gorchakov did not conceal this and said it in conversation with Plessen.

La politique de la Russie est subordinée au grand intérêt, que la Russie a par suite de la situation intérieure, à se tenir le plus longtemps possible, en dehors des complications extérieures.

Si l'Allemagne donne à la guerre, qu'elle entreprend contre nous, ce caractère, la Russie voudra-t-elle intervenir matériellement, dans un moment, où la question de Pologne, doit nécessairement la préoccuper et faire désirer à la Russie de rester dans de bons rapports avec la Prusse? – Plessen asked.[87]

Both Gorchakov and Alexander II thought anxiously about the possibility of Federal Execution as a result of failure by Copenhagen and the Estates of Holstein to agree on a budget for Holstein,[88] and considered that the German demands must

---

83. Bismarck's reports of 27 and 28 January 1861. Raschdau ..., *Bismarck,* vol II, pp. 10, 17-19.
84. Dep. Rus. no. 3, 14 (2) January 1861.
85. *Le Nord.* no. 18, 1861.
86. In a letter to Schleinitz from St. Petersburg on 13 March 1861 Bismarck wrote:
    ... erlaube ich mir in der Anlage nr. 28 des Nord vorzulegen, deren zweiter Leitartikel ungeachtet seines alten Datums um deshalb von Interesse ist, weil ich sichere Anzeichen habe, das er von hier aus entweder direct oder durch Budberg's Vermittelung suppeditirt worden ist.
    Man würde sich irren, wenn man den Fürsten Gortschakow für alles verantwortlich machen wollte, was in Nord steht; aber im Grossen und Ganzen hängt das Blatt von ihm ab, und viele, an ihrem Styl leicht kenntliche Artikel, werden unter seiner persönlichen Leitung und Korrectur redigirt.
    Bismarcks Briefwechsel mit Minister Freiherrn von Schleinitz, 1858-1861, (Berlin, 1905), p. 151.
87. Dep. Rus. no. 22, 1 April (20 March) 1861.
88. Bismarck, 27 and 28 January 1861, vol. II, pp. 10 and 17-19.

be satisfied, because Federal Execution could bring enormous complications,[89] both from the point of view of general European interests and of the Danish monarchy. If war broke out in the north the effects would be 'la plus funeste pour l'avenir de la Monarchie Danoise'.

It emerged from a talk which Gorchakov had with Plessen in the presence of Osten-Sacken that Russia, like Britain and France, would not oppose Federal Execution, and Russia did not have the right to intervene in the Holstein question, whereas the German Confederation did. As far as Schleswig was concerned, in the St. Peterburg cabinet's opinion (this position was shared by the British government – E.H.) the measures taken by the Danish government had been ineffective and tended rather to support the charge that this administration was a burden on the German population. To Plessen's reply that it was very hard to take steps which Germany would receive positively Gorchakov had to answer; 'pour les grandes intérêts qui sont en jeu, nous faisions trop peu et mesurions nos [the Danish] concessions avec trop de parcimonie'.

Gorchakov considered[90] that in principle Germany did not have the right to interfere in the affairs of Schleswig, but to go and see whether the Danish promises had been fulfilled. He was inclined to regard the expression used by Russell, that 'His Danish Majesty is bound by honour',[91] as a minor nuance, and repeated his readiness to join with France and Britain to persuade Denmark to make concessions to the German population of Schleswig in language matters.[92] He admitted that the tone of Prussia's reply to Russell was 'un peu acerbe'.

He had no intention of defending Berlin, and criticised it for rejecting the British proposals, but he thought that the Danes were making trouble for Prussia by their behaviour, and if there was a possible way out with a certain degree of honour he (Gorchakov) was sure Prussia would take it with alacrity.[93] If Denmark came to an agreement with Prussia, Holstein would be more flexible because it did not itself want federal action.[94] The convening of the Estates, Gorchakov thought, was the one measure which could prevent federal action, and the Berlin cabinet would accept this move eagerly to free itself from further involvement.[95]

Budberg suggested that Gorchakov should propose that the great powers make a joint approch to Copenhagen to persuade the Danish government to convene the Estates of Holstein.[96] But this was no longer necessary as a telegram arrived from Copenhagen to say that Hall had proposed the convening of the Estates of Holstein to the King. Gorchakov believed Federal Execution had been postponed.

---

89. Bismarck, 26 February and 21 March 1861, vol. II, pp. 25, 41 ff.
90. Dep. Rus. no. 10, 2 February (21 January) 1861.
91. Dispatch of 8 October 1860 to Lowther. Dep. Rus. no. 15, 27 (15) February 1861.
92. Bismarck, 21 and 26 March, vol. II, pp. 41 ff. and 50.
93. Dep. Rus. no. 15.
94. Dep. Rus. no. 13, 11 February (30 January) 1861.
95. Dep. Rus. no. 10, 2 February (21 January) 1861.
96. Dep. no. 13.

As Plessen reported, in the eyes of the St. Petersburg cabinet this was a wise and provident step, dictated by circumstances and moving in the direction which the Russian government, together with the other major powers, had been intending to recommend. Seeing how highly Gorchakov valued Budberg's opinion, Plessen advised Hall that in all cases when he sought the help of the Russian government Budberg should be informed through the Danish ambassador in Berlin, as Budberg's voice would be very important in St. Petersburg.[97]

Without any prompting from Thun, Gorchakov raised the subject of Danish-German relations with him and said that his government was not interested 'à encourager le Cabinet de Copenhagen dans la fausse route qu'il suit depuis des années'. On the contrary, he wanted to avoid anything that would lead to disagreement between states. In Thun's judgement Gorchakov was concerned to show how extensive Russian influence was in Copenhagen.

Mr. de Hall est au fond bien disposé – said Gorchakov – il cherche des moyens de s'entendre, malheureusement il s'attache à des détails au lieu d'envisager la question en grand, et de proposer des remèdes efficaces.
Il faut absolument trouver un moyen d'arranger cette affaire. Je m'occuperai ces jours-ci à faire des propositions à l'Angleterre et à la France pour engager le Danemarc à des concessions raisonables et suffisantes. Vous et la Prusse vous êtes trop directement interésses comme membres de la Confédération Germanique pour pouvoir vous joindre à une pareille démarche, Gorchakov said to Thun.[98]

Gorchakov regarded the submission of the budget question for discussion by the Estates of Holstein as a concession to the Estates, and assured Bismarck of this.[99] But he doubted whether the steps taken by the Danish government were sufficient, and he reproached Plessen.

'À notre regret Vous parraissez vaciller dans les bons projets que nous aimions à Vous, prêtez, et, comme il est urgent, cette fois-ci, que Vous faissiez une véritable concession,'..
'Prêtez la main au Cabinet de Berlin pour sortir d'une situation, qui pèse sur lui comme sur vous, et ce Cabinet en profitera, j'en suis sûr,...'.[100]

Gorchakov justified his policy towards Denmark by reference to Russia's internal situation and the conclusions the Russian government had drawn from past experience. In the past, said Gorchakov, Russia had involved herself in matters which were not strictly Russian, like the intervention in Hungary, and it had brought her too little benefit. For that reason she had adopted a policy of avoiding direct involvement with Denmark, although, as Plessen described it, she had taken a position 'si bienviellante et si utile' in order not to expose herself to the hatred of the German liberal party, which had demonstrated its anti-Russian position expecially during the Crimean War. Besides, as Plessen recalled, Gorchakov had argued no

---

97. Dep. no. 13.
98. H.H.S.A. P.A.X., Kart. 50, Rus. no. 9 C. 12 February (31 January) 1861.
99. Bismarck, 26 February 1861, vol. II, p. 25.
100. Dep. Rus. no. 15, 27 (15) February 1861.

differently the day after he assumed his post as minister when he said that he would not be able to accompany Denmark on the path she was taking. Gorchakov was weary of Denmark and frequently repeated 'on tenait trop peu des avis et conseils que la Russie dans l'intention la plus amicale nous [Denmark – E.H.] fait parvenir'.[101]

Gorchakov displayed great caution, and in talks with Plessen frequently used expressions like 'Laissez moi examiner toutes les pièces, que je viens recevoir de différentes côtés', or 'D'après mon impression personnelle', as if he wanted to say that he was speaking as a private person rather than Russia's Minister of Foreign Affairs; or he answered in an indecisive way – for example, 'Votre déclaration, emise par le Commissaire du Roi, me semble renfermer les élémens d'un aplanissement'.[102]

Gorchakov did not mean to belittle the difficulties facing Denmark, but he argued that she must bear in mind the fact that the German element in the duchies enjoyed the sympathy of the whole of Germany and the only real road to a settlement was through negotiation and the offer of concessions by Denmark. He continually accused the Copenhagen government of not having a precise plan of action and of lacking clarity and flexibility in many matters, including the question of setting the budget.[103] He was against additional guarantees for Denmark over Schleswig, as they would weaken the force of the Treaty of London.[104] Nor was Gorchakov inclined to exert pressure on Prussia, as Denmark asked him to.[105]

When Federal Execution was hanging by a thread, however, he sent a dispatch to Berlin complaining that the Berlin cabinet had condemned the Danish proposals before the Estates of Holstein had begun to discuss them. Gorchakov supported the proposals from Russell, who appealed to Schleinitz to postpone the Execution. But if it came to it, in Plessen's opinion, Russia – owing to her wish to remain on good terms with Prussia and to her troubles connected with the Polish question – would follow a wait-and-see policy, and the ambassador doubted if she would intervene militarily.[106]

Unable to compel the Danish government to act in the spirit of Russian recommendations, Gorchakov tried to employ other methods, which might lead to the toppling of the government and its replacement by a more compliant one. But for this the agreement of the other powers was needed. First he had to sound out their opinion. For this purpose, Thun reported,[107] Gorchakov organised, as if by chance, a meeting at his house at which the French and British ambassadors and

---

101. On weariness with the Danish question the Prussian diplomat Reuss reported from Paris on 30 May 1861: 'Le Ministre (Thouvenel) ne m'a pas dissimulé qu'il était tant soit peu ennuyé de cette affaire en général'. Schlozer, p. 213.
102. Plessen, no. 27, 13 (1) April 1861.
103. Plessen, no. 25, 6 April (25 March) 1861.
104. A.F. Krieger, 20 May 1861, *Dagbøger*, vol. II, pp. 210-1.
105. Plessen, 6 April (25 March).
106. Plessen no. 25, 6 April (25 March). On Russell's action see Sandiford, p. 51.
107. P.A.X. Kart. 50, no. 16 G. report of 27 (15) March 1861.

Bismarck were present (Thun emphasises that it was no accident that he was not invited, as Gorchakov wanted to show that he was entrusting the matter to Bismarck, i.e. to Prussia) and at this meeting he broached the subject of Holstein. Gorchakov initially set out what Bismarck considered 'une idée parfaitement juste', that in order to put an end to this interminable Danish question the European powers should strive to make the Danish government meet the fair and just demands of the German population in Schleswig. But instead of addressing themselves to the Danish government, Gorchakov proposed writing to Danish ministers who were sympathetical to this kind of demand and helping them to make changes in the government which would get rid of their colleagues who, so to say, took a different position.

Napier saw drawbacks in this procedure and thought that such a letter had to be sent to the Danish government; the government itself could overcome the opposition of certain ministers. Bismarck, in his report to Berlin,[108] said that Napier was against Gorchakov's proposals because it would mean interference in the internal affairs of Denmark. In Napier's opinion such a letter could only be addressed to Hall, who was both Chairman of the Council of Ministers and Minister of Foreign Affairs. Bismarck saw Gorchakov's move as designed to isolate Britain, but the French minister was afraid lest internal intervention led to the government in Copenhagen being taken over by the 'war party'. Gorchakov's proposal, or rather suggestion, lapsed, but it was no accident that it was put forward and for that reason it deserves attention.

The session of the Estates of Holstein from 6 March to 11 April 1861 did not yield the expected results. The Danish government had decided to present the budget to the Estates. Because the Royal Commissioner in Itzehoe, Raasløf[109] (who was at the same time Minister for Holstein Affairs), was not brought into the negotiations which Hall conducted with the great powers, and because the Commissioner's statement did not conform to the declaration Hall had made to the diplomats, there was an atmosphere of mistrust in Itzehoe concerning the real intentions of the Danish government. The Estates rejected the government plan for the establishment of a new state organisation based on the 1855 constitution. The Estates' proposal that the whole Danish budget should be presented to them for confirmation had no chance of success.

---

108. 21 March 1861, Raschdau, *Bismarck ...,* vol. II, p. 42.
109. La conduite tenue par Mr. Raasløff [Harald – E.H.] comme commissaire du Roi à Itzehoe pourrait facilement compromettre le Gouv. Au lieu de suivre les instructions qui lui étaient parvenues d'ici, il a donné des réponses évasives, il a procédé à un ajournement des séances sans aucun motif, enfin il a ouvert la perspective au concessions ultérieures ...
   Hall to the King's Minister in Stockholm, W. Scheel-Plessen, Confidentielle, no. 10, 3 April 1861, Sverige I, Ordrer I, 1861-68. R.A. Copenhagen, H.H.S.A. 21 P.A. XXIV, Dänemark, Hall to Bille-Brahe, 3 April; 1861, Berichte-Weisungen, 1860-61. Cf. also Emil Erbeling, 'Histoire de l'idée d'un partage du Slesvig', in *Manuel historique de la question du Slesvig* (Copenhagen, 1906), pp. 142-3; Møller, *Helstatens Fald,* vol. I, pp. 392 ff.

Here then – wrote Gosch – we have an authentic interpretation of 'autonomy and equality of rights'. Denmark-proper, with 1,600,551 inhabitants, Slesvig with 409,907, Holstein with 544,419, and Lauenburg with 50,147 inhabitants, were, from now on, to contribute to the common expenses of the state in ratio to their population, but to have an equal share in the common legislation and the fixing of the budget.

The Holsteiners thought it incompatible with 'equality of rights' that they were represented in the Council-General of 1855 only in proportion to their numbers and their contributions to the common exchequer, and could therefore only dispose of between one-fourth and one-fifth of the votes of the Assembly. But they did not think it incompatible with 'equality of rights' that Denmark-proper should pay three-fifths of the common expenses, but only possess one-fourth of the legislative power on their application.[110]

A different position was taken by Nicolay, who thought that Hall had made a mistake by not giving the Estates of Holstein the right to discuss problems with a decisive vote and had not treated them like the Rigsraad.[111] The unfortunate course of the debate in the Estates in Holstein and the resignation of Raasløf,[112] with whom Nicolay maintained close relations and whom the ambassador described as 'tout en restant fidèle à son excellent esprit de modération et d'équité', were received badly by the Russian cabinet.[113] But despite that, Nicolay did not consider the situation hopeless and did not attribute great significance to the government's military preparations. He expressed the view that there was nothing to say that war would break out. He wrote in a balanced and responsible way about what was happening in Denmark and depicted the situation without prejudice and with a measure of objectivity. He even managed a detached view of the problem of Scandinavianism, about which Russia was excessively sensitive.[114]

V.

Alarmed by the situation which had arisen as a result of the impossibility of reaching agreement in Itzehoe, the Prime Minister and Minister of Foreign Affairs of Sweden-Norway, Manderström, sent a confidential dispatch to his ambassadors in London, Paris and St. Petersburg on 29 March 1861, setting out his point of view on the Danish-German conflict and how it should be settled. There were three essential points in his plan:

---

110. Gosch, *Denmark and Germany since 1815,* pp. 229 and 263.
111. Report of 29 March (10 April) 1861.
112. Raasløf thought that northern Schleswig should be included in the monarchy and the southern part joined with Holstein in the German Confederation; the frontier should be on the Slie-Husum line. The part joined to Holstein would be independent but connected with Denmark. He opposed Danicisation and any language restrictions. Raasløf favoured Helstat and thought that, as a native of Holstein, he understood the problems of the Duchies best. Equal rights for both nationalities could also be achieved by giving them equal representation in the Rigsraadet or Folketing. *Dansk Biografisk Lexikon,* Vol. XIX, pp. 26-28.
113. Nicolay's reports nos. 23, 25, 26, 31 of 15 (27) March, 18 (30) March), 22 March (3 April), 29 March (10 April), and Particulière 14 (2) April. Bismarck's reports of 21 and 26 March, 1861, vol. II, pp. 41, 43, 50.
114. See reports (Particulière) of 23 February (7 March) and 2 (14) April.

1. Complete administrative separation of Holstein from the monarchy, with only the civil list, foreign affairs, the navy and the post and telegraph remaining in common. The budget could not be changed without the agreement of each part of the monarchy.
2. After the King fulfilled the obligations he had undertaken for the reorganisation of Schleswig and the granting of equal rights to the German and Danish nationalities, the great powers which were signatories to the 1852 Treaty of London were to give assurances that there would be no foreign intervention in the question of Schleswig, nor any talk of the partition of Schleswig.
3. The plan envisaged the complete separation of Holstein from the Danish monarchy (Manderström referred to the example of Holland and the Grand Duchy of Luxemburg in 1839; Luxemburg, like Holstein, was part of the German Confederation) and its neutrality, was guaranteed by the great powers.[115]

Manderström's proposal was equivalent to implementation of the Eider programme, establishing the frontier of Scandinavia where it had been historically, on the Eider.[116]

These proposals met with little interest among the great powers. Russia and Britain were against the neutralisation of Holstein and the weakening of the armed force of Denmark by the exclusion of the Holstein-Lauenburg contingent, and in addition Russell thought that the chances of these proposals being accepted by Germany were slender. Rejecting the Swedish proposals on 19 April, he at the same time put forward his own, which contained the following points:

1. That the quota of the common budget of the Monarchy which affects the Duchies of Holstein and Lauenburg should be submitted to the Estates of Holstein and Lauenburg respectively for their assent, amendment or rejection.
2. That the laws which are to affect the Duchies of Holstein and Lauenburg shall be submitted to the Diets of Holstein and Lauenburg for their assent, amendment or rejection.
3. That the Duchy of Schleswig shall send Representatives to the Parliament of Denmark to vote in that Parliament the common expenses of the Monarchy and to vote on all laws affecting the Monarchy.
4. That the separate Diet of Schleswig shall continue to be elected and meet according to the present law; the functions of that Diet to consist in voting such sums as may be necessary for the maintenance of churches and schools and other local expenses, and in providing by equal laws for the welfare of the Danish, German and other inhabitants of Schleswig.
5. When those terms are assented to, and solemnly proclaimed by the King of

---

115. On the question of Luxemburg see Arthur Herchen, *Manuel d'histoire nationale* (Luxemburg, 1966), pp. 178-92. On the discussion of the subject of giving Holstein a status similar to Luxemburg see Thorsøe, vol. II, pp. 592-3; Møller, *Helstatens Fald*, vol. I, p. 239; Neergaard, vol. I, pp. 161-2. The first plan of this nature was put forward by A. Walewski in 1857.
116. Koht, pp. 70-1; Steefel, pp. 36-7: Hansen, pp. 166ff.

Denmark, the four powers, viz., France, Great Britain, Russia and Sweden, to guarantee to the Crown the possession of the Duchy of Schleswig.

6. That Commissioners should be appointed, one on the part of Denmark, one on the part of Germany, and one on the part of the four Powers, to define the boundary of the Duchy of Schleswig. The guarantee mentioned in a former Article to comprise the Duchy thus defined and bounded.

7. That the Treaty and Engagements of 1852, so far as they are not altered by these Articles should be inviolably maintained.[117]

In a dispatch on 8 May, Russell presented a more specific plan, in order to forestall criticism from the other cabinets.

This plan provided for the separation of Holstein from Denmark, as had been done in the case of Luxemburg in relation to Holland, the merger of Schleswig with Denmark, but the retention of the local Estates in Schleswig as a body guaranteeing the rights and protecting the interests of the Germans living there, 'the neglect of which has given rise to so much complaint'.[118]

Russell believed that Europe would see his proposals as proof that Britain really sought to reconcile the two parties and to save both Denmark and Holstein from the misfortunes of war. But the proposals were rejected by France, Russia and Sweden and the plan was finally abandoned by Russell towards the end of May.[119]

It is interesting to see what arguments Russia used to reject both the Manderström and the Russell plans. As far as the Manderström plan was concerned, Gorchakov's reply took the following line. First of all he expressed solidarity with the Stockholm cabinet and agreed with its opinion that because of the serious complications then threatening northern Europe they should not shirk their obligation to intervene for the purpose of maintaining peace. Experience showed that it was impossible to unite Holstein with the remaining parts of the Danish monarchy and establish a common constitution for them. That was why Manderström had proposed the establishment of a new order based on that existing between the Grand Duchy of Luxemburg and the Grand Duchy of Limberg and Holland, as both these duchies were part of the German Confederation. Without going into whether such a proposal would have a chance of acceptance in the German Diet, Gorchakov argued that there were fundamental differences between the relations between Holland and Luxemburg and those between Denmark and Holstein. There were no common interests between Holland and Luxemburg, but each of them had separate revenues and expenditures which were decided independently. Legislative power was exercised in Holland by the King and the States General, and in Luxemburg by the King as Grand Duke of Luxemburg, but the laws in the two countries

---

117. Russell to Cowley, 19 April 1861, *Correspondence ... Papers presented to Parliament*, LXXIV, (1863), no. 42. Steefel, p. 38; Sandiford, *Great Britain and the Schleswig-Holstein Question, 1848-64*, A study in diplomacy, politics and public opinion, (Toronto and Buffalo, 1975), p. 52.
118. Steefel, p. 38.
119. *Ibid.* pp. 38-9.

were independent of each other. In the Danish monarchy there was no such separation of interests, particularly financial interests. Neither the normal budget nor alterations to it could be implemented except by common agreement. Nor was Holstein an independent country like Luxemburg.

Gorchakov doubted whether the signatories to the Treaty of London would be willing to guarantee the neutrality of Holstein. He also saw procedural difficulties in connection with the fundamental laws in force in the German Confederation (art. 2, 3 and 7). Would not such a change be regarded by some of the federal states as an infringement of federal laws? What would happen to the spirit of the federal act, which it was the duty of the Federal Diet to protect (art. 17 of the Final Act of Vienna, 8 June 1820). In addition, article 7 required a unanimous decision by all thirty-seven states represented in the Frankfurt Diet. There were other difficulties too. If Holstein ceased to supply its contingent to the 10th corps of the federal army it would have to pay an annually determined sum of money instead. The Diet would have to change the federal law. Gorchakov doubted whether something of this kind would have any chance of approval at a time when the Confederation was so busily engaged in a general reform of its military statute.

There is no question but that the reservations which Gorchakov enumerated hid a far more fundamental objection. The legal reservation were only a diplomatic cover. The real point was that the result of the separation of Holstein from Denmark would probably have been the development of a German fleet in the Baltic, based at Kiel. Russia feared this, and her fears were shared by France.

As far as the proposals relating to Schleswig were concerned, the imperial government considered that it would not merely be difficult but in fact quite impossible to draw a demarcation line dividing the two nationalities living there, as the Danes and the Germans were intermixed, and in addition there would be new complications as a result of any extensive population movement, migration and change of place of residence.

Le Cabt. Imp. apprécié hautement la sollicitude que les complications Dano-Allemands inspirent tout particulièrement à Sa M. le Roi de Suède et de Norvége, mais il ne renonce pas à l'espoir qu'au moyen d'efforts communs on réussira à ajouter une nouvelle force aux garanties résultant du Traité du 8 Mai 1852.[120]

Commenting on Manderström's plan in the presence of Plessen, Gorchakov said that in relation to Holstein the plan was not new, and that the originator of the plan himself did not believe that Germany would agree to the imposition of such a solution. He also doubted whether it would satisfy the population of Schleswig. Personally he thought not. It would still have its eyes focused on Germany as before.[121] Plessen was of the same opinion, though he avoided expressing openly his attitude towards Gorchakov's view-point. The Danish ambassador took the posi-

---

120. Observations sur la Dépêche de M. le C te de Manderström du 29 Mars 1861, R.A. Copenhagen, Sverige, Depecher 1856-61.
121. Dep. Rus. Plessen, nos. 25 and 32, 6 April (25 March) and 30 (18) April 1861.

tion that in order to keep the German population in Schleswig calm, Denmark had to find a solution which satisfied the 500,000 Holsteiners and that there was no basis for settlement of the problem other than that provided by the 1852 agreements. Precisely the same view was expressed many times by Gorchakov.

A critical view of the Swedish proposals was expressed by Nicolay. He thought the question of the separation of Holstein had not been clearly formulated. Instead of the neutralisation of Holstein he would have liked to see the whole of Denmark neutralised, and he presumed that if the plan for the neutralisation of Holstein ran into serious difficulties in Germany, then the second plan could include guarantees which would overcome this German objection. Introduction of the principle of neutralisation of the whole of Denmark would become superfluous if the army were divided into two as the Swedish proposal envisaged. Finally, there was the crucial question of Schleswig, which was the centre of interest to both parties; the autonomy of Schleswig should be established in such a way that it could not be included in the programmes of either the Eider Danes or of Schleswig-Holsteinism. Nicolay also thought that the Eider Danes were behind the Swedish plan, and the Helstat or 'whole state' supporters against it.[122]

As for the St. Petersburg cabinet's attitude to Russell's proposal of 7 (19) April 1861, Gorchakov had two basic objections. The first concerned form, the second content. Concerning form, Gorchakov considered that without the participation of the two larger German states the necessary guarantee for Denmark could not be established. In a dispatch to Dashkov on 13 May 1861 we read:

En effet, en laissant ignorer à l'Autriche et à la Prusse les deliberations préalables, en les écartant en quelque sorte des combinaisons concernant le Slesvig, les quatre Puissances non seulement leur fourniraient de justes griefs, mais les mettraient dans l'impossibilité d'influer utilement sur les décisions de la Diète. En un mot, les quatre Puissances créeraient de propos délibéré un obstacle insurmontable à leur propre œuvre de pacification.[123]

In Gorchakov's opinion, as we can see from this passage, co-operation by the major German powers was a *conditio sine qua non*[124] of success.[125] His second objection related to the substance of the matter and concerned point 5 of Russell's proposals. To give Denmark a guarantee concerning Schleswig would, in Gorchakov's opinion, have undermined a clause contained in the Treaty of London. This gave a guarantee in respect of all the lands united under the sceptre of the King. A second, additional guarantee for one part of the monarchy only would weaken the force of the treaty, which spoke of a European guarantee of the integrity of the Danish monarchy. Besides this, Gorchakov thought there was a need for a stronger guarantee for the German element in Schleswig, stronger than that envisaged in the British proposal.[126]

---

122. Nicolay, nos. 39, 26 April (8 May) and (Particulière) 27 April (9 May).
123. R.A. Sverige, Dep. 1856-61.
124. A necessary condition.
125. Bismarck 15 May 1861, vol. II, pp. 95-7.
126. Plessen no. 25 (Secrète) 13 (1) May 1861; Krieger, vol II, 20 May 1861, pp. 210-11; 'Observations sur

L'idée d'une garantie pour la paisible possession du Duché de Schleswig n'est pas nouvelle. En 1715, 1720 et 1727 l'Angleterre, la Prusse, la France, la Suède garantirent successivement cette possession au Roi de Danemark, mais ce fut dans des circonstances tout différentes de celles d'aujourd'hui et par des motifs qui heureusement n'ont plus aucun raison d'être ... Aujourd'hui l'intégrité de la Monarchie Danoise se trouve placée sous la garantie du traité de Londres du 8 Mai 1852 ... Il a donc acquis le caractère d'une transaction Européenne. Le mot de *garantie* [Gorchakov's emphasis] ne s'y trouve pas, il est vrai, mais les Puissances qui ont pris part à cette transaction soit directement soit par leur accession, ont formellement reconnu "que le maintien de l'intégrité de la Monarchie Danoise, lié aux intérêts généraux de l'équilibre Européen, est d'une haute importance pour la conservation de la paix"...

En face d'une manifestation si solonnelle et si imposante, il semble que la combinaison proposés sub. n. 5 aurait des inconvénients plutôt qu'elle n'offrirait une utilité réelle et pratique. Il est douteux d'abord que le Danemark lui-même veuille accepter une garantie pour une seule partie de son territoire, et de la part de quelques-uns seulement des Puissances qui ont concouru au traité de Londres, tandis que le traité lui accorde une garantie morale bien autrement importante.

La combinaison proposée attesterait en quelque sorte le peu la confiance que la France, l'Angleterre, la Russie et la Suède placent elles-mêmes dans l'œuvre de 1852. Elle compromettrait donc aux yeux de l'Europe la haute valeur du traité de Londres sans parler des justes motifs de mécontentement qu'elle fournirait à l'Autriche et à la Prusse.

Quant a l'intérieur de la Monarchie Danoise, la garantie spéciale pour le Schleswig aurait pour effet de raviver les agitations des parties en lutte depuis tant d'années. Le partie appelé *Eyder-Danois* [Gorchakov's emphasis] la saluerait avec foie comme un acheminement vers l'incorporation du Duché dans le Royame proprement dit. Le partie Allemand y trouverait un nouvel défi à l'adresse de sa nationalité et n'insisterait qu'avec plus de force sur l'annexion à la Confédération Germanique. Il n'est nul besoin de faire mention du retentissement qui les tendances opposées auraient en Allemagne. Les Holsteinois enfin, ceux en moins qui ne demandent qu'à vivre sous la domination de leur Roi, ne manqueraient pas de considérer l'acceptation d'une garantie pour le Schleswig comme un moyen de plus de faciliter la séparation complète de l'un et l'autre Duché.[127]

In the Prince's opinion it was impossible for Germany to take any decision without being certain of the intentions of the Danish government in respect of the German population in Schleswig. In this connection he expressed the opinion that almost every government had its difficulties, including even Russia, adding, as if to counter Danish inertia, 'nous mêmes, nous avons la Pologne, et l'Empereur a fait des concessions qui ont de la valeur et qui doivent être éxécutées, selon Sa Volonté'.[128]

When Plessen observed that whilst Russia did indeed have difficulties in Poland, they were not as great as Denmark's because Poland was not so openly supported by other powers as the anti-Danish opposition was, Gorchakov inserted 'pas non plus officieusement dans ce moment' after the word 'ouvertement', which had a special meaning in the context of French policy towards the Polish question, adding that Denmark should take a fundamental step and offer major concessions to Schleswig, as she could not succeed in imposing a solution on Germany by force

---

Raschdau, *Bismarck ...*, la Dépêche de Ld. J. Russell à Ld. Napier du 7 (19) Avril 1861. St. Pétersbourg, le 23 Avril (5 Mai) 1861', in R.A. Copenhagen, Dep. Sverige, 1856-61.
127. 'Observations ...'.
128. Plessen, no. 36, 21 (9) May, S. Kieniewicz, *Powstanie styczniowe,* (Warsaw, 1972), pp. 130-37.

against its will. As for the principles of an agreement with Germany, Gorchakov recommended that Bülow should reach an understanding with influential members of the Frankfurt Diet, and he expressed the belief that it was their wish then to avoid complications. In reality he did not believe the negotiations would succeed, and was concerned that Bülow should conduct them 'académiquement', as he put it, in order to remove the danger that would arise from complications.[129]

The proposals put forward by Manderström and Russell, although not accepted, were not without significance. Some politicians, like Thouvenel, rumour had it, came to the conclusion that the question was more complicated than they thought. 'Plus je lis sur ce différent, moins j'y comprends', the French Minister of Foreign Affairs was supposed to have said. Palmerston was of a similar opinion.[130] Manderström thought that if a congress could be convened in London some solution might be reached, but because of the complicated situation in Europe he expressed doubts about the possibility of convening such a congress.[131]

Gorchakov became convinced that the Danish question could no longer be regarded as a problem which could be solved between Denmark and the Confederation alone, and to avoid extreme complications the great powers would have to intervene. Russia seemed disposed to recognise that the question was a European one, and Sweden-Norway and Britain agreed. But from the beginning there were essential differences between Russia and the remaining states about how the problem should be solved. These derived from their different interests, the internal situation in Russia, and their different approaches to the national question, although Russia appreciated this problem und urged the Danish government to make concessions particularly in the language field. The difference of Russia's position was connected with her negative attitude to the solution of problems in the spirit of liberalism, with her critical attitude to Eider-Danism and the Scandinavianism which was partly concealed behind it, and, finally, with the exceptionally cordial relations between the St. Petersburg and Berlin courts.

The discussion of the Swedish and British proposals gave Gorchakov the idea of a European conference, which he first shared with Brunnow, and to the convening of which all efforts were to be directed.[132] Gorchakov assured Bismarck that if the idea of convening a conference were implemented, the larger German states would not lack support from the Russian cabinet, and Bismarck himself was convinced that on the Danish question Gorchakov would do nothing that could harm Prussia.[133] But Prussia was not convinced by this, and Austria followed her in opposing the idea of a conference, believing that it would tend to favour Denmark's interests. Gorchakov decided not to try to persuade Prussia of the need to change

---

129. *Ibid.*
130. Sybel, vol. III, pp. 126-7; *Istoriya diplomatii,* vol. I, pp. 489-90.
131. W. Scheel-Plessen to Hall, no. 18, 4 June 1861, R.A. Sverige Dep. 1856-61.
132. Nos 36 and 39. 1. June (20 May) and 27 (15) June 1861. See Nolde, *Peterburgskaya Missiya ...,* pp. 268-9.
133. Bismarck, 31 May and 28 June 1861, Raschdau, *Bismarck ...,* vol. II, pp. 103, 108.

her position and said 'Nous ne pouvons pas faire la guerre parce que la Prusse ne veut pas la Conférence'.[134]

In view of the German states' attitude he was also against arranging a meeting of the four non-German states and omitting the German states. 'Telle entente resterait stérile', he said, adding 'Pensez Vous que Lord John Russell veuille faire la guerre à l'Allemagne pour lui imposer le résultat de cette entente éventuelle?' Gorchakov was, however, dissatisfied with the Berlin cabinet's position, accusing it of courting popularity, 'steeple-chase de popularité', but he did not fail immediately to accuse the Copenhagen government of not complying with the 1851-52 agreements and not fulfilling the obligations to which it was committed. If it did so there would not be continual interference from Germany in these affairs.[135]

What gave Gorchakov a feeling of greater confidence than before was the fact that he could cite the opinion of the British government, which, like Russia, was more and more frequently pointing out that Denmark had not fulfilled her obligations towards the population of Schleswig.[136] Osten-Sacken recommended that Denmark should listen to Britain's advice, for, after all, a great deal depended on Britain.[137] Gorchakov criticised Denmark for going around with her head in the clouds ('d'être nébuleux') and not listening to friendly powers. He stressed that the dispute with Germany could not be settled without paying some regard to her demands concerning Schleswig, and added that Denmark should not forget that in 1848 Schleswig was almost totally occupied by Germany and that the war had been over Schleswig.[138]

Schleinitz' plan for partition of Schleswig on a nationality basis was rejected by Quaade, and Copenhagen accepted the position of its ambassador in Berlin. The British suggestion of organising an international conference was rejected by the two larger German states. Thus the matter reached deadlock again.[139]

VI.

In the middle of 1861 there was a noticeable change in Danish policy. For the first time, as Nicolay reported on 4 (16) June, Hall openly presented his programme in the Folketing, a programme which the Russian ambassador called 'Eider-

---

134. Plessen, no. 40, 8 July (26 June) 1861.
135. Dep. Rus. 8 July (26 June) 1861.
136. *Ibid.*
137. Le B-on Sacken me disait, comme avis personnel à lui, que beaucoup si cela n'est tout, dépendrait de l'Angleterre, la puissance la mieux placée et au fond la seule capable pour mener l'idée de conférence à éxecution. Ecoutons l'Angleterre, suivons ses conseils, elle est plus sérieuse que toute autre puissance une fois qu'elle a mis la main à quelque chose ... Plessen to Vedel, 19 June 1861, pk. 12.
138. Plessen to Vedel, 8 July 1861; Schleel-Plessen to Hall, no. 19, 11 June 1861, Sverige Dep. 1856-61.
139. Steefel, pp. 39-40; W. Scheel-Plessen to Hall, 4 June 1861, R.A. Copenhagen, Sverige Dep. 1856-61.

Danois'.[140] It was not a question, he wrote, of immediate and complete exclusion of Holstein, nor of immediate inclusion of Schleswig, as the Dannewirke supporters would have liked, but of legalisation of the principle of partition and establishment of a frontier on the Eider, elimination of constitutional differences between the Kingdom and Schleswig and the introduction of the ultra-liberal Danish constitution. This pointed the way to complete fusion with Schleswig and indicated rejection of the Helstat idea and inauguration of the Eiderstat principle as the only basis for resisting Germany and ensuring the independence of the Danish monarchy. 'J'en doute, pour ma part', whether this programme can be implemented and whether the population of Schleswig is disposed to support this programme. With these words Nicolay ends his dispatch.

Professor Niels Thomsen[141] argued that there was no doubt that the Eider policy was victorious in May 1861 and that this was partly due to the petition in support of this policy organised by the national-liberal press, as a result of which Hall was presented with a petition bearing 71,143 signatures, which was 32.7% of those entitled to vote for parliament. In the petition Blixen, Hammerich, L.C. Larsen and Ploug called for the incorporation of Schleswig in the Danish monarchy in the strict meaning of the word. When he received this delegation Hall really accepted its point of view.[142]

On 19 September 1861, O. Lehman, the leader of the Eider party, became a member of the government: this was no mean success for his party. One of the national-liberal party's organs', *Dagbladet,* commented:

L'entrée de M. Orla Lehman dans le ministère s'explique, selon nous, uniquement comme une garantie offerte à la nation de la sincérité avec laquelle le gouvernement se décide dès à présent à réaliser la solution en question. Aussi fait-il convenir que de toutes nos notabilités publiques, personne n'est plus que lui capable de donner une pareille garantie.[143]

Lehman's entry into the government was not well received in either Germany or Russia, although there was no great surprise. Lehman was known there as a vehement politician, a radical and an ultra-Scandinavianist, the author of the well known saying: 'We will write upon their backs [the Schleswigers'] with bloody swords that they are Danes'.[144] Hall tried in vain to explain to Nicolay that the

---

140. Danish historians disagree about when Hall abandoned the 'Helstaat' aim; Nørregaard dates it in 1861, Møller in August 1862 and Neergaard in March 1863. Steefel and later English historians say 'the Hall ministry had been tending since 1858 towards the Eider-Danes policy', p. 56. In my opinion the ordinances of 6 November 1858 were really the first step in the direction of the Eider-Danes policy.
141. 'Opinion og udenrigspolitik – belyst ved et oprør fra midten 1861', *Nær og fjern. Samspillet mellem indre og ydre politik. Studier tilegnet professor, dr.phil. Sven Henningsen.* (Copenhagen, 1980), pp. 343-96.
142. H.I.A. Raasløf, *Den Halske Politik* (Copenhagen, 1864), pp. 26-8.
143. *Dagbladet,* Revue de la semaine, no. 37, 17 September 1861, no. 216. See also, in defence of Lehman, Revue ..., no. 38, 1 October 1861.
144. Møller, *Helstatens Fald,* vol. I, pp. 430-1; Neergaard, *Under Junigrundloven,* vol. II, pt. 1, pp. 492-4.

Lehman who had been famous for his radical views in 1848 had changed over the years and had become a more experienced politician, very well versed in the internal affairs of the country, and that his talent and influence would make him helpful to the government.[145] If the appointment of Lehman was a guarantee for the national-liberal party, a concession to the supporters of the Eider policy and a guarantee that there would not be foreign action in Schleswig, the appointment of D.G. Monrad to the post of Minister for Church Affairs and Education met with a positive response both abroad and in Holstein.[146] Nicolay showed understanding of the tactics adopted by Hall, who found himself in a difficult situation amid vehemently warring elements, and he appreciated that in this situation Hall was compelled to pick his way carefully.[147]

Faced with the threat of Federal Execution, the Copenhagen government once again took the initiative to start talks with the larger German states, although Hall did not deceive himself about their outcome. Previous efforts had come to nothing because the Estates of Holstein and the cabinet and parliament[148] in Berlin had pursued a two-faced policy, each putting responsibility on the other and saying 'if only the Danish government had put forward concrete proposals'. 'Nous ne pourrons plus nous renfermer dans ce cercle vicieux. Certes nous ne voulons pas de collisions ... Mais l'éxécution fédérale n'est pas le plus grand mal de tout', Hall telegraphed Plessen.[149]

Gorchakov detected positive elements in Hall's May and June dispatches and saw in them the good will of the Danish cabinet, which did not reject the advice of Russia and the other powers but aimed at finding a way of avoiding a collision and sought to eliminate the differences dividing Denmark and the Confederation.[150] In his next dispatch to Nicolay on 11 (23) July, the minister welcomed the declaration the Danish government had made with the aim of averting Federal Execution and paving the way for negotiations. He believed that once the danger to peace was removed (Federal Execution was suspended) there could be talks which might lead to a final and satisfactory result. Gorchakov valued Hall's conciliatory tendencies highly.[151]

The declaration by the Prussian government on 12 July, and especially that by the Danish government on 29 July in which it stated its agreement to holding direct talks with Prussia and Austria and suggested that in the budget for the current financial year the sum for Holstein should be the same as in the normal budget of February 1856, as a result of which the decision in favour of Federal Execution was suspended by the German Diet on 12 August, were received by Gorchakov as evi-

---

145. Nicolay, no. 75, 7 (19) September 1861, vol. 52.
146. Nicolay, no. 73, 4 (16) September 1861.
147. No. 82, (Réservée) 17 (29) October 1861.
148. The *Landtag*.
149. No. 15, 1 June 1861.
150. Gorchakov to Nicolay, 14 (26) May; Privatarkivet 5810, A.F. Krieger, J.9.C, and Sverige Ordrer.
151. Saml. Sager. Den Holst. Forf. vol. 215, R.A. Copenhagen.

dence of both governments' sincere wish to conclude what he described as 'une entente à l'aimable'.

In Berlin the new situation was regarded only as a truce ('une trève'). The Berlin cabinet agreed to this step since it was itself facing a constitutional crisis. It viewed the situation sceptically and understood that an enormous effort was necessary to reach a final agreement before more serious events could occur which might prevent it.

Gorchakov, on the other hand, though that the Danish government was not without cause in fearing that the long summer vacation could mean a loss of valuable time which could be used to settle the question, before the expiry of the current financial year.[152] As Gorchakov was soon to learn, the path to agreement was strewn with thorns.

The greatest difficulty, in the Russian minister's opinion, was Hall's position. Hall still considered that the talks with the German states could cover only Holstein, and never Schleswig, because if the right of the German states to discuss the latter were recognised it would mean questioning the existence of Denmark herself. Gorchakov was unable to appreciate the situation of the Danish minister, who, by making concessions in August, found himself under attack from the Eider-Danois[153] and might not have been able to handle this if he had not brought in O. Lehman, who neutralised the hostile feelings towards the government. Nor did Gorchakov recognise that public opinion was convinced that, in Gosch's words, 'Again it had been the lot of Denmark to make sacrifices for the sake of peace'.[154]

'L'appetit vient en mangeant et le Danemarc en proie à la convoitise de l'Allemagne, dont lui-même aurait reconnu legimité se verrait obligé à adopter un nouveau principe d'existence', Hall complained to Koskull, who was deputising for Nicolay in the latter's absence from Copenhagen.[155] To the Russian diplomat's reply that it was only a matter of Denmark fulfilling the obligations she had undertaken, Hall expressed regret in his own and the King's name at the views of the Russia government, of whose good intentions he had always been convinced and on whose loyalty he could always count. Hall added that there was not a single Dane who whould not prefer war to concessions to Germany, and the surviving part of the nation would not shrink from the prospect of union with Sweden.

This theme, that if Denmark lost Schleswig and Holstein the isolated islands would throw themselves into the arms of Sweden, was frequently repeated by Hall, but Nicolay personally was more sceptical whether such a solution, or even a defensive and offensive alliance between Sweden and Denmark, was at all possible, owing to the anti-Swedish feeling in Norway and unfavourable opinion of Den-

---

152. Gorchakov to Mohrenheim, 21 August. Udenrigs. Samlede Sager. Den Holst. Forf. Vol. 215.
153. Steefel, p. 40.
154. Gosch, p. 243.
155. No. 68 of 4 (16) August 1861.

mark in Sweden. He also though that the youth demonstrations would not have any serious effect.[156]

In a dispatch to Koskull,[157] Gorchakov regretted that recent Danish government dispatches and an account of the Federal Diet session on 12 August had been published in both the German and the Danish press (in *Dagbladet* on 15 August), and wished that both governments would proceed to the agenda and that Copenhagen would send Berlin its terms at an early date, so as to avoid any fortuitous discussion of the kind conducted in the periodical press.[158] Gorchakov appeared very disturbed by the delay in starting talks between Denmark and the larger German states, which was caused by a change of government in Prussia. Schleinitz; place was taken by Bernstorff and the talks did not begin until October, despite the fact that both Russia and the western powers pressed Prussia not to waste time. Mohrenheim had a talk with Sydow, from the Berlin Ministry of Foreign Affairs, on this subject.[159] When Plessen asked Gorchakov whether Russia would defend Denmark during the negotiations, he responded: 'Qu'il ne doutait pas que le Cabinet Russe ne puisse se rendre à cette demande du Gouvernement de sa Majesté but added: 'Il se réserve d'examiner le contenu de la dépêche'.[160] 'Je trouvais le Prince Gortchakoff très fatigué ce matin. La situation intérieure préoccupe', Plessen reported.[161]

In dispatches to Budberg Gorchakov said: 'qu'il serait désirable que les négotiations eussent pour objet la solution définitive de la question'.[162] But because of the situation in which Russia was at the time, Gorchakov's behaviour was entirely passive; he took no initiative at all and even though he had objections relating to Prussia's attitude, he preferred not to criticise her and really directed all his reproaches against Denmark. Specifically, both Gorchakov and Osten-Sacken were concerned about Denmark's attitude to the question of Schleswig, which Gorchakov described as 'la corde sensible' and Osten-Sacken 'le point cardinal'. On the other hand, however, they rejected any analogy between Denmark's behaviour in Schleswig and Prussia's attitude to the Poles.[163]

Gorchakov's attitude and behaviour were showing increasingly clear signs of irritation and dissatisfaction with the lack of progress in the talks between Denmark and Germany. The minister's hypersensitive ambition was offended because the Danish government was not listening to him. Plessen noted this in a letter to Vedel.

---

156. Nicolay, no. 84, 18 (30) November 1861. Cf. A. Bernstorff's view on this subject: 'Skandinavische Union nur möglich und zulässig, wenn mindestens die ganzen Herzogtümer bei Deutschland bleiben', in *Im Kampfe für Preussens Ehre. Aus dem Nachlass des Grafen Albrecht v. Bernstorff,* (Berlin, 1906), pp. 424 and 434-5.
157. 23 August 1861.
158. Udenrigs. Samlede Sager. Den Holst. Forfat. vol. 215.
159. Dep. Rus. no. 53, 10 October (28 September) 1861.
160. Dep. Rus. no. 59, 8 November (27 October) 1861.
161. Plessen to Vedel, 8 November (27 October) Privatarkiv Vedel, pk. 12.
162. *Ibid.*
163. Plessen to Vedel, 29 (17) November.

Mais, je dois observer, que quant à la langue, le point culminant chez nous, on n'admittant par de parallèle, et puis en prenant le caractère de Prince Gortchakov tel qu'il est beaucoup de bonnes qualités mellées à une dose d'amour propre et de vanité-ces parallèles serviront qu'à le provoquer et à l'indisposer.[164]

In a dispatch to Quaade, the Danish ambassador in Berlin, on 26 October 1861, Hall proposed a provisional settlement of the Holstein question to Berlin, reserving the final detailed settlement for the future. The Prussian government delayed its reply, but the Russian cabinet declined to support the Danish proposals and both Gorchakov and Osten-Sacken considered that yet another proposal couched in general terms would be fruitless.[165] As Osten-Sacken said, the Russian cabinet had become convinced that it should not exert any direct influence on Berlin to accept the Danish proposals before Berlin had expressed its opinion on them. Asked by Plessen whether he would support Denmark's proposals, Gorchakov answered that he would recommend Osten-Sacken to study the 26 October dispatch to Quaade, explaining:

Vous savez que, dans Vos affaires j'ai l'habitude de suivre les avis du Baron Sacken. Personne n'est plus de Vos amis, que ne l'est le Baron Sacken, et, certainement, s'il trouve moyen, il sera très disposé à éxécuter Votre demande.[166]

Osten-Sacken found no cause for intervention, and the decisive considerations were not formal ones. He considered that the proposal put to the Estates of Holstein was not very favourable to them, not only where the budget was concerned, but also because it completely isolated Holstein from Schleswig. 'Vous ne voulez peut-être pas incorporer le Slesvig, mais Vous visez à le daniser', which would make every German's blood run cold. Like Gorchakov, he cited the British view that Denmark had not fulfilled her obligations towards Schleswig. He called the Schleswig question 'le clef de voûte de toute la situation' and thought it would be impossible to reach agreement with Germany without reassuring it to a greater degree than hitherto about Denmark's intentions concerning Schleswig. He also criticised the Danish government because there were no Holsteiners in it; the portfolio of the Minister for Holstein Affairs should be held by a Holsteiner, and, as it was not, this was one more piece of evidence against Denmark's system of government in Holstein.

---

164. *Ibid.* In his *Denkschrift*, p. 434, October 1861. Bernstorff described Russia'a policy towards the Schleswig-Holstein problem as follows:
   Russland wird sich gewiss bemühen, Preussen diplomatisch am Vorgehen gegen Dänemark zu verhindern, aber es ist nicht in der Lage diesem Vorsatz materiellen Nachdruck zu geben, geschweige es zu Feindseligkeiten kommen zu lassen.
165. Plessen no. 60, 23 (11) and 29 (17) November, 1861. See no. 15, 27 (15) February 1861.
166. Dep. Rus. no. 60, 23 (11) November.
167. Plessen to Vedel, 23 November 1861, pk. 29 P. Vedels egenhændige uddrag af depecher fra de danske gesandter og notater om begivenheder. R.A. Copenhagen.

During this meeting, Osten-Sacken announced that in view of his age (he was seventy years old) he had decided to retire from political life, and to succeed him he recommended Ewers, who had been secretary of the embassy in Copenhagen in 1846. Plessen regarded this appointment as being to Denmark's disadvantage, since he found Ewers less friendly to her than Osten-Sacken.[167] But the line which Osten-Sacken had laid down on the Danish-German conflict remained in force.

Gorchakov thought the reason for Bernstorff's rejection of Hall's note was the wrong position Hall had taken on the Schleswig question. Gorchakov took the view that Denmark's interpretation of the problem was factually wrong in questioning Germany's rights in respect of Schleswig. These rights were based on the links connecting Schleswig and Holstein, and the King of Prussia had proclaimed them to Europe in 1848. The 1851 agreements had indeed implied that Schleswig-Holsteinism did not exist, but on the other hand they said that the Danish government should consider, and satisfy, the interests of Germany. The purpose of the diplomatic actions of 1851 was to maintain the integrity of Denmark, and Germany had been forced to accept them. For Prussia, in Gorchakov's eloquent phrase, it had been a case of 'passer par le fourches Caudines'.[168] 'N'auriez vous pas pu gagner le Holstein, en traitant autrement le Schleswig'?, the minister asked. By seeking to isolate Holstein Denmark would generate demands which could cause the collapse of the foundations on which the Danish monarchy was based.[169]

Gorchakov also set out his view of the Schleswig question in a dispatch to Nicolay. The question of Schleswig could not be definitively settled unless Denmark fulfilled her promises of 28 January 1851. Besides, Gorchakov recalled in his dispatch to Nicolay, the Danish government had declared to friendly states almost two years earlier that it was ready to make concessions over Schleswig, and Gorchakov had continually urgued it to do so.[170] The same ideas were expounded by Gorchakov in a dispatch to Dashkov on 20 January 1862. This dispatch was in answer to Wedel-Jarlsberg's initiative on 16 January 1862.[171] Gorchakov thought it was necessary to solve the problem of Holstein at the same time, by introducing the essential reforms in Schleswig. Because Copenhagen took a different position, and was supported by Stockholm, the Danish-German differences were in 'un cercle vicieux sans issue'. It would be a good thing if Hall stated clearly, without 'arrière pensée' or 'réservé', what his intentions concerning Holstein and Schleswig were. Gorchakov recognised the right of Prussia and Austria to demand that Denmark fulfil the obligations she had undertaken towards Schleswig, and emphasised this

---

168. Furculae Caudinae, a reference to the defeat which the Samnites inflicted on the Romans, forcing them to capitulate and pass beneath the yoke, (sub iugum) which was such a blow to Roman honour, in 321 BC.
169. Plessen, no. 63, 21 (9) December 1861.
170. 9 (21) December 1861. Udenrigsmin. Samlede Sager. Den Holst. Forf. vol. 216. Vedels papirer, pk. 28, R.A. Copenhagen.
171. Udenrigs. Samlede Sager, *ibid.;* Vedels papirer, *ibid.*

in a talk with Bismarck, adding that Russia had taken this position for two years.[172]

Gorchakov shared Manderström's regret that Hall's first steps towards peace on 26 October 1861 had been rejected by Bernstorff. The severity of Bernstorff's tone was also a surprise for him too and was not a good omen for the future. But, Gorchakov wrote, Hall was still behaving within the bounds of healthy moderation and the speech from the throne had confirmed that Prussia would negotiate. Unlike Manderström, however, he did not think that Prussia alone was responsible for the breakdown in talks. Nor did he share the opinion that the signatories to the Treaty of London should work out an agreement among themselves as that would provoke Germany. He did not share the view that the Danish-German dispute should be made a European question either. He did, on the other hand, share Manderström's opinion that neither Germany nor any other European state had the right to interfere in the problem of Schleswig, although he differed from him on whether Denmark had fulfilled her obligations towards Germany.[173] Both Gorchakov and Nicolay saw a spirit of moderation in Hall's 26 December note, although Nicolay did not believe it would have any practical significance or that Germany would regard it as sufficient.[174]

Gorchakov was aware, and told Plessen frankly that he believed that Hall and his colleagues might have had doubts about Russia's sincere and friendly intentions towards Denmark and about the correctness of her recommendations. But after Russell had rejected Stockholm's proposals and the British government had taken a similar position to the Russian on Schleswig, Gorchakov presumed that the Danish government could no longer think so.[175] Were Russia and Britain asking something impossible of Denmark in connection with the Schleswig problem? Gorchakov assured her that there had been no collusion between the Russian and the British governments over their replies to Stockholm. Thus he advised Denmark to move in the direction both Russia and Britian counselled. His advice was based on a good understanding of Denmark's own interests, and he assured her that he was guided by feelings of friendship towards her.[176]

The pressure on Copenhagen can be partially explained by the disturbing news reaching St. Petersburg from the Danish capital. Nicolay, who had frequent talks with Hall, became convinced that the Danish government could not be expected to depart from its principles concerning Schleswig, in spite of the Russian government's recommendation to carry out urgent reforms and in spite of the fact that he had indicated that settlement of the Holstein question depended on reforms in Schleswig. Nicolay did not share Hall's opinion that the adoption of a liberal elec-

---

172. Bismarck's report of 23 January 1862, in Raschdau, vol. II, p. 168. Cf. Gorchakov's memorandum of 13 May 1861.
173. Dep. Rus. no. 9, 25 (13) January 1862.
174. Nicolay, Particulière, 28 December 1861 (9 January) 1862.
175. Plessen, no. 19, 8 February (27 January) and no. 13, 7 March (23 February) 1862.
176. No. 19, 7 March (23 February) 1862.

toral law in Schleswig would alter the situation there, and that if a liberal representation there replaced the present conservative one, which was hostile to the government, the latter's situation would be improved. Furthermore, he was afraid this was a step towards the merger of Schleswig with the Kingdom, despite Hall's denial. He also had serious doubts whether Danish officials, who frequently exceeded their powers and conducted pro-Danish propaganda, in the hope that their keenness would be rewarded, were capable of carrying out reforms.

It is significant that reservations about the Danish government's intention to introduce changes in the constitution were put forward not only by the Russian government but also by conservative members of the Danish Rigsraad and Conseil Supreme. The leading representative of the conversative camp, Ch. G.N. David, warned the government against abandoning the Helstat programme and implementing the Eider policy. He cited the 1852 agreements and the royal patent of 28 January 1852, from which it followed that Germany had renounced Schleswig-Holsteinism and Denmark had undertaken obligations. In David's opinion the government was not observing this policy, and Denmark's friends abroad were of the same opinion. Denmark was 'bound in honour' and was exposing herself to very 'grave dangers', the effects of which were hard to foresee. 'Un état, qu'il fût grand ou petit, ne saurait sans danger se soustraire aux obligations qui lui ont été imposées par la nécessité'. The Danish concessions in 1851-52 had not deprived Denmark of her independence and, moreover, to make them had been a necessity. History taught that at times even major powers were compelled seriously to restrict their activities, even on their own territory. As an example he instanced Russia, which had been obliged under the Treaty of Paris not to maintain a military presence on the Black Sea and to agree not to construct fortifications there. Thus, Nicolay reported, Russia's arguments and intepretations coincided with those of the leaders of the Danish opposition, who were warning the government that it was taking a wrong and dangerous road, but to no effect.[177]

'Non possumus' was the government's motto. It reacted sharply to the Prussian note of 14 February, which openly declared that the German Diet considered it was entitled to intervene in the affairs of Schleswig, on the basis of the 1851 and 1852 agreements and international agreements. 'La question est entreé dans une nouvelle phase. En Allemagne on a ouvertement prononcé le mot de Slesvig', Nicolay reported on 22 March (3 April) 1862. The Danes protested vigorously against interference by the German Diet, arguing that the talks with Austria and Prussia had not been in the nature of international negotiations. Furthermore, and this was fundamental, the government was continuing work on a change in the constitution, which in turn evoked a protest from Germany.

---

177. 10 (22) February 1862. Tillish told Nicolay that the government was behaving 'C'est comme si le Holstein n'existe plus pour nous'. Nicolay, 19 (31) January 1862. Nicolay reported that during discussion of the plan for changes in the constitution the words 'illégale' and 'intempestive' were used. Nicolay, 25 January (6 February).

Nicolay and his two colleagues, the British and French ambassadors, indicated to the Danish government the dangers which could arise from the proposed constitutional reform and the advantage of dropping the work on it.[178] At this stage of the dispute between the Danish government and the governments of Austria and Prussia Gorchakov took an unequivocally pro-German position. In a dispatch to the Russian ambassadors in Paris and London on 4 (16) April 1862[179] he drew attention to the introductory paragraph of the notes from Berlin of 8 and 14 February, in which the German states reminded the Danish government that the conditions which they agreed in 1851-52 concerned not only the evacuation of Holstein and re-establishment of the royal authority there, but participation by the German states in the European agreements, which was considered very important by the Copenhagen cabinet.

Gorchakov came to the conclusion that owing to Denmark's failure to fulfil her obligations, the German states could feel relieved of the duty to comply with their obligations towards Denmark and the other signatories under the Treaty of London. The firm tone of this note may have been influenced by the memorandum which Brunnow sent to St. Petersburg from London at the end of February or the beginning of March, which Gorchakov gave Plessen to read through,[180] although he would not let him have a copy of it made. This document, which subsequently gained approval from the cabinet,[181] was of especial significance because it came from the pen of Brunnow, who enjoyed a high reputation in diplomatic circles in the capitals of Europe and was furthermore regarded as an expert on the Danish-German problem.

Brunnow considered that the Imperial government's position must meet the requirement of a sound policy and he examined this policy from three points of view:

1. Remplissant les engagements de la Russie envers le Danemark.
2. Dégageant la responsibilité morale de la Russie envers l'Allemagne,
3. Gardant les ménagements que la Russie doit à la Prusse.

Brunnow stated that Russia had stood by her promises to Denmark, steadfastly, loyally and providently keeping within the bounds of justice and reason. Analysing the provisions of the Treaty of London, its joint progenitor judged it an act of European recognition, but pointed out that the obligations of the powers did not go beyond what was contained in the treaty, and argued that this did not include a guarantee. He also recalled that in 1852 the Danish party in London tried to sound out Britain to see if she would agree to include a guarantee in the Treaty.

The ambassador also recalled the public outcry in Germany accusing Nicholas I of infringing German rights. In fact Russia had sought to safeguard Germany's

---

178. No. 24, Nicolay, 22 March (3 April) 1862, vol. 53.
179. Udenrigs. Samlede Sager. Den Holst. Forfat and Ordrer, Rusland, R.A. Copenhagen. No. 27.
180. Dep. Rus. no. 14, 13 (1) March 1862.
181. Dep. Rus. no. 21, 30 (18) April 1862.

rights during the negotiations. Prussia, said Brunnow, had joined the London conference only with the greatest reluctance ('avec une grande répugnance') and hesitated for a long time before agreeing to recognise the principle of the integrity of the Danish monarchy. The Danish Cabinet had thought that without Prussia's accession the conference's work would be incomplete. After analysing what had transpired on 4 July and 2 August 1850, it stated that Prussia's accession to the peace would be of great significance. In order to secure Prussia's agreement to join in the great work of strengthening the integrity of Denmark, the Russian cabinet had taken the position that some satisfaction must be given to German feeling by making certain concessions concerning the administration of Schleswig.

Brunnow's memorandum argued that the Danish government's promises related not only to Holstein and Lauenburg but to Schleswig as well. This was an indisputable fact ('incontestable'), Brunnow emphasised. Referring to the current situation, the memorandum pointed out that in its reply to Stockholm, the Russian cabinet had drawn attention to this state of affairs, and Britain, which had not collaborated with Russia on this matter, had come to the same conclusion. Russell had submitted that Denmark had a duty to fulfil certain obligations to Schleswig, and believed that the Danish government had enjoyed the benefit of recommendations and warnings from its best friends.

Brunnow did not believe that in the current circumstances the conditions existed for convening a European Conference to settle the Danish-German dispute. Such a conference would be a great risk for Denmark and might virtually nullify the significance of the Treaty of London, or at least cast doubt on the sincerity of the states which had signed it, as the guarantee received by one of the signatory states was not directed against the remaining signatories. It followed from this, Plessen added himself, when reading the memorandum prepared by Brunnow, that in the event of war between Denmark and the German states, since the treaty gave no guarantee, everything would again come into question.

If a conference were to take place, however, Brunnow suggested that Germany, or the German Confederation, should take part in it and should be represented by delegates appointed by the Diet. Austria and Prussia had to take part as European powers. Speaking of Prussia, he commented that it was more German than Germany.

In this context this had a special significance. If a conference were convened, Brunnow proposed the appointment of two committees; one, composed of plenipotentiaries from Denmark and the German Diet under the chairmanship of a Swedish plenipotentiary, would deal with the question of Holstein and Lauenburg, and the second, consisting of two plenipotentiaries from Denmark and one each from Austria and Prussia under a British chairman, would examine Denmark's measures in respect of Schleswig. The committees' conclusions would go to a plenary session of the conference. The plenum would meet only to express an opinion of a consultative nature on especially difficult matters.

In Brunnow's view the conference should not be authoritative but should facilitate reconciliation between the divergent opinions. If the efforts of the conference failed to produce results it should note what had occurred and recommend the parties to come to an agreement on the matters in dispute. Finally, he said, on the basis of the 1852 resolutions and agreement, the conference should once again insist on the maintenance of the principle of integrity of the Danish monarchy.

Whilst Gorchakov explained that all this was only Brunnow's opinion, he instructed his subordinates to analyse the document, and Osten-Sacken considered the memorandum 'juste', particularly the third point, which discussed Russian policy towards Prussia. The memorandum won total approval from the Russian cabinet.[182]

As Gorchakov and Brunnow frequently repeated, Russia attached great importance to the documents which she had signed together with the other states in London in 1852, particularly the Treaty of London. Russia regarded this treaty, Plessen wrote, as the work of the dead Tsar and a sacred act, binding the current ruler. The treaty was regarded as inviolable. Russia was afraid that if a conference were held there was no certainty that the powers which had signed the Treaty of London would be willing to maintain the principle of the integrity of Denmark, which Russia considered the basis of any negotiations. The Russian government emphasised what great importance it attached to the Treaty and said reproachfully that it was aware that there was a party in Denmark which would not be sorry if the treaty and the principle of neutrality of the monarchy were abandoned. This party thought it would be able to achieve its aims more easily then. The party Gorchakov had in mind was of course the Eider Danes' party.[183]

Gorchakov spoke to Plessen in an increasingly firm tone, which was undoubtedly influenced also by the reports he was receiving from London about Russell's attitude. In this context it is worth noting what Brunnow wrote:

Je ne Vous parle pas aujourd'hui de l'affaire danoise, mais je crois devoir Vous dire qu'à l'égard de cette affaire, j'observe chez Lord Russell une certaine lassitude. Il est fatigué des refus continuels qu'il éprouve à Copenhague. Que deviendront nos amis les Danois, si le Cabinet Anglais, las de ses constants efforts, se rétire et leur laisse le soin de s'arranger avec l'Allemagne.[184]

Gorchakov paid attention to the British government's opinion, and particularly Russell's.[185] In order to convince Plessen that Russia was right, he drew on Russell's speeches and arguments and quoted them in his efforts to influence the behaviour of the Copenhagen government.

182. Some of the ideas in this memorandum found their way into the memorandum which Brunnow presented to the British government on the eve of the opening of the London Conference in April 1864. Cf. pp. 404 ff. of this work.
183. Dep. Rus. no. 20, 13 (6) April 1862.
184. Vedel, pk. 29, 1861-64. P. Vedels egenhændige uddrag af depecher ...; Dep. Rus. no. 18, 4 April (23 March) 1862).
185. Cf. what Gorchakov said to Plessen on 23 February 1862 and Plessen's letters to Vedel on 1 March and 12 April (31 March) in Vedel, pk. 29 and pk. 12, R.A. Copenhagen.

The Russian government considered that the manner in which Germany was calling for fulfilment of its demands did not relieve Denmark of the obligation to satisfy the German governments in an agreement concerning Schleswig. It was against any Russian intervention in Berlin or Vienna. Like Thouvenel, it was opposed to Russell's proposal on 16 April 1862 for a collective approach to those two capitals as long as negotiations between Denmark and Germany continued, because this would mean 'de mettre l'Allemagne au pied du mur'.[186] It would not even hear of a need 'pour mettre un frein aux ambitions allemandes'.[187] It expressed displeasure at the diplomatic moves undertaken by the Danish government, especially at Bülow's 19 March protest and the spirit of Hall's 25 March note, which seemed to it not far from breaking off the talks with Germany.[188] The vice-chancellor expressed his displeasure in dispatches to Brunnow and Kiselov asking them to draw the attention of the cabinets of St. James and the Tuilleries to the fact that Denmark was in the wrong in refusing to give what he called 'nettes et franchises' explanations concerning Holstein and, particularly, Schleswig. He also regretted that the Danish government did not state its position on the Schleswig problem before settling the question of Holstein, which in his opinion would deprive Germany of the possibility of Federal Execution in Holstein.[189]

The reports coming in to St. Petersburg from Copenhagen reassured Gorchakov that the chances of an alliance between Sweden and Denmark were diminishing, particularly because such a treaty would be beneficial to Denmark, but a burden for Sweden and would impose new obligations on her. And as far as the mood prevailing in Sweden was concerned, Nicolay's reports attached no particular importance to the Swedish King's visit to Denmark. He was pessimistic, however, about the attitude of Danish society, which was following the wrong path owing to illusions about the Eider programme which, in the ambassador's view, was unattainable. Danish society, wrote Nicolay, lacked the courage to break with the past and preferred to surrender the decisions in the dispute with Germany to the great powers. Then they would be able to say that they had been subjected to pressure which they could not resist.[190]

While favouring Germany, Russia continued to make out that she remained uncommitted. This must be the explanation for the fact that she was inclined not to oppose the plan put forward in the spring of 1862 by Palmerston for the partition of Schleswig. It may also have been because she realised that, just as had happened with the similar plan put forward by the same Palmerston in 1848, this plan had no chance of success because of opposition from Austria.[191] Russia continually

186. Dep. Rus. no. 23, 11 May (29 April) and no. 24, 18 (6) May 1862, and A. Thorsøe, *King Frederik ...* vol. II, (Copenhagen, 1899), p. 27.
187. Dep. Rus. No. 18, 4 April (23 March) 1862. Cf. also nos 16-22.
188. Dep. Rus. no. 17, 31 (19) March 1862).
189. Scheel-Plessen to Hall, Udenrigsm. Sverige Depecher 1862-65, no. 18, 14 May 1862.
190. See Nicolay's reports for May to July 1862, vol. 53.
191. See Bismarck, vol. II, 26 February 1862, p. 172, 11 and 15 April 1862, pp. 191 and 196, and 11 July 1862, p. 220. See also Mémoires et documents. Question des duchés. May 1862, vol. 13. A.M.A.E. Paris.

claimed that she was guided by the good of Denmark, she was interested in maintaining the integrity of the Danish monarchy, and her advice was that of a friend. The duplicity of Gorchakov's policy was seen during the conflict in Hessen, when he advised the Danish government to take advantage of a favourable moment, which he compared with the time of the Italian war in 1859, when internal German matters had pushed the Danish-German conflict into the background.[192] Even Manderström could not fathom Gorchakov's intentions, judging by what he said of him in May 1862 in a conversation with the Danish ambassador: 'lui semblait ménager la chèvre et le chou'.[193]

In the spring of 1862 Bismarck, who was then leaving his diplomatic post in St. Petersburg, was convinced that Russia would never oppose Prussia, and if Gorchakov approached other powers with questions concerning the Danish-German conflict he did so only for the purpose of sounding out their opinion. Bismarck believed that Gorchakov wanted to avoid everything that could be unpleasant for Prussia.[194] If the Danish-German dispute were to become a military conflict, there was a conviction that, with regard to Prussia and Austria, Russia must be expected to take a neutral position.[195] This was due, among other things, to the situation of Russia at the time, which Plessen described in the following terms: 'Les événements en Russie ont un cachet horrible. Il y a là les mêmes instincts sauvages qu'en 1848 ont mis Paris en feu et en sang'.[196] Plessen foresaw that in the event of a crisis with Germany, Denmark's situation would be even more difficult than in 1848. There would be no Nicholas I to represent the principle of authority and shatter German liberal aspirations. The principle of solidarity between sovereigns had also vanished.

The August note from Berlin and Vienna in reply to Hall's note of 12 August,[197] in which the central matter was the question of Schleswig, meant the breaking off of negotiations. The German states demanded that Schleswig be returned to the *status quo ante* 1848 in language matters and that the 1855 constitution be suspended in respect of Schleswig, as it was illegal since it had not been approved by the Estates. *Dagbladet* regarded this as unacceptable and *Fædrelandet* called the German demands an affront to the honour of Denmark.[198] The German notes made the resignation of the Danish ambassador in Frankfurt, the distinguished diplomat Bülow, an inevitable fact.[199] They prompted *Dagbladet* to express the view that the

192. Dep. Rus. no. 28, 27 (15) June 1862.
193. Scheel-Plessen to Hall, no. 18, 14 May 1862. Udenrigs. Dep. Sverige. See also Manderström to the ambassador in St. Petersburg, 12 May 1862. Ordrer Russland, R.A. Copenhagen, copy.
194. Bismarck to Bernstorff, 15 April 1862, vol. II p. 195. Cf. Nolde, p. 270.
195. See Hillerbrand, *Bismarck and Gorchakov,* pp. 161-2.
196. Vichy, 9 July 1862, letter to Vedel, pk. 12.
197. R.A. Copenhagen. The Prussian note of 22 August and the Austrian Memorandum of 25 August were published in *Fædrelandet* nos. 217 and 219, (18 and 20 September 1862).
198. Nicolay, no. 16, 14 (26) September 1862. *Fædrelandet,* nos. 221 and 222 (De sidste tydske Noter I, II), 23 and 24 September 1862.
199. Nicolay's Dep. 4 (16) October 1862. V. Sjøquist ed. *Peter Vedels beretning om Danmarks udenrigspolitik fra sommeren 1862 til foråret 1863, Jyske Samlinger,* (Aarhus, 1952-54), pp. 98-9. *Dagbladet,* no. 239, Revue no. 37, 14 October 1862.

demands, particularly Prussia's demands in respect of Schleswig, which had never been part of the German Confederation, were impossible to fulfil, and it saw the real aims of Prussian policy in the words of M. Harkort,[200] to the Maritime Commission in Berlin: 'Kiel, voilà notre vrai port, il faut que le Holstein soit à la Prusse'.[201]

In Denmark the conviction grew that war was inevitable. This was reflected by Gosch in a passionate statement of the position:

The struggle between Germany and Denmark is, as far as the latter is concerned, one of life and death, which can only be prolonged, but not terminated by a compromise. Justice must be done – neither more nor less – but the least that Denmark has a right to demand is the complete vindication of the old verse – Eidora Teutonicum terminat Imperium[202]

In contrast to the view of the German notes prevailing in Denmark, Gorchakov regarded their content as consistent with the main idea of the negotiations with Denmark and urged the Danish cabinet to present its position and speed up the negotiations, since otherwise there would be the danger of a conflict, which was greater for her than for Germany.[203] In a dispatch to Nicolay on 29 September (11 October) he regretted the delay in the negotiations and the tone of the Copenhagen press, which was stirring up public opinion against Germany and magnifying the difficulties. He called on the Danish government to settle the question of Schleswig, repeating the same words he had used previously, and emphasised that if Denmark did not recognise Germany's justification Russia would not give her moral support.[204]

VII

This firm tone on Gorchakov's part was undoubtedly closely connected with the change in Britain's policy towards the Danish-German dispute, which was closely reflected in the well known dispatch from Gotha in which Russell[205] expressed a position in line with German interests. There is a divergence of opinion about the motives which guided Russell. Contemporary historians' views were summed up by Sandiford, who says that the causes of Russell's change of policy were the anti-Danish environment by which he was surrounded during his visit to Coburg and the influence of his secretary, Robert Morier, and, above all, the reports from the vice-consul, Reinals, and also, which appears to be more fundamental, a wish to improve relations with Prussia.[206] In the Gotha dispatch Russell took the position

---

200. A member of the Prussian *Landtag*.
201. These words were quoted in *Dagbladet*, Revue, no. 30, 26 August. See also Revue, no. 31, 2. September.
202. Gosch, *Denmark and Germany*, p. 300.
203. Sverige, Ordrer, R.A. Copenhagen.
204. P. Vedel, pk. 28. Samlinger og sager vedr. historiske begivenheder. Bilag til P. Vedels fremstilling af Danmarks udenrigspolitik 1858-1864, R.A. Copenhagen; Dep. Rus. no. 40, 18 (6) October 1862.
205. W. Czapliński, *Dzieje Danii nowożytnej*, p. 195, wrongly attributes this to Palmerston.
206. Sandiford, pp. 54-5. Cf. Steefel, pp. 43-4; Neergaard, pp. 549ff; J.H. Voigt, *Z.d.G.f.S.H.G.* 1964,

that the 1855 constitution was an illegal act in respect of both Holstein and Lauenburg and Schleswig, as it had not been accepted by the Estates. Schleswig should receive autonomy in matters of religion, education and language and the budget question should be settled in the following way:

The normal budget to be voted in gross for ten years. The distribution or expenditure to be voted yearly. In conclusion, Russell summed up his proposal under four main heads:
1. Holstein and Lauenburg to have all that the German Confederation ask for them.
2. Schleswig to have the power of self-government, and not to be represented in the Rigsraad.
3. A normal budget to be agreed upon by Denmark, Holstein, Lauenburg, and Schleswig.
4. Any extraordinary expenses to be submitted to the Rigsraad, and to the separate Diets of Holstein, Lauenburg, and Schleswig.[207]

Russell's proposals were neither completely new nor original. They were reminiscent of those announced previously by Holstein. If accepted, they would have transformed the Danish monarchy into a 'quadripartite organisation'.[208]

Public opinion in Britain rejected Russell's proposals 'more emphatically than did the Danish government'.[290] Gorchakov, on the other hand, immediately reacted positively to them. As soon as he received news of the Gotha dispatch he wrote to his ambassadors in Copenhagen, Vienna and Berlin, on 29 September (11 October), reminding them that the treaty signed in Berlin on 2 July 1850 had been concluded through the mediation of Great Britain. Britain had played an important role in settling Danish-German affairs and had the right to expect that her recent proposals would be received with due respect in Copenhagen. Russell's dispatch, said Gorchakov, contained proposals which could facilitate the removal of

---

vol. 89, pp. 66ff, and 162-7; Zechlin, *Bismarck ...*, pp. 82-3. The latter emphasises that underlying the change of course was the fear that Britain might be isolated in the face of a Franco-Russian-Prussian alliance. It is interesting to read Klaczko's opinion of the Gotha dispatch, in J. Klaczko, *Études de diplomatie ...*

Dans sa fameuse dépêche du 24 septembre 1862, le chef du *foreign office* commençait d'abord par transcrire une récente note prusienne (du 22 août) pleine de récriminations contre le Danemark; il adoptait comme authentiques les faits allégués dans un document émanant du cabinet de Berlin! (p. 256). Ainsi, par sa missive célèbre du 24 septembre 1862, le comte Russell ne faisait pas seulement un acte manifeste d'intervention dans les affaires intérieures d'un État indépendant, mais il prenait en main la cause de l'Allemagne contre le Danemark, et se prononçait hautement pour les prétentions les plus excessives, les plus injustifiables de MM de Beust et de Pfordten! (p. 258) ... la dépêche de Gotha devint le signal d'une recrudescence violente du *schlesvig-holsteinisme* de l'autre côté du Rhin, et c'est d'elle, à dire vrai, que date diplomatiquement le démembrement de la monarchie danoise. (p. 260).

207. Sandiford, p. 54.
208. Steefel, p. 44.
209. Sandiford, pp. 55-6; Steefel, p. 45.

the existing obstacles. Russell, a minister of a constitutional state, was not pressing for the suspension of the 1855 constitution as Prussia was, but, like Prussia, he saw the necessity of annulling it. His proposals were based on the assumption that the 1855 constitution did not exist. Gorchakov added that in a dispatch to Plessen on 14 May 1861, Hall had declared that his government would submit to proposals which were the product of friendly states. The Danish government should be convinced that the discussions with Germany were becoming more and more irritating and fruitless and, as Russell noted, were only increasing the distance which separated the two sides, instead of bringing them closer. It was time to put an end to the Danish-German dispute, as it was dangerous and, if it were not quickly settled, would be a source of complications of which the Copenhagen cabinet would become painfully conscious.[210]

The position Gorchakov took was greeted with satisfaction by Bismarck, who expressed this in his dispatch to the Prussian ambassador in St. Petersburg on 25 October 1862. He asked the ambassador to inform Gorchakov

que nous nous félicitons sincèrement de l'attitude si conforme à nos rapports réciproques, que le Cabinet Impérial a prise dans la question qui touche de si près les intérêts de la Prusse.[211]

In a conversation with E. Vind, Gorchakov asked the Danish government to give serious consideration to Russell's proposals, because he saw them as a way to end this unfortunate conflict, although he recognised that there were difficulties in accepting the point concerning suspension of the constitution, and in this context he spoke disapprovingly of how the German press was exacerbating the conflict.[212]

Hall's attitude to the Gotha dispatch was unequivocally negative. Acceptance of Russell's proposals was not considered for a fraction of a second in Copenhagen. In Hall's opinion it was impossible and impracticable to agree to the establishment of four assemblies, each with a decisive voice. He categorically rejected the proposals concerning Schleswig, and the suspension of the 1855 constitution.[213] Gorchakov did not abandon attempts to put pressure on Hall and this was reflected in his dispatch to Nicolay on 30 November (12 December). He called on Hall to change his position on the note and to get rid of his dangerous illusions.[214] There was a passage in Gorchakov's dispatch which greatly upset public opinion in Copenhagen. It read as follows:

Mais si l'occasion se présentait d'exposer soit à Mr. Hall lui-même, soit à d'autres hommes d'Etat Danois, les considérations que je viens d'indiquer, l'approbation du Cabinet Impérial est acquise, comme elle l'a été dans tout le cours de telle si regrettable affaire.

210. Vedel, pk. 28.
211. *Ibid.*
212. Dep. Rus. no. 40, 18 (6) October 1862.
213. Nicolay no. 61, 11 (23) October 1862, vol. 53. Neergaard, *Under Junigrundloven*, vol. II, pp. 549ff.
214. Cf. also Paget to Russell, no. 128, 24 December 1862, Rigsark. Danica. P.R.O. London. F.O. 22, 294.

When Nicolay informed Hall of the content of the dispatch he had received, Hall replied shortly that he had nothing to say and was pleased that Nicolay had instructions not to enter into discussion with him. 'I see', Hall said to the ambassador, 'that you have instructions to conduct talks with other statesmen; perhaps they will agree with you. Adieu.'

Nicolay assured him that this was not his intention. But in the meantime it became known that Nicolay had shown the dispatch to Andrae, and Prince Frederick of Hessen received a copy of the same dispatch.[215] News of the dispatch spread and the whole of Copenhagen was in a state of excitement, which was all the greater as it coincided with rumours, 'petit à petit le bruit absurdé s'est répondu' – as Nicolay wrote, 'que j'etais chargé de provoquer une crise, en me mettant en rapports avec *d'autres* hommes d'Etat'.[216] To produce explanations in this affair, which indicated a very great aberration of the idea and concept of diplomatic offices, seemed, the ambassador wrote, beneath his dignity.[217] He therefore ignored these rumours, confining himself, he reported to Gorchakov, to explaining to serious and experienced people what was the truth behind this incident. He did this particularly with those who had regard for the opinion of the Russian government.

Nicolay tried in vain to convince Hall that Russell's proposals contained elements 'd'une entente ultérieure' and to persuade him to give them consideration, as there was an urgent need for negotiations and both sides had to make concessions in these matters where differences existed. But Hall, Nicolay reported, 'prononce son "alea iacta est"'.[218]

Gorchakov did not confine himself to exerting pressure on the Copenhagen government directly, but also decided to involve Manderström. For this purpose he sent a dispatch to Dashkov, dated 1 (13) December 1862.[219] But Manderström did not entirely share Russell's position. As Dashkov reported on 17 (29) December 1862.

Le Ministre ne se dissimile pas les torts que le Gouvernement Danois s'est donnés en n'accordant point toute satisfaction aux voeux des habitants du Slesvig, conduite qui aurait considérablement renforcé sa cause, en ce qui regarde cette province, mais il est d'opinion, qu'en vertu des propositions de Lord Russell, non seulement le Danemark éprouvera d'insurmontables difficultés à se régir avec quatre parlements distincts, mais que la porte resterait toujours encore ouverte à des nouvelles prétentions de la part de l'Allemagne.[220]

Manderström repeated these reservations in his disparch to his ambassador in St.

---

215. Møller, *Helstatens Fald,* vol. I, p. 509. Cf. Nicolay's reports of 3 (15) (Particulière) and 9 (21) January 1863.
216. *Dagbladet,* Revue de la semaine, no. 2, 20 January 1863, called the note interference in the internal affairs of Denmark, and the words used in it, 'd'autres hommes d'état', 'une phrase assez amphibolique', and suggested that Nicolay was meant to establish contact with 'diverses factions oppositionelles'.
217. Nicolay, 3 (15) January 1863.
218. Nicolay, no. 79, 28 December 1862 (9 January 1863).
219. Vedel, pk. 28 and Sverige Dep. 1862-65.
220. Central archive, Moscow. Rigsark. Stockholm, Dep. från Stockholm til Petersb. 14 July – 29 December 1862.

Petersburg, adding that if the British proposal were accepted, the German Confederation would have undue rights in relation to the duchies, greater than it had in relation to the other states forming the Confederation. The minister emphasised that the Treaty of London guaranteed not only the integrity but also the sovereignty and independence of Denmark.[221] Nor should an interpretation be put upon the 1851-52 obligations to which no state could agree.[222]

On 29 December the Danish government discussed the situation which had arisen as a result of Russell's proposals. Monrad, then Minister for Church Affairs and Education, expressed the view that Russell had found strong support in Austria and Prussia, that Russia had joined them in this, and that France had recommended examining the proposals seriously. Hall's assessment was more cautious and he expressed the opinion that it would be too strong to say that Russia agreed with the proposals. She had confined herself to expressing the view that Russell's proposals contained positive elements which could contribute to removing the danger and settling the question.[223]

In a note addressed to Vind on 16 January 1863 Hall, although regretting the differences which had arisen between the St. Petersburg and Copenhagen cabinets on the subject of certain fundamental points concerning the Danish-German dispute, nevertheless could not but recall the sincere sympathy and support which the Russian government had always shown to Denmark. He also cherished the hope and belief that Gorchakov's advice would permit them to come to an agreement on the matter of finding ways and means. He also explained why Russell's proposals were unacceptable to Denmark from both the practical and the formal point of view and in respect of their substance. It was impossible to agree that the German Diet should be the highest arbiter in all constitutional matters in respect of a country which was not part of the German Confederation, and he pointed out what dangers this could bring. He also rejected Russell's position on the question of Schleswig, on the grounds that there was no treaty or agreement in the case of Schleswig, and a non-federal country could not be subordinated to control by the federal Diet. This formal argument by itself was sufficient to show how groundless the German demands were. The Danish goverment, Hall assured him, had a double task to perform; to defend the country's independence and to settle the relations between the different provinces of the monarchy. Its intention was to complete the work it had begun by peaceful means.

In his note, Hall mentioned that Nicolay, who was very familiar with the situation in Denmark, had certainly already informed his government that the whole nation was united behind the King and the government where maintenance of the

---

221. Dispatch to St. Petersburg, 30 December 1862, in Vedel, pk. 28 and Sverige. Dep. 1862-65. Cf. also Scheel-Plessen's report on Manderström's attitude to the Gotha dispatch and Gorchakov's 30 December 1862 dispatch in *Aktstykker vedkommende den dansk-tydske strid. I. Aktstykker, der belyser den svensk-norske regjerings stilling til sagen. (1858-1864)*, (Copenhagen, 1865), pp. 70-75.
222. Manderström to Gorchakov, 30 December 1862.
223. *Statsrådets forhandlinger 1848-1863*, vol. VIII. 8 December 1859 – 29 December 1862. Ed. Harald Jørgensen, (Copenhagen, 1968), pp. 456-7.

independence of the non-federal parts of the monarchy against pressure from the Federation was concerned.[224] Gorchakov did indeed already know the Danish government's position before receiving Hall's note. He was aware of the content of Hall's new note to London and regretted that the Danish government did not regard Russell's proposals as a 'base d'une négociation'. In a talk with Vind, Gorchakov said he had read Hall's reply to Russell on 5 January 1863 with great interest, but the arguments Hall used did not convince him and he had not altered the opinion he expressed previously on the matter. At the same time he repeated his old assurances that he was interested in the integrity of Denmark and sincerely wished the question to be settled definitively in a reasonable and agreeable manner for both parties.[225]

Ewers informed Vind that the Russian government saw the Schleswig problem as the crux of the whole question and that if reforms of the legal provisions concerning language were carried out, Germany would lose the pretext to intervene in its affairs. By voluntarily carrying out a reform, Denmark would gain a victory. If she fulfilled the obligations she had undertaken a situation would be created in which the three great powers would not allow the German Confederation to extend its authority beyond the boundaries defined in the treaties. *En passant,* he threw in the suggestion that in the St. Petersburg cabinet's opinion it would be easier for a government headed by V.C.E. Sponneck, who had been Minister of Finance in the Bluhme government, to reach agreement with Germany than it would for the present Hall government. When he reported this news, Vind stressed that the suggestion had come from Ewers, who enjoyed Gorchakov's confidence and was troughly familiar with the problems involved.[226]

Taken together with the 30 November 1862 dispatch to Nicolay, this suggestion acquires a special significance, showing how much the Russian government would have liked to see a conservative government come to power in Copenhagen.

It may be of interest that, in a conversation with the Danish ambassador in London, the Russian ambassador, Brunnow, was quite critical of Gorchakov's attitude to the Gotha dispatch. He said that he did not attach any importance to what Gorchakov had written on this subject, and the Danish ambassador got the impression from his talk with Brunnow that the latter viewed the dispatch 'comme écrite dans le seul but de plaire à Lord Russell et que le Prince Gortchakoff lui-même n'attendait aucunement qu'elle influerait sur les résolutions du Gouvernement de Roi'. As far as the Gotha dispatch itself was concerned, Brunnow seemed to share the Danish point of view about the impracticality of putting it into effect, and about its unjust nature, or if he thought otherwise then at least he did not counter Bille's cri-

---

224. See Sverige. Ordrer 1861-68, 16 January 1863. Rusland. Ordrer. Cf. Registratur, 1863, no. 69, 2954. Preussen. Ordrer. 1862-67. R.A. Copenhagen.
225. Kabinettet för utrikes brev, Dep. från besk. i Peterb. II, 1863, no. 8, 6 February (25 January) 1863. Wedel-Jarlsberg to Manderström, R.A. Stockholm.
226. Vind no. 5, 3 February (23 January) 1863. See also: R.A. Stockholm, Wedel-Jarlsberg's report, no. 8, 6 February (25 January) 1863.

ticism. Brunnow attributed the document not to hostility towards Denmark on Russell's part but just to impatience and a desire to find *some* solution, and he expressed the opinion that for diplomatic reasons the Danish government should reply in a conciliatory tone.[227]

It would be difficult to say what Brunnow's aim was in criticising Gorchakov's moves at this time. Was it a revival of the old antagonism between them dating back to 1856? Or did he do it in order to ingratiate himself with the Danish government and go some way to satisfy its ambitions by recognising that it was right that the Gotha dispatch could not be implemented for practical reasons, while at the same time persuading it to make a conciliatory reply to the British government? Perhaps both elements influenced the view Brunnow expressed.

The whole episode of the Gotha dispatch only harmed Denmark and helped Germany, as Vedel rightly argued. In Britain it was seen as an attempt to 'pluck in us', and W. Oxholm heard Denmark compared in London to a small boxer who clenched his fists and called 'Come on!'[228] But Vedel added that Europe saw that 'even Britain could not compel us to be silent; and some people observed the rejection of Russell's Gotha dispatch with not inconsiderable satisfaction, 'til viist'.[229] In letters to Paget Russell criticised Denmark for rejecting everything designed to settle the dispute.

In short, the Danes reject everything which would carry into effect the equality between Danes and Germans which is the true policy of Denmark, the obligation by public declaration to allow the fair right of Germans of Schleswig to require ... the only way in which the Germans would agree to it, namely obtaining some security that the Germans would have their share of power – has been rejected by Mr. Hall. I suppose – wrote Russell to Paget on 13 December 1862 – the Danes will one day come to their senses and they will regret their rejection of my propositions.[230]

In another letter to Paget on 21 January 1863 Russell surveyed the current state of the negotiations and said that Denmark could reject his proposals and question Britain's attitude to the problem of her integrity and independence, but he must submit that she had obligations.

These promises constitute an engagement which His Majesty is to fulfil – wrote Russell.
It is not for the interest any more than it is for the reputation of the King to place his German subjects in a situation inferior to that of his subjects of Danish origin, either as to privilege or to favour.[231]

A belief arose, however, in Denmark that Bismarck's accession was an advantage as his hostile attitude to the Schleswig-Holstein movement and the democratic parties in Prussia was well known. It was thought that the opposition in Prussia would

---

227. T. Bille's reports of 5 and 21 January 1863 to Hall. England Dep. 1861-63. R.A. Copenhagen.
228. Sjøqvist, *P. Vedel,* vol. I, p. 161.
229. *Ibid.*
230. Russell to Paget, 30 November and 13 December 1862, P.R.O. 30/22, Sweden and Denmark, Earl Russell, Private, 1859-1865, vol. 102, pp. 10 and 12.
231. Sjøqvist, vol. I, pp. 161 and 247.

make it difficult for him to take energetic measures against Denmark. This caused the Danish Government to feel able to reject Russell's initiative – a step fully approved of by Vedel.[10]

The rejection of Russell's proposals contributed to the chill in relations between London and Copenhagen and between St. Petersburg and Copenhagen. Denmark's situation deteriorated and she found herself almost completely isolated in the international arena.

232. *Ibid.* p. 247.

5. The January Insurrection in the Kingdom of Poland. The Scandinavian Countries and Russia[1]

I

At the beginning of 1863 a chill set in in Russo-Danish relations. Denmark was very displeased by Gorchakov's unequivocal support for Russell's proposals, contained in the so-called Gotha telegram. Both the Copenhagen government and Danish public opinion regarded these as definitely contrary to Denmark's interests, since if they were implemented Denmark would be dependent on the German Confederation. Rumours publicised by *Dagbladet* that the Russian government was seeking to intervene in Danish internal affairs in order to bring about a change of government to one which would be more compliant and would make far-reaching concessions to Germany, exacerbated relations between Russia and Denmark even further.

Everything came to a head with the addresses to the King on 24 December 1862 and 7 January 1863. The Russian ambassador in Copenhagen described these as, on the one hand, manœuvres by the liberal party in an attempt to calm public opinion, and, on the other, assertions of the independence of Denmark and evidence of the categorical rejection of anything seen as an affront to national dignity.[2]

In Copenhagen there was increasing talk of the need to turn to Scandinavianism and more and more emphasis on the need to pursue the Eider policy and abandon the 'Helstat' idea, since the German demands for a change in the constitution, which would mean, for example, that no law in Denmark could come into force if it were not accepted by the Estates of Holstein, would mean in practice paralysis of the legislative and executive bodies in Denmark. The Government's attitude to this matter is illustrated by Hall's instructions to his ambassador in Britain. On 5 January 1863, in his dispatch to Bille, the Danish Minister to London, Hall laid down his plans for Holstein and Schleswig:

D'un côté, il faut subir la nécessité d'accorder aux Etats Holsteinois la position que la Diète de Francfort exige, mais avec les réserves nécessaires pour que cette province ne devienne pas le maître et l'arbitre des destinées du reste de la Monarchie. De l'autre côté, le Slesvig doit rester en dehors de l'action de la Confédération, et conserver ses rapports constitution-

---

1. This is an enlarged version of my book *The 1863 Polish Uprising and Scandinavia. The Year 1863, The Turning Point in Russo-Scandinavian Relations.* (Copenhagen, 1988).
2. 'Le Danemark est un petit pays que l'on croît pouvoir offenser impunément', *Dagbladet*, no. 239, Revue, no. 45, 16 December 1862, in connection with criticism of the Gotha telegram.

nels avec le Royaume pour les affaires communes. Le premier point écartera tout prétexte d'une exécution fédérale dans le Holstein. Le second point est la condition indispensable pour l'existence d'un Etat Danois, et si Lord Russell redoute que le développment de l'état des choses légalement existant pour le Slesvig et le Royaume n'aboutisse à quelque violente explosion, le Gouvernement du Rois est fermement convaincu qu'une telle explosion ne pourrait se produire que par suite d'instigations et des violences étrangères. Et une telle éventualité le Gouvernement envisage avec calme et la résolution que lui inspire la conscience de son bon droit.[3]

But this plan had no chance of success. The session of the Estates of Holstein on 24 January again showed how great was the gap between Itzehoe and Copenhagen.

Meanwhile there was a fundamental change in the international situation. On 22-23 January the Polish uprising broke out. New problems were now piled on top of Russia's previous military, financial and domestic political difficulties. Russia felt threatened at the most sensitive place in her empire, for Poland was, after all, the road to Europe and, furthermore, if the Polish programme for the reconstruction of Poland within its historical frontiers (i.e. those of 1772) were carried out as the Provisional National Government proclaimed, Russia's frontiers, St. Petersburg feared, would be shifted far to the east, to the Dnieper and the Dvina at Kiev and Smolensk. 'This ... destroys her political and geographical unity, pushes her into Asia, sets her back 200 years'.[4] Gorchakov's words to the Swedish ambassador are characteristic here:

... que ce que l'Occident appelle l'indépendance du Royaume [Poland – E.H.], nous le nommons simplement le démembrement de l'Empire. Aucun souverain russe n'y saurait volontairement consentir.[5]

The Franco-Russian rapprochement, of which Gorchakov had been the architect since 1856, and which was designed to help Russia to emerge from the isolation in which she found herself following the Crimean War, and to secure the abolition of the disadvantageous and humiliating clauses in the Treaty of Paris, lay in ruins after the outbreak of the Polish uprising.

For European governments the Convention of Alvensleben, signed by Russia and Prussia in St. Petersburg on 8 February 1863, which again made the Polish question an international one, was of fundamental importance. Poland once more took a special place in the policy both of the occupying powers and of the states of Western Europe – and in public opinion in the West. At the same time, the Polish uprising was a spur to revolutionary struggle throughout Europe, especially in Italy and Hungary. The Convention of Alvensleben accelerated the rise of a new international political constellation. Prussia, which was no less interested in suppress-

---

3. Beskickningens i Köpenhamn arkiv. Handlingar, vol. 8. Question des Duchés, 1848-1864, Riksarkivet, Stockholm.
4. E. Halicz, *Polish National Liberation Struggles and the Genesis of the Modern Nation,* (Odense U.P., 1982), p. 166.
5. Wedel-Jarlsberg, no. 50, 1 May (19 April) 1863, Kabinettet för utrikes brev. Dep. från besk. i Petersburg, 1863, Riks. Stockholm.

ing the uprising than Russia, stood firmly on Russia's side and supported her as her only political and military ally. It depended only on Russia how far active military co-operation between Prussia and Russia would go in the fight against the Polish insurgent forces.[6] If in practice the Convention was less important than it may initially have seemed, this was not only due to the forceful reaction of the Western states but also because Russian national pride did not allow the military and political circles close to Gorchakov in St. Petersburg and the Grand Duke Constantine in Warsaw to treat Prussia as an equal partner. In the Russians' view, to seek military assistance from Prussia would have been equivalent to admitting Russia's military weakness. If anyone gained from signing the Convention (from which, it should be noted, Bismarck soon wanted to withdraw, owing to the reaction in Europe and the fear of possible intervention by the Western States against Prussia), it was in the last resort Prussia – who in fact played little more than a symbolic role in the suppression of the Polish uprising. For it led, after all, to the collapse of the seven-year understanding between France and Russia, leaving Prussia as Russia's sole and indispensable ally at a difficult time.[7]

The situation now seemed advantageous to Denmark,[8] since Europe was absorbed with the Polish question.[9] O. Bismarck had officially stated that he had more important problems than Schleswig-Holstein,[10] and Austria, unlike Prussia, took the Western powers' side, joining in their diplomatic intervention in St. Petersburg over the Polish question.[11] Many Danish ambassadors urged the government

---

6. 'Wir möchten gern, dass in Bezug auf jede polnische *Insurrection,* wie in Bezug auf jede Gefahr vom Auslande her, sich das schöne Wort bewahrheite, welches der Kaiser in Moskau zu Goltz gesprochen hat, dass Russland und der Preussen gemeinsamen Gefahren solidarisch entgegentreten, als ob sie *ein* Land bildeten'. Bismarck to Gorchakov, 2 February 1863. *Werke im Auswahl,* vol. 3, pp. 68 ff. Cf. L. Gall, *Bismarck. Der weisse Revolutionär,* (1983), p. 273; *Krasnyi Arkhiv,* 1933, vol. 61, p. 13.
7. Bismarck had a double purpose in concluding the Convention: to check the liberal and pan-Slavist parties in St. Petersburg and to divide Russia from the Western powers. These aims he achieved. See A. Hillgruber, *Bismarcks Aussenpolitik;* S. Kieniewicz, *Powstanie styczniowe,* (Warsaw, 1979); Gall, *Bismarck ...,* pp. 273 ff. The military convention which Bismarck concluded with Russia, as J. Feldman rightly said, proved to be the germ of the greatness and power of the new Prussia, whose mission was to subordinate the whole of Germany to the Hohenzollern sceptre. In the Polish historian's opinion it was the turning point in the build-up of Prussian power. J. Feldman, *Bismarck a Polska,* pp. 241-4, 266-7; cf. also J. Borejsza, *Piekny wiek XIX,* p. 270 ff. 'Die Konvention hatte jedoch eine grosse politische Wirkung innerhalb und ausserhalb Preussens', said E. Engelberg in his recent work, *Bismarck, Urpreusse und Reichsgründer.* (Berlin, 1985), p. 543. As the well known historian A. Eruzalimsky commented, the political rapprochement between Prussia and Russia in certain matters, particularly the fight against the Polish national liberation movement, went so far that the connections between them were as close as between two sections of the same department. 'Pisma O. Bismarka A.M. Gorchakovu', *Krasnyi Arkhiv,* 1933, vol. 61, p. 5.
8. E. Eyck, *Bismarck,* vol. I. p. 568. N. Neergaard, *Under Junigrundloven,* vol. II, p. I. pp. 597-602.
9. See V. Revunienkov, *Pol'skoe vosstan'e 1863 g. i evropeiskaya diplomatiya,* (Leningrad, 1957), chs. V and VI.
10. C.E.J. Bülow's telegram to Hall from Vienna, 16 February 1863, in Privatarkiv D. C. Hall, Arkiv 3222 pk. 1. R.A. Copenhagen.
11. Despite this, cooperation between the Russian and Austrian police authorities was not interrupted. See E. Halicz, 'L'attitude des autorités militaires autrichiennes de Galicie vis-à-vis l'insurrection polonaise de 1863', *Revue Internationale d'Histoire Militaire* (Paris, 1966), pp. 553-4, and the documents from the Hof-, Haus- und Staatsarchiv, Vienna, published by Halicz in *Studia i materiały do historii wojskowości,* (Warsaw, 1967), vol. XIII, part 2, pp. 294-6.

to use the situation to take a step towards implementation of the 'Dano-Eider' policy. Hall, too, thought that Denmark should take advantage of a favourable international situation: first, there were differences between Prussia and Austria over the Polish question, to which French diplomacy drew particular attention; second, there was the growth of pro-Danish feeling in Britain in connection with the wedding of Princess Alexandra to Edward, Prince of Wales, which tended to neutralise the political moves by Russell at the end of 1863; and third, there was the constitutional conflict in Prussia and Bismarck's troubles with the liberals in the Chamber of Deputies over their opposition to the budget for reorganising the army. In these circumstances, Hall believed, Denmark should proceed to put the relations between herself and Holstein and Lauenburg onto a new footing.

With the support of public opinion, particularly in Copenhagen (which was demonstrated, among other things, by the historic meeting in Casino on 28 March 1863 at which speakers demanded the immediate separation of Holstein and closer union with Schleswig),[12] Hall got the King to sign a Royal Decree[13] on 30 March 1863, to come into force on 1 January 1864, which established new legal regulations for Holstein. The March decree stated that no statute could come into effect in the territory of Holstein without the agreement of the Estates, but also that the Holstein opposition could not annul the legal force of statutes passed by the Rigsraad in the whole of the monarchy and Schleswig. As Hall indicated in his circular to his ambassadors abroad, this decree was a concession to Holstein and was intended to simplify relations between Denmark and Germany.

In order to make the decree more attractive to Holstein, institutions there were to be developed in a more liberal spirit than previously. Holstein was to receive an independent constitution and have its own army, and only the King, foreign policy and the navy were to be common to the Monarchy and Holstein.

Le patente royale est un acte de la volonté souveraine du Roi – we read in Hall's circular to W. Scheel-Plessen on 31 March 1863[14] – qui ne fait dépendre la mise en vigeur de ses dispositions ni du vote approbatif du Rigsraad ni de celui des Etats Holsteinois. C'est que le besoin de la situation exige avant tout une décision catégorique et immédiate. Toute autre manière de procéder que celle que le Roi a choisie, aurait fait perdre un temps précieux, et si le Gouvernement s'était adressé au seul Rigsraad pour arriver avec son concours à une solution, il se serait exposé sans doute au reproche de ne pas avoir demandé également le consentement des Etats Holsteinois. Or, s'il avait fait dépendre l'affaire du vote de ceux-ci, personne qui connaît l'esprit de cette Assemblée, ne saurait douter de ce qui en eût résulté.

C'est cette idée qui a presidé à la rédaction de la patente.

There is no question that this decree marked a step in the direction of the Eider policy, which meant a departure from the 'Helstat' policy and a rejection of the idea of a common constitution for the whole of the Monarchy – one of the under-

---

12. The resolution was published in *Fædrelandet*. See *Denmark and Germany*, no. 2 pp. 28-9, 37-39 and 59-61.
13. The so-called March Patent.
14. Sverige, Ordrer, 1861-68, no. 4. R.A. Copenhagen.

takings Denmark had given in the talks with the German states in 1851-52. Schleswig, however, was becoming undoubtedly closer to Denmark than Holstein. Even the British ambassador in Copenhagen, A. Paget, who favoured Denmark, admitted:

> it is impossible to deny, that as a definitive arrangement, it is contrary to the stipulations entered into by the Danish Government with Austria and Prussia in 1851-52 ... It is, as it were, throwing down the gauntlet to those two Powers, and, as was to be expected, they have not failed to take it up.

Paget saw Hall's decision as a reflection of pressure from the supporters of the Eider party.[15]

Ch. Bluhme, one of the architects of the 1851-52 agreement with Germany, spoke out against the decree. He considered that both the 6 November 1858 and the 30 March 1863 decrees infringed the agreements and the royal decree of 28 January 1852. This 1852 decree, Bluhme argued in his speech in the Rigsraad on 11 May 1863, had been a compromise. The King had undertaken to renounce incorporation of Schleswig and Germany to renounce Schleswig-Holsteinism, that is to say, reconstruction of the old administrative union between Schleswig and Holstein, and it had been laid down that in future Schleswig should have relations with the Monarchy identical to those between Holstein and the Monarchy. If Germany had broken its undertakings, the Danish government should have protested and insisted that the other party fulfil them; by acting in that way it would have earned respect and would not have found itself completely isolated in Europe. By its behaviour the government had jeopardised the country's interests in a most dangerous manner.[16]

The decree, which was undoubtedly intended to be an important step in bringing Schleswig closer to the Monarchy, while not yet incorporating it entirely – as all German and many British historians wrongly claim – caused great displeasure in the German States. The protest movement was headed by the National-Verein, the organisation of German liberals. Austria and Prussia were absorbed in the Polish question and did not want a new crisis in international relations, so they confined themselves to sending identical notes of protest to Copenhagen.[17] Yet on 16 April the matter came up for debate in the German Diet and the committee which it appointed delivered a report, as a result of which on 9 July a majority in the Diet called on Denmark to withdraw the March decree within a period not exceeding six weeks on pain of further consequences as it was contrary to the 1851-52 agreements.

The Russian ambassador in Copenhagen was not surprised by Germany's reaction. In a report on 8 (20) April he said the decree had caused a wave of demonstrations in Holstein and demands for the German Diet to intervene immediately on

---

15. *Denmark and Germany,* no. 2. Sir Paget to Russell, Copenhagen, 29 April 1863, no. 49. pp. 59-61.
16. *Denmark and Germany,* no. 2, pp. 67-9. See also Nicolay's report no. 47 of 2 (14) May 1863.
17. L.D. Steefel, *The Schleswig-Holstein Question,* pp. 57-58.

behalf of Schleswig and Holstein. N. Nicolay also reported that the decree had been criticised in Denmark itself. The conservatives had condemned it as a blow to the integrity of the monarchy, and the national liberal party regarded it as an insignificant and deceptive measure, leaving the field open to all manner of insinuations and interpretations: it thought there should be decisive action to effect the complete separation of Holstein from the Monarchy. Nicolay personally took the view that half- measures and palliatives satisfied nobody and in the longer term could only bring harmful results for the government.

As could be expected,[18] Gorchakov expressed reservations about the decree from the beginning. He asked C.R.E. Vind whether the decree did not mean the incorporation of Schleswig. Their conversation took place at a moment which was not the most propitious for Denmark since it coincided with Gorchakov's complaints concerning the assistance given by Danish sailors to the Polish insurgent action organised by A. Hertzen, N. Ogarev and G. Mazzini, using the *Ward Jackson* to land volunteers and arms in Lithuania.[19] When questioned by Gorchakov, Vind was unable to give any explanation and confined himself to expressions of regret if Danish sailors had really taken part in providing assistance to the Polish expedition under the leadership of Col. T. Lapiński.[20]

Gorchakov's tone in this conversation was different from what it had been during their last meeting, at the reception given by Napier in the British embassy in St. Petersburg on the occasion of the wedding of Princess Alexandra and the Prince of Wales, when Gorchakov had proposed a toast to the health of the Danish King and the newly-weds and expressed the wish that the good relations between Russia and Denmark, going back to Peter the Great, should long continue.[21] The talk which Vind had a few days later with Baron R. Osten-Sacken convinced him that the Russian government was too busy with its own affairs to concern itself seriously with Danish problems. The Russian cabinet, Osten-Sacken declared, was far from approving the petition from the Estates of Holstein, but regretted that the Danish government had not entered into talks with Germany on the basis of Russell's proposals. In his view the decree of 30 March meant neither the complete separation of Holstein nor the incorporation of Schleswig, and he did not consider it contrary to what the King had promised. The German press was going too far in writing of Schleswig as a country which had to be recovered, when it was well known that it had never been part of Germany.

18. 'La Russie, qui en ce moment, attache le plus grand prix à l'alliance prussienne, se rangera probablement du même côté que le cabinet de Berlin', we read in Mémoires et documents. Danemark 1856-63. Question des Duchés II. Vol. 13, April 1863, k. 448-52. A.M.A.E. Paris.
19. Kieniewicz, *Powstanie* ... pp. 410-11; V. Zaitsev, 'Morskaya povstancheskaya ekspeditsíya k beregam Litvy v 1863 g.' in *K stoletiyu geroicheskoi bor'by za nashu i vashu svobodu* (Moscow, 1964), pp. 180 ff.
20. Dep. Rus. no. 10. 10 April (29 March) 1863.
21. Vind. no. 7, 15 (27) March 1863. (According to the Swedish ambassador Wedel-Jarlsberg's account this toast was proposed by Baron Bloudoff. St. Pet. No. 20, 11 march (27 February) 1863. R.A. Stockholm).

Nevertheless, the Russian government had reservations about the fact that the decree had been issued.[22] Gorchakov showed this in a talk with the Austrian ambassador, F. Thun, expressing satisfaction that both of the greater German states were agreed in their view of the decree and hoping that they would continue to cooperate. He himself would miss no opportunity to recommend this to Bismarck.[23] He also showed Thun the text of a dispatch sent to P. Oubril in Berlin and Nicolay in Copenhagen on 13 (25) April which regretted the issue of the decree and criticised the Danish government for it.

As for the motives of the move designed to settle the constitutional position of Holstein, the Russian government did not intend to comment. The Frankfurt Diet was competent to pass judgement on the substance of the matter. By issuing the decree the Danish government was in some sense retreating from the period of genuine reconciliation with Germany, and the fact that there was no mention of Schleswig opened the field for speculation. Gorchakov called on the Danish government to proceed to carry out the 1851-52 obligations, stressed the special importance of an understanding with Austria and Prussia, which both harboured good will towards Denmark, and recommended the government to avoid everything which could further complicate what was already a serious situation.[24]

Hall could not expect the St. Petersburg cabinet to approve his move, but he did not anticipate such far-reaching criticism of the decree from Gorchakov.[25] Hall was particularly stung by two passages in Gorchakov's note:

que nous [Denmark] avons scindé l'objet des négociations avec les cours de Berlin et de Vienne en fixant la position du Holstein par la patente Royale mentionnée

and

qu'il devait avant tout importer aux hommes d'Etat danois de se concillier les *bonnes dispositions* de l'Autriche et de la Prusse.

According to the Russian ambassador's report, Hall saw 'quelque chose d'humiliant pour la dignité nationale' in the words *'bonnes dispositions'*. Hall also tried to convince the ambassador that he was far from the idea of separation and that the Danish goverment wanted at any price to preserve 'le plus de liens possibles' between Holstein and the remainder of the Monarchy.

The French and British governments also regarded the 30 March decree as a dangerous move and both governments urged Denmark to be cautious. E. Drouyn de Lhuys regretted that the decree might unite the German states, which had been split after the outbreak of the Polish uprising, and advised the Danish government to support Austria in German affairs and to make concessions in the direction of

---

22. Vind, no. 13, 25 (13) April 1863.
23. Thun to Vienna, 28 (16) April. H.H.S.A. Vienna. P.A. Russland, Kart. 54.
24. Gorchakov to Nicolay, 13 (25) April 1863. Udenrigsm. Samlede Sager. Den Holstenske Forfat. R.A. Copenhagen.
25. Nicolay, 24 April (6 May) and Hall to Plessen, Ordrer, 18 May, 1863. R.A. Copenhagen.

Vienna. 'Je dois en contester l'opportunité dans le moment actuel-Vous ralliez vos ennemis tout en disséminant vos alliés', the French minister upbraided the Danish ambassador on 27 April.[26] From then on the question of the duchies, and particularly Schleswig, became more and more closely connected with the Polish question.

II

The Polish uprising, which flared up on the night of 22-23 January, met with a lively response in Denmark.[27] Interest in the Polish question had been building up since 1860. The Danish press, especially *Berlingske Tidende* and *Fædrelandet*, devoted a great deal of attention to the problems of Poland and the development of the national liberation movement in the Polish lands. Thanks to the press, Danish society could follow the growing conflict between Polish society and the Tsarist authorities. On the basis of reports in the German, French and Russian press and telegrams from Warsaw and St. Petersburg, the press in Copenhagen kept its readers informed about the course of the patriotic demonstrations in Warsaw, beginning with the events in February and April 1861, the state of siege in Warsaw, the disturbances in Lodz and Kalisz, the peasant movement, and the policy of the local and central Tsarist authorities.

In the autumn of 1861 the Danish papers devoted a lot of space to the church demonstrations and the repression directed against priests, and reported the first cases of long-term exile to Siberia that had been made from Poland. In 1862 they wrote a lot about the revival of the revolutionary movement, the formation of the City Revolutionary Committee in Warsaw and the wave of attacks on leading representatives of the Tsarist administration of the Grand Duke Constantine and A. Wielopolski. Long articles appeared in the press on Poland, her history – particularly since the 18th century – and Polish-Russian relations in the era of the partitions.[28]

In comparison with *Berlingske Tidende*, *Fædrelandet* was involved with events in Poland to a much greater degree. It also took a position of unequivocal solidarity with Poland in her struggle. Its information service was far more extensive and its accounts of events, particularly in Warsaw, beginning with the 25 February demonstration in honour of the 1831 Battle of Grochow, were more detailed. The paper showed great understanding of the demands which the Poles addressed to the authorities, was critical of the unsatisfactory concessions to Polish society which were forced out of the regime, and condemned the repression of demonstrators and the terror employed by the Tsarist authorities in the Kingdom of Poland.

26. No. 42, (Confidentiel), Frankrig. Depecher. 1861-64. R.A. Copenhagen.
27. See E. Halicz, 'The Scandinavian Countries and the January Insurrection', in *War and Society in East Central Europe*. Vol. XIV. (New York, 1984).
28. See *Berlingske Tidende,* 8 April 1861, 'Polen siden dets Deling', 18 June 1862, 'Den polske bevægelse og tydskerne', 18 October 1861, and the series of articles 'Rusland og Polen'.

Fædrelandet quoted the French press, which as a rule favoured Poland, more frequently than *Berlingske*.

Fædrelandet condemned the introduction of martial law in the Kingdom of Poland, and the associated repression and persecution of the Catholic and Jewish priesthood. It wrote sympathetically about Polish secret organisations and their activities and about leaders such as L. Mieroslawski. Thanks to *Fædrelandet,* the Danish reader could understand the various aspects of the situation in the Kingdom of Poland, both political and social, and learn the positions of leading politicians like A. Wielopolski and A. Zamoyski; the attitude of the different social classes and strata to the central problems of the country; and the policy of the Tsarist authorities. Finally, the paper reported the reactions of the societies and governments of Western Europe to events in the Kingdom of Poland. *Fædrelandet* published many articles on a broad range of topics to do with Poland, her history and culture. An article on J. Lelewel (on the occasion of the death of this distinguished scholar and father of Polish democracy, who was also esteemed for his research in the field of mediaeval Scandinavian history), deserves especial mention.[29] Among other things it referred to his eminence in the field of 'nordisk oldkyndighed'[30] and Polish-Danish relations in the seventeenth century, as well as the history of Silesia and Poznan. It stressed that Lelewel's works demonstrated the indisputable Polishness of these western lands, which had been seized and Germanised by Prussia. The drama of Poland from the end of the eighteenth century was presented by J.C. Magnus in a series of articles based on the work of Charles de Mazade.[31]

Following the outbreak of the uprising, the Copenhagen press reported events in the Kingdom of Poland on the basis of information obtained mainly from the German press and the *Journal de St. Pétersbourg*. *Berlingske* reported on the impressment into the tsarist army and the first encounters between the insurgents and Russian troops,[32] predicting that the uprising would soon be lost in a blood bath, whereas *Fædrelandet* was of the opinion that it would gather momentum.[33] The Danish press, especially *Berlingske* and *Morgenposten,*[34] drew attention to the different character of the January uprising in comparison with that of 1830-31. *Berlingske* argued that the uprising was not a national one and bore the marks of a socialist movement. Neither the gentry nor the peasant were joining the uprising to the same extent as the town dwellers.[35] *Berlingske* stressed that the peasants were helping in the capture of insurgents.[36] The conservative periodical *Kronen,* while

---

29. *Fædrelandet,* no. 129, 7 June 1861.
30. *Edda Skandinawska* and *Edda t.j. Ksiega religii dawnych Skandynawii mieszkańców* by J. Lelewel published in 1807 and 1828. See: M. Janion, 'Polish Romanticism and Scandinavia'. In: *The Slavic World and Scandinavia. Cultural Relations.* (Aarhus U.P. 1988, p. 101).
31. *Fædrelandet,* nos. 120-123, 26, 27, 28 and 30 May 1862.
32. *Berlingske,* no. 21, 26 January 1863.
33. *Fædrelandet,* no. 24, 29 January 1863.
34. 29 January and 2 February.
35. See *Fædrelandet,* no. 26, 31 January.
36. *Berlingske,* no. 25, 30 January.

condemning impressment as an old and barbarian practice, also condemned the insurgents who, in its opinion, aimed to make 22-23 January a massacre on a par with the massacre of St. Bartholomew. *Kronen* also maintained that the active groups in the movement were the landless gentry and the urban proletariat, while the peasants, influenced by agitators, had risen against the manors, causing the landowners in many localities to flee to the towns. In *Kronen's* view, the Poles, influenced by Massinism, had rejected the concessions granted them by Alexander II, had set up revolutionary committees linked with terrorist organisations, and had exploited the surge of patriotic feelings during the demonstrations. These had been headed by priests and took advantage of the fact that many Poles serving in the Russian army had joined the movement, to become members of revolutionary committees. In the face of impressment these elements had resolved to start the uprising.[37] It is significant that similar criticisms of the 'ingratitude of the Poles' to their 'benefactor' Alexander II appeared in the reports from the Danish and Swedish embassies in St. Petersburg.

Fædrelandet, however, like *Dagbladet, Danmark* and *Morgenposten*,[38] pointed out that the uprising was aimed at national liberation, and it condemned the barbarity of the Russians. But it was notable that it placed the responsibility for the outbreak of the uprising on the Germans, for the Russians were basically not a fully developed nation and were ruled by the Germans. Since Catherine II, Russia had been ruled by the Holstein-Gottorp dynasty; Germans governed the country, and they oppressed other European nations too.[39] They were ultimately responsible for the plans for the partition of Poland. This emphasis on the special role of Germans in Russian history coincided with the signing of the Convention of Alvensleben. *Fædrelandet*[40] wondered whether this step would not bring Russia more harm than good, as it internationalised the uprising.[41] *Kronen* argued on 28 February that the conclusion of the Convention had changed the constellation of political forces in Europe. Until recently the pattern of the world had been set by the rapprochement between Russia and France and Prussia and France. Now, however, with the Russo-Prussian rapprochement, France, Britain and Austria had moved closed together. But the broad participation by Poles, together with Hungarians, Italians, Russians and Germans, in the European revolutionary movement, together with intensive revolutionary propaganda, would make statesmen (in *Kronens* opinion), disinclined to support the Polish uprising and the attempt to establish an independent Poland. *Kronen* criticised the section of the Danish press which expressed the view that the uprising would be successful. The collapse of the M. Langiewicz dictatorship and the fact that the Polish bands (the paper con-

---

37. *Kronen*, 31 January. The massacre of St. Bartholomew on August 24, 1572.
38. 2 February.
39. *Fædrelandet*, 12 February.
40. No. 45, 23 February.
41. Cf. also *Kronen*, 21 February, 'Preussens Østrigs forhold til opstanden i Polen' and 28 February, 'Det Polske spørgsmaal'.

tinually used such pejorative terms) such as that of A. Kurowski, had not managed to acquire an operating base (in the southern part of the Kingdom of Poland – E.H.) after their initial success nor to control the Warsaw railway line (presumably the Warsaw-Vienna line – E.H.), showed that this prediction was groundless.[42] *Kronen* also made a class analysis of the movement.

What were the great powers demanding from Russia, the paper asked, and answered: the announcement of an amnesty.[43] Russell's demand, on the other hand, that Russia should observe the resolutions of the Congress of Vienna in respect of Poland, as the Berne *Eidgenössische Zeitung* also argued, was farcical. This treaty was archaic and it was well known that it had been broken many times by various states (for example Greece, by Russia after the Polish November uprising, by France and Italy in 1859) and there had been no reaction then from France or Britain. *Kronen* laughed at paper treaties and protocols.[44] It was sceptical about Austria's policy towards the uprising and presumed that Austria, like Prussia, would join Russia in order to protect herself in the face of revolution.[45]

Different conclusions were reached by the weekly *Illustreret Tidende* (Ugens Politik), which favoured Poland. It said that the signing of the Russo-Prussian Convention and the tendency to the reestablishment of the principles of the Holy Alliance had led to a reaction throughout Europe, where the Polish uprising enjoyed universal sympathy and admiration.[46] The paper condemned the Russian troops' action and their barbarous conduct,[47] as well as the murder, arrest and exile of Poles to Siberia.

It welcomed the fact that the uprising had spread to Lithuania and assumed a truly popular character there, as it enjoyed active support from the peasants.[48] Like *Fædrelandet*,[49] the paper was severely critical of the speech in the Rigsraad by the well known Danish politician A.F. Tsherning, who called the insurgents 'bandits'.[50] It was not the Poles but the invaders who were bandits, said *Illustreret Tidende*, and they had destroyed everything that was sacred and dear to the Poles. Rulers, parliaments and ordinary people all wished the Poles success.

As can be seen from the above extracts, the whole of the press in general saw the need to stand up for the Poles on humanitarian grounds. Attitudes to the uprising as a national movement, on the other hand, depended on the political colour of the newspaper, and there were big and fundamental differences in this respect between the national liberal and the conservative papers. Nor can we overlook the fact that the press saw much in common between the Poles' struggle and the problems with

---

42. 'Den polske sags nederlag', *Kronen*, 28 March.
43. *Ibid.*
44. 'Polen og Wienertraktaten', 11 April.
45. *Kronen*, 10 May.
46. 1, 15 and 22 March.
47. 7 April.
48. 10 May.
49. No. 108, 12 May.
50. Røvere – *Illustreret Tidende*, 17 May.

which Denmark was grappling in the duchies. Writing of the outrages committed by the Russians during the uprising and earlier in Poland (1768-69, 1794, 1830-31),[51] comparisons were drawn with Prussia's policy towards the duchies, and it was emphasised that Germany wanted to make Denmark another Poland, while the knightly Estates in Schleswig and Holstein was playing the same role as the Polish aristocracy had once played, thereby betraying its own country. It is significant that even part of the liberal press stressed that the Polish question was not so important a problem for Denmark as it was for Sweden, which feared Russian aggression. The principal question for Denmark was the fate of the Fatherland.[52]

Many Danes, even those friendly to Poland such as C.W. Smith, like many Swedes, did not see a connection between the struggle for progress in their own country and defence against oppression by the invaders.[53] Nor was there any lack of criticism of Poland as a hotbed of anarchy which justified the invaders policy; that the Poles had ruined their country as a result of their inability to agree; and that they were unable to create a culture of their own.[54] Some also said that it was not possible simultaneously to support the Polish uprising and oppose what was happening in Holstein and Schleswig. Finally, Danish views of the events may have been influenced, to some extent, by the fact that Denmark had never had the experience of fighting for its independence. In many circles there was a desire not to antagonise Russia, as her help was still counted on in the dispute with Germany.

The really sharp debate and polarisation of views on what Denmark's attitude to the uprising should be flared up in the Spring of 1863. This debate was closely connected with the central problem pervading Danish society, that of Schleswig-Holstein. The Polish uprising allowed some to cherish the hope that Prussia would turn her attention eastward and cease to take such a keen interest in the affairs of the duchies. This is one of the essential reasons for the strong sympathy which part of Danish society felt for the uprising.[55]

Before the Spring, or more exactly before the second half of April, in the judgement of the Russian ambassador who was sensitive to every sign of pro-Polish feeling, Danish society as a whole was virtually indifferent to the uprising. 'Le public danois avait témoigné jusqu'ici une indifférence complète à l'égard des polonais', Nicolay reported.[56] The French ambassador, Dotézac, was of the same opinion: 'Mais comme les Danois se passionent peu pour les causes qui ne touchent pas immédiatement à leur intérêts politiques, ce mouvement était resté, jusqu'ici, dans les

---

51. *Danmark,* 28 February, 'Russerne i Polen', 4 March, 'Saaledes gik det i Polen', and 17 March, where there was reference to the events in Poland in 1769.
52. *Danmark,* 28 February, C.B. Rimestad, 'Russerne i Polen'.
53. See K. Ślaski, *Tysiąclecie polsko-skandynawskich stosunków kulturalnych,* (1977), pp. 294-5; A. Zaluska-Stromberg, 'Odzwierciedlenie problemów mickiewiczowskich w Szwecji', *Pamietnik Literacki,* vol. XLIX, no. I. pp. 111-55.
54. Ślaski, *Tysiąclecie ...*
55. W. Czapliński and K. Górski, *Historia Danii* (1965) p. 287, T. Cieślak, *Polska-Skandynawia w XIX i XX wieku* (Warsaw 1973) p. 90.
56. Particulière, 24 April (6 May) A.V.P. Rossii, vol. 65.

limites d'une sympathie speculative ...'.[57] But the situation changed at the end of April or the beginning of May. Apart from the fact that despite various forecasts that it would quickly collapse the uprising was in fact spreading, this was to a large extent due to external pressure. On the one hand, there was pressure from Sweden, which was displaying growing interest in the Polish uprising, on the other, there was pressure from the Western states on the Danish government to joint their diplomatic campaign to exert pressure on Russia.

As far as the first point is concerned, an essential influence seems to have been the letter to the editor of *Fædrelandet* written by a Dane living in Stockholm, dated 20 April 1863, and which appeared in the paper on 25 April under the heading *'Danmark og den polske frihedskamp'*.[58] The writer of this letter contrasted the active and friendly attitude of Swedish society towards the Polish uprising with what he called the insensitive attitude of the Danes to the Poles' life and death struggle. This silence on the part of Denmark was giving the country the reputation of being Russophile. How could Denmark ask other nations for help in its fight for Schleswig if it was not prepared to help another nation fighting for freedom. The Danes' indifference could not be justified by the fact that they were a small nation. If we do not commit ourselves, the letter concluded, we shall lose irrespective of whether the Poles lose or win.

The author of the letter thought that Denmark's place was beside France and that this was the only direction in which a constitutional government could go. Russia's friendship was more dangerous than Germany's hostility. There was no reason why Denmark had to thank Russia for bringing about Prussia's withdrawal from Jutland in 1848-49. Now there was no cause to be afraid of her as she was powerless. It was not a question, the writer explained, of going to war for Poland, but of helping her morally and diplomatically. Russia had no chance of victory in the event of war with the coalition of Western states and Sweden and could not defeat that coalition. Denmark could be of great assistance to the coalition. This would create a situation of united action by the Scandinavian countries, the absence of which had been very costly in the past. This applied both to the dispute between Denmark and Germany and to the question of Finland.

The letter evoked an immediate response. A certain 'L.' replied in the pages of *Fædrelandet* on 29 April, expressing astonishment that the author of the letter from Stockholm should criticise the Danes for lack of sympathy for Poland in her struggle. 'L.' submitted that the Danish nation, which was fighting against foreign coercion and was in a similar position to the Poles in Poznan and to the Italians in the Tyrol, was standing by the Poles. He reminded readers that even in 1830-31 the Poles had been admired in Denmark, and only someone who did not know Danish history could doubt whether Denmark would remain neutral if there were a war between the Western coalition and Russia and Prussia. The liberal press

---

57. No. 73, 16 May. Danemark, vol. 243. A.M.A.E. Paris.
58. Denmark and the Polish struggle for freedom.

backed *Fædrelandet's* position,[59] declaring itself in favour of support for the uprising in Poland, and appealed to society in this matter, on the grounds that it had greater freedom of action than the government.[60] But help did not have to take the form of political demands and noisy demonstrations or resolutions, because, *Dagbladet* said, these were not the Danes' custom. Instead it could take the form of the collection of money, regarded as a referendum in which the weak opposed the stronger, as was the case with the Danish question too. No nation could cherish warmer feelings for Poland than Denmark, which knew the truth about Prussian policy towards the Poles and had no doubt about Prussia's hidden intentions in relation to Schleswig. A free Poland on the eastern frontier of Prussia would be the best help in the fight to retain Schleswig.[61]

However, this view met with opposition from conservative circles. The conservative organ *Flyveposten* swung into action against *Fædrelandet*. Its answer to the author of the letter from Stockholm served at the same time as a starting-point for an exposition of the programme of Danish conservatism. In the journal's view, the idea of Scandinavian co-operation implied as a basic aim the conquest of Denmark and the division of its territory between Sweden and Prussia. It also reminded its readers what the outcome of alliance with France had been in the past, in the Napoleonic period, namely the loss of Norway. It also attacked the idea that Russia had played an insignificant role during the last war with Prussia over the duchies. It would be dangerous for Denmark to seek a choice between Napoleon III and Alexander II. It was doubtful whether Britain would support the alliance of France and Sweden militarily. The paper also warned of the consequences of breaking off relations between Denmark and the German Confederation.[62]

The issue of the paper published on 9 May contained a fundamental criticism of the uprising in Poland, accusing the Poles, unlike other nations such as the Dutch, of resorting to insurrection against Russia instead of the peaceful policy initiated by Alexander II. It criticised the links between the uprising and the revolutionary parties in Italy, as well as the social policy of the uprising and the lack of agreement between the Polish parties. As far as the future of Poland was concerned, it was pessimistic and did not believe that Poland could recover lands from Russia, or Poznan and Galicia, and thus act as a buffer against Germany. Poland could, on the contrary, become an instrument in the hands of other (Western – E.H.) states to destabilise her neighbours.

Flyveposten was not, of course, alone in this criticism. It was accompanied by *Kronen,* among others, using similar arguments about Poland. These papers expressed sympathy for the fate of Poland, but they cautioned Danish statesmen not to interfere in Polish affairs, not to antagonise Russia and not to link the country with any European grouping. They believed that with Russia's help 'Helstat' could be maintained and a *modus vivendi* with Germany found.

59. 29 and 30 April.
60. *Dagbladet,* 6 May.
61. *Ibid.* Referendum as a proof of a friendly attitude towards Poland.
62. *Flyveposten,* 5 May.

The conservative press, however, was unable to halt the trend which was becomming increasingly prominent in Danish society. The Danes were afraid of isolation in the face of a united Germany allied with Russia. More and more frequently public opinion began to call for an alliance between Paris, Copenhagen and Stockholm.

Soyez certain – said General F.G. Schoeller, the military commander in Holstein, to the French consul – que nous nous rappelons ce qu'à fait le Comte Cavour lors de la guerre de Crimée. Nous sommes un petit peuple, mais nous avons de grandes ressources et nous saurions les employer de manière à ne point vous être inutiles.

An old Danish diplomat declared:

Vous avez été en Italie sans l'Angleterre, je crois que vous devez agir en faveur de la Pologne sans demander la permission de l'Angleterre. Faitez-vous craindre de vos voisins d'Outre-Manche, c'est le meilleur moyen de vous en faire des amis.[63]

A similar mood prevailed among the officers of the garrison in Kiel.[64]

After the 30 March decree, when the question of the duchies entered a new phase, a wider and wider circle of politicians became conscious that in the event of an international conflict Denmark's place was on the side of the Western powers, particularly France. It was no accident, it seems, that the dailies and weeklies devoted more and more space to the international aspects of the Polish uprising, that they discussed in detail the attitude of the Western states towards the events in Poland, quoted the diplomatic notes sent to St. Petersburg, and wrote extensively about the reaction of the Russian cabinet.[65]

These articles examined the broad historical background of the Polish question from the eighteenth century. They considered the connection between the Polish question and Danish *raison d'état* and the influence of Russian policy on that of Austria and Prussia. They also devoted much attention to the nationality aspects of the Polish uprising, the uprising in Lithuania, Belorussia and the Ukraine, and the Prussian and Austrian policy aimed at Germanising the Polish lands, as well as the exploitation of the national antagonism between Poles and Ukrainians by the Austrian authorities in Galicia. Naturally, this interest in problems posed by nationality was closely connected with the Schleswig-Holstein question, and lasted throughout the uprising.[66]

---

63. A.M.A.E. Paris, Danemark, Kiel, 14 and 22 March 1863. Cf. Bóbr-Tylingo, 'Napoléon III, l'Europe et la Pologne 1863-4', *Antemurale 1863-1963*, (Rome, 1963) pp. 95-6.
64. A.M.A.E. Paris, Danemark, Kiel, 6 May 1863; Bóbr-Tylingo, p. 96.
65. See *Illustreret Tidende.* 19 and 26 April and 3 May. A series of articles on the international aspect of the Polish question appeared in *Berlingske Tidende,* beginning on 23 April.
66. *Fædrelandet* published a number of articles on this problem, of which the following deserve notice for the knowledge and critical value they show: "Den polsk-russiske nationalitetsstrid" (11 June), and some articles concerning the Polish-Russian question. (3 and 4 June, 9 and 23 July).
    The polemics spread to *Dagbladet* (No. 164). The exchange between C. Rosenberg, author of 'Den polske sags retfærdighed', in *Dansk Maanedsskrift,* 1863, vol. II. pp. 361-478, who defended Polish rights to the so-called eastern lands, and L. Rasmussen, author of the treatise 'Westrusland

At the end of April or the beginning of May the former passivity as regards the Polish question ('une indifférence complète à l'égard des polonais'), as Nicolay reported on 24 April (6 May),[67] gave way to considerable activity by various circles in Danish society, not only in Copenhagen but also in the provinces – for example in Odense – in which politicians connected with the national liberal party took the lead. On 6 May *Dagbladet*,[68] following *Fædrelandet,* published a long article calling on Danish public opinion to follow the other nations in Europe and join in providing material help for Poland in its fight for freedom and independence. In the same issue there was an appeal from Odense, written in the spirit of solidarity with Poland and urging society to contribute to a financial collection organised to

    indtil det polske Herredømmes Ophør', in *Dansk Maanedsskrift,* vol. II. pp. 1-75, who defended Russian *raison d'état,* is also noteworthy. Rosenberg defended Polish *raison d'état,* and the liberal policy pursued by Denmark in the duchies, as the opposite of the policy of Russification in the Ukraine and Belorussia, and argued that the parallel Rasmussen drew between Russian policy and Copenhagen's policy in southern Schleswig was groundless. It is also worth noting the treatises by C.W. Smith, particularly 'Preussen og Polen', I and II, in *Dansk Maanedsskrift,* 1864, vol. I, pp. 369-455 and vol. II, pp. 142-99, in which he describes, among other things, the perfidious policy of Prussia towards Poland since the middle of the 18th century, the history of the fight against Polishness, the Polish language and church in the 19th century, finally warning that should Schleswig, and perhaps Jutland too, fall into Prussia's hands the Danish population there would meet the same fate as the Poles.

    It is worth mentioning that two articles with the heading. 'Den polske opstands sande charakter' in *Flyveposten,* 18 and 19 October 1864, reported without comment the publication of the works *Fictions et realités polonaises,* (St. Pétersburg, S, Dufour, 1864) and *La restauration de la Pologne appréciée au point de la science historique et ethnographique,* by Th. de M. et Olricht (Paris, Denty, 1864), inspired by Russia. The author of a review signed R. confined himself to conveying the fundamental criticism directed against old Poland for its intolerant attitude to non-Catholics, and also criticised the attempts of the Polish National Government to restore Poland in its 1772 frontiers, the anti-peasant programme of the Czartoryski party in particular, and, finally, the treacherous methods used by the Poles during the uprising.

    In 1864 the History of Poland by F. Rouse, *Populær skildring af Polens Historie,* was published.

    On Tsarist counter-propaganda see E. Halicz, *'Le Nord* o konflikcie rosyjsko-polskim i jego perspektywach', in *Zeszyty Historyczne* (Paris), 1985, no. 74 and the foreword by T.N. Kopreeva to the volume *Zarys powstania styczniowego opracowany w Warszawskiej Cytadeli,* (Wroclaw and Moscow 1985). But the national question was not the only area in which analogies between Poland and Denmark were sought. *Flyveposten,* 14 and 15 June 1864, attacked *Fædrelandet* for applying the term Targowica to Ch. C. Bluhme. In *Flyveposten's* opinion the analogy was wrong, as Targowica contributed to the partition of Poland and the overthrow of the 1791 constitution and opened the road to foreign intervention. Bluhme's policy, on the other hand, aimed to close the road to foreign intervention, maintain Denmark's independence and preserve her unity. The Polish Targowica was to defend the old privileges of the gentry and was not consistent with the general good. Bluhme, however, aimed to strengthen the constitutional future of Denmark. It was 'Targowica' to support insurrection in Schleswig-Holstein and the appeal by the Estates of Holstein to Prussia against the lawful monarch. *Flyveposten,* no. 157, 10 July 1863, discussed the Instruction of the National Government on partisan warfare.

67. A.V.P.R. Vol. 65. In his report on 9 (21) May Nicolay wrote: 'La petite fraction du public danois qui a jugé convenable d'afficher des sympathies pour la cause polonaise en s'ingéniant à établir une solidarité entre elle et la cause Scandinave ne s'est pas bornée à instituer une collecte qui a atteint jusqu'ici le chiffre d' à près 2600écus; elle a voulu, à l'instar de ce que s'est fait en Suède organiser des démonstrations publiques'. Vol. 53, R.A. Copenhagen.

68. No. 104.

help the uprising. 'We must not forget that the same principles rule in Berlin as in St. Petersburg, and by defending the heroic achievements of the Polish nation the Danish nation is defending its own cause'. On 12 May *Dagbladet*[69] wrote:

Pour recueillir les dons que la sympathie pour l'humanité souffrante fera offrit aux Polonais, il va se former pendant ces jours un comité central à Copenhague. De pareils comités se sont déjà réunis dans plusieurs autres lieux du pays. L'impatience de faire preuve de sa compassion pour la malheureuse nation si cruellement opprimée, a même été si puissante que déjà avant la réunion du comité projeté, des dons assez considérables ont été recueillis et versés dans les bureaux de plusieurs journaux. Les étudiants de l'université de Copenhague comptent se réunir demain dans une séance extraordinaire, ayant pour but de se concerter sur le mode de la manifestation de la vive sympathie que leur inspire la sainte cause des Polonais.

On 15 and 19 May *Danmark* published detailed reports of this university meeting, in which about 600 students and professors took part, as well as prominent Danish politicians, headed by Ploug, the editor of *Fædrelandet,* and the leader of the Polish expedition to Lithuania and Zmudz, Colonel T. Lapiński.

At the meeting there was firm support for Poland in her fight – a fight which was of tremendous importance for civilised Europe and the future of the Scandinavian nations. Speakers maintained that the Poles' battle for freedom was linked to the battle against Prussia in Schleswig. Tscherning's speech in the Rigsraad was criticised. There were calls to contribute to the collection of money which had just begun. A proclamation was adopted – a petition in defence of Poland, which was to be published abroad in French and English in *Moniteur* and *The Times.*

The appeal included the following passages:

... the liberation and restoration of Poland will contribute to secure the safety of our own country and the future of the Scandinavian North. The same people that have oppressed your kindred tribe and prepared your calamity ... that it is now acting in Posen; it is constantly menacing our frontiers, our nationality, and our language; it would if it could prepare us for the fate of Poland. A regenerated Poland is our natural ally against policy of usurpation and love of conquest. And as the Slavonian tribes could only find liberty and safety by attaching tremselves to a regenerated Poland, the Northern tribes seek alliance and union from the same motive.

It ended with the words: 'Poland for ever! God protect and promote her just cause!'[70]

This change of the attitude towards the Polish problem did not escape Dotézac's notice, who reported on May 16 as follows:

'Jusqu'ici les vœux du peuple danois pour la cause polonaise n'avaient pas pris d'autre organe que la Presse, mais s'étaient traduits plus practiquement par l'envoi de secours pécuniaires: la question grecque et la nouvelle organisation du Holstein occupaient trop l'esprit public, pour attirer son attention en dehors; mais aujourd'hui que ces deux faits n'ont

---

69. No. 109, Revue de la semaine, no. 18.
70. *Danmark,* 19 May 1863. The organisers of the meeting included the chairman of the Copenhagen Committee, the well known poet Carsten Hauch.

plus le merité de la nouveauté l'on s'est souvenu d'une question déjà vieille à laquelle on semblait être resté complètement étranger. La présence à Copenhague du colonel Lapinski le chef de la malheureuse expédition maritime, n'a pas peu contribué à ce réveil d'enthousiasme'.

This phenomenon he interpreted in the following terms:

'Mais comme les Danois se passionnent peu pour les causes qui ne touchent pas immédiatement à leurs intérêts politiques, ce mouvement était resté, jusqu'ici dans les limites d'une sympathie spéculative et elle ne les eut pas franchies, n'eussent été les reproches venus de Suède, sur le contraste qu'offrait la tiédeur des Danois avec l'élan des pays frères dont les feuilles apportent journellement ici l'écho'.

The collection of money for the Polish cause was successful and among the contributors were Mrs. Danner and A. Hall. 'Mr. Hall a ignoré cette démarche qu'il regrette, dans sa position officielle'.

Dotézac reported that in these manifestations many politicians were active, especially Ploug, one of the leaders of the Scandinavianist movement.

The increased interest in the Polish cause was welcomed in Sweden. *Aftonbladet*, 12 May, wrote in its 'Revue de la Semaine' No. 6.

... il nous faut bien dire que notre pays continue à se prononcer pour la Pologne. Toujours des démonstrations. Ces jours-ci c'était à Örebro, Askersund, Carlshamn, Arboga, et dans plusieurs localités de la province de Westmanland. Il restait un dernier refuge aux amis de la paix à tout prix; c'était le Danemark, et en effet l'attitude passive de ce peuple-frère, pouvait leur faire espérer qu'il ne se laisserait pas gagner par l'exemple de cette grande émotion. – Helas! Ce dernier espoir leur échappe; voilà les souscriptions que s'ouvrent, même en Danemark, – et avec quel succès! Contenons-nous de dire que parmi les souscripteurs on compte l'épouse morganatique du roi et la femme du ministre des affaires étrangères.

This last point, that it was officially announced in the press that the contributors to the Polish cause included Mrs. L. Danner-Rasmussen, the morganatic wife of Frederick VII, and Mrs. Augusta Hall, the wife of the minister and head of the government, did not escape the notice of the Russian ambassador in Copenhagen and led to quite a vigorous controversy. It became the subject of talks at the highest level in both St. Petersburg and Copenhagen. Perhaps more important was the fact that the news reached Gorchakov at almost the same time as O. Plessen handed the Russian minister a note from his government on the Polish question. Gorchakov broached the subject in a conversation with Plessen without mentioning the two ladies by name, but indicating that husbands were responsible for the actions of their wives – 'Les maris sont responsables des actes de leurs femmes', he claimed.[71]

---

71. Plessen to Vedel, 26 (14) May 1863. Vedel, pk. 12, R.A. Copenhagen. Reporting the collection of money, Nicolay wrote: 'Parmi les noms ... qui figurent sur la liste, j'ai été assez surpris de trouver ceux de la C-m Danner et de Madame Hall! Mr. Vedel m'assuré que personne n'aura été plus surpris que le Président du Conseil de trouver le nom de sa femme sur la liste et cela pour une somme de 50 ecus! La bonne dame, qui je n'ai jamais eu l'occasion de rencontrer est connue pour sa excentricité et il est permis à ce titre d'être indulgent de sa faveur.' (Particulière, 24 April (6 May), A.V.P.R. Vol. 65) Vedel was indeed very displeasé that Mrs. Danner and Mrs. Hall had compromised the government by entering their names of the list ob subscribers, and in a letter to Quaade, the ambas-

Plessen, wanting to make light of the matter in the most obvious way, recalled the November uprising and told Gorchakov that he remembered that the Polish insurgents who had appeared in Copenhagen then had also been the Copenhagen women's favourites, which had evidently displeased the ambassadors of Russia, Austria and Prussia. As a young boy he had heard his parents talk frequently about the demonstrations arranged by the women in Copenhagen in 1830.[72] By this he meant that those demonstrations, like the current ones, were not really very important.

III.

Ever broader circles of Danish society joined the campaign to help the Polish cause, and this coincided with the only official government move addressed to St. Petersburg during the Polish uprising, namely Hall's May note.

Denmark, which had a continuing interest in retaining Russia's friendship, counting on help from the Russian cabinet in the event of a deterioration in her relations with Germany, decided nevertheless on this move – although it was entirely predictable that it would not be well received by Russia, which regarded it as a sign of a pro-Western policy. In view of the nationalism and chauvinism raging in Russia at the time of the Polish events – 'l'enthousiasme qui se manifeste dans toutes les classes en Russie', as Plessen wrote to P. Vedel from Baden-Baden on 8 May[73] – the sending of a note on the Polish question, even apart from its content, could not fail to be seen in St. Petersburg as an unfriendly gesture towards Russia and participation in what St. Petersburg called the European diplomatic campaign against Russia.[74] 'Although', we read, 'some notes were more in the nature of an expression of confidence in the Russian government, taken generally by the very fact that they were presented by the governments, they looked like a European diplomatic campaign against Russia'.[75]

How did it come about that the Danish government, so cautious and concerned to maintain good relations with the St. Petersburg cabinet, decided to send a note to St. Petersburg? The history of this decision and the circumstances accompanying it are very interesting. The documents enable us to understand the real intentions which guided Hall's government in its decision to join the diplomatic campaign inaugurated by the Western governments.

---

sador in Berlin, on 14 May he assured him that Hall had had no idea of this and had only learnt about it from *Fædrelandet*. (Vedel to Quaade, 14 May 1863, R.A. Copenhagen, Quaade, Vol. 6171, pk. 5. See also V. Sjøqvist, *Peter Vedel ...*, vol. I. 1823-64, p. 278). On the same subject Dotézac wrote: 'M. Hall a ignoré cette démarche qu'il regrette, dans sa position officielle'. A.M.A.E. Paris, Danemark, no. 73, 16 May 1863, vol. 243.
72. Plessen to Vedel, 26 (14) May 1863.
73. Vedel, pk. 12.
74. *Ocherki istorii ministerstva inostrannykh del, 1802-1902*, (St. Petersburg, 1902), p. 142.
75. *Ibid.*

Initially, as we know, Denmark decided to remain on the side lines, particularly after Russia and Prussia concluded the 8 February Convention. On 4 March Russell, through Paget, proposed to the Danish government that Denmark should join the powers' diplomatic action, arguing that the states which had signed the Treaty of Vienna in June 1815 were interested in the ending of bloodshed and the observance of the rights granted to the Kingdom of Poland, and that the interests of goverments concerned to maintain peace in Europe demanded this. He expressed the hope that the Danish government would be willing to join in this humanitarian action, an action at which Russia should have no cause to take offence.[76] Denmark, however, declined on the grounds that she was not a signatory to the Treaty of Vienna.[77]

This was of course a pretext, and that was how Russell read Hall's reply. He showed this in a conversation with the Danish ambassador when he assured him that he knew perfectly well that Denmark had not signed the treaty, but had approached her nevertheless, as he had Italy, although her signature likewise was not on the Vienna treaty.[78] The Western countries did not give up, however. They decided to approach Copenhagen again, but this time there was no mention of the Treaty of Vienna. They considered that Denmark should send a note to St. Petersburg, as Sweden had done, calling on Russia to behave humanely towards Poland. Dotézac was the first to approach Hall on the subject, followed by Paget. According to Dotézac, Hall took a positive attitude to the French proposal and said that it was consistent with the view of the problem held both by the King and by himself personally. Nevertheless he could not take a definite position during that talk, which was reported to have occurred on 24 April, as the matter required consultation and Denmark had to be very careful owing to her special position *vis-à-vis* Russia.[79] In his report to Paris, Dotézac mentioned that the Danish government had rejected a similar proposal from London and reported that meanwhile Paget had put a new proposal on the same matter.[80] Of the two notes previously addressed to St. Petersburg by the Western powers, Hall preferred the tone of the French note, expressing the opinion that the British note was too sharp.[81]

Meanwhile the Russian ambassador also intervened, seeking to dissuade Hall from sending a note and to convince him that Denmark, like the majority of the German states, should remain neutral. This argument, as the French ambassador reported, was unfortunate, for if the German states sent notes Denmark would find herself isolated, and by declaring herself on the same side as Austria she would separate the latter from Prussia. During a second talk with Nicolay – which we know from the version of it that Hall gave to Dotézac, who reported it to Paris

---

76. Udenrigs. 1863. A. 3354. R.A. Copenhagen.
77. Registratur. Udenrigsministerium. Tag A 798, R.A. Copenhagen. Hall to the Danish ambassador in London, 1 April 1863.
78. England, Dep. 9 April 1863, R.A. Copenhagen.
79. *Ibid.* no 52.
80. Dotézac's report, no. 60, 29 April. A.M.A.E. Paris.
81. *Ibid.*

– Hall was reputed to have said that Denmark could not remain neutral because Russia had changed her policy towards Denmark in recent years. Faced with the choice of taking Russia's side or that of France and Britain, he had no hesitation. He was also supposed to have added that Russia had been happier with the old cabinet [the Conservative group – E.H.]. Dotézac expressed doubt whether the Danish minister had really said all this to the Russian ambassador, but in his view, too, there was no question that if the Danish government had been headed by Bluhme and [H.C. Reventlov] Criminil, as had been the case in the first year of the Crimean War, relations between it and Russia would have been closer.[82]

A different version of the conversation was given by Nicolay in his report to Gorchakov on 18 (30) April. According to the Russian ambassador's account Hall had said that Denmark, as a small country, was not called upon to intervene. It seemed to him, however, that Dotézac's argument that every country should approach Russia on the matter out of concern for the maintenance of peace, and that Russia could not take offence at such an approach, had made a certain impression on Hall. Nicolay had pointed out to the minister that the fact that the French government had sent identical notes to all states did not mean that they had to share the same point of view, and, as the morning press had reported, the majority of German states had rejected the French invitation.[83] He considered that Hall should reply to Dotézac that Denmark had no interest in intervening on behalf of Poland.

Nicolay initially thought that his arguments had shaken Hall's certainty and that he would not take any decision, at least until Gorchakov's reply to the [April] notes from the Western powers was published, and that this would convince him of the Tsar's honourable intentions in respect of Poland. Nicolay was clearly very concerned to influence Hall and persuade him not to join the diplomatic campaign being staged by the Western states. But from the beginning he had doubts whether he would succeed. This is shown by the text of his dispatch to Gorchakov on 28 April:

En chiffres. Samedi – démarche française, hier – anglaise avec copie des notes remises à St. Pétersburg. J'ai parlé à Mr. Hall dans le sens de la circulaire. Probabilité est que la peur de l'Angleterre et de la France et l'espoir d'en tirer des avantages l'emporteront sur nos arguments. Détermination sera prise au Conseil, lundi prochaine.[84]

Meanwhile a dispatch reached Copenhagen from W. Scheel-Plessen in Stockholm telling Hall about Gorchakov's reaction to the Swedish note to St. Petersburg. The minister now learnt that Gorchakov had received Stockholm's moves ('ouvertures') in the most friendly spirit ('de la manière la plus amicale') and

que ce dernier a rendu pleine justice aux sentiments exprimés par le Comte Manderström et que la réponse du Gouvernement Russe est consignée dans le manifeste accordant une amnestie et une administration locale et nationale.[85]

82. Dotézac, no. 60. A.M.A.E. Paris.
83. Cf. Hans-Werner Rautenberg, *Der polnische Aufstand von 1863 und die europäische Politik* (Wiesbaden, 1979), pp. 231 ff.
84. A.V.P.R. Moscow, vol. 65, R.A. Copenhagen.
85. Scheel-Plessen's dispatch of 21 April 1863, no. 30, R.A. Udenrigsministeriet, Polen, S. 3354.

But, as diplomats accredited to St. Petersburg reported, the reason Gorchakov received the Swedish note 'avec beaucoup de calme' was probably a desire 'pour ne pas irriter davantage l'esprit public en Suède contre la Russie'.[86] When Nicolay asked Hall on 17 (29) April what decision he had taken, he found him greatly troubled. The minister explained that after he had received a further note from London inviting Denmark to join in the three powers' action the situation had become more complicated and Hall could not postpone replying any longer as he did not want to put Denmark at odds with France and Britain simultaneously. Denmark's situation was very difficult and he had to be very careful to avoid everything that could cause differences between her and the Western powers.

There is no question that whether or not to send a note was a difficult dilemma for Hall and Vedel,[87] particularly the latter, the *eminence grise* of the ministry of foreign affairs. Vedel was certainly influenced also by the letters he received at this time from O. Plessen, who was on holiday, and who urged the government to maintain good relations with the great powers, by which he meant Russia, as this was essential in order to make Germany powerless in relation to Denmark and deprive the Holstein opposition of a solid base.[88]

Plessen warned against sending a note to Russia, arguing that Russia was known to be hostile to the liberal party in Germany and that Denmark, in her own interest, should do nothing against Russia, so as not to lose the support she had shown her since the start of the conflict with Germany. He warned that Russia was not really as strong as she had been, but had a great capacity for regeneration, which would enable her to recover from her difficulties.[89] He thought that to send a note to St. Petersburg on the Polish question would be 'assez grave', given Denmark's situation, and he warned against the effects of such a step. 'À mon avis', he wrote to Vedel from Baden-Baden on 8 May, 'la Russie même vaincu exercera toujours une grande influence sur le développement de notre question'. What would happen, Plessen asked, if the Russian cabinet turned against Denmark and switched to Germany's side? Would it not be an enormous moral blow if Russia, on whom Denmark always counted in her secret thoughts, joined our enemies?[90]

Vedel was exceptionally cautious and showed this in talks with Nicolay. He said the Polish question was alien for Denmark and held no interest for her. Yet he did not conceal from the Russian ambassador that it was essential for Denmark to maintain good relations with France, which was on good terms with Austria at that time – a fact which could be useful to Denmark. Anyway, Vedel added, if the government did decide to send a note to St. Petersburg, through Plessen, the latter would explain the true meaning of the note and convey greetings to the Tsar, wishing him

---

86. Report from St. Petersburg, 20 April, Geheimer Staatsarchiv, Russland 1863, S. Bóbr-Tylingo, in *Antemurate 1863-1963*, p. 111.
87. The head of the 1st Department.
88. Plessen to Vedel, from Baden-Baden, 20 April 1863. Vedel, pk. 12 R.A. Copenhagen.
89. Plessen to Vedel, from Baden-Baden, 2 May 1863.
90. *Ibid.*

every success. This could not cause displeasure to the Russian government, Nicolay himself added in his report to Gorchakov.

'He [Vedel] always controls the ministry, and for that reason I have cause to think that the government's decision will conform to the ideals which Vedel expounded', Nicolay explained.[91] The political situation of Denmark was assessed by the moving spirit of the ministry of foreign affairs, Peter Vedel, in the following terms:

Shortly after the start of the uprising two camps were formed in Europe, the Western states and Austria in one and Russia and Prussia in the other. For Prussia this alliance was very dangerous because of the prevailing view that France sought Poland and the seizure of the Rhineland. Reports spread that Bismarck had doubly angered the Emperor [Napoléon III] since by allying himself with Russia he had broken the promise given to the emperor when the Rhine was "bought" in exchange for permission to rule nothern Germany and perhaps for assurance against Austria. For Austria, on the other hand, a particularly favourable situation was created. Outwardly it looked very liberal, and there were also prospects of good will on the part of France and Britain. This gave her advantages in such matters of Italy and Germany and was a better starting point in our [Danish] question. But this, too, was a source of great danger for Denmark. We had to manœuvre so that everything developed without any notable conflict as long as relations between Austria and France did not deteriorate – although in our judgement, that would happen in time, since Austria had no real intention of going to war against Russia. But at the same time we had to associate ourselves to some extent with the anti-Russian action in order to be in good standing with France and not to lose contact with Sweden. These were the two main elements in our policy, which was the product of the current situation.[92]

Here is the most authoritative explanation as to why traditionally pro-Russian Denmark, which still expected Russian help if its conflict with the German states should intensify, finally decided, after two months had passed, to send notes to St. Petersburg.

Ultimately Vedel would have preferred no note to be sent to St. Petersburg. This view was reflected in his letters to Plessen on 29 April and at the beginning of May, the spirit of which was to excuse this move.

Vous aurez sans doute vu par les journaux que les Cabinets de Londres et de Paris ont vivement engagé notre gouvernement à s'associer aux démarches qu'ils ont déjà faites à Pétersbourg. Cette circonstance, jointe à la situation très menaçante que la question polonaise a crée [sic – E.H.] a dû obliger le Ministre à prier V. Exc. [Plessen] de reprendre la gestion de la légation, aussitôt qu'il sera possible. Je me permettrai de parler franchement et sans ambages et détours – je crois connaître V. Exc. assez bien pour savoir qu'avec Vous la voie droite est la meilleure dans toutes éventualités.[93]

In the next letter, when it was a foregone conclusion that a note would be sent to St. Petersburg, Vedel wrote:

---

91. Sjøqvist, *Peter Vedel* ..., vol. I. p. 176.
92. 'Peter Vedels beretning om Danmark udenrigspolitik fra sommeren 1862 til foraaret 1863', in *Jyske Samlinger*, 1952-1954, pp. 149-50.
93. Privatarkiv Plessen, no. 6128 A. I. 2, Otto Plessen VI.I. Letter of 29 April 1863. R.A. Copenhagen.

Pour Vous expliquer notre position dans la question polonaise je Vous envoie copie du rapport qui sera présenté au Roi un des premiers jours. La dépêche sera conçue dans les termes les plus amicaux que nous pourrons trouver. Votre Excellence doit être convaincue que toute cette affaire m'est tellement antipathétique que tout que je pourrai faire pour l'adoucir sera fait. J'ai en l'occasion d'en parler à M. de Nicolay et je crois qu'il apprécie notre manière de voir et d'agir.[94]

As far as the text of the note[95] was concerned, although Hall assured Dotézac that he had decided to keep it in the spirit of the French note,[96] it can be seen from the phrases used that in fact he departed from this intention. Of course it has points in common with the French and Swedish notes concerning such questions as humanitarianism, anxiety about events in Poland, regret at the bloodshed, fear not only on the part of the great powers but on that of the secondary states of Europe too, that the regrettable events in Poland might lead to deplorable consequences and that these in turn might disturb the peace and security of Europe. But the second part of the note contains phrases emphasising

---

94. Vedel to Plessen (May 1863). Copy in Privatarkiv Familien V. Plessen. Otto Plessen, Arkiv. no. 6128. VI. I. A. I. 2. R.A. Copenhagen.
95. The Danish Note of 8 May 1863 read as follows:
   Grâce à la solidarité qui relié tous les jours plus intimement les peuples et les gouvernements de l'Europe, les déplorables événements de la Pologne ont dans tous les Etats profondément remué les esprits et donné de graves préoccupations aux gouvernements.
   Partout l'on forme des vœux pour qu'il soit mis un terme au regretable état des choses qui tend à élever une barrière entre les Polonais et leur Souverain, et la plupart des Cours Européennes ont cru de leur devoir de faire entendre à ce sujet des conseils et de représentations au Gouvernement de l'Empereur.
   Si le Gouvernement du Roi vient aujourd'hui à son tour exprimer ses vœux et témoigner son intérêt pour le bonheur et la prospérité de l'Empire Russe dans tous les territoires que se trouvent réunis sous le sceptre de l'Empereur, c'est avant tout parce qu'il se rappelle combien de foi le Danemark a pu constater l'interêt que le Gouvernement Impérial lui portait et se féliciter de l'efficacité que le pouvoir bien assis de la Russie donnait nécessairement aux manifestations de cet intérêt. Mais à cette considération s'en joint une autre non moins grave et aussi puissante sur l'esprit du Gouvernement du Roi. Il ne se dissimule pas les éventualités qui pourraient résulter de la prolongation de l'état actual des choses en Pologne, il prévoit que de grands dangers menaceraient non seulement les puissances de premier ordre, dont les déterminations peuvent ne dépendre que de leur propre appréciation de ce qu'exigent leurs intérêts, mais encore les Etats secondaires qui, eux ainsi, ressentiraient de mainte manière le funeste contre coup d'une grande commotion, il comprend enfin que parmi ces Etats le Danemark ne serait pas le moins exposé à courir des chances funestes.
   Je prie V.E. de présenter ces considérations à Mr. le Prince Gortchakow et de se faire en même temps l'interprète des vœux que forme le Gouvernement du Roi dans cette occurrence.
   Vous prierez le Prince de croire qu'il n'y a pas un Souverain en Europe qui puisse désirer plus vivement et plus sincérement que le Roi de Danemark de voir la Pologne déposer les armes devant la générosité de l'Empereur et rentrer dans le voie d'un développement tranquille et fécond. Le même esprit qui a déjà suggéré au Souverain d'entreprendre de grandes réformes, réformes dont la conception était aussi noble que l'éxecution a été énergique, ne manquerait pas alors, j'en suis convaincu, de créer au Gouvernement Impérial de puissants titres à la reconnaissance de Ses sujets Polonais.
   J'ai l'honneur d'être C. Hall
   Dispatch addressed to O. Plessen. See Udenrigsministeriet. No. 3332 Polen. A. 3354 and 1863 Registratur Tag A. 798. Journal 753, 3317.
96. Dotézac, no. 65, 9 May, Danemark. Vol. 243. A.M.A.E.

qu'il n'y a pas un souverain en Europe que puisse désirer plus vivement et plus sincérement que le Roi de Danemarc de voir la Pologne déposer les armes devant la géneroșité de l'Empereur et rentrer dans la voie d'un développment tranquille et fécond.[97]

Such expressions and wishes, the sense of which is unequivocally anti-uprising, and such a pro-Russian tone are not to be found in either the French or the Swedish notes, still less in the sharper British one. In essence the Danish government was guided by the principle of keeping the wolf fed and the sheep safe.

At the meeting of the Statsraadet on 8 May the King accepted the contents of the note and it was sent to St. Petersburg the same day.[98] The note was to be handed over by Plessen. He was taking an extended holiday in Germany and Hall asked him if he would go to St. Petersburg and personally hand the note to Gorchakov. In his letter to Plessen on 8 May Hall expressed his request as follows:

Les termes de cet office sont choisis avec assez de soin, je le crois, pour que le Ministre des Affaires Etrangères de l'Empereur ne puisse pas se méprendre sur les sentiments et les motifs qui les ont dictés. Néamoins il me semble qu'il en appréciera encore plus nettement le caractère, s'il lui sont communiqués et commentés par une personne aussi initiée que Vous l'êtes, Monsieur le Baron, dans les pensées des deux gouvernements et dans la tradition, des bons procédés et de l'entente heureuse qui depuis si longtemps caractérisent les relations du Roi avec le Cour de St. Pétersbourg et dont le maintient et la consécration sont dus dans une si grande mesure à Vos soins intelligents et à Votre zèle infatigable.[99]

At the same time Hall's behaviour towards the Western states remained extremely cautious. He was particularly concerned about France's attitude and assured Dotézac that the spirit of the Danish note was close to that of the French note of 10 April,

et que tout en gardant les ménagemens que commande la position particulière du Danemark vis-à-vis la Russie, le Prince Gortchakov ne pourra ne pas voir de quel côté se rangerait éventuellement le gouvernement danois.[100]

But in a letter to the Danish ambassador in Paris, E.C.L. Moltke, on 9 May, referring to his previous letter of 21 April, he wrote:

Vous apprécierez facilement Mr. les considérations qui ont dû motiver le ton de cette dépêche, [the 8 May note] surtout dans un moment, où l'Allemagne se prépare à attaquer le protocole de Londres et où par conséquent, comme Mr. Drouyn lui-même nous le recommande, nous devons nous ménager l'appui de la Russie.[101]

---

97. The text of the note is in Udenrigsm. no. 3332, Polen, 1863, R.A. Registratur 1863. Udenrigsmin. Tag A 798.
98. *Staatsraadets forhandlinger om Danmarks udenrigspolitik 1863-1879*. Ed. Aage Friis (Copenhagen 1936). p. 10.
99. Confidentionale, in R.A. Registratur 1863. Udenrigsmin. Tag A 798. Cf. Ordrer Rus. no. 8, 8 May 1863, R.A. Copenhagen, Cf. also Dotézac, no. 65, 9 May 1863, Danemark. Vol. 243. A.M.A.E.
100. *Ibid*.
101. Registratur. *Ibid*.

In a letter to the Danish ambassador to Britain, Torben de Bille, on 16 May he assured him that the note had been sent only at the repeated request of the British government, and this showed that the misgivings which had caused Denmark not to accede to the first request had been dissipated.[102] In London and Paris it was recognised that Denmark had done what she could in her difficult situation. There was understanding for 'la position difficile et délicate dans laquelle se trouve le Gouvernement du Roi', Moltke reported from Paris, quoting the words of the French minister of foreign affairs

que la dépêche du 8 mai lui paraissait telle qu'elle devait l'être, que les termes dans laquelle elle eut conçue étaient parfaitement choisis, et qu'enfin il ne s'était attendu de la part du Cabinet de Copenhague a ni plus ni moins que ce qui avait trouvé place dans la note en question.[103]

In St. Petersburg there was also no particular irritation on account of the Danish note, although Gorchakov accepted it reluctantly and expressed regret that the note was the topic of the first conversation he had with Plessen after the latter's long absence from St. Petersburg. He certainly felt resentful that a small state like Denmark, which Russia, as he said so often, had protected, had dared to speak about the Polish question. When Plessen observed that it was in the interests of both Russia and Denmark to avoid danger, Gorchakov stressed that Russia had done everything which her interests and honour required and told him how enthusiastically the Russian government's policy was received by all classes of society. If the uprising created a situation in which the honour and interests of Russia were at stake and it became a case of 'd'être ou de non être', Russia would choose war to the bitter end, as she had in 1812, the vice-chancellor said emphatically. He explained that Poland could not be given such freedoms as in 1815 because Russia herself, where serfdom had recently been abolished, was not ripe for such freedoms ('n'est pas mûre').[104] Gorchakov regretted Austria's policy, calling it 'du ton hostile', and argued that an independent Poland would be a vassal of France and its emergence would be contrary to the interests of Austria, Prussia and Britain, which would also not be inclined to make any efforts from which France could derive advantage. As far as Hall's appeal in his note was concerned, Gorchakov pointed out that the Tsar had already responded to that in issuing an amnesty.[105]

Dotézac thought the tone of the conversation between Gorchakov and Plessen showed the exceptional suspiciousness of the Russian government, and he was certainly right.[106] The conversation took place, of course, at the time when the chauvinistic anti-Polish and anti-Western compaign whipped up by M. Katkov and his *Moskovskie Vedomosti* had almost reached its zenith.

---

102. *Ibid.* Cf. also no. 14, Udenrigsm. A 3354 R.A. Copenhagen.
103. Report of 22 May 1863. No. 25. Udenrigsm. A 3354, Journal, no. A. 3332, R.A. Copenhagen.
104. See *Dnevnik P.A. Valueva. I. 1861-1864.* (Moscow, 1961), pp. 34.
105. Plessen to Hall, no. 15, 16 (4) May. Udenrigs. Polen. A 3354.
106. Dotézac, no. 75.

Russia did not attach any particular significance to the substance of the note. But the fact that it was sent could not help her relations with Denmark, especially as Denmark's main enemy, Prussia, was closer to the cabinet in St. Petersburg.[107] Articles began to appear in the semi-official *Journal de Saint Pétersbourg* which Danish diplomats could read as unfriendly to Denmark and which interpreted the situation in the duchies tendentiously. Gorchakov himself had already complained to Denmark that there were Danish sailors, rather than Swedish, as initially believed, on board the *Ward Jackson*, which had carried the Polish military expedition to Lithuania, and, as Nicolay reported, these sailors had piloted the ship through the Danish straits.[108] Gorchakov paid no attention, however, to Nicolay's report[109] that none other than the Danish navy minister, S.A. Bille, had been, *sua sponte*,[110] the first to inform the Russian ambassador of the appearance of the ship off the Danish coast and of its movements.

The sending of the note coincided with visits to Copenhagen by Colonel T. Lapinski and Prince Constantine Czartoryski, who was received at the royal court, and with the wave of demonstrations and collections for the insurgents organised throughout Denmark.[111] In official Russian circles, despite dislike of the fact that Denmark had, as it was described in Russia at the time, joined 'the diplomatic campaign' against her, there was understanding of the Danish situation.

Le jugement qu'on porte sur notre dépêche est favorable. Ceux qui connaissent toutes les pièces se rapportent à ce triste sujet, disent que la notre est la plus convenable, la mieux rédigée, qui dans un langage véritablement diplomatique elle tient compte de ce qui doit être pris en considération. Voilà donc Vos bons et consciencieux efforts récompensés,

Plessen wrote to Vedel on 26 (14) May.[112] Gorchakov's official answer to the Danish note reached Copenhagen very quickly. Hall was struck by the speed of this reply.[113] 'La réponse du Prince', Plessen judged, 'est un peu courte, mais d'après l'appréciation d'ici pas âpre et sèche, comme autres réponses'.[114] The Russian note was indeed perhaps the shortest of any of the replies sent on this occasion. It also in fact tended to make light of the matter. Great Russian pride felt wounded by the fact that a small country like Denmark had sent a note. After acknowledging its receipt, the reply merely emphasised what was most favourable to Russia in it.

Je viens de recevoir de M. le baron de Plessen communication d'une dépêche de M. Hall que je joins ci-près en copie.

---

107. *Monrads deltagelse ...*, p. 25.
108. Udenrigsmin. Polen. no. 10, 10 April (29 March) 1863).
109. No. 19, 14 (26) March 1863.
110. Of his own free will.
111. For more on this see *Wladyslaw Czartoryski. Pamietnik 1860-1864,* (Warsaw, 1960), *Danmark*. No. 125. 2 June 1863.
112. Vedel, Papirer 6498, pk. 12.
113. Gorchakov's dispatch of 3 (15) May. See also Gorchakov to Nicolay, 3 (15) May. Udenrigs. A 3354 Journal no. 3332 and A 3354 Polen 1863, R.A. Copenhagen.
114. Letter to Vedel, 26 (14) May. Vedel. pk. 12 R.A.

Nous apprécions l'intérêt que le cabinet de Copenhague témoigne pour la prospérité de l'empire russe, et surtout le vœu, exprimé au nom de Sa Majesté le roi, de voir la Pologne déposer les armes devant la générosité de notre Auguste Maître et rentrer dans la voie d'un développement tranquille et fécond.

Tel est aussi le plus cher désir de l'Empereur.

Nous comprenons la sollicitude qu'inspire au cabinet de Copenhague le maintien de la paix de l'Europe. Il peut être certain que les périls qui pourraient le menacer ne viendront pas de notre part.

A vehement debate flared up in the Danish press, mainly in the papers published in the capital, concerning Danish policy towards the events in Poland and, in particular, the 8 May note. The liberal national press attacked the government for what it said in the note and called it a shameful and deplorable document.[115] The note could only be interpreted as it had been by Gorchakov, whose reply had expressed appreciation of the Danish government's wish that the uprising should be suppressed as soon as possible and the insurgents submit to the tender mercy of the Tsar. In the paper's view the note should have stressed that small nations respected the value of treaties protecting other nations and wanted to express sympathy for a nation which had played such an important role in history as the Polish nation, and to call for recognition of its national independence. In the name of the Danish nation *Fædrelandet* dissociated itself from the government's position. It did not want a wrong impression of true opinion prevailing in Denmark to be created abroad. The Polish question was a question of conscience for Europe. Thanks to the partitions of Poland, Russia was a power in Europe and Asia. Prussia wanted to take advantage of the fight which Poland was currently waging in order to carry out its aggressive plans in respect of Denmark. Denmark would recognise and welcome the rise of a free Poland. And a free Poland allied with Scandinavia could form a bulwark between Russia and Prussia. Russia and Prussia were threatening freedom in Europe and it was Europe's duty to help Poland. Denmark as such had no interest in war. But her moral help for Poland in her fight, and material help too, were also significant.[116]

Danmark followed the same line, and criticised the government in a similar tone for taking Russia's side instead of expressing sympathy for Poland in her struggle, thereby supporting Tscherning's notorious speech. In its 'Weekly Review' on 2 June *Danmark* attacked the government in the following words:

We have more than once distinctly informed our readers that the Danish Nation generally feels the greatest sympathy in the desperate struggle of Poland for life and liberty. But it must be acknowledged that the above Dispatch of the Danish Government expresses sympathy for the sufferings of Russia, not for those of Poland. Foreign countries will therefore easily conceive the surprise and indignation which this document has excited in Denmark. But it has also called forth great apprehension. We are in a double position. Not only must our noble feelings for a noble land find vent at all hazards, but we must also fix before-

---

115. *Fædrelandet*, 30 May 1863.
116. *Fædrelandet*, 17 and 29 May 1863.

hand the place which we intend to occupy in case a general war flings the European states into two opposite camps. Should anything of this kind occur, the interest of Denmark, its instinct for self-preservation, quite as much as the far higher motives which animate a race so famous and so proud as our own, lead us to join the two other Scandinavian kingdoms in the ranks of those powers which will assist in establishing a free and independent Poland. It would be the greatest possible misfortune for this country if the policy of our ministry, in union with outward circumstances, were, at the decisive moment, to entangle us with powers and operations unfriendly to the chivalrous nations of Scandinavia and the West. We will hope that our cabinet's Dispatch of the 8th of May may not lead to results so disastrous. But it cannot be denied that there is a great danger of this taking place. At all events, in the presence of our foreign readers, we must firmly and decisively and solemnly protest against this Dispatch being considered as expressing the sentiments of the Danish people.

In 'Weekly Review' on 23 June *Danmark* described the political situation as follows:

... the most remarkable step in this direction for us Northmen – for all the Anglo-Scandinavian races – is the mighty movement towards a Scandinavian Union. This, and only this, can save the separate Scandinavian states from impending partition and absorption by Germany on the one hand and Moscovy on the other. This alone can ensure to England an efficient bulwark, a natural ally, a future free from peril. Poland is now struggling for similar consolidation and independence, and with her success is bound up the 'to be or not to be' of our whole Western freedom and civilization. Poland once masticated and assimilated by Russia, by fair means or by foul, Europe becomes inevitably Cossack. But Russia herself is determined to obtain a really national existence, to shake off her traditional slavery under an Imperial German bureaucracy, and to give to her people rights and glory instead of a continuous course of bloody conquest and barbarous legislation.

Even *Danmark,* however, contained some articles[117] seeking to defend the argument that the government's note had been misunderstood since in fact the government had not taken the side of tsarism but of the Western powers, as, among others, Prince Czartoryski said in *Aftonbladet.* The Danish government, however, had not had the courage to express its position clearly in the note. Nevertheless, its wish that there should be accord in the Polish land should not be misinterpreted. The Danish government saw no possibility of the Poles laying down their arms unless the Tsar recognised Polish national demands. The Danish government had also argued that the situation in Poland could bring misfortune for small states. It was not hard to understand that this referred to Denmark's fear of Prussia and Germany.

The paper criticised suggestions that Denmark's attitude to her German subjects was comparable to the treatment of the Poles by the Tsar. It was essential for the government firmly to rebut the outrageous slanders being put about by Germans concerning their alleged persecution in Schleswig.[118] It was also essential for the Danish nation to protest against interpretation of the note as meaning that it equated the Poles' fight for freedom with its own fight against Germany. It must

---

117. See *Danmark,* 27 May and 18 June 1863.
118. Cf. 528 P.A. I. Nachlass Rechberg. 4 Teil. Schl.-Hol. Frage. H.H.S.A. Vienna.

be made clear that the Danish nation had a clean conscience in relation to the Germans. It was also important to appreciate the real motives of the Russian government's behaviour in 1849-50, to which the government referred in its note. Russia was concerned to stop Prussia's attempt to create a Northern Union. Beside this, Russia's dynastic interests were at stake and for that reason she was opposed to the Augustenburg claims backed by Prussia, and to the creation of an independent Schleswig-Holstein. On the other hand, the Tsar did not want to see an Eider-Danish state.[119] Now he was in favour of Helstat, and was supporting the reactionaries in both Denmark and Prussia. Only harm could be expected from Russia. The article expressed the opinion that the majority of Danes supported the government and that the government was fulfilling the wishes of society, which wanted dissolution of the bond between Denmark and Holstein, backing for the Polish cause, the liberation of Poland from the Russian yoke, and support of those European states which took Poland's side.

The conservative press took a different position. An article with the title *'Den polske bevægelse'*[120] in *Kronen* on 17 May expressed disapproval of the fact that, under pressure from the French cabinet, the Danish government had sent a note to St. Petersburg, and warned that the events connected with the Polish question, namely the tone of the liberal national press and the student demonstrations in defence of Poland and in connection with Colonel Lapinski's visit to Copenhagen, could have damaging consequences for Denmark. The paper also criticised *Fœdrelandet* for applying different criteria to the events in Poland from those it used to judge events in Schleswig-Holstein. *Kronen* also defended Tscherning's speech. The differences between such terms as 'opløb' (crowd) 'opstand' (revolt), 'oprør' (rebellion) and 'revolution' (revolution) were just a matter of words, the author of the article said. If C. Ploug's ideas were put into practice the consequences would be that Denmark would lose her independence and be incorporated into a Scandinavia united under the aegis of Sweden. The author could see no other meaning in the movement on behalf of Poland.[121]

On 31 May *Kronen* citicised the government for agreeing to send the May note to Gorchakov at France's request. Other second-rank governments [this was the term used – E.H.] had done the same as Denmark, and only Holland had decided first to hold a debate in the Chamber of Deputies on whether taking part in the diplomatic action would threaten Holland's neutrality in the event of war.[122] *Kronen* was scornful of what it regarded as the unrealistic slogans proclaimed by the liberal national papers *Fœdrelandet* and *Dagbladet,* and the demands addressed to the Danish government by politicians from that camp, who dreamed of the resur-

---

119. L'État Eider-Danois.
120. The Polish Movement.
121. *Kronen,* 17 May 1863, p. 508.
122. Bóbr-Tylingo, pp. 118-20; L. Barzini, *The Europeans,* (New York, 1983) p. 210. ... 'non alignment, non participation in international politics, and strict neutrality, became obsessions' according to J.C. Voorhoeve, the Dutch scholar, in his book: *Peace, Profits and Principles,* p. 31.

rection of the Polish state and a Polish-Scandinavian union which would curb Russia and Germany. The main aim of the Danish note was to try to maintain peace, and Gorchakov had understood this position. On the other hand Denmark could be shown to have taken part in the diplomatic intervention against Russia. Recognition of the principle of solidarity in the maintenance of peace in Europe could prove disadvantageous should Denmark face a conflict.

Kronen subsequently stepped up its criticism of the idea of diplomatic intervention.[123] It expressed the view that the Polish uprising was the work of European revolutionary propaganda, a significant part of the gentry and the peasantry and the population of the old Polish provinces was not taking part in it, and it was only kept going by the pressure of European diplomacy. The paper was sceptical as to whether France and Britain really sought a European conference, or were in a position to induce Russia to participate in one. Besides, what would Britain say if she were called upon to do so during the war against the Sepoys in India?

Finally, the semi-official *Berlingske Tidende*. It defended the content of the Danish note and pointed out that the position Copenhagen had adopted was no different from that taken by Manderström after the outbreak of the uprising in a talk with the British ambassador, Jerningham, when he said that it would be a good thing if the uprising ended quickly because the longer it lasted the less the Tsar would be inclined to grant the Poles concessions.[124] This idea had been repeated in the Swedish note of 7 April, which had expressed the opinion that the uprising would soon be ended because of shortage of arms and ammunition and the hope that the Russian government would treat the insurgents leniently and that peace and order would again ensue. In *Berlingske*'s opinion there was no difference between the attitudes of Copenhagen and Stockholm. The paper attacked *Fædrelandet*'s argument that the Danish note was shabby and deplorable and considered that strong words should not be demanded of weak states, all the more so as they were not to be found in the notes from great powers such as France.[125]

It was also surprising that the criticism in certain circles went further than that in diplomatic circles; even Gorchakov judged the position the Danish government had taken in a more reasonable manner than these circles did. *Berlingske* expressed the same thoughts on 11 June, when it attacked the article in *Fædrelandet* on 30 May. In *Berlingske*'s view it would be unreasonable to ask a small state to phrase the demands it addressed to Russia more sharply than the great powers did, for sincerity not backed by strength led nowhere.

As the reader will see from the extracts I have cited, there were fundamental differences in the Danish press over the country's attitude to the January Uprising. The Conservative groups were essentially pro-Russian and against intervention on behalf of Poland. They regarded the uprising as the work of European revolution and saw the problem as an internal Russian matter. On humanitarian grounds they

---

123. *Kronen,* 14 June 1863.
124. J. Klaczko, *Etudes de diplomatie* ... (Paris, 1866) p. 144.
125. Referring to France's note of 10 April 1863.

expressed sympathy with Poland in its fight. The supporters of Helstat saw Russia as the guarantor of the *Status quo* in Denmark.

The liberal national groups saw a close connection between the Polish question, Scandinavia and freedom in Europe. They warned against Prussia and drew attention to the fact that Prussia was co-operating closely with Russia and that history provided many examples of how dangerous this co-operation could be for Danish interests. In their opinion Russia had changed her traditional policy towards Denmark. The only real help to Denmark would be the rise of an independent Poland on the eastern frontier of Prussia. Allied with Scandinavia this would be a real barrier against despotism. Then Denmark's chances of retaining Schleswig would be increased. These last words, however, reveal a lack of consistency, since sensitivity to the problems of freedom in Poland was not accompanied by a really democratic plan to solve the national problem in Schleswig. This was a source of weakness for both the national liberal party and the government.

It seems to me that the Danish note, the temperature of which – as A. Olsen neatly put it in his article on Denmark's attitude to the Polish uprising[126] – corresponded to the magnitude of the economic assistance given to Poland (up to October 1863 the total collected was 8027rd. 70sk, in other words, not much) and cannot be seen in isolation from the historical circumstances. Nor, as N. Neergaard rightly observed, can it be regarded as evidence of the government's sympathy for Poland, but as a forced move in a great diplomatic game, and a move which the Danish government thought could be helpful to it in the battle for Schleswig. Hall's government faced an increasingly complicated situation and a renewed threat of federal execution in Holstein and tried to pick its way between the Western powers and Russia. Hall personally was closer to a pro-Western orientation, but could not commit himself unequivocally on that side, while his colleagues were becoming increasingly convinced that Russia would soon deal with the uprising, lance the wound, and everything would settle down as before. Whatever happened, Vedel argued in a letter to A.F. Krieger on 10 July 1863, it would be very unwise for Denmark to behave rashly,[127] and by the summer of 1863 he thought that the topic

---

126. Albert Olsen, 'Danmark og den polske Opstand 1863', in *Festskrift til Erik Arup. Den 22. november 1946.* (Copenhagen, 1946), pp. 304-16. Cf. G. Brandes, *Indtryk fra Polen.* (Copenhagen, 1888), p. 177. Neergaard, vol. II, 1, pp. 658 ff.
127. *Danske Magazin,* 1940, 7 Række, 3 B, p. 147. O. Plessen was critical of the insurgent camp from the start of the uprising and continually warned against underestimating Russia. Plessen's dispatches, no. 20, 1 June (20 May) 1863, no. 19, 1 June (20 May) 1863, no. 25, 22 (10) June 1863. Udenrigsmin. A 3354, Journal no. 3332. A 3354 Polen, 1863. In his 11 July (29 June) dispatch Plessen set out his anti-Polish, ultra-conservative *credo.* P. Plessen, and his brother, the ambassador in Stockholm, were criticised in *Fædrelandet,* no. 149, 1 July 1863. Being influenced by the Russian propaganda Plessen repeated indiscriminately all defamations concerning the Polish national movement.

In his dispatch on 1 June he wrote 'Les cruautés que les insurgés commettent sont horribles. Tout dernièrement ils ont perdu des enfants en présence de leur mère et puis la mère elle même, propriétaire d'une terre près de Grodno. Il est vrai que la mère avait averti les autorités de l'arrivée des insurgés par un billet intercepté par eux. Des faites pareils et plus atroces encore, on pourrait en citer beaucoup'. ... 'Irritation contre l'ingérence étrangère est le trait distinctif des ces

of Poland was really already exhausted. But he could not give up the idea that it would come to war if Napoleon III, with support from the north and the west, were willing to take the risk.[128]

Hall took Gorchakov's words about Russia's faithfulness to the provisions of the Treaty of London at face value and continued to count on Russia's diplomatic help, even when Russia was so strongly linked with Prussia. Nor was his policy towards the Western powers consistent, although his leaning in their direction from the middle of 1863 was demonstrated once again in September, when Hall, in order to show that the government favoured the Western states, decided that the Danish King should not go to St. Peterburg to do homage to Alexander II. As Hall explained in a conversation with Dotézac, this was done for a definite political purpose, although he was aware that it would cause unpleasantness for the heir to the throne, Christian, and Princess Louise, whose daughter Dagmar was to marry the heir to the throne in Russia.[129]

The May note could not fail to influence Russia's attitude to Denmark. Nor could the rumours that in the event of war Denmark intended to join the Western coalition, and in particular to support France, fail to have some effect. It was another matter altogether that the rumours were wrong.[130] D.G. Monrad, returning to the history of 1863-64 years later, was right in saying:

Dette Ruslands forhold var atter begrundet i dets hele stilling til Preussen, der havde vist sig som en trofast ven under det store diplomatiske felttog, der foretages mod Rusland i anledning af de polske forhold, og hvori ogsaa Danmark deltog, hvorvel paa en meget mild og beskeden maade.[131]

(Russia's attitude was primarily the result of Prussia's policy towards her during the diplomatic campaign connected with the Polish uprising. Prussia appeared then as the faithful friend of Russia. And Denmark took part in this campaign, though in a modest and mild way).

It is also worth quoting the opinion of someone who was close to the court of the Tsar and the author of a note submitted to Alexander II in 1864.

Die Kopenhagener Demokratie hat die durch die polnische Krisis bewirkte totale Veränderung der Lage Dänemarks so vollständig verkannt, dass sie sich in gradezu unsinniger

> addresses [to Alexandre II]; haine contre les Polonais, de nationalité à nationalité ne s'y manifeste que rarement. En général le Russe, vainqueur du Polonais après des luttes séculaires, ne hait pas le Polonais, comme le Polonais, - le vaincu hait le vainqueur'. In Plessen's reports the Russian troops were brave, orderly and 'magnifiques'. Even M. Muraviev, Governor General in Wilno, the cruel 'Hangman' was praised for his vigorous measures to restore order. (Nos. 19 and 20, 1 June (20 May). Udenrigsministeriet, Polen, A 3354, R.A. Copenhagen).
>
> Plessen continued to exert a strong influence on Vedel's point of view, and their attitude towards the Polish uprising became almost the same.

128. *Danske Magazin,* 1940, 7 Række, 3 B, pp. 149-50, and Privat Arkiver 5810. Politikeren A.F. Krieger, C.I.A. R.A. Copenhagen.
129. Dotézac, 10 September 1863, Danemark, vol. 244, A.M.A.E.
130. Bóbr-Tylingo and Kieniewicz say Denmark did have such an intention, but they cite no source for this.
131. *Monrads deltagelse ...* p. 25.

Weise zu Sympathiebezeugungen für das 'unglückliche Polen' bestimmen liess-ohne auch nur einen Augenblick daran zu denken, dass sie durch eine derartige Lähmung der conservativen Action Russlands das Unglück ihres eigenen Vaterlandes vorbereitete.[132]

And a historian concluded that 'Danish support of Western demands during the Polish uprising had aroused considerable resentment in Petersburg. The Russian government disapproved of democratic tendencies in Denmark.'[133]

But as a matter of fact, the Russo-Danish estrangement was not only influenced by minor episodes connected with the Polish uprising. It was caused mainly by what happened on the Copenhagen-Stockholm axis in the summer of 1863. The contacts between the monarchs of the two countries, and especially between Hall and Manderström, and the advanced stage reached in the talks on a military treaty between Sweden and Denmark greatly disturbed the St. Petersburg cabinet. Every sign of Scandinavianism caused an immediate reaction on the part of Gorchakov.

In the course of 1863, Plessen came to the conclusion that Denmark could not count on Russia to take any initiative to assuage the conflict between Denmark and Germany, nor to speak in defence of Danish policy in the forum of the German Confederation. In contrast to the policy pursued previously by Ch. Nesselrode, Plessen said, Russia would not help Denmark and if a crisis arose Russia's chief concern would be not to antagonise Prussia. She would follow a carefully nuanced policy and her actions would depend on the behaviour of Germany and the cabinets in London and Paris.

L'appréciation du Cabinet Russe, relativement à notre politique, – wrote Plessen on 9 September (28 August) – ne nous est pas favourable. Quelques notions, que j'ai pu soumettre à Votre Excellence dans le courant de cet été, l'indiquent, et une réponse, faite, tout dernièrement, par le Vice-Chancelier au Ministre de Suède, confirme le caractère de cette appréciation. Le Baron Wedel ayant demandé au Vice-Chancelier: s'il y avait du nouveaux dans notre question? Le Prince Gorchakov a répondu: "que nous étions belliqueux: – que la Suède nous encourageait dans ces dispositions – belliqueuses; que c'était au Cabinet de Stockholm de juger de l'opportunité d'une telle politique, et qu'on connaissait chez nous la manière de voir du Cabinet Russe.

Il est-il me semble – de notre intérêt de ne rien faire, qui puisse constater officiellement cette appréciation du Cabinet Impérial et préjuger, par là, l'attitude de la Russie, pour le cas que la crise éclate. – Rien ne m'autorise, il est vrai à penser, que nous puissions compter sur une initiation de la Russie, qui fût favorable aux déterminations récentes du Gouvernement de Sa Majesté du Roi. Le Prince Gorchakov a, toujours, évité – contrairement à la politique de feu le Comte de Nesselrode – de heurter de front, dans notre question, les tendances du libéralisme germanique. Il a un intérêt, si la crise éclate, de ne pas froisser trop la Prusse, seule puissance, qui, dans le débat que la Pologne a fait surgir, se soit montrée amicale pour la Russie; mais, il peut y avoir, je me le figure, des nuances dans l'attitude que prendra la Russie, et ces nuances, plus où moins favorables, dépendront des procédures, plus ou moins âpres et ardentes, adoptées par L'Allemagne et de la position, que prendront les Cabinets de Londres et de Paris'. (No. 49).

132. J.W.A. Eckhardt, *Von Nicolaus I zu Alexander III,* (Leipzig, 1881), p. 236.
133. Steefel, p. 130. Cf. also Dieter Hillerbrand, *Bismarck and Gortchakov: A Study in Bismarck's Russian Policy, 1852-1871.* (Stanford University, 1968; University Microfilms Inc. Ann Arbor, Michigan, 1979) p. 162.

The Italian diplomat, G. Migliorati, brought up in his report on I August the problem concerning the Danish dilemma and the Polish uprising.

> Ce qui inquiète un peu le Gouvernement Danois et paralyse quelque peu sa confiance dans une adhésion de la France et de l'Angleterre à ses vues, c'est la persistance de leur entente avec l'Autriche, qui dans cette dernière phase du conflit a pris une attitude plus décidée que la Prusse, et parait d'après le langage même que tiennent les diplomates autrichiens, vouloir remplir le rôle, que sa rivale a si faiblement joué en 1848-1849.
> La France et l'Angleterre, qui ont réussi à attirer à elles l'Autriche dans la question polonaise ne Lui accorderont-elles rien en retour de cette combinaison dans la question des Duchés? Telle est la demande que se font les hommes d'Etat de Danemark et cet énigme leur semble un sujet des justes appréhensions.
> En ce qui regarde la Pologne Danemark occupe une position bien délicate. Sans compter qu'il se trouve lui-même vis-à-vis des Duchés dans une situation analogue à celle de la Russie vis-à-vis du Grand Duché de Varsovie, il est à remarquer que certains liens dynastiques, et surtout certaines obligations de reconnaissance, qu'il ne peut guère méconnaître, l'enchaînent à cette puissance, d'autant plus que, dans les récentes discussions de la question des Duchés, la conduite du Cabinet russe vis-à-vis du Danemark a été pleine de modération, et de bienveillance. Et cependant en présence d'une lutte contre l'Allemagne, le concours des Puissances occidentales, dont il éprouve le plus impérieux besoin, lui permet-il de repousser leurs sollicitations? Tant que la question polonaise reste dans les limites d'une action diplomatique le Danemark pourra se tirer d'embarras en s'associant avec prudence, et réserve à l'intervention des Puissances et sous ce rapport la note fort modérée qu'il a adressée au Prince Gortchakoff à la demande des Puissances occidentales, n'a pu mécontenter la Russie tout en donnant satisfactions aux vues de ses adversaires; mais si la question prendra des proportions plus graves, d'une rupture ouverte et d'une lutte armée, comment le Danemark pourra-t-il s'abstenir de prendre part à la ligue en présence aussi de l'ardeur belliqueuse de la Suède sa voisine? Il est évident que, si la question de la Pologne dégénérait en guerre européenne et que l'Allemagne fut engagée dans le conflit, l'intérêt du Danemark Lui imposerait de jeter ouvertement dans l'alliance occidentale, mais, tant que la Confédération restera en dehors avec la Prusse, tant que l'Autriche demeurera neutre, le meilleur parti qu'il ait à prendre est, peut-être, de suivre la politique pratiquée pendant la guerre d'Orient; quitte toutefois à savoir si l'appui moral semblerait suffisait aux alliés et si une démonstration armée dans la Baltique ne lui serait pas imposée en compensation de garanties plus ou moins positives, qu'il recevrait dans le sens d'un arrangement satisfaisant du conflit des Duchés.[133a]

The Polish question influenced Danish policy again in 1864. When the Danish-German dispute became an armed conflict the leaders of the Polish uprising expected the conflict on the Eider to influence the future fate not only of Denmark but of Poland too.

The belief that the European complications associated with the Danish war could bring the moment of victory over European reaction nearer was so great that R. Traugutt (the Leader of the Polish National Government) believed the task of the moment was 'to give the strongest possible support to the cause of the freedom of peoples and of justice, and to overthrow the rule of despotism based on brutal force, represented in Europe by Moscow and by the governments of Austria and Prussia, in order to ensure in this way the free develop-

---

133a. Ministerio Degli Affari Esteri, Arkivio Storico-Diplomatico, Rome, Rapporti, pacco 171 (809).

ment of mankind – on the principle of morality ignored and constantly affronted by the forces of despotism.' In the spring the uprising might change from being anti-Russian to being anti-German.[134]

After the operations in Schleswig began, the chief diplomatic agent of the National Government, Wladyslaw Czartoryski, gave considerable thought to the connection between the Danish and Polish questions on the basis of the existing constellation of political forces in Europe.[135] But he quickly became convinced that the fact that the Polish and Danish questions were coupled had led to complete agreement and closer relations between the three northern powers, particularly after the declaration of a state of war in Galicia,[136] and that all the actions of Prussia and Austria in respect of Denmark had the approval of the Tsar and Gorchakov. The only thing Gorchakov was against was the possibility that following partition Denmark might be annexed by Sweden. 'Prussia', we read in Czartoryski's dispatch to the National Government, 'which a hundred years ago was the originator of the plan to partition Poland, is now, true to its history, laying the foundations of a new Holy Alliance on the plunder of Denmark'.[137]

In another dispatch he anticipated that: 'the two great powers, emboldened by Moscow's secret permission, will certainly soon partition Denmark, and the Western powers will probably agree to this rape at conferences in London'.[138] And since during the armed conflict between Denmark and Germany the situation changed so that, of the three states which had spoken up for Poland to Moscow at the beginning of 1863, one had gone over to the enemy camp (Austria), the second was no longer concerned about Poland (Britain), and the third, undeniably the most friendly, was unwilling to do anything to help Poland without the assistance of at least one first rank power (he was referring to France), Czartoryski saw no possibility of further action on behalf of the Polish cause.[139]

Despite this the agent of the National Government in Scandinavia, F. Demontowicz, just after the military action in Schleswig started, approached Monrad with a proposal to form a Polish legion from Poles, Italians and Hungarian

---

134. J. Jarzebowski, *Wegierska polityka Traugutta,* (1939), pp. 21-22, J. Lukaszewski, *Zabór pruski w czasie powstania styczniowego 1863-1864,* (Jassy, 1870), p. 26; Letter from Traugutt to Lukaszewski, (c.) 27 January 1864, in which he envisages the possibility of conflict with Prussia. Halicz, *Polish National Liberation Struggles ...* pp. 74-5, 82.
135. Agencja Paryska, 3 February 1864, in *Polska dzialalność dyplomatyczna w 1863-1864 r.* The collection of documents. Ed. by A. Lewak, (Warsaw, 1937), p. 434; W. Czartoryski. *Pamietnik 1860-1864,* pp. 192-6; J. Zdrada, *Foreign Policy during the January Insurrection.* War and Society in East Central Europe. Vol. XIX, p. 167.
136. *Polska dzialalność dyplomatyczna ...,* dispatches of 17 February, 5 March and 22 April, pp. 437-8, 440, 443, 451-2, 452-63.
137. *Ibid.* p. 440.
138. *Ibid.* p. 463.
139. *Ibid.*

deserters from the German armies, to fight beside the Danish army.[140] The Danish government, however, did not want to annoy Russia and rejected the plan immediately. For this it was attacked by liberal circles, who criticised it for having too little regard for Denmark's natural allies, the Poles, who were linked to Denmark by a common fate.[141]

IV

From 1863 Nicolay began to pay more and more attention to Danish-Swedish relations. He took an interest in royal visits and especially in the progress of negotiations for the conclusion of a defensive treaty between Sweden and Denmark. He assiduously noted any rumours on this subject. But not until the matter seemed to be about to come to a head did he decide to have a serious talk with Hall, trying to convince him of the negative consequences which such a pact could have for Denmark if one day she were compelled to come to Sweden's assistance in a war provoked by the latter's ruler, whose ambitions and plans could not be ignored.

Nicolay was not convinced[142] by Hall's arguments that a link of this kind between the Scandinavian countries, which were already closely connected by their geographical situation and community of interests, excluded any possibility of carrying out any unilateral plans or ambitions by anyone and was purely defensive. Its purpose, if it came into effect, would be to retain Sweden's help for Denmark. In the event of a German invasion the 20,000 troops Sweden would send to Schleswig would be kept under Danish command. Such an alliance would be exclusively defensive and would in fact give Russia a guarantee of security.[143] There was no reason for Russia to be suspicious, Hall claimed, especially as Finland's attitude in recent years had demonstrated to Sweden that any ideas she had about regaining Finland were illusory.

The reports coming in from Copenhagen and Stockholm of a possible alliance between Denmark and Sweden disturbed political circles in St. Petersburg, however. For years Russia had of course been very sensitive to any signs of Scandinavianism. Every indication of Scandinavianism, in every sphere of life, was assiduously noted and in almost every case St. Petersburg reacted, although not always vehemently. This could be observed in the course of the years 1857-63. Yet it seems that after Scheele's well-known reply to Stockholm and the rejection of the proposal put forward by Prince Oscar tension on account of Scandinavianism

---

140. See Demontowicz to A. Sohlman, 3 April, from Hamburg. Kungl. Biblioteket Stockholm, Sohlmans polit. Korresp.; L.K. Ahrenberg, *Skandinavismens inställning*, p. 23; K.G. Fellenius, *Polska frågan år 1863*, (Stockholm, 1936), p. 139.
141. *Fædrelandet*, no. 97, 28 April 1864. Introductory article. Cf. the collection of documents edited by Lewak, vols I (1937) and II (1963); *Le Nord*, 31 October 1864.
142. Report of 12 (24) September 1863.
143. See Møller, *Skandinavisk stræben ...*, pp. 334 ff.

diminished. Scheele's reply, as Dashkov reported,[144] 'paraît être peu goûte ici [in Stockholm] dans les régions gouvernementales que dans le public'. The former saw 'une certaine blâme' in it, and as for the latter, 'elle y produit de pénibles déceptions relativement à l'accomplissement des vœux que plus d'un individu forme en faveur d'une unité scandinave pouvant tenir tête à la Russie'. This confidence did not last very long, however, as in May there was a youth demonstration at the University of Helsingfors, in which students from Uppsala participated, with strong Scandinavian overtones, which, the Swedish ambassador in St. Petersburg reported,[145] gave the ruling circles in St. Petersburg an unpleasant feeling, since the event took place in the capital of the province which seemed to be identified with Russia, something which gave the Russian government much to think about.[146]

Finland was the apple of St. Petersburg's eye and every centrifugal impulse caused a state of agitation in the Tsarist capital, particularly after the experiences of 1854-55.[147] In this context one can understand the Russian reaction to the pamphlet *Finska färhållanden* which was published in 1857 by the well-known Finnish Scandinavianist Emil von Quanten in Stockholm and smuggled into Finland. T. Berg in Finland and Dashkov in Stockholm tried to buy up every copy of it, but to no effect.[148] In 1858-59 tension and fear abour a Scandinavianist policy subsided with the appointment of Manderström as Minister of Foreign Affairs in Stockholm and C. Wachmeister as ambassador in Copenhagen. These appointments, especially that of Manderström, who was known personally to dislike Napoleon III and not to support a pro-French line or to be enthusiastic about Scandinavianism, and to want to normalise relations with Russia, were a certain pledge for Russia that Sweden's official policy would not cause complications between Stockholm and St. Petersburg and that Sweden would not go too far in her efforts to bring the Scandinavian countries together.[149] But although there was increasing recognition on the Neva that it was a long road from the idea of Scandinavianism to its implementation in practice, and that the road was strewn with difficulties connected, among other things, with the problems which the 1857-58 crisis had caused for Swedish trade and industry, the St. Petersburg cabinet did

---

144. No. 18, 15 (27) March 1857 – Rulle 216-217, 1856-57, Central Archive, Moscow, microfilm in R.A. Stockholm.
145. No. 9, 6 June 1857.
146. Kabinett för utrikes brev Depescher från beskickningen i Petersburg 1857-1858, no. 6, 6 June 1857.
147. See: La valeur de la Finlande pour la Russie. 'Elle assure la possession de la fenêtre que Pierre le Grand ouvrit sur l'Europe ... Pétersbourg. La Finlande était nécessaire à la Russie dit le Comte Schouvalov à Napoléon I et tel était le projet de Pierre qui sans cela, n'aurait pas fondé la capitale là où elle existe maintenant.' M. Borodkine, *La Finlande* ... p. 7.
148. Lolo Krusius-Ahrenberg, *Der Durchbruch des Nationalismus und Liberalismus im politischen Leben Finnlands 1856-1863*, (Helsinki, 1934), p. 188.
149. Dashkov, 23 September 1859, and Krusius-Ahrenberg, pp. 166-9. Cf. also pp. 173-4. Cf. also A. Jansson, *Den Svenska Utrikespolitikens historie*, vol. III, 3, 1844-1872, pp. 148 ff.

not cease to be sensitive on the matter even though the situation in Sweden did not favour the adoption of any new political concepts and the prospects for Scandinavianism in Norway were also poor.[150]

Dashkov was aware that Sweden, Norway and Denmark all had different approaches to the problem of Scandinavianism. They were also guided by different aims. Prince Oscar's aim was not to dominate Denmark but to bring the two countries closer together and to form and develop a platform for the purpose of uniting them in those spheres in which they shared common interests – as the Prince Regent defined it to the Belgian ambassador, Beaulieu, who was accredited to the German Confederation and the northern countries. Denmark, however, the Belgian ambassador argued, sought to use Scandinavianism as a useful auxiliary means of achieving specific aims.[151] In Denmark, in Beaulieu's opinion,

on entendait plutôt par ce mot [Scandinavianism – E.H.] une certaine suprématie à exercer sur la Suède si une union devenait un jour possible par suite d'événements imprévus, la richesse, la civilisation et les lumières relatives se trouvant incontestablement du côté de cette dernière puissance.

And although Sweden too had Scandinavianist aspirations, in view of the particular interests of, among others, Norway, it would be hard for the Scandinavian states to reach an agreement.[152]

Dashkov's second in the Russian embassy in Stockholm, Ch. Minciaky, also recognised that too much importance should not be attached to the exchanges of royal visits. Considering for example the Danish King's visit to Sweden in the summer of 1859, he wrote: 'de semblables rêves[153] ont moins que jamais la chance de se réaliser'.[154] The governor of Finland, T. Berg, also gained the impression during his visit to Stockholm in May 1860 that the military's proclivities to rebuild the

---

150. Dashkov, no. 1, 3 (15) January 1858, 14 (26) February 1858, no. 15, 28 February (12 March) 1858, and Berg to Armfelt, 27 July 1859, in Krusius-Ahrenberg, p. 170. As far as Norway was concerned, Dashkov wrote in his report, no. 15, 28 February (12 March) 1858, Reservée:

Ces masquines jalousies [between Norway and Sweden] qui percent chaque fois que les intérêts nationaux sont en jeu, tendent à prouver, en dépit de toutes les belles phrases qui se débitent de temps à autre en faveur du Scandinavisme, qu'on reconnaîtra une immense différence entre la théorie et la pratique si jamais cette idée était appelée à se formuler autrement que par des toasts et des discours d'étudiants. (Rulle 218-220). On 11 (23) March 1858 Dashkov returned to the subject and observed that Scandinavianism rested on shaky foundations because of Norwegian-Swedish trade conflicts ('au sujet des bases fragiles sur lesquelles repose l'édifice Scandinave aussitôt qu'il s'agit d'entrer dans le domaine de la réalité). In many historians' opinion the conflict 'about the vice-regency' between Charles XV and the Swedish nationalists, and the King's abortive attempt to extend Norway's field of authority and abolish the office of viceroy, and the extraordinary increase in the authority and influence of the Council of State, which meant depriving the King – an advocate of Scandinavianism – of a decisive voice in matters of foreign policy, to a significant degree prejudiced the fate of Scandinavianism. See J. Andersson, *Dzieje Szwecji*, pp. 265-6; T.K. Derry, *A History of Modern Norway*, pp. 89-91; A. Kersten, *Historia Szwecji*, p. 318.
151. Dashkov, no. 22, 22 April (4 May) 1858.
152. *Ibid.*
153. (On Scandinavianism – E.H.).
154. Report no. 4, 17. (29) July 1859.

army and use it at the first opportunity were counterbalanced by the existence of pacifist tendencies among influential politicians and statesmen, who realised that a pacifist stance was more appropriate to the geographical position of Sweden and the isolation in which she found herself.[155] But the nation would long retain hostile feelings towards Russia, T. Berg, the Tsar's special emissary to Stockholm for the coronation of King Charles, believed. Sweden disliked Germany, and particularly Prussia, and sympathised with France, while economic interest, in the broad sense of the word, subordinated the country to Britain and the latter's influence was great even though the historical experience of relations with Britain had not always been very favourable for Sweden. (As an example he mentioned that Britain had contributed to Sweden's loss of Finland in 1809, despite which, thanks to Britain, there had been a rapprochement between Russia and Sweden in 1812).

Les tentations d'amour propre et de gloire livreront pendant la règne du Roi Charles XV de rudes combats aux considérations de prudence et de sagesse qui militent en faveur du développement pacifique de la prospérité de ce Royaume ... La Suède prend depuis quelques années un certain essor et un certain développement, qui augmentent ses forces et font, que cette puissance n'est pas à dédaigner. Un série d'habiles mesures administratives ont augmenté ses moyens ... Cet accroissement de ses forces et l'organisation d'une armée de cadres méritent de notre part la plus sérieuse attention,

Berg reported.[156]

As far as Sweden's attitude to Denmark was concerned, Berg concluded that her fondness for the country (Denmark) was not disinterested and her aim was to conquer it.[157]

Dashkov, on the other hand,[158] referring to the feelings generated by the Prussian King's manifesto on the question of the duchies, said that not only Charles XV but the entire Swedish nation sympathised with Denmark. But despite this,

Si l'idée de l'Union Scandinave s'est beaucoup relâchée, – ainsi que le prouve la question Norvégienne, – le Scandinavisme n'en existe pas moins comme bien d'amour propre et de secours mutuels entre les trois nations vis-à-vis des races étrangères.

Dashkov's analysis of the problem was very superficial. He presented only facts and reactions, but did not manage any deep analysis of the phenomenon and of the reasons why the idea encountered great difficulties at various levels. He did not analyse the real conflicts which existed between Sweden and Denmark, namely the differences in economic development; the fact that in both countries there were strong memories of their centuries of conflict for hegemony in the Baltic; and that in Denmark a generation was still living which remembered how in 1814 Sweden

---

155. Reports, 5 (17) and 6 (18) May 1860, Rulle 221-225.
156. Dashkov, 5 (17) May 1860.
157. Cf. Krusius-Ahrenberg, pp. 178-81.
158. Report no. 2, 13 (25) January 1861.

had seized Norway, which had been linked with the Danish Monarchy for centuries.[159] He also underestimated the fact that during the Crimean War the political interests of the two countries clearly diverged, and at the time of the conflict in that part of Europe the Swedes would have preferred their army to be used in the east against Russia, rather than in the south against Germany, as the Danes wanted. There was thus a fundamental clash between the Finnish question, which was of primary importance to Sweden, and the question of Schleswig, which was fundamental for Denmark.[160] Finally, in Sweden it was said that history advised against Nordic unity (Ch. Molbech), and that even a personal union would be a misfortune (M.J. Crusenstolpe); while in Denmark many circles did not believe that the Swedish aristocracy would defend Denmark against Germany.[161] Both in Denmark[162] and in Sweden[163] many people said that a joint Kingdom would never be a great power.[164]

His talks with Manderström convinced the ambassador how alien the idea of Scandinavianism was to the latter personally, and that despite the sympathy he felt for Denmark Manderström very much wanted to avoid having to send Swedish troops to Schleswig in the event of Germany crossing the Eider.[165] In the summer of 1861, when the Swedish King visited France and Britain and rumours were disseminated by the press in the West to the effect that the provisions of the November 1855 treaty were to be implemented, Dashkov, as an experienced diplomat well versed in Swedish affairs, was once again convinced that the rumours were groundless and that there was little probability of a Scandinavian union being put into effect. As so often, the dream was taken for reality.

proprement dit, à ce fantôme de l'union complète des races Scandinaves, dont parlent aujourd'hui quelques journaux étrangers, il dort profondément dans ce pays, à l'ombre des défiances et des jalousies mutuelles des Norvégiens et des Suédois, et ne pourrait se réveiller redoutable qu'au bruit de quelque grand événement à l'étranger.[166]

In spite of this, however, both Dashkov and Russian diplomats generally, and Gorchakov and Alexander II, all reacted sharply to every sign of Scandinavianism, such as support for Finnish *emigrés* in Sweden, and later Polish *emigrés* too, and meetings between Copenhagen students and their colleagues from other univer-

---

159. E. Møller, *Skandinavisk stræben*, pp. 171-2, 178-82.
160. J. Clausen, *Skandinavismen*, pp. 126, 128, and H.E. Pipping, 'Finlands ställning til skandinavismen', in *Skrifter utgivna av Svenska Litteratursällskapet i Finland*, CLVII, (Helsingfors, 1921), pp. 192-3.
161. *Berlingske Tidende*, 27 February 1857; *Flyveposten*, 28 October 1858, 22 February 1859; Møller, pp. 186-99.
162. *Kjøbenhavnsposten*, 22 June 1856.
163. Speeches in the Chamber of Burghers. See also Ludberg's speech.
164. The attitude of society and public opinion to Scandinavianism is discussed by Møller, pp. 198 ff. and T. Jorgenson, *Norway's Relation ...* summary.
165. No. 11, 14 (26) March 1861. Some Swedish politicians began to suggest that a strong Prussia cooperating with Sweden could counterbalance Russian power.
166. No. 15, 25 August (6 September) 1861.

sities in Sweden and Norway.[167] They also reacted sharply to every article in the Swedish papers *(Aftonbladet)* on the topic of the need for coordination, particularly of military policy, between the Scandinavian states.[168] Both Dashkov and Gorchakov showed especial hostility at the news of the arrival of a group of Polish *emigrés* led by Colonel Z. Jordan in Sweden in 1862. Dashkov kept track of their political activities, particularly those connected with the preparation of the ceremony commemorating the approaching anniversary of the battle of Poltava, which was regarded in St. Petersburg as a sign of anti-Russian activity.[169]

Rumours of a political rapprochement, supposedly to be followed by closer military cooperation, between France and Sweden, and of preparations for joint action by them against Russia again increased Gorchakov's distrust of Sweden.[170] His fear of a military alliance between Sweden and Denmark was growing,[171] and on 4 June 1862 he issued instructions that all anti-Russian activity in Sweden was to be carefully watched, and in a talk with O. Plessen he accused Denmark of being aggressive and Sweden of encouraging her.[172]

Dashkov also scrupulously noted Swedish reactions to the announcement by Alexander II in 1862 convening the parliament in Helsinki.[173] On 18 (30) April he reported on Swedish reactions and did not fail to add his own comment:

Mais il n'en pas moins vrais, que tous ceux qui voudraient monopoliser en faveur de la Suède les sympathies nationales du Grand Duché, et c'est le plus grande nombre, n'envisagent point sans un certain déplaisir l'acte Impérial aussi bienveillant que sagement médité.[174]

He said that the news of the restoration of the Finnish parliament, which had been suspended since 1809, had been positively received in Sweden, and observed that this meant that the last remaining link between Finland and Sweden had been broken![175] Two generations had passed since Finland was separated from Sweden and common Finnish-Swedish interests had diminished. This, he added, was the prevailing opinion in Sweden.[176]

---

167. Dashkov's report of 28 May (9 June) 1862.
168. Dashkov's report of 23 June (5 July) 1862. Rulle 226-229.
169. Dashkov's reports of 22 March (3 April), 11 (23) June and 17 (29) June 1862, and Gorchakov's letter of 4 June (old style) 1862. In this letter Gorchakov mentions the unfriendly articles in the French press on the subject of Finland's hostile attitude towards Russia, and adds that such tendencies are not alien to Sweden.
170. Dashkov's reports of 12 (24) March, 11 (23) June, 17 (29) June, 2 (14) July, 9 (21) July and 18 (30) September 1862.
171. Dashkov, no. 25, 23 June (5 July) 1862.
172. Dep. Rusland, no. 49. 9 September (28 August) 1862.
173. This decision by the Tsar was influenced by the events in the Kingdom of Poland. See Ruch no. 2, 8. VII, 1862, in *Prasa tajna z lat 1861-1864,* vol. I. pp. 336-8. This is also mentioned by Krusius-Ahrenberg, pp. 362-5, and by L.A. Puntilla, 'Das Zustandekommen der öffentlichen Meinung in Finnland in den sechziger Jahren des 19. Jahrhunderts', in *Historiallinen Arkisto,* 52, (Helsinki, 1947), and M. Borodkine, *La Finlande comme partie intégrante de l'Empire Russe,* (Paris, 1912).
174. No. 17.
175. Report no. 10 of 24 March 1862. Krusius-Ahrenberg *Der Durchbruch ...,* pp. 336-7.
176. *Ibid.*

The political relations between St. Petersburg and Stockholm deteriorated even more after the outbreak of the Polish uprising, for understable reasons, and the Russian cabinet's suspiciousness increased. This was mainly the result of the pro-Polish mood both in Stockholm and in the provinces, articles in the press, speeches in parliament, and meetings and rallies in support of Poland's cause in her fight against Russia.[177]

As far as Sweden's attitude to the Polish uprising is concerned, a variety of factors influenced her pro-Polish position. For society in Sweden it was primarily humanitarian factors that were important; for the government, however, the reasons were mainly if not exclusively political. The government was in effect continuing the policy initiated during the Crimean War, particularly after the conclusion of the treaty with Britain and France in November 1855, the provisions of which, although not put into effect, had not lost their relevance. Chiefs among the political foundations of pro-Polish attitudes in Sweden were the emergence of France under Napoleon III as the leader of Europe, together with his nationality principle with its implications for Italy and Hungary and then later for Poland; the nationalistic celebrations in Russia in connection with the anniversary of the victory of Poltava; the hostile attitude of Russia towards the idea of Scandinavianism; and, most important for Sweden, the question of her claim to Finland, which was linked to Sweden by several centuries of common history.

Once the uprising broke out, these factors were supplemented by humanitarian considerations, as Swedish society was shocked by the barbarous treatment meted out by the Russian army both to the insurgents and to the defenceless civilian population in the areas affected by the uprising.

An uprising which was regarded initially as an internal Russian affair came to be regarded in Stockholm, as in other European countries, after the conclusion of the Convention of Alvensleben as a question of fundamental significance for the development of European politics. Reports of intended intervention by the European states reached Stockholm and fell on fertile ground.[178]

---

177. Wedel-Jarlsberg's telegram of 17 February, Dashkov, nos. 34 and 36, 3 (15) and 8 (20) April 1863.
    Fellenius, *Polska frågan i Sverige år 1863*, pp. 12 ff. Wedkiewicz, *La Suède et la Pologne*, pp. 34-39. See also articles in *Aftonbladet*, 27 January, 2, 14, 15 February, 6 March, 7, 10, 21 April, 5, 12 May, 29 July, *Nya Dagligt Allehanda*, 27 January, 18 February, 13, 15, 22 April, *Uppsala-Posten*, 25 April.
178. *Aftonposten*, 2 March.
    Jansson: David Lundström, 'Manderström och emigranterna i Sverige 1863' *Historisk Tidskrift*, 1953; Stanislaw Bóbr-Tylingo, 'Do tajnej dyplomacji Napoleona III (1863)', *Teki Historyczne*. (London). Vol. 11, (1960-61), pp. 245-55; W. Czartoryski, *Pamietnik 1860-1864*, Erik Møller, 'Karl XV's og Napoleon IIIs personlige Allianseforhandlinger 1863', *Historisk Tidskrift*, 1934, pp. 281-95; Revunienkov, p. 236. The great interest aroused by the Polish question is shown by the appearance, in a short period of time, of a series of books on the subject of Poland: F.B. Cöster, *Historisk återblick i anledning af senast timade händelser uti Polen*, (Norrköping, 1863); M.J. Crusenstolpe, *Ett sekel och ett år av Polska frågan, (1762-1863)*. *Historisk-kronologisk handbok*, (Stockholm 1863); R. Gustafsson, Polen Blöder, (Stockholm 1863); H.V. Münnich, *Polska frihetskampen 1863. Öfversigt af de Polska krigshändelserna, jemte en historiskinledning om Polens delning*, (Stockholm, 1863). A full bibliography on the subject is given in S. Wedkie-

On 2 March, a committee consisting of representatives of all social groups was created. The members of it were active in collecting money for the Poles, in organizing a press campaign and later in aiding the propaganda campaign connected with the visit of the Polish emissaries, Prince C. Czartoryski and W. Kalinka to Sweden. An American diplomat described the prevailing mood in Sweden as follows:

There appears to be a general apprehension of a general war or revolution all over Europe. A large number of Poles are now in this city, and have been welcomed with great enthusiasm. The Press is very violent, and urges that Sweden should take the initiative; that now is the time to rescue Finland from the Russian bear; that Charles XII saved Poland from the grasp of Peter the Great, and now another and better occasion was offered. It is said that King secretly incited the press and the people; that he is ambitious for military glory, and longs for the opportunity to distinguish himself; that he has set up Charles XII for his model, whom he desires to imitate. One thing is certain, that the King has received the Poles [Czartoryski and W. Kalinka – E.H.] with great consideration.[179]

A few days earlier Napier reported from St. Petersburg:

It cannot be doubted that the Russian cabinet stand in serious apprehension of Sweden. It is believed that Sweden would follow France with great alacrity into hostilities against Russia and would furnish a most formidable basis for offensive operations as well as useful military auxiliaries.[180]

But while public opinion overwhelmingly displayed its pro-Polish attitude and sometimes its readiness for active involvement in anti-Russian action, and while this was supported by King Charles XV personally, the position of the government and, above all, of the minister of foreign affairs was from the start restrained. He was disturbed by the outburst of pro-Polish demonstrations throughout Sweden, which went far beyond humanitarian aid, and by the participation of politicians, intellectuals and people from various walks of life, and he regarded them as unpleasant and even dangerous for the country. Manderström picked his way adroitly between the presure of public opinion, the demands of the Western countries and

---

wicz, *La Suède et la Pologne. Essai d'une bibliographie des publications suédoises concernant la Pologne,* (Stockholm, 1918); see also *Bibliografia Historii Polski XIX wieku. II, 1832-1864,* part III, vol. 3 (Warsaw, 1979).

In 1918 Anton Nyström wrote a paper: Resningen i Polen och Sympatierna i Sverige, and Jens Raabe: Norge och Polen. *Polonica. Kulturbilder från det åldre och nyare Polen.* (Stockholm, 1918), pp. 121-9, 141-8.

A small group of Swedes joined the Polish partisan groups. The most notorious later on were the military historian Julius Mankell and Wilhelm O. Unman, who in 1921 was promoted to Second Lieutenant by the Polish government and decorated with the order *Virtuti Militari*. During the uprising Unman and the two other Swedish students, Johann Erickson and Gabriel Jacobson, were taken prisoner; in February 1864 they were pardoned by General T. Berg.

179. Haldemar, Stockholm, à Seward, 24 April. Diplomatic Correspondence. Bóbr-Tylingo, *Antemurale* ... p. 110. Jerningham, 2 March. T. Filipowicz, *Confidential Correspondence of the British Government respecting the Insurrection in Poland 1863,* (Paris, 1914), p. 161.

180. P.R.O. F.O. 65/630 Russia.

a dangerous course which might became a challenge to Russia. Hence the Minister's personal statements intended to placate the Russian government, which was very hostile to all demonstrations in support of Poland, and his assurance to Russia that any statements in Western periodicals about an inevitable break in relations between Sweden and Russia were incorrect and that the Swedish government did not want its relations with the government in St. Petersburg to deteriorate. The Minister did not wish the Polish question to go beyond diplomatic and general humanitarian intervention. He continually instructed the Swedish Ambassador to St. Petersburg, Wedel-Jarlsberg, to this effect. In a telegram on 2 March 1863, for example, setting out his point of view, he asserted that the pro-Polish demonstrations taking place in Stockholm and other cities in Sweden were distasteful to the government and that he maintained unbroken faith in the best intentions of the Tsar:

Nous avons trop de foi dans les motives élévés et généraux de cet Auguste Souverain pour n'être point persuadés qu'il ne laissera point s'arrêter par *cette regretable* insurrection, dans la marche noble et éclairée que, depuis Son avènement, il a suivie a l'égard du Royaume de Pologne.[181]

In a conversation with the Russian ambassador, Dashkov, Manderström maintained that since he had resided in Stockholm for so many years the ambassador should know perfectly well that the goverment was not in a position to do anything to prevent the demonstrations. The Swedish ambassador, Wedel-Jarlsberg, delivered a similar declaration to Alexander II.

Caution was the motto of Manderström's policy, because, as he himself said, although he was for Poland he considered that lack of caution could lead the country into dangerous entanglements.[182]

The position taken by the minister of foreign affairs contrasted with the complete commitment of the King, something which did not escape the notive of the British ambassador, G.S.S. Jerningham, who perceived the duality in Swedish policy towards Poland.

On 24 February the British Ambassador reported: 'Count Manderström ... once remarked to me that he considered the restoration of Poland to be undesirable for the general interest of Europe, on account of the perturbatory nature of the Poles, whom his Excellency seemed to look upon as incorrigible European 'mauvais coucheurs', an opinion which history perhaps, partially sustains ...'.

As Jerningham reported, the Swedish Minister considered 'la promte supression de l'insurrection comme un bonheur pour la Pologne'.[183]

As a matter of fact, Manderström repeated the opinions formulated by Wedel-Jarlsberg in his dispaches, in which the Ambassador expressed his negative attitude

---

181. Skrivelser från Stockholm til Petersburg, 1863. R.A. Stockholm.
182. Dashkov, no. 12, 20 February (5 March) 1863.
183. Jerningham to Russell, Filipowicz, *ibid.* p. 79, Klaczko, *Études* .. p. 144. See also Jerningham, 17 February and 2 and 10 March, P.R.O. F.O. 73 Sweden.

regarding the Poles, and the Polish uprising, while praising Alexander II for his friendly and liberal policies towards the Kingdom of Poland.

It was the Ambassador's opinion that only a small democratic party and the fanatical clegy supported the uprising. He reported that the Polish political programme, especially the demand for 1772 borders, was unrealistic and that Russia would never agree to accept it.

'De pareilles prétentions équivaudrait à un suicide' and as he stressed in his report of 20 (8) February, 'aucun souverain Russe, n'y saurait consentir sans léser gravement les intérêts russes et susciter profond mécontentement dans les masses et ses sujets de la dite cathégorie'.[184]

It must be said, to Manderström's credit, that all the Chambers (of nobles, clergy, burghers, peasants) rejected resolutions demanding co-operation between Sweden and the Western powers with the aim of reconstructing the Polish state.

His speech in the Chamber of Nobles, on 14 March, in which he admittedly praised the Poles and appealed for caution, may, perhaps be considered a masterpiece of diplomacy in regard to a difficult question.[185]

On 16 March Scheel-Plessen reported:

Le même jour (samedi dernier) Mr. le Baron Stael v. Holstein, ancien capitaine dans la garde et frère du baron Stael v. Holstein, Directeur général des Postes, a fait une motion tendant à inviter la Diète à engager par une adresse le Gouvernement du Roi à faire des démarches diplomatiques en faveur des Polonais d'accord avec les autres Puissances, signataires des traités de 1815. Cette motion, reproduite dans le coupon de journal ci annexé, a été declarée restante sur la table dans la maison des nobles. Une motion identique a été faite dans l'ordre des bourgeois par M. Bjorck avec le même résultat. Si je suis bien informé Mr. Stael v. Holstein n'est pas un homme de paille, l'idée de cette motion ayant été conçu dans la tête de M. Lallerstedt qui, pour donner plus de poids à cette mesure a décidé Mr. Bjorck à s'en charger, probablement en lui offrant en échange des services lors du vote sur une autre question, pour laquelle s'intéresse Mr. Bjorck.

Le Gouvernement voit d'un mauvais œil cette proposition, propre à lui créer des embarras; les débats à ce sujet aurait lieu dans une des premières séances plénières, M. le Comte Manderström prendra alors la parole, principalement pour porter d'une manière officielle à la connaissance du Comité qui sera saisi de cette question, les vues du Gouvernement à cet égard. Personne ne s'attendait à une pareille interpretation qui a fait l'effet de l'éclair par un ciel serein; quant aux motifs allégués par les motionnaires, il faut avouer qu'ils sont passablement tirés par les cheveux; car si un de la Constitution préscrit qu'il faut un événement pour admettre une motion particulière en dehors d'une époque, pendant laquelle elle doit être mise en avant, on a certainement eu en vue événement qui s'est passé à la Diète.

In his despatch no. 17 of 7/19 March Dashkov wrote:

---

184. See Wedel-Jarlsberg's dispatches of 27 January to the end of May 1863 and Manderström to Wedel-Jarlsberg, 16 March. Koncept, 1863. Vol. 5.
185. Filipowicz, *ibid*. s. 265. See Dashkov's dispatches of 23 April (5 May) and 26 April (8 May) 1863. On 23 April (5 May) he reported that Manderström aided 'pour triompher des idées plus pacifiques'. See 'Krig og fred'. The Danish envoy, Scheel-Plessen, suggested that his article was inspired by Manderström. Depecher Sweden, n. 28, 17 April 1863.

Partant ensuite du principe de non-intervention, il (Manderström) rappelle le souvenir des malheurs causés autrefois à la Suède par l'immixtion des Puissances étrangères dans ses affairs. Il admet qu'une Chambre fasse des vœux pour la solution d'une question mais non qu'elle impose au Gouvernement le mode de la trancher ... il prend un vif intérêt aux malheurs de la Pologne, il en désire la prompte terminaison, mais il ne veut et ne doit pas s'aventurer dans les voies qui pourraient non seulement contrarier le but qu'on se propose ou bien de le faciliter, mais entraîner même des suites qui dépasseraient vraisemblablement les prévisions de la représentation nationale ...'.

'... il reconnaît pourtant que dans certains cas une opinion exprimée par les Chambres sous forme de vœux peut assurer au Gouvernement un appui important dans quelques affaires extérieures, mais il insiste sur la nécessité de laisser le dernier, seul juge de l'opportunité comme la direction de son action à l'étranger.

Il appuya ensuite sur le tors qu'aurait la Diète de vouloir obliger le Roi à faire, au risque d'eprouver des refus, une proposition dans ce sens aux autres Puissances ...

'Je réussirais à écarter la motion dans la Chambre des Nobles, je ne saurais assurer ce même dans celle de Bourgeoise', Manderström informed Wedel-Jarlsberg on 16 March.

'La Suède n'avait nullement garanti l'indépendance de ce pays', Manderström stated during the session of the *Ordre des Nobles.* And on 23 April (5 May) Dashkov sent a report *'Rejet de la motion pour la Pologne par les Quatre Ordres'.*

Daskov was right stressing that Manderström's peaceful policy prevailed over the warlike ideas promulgated by Quanten. And all the Estates, The *Ordre des Nobles, des Prêtres, des Bourgeois,* and *des Paysants* voted in favour of Manderström.

'Animés d'une vive sympathie pour les malheurs du people polonais et affligés des injustes auquelles l'expose sa nationalité opprimée, les Etats du Royaume sont persuadés que le Gouvernement ne manquera pas, d'accord avec les Puissances Etrangères conformement aux exigences du droit des gens de l'humanité, de se prononcer en faveur de la Pologne, mais sans troubler la paix en tant que cela pourra être compatible avec notre indépendance, notre honneur et notre considération'.

The minister's cautious policy was influenced both by sceptical reports from C. Wachmeister in London and C.N. Adelswärd in Paris, saying there was little hope of joint military intervention by the Western powers against Russia, and by information from Swedish military circles which indicated fundamental gaps in the army's equipment in the event of a conflict.

And Wedel-Jarlsberg reported:

l'armée russe est sur le pied de guerre et pouvoir à l'armement complet de la forteresse de Cronstadt. Les motifs de cette détermination subite sont à chercher, d'abord dans les très sérieuses appréhensions qu'on a ici, que les nombreux meetings à l'étranger en faveur de la Pologne aboutirent pourtant un jour à une intervention plus ou moins directe de la part de l'Europe. Et, sous ce rapport, j'ai plus d'une fois en lieu de m'apercevoir que les craintes de la Suède ne figurent pas au dernier plan. Le souvenir de notre traité de Novembre et du poids réel que nous jetâmes alors dans la balance politique et loin d'être oubliée ici – et si, d'un côté, la mise d'embargo sur le *Ward Jackson* a été accueillie avec reconnaissance par le Gouvernement Impérial, des dernières ovations à Stockholm en faveur du Prince Czartoryski et les attentions royales au Chatêau de Stockholm et à Ulriksdal pour cet illustre voyageur l'ont, de l'autre, très visiblement inquiété.

Why you have decided to rearm Kronstadt – Wedel-Jarlsberg asked Gorchakov. Nobody would like to attack you – he asserted. Gorchakov replied 'qu'il ne fallait pas se laisser prendre à l'improviste et que, d'ailleurs, l'attitude récemment prise par le vieux parti Moscovites et les adresses aussi patriotiques que belliqueuses des Assemblées de Noblesse obligeaient le Gouvernement à ne pas rester sourd à ce réveil national'. (No. 37, 7 April, (26 March) 1863.

Under the influence of the government, and in particular at the instigation of the minister of foreign affairs, articles appeared in the conservative press (Posttidningen) warning against an adventurist policy and agitation for war. There was no shortage of voices in society warning against Swedish involvement in a war against Russia, especially when the increasing wave of pro-Polish articles agitating for war caused panic on the stock markets and a collapse in the value of Swedish securities.

The Swedish authorities' attitude to Polish affairs was put to the test again during the famous expedition by Col. T. Lapinski on the *Ward Jackson*. On board the *Ward Jackson*, which sailed from Britain on the night of 21-22 March, there were 185 volunteers of various nations and a large quantity of arms destined for the insurgents in Lithuania. A Herzen, M. Ogarev, G. Mazzini and K. Marx, among others, were involved in the preparations for the expedition. M. Bakunin joined it in Helsingborg. On 30 March the ship put into Malmö. The Swedish authorities, wanting to demonstrate their neutrality to Russia, despite progressive public opinion in their own country, complied with Russian demands for the confiscation of the vessel and its cargo.[186]

All the same, under pressure from public opinion and asked by Russell to join the diplomatic intervention, the government despatched notes to Gorchakov defending the Polish nation and its rights according to the provisions of the Treaty

---

186. See Central Archive, Moscow. Microfilms and photocopies, R.A. Stockholm. Depescher från Stockholm, nos. 23, 24, 25 and 31, 20 March (1 April), 21 March (2 April), 25 March (6 April) and 28 March (9 April) 1863. Manderström's instructions to Wedel-Jarlsberg, Skrivelser från Stockholm til Petersburg, 1863. Kabinet för utrikes brevväxlingen. Koncept 1863, vol 5. Wedel-Jarlsberg to Manderström, no. 44, 19 (7) April. Depescher från besk. i Petersburg, 1863. Rosenberg to Bismarck, 26 April 1863. Rosenberg to Bismarck, 26 April 1863, APP III, p. 516. Among the printed literature the following deserve notice: Einar Hedin, 'Sveriges ställning i förhållande till Ryssland och våstmagterna år 1863', *Historisk Tidskrift*, 1922; Carl Hallendorff, *Illusioner och verklighet*. Studier öfver den skandinaviska krisen 1864, (Stockholm, 1914), pp. 102 ff. L. de Geer, *Minnen upptecknade*, förra delen, (Stockholm, 1892), pp. 242 ff. J.W.A. Eckhardt, *Von Nicolaus I zu Alexander III* (Leipzig 1881) pp. 155-160; F.G. Fellenius, *Polska frågan i Sverige år 1863*, (Stockholm, 1936); Lolo Krusius-Ahrenberg, 'Skandinavismens inställning till den slesvig-holsteinska frågan och Rysslands hällning till bägge vid det dansk-tyska Krigets utbrott', *Historisk Tidskrift for Finland*, 1942, Arg. 27, H 1-2; L. Posten, *De Polska emigranternas agentverksamhet i Sverige 1862-1863*, (Lund 1975); A. Jansson, *Den Svenska utrikespolitikens historia*, III. 3 (Stockholm 1961); E. Halicz, *The Scandinavian Countries and the January Insurrection*, (NY, 1984); W. Czartoryski, *Pamietnik 1860-64*, (Warsaw, 1960). E. Zaitsev, Morskaya povstancheskaya ekspeditsiya k beregam Litvy v 1863 g. *K stoletiyu geroicheskoi bor'by*, (Moscow, 1964). Bibliotèque Polonaise, Paris, Rkps. p. 531, 39,.2, 4, and 6 April, 1863.

of Vienna. It called for the protection of peace in Europe and declared itself opposed to bloodshed in Poland.[187]

Gorchakov was concerned not to irritate and exacerbate relations with Stockholm 'Je fus agréablement surpris de la manière vraiment bienveillante, dont le Prince Gorchakov reçut ma communication en faveur de la Pologne-reported Wedel-Jarlsberg, mais l'explication se trouve sans doute dans la crainte *réelle* que nous inspirons en ce moment et les ménagements qu'en sont la *conséquence*'.

Gorchakov's reply to the basic Swedish note of 7 April[188] ran as follows:

Dispatch from Gorchakov to Dashkov, St. Petersburg, 14 April 1863.

M. le ministre de Suède et de Norvége m'a donné lecture d'une depêche de M. le comte de Manderstroem, relative aux préoccupations qu'inspirent à la cour de Stockholm la situation actuelle de la Pologne et l'influence qu'elle peut exercer sur le repos de l'Europe.

M. le Comte de Manderstroem a rendu justice aux sentiments qui animent notre Auguste Maître, en exprimant la conviction que Sa Majesté trouverait, dans ses propres inspirations, les paroles de clémence et les perspectives de progrès propres à faire cesser l'effusion du sang et à ramener l'ordre et la tranquillité dans le royaume.

Le manifeste Impérial du 31 mars témoigne que la sollicitude de l'Empereur s'était déjà portée dans cette direction.

On ne saurait, toutefois, meconnaître que l'agitation puise dans les instigations permanentes du dehors ses principaux aliments.

187. Dispatch from Manderström to Baron-Wedel-Jarlsberg (the Swedish note) 7 April 1863.
   Les nouvelles qui parviennent du theâtre de la guerre en Pologne, paraissent établir, malgré les contradictions dont elles fourmillent, que l'autorité de l'Empereur tend à se rétablir et que ce ne sont que des rassemblements partiels qui lui opposent encore de la résistance. Les insurgés manquent d'armes et de munitions, et il leur sera sans doute presque impossible de s'en procurer. Dans cet état des choses, et nous fondant non seulement sur l'intérêt qui nous prescrit impérieusement d'employer tous nos efforts pour amener la cessation d'une situation qui pourrait dans ses conséquences menacer la paix de l'Europe, mais aussi sur les principes d'humanité et de générosité dont nous savons que le cœur de S.M.L.'Empereur est trop empreint pour ne pas désirer vivement d'en donner des témoignages éclatants, nous pensons devoir joindre nos représentation à celles, offertes déjà par d'autres Etats, appelés au même titre que nous à émettre leur opinion, pour tâcher d'arrêter l'effusion du sang, et d'amener pour la Pologne une situation plus conforme aux légitimes aspirations des hommes de bien de ce pays, dont le nombre dépasse incontestablement de beaucoup celui de ceux que des réformes équitables ne sauraient contenter. Nous nous tenons assurés que des paroles de clémence et d'oubli, et la perspective d'un régime propre à assurer une sage liberté, suffiraient pour ramener complètement l'ordre et la tranquilité. Nous ne nous permettons pas d'indiquer plus spécialement les moyens d'y parvenir, - à cet égard la France et la Grande Bretagne ont déjà exprimé leur avis, - et nous sommes certains que Sa Majesté Impériale trouvera dans Ses propres inspirations tout ce qui conduirait le plus sûrement à un but, qui ne saurait que former l'objet de Ses vœux.
   Vous devez, Monsieuer le Baron, Vous prononcer dans ce sens dans les entretiens que Vous aurez l'honneur d'avoir avec Mr. Le Prince Gortchakoff qui ne saurait y voir que l'expression de l'intérêt amical du Gouvernement du Roi. Agréez etc.
   Central Archive, Moscow. Skrivelser från Petersburg til Stockholm. H.W. Münich, Polska frihetskampen, 1863, pp. 164-65.
   Hedin named the 7 April note 'une étourderie digne du plus sévère blâme'. Cf. Stück-Warburg, *Illustrerad svensk litteraturhistoria*. 1915. IV. I. p. 62. See Wedel-Jarlsberg's dispatches no. 43 and 45, 19 (7) and 20 (8) April, 1863.
188. In *Sbornik izdanyi v pamyat' dvadtsatiletiya upravl. min. in. del gosud. Kantslera A.M. Gorchakova 1856-1881*. (St. Petersburg, 1881), pp. 25-26.
   Aftonbladet, 12 May pointed out: 'ce que n'aura point passé inaperçu à l'étranger c'est le ton glacial sur lequel la Russie nous répond'.

Nous y avons rendu attentifs les cabinets qui nos ont adressé des communications analogues à celle dont vient de s'acquitter M. le ministre de Suède et de Norvége.

Vous en trouverez ci-près les copies, ainsi que les réponses que j'y ai faites, d'ordre de notre Auguste Maître.

Désirant constater le prix que nous attachons à conserver des rapports de confiance avec la cour de Stockholm, Sa Majesté vous autorise à communiquer à M. le comte de Manderstroem la présente dépêche, ainsi que ses annexes.

As the reader can see, its tone was mild and conciliatory.

But at the end of April (on 29), disturbed by rumours that Napoleon III was in favour of a military expedition against Russia, Manderström sent a more resolute note to St. Petersburg in which he called Russia's attention to the fact that assurances given by her were not enough to restore order and peace in Poland. The Russian government was asked to take additional measures. At the end of this note Manderström wrote that he had no doubts of the motives of the Russian government.

The note was ignored by Gorchakov, who told Wedel-Jarlsberg on 6 May that the Polish rebels were only continuing their struggle because of the support from abroad. He assured him that the best way to restore order would be not to encourage the Poles.

Selon lui-reported Wedel-Jarlsberg – rien n'entretenait l'agitation en Pologne autant que les instigations permanentes du déhors ... rien ne serait plus propre, pour atteindre le but de pacification qu'on se propose, que de s'appliquer à écarter *les excitations du dehors,* se traduisant non seulement par des phrases, mais aussi par des envois d'emissaires, d'armes, d'argent etc. Ce serait là un service réel que les puissances étrangères rendraient non seulement au Gouvernement Impérial et à la Pologne, mais aussi à l'Europe, au profit de la cause de l'ordre, directement ménacé par le mouvement qu'on s'efforce d'acclimater en Pologne. Une marche semblable accélérerait infailliblement et plus que toute autre chose, le développement des idées libérales, qui sont toujours dans les généreuses intentions de l'Empereur.[189]

Despite the fact that the Stockholm cabinet's April notes to Gorchakov on the Polish question did not go beyond calls for the maintenance of peace in Europe and mainly put forward demands of a humanitarian nature, Gorchakov as in the past did not trust Sweden and issued instructions that events there should be most carefully followed. 'Redoublez viligance en tout ce qui concerne Pologne', he recommended on 9 March.

On 13 May Gorchakov sent a telegram: 'Informer exactement et en tout utile nos Ministres de la Défence et de la Marine de tout les préparatifs de guerre qu'avaient lieu en Suède'.

Two months later on (13 July) a following telegram was dispatched to Stockholm: 'Tâchez de pénétrer s'il n'y a pas entente contre nous entre France et Suède'.[190]

---

189. C. Hallendorf, *Illusioner och verklighet,* (Stockholm, 1914), p. 96.
190. Gorchakov to Dashkov, 9 March, 27 March, 13 May, 4 July and 13 July 1863, Central Archive Moscow, R.A. Stockholm. Cf. also Jansson, pp. 180-88, 306-7.

These telegrams reveal something of Gorchakov's thought and illustrate his fears of the Stockholm cabinet's military and diplomatic activities. But there was no reason to be in fear.

Even the well-known radicals C.H. Anckarsvärd and F.A. Dalman, actively engaged in the national-liberal movement, warned against Swedish military intervention. Dalman was of the opinion that intervention in Poland's favour was unjustified 'ni par des antécédentes historiques, ni par les intérets du pays, qui, dans presques toutes luttes avec la Russie, a eu la Pologne contre lui.' These were the words used by Dashkov in his despatch of 26 April (8 May).

And the organ of the liberal party Aftonbladet wrote:

'Pendant que les plusieurs journaux du continent entretiennent leurs lecteurs de nos velléités belliqueuses et d'une rupture imminente entre la Suède et la Russie, – bruit qui a causé même quelque émotion à la Bourse de Paris, – nous vivons dans le calme le plus parfait et nous n'entendons parler ni de préparatifs de guerre, ni de la moindre mesure qui, de la part de notre gouvernement puisse provoquer une tension quelconque avec aucune puissance étrangère.

Il y a plus, on pourrait conclure, du langage qu'il tient officiellement, que notre gouvernement ne désire pas le moins du monde s'occuper de la question polonaise, même par la voie diplomatique, et qu'il désire vivement opérer une réaction dans les sympathies qui se manifestent si généralement pour la Pologne, et encore en ce moment, par des meetings et autres manifestations publiques.'[191]

But as time went on Swedish public opinion became indifferent towards the Polish problem. The Russian Ambassador took notice of this and in his dispatches of 12 (24) August and 13 (25) September tried to explain it in the following terms.

Le calme politique que je signalais dernièrement à Votre Excellence paraît se consolider de plus et l'on dirait même que, fatiguée par les excitations passées, l'opinion trahit des symptômes d'indifférence au sujet des Polonais...

Du reste wrote Dashkov on 13 (25) September, la sollicitude pour la Pologne a presque totalement cédé la place ici aux inquiétudes causées par la perspective d'une crise prochaine dans la question du Holstein.

The 7 and 29 April notes to St. Petersburg were really the end of the Swedish government's official involvement in the Polish question. A policy of non-intervention gained the upper hand and from then on the government displayed even greater caution. For this there were many reasons. For one thing, there was fear that the economy would collapse because of the abrupt fall in the value of Swedish securities on the exchanges, particularly in Hamburg (which incidentally was Russia's doing). Then there was the shortage of funds to re-equip the army unprepared for military action.[192]

There was a clear lack of enthusiasm for Stockholm's military plans in Norway, which had no interest in strengthening Sweden. There was opposition in Finland too, where the people showed not the slightest enthusiasm for the Finnish Scandinavianists' plans and where anti-Russian feeling was very weak. 'Finland was,

---

191. Revue de la semaine, nos 3 and 5. 21 April and 5 May.
192. I. Andersson, *Dzieje Szwecji,* pp. 267-68.

as many Swedes perceived, developing along lines that precluded reunion with Sweden'.[193]

The separate policy carried on by the King behind the back of the government was another question. He linked it with opportunities to implement his own political plans, which aimed at uniting the Scandinavian states, recovering Finland and also increasing his own power. The King's dislike of Russia and his awareness that the reconstruction of Poland was in the interests of Sweden were the main reasons for the increased contacts between the King and representatives of the Polish political *emigrés,* beginning in 1862. The frequent contacts between the King and court and representatives of the various political groups among the *emigrés* in 1863 were based on the common purpose of persuading France to go to war against Russia. It is hard to say, however, how far these plans really aimed at coordination of the two countries' efforts and how far they were merely soundings, particularly on the part of Napoleon III. There is a lack of new archival evidence here – apart from the documents published by Bóbr-Tylingo in *Teki Historyczne,* 1960-61. At any rate, in the second half of 1863 the King returned to the idea of starting a war jointly with France against Russia and he thought it could be launched in the spring of 1864.[194]

If all these plans came to nothing, the chief responsibility, as Swedish historians correctly stress, lies with France and Britain, since these powers were incapable of reaching agreement and acting in defence of Poland.[195] Even the cautions Manderström saw Sweden's place as beside the Western powers in the event of armed action by them in the Baltic. Sweden could not act on her own but would be obliged to follow their lead.

Towards the end of 1863 Manderström did not hide the great danger threatening the country from Russia. He feared a surprise attack on Sweden in revenge for the policy pursued by Sweden towards the end of the Crimean War and in 1863. Faced with the prospect of an alliance between Russia, Prussia and Austria, he severed the Swedish alliance with Denmark at the end of 1863, at the moment when Denmark was facing mortal danger and was under diplomatic and military pressure from the coalition of German states.[196]

Norwegian society viewed Polish events from the point of view of its own interests. Norway did not feel the Russian threat in the same way as Sweden and had no territorial claims against Russia. Only a small group of Norwegian Scandinavianists felt any solidarity with the anti-Russian disposition of the Swedes. Liberal

---

193. R.M. Hatton, 'Russia and the Baltic', in *Russian Imperialism* ... p. 127. Wedel-Jarlsberg's dispatches of 16 June and 3 August.
194. The King of Sweden had offered The Emperor Napoleon III to assist with 100.000 men in the restoration of the Kingdom of Poland. F.O. 27 France. Bóbr-Tylingo, *Teki Historyczne,* XI (1960), pp. 248-52. Jerningham on 3 July reported that the King promised only 50.000. *Den skandinaviska alliansfrågan 1857-63.* pp. 196-97.
195. Cf. Hedin, Jansson. The same point of view was expressed in 1863 by A. Sohlman, M.J. Crusenstolpe, H.W. Münich, J.G. Carlén.
196. J. de Coussange, *La Scandinavie,* (Paris, 1914), p. 19.

circles supported the Polish nation's struggle for liberation chiefly from fear of states that trampled on the right of others to political independence.

The Polish question was used by the liberal opposition to advance its political programme, which aimed to abolish the office of governor, strengthen the parliamentary system, make the government subject to Parliament, and thus ultimately strengthen democracy in Norway. Solidarity with Poland was expressed by leading representatives of the liberal camp in the press and by meetings in Christiania and other towns, especially in April 1863.

At the largest of the solidarity rallies in Christiania 3000-4000 people took part. The meeting was opened by L. Daa, a professor at the university. The other speakers, in order of speaking, were Nissen, the rector, Frölich, a bank director, Kildal and Steen, members of the Shorthing, and Ebbel, the representative of the students. The main elements in the speeches were humanitarian demands and the need to fight tyranny. These was recognition for the Polish nation's hundred-year struggle for freedom and calls for solidarity with it. Small nations should draw conclusions from the Poles' experience. This applied particularly, speakers said, to Denmark, where Prussia wanted to follow the same policy as Russia was pursuing on the Vistula.[197]

The unanimously adopted resolution, in which solidarity with the Polish struggle for freedom, national independence and human dignity had been expressed, was sent to Wladyslaw Czartoryski, the Main Agent of the Polish National Government in Paris.

The Christiania meeting did not escape Dashkov's notice. 'À Christiania – he reported on 13 (1) April – où l'on n'est pas mieux disposé pour nous qu'on est en Suéde, on ne s'est pas fait faute d'organiser dernièrement un meeting en faveur de la Pologne. Un millier des personnes y assistaient et il n'a manqué ni les discours ni des acclamations d'usage'.

The Christiania meeting was a new phenomenon in the history of Norway: for the first time, an international problem had been a matter of public debate in the country.

The position taken by supporters of Scandinavianism in Norway coincided with that of fellow Scandinavianists in Sweden, but it was realized that there was a difference in national interests and aims between the two countries.

They considered that diplomatic endeavours, unsupported by force of arms, would not free Poland. If France and Britain declared war against Russia, they argued, Sweden and Norway should take part in it. Such a war was in the interests of the whole of Scandinavia, which was threatened by Russia. Russia had already

---

197. Report of the rally on 7 April in *Morgenposten,* (Christiania) 9 April. See *Norge og den polske frihetskamp,* (Oslo, 1937), pp. 141-8, 210-24. Cf. Dashkov's report, no. 33, 1 (13) April 1863, Cent. Arch. Moscow, in Dep. från Stockholm til St. Petersburg, 28 March – 11 May 1863. On the revival of the pro-Polish movement in Norway see also *Aftonbladet,* Revue de la semaine, no. 2, 14 April 1863. Cf. L. Kowalska-Posten, *Norwegowie a sprawa polska w roku 1863,* Komunikaty Instytutu Baltyckiego, (Gdansk, 1979), z. 30, p. 17. *Dagbladet* (Christiania) 18 June 1863.

swallowed up Finland and threatened to invade Sweden and northern Norway. The main aim of action by the Scandinavian states must be the liberation of Finland, and the situation which had arisen in the Polish lands should favour that. Even if the attempt to free Finland failed, the very fact of the rise of an independent Poland would be of enormous importance for the Scandinavian countries. The rise of Poland would push Russia eastward and force it to switch to a defensive policy towards the European states. This would be important for Denmark, too, since the revival of a strong, free Poland could draw the Germans' attention away from Denmark. Starting from these premises, it was argued, the Scandinavian states ought to support the struggle for the liberation of Poland.[198] The majority of Norwegian society, however, regarded these principles with scepticism. It thought that war with Russia was mainly in the interests of Sweden, which sought to regain Finland. Norway was not interested in strengthening Sweden.[199] Thus pro-Polish sympathies there did not gather the same momentum as in Sweden, chiefly because of differences in political objectives.

In correspondence with the Norwegian Minister of State in the Swedish government, G. Sibbern, the Norwegian government, and especially the Prime Minister, F. Stang, praised Manderström's restraint and requested Sibbern to spare no effort to persuade Charles XV to abandon his scheme with France if Britain did not join them too.[200] Stang was sharply at odds with the Polish committee in Christiania and for that reason Prince Constantine Czartoryski did not pay him a visit during his stay in Christiania in May 1863.[201] The policy of the government and the Norwegian conservatives was not to annoy Russia and not to help to stiffen the Danish position in the dispute with Germany.

V

The Polish Uprising and the Beginning of the Reform Era in Finland

The reign of Alexander II began auspiciously for Finland with the opening in 1856 of the Saimaa Canal, which linked eastern Finland more closely with St. Petersburg but also opened up its forests for the timber trade to western Europe. Finland had given no trouble to Russia during the Crimean War, despite the Anglo-French naval attack on the Åland Islands and the bombardment of Sveaborg. Some exiles in Sweden had made anti-Russian propaganda, but the failure of Sweden to take part in the war had made anti-Russian action in Finland impossible. Alexander II had thus no reason for resentment against Finland, but had perhaps some reason to favour the Finnish majority, against the Swedish minority, which comprised the

---

198. *Dagbladet,* 18 June 1863. *Norge og den polske frihetskamp,* pp. 244-53.
199. *Aftonbladet,* 8 July 1863; *Dagbladet,* 11 July 1863; Russer og Polakker, Jorgenson, p. 350 ff.
200. Letters in Alf Kaartvedt, *Frederick Stang og Georg Sibbern,* I. 1862-1871, (1 January 1862 – October 1863), (Oslo 1956), pp. 15, 20, 22, 27, 340, 353, 358, 367-8.
201. *Ibid.* p. 403.

whole landowning and upper business class, as well as a share of the lower social classes.[202]

Even so, in the so-called April Manifesto of 1861 the Tsar postponed the convening of the Finnish Diet indefinitely.

In Finland, the question of the attitude to the Polish national liberation movement was different than in other Scandinavian countries. Initially the Tsarist regime was afraid the example of the Kingdom of Poland might spread to Finland. The Tsarist authorities were also worried about the internal situation in Finland, owing to the revival of political life in connection with hopes of reform. They were also concerned about possible growth in the Scandinavianists' influence in Finland and their international contacts, and finally about the possibility of intervention in defence of the Polish uprising by Napoleon III, in which case the military action might involve Finnish territory too.

'The interest of the Finns in the new Polish revolt was quite different from their passivity during the revolt of 1830-1. However they were not interested in the new revolt because the Poles had the same kind of autonomous status as Finland, but above all as an expression of the idea of nationalism. The attitude to the Polish revolt in its entirety constituted for the Finns a political-moral problem. They were faced with two alternatives: should they demonstrate loyalty to the empire, and so think primarily of the inviolability of Finland's position, or was sympathy with an oppressed nation seeking freer conditions more important?' ...

'The liberals – J. Paasivirta stressed, represented a clear westward orientation, which seemed to free them in a remarkable way from political commitments, and led them to the view that Russia was "remote" from Finland. Their purpose was above all to liberalise Finland's position in relation to Russia. Their endeavour to loosen the relationship between the two was shown, for example, when they began to speak of Finland's "union" with Russia in connection with the international crisis of 1863.'

In their political attitude the fennomans differed from the liberals, in that they declared their loyalty to the empire, and sought to tranquillise public opinion against rumours of war ... Snellman (the leader of the fennomans – E.H.) feared that Poland's fate could befall Finland if war ever touched her territory. He also assumed that Finland had the possibility of national development within the imperial framework.[203]

The attempt to protect Finland from war and crisis was also aimed at developing the 'large perspective', that is the strengthening of national consciousness and peaceful progress, and the aspirations for reform those elements contained within them.[204]

202. H. Seton-Watson, *The Russian Empire,* (Oxford, 1967), pp. 415 ff. M. Borodkine, *La Finlande comme partie intégrante de l'Empire Russe,* (Paris, 1912), pp. 7, 44-45, T.K. Derry, *A History of Scandinavia,* (London, 1979), pp. 233, 275-76.
203. See Snellman's article "Krig og fred" (War or Peace) in *Litteraturblad* at the beginning of July 1863.
204. J. Paasivirta, *Finland and Europe, International Crises in the period of Autonomy 1808-1914,* (Minneapolis, 1981), pp. 121 ff.

In the spring of 1863 the Russian authorities tightened up the supervision of foreigners in Finland, since they were afraid Finnish territory might be used to get supplies of arms to the insurgents, especially those operating in Lithuania.

'En Finlande – wrote *Aftonbladet* in the Revue de la semaine No. 10 on 9 June, – non seulement les armements continuent, mais ils deviennent de jour en jour plus formidables' ... 'L'armée d'occupation en Finlande ... va être portée au triple ou au quadruple' – *Aftonbladet* reported in the Revue de la semaine No. 11 on 16 June. This was done even though both A. Armfelt and P. Rokassowski assured St. Petersburg that although there were people in Finland sympathetic to Poland, and those who would gladly transport arms for her for material advantage, there was no mood of insurgency there and anything of that kind was impossible as the inhabitants of Finland without exception ('ohne Ausnahme') were sincerely devoted to His Highness.[205] Such feelings did indeed predominate, although some young liberals, who favoured Scandinavianism, cultivated contacts with the circle of people around E. Quanten, Librarian to the King of Sweden, which had connections with Polish *emigrés*. But no one thought about an uprising in Finland and it was recognised that the liberation of Finland and its inclusion in a Scandinavian union could only come about in the event of a major European war. The influential Young Finnish party, which was growing in strength, argued that the Finns had their own state and national interests, which were contrary to Scandinavianism. There was also awareness that many Finnish peasants were devoted to the Tsar.

Finland, however, did not join in the display of servility to Alexander II, and in the face of a possible European war over the Polish question some Finnish politicians would have liked to adopt a position of neutrality. This idea, which was born among a small group of radicals around the *Helsingfors Dagbladet,* met with criticism from many directions. M. Katkov attacked it because he considered that Finland, as it was not a sovereign state but part of the Empire, had no right to put forward such ideas.[206]

It was attacked by the leader of the Finnish party, J.V. Snellman, who opposed the idea that Finnish vessels should be neutral during the Polish uprising as such a position would damage good relations with Russia, on which, in his opinion, the programme of reforms being carried out in Finland depended. It would be bad, Snellman considered, if Russia had doubts about the loyalty of Finland.[207] According to Dashkov, these ideas were put out by a narrow group of radicals with no influence among the Finnish population, which was loyal to Russia, and its emergence was the work of the Poles and Scandinavianist who, having failed to revolutionise the Finns, sought to cause new difficulties for Russia in this way.[208]

---

205. 31 March 1863. K. Ahrenberg, p. 34.
206. 15 April, 28 May, 10 and 24 July 1863. This idea of neutrality was put forward for the first time in 1859. Borodkine, *La Finlande* ... pp. 52-54.
207. 'Krieg oder Frieden für Finland?', *Litteraturblad,* no. 5, 9 July 1863. Cf. P. Airas, *Die Geschichtlichen Wertungen Krieg und Friede* ..., p. 320, L.K. Ahrenberg, p. 385.
208. Reports of 16 and 29 April, 11 and 15 May, and 16 June 1863. Cf. Ahrenberg, pp. 380, 385, V.V. Pokhlebkin, in *SSSR-Finlandiya,* pp. 99-100, regards the neutrality plan as a hostile act towards Russia from the point of view of her military strategic interest.

Towards the end of the spring the situation in Finland appeared to be hopeless. There was no sign that the expected reform would be introduced soon by St. Petersburg. Nor would military intervention in the Baltic by the Great Powers bring a positive solution for Finland. The Finnish dilemma was impartially described by O. Plessen in his dispatch on June 1 (20 May).

De Finnlande jusqu'ici aucune adresse [i.e. servile address to the Tsar - E.H.] que je sache. Cependant on me dit que là aussi s'en préparent. La Finnlande - he stated - est dans une situation qui me semble fort pénible. Hétérogéne au reste de l'Empire, moins confondue avec la Russie que les provinces Baltiques allemandes qui n'ont pas d'administration et de constitution distinctes, les habitants de la Finnlande ne peuvent guère éprouver ce qu'éprouvent les Russes. Si la guerre éclate le Grand-duché soufrirra de nouveau le premier de tous les pays appartenant à la Russie. Son commerce, unique source de son bien-être sera détruit, ses bâtiments capturés, ses côtes dévastées et pillées, comme pendant la guerre de Crimée. En temps de guerre la Finnlande ne retira aucun avantage de sa qualité de province d'un vaste et riche Empire. D'un autre côté, si la Finnlande cherchait à se rallier à la Suède, qui n'est pas assez riche pour la nourrir dans ses fréquentes disettes, et qui, ce que la Russie ne fait pas, l'absorberait administrativement et politiquement, quel avenir se préparait la Finnlande? Elle deviendrait, à moins que la Russie ne soit entièrement refoulée, que Pétersbourg cesse d'être capitale, l'objet indispensable de la convoitise de la Russie."[209]

It is not easy to establish the attitude of Finnish society to the Polish uprising on the basis of the contemporary press in Finnish and Swedish in Finland. It was of course subject to strict censorship and during the uprising it was forbidden to publish any news other than from Russian sources.[210] The total amount of reporting on the uprising is meagre. There was something on the M. Langiewicz party,[211] on the uprising in the Ukraine and Belorussia,[212] and here and there expressions of sympathy for Poland and the fight for freedom. One of the articles expresses the opinion that an uprising does not take place without reason. Nations cannot be torn and divided by force. Finland has also been treated as an article of commerce. But Finland has been united as a nation and so it must continue. Dissension was the undoing of Poland.[213] The article 'Kansan miehille ja kansan ystäville' (To men of the people and to friends of the people) which appeared in *Kansakunnan lehti*, 29 October 1863, deserves notice: the author criticised the attitude of the Polish gentry to the peasants, as a result of which the social base of the uprising was narrow.[214]

---

209. Udenrigsministeriet A 3354, R.A.
210. *Helsingfors Dagblad,* no. 168, 24 July 1863.
211. *Helsingin Uutiset,* no. 26, 30 March. Article 'Ulkomailta', Puola, (From Abroad, Poland).
212. *Ibid.* no. 45, 8 June. Article "Ulkomailta".
213. See the articles "Ote Mehiläisesta" in *Mehiläinen* (a literary review), and 'European tila 1863' (The Situation in Europe 1863) in *Praivätär*, 2 January 1864 in which words of praise about Poland's bravery were expressed. 'There are many friends among nations ... the governments have given no aid.'
214. I would like to thank Aila Lassila of Helsinki University Library for information concerning the Finnish press.

Summing up Finland's attitude to events in Poland in 1863 L.A. Puntilla expressed the opinion that there was great sympathy for Poland, but those who wanted to rebel actively were not so many. As the Polish uprising was quenched in its beginnings, the possibility of a conflict in Finland had passed. The new Russian regime had been fairly peacefully settled in Finland.[215]

The idea of a link between the events in the Kingdom of Poland and the reforms carried out by Alexander II in Finland in 1863 was developed by G. Lindström. Lindström thinks that the call to the Diet of 1863 was finally sent by the Emperor because he was afraid the Finns could join the Poles to free their country completely. The same opinion was expressed by M.G. Schybergson and L.A. Puntilla.[216]

The programme of reforms put forward by the Young Finns, who broke away from the old conservative party, sought equal rights for the Finnish and Swedish languages, freedom of the press, autonomy in the economic sphere, the introduction of the Finnish mark as legal tender, and also the reconstruction of the Finnish army, gradually gained the approval of Alexander II and many of his closest advisers, but it was only slowly put into practice, and events in Poland exerted an influence on the Tsar's decisions and once again demonstrated the special strategic role of Finland in the event of armed conflict between Russia and the Western powers.[217]

On 18 September Alexander II summoned the Diet in Helsingfors for the first time in fifty-four years. The Diet passed legislation on currency, railway building, and education. But the most important act was the Language *Ordonnance* of 1 August, which laid down that within twenty years the Finnish language must be introduced into all public business on a level of equality with Swedish. The result had been the fuller development of the indigenous Finnish culture, which had been for so many centuries subordinated to the Swedish.

New reforms were introduced in 1865 and 1869.

Alexander II's reforms met with a mixed reception in Russia itself. Katkov opposed and criticised them. He expressed this in a letter to the Minister, P.A. Valuev, on 2 December 1863. He considered that granting autonomy to Finland would create a dangerous precedent for Russia, for Finland would be the archetype of federalism. With only a dynastic link to the Russian state, Finland would be a model for the dismemberment of the organic Russian state. He was also indignant that the possibility of expressing this opinion publicly in Moscow itself was limited.

215. In *Historiallinen Arkivisto*, vol. 52, 1947, pp. 455-521.
216. M.G. Schybergson, *Finlands Politiska Historia, 1809-1919*, Helsingfors, 1923), pp. 171-72, G. Lindström, Vuoden 1863 valtiopäirväkutsumusta odetettaessa. (When waiting for the Call to the Diet of 1863. *Nuori Suomi.* XIX joulualbumi. Helsinki, 1909. L.A. Puntilla, *Histoire politique de la Finlande de 1809 à 1855.* (Neuchâtel, 1964); p. 53. See also B. Estlander, *Elve Årtionden ur Finlands historia.* I. 1808-1878. (Helsingfors, 1919), pp. 171 ff. and K. Ahrenberg, p. 425.
217. *Helsingfors Dagblad*, 11 July 1863. See Wedel-Jarlsberg's report to Manderström on his conversation with Gorchakov no. 67 on 2 June (21 May) 1863, and on Alexander's II visit to Finland in July 1863. (No. 88, 3 August 1863). See also: Borodkine, *La Finlande* ... pp. 44-45, E. Jutikalla with K. Pirinen, *A History of Finland*, (New York, 1962, pp. 203 ff.). J.H. Wuorinen, *A History of Finland*, (London, 1965), pp. 159-79; Puntila, *Historiallinen Arkisto* 52, 1947, p. 522.

You find it unsatisfactory to permit me to wage a polemic on the Finnish question with the Helsinki press – wrote Katkov – My God! What kind of position is this! It is possible to speak Swedish in Helsingfors against all of us, that is permissible; but the government itself forbids us in Moscow in the very center of the Russian state, to voice ourselves in Russian.[218]

But another Russian publicist, the Slavophile I.S. Aksakov, welcomed the reforms introduced in Finland, arguing that convening the parliament in Helsinki had made an enormous impression not only in Finland and Russia but throughout Europe, and showed that such nations, which did not have very much in common with Russia and were under a Russian protectorate, were receiving freedom. This gave the lie to foreign propaganda concerning Russia's policy towards the nations which made up the empire.

Combien il y a peu de tendances en nous Russes, à russifier les non-russes! Au contraire, on peut faire le reproche à la Russie de s'être par trop facilement laissé approcher "par la propagande étrangère. Effectivement, la Finlande ne fut jamais soumise à une politique de russification violente". "Nous devons espérer – Aksakov wrote – que la Diète de Finlande fixera enfin son attention sur la situation des Russes dans le Grand-Duché, et qu'elle leur donnera la possibilité de jouir des droits réservés aux Finlandais d'origine".[219]

Helsingfors Dagblad and *Åbo Underrättelser* set themselves to rebuff Katkov's attacks on Finland. They began by claiming that he did not understand Finland's special status, and pointed out that his views were representative of only a narrow circle among the Russians.

Dissatisfaction with the interpretation of the Finnish liberals, that the relations of Finland and Russia were 'contractual' and to be classified as 'a genuine union', also appeared in the Russian foreign ministry. Alexander II in his closing speech to the Finnish Diet on 15 April 1864, criticized 'errant ideas' expressed by the liberal Finnish circles about the relationship of the Grand Duchy to the empire. The Tsar pointed out that it was in Finland's interest try 'to strengthen, and in no way weaken her close ties with Russia.'[220]

VI.

The problem concerning the relationship between the January Uprising and the Scandinavian countries, which in my opinion has not hitherto received the attention which it is due, played a far from trivial role in the history of Scandinavia. I am thinking here both of the direct and indirect importance of the Polish events.

---

218. M. Katz, *M. Katkov. A Political Biography 1818-1887.* (The Hague and Paris, 1966), p. 134; M. Katkov, *Sobranie* ... 1863, nos. 209, 210-A, 238, 258. Borodkine, *La Finlande* ... pp. 53-54, Schybergson, *Finlands politiska historia,* pp. 180-81.
219. N. Barssoukov, *Vie de Pogodine,* Vol. XX, pp. 232-34; Borodkine, *La Finlande* ... pp. 52-53. See also: Le Scandinavisme et le droit nouveau. *Le Nord,* 6 July 1863.
220. Paasivirta, *Finland and Europe* ... p. 135.

As far as their direct importance is concerned the principal facts to be mentioned are the influence of the uprising in activating the supporters of Scandinavianism in all three Scandinavian countries, the growth of anti-Russian feeling, especially in Sweden, and the popularisation of both Poland's national liberation struggle and her history and culture throughout the Scandinavian lands. Scandinavian society witnessed once again what Russia was like, what atrocities the Russian apparatus of coercion was capable of: the governments of the Scandinavian states could also see once again just how much importance Russia attached to the Polish question and just how sensitive she was on the matter, especially when she felt herself threatened from this quarter.

It must be said to the men of letters credit, that they defended the Polish cause and informed public opinion in Denmark and Sweden – Norway impartially about the Polish events. Among the poets, Carl Snoilsky – the bard of the Polish uprising – made the greatest contribution to the popularization of the heroic struggle of the Polish nation for independence and human dignity. Among the journalists Carl Ploug, August Blanche, Viktor Rydberg, Karl Gustaw Wetterhoff, Fredrika Bremer, Anton Nyström, Henrik Wergeland, Sylvester Sivertson and Bjørnstjerne Bjørnson were the most active spokesmen for the Polish cause.

The political changes which occured in Europe as a result of the Polish uprising had a more fundamental influence on the history of the Scandinavian countries. Sweden, faced with the new constellation in Europe (France was now isolated on the continent of Europe and Russia thanks to Prussia's attitude in 1863 slightly reestablished her international prestige), abandoned the plans for close co-operation with France and military alliance with Denmark and also gave up her attempts to put the idea of political Scandinavianism into effect. The uprising influenced Russia's attitude to the Scandinavian states directly, but differently in the case of each country. Russian relations with Sweden deteriorated to such an extent that towards the end of 1863 the Swedish government did not rule out the possibility of Russian military intervention. On the other hand, there was quite a fundamental change in Russia's attitude to Finland, where Alexander II initiated a policy of concessions. As far as Denmark was concerned, although Russo-Danish relations apparently did not change much in comparison with what they were at the turn of the year 1862-63, in fact the influence on the future of Denmark of the political transformations in Europe associated with the Polish uprising was immense. By his continual manoeuvring Bismarck succeeded in avoiding the consequences which the signing of the Convention of Alvensleben had at first seemed to threaten, and in ensuring Russia's continued friendly attitude to Prussia. At the same time he secured the isolation of Austria, which by oscillating between Paris and St. Petersburg during the Polish uprising, ended in alienating both Napoleon III and Alexander II. Bismarck was able to use her as a tool in Prussia's hands to carry out his plans for starting a war with Denmark under the most favourable conditions for Prussia.[221]

221. Józef Piłsudski o powstaniu 1863 roku, (London, 1963), pp. 157-58, 201-2, 218.
    See M. Żywczyński, *Historia powszechna 1789-1870,* pp. 426-7. Von Schweinitz offers some in-

Europe left Denmark to fight a lone duel against the consolidated power of the German states.

The Danish-German war could break out only because the Polish uprising had come to an end. The Polish uprising, by weakening France diplomatically, and Russia both diplomatically and militarily, had created conditions in which both powers had given their consent to Austria's removal from Germany and Prussia's triumph.

The adverse political situation in Europe, which was the consequence of the collapse of the uprising, was a major cause of Denmark's defeat. J. Klaczko quotes Sir Andrew Buchanan's letter to Russell on 28 November, 1863, as follows: 'Les événements qui se passent en Pologne, malgré la réprobation des trois grandes puissances, ont améné les Allemands à croire que personne ne s'opposerait par les armes à une œuvre de spoliation contre le Danemark ...' Klaczko adds his own comment on this quotation: 'Si, au lieu d'être divisées et méfiantes l'une envers l'autre, les deux puissances libérales de l'Occident avaient été unies en ces années 1863-64, que de bien on eût pu faire, que de mal on eût empêché sur les bords de la Vistule, de l'Eider, et peut-être même du Potomac!'[222] Polish *emigré* papers said 'the Prusso-Austrian attack on Denmark is the natural consequence of the abandonment of Poland in 1863'.[223] These contemporary judgements agree with the assessment given many years later by F. Engels in his essay *The Foreign Policy of Russian Czarism*, where he wrote:

During the Polish uprising of 1863 he (Bismarck) took the side of Russia, opposing Austria, France and England, in a theatrical manner and did everything to bring about victory for Russia.[224] That secured him the defection of the Czar from this usual policy in the Schleswig-Holstein question: in 1864 the Duchy was wrested from Denmark with the Czarist permission.[225]

---

teresting observations on this subject: Wenn nun jene Stimmung, welche der Austausch von Höflichkeiten beim Pariser Kongress und in Stuttgart genährt hatte, zur Zeit des dänischen Krieges noch fortgedauert hätte, so wäre die Lostrennung der Herzogtümer unmöglich gewesen, aber der polnische Aufstand hatte die ganze Situation verändert, und Bismarck hatte dies augenblicklich verstanden und gründlich ausgenutzt.

Denkwürdigkeiten des Botschafters General v. Schweinitz, vol. I. (Berlin, 1927), p. 176.

Herr V. Bismarck aber erkannte, was sich Europa bieten liess, und hermit sowie mit dem Bewusstsein, Russland sich verpflichtet zu haben, schloss er die Rechnung des Jahres 1863 ab, als der König von Dänemark, Friedrich VII, die Augen zumachte, und Europa nun zeigen sollte, ob es den Willen habe, sein Londoner protokoll von 8 Mai 1852 durchzuführen.

Ibid, p. 179. Cf. *A. Kriegers Dagbøger*, vol. III, 5 December 1863, pp. 7-8.

222. J. Klaczko, *Études de diplomatie contemporaine. Les cabinets de L'Europe en 1863-1864*, (Paris, 1866), pp. 447-8.
223. *Der Weisse Adler*, no. 66 and 81, 7 and 11 July 1864, and *Glos Wolny*, 20 May 1864. See H. Wereszycki, Sprawa polska w XIX wieku. *Polska XIX wieku*, (Warsaw, 1986), p. 137.
224. Cf. J. Klaczko's point of view: 'L'État qui devrait le premier et le plus douloureusement se ressentir bientôt des suites de l'abandon de la cause polonaise et du rapprochement opéré par cet abandon entre les trois puissantes co-partageantes, le Danemark, ne songeait alors qu'à s'assurer les bonnes grâces du tsar'. *Études* ... p. 144.
225. *The Russian Menace to Europe*, (Glencoe, Ill. 1952), p. 48.

VII

Gorchakov, like Alexander II,[226] regarded Denmark's situation as very difficult in the face of Germany's uniform attitude.[227] 'Vous n'êtes pas soixante dix millions comme nous', he stressed in a talk with Plessen,[228] but despite this, the minister said reproachfully, Danish-German relations had been exacerbated to a point where they were more tangled and bitter than Russia's relations with the powers which had intervened in the Polish question. He foresaw the possibility of a situation arising in which the London protocol, to which Russia attached such an important role, could not be enforced.[229]

Gorchakov told Plessen that it was in Denmark's interest to maintain a conciliatory position, but to Germany he said that a peaceful settlement of the conflict, in which he personally believed, would be possible if her demands were not too excessive.[230] Gorchakov considered the German Confederation's decision of 9 July to demand that the Danish government revoke the warrant of 30 March as legal, as he did the possible Federal Execution which was threatened in the event that Denmark did not comply with the 9 July resolution and withdraw the warrant within six weeks. Like the Tsar, Gorchakov expressed his satisfaction that Denmark was disposed towards negotiations and a peaceful settlement of the dispute with the Confederation on the basis of independence and autonomy for Holstein, but he regretted that, irrespective of what the Confederation's legal rights were, the Danish government would not simultaneously give it certain assurances concerning Schleswig, which in Gorchakov's opinion could cause it to turn away from the course it was following.[231]

Gorchakov did not share the Danish government's point of view or its fears that the Federal Execution might exceed the legal competence of the German Confederation. The truth was, he argued in an instruction to Budberg in Paris, that the 1851-52 agreements had made Schleswig a source of discord and the seeds of this had not disappeared and were acting on minds and public opinion in Germany, just as it was true that sending federal forces to Holstein could give the Confederation additional means to exert pressure beyond the federal boundary, in Schleswig, Holstein's neighbour. But Germany did not overlook the fact that the Schleswig question was an international one, and the German powers were equally as interested as Britain and France in maintaining the independence and integrity of the Danish monarchy. For that reason he would also be glad to see co-operation between Nicolay and those power's ambassadors in Copenhagen.[232] In talks with

226. Dep. Rusland, no. 17, 22 (10) 1863.
227. J. Daebel, *Die Schleswig-Holstein Bewegung in Deutschland 1863/64*, (Cologne, 1969).
228. Dep. no. 38, 5 August (24 July) 1863.
229. Dep. no. 21, 1 June (20 May) 1863.
230. See Thorsøe, vol II, pp. 945-6.
231. Plessen, no. 58, 5 October (23 September) 1863. Cf. dispatch to Nicolay from St. Petersburg, copy, no. 49, 31 August 1863, in H.H.S.A. Vienna, 23 P.A. Dänemark, XXIV.
232. Copies of the dispatches from Gorchakov to Budberg and Nicolay may be found in R.A. Co-

the Danish ambassador Gorchakov displayed greater impatience and displeasure with Danish policy than previously, which later, as Plessen described in letters to Vedel, gave way to silence.

Comme il est constamment très bon pour mois – Plessen wrote to Vedel on 26 (14) October 1863 – en me mettant à même de fournir des renseignements qui pouvaient avoir de l'intérêt pour nous, Son [Gorchakov's – E.H.] silence dans une crise aussi grave me surprend ... Il sent de dire "plus la question danoise s'engage, plus la situation de la Russie se dégage". Il sent aussi, je crois que Vous me l'accorder, se dire, que la Russie en penchant du côté de l'Allemagne, y trouvera des compensations, que nous ne pourrons pas lui offrir. N'est-il pas de notre intérêt d'eviter tout ce que peut le pousser dans cette voie?[233]

It was certainly no accident that the semi-official *Journal de St. Pétersbourg,* which was under Gorchakov's control, published a telegram reporting that the Danish government had fixed a budget, including for Holstein, without reaching agreement with the latter, when in fact this was not the budget but only the draft budget. This was the subject of a protest to Gorchakov by Plessen.[234] Gorchakov claimed that Russia had no wish to exploit others' troubles and such conduct was not in her nature. But really he did nothing to alleviate the conflict. On the contrary, he did not support British efforts to block German action in Holstein and even expressed surprise that Russell, in contrast to the position he had taken previously in the autumn of 1862, was now opposed to Federal Execution, which could offend 'l'amour propre' of the German Confederation and have the opposite effect to what Russell intended.[235] Far be it from him to influence the decisions and behaviour of Germany, as he did not want to annoy the German states, above all Prussia and Austria, and was afraid that the bellicose tone of the Hall government could make Berlin and Vienna more determined than before. Gorchakov tried to persuade both Denmark and Sweden that the Federal action would not go beyond the boundaries of the federation and that really everything depended on whether Denmark, faced with this action, would withdraw her army beyond the Eider.[236]

When the Swedish ambassador enquired whether he was not inclined to intervene once again in Frankfurt to avert the storm, Gorchakov, without pausing for reflection, answered in the negative. 'À quoi bon'? he asked. That would be nothing more than repeating old moves. He advised that the question should be settled in accordance with the treaties, in a peaceful way, and, as he put it, Russia would not disappoint anyone. Gorchakov felt an increasing dislike of the Danish government, and especially of Hall. He still looked to the conservative politicians. This explains why he had long talks with Sponneck, the Conservative Danish politician,

---

penhagen, in A.M.A.E. Paris, Russie, in H.H.S.A. Vienna, 23 P.A. Danemark XXIV, and Blue Books, *Denmark and Germany,* no. 3, N. 129, pp. 133-4.
233. Vedel, p.k. 12, R.A. Copenhagen.
234. Plessen no. 59, 5 October (23 September) 1863.
235. *Ibid.*
236. Wedel-Jarlsberg, 28 (16) September 1863, R.A. Stockholm. Kabinett för utrikes brevväxlingen, Depescher från beskickningen i Petersburg 1863.

who also enjoyed the respect and esteem of the Tsar, during a visit Sponneck paid to St. Petersburg.[237] Was one reason for Gorchakov's extremely cautious policy perhaps that even among the people around him there were fears towards the end of September that the state of relations with the Western powers over the Polish question was still so unclear that the danger of war might not have been averted?[238] Was he further annoyed by the news continually coming in of negotiations between Denmark and Sweden, which he regarded mainly as an anti-Russian action undertaken by Sweden?[239] The Swedish Minister of Foreign Affairs tried to sum up Gorchakov's position at this stage in a letter to Hamilton, his ambassador in Copenhagen, on the basis of the reports from his ambassador in St. Petersburg:

Le caractère du Protocole de Londres est pour la Russie sacré et son maintien obligatoire. La question du Slesvic est à ses yeux toute internationale. Il [Gorchakov] ne méconnait point la gravité de la situation, mais il espère que ni d'un côté ni l'autre, on se laissera aller à des déterminations extrêmes. On lui a donné l'assurance tant à Vienne qu'à Berlin que les troupes allemandes ne dépasseront point les limites fédérales. À la demande de notre ministre, si le Cabinet de St. Pétersbourg ne serait pas disposé à faire une toute dernière tentative pour conjurer l'orage, le Vice-Chancelier a repondu: à quoi bon? Cela ne pourrait être qu'une répétition des demarches déjà faites; mieux vaut maintenant voir venir, - et régler sa conduite en conséquence: elle est du reste tout tracée par les Traités, et pour notre part, nous n'y faillirons pas.[240]

What the defence of the sacred rights guaranteed in the Treaty of London, as Gorchakov called it, was to mean in practice the minister did not explain. But Wedel-Jarlsberg understood full well:

Nul doute – the ambassador reported – que les questions de l'intégrité de la monarchie et de la succession, l'appui moral et l'action diplomatique du Cabinet de St. Pétersbourg seront acquis au Danemarc, mais je suis également convaincu que ce bon vouloir ne sera appuyé *ni par un soldat, ni par un vaisseau, ni par un écu*. Pour le paralyser, il suffira des ménagemens à garder envers la Prusse, sans parler de l'état déplorable des finances Russes, des soins à donner à la propre défense de l'Empire et de l'impossibilité où on se trouve de détacher, pour l'assistance matérielle d'une autre Puissance, la moindre partie de ses forces soit de terre soit de mer. Il n'y a sous ce rapport qu'une seule éventualité, – et ce serait encore là du "self-conservation" ou l'immense danger d'un contre-coup en Pologne – dans laquelle on se deciderait, je crois à passer outre.[241]

---

237. *Ibid.*
238. See A.V. Nikitenko, *Dnevnik,* vol. II, 1858-1865 (Moscow, 1955), pp. 367-8.
239. For Plessen's reports of Gorchakov's interest in the talks between the Western Powers and the governments of the Scandinavian states see no. 62, (Réservée) 2 November (21 October) and no. 65, 11 November (30 October). Cf. the reports by Dashkov and Minciaky from Stockholm, 12 (24) August, 30 August (11 September), 8 (20) October, 29 October (10 November), 18 (30) November, 7 (19) December, 12 (24) December and 17 (29) December 1863. Central archive Moscow, II, in R.A. Copenhagen, Cf. also A.F. Krieger, *Dagbøger,* vol. II (Copenhagen and Christiania, MCMXXI) p. 341. See Nicolay's report no. 82 (Reservée) of 12 (24) September 1863).
240. Henning Hamilton, *Anteckningar rörande förhallandet mellan Sverige och Danmark 1863-1864,* eds. Aage Friis and Einar Hedin (Stockholm and Copenhagen, 1936), p. 46.
241. Wedel-Jarlsberg, dispatch of 3 December (21 November) 1863. Cf. *Anteckningar ...,* p. 113.

Towards the end of the summer the Danish government found itself in a very disadvantageous situation. It was being attacked by the Ultradanois, both in Denmark itself and in Schleswig, for not going far enough and not finally settling the Schleswig question, i.e. by merging Schleswig with the monarchy in the narrow sense of the word, and by the conservatives for abandoning the 'Helstat' (Whole-State) policy. In talks with Koskull Hall obstinately maintained that the March warrant, by linking Holstein more closely with the German Confederation, did not harm Germany, and that there was no legal basis for Federal Execution.[242] As far as any kind of legal intervention by the Confederation was concerned, it could relate only to Holstein; any other objectives could only be of an international nature. Of course he had Schleswig in mind here. As for the latter, Hall was aware that there was indeed opposition to Copenhagen's policy in the Estates of Schleswig, but he counted on the liberal elements and the introduction of concessions in future relating to the law of petition, freedom of religion and reform of the electoral system to enable him to defeat the opposion and gain the support and approval of enlightened opinion for Danish policy.[243] This optimistic forecast was shared neither by Koskull nor by St. Petersburg.

The Federal Diet in Frankfurt rejected the Danish proposal of 27 August and as a result adopted a resolution on 1 October on Federal Execution, to be carried out by Hannover and Saxony. Hall was aware that, as he described it in a letter to Bille in London on 3 September,

Une crise parait imminente, mais le Gouvernement du Roi ne la craint pas. ... le Gouvernement est allé plus loin encore dans la voie de la conciliation. Il s'est declaré prêt à entrer dans des négotiations avec La Diète si, après un examen un peu plus approfondi de la Patente que celui qu'elle avait entreprise jusqu'ici, cette Assemblée devait encore arriver à ce résultat qu'il reste des points où la Patente n'a pas suffisamment sauvegardée les intérêts Holsteinois.

Dans ces circonstances on conçoit facilement que tout occupation du Holstein, à laquelle la Confédération pourrait vouloir procéder, manquerait du prétexte même d'une acte fédéral ... Si les armées de l'Allemagne franchissent l'Eider, tout le monde reconnaîtra la nature internationale d'une telle démarche.[244]

With the matter about to come to a head, Hall undertook preparatory work for the adoption of a new constitution, which would apply both to the monarchy proper and in Schleswig. He expected the Confederation to greet it with a storm of protest, as usual, but to go no further. For its authority did not extend to Schleswig, the future of which Denmark had the right to decide. Besides, all the powers emphasised that Schleswig was not a German matter but an international question. Gorchakov had continually repeated this, and Russell confirmed it in his instruction to Grey on 16 September 1863 setting out his view of the dangerous situation created by the impending Federal Execution, which he wished to counteract.[245]

242. Koskull's report no. 61, 21 June (3 July) 1863, vol. 53.
243. Koskull's report no. 62, 4 (16) July 1863.
244. *Denmark and Germany*, No. 2, pp. 125-6.
245. Ibid no. 125, 16 September, pp. 129-30.

In his assessment of the international situation Hall saw features favourable to Denmark. He felt that these included: 1.) the differences between Austria and Prussia had been clearly demonstrated again in connection with the Austrian plan for reorganisation of the German Confederation and the proposed congress of princes and rulers in Frankfurt in August, to which Bismarck was vehemently opposed,[246] 2.) the firmly pro-Danish attitude of Britain, especially of public opinion, parliament and the government, as shown by Palmerston's speech in the House of Commons on 23 July in which he gave an assurance that in the event of armed conflict with Germany Denmark would not be isolated, which was wrongly interpreted, on account of its ambiguity, as evidence that Britain would be ready to help Denmark, 3.) the prospect in the summer of 1863 of a rapprochement between Denmark and Sweden, which was seen in the visits of Charles XV and Prince Oskar to Skodborg and Frederick VII's return visit and the progress of the talks between Manderström and Hall on the conclusion of a military alliance between Denmark and Sweden – an alliance which would provide that, in case of war between Denmark and Germany, the Danish frontier on the Eider would be defended not only by the Danish army but also by a corps of 20,000 soldiers sent from Sweden.

Lord Palmerston's speech in the House of Commons on July 23rd seemed to signify something more than 'a gesture' as the phrase is in the relations of Great Britain to the Schleswig-Holstein question, for he stated his conviction that, if any violent attempt were made to overthrow the rights and interfere with the independence of Denmark, 'those who made the attempt would find in the result, that it was not Denmark alone with which they would have to contend'.

Le discours que Lord Palmerston – a tenu, dans le séance du 23 juillet, à la Chambre des Communes a produit en Danemark une satisfaction aussi vive, que la dépêche de Lord Russell, sous la date du 24 septembre 62, avait produit un profonde découragement – the Italian Ambassador wrote on 1 August. Le Gouvernement Danois croit pouvoir se flatter aujourd'hui, que l'appui de l'Angleterre ne lui fera pas défaut dans la situation critique où le place une lutte imminente avec l'Allemagne.

Maintenant, me disait, il y a quelques jours un haut fonctionnaire Danois nous sommes sûrs que l'Angleterre envisage la question du Slesvig comme une question internationale, jamais Elle ne l'avait déclaré aussi nettement en face de l'Europe. Elle ne peut plus se dédire. Quant à la France, nous avons tout bien de croire, que son appui sera plus énergique encore.[247]

Hall believed that Denmark would not be left alone in the event of a conflict, either in the diplomatic or the military sense. 'His Excellency', Paget reported to

---

246. Cf. E. Franz's point of view concerning the German problem and the place of the Schleswig-Holstein problem: 'Die Enscheidung der Deutschen Frage lag in steigendem Masse seit 1860 und erst recht in Zukunft nicht in Schleswig-Holstein, nicht im Bundestag, nicht in der Einheitlichkeit von Gesetzbüchern und Prozessverfahren, sondern in allererster Linie in dem Ausgang der Zollunionsfrage'. *Der Entscheidungskampf* ... p. 215.
247. Migliorati to Turin, 1 August 1863. A.S.-D. Pacco no. 171 (809). Danimarca. Seria politica 1861-64. Min d. E.A. Rome.

Russell after a conversation with Hall,

> went on to observe that although a war with Germany would undoubtedly be a misfortune now as at any time, the present moment was perhaps as favourable for Denmark and as unfavourable for Germany as any that would occur; that it was impossible for Denmark to live under continual menace of hostilities; that Sweden was with her; that the public feeling of England, France and Europe in general was roused in favour of Denmark at this moment; that there was a more complete comprehension of the rights of the question now than was perhaps to be hoped for at any future time; in short, that there was a combination of circumstances highly advantageous to Denmark at the present time which might very likely never occur again. If, therefore, His Excellency continued, the question must be settled by an appeal to arms, it had better be so now, and he felt convinced, he said, that Denmark and Sweden would not stand alone.[248]

During a talk with Paget, Hall said he could possibly withdraw the warrant, but on one condition only, namely that Britain and France gave a formal promise that there would be no more demands of any kind from Germany.[249]

Hall, as the former French consul-general in Russia, A. Valois, said, thought it impossible that France, Denmark's old ally, and Britain, which was linked to Denmark by family ties, should desert her. La Russie,, Valois wrote, – in Hall's opinion –

> est intéresée à maintenir notre existence, qui garantit sa puissance maritime dans la Baltique. Elle doit vouloir nous servir comme elle l'a fait lors la primière révolte des Duchés en 1848. ... Nous somme faible, mais notre cause est juste ... et l'Europe ne peut nous laisser anéantir...

These were illusions, Valois concluded.[250]

Hall also cherished certain hopes that after she had rid herself of the spectre of diplomatic intervention and disturbances, Russia would be more kindly disposed towards Denmark. He expressed these hopes in his letter to Plessen on 1 October 1863, in which he wrote:

> nous sommes en droit d'espérer que les leçons ne manqueront pas d'exercer une heureuse influence sur son appréciation des difficultés que l'opposition des états holsteinois et l'ingérence de la diète germanique suscitent sans cesse au gouvernment du Roi.[251]

He expected something, the more so since Gorchakov could see for himself that the German Confederation had rejected the Danish proposals for peace negotiations, thereby disappointing the expectations of Russia, which had urged both the parties involved in the conflict to hold talks.[252] At that time Hall could not yet foresee the the course of events on either the German or the international scene. He certainly did not realise that the two great German powers, which were in conflict with each

---

248. *Denmark and Germany,* No. 2, no. 165, pp. 159 ff. Paget to Russell, 14. October 1863.
249. *Ibid.* p. 161.
250. A.M.A.E., Mémoires et documents, vol. 14. Mémoires sur les événements des Duchés de l'Elbe (de 1863 à 1866).
251. Udenrigsmin. no. 3332, R.A. Polen, Registratur, 1863, Tag. A 798.
252. *Ibid.*

other for supremacy in Germany after Prussia torpedoed Austria's plans for reorganisation of the Confederation in the summer of 1863, would very quickly come to an understanding on the Schleswig-Holstein question, thanks to Bismarck's ruthlessness, and that Bismarck would propose to the Austrian ambassador Karolyi that the two great German states should co-operate in the German Diet in order to carry out a quick Federal Execution against Denmark. This agreement was concluded on 24 November. Nor did Hall foresee that the Anglo-French alliance would finally collapse and that Austria would incline more and more towards improving her relations with Russia, or that he would meet with such a disappointment from Sweden, which decided on 8 September to make help for Denmark in a conflict with Germany conditional on participation by either Britain or France as well, of which he was officially informed in 13 October.[253]

Hall underestimated Bismarck's diplomatic skill, as incidentally did many other diplomats and politicians, and saw him as a man of moderation.[254] Nor could he know that from the end of 1862 Bismarck was convinced that the whole Danish business can be settled in a way desirable for us only by war, that it was not in Prussia's interest to install in Schleswig-Holstein a new Grand Duke, and that from that time on H. Moltke had been working on plans for war with Denmark.[255]

Anticipating German intervention, the Danish government did not neglect defence preparations. On 1 July it raised a two-year levy and called up reserve officers, began fortification works at Dannewirke, placed the garisons in the towns on the alert and augmented the navy with a new vessel, the *Rolf Krake,* built in England. None of this escaped the notice of the Russian ambassador, Nicolay.[256]

The press, as he reported on 19 (31) July, had been whipping up war fever. In his talks with Hall, Nicolay tried to calm the warlike mood and argued that Denmark should do everything to avoid such an unequal fight. He tried to restrain Hall and persuade him to hold further talks, as the chances of agreement with Germany, he thought, had not been exhausted and the Prussian government was offering a guarantee of conciliation of which Denmark should take advantage.

Hall, as his discussions with Nicolay showed, was well aware how unequal the battle would be, but he pointed to the fever gripping the nation and expected a stubborn fight if Schleswig and Jutland were attacked. He believed Palmerston's words, repeating: 'il est probable que nous ne serions pas seules à combattre'.

---

253. Steefel, pp. 62-68. Cf. the list of events prepared by Vedel, R.A. Copenhagen.
254. The view that Bismarck was a politician of moderate views was expressed by, among others, the Danish ambassador in Berlin, Quaade, in reports on 21 October and 20 November 1863, (Udenrigs. Preussen, Dep. 1860-1866) and Sibbern in a letter to Stang on 31 October 1863 *(Frederik Stang og Georg Sibbern ...* vol I, Oslo, 1956, p. 616).
255. Sybel, vol. III, p. 118; Seton-Watson, *Britain in Europe 1789-1914. A Survey of Foreign Policy,* p. 445; Moltke, Militärische Korrespondenz, nos. 1, 2, 1864, Militärische Werke, I, in A. Klein-Wuttig, *Politik und Kriegsführung in den deutschen Einigungskriegen, 1864, 1866 und 1870/71* (Berlin, 1934), pp. 6-7.
256. Cf. Defence expenditure in 1860/61-1863/64. H. Chr. Johansen, *Danish Historical Statistics 1814-1980,* (Copenhagen, 1985, p. 345).

The King too, in a talk with the ambassador after his return from Sweden, declared firmly: *'si vis pacem, para bellum'...*[257] 'oui bien certainement, je désire la paix, mais si on m'attaque, je me défends'.

The King's language, the ambassador explained in his report, like that of Hall and the press, reflected the mood of society and was the result of the fact that they saw little chance of maintaining peace in northern Europe. In Nicolay's judgement this was not just a manœuvre designed to frighten Germany but a conviction that war was in fact the only way to resolve the dispute in Denmark's desperate situation – and Nicolay agreed that her situation was indeed desperate. 'Il ne serait pas prudent d'exclure la possibilité d'un conflit du calcul des probabilités' he reported on 25 July (6 August). If the German Diet insisted on the revocation of the 30 March patent this would bring to power a new government which was bound to be far more ultra-nationalistic that the Hall government. The Hall government had no intention of abolishing the patent, but would be willing to provide full information and explanations for the German Confederation and believed that this could help to revise the Confederation's judgement of the patent.

Working on the adoption of a new constitution, Hall was aware that it infringed the 1851-52 agreements and was conscious that if Prussia and Austria had protested in 1856 and later, but particularly on 14 February 1862, against partial changes in the 1855 constitution, they would protest all the more strongly if a constitution were adopted which would not in fact alter the internal situation in Schleswig but would lead to a final break with the 'Helstat' policy, which the Danish government had undertaken to follow in 1851-52. It would also change both the place of Holstein in the monarchy and the relations between Schleswig and the monarchy and between Schleswig and Holstein. Schleswig would receive a fundamentally different status from Holstein and cease to be a link between Holstein and Copenhagen.

Hall intended the new constitution to be the logical consequence of the step taken in March 1863, and a victory for the Eider party's programme,[258] although it did not take this to its ultimate conclusion as it would not be followed by incorporation of Schleswig, and Schleswig was to retain its local self-governing institutions.

From the formal and state point of view, the government saw this as the most appropriate solution as it created the preconditions for preservation of state and national independence within the historical borders north of the Eider and for normal functioning of the government, while it in no way infringed the authority of the Federal parliament in respect of Holstein and Lauenburg as members of the German Confederation.[259] But from the international point of view it did infringe the provisions of 1851-52, and was regarded as such not only by Germany but also by neutral states and diplomats friendly to Denmark, like Paget. It was, in effect, throwing down a challenge to Germany.[260]

---

257. Let him who desires peace, prepare for war. See Report no. 71 of 25 July (6 August).
258. Steefel considers that it 'legally established the Eider-Denmark', p. 72.
259. Troels Fink, *Otte foredrag om Danmark Krise, 1863-64,* (Aarhus, 1964), p. 9.
260. Paget to Russell, 13 and 14 October 1863, *Denmark and Germany,* no. 2, pp. 158-62.

Following the progress of work and discussions in the Rigsraad on the new constitution, Nicolay regarded Hall's determination as a regrettable fact, and he found it hard to understand how Hall could reconcile his inclination to a definitive agreement with Germany with such an unceremonious and obvious rejection of the 1851-52 agreement.[261] Nor did he succeed in convincing Hall that the well-being of Denmark, and negotiations with the German Confederation, were impossible without the suspension, 'pure et simple', of the March warrant. Hall stoutly defended this step because previously, he argued, there had been an intolerable situation – no law concerning general matters could be adopted without the agreement of the Estates of Holstein, and it was not possible to be dependent continually on their caprice.[262]

After 1 October Hall no longer had any illusions about the German Confederation's plans. But he still thought, as incidentally did Russell too, that matters not concerning the duchies belonging to the Confederation would have a chance of successful settlement by means of mediation involving the signatories to the Treaty of London.[263]

In view of the fact that the mandates of the deputies in the Rigsraad were about to run out, Hall thought that the matter of the constitution should be brought to a conclusion as quickly as possible.[264] Nicolay saw his task as recommending restraint and seeking means of reaching the desired result. He thought more direct intervention was essential and that a definitive solution of the differences between Denmark and Germany could not be achieved by mediation alone.[265]

There was not really any government which would have approved the introduction of the new constitution at that juncture and Nicolay was not the only one to warn against the consequences. Russell and Paget did so, as did the Prussian ambassador, Balan. From Berlin the Danish ambassador, Quaade, also warned of the consequences of such a step. Despite this, Hall decided to carry out his plans. On 14 November the Rigsraad approved the text of the new constitution. There was some opposition to it in the debate, however, and a politician of the calibre of Bluhme regarded it as an unfortunate move and spoke against its adoption because it was not consistent with the royal promises of 1851-52 and could have adverse consequences.

The situation was then complicated by the sudden death of Frederick VII. Hall was the only person who could have the signing of the constitution by the new monarch, Christian IX, postponed. But even if the signing of the constitution by the new King were to bring incalculable harm both to Denmark and to the monarch, and put in question both the integrity of the monarchy and the right of

---

261. Nicolay, no. 88, 9 (21) October 1863, vol. 53.
262. Nicolay, no. 89, 10 (22) October.
263. Nicolay, no. 91, 17 (29) October.
264. Nicolay, no. 93, 31 October (12 November). M. Florinsksy said: 'The Danes meanwhile pursued an increasingly intransigent policy'. Vol. II, p. 962.
265. Lettre particulière. 10 (22) October.

Christian IX to the succession in the duchies, Hall nevertheless pressed him to sign it immediately. The new ruler found himself in a difficult situation. Theoretically the King could appoint a new government, led by a politician other than Hall, but in view of the situation in the country and the great political tension, particularly in Copenhagen, where a truly revolutionary situation was developing and the population was demanding the introduction of the new constitutional law at any price ('Strassendemokratie', as Bismarck called it),[266] no one from the conservative 'Helstat' party, to whom the King turned, would dare to set about forming a new government. The King was conscious that signing the constitution was a mistake and that by doing so he deprived himself of the possibility of help from abroad. But if he pursued a policy which satisfied the great powers and Prussia, his position in a country in which he was not yet accepted, and in a city where he was regarded as a German, would be doomed. He therefore decided after much vacillation to take the risk with the government and sign the constitutional act.[267]

Gorchakov, alarmed by the situation in Denmark, at the last moment sent a telegram to Nicolay asking that the constitution should not be signed, as this could cause great difficulties.[268] Hitherto Prussia had been well disposed towards the problem, Gorchakov considered, but if the King signed the constitution she would find herself in a situation where she would be compelled no longer to recognise the London protocol.

Gorchakov urged Plessen to promise to try and ensure that the King did not sign the constitution. In a talk with the ambassador he said he appreciated the difficulties and the pressure from the population in the capital which was demanding that the constitution be signed, but he could not understand the government's purpose in forcing through the new constitution. He would not accept Plessen's explanation that the government had done it in order to consolidate the monarchy and preclude foreign states from interfering in the non-German parts of Denmark, arguing for his part that while it would have been difficult to achieve these aims when Frederick VII was alive, now, when the London protocol concerning the succession to the throne was to be put into effect, to approve the constitution could only provoke Germany and risk the integrity of the monarchy. Gorchakov also expressed

---

266. Eyck, *Bismarck,* vol. I, p. 585.
267. See Fink, *Otte foredrag ...,* ch. 4, 'Risiko for Revolution; Tronskiftet i 1863', pp. 39-49. Cf. also Dronning Louise til Baron Otto Plessen, 24 November 1863, Plessen, Privat arkiv. 6128, R.A. Copenhagen.
268. 'Vous connaissez', Gorchakov's telegram of 7 (19) November ran

protestations soutenées par diverses cours allemandes à l'occasion du changement de règne, toutes dirigées contre protocole de Londres et tendant au démembrement du Danmark. Augustenbourg à déjà annoncé à Oldenbourg son avènement comme duc Holstein-Slesvig. Bismarck, du reste favourable disposé nous supplier d'engager Roi Chretien a ne pas se hâter de confirmer constitution générale, qui empêcherait Prusse à son grand regret d'insister à trancher sur protocole Londres. Rendez Hall attentif a forte crise que traverse Danmark et signalez absolue nécessité de beaucoup de prudence.

L'Empereur Vous ordonne d'exprimer au Roi les vœux de S.M. pour la prospérité de son règne.
A.V.P.R., Fond Kantselariya, delo 34, Danica, archive no. 485, no. 66.

fears that because the German Confederation wished to transfer Holstein to Prince Frederick Augustenburg, and in view of the new situation that had arisen in Copenhagen, Prussia would not be able to oppose the German states and would therefore be unable to adhere to the London protocol.[269] Gorchakov advised avoiding everything which could give the German states a pretext for exempting themselves from the provisions of the Treaty of London.[270]

The emphasis was similar in Gorchakov's dispatch to Nicolay on 7 November (old style). He warned against the consequences if the King signed the constitution, and called for reflection.

Elle ajouterait des difficultés insurmontables à celles que les Cours amies du Danmark ont eu a combattu jusqu'à présent dans l'intérêt de la paix du Nord de l'Allemagne. Je dirais plus M. le Baron, elle plaurait les plus principales puissances Allemandes qui ont concouru avec la Russie, la France, l'Angleterre et la Suède au traité du 8 mai 1852, dans la presque impossibilité de soutenir les droits qui résultent de cette transaction pour le Roi Chrétien IX et Sa dynastie ... Plus que jamais, nous l'avons dit souvent et je le repète une fois de plus, plus que jamais le Cabinet de Copenhague a besoin de concillier l'appui de l'Autriche et de la Prusse. Vous ne sauriez assez clairement Vous prononcer dans ce sens envers les hommes d'Etat que le Roi honore de Sa confiance.[271]

He gave Nicolay permission to give Hall a copy of this dispatch, which was, he said

une preuve de l'amical et très sincère intérêt que le Cabinet Impérial a pris de tout temps, et qu'il prend surtout dans le moment actuel à la conservation dans son intégrité et au bien être de la Monarchie Danoise.[272]

Gorchakov's telegram and his letter reached Copenhagen too late, however, after the King had signed the constitution. Gorchakov regretted this deeply.

Nicolay, who was following the situation in Copenhagen at this time with bated breath, although his attitude to the problem was unequivocal, came to the conclusion that it really would have been impossible for the King to refuse to sign the constitution as the government and the population demanded.[273] He wondered whether further hesitation would not have reflected on the dignity of the King and the future of the dynasty, which had not yet put down roots in the country. In the event of opposition from the population the King would not be able to count on any support. Similar conclusions were reached at this point by other ambassadors accredited to Copenhagen.[274]

---

269. Dep. no. 66, 19 (7) November 1863. Cf. also Quaade on his talk with Bismarck, Dep. Preussen, no. 30, 20 November 1863.
270. Plessen, no. 66, 19 (7) November 1863.
271. Ordrer. Rus. R.A. Copenhagen, and Udenrigs. Samlede Sager. Krigen 1864. Gruppen no. II.
272. *Ibid.*
273. Nicolay's report no. 102 of 9 (21) November on the pressure from, among others, the City Council in Copenhagen and the situation in the city on 5 (17) and 6 (18) November, vol. 54. (Nos. 98 Secrète and 99).
274. See the excerpts from ambassadors' reports collected by A. Friis in Privatarkiv 5424, R.A. Copenhagen, C.N. David, 'Christian IX og Sir Augustus Paget i november 1863' by A. Friis, *Hist. Tids.*, 6 (1928).

If the King had refused to sign, the ministers would have resigned and it would have been impossible to find any politician who would undertake to form a government, agitation would have grown and there would have been the threat of demonstrations in defence of the constitution. As we know from another source, the chief of police, Crone, entered into negotiations with the students to secure from them a promise that they would remain peaceful for a further two days, in order to ensure calm in the capital for the moment. But in the longer term, he said, he could not guarantee security in the capital in this situation.[275]

In Paget's report to Russell,[276] written literally at the moment the King was putting his signature to the constitution, we read

> The only possible transaction would be if Monsieur Hall would take the responsibility upon himself of announcing to the Rigsraad that under present circumstances, and in order not to prejudge the result of the coming negotiations, he had advised the King temporarily to suspend his signature, but in view of His Excellency's declaration in the Rigsraad and of the clause which he recently inserted in the Constitution giving it force from the 1st of January next, it is almost impossible that he should adopt this course, and perhaps indeed it is now too late that even this should be successful.
> P.S. Since this Despatch was written, the King has signed the Constitution as your Lordship will have learnt by the telegram just sent.[277]

In his dispatch on 20 November,[278] however, the ambassador said that although he regretted that the King had signed the constitution, 'it is possible that in the circumstances this step could not be avoided'. Dotézac wrote of the circumstances surrounding the signing of the constitution: 'il faut que le Prince Christian declare nettement s'il est danois ou allemand. La réponse, c'est la sanction'.[279]

Immediately aften receiving his instruction from St. Petersburg, Nicolay went into action and appealed to Hall to act with greater caution in view of the difficult situation in Holstein, the activities of Prince Augustenburg and the increased political temperature in Germany.[280] Hall, like the King, argued that the changes in the constitution were essential. He was very concerned to convince the imperial government that the King could not act in any other way and hoped the Russian government would use its influence at this difficult moment to avert the danger. Hall also assured him that there was no question of incorporating Schleswig, which would retain its administrative and legislative independence.[281]

---

275. See Nicolay, no. 102 of 9 (21) November, and 'Arup. David og Hall', *Scandia*, vol. I (1928). Cf. also Håndskrift Samlinger I Aage Friis Samlingen, R.A. Copenhagen, copies of reports by Paget, Balan and Krüger, the ambassador from Hamburg, in Privatarkiv no. 5424, and also in the same collection the reports by the Belgian ambassador, M. Bosch Spencer, nos. 203, 204, 18 and 19 November, to his minister, Charles Rogier.
276. No. 251, 18 November 1863.
277. *Denmark and Germany,* no. 2, p. 214.
278. Paget to Russell, Danica Fotografering, R.A. Copenhagen. F.O. 22/299.
279. No. 186, 25 November, Håndskrift Samlinger I. Aage Friis Samlinger pk. no. 2, Afskrifter af akter i franske arkiver 1863-95, A.M.A.E. Paris, Danemark, vol. 245. Cf. also no. 176, 18 November, the petition from the city Council of Copenhagen.
280. No. 103, 9 (21) November 1863.
281. Nicolay, no. 106, 12 (24) November 1863.

In a letter to Plessen[282] Hall once again set out his reasons and his hopes that, just as before, the Russian government, which was familiar with the course of the previous negotiations with Germany, would understand the step Denmark had taken, a step which meant only that it

revendique pour les parties de la Monarchie qui n'appartiennent pas à la Confédération la liberté de se développer les conditions de leur existence constitutionelle.
Si la Confédération veut s'attaquer à ce principe il n'est pas en notre pouvoir de l'en empêcher, il ne nous restera qu'à la rendre responsable des conséquences de sa résolution et des voies nouvelles où son agression pourrait nous jeter.

Nicolay urged Hall to remain calm about the Federal Execution in Holstein and at all costs to avoid an armed conflict, for only if he did so would the friendly states be able to exercise a salutary influence and bring the present crisis under control ('à maîtriser'). The ambassador did not anticipate, incidentally, that the Danes would resist armed federal action and let themselves be drawn into an unequal war with Germany which would have catastrophic results for Denmark.[283] Nicolay talked to Monrad in a similar spirit. The latter, like Hall, tried to prove that the new constitution was better than its predecessor and would facilitate the conduct of talks with Holstein. The new constitution could not be changed.[284] In Monrad's opinion the mission by Ewers and Wodehouse, which had just been announced, would open the way to negotiations, which had not been possible hitherto as both Holstein and the German states had rejected all the Danish proposals. Now, however, the German states must put forward their ideas. Nicolay, in his opinion, could be helpful in these negotiations.[285]

The same opinion was shared by the King, with whom Nicolay had talks on this subject. The King also said he saw no possibility of suspending the constitution at the moment of his accession to the throne and was convinced of the necessity of accepting the 1851-52 agreements as the starting point for talks. The King could not be asked, Nicolay argued, to suspend the constitution 'pure et simple', but means had to be found to get out of the difficulties and come to an agreement with Germany.[286] The King assured the ambassador that the War Minister, by agreement with Hall, would issue instructions not to oppose the federal forces if they entered Holstein.

On the eve of Ewers' arrival in Copenhagen *Fædrelandet* published an article[287] expressing its regret that a treaty between the Scandinavian states had not been signed.[288] Nicolay received this news with satisfaction.[289]

282. No. 34, 2 December 1863. Udenrigsm. Samlede Sager. Krigen 1864. Gruppe no. 11, vol. 447, and Registratur no. 2116, 143v.
283. No. 109, 22 November (4 December), no. 112, 9 December (one date only – E.H.).
284. No. 111, 25 November (7 December).
285. *Ibid.*
286. Nicolay, no. 113, 30 November (12 December).
287. 12 December 1863.
288. Between 11 and 24 December 1863 *Dagbladet* published a series of articles under the tittle 'Sverige-Norges forandrede holdning'. Cf. also J. Clausen, *Skandinavismen ...*, pp. 184ff.
289. Nicolay, no. 114, 2 (14) December, 1863, vol. 54.

Part II

Part II

6. The Federal Execution and the Ewers Mission

I

On receiving the news that the Rigsraad had adopted the new constitution for the Kingdom of Denmark and Schleswig, Gorchakov sent a telegram warning the King of the consequences if he signed it. But this telegram, sent to Nicolay, was too late, arriving after the King had signed the constitution. When Gorchakov learnt this he expressed regret but at the same time conveyed Alexander II's sincere sympathy for King Christian IX.[1] He did not conceal how much he wished the government would find a way out of the new and dangerous situation and the complications caused by the approval of the constitution. When Plessen tried to defend the step the King had taken, citing the domestic factors which had led to the decision, Gorchakov disagreed, contrasting them with the international implications. Russia's future position would depend on the attitude of France and Britain, and he sent a telegram to Brunnow instructing him to maintain close cooperation with the British government on the matter.[2] Two days later, after receiving Hall's instruction (of 20 November), Plessen asked Gorchakov to instruct Ungern-Sternberg – then the Russian Minister in Frankfurt – to intervene against the taking of a vote on the question of possible federal intervention in Holstein. Gorchakov refused this request and at the same time reproached the Danish government for not following Russia's friendly advice. He also submitted that, as the helmsman of Russian policy, he could not be guided by the domestic aspects of the Danish question which Plessen had mentioned. As Russia's minister of foreign affairs, he could not overlook the fact that by adopting the new constitution Denmark had broken its obligations to Germany. He reacted negatively to Plessen's comment that Germany had also broken the agreement by seeking to extend its authority to the non-German parts of the Danish monarchy.

After what he had heard, Plessen considered how Russia would now behave towards Denmark, and came to the following conclusions: Russia would act within the limits of what her own situation allowed, and she would try to keep within the framework of the London protocol. He did not question Alexander II's sympathy for King Christian IX. As for Gorchakov, he firmly rejected Hall's justification of the Danish government's behaviour in the past few days, the effect of which had

---

1. See Gorchakov to Nicolay, 7 November 1863 (old style). 'Leurs Majesté Vous chargent d'offrir leurs vœux au Duc et à la Duchesse de Glücksbourg à l'occasion du 25 anniversaire de marriage'. A.V.P.R. Fond Kantselariya, delo 34-38, Vol. 66.
2. Plessen, no. 67, 22 (10) November, 1863.

been the adoption and promulgation of the 18 November Constitution; but despite this he assured Plessen of his interest in preserving the integrity of Denmark and promised that as the situation developed he would neglect nothing which could be useful for Denmark.[3]

When Plessen presented his credentials, following the accession of Christian IX to the throne, Alexander II addressed many kind words to the Danish King and said that he was doing what he could in Denmark's interest, but for some time, he reproached the ambassador, 'Vous tendez trop la corde. Nous serons conséquents'. Besides, he added, Russia's capacity was limited and the most appropriate form of action for her would be diplomatic action. Like his minister of foreign affairs, the Tsar would take no notice of Plessen's remarks about the domestic difficulties Denmark was experiencing and even tried to minimize the significance of the revolutionary movement in Germany, admitting that the movement existed but claiming that it was only to some extent revolutionary and was confined to the second-rank states. It did however cause certain difficulties for Vienna and Berlin, of which Denmark should be aware. Alexander II expressed regret at the signing of the new constitution, which had complicated the issue still further, and he backed up his protest with a reference to the British cabinet, which took the same view of the Danish government's action. He did not accept Plessen's assertion that the 18 November Constitution did not alter the general attitude of Denmark to Germany.

Referring to the plan to send Ewers on a special mission to Copenhagen, the Tsar explained that its form had been changed. Initially the aim was to combine the efforts of all the signatories to the Treaty of London, but this idea had had to be altered as representatives of the two German powers were not participating in it because their aims differed from the aim of the mission. But since Britain and France had accepted the Russian principles, an opportunity had arisen which Denmark should use. If war broke out between Denmark and Germany, however, said the Tsar, 'Je ne pourrais pas m'y associer. Au reste, Vous [Plessen] qui connaissez notre situation, Vous devez le comprendre'. Plessen replied that Russia was now free of the dangers which had seemed to exist during the summer and he therefore hoped she would take up the position of Denmark's protector, as Nicholas I had done, to which he received the answer that although the situation in Poland had improved, nevertheless, as the question of the congress proposed by Napoleon III had not been finally settled, the position was unclear and no one knew what the outcome would be.[4] The Tsar summed up his position by saying that a sharply anti-Danish

---

3. Plessen, no. 68, 24 (12) November, 1863.
4. The Tsar did indeed see the international situation in gloomy colours, as is shown by his correspondence with his close acquaintance Prince A.I. Baryatinsky. On 22 November (4 December) 1863 he wrote from Tsarskoe Selo:
Malheureusement l'horizon politique qui est encore bien sombre nous oblige de nous préparer aux plus mauvaises chances; aussi nos préparatifs militaires sont poussées avec la plus grand vigeur.
The politics of Autocracy. Letters of Alexander II to Prince A.I. Bariatinskii, 1857-1864, ed. with an historical essay by Alfred J. Rieber (Paris, Mouton and Co. The Hague, 1968), p. 151.

movement was indeed developing in Germany but that there were tendencies to excess in Denmark too.[5]

Gorchakov received the news that, under pressure from London, the Danish government had revoked the 30 March warrant on 4 December, without much enthusiasm, for he considered the move too late.[6] Other diplomats accredited to Copenhagen were of a similar opinion. The Belgian ambassador, Bosch-Spencer, wrote in his report to his minister, Charles Rogier, on 6 December:

> Vient d'apprendre que le Gouvernement a retiré la patente du 30 mars 1863. Cette mesure a été précédé d'une proclamation du Roi aux habitans du Holstein, le retrait de la patente du 30 mars est le seul moyen pour le Danemark d'enlever à l'exécution fédérale sa base légale, et lui était commandé par ses embarras intérieures et extérieures. Mais il est douteux que cette concession satisfasse l'Allemagne.[7]

It was a concession of little meaning so long as the November Constitution remained valid.

Two days later, on 8 December, the ambassador informed his minister of the fiasco following the revocation of the warrant.

> Pénible impression causée par le retrait de la patente du 30 mars, que la presse considère comme une concession inutile et malheureuse, faite sous la pression de l'Angleterre. La Russie aurait sérieusement proposé aux Puissances signataires du traité de Londres de faire une démarche collective auprès de la cour de Copenhague pour l'engager au retrait ou à la suspension de la constitution du 18 novembre. Le succès de cette démarche entraînerait la chute du ministère Hall. Elle n'a arrêtera pas l'Allemagne et le Danemark n'a plus qu'à se défendre par les armes. Il s'y prépare de toutes ses forces.[8]

It is true that when talking to Plessen[9] Gorchakov did not argue that the new constitution implied the incorporation of Schleswig, but it followed from his comments that he regarded it as a means to that end. The approval of the constitution, in his opinion, had inflamed feelings in Germany, complicated the situation and made it more difficult for the other German states (i.e. Prussia and Austria). Moreover, all this could not be justified even if it were accepted that the move had been a positive one as far as the internal situation in Denmark went. Gorchakov did not approve the excessive German demands but he criticised Denmark for not fulfilling the obligations she had undertaken in 1851-52, and if the Treaty of London, which Russia supported, collapsed the responsibility would lie with Denmark.

Referring to the Ewers mission,[10] Gorchakov explained that its purpose was to

---

5. Dep. Rus. no. 72, 10 December (28 November) 1863.
6. Dep. Rus. no. 73, 14 (2) December 1863.
7. No. 216, 6 December 1863. Afskrifter og fotokopier fra udenlandske arkiver vedr. dansk udenrigspolitik pk. II. Privatarkiver historikerens Aage Friis, 5424, R.A. Copenhagen.
8. No. 217. Afskrifter af akter i det belgiske udenrigsministeriums arkiv 1863-64. A. Friis, Privatarkiv 5424, II. R.A. Copenhagen.
9. Plessen, no. 73, 14 (2) December 1863.
10. In a letter to Vedel on 3 December Plessen said that Ewers exercised a great influence on Gorchakov's decisions on the Danish question. Vedels papirer, pk. 12.

uphold the idea of the Treaty of London, and he was confident that both Wodehouse, the British emissary, and France, as he concluded from a conversation with Massignac, would take a similar position to Russia and Britain. 'Dieu veuille que Vous empêchiez que la guerre n'éclate. Sur qui comptez Vous dans le cas de guerre, le savez-vous?' Fait-on grand fond chez Vous sur la France?' asked Gorchakov.

Gorchakov advised doing everything to avoid war and said that it would not be to Russia's advantage to join in such a war. Russia would maintain her previous position, i.e. she would support a peaceful solution of the dispute.[11]

In subsequent talks, Plessen concluded that Gorchakov was rather in favour of the proposal put forward by Britain to convene a conference in Paris to settle the Danish-German dispute. But he was both against the application of the French idea of nationality and the idea of Scandinavian union. He approved of the larger German states' policy, and the fact that they did not join in sending condolences on the death of Frederick VII showed how essential it was to take account of the anti-Danish feeling prevailing in Germany, though he was annoyed by the attitude of Bavaria and Saxony. He wanted it to be known in Frankfurt that Russia disapproved of the actions of the lesser German states, although he was against sending an official note from the St. Petersburg cabinet to Frankfurt.[12]

In Gorchakov's opinion, Napier reported to Russell on 1 December 1863,

M. de Bismarck is moderate in this question, and that he restrains the King of Prussia, who is urged to more extreme measures by persons of strong German sympathies and aspirations in His Majesty's confidence. Mr. Bismarck, however, considers the engagements of 1852 respecting the Danish succession to be strictly contingent, as far as Prussia is concerned, on the fulfilment of the previous promises of Denmark respecting Schleswig. Both Prussia and Austria insist on Federal Execution in Holstein in the limits heretofore prescribed by the Diet, and with the design to keep the interests of Constitution and Succession separate. Prince Gortchakoff – the ambassador reported – is disposed to see in the Federal Execution, if properly managed, a conservative measure, – a means of giving satisfaction to the legitimate claims of the more moderate parts in Germany, and of thus discouraging the designs of the Revolutionary section. Acting under judicious orders, in the opinion of the Prince, the Federal troops might preserve order, and maintain the due distinction between the legislative and dynastic questions.[13]

Napier took a different position. He was afraid that if troops belonging to the lesser German states took part in the Federal Execution it could contribute to the growth of democratic and national agitation and could be more of a revolutionary than a conservative measure.[14]

The so-called Ewers mission was really the only initiative the St. Petersburg cabinet took in connection with the long-running Danish-German conflict. Gorchakov proposed it immediately after Christian IX signed the constitution. Its aim was to make use of the courtesy mission which was to be sent to Copenhagen on the oc-

11. Plessen, 14 (2) December.
12. No. 75, 25 (13) December.
13. *Denmark and Germany,* vol. 1, no. 359, p. 312.
14. *ibid.*

casion of Christian IX's accession to the throne for political purposes. Special representatives of the states which were signatories to the Treaty of London were to persuade the Danish government to withdraw those provisions in the constitution which concerned Schleswig. For not only German opinion, but also politicians and diplomats regarded as pro-Danish, like Paget for instance, regarded the adoption of the new constitution as an infringement of the obligations undertaken by Denmark in 1851-52, which handed the German states an argument to use against Denmark.

In a talk with the Austrian ambassador, Thun, Gorchakov described his intention and set out his position.

Il a vue avec plaisir que les deux Cabinets Impériaux se rencontraient dans le désir de distinguer entre la question de la succession et celle de la constitution danoise – Thun reported to Vienne. Il pense qu'il serait difficile de ne pas accepter cette dernière puisq'elle est, pour ainsi dire, un fait accompli, mais il croit qu'une action commune des grandes Puissances ou de plusieurs d'elles pourrait amener le Cabinet danois à l'adaption de quelques articles additionels et explicatifs, qui tiendraient compte des promesses faites à l'Allemagne et aux Duchés.

In order to achieve this aim, Gorchakov explained, special missions needed to be sent to Copenhagen, and he had proposed to the Tsar to send one, as he put it,

chargé de Sa réponse, non par "une paire d'épaulettes" mais un diplomate versé dans les affaires danoises. Son choix – Thun reported – est tombé sur un des employés supérieurs du Ministère des Affaires Étrangères, qu'il ne m'a pas nommé.

Gorchakov thought the other states should follow the same course, and that four or five envoys 'pourraient agir avec succès sur l'esprit du Cabinet de Copenhague pour atteindre le but indiqué'.

Comme le Roi de Danemarc a déclaré vouloir soumettre le règlement du conflit avec l'Allemagne à un congrès, le Prince Gorchakov serait enclin à prendre acte de cette déclaration, mais il voudrait que ce fut plutôt une conférence ministérielle ad hoc qu'un véritable congrès.
"Il pense que Londres serait peut-être le lieu le plus propice pour le siège de cette conférence, Vienne et Berlin pouvant offrir des inconvéniens."

Thun judged that the Russian cabinet would stand by the London protocol, as it did not wish to find itself in opposition to Britain, with which it wanted a rapprochement, since its distrust of the cabinet in the Tuilleries was growing day by day. But if London rejected his proposals, Gorchakov would turn to France again, 'car l'isolement, qu'il acceptait naguère presqu'avec satisfaction, lui devient de plus en plus difficile à supporter'.[15] These last words show that Thun understood Gorchakov's weaknesses well and knew that what Russian politicians feared most was isolation.

Gorchakov considered that the success of the mission depended on joint action

---

15. Thun to Rechberg, no. 41, B. 25 (13) November 1863, H.H.S.A. Vienna, P.A. Russland, vol. 54.

in Copenhagen by emissaries of all five states which were signatories to the Treaty of London. He was especially anxious that there should be an envoy from France in Copenhagen.[16] Meanwhile, Austria and Prussia had rejected this suggestion on the spot, not wanting, for reasons of principle, to send a courtesy mission to Copenhagen – but Gorchakov made no effort to persuade them. It may be noteworthy that, as Steefel observed, the correspondence between Gorchakov and Bismarck apparently stopped abruptly; at any rate Steefel found no trace of it in the Prussian archives.[17] Sweden also declined to take part in joint action with the St. Petersburg cabinet, though of course for different reasons from those of Prussia and Austria. She did not want to put pressure on the Copenhagen government. France agreed to send a special envoy – he was to be the personal friend and adjutant of Napoleon III, General Fleury – but since her authority had been hit by Britain's rejection of Napoleon III's idea of convening a European congress, she had no intention of collaborating with Britain, even though E.F. Fleury's instructions were no different in substance from those of Ewers and Wodehouse. France decided to act separately in Copenhagen. So the only possible joint action was by the envoys of Russia and Britain.[18]

On 19 November (old style), at Gorchakov's suggestion, Alexander II decided to send Ewers on a special mission to Copenhagen. Ewers was one of the most experienced Russian diplomats, had been secretary of the Russian embassy in Copenhagen in 1848-49, and had dealt with Danish-German and Scandinavian problems in the Russian ministry of foreign affairs for many years. The very fact that, in contrast to Russian tradition, a non-military person was to be sent on a courtesy mission on the accession to the throne of a monarch of a friendly state, spoke for itself. Before Ewers' departure, a memorandum of instructions was drawn up setting out the Russian government's position.[19] This memorandum, dated 19 November 1863, stated that:

The accession of Christian IX to the throne had been the cause of violent agitation in Germany, while the signatories to the Treaty of London were in favour of maintaining the integrity of the Danish monarchy in the interests of the balance of power in Europe and the preservation of peace. It was not for Russia to prejudge what decisions Denmark would take in connection with the events which had occurred there following the death of Frederick VII and his successor's acceptance of the constitution passed by the Rigsraad. But it was indisputable that by not opposing the government, and signing a constitution which aimed at the incorporation of Schleswig into the Danish monarchy in the narrow sense of the word, the King had piled additional complications on top of the already serious difficulties be-

---

16. A.M.A.E. Russie, vol. 232, 14 December 1863, no. 2 and the telegraph dispatch of 9 December in the same place.
17. Steefel, p. 132.
18. Brunnow and Russell played a positive role in co-ordinating their positions. See Russell to Napier, 2 December 1863, in *Denmark and Germany,* in P.A. XXIV. 24 Dänemark, H.H.S.A. Vienna.
19. Memorandum destiné à servir l'instruction au Conseilleur d'État actuel Ewers. Delo 32, vol. 65.

queathed to him by his predecessor. The memorandum cited article III of the Treaty of London and referred to the Danish King's proclamation of 28 January 1852 and the 'exhortations' addressed to Denmark seeking to persuade her to fulfil the obligations she had undertaken. By acting in this way – we read in the memorandum – the Imperial cabinet had continually shown its concern. Guided – the document said – by friendly intentions towards Denmark, the Emperor of Russia had not hesitated to take action to secure approval of the Treaty of London by those states in the German Confederation which had not yet recognised it.

A gathering in Copenhagen of representatives from the states which were signatories to the Treaty of London, for the purpose of offering their congratulations to the King, would seem to be a natural opportunity to convey these states' position to the Danish government and advise it on how it should act. The representatives should act together and express their views in an identical manner. In order to reach an agreement it was necessary to separate the two essential issues in the present Danish-German conflict: the question of the succession and the new constitution approved by the King.

The former had been decided by the signatories to the Treaty of London, who wanted to remain faithful to it. The German Confederation had to be persuaded to follow the example of Prussia and Austria and accede to this treaty, which was an international act. This aim could only be achieved if the Copenhagen cabinet carried out its obligations to Germany with the same faithfulness as the signatories to the treaty had carried out theirs to Denmark. The Danish government should be reminded of the dead King's promise never to incorporate Schleswig, to which the two German powers which had signed the treaty had agreed, and the representative must explain to the government how difficult it was for the states friendly to Denmark to demand that the German Confederation recognise the provisions of the London protocol if they continually received negative replies to their complaints.

Justice – the memorandum continued – as well as the interests of Denmark, demanded prompt modification of the 18 November Constitution. But far from imposing on King Christian IX the obligation to revoke a constitution he had approved, the powers would be inclined to leave the Danish cabinet complete freedom in the choice of means by which it gave the German Confederation and the duchies assurances of its sincere intentions not to infringe the legal and international documents relating to the incorporation of Schleswig, together with effective guarantees of the loyal discharge of the obligations contained in the royal manifesto of 28 January 1852. The Danish government – the memorandum said – should know that if it ignored or absolutely rejected the path of conciliation, the powers would be compelled to make it bear the responsibility for such behaviour.

If negotiations were undertaken in a spirit of conciliation the signatories to the Treaty of London would support the Danish cause in the Frankfurt Diet. Apart from Austria and Prussia, which were signatories to the treaty, some other German states, like Württemberg, Hannover and the Electorate of Hess, which had signed the treaty but reserved to the German Confederation the right to ratify it, would gladly accept this. Furthermore, the treaty which settled the order of succession to the Danish monarchy was not the first example of European intervention in such a question. A similar type of treaty, the memorandum recalled, had been signed by Austria, Britain, Prussia and Russia in Frankfurt on 19 July 1819 in respect of the succession to the Grand Duchy of Baden.[20]

Ewers was instructed to make his way to Copenhagen via Berlin in order to have talks there – in the first place with Bismarck – to find out what position the Berlin cabinet took on the conflict with Denmark. Gorchakov was aware that the key to solution of the conflict lay in Prussia's hands. He also knew that Austria was behaving with restraint in the matter, and this met with his approval. He expressed his satisfaction with Austria's attitude during his next talk with Thun, when he informed the ambassador that Ewers had been entrusted with a special mission and charged with finding out in Berlin, on his way to Copenhagen, what the vice-chancellor described as

des intentions exactes du Cabinet de Berlin au sujet de cette question. M. De Bismarck lui avait répondu qu'il ne pouvait formuler un programme définitif avant de s'être concerté avec le Cabinet de Vienne, mais il parla à l'Envoyé russe de l'utilité d'une pression exercée par lui sur le Roi Chrétien pour obtenir le renvoi du Ministère.

Le Prince Gorchakov m'a dit à cet egard – Thun reported – "Vous comprenez que M. Ewers ne pouvait se charger d'une semblable commission, puisque ses instructions lui enjoignent avant tout d'entrer en pourparlers avec M. Hall, afin de le ramener à des idées plus conciliantes. Ce qui du reste n'est exclut pas qu'il s'entende avant d'agir avec les représentans de l'Autriche et de la Prusse à Copenhague".[21]

It was this conversation that prompted Thun to have second thoughts about Gorchakov's real intentions. The same day he sent another report to Rechberg-Rothenlöwen, in which he expressed his doubts:

Il me parait fort difficile de découvrir dans le dédale de bonnes paroles et de promesses satisfaisantes les véritables intentions du Cabinet russe dans la question du Schleswig-Holstein.

Tous ces témoignagnes de bienveillance à l'égard de l'Allemagne ne me semblent guère être appuyés suffisamment par des faits pour m'inspirer une confiance absolue.

Je suis loin de penser que le Prince Gortchakov ait contribué pour la moindre part à embrouiller cette question, mais il n'est pas moins vrai que le Cabinet russe a laissé échapper jusqu'ici mainte occasion pour détourner le Gouvernement danois de sa voie néfaste.

C'est ainsi que rien n'a été fait pour soutenir le Roi Chrétien contre la pression du parti de l'action, et qu'on s'est borné à *déplorer vivement* la promulgation de la fameuse constitution, et maintenant encore, où le changement du Ministère danois parait indispensable pour arriver à l'applannissement des graves difficultés qui menacent de faire éclater la tempête qui gronde en Allemagne, le Prince Gorchakov parait exclure une semblable demande de son programme. On veut bien prendre des mesures, mais on les prend trop tard et l'on n'en choisit point d'efficacer.

Le Vice-Chancelier a donné trop de preuves de la fécondité de son esprit, si riche en combinaison, pour qu'il soit permis d'attribuer à la lenteur de son jugement le manque de précision qui caractérise son action dans une question aussi simple.

20. A.V.P.R. Danica. R.A. Danica. R.A. Copenhagen, copy in A.M.A.E. Paris, Russie, vol. 232, p. 245-55.
21. H.H.S.A. no. 42B, 11 December (29 November), P.A. X Russland, Kart. 54.

On serait presque tenté de supposer que le Prince Gortchakow voit dans une complication qui détournerait les regards de l'Europe des affaires de Pologne, un avantage pour un pays qu'il pourrait bien désirer lui assurer sans trop y paraître lui-même.[22]

I have quoted this report in detail because it is very significant, illustrating the extent of the uncertainty in diplomatic circles about Russia's real attitude to the conflict at this stage, and how far Gorchakov was mistrusted. Thun had doubts whether Gorchakov really took a pro-German position.

Gorchakov himself claimed to be neutral in the conflict. In a talk which he had with Massignac about convening a congress in the spirit of Napoleon III's proposal, he asked the French *chargé d'affaires* what the latter thought about Prince Augustenburg's declaration, saying 'C'est une fâcheuse affaire', and adding that it was causing the two larger German states much concern. When he did not receive a positive reply, since Massignac did not know Drouyn de Lhuys' intentions, he declared:

'Nous avons signé avec la France, au sujet de ces affaires, un traité dont l'ancre n'est pas encore sèche. Nous le maintiendrons – he assured him – cela me parait à la fois sage et équitable'.[23]

But in a letter to Olga Nikolaevna on 24 November, concerning the Ewers mission and Russia's attitude, Gorchakov wrote:

Les instructions dont a été muni Mr. d'Ewers, chargé de complimenter le Roi Chrétien IX sur son avènement au trône et d'éclairer les Ministres Danois sur les périls de la marche qu'ils suivent. Nous ne faisons pas particulièrement mystère de ces instructions et Votre Altesse Impériale peut en faire l'usage confidentiel qu'Elle jugerait convenable. Nous avons cherché à tenir entre les deux parties une balance égale tout en confirmant notre fidélité aux obligations contractées par le Traité de Londres quant à l'ordre de succession et à l'intégrité de la Monarchie Danoise, nous insistons pour que le Cabinet de Copenhague remplisse de son côté les engagements qu'il a pris au 1851-52 vis-à-vis des deux Grands Cours Allemandes et à l'égard de l'Allemagne. Notre proposition a trouvé le meilleur accueil près toutes les Cours signataires de Traité de Londres, sauf la France dont nous ne connaissons pas encore les intentions. Le succès de la démarche dépendra de l'unanimité et de l'énérgie du langage.

... En lisant les instructions à Mr. Ewers, Votre Altesse Impériale verra que nous nous plaçons sur le terrain de l'équité tout vis-à-vis le Danemarc que vis-à-vis l'Allemagne et que, si notre démarche est vigoureusement soutenue, les buts que l'Allemagne peut avoir rationnellement en vue seraient atteints, c.à.d. des rapports plus avantageusement définis dans les sens des vœux de la Confédération, entre les Duchés et la Monarchie, mais non le démembrement de cette dernière et l'exaltation de P-ce d'Augustenburg qui, sans mentionner la renonciation très positive du père pour lui et ses descendans, nous semble, sous plus d'un rapport, hors de question.[24]

Thus even in a private letter, Gorchakov described his attitude to the conflict as impartial and expressed his clear opposition to the partitioning of Denmark and to

22. *ibid.*
23. A.M.A.E. Russie, vol. 232, p. 59, 29 November 1863.
24. H.S.A., Stuttgart, G 314 Bü. 7, no. 83.

any claims by Prince Augustenburg. He argued that Russia was seeking a balance between maintenance of the provisions of the Treaty of London and pressure from Germany.

How did diplomatic circles in St. Petersburg – the ambassadors of the neutral states – regard the Ewers mission? The British ambassador in St. Petersburg, Napier, wrote on the subject as follows:

The special envoy designated by the Emperor of Russia to carry His Majesty's congratulations to the King of Denmark is M. d'Ewers, formerly employed in the Foreign Diplomatic Service, but now placed in the Foreign Department here, a gentlemen of excellent character and abilities, who is particularly versed in the questions now under discussion. M. d'Ewers will leave St. Petersburgh[!] for this destination on the 4th or 5th instant. Prince Gortchakoff was so kind as to make me acquainted with the instructions adressed to the Russian Envoy. They will be sent to Baron Brunnow along with this dispatch, and will be imparted to your Lordship.[25]

The Swedish ambassador, Wedel-Jarlsberg, described Ewers in his report of 30 (18) November, calling him a diplomat very well versed in the problems of the Danish-German dispute, and familiar with conditions in Copenhagen, too, as fifteen years before he had been secretary of the Russian embassy there. He had worked in the ministry under the direction of the old Baron Osten-Sacken. 'C'est un homme aussi capable que conciliant et fort en avant dans la confiance du Prince Gortchakov'.[26] In his next report, on 3 December (21 November), the Swedish ambassador noted Ewers' departure for Denmark via Berlin and the essence of the instructions which he had been given, observing that whilst he did not really suspect Gorchakov of harbouring unfriendly intentions towards Denmark, he did detect 'd'un peu de partialité pour l'Allemagne' and it was impossible to overlook the fact that

le P-ce Gortchakov n'a jamais eu le temps d'étudier à fond le différent Dano-Allemand et que ses principaux conseilleurs dans cette affaire sont tout d'origine allemande et ayant conséquemment plus ou moins de prédilection pour "Vor grosse Vaterland". De même ils n'ont pas encore renoncé à leurs idées sur la possibilité et l'excellence du Helstats forfatningen.

Plessen, the ambassador added, had expressed a similar opinion.

Wedel-Jarlsberg took a different view of Gorchakov's role in the Danish-German conflict to that of Thun. He recognised[27] that Gorchakov favoured preserving the integrity of Denmark and upholding the existing succession, and as far as his attitude to the London protocol was concerned he was 'aussi correct et aussi categorique que possible'. He would also give Denmark moral support on these questions. But the ambassador was also convinced 'que ce bon vouloir ne sera appuyé *'ni par un soldat, ni par un vaisseau, ni par un écu'*. He attributed this to the

---

25. Napier to Russell, 1 December 1863. *Denmark and Germany,* vol. 1, no. 359, p. 312.
26. R.A. Stockholm. Skrivelser från Petersburg til Stockholm.
27. Dispatch of 3 December (21 November), Friis-Hedin, p. 113. Thun's dispatch no. IB, 26 (14) January 1864. P.A.X. Kart. 55.

fact that Russia had to be careful to keep on good terms with Prussia – not to speak of the lamentable state of Russian finances, her own defensive capacity, and the impossibility of allocating part of her land or her naval forces to provide military help. At the roots of Russia's policy lay concern with 'self-preservation' together with fear of a counter-coup in Poland, of the revolutionary movement in Germany, and of the Berlin government finding itself in a similar situation to that of 1848.

Wedel was convinced that when Ewers went to Berlin he would try, in his talks with Bismarck, to find ways of establishing good relations with Denmark and at the same time guard against the storm which the democratic elements in Germany might cause to blow up. The ambassador thought that whilst there was no certainty that Russia would send troops to Berlin to maintain the authority of the King in the common interest of both countries, it was more certain that the Tsar could issue a declaration similar to that issued by Nicholas I in 1849. But times had changed. In the ambassador's opinion, Gorchakov had been strongly impressed by the signs of weakness displayed by Bismarck in his last speech. In his report on 6 December (24 November) Wedel wrote that he had come to the conclusion that Gorchakov was neither 'ultradanois' nor 'ultraallemand'. He was in favour of maintaining the London protocol but he considered that Denmark had not discharged her 1851-52 obligations to Germany and consequently feared that Prussia and Austria would announce that they felt themselves relieved of their obligations under the 8 May 1852 Treaty.

Gorchakov regretted that it was not certain whether united action by all the signatories to the Treaty of London could be achieved. He doubted whether Hall would heed his advice but he considered it axiomatic that Denmark could not count on any material help from Russia. 'Le sang de la Russie', he declared, 'ne doit en principe selon lui être répandu que pour des intérêts purement russes', and the Copenhagen cabinet should not claim the benefits of the London Convention without at the same time bearing any of the burdens stemming from it. Running through all Gorchakov's interpretations and arguments Wedel perceived a partiality in that when he spoke of obligations he saw only the Danish side and overlooked the duties and obligations undertaken by Austria and Prussia in their notes of 26 and 30 December 1851.

Wedel's doubts about Gorchakov's impartiality did not diminish. On the contrary, in a telegram on 6 December (24 November) he expressed them as follows:

Malgré la profession de foi de l'impartialité du Prince Gorchakow je n'en continue pas moins à croire à une politique que de ménagement envers l'Allemagne et surtout pour la Prusse. La crainte du countrecoup en Pologne pouvant résulter du débordement des éléments démocratiques n'est pas étrangère peut-être. Même en cas d'acception des conseils Russes le Denmark ne saurait guère, je pense, compter sur une assistance matérielle quelconque venue d'ici facilement. "Uti in utteris humillimis."

There was no sign of the rise of a coalition against France, Wedel-Jarlsberg reported on 12 December (30 November), and in his opinion the Fleury mission was evidence rather of a tendency to a revival of the alliance with France. It was not impossible that Fleury would go to St. Petersburg. An alliance with Austria, however, was a real possibility, in the interests of both countries. Gorchakov treated the Danish question, in the ambassador's opinion,

> avec une grande légérité et comme si les intérêts russes n'y étaient pas sérieusement engagé. L'autre jour il a même en l'air de faire bon marché des observations d'une personne fierce qui essayait de lui faire comprendre qu'en abandonnant le Denmarc à ses propres ressources on arrivera infailliblement en dernier analyse à la réunion des trois couronnes dans une forte Scandinave.
>
> Je suis cependant très tenté de croire que cette indifférence du Prince Gorchakov *n'est qu'apparante* [W.J.] est que nous entendrons un autre langage le jour quand la supposition éventuelle aurait des chances réeles d'aboutir.

Gorchakov was pleased to received the information that Sweden had finally withdrawn from negotiations with Denmark. Apart from fundamental considerations, he was of the opinion that the fact that Denmark could no longer rely on Swedish help meant she would bow to pressure from Ewers and Wodehouse and suspend the points in the constitution relating to Schleswig.[28] Gorchakov believed this, although the Swedish ambassador assured him that Denmark would bow neither to the threat from Germany nor to the pressure of friendly advice, because if she did so she would only expose herself to still greater danger.[29]

Sweden's withdrawal from the talks with Denmark should not have been a great surprise to Gorchakov, since, in contrast to the earlier reports reaching St. Petersburg from Stockholm, which indicated the possibility that a defensive treaty might be concluded between the two conuntries,[30] the reports being sent by the end of October said that Manderström was delaying signing the treaty and that both in military circles and in society at large there was no enthusiasm for it. Among other reasons, this was because of financial difficulties, together with a belief that Britain and France would not pledge help in case of need. Calls for a restrained policy towards Denmark were multiplying.[31]

> Une des causes de cette indifférence actuelle pour la question Danoise prouvait évidement de la crainte de se trouver engagé dans une querelle étrangère au moment où, peut-être, se résoudra la question polonaise.[32]

The Scandinavian countries did not want to become involved in a war.

> Si donc les événements améneront une action militaire en faveur du Danemarc, ce sera plutôt la conséquence d'un point d'honneur que d'un entraînement national,[33]

Dashkov reported. The King was also acting in a way designed to preserve peace.

---

28. Wedel-Jarlsberg, no. 136, 22 (10) December 1863.
29. *Ibid.* 25 (13) December.
30. See for example Minciaky's report, no. 79, 30 August (11 September) and Dashkov's report, no. 84, 8 (20) October 1863.
31. Report no. 63, 8 (20) October.
32. Report no. 88, 18 (30) October.
33. Dashkov's report, no. 89, 29 October (10 November).

The idea of Scandinavian co-operation had become a fiasco, and, apart from a group of students from Christiania and *Aftenbladet,* public opinion not only accepted that the government had abandoned the Danish cause but the majority approved of their government's decision, the ambassador reported.[34] Gorchakov could thus see what shaky foundations the so-called Scandinavianism policy was based on and how exaggerated his fears of possible military co-operation between Sweden and Denmark had been.

Dashkov reported[35] that Manderström had used very moderate language ('moins belliqueux') in a talk with him and had explained that Sweden herself could not help Denmark and was awaiting developments. The reason for this, among other things – Scheel-Plessen reported – was that Manderström was afraid that now Russia had dealt with the Polish uprising and was seeking an alliance with Prussia and Austria – and even a rapprochement between Russia and France could not be ruled out – Sweden could expect retaliation for her policy during the Crimean War and the Polish uprising in the form of a Russian raid on Sweden's coast.[36] Towards the end of 1863, Dashkov came to the conclusion that Scandinavianism had sustained a shattering blow and the plans of the Scandinavianists had come to nothing.[37]

Nevertheless, despite Gorchakov's insistence, the Swedish government did not decide on any joint diplomatic action with Russia and Britain to put pressure on Denmark.[38] Nor did France want to join the Ewers-Wodehouse duet. In a talk with Massignac Gorchakov said he favoured simultaneous ('commune et iden-

---

34. Nos. 97 and 100, 7 (19) and 12 (24) December.
35. No. 102, 17 (29) December.
36. Dep. Sverige 1862-65, R.A. Copenhagen, nos. 57, 60 and 62, 27 November, 4 and 10 December. Cf. J. de Coussange, *La Scandinavie* ...(1914), p. 19.
37. Møller, *Skandinavisk stræben;* J. Clausen, *Skandinavismen,* pp. 176-9; Janson, *Den Svenska Utrikespolitikens Historia,* Jorgenson, *Norway's Relation to Scandinavian Unionism,* pp. 353, 381. A typical illustration of the feeling that earlier prevailed in Sweden is perhaps the article by Auguste Blanche in *Dagligt Allehanda,* no. 239, (October 1863), in which the author points out the impracticality of the idea of Scandinavianism from the point of view of the key interests of Sweden, whose enemy no. 1 was Russia, and Denmark, whose enemy no. 1 was Germany. She also comes to the conclusion that if Sweden were to find herself in conflict with Russia again Denmark's help would not mean much.

Bismarck, in a conversation with J. Hansen during an audience in Berlin on 16 December 1864, described Sweden's attitude to Denmark during the latter's conflict with Germany in the following manner:

'Si les Suédois se sont abstenus de prendre part à la guerre dano-allemande, cela vient d'abord de ce qu'ils ont vu l'impossibilité de défendre la presqu'île du Jutland, mais aussi de ce que l'aristocratie suédoise ne veut rien avoir à faire avec la démocratie danoise, elle a assez de la démocratie norvégienne. Le Danemark ne trouvera de sympathies en Suède que chez la famille royale et dans les universités'. (J. Hansen, *Les coulisses de la diplomatie* ..., p. 42).

The Norwegian historian Koht blamed the Danish government for lack of foresight and misjudgement of the Scandinavian states' possibility of coming to the aid of Denmark with military help. 'Die dänischen Illusionspolitiker müssen indessen auch ihren Anteil an der Verantwortung tragen,... Eine Politik, die beiderseits auf solchen Fälschungen bewusst und unbewusst gebaut war, musste unumgänglich zur Niederlage führen. (pp. 250-1).
38. Wedel-Jarlsberg, Report no. 1, 1 January 1864 (20 December 1863).

tique') action by the great powers, considering that 'la présence simultanée des agents donnât plus de force aux conseils qu'on allait donner au Cabinet Danois'.[39] But despite the fact that, as he said, he detected a certain nuance in the policy of France, which had decided to act independently, he saw the fact of sending General Fleury to Copenhagen as a positive move and expressed his satisfaction on that account. He was especially pleased by the sending of Wodehouse, which was a break with British tradition.[40]

As Ewers was leaving St. Petersburg, Dotézac was considering what it would mean in essence if the Danish government were to accept Gorchakov's proposal. This move, 'pleine d'habilité' (joint action by the signatories to the Treaty of London) would deprive the present government of all the prestige it enjoyed and give the King the opportunity to appoint a new government 'selon son cœur'. In Dotézac's opinion this view was shared by Hall. Dotézac repeated Hall's opinion that Gorchakov's suggestion had been put forward in this form with the knowledge of the King, and that the Danish ambassador in Russia, O. Plessen, was behind them. Plessen was devoted to the King, associated with his brother Carl Scheel-Plessen, a former chairman of the Estates of Holstein, and close to both Russia and Germany. This move was untypical of the St. Petersburg cabinet, including the fact that it was not a military mission that was going to Copenhagen, which would have been consistent with Russian practice, but Ewers – a diplomat. Dotézac saw a conspiracy there, involving St. Petersburg, the King and O. Plessen, the Estates of Holstein and Prince Frederick of Hess.

The conciliatory tone Russia adopted towards Austria and Prussia, the close relations between Russia and Prussia, Gorchakov's satisfaction at the cooperation between the two larger German powers, the content of Gorchakov's 4 April 1862 note and the choice of Ewers as special envoy, taken together pointed to pro-German sympathies on the part of Russia and suggested that the Ewers mission could also be important for the future internal development of Denmark. Russia, Hall thought, would like the King and Queen, who were pro-German, to give way to Germany and break with Scandinavianism. These were the dual aims of Russian policy.

Even if there was an element of exaggeration in this assessment, Hall was in no doubt that this was the ultimate aim of Gorchakov's policy. Fulfilment of this aim would be equivalent to a personal defeat for Hall and would mean abandonment of the principles of the 18 November Constitution and a change in the direction of Danish policy. If there were certain doubts about this, Dotézac argued, it was sufficient to note the tone of the speech by Prince Frederick of Hess, the brother-in-law of the King and Alexander II, who laid the responsibility for everything that had happened in Denmark on the present Danish government.

Prince Frederick had not concealed his views from Dotézac. He glossed over

---

39. A.M.A.E. Paris, Dep. teleg., 9 December and no. 62, 14 December, Russie, vol. 232.
40. *Ibid.* 17 December.

the position taken by Prussia and Austria on the succession to the throne, spoke of the Danish government with contempt, blaming it for the growth of anti-Danish feeling in Germany, and pressed for the dismissal of the cabinet. He also urged Dotézac to adopt the same position. Dotézac protested ignorance of Russia's proposal and lack of instructions. Nor, said the ambassador, could he interfere in the cabinet's affairs. Paget also viewed Prince Frederick with suspicion. He too said that the latter was doing a great deal of harm by his intemperate language, although he thought he was acting for the King. To bind Denmark to Germany, in accordance with the King's feelings, break the links between Denmark and Sweden, and maintain a King with anti-Scandinavian views, in Dotézac's opinion, were the main aims of Russian policy. Russia had worked patiently in this direction during the reign of Frederick VII, but had not achieved any results. The new King had opened the gates for Gorchakov to carry out his plan.[41]

Referring to Gorchakov's proposal, the helmsman of Danish policy, Hall, said in a circular to Berlin, Frankfurt, London, Paris, Vienna, St. Petersburg and Stockholm:

Il parait que le prince Gortchakov propose qu'en félicitant Sa Majesté on déclarera reconnaître pleinement la validité du Traité de Londres, mais qu'on engagera en même temps vivement le Gouvernement du Roi à remplir les transactions de 1851/52,... Nous ne récuserons point la base de 1851-52, mais nous demanderons nécessairement à en arriver enfin à une interprétation claire et précise des obligations réciproques, résultant de ces négotiations. La nécessité d'une réunion des puissances signataires du traité de Londres à cet effet deviendra aussi évidente.[42]

II

Ewers began his mission with a visit to Berlin. Wodehouse, incidentally, did the same.[43] On 24 November (6 December) Ewers arrived in Berlin and had a talk with Bismarck.

Ce n'est plus cet homme ardent, au verbe haut, et qui se complaisait dans les combats politiques, c'est maintenant un homme aigri, fatigué et presque brisé par la double lutte qu'il a soutenir contre les chambres et contre le Roi, qui, sur la question holsteinoise diffère complètement de sentiment avec son Ministère.

In his report to Gorchakov Ewers followed up this impression of Bismarck with an account of the battle Bismarck was fighting, which he compared with the punishment of Sisyphus.[44] He was fighting against the German princelings, who, Bismarck said, had organised a real conspiracy, inundating the King with letters

---

41. A.M.A.E. Danemark, vol. 245, no. 192, 4 December 1863.
42. Hall to Scheel-Plessen, 7 December 1863, Ordrer, Stockholm, 1861-68, R.A. Copenhagen.
43. A.V.P.R. Delo 32, vol. 65; Wodehouse to Russell, *Denmark and Germany*, I, no. 434, Berlin, 12 December 1863, pp. 375-7.
44. On the anti-Bismarck *fronde* see Engelberg, *Bismarck*, pp. 550-1.

urging him to lead the fight against Denmark. The effect of this pressure on the King was greater and greater. Seeking an ally in Ewers, Bismarck had suggested that he should have a talk with the King himself, which Ewers had accepted. Bismarck had declared himself in favour of a peaceful solution to the dispute and asked Ewers to make the following points to the King:

1. The Imperial Cabinet was convinced that the claims of Prince Augustenburg had no legal basis.
2. The Imperial Cabinet was afraid that if the King renounced the Treaty of London he would be drawn into an alliance with France and a revolutionary policy.
3. The Tsar believed that the differences between Denmark and Germany could be settled by diplomatic means.

Ewers would not let himself be completely entangled by Bismarck, as he said that the second point was unacceptable to him because it was contrary to the deeply-held conviction of the Tsar, who would never believe that the Prussian King could be drawn into a situation in which he would follow a revolutionary policy. During his audience, Ewers found the King just as he expected after what Bismarck had said. The King told him that whilst Prussia and Austria were indeed bound by the Treaty of London, there was also the German Confederation, which did not recognise it, and if his mission were successful both the larger German states might be satisfied, but it would not suit the rest of Germany. He could not feel himself bound by the treaty, however, if Denmark did not fulfil her obligations to the Confederation and if Federal Execution were met with armed resistance. In his report to Gorchakov, Ewers noted that it was clear from this how heavily the Treaty of London weighed on the King, and that he would repudiate it if circumstances permitted.

When he said to Bismarck that the two German states should define what they wanted in connection with the Danish obligations of 1851-52, Bismarck replied that he had not yet discussed this with Austria, but that what he wanted above all was a change of government in Copenhagen, greater power to be given to the King, and a declaration that the fortress of Rendsborg was federal. When Ewers said that whilst he did not deny that these demands could be useful, they did not follow from Copenhagen's obligations, Bismarck agreed, saying that he had thrown them in 'au hasard', and that the most important thing for him was agreement with the Vienna court on settling what Denmark must do to fulfil the promises she had given.

Summing up, Ewers said he had found a constitutional country in which the chairman of the council of ministers was engaged in an open battle with the Chambers and some of his colleagues, and in which there were deep and all-pervading differences of opinion between him and the King. Such an abnormal situation could not last long, and a change of government would bring about an immediate war with Denmark.

Ewers' visit to Berlin undoubtedly influenced the course of his mission in Copenhagen. Bismarck's comments presumably influenced his attitude to Denmark, and to some extent modified his views, and this was reflected in his actions in Copenhagen. When he reached Copenhagen, Ewers received an additional report from Nicolay on the current situation in Denmark, and began his mission without waiting for Wodehouse's arrival.[45] Everything pointed to cooperation being possible only with Wodehouse, whilst there seemed little likelihood that General Fleury, or the Swedish representative, Hamilton, could be drawn into joint action.

Hall's attitude to Gorchakov's initiative was negative from the start. He could not accept the Russian point of view that Denmark had broken the 1851-52 agreements and that the adoption of the 18 November Constitution was an infringement of these obligations. Hall took it for granted that his government would not yield to pressure from the great powers. He regretted that Napoleon III's idea of convening a congress had been torpedoed by Britain. For if a congress had been held, Gorchakov's initiative would not have been necessary, and putting the Danish question to a congress, Hall believed, would have saved Denmark. Krieger also thought that it would have been good for Denmark if there had been a European conference.[46] The leading Danish politicians had no confidence in Ewers. Hall called him 'en Tysker en rigtig Dänenfreser' (A German, a real Dane-eater),[47] and Krieger, whilst not questioning his diplomatic skills, saw him as 'en hensynsløs kold Tysker' (A ruthless cold-blooded German),[48] and wrote of Russian policy on 14 December 1863: 'Rusland vilde være »conséquent« i sin tydsk-heldende politik, det var alpha og omega' (Russia wants to be »consequent« in her pro-German policy and it was alpha and omega).[49] Their judgement was not mistaken, as Ewers himself said of himself in a letter to O. Plessen on 19 June 1864: 'Für die Dänen habe ich keine Sympathie, aber unendlich Leid thun mir die Königin und der König, denen ich aufrichtig ergeben bin'.[50]

During his first talk with Hall, Ewers believed that Hall realised what a difficult situation Denmark was in, and that he was convinced of the need to avoid armed confrontation at the moment of the Federal Execution by German troops in Holstein.[51] In Ewers' opinion, Hall's assurances had removed a certain danger, at least for the moment, and in this way Copenhagen could gain the time which was necessary for negotiations with Berlin and Vienna.

During an audience with the King on 10 December[52] when Ewers handed over a letter of congratulation from Alexander II, and Nicolay simultaneously presented

45. Nicolay to Gorchakov, 28 November (10 December), Fond-Kantsel, delo 38, vol. 65, A.V.P.R.
46. A.F. Krieger, *Dagbøger*, 31 July 1866, vol. III, p. 385.
47. Møller, vol. I, p. 616.
48. 11 December 1863.
49. *Dagbøger*, vol. III, pp. 12, 14.
50. Privatarkiv O. Plessen, Arkivn. 6128, A. 1.2. R.A. Copenhagen.
51. 28 November (10 December), Delo, vol. 65. On 24 December German troops under the command of the Saxon lt. Gen. von Hake entered Holstein. Austrian and Prussian troops remained in reserve in Hamburg and Lübeck.
52. See reports by Ewers, 3 (15) December, Nicolay, 28 November (10 December) and 30 November (12 December), and Dotézac, no. 200, 12 December.

his credentials, Ewers acquainted the King with the purpose of what he called his peace mission ('un mandat de paix') designed to facilitate an agreement between Denmark and Germany. Reporting the course of his talk with Bismarck, Ewers emphasised how very important it was for future negotiations to support Bismarck,

le plus modéré des hommes d'État, mais il a contre lui tous les partis et le Roi lui-même dans cette question. Il [Bismarck] ne voit pas une difficulté insurmontable dans la nouvelle constitution, car on peut la modifier.

St. Petersburg regretted that the King had approved the constititon, but understood that he could not have acted in any other way.

Ewers also informed the King that the Tsar was firmly committed to maintaining the Treaty of London and regarded it as separate from the agreements concluded between Denmark and the larger German states. Finally, he declared that the aim of his mission was, in conjunction with the representatives of the other powers, to arrange for the opening of negotiations between the two parties in dispute.[53]

Ewers' language, Dotézac reported to Paris on 12 December, was moderate and conciliatory, but

la Russie n'a pas l'habitude de se démasquer avant l'heure. Il est certain qu'elle n'aime pas ce ministère, ni les tendances qu'il représente. Ce qu'il veut, c'est dégager le Roi sans trop le compromettre aux yeux des Danois, en s'associant les autres puissances, car c'est sur le Roi qu'elle fonda l'avenir de sa prépondérance en Danemark.[54]

Ewers assessed the situation at the moment of his arrival as more complicated and worse for Denmark than previously, since Prussia and Austria were acting together against Copenhagen, and he could probably only count on cooperation with Wodehouse. He was aware that he faced great difficulties, but he hoped that coordinated action with Wodehouse could produce positive results. At dinner with the King, Ewers emphasised that he had found Hall 'assez modéré et très désireux de chercher une issue pour sortir de la position difficile où la Denmark se trouvait engagé'.

Wodehouse arrived in Copenhagen via Berlin. The next day he met Ewers. He reported with satisfaction that Ewers and Nicolay were interested in cooperating with him.[55] In the course of their talk it became apparent that the gist of their instructions was similar. The British instructions, however, went further in addressing demands to the Danish government, as they called on Denmark to suspend that part of the constitution which concerned Schleswig. Although Ewers

---

53. Ewers, 3 (15) December, vol. 65. See also. M. Bosch Spencer's dispatch of December 15. Privatarkiver A. Friis, 5424.
54. Dotézac, no. 200, 12 December. The content of this report does not differ from Nicolay's account (3 (15) December) of his and Ewers' audience with Christian IX.
55. Wodehouse to Russell, 16 December. F.O. Denmark 22/306 (13). On Wodehouse's mission see Keith A.P. Sandiford, *Great Britain and the Schleswig-Holstein Question, 1848-64. A Study in Diplomacy, Politics and Public Opinion.* (Toronto and Buffalo, 1975), pp. 78 ff. Also H. Voigt. 'Englands Aussenpolitik'. In *Z.d.G.f.S.H.G.* vol. 89, (1964).

was not directed to give such advice to the Danish Government, he had no hesitation in associating himself with me [Wodehouse - E.H.], in the step which I proposed to take, as such a step would be in conformity to the spirit of his instructions.[56]

Ewers considered that collective action in relation to the Danish government was most appropriate and was the only thing likely to produce results. He was also sure that his approach would meet with Gorchakov's approval, and he was not mistaken.[57] But new attempts by Ewers to persuade Fleury and Hamilton to join in collective action came to nothing.[58]

As far as Fleury was concerned, however, whilst he refused to co-operate because of the state of relations between Paris and London, he unexpectedly questioned Ewers about a different matter. He suggested that if, as was being said in St. Petersburg, national agitation had subsided, the time had come, as he put it, 'pour un rapprochement entre nous'. 'Vous ne sauriez nous reprocher nos sympathies pour la Pologne, elles s'expliquent par toute notre histoire', said the general, wanting as it were to justify France's policy during the uprising. This passage in Ewers' report of 7 (19) December was subsequently annoted in the margin by the Tsar, 'quel cinique'.[59]

The initiative, however, should come from Russia. Negotiations could begin in Paris if the Tsar sent someone trusted - Ewers himself for example. Ewers did not reply to this and showed no interest in these unexpected overtures from Fleury.[60]

On 20 December Wodehouse and Ewers met Hall. At Ewers' request, Wodehouse presented their point of view on the necessity of suspending those parts of the constitution concerned with Schleswig, since by adopting them Denmark had broken its obligations to the German states.[61] After this talk[62] Ewers and Wodehouse came to the conclusion that Hall, as Ewers reported, 'avait fini par comprendre la gravité de la situation' in which Denmark found itself, and had decided to advise the King to appoint a new government, which would be more favourable to a proposal for the suspension of the 18 November Constitution.[63] When the session of the Rigsraad closed for the holiday, however, the King did not mention the recommendation of Ewers and Wodehouse, which was equivalent to rejecting their advice.

56. Wodehouse to Russell, 19 December, no. 504, *Denmark and Germany,* vol. I, p. 415.
57. On 5 (17) December he sent the following telegram to Gorchakov: 'Wodehouse a ordre de conseiller abrogation de la nouvelle constitution. C'est conforme à l'esprit de mes instructions, mais contraire à lettre. Puisse-je me joindre à sa démarche. Si non, l'Allemagne menace de guerre.' (A.V.P.R. vol. 65) 'Se joindre à la démarche de Wodehouse quant à l'abrogation de Constitution générale', was the reply, approved by the Tsar on 6 December (O.S.) and dispatched by telegraph by Gorchakov on 7 (19) December. (A.V.P.R. delo 32, vol. 65).
58. Ewers, 8 (20) December, vol. 65.
59. Vol. 65.
60. In *Souvenirs du Général C-te Fleury,* vol. II, 1859-67 (Paris, 1898), the author does not mention a word of this matter.
61. Ewers' report of 8 (20) December, vol. 65; Wodehouse to Russell, no. 507, 21 December, *Denmark and Germany,* vol. I, pp. 416-8.
62. Cf. Hall's report on the talk, 21 December 1863, *Statsraadets Forhandlinger 1863-1864,* vol. IX (Copenhagen, 1970), pp. 236ff.
63. Ewers' report, 10 (22) December, vol. 65.

This rejection did not surprise Russell. In a letter to Wodehouse on 17 December, quoting the opinion of Col. Raasløff, he wrote:

He hoped [Raasløff] the King would not be asked to force the Parliament to revoke the constitution. Such attempt might cost him his Crown. ... But we cannot give active support to a Government which puts itself so manifestly in the wrong ... Germany puts herself still more in the wrong than Denmark. The Germans are so hot ... they set aside all prudential motives.[64]

Wodehouse held similar opinions of the attitudes of both parties. In his report to Russell for 16-22 December he wrote: 'Will try to find some middle way but both parties are blinded with passion. Hopes to discover some way of "moving this stiff necked race".' [This was how he described the Danes.] Wodehouse consulted with Paget about what to do to save Denmark from the 'impending ruin' and they concluded that in the first place the constitution had to be suspended and Schleswig given complete autonomy and authority in local matters.[65] In contrast to Ewers, however, Wodehouse was involved not only officially but also emotionally.[66]

It must be admitted that the talks with Hall were not easy for the two diplomats. Hall continually claimed that in the past Denmark had fulfilled German demands, but that every move to meet demands made by Germany had been followed by new demands from the latter.[67]

Ewers expected Hall to reject their proposals concerning changes in the constitution. He appreciated that Hall enjoyed support from a variety of quarters. Some of his supporters said that if war broke out one or other of the great powers would help Denmark materially, and they believed it. Others maintained that if the monarchy were partitioned the remaining part, which was not absorbed by the German monarchy, would join a Scandinavian Confederation in which Denmark would play the primary role. Ewers did not know to which of these groups Hall inclined. But it was indisputable that Hall had the support of public opinion in Copenhagen, although other regions of the country were against a violent solution to the conflict and a mass of letters had been sent to Copenhagen in which the population spoke out against war.

As far as the population in Schleswig was concerned, however, it was devoted to the King. But it submitted that for fifteen years the Danish administration in Schleswig had been guilty of a series of wrongs and arbitrary acts. Whereas in Copenhagen an exaggerated respect was shown for constitutional forms, in Schleswig rights were trampled under foot.[68] Ewers also drew attention in his report to *Fædrelandet's* opinion that France and Sweden differed from Russia

---

64. P.R.O., vol. 102.
65. Report to Russell, 22 December 1863. P.R.O., vol. 102.
66. See Wodehouse to Russell, 21 December 1863, no. 28. Confidential. F.O. 22/306/28.
67. At the session of the Statsraadet on 17 December Hall expressed the opinion that the German side's aim was to merge Schleswig with Germany. *Statsraadets Forhandlinger 1863-1864,* vol. IX, p. 227.
68. Cf. Russell to Wodehouse: 'The greatest fault in my eyes of the new constitution is that is sets aside the rights of Schleswig without their consent'. P.R.O., 30/22 vol. 102.

and Britain in their attitude towards Denmark, on which he offered the following comment: 'Je dois regarder cette assertion comme un mensonge imprudent, si je ne veux admettre que le général Fleury ait usé envers nous de la plus sincère fausseté'.[69] Ewers' reports were shorter and less exhaustive than those supplied to London by Wodehouse. Ewers himself pointed this out to Gorchakov, explaining it by the fact that Wodehouse had colleagues with him whereas Ewers was on his own.[70]

Parallel to the official mission to put pressure on the Hall government which was organised jointly with Wodehouse, Ewers tried independently to sound out the prevailing situation and familiarise himself with the pattern of political forces in Copenhagen. It was presumably no secret to him that the British government would also have been glad to see a change of government in Denmark headed by one of the conservative politicians, or even Bluhme.

Bluhme's name as an alternative was repeated in Russell's dispatches to Paget. On 2 December Russell wrote:

It may be found on trial that the King is unable to induce his present Ministers to draw a single foot back from the position they have taken. In that case I hope H.M. will try M. Bluhme or some respectable politician and get them to form a Ministry.

Bluhme's name was also mentioned in the letter informing Paget of Wodehouse's mission:

It is my persuasion that Hall is too much committed to the Constitution of 18th November to give way upon it. Yet if it remains no good can be done and the Danish promises of January 1852 are clearly violated. The only thing then is that the King should take the advice of his allies, and send for M. Bluhme to form a Ministry ... new Ministry under Bluhme should replace Hall's.[71]

Ewers also certainly knew that the Austrian government was annoyed that Gorchakov had done nothing to bring about the removal of the Hall government and its replacement by a conservative one. Ewers would undoubtedly have been glad to see a change of government in Copenhagen. But being more and more aware of the mood in the capital, and knowing the personality of the King, who had a noble but weak character and who was the spirit of integrity but lacked inspiration, he did not see him as a ruler who was capable of carrying out a coup d'état in these circumstances. Ewers recognised the risk the King ran if he sought to change the government and placed a conservative politician at the head of it. For this reason Ewers was unusually cautious in this matter.

It is true that for a moment it seemed to him that it would be possible to form a new government under Andrae, and he put this suggestion to the King.[72] But when Andrae declined, Ewers did not propose any new candidates, as he understood that the man he would have liked to see as head of the government, or at any

69. Ewers' report of 10 (22) December 1863.
70. *Ibid.*
71. P.R.O. 30/22, vol. 102.
72. Ewers' report of 12 (24) December.

rate in the government, Bluhme, could not be appointed under these circumstances.[73] But he did not give up having talks with the leaders of the conservative opposition. He also had discussions with Bluhme and David, who was close to the King, and with members of the royal family, Prince Frederick of Hess and Prince Glücksburg, the King's elder brother. But he was very cautious in his talks, particularly with the latter, and in any case the initiative for them came from the members of the royal family. They wanted to sound out the Russian diplomat's opinion of the internal situation in Denmark and what possibly should be done to change it.

As an experienced diplomat, Ewers preferred not to say anything on these topics during these conversations, on the grounds that as a foreigner he was not entitled to do so. He considered this a very delicate matter, particularly as he had such a difficult mission to perform. On 12 (24) December Ewers was invited to a meeting by Prince Glücksburg, who wanted to consult him on what should be done in connection with the crisis in the country. Ewers said he could not give the King and the government any advice other than what he had received from the Tsar. He also said that anything in the nature of a coup d'état should be rejected, because it would compromise the King. He, Ewers, would then bear responsibility for the behaviour of the government, and suspicions would arise that these decisions were provoked and that foreign powers were behind them. The whole of Europe was aware that the missions sent by the Russian, British and French governments had arrived in Copenhagen.

It was essential, he said, that it should be seen that the King had consulted no one other than his own ministers, and that if the government would not do what the King considered desirable he should turn to Danish statesmen only, and take their views into consideration. This was the best way to form a new government. Asked by the princelings present at this reception about a person who could form a new government, Ewers countered that the friendly powers had no intention of interfering in the internal affairs of the country. Moreover, he had left Copenhagen so long ago, he no longer knew people. Nicolay and Paget, however, had often mentioned Andrae, who combined the necessary qualifications, and the King would not compromise himself by talking to him about the possibility of his forming a government and could find out whether Andrae would take the measures which the three powers had advised the King to take.[74]

When the princelings asked whether it would not be convenient if the King were to abdicate in favour of his son, who had been born in Copenhagen and might therefore be more popular than his father, and for whom it would be easier to abolish the 18 November Constitution as he had not approved it, Ewers said that not

---

73. The Hamburg representative, Krüger, reported in more detail on these plans to the Syndic of Hamburg, Merck, nos. 107 and 108, 29 and 30 December 1863, in Privatarkiv A. Friis, 5424, R.A. Copenhagen. On Bluhme's views see no. 80, 24 November and Balan to Bismarck and the King, 20 November, no. 276.
74. As we know, the King had in fact approached Andrae on 23 December, but the latter had declined. Ewers to Gorchakov, 12 (24) December.

only was this a question which he was not entitled to discuss but that members of the royal family had no right to propose this to the King. Wanting to be loyal to Wodehouse, Ewers said he would like to tell the British diplomat about the course of the meeting, with the exception of this last matter. To this they all expressed their agreement.

A different view of Ewers' behaviour is given in Ch. G.N. David's account. According to David, Ewers said at a dinner at Nicolay's that all this talk of a Copenhagen revolution (which seemed a threat in the historic days after the accession of Christian IX, when the question was whether he would sign the constitution) was exaggerated, for every government had the means to suppress such a revolution, as Russian experience showed. As a Russian, David added, Ewers had experience of how a revolutionary movement could be suppressed with the help of armed force. David had tried to convince Ewers that Denmark was not Russia, and that he (Ewers) was not familiar with the circumstances and did not understand the King's situation.[75] It follows from this that Ewers allowed himself greater sincerity in conversation with David than with the princelings.

The pressure from Ewers and Wodehouse, and Denmark's deteriorating situation, could not fail to exercise some influence on the attitude of the King and the government. But Hall, who was rather a cautious politician, prefered to stand by his decisions. The King, who in essence had a different view of the matter from his government, was, on the other hand, an irresolute person. He was also undoubtedly under pressure from members of his family. Thus when he met Ewers at Prince Frederick's he told him that he was inclined to suspend the constitution, on the condition that the larger German states gave a guarantee that they would demand nothing more than fulfilment of the 1851-52 promises. Ewers had doubts whether such guarantees would not be too indefinite ('vague') as there were different interpretations of how these obligations should be discharged. Unfinished negotiations were going on on precisely this question, and it might be better if the King indicated specifically to what concessions he would agree.

To this the King replied that he wanted to carry out the obligations undertaken in 1851-52 loyally and fully, but on the condition that he would not be required to link Schleswig and Holstein more closely, because to that he neither would nor could agree. If this were accepted, he wanted Ewers and Wodehouse to intervene in Berlin and Vienna to persuade these two governments not to pursue their demands any further. If such guarantees were obtained, he would insist that Hall took steps to suspend the constitution, and if Hall refused he would appoint another government.

Ewers for his part assured the King that both he and Wodehouse would take such steps in both Berlin and Vienna and that General Fleury would join them, but he warned that they must be careful not to incur the charge of ignoring constitutional

---

75. 'David og Hall. Krisen i Danmarks historie 1863. Kritisk studie by Erik Aarup', in *Scandia,* vol. I, (February 1928) pp. 164-5.

forms. Being cautious as usual, Ewers recommended the King to agree the whole matter with Wodehouse, who was well versed in constitutional questions and would be able to make many practical suggestions. In addition, Wodehouse would feel flattered that the King treated him with the same confidence as he did Ewers. The King did in fact have a conversation with Wodehouse on this subject the next day.

Insister auprès du Gouvernement prussien pour qu'on ne précipite rien. Il se prépare ici quelque chose qui contentera, peut-être l'Allemagne.

This was the telegram Ewers sent to Oubril on 13 December (old style), and a corresponding one went to Knorring in Vienna.[76]

Hall rejected the King's proposal to suspend the constitution. The King's talk with Andrae produced no result. The King planned to approach other statesmen and to recall the Rigsraad, which had gone into recess four days before. This, Nicolay thought, would be the best proof for the German states that the King had conciliatory intentions.[77]

Hall took an uncompromising position in these crucial days.[78] This was not the product of stubbornness, but of a deep conviction that Germany was not interested in Federal Execution but in something much greater, and that this was no longer a secret to anybody. Nor was Germany concerned about ensuring constitutional rights for Holstein, since Denmark had agreed in October to satisfy all the demands concerning Holstein presented by the federal Diet. 'Il ne s'agit plus de tout cela', said Hall in a document sent to O. Plessen on 24 December, when he was certainly already aware that he would be leaving office.[79]

Il s'agit tout simplement d'une invasion dans la monarchie Danoise. L'invasion n'est pas un moyen, main le but même, elle se fait pour donner une satisfaction à l'esprit révolutionnaire qui éclate aujourd'hui en Allemagne avec toute la même faveur qui a caracterisé les mouvements de l'année 1848. Les conséquences prochaines de cette fatale complicité des Gouvernements ne sont que trop évidentes. L'esprit qui agite l'Allemagne ne se contentera pas de l'invasion des provinces allemandes de la monarchie Danoise. Dans ses vagues et folles aspirations, son véritable but, si tant est qu'il est conscience d'un but précis et réfléchi, est d'envahir et de conquérir les provinces Danoises de la Monarchie, ou, tout au moins le Duché de Schleswig. Loin de satisfaire, par l'invasion du Holstein, les esprits montés à un pareil degré de passion, les Gouvernements se trouveront irrésistiblement entraînés plus loin par le courant. Ils seront poussés a là guerre contre le Danemarc et pris entre l'esprit de subversion, toujours croissant en Allemagne, et l'agitation, qui ne manquera pas de se produire dans le Holstein par suite de l'occupation, ils deviendront forcément les promoteurs des desseins d'un prétendant dont ils reconnaissent eux mêmes le manque de tout droit. Ce dont il s'agit, c'est donc, à bien y regarder, du renversement de l'arrangement dynastique consacré par le traité de Londres, et de l'anéantissement de la Monarchie Danoise comme faisant

76. Vol. 65.
77. *Ibid.*
78. 'C. Hall, the leader of the Eider-Dane party, a politician of both capacity and daring and supple as well as pertinacious'. *The Cambridge History of British Foreign Policy 1873-1919*, vol. II, 1815-1866, Ed. Sir A.W. Ward and P.G. Gooch (Cambridge, 1923), p. 543.
79. The same day federal troops entered Altona and Prince Augustenburg issued his proclamation.

partie du système politique Européen. La question ainsi posée, chaque concession ne fait qu'ajouter au péril de la situation.

The Danish government, Hall informed the ambassador, had decided not to resist Federal Execution and to withdraw Denmark's forces to the Eider.

Si nous avons pris cette résolution, c'est uniquement pour nous rendre aux conseils et aux insistances de puissances Gouvernements amis et pour différer aussi longtemps que possible une collision à main armée, collision qui, néanmoins nous semble inévitable, tant que l'Allemagne persistera dans ses visées et ses aspirations actuelles.[80]

This document explains why Hall was not prepared to make concessions and suspend or arrange for the suspension of those points in the constitution which related to Schleswig. Many years of experience had convinced him that no concessions on Denmark's part would satisfy Germany, and that the latter's only aim was to detach Schleswig from Denmark. The most he would do, as he admitted, was to agree not to resist the Federal Execution, and he only took this step at the wish of friendly powers.[81]

Ewers' and Wodehouse's last meeting with Hall took place on 26 December, after the latter had effectively left office though formally he was still in power. The purpose of this meeting was to inform him that the British government had agreed to the convening of a conference of the signatories to the Treaty of London together with a representative of the German Confederation, in Paris. Although Ewers had not yet received instructions on this matter he decided to accompany Wodehouse, wanting to provide new proof of cooperation between Britain and Russia. (Later, instructions came from Gorchakov expressing agreement, telling him to cooperate with Wodehouse, and adding that if the latter had not received instructions he, Ewers, should act on his own as time was pressing - 'insinuez seul, temps presse',[82] said the telegram from St. Petersburg on 17 December (old style). Wodehouse informed Hall that Prussia had decided to go to war if the constitution had not been suspended by 1 January 1864 and Bismarck, although in favour of upholding the Treaty of London, was not in a position to resist public opinion.[83] The meeting was brief, and Hall received Ewers and Wodehouse coldly, although

---

80. Circulaire no. 39. Fond Kantselariya, god 1863, Delo 41, vol. 65.
81. Neergaard suggested that since the sudden death of Frederick VII, Hall was governed by a sort of fatalistic belief that a serious crisis was inevitable and he had come to regard himself less as a leader who could choose his paths and direct his country's policy towards a definite goal, than as an instrument in the hands of a mightier power. (Vol. II, p. 883). His argument is much more convincing than E. Arups opinion. Arup interpreted Hall's policy after the death of Frederick VII as an attempt to create a domestic crisis for the purpose of bringing about a "Scandinavian revolution". 'David og Hall ...', pp. 166ff.
82. Gorchakov's telegram to Nicolay, the text of which was approved by the Tsar, ran as follows: 'Insinuez au Danemark demander Conférence, exclusivement sur question Danoise, composé des Représentantes de Puissances ayant signé Traité de Londres, avec adjonction de délegué de Confédération Germanique. Nous n'objectons pas à Paris'. (Vol. 65).
83. See Russell's instructions of 26 December, no. 521, *Denmark* ... vol. I, pp. 426-7, and Wodehouse to Russell, 26 December, no. 555, *ibid.* p. 446.

he described the proposal as 'une dernnière planche de salut offerte au Denmark'. The reason for this seems to have been that Hall was afraid Russell's proposals to convene a conference in Paris would be ill received by the country (France) whose own proposal to convene a European conference had recently been rejected. Ewers soon saw that Hall was right, for France opposed a conference 'pour un but spécial', as Fleury said.

Hall promised to inform the King about the suggestion of convening a conference. After Hall's departure, Ewers expressed the following opinion of him in his report to Gorchakov on 16 (28) December. He considered that, by his behaviour, Hall had made his successor's task more difficult, to such an extent that a man with a courage rarely met among statesmen would be needed to take on the post of head of the government. Hall, in Ewers' opinion, had done everything he could to make it impossible for the King to entrust the formation of a government to people of a different political colour. He had also entrusted the position of chief of police to someone (Crone) who would not ensure order in the capital if the King suspended the constitution.[84]

A new government had not yet been formed, so Germany could not be shown evidence that Denmark's policy would change. But, in Ewers opinion, the diplomatic action had not been fruitless. The idea of recalling the Rigsraad was being seriously discussed, the old government had gone, and the situation had changed to such an extent that further pressure could compromise the King. For that reason Russia should refrain from any extreme action before a new government was formed which would be more inclined to listen to the advice of friendly governments. That moment, in Ewers view, was not far off.

After the fall of Hall, the King appointed a government headed by D.G. Monrad. This change, Ewers thought, should facilitate the peaceful solution of the dispute with Germany. On the other hand, however, because the Rigsraad was in recess the new government could not immediately suspend the constitution, or abolish it. For this reason, too, Ewers concluded that pressure on the government at that juncture could not produce any result, and that his and Wodehouse's presence in Copenhagen could only be harmful, as suspicions might arise that they wanted to influence the King's advisers in an anti-constitutional direction.[85] Ewers thought that Nicolay could solve any problems that arose and would be able to exercise a healthy influence on the government. If Gorchakov agreed, he would

---

84. This assessment is balanced in comparison with the view of Hall given by Queen Louise at this point.

Sie beurtheilten die Sache ganz wie der König u. ich, nur banden die Umstände ihm sehr die Hände, aber mit Hall war nichts zu beginnen er ist nach meiner Ansicht ein gehährlicherer Mensch gewesen als alle andern u. *ein Verräther seines Vaterlandes* indem er alles *unbemerkt* zu dessen *Auflösung hin lenkte* u. nur der *schnelle* Todt des K. Fried. verhinderte die Ausführung des mit *Schweden* gefassten Planes, nämlich durch *Krieg,* da er die Execution als Kriegserklärung nehmen wollte, u. Schweden als Hülfe *die Inseln* besetzt natürlich als Eigenthum nach her behielte ...

Letter from Queen Louise to O. Plessen, 6 Januar 1864 (emphasis in the original). O. Plessen, Privatarkiv, no. 6128, A I 2, R.A. Copenhagen.

85. Ewers, 19 (31) December 1863.

like to depart at the same time as Wodehouse, who had asked Russell for permission to leave Copenhagen.[86] Ewers' telegram crossed with a telegram dispatched from St. Petersburg on 19 (31) December in which Gorchakov instructed him to exert pressure on the Danish government to agree to participate in a possible conference which was to be held in Paris to settle the Danish-German differences.

Ewers then went with Wodehouse to Monrad, the head of the new government, to suggest that he should propose the convening of a conference, and if Monrad were to propose Paris as the venue for it Russia would have no objection. 'He' (Ewers) – we learn from Wodehouse's report to Russell – 'pointed out forcibly that in critical situation of affairs the Danish Government should lose no time in determining what course they should pursue'.[87] Monrad, Ewers reported on 19 (31) December, said that personally he was not against this proposal, but he had doubts about what position France would take, as he had learned from Dotézac that the proposal did not suit France, and besides that the cabinet had not yet been formed and he would have to consult Quaade (who was returning from Berlin to take up the post of minister of foreign affairs) and other colleagues. The next day Wodehouse reported that he had learned from Vedel, who had it from the Danish ambassador in Paris, that the Emperor of the French 'will not consent to a Conference on the affairs of Denmark unless it is attended by all the Powers of Europe. In these circumstances it does not seem probable that Denmark will make any proposal for a Conference', Wodehouse concluded.[88]

However, Monrad returned to the question of a conference immediately the cabinet was formed. He asked Ewers and Wodehouse to call on him,[89] informed them of the appointment of Quaade to the post of minister of foreign affairs, and said that he wanted to ask the signatories to the Treaty of London to organise mediation, whether in the form of a conference or a congress. In this he would like to base himself on the decisions of the Congress of Paris in 1856, which provided for the use of mediation rather than resort to war in cases of dispute between states. Denmark no longer had diplomatic relations with Berlin and Vienna and it was not possible to ask the German Confederation to take part in mediation, although he was not opposed to this if some way could be found to arrange it. But at the same time he insisted that the *status quo* before 1 January 1864 (i.e. after the date of the Federal Execution in Holstein) must be preserved during the negotiations. Monrad emphasised that if German troops entered Schleswig this would be regarded as an act of war 'which must at all hazards be resisted by force',[90] and that the King could not change the constitutional statute without the agreement of the Rigsraad. Although the government would like it to, the Rigsraad could not reassemble before 1 April.[91]

86. *Ibid.*
87. No. 592, 30 December 1863, p. 471. See also Napier to Russell, nos. 610, 611, 29 and 31 December, in *Denmark ...*, vol. I, p. 483.
88. No. 593, 31 December 1863, pp. 471-2.
89. Ewers, 24 December 1863 (5 January 1864).
90. Wodehouse to Russell, 4 January 1864, F.O. 22/306.
91. Wodehouse to Russell, 5 January 1864, F.O. 22/306.

It is also worth noting the views of the new head of government on Denmark's chances in the event of war.

The Bishop said he thought I underestimated the power of Denmark to resist Germany. He must admit indeed that, however brave a resistance the Danish Army might offer to the invasion of Schleswig and Jutland, the superior numbers of the Germans must ultimately prevail, but Denmark might carry on the war for two or three years from the Islands, harassing Germany by sea, while eventually, revolutions at home might compel the Germans to evacuate the Danish Peninsula, as in 1849.

Wodehouse expressed his doubts about this reasoning and these optimistic predictions:[92]

I knew well that the Danes were a gallant nation – and would oppose an obstinate resistance to any invading force however overwhelming – said Wodehouse – but it was unnecessary to discuss the chances of war if we were agreed that it was a wiser policy to endeavour to avert the war by negotiation. The Bishop – concluded Wodehouse – is, I believe, really disposed to be more conciliatory than Mr. Hall, but such is the excited state of public opinion in this country, that no Minister ventures to admit the necessity for abandoning the uncompromising policy, which has brought the Monarchy into such imminent peril.[93]

The idea of a conference of European states conformed to the wishes of the British and Russian governments. Wodehouse and Ewers therefore supported it and asked Monrad not to waste time.[94] At this point Ewers thought his mission was concluded. He expected his request to leave Copenhagen at the same time as Wodehouse to be answered in the affirmative.

Owing to the fact that the King was going to visit the army in Schleswig for a week, Ewers and Wodehouse asked for a farewell audience, during which the King spoke about the formation of the new government, the scandalous behaviour of Prince Augustenburg and the chaos in Holstein, while thanking Ewers for his mission and the Tsar for his interest in the problems of Denmark. He said he wanted to confer Le Grand Croix de Ordre du Danebrog on Ewers and would ask for Gorchakov's agreement.[95]

On 24 December 1863 (5 January 1864) Nicolay received a telegram in code which ran as follows:

Pour Ewers. A moins de raisons très concluantes que Vous expliqueriez, ne prolongez pas Votre séjour au delà de celui de Wodehouse et revenez ici. Il ne nous convient pas de rester seuls en première ligne. Gorchakov.

On 26 December (7 January) Nicolay reported to Gorchakov that Ewers and Wodehouse had left that evening.[96] The same day Wodehouse reported to London:

92. See Johan Schioldam Nielsen, *D.G. Monrad. En patografi* (Odense, 1983).
93. Wodehouse to Russell, 2 January 1864. F.O. 22/306.
94. Ewers, 24 December (5 January), vol. 65: Wodehouse to Russell, 3 January 1864, no. 632, *Denmark...*, vol. I, pp. 494-5.
95. Ewers, 23 December (4 January). He was awarded this cross on 31 December 1863. *Kongelig Dansk Hof og Statskalender for Aaret 1866*, p. 11.
96. Vol. 67, Delo, 212.

I have the honour to report that M. d'Ewers has received orders from the Russian Government to leave Copenhagen at the same time with me, and he will accordingly take his departure to-day.

I cannot omit this opportunity of acknowledging the advantage which I have derived from his cordial and efficient co-operation with me throughout my mission to this capital.[97]

III

The Ewers and Wodehouse mission took place at an important moment when a turning point was looming in the history of Europe. As a result of the collapse of the Polish uprising, fundamental changes in the European constellation ensued, and towards the end of 1863 the pattern of forces which arose after the Crimean War was finally broken, although it should be noted that for some years it had been only partially sustained, more by inertia than anything else.

The Ewers mission came at the moment when Danish society and the Danish government had become convinced that it was not possible to capitulate politically to a Germany which was not concerned about the German duchies but only in detaching Schleswig from Denmark.

Gorchakov's initiative in sending a special mission to Copenhagen was indeed accepted by France and Britain. In Copenhagen co-operation with Britain proved possible and effective for Russia. Britain, like Russia, was interested both in preserving the integrity of Denmark and in maintaining the balance of power in the north, which meant not allowing the formation of a Scandinavian union, which would probably have followed the defeat of Denmark and the detachment of the duchies. Britain and Russia were anxious that the emergence of such a union under the aegis of Sweden would lead to an increase in French influence in that part of Europe and would upset the previous balance of power in the Baltic.

Although Gorchakov stressed his neutrality in the conflict, it is impossible not to notice that from the very beginning the mission took the line of satisfying Germany's, or, more precisely Bismarck's, aspirations.[98] Even Wodehouse, who valued his cooperation with Ewers highly, observed that Ewers did not take a completely objective position, and he was of the opinion that during his stay in Berlin. Ewers had been excessively influenced by Bismarck.[99] He finally concluded that

> Mr. d'Ewers, on the other hand, and Mr. de Nicolay are evidently in earnest in their desire to arrive at some understanding with their colleagues, but in their anxiety to prevent the outbreak of war, they seem disposed to counsel Denmark to yield everything to the German demands.

---

97. No. 661, *Denmark* ... vol. 4, pp. 512-13. Cf. P.R.O. F.O. 30/22. Denmark 1859 to 1865, vol. 51. Wodehouse to Russell, 22 December. "Ewers has acted most cordially with me!"
98. D. Hillerbrand, *Bismarck and Gorchakov,* chapter 5.
99. Wodehouse to Russell, P.R.O. F.O. 22/306, 16 December 1863.

Hall and Monrad too took a similar view of Ewers from the start. Hall was deeply convinced that Germany was out to destroy the Danish monarchy. Russia, he argued, claimed that she did not see what Germany's intentions were. How could she have been so obtuse as not to see through German plans? The Ewers mission only served to convince him on which side Russia stood and what her aim was.

From the beginning, before his arrival in Copenhagen, Wodehouse had doubts as to whether the mission would achieve positive results. He doubted if it would succeed in convincing the Danish government to accept the German demands. If a common constitution proved unacceptable owing to lack of agreement between the monarchy and the duchies, then by the same measure the Danes would feel that they could not be compelled to create an absolutely independent Schleswig, connected with the monarchy only by personal union. Therefore, he wrote to Russell on 16 December, 'some middle way' had to be found.[100] But how to find it, if 'both parties are blinded with passion', and how to 'discover some way of moving this stiff necked race' (the Danes)?

> These people here are so stiff-necked and so ready to imagine that by sheer obstinacy they may get out of the scrape without making any concession that I attach importance to a step which binds them to accept negotiation upon the whole matter.[101]

If Schleswig were attacked, however, said the British diplomat, King, government and people were unanimous that they should fight. As far as Monrad was concerned, Wodehouse's opinion of him did not differ from Ewers'.

> Monrad is more pleasant and reasonable in his manner than Hall, and he has the reputation, which he seems to deserve, of a man of ability but when we come to arranging the terms of a definitive settlement we shall find him, I suspect, not much more tractable than other Danes.[102]

Reflecting on the mood in Denmark, he observed that the hopes placed on the Scandinavian party had diminished somewhat because of Sweden's behaviour, but pro-Scandinavian feeling was still strong. He realized that the violent language he heard struck him more forcibly since he was a newcomer to the situation, but no one was able to answer the question which he put continually.

> What Denmark can gain by the present policy? The only defence offered for it is that nothing is now left for Denmark, but to perish after a desperate resistance. This may appear a mere exaggeration, but in sober seriousness I am convinced that this idea has penetrated deep into the heart of the people, and it is the knowledge of this feeling which makes it so difficult to induce anyone to undertake to form a Cabinet with a basis of a pacific policy.
>
> I endeavour to prove that the chances of negotiations are infinitely preferable to the continuity of a war against an overwhelming force, but it is a hard task to drive any idea into the heart of their people. I admire the patriotism, but I cannot say much for their political intelligence.[103]

100. P.R.O. The Russell Papers. Vol. 51.
101. *Ibid.* 5 January 1864, p. 200a.
102. *Ibid.*
103. *Ibid.* Wodehouse to Russell, 29 December 1863, p. 289.

Ewers was presumably of a similar opinion.

There was great interest in the Ewers-Wodehouse mission in Copenhagen at the time. Dotézac saw Ewers' action as mainly or solely an attempt to compel the government to make unilateral concessions to Germany at any price; when he ran into objections he sought the overthrow of Hall's government, because of its inflexible and uncompromising attitude, and its replacement with a government whose policy would be closer to the King's heart and the line being followed by the Russian cabinet. The Belgian ambassador, Bosch, had no doubt that Hall's dismissal was 'causée par la pression exercée par les envoyés speciaux de la Russie et de l'Angleterre'.[104] After the end of the mission he reported to Brussels on 7 January 1864:

Le résultat des négociations semble satisfaire également toutes les parties. La France n'a en aucun rôle en cette affaire. La Suède semble s'être également tenue à l'écart.

While the mission was still in progress, Gorchakov himself assessed it as follows:

Il est après cela fort satisfait de la manière dont M. Ewers s'est acquitté de la délicate mission, qui lui à déjà confiée à Copenhague, mais ne cache pourtant pas que le premier succès (la démission du Ministère Hall) de cet Envoyé est encore loin de résoudre les nombreuses et sérieuses difficultés inhérentes à la situation. De mon côté, j'ai franchement avoué mes doutes sur la possibilité de faire accepter par le Rigsraad et la nation les concessions en sens allemand, dont il s'agit et l'heure où j'écris le Cabinet de Copenhague doit déjà avoir pris son part dans un sens, ou dans l'autre, car le Prime Ministre me dit savoir de source certaine, que l'Allemagne n'attendrait que jusqu'au 1 janvier pour agir d'une manière plus active et déterminée.[105]

Thus, according to this Swedish diplomat's report, the greatest success of the mission in Gorchakov's view was its contribution to the dismissal of Hall and the fall of his government. But the Vice-Chancellor still had great doubts as to whether the newly appointed government in Copenhagen would comply with Russia's wishes.[106]

---

104. No. 230, 25 December 1863. Afskrifter af akter i det belgiske udenrigsministeriums arkiv 1863-64. Vol. II. Afskrifter og fotokopier fra udenlandske arkiver vedr. dansk udenrigspolitik, p.k. 11. Privatarkiver historikerens Aage Friis, 5424, R.A. Copenhagen.
105. Wedel-Jarlsberg, no. 1, 1 January (20 December).
106. Scheele-Plessen's report to Hall on 31 December 1863 has the following to say on Russia's attitude to Denmark. (It may be presumed that this was the opinion of Dashkov or another of the Russian diplomats in Stockholm).
    Nous croyons Vous rendre service en Vous engageant à agir de façon à ôter à l'Allemagne tout prétexte pour dépasser les limites d'une exécution générale. Quant à cela je réplique [this was the Danish ambassador's reply] que dans d'autres temps la Russie certes n'aurait pas tenu un pareil langage, j'entends de nouveaux le refrain: "Que voulez-Vous, les temps ont changé". Helas?
    Sverige. Dep. 1862-65, no. 67, 31 December 1863.

7. Gorchakov and the Outbreak of the Danish-German War

I

By the autumn of 1863 the Polish question had ceased to be a real threat to Russia, although Gorchakov continually referred to it in the context of a threat to the Empire and frequently used this argument as a justification for all kinds of Russian diplomatic moves.

Comme tous les Russes, M le Ministre, – wrote Massignac – le Vice-Chancelier perd son calme lorsqu'on prononce devant lui le mot »Pologne«. »C'est que Vous me dites« – m'a-t-il répondu avec vivacité, M de Lhuys l'a déjà dit à M de Budberg, mais la Pologne est pour nous une question vitale, et à côté d'elle, toutes les autres sont secondaires.[1]

It is true that, unlike the Polish question and its place in Russian policy, the Danish question did not play a crucial role in Russian strategy. But in the context of the general principles of the St Petersburg cabinet's policy, which aimed to maintain peace and preserve the *status quo* in Europe, the Danish-German dispute and its possible consequences could have incalculable effects on the peace of Europe.[2] 'Malheureusement l'horizon politique qui est encore bien sombre nous oblige de nous préparer aux plus mauvaises chances; aussi nos preparatifs militaires sont poussées avec la plus grande vigeur', the Tsar wrote to Prince A.I. Baryatinsky from Tsarskoe Selo on 22 November (4 December) 1863, when he received news of the worsening conflict on the Elbe.[3] A few weeks later, in another letter to Baryatinsky, Alexander II wrote as follows: 'En Pologne les affaires s'améliorent décidément et depuis les complications du Holstein, cette question se trouve reléguée sur le second plan, ce qui pourtant ne diminue nullement notre vigilance'.[4]

Towards the end of 1863 and during the early months of 1864, diplomats and politicians were considering what position Russia would take in the Danish-German conflict. Political circles in both France and Britain came to the conclu-

---

1. A.M.A.E., Paris, no. 59, 29 November, Russie, no 232. k. 230 v.
2. Clarendon was right when he said: 'It is not the Polish torch that frightens me, but the Holstein match'. R.W. Seton-Watson, *Britain and Europe, 1789-1914. A Survey of Foreign Policy.* (Cambridge, 1937), p. 445. See also Russell's circular of 28 December 1863 in *The Cambridge History of British Foreign Policy 1783-1919*, vol. II, 1815-1866, ed. Sir A.W. Ward and P.G. Gooch (Cambridge, 1923), Chapter XIII, 'The Schleswig-Holstein Question, 1852-1866', p. 522.
3. A. Rieber, *The Politics of Autocracy. Letters of Alexander II to Prince A.I. Bariatinskii, 1857-1864* (Paris and The Hague, 1966), p. 151.
4. Letter of 10 (22) February 1864, Rieber, *The Politics ...* p. 152.

sion that owing the the internal difficulties she had been going through since the Crimean War, her exceptionally difficult financial situation, and the trouble over the Polish question, Russia would not enter the war. This view was expressed in December by the Danish ambassador in Paris, Moltke, citing the opinion of Drouyn de Lhuys.[5] A similar view was expressed by the Danish ambassador in London, T. Bille, in a memorandum written somewhat later at the request of his minister, Quaade: 'La Russie impuissante pour le moment d'intervenir dans les affaires de l'Europe se garderait surtout de contrecarrer de quelque manière que ce soit les intérêts de la Prussie'.[6]

The same conclusions were reached by the anonymous author of a note on the military state of Russia sent from St Petersburg to Paris, which emphasised the impossibility of Russian intervention because of her financial difficulties and consequent inability to equip a modern army; the problems connected with the situation in Poland, and the backwardness of the country, reflected particularly in the bad state of the railways.[7] Finally, A. de Valois, a former French consul-general in Russia, argued that Denmark, as a small state and, in addition a democratically governed one, could not count on help from Russia. 'On devait penser que la Russie ne voudrait jamais se brouiller avec l'Allemagne pour protéger un petit Etat, qui n'avait pas à ses yeux, le mérite d'être gouverné par de hommes imbus de saines doctrines professées au Palais d'Hiver'.[8] They all correctly judged that the Russian cabinet had no intention of allowing the country to be drawn into the war.

Starting from her overriding aim of maintaining peace in Europe, Russia was interested in strengthening the alliance between the two great conservative German states and also in a rapprochement between the three northern powers and Britain, in order to prevent the latter joining up with France. Faced with the deteriorating situation in northern Europe, and the break-up of the London-Paris axis, Gorchakov aimed to set up an alliance of the conservative states, Russia, Austria and Prussia, and to persuade Britain to join it, since she was no less interested than Russia in maintaining peace and feared that the plans of Napoleon III would undermine the *status quo* in Europe.

The tsarist autocracy was afraid of France's entry into the war, whether on Prussia's side or against her, among other things because this could lead to the revival of nationalist and revolutionary movements in Europe. Furthermore, France's involvement would once again put the Polish question on the agenda and would strengthen French influence in Germany and Scandinavia. If Austria and Prussia were to be defeated, Russia would find herself confronting France. And again the

---

5. Lettre confidentielle, Paris, 5 December 1863. Udenrigsmin. Dep. Frankrig, R.A. Copenhagen.
6. Confidential, no. 28, 1 March 1864, Udenrigsmin. England Depecher, 1864, R.A. Copenhagen, in reply to Quaade's dispatch no 13, 16 February 1864.
7. A.M.A.E. Russie, vol. 232. Annexe to political report no. 63, 19 December 1863. W. Wolowski also wrote of Russia's inability to go to war because of the bad state of her finances, 'Les Finances de la Russie', *Revue des Deux Mondes,* vol. 49, (1864) pp. 431-52.
8. A.M.A.E. Mémoires et documents. Danemark 1864-1866. Question des Duchés, III. vol. 14.

Polish question would be revived. These fears of French intervention and help in the defence of Denmark were deliberately inflamed by Bismarck, who sought to use this trump in his diplomatic game. He frightened Russia by claiming that Napoleon III was preparing to implement his plans for the Rhineland, and, furthermore, that his plan included landing French troops in Gdansk in support of the Polish cause. Bismarck said this even though he was personally convinced that France did not intend to intervene in defence of Denmark.

Britain's accession to the alliance of the three northern powers, in Gorchakov's opinion, would be very important in facilitating the settlement of the Danish-German conflict, which was being transformed from a diplomatic and political conflict into a military one. It would mean the isolation of the national-liberal elements in Germany, which were very much alive, and relying on the two great conservative German powers in the Danish-German dispute, which continued to declare their support for the Treaty of London. It would mean, too, the isolation of the German 'Triad' created by Beust, Pforden and Dalwigk (Saxony, Bavaria and Hesse-Darmstadt)[9] and would prevent France from subordinating the lesser German states to herself and transforming them into something in the nature of a French prefecture, Gorchakov wrote to Olga Nikolaevna.[10] It would also mean preservation of the balance of power in the north and would block the creation of a Scandinavian union, which Napoleon III was very concerned to bring about.

But at the same time it would mean giving the larger German states, and particularly Prussia, a free hand in their conflict with Denmark. As Lenz wrote later, however friendly Russia's feelings towards Denmark might have been, she was not in a position to risk a loosening of her relations with Prussia, and furthermore, she took care to try to persuade both Britain and Austria to take a favourable attitude towards Prussia.[11] This was precisely how both Wilhelm I and Bismarck interpreted the idea of a four-way entente when they received a report about it from Redern and learned that Gorchakov was urging the idea on Prussia.[12]

Russia's relationship with Prussia occupied a central place in Gorchakov's entire conception of affairs. There can be no question that Gorchakov, an experienced diplomat who had lived in Germany for many years, was already aware then, on the basis of the reports sent to St Petersburg,[13] that the dispute over the duchies was about something more than just taking them from Denmark. He knew that the central problem to be solved was the unification of Germany. He had, after all, spent the turbulent years 1848-49 in Germany and had followed the struggle

---

9. In many works the Triad is said to comprise Saxony, Bavaria and Württemberg.
10. Letter of 13 March 1864 (old style) in H.S.A. Stuttgart, G 314, Bü 7, dokument n. 84.
11. M. Lenz, *Geschichte Bismarcks*, (1913), p. 233.
12. APP IV, pp. 183-4, Redern to Bismarck, 20 November 1863. *Die Auswärtige Politik Preussens.*
13. It is worth quoting the opinion of the King of Württemberg, William I, expressed to the Russian ambassador, Titov, at the end of 1863: Querelle danoise, n'est qu'un point de transition pour en venir à l'unité nationale représentée dans un parlement germanique'. Titov to Gorchakov, 31 (19) December 1863. H.S.A. Stuttgart, E 73, Gesandtschaftsakten, Württembergische Gesandtschaft St Petersburg, 1808-1893, Fasc. 86, 1860-1865.

between the different political tendencies and the accompanying rivalry between Austria and Prussia, as well as the battle between the progressive and conservative forces about the character and means of unification of Germany. In the summer of 1863 there had even been serious differences of opinion over the reorganisation of the German Confederation between Austria and Prussia, or, more precisely, between Austria and Bismarck.

Gorchakov, therefore, faced with the political crisis at the close of 1863, must certainly have pondered about how the dispute with Denmark, into which virtually the whole of Germany had been drawn, might influence the tendencies towards unification which were so strong in all German circles. Gorchakov must have been presented with a dilemma: what was better for Russia – the *status quo*, that is, the continuation of the German Confederation, or the unification of Germany under the aegis of Prussia. But unification of Germany was not in the Russian tradition, nor in the interest of Russia. In the past Russia had tried to maintain the federal form of organisation in Germany as an important element in her own security and something necessary for the balance of power in Europe. In 1815 Russia had supported the existence of Germany in this form, but at the same time she had been concerned to preserve a balance between the two larger German states. This had been Russian policy since the Congress of Vienna, under Alexander I and Nicholas I, right down to the outbreak of the Crimean War.

On the other hand Gorchakov presumably recognised that in 1812 and 1853 a defeated Germany had been in no position to protect Russia against French aggression. It may be that these experiences, and the more recent one during the Polish uprising, inclined the Vice-Chancellor to think that it would be better if a conservative Prussia, on friendly terms with Russia, strengthened its position in Europe. This may have led him to support Bismarck's policy, the more so as he was convinced, both during the Crimean War and in 1863, that Russia could count only on Prussia, with which she had so many ties.[14] And he was not alone; Palmerston, as we know, also favoured strengthening Prussia's position in Europe, seeing it as an important element in restraining the aspirations of Napoleon III.

It is true that Gorchakov could not know Bismarck's short or long-term plans since, as we know, Bismarck changed and adapted them to suit the situation, but Bismarck did not hide the fact that his aim was to bring about a fundamental change in the constellation of forces in Germany and Prussia's place in it. In a talk with Oubril in September 1863 Bismarck uttered the following words: 'You are accustomed to a Prussia that lives quietly between Berlin and Sans Souci and goes, if necessary, to Olmuntz. The time for that is absolutely past'.[15] But Gorchakov disregarded this and other comments and doubts expressed by Oubril about Bismarck's policy.

---

14. See Gorchakov to Saburov, 8 (20) January 1880, no. 60. pp. 256-7; in V.G. Revunienkov, *Pol'skoe vosstanie 1863 i evropeiskaya diplomatiya*, (Leningrad, 1957), p. 350.
15. Oubril's report, no. 297, 15 September 1863; see R.H. Lord, 'Bismarck and Russia', *American Historical Review*, vol. 29, (1923), pp. 47ff; Steefel, p. 257.

There were, however, many among Gorchakov's closest colleagues who were uneasy about the attitude of the Prussian government. I. Tyutchev, for example, told A. Nikitenko he believed that while Prussia did indeed incline towards Russia, which he regarded as quite natural, her current government was behaving in an absurd manner. ('No idiotskie nyneshnee pravlenie v nei delaet iz nee chto-to nelepoe'). 'German unity', Tyutchev added soon afterwards, 'is a complete and utter fantasy' ('Germanskoe edinstvo – chistaya i pustaya fantaziya'.)

Other diplomats accredited to Berlin also had doubts about Bismarck's intentions. This is what Buchanan wrote:

Es ist schwer zu sagen, was Bismarck schliesslich tun wird. Er ist ein Politiker nach der L(ouis) (Napoleon?). – Art und offentsichtlich zu allen Eventualitäten bereit, treu allein der Vergrösserung Preussens mit allen nur möglichen Mitteln – ein würdiger Schüler des Grossen Friedrich'.[16]

Gorchakov also disregarded suggestions by Bismarck in December that maintenance of the provisions of the Treaty of London could prove problematical as the provisions might turn out to be unsatisfactory.[17] He was satisfied with the fact that Bismarck spoke generally in favour of maintenance of the treaty, saying 'honour and wisdom dictate that there should be no doubt about our [Prussia's – E.H.] faithfulness in adhering to our obligations'. Gorchakov surely knew that Bismarck took this position mainly because, by adhering to the provisions of the treaty, Prussia could intervene in the Schleswig question and at the same time keep both the German Conferation and the lesser German states out of the dispute with Denmark.[18] Bismarck had no fears about the attitude of Russia, which in his view occupied the key position in the whole matter. As Goltz reported from Paris after a talk with Budberg and, more important, Redern confirmed after a conversation with Gorchakov, Russia had no intention of coming to the material aid of Denmark in the event of the dispute deteriorating into an armed conflict. Russia merely emphasised that she favoured maintenance of the provisions of the Treaty of London and the integrity of the Danish monarchy. Gorchakov stressed that preservation of the Danish monarchy was essential, for if it were weakened this would lead to the strengthening of Sweden. The Vice-Chancellor considered that Denmark should meet the demands of the German Confederation and make changes in the constitution. He saw Federal Execution as a legal step, but he saw it also as the first step towards the break-up of Denmark, because the population of Holstein would make use of the shield provided by the execution armies to proclaim the separa-

---

16. Buchanan to Wodehouse, 25 December 1863, also Buchanan to Russell, no. 630, Confidential, 22 December 1863. F.O. 64/547, in Voigt, pp. 91-92, 173-5.
17. *G.W.IV,* (Berlin, 1929), p. 223.
18. 'Er musste vielmehr den Weg des Londoner Protokolles wahlen', we read in E. Marks' work, *Kaiser Wilhelm I,* 'weil nur dieser ihn gegen das drohende Ausland sicherte und ohne internationale Schwierigkeiten auch die Besetzung des nicht zum Bunde gehörigen Schleswigs erlaubte'. (p. 236). See also Z. Grot, *Pruska polityka narodowościowa w Szleswigu, 1864-1920,* p. 60.

tion of Holstein from Denmark.[19] But Gorchakov did not accept the Danish point of view that the German side was also not without blame, although there was no lack of voices among Russian diplomats saying that Denmark was not the only party responsible for the conflict.

One example was Ivan Petrovich Ozerov, Russian ambassador to Bavaria from 1863 to 1880.[20] On 24 (12) December 1863 Ozerov handed the minister a memorandum in which he set out his view of the Danish-German conflict.[21] In his memorandum,[22] Ozerov described both the historical background to the dispute over Schleswig and the current state of affairs and the attitudes of the great powers to the problem. In the historical section he said that since time immemorial Schleswig had been an integral part of Denmark, guaranteed by treaties with France, Britain, Sweden and Russia in 1720 and 1773, and that a process of Germanisation of Schleswig had been deliberately carried out by the Germans living in Holstein, with the aim of gaining political influence and extending the power of the Holstein aristocracy over the Danish monarchy. Basing itself on the 'nexus socialis', the Holstein aristocracy had worked for many years to make the administration of the two duchies not only common and indivisible but also different from that of the Danish monarchy in the narrow sense of the word.

These tendencies could be recognised in 1848-49. But then, when General Wrangel entered Jutland, Nicholas I had taken energetic and effective counteraction *vis-à-vis* Berlin. As far as the basic promises and obligations contained in the Danish declarations of 9 December 1851 and 29 January 1852, and the Austrian and Prussian declarations of 26 and 30 December 1851, were concerned, he saw them as follows.

On the Danish side:

1. To establish a common constitution for the whole of the monarchy, while retaining the provincial estates, which would deal with the special affairs of each part of the monarchy.
2. Not to incorporate Schleswig into the monarchy in the narrow sense of the word.
3. To give equal positions, rights and privileges to the Danish and German elements in the monarchy.

The larger German states had declared that:

1. The problem of Schleswig-Holstein would never arise again.
2. There would be no political relations between the two duchies.
3. The Diet in Frankfurt would never seek to extend its competence to, or inter-

---

19. See Goltz' report of 27 November and Redern's of 1 December 1863 to Bismarck. APP IV, pp. 217-8 and 246-7.
20. *Ocherk istorii ministerstva inostrannykh del, 1802-1902,* (St. Petersburg, 1902).
21. A copy was appended to Wedel-Jarlsberg's report, no. 2, 2 January 1864 (21 December 1863). St. Stockholm. Bes. från Petersburg, 1864.
22. Aperçu historique, mêlé observations, de la quéstion Dano-Allemande.

fere in, the internal affairs of any country which was not a part of the German Confederation (this mainly concerned Schleswig).

Germany was accusing Denmark of not carrying out her obligations scrupulously. Ozerov admitted that the Copenhagen cabinet could have been more inspired in setting about the prompt establishment of complete equality between the two national groups residing in the monarchy. But Germany for its parts could not enjoy all the benefits (les bénéfices) without bearing any of the costs (les charges) and, to be fair, it had to be recognised that Germany, too, was at fault and the illegal pressure (extralégal) from the German states, and particularly the Frankfurt Diet, should be taken into account as well. This pressure had been exerted on Danish governments from Bluhme and Ørstedt to Scheele and Hall. The Frankfurt Diet in 1858 had threatened Federal Execution because it judged that the moment was ripe to overthrow the common constitution of 29 July 1852 on the pretext that the estates of Holstein did not want it.

'... c'est encore par cette raison, dis-je, que le Ministère actuel a dû abandonner l'idée du 'Gesamtstatt'[23] – et en venir à la proposition de 'l'Eyderstatt', avec une espèce d'union personelle pour le Holstein, c'est à dire, que ce Duché aurait une administration et une législation autant que possible distinctes'.

This showes distinctly that Ozerov blamed the Frankfurt Diet for the crisis and for the deterioration of the relationship between the Duchies and Denmark.

In Ozerov's opinion, the idea of a close link between Denmark and Schleswig had been born out of the difficulties and troubles which Denmark had experienced in this situation, and he saw this as the genesis of the 18 November Constitution. As for Denmark's prospects in the event of war, he considered that her army was well organised, courageous and capable of resisting and holding the German forces behind the Dannewirke line. Help from outside, on the other hand, was only a possibility. Although Russia's situation was fundamentally different from what it had been in 1849, when Nicholas I had supported intervention in the Danish-German dispute on Denmark's side, he thought that Russia should not be indifferent towards German claims against Denmark, because the principles which the democratic elements in Germany were proclaiming were dangerous, especially on account of the Polish question. Furthermore, and to this he wished to draw Gorchakov's special attention, by backing the German demands, Russia would help to bring about results which were diametrically opposed to her own interests. The weakening and partitioning of the Danish monarchy would lead to the creation of a stronger Scandinavia and a stronger German naval power.[24] 'Or, ni l'une ni l'autre de ces éventualités ne conviendrait certes à la Russie', said Ozerov.[25]

23. I.e. The Whole-State.
24. K. Döhler, *Napoleon III und die deutsch-dänische Frage,* considers that the possibility that Kiel would become a German port was seen even earlier in France. See Oscar I to Manderström, 6 December 1856, Ep. M.1, K.B. Gullberg ..., p. 36.
25. La Russie. La réorganisation complète de l'Empire, avec les vastes réformes administratives et

As far as Britain's position was concerned, he thought that in the last resort Denmark could count on her help, as British interests were involved in the whole affair. In the case of France, however, he wondered whether Napoleon III might not want to take advantage of the situation to carry out his Rhineland plans. As for the attitude of Sweden-Norway, it was as usual urging Copenhagen to be conciliatory and restrained, and to make concessions to the Germans in Schleswig. It was not interested in Holstein, which lay within the competence of the German Confederation, but would not be able to remain an observer if Schleswig were attacked – and this for two reasons: the necessity of defending a just cause and loyalty to tradition.

As far as the attitudes of Austria, Prussia and the German Confederation were concerned, however, Ozerov stressed that when the Germans spoke about Holstein they always had Schleswig in mind, were secretly aiming to acquire ports on the Baltic Sea, and were continually returning to the plans frustrated in 1848-49. He stated without reservation that Prussia's aim was the division of Denmark. Hitherto Rechberg and Bismarck had stood up to the democratic elements, but, as the King of Bavaria said, Hannover, Saxony and other sovereigns of lesser German states, as well as the cabinets of Vienna and Berlin, could be expected to find themselves in dire straits and Denmark would benefit from this.

Thus Ozerov's point of view on the Danish-German conflict, as we can see, was much more objective on some points, including fundamental ones like the origin and development of the conflict, than that of his government. He was also able to look the truth in the eye where the real aims of Germany, and particularly Prussia, were concerned. He warned the Russian government that one-sided support of Germany and approval of the weakening of Denmark and the partitioning of the Danish monarchy were incompatible with Russia's interests. He also warned that if Russia followed such a policy, which was against her interests, a Scandinavian and a German naval power would appear in the Baltic – presumably he meant Prussia. But this memorandum was consigned to the archives.

sociales à y consacrer, – la crise financière du moment, – les embarras de la question Polonaise et la nécessité qui en découle de ne point occuper ailleurs les forces défensives du pays, – voilà autant de motifs pour que le Danemarc ne puisse guère s'attendre à une assistance matérielle Russe analogue à celle de 1849. – Mais s'il en est ainsi, les intérêts *positifs* de l'Empire n'en sont pas moins restés les mêmes que par le passé. – D'autres, que je qualifierai de passage, sont même venus s'y joindre. – C'est ainsi qu'il ne saura être indifférent à la Russie si les éléments démocratiques en Allemagne prennent le dessus; – car le countrecoup pourrait facilement se faire sentir en Pologne, juste au moment où l'Auguste volonté Impériale, après avoir réprimé l'émeute, se dispose à pacifier le Royaume, au moyen de la liberté, et de réforms civilisatrices sur une large échelle. – Une autre considération, basée sur le même ordre d'idées, est celle qu'en insistant aujourd'hui à Copenhague pour que le Danemarc contente l'Allemagne, le Cabinet de St. Petersburg se déclare dans le fait pour les nationalités. – Or, ce language pourrait facilement, il me semble, avoir des inconvénients, surtout si l'on n'est pas très-disposé à admettre le principe également chez soi et pour ses propres affaires.

Après celà-et j'en ai souvent loyalement fait l'observation à Monsieur le Vice-Chancelier – en favorisant plus ou moins les prétentions Allemandes, le Cabinet de St Pétersburg pourrait, en dernière analyse et en cas de réussite des dites prétentions, arriver à un résultat diametralement opposé à ses véritables intérêts; car l'affaiblissement et le démembrement de la Monarchie Danoise mène forcement, un jour ou un autre, à une forte Scandinavie et á une Allemagne-Puissance de Mer. Or, ni l'une, ni l'autre de ces éventualités ne conviendrait certes à la Russie.

II.

Alexander II and his minister favoured Bismarck, and did so all the more effectively beneath the cloak of neutrality (Klaczko). Fleischhauer called their conduct 'wohlvollende Neutralität'. Gorchakov, like the Tsar, accepted Bismarck's point of view on Federal Execution, arguing that it would restrain the growth of the revolutionary movement and was in a certain respect a recognition of Christian IX as Prince of Holstein and a member of the German Confederation, while at the same time it barred the way to Prince Augustenburg.[26] He defended Bismarck's behaviour to Russell and Napier. On 1 December, Napier reported to Russell:

Le langage du Prince Gortchakof me fait croire qu'il est persuadé que M de Bismarck a des *vues modérées* dans cette question. Le Vice-Chancelier est disposé à considérer une exécution fédérale, si elle est bien conduite, comme une *mesure conservatrice*. Dans son opinion, les troupes fédérales, agissant d'après des instructions judicieuses, assureraient l'ordre, et maintiendraient la distinction nécessaire entre la question législative et la question dynastique ...[27]

'Le Prince Gortchacow trouve qu'il y a péril en la demeure ...' reported Thun. 'Le Vice-Chancelier craint que les commissaires hanovrien et saxon dans le Holstein, n'aient pas l'autorité nécessaire pour s'opposer à un movement populaire et cela d'autant plus que les troupes saxonnes ne lui paraissent guère disposées à le réprimer. Il regrette en conséquence que ce ne soient des troupes autrichiennes ou prussiennes qui fussent chargées de l'éxécution fédérale'.[28] The whole expedition, as Bismarck intended, was interpreted by Russia as a military expedition for the purpose of defending the decision taken in London in 1852, rather than as an attack on the integrity of Denmark. Russia's emphasis on the integrity of Denmark as a *conditio sine qua non* of support for Austria and Prussia made an impression, particularly in Britain, where public opinion was on Denmark's side, and where the opposition did not conceal its dislike of Austria and Prussia, seeing the Prussian demands as a growing threat to Denmark.[29]

Towards Denmark, Gorchakov showed less and less tolerance and growing impatience, and he addressed her from the position of a great power, stressing that as a small state Denmark could not expect to do what Russia could do.[30] He would pay no attention to the Swedish ambassador's comments that the 1851-52 obligations were binding on both sides.[31] If Denmark did not listen to Russia and fulfil the obligations undertaken in 1851-52, derived from the provisions of the 1852 treaty,

---

26. See Oubril to Gorchakov, 30 (18) October 1863. APP IV, no. 161, pp. 234-5.
27. Quoted from J Klaczko, *Deux Chanceliers. Le Prince Gortchakof et le Prince de Bismarck* (Paris, 1876), p. 197.
28. Thun's report of 1 January (20 December), H.H.S.A., P.A.X. Kart. 55.
29. As Sandiford put it, 'Despite this strong anti-German feeling, however, the British people recognised the need for moderation and peace' (*Great Britain and the Schleswig-Holstein Question*, pp. 72-75).
30. This theme, that Denmark, as a small state, must make concessions to the united German forces, was also emphasised by Palmerston in a talk with the Danish Ambassador in London in January 1864.
31. 25 (13) November 1863. R.A. Stockholm.

Gorchakov repeated, she would expose herself to danger, adding that she could not rely on material help from Russia. Russia would shed blood only in her own interests. The Danish government could not claim any benefits deriving from the London convention if it did not carry out its obligations.[32] Gorchakov treated the whole problem 'avec une grande légèreté', as if Russian interests were in no way involved, stressing that the Danish-German dispute was of secondary importance for Russia.

Gorchakov could not really be satisfied with the results of the Ewers mission. But he also saw positive aspects in it. Hall's government, which had been so inflexible and disinclined to compromise, had fallen and been replaced by one led by Monrad which was almost universally regarded as more willing to offer concessions. Furthermore, Ewers' close co-operation with Wodehouse during the course of his mission had demonstrated that there was a possibility of increased co-operation with Britain, and thus, of implementing Gorchakov's conception of four-power collaboration. The Russian view that Monrad would prove more flexible seemed to be confirmed by the first document which he sent out to Danish diplomatic posts, on 5 January 1864, the day after he had formed his government.

In a letter to Plessen, Monrad expressed his positive attitude towards Gorchakov's ideas and Ewers' mission. Referring to the protocol of 14 April 1856 signed by the signatories to the Paris peace treaty and to the Treaty of London, Monrad put forward the suggestion of mediation, indicating that he wanted to defend Denmark's rights 'devant une réunion plus ou moins restreinte des puissances impartiales'.[33] But Gorchakov thought Monrad's proposal was vague, dull and not sufficiently concrète.[34] Quaade, who had been appointed minister of foreign affairs, also admitted that the 5 January despatch was not really clear, but he explained that in its first move the government could not give it a very precise form. The purpose of the dispatch was to show that the government aimed to settle the dispute with the participation and help of the other powers. He explained that the move had been co-ordinated with the extraordinary envoys of Russia and Britain and that the government would accept every form of intervention which would contribute to achieving this aim.[35]

Gorchakov now hoped that the Danish government would suspend the constitution and succeed in finding a way to satisfy Germany on the basis of the Treaty of London,[36] and that there would be no events in Germany like those of 1848. When, at the end of December, Britain proposed a conference to deal purely with the Danish question, and suggested that it should be held in Paris, Gorchakov took a positive attitude, not knowing that France would respond:

---

32. Wedel-Jarlsberg, 25 (13) November and 6 December (24 November), 1863.
33. R.A. Registratur, 1863-1864. Udenrigsmin. Tag. A. 798 and Sverige ordrer 1861-64.
34. Neergaard, op.cit. Vol. II, p. 1000. See Plessen's report, no. 6, 27 (15) January 1864.
35. Nicolay, no. 3, 12 (24) January 1864, vol. 54.
36. Massignac to Drouyn de Lhuys, 31 December 1863, A.M.A.E., Russie, vol. 232, no. 66. Cf. *Origines,* I, pp. 53-55.

C'est un Congrès général que nous désirons, et non pas une Conférence spéciale. L'insuccès de 1852 n'est pas de nature à encourager une tentative du même genre. En tout cas, nous ne voudrions point que la Conférence se tînt à Paris.[37]

It is worth noting that Gorchakov was unable to reply when Massignac questioned him about what line Russia would take if a conference were convened. The vice-chancellor confined himself to saying that in his opinion the resolution of the London Conference should be taken as a starting point and 'ne se montrer ni trop Danois ni trop Allemand'. When Massignac observed that the situation had changed, Gorchakov said that as soon as the conference commenced spirits would be calmed and there was no need to be alarmed, either by the presence of Danish troops on the Eider or by the measures decreed by the German Diet. 'Agir vite et d'accord contre l'esprit révolutionnaire'. But the French government could render a great service to the peace of Europe if it joined with the other states in order to calm the revolutionary spirits in Germany. To this, Massignac observed that France disliked revolutionaries no less than Russia.[38] Napier, on the other hand, reporting to Russell on 30 December, portrayed Gorchakov's view as follows:

Prince Gortchakow affirms that the Imperial Government of France allied with the revolutionary forces in Europe is a constant source of anxiety and disturbance to the other Powers. The bulwark against French ascendancy in the Monarchies of Austria, Prussia and the German Confederation is profoundly shaken and may at any moment be laid in ruins. It therefore behoves England and Russia to lay, cautiously and quietly, the basis of a common policy the objects of which should be to support the two Great German Powers and give them courage to resist the elements of internal dissolution and the menace of foreign aggression. He merely proposes that the four powers should mutually acknowledge their common interests in this matter and avow to each other the formation of a sort of a moral coalition against revolutionary conspiracy, ultra-democracy, exaggerated nationalism and military Bonapartist France.[39]

At the beginning of January, Gorchakov was in favour of convening a conference, even if the German Confederation refused to take part in it.[40] What he categorically did not want was any kind of intervention by the signatories to the Treaty of London to persuade Austria and Prussia, especially Prussia, to stop the hostile action taken against Denmark by Germany.[41] For if Britain and Russia were divided from Austria and Prussia, this could lead to the end of France's isolation, because it would split Europe into two camps and would set the non-German states against the German states. He aimed to avoid anything which could be unpleasant for the

---

37. Drouyn de Lhuys to Dotézac. Teleg. Minute à chiffrer. A.M.A.E. Danemark. vol. 245, Paris, 27 December. *Orig.* I. pp. 25-26. See also Drouyn de Lhuys to Fournier (Confidentielle), 29 December, A.M.A.E., Suède, vol. 333, no. 25. *Orig.* I, pp. 35-36; Russie, vol. 233, *Orig.* I p. 116.
38. A.M.A.E. Russie, vol. 232, no. 66, 31 December. *Orig.* I, p. 54.
39. Napier to Russell, no. 823, most confidential, 30 December 1863. R.A. I, 92/175, copy. Some days before this Gorchakov had proposed to the British government that they should support Bismarck, seeing this as the only barrier against the outbreak of war with Denmark and revolutionary agitation. R.A. I, 92/127, 24 December 1863.
40. *Ibid.,* I, 93/17 12 January 1864.
41. Napier to Russell, 11 January 1864, P.R.O. 30/32, Russia, 1863 to 1865, vol. 84, pp. 166-70.

German powers:[42] 'ne pas séparer l'Autriche et la Prusse de l'Angleterre et de la Russie et de ne pas donner à la France l'occasion de sortir de son isolement'.[43] Plessen was sure that Gorchakov preferred a conference to mediation, as the latter would lead to the isolation of Austria and Prussia and push them towards the lesser German states.[44]

It had been realised in diplomatic circles since the late autumn that immediately after the Federal Execution in Holstein, the question of Schleswig would come onto the agenda. In a talk with Buchanan towards the end of December, Bismarck made no effort to conceal that Schleswig would quickly be occupied: 'M. Bismarck having said that a few cannon shots would settle the question'.[45] In a talk with Oubril a month later he confirmed his intention, using the following words: 'let us exchange a few cannon shots with Denmark'. The Russian ambassador concluded that Bismarck had thought the whole matter through carefully and saw his words as a sign of determination.[43]

As before, Gorchakov was opposed to any steps by the Confederation in respect of Schleswig, because in his opinion it had no rights in the matter. But he saw things differently in the case of Austria and Prussia. He did not deny the latter the right to intervene since, as he put it to Thun, this stemmed from the international obligations undertaken by Denmark.[47] Gorchakov was so sensitive about relations with Vienna and Berlin that if Britain had organised a naval demonstration in the Baltic he would have informed the two German governments that it was directed exclusively against the German Diet, so that, as he put it, co-operation between the signatories to the Treaty of London should not be impaired.

Yet while Russian diplomacy supported Bismarck's point of view, it had certain fears about the possible consequences of Bismarck's behaviour. These doubts were shown by a talk at the end of December between Mohrenheim, the Russian *chargé d'affaires* in Berlin, and Bismarck. Mohrenheim warned Bismarck that if German troops crossed the Eider it would be seen as open war in Denmark, and could have unforeseen consequences from the European point of view, as such a step could help to unleash a revolutionary war in both Germany and Europe. 'Il ne s'agit pas du Schleswig, mais du monde', said Mohrenheim. 'La seule digue morale à opposer au flot [the revolutionary movement in Germany] qui monte est la solidarité des puissances conservatrices' he added. In view of Britain's negative attitude to the occupation of Schleswig, he also spoke of the possibility of a rapprochement between France and Britain. Gorchakov also shared this belief, but in view of the bad relations then prevailing between London and Paris, this judgement did not indicate great shrewdness or foresight on the part of either Gorchakov or Mohrenheim.

42. Wedel-Jarlsberg, no. 5, 6 January (25 December), R.A. Stockholm.
43. *Ibid.,* no. 6, 8 January (27 December).
44. Krieger, *Dagbøger,* vol. III, p. 99.
45. Buchanan to Russell, no. 630, 22 December 1863, F.O. 64/547, in Voigt, p. 175. On Bismarck's views on how to resolve the conflict, see Gall, *Bismarck,* pp. 306-7.
46. Oubril to Gorchakov, 31 (19) January 1864. *Krasnyi Arkhiv,* 2 (93), (Moscow, 1939), p. 74.
47. Thun's report, no. 1, 26 (14) January 1864. H.H.S.A. P.X. Kart. 55.

Bismarck immediately counter-attacked, refuting Mohrenheim's arguments as follows:

Mais il faut me venir en aide. Je suis seul à lutter, et j'ai de nombreux et de puissants adversaires ... La moitié de la pression que l'on a exercée contre nous eut suffi pour ramener le Gouvernement danois à une saine appréciation de ses devoirs. Je Vous répète, obtenez la révocation de la Constitution du 18 novembre. Vous êtez en mesure de l'exiger. Il n'y a hors de là, qu'occupation du Schleswig ou abandon du traité de Londres ... La guerre, si on nous y force, [Bismarck's cynicism – E.H.] n'exclut pas les négociations.[48]

This line of argument by Bismarck led Mohrenheim to conclude in his report that 'la Constitution du 18 Novembre doit être retirée à tout prix'.

Gorchakov adopted Bismarck's point of view as his own and sought to urge it on Napier. 'Le Vice-Chancellor russe m'a fait ce matin la suggestion' – Napier reported to Russell on 11 January 1864 – 'qu'on devrait engager le Danemarc à *admettre* l'occupation du Schleswig par des forces de l'Autriche et le la Prusse, à titre de *garantie* donnée à ceux Puissances par rapport à la population allemande du duché'.[49]

Gorchakov initially intended to associate himself with the note to Frankfurt from the Western powers and Sweden to restrain any moves the Confederation might make to cross the Eider, as this would be an infringement of non-federal territory and an act of war against Denmark. But he would not agree, as the British and French governments wanted, that the protest should first be sent to Vienna and Berlin and only thereafter, and in a milder form, to Frankfurt. He also refused to join the note of protest from Britain and France against the results of the vote in the German Diet on 14 January and the fact that Austria and Prussia took up the Schleswig question and decided to send a 48-hour ultimatum to Copenhagen. The two German states declared that if this were rejected their forces would enter Schleswig, as signatories to the Treaty of London.[50]

When, during the course of an audience with ambassadors, Gorchakov received the news of the military steps taken by Austria and Prussia he was clearly in consternation. 'Ceci change et déplace la question. Elle ne se trouve plus à Francfort, mais à Berlin et à Vienne. Que faire à présent?' But he quickly controlled himself and replied to the British proposal to send notes to Berlin and Vienna by saying to Napier:

Jamais la Russie ne se prêtera à une démarche qui serait de nature à blesser la Prusse et l'Autriche. La Russie désire entretenir avec la Prusse, l'Autriche et l'Angleterre les meilleurs rapports ... Je déplore la résolution que la Prusse et l'Autriche viennent de prendre [the 48-hour ultimatum – E.H.]. Je n'y comprends plus rien. Occuper le Schleswig et declarer en même temps ne pas vouloir s'écarter du protocole de Londres'.

---

48. Mohrenheim's report, 27 December 1863 (8 January 1864), APP vol. IV, pp. 416 ff. In the text the date is wrongly given as 27 Novembre. See also Guldencrone's telegram no. 878 in code from Berlin 13 January 1864. Preussen, Dep. 1864. R.A. Copenhagen.
49. Quoted from Klaczko, Deux Chanceliers, p. 198.
50. On 16 January an Austro-Prussian entente on military intervention in Schleswig was concluded. The same day the ultimatum was sent to Copenhagen. On 1 February the forces of both states crossed the Eider. See Gall, *Bismarck*, pp. 301-2. *Deutsche Revue*. Stuttgart a. Leipzig, (1903), pp. 2-4.

And he turned to Ewers as if looking for help: 'Car, n'est pas Mr Ewers c'est bien ce que M de Bismarck Vous a dit l'autre jour à Berlin? Répétez nous ce qu'il Vous a dit'. 'Herr von Ewers wiederholte hierauf - reported Redern, who was present at the audience -

dass Ew. Exzellenz ihm die bestimmte Versicherung gegeben habe, dem gedachten Protokolle treu bleiben zu wollen. "Cette assurance est à la vérité très satisfaisante et en tout cas il vaut mieux que ce soient la Prusse et l'Autriche qui occupent le Schleswig et pas les états secondaires qui réproduiraient les scènes revoltantes dont le Holstein vient d'être le theâtre" declared the prince. Le Roi Chrétien risque sa couronne, fuhr er fort, s'il cède. Il a prouvé qu'il comprend les dangers de sa position en changeant son ministère et en proposant la conférence pour en arriver à une solution pacifique. Et après toutes ces preuves de bon vouloir Vous lui posez un terme de 48 heures etc. etc.

These words were adressed to Redern and were uttered reproachfully.[51]

Gorchakov clearly found it hard to control his astonishment at the behaviour of the larger German states and he mastered himself with difficulty. But he refrained from openly condemning them. He was blackmailed by Bismarck, who, Oubril telegraphed from Berlin, was threatening that if the occupation of Schleswig were obstructed the King would either abdicate or appoint a liberal government, whereas he intended to complete the occupation on conservative principles, preserving the integrity of Denmark and the provisions of the Treaty of London. 'C'est parfaitement correcte, pourvu qu'il parvienne à le faire accepter', Alexander II commented on the margin of the report.[52] Oubril was disturbed, not so much by the invasion of Schleswig itself, as by the possibility that Britain might break with the German states, in which case, he assumed, France would join up with Britain 'sans aucune doute'. 'Cet état de choses compromettrait les intérêts généraux et particuliers, ainsi que l'espoir d'un meilleur avenir pour l'Europe en étouffant dans son germe'.[53]

Oubril's correspondence to Gorchakov[54] shows that Bismarck's blackmail made an impression on both the Tsar and Gorchakov. Bismarck frightened them with the prospect of a French landing on the north coast of Prussia and in Gdansk, and by suggesting that if he abandoned the occupation of Schleswig his government could be expected to fall because the King, who would never agree to giving it up, would appoint a government of liberals, who were backed by France. Another variant of Bismarck's blackmail had it that the King himself wanted to abdicate.[55] Oubril himself was afraid of new complications, writing:

We cannot lose sight of the fact that the defeat of Prussia and Austria (by France) would put us (Russia) face to face with France, and Napoleon's attitude towards the Polish question can leave no doubt about what such proximity would mean if it occured.

51. Redern to Bismarck, 16 January 1864. APP, IV, pp. 442-4.
52. *Ibid.*, p. 490.
53. *Ibid.*
54. Oubril, 20 (8), 23 (11), 25 (13) and 28 (16) January 1864.
55. APP, IV, p. 490.

In a letter to Oubril on 28 (16) January, Gorchakov wrote that the Tsar wanted to make things easier for both the German courts in the sphere of international affairs as well as in internal German matters. As for Bismarck's suggestion about France's policy as a threat to Prussia, Gorchakov was of the opinion that the Tuilleries cabinet would continue to bide its time and would not repudiate its obligations under the Treaty of London; he wanted to have freedom of action in the event of Britain proposing co-operation with Russia. France, Gorchakov judged, was not convinced that an entente between the four powers was a serious prospect and would seek allies among the ultra-liberals and revolutionary elements. Their position would depend on how the situation developed. It was therefore in Prussia's interest that the German states should not break with Britain. If they repudiated the Treaty of London the result might be an Anglo-French alliance. This would lead to the division of Europe into two camps and would produce a dangerous situation.

Fearing new international complications, Gorchakov turned to the cabinets in Vienna and Berlin and asked them to give the Danish government more than 48 hours. Gorchakov asked Russell that his government should take the same position and Nicolay received instructions to consult with Paget and jointly to urge the Danish government to convene the Rigsraad and repeal the November Constitution.[56] At the same time he instructed Brunnow to propose to the British government joint action to recommend Denmark to agree to the occupation of Schleswig in exchange for the removal of Prince Augustenburg from the teritory of Holstein.

Owing to the new circumstances brought about by the behaviour of the German states, Gorchakov found himself under pressure from Napier, Wedel-Jarlsberg and Plessen, who were demanding that he should protest energetically to Vienna and Berlin. Massignac reported that it seemed for a moment that Gorchakov would send notes to Austria and Prussia, but that if he did so they would amount to no more than 'des conseils de modération très reservés. Il est certain que la Russie n'est point en état d'intervenir le pour Danemark et que les inquiétudes y sont vives'.[57] Massignac indicated that Alexander II was anxious about what would happen in the spring. There was the threat of a blaze in Schleswig, while in the Danube principalities and Poland, although the uprising was dying down, it might flare up again in the spring.

La Russie ne peut pas approuver qu'on dépouille le Danemark, elle ne peut pas accepter en silence que l'esprit national ajoute un nouveau fleuron à sa couronne – Pepoli reported on 31 January. La question du Holstein resolue dans le sens Allemand, est une nouvelle condamnation de l'occupation de la Pologne, c'est une consacration du principe des nationalités, que repousse *l'union personne* comme douloureuse utopie et une déplorable mystification.[58]

56. Telegram of 18 January, I, 93/117.
57. Report of 18 January 1864, A.M.A.E., Russie, vol. 233, no. 4, *Origines,* I, p. 159.
58. 'Le Ministre ... m'a fait seulement observer que, selon lui, il fallait distinguer quant à l'occupation du Schleswig entre les troupes fédérales et les troupes austro-prusiennes. En effet il part toujours du principe que la Confédération germanique n'a nullement le même droit de se mêler des affaires du Schleswig qu'en vertu des engagemens internationaux les deux grandes puissances allemandes pouvaient réclamer ...'. Rapporti Della Legazione i Pietroburgo, no. I, (Confidentielle), Pacco 205 (843) A.S.-D. Rome.

The Tsar also feared disturbances in Russia itself. He wanted to maintain a first-rate army but was encountering financial difficulties in doing so. Despite his sympathy for Denmark it was hard to believe that a single ruble would be spent, or the life of a single Russian sacrificed, for this purpose. This was why the Russian government attached such importance to the position of the French government and Gorchakov pressed Paris to agree to a conference: 'une conférence, une réunion, une médiation, le nom importe peu'. Gorchakov also spoke of the treaty of Warsaw as a Russian 'reserve', which would enable her to reclaim Russia's rights to Holstein. He mentioned this in the context of Prince Augustenburg's circular addressed to the free German towns and governments maintaining that the rights of the imperial house of Holstein had expired.

This question of Russian rights revived, for understandable reasons, at the beginning of 1864. On 28 December 1863 (9 January 1864), the semi-official *Journal de St Pétersbourg,* at Gorchakov's behest, published the text of the 1851 Warsaw protocol in which the Tsar, as the representative of the senior Holstein-Gottorp line, renounced his rights to Holstein in favour of Prince Glücksburg and his male heirs in order to preserve the integrity of the Danish monarchy. But he reserved the rights to himself in the event of the male line descending from Prince Glücksburg becoming extinct.[59] As Napier reported:

Russia in so doing was, however, moved by no selfish design. She desired to recall to Germany and Europe that the principle in which all these transactions have been based was the desire to maintain the integrity of the Danish monarchy.[60]

Thun quoted Gorchakov's words to Napier:

Nous pourrions parler, lui-a-t-il dit, plus énergiquement à Copenhague, mais comme l'Empereur est décidé à ne faire marcher un homme ou à dépenser un sous ni pour ni contre le Danemarc, je dois me borner à des conseils.

But in his opinion 'une trop grande valeur' should not be ascribed to this declaration.[61]

The Swedish ambassador sent the following report on Gorchakov's policy at that time:

Je crains que le Prince Gortchakov (N.11, 20/8.I.1864 – En Chiffres) ne joue un peu double jeu et que son langage aux Ministres de l'Autriche et de Prusse ne diffère de celle à Lord Napier, au B. Plessen et à moi. Il veut certainement du bien au Danemarc, mais à condition de ne pas indisposer la Prusse, dont l'appui lui parait indispensable dans la question polonaise, qu'un débordement démocratique ou une guerre générale pourrait si facilement réussir. C'est là son premier souci et il y sacrifiera au besoin les intérêts du Danemarc. Sa pression amicale à Copenhague n'ayant point abouti la suspension de la loi du 18 Novembre

---

59. See 'Protokoll mellem Danmark og Russland, det Warschau, 24 mai/5 juni 1851', in *Danske Traktater efter 1800. Første Samling. Politiske Traktater. 1800-1863,* (Copenhagen, 1877), pp. 220-3.
60. Napier to Russell, 10 January 1864, Denmark, no. 2, no. 704, p. 538, and the appended protocol, pp. 538-41.
61. H.H.S.A., P.A. Rus: Kart. 55, Thun to Rechberg, no. 18, 26 (14) January 1864.

il voudrait maintenant et toujours pour éviter le conflit que le Danemarc consente à l'occupation pacifique de Schleswig par les troupes Austro-Prusiennes. Dans ce but employé comme pression d'un autre genre, j'ai lieu de craindre que, contrairement aux idées du Lord Napier, il ne travaille à Londres pour que le Cabinet Anglais ne pose pas le cas de guerre au passage de l'Eyder par troupes allemandes.[62]

In talks with Plessen Gorchakov justified the behaviour of the larger German states, which, Napier reported, he regarded as 'unavoidable'.[63]

Selon l'appréciation du Prince Gortchakow – Plessen reported[64] – la détermination de l'Autriche et de la Prusse renferme de la part de ces deux Puissances une rupture avec la politique révolutionnaire de l'Allemagne et inaugure une politique à leurs risques et périls comme grandes Puissances, que le Prince qualifie de "hasardée", mais dont Il ne conteste pas aux Cabinets de Vienne et de Berlin la légalité, parce que ces deux Cabinets font cette politique à titre de Grandes Puissances, et pas de Puissances Allemandes.[65]

Le Vice-Chancelier – Plessen's report goes on – dans cette occurence, s'abstient de donner au Gouvernement de Sa Majesté des conseils. Il m'a dit

nous ne tirerons pas l'épée, Vous le savez. C'est à Vous de calculer les chances et de Vous arrêter à la détermination, qui Vous paraîtra commandée par vos convenances.

... Malgré la décision de l'Autriche et de la Prusse, le Vice-Chancelier maintient ses idées à l'égard d'une réunion à effectuer, conformément aux idées de la dépêche du Président du Conseil, du 5 janvier.

Plessen sent a similar report to Vedel.[66] In his report to the minister of foreign affairs, Quaade, Plessen gave further details about the arguments Gorchakov had used in his talk with him.[67]

L'Autriche et la Prusse veulent, selon le Prince Gortchakov quant au Danemarc, ce que veulent l'Angleterre et la Russie "le maintien du traité de Londres". En écartant leur Confédérés allemands qui proclament l'abandon du traité de Londres, elles agissent en vue d'un but qui est celui de la Russie et de l'Angleterre, la conservation et l'intégrité de la Monarchie Danoise. Le Vice-Chancelier n'approuve pas les moyens à cet effet, auxquels l'Autriche et la Prusse semblent décidées à avoir recours, mais il excuse en quelque sorte la détermination des deux grands cabinets allemands par la nécessité dans laquelle elles se trouvent en face de l'excitation extrême de l'Allemagne. La détermination de l'Autriche et de la Prusse divise l'Allemagne en deux camps, c'est en vue du maintien de l'intégrité de la Monarchie, un avantage, selon le Vice-Chancelier qu'il ne faut pas compromettre en poussant l'Autriche et la Prusse par une démarche inconsidérée dans le camp de leurs confédérés, ce qui nous mettrait en face d'une Allemagne unie. Ceci est le raisonnement du Prince Gortchakov.

---

62. No. 11, 20 (8) January 1864.
63. Napier to Russell, 20 January 1864. P.R.O. 30/32, vol. 84, pp. 175-7.
64. 16 (4) January, no. 3.
65. The same wording is to be found in Wedel-Jarlsberg's report, no. 9, 18 (6) January 1864.
66. See no. 4, 18 (6) January.
67. No. 4 18 (6) January.

Gorchakov rejected Plessen's argument that as events unfolded, the larger German powers could change their attitude to the Treaty of London, stressing the role of Britain, with which country Russia had recently enjoyed, as he put it, 'excellentes rapports', and which was so involved in the defence of Denmark.

In his next talk with the Danish ambassador Gorchakov defined Russia's position as follows:

Nous ne nous mettrons pas entre le Danemark et les Cours Alemandes; mais, si Vous nous en donnez l'occasion, nous travaillerons de notre mieux pour maintenir le traité de Londres, que ces cours veulent également maintenir.[68]

Gorchakov, Plessen reported, had indeed said he regretted that the actions taken by the signatories to the Treaty of London to secure a six-week postponement from Austria and Prussia had been fruitless, but he had immediately found excuses for them and explained their behaviour by the urgency brought about by the situation which had developed in Germany and the need to do something to satisfy the passions which had been aroused.[69] The aim by which Russia was guided, namely maintenance of the integrity of Denmark, could run into difficulties if the very determined German states' execution met with resistance and developed into a conflict with Denmark; for this reason, too, Gorchakov recommended Denmark to do everything in her power to avoid bloodshed, all the more so as he personally did not believe that Denmark was capable of resisting the stronger and better equipped German armies.[70] Hence he advised Denmark to agree to the occupation of Schleswig, while he would try to obtain agreement from Vienna and Berlin that the German forces would occupy only the southern part of Schleswig and not attack Dannewirke. Gorchakov hoped that in this way he would be able to save the Treaty of London.[71] But just as with the proposal to extend the ultimatum, Bismarck now rejected the suggestion not to attack Dannewirke, which was regarded by Denmark as the bastion of her independence and which, Gorchakov thought, the government could not surrender without infuriating public opinion. In a talk with Oubril, Bismarck categorically demanded that he be allowed an exchange of artillery fire. He really repeated the position he had taken long before, that the dispute with Denmark must be settled on the field of battle, and now he had concluded that an opportune moment for this had come.[72]

---

68. Plessen, no. 5, 19 (7) January 1864.
69. On 20 January Napier reported that Gorchakov did really consider that Austria and Prussia had behaved too sharply, but their action 'gave faith' as it would be carried out in the spirit of the principles contained in the treaties of 1851 and 1852. P.R.O., 30/32, vol. 84. *ibid.* He was also against using the wording proposed by Russell, 'Austria and Prussia should be urged to give time for the Danish Rigsraad to meet', in dispatches to Vienna and Berlin on the question of postponing the date for the invasion of Schleswig, as he considered it too categorical. 24 January, no. 847, *Denmark and Germany*, no. 5, 1864, p. 621. Plessen, no. 6. 27 (15) January 1864.
70. See Plessen's telegram, no. 1358, 29 January 1864.
71. See Krieger, vol. III, 27 and 30 January 1864, pp. 61-62 and 65.
72. See Bismarck's letter of 22 December 1862 in Sybel, *Die Begründung ...*, vol. III, pp. 118-19, 172; R.W. Seton-Watson., *Britain in Europe. 1789-1914,* (1937), p. 445; the correspondence between Gorchakov and Oubril of 28 (16) and 31 (19) January 1864, *Krasnyi Arkhiv,* vol. 2 (93), (1939), pp.

In his report to Gorchakov, Oubril expressed his own opinion that the Danish government could not honestly be advised to agree to the peaceful occupation of Schleswig and surrender with bound hands to the tender mercies of the German states, when there was no real guarantee that the latter wanted to preserve the integrity of the Danish monarchy.[73] Knowing Gorchakov's views, however, he did not fail to add immediately that the declaration issued by the Prussian and Austrian governments could provide a basis for saying that their contention that the occupation of Schleswig would ensure its security had not ceased to be relevant.[74] It is more than doubtful whether Oubril, watching Bismarck's moves in those eventful days, could really have believed this.

In these closing days of January 1864, the game Bismarck played against Russia was exceedingly subtle. He claimed that he found himself in a tragic situation, asked whether Russia could remain an indifferent onlooker if France entered Gdansk and, furthermore, even pretended to ask Gorchakov for material help from Russia. He did this so that Russia did not feel humiliated and to give her limited scope for independent action, for he certainly realised that this was a demand which the St Petersburg cabinet could not meet. At the same time it was a form of diplomatic pressure on the St Petersburg cabinet designed to procure its complete approval of Berlin's actions.

Bismarck also said that he shared Gorchakov's point of view on the need to maintain co-operation between the three northern cabinets and Britain, that both he and the King supported the Russian view of the French cabinet's policy, and that he would not oppose the idea of initiating a conference even while the military action was going on. But he categorically rejected the idea that he should limit himself to occupying southern Schleswig and stopping at the Dannewirke line.

It is significant, and certainly no accident, that not only Bismarck but General Gablenz also talked about an alliance between Prussia, Austria and Russia in a conversation with Oubril. Oubril was struck by the similarity of their words and their emphasis 'on the possibilities which existed for a brotherhood in arms'.[75] In the margin of his account Oubril addressed a question to Gorchakov, asking whether he did not think that Prussia only turned to Russia when she felt threatened and uncertain, seeing that Russia was both inactive and silent.

Alexander II wrote a note on the report: 'As usual, they remember us when they feel in danger'.[76] Both the Tsar and his minister, and Oubril, were undoubtedly

---

68 ff. Bismarck's confidential letter of 22 December 1862 shows that even then his plan was clear in his mind: ... es ist gewiss, das die ganze dänische Angelegenheit nur durch den Krieg in einer für uns erwünschten Weise gelösst werden kann. Der Anlass zu diesem Kriege lässt sich in jedem Augenblick finden, welchen man für einem günstigen zur Kriegführung hält ... Den Nachtheil, das Londoner Protokoll unterzeichnet zu haben, theilen wir mit Österreich, und können uns von dieser Unterschrift ohne kriegerischen Bruch nicht lossagen. Kommt es aber zum Kriege, so hängt von dessen Ergebnis auch die künstlige Gestaltung der dänischen Territorialverhältnisse ab.

73. Oubril, 31 (19) January 1864, *ibid.* pp. 72ff.
74. *Ibid.*
75. Oubril's reports of 20 (8) and 23 (11) January, *ibid.*
76. *Ibid.*

thinking of the behaviour of Prussia, and especially of Wilhelm I, in the spring of 1863, when he rejected the proposal by Alexander II to conclude an alliance between Russia and Prussia.[77] But despite all these circumstances Gorchakov did not alter his policy and still saw Russia's place as the link between the German states and Britain.

The Russian government continued to try and persuade Denmark to forbear from resistance.

Il est pour le Danemark de la dernière importance que l'Autriche et la Prusse soient maintenus dans leurs fidelité au traité de Londres. Jusqu'ici promis. Une résistance armée à l'occupation du Schleswig menaçaient de briser immédiatement ce bien.[78]

On 28 January, Gorchakov addressed the following telegram to his ambassador in Copenhagen: 'Engagez Mr Quaade à réitirer sans délai invitation, dans les terms indiquées par Plessen. Nous l'appuyons partout chaleureusement'.[79] Gorchakov appealed to the Danish government to agree to the occupation of Schleswig. This step would be a guarantee for the German states to compel Denmark to fulfil her 1851-52 promises and not only would not harm Denmark but would safeguard the Treaty of London.

The Vice-Chancellor – Napier reported to Russell on 1 February 1864 – told me that he had not advised the Danish Cabinet to take any course whatever; he had merely placed their position plainly before them, pointing out if they should resist, the two German Governments would not consider the stipulations of 1852 as any longer binding.[80]

Gorchakov called on Brunnow to convince Britain about Bismarck's policy, and he also asked Redern and Thun that their governments should take similar action. Gorchakov himself, in a talk with Napier, asked that the British cabinet should not make difficulties for Bismarck over the occupation of Schleswig because by acting in this manner Bismarck was barring the way to Prince Augustenburg.[81]

La conduite que Gortchakoff recommendait au Danemark – wrote François Charles Roux – touchait en effet au ridicule: il lui conseillait de considérer l'invasion des troupes austrio-prussiennes dans les duchés comme une simple occupation, afin de sauvegarder jusqu'au bout les apparences de la paix.[82]

In view of the fact that London did not trust what Vienna and Berlin said about the occupation of Schleswig, Gorchakov advised the German governments to give assurances to the British government. Gorchakov assured Berlin and Vienna of his devotion to the German governments and hoped that the matters arousing

---

77. See the correspondence between Alexander II and Wilhelm I of 20 May (1 June), 17 June and 30 June (12 July) 1863, in B. Nolde, *Ryssland, Preussen och Polen 1861-1863*, (Stockholm, 1916), pp. 36ff; also Friese, pp. 374-9.
78. Gorchakov to Nicolay, A.V.P.R., vol. 68, telegram of 21 January (old style).
79. *Ibid.*
80. *Denmark and Germany,* no. 5. *ibid.* no. 909, p. 661.
81. Gorchakov to Oubril and Brunnow, 17 (29) January 1864.
82. François Charles-Roux, *Alexandre II, Gortchakoff et Napoléon III,* (Paris, 1913), p. 371.

passions on the Eider would not stifle something far more important, namely the four-power entente between Russia, Austria, Prussia and Britain for which Gorchakov was striving. Gorchakov's aim, as he himself wrote to Oubril, was to strengthen Bismarck's position in his country, convince Britain of the correctness of his behaviour, and induce Denmark to agree to the occupation of Schleswig, promising in return that Prince Augustenburg would be banished from Holstein. As Klaczko argued,

Le Prince Gortchakof n'a cessé de favoriser le ministre prussien par tous les moyens, de lui tendre avec empressement, et le plus souvent à la dérobée, une main secourable à chaque traversée difficule. Son concours fut absolu et d'autant plus efficace qu'il prenait les dehors d'une neutralité affairée en quête d'un arrangement pacifique.[83]

When the declaration which Gorchakov had urged them to make was issued by the two German governments, there was no mention in it of the Treaty of London, nor a word about the integrity of Denmark, but only reference to the Danish obligations of 1851-52. Napier drew Gorchakov's attention to this, but he took no notice. When he informed Napier of the *communiqué* issued by the governments of Austria and Prussia at the moment their armies entered Schleswig, Gorchakov added as his own commentary:

that the two Governments had not distinctly pronounced the words "Treaty of London of 1852" or the terms "the integrity of the Danish Monarchy", but in citing the engagements of 1851-52 they implied the principle of that integrity.

He preferred not to accept Napier's reservations about the intentions of the German states and their possible plans to detach Schleswig from Denmark, join it with Holstein and form a personal union of the two duchies and Denmark.

Prince Gortchakov replied that it was no use speculating on future contingencies, we must deal with them as they arose. In the meantime he must accept and record the assurance of the German Cabinets in the sense most conformable to his views and wishes. He recognised in this declaration the principle of the integrity of the Danish Monarchy and that of a Conference both of which he had at heart.[84]

As Napier reported to Russell on 4 February 1864,

Prince Gortchakov continues to feel or to affect a perfect confidence in the German powers. In his eyes they make war on Denmark for Denmark's good to establish her integrity and to protect her from the more dangerous danger of German Democrats and Nationalists. He would have sincerely preferred that Austria and Prussia had granted the reasonable respite proposed by Her Majesty's Government. Failing that he would have denied that the Danes should have evacuated their entrenchments and admitted the benevolent enemy. Even [?] that the Austro-Prussian army advanced and the Danes do not retire he hopes that the weaker party will be rapidly overcome, that an armistice will ensue and that the Austrian and Prussian ministers satisfied with their victory and provided with their "material guarantee" will

---

83. Klaczko, *Deux Chanceliers* ..., p. 196.
84. Napier to Russell, 4 February 1864, no. 913, *ibid.* pp. 662-3.

retire on reasonable terms eventually. I confess – Napier added – I am less confident.[85]

As this passage shows, Gorchakov took on himself the function of defender of the German actions and spared no effort to convince Britain that Bismarck still held to the provisions of the Treaty of London, while the facts clearly contradicted this contention. Bismarck had no intention either of guaranteeing the principles laid down in the treaty or of promising to preserve the integrity of the Danish monarchy. His behaviour showed clearly that there could be no question of a return to the *status quo ante*. Furthermore, Gorchakov did not conceal from Napier that he hoped the stronger army would quickly triumph and when satisfied with victory would agree to reasonable terms. Napier was less convinced. He still entertained some hopes that Russia could be persuaded to change her policy: 'A decided step on the part of Her M's Government would probably still lead on the Russian to some extent', he wrote to Russell.[86]

III.

From the end of 1863, Gorchakov strove to maintain good relations with Britain, although this took some effort in view of their growing differences of opinion about the German states' moves, which did not meet with the approval of British public opinion in particular. Anglo-Russian conflicts in Asia were another obstacle. The desire for co-operation prevailed however, to some extent helped by the fact that both Brunnow in London and Napier in St Petersburg were advocates of such a rapprochement.

Les relations entre les Cabinets de St Petersbourg et Londres deviennent de jour en jour plus intimes – Thun reported on 26 (14) January – Le Prince Gortchakov qui, il n'y pas longtemps, semblait voulour laisser au Danemarc seul la responsabilité de sa mauvaise fois dans ses rapports avec Allemagne, en est maintenant, grâce à l'influence de Lord Napier, à considérer l'intégrité de la Monarchie danoise comme une nécessité europénne de laquelle il fallait tenir compte n'importe que ce pays remplisse au nom ses engagements internationales ...[87]

Gorchakov even turned out to be disposed to consider British proposals going beyond merely moral aid for Denmark, judging by Napier's report to Russell a day later:

If your lordship takes a decision, if you express it with the plainness which you used recently towards France, and if you make a commencement or demonstration of action by putting the fleet in motion, then I think Russia may be drawn into something. Sweden will join at once.[88]

85. P.R.O. 30/32, vol. 84, pp. 187-9.
86. 4 February 1864, Private. P.R.O., 30/32, K. 187-9.
87. No. 1B. See also the view of the Anglo-Russian rapprochement in Lord Redesdale, *Memories,* vol. I. (London, 1915), pp. 243-5.
88. P.R.O. 30/32, vol. 84. Cf. Johannes H. Voigt, 'Englands Aussenpolitik während des deutschdänischen Konflikt 1862-1864', *Zeitschrift der Gesellschaft für Schleswig-Holsteinische Geschichte,* Vol. 89, (1964) p. 101.

Thun became convinced that Britain's influence on Gorchakov was immense.

En général le Vice-Chancelier se montre de plus en plus partisan chaleureux de l'Angleterre, l'appui qu'il a prêté à la proposition de l'armitrice sans savoir si cet arrangement était agréé par le Cabinet danois en est une preuve ... Je ne crois pas me tromper très fort en supposant que l'Allemagne ne poura guère compter sur l'appui du Cabinet russe au Conférence que le Vice-Chancelier continue de considérer comme le seul moyen pour sortir des grandes complications causées par le différend dano-allemand ... Il m'a lu – Thun reported to Vienna – une longue dépêche qu'il a adressé à Mr de Knorring dans laquelle il s'efforce à démontrer la nécessité pour nous de satisfaire autant que possible le Cabinet Anglais, qui, selon lui, n'est nullement rassuré par nos déclarations.[89]

In reality Gorchakov's aim was to halt any British activity, other than diplomatic, and to paralyse any action which could harm the German states. Thus when Napier, on the instructions of his government, asked Gorchakov on 26 January to state his position on the possibility of Russia joining Britain, France and Sweden to give material help to Denmark, Gorchakov refrained from replying, even though Napier had stipulated that such help would not be given as long as Austria and Prussia confined themselves to execution of the Danish obligations of 1851-52 and did not detach the Elbe duchies from Denmark.

The proposal to send an Anglo-Russian naval squadron to Copenhagen, which Britain put forward because she was alarmed by the advance of the Austro-Prussian armies, was received with great caution by Gorchakov. When Napier questioned him on what he thought about a possible joint demonstration of this kind and what position Russia would adopt, he told the ambassador that he would ask the Tsar's opinion. He also requested Napier to ask the British government what it had in mind when it spoke of 'concert and co-operation'. He was interested in two questions:

What was the nature and what the extent of the armed assistance which Her Majesty's Government proposed in certain contingencies to afford to Denmark; and whether Her Majesty's Government proposed to afford such aid only in combination with all the powers signatories of the Treaty of London, or with some of them or even alone.

He was unwilling to give a concrete answer about Russian participation until he knew the intentions of the remaining signatories to the Treaty of London, but, Napier reported to Russell,

His Excellency did not, however, say that in no circumstances would Russia interfere by force of arms to preserve Denmark from dismemberment.[90]

Gorchakov explained that the Gulf of Finland was frozen until the middle of May and that no Russian squadron could show itself in Danish waters before then. To Napier's suggestion that Russian vessels currently in American ports could be used for the purpose, the reply came that it would be two months before they could

---

89. Resérvé, no. 3, 20 (8) February 1864.   H.H.S.A., P.A. X Rus. Kart. 55.
90. Napier to Russell, no. 1033, 17 February. *Denmark and Germany*, no. 5. p. 729.

reach the Baltic and, besides, they were of poor quality; if Russia were going to show herself in Copenhagen she had to appear in all her splendour.[91]

In a letter to Brunnow telling his ambassador about his talk with Napier, Gorchakov informed him that both the British and the French governments had reached the conclusion that the time had come to send a squadron to Copenhagen. This however was only a proposal and the three courts' action would not go beyond the role of intermediaries. Gorchakov repeated what he had said previously, that Russia's position depended on the will of the Tsar, but he, Gorchakov, would like to move together with Britain.

In Gorchakov's opinion they should aim to avoid the prospect of such partly moral and partly material action creating dangerous illusions in the Danish government's mind. The latest news from Copenhagen was that a mood of readiness for war prevailed there and they wanted neither a conference nor a truce, nor to listen to anyone's advice. The Russo-British action was designed as a step towards mediation in itself, and the Danish government was being pressured to accept mediation.

For his part Gorchakov wanted to know from the British government:
1. the number and tonnage of the British vessels in the expedition,
2. what reply France had given.

Gorchakov did not regard the question of sending a squadron as settled, and perhaps still hoped to avoid it. Alexander II's reaction to Russell's telegram was symptomatic of his way of thinking: 'I cherish the hope that by that time the situation will have improved.'

Gorchakov personally assumed that there was a difference between Napier's attitude to the matter and that of the British government. Napier was pressing the government to take this action, while the goverment remained calmer. Considering the state of affairs concerning Denmark, Gorchakov emphasised that Russia must not lose sight of the immense importance of preserving the best possible relations with Vienna and Berlin. If Russia decided to take part in a show of naval strength it would be mainly to prevent the rise of a coalition against the two German states, and to increase her influence in Denmark and support the government there in its fight against local demagogy.[92] In the end, the expedition did not take place and on 25 February Napier informed Gorchakov that, in view of the satisfactory assurances from the cabinets in Vienna and Berlin, his government had decided not to send an expedition to the Baltic.[93]

The real reason for this was the withdrawal of France and Russia. 'But Denmark unsupported by France and Russia must not count upon England acting alone in her behalf', Russell wrote to Paget on 10 February.[94] 'Sowohl Gortschakows dop-

---

91. Napier, 23 February; Steefel, pp. 198ff; Gorchakov to Brunnow, 24 (12) February, *Krasnyi Arkhiv, ibid.* pp. 79-80; Plessen, no. 10, 25 (13) February, R.A. Copenhagen.
92. See Mosse, *The European Powers ...*, pp. 184-5.
93. Napier to Russell, no. 132, 25 February, R.A. I, 95/II. Copy.
94. P.R.O. 30/32, 102. Cf. Sandiford, pp. 100-2 and Voigt, pp. 118-9.

pelzüngige Politik als auch seine Haltung in der folgenden Tagen zeigten Russell, wie der Wind in Petersburg wehte', Voigt argued.[95] But the cynical Gorchakov treated the British government's decision with irony: 'Alors milord, je mets de côté la supposition que l'Angleterre fasse jamais pour une question d'honneur'. 'Pretty words for an English Ambassador to listen to', was Redesdale's comment.[96]

In his coded report to Stockholm on 25 (13) February, Wedel-Jarlsberg reported as follows:

The recent declaration by Austria and Prussia agreeing to take part in a conference led to the decision not to send a British fleet to the Baltic. Gorchakov was pleased by this and defended the calling of a conference in Copenhagen. ('le plaide à Copenhague Conférence'). The Vice-Chancellor was opposed to any active intervention in favour of Denmark, and in order to achieve this aim 'Il s'efforce constamment de retenir la Prusse et de modérer ses aspirations ambitieuses'.

Napier, who was in close contact with Gorchakov and followed the policy being pursued by the Russian cabinet carefully, came to the conclusion that Gorchakov was in favour of close co-operation with the British cabinet, but only of the kind which he himself called 'moral concert and co-operation' for the purpose of settling the conflict between Denmark and Germany. In order to achieve this he was sending frequent telegrams 'of an admonitory character' to the cabinets in Vienna and Berlin, calling on them to be true to their international obligations and warning them of the dangers to which they could expose themselves if they seriously antagonised Britain.

I am bound to submit – wrote Napier – my impression to your Lordship, in justice to Prince Gortchakoff, that nothing could be more zealous and well-intentioned, than the course pursued by the Vice-Chancellor in this matter ...

He could only do more by using the language of direct menace to the German Powers and by promising material aid to Denmark; but the position of Russia justifies Prince Gortchakoff in pausing on the threshold of such a policy, and His Excellency has never as yet held out to Her M's government any expectation that he would proceed to such extremities.[97]

Wedel-Jarlsberg, also an observer of Russian policy, summed up Gorchakov's policy and the reasons for it as follows:

Sans certes désirer la guerre, on en est, je crois, arrivé ici à la considérer comme un mal à peu inévitable, afin d'empêcher le débordement des éléments démocratiques. Ensuite les embarras financiers sont arrivés à tel point qu'on ne voit plus d'autres remède pour en sortir et éviter une banqueroute. Pour fortifier sa position en Pologne le Gouvernement Imperial s'approche visiblement de l'Autriche, les anciens griefs sont oubliés au moins mis de côté et tout porte à croir que, les cas échéant, on verra une triple alliance offensive et défensive entre la Russie, la Prusse et l'Autriche et quoique le Prince Gortchakov la nie toujours, les personnes ordinairement bien informées assurent même que un tel arrangement existe déjà avec la Prusse. Il reposerait, il me semble, sur une base bien fragile, vu l'improbabilité du maintien

---

95. Voigt, p. 119.
96. *Memories,* vol. I, pp. 244-5.
97. Napier to Russell, 17 February. *Denmark and Germany,* no. 5, no. 730, p. 1035.

à la longue du Ministère Bismarck et le revivement de politique complet auquel sa chute pourrait donner lieu. Dans une telle éventualité il ne serait pas même impossible qu'on vît la Russie prendre à l'égard du Grand Duché de Posen et de la Prusse une attitude analogue à celle de l'année 1849.[98]

Wedel-Jarlsberg's report reflects the atmosphere prevailing in St Petersburg and shows what fear there was there about the growth of the revolutionary movement in Germany, and that there was still great uncertainty about the future of the Polish lands. St Petersburg even reckoned on the fall of Bismarck and the necessity for Russian intervention in Germany if the situation in 1849 were to recur.

This report caused a stir in diplomatic circles in Stockholm and elicited numerous comments. This is shown by, among other things, Scheel-Plessen's report to Quaade on 17 February 1864,[99] in which the Danish ambassador posed the following questions concerning the possibility of a defensive-offensive alliance being concluded between Russia and Prussia, which Austria would supposedly join, and the aim of which would be to crush the revolutionary movement in Germany:

Est-il permis de supposer que le but [to fight the revolution in Germany – EH] puisse être atteint, sans qu'une guerre Européenne n'en résulte? La France, l'Angleterre, l'Italie resteront-elles spectatrices de la lutte qui va éclater? Ou seront-elles poussées par la force des choses à prendre une part active dans ce demêlé des nations? Sera-t-il loisible dans les circonstances actuelles aux Danemarc et aux Royaumes – Unis de Suède et de Norvège de garder la neutralité comme ils n'ont fait à d'autres époques?

Rumours of this kind, which were repeated into the summer of 1864, formed a sort of explanation for the policy pursued by Gorchakov and justified his actions supporting the policy adopted and implemented by Bismarck. Wedel-Jarlsberg's observation about a Russo-Austrian rapprochement, however, was confirmed by the facts.

The signs of this rapprochement date from October 1863. When the Russian *chargé d'affaires* informed him of the position taken by the Russian cabinet on the worsening conflict between Denmark and Germany, Rechberg sent a letter to the Austrian embassy in St Petersburg which included the following passage:

M le chargé d'affaires est invité à témoigner au Cabinet de s. Pétersbourg la satisfaction que nous ont causée l'attitude qu'il a observé dans la question dano-allemande et les sages conseils qu'il a fait parvenir à la cour de Copenhague.[100]

In November, the two governments, Austrian and Russian, consulted each other about their position in the Danish-German dispute.[101]

Great store was set by Russian opinion in Vienna, all the more so in view of the

---

98. In code, 30 (18) January 1864.
99. Confidentielle, no. 20. Sverige Depecher 1862-1865, R.A. Copenhagen.
100. H.H.S.A., P.A.X. Rusland, Kart. 54, no. 4. 15 October 1863. See also Rechberg to Thun, 29 January 1864. Kart. 55.
101. Rechberg's telegrams to Thun on 20 and 23 November, *ibid*. 'Fürst Gortchakow attacherait grand prix à connaître le plus possible les intentions des K K Cabinets in des Schl.-Holsteinische Frage'. See also Thun's Telegram in code from St. Petersburg.

close relations between Russia and Prussia. Vienna was aware that these connections had a bearing on mutual relations between the two German states. The Austrian government was satisfied with the position taken by St Petersburg on the conflict over the duchies, and Rechberg expressed this in his telegram to Thun on 29 January 1864 asking him to convey his gratitude to the Russian cabinet for the conciliatory ('conciliante') attitude it had displayed over the Danish question.[102] Gorchakov in turn, Thun reported,[103] thanked the Austrian government for the line it had taken and for its positive attitude to the integrity of the Danish monarchy and the understanding it had shown for the importance of a four-power alliance.

Rechberg's telegram to Thun on 17 February 1864 was couched in a similar friendly spirit:

Nous avons constaté avec une vive satisfaction en prenant connaissance de cette pièce[104] que les vues du Cabinet Impérial de Russie tant sur l'affaire du Schleswig-Holstein en particulier que pour autant qu'elles s'appliquent à la situation générale se trouvent dans la plus parfaite harmonie avec la nôtre.[105]

On 2 March (19 February) Gorchakov expressed his satisfaction that Austria had declared herself in favour of a conference.[106] 'Vous vous êtez toujours conséquents et modérés, l'acceptation de la conférence en est une nouvelle preuve'.[107]

There can be no question that the improvement of relations on the Vienna-St Petersburg axis was helped by the change in the Austrian government's policy towards the Polish uprising. This change occurred at the close of 1863 and led to the decision to declare a state of emergency in Galicia, which was taken by the cabinet in Vienna on 18 February and proclaimed in Lvov on 29 February.[108]

The state of emergency in Galicia could not deliver a *coup de grâce* to the uprising, which was in any case on the ebb. The Austrian government's action did not fundamentally alter the course of the insurrection. It is doubtful if it even curtailed it much. From the viewpoint of the Austrian government, H. Wereszycki wrote,[109] the state of emergency was an unnecessary and even harmful step in its domestic policy. But its purpose was to aid the reconciliation with Russia. The Polish argument was intended to remind the Tsar that Austria was interested in defeating revolutionary movements in Europe and to undermine Alexander II's trust in Napoleon III's policy. *'Hodie mihi - crass tibi'*. Italy today - Poland tomorrow. The declaration of a state of emergency in Galicia was received in St Petersburg, Wedel-Jarlsberg reported,[110] with all the more satisfaction because it was expected

---

102. H.H.S.A. *ibid.* Kart. 55.
103. No. 2 B, 4 February (23 January) 1864, Kart. 55.
104. After Knorring had acquainted him with the content of Gorchakov's telegram to the Russian chargé d'affaires in Berlin.
105. *Ibid.* Kart, 55.
106. *Ibid.*
107. *Ibid.* Cf. Wedel-Jarlsberg, no. 33, 15 (3) March 1864.
108. S. Kieniewicz, *Powstanie styczniowe* (Warsaw, 1972), p. 706.
109. H. Wereszycki, *Austria i powstanie styczniowe* (Lvov, 1930), pp. 301-2.
110. No. 28, 3 March (20 February) 1864.

to make things more difficult for the Polish revolutionaries. And although Plessen thought the declaration of a state of war was not the result of an *entente* between the two courts, he submitted that the move would serve the interest of Russia as it would make it harder for new groups of insurgents ('des bandes') to form and penetrate the Kingdom of Poland. This fact showed the two powers' solidarity of interest in the Polish question.[111]

The matter was widely discussed in diplomatic correspondence, particularly the French, and in the European press. The French ambassador in Stuttgart, le Comte de Damrémont, assessed the Austrian government's move as follows in a report on 3 March:

La mise en état de siège de la Galicie est généralement regardée comme le prélude d'une série de mesures réactionnaires qui tiendraient à rétablir l'intimité des relations entre les Cours de Vienne et de Saint-Pétersbourg. Ce fait, M le Ministre, ne renfermerait - il pas le germe d'une triple alliance qui offrirait à la Russie le moyen d'éteindre l'insurrection polonaise, à l'Autriche l'espérance d'une revanche de Magenta et de Solférino, et à la Prusse la perspective d'une agrandissement de territoire?[112]

Le Prince de la Tour d'Auvergne, the French ambassador in London, regarded the step taken by Vienna in Galicia as a sign of Russo-Austrian rapprochement, a blow at the uprising, and thus a help to Russia. In a report to Paris on 5 March he quoted the opinion of Russell, who seemed to him not to attach too much importance to the event and thought the rapprochement of the three northern powers was largely a matter of chance intended only to stem the revolutionary movement in Germany, which sought to take advantage of the tensions created by the question of the duchies. But in Russia's view the two larger German states would frustrate these plans. That was why, in Russell's opinion, Gorchakov would show indulgence towards the policy pursued by Austria and Prussia *vis-à-vis* Denmark.[113]

On the other hand, Baron Forth-Rouen, the French ambassador in Dresden, thought that as a result of the rapprochement between Austria and Russia, Gorchakov had secretly given his approval to the political line taken by Austria in respect of Denmark. This plan tallied with Russia's views. St Petersburg not only approved of it but boasted that it had won approval in London too. In this context it was to be noted that there were reports of fears in both St Petersburg and Vienna that Prussia would ally herself with the second-rank German states and that Berlin was planning to create a new Confederation of the Rhine.[114] The French ambassador in Vienna, Le Duc de Gramont, reported on 11 March, on the basis of information and explanations from Rechberg, that the minister had told him the state of war in Galicia had been declared as a result of increased activity by the clandestine government in Galicia, and that Russia had not influenced his government's decision in any way.[115]

---

111. No. 13 14 (2) March 1864. Cf. *Galicja w powstaniu styczniowym* (1980) pp. 362ff.
112. Damrémont to Drouyn de Lhuys, 3 March 1864. *Orig.* II, p. 75.
113. A.M.A.E. Angleterre, 728 no. 44. *Orig.* II, pp. 88-9.
114. 9 March, *Orig.* II, pp. 101-3.
115. A.M.A.E., Autriche, 486 no. 24, 5 March 1864, *Orig.* II, pp. 115-6.

In a dispatch to Vienna, Drouyn de Lhuys described the declaration of a state of war in Galicia as evidence of rapprochement between the St Petersburg and Vienna cabinets, but he found it hard to understand the logic of the decision in the light of the fact that Austrian troops were fighting in Schleswig in the name of the nationality principle.[116] In his opinion, and he had secret knowledge of this, there had been no agreement on the subject between Vienna and St Petersburg, and Vienna's decision had been taken independently. And he was right.[117]

Russia did indeed reconcile herself to the idea that the German armies' operation would not stop at the Dannewirke line, but Gorchakov began to become more and more conscious of the wretched role Russia was playing compared with the steps taken by Nicholas I, when Prussia invaded Jutland. He showed this during a talk with the Saxon ambassador in St Petersburg.

> Le Prince Gortchakoff rappelait ... que, lors de la première occupation du territoire danois par le Maréchal de Wrangel, l'Empereur Nicolas avait fait savoir à Berlin que, si le troupes prussiennes ne se retiraient dans un délai de ..., il prendrait à son tour possession du Duché de Posen. Les menaces de la Russie à cette epoque étaient plus écoutées que ne le sont, pour le moment, celles de l'Angleterre, qui, en abusant de cette arme, comme elle le fait, sans jamais y donner suite, provoque plutôt la résistance qu'elle ne l'écarte, ainsi que cela a eu lieu dans toutes les phases de la question danoise et *particulièrement encore aujord'hui*. Le Prince Gortchakoff faisait encore observer à M de Koenneritz que la France ne désirait que la confusion en Allemagne et une guerre en Danemark, pour pouvoir donner ensuite la main à l'insurrection polonaise.[118]

The news that the German forces under the command of General Wrangel had crossed the Eider, and the news of the first fighting and the resistance by the Danish army, initially made a great impression on Gorchakov. Up to the last moment he had deluded himself that the Danes would accept his advice and agree to the occupation of southern Schleswig.[119]

Gorchakov's unease could have been caused partly by the fact that, as Wedel-Jarlsberg reported,[120] the German aggression had met with universal disapproval in Russia, and the news that the Danes were fighting bravely was welcomed and applauded both by the court and by society, which hoped the Danes would succeed in repulsing the German attack.

---

116. A.M.A.E., Autriche, 486 no. 23, Minute. *Orig.* II, pp. 85-7.
117. See also Drouyn de Lhuys to Gramont and to the ambassadors to London, Vienna, St. Petersburg, Berlin and Frankfurt, 10 March 1864. Confidentielle. Minute, Angleterre. 728 no. 50. *Orig.* II pp. 106-8, especially p. 108. Rumours about the reconstruction of the Holy Alliance were denied by Gorchakov: 'La Sainte Alliance, telle qu'on l'entendait autrefois, a ajouté le Prince, est *morte* et *enterrée*', he said to Massignac, assuring him that Russia had not given Austria any advice in connection with her decision to introduce a state of war in Galicia. Massignac, 14 March, Confidentielle, Original, Russie, 233 no. 14, *Orig.* II, pp. 123-5. On 14 March the *Journal Officiel de St Pétersburg* published, as Gorchakov pointed out, an official denial of the rumours about the renewal of the Holy Alliance.
118. Baron Forth-Rouen, ambassador in Dresden, to Drouyn de Lhuys, Dresden 27 January 1864. *Orig.* I, pp. 216-7.
119. Wedel-Jarlsberg, no. 18, 4 February (23 January) 1864.
120. No. 20, 6 February (25 January) 1864.

L'Empereur même paraît plus sympathique à la cause Danoise que son Ministre. Il en est en général de même de la cour et de la société qui applaudit hautement à la vaillante résistance des Danois et fait des vœux pour que les agresseurs soient rejetés...

L'impression est immense ici – reported the Swedish ambassador – et plus que jamais l'opinion publique se prononce en faveur du Danemark.[121]

Napier also reported the change in mood and the pro-Danish attitude.

The sympathy for the Danes is certainly rising here though it has not reached the Foreign Department. The Emperor, the court, the government generally and the public are more Danish than Prince Gortchakof. Their influence – Napier hoped – might gradually move the Minister onwards.[122]

The main reason, however, for the striking difference between the position of Gorchakov and those around him was his fear that in view of the new situation, his conception of a four-power *entente* might collapse and that after the first exchange of shots in Schleswig the German states could retract the support they had only recently given to the Treaty of London. Gorchakov was aware that even before the German armies entered Schleswig, Bismarck had only conditionally agreed to maintain the Treaty in force, and that under pressure, and even then he had sounded out Oubril about a personal union of the duchies with Denmark. After the armies had entered Schleswig, and particularly after the capture of Danewirke,[123] Redern made it clearly understood that in the current circumstances Prussia would not return the duchies and would not agree to a personal union either.[124] Gorchakov had been afraid since the beginning of February that after the occupation of Schleswig the German states might repudiate the Treaty of London and that the result might be an Anglo-French rapprochement. 'C'est donc la guerre générale que Vous voulez', the vice-chancellor argued emphatically in his talk with Redern on 3 February.[125] Certainly, Gorchakov said, no one could prevent Prussia from declaring war against Denmark, but neither could anyone prevent France, Britain and Sweden from coming to Denmark's aid. At the same time this was an opportunity to demonstrate his pro-Prussian feeling yet again. 'La Russie ne fera jamais', Gorchakov declared, 'rien contre la Prusse, mais Vous aurez les trois autres sur les bras et Vous aurez ramené l'entente entre la France et l'Angleterre'.

Redern's cynicism showed in his immediate reply that it was not Germany that had declared war on Denmark but Denmark that had declared war on Germany, and many times at that, and he doubted whether Britain would help Denmark or whether Napoleon III would move together with Britain. 'Mais ce n'est pas pour les beaux yeux des Danois que l'Europe est convenue de son integrité, c'est dans un intérêt Européen que le protocol a été signé et cet intérêt prévaut encore aujourd'hui et nous est commun', cried Gorchakov, who was even more agitated when a courier

---

121. *Ibid.* and no. 21, 7 February (26 January) 1864.
122. Napier to Russell, 4 February, Private, P.R.O., vol. 84, pp. 187-9.
123. The Danish army abandoned the Danewirke on 5 February.
124. Wedel-Jarlsberg, no. 21, 7 February (26 January).
125. APP vol. IV. p. 513.

came in with a telegram from Kiel informing him that the Prussians had repulsed the Danes at Casel and Missunde. 'C'est la guerre générale', shouted Gorchakov, who was well known for this theatrical gestures. 'Vous aurez la France, l'Angleterre et la Suède contre Vous. La Russie jamais. Jamais elle ne marchera contre la Prusse'.[126]

The next day, however, Redern reported, Gorchakov changed his tone and expressed satisfaction with the declaration by Austria and Prussia that they would not abandon the principle of the integrity of Denmark, and he even urged Redern: 'Prenez le Dannewerk', 'le plus tôt possible, pourvu que cela ne coûte pas trop de sang'.[127] Basically he was satisfied with the course of events, thinking that it would hasten Copenhagen's agreement to the calling of a conference. After all, both Bismarck and Rechberg had indicated the possibility of convening one, despite the continuation of military operations.

Gorchakov, who was opposed to the policy of the Danish government but at the same time was concerned about the interests of Christian IX, must have been aware that the defeats at the front had caused a strong reaction in Copenhagen and that public opinion held not only General Meza but also the King responsible. 'Le Roi n'est pas un roi danois. Il est avant tout russe et allemand. Sa famille, son entourage sont dans les mêmes sentiments' ... 'Les intérêts de la Russie et du Roi Christian sont identique, et leur accord est complet'.[128] It was already being said, Dotézac reported, that Prussia and Austria would demand the union of Schleswig and Holstein, and that the King, who favoured the German element in the monarchy and wanted to please Prussia and Austria, would not oppose this, even though he had declared himself against it, since Russia favoured this solution, which 'réussissant, placerait le Danemark dans les mains de l'Allemagne, et surtout de la Russie, qui verrait ainsi s'accomplir, sous un Roi son satellite, la pensée pérsévérante de sa politique'.[129]

Plessen, however, saw no change in Russia's attitude towards Denmark after the German invasion. 'Je dirais qu'elle [Russia – EH] cherche à maintenir les deux puissances allemandes dans la fidelité à leurs engagements et qu'elle saisira toute occasion qui pourrait offrir des chances pour mettre un terme à l'état des hostilités.[130] In Plessen's opinion, Gorchakov had continually made efforts, but he had not used any threats against Vienna and Berlin. Gorchakov was also greatly disturbed by the demonstrations in Schleswig in support of Prince Augustenburg, which were staged in the face of the allied forces. In Gorchakov's opinion these could undermine the British cabinet's confidence in the allies and put their fidelity to the 1851-52 agreements in question. This could push Britain in a direction con-

---

126. Redern to Bismarck, 3 February, 1864, *Ibid.* pp. 513-514.
127. *Ibid.*, 4 February, p. 518.
128. Dotézac to Drouyn de Lhuys, 8 February 1864, A.M.A.E. Danemark, 246, no. 22. *Orig.* I, pp. 273-5.
129. *Ibid.*, p. 275.
130. No. 8 15 (3) February.

trary to the German states' interests and might have fatal effects for peace and the balance of power in Europe.[131]

Gorchakov's own assessment of the political situation and the place of Russia is to be found in the *Mémoire Confidentiel* which he drew up on 5 February 1864.[132] This memorandum stated that the new element in the political situation was the fact that the Polish question had ceased to be a problem of primary importance and its place had been taken by the Danish question, which was becoming more and more ominous each day. For Russia there were three aspects to the problem:

1. There were traditions and obligations from the past concerning the integrity of Denmark.
2. Russia had a great interest in ensuring that the partitioning of the monarchy did not lead to its absorption into a Scandinavian union.
3. It was in Russia's interest that the alliance envisaged between the conservative governments against demagogic infatuations should not be weakened, and that the current problem should be settled by the existing governments.

The impartial position adopted by Russia from the beginning of the conflict would make it easier for her to perform a conciliatory mission.

As far as Russia's attitude was concerned, we read in the memorandum, ever since the start of the conflict she had unceasingly urged Denmark to respect the obligation undertaken *vis-à-vis* Germany and, above all, to exercise restraint. This contrasted with Britain's agitation and contradictions, and the reserve maintained by France. Russia had first supported schemes designed to warn against the conflict, then to postpone it, and finally to find a way out of the situation and resolve it.

Russia had therefore supported the idea of taking advantage of the opportunity to send an extraordinary mission to King Christian IX, the object of which was to bring about the suspension of the 18 November Constitution in respect of Schleswig, while the Federal Execution in Holstein would simultaneously be revoked. Next, proposals had been put forward to convene a conference, and finally efforts had been made to secure agreement to postpone the occupation of Schleswig for a period of six weeks, so that Denmark would have time to convene the Rigsraad and present proposals to it for the repeal of the common constitution. Recently, a truce between the warring parties had been proposed, with the simultaneous opening of negotiations at a conference. Russia had striven to ensure that the German states upheld the provisions of the Treaty of London and, above all, she had sought the agreement among the conservative states which was so necessary for the preservation of peace in Europe.

Because the second-rank German states inclined in the direction of democracy, said the memorandum, *we urged* [my emphasis - EH] the larger German states

---

131. See Knorring to Rechberg, Particulière, Vienne, 31 January (12 February) 1864. H.H.S.A. P.A. Rus. Kart. 55.
132. A.M.I.D., vol. 68.

to take the matter into their own hands. Russia had brought her influence to bear on Britain to give them [Austria and Prussia - EH] the confidence to join together in the name of their honour and interests and to fulfil their obligation.

In Gorchakov's opinion, Britain found herself in a delicate situation because of family links (the marriage of the Prince of Wales to the daughter of Christian IX), and the Russian government therefore urged both the German powers to include in their declarations a promise to preserve the integrity of the Danish monarchy. Russia had pointed out the possible consequences if Britian joined up with Germany's enemies. Russia sought to strengthen the influence of the moderates in Berlin and Vienna against revolutionary infatuations. Despite her efforts, the memorandum said, she had failed to halt the course of events and all that she had been able to do was to slow them down and bring about the start of negotiations, even though the fighting continued. This nevertheless remained Russia's aim. On the one hand she was pressing the Copenhagen government to state its willingness to take part in a conference, and on the other she was urging the German governments not to cause a more dangerous situation in Europe. Russia was co-operating with Britain to preserve peace and stave off extreme decisions which would lead to a war with Germany, and to persuade the government in Copenhagen, in its own interests, to act wisely in accordance with circumstances and necessities.

The near future would show how far diplomatic methods would succeed in obtaining results, thus pre-empting the threat of complications which could be caused by elements already prepared for this. If the Danish-German question went in the same direction as the Polish question it could lead to a surge of revolutionary fervour in Europe and, in the end, to world revolution. The centres of trouble, in Gorchakov's opinion, were the Polish, Italian and Hungarian emigration. Beside this, Gorchakov stressed the dangers threatening from the Danube principalities on account of the policy of Prince A. Cuza, whose programme of secularisation of lands appeared to be not only revolutionary but also a dangerous political device aimed at the complete independence of the country. For this reason events in northern Europe could cause repercussions in Europe as a whole - especially in the Danube principalities - as well as in Serbia and Montenegro, lands belonging to Turkey.[133]

The memorandum is an apotheosis of Russian policy. It portrays it as a consistent policy aiming to preserve peace in Europe. It goes out of its way to claim that this policy was objective and impartial. Gorchakov ascribed all the initiatives from November to February exclusively to himself, whereas we know that only the first, connected with the Ewers mission, was his work. In the case of the others he joined them rather under the pressure of events, and supported them at times reluctantly and usually only half-heartedly. The document makes it appear that only Russia fought actively and agressively to preserve peace. This was of course a highly subjective view of the situation.

133. The situation in this part of Europe is discussed more broadly in Ch. and B. Jelavich. *The Establishment of the Balkan National States 1804-1920, A History of East Central Europe*, vol. VIII, (University Press, Washington 1977).

On the other hand, however, the efforts of British diplomacy were just as ineffective. 'At no period in the history of this question had British diplomacy been more active, and at no time had it been of less effect', say British historians.[134]

Contrary to the facts, Gorchakov's memorandum claimed that Russia had behaved impartially during the developing Danish-German conflict, which was of course at variance with her *de facto* commitment to Bismarck's Prussia. The document acknowledged, however, that Russia had not opposed the entry of Austro-Prussian troops into Schleswig. The Tsar, the memorandum states, had confidence in the declarations and policy of the German states and considered that the just demands of Germany should be met. He was also in favour of restraining revolutionary agitation in the Elbe lands, as a means of arresting the dangers which threatened European peace. Peace and the social order could be guaranteed only through co-operation by the conservative states. As far as Britain was concerned, we read, she was disposed to peace and wanted to avoid a conflict with Germany, but had reservations about the latter's intentions. It was necessary, therefore, to calm her fears, which increased after the German armies entered Schleswig, and to support her plan for a truce. Rechberg had spoken in favour of the British plan, but on condition that Denmark evacuated the whole of Schleswig and the island of Als. Russia supported this plan and urged Berlin to do so too. Gorchakov invited Napier to call on him so he could inform him that the Tsar had recommended support for the planned truce 'with the full weight of his Majesty's personal authority'.[135] Mohrenheim had received instructions to support it in Berlin and to co-operate with the British ambassador over the matter.[136]

At any rate, Gorchakov said with satisfaction, Germany had already achieved a positive result, and this applied both to the independence of Germany and to the balance of power in Europe. The Tsar was pleased with this result. The alliance of the two larger German states had been strengthened by brotherhood in arms. The Tsar hoped that it would be extended in glory and strength and would now overcome other problems which had hitherto divided them. He welcomed the Austro-Prussian alliance and wished it success in the future, in accordance with the great purpose by which it was guided.

After the German armies entered Schleswig, the Danish government turned to the Russian cabinet with a request for material help citing the old Russian guarantees of 1767 and 1773 concerning Schleswig and the 1851 Warsaw protocol and 1852 Treaty of London. Gorchakov and Alexander II refused such help.[137] Alexander's marginal note on this document demonstrates the cool and impersonal attitude taken by the Tsar. 'We have done and will do morally everything possible to defend Denmark. As to actual intervention, that is out of the question.'[138]

---

134. *The Cambridge History of British Foreign Policy,* vol. II, 1815-1866, p. 570.
135. Napier to Russell, 10 February 1864, *Denmark and Germany,* No. 959, p. 687.
136. Napier, 9 and 10 February, *ibid.,* nos. 958 and 959, p. 687.
137. A.M.I.D., vol. 68. Plessen's note of 1 (13) February 1864.
138. *Krasnyi Arkhiv,* vol. 2 (93) (Moscow, 1939), p. 77.

In a talk with Plessen, Gorchakov said the Danish note had not used the word 'matérielle' and had said nothing about active help ('secours actif'). He said the same thing to Napier, 'that the Danish note did not ask for material assistance, the word "material" was not in it', although the latter tried to demonstrate that the Danish telegram had contained an implicit request for military assistance. Referring to the recent conversation between Brunnow and Russell, Gorchakov observed that his aim, like that of the British government, was

> the preservation of Denmark in conjunction with the satisfaction of Germany ... The question at issue between Germany and Denmark must be brought under the control of all the parties interested. Only by a conference could such control be attained.[139]

The Vice-Chancellor, Wedel-Jarlsberg reported, 'n'a donné le moindre espoir d'une assistance matérielle de la part de la Russie'.[140] And he complained

> une fois de plus de la position précaire, politique et militaire dans laquelle l'intervention de l'Europe en faveur de la Pologne a placée la Russie, et, partant de là, pour contester le droit des co-signataires du protocole de Londres de s'attendre ou de compter sur une initiative rigoreuse quelconque de sa part.[141]

What was to be done now? In Gorchakov's opinion, 'insister sur une réunion au plus vite de la conférence proposée'. The Austro-Prussian armies' entry into Schleswig Gorchakov called a military demonstration, and their subsequent invasion of Jutland 'un movement motivé par les operations militaires', and, he added, 'et n'invalident en rien les déclarations allemandes'.[142] Napier wrote:

> He told me that he regarded the invasion of Jutland merely in the light of a military operation which did not invalidate in the least degree the political pledges given by the Governments of Austria and Prussia in regard to the integrity of the Danish Monarchy.[143]

As Massignac reported, Gorchakov tried to play down the significance of the Austro-Prussian troops' movements, describing the capture of Kolding as a strategic manoeuvre, whereas in 1849 as soon as the Russian government had learned of the Prussian plan for a show of military force on the Jutland frontier it had threatened Prussia with invasion of Poznan. On 8 May 1849, Nesselrode had sent a note to Berlin in which he threatened that if the Prussian troops entered Danish territory the St Petersburg cabinet would regard it as a hostile act.[144]

All the same, Massignac sensed unease in Gorchakov's attitude. In a talk with Massignac he had argued emphatically that it was essential to convene a conference in which a representative of the German Confederation would also take part, 'même sans armitrice conclu', and that the absence of a representative of the Con-

---

139. Napier to Russell, 16 February. *Denmark and Germany,* no. 1032, p. 728.
140. No. 24, 16 (4) February.
141. Wedel-Jarlsberg, *ibid.,* no. 22, 9 February (28 January) 1864.
142. In code, 20 February, and Massignac, A.M.A.E., Russie, 233, nos. 7 and 8, 22 and 23 February. *Orig.* II, pp. 5 and 22.
143. Napier to Russell, 20 February, no. 1054. *Denmark and Germany,* vol. 5, p. 740.
144. Massignac. *Orig.* II, p. 5.

federation during the London negotiations in 1852 had weakened the final resolution of that conference. He added that he did not understand why Denmark was unwilling for a conference to be called. And, most important, he put responsibility for what was happening on France, saying:

> Vous nous avez mis dans une telle situation par suite de Votre ingérence dans les affaires de Pologne, que nous ne pouvons agir d'une manière active et que nous devons attendre le développment des événements.

Gorchakov thus struck a different tone from his previous one, showing that basically he did not much like the situation in to which Russia was being drawn by events, since this meant a loss of initiative.[145]

It seems that in reality Gorchakov was greatly disturbed by the German armies' invasion of Jutland. On 22 February, Knorring reported to Rechberg:

> Les nouvelles reçues à St Pétersbourg de Londres et de Paris signalent une irritation fort vive produite par l'annonce de l'entrée des troupes austro-prusiennes en Jutlande.
>
> M le Prince Gortchakoff m'exprime l'appréhension que les avantages que cette mesure pourra avoir momentanément sous le rapport militaire ne soient contrabalancés par de sérieux inconvéniens politiques. Il croît d'ailleurs devoir abandonner à la sagesse des deux Cabinets alliés de peser les conséquences de la résolution qu'ils viennent de prendre.[146]

And Thun telegraphed in code on 22 February that Gorchakov regarded the entry into Jutland as

> Très grave, il m'a dit, Mr de Bismarck se fait des illusions sur l'attitude de la France et l'Autriche en sera la victime innocente.[147]

As we can see from these reports, Gorchakov was not indifferent to the turn of events and was aware that Bismarck was the *spiritus movens* (moving spirit) behind these decisions and that, while Austria had no interest in such a course of action, it could in the last resort fall victim to the policy pursued by Bismarck.[148]

In addition, disturbing reports about Bismarck's behaviour were reaching St Petersburg, indicating a growing discrepancy between what the helmsman of Prussian policy said and what he did. Oubril and Mohrenheim in Berlin and Brunnow in London trusted less and less what Bismarck said about his intentions. In February these doubts were further increased.

History, Mohrenheim philosophised in his report on 15 (3) February 1864, had condemned the compromise of 1851-52, the war had changed the situation, and the agreements concluded with Denmark no longer existed. The war had put an end to them and Germany was not bound by them. Any indecisive action would only encourage disorder in Germany. Only the London declaration on the territorial

---

145. A.M.A.E., Russie, vol. 233, 22 February 1864. *Orig.* II, pp. 4-5 contains only a fragment of this conversation.
146. Particulière, H.H.S.A... P.A. Rusland. Kart. 55.
147. *Ibid.* No. 3 (Chiffre).
148. 'He (Bismarck) was wise enough to keep Austria in tow', wrote C.W. Clarke, *Franz Joseph and Bismarck,* (Cambridge, Mass., 1934), pp. 61-2.

inviolability of the territory of Denmark remained in force, and it was necessary to agree on new arrangements which would be appropriate in view of recent developments.

The Russian *chargé d'affaires* had found Bismarck's course correct and made no reply to these words. He confined himself to warning Bismarck that he should be careful about Britain, so as not to produce a situation in which Britain threw herself into the arms of France.[149] In order to create a favourable disposition on the part of Russia, Bismarck in turn declared himself categorically against Prince Augustenburg and in favour of Prince Oldenburg, who was close to Russia, as a possible candidate to rule in the duchies.

Then, on 11 (23) February, Oubril reported that he was worried about Bismarck's intentions and was not certain what his plans really were. This time Bismarck had gone further than during his talk with Mohrenheim, putting forward demands such as a personal union of the duchies with Denmark and also demanding the transfer of the fortress of Rendsborg to Germany as a guarantee that Denmark would stick to her obligations. From Oubril Bismarck got only a warning, or rather friendly advice, on 26 February (9 March)[150] not to neglect the danger from Britain and France. Bismarck treated this lightly, saying he did not believe a situation existed in which co-operation would be possible between those two powers in the same way that he acted jointly with Austria.

Tels sont, mon Prince – wrote Oubril – les arguments dont se sert Mr de Bismark pour répudier nos salutaires conseils ... je ne puis que déplorer la légèreté avec laquelle il continue à envisager une situation dont la gravité ne devrait pas lui échapper

Bismarck played a cunning game with Russia, always using the same methods, complaining about the very difficult domestic situation, the difficulties of maintaining proper relations with the lesser German states, the differences among Prussian diplomats over her foreign policy (he was referring to the views of Goltz, who advocated alliance with France), the objections from the King, who was dissatisfied with his minister's moderation and threatened to abdicate or to appoint a new cabinet. He knew how to flatter Gorchakov, asking Oubril to assure him that as far as he (Bismarck) was concerned

le gouvernement prussien était très sincèrement reconnaissant de l'attitude de la Russie dans l'affaire danoise, qu'il etait charmé de pouvoir me le déclarer et que sous ce rapport il se reconnaissait en effet notre débiteur.[151]

The effectiveness of Bismarck's action is shown by the fact that Oubril came away with the impression that he had achieved his purpose and that he had convinced Bismark, as he explained to Gorchakov, 'de maintenir le Cabinet de Berlin sur une

---

149. *Krasnyi Arkhiv*, vol. 2 (93) (Moscow, 1939), pp. 77-9.
150. APP IV. pp. 651-2.
151. Bismarck had previously asked Redern on 2 February 'to express our trust in and gratitude for the continued friendly attitude of the Imperial Cabinet'.

ligne de conduite correcte et favorable dans des questions qui se rattachent à des intérêts majeurs pour la Russie'.[152] In reality, Bismarck treated the Russian advice indulgently and achieved what had always been his aim – the strong backing of Russia for his policies.

Officially, Gorchakov did not manage to address even a word of criticism to Austria and Prussia about the behaviour of the Austro-Prussian troops in the occupied duchies. When Plessen, after receiving a dispatch from Quaade on 15 March, gave him an account of events in Schleswig, of the destruction of the emblem of royal authority, the arrest of Danish officials and priests, the compulsory introduction of the German language in offices and schools and the desecration of graves and monuments to the events of 1848-49, all this made no impression on Gorchakov, who confined himself to saying he 'se réservait de méditer le sujet',[153] or Alexander II, who recorded his reaction on the report: 'highly exaggerated but probably partly true'.[154]

In view of the bad impression which the memorandum drawn up by Quaade might make in Britain, Gorchakov advised Thun (who tried to make light of the facts presented by the Danes, saying that three-quarters of it was slander and one-quarter insignificant trivia) not to neglect the matter, and was satisfied with the report he received in connection with it from Knorring.

Gorchakov also expressed concern about Prussia's attitude after the capture of Düppel:

Malheureusement – a-t-il ajouté – je ne puis pas dire la même chose [he was talking about Austria's moderate attitude, which he praised] de la Prusse, et je crains que le fait d'armes de la prise des fortifications de Düppel ne lui monte à la tête et qu'elle vous causera encore bien des embarras.[155]

Gorchakov, however, no longer had any doubt that Prussia was trying to turn the whole affair in a different direction from the one she stated in public. He also began to realise that it would be difficult to restrain Bismarck's aspirations. He started to warn Austria, about whose policy in the conflict with Denmark he felt increasing confidence, convinced that she would stay loyal to the provisions of the Treaty of London. Gorchakov began, moreover, to perceive how Austria might suffer more from Bismarck's miscalculations.[156] He did not find this hard, since from the beginning Austria had accepted Bismarck's plans with great hesitation.[157] During the following weeks, Gorchakov tried to use the same method, supporting Austrian conservative inclinations and attempting, unsuccessfully, to strengthen Austria's influence in Berlin.

---

152. APP, IV, pp. 685-7, Oubril to Gorchakov, 18 (30) March 1864.
153. Plessen, no. 15 30 (18) March 1864.
154. *Krasnyi Arkhiv, ibid.* p. 82.
155. H.H.S.A., P.A.X, nos. 7 A-9, 30 (18) April 1864, Kart. 55.
156. Thun to Rechberg, 22 February 1864, H.H.S.A. P.A.X., Kart. 55.
157. A. Klein-Wuttig, *Politik,* pp. 14-18; *Origines,* I, pp. 322ff.

Gorchakov took care to maintain the *entente* between Austria and Prussia, but at the same time he sought to build up Austria's firmness *vis-à-vis* Prussia. He also saw that Austria followed his advice more willingly than Prussia. He perceived, too, that Austria was beginning to realise more and more that Prussia's policy was increasingly a source of trouble for her. Austria was afraid of being exposed to great dangers if Prussia's actions led Britain to change the direction of her policy.

However, in trying to use Austria's influence on Bismarck to restrain his ambitions, Gorchakov's main concern was to help Bismarck avoid a dangerous new international situation.[158] Guided by this, Gorchakov advised Bismarck, through the Prussian *chargé d'affaires,* to issue a suitable public statement in order to placate British opinion, which had been disturbed by the actions of the German armies in Schleswig.

IV.

While restraining, or rather trying to restrain, Bismarck's ambitions, Gorchakov never for a moment ceased to press the government in Copenhagen to make concessions. The Russian government was very displeased by the prevailing mood in the Danish capital. And its dislike of the Danish government was only intensified by the latter's uncompromising attitude towards proposals that Denmark should express her willingness to enter into talks with Germany, while Russia simultaneously looked after the interest of the dynasty and the King. The Russian government thought Denmark had no chance on the battlefield in the face of the military superiority of the armies of the alliance and that time was not on Denmark's side.

Whereas in his dealings with the German states Gorchakov employed persuasion and warnings of the dangers of creating a Franco-British coalition, as far as Denmark was concerned he used pressure and behaved like a Russian grandee offended at the rejection of his advice by such a small country. It was no accident that diplomats knowing Gorchakov's vanity (M. Perglas, for instance) called him 'the Peacock', and that many Russians who had met him personally (D. Milyutin, V. Meshschersky) were of the same opinion. This element in the explanation of his behaviour towards the Danish government must not be left out of the reckoning.

In the middle of February the pressure on the Danish government came from two directions: firstly, it was urged to abandon its naval operations and the blockade of ports and, secondly, to agree to take part in a conference. In this connection, Gorchakov sent the following telegram to his embassy in Copenhagen on 4 (16) February:

Recommandez au Gouvernement Danois, dans son intérêt prudence surtout dans mesures maritimes. Nous regrettons son refus d'entendre le délai convenu par la saisie de navires

---

158. K. Schach, *Russian Foreign Policy Under Alexander Gortchakov. The Diplomatic Game Plan Versus Austria,* 1856-1875. (Ann Arbor, 1974), pp. 279ff.

Austrio-Prusiennes dans le ports à ceux dans la haute mer et redoutons que s'il procède à une saisie de navires Allemandes, il n'en résulte une guerre avec toute la Confédération. Nous appuyons partout chaleureusement la réunion immédiate de la Conférence.[159]

The blockade of Baltic ports by the Danish fleet also hit Russian trade. Russian merchants were calling on Gorchakov to secure the lifting of the blockade of Memel, as this port was used exclusively for shipping Russian exports.[160] As a result of Nicolay's intervention with the Danish government, the blockade of Memel was lifted for a period of three months, and Monrad did not rule out the possibility of an extension, or that by then the situation would have changed so that the blockade would no longer be necessary. But Monrad preferred to retain freedom of action for himself.[161]

Napier could not understand why Gorchakov took such a one-sided and unfavourable attitude towards Denmark and saw her as the sole aggressor. During a conversation on 16 February, when Gorchakov vehemently criticised Denmark's naval activity, Napier observed that it was the Confederation that had attacked Denmark and Austrian and Prussian troops that had invaded Danish Schleswig. It was doubtful whether Denmark's situation could deteriorate much more even if Danish naval actions led to the Confederation armies joining in the war.

The Prince contended in reply that it was idle to discuss whether the Germans were in principle engaged in hostilities against Denmark or not. We were not obliged to discover and affirm that such was the case. Our duty was to mitigate and diminish the causes of provocation as much as possible; nor could it be indifferent to Denmark even in a military point of view if the troops of the Confederation should be added to the forces now before the entrenchments of Düppel and Alsen.[162]

At this stage, Gorchakov's dislike of the Danish government increased because it refused to agree to immediate participation in the conference proposed by Britain and strongly supported by the Russian cabinet.

Gorchakov set out his view of the problem in a letter to Brunnow:

Prince Gorchakov believes – Brunnow informed Russell – that the determinations of Prussia and Austria are not finally settled, they depend most likely on the course of events. He quite agrees with you upon the necessity of bringing about, as soon as possible, an arrangement which could maintain, on the one hand, the existence of the Danish Monarchy, and, on the other, afford to Germany reasonable concessions within the limits of what may be considered as fair and just. With this view, Prince Gorchakov is desirous of removing the diffi-

---

159. A.V.P.R., vol. 68.
160. See the letter from Jewish merchants in Minsk to Gorchakov, March 1864, in A.V.P.R., vol. 68.
161. Nicolay, telegram to Gorchakov, 2 (14) April, A.V.P.R., vol. 67, and Nicolay to Gorchakov, report of 3 (15) April, *ibid.* On 27 April, in reply to Gorchakov's note of 1 (13) April, Monrad, in a letter to Nicolay, gave 'la garantie contre tout empiétement sur les droits d'une puissance neutre et amie'. R A Copenhagen, (661) (3). On the blockade see Correspondance Commerciale, Copenhague 1864-1869, vol. 15, A.M.A.E. W. Konopczyński, a distinguished expert on Baltic problems, considered the blockade an effective defence against Prussia. *Kwestia bałtycka do XX w.* (Gdansk, Bydgoszcz and Szczecin, 1947), p. 178.
162. Napier to Russell, no. 1034, 17 February 1864. *Denmark and Germany,* p. 729. Cf. Plessen's despatch of 10 May (28 April) 1864.

culties which stand in the way of the meeting of a conference. He is of the opinion that representatives of the Powers who signed the Treaty of 1852 would be able, in conference, to moderate the exaggerated pretensions of both parties. The main point, which Prince Gorchakov recommends me to bear in mind, is the need to strengthen the link which attaches Prussia and Austria to the London Treaty. This link is stronger in Vienna than in Berlin. In conference it would become more solid. Unfortunately, the latest intelligence received from Copenhagen tells that the Danes will fight and not enter into negotiation.[163]

Neither Plessen nor Nicolay helped ease the tensions between Copenhagen and St Petersburg. The former[164] discharged his function in a very formal manner, without involving himself in the defence of his government's policy, since he was not personally convinced that it was right and effective, and he was in essence closer to the political line represented by Gorchakov than to that being pursued by the Copenhagen government which he represented. Nicolay had little sympathy with, or confidence in, Monrad or the members of his government; if he singled out any one of them positively it was the minister of foreign affairs, Quaade, who was well known for his moderate views. In private talks he frequently recognised that the Russian ambassador was right, but simultaneously explained that on account of the tense situation in the country, and indeed the national movement in defence of the November Constitution, 'nous ne pouvons pas'.[165] But Quaade was not a personality who would have been able to oppose Monrad and public opinion then prevailing in the capital. The reason for this may have been that Monrad was, on the one hand, an exceptional personality but, on the other, a person with whom it was hard to work, as he suffered from manic depression, and from a psychologist's point of view was a veritable 'mine which would repay study', as his close colleagues P. Vedel and A. Krieger wrote of him.[166]

Nicolay was disturbed by the fact that the Danish government had decided to resist the occupation of Schleswig.[167] and that after the initial defeats and the

---

163. Saturday morning [before 14 February – EH]. P.R.O. 30/32, vol. 78 k. 317-8.
164. Plessen put forward the argument that the key to the international situation lay in the hands of France. France, which was reserving her position, might take Denmark's side, leading to the mobilisation of the whole of Germany, or she might propose peace to Germany at Denmark's expense. If the war became general there was a possibility of an alliance between Britain and France, but would Britain agree to France's territorial claims? As far as Russia was concerned, Plessen reasoned, it was impossible to say how she would behave in the event of a general war. But because of her internal situation she would keep her distance as long as the interests of her security were not involved – keeping her army in readiness on the Danube and in Poland and giving neighbourly assistance to Austria and Prussia against the revolutionary movements in Italy and Poland.

Summing up, Plessen thought that 1) revolutionary principles could not help Denmark; 2) a general war was not in Denmark's interests and it was hard to say what its consequences might be; 3) Germany's complaints were partially justified; 4) the Danish policy which had led to the war had been condemned by Britain and Russia; and 5) the interests of the King and the monarchy demanded caution and settlement by diplomatic means with the help of friendly states rather than continuation of the war, which would not bring positive results for Denmark. Plessen, no. 11, 2 March (19 February) 1864.
165. No. 1, 1 (13) January; no. 5, 6 (18) January and 12 (24) January.
166. Recently this question has been studied more fully by Johan Schioldan Nielsen in his work *D.G. Monrad. En Patografi,* (Odense U.P., 1983), pp. 386, 370, 569-72.
167. Lettre partic, 13 (25) January 1864.

army's retreat from the Dannewirke line the whole country was seized by the will to fight to the end.[168] In talks with Quaade, Nicolay said that he was unpleasantly surprised, and regretted that the Danish government would not begin negotiations as long as Austria and Prussia occupied Schleswig. He rejected as illusory the government's claim that it possessed sufficient resources to continue the fight and compel Austria and Prussia to leave Schleswig. In Nicolay's opinion, fears about the attitude of Danish society after the loss of the Dannewirke and the faith – which both the government and national liberal circles in Copenhagen continued to cherish – that Denmark had to fight on because, by prolonging the conflict, it could and would create favourable conditions for herself, were vain. The government was counting, among other things, on help from abroad, on some state, be it France, Britain or Sweden, coming to Denmark's aid.[169]

Seeing no chance of a peaceful solution to the problem while the occupation of Schleswig continued and Monrad intended to fight to the 'dernière extrémité', the ambassador reported as follows on 7 (19) February:

Il est nécessaire que ce pays – Nicolay argued – traverse une plus rude épreuve que celle qu'il a eue à subir jusq'ici avant qu'il y ait quelque chance pour un gouvernement quelconque de pouvoir aborder la voie plus pacifique des négociations. Il y a d'ailleurs de l'intérêt personnel du Roi et de tout l'avenir d'une dynastie, qui n'a pas encore poussé de racines assez profondes dans ce pays pour pouvoir risquer se suivre une direction si impopulaire. La Roi ne se fait pas d'illusions à ce sujet. Il est, à ce que me revient de bonne source, profondément éprouvé par l'état des choses et son impuissance d'y remédier. Une réaction ne saurait manquer de s'établir avec le temps. Il faut souhaiter que ce moment ne tarde pas trop à arriver.[170]

During his next talk with Quaade, Nicolay, wanting to persuade him to act promptly in support of a peace conference, argued that if he rejected this proposal it would make the worst possible impression on the cabinet in St Petersburg. He pointed out that there were precedents for holding talks about ending a war during the course of the fighting; an example of this might be the conference which took place in Vienna during the Crimean War.[171] On 24 February, Nicolay sent the following telegram to Gorchakov:

---

168. Nos. 17 and 18, 25 January (6 February) and 26 January (7 February) 1864, vol. 54.
169. Particulière, 4 (16) February 1864. Paget described similar reasoning by Monrad in his report to Russell on 23 February, no. 1066, pp. 745-6. In a letter to Paget Russell warned that Denmark would have to fight 40 million Germans and should therefore agree to a conference. 9 March, no. 1140, pp. 780-1.
170. No. 23.
171. No. 26, 11 (23) February 1864. Monrad took a different position on this matter.

Bishop Monrad was convinced, he [Quaade – E.H.] said, that no terms to which Germany would consent could be accepted by Denmark now, and he did not therefore see the point of entering a Conference for the purpose of leaving it. He said too, with reference to the negotiations that had taken place at Vienna [in 1854-55], that the case was quite different. None of the Powers there represented were engaged in the struggle for life or death, as Denmark was at the present moment; and the fact that negotiations for peace were going on during hostilities was not calculated to produce the same effect on the public mind, because no national existence was at stake. Paget to Russell, 26 February. *Aktstykker vedkom. den dansk-tydske strid. II. Akst. ved Londoner conf.* (Copenhagen, 1866), pp. 21-23.

Proposition anglaise d'une conférence sans armitrice. Faible espoir de voir le Cabinet danois y accéder. Conseils donnés par la Russie sont transmis à Mr Quaade. Dangers menaçant le Ministère et la dynastie. Esprit belliqueuse de la nation. Hésitations du Gouvernement[172]

In reply he received this telegram from St Petersburg, dated 13 February (old style):

L'Autriche, la Prusse et nous acceptons la conférence immédiate proposée par l'Angleterre. L'Empereur désire vivement que le Gouvernement Danois ne décline pas cette combinaison. Les intérêts vitaux de la Monarchie sont en jeu. C'est le moment d'écarter les illusions et de savoir restreindre même les aspirations d'un sentiment national, que nous comprenons, pour sauvegarder le présent et un avenir du pays [un avenir de paix]. Le Roi peut-être persuadé, que dans cette conférence, Il trouvera de chaleureux défenseurs de Son honneur, de l'intégrité de la Monarchie et des intérêts de la dynastie. Nous regretterions profondément, si notre voix amie, n'était pas écoutée. Nous renouvelons instamment le conseil de révoquer l'ordre de saisie des vaisseaux [navires] allemandes.[173]

Alexander II put forward similar demands in a conversation with Plessen,[174] and on 18 February (old style), Gorchakov telegraphed:

Danemark agit diametralement contre ses intérêts en mandant sursis de quinze jours pour sa réponse. Aujourd'hui les dispositions ont favorables pour la réunion de Conférence. Personne ne peut garantir ce qu'elles seront dans quinze jours. Ditez celà à Quaade et pressez acceptations.[175]

Napier reported on 28 February[176] that Gorchakov considered that

the delay desired by the Danish, and advocated by Her M's Government, was impolitic. The meeting of the Conference might be an unpalatable remedy, but its was necessary for the welfare of Denmark. That remedy ought to be taken at once by a bold resolution; if deferred, its acceptance might be rendered more difficult. Time in this matter was more than usually precious, and every delay exposed us to the hazards of some unknown contingency. In his opinion the Cabinet of Copenhagen ought rather to have been pressed to assent at once.

On 29 February Gorchakov informed Nicolay by telegraph that Austria and Prussia had declared that they were ready to conclude an armistice with Denmark if there were

d'evacuation réciproque des positions de Düppel et l'Alsen par les troupes Danoises et du Jutland par les Austrio-Prussiens, soit de l'*uti possidetis* militaire ... Conditions de cet armitrice: suspension des hostilités sur mer avec restitution des prises faites de part et d'autre et levée de l'embargo sur les bâtiments dans les ports.

172. A.V.P.R., Missiya v Kopenhagen, vol. 67, in R.A. Danica ...
173. This text, with minor changes [...], is to be found in *Aktstykker* II, 1866, pp. 17-18.
174. Plessen's telegram of 27 February.
175. A.V.P.R. vol. 67. Cf. Thun's report no. 4 A-C of 2 March (19 February).
   "Le Vice-Chancelier m'a parlé hier – Thun reported – dans le même sens en me disant, qu'il ne partageait nullement l'opinion du Cabinet Anglais qui paraissait vouloir appuyer la prétention du Gouvernement danois qui demande quinze jours de réflexion avant de ce prononcer. Il m'a dit avoir télégraphié au Ministre de l'Empereur à Copenhague pour le charger de faire valoir que l'acceptation immédiate et sans conditions des conférences était commandée par l'intérêt même du Danemarc ....".
176. Napier to Russell, Aktstykker ved. London conference, p. 27.

Furthermore, the German courts announced their readiness to participate in a conference with interested states to consider ways of restoring peace. Gorchakov instructed Nicolay to inform Quaade of this.[177]

Under the pressure of these telegrams Nicolay stepped up his activities. In a talk with Quaade he submitted that if Monrad's authority were not sufficient to rein in the mood of national exultation then the question of maintaining the government in office should be of secondary importance. What was of primary importance was to uphold the position of the King and the future of the dynasty, and he doubted if the government was interested in anarchy.[178] 'Je constate avec un sincère regret l'impossibilité *pour le moment* de faire prévaloir ici l'influence des conseils de prudence et de conciliation', Nicolay reported, almost with resignation, when he learned from Quaade that his efforts to persuade the government to agree to the conference proposed by the cabinet of St James were fruitless and that no one in the government would support him in this matter.[179]

The anti-peace mood in Denmark was reinforced by a number of factors:

The elections to the Folketing, the increased political activity, the press campaign in the pages of *Dagbladet* and *Fædrelandet,* Hall's speeches to the electorate and his argument that the German demands for the abolition of the 18 November Constitution were only a pretext on Germany's part (since the German troops had entered Schleswig despite the fact that the Danish government had promised to convene the Rigsraad and change the constitution), and Hall's claim that it was not true that Denmark had failed to fulfil her 1851-52 obligations.[180]

Nicolay tried to influence the King. The latter held Alexander II in the highest respect. He said that he recognised how much damage the country would sustain because of the prolonged and unequal fight, but maintained that the chances of peace were small since the nation was resolved to continue the desperate battle irrespective of the results.

Tout le langage du Roi était empreint d'une profonde tristesse, d'une pénible conviction de Son impuissance, et je ne puis que constater à mon sincère regret, que la position du Roi, Son isolément, l'absence de toute initiative énergique de la part de ceux qui sont les soutiens naturels du principe Monarchique, et les excitation du part démocratique, qui a exploité à son profit les sentimens d'indépendence et d'amour propre national, – sont des considérations qui doivent réagir sur toute attitude et les déterminations d'un Gouvernement surtout lorsqu'il est entre les mains d'hommes qui sont à chaque instant forcés de tenir compte des influences de l'opinion publique.[181]

In his telegram on 4 March (old style) Gorchakov instructed Nicolay: 'appuyez chaleureusement Paget décider Cabinet de Copenhague à autoriser ses plénipotentiaires à consentir à armitrice'. He urged the Danish government to be satisfied

---

177. Danica ... R.A. Copenhagen.
178. No. 27, 15 (27) February 1864.
179. No. 31, 19 February (2 March).
180. Nicolay, no. 34, 24 February (7 March).
181. Nicolay, no. 36, (Reservée) 26 February (9 March).

with the Austro-Prussian declaration concerning the integrity of the Danish monarchy. 'Les amis du Danemark ne peuvent agir avec quelque efficacité que dans le sein de la Conférence', and finally 'Danemarc agirait contre ses intérêts vitaux, si ne facilitait pas tâche de ses amis'.[182] Two days later Gorchakov sent the following warning:

Insister sur l'acceptation d'armitrice. Le Danemarc en donnant une réponse dilatoire, joue le jeu de ses adversaires et paralyse les efforts de ses amis. Les cours Allemandes paraissent n'avoir proposé l'armitrice que pour donner une preuve de conciliation aux autres Cabinets. Si le Danemarc persiste à décliner elles pourront se croire dégagés de toute résponsibilité. Ce serait une très mauvaise position pour le Gouvernement Danois.

Il sait aujourd'hui ne pouvoir compter sur aucune assistance matérielle de l'Angleterre.[183]

This telegram reinforced the one sent by Russell to Paget on 15 March:

Denmark, by delaying to agree to a Conference, incurs the risk of events occuring which might alter much to her disadvantage her present position and therefore it is that Her M's Government recommend the Cabinet of Copenhagen to give an early answer not only on the point of a Conference, but that also of an armitrice of which the military *status quo* should be the basis.[184]

On 5 (17) March Nicolay received instructions to back up the British government's recommendation for a suspension of the fighting on the principle of the *status quo*.[185]

Plessen was also working to persuade the government to announce Denmark's willingness to participate in the planned conference. On 14 (2) March[186] he addressed a long report to Quaade on his talk with Alexander II.[187] From it we learn that twice during the talk the Tsar appealed to the King to find a way to an agreement, that is to say, to bring the Danish government to express its willingness to participate in a conference. Gorchakov referred to the Tsar's wishes and explained that they stemmed from the conviction that, serious as Denmark's situation was, if the fighting were prolonged it could only deteriorate further and Danish integrity

---

182. Danica, Rus. Film. R.A. Copenhagen.
183. Telegram coded, 6 March (O.S.), Danica, R.A. Copenhagen.
184. Denmark ..., no. 5, no. 1172, p. 797. See also Buchanan to Russell, 19 March: 'The Danes have rendered Bismarck a great service by rejecting the armistice', P.R.O. 30/32 vol. 82, Voigt, p. 127 and General Grey to Queen Victoria, 17 March: 'The refusal of an armistice seems nothing short of madness, particularly after the miserable resistance they seem to have made in Jutland,' Voigt, *ibid.*
185. Nicolay, no. 42, 5 (17) March. Cf. Thun's dispatch no. 5 A-B of 14 (2) March. Kart. 55.
186. No. 12.
187. According to Redesdale, in a talk with him Plessen criticised the attitude of the public in Copenhagen, which continued to delude itself that Britain and France would send their fleets to the Baltic to help Denmark. It was this belief 'which caused the Danes so stubbornly to refuse an armistice which would have saved Düppel and spared thousand of lives ... Obviously', said the British diplomat, 'Baron Plessen disapproved of the action of his government in "prolonging their obstinate resistance" at the bidding of the Copenhagen mob, whom they feared, and, much as I admired the gallant defence of Düppel, I could not help sharing his view ... Baron Plessen', wrote Redesdale, 'was a man of great ability, calm, just and moderate in his views,' *Memories,* vol. I, pp. 274-5.

would be put at risk. In order to convince the Danish government that this was the only course for Denmark to follow, Gorchakov showed Plessen a report he had received from a courier on 12 March (29 February) of a conversation between Brunnow and Palmerston.

Before proceeding to discuss the current state of the Danish-German conflict, Palmerston had spoken of the mistakes Denmark had made previously, as well as accusing Austria and Prussia of turning the conflict into a war. He expressed recognition of the role Russia was playing, and of the restrained – as he called it – role of Prussia, which seemed to have remained faithful to the Treaty of London. Britain supported the integrity of Denmark and wanted to use peaceful means to preserve it. Palmerston expressed the opinion that prolongation of the fighting would not improve Denmark's situation, quite the opposite, the complications would multiply and Denmark could meet the same fate as Holland. (He was thinking of the events of 1830 and the birth of Belgium as a result of its detachment from Holland).

In his report Brunnow quoted Palmerston's words:

Je me souviens – said the British prime minister – d'un mot fort remarquable de Mr de Talleyrand, "En toute choix examiner bien si le temps est pour Vous, ou contre Vous. S'il Vous favorise, soyez lent. S'il Vous est contraire, hâtez Vous". Il est évident qu'une saine politique doit recommander aux Danois de mettre fin sur hostilités, sans le moindre délai. Chaque jour est perdu, augmente leurs dangers. Leurs forces militaires s'épuissent, tandis que leurs ennemis sont en mesure de reçevoir des renforts qui comblent sans cesse le vide que la guerre fait dans leurs rangs. Malgré la défense la plus opiniâtre, Frédéricia tombera, – les positions de Düppel finira par être emportée. Lorsque les choses en viendront là, le Danemarc sera récruit à subir des conditions infiniment plus dure que celles qu'il peut espérer encore aujourd'hui.

Il est impossible, mon Prince – Brunnow added his own comment – de rendre la force des expressions avec laquelle Lord Palmerston a énoncé ces vérités. Je crois que tout homme d'Etat Danois, quelque prévenu, ou exalté, qu'il fût, aurait compris, en écoutant les paroles du Premier Ministre, que le salut du Danemarc dépend de la promptitude et de la bonne fois avec laquelle la Cour de Copenhagen acceptera les conseils qui lui viennent en même temps de St Pétersbourg et de Londres. Si les conseils tardent à être suivis, le malheur sera accompli; sans qu'il soit en notre pouvoir de la réparer.

In order to facilitate the start of talks Palmerston intended to put pressure on both Denmark and the German states.[188]

Palmerston's ideas were identical to what Gorchakov was saying. Neither gave Denmark any chance militarily, and they had no illusions about the great powers' policy towards Denmark. It was not in the least surprising that Plessen should have been given access to Brunnow's report, since it was an additional and very important factor in the diplomatic manœuvres designed to compel the Danish government to take its place at the conference table.

At the session of Statsraadet on 12 March Quaade informed the members of the council that fourteen days before he had received proposals from the British government for convening a conference. The Russian government was demanding

---

188. A copy of Brunnow's letter dated 11 (23) March 1864, no. 56 is to be found in A.M.I.D., vol. 68.

insistently, said the minister, that Denmark should express her agreement to this.[189] Britain had said that she could not help Denmark on her own.[190] Nor could help be expected from France. As for Russia, he had reliable information that she was allied with Prussia. Monrad had received the information from Paget, who had said that Russia and Prussia had long ago concluded a treaty, so there was no prospect of help from Russia.[191] And as far as Sweden was concerned, said Quaade, her behaviour would depend on the circumstances.

In view of the difficult situation, both on the battlefield and in the diplomatic sphere, the Danish government agreed after a week of strong pressure from Russia and Britain and, as we know, after deep and prolonged hesitation, to accept the British proposal and take part in a conference without a prior truce, on the basis of the 1851-52 negotiations as a *sine que non* of its participation. Gorchakov was immediately informed of this by Nicolay.[192]

The question was, why did Gorchakov apply so much pressure on the Danish government to persuade it to participate in the conference? It was mainly, of course, because he was afraid that as the Danish-German conflict assumed ever broader dimensions and the territory of the battle was extended to Schleswig, Jutland and the Baltic, a local conflict would be transformed into a general war, '... dans une lutte ouverte entre le principe de l'autorité et celui de la révolution', as Gorchakov wrote to Olga Nikolaevna on 13 March (old style),[193] if France entered the war. Gorchakov also feared that Denmark, utterly defeated, stripped of the duchies and confined to the island territories, would throw herself into the arms of Sweden and create the Scandinavian union which for decades Russia had violently opposed. In his opinion this would have been equivalent to establishing French influence in that part of Europe and destroying the achievements of Russian policy going back to the time of Peter the Great. The closure of the Sound in the event of war would mean cutting Russia off from Europe. The Baltic would have become a second Black Sea.

The German historian, Cierpinski, wrote of this:

Es zeigten sich auch die ersten Spuren der Skandinawischen Bewegung, die den Russen in ersten Linien sehr unsympatisch war, weil sie den Ausgang der Ostsee nicht in einer Hand vereinigt sehen wollen, und weil ihre eigenen Pläne auf Dänemark dadurch gestört werden.[194]

Russia acted firmly against any change in the political system of Denmark. For the same reason she stressed the need to maintain the integrity of Denmark and

---

189. Neergaard, vol. II, p. 1134; *Statsraadets forhandlinger* ..., pp. 94-5.
190. Russell to Paget, 9 March 1864. Aktstykker, vol. II, p. 32.
191. *Statsraadets forhandlinger*, pp. 96-9. All this was based on the so-called Polish papers, published in the *Morning Post*, which were forgeries of diplomatic documents perpetrated by Polish emigrés and used by Palmerston.
192. Nos. 43, 7 (19) March and 46, 11 (23) March 1864.
193. H.S.A. Stuttgart, G 314 Bü 7.
194. *Zeitschrift der Gesellschaft für Schleswig-Holsteinische Geschichte*, vol. 44 (1914), p. 221.

defended the rights of the Glücksburg dynasty and Christian IX to the throne in Copenhagen. Russia was afraid that if the Danish army were routed, Christian IX would lose the throne and the population would hand the country over to Sweden, to which Britain and France would not object, and then Russia might lose Finland to Sweden. Hence she was also opposed to the stirring up of feeling in favour of Denmark in the territory of the Grand Duchy of Finland.[195]

The Russian cabinet was pleased to learn of the collapse of Danish-Swedish negotiations for a defensive treaty between the two countries. But Russia did not trust Sweden even for a moment and kept a careful watch on the reactions of both government and public opinion to the events in nearby Denmark during the Danish-German conflict.[196] Since December the reactions had in fact been calm, both on the part of the government and of Swedish society. Dashkov reported accordingly to St Petersburg, saying that Manderström had ceased making suggestions for armed intervention on behalf of Denmark, the demonstrations in favour of Denmark at the turn of 1863-64 had stopped, and Napoleon III was no longer urging the Swedish government to give material assistance to Denmark as categorically as before.[197] Sweden was unable to make up her mind about taking action to help Denmark in the face of the passivity displayed by the Western powers and her fear of Russia.[198]

Cette situation est pour nous très-penible, mais une nécessité politique nous commande, en cet état de choses, la plus grande réserve, que présent ultérieurement encore l'incertitude dans laquelle nous nous trouvons à l'égard des véritables intentions de Sa M le Roi de Danemark et son Ministère,

Manderström wrote to Hamilton, his ambassador in Copenhagen.[199] 'Que faite la Russie de la remise de l'ultimatum à Copenhagen?', was the gist of a telegram Manderström sent on 18 January to his ambassador in St Petersburg. And when the German armies went into Jutland he telegraphed: 'Cette nuit les allemands sont entrés à Jutland, qu'en dit la Russie?'

When the German troops crossed the Eider Manderström confined himself to a protest and public opinion expressed satisfaction with the government's attitude.

Je penche vers l'opinion – Dashkov reported – que la masse du pays est fort opposée à voir la Suède figurer dans une guerre, en risque de compromettre pour longtemps encore la vie de progrès matériel dans laquelle le pays se trouve engagé.[200]

195. Massignac's report, Russie, no. 233, no. 6, 16 February 1864, *Origines,* vol. I, pp. 315-7; Klaczko, *Études ...,* p. 371.
196. See Krieger, *Dagbøger,* vol. II, p. 341.
197. See Dashkov's reports, no. 97, 7 (19) December 1862, no. 102, 17 (29) December, no. 104, 26 December (7 January) and no. 2, 10 (22) January 1864.
198. See Gulberg, *Tyskland i svensk opinion 1856-1871,* (Lund, 1952), pp. 99, 102-3; Hallendorf, *Illusioner ...,* p. 104. See also the report from the Prussian ambassador, Adelbert Rosenberg, to Wilhelm I, 2 November 1863, APP, vol. IV, no. 51, p. 103, and the reports from the French ambassador, Fournier, to Drouyn de Lhuys, 9 January and 10 February 1864, A.M.A.E., Suède, vol. 334, *Origines,* vol. I, pp. 117-9, 286-7. See also 'Kong Oscar IIs Breve til Henning Hamilton', ed. Aage Friis, *Danske Magazin,* (Copenhagen, 1940), Series 7, vol. 2, pp. 169ff.
199. Beskickningen i Köpenhamn arkiv. Ankomna skrivelser. 1864 II. Från svenska regeringen, 1864, no. 5, Stockholm, 7 January 1864.
200. No. 3, 21 January (2 February) 1864.

And despite the consternation after the fall of the Dannewirke, the ambassador reported:

Aujourd'hui ce n'est pas plus à la Russie, c'est à la France et à l'Angleterre que l'on attribue la principale cause de l'état de délaissement dans laquelle se trouve le Denmark. Le fait est que le prestige de la France et celui de l'Angleterre n'ont pas gagné actuellement.[201]

In spite of demonstrations in Stockholm against the King and particularly against Manderström and 'contre les Allemands et les Russes', organised by Scandinavianist agitators after the German forces entered Jutland, they did not succeed in changing the direction of the government's policy.[202] As Dashkov reported,[203] everyone regretted the injustice meted out to Denmark, but the predominant view was:

La Suède aime la paix, elle espère son maintien combiné avec le triomphe du bon droit du Danemarc. L'Europe ne permettra pas que les droits les plus sacrés soient impunément méconnus.

The Norwegian Storthing, contrary to what the King anticipated, expressed doubt whether, in view of Norway's difficult economic situation and the lack of allies, assistance from the Scandinavian countries alone could be sufficient for Denmark. It passed a resolution that in the current situation the country should not involve itself in the war and that 'la grande majorité du peuple norvégien ne désire sûrement pas une union plus étroite avec le Danemarc'. This resolution, as the King correctly foresaw, also influenced the anti-war attitude in Sweden.[204]

After the fall of Dannewirke, Manderström emphasised that it was no longer a question of defending Schleswig but of regaining it, and the Swedish forces were too weak to do this.[205] At the same time Manderström asked the neutral Western states to help Denmark.[206] London answered that Britain would not co-operate with Sweden by herself and Drouyn de Lhuys gave the non-committal reply that he did not intend to intervene now but reserved his freedom of action.[207] After receiving these replies, and being afraid of Russia, Sweden decided to step up her level of military preparation but to do nothing to defend Denmark.[208] Fear of a possible Russian invasion increased when the King received reports from Finland that Russia was concentrating forces and preparing for action in the region of Helsingfors, Sveaborg and Abo.[209]

Wedel-Jarlsberg received instructions from Stockholm to prepare a report on

---

201. No. 4, 28 January (9 February).
202. No. 11, 25 February (8 March) and no. 16, 6 (18) March).
203. No. 14, 3 (15) March.
204. Dashkov, no. 18, 13 (25) March, no. 19, 20 March (1 April), and no. 20, 24 March (5 April).
205. Koht, *Die Stellung ...*, pp. 216ff; Drouyn de Lhuys to Fournier, 23 February. Minute. Suède, 334, no. 6. *Origines,* vol. II, pp. 12-14.
206. Fournier, Confid. Orig. Suède, 334, no. 52, 3 February 1864, *Origines,* vol. I, p. 253.
207. Drouyn de Lhuys to Fournier, 23 February, and in *Origines,* vol. II, pp. 12-14.
208. Koht, pp. 216ff; Neergaard, vol. II, pp. 1123ff.
209. Fournier to Drouyn de Lhuys, (Confid.coded) 26 March, Suède, 334, no. 71, *Origines,* vol. II, pp. 178-81.

the state of affairs in Russia.[206] In his report the ambassador analysed the international and the domestic situation of Russia in 1863 and at the beginning of 1864. Comparison of Russia's situation in these two years led him to the following conclusions: from the point of view of the international situation, Russia's position had improved as, while in 1863 she was virtually isolated, at the beginning of 1864 she had recovered her natural allies ('ses deux alliés naturels'), Prussia and Austria, and they were bound together by a common interest, namely the fight against democratic elements in Germany and Poland. In addition, Britain was taking a more friendly attitude towards Russia. From the domestic point of view the situation had quietened down after the disturbances connected with the emancipation of the peasants and the revolutionary agitation reminiscent of the revolutionary propaganda in France in 1789, which had even penetrated the ranks of the civil service and the army.

Le sentiment national s'est enfin retrempé et le patriotism russe ne laisse plus rien à désirer ... la nation est aujourd'hui disposé aux plus grands sacrifices pour défendre l'intégrité de l'Empire contre l'étranger et ce qu'on appelle ses injustes prétentions.

From the military point of view, too, the situation had improved in comparison with 1863. A process of modernisation was under way in the army, which numbered effectively 1,200,000, of whom 800,000-900,000 were capable of fighting, not counting the rural militia. Following the reorganisation of the garrison and the strengthening and re-arming of the infantry and artillery, approach to the fortress of Kronstadt and the shores of the Baltic from the Gulf of Bothnia was much more difficult.

Il est facile de comprendre que l'Europe trouverait aujourd'hui à qui parler et que l'entreprise d'une attaque serait maintenant hérisée de difficultés tout autres qu'il y a un an.

Only the financial situation of Russia was worse in 1864 than it had been in 1863. As far as the Kingdom of Poland was concerned, on the other hand, Russia was in a much better position there than she had been a year before.

La conservation de la Pologne lui tient essentiellement à cœur - et, pour atteindre ce but et ne pas avoir à compter avec le débordement démocratique de l'Allemagne, il laissera faire l'Autriche et la Prusse, et sacrifiera maintes fois le Danemarc - même avec la perspective d'une Scandinavie forte.

And Wedel-Jarlsberg's final conclusion was:

De tout ce qui précéde il est évident que la position de la Russie est infiniment meilleure aujourd'hui qu'il y a un an. De faible et misérable qu'il fut alors, le pays est maintenant fort, uni, régénéré et bien préparé. Ayant retrouvé ses anciennes alliances naturelles, le Cabinet de St Pétersbourg attend avec calme et résignation les événements et tout indique qu'il per-

---

210. Depecher från beskickningen i St. Petersburg. E. II, f. no. 29, 10 March (27 February) 1864). See also Fournier to Drouyn de Lhuys, 26 March. *Origines,* vol. II, pp. 180-1.

sévéra longtemps dans cette politique expectante. En principe, il se prononcera certes pour le maintien de tous les traités dont il est signataire, mais en réalité il fera – j'en suis persuadé – les plus sacrifices pour ne pas se mêler activement des affaires d'autrui.

The situation could change in the spring, however, since the revolutionary wave which was anticipated in Hungary, Galicia, the Danube principalities, Poland and Italy could create the right circumstances for France to liberate Denmark, and if this were to come about Sweden would soon be able to join in and come to the aid of Denmark. Turkey, too, might then serve as an ancillary anti-Russian force.[211] The ambassador's report could only say that the Stockholm cabinet's cautious policy was correct and justified in the circumstances. This was confirmed by a telegram from Napoleon III to King Charles XV on 19 April: 'Dans l'intérêt de Votre Majesté, je crois qu'il est maintenant trop tard pour faire une manifestation armée en faveur de Danemark'.[212]

Both sides appear to have made similar mistakes in their assessments of the situation and of Russo-Swedish relations. The Russian government had exaggerated fears of Swedish intervention and its possible effects, which might lead to a general war, something Russia wanted to avoid at any price.[213] On the other hand, rumours that Russia was planning to attack Sweden and draw her into the conflict, 'à la guerre générale', as Nicolay said, which could lead to unforseen consequences, were certainly incorrect, as were the stories that if Sweden-Norway stood by Denmark she would risk war with the three powers since, according to the rumours circulating at this time, Russia had confidentially assured Berlin that in all cases she would co-operate with the Berlin cabinet.

The argument that Russia played a double game, officially neutral but unofficially, and secretly pro-German, with the intention of compelling Sweden to adopt a passive attitude, was set out by C. Bååth-Holmberg[214] on the basis of articles on the subject, which were published in the Norwegian *Morgenbladet* in October 1890. In the Public Records Office in London I came across a hitherto unknown report from Napier to Russell, dated 22 June 1864,[215] dealing with this question.

I have heard and two of my colleagues here have heard – reported Napier – that Russia gave positive assurances to Prussia and Austria that in the event of war for Denmark, Russia would stand by German powers and particularly that, if Sweden drew the sword for Denmark, Russia *would send* an army of observation into Finland. If it is not stated that Russia has promised to go to war for Germany against Denmark, England and Sweden until to,

---

211. Report no. 29, 10 March (27 February) 1864. Depescher från beskickningen i St. Petersburg, 1864, E II, f.
212. See Drouyn ne Lhuys to Fournier, 21 April, *Origines,* vol. II, no. 448, pp. 280-1, and vol. III, pp. 366-372. (Mémoire par Lefebvre de Béhaine). See also Koht, *Die Stellung* ..., pp. 210ff. Hallendorf, *Illusioner* ..., pp. 127ff, Steefel, pp. 170-1, Allan Jansson, *Den svenska utrikespolitikens historia,* vol. III, part 3, 1844-1872, pp. 219ff; W Mosse, 'England and the Polish Insurrection of 1863' *The English Historical Review,* vol. LXXI, no. 278 (January 1956) pp. 38, 51.
213. See Dotézac to Drouyn de Lhuys, A.M.A.E., Danemark, vol. 246, no. 26, 12 February, *Origines,* vol. I, pp. 298-9.
214. C. Bååth-Holmberg, *Carl XV,* (Stockholm, 1891), p. 444.
215. P.R.O. 30/32, vol. 84. k. 230-2.

it is asserted that Russia is determined to throw her moral weight and influence into the apposite scale and *said she would do so.*

Napier was concerned to explain this matter and reached the following conclusions. Referring to previous corresponence about the question of troop concentrations on the Finnish border, he assured Russell that Gorchakov had stated that these rumours were without foundation:

The forces in Finland are being reduced not augmented and Russia is at this moment disarming, not arming.
Prince Gortchakow never pretended that he would take up arms for Denmark, but he incessantly expressed his regret and reprobation at the course taken by Germany and Prussia and he incessantly sent dispatches to Austria and Prussia advising moderation and pointing out the dangers on which they were running.

If the war had broken out, and if Sweden had entered the lists against Germany, it was open to Russia to take the course which it considered conformable to its interests and safety.

But if Prince Gorchakov, in *anticipation,* told Prussia and Austria that in the event of war he would stand by them and intimidate Sweden, then he undid secretly the work he pretended openly to effect; he neutralised his avowed counsels and encouraged Russia to continue on the course which he pretended to denounce, and did denounce to Brunnow, Knorring and Oubril over and over again.
The Russians might determine on any policy that suited them, but they were not justified in communicating it to Germany. Germany might *guess* that the course of Russia would for natural reasons be so or so, but they ought not to have received an assurance to that effect.

This line of reasoning by the British ambassador was correct. In addition he was able to report that Mukhanov, deputising for the absent Gorchakov, had assured the French *chargé d'affaires* 'that no such assurances had been given, no such declaration had been made'.[216]

One thing is certain, that, faced with a choice between Germany and Scandinavianism, Russia's place was always with Germany. Consequently, she covertly torpedoed any steps designed to tighten co-operation between the Scandinavian countries.[217] To his diary entry for 27 March 1864[218] Krieger added some characteristic words in 1869 about Russia's position in 1864, saying that since 1863 she had been unswervingly anti-Polish and anti-Scandinavian.

Pirch, Bismarck's personal envoy, observed in a report to Berlin from St Petersburg dated 11 May 1864.

Der Fürst Gortchakow seinerseits geht von dem Grundsatze aus, dass die Integrität der dänischen Monarchie für Russlands auswärtige Politik von der höchsten Wichtigkeit sei, denn er fürchtet in einer Dismembrierung derselben den Anfang der Skandinavischen Union und hat wiederholt geäussert: "Jamais la Russie ne pourra souffrir que le Belt devienne

---

216. Napier to Russell, Private, 22 June 1864. PRO 30/32, vol. 84, k. 230-2.
217. E. Møller, *Skandinavisk stræben og svensk politik omkring 1860,* (Copenhagen, 1946).
218. Vol. III, p. 105.

un second Bosphore!" Und strebt deswegen dahin, die Machtstellung Dänemarks so wenig als möglich schwächen zu lassen.[219]

Russian and British interests coincided in policy towards the Baltic, as both powers were opposed to any third power becoming strong enough to be able to close the access to the Baltic.

I told Brunnow yesterday – Russell wrote to Napier on 30 March – that question was approaching equally connected England and Russia, that a power like Germany with a pretended Scandinavian Kingdom would have in their power to close the Baltic; and this was the interest both of Russia and of England to prevent. He quite agreed with me.[220]

'Rusland-England frygtede for Skandinavien af de samme grunde (considered the Swedish ambassador in London, Wachmeister) som bragte Frankrig til at ønske det',[221] Krieger wrote from London to Vedel.[222] And in a letter to Gorchakov on 1 June (20 May) 1864[223] Brunnow expressed the fear that Bismarck's lack of restraint and the absence of any assurance from him that he did not intend to destroy Denmark could lead to serious consequences. If Bismarck, wrote Brunnow, gave suitable guarantees of the national independence of Denmark and declared that he did not intend further occupation of the country, he would prevent Swedish action in support of Denmark and avoid the Baltic fleet putting to sea. 'In a word, he will not repay us with bad for good. He would do us a poor service if he caused Denmark to join a united Scandinavia. I foresee just such an outcome if Bismarck does not stop in time', Brunnow concluded.

The ambassador's concern was fully shared by both Alexander II and Gorchakov. 'Votre pensée "d'isoler les îles pour que le Danemarc ne devienne pas Suèdois" est celle de S.M., qui l'a exprimé elle-même au Roi de Prusse et l'Empereur d'Autriche,' Gorchakov telegraphed to Brunnow from Kissingen on 13 (25) June 1864.[224]

It is highly significant, although understandable, that Scandinavianism found support in Germany among democratic and liberal elements. In their fight against the Treaty of London, and particularly the 1851 Warsaw protocol, behind which they saw Russia's hand, and against what they called annexationist tendencies in Denmark on the one hand, and the feudal party in Germany on the other, they wanted the support of Britain and Sweden. In their opinion a union of the German Union and Scandinavia would guarantee freedom in the Baltic and would be in the

---

219. APP, 1858-1871, vol. V, p. 94.
220. P.R.O. Russia, 30/32. Earl Russell, Private, 1859-1865, vol. 114.
221. Krieger reported that Russia and Great Britain were frightened for the same reason at the idea of the Scandinavian Union, but France was in favour of it.
222. Krieger to Andrae, 17 April 1864. *Historisk Tidsskrift,* 1895-95, pp. 132-33. Krieger to Vedel, 18 April 1864, *Danske Magazin,* 1940, vol. 3, p. 166. See also Kriegers remarks on Russian attitude towards Denmark in 1864, made on 27 March, 1869. *Dagbøger,* vol. III, p. 105.
223. *Krasnyi Arkhiv, ibid.,* pp. 95-6.
224. AMID, vol. 68.

interests of Germany, Scandinavia and Britain.[225] The following excerpt from a document written in February 1864 is characteristic of these circles' line of argument.

Das Interesse Deutschlands und Englands war, dass durch unbeugsames Festhalten an dem schleswig-holsteinischen Staats- und Erbrecht von Seiten Deutschlands Dänemark bestimmt worden wäre, die einzige ihm noch übrige Wahl rasch zu ergreifen, nämlich ein bescheidenes Glied einer skandinavischen Union zu werden, und dass diese Union mit den anderen germanischen Staaten im Bund die Freiheit der Ostsee gewahrt hätte. Statt dessen hing man an dem Phantome der europäischen Nothwendigkeit eines starken Staates am Sund; man sah nicht oder wollte nicht sehen, wie damit nur für russisches Interesse gearbeitet war; man besiegelte im Londoner Protokoll das Attentat, welches Russland mit dem Warschauer Protokoll auf die Interessen Deutschlands und Skandinaviens gemacht hatte.[226]

Bismarck was right when he stressed in a talk with the French ambassador in Berlin, Talleyrand, on 23 February 1864, how important the question of Scandinavianism was for Russia and how sensitive she was to any sign of it, especially in Sweden, which Gorchakov continually suspected of seeking to take advantage of the situation connected with the Danish-German conflict to recover her former domination of the Baltic. Bismarck commented on Russia's anti-Scandinavianist obsession: '... la Russie, par crainte de l'idée scandinave, insiste en faveur de l'armitrice, de la Conférence, et de l'intégrité de la Monarchie danoise'.[227] His reasoning ran as follows:

Si l'intégrité de la Monarchie danoise ne triomphe pas en dernière analyse, il faut s'attendre à voir un jour ou l'autre le Danemark diminué faire retour à la Suède pour retrouver dans l'union scandinave la force vitale qui lui serait ôtée: or, rien ne serait plus contraire aux intérêts de la Russie que de tolérer l'accroissement de cette nationalité hostile qui dominerait la Baltique et en tiendrait les clefs.[228]

---

225. These tendencies and contacts in the years 1856-63 have been discussed by, among others, Gulberg and Jansson.
226. Eidgenössische Correspondenz für Deutschland. I. Die Pflicht Westdeutschland gegen Deutschland und Europa. (Anfang Februar 1864). (Als Manuscript gedruckt) H.H.S.A. P.A. Nachlass Bernard, Graf Rechberg, 1859-1864, no. 528, Teil 4, Schleswig-Holsteinische Frage, Kriege 1864-1866.
227. A.M.A.E., Confid. Prusse, no. 30, *Origines,* vol. II, p. 15.
228. Talleyrand to Drouyn de Lhuys, 20 February 1864, *ibid.,* no. 29, *Origines,* vol. I, p. 342.

8. From the London Conference to the Treaty of Vienna April – October 1864

I

Both sides, Denmark and Germany, finally agreed to take part in a conference, which was to be held in London. The signatories to the 1852 Treaty of London would participate, and there would also be a representative of the German Confederation. Over a month passed, however, before the first session of the conference. Towards the end of March the hosts issued official invitations, and the first formal meeting of the conference took place on 20 April.

The invitation was signed by Russell, and drawn up jointly by him and Brunnow. The latter was responsible for giving it a more flexible form.[1] There were many reasons for the delay in the start of the conference. Initially it was expected that a cease-fire[2] could be achieved before the discussions opened. But Denmark was in no hurry to come to the conference. Both the Danish government and public opinion, particularly in Copenhagen, realised the gravity of Denmark's situation and how difficult her position would be at the conference. They continued to believe that France, faced with the prospect of co-operation between Russia, Prussia and Austria, would take up arms and, together with Italy and Sweden, attack Germany and that Britain would then join in with them. There were also difficulties over the choice of a representative of the German Confederation, and the preparation of instructions for him. Finally, Bismarck was in no hurry either. He was aiming for another victory on the battlefield before the work of the conference began, namely the conquest of Düppel, which was eventually taken by the Prussian army on 18 April.[3]

Prussia's victory there made Denmark's position even more difficult. All the neutral countries, whatever they said officially, had to recognise that however much they might declare themselves in favour of the maintenance of the provisions of the Treaty of London, there was no longer any question of a return to the *status quo ante*. But only one of them spoke out soberly and rationally, starting from the principle that the Danish-German conflict should be settled in accordance with the spirit of the times. That country was France.

---

1. H.H.S.A., P.A. VIII, England, vol. 63, no. 20B. Apponyi to Rechberg, 19 March 1864.
2. In Danish there are two terms: våbenhvile (Cease-fire) and våbenstilstand (Suspension of the Fighting, Armistice, Truce).
3. A. Klein-Wuttig, *Politik and Kriegsführung*, pp. 20ff. According to Klein-Wuttig, both Moltke and Bismarck and the King were in favour of a military solution. pp. 26-27. J. Nielsen, *1864 Da Europagik af lave*, (Odense, 1987), ch. 12.

French diplomacy was based on the principle that the southern part of Schleswig should be joined with Holstein, since it was inhabited by a mainly German population. The northern part of Schleswig would remain part of Denmark, and there the 18 November Constitution would continue in force.[4] If these conditions were fulfilled, peace could quickly be restored. The only doubtfull question would be the so-called mixed districts, inhabited by Danish and German populations, and in this part of Schleswig France proposed that a plebiscite should be held to enable the population to express its view about the future,[5] i.e. whether they should remain part of Denmark or not.

Regardless of what intentions lay behind the policy of Napoleon III at this time, the idea, based on understanding of the importance of the national question, was essentially modern and correct. In practice it meant reduction of Denmark's territory.[6] It was opposed by the conservative countries, in which the application of this principle could have incalculable consequences. I am thinking here primarily of Austria, torn by nationality conflicts, and Russia, the 'prison of nations'.

Gorchakov was the first to reject the French proposal categorically, both on grounds of principle and for practical reasons, arguing that under the conditions created by the military occupation of Schleswig the population there could not express itself freely about its future, and it was improbable that the Austro-Prussian army would withdraw for the period of the voting. Gorchakov was perfectly well aware[7] that the differences between Denmark and the German states, and particularly between Denmark and Prussia, were of such an order that it would be hard to reach any agreement. He realised that Bismarck's ambitions were continually growing as his army won new military victories, and that there was an ever larger gulf between his real aims and what he said officially. Reports were coming in to St Petersburg from Oubril and Brunnow that after the recent victories in Jutland Bismarck's language had changed. Gorchakov was extremely anxious that the aggressive position being taken by Bismarck could lead to a violent reaction on the part of Britain, and especially France, and that as a result the balance of power in Europe would be disturbed.

In spite of this, however, he did not alter his position on the fundamental question. This is shown by a letter to Olga Nikolaevna on 13 March (old style), in which he expressed himself firmly in favour of a union ('d'une union') of the German states with the two great German powers, since this was essential for a strong Germany. He was against the dreams of Pfordten and Beust, as, if they were fulfilled,

---

4. Apponyi reported from London on 4 April that Lord Russell saw the French proposal to consult the population of the duchies as an attempt to undermine the conference. 'Baron Brunnow juge ce mode inadmissible. Selon lui les grandes Puissances ne subordonnent leur opinion à celle des maîtres d'école de Schleswig et à ce prix il voudrait mieux que la conférence ne se réunit plus'. No. 25 C, Chiffre. Kart. 63, H.H.S.A., P.A. VIII.
5. Russell to Paget, 23 March 1864, P.R.O. vol. 102.
6. According to Moltke's report to Hvitfelt on 12 April 1864, Drouyn de Lhuys said: 'If a country is sick, amputation is necessary.' Dep. Frankrig.
7. Gorchakov to Brunnow, 24 March 1864. A.M.I.D., vol. 68.

the second-rank German states would be transformed into something like French prefectures.

Les rêves de MM.v.d. Pfordten and Beust, s'ils pouvaient se réaliser, aboutirait à un résultat diamétralement opposé. Sous des noms plus ou moins pompeux ils convertiraient des Souverainetés Allemandes du second ordre en quasi-Préfectures françaises. Je crains que dans la marche qu'on suit aujourd'hui on ne perde de vue ce résultat,

said Gorchakov. Referring to Prussian policy, he wrote:

Si la Prusse a des convoitises, elles seront contenues par l'attitude de l'Autriche. Cette dernière veut de l'influence, mais certes aucune idée d'absorption n'entre dans ses prévisions.

This assessment of the aims of Austrian policy was correct, but – like the other powers – he over-estimated her capabilities in comparison with the strength of Prussia. The threat he feared was not Prussian demands but French involvement in the conflict. 'Voilà, ce qu'il faut éviter ...', wrote the vice-chancellor.

Certes, nous ne demandons pas que l'Allemagne verse son sang pour conserver au Danemarc les Duchés de l'Elbe, mais nous ne voyons aucune raison qu'elle le répande pour les lui enlever et porter ainsi à la Monarchie Danoise des coups qui finalement atteindraient les autres Souverainetés secondaires ... Quand on allume soi-même un phare, on se ménage la meilleure chance de ne pas se heurter contre l'écueil.

In view of the fact that there were so many difficulties, Gorchakov expressed fears about the outcome of the approaching conference: 'J'hésite à énoncer une espérance positive'. But Gorchakov believed that it was the only chance and at the same time respite which would allow passions to be tamed.[8]

Gorchakov considered that the primary aim must be to secure a suspension of the fighting, and that once the action subsided it would be easier to conduct negotiations. When the Swedish ambassador asked him what position Russia intended to take at the conference and what view of the Danish-German problem she would present, Gorchakov replied:

s'il m'autorisait à dire à mon Gouvernement, qui certes attacherait un haute prix à une telle assurance, qu'à la conférence future la Russie se prononcerait strictement pour la maintien des stipulations de 1851 et 1852. C'est plutôt repondit-il 'élastiquement' qu'il faudra dire. Le traité de Londres ne parle que de l'intégrité de la monarchie danoise et de l'ordre de succession, et ce sera la nôtre base.

Quant à l'application ultérieure des dits principes, ce sera l'affaire de la conférence. L'essentiel est qu'elle se réunisse au plus vite et tout ce que je peut dire pour le moment, c'est que nous nous attacherons à y obtenir au Danemarc des conditions aussi avantageuses que possible. Mais, lui répliquai-je – the ambassador reported – en admettant tout cela, êtez-vous également sure que l'heure de la France ne sonnera pas bientôt et que son invervention ne modifiera pas sensiblement les choses?

J'admets parfaitement-dit-il, cette éventualité et qu'en pareil cas, la question Dano-Allemande sera momentanément reléguée au troisième ou au quatrième plan, mais, sans vouloir hazarder aucune prédiction sur l'issue définitive du grand drame Européen qui se

8. H.S.A. Stuttgart, G 314, Bü 7, Dok. 84.

jouera alors, je pense de même qu'en dernière analyse le Danemarc n'y gagnera rien.

Le Prince – Wedel-Jarlsberg ended – est en un mot convaincu que ce le Danemarc a de mieux à faire – c'est de faire la paix au plus vite, et il n'admet pas que les pertes influgées au commerce allemande puissent jamais rendre les alliées plus traitables au contraire![9]

Wedel-Jarlsberg expected Russia to support the old British idea of division of Schleswig, which Russell was said to have put forward again. If it was rejected Britain would propose an actual union (l'union réelle') of the duchies and a personal union between the duchies and the Danish monarchy.

D'après toutes les probabilités – the ambassador reported – la Russie prononcera de la même manière, car plus que jamais ceux deux puissances semblent être d'accord pour étouffer coûte que coûte, et probablement aux dépens du plus faible, le conflit Dano-Allemande, et empêcher ainsi, au du moins ajourner une conflagration générale.[10]

Gorchakov said the same thing to Napier the next day. He argued that Denmark was not in a position to resist the forces at the disposal of Austria and Prussia for long; that there was no possibility of co-operation with any of the great Western powers; and Britain was more than ever determined not to intervene.

There was one significant feature in what Gorchakov said. I refer to his interpretation of, and his attitude to, the Treaty of London. Until then, as he himself said, it had been the corner-stone of his policy. Now, in view of the new situation, he was compelled to say that basically the provisions of the treaty were of a general nature and that the formulations it contained really only applied to two questions: the integrity of Denmark and the succession to the throne. Russia did not intend to cling to the provisions of the Treaty literally and would pursue a flexible policy. Gorchakov realised that the chances of keeping the provisions of the Treaty in force were not great.

During talks with Massignac, according to the Swedish ambassador's account, Gorchakov was 'très pacifique'. 'Il s'y est appliqué – Wedel-Jarlsberg reported[11] – à faire ressortir tout l'intérêt pour l'avenir comme pour le développement intérieur de la Russie, du maintien de la paix et des bonnes relations avec le reste de l'Europe'. The best evidence of this was Gorchakov's attitude towards the planned celebrations of the fiftieth anniversary of the Russians' entry into Paris. In spite of the position taken by the Tsar and military circles, Gorchakov sought to make his view prevail. In his opinion the anniversary should be observed in an atmosphere which would not annoy France.[12]

9. No. 35, 19 (7) March 1864.
10. No. 39, 30 (18) March 1864.
11. No. 40, 5 April (24 March) 1864.
12. As the Minister of Internal Affairs, P.A. Valuev, recorded in his diary, the Council of State resolved on 16 February that on 19 March there would be a march-past on the anniversary of the Russian army's entry into Paris. The Vice-Chancellor, the War Minister and Prince Dolgorukii had asked previously (the week before) that the march-past should be abandoned, since to hold it on precisely that day would be an affront to the Emperor of the French. The Tsar evidently agreed with their point of view and decided to give a reception instead. The reception was to be held on 18 March, but there would also be a parade on 19 or 20 March, which was said to be at the request of the officers of the guard and Grand Duke Nikolai Nikolaevich. So much for Valuev. (*Dnevnik P.A.*

Thanks to Gorchakov, the anniversary passed off in an atmosphere which both Plessen and Wedel-Jarlsberg judged 'n'a présenté aucun caractère blessant, ni même malveillant, pour la France et son Souverain',[13] and Plessen reported: 'Des démonstrations hostiles pour la France n'ont pas eu lieu, que je sache...'[14] On peut se dire, du point de vue de le politique Russe, que les souvenirs humiliants pour la France fortifient l'Empereur Napoleon III, et de le fortifier n'est certainement pas dans les dispositions de la Russie'. In connection with the march-past which was to take place in St Petersburg, and the reception in the Winter Palace, Gorchakov – Plessen reported – gave instructions to Budberg to explain in Paris that these celebrations were being held only because it was in the Russian tradition to commemorate great anniversaries in this way, whereas in France great victories were honoured by conferring titles and naming public monuments.[15]

'Gorchakov [the eternal actor – EH] se montre toujours très optimiste à l'égard du résultat de la future conférence à Londres'. He expected that its results would be no less satisfactory for Denmark than for Germany, and even the choice of Beust as the representative of the German Confederation did not discourage him. 'Nous verrons bientôt', he said to the Swedish ambassador.[16]

J'observerais encore qu'on est au fond très-peu satisfait ici de l'obstination de la politique de Mr de Bismarck et que malgré les ménagements envers la Prusse dictés par la reconnaissance, c'est bien plutôt vers l'Autriche qu'inclinent en ce moment les sympathies du Gouvernement Russe. On lui sait non moins gré de sa modération rélative dans la question Danoise, que de l'énergie de sa conduite en Galicie.[17]

Not only Gorchakov, but other ministers too, like Valuev, for example, had had no illusions for some time about Prussia's attitude to the conflict with Denmark.[18]

Their fears increased on the news of Prussia's capture of Düppel.[19] But Gorchakov's cynicism exceeded all expectations when he expressed the opinion

qu'il facilitera une prochaine solution pacifique ...,[20] que le succès de Düppel aurait diminué ces dernières (des prétensions surtout de la Prusse), mais c'est le contraire qui est le cas. Aussi sa fois dans les assurances de conciliation de M de Bismarck, n'est-elle plus aussi robuste que par le passé et Son Excellence commence à la fin de s'apercevoir que, comme je le disais dans le temps, le rénard se trouve dans le colombier et qu'il ne sera pas facile de l'en faire déguerpir.[21]

Valueva, ministra vnutrennykh del, 1861-1864, vol. I (Moscow, 1961), 16 March 1864, p. 274. The diplomatic corps in St Petersburg wrote at length about the march-past and the difference of opinion on the subject. Thun reported on 30 (18) March that he knew there was a difference of opinion about this matter between Gorchakov and the Tsar. Gorchakov knew 'que cette fête pourrait donner de l'ombrage à la coeur de France, mais l'Empereur n'a pas cru devoir tenir compte de cette observation'. H.H.S.A. no 6B. P.A. X. Rusland, Kart. 55.

13. Wedel-Jarlsberg, no. 40, 5 April (24 March) 1864.
14. Plessen, No. 17, 11 April (30 March) 1864.
15. *Ibid.* See also Pepoli's report, no. 10, 24 March 1864. Pacco 205, A.S.-D. "Gortchakow avait en vain lutté contre le parti militaire qui entoure et entretient l'Empereur".
16. Wedel-Jarlsberg, no. 46, 18 (6) April 1864.
17. *Ibid.*
18. Valuev, *Dnevnik ...,* vol. I, p. 274.
19. Wedel-Jarlsberg, no. 47, 20 (8) April. The bombardment of Düppel had begun on 15 March; the Prussians captured it on 18 April.
20. *Ibid.*
21. *Ibid.* no. 53, 4 May (22 April) 1864.

'J'espère enfin que c'est la paix', Gorchakov said to the Prussian *chargé d'affaires* after the capture of Düppel.[22]

L'attitude du Cabinet Impérial – Wedel-Jarlsberg reported[23] – est en effet (en ce moment) invariablement la même, savoir appui *moral* au protocole de London, mais abstention matérielle complète. Du reste, tout pour soi et rien pour les autres, et entente Austro-Prusso-Russe pour rester maître de la question de Pologne, prévenir le débordement démocratique et éviter une guerre générale. À telle fin on n'était pas non plus fâché du refroidissement de l'entente Anglo-française.[24]

In his letter to Vedel on 16 (28) April 1864 Plessen referred to his report no. 22, in which he had touched on the question of a personal union. Gorchakov had raised this, and the Vice-Chancellor regarded it as an open question. Plessen described Russia's position the day before the London conference opened as follows:

La Russie entre dans la Conférence avec le désir de la voir aboutir à une solution pacifique. Elle écoutera toujours les propositions et se prononcera en faveur de celle qui lui semblera réuni le plus des chances et mener au résultat qu'elle a en vue, 'La paix et la conservation de la Monarchie'. La Russie fera tout son possible pour obtenir dans les modalités celles que nous ameneront les meilleurs chances, c'est une chose dont je suis convaincu ... Mais je crois que dans le cas que le partage fût adopté comme sorte de solution, il serait en vain de nous flatter de l'espoir que nous puissions obtenir la ligne de Dannewirke. Cette ligne sera tracée bien plus au nord Dannewirke, ce que je regarde comme impossible.[25]

Thus although Plessen did not doubt that Russia would defend Denmark's interests at the conference, he warned his government that Denmark would not succeed in keeping a significant part of Schleswig, and that the frontier line would probably be drawn somewhere to the north of the Dannewirke.

Gorchakov himself, in a letter to Olga Nikolaevna in April, in reply to her letter of 25 March (6 April), adjudged the convening of a conference in London and Constantinople as a slight change for the better, 'une petite éclarcie sur l'horizon politique', which, if successful, could have a positive influence for peace in Europe ('sur la paix générale'). 'J'espère qu'avec beaucoup de calme et de conciliation on parviendra aussi à dénouer ce noeud. Nous y apporterons la meilleure volonté ...' He wrote in complimentary terms of Russia's representative at the conference: 'par sa position le B- on Brunnow est appelé à être le trait d'union être les partis extrêmes. Ni l'expérience ni l'habilité ne lui ferons défaut. L'Empereur a jugé un second plénipotentiare inutile'. And this was Gorchakov's opinion of Prussia and Bismarck.

La prise de Düppel *devrait* faciliter les négociations. L'amour-propre militaire de la Prusse est satisfait. Si Bismarck entend son intérêt il sera modéré. Quoi qu'il en soit, un grand pas est fait. Les positions se defineront plus nettement autour du tapis vert et les arriére-pen-

---

22. Redesdale, *Memories*, I, p. 274.
23. Wedel-Jarlsberg, no. 51, 27 (15) April 1864.
24. See no. 55, 11 May (29 April).
25. Plessen to Vedel, pk. 12. R.A. Copenhagen.

sées, s'il y en a, oseront difficilement se produire au grand jour.[26]

As we can see from this letter, Gorchakov basically was not convinced that the conference would succeed in resolving the difficult tangle of problems connected with the Danish-German conflict. Everything, he wrote, depended on Prussia and Bismarck. The praise which he lavished on Brunnow is also significant. Gorchakov was not in the habit of writing in this way about people whom he saw as rivals for his position.

An official exposition of Russian policy is to be found in the instructions for the Russian plenipotentiary, the ambassador in London, Brunnow. These instructions, dated 28 (16) March 1864, said that the Russian government had accepted the British government's proposal to convene a conference in London on 12 April (old style) in order to settle the conflict between Denmark and the German states, although it had no illusions about the prospects for such a conference. The fact that it had been convened, however, was regarded as positive. The problem was shifting from the sphere of military operations to the sphere of diplomacy and this would compel both sides to formulate their positions. The countries that were not involved would have the opportunity for diplomatic activity with the aim of finding a basis of understanding. In view of the fact that Brunnow was perfectly familiar with the complicated nature of the problem, he did not need directives, and Gorchakov confined himself purely to general considerations.[27]

The general part of the instructions stated that, from the beginning, the Russian government had taken the position that the 1851-52 obligations should be upheld. With a view to the balance of power in Europe, Russia had, 1) recognised Denmark's rights, and, 2) not rejected German claims, which were in part justified. Russia's position was identical to Britain's, and aimed to forestall, limit and ultimately settle the conflict. Russia trusted Austria and Prussia, and saw their military actions as beneficial, as they were intended to support conservative policies and were directed against revolution. Russia was making efforts to explain the positive side of the larger German states' actions to Britain. Now Russia, together with other states – and here co-operation primarily with the British cabinet was

---

26. H.S.A. Stuttgart, G 314, Bü 78, no. 85.
27. In a talk with Massignac, Gorchakov told him he had given Brunnow instructions and 'les pouvoirs les plus étendus, toute la liberté d'action, en un mot, que justifie la parfaite connaissance qu'il a de la question Danoise et des grandes intérêts qui s'attachent'. Gorchakov also said he had given him complete freedom 's'entendre en toute liberté avec les autres plénipotentiares'. 7 May 1864, no. 29, A.M.A.E., Russie, vol. 233. See also Plessen to Monrad, 10 May (28 April) 1864. Ges. Ark. London. Samlingspakke 29. R.A. Copenhagen.

'Selon le Vice-Chancelier, l'Ambassadeur de Russie qui aime a s'appeler' amicus Daniae mettra à profit toutes ses capacités et ses grandes ressources d'esprit pour nous obtenir les meilleures conditions possibles, en égard des circonstances politiques générales et la situation que nous a faite le sort de la guerre.

Le P-ce Gortchakow pensa – Plessen reported – que les Plénipotentiares du Roi trouveraient auprès du B-on Brunnow un véritable appui et le désir de leur être utile, et il m'a assuré que de Berlin il lui parvenait – et même de Vienne, qu'on trouvait l'Ambassadeur de Russie à Londres 'trop Danois'.

Plessen to Monrad, 10 May/28 April 1864. Ges. Art. London R.A. Samlingspakke 29.

mentioned – was aiming to reach a settlement of the conflict through talks, soundings and seeking points of common ground between the opposing parties.

Russian policy, we read, was dominated by the principle of the integrity of the Danish monarchy and the succession to the throne. But the foremost principle was the cause of peace and the balance of power in Europe. It was best ensured by the Treaty of London. This was a basic and inviolable principle. But it would be an illusion to believe that there was any possibility of returning to the position before the war. The result of the military action, the attitude of the forces involved and the mood reigning in Germany would not permit this. And even from the point of view of justice it was not possible to deny the fundamental grievances which the German states had against Denmark, which for twelve years had failed to fulfil its obligations.

The question was what guarantees should be given 1) to satisfy German claims, 2) to safeguard Denmark's rights, and 3) to ensure that they were consistent with the interests of Europe.

In Russia's opinion, the only option which met the conditions was that of a personal union which, however, the Danish government rejected, seeing it as the first step towards the partition of the country. The lesser German states regarded this measure as insufficient; Prussia and Austria would possibly agree to it, but not without modifications, and they were as yet undecided. The other states had not yet expressed a view on the matter. As far as Russia was concerned, it was well known that during the discussions on the Danish-German question in 1851-52, Nesselrode's dispatch (a copy of this was appended, but the microfilm in the possession of the Rigsarkiv in Copenhagen does not include it) mentioned a personal union as a possibility. This was what had been done in the case of relations between Sweden and Norway, and there was no reason to reject it *a priori*. With certain modifications, it could be put to the conference and agreement on it sought.

However, the problem of implementing such a union was complicated and undefined, though the administrative union of the two duchies, together with a personal union involving more or less co-operation with Denmark in financial and military spheres, could be adopted.

Two questions, Gorchakov argued, could not be overlooked. The first concerned a truce. From a humanitarian point of view, an end to the military action was of prime importance. The second point he wished to draw to Brunnow's attention was, however, no less fundamental. If, despite Russian wishes and efforts, the Treaty of London were annulled, the Tsar would demand the restoration of his old rights, which he had ceded to Christian, Prince of Glücksburg, under the Treaty of Warsaw, and would submit this matter for decision by the European states. If a new situation of this kind arose, Brunnow would receive instructions to present this question as a matter of principle in the name of Alexander II.

So, to sum up:

1) the question of a truce was, if not absolutely the first, then a very important point for discussion;

2) the Treaty of London was the starting point of the conference and should be maintained in force, if not absolutely, then in essence in the context of the balance of European power and the associated question of the integrity of the Danish monarchy and the succession to the throne in Denmark;[28]
3) personal union, as a possible solution, could meet the conditions enumerated above. In connection with this, measures should be adopted designed to maintain a strong link between the duchies and the Danish monarchy;
4) finally, in the event of the annulment of the Treaty of London, the question of the preservation of Russian rights to part of Gottorp-Holstein must be raised.

The Emperor had confidence in Brunnow, knowing his experience and perspicacity in the fulfilment of his duties. In conclusion, the instructions said, the Emperor would welcome participation in the conference by a representative of the German Confederation, but this was not an essential condition for opening the conference.

These instructions were supplemented by Gorchakov's dispatch to Brunnow on 5 April (24 March), in which the Vice-Chancellor categorically instructed him to reject the French idea of conducting a plebiscite in Holstein and Schleswig. Gorchakov used the same arguments in his instructions as he had in his talk with Massignac.

Apart from the principle of participation by the population of the duchies in political decision-making, which Gorchakov had preferred not to speak of in his talk with the French *chargé d'affaires,* Gorchakov recalled that France had signed the Treaty of London concerning the integrity of the Danish monarchy. He also pointed out that Holstein and Schleswig were occupied by the Austro-Prussian armies and there was no possibility of removing them, nor of removing the pretender to the throne (Prince Augustenburg) and restoring the authority of the King and his officials. In view of the situation which existed, and the one-sided moral and material pressure being exerted on the population of the duchies, no plebiscite could guarantee that the problem would be solved in a just manner, which was the concern of the great powers.[29]

---

28. E. Møller is right that, from the political point of view, the fight to defend the integrity of the monarchy was deception. London-Konferencens Hovedproblem ... in *Festskrift til Kristian Erslev,* (Copenhagen, 1927), p. 517).
29. Le Baron de Nicolay – Monrad wrote – vient de me faire le récit suivant d'un entretien que le Chargé d'affaires de France à St.Pétersbourg a eu dernièrement avec le Prince Gortchacow au sujet de notre question. Le diplomate Français a expliqué comment, d'après les vues de son Gouvernement, une solution durable et satisfaisante de cette question ne serait guère à trouver que dans l'application du principe des nationalités et du vote universel des populations dans les deux Duchés. Aussi son Gouvernement proposait dans les conférences cette manière de résoudre les difficultés, et il espérait que le Cabinet de St. Pétersbourg s'associerait à cette proposition.

Le Vice-Chancelier a répondu que, même en admettant que le principe susmentionné fût de nature à être suivi dans des questions internationales, il ne pourrait en aucun cas trouver son application dans cette occasion, puisque l'intégrité de la Monarchie Danoise était déjà établie d'une manière définitive par le Traité de Londres que le Gouvernement Français avait signé dans le temps conjointement avec les autres grandes Puissances. Le Prince a fait observer ensuite que dans les circonstances actuelles toutes les conditions feraient défaut qui eussent pu permettre de voir dans

The two documents cited above formed guidelines for Brunnow. Gorchakov's ideas were developed more fully in his next writing, the 'Mémoire très confidentiel sur la situation politique générale au 5 Avril 1864'. The London Conference, the introduction to the 'Mémoire' said, had been agreed upon and was to meet on 8 (20) April.[30] In order to reach positive results the basis for discussion had to be settled and means had to be found to establish peace between Denmark and Germany. The Copenhagen court had insisted that the starting point should be the outcome of the 1851-52 talks, but was not against taking part in discussions designed to find another common basis.

Speaking of the role Russia had played up till then, the documents used phrases such as: 'Notre influence conciliante a contribué à établir de transaction, le seul où pourraient se rencontrer les intérêts divergents'. The Russian government was aware that there were deep differences of opinion between the parties and among the states which were signatories to the Treaty of London. Britain expressed herself in favour of maintaining the 1852 Treaty of London; France was for a 'vote populaire'; Denmark wanted to keep the Treaty of London in force; and the German Confederation rejected it absolutely. The larger German powers, on the other hand, recognised the agreements concluded in 1851-52 as the starting point for the talks, but only conditionally. Russia was in favour of upholding the 1852 agreements.

Nous maintenons – we read – les engagements de 1852, dans leurs principes fundamentales, intéressant l'équilibre Européen, c-à-d l'intégrité de la Monarchie Danoise et l'ordre de succession établi pour la garantir.

Toute solution qui pourra concilier ces principes avec les exigences de la situation actuelle et la conservation de la paix générale rencontrera notre adhésion ...

Dans cette ordre d'idées, nous avons rejeté le recours au vote populaire, non seulement comme une doctrine qui n'a pas acquis droit de cité dans la domaine politique, mais comme impracticable dans les conditions auxquelles l'occupation militaire, la guerre et les intrigues de parti ont réduit les Duchés.

Telles sont les dispositions que le Cabinet Impérial apportera à la Conférence qui va s'ouvrir.

Sa seule réunion à laquelle nous avons contribué de tous nos efforts, et un élement favorable au maintien de la paix. Il ne dépendra pas de nous qu'elle n'aboutisse à ce résultat.[31]

---

un vote universel des populations des Duchés l'expression d'un véritable vœu populaire. L'autorité du Roi est en effet suspendue, les employés loyaux sont destitués, la population fidèle est découragée et tourmentée par l'agitation et la crainte. Quelle foi pourrait-on ajouter à un vote emis par une population placée dans une telle situation? Et même si le pays était évacué par les troupes étrangères et l'autorité du Roi restituée, l'agitation des esprits se conserverait encore longtemps et rendrait parfaitement illusoire toute expérience d'un vote universel.

Par ces motifs le Vice-Chancelier a déclaré au Chargé d'affaires de France que le Cabinet de St. Pétersbourg ne saurait nullement s'associer à l'idée qu'il venait de lui soumettre, et Mr. de Nicolay m'a dit que le Prince avait écrit dans ce sens à Mr. le Baron de Brunnow.

(Monrad à Messieurs les Commissaires du Roi à la Conférence de London, 13 April. Ges. Ark. London. Samlingspakke 28).

30. The Conference was in fact opened on 20 April, but the first session took place on 25 April. Lord Russell chaired the conference.
31. A.M.I.D., vol. 68.

The three documents discussed above formed the guide-lines which Brunnow was to follow and provided an exposition of Russian policy on the eve of the opening of the London conference. They met with an immediate reaction in diplomatic circles and the diplomatic correspondence devoted a relatively large amount of space to them. Austria reponded favourably to the position taken by Russia. In a dispatch to Thun, Rechberg emphasised that in his instruction to the Russian plenipotentiary, Gorchakov had recommended him to maintain good relations with Britain, and had expressed himself

avec la plus grande confiance à l'égard du Cabinet Impérial (i.e. Austria), avec lequel il désire également entretenir la meilleure entente dans cette question.

Quant à Prusse – said Rechberg – le Prince Gorchakoff ne paraît pas rassuré sur les intentions qui guident cette puissance avec l'affaire du Holstein et du Schleswig; il reconnaît toute fois la nécessité pour les deux grandes puissances allemandes de conserver l'accord qui est établi entre elles, tout en ne cachant pas ses appréhensions.[32]

Rechberg was also pleased that Gorchakov was against 'd'admission du suffrage universel dans le règlement de la question du Schleswig-Holstein', as on this Russia's position was identical to Austria's.[33]

What suited Austria, however, did not suit Bismarck. Bismarck vigorously attacked Gorchakov's argument that is was impossible to take into account the opinion of the population of the duchies because of the prevailing conditions of war.

In a talk with Oubril, he did not conceal his displeasure that Gorchakov could consider leaving the duchies as dependent on Denmark as they had been before the war. He was particularly incensed by the very idea that, if there were to be a vote, the withdrawal of the German forces from the duchies would be considered a prerequisite.[34] When he received the news of Bismarck's reaction, Alexander II wrote in the margin of Oubril's report: 'I fear that Bismarck may, possibly create a more complicated situation'.[35]

Berlin and Paris were united in their attitude to the possibility of a plebiscite in the duchies, but Paris and St Petersburg were divided. During his talk with Massignac on 4 April, and after he became acquainted with Drouyn de Lhuys' *circulaire* of 29 March,[36] which set out the view that

La lutte actuelle est la conséquence de l'antagonisme des populations, rien ne nous semble donc plus équitable et plus juste à la fois, pour l'Allemagne comme pour le Danemark, que d'avoir égard au sentiment national dans les arrangements qui interviendront,

Gorchakov once again objected and declared emphatically:

---

32. Rechberg to Thun, H.H.S.A., P.A. Rus. Kart. 55, 22 April 1864.
33. *Ibid.*, no. 7, A-G, 30 (18) April 1864.
34. *Krasnyi Arkhiv*, 2 (93) (Moscow 1939) pp. 87-88, Oubril to Gorchakov, 21 (9) April 1864.
35. *Ibid.*
36. *Origines,* vol. II, p. 188.

qu'à son point de vue il serait fort difficile de connaître en ce moment d'une manière certaine le voeu des populations des Duchés, si on les consultait pendant qu'ils sont occupés par des troupes étrangères; que les instructions qu'il avait lui même envoyées à M de Brunnow l'invitaient à faire ses efforts au sein de la Conférence pour qu'on s'éloignât le moins possible de l'esprit du traité de Londres, sans toutefois trop s'attacher à la lettre, et qu'en somme il devait chercher à faire prévaloir une combinaison qui, tout en sauvegardant l'intégrité de la monarchie danoise, donnât cependant satisfaction aux voeux légitimes de la population des Duchés.

Massignac thought Drouyn de Lhuys might consider that Gorchakov 'a été un peu vague dans ses explications', but the reason for this was that Gorchakov did not want to admit that he had left Brunnow, the complete expert on the subject, considerable freedom of action. Gorchakov was concerned above all that the war should not be prolonged and that the question of the duchies should be settled as quickly as posssible.[37]. Later, on May 7, Gorchakov admitted only that Brunnow had been given broad plenipotentiary powers.[38].

Thus the fact that France was not prepared to support the Treaty of London, and, more importantly had raised the nationality principle which was at odds with the conservative foundations of Russian policy, led in the end to discord between St Petersburg and Paris on the question of the duchies.[39]

Tout ce qui touche à l'intégrité de la Monarchie et à la personne du Souverain constitue, aux yeux du Gouvernement danois, l'intérêt principal, et la logique cède devant cette considération – said Dotézac.
... Les instructions données à M le Baron de Brunnow corroboreraient, s'il en était besoin, cette confiance. Le Plénipotentiaire russe a l'ordre, c'est du moins ce que le Roi a dit à une personne haut placée qui me l'a répété, non seulement de combattre énergiquement toute atteinte à l'intégrité du Danmarc, sous quelque forme qu'elle se produise, mais encore de quitter la Conférence si cette intégrité était menacée, et, dans le cas où le nom du Prince d'Augustenbourg serait prononcé, d'opposer hautement les droits de la Russie.[40]

The French ambassador in Stockholm, Fournier, on the other hand gave a different view of Russia's intentions. On the basis of what Manderström had said, Fournier repeated that Russia would represent mainly Prussia's interests at the conference, while Britain, owing to family links with the ruling house in Copenhagen, would support the Treaty of London, but

selon les conditions mises au maintien de cette intégrité et de cet ordre de succession par l'Allemagne, il peut en découler, en dépit des apparences momentanées, la ruine du Danemark et sa germanisation certaine avec le temps.
A ce prix, la Russie payerait à la Prusse les services qu'elle en a reçus, l'Angleterre conserverait la paix dans le présent, sans trop se soucier de l'avenir, et Christian IX garderait une royauté qu'on lui suppose plus le penchant de voir appuyée sur l'Allemagne et la Russie que sur les idées de son peuple et sur les idées scandinaves.[41]

37. A.M.A.E. Russie, vol. 233, no. 20, 4 April 1864. *Origines,* vol. II, p. 215.
38. See p. 386 of the present work.
39. Dotézac to Drouyn de Lhuys, 25 April 1864, *Origines,* vol. II. pp 289ff, and A.M.A.E. Danemark, vol. 247, no. 89.
40. Dotézac, *ibid.,* pp. 289-90.
41. A.M.A.E., Suède, vol. 334, n o. 76. (Confidentielle), 25 April 1864. *Origines,* vol II, pp. 294ff. 299.

As far as British diplomacy is concerned, Russell appreciated the difficulties the Monrad government would encounter during the conference. He was aware that the Danish government would not agree to the proposal to divide Schleswig in accordance with the French plan. T. Bille, to whom Russell had put the plan, objected strongly to Rendsborg and Kiel becoming federal fortresses. 'In this there would be no excuse and I would think Russia would oppose it'. It is characteristic that, according to Russell, the Russian diplomats also agreed that part of Schleswig, the so-called Southern Schleswig, should be detached and merged with Holstein. Did Brunnow agree too? On the other hand, Russell could not imagine a situation in which 35,000 Danes could oppose the 150,000-strong forces of Austria and Prussia. Hence he wished that negotiations, which were taking some time, should be started as quickly as possible. In a letter to Paget, Russell referred to the opinion of Brunnow, who preferred that Denmark should not be represented by Bille, as it would not be easy to reach an agreement with him. Russell would have been happy if Denmark were represented at the conference by Quaade or Blome. [i.e. Bluhme? – E.H.][42]

Napier, on the other hand, assessed Russia's position as follows:

The instructions sent to Brunnow concerning the Danish affairs must necessarily be very vague. I believe that the Vice-Chancellor tells him that his chief objects must be the settlement of the succession and the integrity of the Monarchy and if it be necessary in order to arrive to those results that mention should be made of the eventual reserved rights of the Russian Reigning House and of those of their German Princes in the Duchies, Baron Brunnow will be empowered to make such mention.

The *apparent* unity of the Monarchy will satisfy Russia. No great difficulty will be made about details. The severance of Schleswig or any other expedient will be accepted. I do not think that Prince Gorchakow has any practical suggestion in store. He trusts to the supple and fertile intelligence of his ambassador who is expected to take a leading part in the Conference and who is charged to open himself to your Lordship particularly with all the sincerity compatible with his character. The Russian Government is most anxious to close this question and will make any concession compatible with the maintenance of the apparent union of the provinces not constituting the Danish Monarchy. If the German Powers should aim to destroy the Danish Monarchy and separate the Duchies from it then I think the Russian Government could be brought almost to the verge of hostilities on that account.

No doubt very strong language would be used both at Berlin and Vienna to prevent such an extremity, a naval demonstration would perhaps be made in conjunction with England, every thing would be done short of war and I am sure that the Emperor would fret that he could not speak and act like his father in the question, for the Emperor and the Empress are both decidedly Danish in their sentiments, but with such embarassements in Poland this government could not make war against Germany for the sake of Denmark and really ought not to do so.[43]

In his report on 13 April Napier informed Russell that he had not so far talked with Gorchakov about the question which was the common concern of Britain

---

42. Russell to Paget, 23 March 1864, P.R.O. 30/22, vol. 102. See also 30/32, 102; Voigt, p. 134.
43. Napier to Russell, Private, 30 March 1864, P.R.O. 30/22, vol. 84, k. 195-198.

and Russia; that the Sounds should not pass into the hands of either 'a strong Germany or a strong Scandinavia'. 'Up to recent time', Napier observed, 'the Prince seems to be acting wisely and fairly in the Danish question', but 'that the Emperor and Empress are still better disposed towards Denmark than the Minister'. He believed that Gorchakov sincerely supported the integrity of Denmark, and he wrote –

> I am convinced that the Emperor shares the same policy strongly ... I do not think that any defensive alliance has been signed between the three Northern Courts as yet because no necessity has as yet arisen. I think, however, that the three Courts will act together for certain important purposes ... though on the Danish question they are seriously divided. I am using every means at my disposal to discover the existence of a Convention. I have found nothing yet and I believe that nothing exists ...[44]

So much for Napier.

It is also worth quoting a passage from the report of the Italian ambassador, Pepoli, who looked at Russian policy from the point of view of a struggle between conservative and liberal forces in Europe.

> ... il (le Cabinet de St. Pétersbourg) gronde ouvertement les grandes Puissances Allemandes, mais secrètement il les flatte. Il agite continuellement aux yeux de la Prusse et de l'Autriche le drapeau rouge pour leur arracher des concessions qui puissent satisfaire l'Angleterre et permettre à l'entente cordiale de la former. La coalition contre les idées nouvelles representées par la France, voilà son but avoué, persistant et pour atteindre ce but il demande à grands cris les Conférences, parce qu'il flatte qu'autour d'un tapis il pourra battre la Démocratie, et cet esprit national qui passionne les masses et qui menace de lui arracher la Pologne ...
>
> ... Tout le terrain gagné en Pologne – Pepoli predicted – serait perdu si la Démocratie triomphe en Allemagne. L'œuvre est difficule mais la Diplomatie est si habile ... elle n'a qu'à vouloir pour réussir.
>
> En effet elle a imaginé l'union personelle. Cette proposition patronée par la Russie par l'Autriche et par l'Angleterre est selon moi – Pepoli argued – un point de réaction, un manœuvre très habile. Il est vrai que la Prusse n'est pas tout à fait d'accord mais on espère entrainer le Roi Guillaume en lui montrant que c'est le seul moyen de battre la Démocratie qui menace le trône et l'autel ... Qu'est ce que c'est l'union personelle – he asked. C'est la négation du principe national. C'est la consecration du Droit Divin. L'union personale est en politique ce que la polygamie est dans le marriage. L'histoire a enfanté la révolution''.

Pepoli categorically opposed the idea of a personal union. It was not a solution – he argued – but only paved the way for revolution. The 1830 Belgian and the 1830-31 Polish Insurrection were the best proof of this. And the envoy concluded: "Ce n'est pas une solution, ce un expédient. Ce n'est pas la paix une trêve armée. En dernière analyse cette solution constituant une grave danger pour le parti libéral, elle lui impose de grandes devoirs''.[45]

As far as the Danish government's attitude to the basic principle of Russian policy is concerned, Nicolay's account, dated 1 (13) April 1864,[46] presented the fol-

---

44. *Ibid.* k. 199-200.
45. 2 March. Rapporti Della Legazione in Pietroburgo. Pacco 205.
46. Nicolay, no. 56, vol. 54.

lowing picture. According to Nicolay, the arrival of Gorchakov's 24 March dispatch to Brunnow coincided with the battles being fought by the Danish army around Düppel and along the Als-Sund and with the publication in the French press of the call for a plebiscite in the duchies in order to help to make clear the population's wishes concerning the future. For this reason, Nicolay reported. Monrad 'a été très sensible à cette communication [the instructions to Brunnow] et m'a prié de vous offrir tous ses remerciements'. Monrad also said that the British government fully shared the point of view of the Imperial Cabinet, and also doubted whether Austria would associate herself with a principle which she would not allow to be applied in her own territories. He therefore expected the French proposal to be rejected if it were presented at the conference. In Nicolay's opinion there was no doubt that the King, who as usual looked towards Russia, fully accepted the position taken by the St Petersburg cabinet.[47]

National liberal circles in Copenhagen had no doubt about Russia's real attitude towards the Danish-German conflict on the eve of the London Conference. *Fœdrelandet* reflected the opinion of these circles in its issue of 28 April,[48] criticising both those in Denmark who expressed the belief that Russia would support Denmark during the conference and the nationalist elements of the German press which were once again accusing Russia of talking an anti-German stance. What could the Russians fear from the existence of a German fleet in the Baltic, a fleet which would strengthen Russia's position and make Scandinavianism impossible? What – *Fœdrelandet* asked – could Russia have against Denmark becoming a part of the German Confederation? Hence – the paper observed – Russia had no real interest in taking Denmark's side at the conference. The facts were the best indication of Russia's true pro-German attitude. And the paper cited the following to show Russia's pro-German position: Russia was providing Russian documents for vessels belonging to the Hanseatic towns (Hamburg, Bremen) in order to protect them against Danish ships; in Finland the Russian authorities were suppressing any sign of pro-Danish sympathy; they were taking action against those who were preparing to go to Denmark's aid as volunteers; and prohibiting the collection of money for Denmark in Helsinki. What sort of friendship towards Denmark was that, the author of the article asked.

The paper did not deny that Russia might want to appear at the conference in the role of defender of Denmark. This might be due merely to a desire (in the situation existing in the duchies and in view of the position adopted by Austria and the demands of Prussia) to create a state of affairs in the duchies which would weaken Denmark and tie her to Germany to such an extent that it would become impossible for her to join a Scandinavian union. The latter was what Russia wanted above all to avoid, because it would mean a reduction of her influence in the Northern Countries. In a situation where the whole of Schleswig was in the hands of Prussia and Austria, Russia's task would be confined to modifying a personal union to make it

---

47. Nicolay had expressed a similar opinion previously, for example in no. 36, 26 February (9 March) 1864.
48. *Fœdrelandet*, no. 97, 28 April 1864.

a weak union, which in reality would extend independent provincial status in Schleswig, in a way that would satisfy Germany and pave the way for a merger with Germany at the first sign of upheaval in Europe.

In the present situation only Russia could really take action, but what was the use of that if she was on Germany's side? Russian troops were not standing by on the frontier in order to compel Austria and Prussia to do something, but to come to their assistance in case of need. The constellation of forces in Europe was such that on one side there was an alliance of Russia, Austria and Prussia, which would put its stamp on the future peace, while on the other there was only a kind of 'poor' *(fattig)* entente, weak and helpless. The rapprochement between Russia, Prussia and Austria had gone so far that, although no 'Holly Alliance' had been definitely concluded, in practice it existed. For this reason there was cause for fear about the future peace, which could be concluded in the spirit of the treaty of Warsaw, leading to the fulfilment of Russian aspirations to make Denmark a vassal state of the Eastern empire. Such a solution, in the form of the so-called 'Helstat', would be equivalent to loss of independence and the end of Denmark. Consequently it was necessary to bear great and heavy sacrifices rather than agree to such a solution, *Fædrelandet* concluded.

II.

The Russian plenipotentiary at the London conference, Philipp Brunnow, had played a special role in the Danish-German conflict ever since the end of the 1840s. Brunnow (1797-1875) who came from an old Courland gentry family, was born in Dresden and educated there and then at the University of Leipzig. He entered the Russian diplomatic service as a young man in 1818. He took part in the congresses of the Holy Alliance in Opawa, Ljubljana and Verona and then went to work as secretary to the Russian embassy in London. In 1828-29 he participated in the war with the Turks as a civilian official. As one of Nesselrode's closest colleagues, he was appointed chief editor in the ministry of foreign affairs. The *Memoires* he wrote concerning numerous international affairs, including the Danish, Greek, Near East, French and German questions, date from this period.[49] When preparing his memorandum on the Danish question, he made the following observation:

Chaque affaire devient plus facile, lorsque peu de monde s'en occupe. Le malheur de la question Danoise est que trop Conseillers à la foi cherchent à la compliquer.[50]

He was able to see for himself how right this conclusion was when he became more closely involved with the problem in the 1850s and 1860s.

Brunnov's note on Russia's foreign policy after the conclusion of the Berlin Convention on 3 (15) October 1833, written in 1838 under the title 'O obshchikh nachalakh sluzhashchikh osnovaniya nashei vneshnei politiki', (Aperçu des trans-

---

49. F. de Martens, *Recueil des traités et conventions,* vol. XII, *Traités avec l'Angleterre 1832-1895* (St. Petersburg, 1898), p. 274.
50. *Ibid.*

actions politiques du Cabinet de Russie. Aperçu des principes du Cabinet de Russie sous les regnès de Catherine II, Paul I et Alexandre I), made him well known. In Vienna he was called 'the Russian Gentz' (a reference to Friedrich Gentz, Metternich's colleague) and his text was included in the course in history prepared for the heir to the throne, Alexander.[51] The principal thesis of the document is in line with Nesselrode's policy based on co-operation between Russia, Austria and Prussia as a guarantee of the maintenance of peace in Europe and the best way to counter the ambitious plans of both France and Britain, which aimed to dominate other countries.[52]

In a note written in 1839, Brunnow came to the conclusion that Russia should seek an entente with Britain, rather than France. In his opinion the age-old dislike of Russia on the part of the British government and society was based on misunderstanding. There were prejudices there about Russia's 'aggression' in the east.[53]

From 1839 Brunnow's career took him to Stuttgart and Darmstadt, and in the autumn of 1840 he was sent to London as a special plenipotentiary for the purpose of securing close co-operation between the St Petersburg and London cabinets on eastern matters. On 15 July 1840, a treaty on the eastern question was signed, as well as a convention on Egypt and the straits (1841), in both of which he was an active participant. These were considerable achievements for Russian diplomacy, since they succeeded in dividing Britain and France while at the same time strengthening co-operation between the states of the north. The rapprochement between Russia and Britain was also enhanced by the 1849 treaty on trade relations between the two countries.[54] Anglo-Russian co-operation for the purpose of settling the conflict between Denmark and Germany culminated in the 1851 London protocol and the 1852 Treaty of London, which were concluded by the two parties thanks to the efforts of Palmerston and Brunnow. He was compelled to leave London in 1854 because of the outbreak of the Crimean War, and after a year's interval was sent to Frankfurt as Russian representative to the German Confederation, and to Darmstadt and Kassel. After that he is to be found in Paris as the second Russian representative, beside Orlov, at the negotiations which led to the signing of the treaty of Paris. In 1856-57 he was ambassador in Berlin, and from 1858 he was posted to London. He was ambassador there from 1860 to 1874, with a break from May to November 1870 when he was accredited to Paris and his place in London was taken by Nikolai Orlov, who was not accredited.[55]

This Nestor of Russian diplomacy,[56] one of the wisest Russian diplomats of

---

51. S.S. Tatishchev, *Vneshnyaya politika Imperatora Nikolaya Pervogo* (St. Petersburg, 1887), p. 27. The text of the note is in Martens, *Recueil ...*, vol. IV, pt 1, pp. 460-2; Tatishchev, p. 30 and note. Documents relatifs à l'Histoire de Russie. XXXI. (St. Petersburg, 1881), pp. 197ff.
52. H. Treitschke, *Deutsche Geschichte im Neunzehnten Jahrhundert*, vol. 5 (Leipzig, 1894), pp. 761ff. *Policy in Action. Russia and the European Political System*, p. 385.
53. Tatishchev, pp. 475-81.
54. Joseph L. Wieczynski, *The Modern Encyclopedia of Russian and Soviet History*, vol. 5, (1977), p. 201.
55. *Entsiklopedicheskii slovar'*, vol. IV. A, (St. Petersburg, 1891) p. 755; *Ocherk istorii Ministerstva Innostrannykh Del*, (St. Petersburg, 1902).
56. See Wieczynski; B.E. Nolde, *Vneshnyaya politika. Istoricheskie Ocherki*, vol. II, Bosfor i Dardanele, (Petrograd, 1915) p. 67.

the nineteenth century, 'Le type du diplomate irréprochable' – as Ollivier described him,[57] a distinguished dialectician and a fine linguist, widely read in classical literature, a lover of Cicero, with an encyclopaedic knowledge of diplomacy and, finally, a complete expert on Britain, did not always enjoy the best of reputations, especially among his countrymen. Contemporary accounts of Brunnow's personality are contradictory, although none denied that he was a talented and highly educated man.[58] Russians accused him of becoming cut-off from his country owing to his twenty-year stay in London; he was unfamiliar with Russia's problems, they said, and had a picture of some fictional Russia rather than the real one. Some, like Meshchersky, called him an 'old crank', accusing him of being an egoistic German, to whom Russian feelings were alien.[59] Others, like Chicherin,[60] criticised him for making fundamental errors in his assessments of British policy during the time he was in the embassy in London. In 1853 he had been sure that war would not break out and in 1863 he had been certain that Britain wanted war with Russia because of the Polish uprising, when in fact she was only concerned to separate Russia and France. Polovstev, on the other hand, said that Brunnow had helped Gorchakov in 1863 by assuring him that Britain would not move; only then did Gorchakov send out his notes, which had brought him so much popularity in Russia.[61]

In diplomatic circles in the West, Brunnow enjoyed a very high reputation:

Unter den Botschaftern hatte er das weitaus grösste Ansehen, er war eine Fundgrube diplomatischen Wissens ... er hatte die Pose des weisen Mannes, aber zugleich auch einen überlegenen Humor, der für die andern nicht immer bequem war. Seine Formen waren jedoch ausserordentlich verbindlich und selbst für junge Leite artig und liebenswürdig. In seinen Mussenstunden las er den Cicero.[62]

Among German diplomats, we find a firmly negative picture in the memoirs of his antagonist at the time of the 1864 London Conference, Beust: *'Capacité trop connue* und deshalb *trop vanté'* (emphasis in the text!).[63]

---

57. E. Ollivier, L'Empire libéral, vol. VII, (1911), p. 83.
58. V.P. Meshchersky, *Moi vospominaniya,* vol. I. p. 303, vol. II. pp. 238-9 (St Petersburg, 1897 and 1898), B.N. Chicherin, *Vospominaniya* (Moskovskii universitet, Moscow, 1929), vol. I, p. 255. (See also A.F. Krieger, *Dagbøger,* vol. III, p. 119.
59. Meshchersky, vol. II, p. 303.
60. Chicherin, pp. 99-100.
61. A.A. Polovtsev, *Dnevnik gosudarstvennogo sekretarya,* vol. I, 1883-1886 (Moscow, 1966), see entry for 3 March 1883, p. 87. The historical literature on Brunnow includes works by Nolde, *Vneshnyaya politika ...,* who assessed him highly as a diplomat and criticised A. Goryanov, who accused, Brunnow of doing well for Britain but not understanding Russia's interest, since he was cut off from the country and only tenuously connected with the Ministry of Foreign Affairs.
62. *Errinerungen von Ernst Freiherrn von Plener,* (Stuttgart, 1911), p. 113. Cf. Franco Valsecchi, *Il Risorgimento e l'Europa: l'Alleanza di Crimea,* (Verona, 1948), p. 211; *Die Technik der Diplomatie. L'Art de négocier von Heinrich Wildner* (Vienna, 1959), p. 51. Cf. also Gordon A. Craig, 'Techniques of Negotiation' in *Russian Foreign Policy ...,* ed. I.J. Lederer, (New Haven and London, Yale UP, 1962), p. 357.
63. F.F. von Beust, *Aus Drei Viertel-Jahrhunderten,* vol. I, 1809-1866 (Stuttgart, 1887), p. 364, vol. II, 1866-1885, p. 547. Beust gave the following example, among others, to show Brunnow's vanity. In order not to interfere with the ceremonies connected with the entry of the Princess of Edinburgh,

After the resignation of Nesselrode many Russian diplomats thought that Brunnow might be a better candidate for the post of minister of foreign affairs than Gorchakov. And not only Russians.[64] Gorchakov, who was very suspicious and always nervous about his position, was aware of this.[65] At the turn of the year 1857-58, Esterhazy reported, Brunnow changed from an antagonist to a supporter of Gorchakov.[66]

Ce revirement fait assurément plus d'honneur à l'esprit du Baron Brunnow qu'à Son caractère. Toujours est-il qu'il semble avoir entièrement réussi jusqu'à présent à captiver le Ministre actuel, et qu'il y est surtout parvenu par l'habilité extrême avec laquelle il sait développer ses vues et lui suggérer et pour ainsi dire lui substituer ses propres idées de telle façon que le Prince Gortchakoff, tout en les [E.H.?]empruntant et se les identifiant, s'en croie toujours le seul et véritable auteur.

Le succès dont cette tactique continue à jouir s'est révélé dernièrement par les paroles suivantes que le Prince Gortchakoff avait adressé à quelqu'un au sujet de cet agent diplomatique. Depuis que j'ai *'russifié'* le Baron Brunnow il est devenu excellent ...

Ce diplomat (Brunnow) se flatte évidemment de retrouver à Londres la même position éminente qu'il y avait occupée avant la rupture des relations diplomatiques entre la Russie et la Grande Bretagne.[67]

There can be no doubt that Brunnow played his part well in order to gain the minister's confidence and attain the position in London of which he dreamed. In 1863, when for a moment Gorchakov's position was shaky, Brunnow's name came up again, alongside that of Budberg, as possible successor to Gorchakov. But although he enjoyed the Tsar's confidence, Budberg was said to be too pro-French, while Brunnow was alleged to be too cut off from the domestic affairs of the country.[68] The next year, as Massignac reported,[69] Gorchakov had more troubles as, just as during every crisis, Budberg was put forward as a successor to the minister, while Brunnow in London showed his unfriendly attitude to Gorchakov so that the antagonism between them was visible on every occasion ('à chaque occasion').

Brunnow really entered the history of Russo-Danish relations in the years 1848-52, during the Danish-German conflict and the first Schleswig-Holstein war. With Palmerston, he played a prominent part in the Danish-German negotiations,

---

Brunnow delayed announcing his wife's death for three days and preserved the body in ice, (vol. I, p. 365). Sybel, on the other hand, wrote of Brunnow's attitude at the 1851-52 London Conference: 'ein stets milder und gefühlvoller und zugleich recht schlauer Herz'. (Sybel, vol. III, p. 78).

64. Budberg, the ambassador in Berlin, to Dimitrii Nesselrode, 20 April 1856. *Lettres et Papiers du Chancelier Comte Charles de Nesselrode, 1760-1858,* ed. Comte A. de Nesselrode, (Paris), vol. XI, p. 132. Buol to Esterhazy, 9 May 1856, H.H.S.A. P.A. Rus. vol. 43.
65. According to Chicherin, Gorchakov was 's nim v razladie i malo emu doveryal', (disagreed with him and hardly trusted him), Chicherin, vol. I, pp. 99-100.
66. Il (Brunnow) est progressivement arrivé à se constituer le champion le plus zélé du Prince Gortchacoff, dont pourtant il avait été autrefois l'antagoniste. Changement sensible qui s'est opéré dans les opinions du B – on Brunnow qui est parvenu à gagner la confiance du P – ce Gortchakoff.
67. In place of Khreptovich. Esterhazy to Buol, H.H.S.A. P.A. Rus. Weisungen, Varia, 1857, Berichte 1858, I-V, Kart 45, no. 2E, 8 January 1858 (27 December 1857).
68. Thun to Rechberg, no. 16, 5 May (23 April) 1863. H.H.S.A. P.A. X. Kart. 54.
69. A.M.A.E. Russie, vol. 233, no. 42, 21 September 1864.

which lasted from 1849-1852. They were both 'fathers' of the 1851 London protocol and the 1852 Treaty of London. This treaty, of which Brunnow was so proud, was a masterpiece of diplomatic art, containing provisions which could be accepted by Denmark and the two larger German states, and by Britain, France, Russia and Sweden. But the problem itself was only postponed and still required solution.[70]

Brunnow earned recognition and gratitude from King Frederick VII who gave him a *daase*[71] a with the inscription 'Rex Daniae amico Daniae', of which Brunnow was exceedingly proud. He often used this royal recognition as an argument in his talks with Danish diplomats, particularly during the 1864 London Conference.[72]

From the end of the Crimean War to the outbreak of the war in 1864, Brunnow was frequently questioned by Danish diplomats and thus had occasion to express his views on the conflict between Denmark and Germany. In 1857 in Berlin he warned B.E. Bülow that the situation in Europe had changed to the disadvantage of Denmark and advised her to regard the dispute as a specifically German matter rather than treat it as a European question, and to come to an agreement with Austria and Prussia as quickly as possible. He repeated essentially the same advice a month later during a talk with F.P. Bille-Brahe. He warned that, owing to the unfavourable international situation for Denmark (Russia had moved closer to Prussia after the Crimean War, Britain would confine herself to sending notes in the event of a conflict, and France would not risk war on Denmark's account), she would be completely isolated. He therefore advised her to follow Russia's example and seek peaceful ways of solving the dispute, just as Russia had by concluding the Treaty of Paris in 1856, in order to avoid misfortunes.[73]

Similarly, at the beginning of 1860, in talks with Ch.F. Falbe, he argued that really only Sweden maintained a truly loyal and disinterested attitude towards Denmark. She could not count on the great powers, and guarantees and international treaties were often ignored. He therefore considered that she should not turn to the great powers but should come to an understanding with the aristocracy in the duchies, who enjoyed authority there; the more tactfully and courteously Denmark behaved towards them, the more easily she would achieve good results.[74] Brunnow's attitude stemmed from his conviction that Britain would refrain from any involvement in the dispute between Denmark and Germany, and the Francophile Gorchakov had no intention of coming into conflict with Prussia.[75]

---

70. Sybel, vol. III, pp. 78-80; Neergaard, vol. I, pp. 742-5; Alexander Scharff, *Schleswig-Holstein in der deutschen und nordeuropäischen Geschichte* (Stuttgart, 1969), the article 'Das Erste Londoner Protokoll. Ein Betrag zur europäischen Problematik der Schleswig-Holsteinischen Frage', pp. 189-216. Scharff considers that the first variant of the London protocol, dated 21 April 1850, was the work of Brunnow, p. 217; Jens Engberg, *Det slesvigske spørgsmål 1850-1853,* (Copenhagen, 1968).
71. A snuff-box.
72. Neergaard, vol. II, p. 139. On 18 November 1848 Brunnow received the order of Danebrog. (First class) *(Kongelig Dansk Hof og Statskalender for aaret 1849,* p. 10).
73. See *Danmarks historie,* vol. XI, by Roar Skovmand (Copenhagen, 1964), p. 441.
74. Confident. Falbe to Blixen-Finecke. Dep. England, 1856-60, no. 8, 24 January 1860.
75. Torben-Bille on his talk with Brunnow on 20 November 1860. *Ibid.*

At the point when Federal Execution was impending in Holstein (towards the end of 1860), Brunnow advised Denmark not to resist it. He did not share the Danish government's fears that the Execution would assist the rise of the Schleswig-Holstein party under the aegis of the German Confederation and would be a stage in preparations for the invasion of Schleswig.[76] He was critical of the royal decrees concerning matters of language and schooling in Schleswig, considering them insufficient concessions to the population, but he stipulated that these comments should be regarded as his personal opinion.[77]

At the beginning of 1861, Falbe reported, Brunnow began to incline somewhat towards Palmerston's idea of partitioning Schleswig as the most practical way of solving the conflict with Germany.[78] On 16 April, the Danish ambassador reported, Brunnow informed him in his own distinctive way, 'par des demi-mots et d'une manière détournée comme d'habitude chez lui', of the new effort the British government had made to restrain Prussia from any extreme actions. He had congratulated the ambassador, but at the same time asked him to warn his government not to put too much store by the pro-Danish demonstrations in Britain and not to delude itself that in the event of a conflict Britain would give Denmark anything more than 'un appui purement moral et diplomatique'. He repeated that, in contrast to what Lord Russell said, he did not think the execution could lead to war between Denmark and Germany; on the contrary, he believed Germany was interested in avoiding war.[79]

Towards the end of 1862 Torben Bille was in frequent contact with Brunnow in order to find out more about the commotion connected with the Gotha Dispatch, since he saw him as a diplomat extremely well-versed in both the Danish-German dispute and the policy being pursued by the British government. It emerged from T. Bille's talks with Brunnow at the beginning of 1863 (on 3 and 21 January)[80] that the latter took a slightly different view from his minister, Gorchakov, (although only superficially) of Russell's moves the previous autumn and their consequences for Denmark. Brunnow did not agree that Russell's recent moves had essentially exacerbated Denmark's situation and threatened her with the real danger of war with Germany. He considered that Russell was still well disposed towards Denmark and had been motivated only by impatience and a desire to put an end to such a long-running conflict. He was looking for new tactical solutions and trying to find support in Germany.

Brunnow, T. Bille reported, seemed to share the Danish government's opinion that from the practical point of view Russell's proposals were unacceptable and that they were unjust; at least, he had not denied it when Bille expressed that view.

76. Falbe to Hall, 26 November 1860. *Ibid.*
77. Confident. Falbe to Hall, 20 December 1860, *Ibid.*
78. Dep. England, 1861-63, no. 1, 3 January 1861. On the subject of partitioning Schleswig see E.L. Petersen, 'Martsministeriets Fredsbasisforhandlinger', *Historisk Tidsskrift,* 11, R. 4B; E. Erbelling, 'Histoire de l'idée d'un partage du Slesvig', in *Manuel historique de la question du Slesvig,* (Copenhagen, 1906).
79. Dep. England, no. 20, 16 April 1861.
80. Reports to Copenhagen no. 1 and no. 5, 3 and 21 January 1863.

But he did not share the ambassador's opinion that Russell was about to reach for his pen again and propose something anti-Danish in spirit.

Brunnow hoped that Hall would reply to Russell in a conciliatory spirit, as Denmark had nothing to gain by doing otherwise, and would only present the British government as unfriendly to Denmark. That would be a mistake. On the contrary, Brunnow argued, Hall should thank Lord Russell for his strenuous efforts and his goodwill and keen interest in Denmark's cause, and regret that she could not act according to his advice. He advised Bille, 'en bon ami et collègue', to be cautious and not to associate himself with the leaders of the opposition in the British parliament who were attacking the government over its policy on the Danish question.[81]

After he learned of the exchange of dispatches between Gorchakov and Nicolay and Hall's reply of 16 January, with which he was quite satisfied, Brunnow[82] expressed the view that Denmark must not be in a hurry to do anything precipitate, but should act calmly as events unfolded. Brunnow did not agree that the course of events was bound to lead to the constitutional separation of Holstein, and thought the results of this would be fatal for Denmark. He was even reluctant to grant that something of the kind was being seriously considered. But when Bille asked what Denmark should do, he was unable to give a concrete reply and confined himself to vague remarks ('n'a su répondre que par des observations vagues'), speaking of moderation and concessions to satisfy the members of the *Ritterschaft* in the two duchies. He also submitted that he saw no reason why the dispute, which had already lasted over ten years, should not continue indefinitely. Denmark, said Brunnow, was prospering, the Holsteiners were happy, so why take risks and seek to end a dispute which was harming nobody. 'Laissez donc les choses aller leur train et n'oublier pas que le mieux est l'ennemi du bien'. This was no off-the-cuff opinion, as we know from Russell's letter to Loftus on 6 August 1862 that Brunnow was already of a similar opinion then.

Brunnow I am told is of the opinion that the Holstein question sh(ould) be allowed to *cuire dans son jus* [emphasis in the original – E.H.]. Such however is not my opinion – said Russell – tho' France and Russia seem both to have adopted it. But I am disheartened by the wrongheadedness of both sides. I will endeavour still in this private form to see whether any ray of light can be perceived in this dense darkness.[83]

Quant à la depêche du Prince Gortchakoff – reported Bille – le Baron Brunnow n'y attache aucune importance. Sa manière d'en parler me donna l'impréssion qu'il regardait cette dépêche comme écrite dans le seul but de plaire à Lord Russel et que le Prince Gortchakoff lui-même n'attendait aucunement qu'elle influerait sur les résolutions du Roi.

How should we interpret the fact that Brunnow expressed approval both of Hall's reply to Russell's latest dispatch, which had incurred the displeasure of the St Petersburg cabinet, and of Manderström's note in response to the Gotha dispatch,

---

81. See p. 216-7 of the present work. Sandiford. *Great Britain* ..., ch. 4.
82. Report no. 5, 21 January 1863.
83. Russell to Loftus, 6 August 1862, P.R.O. 30/32, vol. 112 P(embroke) Lodge. Cf. Voigt, Englands Aussenpolitik ... *Z.d.G.f.S.-H.G.* vol. 89, (1964), p. 162.

adding that 'une importance toute particulière' was attached to the latter in London, while he spoke slightingly of Gorchakov's dispatch?[84] Extravagance, cynicism, deliberate disinformation, perhaps dislike and contempt for Gorchakov – it is hard to evaluate Brunnow's true attitude at this time solely on the basis of the Danish ambassador's reports.

Towards the end of November 1863, Gorchakov used Brunnow to sound out public opinion, and particularly the attitude of the British government, towards Russia in the face of the increasingly serious and threatening Danish-German conflict.[85] The diplomats from the German countries, on the other hand, especially Apponyi, sought contacts with Brunnow in order to sound out his opinion about the conflict and find out more about what position Russia would take. Apponyi's report to Rechberg[86] shows that Brunnow's opinion at this time was the same as the one the diplomats in St Petersburg were hearing from Gorchakov. Brunnow defended the Treaty of London and boasted of his role in drawing it up, spoke of the positive feelings of both the German states, and expressed himself in favour of peaceful settlement of the dispute on the basis of the provisions of the 1852 treaty. He considered that the signatories to the treaty should sign an additional protocol, on the basis of the treaty, stating that the German states recognised the new law of succession and Denmark undertook to fulfil the obligations towards the German states entered into by Frederick VII. Brunnow was sure the British government would accept his suggestion and expressed doubts only about France's attitude. He attributed great importance to the fact of sending state delegations to Copenhagen, and was confident that Christian IX and his government could be persuaded to modify the provisions of the 18 November Constitution in ways that could satisfy the German cabinets, especially in respect of Schleswig, and to discharge the obligations Denmark had undertaken in 1851-52.

There can be no question that Brunnow had an important role to play in the Danish-German conflict. It fell to him to carry out Russian policy in Britain. This was a matter of skilfully co-ordinating Russian and British efforts and not allowing the conflict to spread. Gorchakov's conception of a four-party entente would have been impossible to implement without the active participation of Britain.

It so happened that Brunnow in London and Napier in St Petersburg both had more friendly attitudes towards Denmark than their own governments did, and they had to make considerable efforts to persuade both their own governments and the governments to which they were accredited to take more positive action on behalf of Denmark. Of course they could not go against the instructions they received. But within the framework of their instructions they could achieve more positive results by appropriate interpretation of those instructions, not to speak of the suggestions they themselves could put forward. Brunnow played an especial role in

---

84. T. Bille to Hall, no. 5, 21 January 1863.
85. Apponyi to Rechberg, no. 93C, London, 19 December 1863, H.H.S.A., P.A. England, Berichte VIII, Kart. 61, and Russell to Napier, 2 December 1863, *Denmark and Germany*.
86. No. 89 A-D, 2 December 1863, H.H.S.A. *Ibid*.

this matter, as the diplomats accredited to the Cabinet of St James, particularly Apponyi and La Tour d'Auvergne, noted.[87] On 13 January 1864 the latter reported to Drouyn de Lhuys:

'L'activité, tout au moins un peu confuse, que Lord Russell déploie à propos de l'affaire des Duchés' semble d'ailleurs encouragée par le Baron Brunnow, Ministre de Russie à Londres, qui se montre à la fois défenseur zélé du traité de 1852 et grand partisan de la Conférence. On dit même qu'il pousserait le Gouvernement anglais à employer la menace pour vaincre les résistances de l'Allemagne. Mais Lord Russell s'est abstenu de faire, auprès du Comte de Bernstorff et du Comte Apponyi, aucune allusion aux mesures que l'Angleterre pourrait adopter pour empêcher un démembrement du Danemark. C'est uniquement, semble-t-il, dans ses rapports avec les États secondaires de l'Allemagne que se montre sa mauvaise humeur.[88]

Like Russell, Brunnow's assessment of the Danes' possibility of resistence was very low.[89]

They [the Danes] cannot drive the 250,000 men of Austria and Prussia out of Schleswig alone.

Prince Gortchakoff tells me – Brunnow informed Russell[90] – that our poor friends the Danes are bent upon fighting, and that the prospect of their accepting a conference appears doubtful. This circumstance explains to me the reason of the delay they have asked, as you mentioned it to me in your note yesterday.

I am afraid this is, on their part, a very short sighted policy! I make great allowance for their feeling under the present trying circumstance, but *fighting* can do them only harm, and no good whatever, 'victa causa placuit Catoni' is a bad precedent.[91]

Had Cato – Brunnow ended – been a bishop at Copenhagen [the allusion was to Monrad], I believe he would have had the good sense of advising the King to accept the Conference.

In a second letter to Russell dispatched the same day[92] we read:

Prince Gorchakoff believes that the determinations of Prussia and Austria are not finally settled. They depend most likely on the course of events.

He quite agrees with you upon the necessity of bringing about, as soon as possible, an arrangement which would maintain, on one hand, the existence of the Danish Monarchy, and, on the other afford to Germany reasonable concessions, within the limits of what may be considered as fair as is just. With these views, Prince Gortchakoff is desirous of removing the difficulties of a conference. He is of the opinion that the representatives of the Powers, who signed the Treaty of 1852, would be enabled, in conference, to moderate the exaggerated pretentions of both parties. The main point, which Prince Gortchakoff recommends me to bear in mind, is to take care to strengthen the link which attaches Prussia and Austria to the

---

87. H.H.S.A., P.A. VIII, England, Kart. 61, no. 93C.
88. A.M.A.E., Angleterre, 728, no. 7. *Origines,* vol. I, pp. 121-2. See also Carl Friedrich, Graf Vitzthum von Eckstädt, *St. Petersburg und London in den Jahren 1852-1864,* (Stuttgart, 1886), vol II, London, 24 January, 1864, pp. 309-10.
89. Russell to Paget, 10 February 1864, P.R.O. 30/22, vol. 102.
90. February 1864, Saturday morning, P.R.O. 30/32, vol. 78 K. 314-316. [No date – E.H.].
91. Brunnow refers to Cato Uticensis junior, who during the war between the Senate and Caesar gave backing to the Senate. After the defeat at Thapsus, Cato committed suicide. Cf. *Victrix causa deis placuit, sed victa Catoni.* (Lucanus Pharsalia, I, 128). *Dei* means here fate, and *Cato*-virtue.
92. *Ibid.,* K. 317-319.

London Treaty. This link is stronger in Vienna than in Berlin. In conference it would get more solid.

Unfortunately – concluded Brunnow – the last intelligence received from Copenhagen tells that the Danes will fight, and not enter into negotiation!«[93]

Finally, in his letter to Russell on 24 February, Brunnow expressed his position as follows:

The Times of this morning states that Austria and Prussia have accepted your proposal of a Conference. Is it true? Should this be the case, I can assure you that no one would rejoice more sincerely than myself at a result obtained by your persevering efforts, and so completely satisfactory to both our governments ...

Brunnow received the news that both the Danish and German parties had finally agreed to take part in a conference with great satisfaction, but he did not conceal his fears about the course it would take and the possibility of settling the matters in dispute. Consequently, when he went to see Russell for the purpose of drawing up the formal invitation to the participants in the coming conference he was of the opinion that the more flexible the text was the better.[94] Brunnow's scepticism and unease increased when he learned of the French proposal to consult the population of the duchies about their future. Russell, for his part, Apponyi reported to Vienna, regarded this plan as an attempt to frustrate the convening of the conference, and Brunnow considered it inadmissible. The great powers, he said, could not subordinate themselves to the opinion expressed by headmasters in Schleswig, and if this was the price that had to be paid it would be better if the conference were not held at all.

Fearing that the conference might end in a fiasco because of the differences of opinion between the parties involved in the conflict and between the neutrals on the ways of resolving the questions in dispute, Brunnow prepared a memorandum on 26 March (6 April) and sent it to Russell. In it he set out both his own point of view on the conference itself and some proposals of a technical nature, and suggested a preliminary discussion of them at his next meeting with the British minister.[95] In Brunnow's opinion the questions to be settled at the conference could be divided into two parts: one of these was of European significance, the other was a federal matter. It was important to distinguish between them and to settle them at the conference in a logical manner and a friendly spirit.

The first problem included the general question of peace and the balance of power in the north. These matters ought not to be controversial. Austria, Prussia, Denmark, Britain, France, Russia and Sweden regarded it as a long-term question and had unanimously recognised the act concerning the succession to Frederick VII in order to maintain the integrity of the Danish monarchy. The conference should merely confirm the agreements which had been in existence since 1852. The

---

93. *Ibid.,* K. 324-326.
94. Apponyi to Rechberg, 19 March 1864. H.H.S.A. P.A. VIII, England, Kart. 63.
95. P.R.O. 30/32, vol. 15 B, K. 22-29.

German Confederation had been asked to take part in the conference in the cause of peace and to become a party to the Treaty concluded in London.

In Brunnow's opinion the wording of the general treaty should be simple and cover matters such as:

1. maintenance of the integrity of the Danish monarchy;
2. recognition of the existing law of succession;
3. settlement of the rights and mutual obligations of the King of Denmark and the German Confederation from the point of view of federal law - a settlement which should be the subject of a special convention between Denmark and the Confederation and be an appendix to the Treaty of London.

If these outline suggestions were accepted, the work of the conference would move on to a new stage. Therefore,

1. First the general treaty should be signed.
2. After this the special convention governing federal relations should be signed. This convention, signed by the plenipotentiaries of Denmark and Germany, would become an appendix to the general treaty.

The neutral states could use their good offices to contribute to a rapprochement and bring about a sincere and lasting agreement between Denmark and Germany.

This way of proceeding seemed to Brunnow simple, precise and correct. The neutral countries should not intervene in purely German matters, and should not impose obligations on Denmark which were contrary to her feelings of propriety. Their role should be confined to facilitating an entente which in the nature of things would be consistent with the maintenance of peace and the general balance of power.

The matters of federal interest included ending the conflict between Denmark and the larger German powers. If a bilateral agreement to suspend the fighting on land and sea could be obtained, that would be a step forward in the work of the conference. But, in order to ensure success, they should proceed very cautiously and begin with confidential talks with the plenipotentiaries to sound out their opinions and make an effort to avoid the first proposals presented at the conference being rejected. That would be a serious moral blow to the future course of the negotiations. If matters advanced favourably, the two parties should then present in writing the views of their governments on the federal questions to be settled between Denmark and Germany.

Up till then, after all, there had been complete uncertainty about the matter, which made it totally impossible to form a view of what the German Confederation, Austria and Prussia wanted, or of what Denmark was disposed to agree to. Chance situations should be avoided in the negotiations. For this reason they should begin by obtaining a clear picture of what both sides wanted. Once their positions were clear it would be possible to act so as to reconcile their views. The whole matter required a patient approach. To obtain a result nothing must be forced. The plenipotentiaries should be given time at each stage to get new instructions in order to overcome difficulties which might arise. Finally, the two parties' demands would have to be moderated by a friendly reminder that the party who caused a breakdown in the negotiations would bear the full responsibility for it and would have to do so before the eyes of the whole of Europe.

On 8 April, in a letter to Russell, Palmerston commented on Brunnow's memorandum. He was complimentary about the first part of the document, describing it as very logical and practical, but he expressed reservations about the second part, as he did not understand what it meant by saying that relations between Denmark and the German Confederation should be settled in a special way. Relations with the Danish King as Duke of Holstein could be settled in accordance with the laws in force in the Confederation. Probably Brunnow would be able to explain in more detail what he meant by this special settlement. Palmerston expressed the view that Denmark, unless she had her back to the wall, would never agree to include part of Schleswig with the parts of the Danish monarchy which were to be part of the Confederation.[96] If it were necessary for the southern part of Schleswig to be administratively merged with Holstein, this could be done in such a way as not to involve incorporation of part of Schleswig in Holstein, so that it became part of the German Confederation.[97]

As we can see, the first part of the document composed by Brunnow, was merely a confirmation of the provisions of the Treaty of London, except that the number of signatories was augmented by the inclusion of the German Confederation. The only point of note in the second part is the practical remarks he found it necessary to make in order to prevent the conference from becoming a fiasco from the very beginning in view of the great difficulties it faced. Substantively, this part of the memorandum offered nothing new either, and its content was opaque. It is not surprising, therefore, that a seasoned diplomat like Palmerston had nothing to say for it.

III.

Brunnow was undoubtedly right to see the immense difficulties looming over the conference from the very start. He had no particular regard for the Danish delegation as a whole. It consisted of Quaade, hitherto Minister of Foreign Affairs in the Monrad government (on his departure for London he handed his portfolio over to Monrad), a politician with a reputation for moderation and a readiness to compromise but not considered very important in the government itself, A.F. Krieger,

---

96. I.e. Holstein-Lauenburg.
97. P.R.O. *Ibid.*, vol. 15B, K.30-31.

professor of law at Copenhagen University, one of the leading figures in the national-liberal party, who enjoyed great authority in the government and among public opinion in Copenhagen, and the ambassador in Britain, Torben Bille. As far as Bille was concerned, Brunnow thought that it was impossible to reach any agreement with him.[98]

The Chairman, Quaade, made a positive impression on Brunnow, according to the reports received from Nicolay. 'Les principes et le caractère de Mr Quaade', Nicolay reported,[99] 'offrent de garanties, dont V E (Gortchakoff) saura apprécier d'avance toute la valeur'.[100] Brunnow was certainly familiar with this judgement.

Dotézac's comments on the choice of Quaade are interesting.

On peut être assuré que M Quaade, par ses tendances politiques et sur la volonté expresse du roi et de la reine, acceptera l'influence de M de Brunnow, pour lequel il professe d'ailleurs une profonde admiration.[101]

Precisely because this was well known, Dotézac wrote to Paris, Quaade asked for a representative of the national party to be appointed to the delegation.[102]

What Nicolay wrote about Krieger, on the other hand, was certainly not very enthusiastically received by Brunnow. And Krieger had *de facto* the decisive voice and was trusted by Monrad.

M Krieger – Nicolay reported – est une personalité moins connue à l'étranger; moi-même, je ne le connaîs que de vue son extérieur ne prédispose pas en sa faveur. Tout le monde ici est toutefois d'accord pour rendre justice à ses talents, à son esprit et sa profonde érudition. Personne ne connaît mieux que lui tous les détails de l'organisation constitutionnelle de ce pays. Apartenant à l'école des doctrinaires, il est lié au parti national et s'est identifié avec ses intérêts ... Il est toutefois séparé un peu de ses anciens amis politiques, et a cherché à tenir le milieu entre les tendances séparatistes du parti ultra-Eider-Danois et les aspirations des hommes désirés de rétablir le Helstaat. Nommé raporteur au comité chargé de l'examen de la Constitution du 18 Novembre, il s'est prononcé en faveur de cette loi, de l'union constante du Schleswig avec le Royaume, comme d'une conséquence naturelle de la situation- tout en se déclarant prêt à y introduire avec temps les modifications que réclamerait la rétablissement d'une union avec le Holstein lorsque les Etats de ce Duché témoignerait le désir de s'entendre à ce sujet avec le nouveau Rigsraad.

Il se rapproche ainsi des idées de l'Evêque Monrad et c'est sans doute son sentiment d'estime personnelle pour lui, l'espoir de pouvoir tirer parti de sa popularité pour calmer les inquiétudes de l'élément national au sujet des négociations, et couvrir aussi la responsibilité de Mr Quaade, qui aura engagé le Président de Conseil à envoyer Mr Krieger à Londres. Sa présence à la Conférence me paraît devoir offrir un avantage. Elle mettra un des hommes les plus intelligents du parti national au contact avec les hommes d'État d'autre pays, il aura ainsi l'occasion d'examiner la situation d'un point de vue moins exclusif, d'apprécier mieux

---

98. The secretary to the delegation was Baron Ehrenreich Gyldenkrone. As far as Torben Bille was concerned, Russell said in a letter to Paget on 23 March 1864 that it was impossible to reach an agreement with him. P.R.O. vol. 102. Cf. Nielsen, *1864. Da Europa...*, ch. 14.
99. No. 50, 23 March (4 April) 1864.
100. 'Quaade ist der beste Mensch der Welt, versöhnlich und vernünftig,' wrote Queen Louise in a letter to O. Plessen on 6 May 1864. Privatarkiv O. Plessen, 61824, A1, 2, R.A. Copenhagen.
101. Dotézac anticipated that Ewers would take part in the conference as well as Brunnow.
102. Dotézac to Drouyn de Lhuys, A.M.A.E., Cor. politique, Danemark 1864, vol. 246, no. 71. 30 March 1864. *Origines,* vol. II, p. 193, contains a summary of this report.

les risques et les périls du système que ses amis ont poursuivi jusqu'ici, et l'expérience qu'il aura ainsi acquise ne pourra que profiter aux intérêts de son pays.[103]

We know how much difficulty Britain and Russia had in persuading the two sides to agree to begin negotiations. The Danish government eventually accepted the British proposals to hold a Conference in London on condition that the 1851-52 negotiations would be a *conditio sine qua non* and the starting point for the new negotiations.[104] At the same time both Monrad and Quaade stubbornly argued that they could not agree to a truce ('armitrice').

Mr de Quaade m'a dit – reported Nicolay – que si les Puissances Allemandes s'étaient bornées, comme l'avaient annoncé au début, à une simple occupation militaire du Schleswig, le Gouvernement Danois aurait pu accepter l'armitrice, mais depuis qu'ils y avaient complètement modifié l'organisation administrative et supprimé tout vestige de l'autorité Royale, le Gouvernement Danois ne pourrait pas consentir à la conclusion formelle d'un armitrice, qui impliquerait en quelque sorte de sa part une admission en faveur d'un semblable ordre des choses. Il a ajouté, qu'une simple suspension d'armes momentanée, qui n'avait qu'une valeur purement stratégique, n'offrirait pas les mêmes inconvénients. Tout en faisant cette distinction, Mr de Quaade n'a pas voulu prendre sur lui de me dire que le Gouvernement consentirait à un pareil arrangement, mais il n'y aurait pas en lieu pour lui d'en faire mention, s'il n'y avait rattaché quelques espérances. Ces indices ne sont pas favorables.

This was the conclusion reached by Nicolay.[105]

Monrad referred to this question two weeks later during a talk with the Russian ambassador.

---

103. Finally, it is worth quoting Clarendon's opinion of the Danish delegation:
Quaade war gemässigt und übervorsichtig, Krieger war fest und doctrinär, Bille tat nicht einmal den Mund auf. Alle drei zusammen erschienen mir wie die Inkarnation des passiven Widerstandes.
Clarendon to Russell, 12 April 1864, P.R.O. 30/32, 26, as cited in Voigt, p. 136; see also Steefel, *The Schleswig-Holstein Question,* p. 227; Troels G Jørgensen, *Andreas Frederic Krieger, Juristen – Politikeren – Borgeren* (Copenhagen, 1956), pp. 133 ff. Paget expressed the following opinion when he learned of Krieger's appointment:
I confess when I heard of the intention of appointing him I was rather painfully surprising and I had intended astray [E.H.-?] asking Monrad to reconsider his idea – but I have been reasoned by Quaade. My notion of Mr Krieger was that he was a dogmatical professor, unyielding and controversial and deeply imbued with ultra Danish principles, – but Quaade assures me I am mistaken. He speaks of him on the contrary as a man of reasonable and moderate views, of great ability and with the exception perhaps of not very polished manners as being a man he will be very glad to have associated with him. He has undoubtedly a good deal of political influence here and this of course is the reason why Monrad has fixed upon him.
P.R.O. 30/22, vol. 51, K. 238.
Dotézac gave a similar description of Krieger's personal characteristics.
l'un des hommes le plus considérables de ce pays. Sa capacité est incontestée, son caractère honoré et par ses opinions il offre au parti national dont il est l'un des chiefs toutes les garanties désirables, et que M Quaade recherchait dans son alter ego. Dotézac, *ibid.,* vol. 247, 3 April 1864. Summary in *Origines,* vol. II, p. 207.
104. Nicolay, no. 43, 7 (19) March 1864. See: Foreløbig Instruction for de Kongelige Befuldmægtigede ved Londoner-Conference 1864. In: Udenrigs. Ark. London, Samlingspakke 28, 29. R.A. Copenhagen.
105. No. 51. Réservé, 25 March (6 April) 1864, vol 54.

Il maintien – the ambassador reported[106] – qu'un armitrice, sans aucune garantie que les négociations aboutiraient à une paix acceptable pour le Danemarc, et avec la perspective, dès lors, de pouvoir les rompre lorsque la saison redeviendrait défavorable à l'action de la flotte Danois, se présentait dans des conditions trop favorables pour l'Allemagne et trop défavorables pour ce pays-ci, pour que le Gouvernement Danoise puisse l'accepter.

This was Monrad's argument for refusing to agree to a truce.

The Copenhagen governement's position incurred the disapproval of the St Petersburg cabinet. Gorchakov advised Nicolay to persuade the Danish government to send new instructions to its plenipotentiaries in London, to induce them to conclude a truce ('armitrice') with the German states, rather than a 'suspension of hostilities'.[107] Formally Gorchakov did not urge, however, but only advised. As he wrote to Brunnow,[108] only Christian IX and his government could judge what was in the interests of his country, and Russia would not put any obstacles in the way. Any initiative or means of solving the problems could not and should not be Russia's doing.[109]

A difficult problem was to establish the principles and conditions on which the suspension of hostilities was to be based. This question was posed at the first real session of the conference, but the efforts to settle it immediately ran into difficulties. Two matters in particular proved troublesome – the question of the German troops evacuating Jutland, which the Danish side demanded, and the lifting of the blockade, which both the larger German states demanded,

Gorchakov was for ending the blockade. He tried to persuade the Danes that it would lead to nothing. In a conversation with the Danish envoy on 10 May/28 April Gorchakov questioned the efficiency of the blockade because the Danish navy was too small to blockade the whole Prussian coastline. He warned the Danes against runing the blockade because it would also estrange the allies from Denmark.[110] The essence of this conversation Plessen reported to Copenhagen in the following terms: "Que le maintien du blocus ne ferait qu'irriter d'avantage les Allemandes et finirait peut être, à cause des inconvenients qu'en ressentent les neutres d'attiédir à notre détriment ceux qui ont de la sympathie pour notre cause".[111]

At the meeting on 25 April Brunnow appealed for an end to the bloodshed.[112] The tactics Brunnow adopted were as follows: in talks with the Danish delegation[113] he urged them to conclude a truce as quickly as possible, arguing

---

106. No. 59, 8 (20) April 1864.
107. Brunnow to Russell, 18 April 1864, P.R.O. vol. 78.
108. 2 (14) April 1864.
109. *Ibid.*
110. As a matter of fact Gorchakov pleaded for Prussia whose affairs were, in the first place, jeopardized because of the blockade. See next note.
111. Cf. Russell to Lytton: Duly the Danes should, if the war goes on, rescind their order to capture German Vessels (not Prussian and Austrian). (P.R.O./32. Sweden and Denmark. Earl Russell. Private 1859-1865. vol. 102. p. 80).
112. *Aktstykker vedkommende tydske strid. II. London Konferencen* (Copenhagen, 1866), p. 64.
113. 'Krieger to D.G. Monrad, 1 May 64', *Dansk Magazin*, (1940), pp. 118-90.

that after the fall of Düppell and the surrender of Fredericia it would be impossible to hold Als.[114] He considered the position taken by the Danish government to be a mistake. The Danes would soon have to lift the blockade, as they could not count on any external help, but by concluding a truce Denmark could at least save Jutland from devastation.[115] Brunnow urged the Danish delegation to ask Monrad as soon as possible to give them a free hand to conduct the negotiations. He appealed to the delegation as 'amicus Daniae' – as he called himself – and stressed that he was only telling them the truth, and that as long as there was no truce they could not count on Britain's help.

At the plenary sessions of the conference, however, Brunnow, like the Swedish delegate, Wachmeister, took the position that

Le devoir des Puissances neutres est de concilier les opinions extrêmes, et de conseiller un système de compensation équitable.[116]

M le Brunnow pense également – reported the French representative, La Tour d'Auvergne – qu'il faudrait tenir compte du sacrifice que tenait le Danemark en se désistant du blocus, et que les compensations devraient être plus larges.[117]

Seeing the uncompromising attitude of Germany and knowing the position of his own government, Brunnow strove to persuade the British government to take firmer action to help Denmark and force Germany to adopt a more flexible attitude. But he was unable to do much in this respect. Eventually, with Brunnow playing a prominent role, the two sides agreed rather unwillingly on 9 May to sign a suspension of hostilities for a period of four weeks from 12 May.[118]

When Brunnow informed Gorchakov of the suspension of hostilities agreed on 9 May, and that the blockade would be lifted, he expressed regret that the Danish goverment had not accepted the proposals for a truce put forward by Russia. The Danes might then have been able to secure the evacuation of German troops from the whole of Jutland, and at least from the fortress of Fredericia, if they had agreed to leave the island of Als (which was part of Schleswig) and some small islands of no great importance. But they had preferred to conclude a suspension of hostilities, reserving the right to come to a truce later, once they knew what the German plenipotentiaries' terms for the conclusion of peace would be.[119]

Monrad was very sceptical about the suspension of hostilities and, knowing the German attitude, did not expect any further positive results. He expressed this in a *circulaire* to Plessen on 18 May[120] (six days after the suspension of hostilities took effect), predicting that action at the front would resume after the month, in which case the blockade would be reimposed. He asked Plessen to inform Gorchakov that,

114. See Voigt, p. 129.
115. *Ibid.*
116. *Aktstykker* ... p. 69.
117. .*Ibid.* p. 70. Cf. also F.F. Beust, *Aus Drei Viertel-Jahrhunderten* ... vol. I. 1809-1866. Appendix to Chapter XXVII, (Stuttgart, 1887), pp. 378-9.
118. *Ibid.* p. 73. Cf Vitzthum von Eckstädt, vol. II, p. 330; Voigt p. 129; on Moltke's reluctance to agree to the suspension of hostilities, see Klein-Wuttig, pp. 25-26.
119. A.M.I.D. Dispatch of 27 April (9 May) 1864, vol. 68, no. 104.
120. No. 35.

in the interests of general trade, vessels of neutral states would not be apprehended.[121]

Gorchakov took a positive view of the fact that a decision to suspend hostilities had been agreed, but did not deny that the final outcome of the conference was still a matter for the future, and that what he called 'la tâche réelement épineuse de la Conférence' was only just beginning.[122] What filled him with anxiety? In the first place the increasingly aggressive policy of Bismarck and the complications to which it could give rise in Europe. Secondly, like Brunnow, he was disturbed by the lack of flexibility displayed from the start of the conference by the Danish side.

Wedel-Jarlsberg felt that, while it criticised the behaviour of the German powers, the Russian cabinet would not cease to regard them as its only true allies, who had to be spared in spite of everything ('quand-même').[123]

Dieu veuille que les difficultés inhérentes à la Pologne ne rejaillissent pas trop sur l'attitude de la Russie à Londres et qu'elle ne s'y montre pas trop partiale pour l'Allemagne surtout en ce qui concerne le projet d'Union personelle[124]

This, however, does not alter the fact that uncertainty about Prussia's behaviour was growing. Towards the end of April (23/11), Oubril was sending telegrams of alarm to Gorchakov, urging him to cool Bismarck's aspirations and to persuade Bismarck to make clear what his intentions were. He considered that the unease and displeasure about Bismarck's policy shown in London was justified. Alexander II wrote the following comment in the margin of this telegram: 'I am very much afraid that he may complicate matters even further'.[125]

In a special communication dated 26 (14) April, in which Oubril reported on a talk with Bismarck, he informed Gorchakov that Bismarck had said the preservation of the King's and his own position depended on the settlement of the conflict with Denmark. In contrast to the recommendation of Gorchakov, who thought that after the success of the victory at Düppel Bismarck should calm the members of his cabinet and exercise moderation,[126] Bismarck was demanding further successes, including territorial gains, which, Oubril observed, had previously been officially denied.

As we know, Bismarck presented four alternatives for settling the problem:

1. a personal union;
2. to give the duchies to Prince Augustenburg;
3. or to Prince Oldenburg;
4. or to merge them with Prussia;

although he considered that annexation of a territory with a population of 500,000

---

121. A.M.I.D. vol. 66.
122. Wedel-Jarlsberg, no. 55, 11 May (29 April) 1864.
123. *Ibid.*
124. *Ibid.*
125. A.M.I.D. vol. 66, *Krasnyi Arkhiv*, 2 (93), (1939), p. 116.
126. *Ibid.* pp. 88-90, see Gorchakov's telegram to Oubril, 19 (7) April 1864.

was insignificant as far as the Prussian monarchy was concerned. In view of the growing hostility of Britain, he would be inclined to accept the French proposal for a plebiscite.[127] How Bismarck's tone had changed, said Oubril, compared with his talk a month before?[128]

When Bismarck realised during the course of their talk that everything he was saying about his policy was producing a negative impression on Oubril, he hastened to thank the Russian government for its attitude to the Danish-German conflict and, the ambassador reported, 'que sous ce rapport il (Bismarck) se reconnaissait en effet notre débiteur'. He did this so skilfully that for a moment Oubril thought he had achieved the aim of his talk and had succeeded 'de maintenir le Cabinet de Berlin sur une ligne de conduite correcte et favorable dans des questions qui se rattachent à des intérêts majeurs pour la Russie'.[129] As a result of this last talk Oubril asked Gorchakov to get Bismarck to declare his intentions, and Alexander II wrote the following comment in the margin of this 26 (14) April report: 'I find Bismarck's language less than reassuring' ('Nakhozhu yazyk Bismarka malo uspokoitel 'nym').[130]

Prussia had been exploiting her victory from the moment she captured Düppel and occupied Jutland, Brunnow reported,[131] recounting her behaviour during the first days of the Conference, when the question of a suspension of hostilities was under discussion. She did not want Denmark to remain a single entity, she had withdrawn her proposals for a personal union, she wanted the duchies to be completely independent and separate from Denmark. Prussia no longer wanted what she had been demanding the day before. To tell the truth, even Austria did not know what Prussia wanted, and Austria's role in the whole affair was a miserable one. She had to go along with Germany in order not to lose popularity there. And the representative of the German Confederation, Beust, was negotiating with the help of Prussian bayonets.[132]

Chester Wells Clark, the author of *Franz Joseph and Bismarck. The Diplomacy of Austria before the War of 1866,* summed up the situation as follows:

With consummate skill, Bismarck exhausted all the arts of diplomacy to drag Austria farther and farther into the enterprise ... But Rechberg did not visualise a very bold policy, in view of Austria's precarious situation. The Emperor and Rechberg accepted Bismarck's terms ... No one but Freiherr von Lasser in the Austrian Cabinet was as far-sighted as Bismarck. But Rechberg and Franz Joseph were too paralysed with fear of French intervention to perceive

---

127. See Oubril to Gorchakov, 16 (28) May 1864, APP, V, p. 169.
128. See Oubril to Gorchakov, 18 (30) March, 1864, APP, IV, pp. 685 ff.
129. APP, IV, p. 687. "Je l'espère bien" – wrote the Tsar in the margin of the report.
130. *Krasnyi Arkhiv, ibid,* p. 90. On 24 April C. Spitzemberg, the Württemberg ambassador in St Petersburg, reported that the Tsar, for whom Bismarck was 'persona gratissima' (see his report of 13 July 1861), had great doubts about the 'abenteuerliche Politik des Herrn von Bismarck'. H.S.A. Stuttgart. E 73, Gesandtschaftsakten. (Württembergische Gesandtschaft St Petersburg. Facs. 86, 1860-65). See Sten Martenson, *Württemberg und Russland im Zeitalter der deutschen Einigung 1856-1870. Die diplomatischen und dynastischen Beziehungen eines deutschen Mittelstaates,* (Göppingen, 1970), p. 124.
131. 4 May (22 April).
132. *Krasnyi Arkhiv, ibid,* pp. 92-95.

that Bismarck needed them at this time more than they needed him and that they might have stolen the king away from the policy of his minister-president ... As Austria was the more passive partner in the Danish campaign, so her envoys at the Conference limited themselves largely to assenting to declarations given in the name of the allies by the Prussian delegates.[133]

As far as Denmark was concerned, Brunnow reported, she had already lost much, but would listen to no one, 'and suffered advice only out of despair' ('iz svoego otchayaniya'). Even if it were possible to secure an honourable compromise for the Copenhagen court, with the duchies remaining connected with Denmark by personal union, Denmark's plenipotentiaries did not have the authority to agree to it.[134] They were saying that if that happened, if national interests were sacrificed to dynastic considerations, Christian IX would bring about his own ruin. That might be correct, observed Brunnow, but this attitude in London only paralysed the progress of the talks. One question alone, namely that of the compensation the German states were demanding, would be enough to break up the discussions. Oubril had reported that the German states were demanding a contribution amounting to seventeen million florins, of which seven would go to Austria. And for Franz Joseph the financial question was of fundamental importance.

Brunnow was very pessimistic about the future course of the conference. He doubted whether the neutral states would be willing or had the means to make Prussia relinquish Jutland and Schleswig and Germany give up Holstein. France did not want to, Britain could not, and Russia had entered the negotiations with the idea of an entente based on maintenance of the integrity of Denmark, for which Prussia and Austria had declared their support. Now that the Prussian plenipotentiary, the ambassador in London, A. Bernstorff, had come out against the integrity of Denmark, Brunnow questioned whether it would not be better to withdraw from the conference with honour then, rather than let Russia find herself in a difficult situation and abandon her principles without the least hope that it would bring Denmark any benefit. Brunnow also asked Gorchakov to explain precisely to him how the clause (reservation) designed to protect the rights of the Imperial house should be formulated for inclusion in the minutes of the conference. No amount of caution over this question would be too great, as he anticipated an immediate response from Beust. As for Russian rights to Kiel, while Bismarck insisted on this, urging Russia to raise the issue in Frankfurt, Brunnow saw that as hypocrisy on Bismarck's part, since Bernstorff declared that Russia had no such

---

133. Chester Wells Clark, *Franz Joseph and Bismarck. The Diplomacy of Austria before the War of 1866,* (Cambridge, Harvard UP, 1934), pp. 56, 57, 64, 66, 69. Cf. George O. Kent, *Bismarck and His Times,* (Southern Illinois UP, 1978), p. 50, 'Prussia under Bismarck's skillful leadership had outmaneuvered Austria.'
134. According to Møller, basing himself on the text of Bismarck's dispatch to Goltz on 19 May 1864 (*Gesammelte Werke,* vol. IV, 1927, no. 372), Bismarck could accept a personal union without division of Schleswig. Møller also attacks the argument that there were differences between Bismarck and Wilhelm I on the question of the frontier. London-Konferencensproblem Hovedproblem, *Festskrift til K. Erslev,* (Copenhagen, 1927), pp. 521, 523.

rights, as she had received indemnity for the house of Oldenburg. If Russia claimed her rights, Bernstorff said, it would mean she wanted to be recompensed a second time for something for which she had already received the equivalent. Russia's reservations, Brunnow observed, were more a problem of law than they were an actual fact. For without a victorious war neither Germany, nor Britain nor Sweden, would wish to see the Russian flag flying over Kiel.

This document is one more proof that Russian diplomats, particularly those like Brunnow, had no illusions about Bismarck's behaviour and the methods he used. He was really master of the situation and was doing everything, per *fas et nefas*,[135] to attain the maximum advantage for Prussia.

One of the matters touched on in Brunnow's letter of 4 May (22 April) deserves special attention, namely his suggestion of possibly leaving the conference. On this, Alexander II resolved: 'if matters take this course there will be no alternative left for us other than to do that'.[136] This matter became known in diplomatic circles, and the Saxon ambassador in London, Vitzthum von Eckstädt, wrote of it:

Der russissche Bevollmächtigste hat ausserhalb der Conferenz sehr kategorisch erklärt, er werde den Sitzungssaal sofort verlassen, wenn die Integrität der dänischen Monarchie in Frage gestellt werden sollte. Dem französischen Botschafter, der mir diese Drohung hinterbrachte, erwiderte ich: 'So lange England und Frankreich bleiben, ist darum die Conferenz noch nicht gesprengt; auch könnte man den Russen das Protokoll offen halten.

Ist Baron Brunnow zu einer solche Sprache ermächtigt? Wird er vorkommenden Falles seine Drohung ausführen? Ich möchte beides stark bezweifeln. Wie die Dinge heute liegen, dürfte die Hauptfrage in der Conferenz nicht so bald zur Sprache kommen und die auf nächsten Montag anberaumte Sitzung wieder ohne Abschluss des Waffenstillstandes auseinandergehen.[137]

If Brunnow presented such a drastic conclusion to the cabinet as to suggest the possibility of withdrawal from the conference, it was not because of a passing mood or on the spur of the moment. My impression is that he did it after carefully thinking over the whole situation which had arisen at the conference at the beginning of May. He was not the only one to be influenced by the new situation created as a result of Bismarck's behaviour. Russell responded to Bismarck's conduct with a sharp speech delivered in parliament in April, Garibaldi was ceremonially received in London, which was associated with anti-Austrian feeling, and finally there was Clarendon's mission to Paris, which, it was rumoured, had opened up the possibility of a Franco-British alliance being concluded. There was again talk in political circles in London of the need to counter the possible dispatch of an Austrian squadron, which the Austrian government was said to be intending to send to the Baltic to protect the German ports threatened by the Danish blockade. In this context, and in view of the difficulties accumulating at the conference itself, the tone of Brunnow's letter may be understandable.

135. By fair means or foul.
136. *Krasnyi Arkhiv, ibid.* pp. 92-94.
137. Von Eckstädt, vol. II, p. 331.

Something in the nature of a crisis of confidence in Russo-Prussian relations was beginning to come to a head. Gorchakov's fears about how the situation would develop were growing; uncertainty about Bismarck's plans was increasing. He wanted to know what Bismarck's intentions were. Bismarck, too, began to realise the mood in St Petersburg, and decided to send his special envoy, Pirch, there with the task of arranging a rapprochement between Russia, Prussia and Austria. The talks Pirch had in St Petersburg with both Gorchakov and Alexander II show that Gorchakov was aware of the aims of Bismarck's policy in general terms, particularly since, despite the restraint in what he said, Pirch did not conceal that Bismarck (as Pirch explained), in view of the political authority of the King, would not let the blood of Prussian soldiers be shed in vain, and made it clear that he would not be satisfied with fruitless laurels. But general statements no longer seemed sufficient to Gorchakov, and he insisted that he wanted to know Bismarck's plans 'ganz offen und deutlich', and asked him to take him into his confidence, which Gorchakov promised to keep absolutely secret.

We only want to ease the situation for him. We attach enormous importance to the maintenance of friendly relations between us, but in order to have the opportunity of being useful we must know in what direction Mr Bismarck aims to gain an advantage. I have spelled out exactly what I mean – Gorchakov said to Pirch, ending with these words – one should not set riddles for friends[138] (Druz'yam ne sleduet zadavat' zagadok).[139]

This is what Gorchakov wrote to Oubril after his first meeting with Bismarck's envoy.[140]

Gorchakov received no answer to the questions he asked Pirch, such as: what were Bismarck's aims, particularly at the conference; what did he understand by a personal union; what did his army really want? Were Prussia's demands not excessive or too egoistical if one of the possibilities mentioned by Bismarck was annexation of the duchies and their 500,000 inhabitants, which, Gorchakov feared, could arouse strong opposition? Gorchakov assured him that he shared Bismarck's opinion that the Danish question was in principle a secondary matter,[141] but he argued that it should not compromise or infringe the general interests of Europe and lead to the rise of two blocs, a western bloc and an opposite conservative one, since then the Danish question could cease to be secondary and the effects of such a division

---

138. 'Welche Ziele er [Bismarck – E.H.] der preussischen Politik jeweils setzte, hing für ihn immer davon ab, was gerade Erfolg versprach – S. Haffner wrote. Mit Bezug auf den Dänischen Krieg von 1864 zum Beispiel hat er das in einer Rede einmal ausführlich ausgeplaudert: 'Ich habe stets an dem Klimax festgehalten, dass die Personalunion (Zwischen Dänemark und Schleswig-Holstein) besser war als das, was existierte, dass ein selbständiger Fürst besser war als die Personalunion, und dass die Vereinigung mit dem preussischen Staate besser war als ein selbständiger Fürst. Welches davon das Erreichbare war, das konnten allein die Ereignisse lehren!' (*Preussen ohne Legende* pp. 337, 361).
139. *Krasnyi Arkhiv, ibid.* p. 91.
140. 30 (18) April 1864. Cf. Pirch to Bismarck, 20 April 1864, Ganz Vertraulich. APP, IV, pp. 725-6. See also *Krasnyi Arkhiv, ibid.*, pp. 90-92.
141. Gorchakov had expressed this idea previously in a letter to Olga Nikolaevna on 13 March (old style).

of Europa would be disastrous. Therefore Gorchakov appealed, through Pirch, for the London conference to be imbued with a spirit of reason and moderation and readiness to reach agreement.[142]

During Pirch's audience with Alexander II, the Tsar, who incidentally a few days before had, like Napoleon III (NB without the knowledge of Drouyn de Lhuys), sent congratulations to Wilhelm I on the capture of Düppel,[143] assured the Prussian envoy of his love for King Wilhelm I and did not stint in his praise of the Prussian army.

Ich wünsche von Herzen dass es Herrn Bismarck den ich liebe, achte und hochschätze und in dessen Charakter und Tendenz ich das vollste Vertrauen setze, gelingen möge, aus diesen von mir angedeuteten Klippen einen Weg zu finden zum Frieden den ich sehnlichst herbeiwünsche und dessen wir alle bedürfen, und zu einem Erfolge, der Preussen genügen könne. Mein Herz und meine Wünsche sind mit Preussen und seiner Sache und werden es stets bleiben.[144]

But after these declarations and wishes for Bismarck and Prussia, the Tsar added that he was disturbed by the nervousness Britain was displaying on account of Prussia's behaviour, and by the thought of the possibility of an alliance between Britain and France, which would be a threat to Europe. On the other hand, the Tsar said, the French Social-democratic idea of a popular vote in the duchies also seemed 'gefährlich' to him.

Alexander's thoughts were developed by Gorchakov during his next meeting with Pirch.[145] He warned Prussia not to let Britain follow France, as he put it, 'qu'on lui arrondisse les angles', and expressed the wish, 'England einem Ausweg aus der dänischen Frage möglichst zu erleichtern'. Prussia, in Gorchakov's opinion, should move closer to Austria and Britain. 'Pour la Russie', he assured him, 'elle vous est acquise d'avance'. Gorchakov informed Pirch that he had received instructions from the Tsar to support Prussia's interests in the Danish question. He himself appreciated that the Danish-German conflict was a vital problem for Prussia and he wanted to be as helpful as possible to Bismarck. But it would be easier for him to do so if he knew Bismarck's plans and the specific position he took. Like the Tsar, Gorchakov was against a vote in the duchies, particularly under current conditions, and he demanded to know whether Bismarck still supported the integrity of Denmark. If so, it would be possible to find a solution. But if not, he would like to know. Russia would then have to consider if she could support Prussia at the conference.

This conversation led Pirch to conclude that as far as Russia was concerned only

---

142. Pirch to Bismarck, APP, IV.
143. APP, IV, no. 599, 19 April 1864.
144. Pirch to Wilhelm I, 2 April, APP, IV. pp. 758-9. In his dispatch to Hügel on April 26, 1864 C. Spitzemberg wrote that Prussia was sure that 'Russland nichts Feindliches gegen Preussen unternehmen und sich von jeder Demonstration fernhalten wurde, welche dem König von Preussen Verlegenheiten bereiten konnten'. H.S.A. Stuttgart, E. 73. Württemb. Gesands. St. Petersburg, 1864.
145. APP, vol. V, 3 May 1864, pp. 75-77.

Alexander II really supported the German side in the Danish-German dispute. The Tsarina, and the heir to the throne, in view of his marriage to Dagmar, took Denmark's side, and Gorchakov firmly defended the integrity of Denmark because if Denmark were weakened she would throw herself into the arms of Sweden and the consequence would be a Scandinavian union.[146] 'Jamais la Russie ne pourra souffrir que le Belt devienne un second Bosphore'',[147] Gorchakov kept repeating, suffering like almost all Russian politicians from a claustrophobic concern about Russia's isolation and the closure of the straits. Pirch thought that Gorchakov would support Prussia for as long as she was useful to him in carrying out Russian policy on the Polish and the Eastern questions. The aims of his policy were the integration of Denmark, to earn Denmark's gratitude for the marriage of Dagmar to the heir to the Russian throne, strengthen the alliance with Denmark, reach a four-power entente with the help of Prussian concessions, and ultimately to use these connections to achieve success in his Eastern policy.[148] Pirch also noted that Napier, who was meeting Gorchakov almost daily, exercised a considerable influence in his policy. 'Der Fürst möchte gern die *societas leonina* mit Preussen fortsetzen, d.h. Hilfe beanspruchen ohne Gegenleistungen'.[149]

This, however, was not British diplomacy's view of Gorchakov's position. Britain therefore warned the St Petersburg cabinet against Bismarck's policy of intrigue and his annexationist tendencies. Buchanan, the British ambassador in Berlin, warned Oubril:

Yet as it was now evident that his [Bismarck's] own interest and the aggrandizement of Prussia would be best promoted by the separation of the Duchies of Holstein and Schleswig from Denmark and their subjection directly or indirectly to Prussia, I thought it was prudent to receive with some doubt any assurances which he [Bismarck] might offer of the disinterestedness which would animate the Prussian Government in their treatment of the questions brought before the Conference in London ... I have endeavoured to present Mr Bismarck's views from being too favourably represented at St Petersburg.[150]

But Clarendon, whom the Danish ambassador in Paris met at Cowley's house, expressed the opinion that the Russian government would probably favour 'd'union purement personal, analogue à celui qui existe entre la Suède et la Norvegè', so as not to give Germany the opportunity to find a pretext for intervention in Danish affairs. Clarendon was of the opinion that Russia would defend the principle of the integrity of the Danish monarchy at the conference, while at the same time reserving to herself the right to certain parts of Holstein.[151]

There were some differences of opinion among British politicians about the Russian policies. Napier, at first, really believed that Gorchakov, and the Tsar, were sincerely in favour of the integration of Denmark, and that there was no defensive

---

146. APP, vol. V, 11 May 1864, pp. 94-95.
147. *Ibid.* p. 94.
148. *Ibid.* 21 May 1864, pp. 144-6.
149. *Ibid.* 11 May, p. 95. See Colonel v. Loën to Manteuffel, 22 May, p. 150.
150. Buchanan to Russell, 14 May 1864. APP, ibid. p. 114.
151. Dep. Frankrig no. 31, 17 April 1864. Moltke to Copenhagen. R.A. Udenrigs.

treaty between the three Nothern powers. But Russell was in no doubt as to the Russian position, all the more so since he detected differences between the attitudes of Gorchakov and Brunnow towards Denmark.

I don't know at all what to make of the Russians. Brunnow is always urging me to send ships to the Baltic, saying that he thinks Russia will join us there, but Gortchakoff seems more disposed to join Bismarck,

Russell wrote to Napier on 4 May.[152]

Brunnow advocated joint action by the British and Russian fleets,

car ni la Russie ni la Suède ne pourraient permettre qu'on vînt, suivant l'expression de M le Baron de Brunnow, *faire du tapage dans la Baltique,* et que, le case échéant, elles prendraient sans doutes des mesures pour s'y opposer.[153]

Gorchakov, on the other hand, was making efforts to persuade Vienna to abandon the idea of sending an Austrian squadron to the Baltic as it would not be 'ni du goût, ni dans les intérêts de l'Allemagne'. Asked by the Swedish ambassador what he intended to do if the squadron appeared in the Baltic, he responded: 'nous aviserons, c'est tout ce que je puis Vous dire pour le moment'.[154] Furthermore, it became a generally accepted belief that, as Wedel-Jarlsberg wrote, there had been a consolidation between Austria, Prussia and Russia and that, as Napier said to Wedel, there was less hope then of drawing Russia into joint action than there had been two months earlier.[155] Gorchakov answered questions with 'nous verrons, nous aviserons'. Wedel, however, came to the conclusion that: 'En définitif, le Prince Gortchakoff me parait en dernier lieu plutôt se réfroidir pour la cause Danoise', and bore the Danish cabinet ill will because it would not listen to his advice and was not prepared to make sacrifices to avoid trouble, 'des embarras au Grand Europe'.[156] 'Le Gouvernement Imperial avisera, peu d'espoir d'un commun matériel', he telegraphed on 23 (11) May, but to Gorchakov's satisfaction the question of an Austrian squadron to be sent to the Baltic ceased to be an immediate concern.

Napier reported on 11 May that Brunnow was more pro-Danish than the Russian cabinet. Gorchakov was becoming increasingly cool towards Denmark, and

---

152. P.R.O. Russia, Earl Russell, Private, 1859-1865, vol. 114, K. 138; Cf. Voigt, pp. 132-3.
153. La Tour d'Auvergne to Drouyn de Lhuys, 28 April 1864, *Origines,* vol. II, p. 317.
154. Wedel-Jarlsberg, no. 56, 14 (2) May 1864.
155. *Ibid.* The Swedish ambassador commented:

Quoique le Prince ne fit aucune observation sur l'opportunité de la prochaine sortie de l'escadre Suèdo-Norvégienne, je crois pourtant qu'une immobilité complète de notre part lui eut été plus agréable. C'est que tout novel élement, quelque petit qu'il ait, jetté dans la balance est considerée par lui comme un danger de plus pour la paix générale. Or essentiel à ses yeux c'est la Russie ne soit entrainée dans les complications Européennes, le reste y compris les intérêts vitaux de la Danemark, ne viennent qu'ensuite, sur le second, troisième ou même quatrième plan.

Pour la même raison, il est contraire et verrait d'assez mauvais oeil l'entrée d'une flotte Autrichienne dans la Baltique, - et tout ses moyens de persuasion amicale seront employés à Vienne pour écarter la réalisation d'un projet éventuel de ce genre.

156. *Ibid.*

towards links with Britain. Even before this, the Saxon ambassador had observed that the more pro-Danish Britain became, the more Russia became pro-German.[157] Napier said he was convinced that Gorchakov would do everything to warn Bismarck to follow a restrained and moderate line. He thought Gorchakov would behave in this spirit at the meeting between Alexander II, Wilhelm I and Franz Joseph at Kissingen, which was expected soon. Gorchakov's views were gradually adjusting to links with Germany, and he had come to the conclusion that this course was the safest one for Russia in view of the need to subdue Poland.[158]

Napier seems to have judged Gorchakov's true intentions much more accurately than Pirch. Pirch's dissatisfaction with Gorchakov's attitude stemmed from the fact that the vice-chancellor was not willing to go as far as Bismarck wanted, and Bismarck employed various means to bind Russia to Prussia. This time he tempted her with the prospect of building a canal thorugh the duchies linking the North Sea and the Baltic, which could have been important for Russia, as it would have ended the monopoly of the Sound, and Russia could have derived both political and economic advantages from the canal.[159] It is worth mentioning that the idea of building such a canal goes back to the time of Peter the Great.[160]

In a talk with Redern, Gorchakov remained cautious about this proposal, which had been put to him by Pirch. According to Wedel-Jarlsberg's report,

Gortchakoff se borna alors à répondre que, selon lui, la construction d'une tel canal était une question de détail, dont la solution devait être réservée à l'avenir. En ce moment – ajoute le Prince, il s'agit avant tout à nos yeux de la consécrative d'un grand principe, savoir – le main pièce de l'intégrité de la Monarchie Danoise, et c'est cette question là réclame principalement notre attention.

He thus made it clearly understood that in spite of the benefits the canal would bring Russia, the idea was not acceptable to him at that moment. The question of the balance of power in the north was more important. The Swedish ambassador concluded that Gorchakov was concerned not to undermine the authority and standing of the Danish King and not to infringe the principle of the integrity of the monarchy.[161]

Bismarck did not achieve everything he expected from the Pirch mission, but on one thing he could be sure: there was no threat of any danger from Russia, quite the contrary. She would never join the anti-Prussian camp.[162] And once he was

---

157. Von Eckstädt, vol. II, p. 323.
158. Napier to Russell, 11 May, P.R.O. vol. 84.
159. *G.W.* vol. IV, no. 340, Bismarck to Pirch, 20 April 1864.
160. See W. Mediger, *Der Ostseeraum im Blickfeld der deutschen Geschichte* (1970), pp. 150ff on Peter's plans and the efforts of Holstein-Gottorp; Mecklenburg-Schwerin, however, was against it.
161. Wedel-Jarlsberg, no. 54, 3 May (26 April) 1864.
162. The Prussian chargé d'affaires in St Petersburg assured C. Spitzemberg that Russia's friendship for Prussia was far-reaching. But he also said that Gorchakov had continually advised him not to demand anything more from Denmark than a personal union of Denmark and the duchies. Prussia believed 'dass Russland nichts feindliches gegen Preussen unternehmen und sich von jeder Demonstration fernhalten würde, welche dem König von Preussen Verlegenheiten bereiten könnten'. H.S.A., Stuttgart, report of 21 May 1864.

certain of this, there was nothing more to fear. Gorchakov, on the other hand, had no particular cause for satisfaction, as he had failed to obtain answers to the questions about Prussia's future plans which were troubling him. Pirch could not give him an answer to his questions, – what did Prussia mean by saying she wanted to be freed of the 1852 obligations, and on what terms did she plan to negociate a peace? Nor could he persuade Bismarck to relinquish the idea of a plebiscite in the duchies, despite appealing to his monarchist principles.

Massignac did not believe St Petersburg would be pleased at the prospect of an increase in the power of Prussia or Germany. Nor would it like to see Rendsborg become a federal fortress, or Kiel a German port. If it came to that, Gorchakov had been obliged to say, Kiel should belong to Russia ('à l'Empereur de Russie'), Massignac reported. Gorchakov still did not believe that it could go to Prussia. That, wrote the French *chargé d'affaires,* was Gorchakov's attitude to the growth of German power in the north.[163] And this was at a time when there was a growing number of reports from diplomats that Prussia was not vacating the duchies she had occupied,[164] while Bismarck's official envoy was saying that Prussia would not give up the gains she had won so dearly in the war.[165]

On 12 May, at the first session of the conference after the conclusion of the four-weeek suspension of hostilities, when the question of the future peace treaty was on the agenda, Bernstorff renounced the Treaty of London in the name of the larger German governments. This move, especially coming from Prussia, could not be a surprise for any of the participants at the conference. For many months Bismarck's behaviour had indicated that he regarded the treaty purely as an historical document, and even in February he had really only agreed to conditional observance of the 1851-52 obligations.[166]

In his instructions to Brunnow on the eve of the opening of the conference, Gorchakov foresaw the possibility of the annulment of the treaty. He therefore spared no effort during April and at the turn of the month in attempting to persuade Bismarck to observe the 8 May 1852 provisions, the principal idea of which was the

---

163. A.M.A.E., Russie, vol. 223, 22 May 1864. *Origines,* vol. III, p. 90.
164. See Cintrat, Ministre à Hamburg, to Drouyn de Lhuys, 7 May 1864, and Méroux de Valois, Agent consulaire à Kiel, to Drouyn de Lhuys, 7 May 1864. *Origines,* vol. II, pp. 349-52.
165. See his (Pirch's) first talk with Gorchakov, and his talk with Massignac. Report to Drouyn de Lhuys, 22 May 1864. *Origines,* vol. III, pp. 89-90.
166. On 18 March Bloomfield, the British ambassador in Vienna, wrote to Russell:
He (Rechberg) regretted to say that the opinion in Germany was as much opposed as ever to the Treaty of London, and that, in spite of the efforts of Austria and Prussia, no serious impressions had yet been made and without the concurrence of the Confederation a permanent settlement of the Danish question was impossible. *Aktstykker ved London Konferencen* (Copenhagen, 1866), p. 48.
On 19 March Buchanan, the British ambassador in Berlin, wrote to Russell:
M de Bismarck said that the Danish Government ought, however, to understand that the events of the war had abrogated the engagements of 1851-52, and that they could not expect to obtain the same conditions of peace in 1864 which had been granted to them at the termination of the war of 1848. *Ibid.,* pp. 49-50.

integrity of the Danish monarchy – 'Seine Lieblingsidee', as Pirch ironically called it in a letter to Bismarck.[167] Gorchakov regarded maintenance of the Treaty of London as an important step in preserving peace in Europe, and as a fundamental element cementing an entente between the four powers.

Brunnow also expected the renunciation of the treaty. Krieger reported to Andrae that during his talk with Brunnow on 9 May the Russian delegate had spoken of the idea of a personal union, but also of the possibility of separating Holstein and part of Schleswig from Denmark (the letter is dated 11 May) and transferring them to some German prince. To Krieger's comment that Europe had not fallen so low as to dance to Frankfurt's tune, Brunnow replied: 'Mein Lieber Herr v Krieger, es scheint fast so'. 'It looked as if only he and Palmerston were of a different opinion, and we [i.e. Russia] would be better to withdraw from the conference'. In a talk with Quaade and Krieger, Brunnow was compelled to admit that the German states were playing the decisive role at the conference.

He viewed the situation at the conference more and more pessimistically. The German demands included separation of Holstein and Schleswig from Denmark and their personal union under Christian IX, surrender of the fortress of Rendsborg to the German Confederation, and construction of a canal from the North Sea to Kiel, and Austria was demanding an enormous sum in damages. Meanwhile Gorchakov, wrote Krieger, complained that Russia could do nothing for Denmark because Russell had weakened her so much by his behaviour and his speeches on the Polish question.[168]

Brunnow himself did not conceal his displeasure at the conduct of his government, which, as he put it, no longer trusted him and left him to his own devices. Sometimes, Brunnow admitted, he could hardly wait two weeks for instructions, and then he felt very frustrated and aware of his own impotence.[169] Although he expected it, the renunciation of the treaty of which he was the joint creator and of which he felt very proud, nonetheless had a great effect on Brunnow. He felt as if he had been personally wounded. He also realised how the authority of the state he represented had fallen, and thus how his own prestige had declined, too.

Le Baron Brunnow se plaint beaucoup du peu de cas que la Conférence de Londres semble faire des opinions de la Russie. La position de Monsieur l'Ambassadeur doit en effet être beaucoup moins prépondérante qu'autrefois et ses avis accueillis avec infinitivenent moins de respect et de condéscendance.[170]

Krieger observed this much earlier, writing to Andrae on 17 April that the options open to Brunnow were even fewer than gossip had it. He had great sympathy

---

167. APP, V, 28 May 1864, p. 166.
168. *Danske Magazin* (1940), pp. 143 ff.
169. A.F. Kriegers, D G Monrads og P.V. Vedels indbyrdes brevveksling (1864-1866)', 11 May 1864, *Historisk Tidsskrift*, 7, Series 3B, (Copenhagen, 1940), p. 204.
170. Wedel-Jarlsberg, no. 61, 6 June (25 May) 1864.

for Denmark, but could not help her much. Krieger compared it to the sympathy for Garibaldi in London and its influence on help for Italy in the liberation of Venice. And in his letter to Andrae on 20 April he said that Russia at that moment was not much more influential than Sweden. Even if there was an element of exaggeration in this, it certainly reflected the climate prevailing at the conference.

To try to convince the Danish delegation of the need to alter its inflexible position, Brunnow referred to Russia's attitude after the fall of Sebastopol, and cited her conciliatory and flexible policy, her readiness to compromise, as an example which he urged Denmark to follow too.[171]

At the conference sessions on 12 and 17 May, Brunnow was involved in frequent arguments with the German plenipotentiaries, particularly Bernstorff and Beust.[172].

'M le Baron de Brunnow maintient – we read in the minutes for 12 May[173] – qu'avant d'abandonner un Traité qui a été ratifié par les Puissances signataires dans l'intérêt général de l'Europe, il faudrait donner des raisons juges satisfaisantes d'un commun accord. Ces raisons devraient être bien graves. Le Traité de 1852 a eu pour objet de consolider la paix du Nord, et de sauvegarder l'équilibre Européen. Il a été conclu non seulement entre les Puissances actuellement en guerre, mais entre toutes les Puissances qui y ont participé.

M le Baron de Brunnow fait observer qu'il n'a pas parlé de bases, mais que selon lui le principe du Traité de 1852 subsiste toujours, car l'intérêt général, dans lequel cet Acte a été conclu, reste le même.'[174]

Brunnow denied that the German Confederation had the right to discuss the subject of the treaty, since, 'quoique la Russie soit liée par le Traité, la Confédération ne l'est pas'.[175] He personally regretted that at the time the Confederation had not been informed of the treaty, although he explained, 'qu'un Article du Traité a expressement réservé les droits et les obligations établis par l'Acte Fédéral'.[176]

Brunnow also emphasised that the Confederation had rights relating to Holstein, but 'que les actes (les Actes Fédéraux) ne s'étendent nullement en Slesvig'.[177] Russia was aiming

d'amener entre le Danemark et l'Allemagne une réconciliation sincère et durable, dans l'intérêt général du rétablissement de la paix ... par une transaction honorable, librement consentie par les deux parties ... d'écarter les résolutions extrêmes et de tâcher d'ouvrir la voie à une entente à l'amiable. Je désire d'une part que l'arrangement qui interviendra soit; placé sous la protection de garanties efficaces, satisfaisantes pour l'Allemagne, et destinées

---

171. Krieger's letters to Vedel, 26 April and 4, 8, 9 and 19 May, 2864. Krieger, *Dagbøger,* vol. III, pp. 119,131, *Danske Magazin* (1940), pp. 195, 200. Krieger's letters to Andræ, 17 and 20 April. *Historisk Tidsskrift*, vol. 5 (Copenhagen, 1894-5), pp. 132-5.
172. See the minutes of the conference, and Beust, vol. I, pp. 380ff.
173. p. 79.
174. Minutes, p. 80. and Protocols of Conferences held in London relative to the Affairs' of Denmark, Presented to both Houses of Parliament by Command of Her Majesty. 1864. Ad. 4, 12 May 1864, p. 22 and Minutes, p. 84, in A.M.A.E. Paris.
175. Minutes, p. 82.
176. *Ibid.*
177. Session on 17 May, p. 90.

à prévenir le retour de nouvelles complications, de l'autre je dois veiller à ce que la Monarchie Danoise conserve parmi les Puissances de l'Europe le rang, la dignité et l'indépendance nationale que le Cour de Russie regarde comme un élément nécéssaire de l'équilibre général et du maitien de la paix du Nord.[178]

La question qui nous occupe – said Brunnow, summing up – se résume à savoir que celles garanties seront jugées de nature à satisfaire à la fois aux réclamations de l'Allemagne, aux droits du Danemark, aux intérêts de l'Europe.[179]

M de Brunnow a défendu le traité de 1852 avec chaleur, comme un père défend son enfant', was the *Revue des Deux Mondes,* view of his attitude.[180].

After the Treaty of London was formally renounced by the German states, consternation reigned for some days in the Russian ministry of foreign affairs while they considered what to do.[181]

Dänemark erfreut sich überall der grössesten Sympathien, und wenngleich ein grosser Teil der älteren Offiziere unserem Waffenruhm gebührende Anerkennung zollt, so bedauert man Dänemark als den Schwächeren, der ungerecht leiden müsse ...[182]

Ich höre jetzt aus bester Quelle, dass vor wenigen Tagen, als die Erklärung Preussens und Österreichs, dass sich beide nicht mehr an den Traktat von 1852 gebunden hielten, in den hiesigen Auswärtigen Amt bekannt wurde, dass grosse Bestürzung geherrscht und man sich viel damit beschäftigt habe, welche Antwort darauf gegeben werden könne. Seine Majestät der Kaiser, den ich eben einen Augenblick bei einer aus Warschau angekommenen Kompanie gesehen habe, sagte mir darüber nichts. – Napier und Gortschakow hängen jetzt ganz zusammen, und letzterer sucht nun sein Heil bei England ebenso, wie bisher bei Frankreich; es wird ihm aber unmöglich werden gegen Deutschland handelnd aufzutreten, denn hier will niemand Krieg, alles schreit nach Frieden, und die Finanzen bedingen denselben. Nur in der Absicht, den Frieden zu sichern, könnte Russland mit Krieg drohen wollen. Es wird aber begreifen, dass sich daran doch niemand kehrt und wird hoffentlich auch das unterlassen.[183]

Gorchakov, who relied on Brunnow's opinion, was waiting for a report from him because he did not know how he should react in the new situation.[184]

Meanwhile, having discussed Denmark's position at the conference, the British cabinet came to the conclusion that since really no power saw any possibility of maintaining the Treaty of London, the conference should discuss the question of separating Holstein and the purely German part of Schleswig from Denmark. Russell proposed to Brunnow on 14 May that before the next meeting of the commission, i.e. before 26 May, the representatives of the neutral states should hear Bernstorff's views. He himself thought that in exchange for agreeing to it, Denmark would have a guaranteed peace, and her compensation for the territorial losses would be freedom from interference in internal Danish affairs by the German Confederation.[185]

178. p. 96.
179. *Ibid.*
180. *Revue des Deux Mondes,* 14 June 1864 (vol. 51). 'Chroniques de la quinzaine', p. 1018.
181. Oberst Loën to Manteuffel, 22 May 1864. APP, V. p. 150.
182. *Ibid.*
183. *Ibid.*
184. Pirch to Bismarck, 26 May 1864, APP, V, p. 160.
185. P.R.O., 30/22, vol. 114, R. 140-42.

In his reply to Russell on 15 May[186] Brunnow expressed the opinion that Alexander II appreciated the frankness with which Russell had explained the British government's view. As was well known, he said, the Russian government had instructed him to make efforts to preserve the integrity of Denmark and the law of succession. Berlin and Vienna had been in favour of a personal union of Holstein and Schleswig under one sceptre. Vienna still wanted that. Prussia, on the other hand, had added a series of new conditions which were unacceptable to Denmark, such as the possession of fortresses and ports, and indemnities. It was a foregone conclusion that Copenhagen would reject these demands. Prussia in turn had proposed the separation of the duchies from the monarchy.

In Brunnow's opinion Denmark should be given the right to state her position, so that Christian IX could declare whether he wanted a personal union with onerous conditions ('avec les conditions onéreuses') or whether he preferred renunciation of Holstein and the southern parts of Schleswig without such conditions. In order to minimise future sacrifices he, Brunnow, considered that King Christian should relinquish the dynastic interests in the German duchies. This would be significant and would reinforce the authority of the King. The neutral countries should not, however, exert pressure on Denmark. The Tsar would certainly not wish the results of an agreement to be contrary to the will of the King.[187]

Brunnow summed up as follows: Denmark had gone into an unequal war without examining her own capabilities, and the consequences had been dire. The German states were exploiting their victory by imposing heavy sacrifices on Copenhagen, and the neutral countries were not in a position to prevent them. The role of Denmark's friends should be to respect her freedom of action and to pave the way to agreement and to Denmark's continuing existence as an independent European country assured of its security and stability. This should be an act of a European nature.[188] For this purpose Denmark must be assured of the advantage stemming from the principle of permanent neutrality, already recognised by Belgium [in 1831 – E.H.]. By agreeing to that, the German states would be giving Denmark compensation, and the cabinets which were signatories to the 1852 Treaty would guarantee Denmark the security which the Treaty of London had guaranteed, as that was necessary in order to ensure peace in the north in the interest of maintaining the balance of power. Brunnow would present these preposals to the Imperial cabinet, but until he received an answer he would adhere to his previous instructions.[189]

Brunnow spoke in this spirit at the meeting of the Conference on 28 May, emphasising particularly that Christian IX had to decide on the solution. Speaking during the discussion he defended the Treaty of London. He left open the dynastic

---

186. P.R.O., 30/22, vol. 78, K. 340-47.
187. P.R.O., 30/22, vol. 78.
188. Recognised by the Powers.
189. *Ibid.* Cf Krieger to Andrae, 11 May 1864. – Brunnow on the alternative of separating Holstein and a small part of Schleswig from Denmark, and the question of Prince Augustenburg and Prince Oldenburg.

question that would arise in the event of separation of the duchies from Denmark, but mentioned the candidacy of Prince Oldenburg as well as the aims of Prince Augustenburg.[190] There was also an argument between Brunnow and Beust. At this session Quaade recognised that the question of the frontier was, as he put it, 'un point capital'.[191] Brunnow also appealed for an extension of the truce ('de la suspension d'hostilités').

Reporting to Gorchakov, Brunnow explained[192] that the German representatives had accepted Russell's plan in principle but had reserved the right to discuss the details, particularly concerning problems such as 'la trace de la frontière, et la restriction imposée à l'Allemagne relativement l'établissement de forts et de ports de mer'. It was likely that the Danish side would agree in principle,

> 'mais avant d'y consentir, en principe, ils voudraient acquérir la certitude que les détails de cet arrangement obtiendront d'adhésion positive de Cours d'Allemagne. La question de la délimitation forme, comme de raison la difficulté principale à ressoudre'.[193]
>
> La question dynastique a été tranchée par les Plénipotentiares Allemands dans un esprit entièrement favorable au prétentions du Prince d'Augustenbourg.
>
> Enfin je me suis fait un devoir de réserver expressément les droits de le Grand Duc d'Oldenbourg ... Tous les deux (Russell and Palmerston) ont rendu le plus juste hommage aux intentions de l'Empereur.

In a letter to Nicolay, Gorchakov set out the position of the Russian cabinet, which was identical to Brunnow's.[194] This position had been approved by the Tsar. The Copenhagen cabinet, Gorchakov said, was familiar with Russell's view. Brunnow had associated himself with it on condition that Christian IX agreed to the British proposals. The Imperial cabinet had no intention of exerting any pressure on the Copenhagen government. No effort had been spared by Russia to maintain the provisions of the Treaty of London. That must be well known in Copenhagen. According to the information at his (Gorchakov's) disposal, Prince Augustenburg's chances had increased and it seemed that he was almost certain to be chosen, as the Vienna and Berlin cabinets had agreed to it.[195]

190. Minutes pp. 101, 108-12.
191. p. 108.
192. No. 125, 19 (31) May. A.M.I.D.
193. See E. Møller, London-Konferencens Hovedproblem. *Festskrift til Kristian Erslev.* (Copenhagen, 1927), pp. 515-36.
194. 19 (31) May, A.M.I.D, vol. 66.
195. Apponyi declared Augustenburg's candidacy for the German duchies in the name of Austria at the session of the conference on 28 May Minutes (p. 98). Austria was the proposer because she wanted to please public opinion in Germany and counter Prussia's aggressive plans.
1661, Privatschreiben des Grafen Apponyi an den Grafen Rechberg, London 19.V.1864.
Notre position à la conférence devient de jour en jour plus difficile; nous y sommes entièrement isolés. Personne ne veut de notre programme de l'union personnelle. Les Danois le rejettent comme inadmissible, les duchés comme insuffisant; les neutres le considèrent comme une solution incomplète et impracticable; Beust, en pleine séance, le déclare inacceptable pour l'Allemagne et la Prusse ne cache pas ses répugnances et fait son possible pour s'y soustraire ...
Même le Baron de Brunnow dans sa déclaration écrite et soigneusement rédigée d'avance n'a plus prononcé le mot d'intégrité, qui avait été jusqu' ici son cheval de bataille ... Si donc l'Angleterre, la Russie et la France semblent disposées à abandonner le terrain du traité de Londres, si la Prusse

In order to make it easier for Denmark to conclude peace with Germany and eliminate a candidate

dont le choix blesserait plus particulièrement les susceptibilités nationales Danois, et pour ménager à ce pays un voisin pour le moins inoffensif, l'Empereur a ordonné à Son Ambassadeur à Londres, de rappeler les droits de la Maison de Russie, que reprennent toute leur valeur dans le cas d'abandon du traité de Londres, et de déclarer dans la séance du Jeudi, 2 juin, que Sa Majesté a fait cession de ces droits au Grand duc d'Oldenbourg, qui aurait alors à faire valoir lui même ses titres personnels et ceux de la Maison Impériale dont il serai investi.

Le Roi y reconnaîtra, nous ésperons, une preuve du désir de Notre Auguste Maître de rendre moins pénible le sacrifice qu'on Lui demande. Il appartiendra à la sagesse du Roi de décider la ligne de conduite à suivre. L'Empereur, nous le répétons, lui réserve, pour Sa part la plus complète liberté d'action, mais Sa Majesté Impérial croirait manquer à un devoir d'amitié, si Elle dissimulait la gravité des circonstances résultant des dispositions générales de la Conférence, et si Elle encourageait l'illusion de la possibilité du maintien des stipulations du Traité de Londres.[196]

In his letter to Brunnow on 23 May 1864, Gorchakov developed his idea more fully.

Un candidat conservateur est un opposé sur la base historique au candidat de la démocratie. Bismarck ne lui pas défavorable. Rechberg hésite; l'Angleterre et le Danemark devraient lui donner la préference. Beaucoup dépend de la valeur des titres que produira le Grand Duc. Il en a religion. Nous autres gens du Nord, nous sommes à peine juges compétents, pour débrouiller le dédale juridique des Allemandes. L'examen du reste sera leur affaire. Le Grand Duc en tout cas agirait à ses risques et périls ...

Napier, with whom Gorchakov discussed Prince Oldenburg's candidacy, personally had nothing against it, but observed that

ce nominé [of Russia] serait un satellite toujours à notre disposition etc. puis il ajoute que personnellement il n'y voit pas de mal.

Bien que cela fut inutile, j'ai essayé de lui prouver que politiquement la personalité du Souverain de Holstein pouvait être indifférent à la Russie, que personnellement nous avions une estime bien fortifié pour le Grand Duc d'Oldenbourg, mais aucun sympathie extrême, que nous n'avions aucune prétention de nommer qui ce soit au trône de Holstein, qui investi de droits dynastiques, l'Empereur s'était borner à les céder au Grand Duc, afin d'être hors de cause de Sa personne etc. Mais que nous croyons venir au secours de la dignité gravement compromis des grandes Puissances, en leur ouvrant la chance de ne point fléchir devant les cris de la multitude et de la démocratie par une aveugle acceptation du candidat que celles-ci reculent imposer. En même temps nous croyons diminuer les périls géographiques et ménager les justes susceptibilités de Danemark par la perspective d'un voisin inoffensif et plus acceptable.[197]

> déchire ce traité et si la Conféderation le renie, pourquoi resterions nous seuls à le maintenir, même envers le Danemark, qui repousse nos propositions conciliantes et leur préfère la cession d'une partie de son territoire? Je crains que dans ces circonstances un changement de front ne soit devenu pour nous une nécessité inévitable. Plus nous le retarderons, plus nous augmenteront les chances de la Prusse, car les velléités d'annexion et ses intrigues dans les duchés ne sont plus un secret pour personne. H Ritter von Srbik, *Quellen zur deutschen Politik Österreichs, 1859-1866,* vol. IV, (Osnabrück, 1967), pp. 126-7.

196. A.M.I.D. vol. 66.
197. A.M.I.D. vol. 68.

Gorchakov regarded Russia's abandonment of the Treaty of London as a momentous event and basically as a great political defeat for Russia. In a 'Memoire très confidentiel', dated 28 May 1864,[198] he explained and justified this step by saying that it had been taken only when it was obvious that none of the great European powers had any intention of recourse to arms in defence of the treaty's provisions. The German states had renounced the 1852 Treaty and declared themselves in favour of separation of the duchies, which should be merged administratively, preserving only a personal link with the Danish King and leaving the question of the succession to be decided in Frankfurt. Denmark had firmly rejected a personal union. Britain, on the other hand, would have preferred the division of Schleswig and the formation of a German state consisting of the German part of Schleswig, Holstein and Lauenburg, with the Danish part of Schleswig being joined with Denmark, giving her European guarantees. The German states had accepted this plan but left three question unresolved:

1. the sovereignty of the duchies,
2. the demarcation line between the duchies and Denmark,
3. the strategic benefits.

Austria's position had changed fundamentally by the time she put forward the proposal to transfer the duchies to Prince Augustenburg.[199] And when, in addition, France came out with the idea of a plebiscite,[200] it was clear to Russia that there was no way of maintaining the Treaty. Russia had then proposed Prince Oldenburg as a candidate.[201] As far as the demarcation line between the two parts of Schleswig, which Germany was to demand, Russia did not intend to make any absolute pronouncement. Like Britain, Russia emphasised the necessity of guaranteeing Denmark a strategic frontier which would guarantee her security and lasting peace.

Nous soutenons avec l'Angleterre la nécessité d'une frontière stratégique qui garantisse la sécurité du Danemark et le maintien d'une paix durable, nous ne reconnaissons pas pour l'Allemagne l'urgence de fortresses sur une frontière qu'aucun danger sérieux ne ménace, mais nous n'avons pas non plus d'intérêt majeur à empêcher le développement maritime

---

198. A.M.I.D. vol. 68.
199. Drouyn de Lhuys wrote to La Tour d'Auvergne on 25 May 1864 that Austria would prefer not only the incorporation of the duchies but the inclusion of the Danish Monarchy in the German Confederation. A.M.A.E. Minute, Angleterre, 729, no. 103 Origines, vol. III, pp. 104-5.
200. On 22 May 1864, Massignac reported that Gorchakov was doing everything he could to dissuade Bismarck from supporting the idea of a vote, as he believed the outcome of a vote would be a popular demand for annexation. The Russian government was not in favour of increasing Prussia's power, was against giving the fortress of Rendsborg and the port of Kiel to the Federation; if the status of Kiel had to be changed, Gorchakov assured him, 'il devrait appartenir à l'Empereur de Russie'. Origines, vol. III, pp. 89-90.
201. 1688. Erlass an den Grafen Apponyi and Herrn von Biegeleben in London. Vienna, 9 June 1864, and Bericht des Grafen Apponyi and Herrn Biegeleben, London, 15 June, 1864, in Srbik, Quellen ..., vol. IV, pp. 166-7 and 174-6. 'He (M. Biegeleben) was ... the only Austrian official to appreciate Bismarck for what he really was.' E. Crankshaw, The Fall of the House of Habsburg (N.Y., 1963), p. 223. See also Palmerston to Russell, 31 May 1864, P.R.O. 30/22, vol. 15; Voigt pp. 187-8.

que la Prusse en particulier a toujours poursuivis de ce côté. Nos efforts – added Gorchakov – sont consacrés à donner à ces questions la meilleure issue possible dans les voies de la conciliation.[202]

In a talk with Plessen,[203] Gorchakov stressed that after Britain had been the first neutral country to decide to abandon the Treaty of London, and France had not opposed this step, Russian opposition had been too weak to uphold the Treaty.[204] The Tsar had then decided to put forward Prince Oldenburg as a candidate and to transfer his rights to him, as he would be

un voisin moins pénible, blessant moins l'amour propre du Danemark que le Prince d'Augustenbourg, sujet rebelle en quelque sorte et ayant pris une attitude directement hostile au Danemark.

The day before, Wedel-Jarlsberg reported,[205] Alexander II had condemned the occupation of Schleswig and the abandonment of the Treaty, in consideration of his father Nicholas I, as 'ses vœux personelles sont certes pour sa Majesté Danoise', and declared his support for the 1852 Treaty; whereas, the ambassador reported, there were reservations about the British plan for the division of Schleswig, and Russia was waiting to hear what Denmark would have to say.

It is true that Russia stuck to the Treaty of London a few days longer than the other states, but in view of the accumulating difficulties she eventually decided to abandon it. She abandoned not only the letter but also the spirit of the treaty. In fact, the treaty had been a dead letter for a long time. But Gorchakov continually talked about it as an act of fundamental importance: he could not replace it with anything concrete which would satisfy Prussia's demands, while simultaneously maintaining the principle of the integrity of Denmark. There was no way of combining the two. This adherence to a Treaty which was already a dead letter, when all the other states had abandoned it, was a tactical ploy on Gorchakov's part designed to create a propaganda effect and show that Russia stuck to treaties when others broke them. Not six years later, the same Gorchakov took advantage of a favourable international situation to renounce unilaterally the Treaty of Paris, which contained a number of provisions which he considered inconsistent with Russia's interests.

It is also true that Russia most consistently opposed the candidacy of Prince Augustenburg. This, however, was not because she wanted to defend the Danish King's rights to the duchies, but because she was fighting against a candidate who was backed by liberal and democratic groups in Germany. Wishing to oppose him, she proposed Prince Oldenburg, a representative of conservative forces, as a can-

---

202. A.M.I.D. vol. 68.
203. Plessen, no. 26, 1 June (20 May) 1864.
204. "que l'Angleterre, parmis les puissances neutres, ayant pris l'initiative de l'abandon du traité de Londres, détermination que la France voit sans déplaisir, l'opposition de la Russie seule n'aurait pas été à même de maintenir ce traité".
205. Wedel-Jarlsberg, no. 58, 31 (19) May 1864.

didate. Peter, Grand Duke of Oldenburg, was furthermore a favourite of the court of the Tsar. By putting him forward, Russia was basically carrying out a suggestion made by Bismarck. Monrad was right when he argued that Russia had done it because it was in Prussia's interests to thwart Augustenburg's plan.[206]

A few days afterwards, however, when Russia, too, had officially abandoned the treaty, Alexander II explained the circumstances which had compelled Russia to take this step in a talk with the Swedish ambassador.

Je déplore – said the Tsar – que le maintien de cette integrité ait été jugé impossible – et il ne servirait à rien que, *Seul*. Je me prononce en faveur des stipulations de 1852 – car les choses en sont malheureusement arrivées au point que, lors même que le Cabinet de Copenhague voulut en ce moment accepter l'Union personelle, on lui opposerait un-*trop-tard*. Ne voulant toutefois pas que *Ma Maison* profite en rien de cet état des choses, Je cède tous mes droits éventuels sur la partie Gotorpienne dans le Holstein au Grand Duc d'Oldenbourg.[207]

J'apprends – wrote Wedel-Jarlsberg – encore que, pour ce qui regarde le refus d'accorder à l'Allemagne la faculté d'ériger des fortéresses et des ports fédéraux dans le Holstein, le Prince Gortchakow, S'énonce à peu-près ainsi: tant que l'intégrité Danois restait débant et que l'Union personelle devait rattacher les Duchés au Royaume proprement dit, nous aurions pû être plus coulants au sujet des désirs allemands.

Tel n'est plus le cas aujourd'hui – car il s'agit d'établir un nouvel ordre des choses sur les bords de l'Eyder. Or, cet ordre des choses ne pouvant être inauguré qu'avec le consentement des Puissances Européennes, celles-ci sont parfaitement fondées à faire leurs conditions préalables.

And when Napier, the Swedish ambassador reported, pressed Gorchakov and spoke of the necessity of joint action against Germany's excessive demands, Gorchakov replied: 'Vous parlez de résistance, My lord, – mais ce mot n'existe plus dans le vocabulaire Anglaise'.[208] Thus Gorchakov, in a way that was typical of him, put the blame for his own passivity on other powers, this time Britain.

The question of the renunciation of the Tsar's rights in favour of Prince Oldenburg, which was formally announced by Brunnow at the session of the conference on 2 June 1864,[209] requires particular comment. In a letter to Andrae on 3 June, Krieger called this 'den storartede russiske Comedie, som opførtes af Brunnow og colleger er i sin genre masske den Allerskandaleuseste'.[210,211] To the surprise of everybody, Brunnow declared that, as a result of the collapse of the Treaty of London, the Tsar had decided, on the basis of the 1851 Warsaw protocol, to transfer the rights which derived from his rights to the house of Gottorp to Prince Oldenburg. Sybel called Brunnow's announcement a comedy,[212] and in a letter to Krieger on 16 June 1864 Vedel described it as follows:

---

206. *D.G. Monrads Deltagelse i Begivenhederne 1864, En efterladt redegørelse udgivet ved Aage Friis,* (Copenhagen, 1914), pp. 24-25, 40, 125-6, 150. Cf. E. Eyck, *Bismarck,* vol. I, p. 620.
207. Wedel-Jarlsberg, no. 61, 6 June (25 May) 1864).
208. *Ibid.*
209. Protocols, pp. 129-30.
210. The greatest and maybe the most scandalous comedy performed by Brunnow and his colleagues.
211. *Historisk Tidsskrift,* 6.R.5, (1894-95), pp. 157-59. Neergaard. *Under ...,* vol. II, pt 2, pp. 1255-56.
212. Sybel, vol. III, p. 333, wrote of Brunnow's announcement as follows:

Cessionen til Oldenburg er en perfidi 1/ fordi den gjorde det muligt at opgive Londoner Traktat uden at man risikerer at see Rusland komme selv paa Tapetet. 2/ fordi den erkjender udtrykkelig forbundets competence til afgjorelsen af arvespørgsmaalet for Holstein og Lauenburg. 3/ fordi det giver Preussen et udmærket vaaben imod Augustenburg's uafhængighedsanstød.[213,214]

In the course of his speech, Brunnow referred to the Warsaw protocol. The Russian government's intention to make use of this particular diplomatic document may be shown by the fact that, on Gorchakov's instructions, it was published in the *Journal de St Pétersbourg* on 9 January 1864. Evidently, he was concerned to remind diplomatic circles and public opinion that the Imperial house remembered its rights to Gottorp-Holstein. It should also be emphasised that, in talks with Oubril, Bismarck had more than once mentioned the name of Prince Oldenburg as a candidate to counter Prince Augustenburg who was being pushed by liberal circles in Germany and by the German Confederation.[215]

Before Russia put the Grand Duke of Oldenburg forward as a candidate, Oubril had a talk with Bismarck in which the latter explained that it had been the King's decision to support Prince Augustenburg's candidacy, which had been proposed by Austria. He himself, when Denmark had rejected the idea of a personal union and Britain and France had come out in support of partition of the duchies on the principle of nationality, had proposed the dynastic separation of the duchies to Vienna, anticipating that this would not be opposed by London and Paris. He had consequently agreed to Prince Augustenburg's candidacy[216] as proposed by Vienna, which preferred Augustenburg to Oldenburg or Frederick of Hesse, or annexation of the duchies by Prussia. Bismarck could not oppose this, although, he explained, he was against it.[217]

During his next talk with the Russian ambassador, Bismarck came out in support of Oldenburg:

> Sofort nahm Brunnow das Wort, und mit gewohnten sentimentalem Pathos seine schmerzliche Überraschung über die deutscher Seits begehrte Zerreissung der dänischen Monarchie auszusprechen, den Antrag mit lebhaftem Bedauern abzulehnen, allem Mitbewerben Augenstenburg's, inbesondere dem Grossherzog von Oldenburg, alle Rechte vorzubehalten.

213. The ceding to Oldenburg is an act of perfidy: 1/ Because it made it possible to abandon the Treaty of London without the risk of putting only Russia on the carpet. 2/ Because it explicitly recognised the right of the Confederation to settle the problem of the inheritance of Holstein and Lauenburg. 3/ Because it gives Prussia a perfect weapon against Augustenburg's independent position.

214. *Danske Magazin*, (1940), p. 251; Neergaard, vol. II, pp. 1255ff. and 1370.

215. Steefel, pp. 219, 222-3, 231-4, 241; Sybel, vol. III, p. 338. On Bismarck's attitude to this question see Lenz, *Geschichte Bismarcks*, p. 251. Steefel thinks that 'the initiative may have been Bismarck's (p. 234). According to Oncken, *Grand Duke Peter of Oldenburg*, the Tsar promised in 1860 to transfer his rights to Oldenburg if the treaty of London were 'abrogated' (p. 69). According to the British and French diplomats the decision to cede the rights to Oldenburg was taken in 1862. Napier to Russell, no. 282, 30 May 1864. P.R.O. Confid. *Origines*, vol. III, no. 600. Gorchakov assured Lord Napier that the announcement at the conference was not based on previous agreements with Prussia. Steefel, pp. 234, 241.

216. On Bismarck's attitude to Prince Augustenburg see E. Brandenburg. *Die Reichgründung*, vol. 2, pp. 102-5; M. Lenz, *Geschichte Bismarcks*, pp. 239ff.

217. APP, vol. V, pp. 168-171, Oubril to Gorchakov, 16 (28) May 1864.

Mr de Bismarck – Oubril reported[218] – voit de plus avec satisfaction la solution éventuelle de l'affaire des Duchés rentrer dans une voie plus conservatrice.

Oubril came to the conclusion that Bismark wanted

des facilités maritimes qui lui semblent indispensables pour la Prusse comme pour l'Allemagne[219] ... Son but principale reste donc d'amener, par la séparation des Duchés, une solution définitive conforme aux vœux de l'Allemagne, ne se réservant d'ailleurs, pour les sacrifices supportés par la Prusse, que l'avantage d'influences morales et des facilités maritimes. La portée de ces derniers reste encore à préciser.

'Je suis content de voir notre ami Bismarck revenu sur la bonne voie', commented Alexander II on Oubril's report.[220] Meanwhile, Knorring informed Gorchakov that Vienna, too 'par égard à la Russie' was not against Prince Oldenburg's candidacy.[221]

In Copenhagen, Dotézac reported on 10 June, Brunnow's declaration of the transfer of the Imperial house's rights to the house of Oldenburg produced

un doloureux étonnement parmi les partisans de la Russie. On est frappé aussi de la façon dont la renonciation a été faite, et qui semble admettre la compétence de la Diète germanique sur la question de succession, puisque le Duc d'Oldenbourg doit s'entendre avec la Diète.

But the King, Dotézac said, showed no less sympathy for Russia; this was partly because he expected Dagmar to marry the heir to the Russian throne, Nicholas, the eldest son of Alexander II,[222] and this was his sole wish. This act of compliance, for that was how Russia's move was seen, in contrast to the position she had taken on the treaty of Warsaw, showed how very dependent the St Petersburg cabinet was on Germany.[223]

The Danish delegates at the conference were full of bitterness towards Russia.

Les plénipotentiares de Danemark seuls, comme il fallait s'y attendre, n'ont pu s'empêcher d'éprouver un sentiment de regret en voyant la Cour de Russie se dégager d'une position devenue impossible depuis que la Traité de Londres a cessé d'être exécutable en réalité,

Brunnow wrote to Gorchakov,[224] explaining that after first Prussia and then Austria and the German Confederation had renounced the Treaty, and the German countries had declared that Christian IX was no longer ruler of Holstein, a situation had arisen in which no one was capable of upholding the legality of the Danish

---

218. *Ibid.* pp. 185-86. 22 May (3 June) 1864.
219. APP, vol. V, p. 186.
220. *Ibid.*
221. Pirch to Bismarck, telegram dated 4 June. Similar telegram from Bismarck to Pirch, 5. June. APP, vol. V, p. 186, Oubril to Gorchakov, 22 May (3 June) 1864. See also Bismarck's telegram to Pirch dated 6 June (26 May). A.M.I.D.
222. Nikolai Aleksandrovich died in 1865 and Dagmar maried his brother Alexander, later Alexander III.
223. A.M.A.E., Corr. polit. Danemark, vol. 247, no. 113. *Origines,* vol. III, p. 210.
224. 26 May (7 June) 1864, no. 129, A.M.I.D., vol. 68.

King's position as ruler of Holstein. The Frankfurt Diet had decreed that the King had ceased to be Duke of Holstein, and before that Holstein had been occupied by federal troops. No one was in a position to oppose these events. There was nothing left for the states which were friendly to Denmark except to make efforts to put forward a just arrangement. Britain had done this by proposing the separation of Holstein from Denmark, with the agreement of Russia, France and Sweden.

This report shows that Brunnow was well aware of how weak the position of Russia and the other neutral states was in the face of the aggressive attitude of Germany, and particularly Prussia.

In the course of the Conference all the participants began to realise that, as Quaade put it, 'la question de frontière est un point capital',[225] and Krieger recognised that 'le principe de nationalité est un élément très essentiel de la question, mais non pas le seul à être prise en considération'.[226] Brunnow was aware that it would be hard to find some common denominator, and as time passed he ceased to believe that the German states would agree to the Slie-Dannewirke frontier line proposed by Russell, or the Eckernförde-Schleswig-Friedrichstadt line suggested by Quaade.[227] Denmark in turn rejected the German states' proposal for a frontier on the line from Åbenrå to Tønder,[228] as then not only the part of Schleswig in which the German population was predominant, but also the part where a large percentage of Danes lived, would come under German rule. In a letter to Gorchakov on 1 June (20 May) 1864, Brunnow warned that if Denmark refused to reach a compromise despite Russia's advice she would provoke a renewal of military operations, and Prussia would exploit new victories to go beyond the limits of a reasonable policy. In Brunnow's view the planned visit to Kissingen by Alexander II should aim to persuade Berlin to moderate its demands. Brunnow knew the key to the question of peace was in Prussia's hands. He expressed this in a report to Alexander II during the Tsar's June visit to Berlin in the words 'von allem ja fast allein in Preussens Händen läge'.[229]

In the first few days of June, Brunnow expressed deep unease to the Danish delegation because the suspension of hostilities was due to expire shortly. 'Den miskjendte',[230] 'amicus Daniae', as Krieger ironically called him, assured them that he would go 'a pied et à la nage' to Copenhagen to entreat the Danish government to

---

225. Protocols, p. 108. Telegraph Copi Bog 1864. Nr. 2. Ges. Ark. London 1864. Samlingspakke 28, R.A. Copenhagen.
226. *Ibid.,* p. 118.
227. *Ibid.,* p. 122.
228. *Ibid.,* p. 115.
229. Aufzeichnung des Auswärtigen Amtes über die Unterredung Bismarcks mit Kaiser Alexander II and Fürst Gortchakow, 11 (23) June 1864, APP, vol. V, p. 209. What did Prussia want, Brunnow asked, and answered: the destruction of the remaining parts of the Danish monarchy. If Bismarck, who had already achieved his purpose of freeing the German population from the Danes, did not give up further aggression he would cause Sweden to enter the war, bring the British fleet to the Baltic, and further reduce Denmark to be merely the frontiers of Scandinavia. This would be no service to Russia.
230. Unappreciated.

agree to a continuation of the truce,[231] irrespective of where the frontier line in Schleswig would run or of military rights (easements).[232] When Denmark agreed to a fifteen-day extension of the suspension of hostilities, Brunnow expressed his satisfaction at the Conference session on 9 June and appealed to both sides not to make accusations against each other, but, on the contrary, to seek to settle their disputes. He expressed the hope that during the continuing suspension of hostilities they would succeed in finding a peaceful solution.[233]

Although Brunnow continually presented himself as the friend of Denmark, and although at the conference sessions he argued with the German delegates, particularly Beust, maintaining that the German Confederation had no right to speak except on the question of Holstein,[234] Krieger did not trust either Brunnow or Russia. In a letter to Vedel on 8 June 1864 he urged him to expose Russia's lies, such as, for example, the Tsarina's letter to the Danish Queen many weeks earlier saying that Russia was working to uphold the Treaty of London.[235]

Fearing further international complications, Brunnow made one more attempt to persuade the Danish government to agree to concessions. He prepared a set of 'Articles préliminaires' and, after consulting Russell and the French and Swedish plenipotentiaries, presented them to the Danish plenipotentiaries, requesting that they give them serious consideration. Unable to obtain concessions and agreement to the new proposals from them, because they did not have instructions, he decided, on Quaade's advice, to send the document to Nicolay, requesting the ambassador to hand it to the Copenhagen government with a warning about the situation which could arise if the conference were broken off and hostilities resumed. In his dispatch to Gorchakov on 22 (10) June, Brunnow explained the history of this document and the circumstances surrounding it.

Although, as he had already reported on 27 May (8 June), the conference was drawing to an end, he, Brunnow, was not without hope and had persuaded Russell to invite the Danish delegation, the French and Swedish ambassadors, and Brunnow himself, to his house for a friendly meeting on 11 June. At this meeting Brunnow summed up the state of the conference and proposed the preparation of a set of principles which would form the preliminary terms for the conclusion of peace.

The Danish delegation did not have plenipotentiary powers and so was unable to accept these terms. The Danes were evidently afraid peace might be quickly concluded, from which one could deduce that they were seeking a resumption of military operations as soon as possible.

Brunnow said that he could not reproach Bille, Krieger or Quaade, who had asked him after the meeting for the draft of the preliminary peace terms he had drawn up, in order to send it confidentially to Copenhagen. Loyal, but timid,

---

231. Krieger to Vedel, 7 June 1864, *Danske Magazin*, (1940), pp. 232-3.
232. See Klein-Wuttig, *Politik ...*, p. 29.
233. Protocols, pp. 147, 153 and 168.
234. *Ibid.*, pp. 162, 163, for the session on 9 June.
235. *Danske Magazin*, (1940), p. 237.

Quaade had once again gone out ahead of his government in the role of defender of the peace.

For his part, Brunnow thought the position was hopeless if the extremist tendencies in the royal council gained the upper hand. As far as he himself was concerned, conscience bade him to do his duty by that state and point out the consequences which were to be expected if Denmark let herself pursue a course which would lead the monarchy to ruin. 'If Your Highness', Brunnow wrote to Gorchakov, 'reads the dispatch sent to Nicolay, you will agree that I have presented everything openly to the Danish cabinet. It must make the choice between peace and war. If something happened, it would not be able to complain that the Emperor's plenipotentiary failed to point out the danger threatening the monarchy'. Alexander II commented on the document: 'if military operations are resumed, it will be mainly the Danes' fault.'[236]

In a letter to Nicolay, Brunnow anticipated that if hostilities were renewed the chances of a peaceful solution to the conflict would vanish.[237] Denmark had no chance of victory and her ability to impose a blockade would decrease. The German states would advance further, and impose a heavy indemnity on Jutland in compensation for Denmark's restriction of their maritime trade. The end of the war would be very unfavourable for Denmark, as she would lose Schleswig, whereas at the moment she would be able to retain at least a part of it. Jutland would suffer prolonged occupation, and the allies would demand an enormous indemnity. All this together would be a disaster for Denmark. The peace that would eventually be concluded would not be honourable but humiliating. As a friend of Denmark, Brunnow was not afraid to speak the truth. An unsuccessful resumption of the war threatened the extinction of the monarchy, while a bravely concluded peace would save the throne and ensure the independence of the country. He was writing to save Denmark from danger. He appealed to Monrad to agree to the British initiative and let a court of conciliation settle to which states the disputed ('mixtes') territories belonged.

In his 'Articles Préliminaires de Paix'[238] Brunnow proposed that the Danish monarchy should be maintained as an independent state, something essential to the balance of power in Europe, He proposed that the Danish King should agree to relinquish Holstein and accept the Slie-Dannewirke frontier line as the best option, in accordance with the conclusion presented by the British delegation at a session of the conference. The German delegates, on the other hand, proposed a demarcation line running from Flensborg to Tønder, and drawn so that the town of Schleswig was in the part which would pass to Germany. Brunnow proposed that, for a period of three years, the inhabitants living north and south of the demarcation line should have the opportunity of resettlement and the choice of

236. A.M.I.D. Kantselariya, 1864, no. 79, *Krasnyi Arkhiv,* p. 98.
237. 13 (1) June 1864. *Krasnyi Arkhiv,* pp. 96-97.
238. *Statsraadets Forhandlinger om Danmarks Udenrigspolitik 1863-1879,* ed. Aage Friis, (Copenhagen, 1936), pp. 420-30. A somewhat different version of the Article is in *Origines,* vol. III, pp. 166-68.

place of residence. He considered that Christian IX should renounce the duchy of Lauenburg and make a concession to the German Confederation in order to facilitate the conclusion of an agreement by ceding the fortress of Rendborg to the Confederation. In exchange for this, the German courts should agree not to interfere in internal Danish affairs. Holstein and the part of Schleswig which Christian IX would give up would join the German Confederation and the remainder would become part of the Danish monarchy. The great powers would have to guarantee the independence of Denmark.

Brunnow's proposals, like the new Russian initiative of which the Danish ambassador in St Petersburg was also to be the champion and spokeman, were rejected by the Danish government. Both fell on infertile ground in Copenhagen. The military defeats and diplomatic reverses had led to a conviction on the part of the government and among Danish society that her allies had let her down, and this had caused great disappointment, bordering on despair. As Nicolay reported,[239] there was general dissatisfaction in Copenhagen that her allies had abandoned the Treaty of London, which had been the basis for negotiations, and general opposition to the scheme for partition of the Danish monarchy.

Les feuilles conservatrices se refusent de croire à la possibilité d'un pareil abandon, et voient la ruine complète du pays dans un ordre des choses qui ne saurait qu'être un triomphe pour l'Allemagne, et consolider ici, en Danemark l'ascendant du parti démocratique. Rien ne s'opposerait plus à la rentrée de M M Hall, Orla Lehman, et de leurs associés politiques.

J'ai engagé toutefois vivement – the ambassador reported – Mr Monrad à ne pas se laisser aller à des illusions sur la possibilité de revenir aux stipulations du traité de Londres et d'être bien convaincu, que ce n'est qu' après mûr examen et en présence d'une conviction bien arrêtée de l'impossibilité de maintenir cette base, que le Gouvernement Imperial avait pris la résolution de recommander à la sérieuse considération du Gouvernement Danois la seule voie pratique à suivre dans ce moment.[240]

In this atmosphere of disappointment and exasperation neither Brunnow's proposals nor the conception of a personal union of the duchies and Denmark put forward almost simultaneously by Plessen had any chance of success, the more so since the Danish government was convinced that no concessions by Denmark would achieve anything and that it was impossible to go further than the Slie-Dannewirke line. The government was still under the illusion that Denmark could rely on help from Britain. Brunnow's suggestion not to break off the negotiations was rejected by the Staatsrådet (State Council)[241] although, as Monrad wrote later, they all appreciated Brunnow's pro-Danish attitude in the past ('gamle, trofaste vilvilje mod Danmark'[242]).[243]

---

239. Nicolay, no. 73, 21 May (2 June) 1864.
240. Nicolay, no. 75, 27 May (8 June) 1864.
241. *Statsraadets Forhandlinger ...*, 16 June 1864, pp. 177ff.
242. Old faithful good-will to Denmark.
243. *D.G. Monrads Deltagelse,* pp. 150-51.

IV

Brunnow's initiative coincided with rumours, which were especially odious to Danish progressive circles, that the whole of the Danish monarchy was to join the German Confederation, so as to save the monarchy and the integrity of Denmark and make her the admiral of the Confederation. This idea, too, rumour had it, had been engendered in St Petersburg. Nor was it a new idea. The documents which I have studied show that it was being discussed in diplomatic circles as early as the end of 1863.

The Bavarian ambassador in Vienna, Otto Bray-Steinburg, had reported to King Maximillian II,[244] in connection with the conflict between Denmark on the one hand, and the duchies and the German Confederation on the other, that Rechberg had conceived a plan for the admission of Denmark to the Confederation. There had been rumours that in the event of conflict Denmark, if deprived of the German duchies, would become a Scandinavian state, and that was not in the interests of either Russia or Britain. Bray, however, thought that this plan should be avoided.[245] There was a possibility, the ambassador wrote, of solving the German problem in Denmark on the basis of the British proposal - which was not new - for the partition of Schleswig, with the southern part going to Holstein and the northern part to Denmark. In the ambassador's opinion, however, the time was not yet ripe for this solution.

At that time the rumours concerning Denmark's admission to the German Confederation spread over Europe. The Italian government was very concerned about them. Letters and telegrams were sent to St. Petersburg.

Votre dépêche télégraphique du 29 janvier me renouvelle avec instance la demande que vous m'avez déjà posé dans plusieurs de vos lettres, si une coalition des trois puissances du Nord est sur le point de se former ou même si elle est déjà formée.

Je crois pouvoir vous répondre négativement pour le moment - Pepoli, the Italian envoy, reported. La politique de la Russie tient à se rapprocher plus de l'Angleterre que des deux puissances Allemandes, et la question des Duchés n'est pas de nature à resserer les liens entre le Cabinet de St. Pétersbourg et les Cabinets de Vienne et de Berlin. Si cette question est applanie, si le movement national Allemand est écrasé, peut-être vos craintes se réaliseront-elles, et nous verrons alors les faisceaux brisés de la Sainte Alliance se réunir et se serrer intinement. Dans l'entrevue que j'ai eu dans le temps avec l'Empereur Alexandre et dont je vous ai rendu compte vous vous souviendrez, Monsieur le Ministre, que le fantôme qui troublait son esprit était le fantôme révolutionnaire.[246]

These ideas revived again in May 1864 in Vienna, and they were basically connected with Gorchakov's anti-Scandinavianism. As Fournier reported, Rechberg

---

244. Vienna, 14 December 1863.
245. *Quellen zur deutschen Politik Österreichs, 1854-66.* Unter Mitwirkung von Oscar Schmid herausgegeben von Heinrich Ritter von Srbik, vol. III. January 1863 to March 1864 (Osnabrück, 1967), p. 501, no. 1352.
246. Rapporti Della Legazione in Pietroburgo, Pacco 205. Pepoli's report no. 1, on January 31, 1864. Confidentielle.

learned from Knorring that Gorchakov was inclined to separate Schleswig and Holstein from Denmark and transfer them to Prussia or the German Confederation. St Petersburg preferred this solution to the rise of a Scandinavian fortress. This was to be connected with Gorchakov's other plans, at the root of which lay the desire to torpedo the rapprochement between Britain and France by strengthening the good relations linking Russia with Prussia and Austria.[247]

On 20 May 1864 Gramont, the French ambassador in Vienna, reported to Drouyn de Lhuys that one of the ideas which had arisen in Vienna was that the whole of the Danish monarchy should join the German Confederation.[248] On 25 May Drouyn de Lhuys informed his ambassador in London that the Vienna government would not only prefer the incorporation of the duchies, but of the entire Danish monarchy, into the German Confederation.[249] This atmosphere of uncertainty was considerably reinforced by the affair of the so-called Polish Papers,[250] faked documents which were published in the *Morning Post*, Palmerston's semi-official organ, which made clear just how far Gorchakov, obsessed by his anti-Scandinavianism, had moved closer to Austria and Prussia and the extent to which he supported their plans for the ruin of Denmark.[251]

At the beginning of June there was an avalanche of rumours that Russia had proposed that Denmark should join the German Confederation, although both Gorchakov and Nicolay, on his behalf, categorically denied that Russia was the source of the rumours. On 5 June Manderström sent a warning telegram to Adelswärd in Paris in which he asked the ambassador to inform Drouyn de Lhuys that Russia had proposed that Denmark should join the German Confederation. 'Employez tous vos efforts pour faire ressortir combien une telle solution serait désastreuse pour le Danemark et pour nous'.[252] On 6 June Russell had a talk with Quaade and

---

247. A.M.A.E. Suède, vol. 335, no. 79, Stockholm, 2 May 1864. *Origines,* vol. II, p. 337. The creation of a greater Scandinavia would have been against the interests not only of Germany and Russia but of Britain too. See Koht, *Die Stellung ...,* pp. 231-2, 243, 251; see also Krieger to Andrae, 17 April 1864. Russia was opposed to Napoleon III and hence did not want to see a union of the three Scandinavian states because she did not want to let France have such a strong ally in the north. *Hist. Tidss.,* (1894-95), pp. 132-33.
248. A.M.A.E., Autriche, 486, no. 39. *Origines,* vol. III, p. 63. Migliorati to Visconti-Venosta no. 64 Confidentielle. Archivio Storico Diplomatico, Rome, Rapporti Della Legazione in Copenhagen, Pacco 171 (809). *The Cambridge History of British Foreign Policy,* vol. 2. (Cambridge, 1923, p. 589).
249. A.M.A.E., Angleterre, 729, no. 103. *Origines,* vol. III, pp. 104-5.
250. *Origines,* vol. III, pp. 139-41.
251. See Koht, p. 243 and appendices, which contain the texts of these documents. Doria f.e. took this dispatch on trust. Report, 10 May, Pacco 171, A.S.-D.). On 15 May Gianotti, an Italian diplomat in St. Petersburg, reported to Turin: 'Le Chargé d'affaires de Russie à Vienne vient d'informer le Prince Gortchakoff que M. de Rechberg lui a dit tenir de la bouche de l'Ambassadeur de France, revenu récemment de Paris, que Mr. Pepoli a dit avoir vu à St. Pétersbourg le Traité d'alliance entre la Prusse, l'Autriche et la Russie. Le Prince Gortchakoff a dit qu'il était étonné de voir le Duc de Grammont plaidir le faux pour savoir le vrai, puisqu'il devait savoir que Mr Pepoli n'a pas pu affirmer une pareille nouvelle'. Annexe à la dépêche no. 13 A-C. Pièce chifrée. Pacco 205 (843). A.S.-D.
252. A.M.A.E., Suède, 335, *Origines,* vol. III, p. 170. Koht. pp. 343-45.

asked him if Denmark would agree to a frontier running along the line from Kappeln to Flensborg and Husum; he informed him that this was Britain's and France's proposal and that if the German side rejected it Denmark would receive material assistance. On the same day Wachmeister, in London, received similar information from Stockholm as Adelswärd in Paris had the day before, that the Russian government, via the Danish ambassador to the cabinet in St Petersburg, had expressed its agreement to Denmark joining the German Confederation. Manderström was greatly alarmed by this, because if the plan were really put into effect Sweden would find herself in a very difficult situation between Russia and Prussia, and the freedom of the Baltic would be threatened by Germany. If Denmark in turn demanded help, Sweden would likewise be in a very problematical situation.

For the next few days this question absorbed the attention of the governments and diplomats of Europe. Drouyn de Lhuys reacted immediately to the news received from the Swedish ambassador in Paris and confirmed by Fournier, although the latter added in his telegram on the matter that he had told Manderström he personally did not believe anything of the kind was possible in Copenhagen. On 6 June Drouyn de Lhuys sent telegrams to Massignac in St Petersburg and to Dotézac in Copenhagen to clarify the matter. 'Vérifiez l'exactitude de ce renseignement', was the instruction Massignac received.[253] 'Nous sommes résolus à combattre la réalisation d'un pareil projet. Demandez au Cabinet de Copenhague des explications catégoriques sur la réponse qu'il compte faire à cette étrange proposition', Drouyn de Lhuys instructed Dotézac.[254] Talleyrand in Berlin was told to inform Bismarck that France was against the Danish monarchy becoming part of the Confederation. The French ambassador in London, on the other hand, received instructions to inform Russell of France's position and to state 'que la France serait disposée à unir ses forces de terre et de mer à celles de la Grande-Bretagne pour empêcher l'accomplissement d'un pareil projet, si telle était la pensée du Cabinet de Londres'.[255]

It soon turned out, however, that the rumours were not correct. On 6 June Dotézac was already telegraphing that there had been no such proposal from Russia. Monrad had told him he would rather agree to the indépendance or annexation of Schleswig and Holstein than to a union between Denmark and the German Confederation. If he knew anything about this plan, it had come from Vienna. Copenhagen did not take the matter seriously, and the idea would be opposed by the German countries. Gorchakov, Massignac telegraphed, had categorically denied that the Russian government had proposed that Denmark should join the Confederation.[256] Gorchakov had also said that Russia's position *vis-à-vis* Prussia and Denmark was exceptionally delicate, and he had taken the opportunity to

---

253. Chiffre, A.M.A.E., Russie, 233. *Origines,* vol. III, p. 174.
254. A.M.A.E., Danemark, 247, *Origines,* vol. III, p. 171.
255. A.M.A.E., Angleterre, 730, no. 113. *Origines,* vol. III, p. 172.
256. A.M.A.E., Russie, 233, *Origines,* vol. III, p. 183, and the dispatch of 8 June, p. 193.

to inform Massignac that Alexander II was going to Germany on 7 June and that he would join him there shortly. The minister in charge in St Petersburg would be N. Mukhanov.

On 7 June Manderström telegraphed to Adelswärd, on the basis of information received from Wedel-Jarlsberg, that Russia's move had been highly confidential: 'elle pourra la nier, mais elle existe'. According to the report from Copenhagen, Manderström informed him,

> La Russie n'a point fait de proposition directe, mais le Prince Gortchakoff a fait entendre au Ministre danois à St Petersburg que la Russie ne s'opposera pas à l'entrée du Danemark et de toutes ses possesion dans la Confédération Germanique. M. Monrad, en portant ce fait à la connaissance du Ministère de Suède et de Norvège, a ajouté que les relations dans lesquelles se trouve le Baron Plessen à Saint Pétersbourg lui donnent une garantie suffisante qu'il avait exprimé la pensée intime du Cabinet russe.

Manderström was also convinced that Britain and France would not permit such a solution. 'Une fois la mine éventée, il me paraît probable que la Russie niera le fait, mais les données sont trop sérieuses pour que je puisse le mettre en doute'.[257]

Drouyn de Lhuys had a talk with Budberg on the subject of Denmark joining the Confederation, without mentioning the originator of the idea. Budberg confined himself to saying that for both Denmark and Germany the idea could be a way out of the current difficulties. The French minister was of a different opinion, arguing that a solution of this kind would be contrary to the aspirations of the Danish and the German population, as well as against the best interests of European peace generally and counter to the provisions of the Congress of Vienna, which stated that only countries which had formally been part of the German empire could belong to the German Confederation.[258] After Drouyn de Lhuys received, among others, a telegram from London saying that Britain, like France, was opposed to this arrangement as it was no less disadvantageous for Britain than for France, and that the creation of a large Scandinavian state appeared no less dubious than Danish entry into the German Confederation,[259] he consequently sent a telegram to Dotézac on 9 June expressing his view of the problem as follows:

> J'avais été tout d'abord frappé du caractère d'invraisemblance d'un tel projet, aussi antipatique aux vœux des pays scandinaves que contraire aux intérêts manifestes de la Russie et aux exigences de l'équilibre européen. Personne ne pouvait songer sérieusement à un plan qui aurait dénaturé complètement le caractère de la Confédération, et qui n'aurait pas manqué de soulever de la part des Puissances neutres la plus énergique résistance.

Drouyn de Lhuys informed Dotézac that Gorchakov had formally denied ('nie formellement') that the Russian government had made such a proposal and that the

---

257. *Origines,* vol. III, pp. 183-4; Koht, p. 345.
258. Drouyn de Lhuys to Massignac, 8 June, A.M.A.E., Russie, 233, no. 37. *Origines,* vol. III, pp. 184-6.
259. *Origines,* vol. III, pp. 191-2.

Berlin cabinet had declared: 'si une telle idée était mise en avant, l'opposition qu'elle recontrerait infailliblement aurait toutes les sympathies de la Prusse'.[260]

Dotézac's telegrams of 9, 10 and 12 June would seem to have helped to clarify the matter further:

> Il n'y a pas de proposition russe; ce sont des idées émises, dans sa correspondance, par le Ministre de Danemark à Pétersbourg, attendu ces jours – ci. Le Président du Conseil ne déclare qu'en aucun cas ni lui ni ses Collègues n'y prêteraient les mains.[261]

Monrad assured Dotézac that there had been no Russian proposal for Denmark to join the German Confederation. In the dispatch which had come to Copenhagen, Plessen had mentioned the proposal, without saying anything about Gorchakov but mentioning Austria, which seemed to have been its originator.[262] In Monrad's opinion there were two parties in Denmark with opposing ideas. One sought a Scandinavian union, the other would prefer a closer link with Germany. If Denmark lost the greater part of Schleswig, the advocates of the second school of thought would aim for this solution, 'mais ce n'est pas moi qui l'y conduirai'.[263] When Monrad had mentioned the idea of Denmark joining the German Confederation at the last meeting of the Statsraadet, the King had declared: 'Je ne veux être ni scandinave, ni allemand, je veux être un Roi danois indépendant'.[264]

On the basis of the information which he had collected on the subject Dotézac deduced that the plan had originated in Vienna, had then been passed to the St Petersburg cabinet, and the latter had used Plessen to sound out reaction to the plan in Copenhagen. The prince could not have found a better assistant than Plessen, whose brother was the leader of the feudal opposition in the Estates of Holstein and who, like him, 'est dévoué corps et âme à l'alliance russo-allemande, et son marriage avec une princesse russe[265] n'a pu que fortifier ces tendances de famille et de caste. Il est – Dotézac added – particulièrement hostile à la France'.[266] In the ambassador's opinion, Plessen had the backing of Austria and Russia. Dotézac was also doubtful whether the words of Christian IX quoted above were sufficient guarantee against a plan which was such a threat to French interests. Dotézac also shared Monrad's opinion ('l'expression pittoresque') that 'les Danois suivraient le Slesvig en enfer'. The King would probably be willing to accept the plan for a personal union, but the government and society were against both these plans.[267]

Two days later, after Vedel, with Monrad's authorisation, had acquainted him

---

260. A.M.A.E., Danemark, 247. *Origines,* vol. III, pp. 197-8.
261. 9 June, A.M.A.E., Danemark, 247. *Origines,* vol. III, p. 199.
262. *Ibid.,* pp. 205-9, 215, Dotézac's reports of 10 and 12 June.
263. *Ibid.,* p. 207.
264. *Ibid.*
265. Princess Barbara Sergeevna Gagarina, daughter of the major-domo.
266. *Origines,* vol. III, p. 208.
267. Dotézac to Drouyn de Lhuys, 10 June 1864. A.M.A.E., Danemark, 247, no. 112. *Origines,* vol. III, pp. 205-9.

with the contents of Plessen's dispatch on the question of Danish entry into the German Confederation, Dotézac reported that Plessen had mentioned only Austria as a country which would be pleased to see such a solution, and had not referred to Russia at all, although the plan had originated during the course of talks between Gorchakov and Plessen. Of that Dotézac had no doubt. Plessen had listed the following advantages for Denmark in his dispatch:

1. maintenance of the integrity of the monarchy,
2. an honourable position in the German Confederation,
3. the existence of an army which served to defend the members of the Confederation,
4. the assurance of peace in the north,
5. the creation of conditions for the renewal of the friendly relations which had existed between Sweden-Norway and Germany before 1848.

Plessen concluded that, with the exception of France, all states would gain by this proposal.[268]

The Vienna cabinet, however, did not admit authorship of the plan. In Gramont's opinion it was an old idea dating back to 1851, when there had been an attempt to settle the Danish-German conflict in this way in order to preserve the integrity of the Danish monarchy and counteract Scandinavianism. At present, Rechberg said, the idea did not exist, or perhaps only in a form 'tout académique'. In any case it had never gone beyond the realm of abstraction and general discussion, and no trace of it would be found in any official form or in diplomatic correspondence. Nor did Rechberg believe that the idea could ever win the approval of St Petersburg.[269]

Rechberg seems to have taken this attitude towards the question because he was already aware that Bismarck was opposed to Danish entry into the German Confederation, from practical considerations.

Den Gedanken der Aufnahme Dänemarks in den deutschen Bund erklärt Bismarck für unpraktisch. Wäre dabei die Voraussetzung das Dänemark mit dem Herzogtümern verbunden bliebe so wäre der Streit der Nationalitäten nicht geschlichtet, und der Bund könnte demnächst in die Lage kommen, dem Könige gegen seine deutschen Unterthanen Hülfe leisten zu müssen. In andern Falle käme es zum ersten Male vor, das ein völlig undeutsches Territorium in den Bund einträte, was in keiner Weise wünschenswerth erscheinen könnte. Auch sei Frankreichs Widerwille dagegen bekannt.[270]

Although there were doubts about this problem from the very beginning, it caused no small commotion.

It is perhaps worth quoting a passage from the report by the Italian ambassador, Doria, who, although he did not really consider the idea of Denmark joining the

---

268. 12 June, A.M.A.E. *Ibid. Origines,* vol. III, p. 215.
269. Gramont to Drouyn de Lhuys, 14 and 16 June 1864. A.M.A.E. Autriche, 486. *Origines,* vol. III, pp. 225, 233-5.
270. Sybel, vol. III, p. 363.

German Confederation seriously and regarded it as a dream on the part of the Germans, nevertheless did not completely reject the possibility of its implementation. Viewing it from the Italian position, he saw potential dangers in it for Italy.

Selon moi le projet – the ambassador reported on 12 June – d'une union intime entre les États Scandinaves n'est pas encore mûr, il se realisa pourtant dans un avenir plus ou moins éloigné, mais l'idée de l'entrée du Danemark dans la Confédération Germanique ne parait tout bonnement une absurdité. Le Danemark deviendrait peut-être l'État Amiral de l'Allemagne mais il se transformerait en même temps en Province Allemande gouvernée par la Diète Germanique et esclave de ses volontés. Le jour pourrait alors arriver où la flotte Danoise serait non seulement l'avant-garde de l'Autriche dans les mers du Nord, mais aussi dans l'Adriatique. Je mentionne l'idée émise par la feuille en question parce que je sais positivement que l'on s'en est occupé à Pétersbourg. La Russie, comme de raison ne pourrait qu'applaudir et que prêter son concours au projet de l'entrée du Danemark dans la Confédération Germanique car la réalisation serait un coup mortel porté au Scandinavisme, qu'elle redoute quant à la France et à l'Angleterre elles ne pourront jamais y consentir car si le Danemark devait un jour faire partie de la Confédération Germanique, la création d'une puissante flotte Allemande cesserait d'être un rêve inoffensif pour devenir une realité dangereuse.

--- quant au Danemark lui-même, j'étais dans l'erreur en Vous écrivant que personne ici ne voudrait du maintien de l'intégrité de la Monarchie au prix de son entrée dans la Confédération. Des renseignements ultérieurs me permettent d'affirmer – Doria argued on 16 June, que plusieurs personnes à commencer par le Roi n'hésiteraient pas à souscrire à une telle condition.[271]

Right from the start Gorchakov categorically denied authorship of the plan for the inclusion of Denmark in the German Confederation. But, despite his denial, Wedel-Jarlsberg concluded that 'il me serait cependant pas impossible que, dans les circonstances du moment, une telle solution lui paraît de même être la moins desavantageuse pour la Russie'.[272] There was unease in Russia about the European situation and Russia was making efforts to prevent any intervention in the Danish-German war. She was therefore maintaining a defensive entente with Austria and Prussia, the reason for which was the Polish question and the desire to counter the democratic elements in Germany.[273] If Gorchakov had to choose whether Denmark was to be Germanised or Scandinavianised, 'plus ou moins compacte', he would also decide in favour of the first option.[274] Finally, the ambassador concluded that the suggestion that Denmark should join the German Confederation was rather a wish on the part of Gorchakov than advice in the strict sense of the word. Rechberg was in favour of the plan, but Bismarck had categorically rejected the idea.[275]

---

271. Dep. no. 48 and 50, 12, 16 and 18 June 1864. Privatarkiv no. 5424, A Friis' Historiske Samlinger. Afskrifter af akter i italienske arkiver 1863-79. R.A. Copenhagen.
272. Report of 7 June 1864.
273. No. 63, 13 (1) June 1864.
274. *Ibid.*
275. Wedel-Jarlsberg, no. 64, 20 (8) June, no. 66, 27 (15) June, no. 69 (17) (29) June and no. 74, 25 (13) July.

In the final stage of the question of Danish entry to the Confederation, Christian IX played a special role. From the beginning the Danish king took a very realistic attitude, realising that there was little chance of a military victory by the Danish army, which would involve driving the Germans first out of Schleswig and then Jutland. Likewise he was aware that the blockade could hardly be maintained once the Austrian fleet appeared in the Baltic, and that there was not much likelihood of some other power coming into the war on Denmark's side.[276]

Unlike Monrad, the King was against the partition of Schleswig and in favour of personal union of the duchies with the monarchy.[277] Officially he was against Denmark joining the German Confederation. But in fact he saw it as one solution and consequently decided in June to send his brother Hans to Leopold I, King of Belgium, with a request that the latter should contact the King of Prussia, Wilhelm I, about the matter. Leopold reported on 16 July that Wilhelm had taken a negative attitude to the problem. This was then the end of the matter.[278]

Massignac took up the question of Danish entry into the German Confederation with Gorchakov again in July, after the latter's return from Germany. Gorchakov once more denied that he had had anything to do with this suggestion and explained that such a move would upset the balance of power in Europe because it would mean expansion of the German Confederation. Russia could not allow the key to the Baltic to be given into German hands as this would be against her interests. Gorchakov's words implied, Massignac reported, that Rechberg was in favour of Denmark joining the Confederation, but this was a dream that could not be fulfilled.[279]

La France ne pourrait permettre l'absorption du Danemark dans la Confédération germanique, la Russie ne permettrait point l'union scandinave. De l'une ou l'autre de ces absorptions naîtrait infailliblement une guerre européenne,

wrote the *Revue des Deux Mondes* on 14 July 1864.[280]

Gorchakov was connected with the re-emergence of the question of a personal union of the duchies with Denmark, which was taken up by Plessen when it was not possible to find a compromise between the parties at the London Conference about the frontier line to be drawn through Schleswig. It was no accident that the idea of a personal union was put forward at that moment by Plessen, who was a conservative politician, a firm opponent of the Eider policy, and closely connected with the Holstein aristocracy and the royal court. Plessen regarded the rejection of the idea

---

276. Statsraadets Forhandlinger, ed. A. Friis, pp. 74-5, 113, 129, 132, 136 and 141.
277. 23 May 1864. *Ibid.*, pp. 150-1.
278. See Wedel-Jarlsberg's 25 June telegram on the sending of Hans to Leopold I, Talleyrand's 9 July report to Drouyn de Lhuys, *Origines*, vol. III, p. 311, Queen Louise's 3 July letter to Plessen, Arkivn. 6128 A 12, and *Statsraadets Forhandlinger, ...,* pp. 431-4. In his letter to Christian IX, Leopold wrote: jetzt scheint man in Preussen der Idée nicht mehr günstig zu seyn. (p. 431).
279. A.M.A.E. Russie, 233. Massignac's reports to Drouyn de Lhuys, 7 and 19 July 1864. See also Wedel-Jarlsberg's report no 75, 1 August (20 July) 1864.
280. *Revue des Deux Mondes*, 'Chronique de la Quinzaine', vol. 51, p. 1020.

of a personal union as a mistake, and in expressing this opinion he also referred to the view of the matter prevailing in government circles in St. Petersburg. 'D'après la manière de voir ici, l'intégrité de la Monarchie est sacrifiée à des convenances de politique intérieure, les nécessités de politique extérieure n'en auraient pas fait une condition absolue'.[281] In his next report Plessen returned to the subject and openly referred to the opinion of Gorchakov, who was advising taking action to maintain the integrity of the monarchy by means of an agreement with the leading Holstein politicians, who had not previously sought separation from Denmark and had stood aside during the demonstrations in honour of Prince Augustenburg – if, of course, the King's cabinet would support action of this kind.[282]

Having obtained the King's agreement to come to Copenhagen,[283] Plessen set off by the same train as that which took Gorchakov to Kissingen, via Berlin. On 14 June he was in the Danish capital. After having talks with the King, Danish politicians and Nicolay, Plessen put his plan for a personal union to the Royal Council (Rigsraadet). Despite support and commitment by the King, Monrad and his government rejected it categorically.[284]

For the Russian ambassador, who was perfectly *au fait* with the situation, this outcome was no surprise. Judging by the phrase he used in the account he sent to Gorchakov, Nicolay expected this result after the first talk he had with Plessen:

... le Bn O. Plessen partage entièrement la manière de voir de V E quant à l'utilité du moins d'une tentative de la part du Roi de sauvegarder un principle sur lequel reposent Ses droits à la Couronne. La difficulté est de trouver à Copenhague un individu qui voulait assumer la responsibilité d'une détermination aussi antipatique au sentiment national surexcité.[285]

Nicolay, who followed Plessen's mission with unflagging interest, thought that if the King had had the necessary personal qualities and could 'tenir tête à une pression populaire', the plan could have succeeded.[286] The idea could have been put into effect if the King had displayed energy and tenacity and, knowing what attitude Monrad would take, had got rid of that government and formed a new administration which would have steered public opinion in the right direction.

C'est avec le plus vif et sincère intérêt que j'assiste à cette tentative – wrote Nicolay – sans de dissimuler toutes les grandes difficultés qu'il s'agit de surmonter, et qu'il faut tant le dévouement et le courage du B-on Plessen pour affronter. Mon rôle pour le moment me paraît devoir être passif. J'observe ce qui se passe, et je ne crois pas appelé à donner des conseils.[287]

Plessen's plan collapsed, the government submitted its resignation and even personalities such as Andrae, Bluhme and David, who favoured the solution advocated

---

281. Dispatch no. 26, 1 June (20 May) 1864.
282. No. 27, 3 June (22 May) 1864.
283. No. 880, telegram, 8 June 1864. 'Le Roi désire que le B -on Plessen vienne ici tout de suite'. P.A. Registratur 1864. Sag Register til Archiv journalen. R.A. Copenhagen.
284. Many years later Monrad admitted that Plessen had been right. *Monrads Deltagelse*, p. 130.
285. Nicolay, Lettre particulière, 4 (16) June 1864, vol. 54.
286. *Ibid.*
287. *Ibid.* No. 78, 7 (19) June 1864.

by Plessen, were not able to undertake to form a new government on account of the atmosphere prevailing in the country, and particularly in Copenhagen. The King finally succumbed to the pressure in the capital and appointed Monrad to head the government once again.[288]

With reference to Plessen's mission it should be emphasised that this was an important political event, and even before Plessen appeared in Copenhagen it had generated a lively discussion both in Danish government and diplomatic circles. Above all, the question was whether Plessen was coming on his own or on Russian initiative. Monrad was puzzled, and questioned Nicolay about whether he had received any instructions in connection with Plessen's arrival. Nicolay's answer was in the negative, which incidentally was the truth.[289]

The whole affair acquired a special notoriety after *Dagbladet* published an article on 20 June[290] in which it reported that Plessen had presented the case for a personal union at a session of the Royal Council and that Gorchakov was behind the plan and had sent corresponding instructions to Nicolay. According to the article, the instructions emphasised that Russia stood for the integrity of the Danish monarchy, provided that Schleswig and Holstein were joined with it on the basis of a personal union. This had led to a conflict between the King, who was in favour of it, and the government, which rejected the idea. In the name of national as opposed to dynastic interests the paper declared its support for a frontier on the Eider, or at least along Dannewirke, and appealed to the King not to listen to Russia's false advice. *Dagbladet* argued that the merging of Schleswig-Holstein in Germany as well as the personal union with the Monarchy would mean the same, the loss of Schleswig and the fall of Denmark.[291] A few days later *Dagbladet*[292] published the text of Gorchakov's 7 (19) November 1863 dispatch in order to show that the Imperial cabinet had been co-operating for a long time with Prussia and Austria and, while proclaiming its support for the preservation of the integrity of Denmark, was in reality working for Schleswig-Holsteinism.[293]

Nicolay, who generally did not attribute too much importance to newspaper articles, on this occasion protested to the ministry of foreign affairs. As a result of his intervention Vedel agreed that the semi-official *Berlingske Tidende* would publish a denial on the subject of Russia's role in the episode of the proposal put forward by Plessen, and that the announcement of the events of the past few days would be phrased in such a way as to calm excited spirits and inform society that the differences of opinion between King and government had diminished.[294]

---

288. Nicolay described the crisis in his reports on 4 (16), 7 (19), 8 (20) and 9 (21) June.
289. No. 78, 7 (19) June.
290. *Dagbladet*, no. 142, 20 June 1864.
291. On the differences between the King and the government see *Statsraadets Forhandlinger ...,* pp. 147 ff, 174-7, 177-83, 183-7; the stenographic record of the sessions of the Royal Council on 23 May, 7 June, 16 June and 20 June 1864. *Dagbladet,* no. 142.
292. *Dagbladet,* no. 151, 30 June 1864.
293. Nicolay, no. 83, 18 (30) June 1864.
294. Nicolay, no. 80, 8 (20) June 1864.

Diplomats from the Western countries in Copenhagen, and particularly the French ambassador, speculated about the role the Russian cabinet had played in Plessen's mission. Dotézac wondered 'a-t-il agi de son propre chef ou bien était-il l'instrument de la Russie?' Monrad told him that he favoured the first alternative and assumed that 'le Prince Gortchakoff, sans vouloir décourager M le Plessen, ne l'a pas autorisé à se prévaloir de l'adhésion de la Russie', arguing that since Russia had spoken at the Conference in favour of the idea of partition she would not simultaneously seek to torpedo it in Copenhagen. Dotézac personally was not convinced, however, of what he called in his report 'l'innocence de la Russie dans cet incident'. He did not believe that Plessen would have put his plan forward without having external support, nor that the King would have advocated a personal union without being certain of St Petersburg's position on the question. Russia had always regarded a personal union as the best and most advantageous solution from the point of view of her own policy.

Si elle a fléchi, c'est guidée par le désir de resserrer ses liens avec l'Allemagne. N'est-il possible – asked the ambassador – d'admettre que le Cabinet de Saint-Pétersbourg ait agi dans ces derniers temps auprès de la Cour de Vienne, peu portée dans le fond du cœur au démembrement du Danemark, et qu'il ait espéré de rallier également la Prusse, en faisant envisager à Vienna et à Berlin, l'union personelle comme le prélude de l'entrée du Danemark entier dans la Confédération germanique, sous un Roi dont la reconnaissance viendrait s'ajouter à ses sentiments personnels?

Dans tout les cas, cette tentative en faveur de l'intégrité danoise avait pour la Russie ce bon résultat d'effacer l'impression qu'aurait pu produire sur le Roi le cession qu'elle a faite de ses droits au Duc d'Oldenburg.

The basis of this reasoning was the fact that, in a talk with Paget, the King had spoken of the whole of Denmark joining the German Confederation as a solution 'qui pourrait tout arranger', but Paget had firmly rejected the plan.

Malgré l'assurance donnée par un journal officieux [*Berlingske Tidende – E.H.*] qu'aucune dépêche n'était venue de Saint-Pétersbourg pour recommander la combinaison, l'opinion publique n'en associe pas moins la Russie à l'œuvre de M de Plessen.[295]

The affair caused a great stir in international circles and there was a general belief that the question of a personal union was the work of Russia.[296]

---

295. Dotézac to Drouyn de Lhuys, no. 118, 22 June 1864, *Origines,* vol. III pp. 262-6. On the crisis at this time see also *Ibid.,* no. 131, 6 July, pp. 306-11.
296. Among Danish historians, Møller has written at length on the subject. In *Skandinavisk stormagterne og allianceforhandlingerne. Stræben og svensk politik,* p. 397, he saw something mysterious in Plessen's mission, and in his fundamental work *Helstatens Fald,* vol. II, p. 128, he said that the idea for the mission and the initiative were undoubtedly Plessen's own, but that Gorchakov had been its father. The Danish court had also been behind the mission.
It is worth quoting a passage from a letter by Marx to Leon Philips on 25 June 1864, immediately after the events in Copenhagen:
Am 19-21 Juni war Kopenhagen auf dem Punkt einer Revolution. Der König [Christian IX] hat eine *russische* Depesche erhalten, worin ihm empfohlen ward, sich für Personalunion der Herzogtümer mit the Danish Crown zu erklären. Der König, eine Kreatur der Russen (die seinen Sohn [i.e. Wilhelm, – King George I of Greece – EH] nach Athen, seine Tochter [Alexandra – E.H] nach

In the light of the A.M.I.D. documents for 1864, I have succeed in investigating this question exhaustively and I have come to the conclusion that Gorchakov was indeed the initiator of the idea. He persuaded Plessen to go to Copenhagen, while Plessen fully accepted the idea suggested by Gorchakov. The way Gorchakov conducted his talk with Plessen and the nature of the mission he was to carry out in Copenhagen made it obvious to Plessen, an experienced diplomat, that in no event could the name of Gorchakov be mentioned. Plessen's mission was in essence Russian interference in the political life of Denmark, designed to change the direction of Danish foreign policy by engineering the overthrow of the legal, national-liberal government and replacing it with a conservative one. In this way Russia would achieve something she had been aiming at for many years. This explains why the diplomatic mission was not entrusted to Nicolay.

The fundamental aim of Plessen's mission was to bring about the fall of the existing government. With the experience of recent years, Gorchakov could not risk using the Russian ambassador in Copenhagen for this purpose. Consequently he preferred to use O. Plessen.[297] An attempt by a Danish diplomat who was close to the King and to conservative circles in the capital and in Holstein to bring down the government seemed to have a chance of success. My conclusion on this question is founded on Gorchakov's correspondence of the time, and especially his letter of 28 May 1864 (old style) to Brunnow.[298]

In this letter Gorchakov first summed up Russian policy at the London conference and explained the circumstances and the reasons why Russia had abandoned the 1852 Treaty of London and decided to put forward Prince Oldenburg as a candidate to rule the duchies. He then informed Brunnow about the course of his confidential talk with Plessen ('qui est une parleur de bons sens et de tact') and how he had persuaded him to set out on a special mission to Copenhagen. This talk, the vice-chancellor said, had been about the fate of Holstein when Denmark lost it. It was clear, Gorchakov had argued, that with few exceptions the Holstein elite and the large, prominent landowners ('des hommes de nom') were against Prince Augustenburg. At the moment they were standing aside and being terrorised. Did Plessen not think, Gorchakov had asked, that they would prefer a tried and tested

---

England brachten und ihn selbst auf den dänischen Thron gesetzt haben), erklärte sich für den russischen Vorschlag. Minister Monrad dagegen. Erst nach zweitägigen Debatten, Resignation des Monrad, Demonstration in the Street of Copenhagen, zog der neugebackne King die Hörner ein, but in this way Russia has again shown the cloven hoof. *Werke,* vol. 30, pp. 666-7.

Engels, who was following events carefully, wrote of Russian intrigues in a letter to Marx on 2 September 1864:

Die Dänen glauben oden vielmehr fürchten noch immer, dass die Personal-Union hergestellt wird, und da die Redaktoren Bille vom 'Dagbladet' und Ploug vom 'Fædrelandet' beide Deputierte sind und sicher gute Quellen haben, auch die jetzigen Minister gute Russen sind, so bin ich überzeugt dass starke Intrigen in dieser Richtung von Rusland gespielt werden. *Ibid.,* p. 425.

I quote these passages because the whole of democratic public opinion assessed Russia's policy towards the Danish-German conflict in the summer of 1864 in the same way as Marx and Engels.

297. Monrad wondered why Gorchakov had used Plessen rather than Nicolay. *Monrads Deltagelse ...,* pp. 151-52. Cf. C. Th. Sørensen, *Den anden slesvigske Krig,* vol. III, (Copenhagen, 1883).
298. A.M.I.D., vol. 68.

prince who was already their ruler. Did he not think that if this influential section of the population spoke out in these terms it might influence the people. Did he not also think, Gorchakov had asked the ambassador, that a personal union might have a chance of success if Holstein were assured of European guarantees against infringement of its rights by the democratic authorities in Denmark. The German population, and particularly the educated classes, Gorchakov argued, as before, were demanding assurances that they would be able to enjoy their rights, rather than separation from the Danish monarchy. If they received assurances concerning their rights, guarantees concerning a separate administration, and also that the population of the German part of Schleswig would not have to defend itself against the whims of Danish democracy, would the German population not be willing to take advantage of the opportunity and seek to maintain a personal tie with Denmark? The aim should be a solution about which the German population could have no real cause for complaint. It was already late, of course, said Gorchakov. But if he were ambassador for King Christian IX he would advise him to make a final attempt to present the conference with a plan which recognised all the demands of his German subjects, 'pour la mettre à même de prononcer sur le destinée de la Monarchie sous de conditions qui jusqu'alors n'avaient pas été soumises à son examen'.

In this conversation Gorchakov once again showed his hand to Plessen and once again declared himself an advocate of a conservative approach to settlement of the conflict. Once more he spoke out clearly and explicitly on the side of the German conservative groups and stressed emphatically that their grievances were justified and that the blame for the conflict lay with a Danish government which represented democratic and liberal forces in Denmark. This assessment differed in no way from Plessen's.

Gorchakov made it clearly understood to Plessen what the whole thing was about, and he could have complete confidence that the latter, with whom he had been in contact for many years and whose views and personality he knew well, would not on any account mention his name in connection with the mission which he had suggested Plessen should undertake. In his letter to Brunnow, Gorchakov described his relations with Plessen in the following terms:

Nos rapports ont été des plus intimes. Depuis huit ans qui le portefeuille m'est confié, j'ai invariablement trouvé dans ce Ministre du Danemark près notre Cour un grand sens, une parfaite loyauté et un tact pratique remarquable. Aussi une causerie avec Lui Vous renseignera presque aussi complètement qu'un tête à tête avec moi.

The collapse of Plessen's mission contributed to a decline in the authority of the King[299] and to a deterioration in relations between Monrad and the King and between the Danish and Russian governments, especially when Denmark rejected Brunnow's 'Actes Préliminaires', saying that she could make no further concessions

---

299. Dotézac, 22 June and 6 July, nos. 118 and 131, *Origines,* vol. III, pp. 262-6 and 306-11; Nicolay, 6 (18) and 7 (19) June.

beyond agreeing to the Slie line.³⁰⁰ In a letter to Gorchakov, Brunnow complained about the behaviour of both the Danish government and its plenipotentiaries, who were acting in an incomprehensible manner in a situation which was difficult for them. They were refusing to make clear to their friends what the intentions of their government were. 'C'est absurde!'³⁰¹

Gorchakov regarded news of the collapse of Plessen's mission and the resignation of Plessen himself as a personal failure.³⁰² 'La noble conduite du Bn Plessen a été hautement appréciée par notre auguste Maître', he wrote to Nicolay from Kissingen on 15 (27) June.³⁰³ Referring to Nicolay's recent dispatches of 7 (19) and 9 (21) June, Gorchakov informed the ambassador that they had interested the Tsar keenly and that

il n'y a rien à espérer de ce côté (Denmark) en fait de raison pratique. Nous plaignons ce pauvre Roi, jouet d'un parti qui le mène à sa perte et qui achève la ruine du pays. Aussi nous bornant aux avertissements que nous avons donnés aux Ministres Danois dès le commencement de la crise et qui sont toujours tombés sur un terrain aride –, nous ne Vous chargeons d'aucun conseil pour des gens, qui non seulement ne veulent pas les suivre, mais qui poussent l'aveuglement jusqu'à faire ostensiblement mystère de leurs vues aux seuls amis qui les soutiennent sous arrière-pensées.³⁰⁴

On 16 (28) June Gorchakov sent a very sincere letter from Kissingen to Plessen, who was on holiday in Baden, acknowledging receipt of his letter dispatched while he was still in Copenhagen, thanking him, in the name of the Tsar and on his own behalf, for his many years of co-operation, expressing his regret at the failure of

300. Nicolay, nos. 77 and 78, 6 (18) and 6 (19) June.
301. A.M.I.D., vol. 68, letter of 20 May (1 June) 1864.
302. In O. Plessen's private papers there is a copy of a letter from Ewers, dated 19 June (old style), from St Petersburg, which is a reply to a letter Ewers had received from Plessen the previous day. We do not know the content of Plessen's letter, but it is significant that the Danish ambassador considered it appropriate to inform the Russian diplomat about the course of his unsuccessful mission immediately. Ewers' reply throws light on his attitude to the Danish nation and government, on the one hand, and to the King on the other. (Arkivn. 6128, R.A.).

St. Petersburg d. 19ten Juni 1864.

Liebster Freund.
Ihr Brief den ich gestern erhielt hat mich betrübt, aber nicht überrascht. – Was Sie in Kopenhagen finden würden, war nicht schwer vorauszusehn; nämlich dasselbe wie ich, nur durch den Gang der Ereignisse noch verschlimmert. Dieselbe Minister Krisis, wenn man dem Könige den Weg zeigt auf dem seiner Minister gehn, dieselben Berathungen mit Bluhme, David, Tscherning etc. Dieselbe richtige Einsicht über das verderbliche der bis jetzt befolgten Politik, aber natürlich auch dieselbe Ohnmacht eine neue Regierung zu bilden die ein Programm durchführen könnte, welches ausser einigen wenigen personen kein Mensch will. Täuschen wir uns doch nicht, die Dänen wollen die Herzogthümer nur unter der Bedingung sie zu danisiren und wie eroberte Provinzen behandeln zu können, sonst wollen sie dieselben lieber nicht. In den Herzogthümern will die überwiegende Majorität überhaupt unter gar keiner Bedingung mehr zu Dänemark gehören, und sich von einem Könige regieren lassen, der durch die Gewalt der Verhältnisse gezwungen, immer unter dem bestimmenden Einflüsse der ultra-dänischen Parthei stehen wird. – Unter solchen Umständen ist an kein Gesammtstaatliches Ministerium zu denken. – Für die Dänen habe ich keine Sympathie, aber unendlich leid thun mir die Königin und der König, denen ich aufrichtig ergeben bin. Aus diesem Grunde bedaure ich es auch dass Sie Ihren Abschied verlangt haben, obgleich ich den Schritt an sich nicht tadeln kann! Verhältnisse gezwungen.

303. A.M.I.D., vol. 68.
304. *Ibid.* vol. 67, delo 37.

his mission and his resignation.[305] In this letter Gorchakov told Plessen that Alexander II was aware of the contents of his letter and had authorised Gorchakov to express the Tsar's appreciation personally and to inform Plessen how highly he regarded his 'noble conduite'.

Elle ne saurait rien ajouter à l'estime que l'Empereur a toujours vouée à Votre caractère et n'a fait que confirme. Sa Majesté n'a jamais cessé d'entretenir. Ces lines suffisent pour Vous donner la certitude du regret que nous ferait éprouver la cessation de nos rapports officiels avec Vous. Nous nous réjouirions si cette nécessité pouvait être écarté sans porter atteinte à vos principes.

On the basis of the reports received from Nicolay, Gorchakov now considered Denmark's situation deplorable ('deplorable au plus haut degré').

Il est impossible de venir efficacement au secours de ceux qui ne paraissent pas vouloir être sauvés et se renferment dans des réticences vis-à-vis d'amis dont la sympathie désinteressée ne saurait être douteuse.

Nous ne tarderons pas à connaître les conséquences immediates de la rupture des Conférences et de la reprise des hostilités. L'attitude du Gouvernement Anglais se définera plus nettement devant les Chambres que dans la correspondance diplomatique.

La nôtre Vous est connue, elle ne sera plus altérée. Nous conserverons malgré tout ce qu'on a fait nos sympathies traditionnelles, mais notre soutien matérielle ne serait engagée que *du moment où les intérêts directs de la Russie nous en imposerait l'obligation.* [Emphasis added – E.H.].

Adieu, mon cher B-on ne me laissez pas ignorer ce qui aura été décidé personnellement à Votre égard. Je n'ai pas besoin d'ajouter que la décision qui répondrait à nos vœux serait celle qui Vous maintenant dans les fonctions que depuis nombre d'annees Vous avez rempliés avec une invariable loyalité.[306]

In the margin Alexander II added 'très bien'.

V

As we have already mentioned, Gorchakov and Plessen left St Petersburg on the same day, 5 June, and by the same train. Plessen was bound for Copenhagen, Gorchakov for Kissingen. Gorchakov was to join Alexander II, who had left for Berlin a few days before. The Tsar and his minister were to have talks with Wilhelm I and Bismarck in connection with the impasse at the London Conference and the growing rumours of possible joint action by Britain and France, about which Brunnow, among others, sounded the alarm in his report, on 8 June.

Anglo-French talks were under way and Gorchakov was trying by every means at his disposal to frustrate British endeavours. When Russell proposed to Gorchakov, before his departure for Kissingen, that Russia should join the Western

---

305. When Bluhme came to power he asked Plessen to return to St Petersburg as quickly as possible in connection with the peace talks. P.A. Registratur 1864, R.A. Sag, Register til Archivjournalen.
306. A.M.I.D. vol. 67, delo 37.

states' action in order to restrain the eagerness of the great German states, Gorchakov - as Redern later reported[307] - replied

Que la situation géographique de l'Angleterre était différente de celle de la Russie, qu'un blocus des ports Allemands par l'Angleterre et la Russe, amènerait la guerre générale et y entraînerait la Russie; une pareille éventualité n'entrait pas dans les vues de l'Empereur.

Disquiet at Prussia's uncompromising stance, and fear as to how far her aggressive plans extended, were increasing among Russian diplomats. At the same time it seemed to the Tsar, Gorchakov and Brunnow (who persuaded Gorchakov to make the trip) that the Tsar and his minister would be able to influence the King of Prussia and Bismarck so as to improve the situation. Brunnow also hoped that the impasse at the London Conference would be resolved after these talks.

The purpose of the meeting was an exchange of views on problems of interest to both parties, and Gorchakov had been preparing for it for a considerable time. As early as 11 May Napier reported that a meeting would shortly take place in Kissingen.

There will probably be a meeting of the three Sovereigns at Kissingen, at least a meeting of the two Emperors ... I firmly believe that it is nothing preconcerted yet, ... a personal rapprochement between the Sovereigns of Russia and Austria may have some effect on the political relations of the Governments. In all this there are compensations for disadvantages. If we lose on the side of Denmark by the good understanding between Russia and Germany, we gain in the East by the friendly relations of the Russian and Austrian Cabinets. As long as Russia is well with Austria, she will not be ill with Turkey.
The story that Marquis Pepoli saw the Triple Alliance in the hand of Prince Gorchakov is a pure invention. I am confident that Pepoli never said anything of the kind.

Elsewhere in the report Napier wrote:

I find Prince Gorchakov rather colder towards Denmark and the English connection than he formerly was. His views are being gradually circumscribed by the German connections which he now believes to be consolidated and which he finds a security for the subjection of Poland. I am confident, however, that the Prince will do all he can in the admonitory way to keep de Bismarck moderate and straight.[308]

Russia's intentions at the meeting were judged correctly by Napier. As far as Russian policy towards Denmark was concerned, the ministry of foreign affairs in St Petersburg was convinced that Russia had done the maximum possible for Denmark, and that if she had not done more it was not Russia's fault.

Referring to this report the day before Gorchakov's departure for Kissingen, Napier informed Russell that N. Mukhanov, Gorchakov's deputy, had expressed the belief that the British government could be satisfied that the Russian government had on the whole been sincere and well intentioned in the Danish Correspondence.

N. Mukhanov expressed this in a talk with Napier, saying that

---

307. Redern to Bismarck, 2 August 1864. APP, vol V, p. 349.
308. P.R.O. 30/22, vol. 84, k. 202-4.
309. Napier to Russell, 4 June 1864, ibid., k. 218-9.

in the limits of their present position and policy they [Russia] have done their best. They would have done more if they had been sure that England would or could have given more effectual support for Denmark, but Baron Brunnow took a just estimate of our [British] political position and necessities.

In any case the intervention of Russia would have been limited to advice and demonstration. They might have been more strenuous and public if Her M's Government had been more energetic but they might not have been effectual.[309]

Napier, who was undoubtedly more favourably disposed towards Denmark than was his government, saw a link between the Russian government's policy and the indecisive and non-committal attitude of the British government.

At the time of his departure for Kissingen,[310] the helmsman of Russian policy no longer had any illusions about the real aims of Bismarck's policy, and he showed this in a dispatch sent to London on 23 May (old style), the day before he left St. Petersburg.

Quant à Bismarck on ne saurait lui refuser une énergie persévérante et une fixité d'intention. Dès le début il a poursuivi invariablement l'idée de faire ressortir pour la Prusse soit matériellement, soit moralement le plus d'advantage possible du conflit actuel, et c'est le seul qui jusqu'ici a progressé, dans le sens du but qu'il s'était proposé. Il est vrai que la conduite du Ministre Anglais diminue le mérite de cette énergie.

He had no doubt that his task would not be an easy one.

Bien que nous ne cesserons pas de prêcher la modération [du - E.H.] Berlin, il nous sera difficile de continuer à nous servir de l'argument que la temérité Prusienne peut lasser la patience Britannique.[311]

The Russo-German talks were held first in Berlin, then in Kissingen,[312] where Franz Joseph joined them, and finally in Carlsbad. The accounts of these talks which are available[313] show that the attitude of both the Tsar and his minister towards their hosts was clearly defensive,[314] and the approach they adopted in their talks with Wilhelm I, and particularly with Bismarck, was one of persuasion. The Russian party was aware that the question of peace, as Brunnov correctly judged, 'die Erhaltung dieses Friedens vom allem, ja fast allein in Preussens Händen läge'.[315]

Bismarck virtually ignored the remarks by Alexander II and Gorchakov about the British threat and the possibility of France joining her in the event of a German

310. Bismarck's meeting with Alexander II took place on 10 June, that with Gorchakov on 12 and 13 June.
311. A.M.I.D., vol. 68.
312. See p. 444 of the present work.
313. The Prussian ministry of foreign affairs account in APP, vol. V; Oldenburg, (1933), pp. 208-11; Gorchakov's dispatch to Brunnow on 13 (1) July 1864. *Krasnyi Arkhiv, ibid,* pp. 101-5; the account of a conversation between Alexander II and minister R. Dalwigk on 13 June 1864, in *Die Tagebücher des Freiherrn Reinhard v Dalwigk zu Lichtenfels aus den Jahren 1860-71,* ed. Wilhelm Schüssler (Osnabrück, 1967), pp. 139-40; Horst Kohl, *Bismarck-Regesten,* vol. I, p. 232; Sybel, vol. III, pp. 342ff.
314. Eyck, vol. I, p. 627.
315. Aufzeichnung des Auswärtigen Amtes über die Unterredung Bismarcks mit Kaiser Alexander II and Fürst Gortschakov, Berlin den 11/13 Juni 1864, APP, vol. V, p. 209.

attack on the island of Funen. His reply, that there was something worse than such a war, namely the development of a revolutionary movement in Germany, was designed to frighten his interlocutors. If Napoleon III went to war, Bismarck said, he would have the whole Germany against him, and it was obvious to him that then Russia, too, would be compelled to enter the war.

Alexander II thanked Prussia for her friendly attitude towards his proposal of Prince Oldenburg as a candidate for the duchies, and, like his minister, described the Treaty of London as obsolete. The Tsar attached special importance to cooperation between Prussia and Austria and called on his hosts not to come to a separate entente between Prussia and France. During his stay in Potsdam from 9 to 11 June, Alexander II decorated Prussian generals and officers with 'des distinctions honoriques'[316] as a sign of friendship.

Gorchakov assured his hosts that Russia regarded Prussia as a genuine friend and intended to maintain that alliance. War between them, which Gorchakov called fratricide, was absolutely out of the question, irrespective of the course events took. Gorchakov also regretted that if the British fleet were to appear in the Baltic the Russian fleet would be unable to be at the side of the Prussian fleet, even though – he said in answer to a question put by the Prussian King – it would not fire on it. However, the mere fact that it could not support Prussia was a cause for regret.

'You would not, of course, shoot at us?' the King asked. 'No, Your Majesty', replied Gorchakov, 'but the very presence of our flag among your enemies would be a sufficiently sad proof that from the political point of view, we cannot favour the issues which you support. It would be an extreme inconsistency if we should act otherwise'. 'I understand' replied the King.[317]

Everything Gorchakov said was in the nature of good advice about what Prussia should do to avoid getting into a difficult situation. Gorchakov tried only to moderate Bismarck's position and persuade him not to cause a conflagration in Europe on account of what he considered a matter of secondary importance, such as the Danish question. He appealed to him to help maintain an alliance of conservative states, and to draw Britain into it and turn her against the revolutionary movement. He considered that it was in Europe's interest to find a compromise to settle the disputed question of the frontier, with a solution lying somewhere between Prussia's demand for the establishment of a frontier along the line from Flensborg to Tønder and the Slie-Dannewirke line proposed by Britain. If Denmark were left Flensborg it would help the British government in its struggle with the parliamentary opposition and then the subject of the Slie would cease to be a pretext for the opposition to attack the government.

Prussia had won militarily, Gorchakov argued, so was it worth risking the peace of Europe for the sake of a few dozen square miles? Gorchakov asked Prussia to be satisfied with her military victories, but Bismarck countered this, saying that

---

316. Talleyrand to Drouyn de Lhuys, 21 June 1864, A.M.A.E. Prusse, 349, no. 68. *Origines,* vol. III, p. 260.
317. Gorchakov to Brunnow, 13 (1) July 1864, A.M.I.D. vol. 68. Krasnyi Arkhiv, 2 (93), (1939), p. 104.

they were exaggerated, which was only natural in view of the fact that they related to a nation which had not been to war seriously for fifty years. Bismarck also thought that Gorchakov's attitude to the question of the frontier between Denmark and the German Confederation was more friendly than that of his ambassador in London and

qu'il s'est montré de meilleure composition que son Ambassadeur à Londres et admis sans difficulté une ligne plus avantageuse pour l'Allemagne que celle proposée par les plénipotentiaires anglais.[318]

When Talleyrand enquired whether the Tsar and Gorchakov had asked him to exercise moderation towards Denmark, Bismarck replied in the affirmative.

Il m'a répondu affirmativement – Talleyrand reported to Drouyn de Lhuys – en ajoutant néamoins que, chaque fois que la question danoise venait à être touchée avec les hommes d'État russe, on voyait leur politique se présenter sous trois aspects différents: ainsi l'Empereur était presque *allemand,* le Prince Gortchakoff presque *neutre,* et le Baron de Brunnow tout à fait *anglais et danois.*

Bismarck took a rather dismissive attitude to Gorchakov's comments about the threat to Prussia of war with Britain and France,[319] though he did not disagree as to the necessity of settling the dispute over the frontier with Denmark by means of compromise. The King, on the other hand, while not expressly rejecting Gorchakov's suggestion, spoke of the honour of the country and the army, which, coming from him, sounded like rejection rather than approval. Nor did Bismarck omit to mention that Russia should be grateful to Prussia for the position she had taken in 1863. He also wanted to persuade Gorchakov to support Prussia's demands for a reduction in customs duties on Prussian goods exported to Russia; to this Gorchakov replied that it was a question for the finance department.[320]

This is how Gorchakov described the course of the talks and the position taken by Alexander II in a telegram to Brunnow on 7 (19) June 1864.

Tant à Berlin, qu'à Kissingen, notre A M a appuyé énergiquement et en premier lieu sur l'impérieuse nécessité de ménager le Gouvernement Anglais dans l'intérêt de la paix générale, afin qu'il ne soit pas forcé à chercher ailleurs un appui. Empereur d'Autriche est profondément convaincu de cette verité et agira dans ce sens à Carlsbad. Confiez à Russell et Palmerston.[321]

We know from the telegram sent to Brunnow on 13 (25) June that the possibility of Denmark joining a Scandinavian union was raised in the talks:

Votre pensée: isoler les îles pour que le Danemark ne devienne pas Suédois, est celle de S M, qui l'a exprimé Elle-même au Roi de Prusse et l'Empereur d'Autriche. Au clair. S.M. approuve Votre langage et attitude aux Conférences.[322]

318. 15 June, A.M.A.E., Prusse, 349, no. 63. *Origines,* vol. III, pp. 227-8; Damrémont to Drouyn de Lhuys, 28 June, *Origines,* vol. III, pp. 290-1.
319. See A. Memor, *L'Allemagne nouvelle, 1863-1867,* (Paris, 1879), pp. 156-7. See also: Knorring to Rechberg, no. 341, 2 (14) July 1864. H.H.S.A. P.A. X. Kart. 55.
320. *APP,* vol. V, p. 211.
321. Chriffres, A.M.I.D., vol. 68.
322. A.M.I.D. vol. 68. Chiffres. See *Die Tagebücher des F.R. von Dalwigk ...,* p. 739.

Gorchakov was unable to report any success in his talks with the Vienna court either.[323] Nothing could save the London Conference. 'Russian diplomacy could do no more'.[324] Gorchakov, however, later tried to prove that, thanks to his activities in Berlin and Kissingen, he had succeded in averting a European war and had an essential influence on Prussia's adoption of a more restrained policy. In a conversation with Massignac after his return from Germany, Gorchakov painted a very positive posture of his role during the talks in Kissingen.

> Le Prince Gortchakoff qui ne peut pas vivre sans aimer à croir et tâcher de persuader à son entourage qu'il a toujours un succès dans les questions dont il s'occupe, dit, qu'il a beaucoup parlé à Kissingen de l'affaire du Danemark et il ajoute que ses conseils de modération ont été pris en sériuese considération par les Cabinets de Vienne et de Berlin, – que son influence a puissament contribué à la signature des préliminaires de paix, enfin que si le Danmark est traité un peu durement, c'est pour n'avoir suivi dans le principe des sages conseils qu'il avait fait entendre à Copenhague.[325]

But Massignac did not trust the Russian minister's boasts:

> Je ne cacherai point à Votre Excellence,[326] qu'une partie du Corps Diplomatique ne prend pas au sérieux les éloges que ses décerne le Vice-Chancelier mais les Russes, tout en trouvant que le Danemark est fort maltraité, pensent que sans intervention du Prince Gortchakoff il l'eut été encore davantage.[327]

Gorchakov took a similar attitude towards B.N. Chicherin, a professor at Moscow University, telling him: 'people ask why the Chancellor was in Kissingen. The reason is, because thanks to the chancellor's presence in Kissingen a European war was averted'. But Chicherin too did not trust Gorchakov's version.

> Denmark was handed over to be swallowed up by her enemies, and Prussia had her hands unbound. This was a fatal move which led to a succession of events. Prince Gorchakov foresaw nothing. ... Impressionable and vain, he had no properly thought-out policy and did not understand Russia's real interests. He was guided by his mood to favour one state or another ... After the outbreak of the Polish uprising the French became the object of his indignation, although Louis Napoleon had warned the Tsar in his time that there were differences between them over the Polish question. Prussia, which was no less interested than we were in suppressing the Polish revolt, was the only country to give us diplomatic support, and for this service, which cost her nothing, she has now gained a substantial (*sushchestvennoe*) reward.[328]

---

323. Alexander II and Franz Joseph met in Kissingen. See Sybel, vol. III, (1890) pp. 340 ff. Clark pp. 123-4, says that Revertera had no doubt that Austrian influence on the Neva had increased in comparison with the previous period 'yet basically Russia's interest in the smaller German states (the Tsar had family ties also with Stuttgart and Darmstadt) coincided more closely with Vienna's federation than with Berlin's annexationism, and offered some ground for co-operation during the following months'. From 16 to 21 June the Tsar travelled to Munich and Kissingen, where he met Franz Joseph.
324. Mosse, *The European Powers*, p. 201. See also Bericht des Legationsrates Grafen Chotek, Berlin, 14 June 1864; H. Srbik, *Quellen ...*, vol. IV, pp. 172-4, Written on the basis of Bismarck's account of his talk with Gorchakov and Alexander II.
325. A summary of the conversation is to be found in *Origines*, vol. IV, pp. 16-17.
326. Drouyn de Lhuys.
327. Massignac to Drouyn de Lhuys, 5 August 1864, A.M.A.E., Russie, 233, no. 37.
328. *Vospominaniya Borisa Nikolaevicha Chicherina,* Moskovskii Universitet, (Moscow, 1929), p. 130.

In essence, said Chicherin, at this kind of congress in Kissingen, where the heads of the three northern states were accompanied by their ministers of foreign affairs, and King Ludwig II of Bavaria and numerous Russian diplomats and senior officials of the ministry of foreign affairs were also present, Gorchakov was most struck by Budberg, the ambassador in Paris, who opposed him and loudly criticised him for pursuing an unthinking policy. Gorchakov made no bones about this after his return to St Petersburg. Gorchakov, of course, could not bear Budberg, mainly because it was always being said that the latter would succeed to Gorchakov's post. And these rumours were an ominous reminder to Gorchakov that Budberg was on good terms with Alexander II.[329]

As far as the significance of the Kissingen meetings was concerned, in essence they achieved nothing positive. They only assured Prussia that she had nothing to fear from Russia and that there was nothing to stop her dealing finally with Denmark. Despite Russia's intentions, the talks had no influence on the course of the London Conference.[330]

Diplomats and the European press were initially convinced that some entente concerning the Holy Alliance had been concluded at the Kissingen meetings – a formal treaty guaranteeing each of the three powers its sector of Polish territory, and a secret agreement allowing Russia to intervene in German affairs, as if this were quite natural.[331] Others, like Dalwigk, did not believe this and regarded Kissingen 'comme une rencontre vaine, sans plan déterminé, sans portée aucune'.[332] Russian diplomats denied the rumours about the conclusion of an entente most categorically.[333]

It is significant that, even before leaving Kissingen, Gorchakov visited the wife of the British ambassador, Napier, who was taking a cure there, and asked her to tell her husband that he had never written letters such as the *Morning Post* claimed[334] and that at the conferences in Berlin and Kissingen not even the word Poland had been mentioned.

Before the Russian Court left Kissingen – Napier reported to Russell on 20 July – Prince Gortchakow called on my wife and requested her to state to me emphatically:

---

329. *Ibid.* pp. 129-30. See also: Baron de Franckenstein's report to Vienna, no. 14, 27/ 15 August 1864. H.H.S.A. P.A.X. Kart 55.
330. In a memorandum presented to Alexander II on 3 September 1865 (old style) Gorchakov admitted that the meetings in Berlin and Kissingen had ended in failure. *Krasnyi Arkhiv,* pp. 107-111; Cf. the view of A. Memor, *L'Allemagne nouvelle* ..., p. 156, 'Ainsi au point de vue politique il n'était rien sorti des entrevues souveraines à Kissingen'.
331. Le Comte de Damrémont from Stuttgart to Drouyn de Lhuys, 18 June 1864, *Origines,* vol. III, pp. 247-50.
332. Le Comte d'Astorg, ministre à Darmstadt, to Drouyn de Lhuys, 20 June 1864, *Origines,* vol. III, pp. 256-58, Le Comte de Salignac-Fenélon from Frankfurt to Drouyn de Lhuys, 18 June 1864, *Origines,* vol. III, pp. 242-44.
333. Napoléon III in a talk with Austrian Ambassador, R. Metternich, presented his point of view about the meetings at Kissingen and Carlsbad:
    'que les trois souverains chercheraient à toucher d'accord sur une entente intime impliquement la garantie réciproque de leurs possessions plus ou moins nenacées par la révolution'.
334. He was referring to the so-called Polish papers.

First that he never wrote the letters attributed to him in the *Morning Post.*

Second that in the various conferences and discussions which had recently taken place at Berlin and Kissingen the name of Poland had never been mentioned.

... It was a spontaneous personal declaration and Prince Gortchakow according to my wife seemed to attach that I should believe him. I believe him about the dispatches. I am perfectly convinced that he never wrote those which are atttributed to him by the *Morning Post.* I do not know what to think about Poland. It is possible that the Emperor of Russia, feeling hate of Poland now, determined not to make this country the subject of discussion with any power and especially not with Austria which had been against him in the outset of the revolution.[335]

This whole episode shows how very concerned Gorchakov was about Britain.

Just before Napier's departure for Germany on holiday, Alexander II personally returned to the subject of the Kissingen meeting and asked the British ambassador 'to inform the British government and assure it that there had been no talk of a Holy Alliance during his German tour', 'il n'avait jamais été question ni de la *Sainte Alliance* ni d'aucune espèce de *garantie territoriale*'. These words, added Massignac, reporting to Paris on Napier's visit to the Tsar, 'were in complete accord with what Gorchakov told me a few days ago'.[336] During his talk with Massignac on 28 July, Gorchakov called the rumours about the conclusion of a new Holy Alliance absurd.

C'est moi qui à Vienne a déchiré la Sainte-Alliance, voulez vous que je me prête à en rassembler les morceaux? J'en suis l'ennemi ... – said Gorchakov – je vous donne ma parole d'honneur – he continued – que pas une fois le mot de *Pologne* n'a été prononcé dans nos entretiens.[337]

From Kissingen, Gorchakov sent telegrams to Brunnow. The London Conference was at an impasse, for the only thing which had been achieved in June was an extension of the suspension of hostilities, but that was only for two weeks, as Denmark refused to agree to a longer period. On the central issue, the establishment of the frontier line between Denmark and the German Confederation, the negotiations had made no progress at all. There had been a variety of proposals for the frontier. The British proposed a line running Schleswig-Slie-Husum, the French Eckenförde-Husum, Bismarck Åbenrå-Tønder and Denmark Eckenförde-Friedrichstadt (from defence considerations).

The Danes had agreed to accept a division of Schleswig at the Schlei-Dannevirke line. From the national point of view, that would include in Denmark all the Danish-speaking populations and also a district of Angeln which had been completely Germanised only in the nineteenth century. From the historical point of view, it was almost as satisfactory. The Eider had been the historical frontier of Denmark, but the Dannewirke had been its defensive one. This frontier was the Danish ultimatum.[338]

335. P.R.O. 30/22, vol. 84, k. 236.
336. A.M.A.E. Russie, 233, no. 37, *Origines,* vol. IV, p. 16, 5 August 1864; Cf. Massignac's dispatch of 28 July, A.M.A.E., Russie, 233, no. 36, *Origines,* vol. III, pp. 364-6.
   See also: Rechberg to Metternich and Apponyi, 26 July 1864. 'Aucun engagement ni ostensible, ni secret n'a été contracté dans aucun de ces entrevues'. H.H.S.A. P.A. IX, vol. 80.
337. *Ibid.,* pp. 364-6.
338. Steefel, p. 242.

But aside from the fact that the Schleswigers themselves were opposed to a division of the duchy, a Schleswig north of Flensburg did not in those days seem of special value; not dynastic to the Royal House, not historical or cultural to the 'whole state' party, not legitimate or economic to the Eider-Danes, and not even national to the advocates of partition.[339]

On 15 June the French made a new proposal: Kappeln-Husum. This was more favourable to Denmark, but Monrad rejected it and built up hopes of a better future, referring to the Thirty Years War, when after many years the enemy had been driven out of Jutland.[340] As Dotézac reported, Monrad was unyielding and opposed to compromise; in a talk with the French ambassador he described the situation as follows:

Nous avons fait cinq mois la guerre: qu'est-ce que cinq mois pour le Danemark? On nous prendra le reste du Jutland: Wallenstein a occupé le Jutland pendant trois ans, et on nous l'a rendu. On nous prendra Alsen, et peut-être, quoique cela soit bien difficule, l'île de Fionie, mais nous sommes invulnérables dans la Séelande: là nous attendrons les événements. Je ne vois pas l'avenir aussi menaçant que vous. Ne ne perdrons pas tout le Sleswig, quoi qu'il arrive. Les Danois, je vous le répète avec conviction, préféreraient encore, malgré leur répulsion profonde pour l'Allemagne, entrer dans la Confédération germanique, plutôt que de renoncer à un territoire arrosé de leur sang depuis tant de siècles.[341]

The proposal put forward by France, that in the so-called 'mixtes districts' a popular vote should be held, was rejected by Denmark. Among the neutral states it was most sharply opposed by Russia. Brunnow criticised the French plan and at the same time criticised Prussia, which supported a plebiscite.[342]

Je regrette – he argued on 18 June 1864 – de me trouver dans l'obligation de déclarer que je diffère entièrement de l'opinion énoncée par MM les Plénipotentiaires de la Prusse. Le sentiment de regret que j'éprouve est d'autant plus vif qu'il m'est pénible d'être en désaccord avec les Représentants d'une Puissance unie à la Russie par les liens d'une amitié intime ...
Je m'éloignerais de ces principes si j'admettais l'appel que MM les Plénipontentiaires de la Prusse proposent de faire aux populations du Slesvig...
Aujourd'hui, après avoir militairement occupé ce Duché, la Prusse, loin de restituer ce gage à son Souverain, propose d'en appeler aux habitants afin qu'ils décident à qui ils veulent appartenir.
C'est aux paysans de Slesvig qu'on adresse pour qu'ils tracent la frontière d'une contrée qui forme en ce moment l'objet des délibérations de la Conférence à Londres? Est-ce-là le but dans lequel les Représentants des grandes Puissances ont été appelés à se réunir à Londres? Le Plénipontiaire de Russie est loin de l'admettre. Dans son opinion les Puissances alliées ont reconnu la nécessité de se concerter avec les autres puissances signataires du Traité de 1852 sur les arrangements qu'il conviendrait de substituer à cette transaction, après une

---

339. M. Rubin, *Historisk Tidsskrift,* 8 Series, V, p. 123.
340. Graef, pp. 325-6. Cf. p. 367 of the present work. Cf. also A Scharff, 'Bismarcks Plan einer Volksbefragung im Herzogtum Schleswig 1864', pp. 236-50, and 'Vom übernationalen zum nationalen Staat', pp. 218-35, in *Schlesswig-Holstein in der deutschen und nordeuropäischen Geschichte* (Stuttgart, 1969).
341. Dotézac to Drouyn de Lhuys, 15 June 1864. A.M.A.E. Danemark, 247, no. 116, *Origines,* vol. III, p. 230.
342. 10th session of the conference, pp. 171-2.

entente établie d'un commun accord. Aujourd'hui, au lieu d'arriver à cette entente par les efforts, par les conseils réunis, des Représentants des Grandes Puissances de l'Europe, voudrait – on consulter les populations de Slesvig, pour subordonner à leur avis les actes de la Conférence! Le Plénipotentiaire de Russie, pour sa part, ne saurait donner son assentiment à cette proposition.[343]

Brunnow supported the position taken by Clarendon, who disagreed with Bernstorff on the meaning and importance of the Treaty of London.[344] He criticised Bernstorff, who defended the idea of a plebiscite in Schleswig, cited past precendents and pointed to the examples of the Ionian Isles, Naples, Tuscany, Savoy and Nice, where the principle of holding a vote had been applied. Brunnow pointed out that the situation in the Ionian Isles had been fundamentally different from that in Schleswig. It had not been a question there of detaching them from their sovereign, but only of whether they wanted to remain as a British protectorate and retain independence, or relinquish this and merge with Greece. Nor did he understand the comparison with Greece, because Greece had not been occupied by Russia as Schleswig was by Prussia, and had not been treated as a pledge;[345] the Russian government had recognised the new sovereign chosen by the National Assembly of Greece, but had not sought to use the opinion of the inhabitants in order to deprive the ruler of his throne.

As far as Prussia's complaints about the blockade of the Baltic ports were concerned, on the other hand, Brunnow agreed that the safety of navigation in the north could be endangered in the event of a blockade: 'les questions maritimes sont basées sur certaines principes qu'il serait très graves de remettre en doute'.[346]

At the session of the conference on 22 June, on the basis of new instructions received from St Petersburg, Brunnow confirmed his opposition to the Prussian plan for conducting consultations among the inhabitants of Schleswig.[347] As far as the French proposal to hold a vote in the 'districts mixtes' was concerned, he thought the districts with a mixed population should remain under Christian IX as compensation for giving up Lauenburg.[348] To give the peasants the right to vote and decide their fate was contrary to the Russian sense of justice.[349]

Realising that pressure on Bismarck would have no effect, Gorchakov attempted once again to settle the question of the frontier by instructing Brunnow to try to influence the Danes. On 15 June he sent the following telegram from Kissingen: 'Si le Cabinet de Copenhague acceptait immédiatement la dernière concession de la Prusse, la ligne Flensbourg-Tondern, il mettrait ses adversaires dans un grand em-

---

343. *Ibid.*, p. 172; Beust, London, 20 June 1864, pp. 391-2; F. Lecomte, *Guerre du Danemark en 1864* (Paris, 1864), pp. 391-2; M.N. Pokrovsky, *Diplomatiya i voiny tsarkoi Rossii v 19 stoletii*, Sbornik statei, (Moscow, 1923), p. 236.
344. Protocols, pp. 175-6.
345. i.e. By Prussia during the War.
346. *Ibid.*, pp. 199, 201.
347. *Ibid.*, p. 212; Steefel, pp. 241-2.
348. Protocols, p. 212.
349. Beust, vol. I, pp. 392-3.

barras'. The Danes rejected this proposal. Nor did Brunnow succeed in persuading them to agree to arbitration by a neutral country in order to establish the demarcation line in the so-called mixed nationality districts. 'The Danes', wrote Steefel, 'flatly rejected it and demanded either the Schlei-Dannewirke line or the maintenance of the Treaty of London. Again, as in December, the Danes had done Bismarck's work for him'.[350] The rejection of this proposal meant a resumption of hostilities by the German side.

A few days before the end of the conference Brunnow sent a 'Lettre particulière' to Gorchakov, dated 20 June (1 July),[351] in which he gave his own summary of his role in the work of the conference and tried to indicate the reasons why it had ended in a fiasco. In both content and form this is a special kind of document, such as one rarely finds in diplomatic correspondence. The letter begins with the words the author had adressed to Quaade, who enjoyed Brunnow's confidence: 'Il est impossible de servir des amis qui ne Vous disent pas ce qu'ils veulent'. A situation had arisen, said Brunnow, in which really no one, neither Nicolay in Copenhagen nor the Vice-Chancellor in St Petersburg nor Brunnow himself in London, knew what Copenhagen wanted. Did it want peace? If so, why did it not state openly and honestly on what terms? Why did the Danes not say this 'à de vrais amis, comme nous!'? 'Veut-on reprendre les hostilités, par obstination, par désespoir?', Brunnow had asked Quaade. 'Pourquoi négocier alors, sans but, sans raison, et pour tout dire sans franchise?'

Brunnow's letter took a critical view of Hall's policy. He had made a great mistake by drawing the country into war. Monrad had made another mistake by refusing to accept peace when it could have been obtained. He was really no statesman if he could say to Paget that he would let Napoleon protect the country and that that would be a blow to Britain. Russell and Clarendon had not been frightened by this threat, and its effect had been to dull rather than sharpen the keenness of the British government.[352] 'Just when we were striving to secure the greater part of Schleswig from Germany', wrote Brunnow, 'Bille received instructions to state that if the negotiations did not finish by 12 June Denmark would renew the blockade. How could results possibly be obtained by such clumsy behaviour?'

In spite of this, Brunnow assured Gorchakov, he had continued to work for peace in accordance with the wishes of the Tsar. He had met Apponyi, Bernstorff and

---

350. Steefel, p. 242. Cf. J.H.S. Birch, *Denmark in History,* (Westport, Connectitut, 1975), p. 368; A Jansson, p. 230. On this last question the under-secretary of state at the British Foreign Office, A.M. Layard,, sent the following telegram to Paget:
Tell the Danish Minister that in the opinion of Her Majesty's Government an acceptance of the arbitration proposed would, whether accepted or refused by German powers, tend to establish the security and independence of Denmark for the future. A war unsupported might weaken and cripple Denmark for ever. She ought to embrace the fair and reasonable proposal made yesterday in Conference by Her Majesty's Government.
Statsraadets Forhandl. 1863-1870, ed. A. Friis (Copenhagen, 1936), p. 430.
351. A.M.I.D., delo 25.
352. In a letter to Russell after Denmark's rejection of the 'Articles' Brunnow called Monrad 'warlike'. June 1864, P.R.O. vol. 78.

Beust privately to try to reach agreement on the establishment of the frontier. The Germans would not agree to the Slie line. They had agreed, under strong pressure, to propose the Flensborg-Tønder line. The Danes, however, still demanded a line along the Slie. There were perhaps 100,000 inhabitants living between these two lines. Was this a reason to jeopardise a population of 3 million, the throne and the monarchy, to cause the resumption of hostilities in a war in which Denmark had no rational chance of success: 'c'est de la démence'.[353]

The private meeting with the Danish plenipotentiaries which Brunnow organised on the day he sent the letter was the last, and unsuccessful, attempt he made to get them to report the state of affairs to their government and obtain a final decision. Of himself Brunnov wrote that he was disheartened.

> Je me suis souvenu qu'avant le désir de plaider la cause du Danemark, vient le devoir de servir les intérêts de la Russie! Comme le duc de Wellington le disait: 'avant tout le service du pays'.
>
> J'ai mis en sûreté les intérêts de l'Empereur, j'ai dégagé la cause de la Russie pour ne pas la laisser compromettre par les Danois, si ceux-ci ceulent absolument courir à leur perte. Bourgeoisement parlant, j'ai tiré notre épingle du jeu. Je l'ai fait résolument mais avec probité et avec ménagement envers nos amis les Danois. ...
>
> Chacun sert son pays. Moi j'ai la conscience d'avoir servi le mien, comme je le devais.

On the one hand, this document is a shattering criticism of the policy pursued by the Danish government, but, on the other, Brunnow presented himself as the great friend of Denmark who had made every effort to help her and steer her policy in the

---

353. It is worth comparing Brunnow's opinion of Denmark's policy and behaviour with British views: 'I admire their patriotism but I cannot say much for their political intelligence' and 'Stiff necked race' are two of the expressions we find in Wodehouse's dispaches to Russell at the end of 1863. (P.R.O. 30/22, vol. 51, 22 December and 29 December. See Voigt, p. 89). On 13 February 1864 Queen Victoria wrote to Gen. Grey (RA-I 94) as follows:
It is hardly possible to conceive such utter folly and insanity. But it must have the good effect of convincing those who w(oul)d wish to assist them, of the impossibility of saving a people who *will* [emphasis in the original – E.H.] not be saved. (Voigt, p. 120).
General Grey to Queen Victory, 17 March 1864:
The refusal of an armitrice seems nothing short af madness, particularly after the miserable resistance they seem to have made in Jutland. (R.A. – I 95, Voigt, p. 127).
Russell to Lytton, 4 May 1864:
We find our Danes to be of the sternest stuff of which ambition was ever made. They will very soon have nothing but Copenhagen with its mob and its press to govern, or rather to govern them. (P.R.O. 30/22, vol. 102, 11 May 1864).
I cannot see any hope for them for renewed war, either in their own resources or from their allies of whom England alone is disposed to fight if France and Russia join. Austria gave up Lombardy when she was beaten...
Russell called the policy of the Danish plenipotentiaries at the conference 'temporary insanity'. Review by Scharff, *Z.d.G.f.S.-H.G.* vol. 85/86, (1961), p. 358.
Russell to Paget, 6 July 1864:
I am very sorry for Denmark, but Danish statesmen have destroyed their country. (P.R.O. 30/32 vol. 102, 13 July 1864).
But the Danish misfortunes are owing to such Danish patriots as Hall and Monrad. (P.R.O. 30/22, vol. 102. Voigt, p. 155).
These Danish affairs have ended very ill, but I don't know that we could have done better. We could not have espoused the Danish cause without obliging Hall and Monrad to behave with justice to the German subjects of the king, and that they were determined not to do. (Russell to Paget, 10 August 1864, P.R.O. 30/22, vol. 84, k. 92).

right direction. He described the situation which eventually arose and explained why he decided to abandon the position he had adopted until then, or, in other words, why the conference had achieved nothing.

It is significant that he laid the blame exclusively on the Danish side and said nothing about the more and more uncompromising and aggressive attitude of the Prussian delegation at the conference. The ending of the letter is astonishing. Brunnow assured Gorchakov that he had done everything in his power to be equal to the task and the purpose which guided him above all else – the service of Russia. It was as if he were justifying himself and explaining himself to his superior.

This passage is intriguing. Was he in trouble again, was he being criticised in St Petersburg for being cut off from his country and not understanding its needs, or for not having done his job properly? Or might there have been new misunderstandings between Brunnow and Gorchakov?[354] We shall not find an unequivocal answer to these questions.

When it became obvious that the conference had ended in failure, Brunnow sent a telegram to Gorchakov informing him that Palmerston wanted to issue a final document in the name of the neutral states indicating the efforts which they had made for the purpose of restoring peace and the reasons why these efforts had been unsuccessful. He had further proposed that the neutral states should declare that they would insist that Denmark continued to exist, as an essential element in the balance of power in the north. Finally, they would state that in spite of the fact that they were not involved in the fighting on land, they wanted to make clear that they did not wish to see the war spread to the islands and threaten Copenhagen. Palmerston expected that France would refuse to join in this declaration, but it would be sufficient if Britain and Russia did so. The purpose of the declaration was to contribute to the security of Denmark and protect her from serious complications. In conclusion, Brunnow asked to be informed of the Tsar's decision on the mater.[355]

In his reply[356] Gorchakov expressed no objection to a declaration giving prominence to the efforts directed towards preserving peace, and also agreed to the mention of the question of maintaining the Danish monarchy and of the security of Copenhagen, for these were matters of cardinal importance to the neutral states. But he demanded that there be no reference to the question of material naval assistance. His reasoning here was that Britain had already shown her changeability, so that he had no confidence that she would not back out. Furthermore, she was strong enough at sea to be able to ensure the security of Copenhagen and the Islands on her own. If she announced that she intended to intervene on land, it would mean she intended to take only limited action, while a conflict at sea could easily draw Russia into the war on land. The two powers' participation would not be equal. Russia's role was to preserve general peace, Gorchakov concluded, and she saw her place

---

354. Massignac reported that antagonism could be observed again between Brunnow and Gorchakov, as, incidentally, on many other occasions. The reason for this was the reappearance of Brunnow's name, and of Budberg's as possible candidates to succeed to Gorchakov's post. A.M.A.E., Paris, Russie, 233, no. 42, 21 September, 1864.
355. Telegram of 10 (22) June 1864. A.M.I.D. vol. 68.
356. From Kissingen, 11 (23) June 1864. A.M.I.D. *ibid.*

as a link between the extreme parties ('à être le trait d'union entre les parties extrêmes'). This point of view was approved by Russell at the closing session of the conference and Brunnow was able to telegraph to Gorchakov on 13 (25) June: 'Pressant ordre y contenu et pris nul engagement matériel'.[357]

At the time the London Conference was convened Brunnow appeared to be the person perhaps most predestined to play an important role as mediator. Completely familiar with the problem, close to the leading British politicians, and also well respected by Danish politicans as a long-standing friend of Denmark, it seemed that he would also be able to find a common cause with some of the German politicians, in view of the ties linking Russia and the larger German powers. But in practice these predictions proved unavailing. Brunnow's reputation as, in Beust's words, 'Vorkämpfer für die dänische Sache',[358] a view shared by Bernstorff too,[359] was only reinforced during the conference, while the Danish side, and particularly the central figure in the Danish delegation at the conference, A.F. Krieger, did not trust Brunnow from the beginning and in his letters to Andrae, Vedel and Monrad questioned the view of Brunnow as a politician devoted to Denmark.[360]

Instead of co-operation between the Danish delegation and Brunnow there was dislike, increasing disagreement and finally exasperation. The reason was the lack of understanding between the two parties stemming from their differing views of the Danish problem and the possibility of solving it. The two delegations had different assessments of Denmark's chances and of the political climate surrounding the Danish-German conflict, particularly in Britain. Knowing Russia's attitude and also being in very close touch with British politics, Brunnow saw no other or better solution than for Copenhagen to compromise, whereas Krieger, and Monrad too, were really against negotiations from the start and would have preferred to go on fighting, since they overestimated Denmark's military strength and continued to believe that help would be forthcoming from abroad, especially from Britain.

The National Liberals who still controlled Danish policy, and especially Krieger, their representative at the Conference, had never really liked the negotiations. They felt, that they were being dragged from concession to concession and that it would be better to keep up the fight. Untaught by the experience of the first stages of the war, they overestimated the strength of Denmark's military position and they still hoped for foreign aid.[361]

The majority of Danish historians follow Neergaard's view[362] that the choice of Brunnow as Russia's representative was, in principle, to Denmark's benefit. He supported Denmark as long as possible, and the maintenance of the provisions of the

---

357. A.M.I.D., *ibid.*
358. Beust, vol. I, pp. 364-5.
359. *Im Kampfe für Preussens Ehre. Auch dem Nachlass des Grafen Albrecht v Bernstorff,* Ed. Karl Ringhoffer (Berlin, 1906), pp. 560-1.
360. See 'A.F. Kriegers, D G Monrads og P V Vedels indbyrdes brevveksling 1846-1866'. ed. Aage Friis and Just Rahbek, *Danske Magazin,* (1940), pp. 131, 188-90, 195, 200 and 258 and also Kriegers Dagbøder, vol. III, pp. 119, 127-8, 225.
361. Steefel, p. 243; *Kriegers Dagbøger,* vol. III, pp. 140, 155, 156ff., 163 and 167.
362. Neergaard, vol. II, pt 2, p. 1160.

Treaty of London was a question of honour for him. Others, like Møller, say that although Brunnow was well-versed in the legal and diplomatic aspects of the problem, he did not understand the national aspect, and this was the source of misunderstandings with the Danish party at the conference. This view of Brunnow's positive role as defender of the integrity of Denmark for as long as he could has also been characteristic of French and British historiography.[363] German historians on the other hand, starting with H. Sybel, K. Jansen and K Samwer, and followed by Cierpinski and Heinze, see Brunnow as a politician who 'sehr deutschfeindlich war', and Cierpinski thought that in London Brunnow 'mehr gesagt hat, als man in Petersburg gut hielt'.[364]

The general view of Brunnow from the point of view of relations with Denmark may be positive, and historians inclined to say that he made the maximum effort possible within the framework of the general instructions he received from St Petersburg to help Denmark, and moreover was able to do so since he enjoyed considerable freedom of action within that framework, but as far as detailed solution to the problems is concerned[365] the general opinion about the Danes is uncomplimentary. The majority of Danish historians, like Neergaard, Povl Engelstoft, the authors of Schultz's *Danmarkshistorie* and the authors of works on Monrad – P. Svanstrap, P. Lauristen, A. Nyholm and J.S. Nielsen, were very critical of the conduct of both Monrad's government and, in particular, of the head of the government himself, as well as of Krieger, during the London Conference, accusing them of being doctrinaire, inflexible and excessively optimistic about Denmark's military and political capacity, and throwing away the last chances Denmark had.[366] It is not possible to attribute this entirely to Monrad's state of health.[367] Many years afterwards, Monrad himself was also critical of his own conduct, saying that Denmark had been a small country in a great storm and that her lack of a political genius had contributed to her defeat.[368]

François de Callières wrote in a treatise in 1716: The art of negotiation ... is so important

---

363. See J. Klaczko, E. Ollivier, Pierre de la Gorce and contemporary French historians; in British and American historiography see A.W. Ward, P.G. Gooch, S. Wilkinson and Steefel.
364. *Z.d.G.f.S.H.* vol. 44 (1914), pp. 255-66. (Cierpinski, 'Die Politik Englands ...').
365. See Pirch to Bismarck, 26 May 1864, APP, vol. V, p. 160.
366. Troels G. Jørgensen, *Andrew Frederik Krieger. Juristen, Politikeren, Borgeren* (Copenhagen 1956), tries to revise this view on the basis of a letter from the British diplomat Edward Robert Bulwer-Lytton (1831-91), who was secretary of the embassy in Copenhagen, to Vedel in June 1864, in which he says that Russell and Clarendon had a very favourable opinion of Krieger. According to Bulwer-Lytton, Russell was supposed to have spoken of Krieger 'in the highest term as being both very able and very conciliatory'. Clarendon was quite enthusiastic in praise of him and says that everybody finds him not only exceedingly courteous and agreeable to do business with but that Mr Krieger has made some statements in Conference defence and explanations of Danish policy and interests, which were very effective, and have given him (Clarendon) a very high opinion of Mr Krieger's ability, See also J. Nielsen, *Da Europa gik af lave.*
367. See J.S. Nielsen, *D.G. Monrad. En patologi,* (Odense, U.P., 1983). There is an interesting review of this work by T. Kaarsted, 'Var D.G. Monrad manio-depresiv?'. *Historie,* vol. XV, no. 2, 1984, pp. 263 ff.
368. *Monrads Deltagelse ...,* p. 22.

that the fate of the greatest states often depends upon the good and bad conduct of negotiations and upon the degree of capacity in the negotiators employed ... in a word, one may say that the art of negotiation, according as its conduct is good or evil, gives form to great affairs and may turn a host of lesser events into a useful influence upon the course of the greater.[369]

Or, in Erich Ewerth's words,

Die Politik ist eine Kunst des Möglichen, nicht eine Wissenschaft des schon Wirklichen. Politik will und muss oft etwas Bestehendes umstürzen, um Anderes aufzubauen.[370]

The Danes lacked these qualities and skills in the difficult days of 1864.

Against this background Brunnow's attitude is indeed distinctive. When we analyse his position at the Conference we may have serious reservations about the description German politicians and historians applied to him, and the view that his actions were hostile to the interests of Germany. It is true that he opposed the views of Beust, who represented liberal-national circles,[371] but in principle he was sympathetic to Austrian and Prussian views, and sought only to moderate them, because the audacity and lack of restraint of the Prussian delegation in particular, might have led to new complications in Europe, which Russia wanted to avoid at any price.

Within the limits of what was possible for him, he suggested various solutions in his quest for peace on terms which Denmark could accept with honour. In this effort he showed much goodwill and looked for tactical solutions within the framework of the general strategy dictated by Gorchakov. There were differences between him and Gorchakov concerning the solution to certain problems. And the 'amicus Daniae' and joint creator of the Treaty of London, which was the greatest achievement of his life,[372] had a better feeling for the situation than his minister. These differences might not be fundamental, but they were noticed. Brunnow had been rather more pro-Danish than his government, Napier reported to Russell.[373] Such an opinion was shared by many Danish politicians.[374]

---

369. *The Practice of Diplomacy,* being an English rendering of François de Callières, 'De la manière de négocier avec les souverains', presented with an introduction by A.F. Whyte (London, 1919), pp. 7, 16; cf. *War, Politics and Diplomacy,* selected by Gordon A. Craig (New York and Washington, 1966), p. 220.
370. Erich Ewerth, *Die Öffentlichkeit im Aussenpolitik von Karl V bis Napoleon,* (Jena, 1931), p. 207.
371. Beust, pp. 389, 396.
372. 'Baron Brunnow, the most ardent and staunch supporter of the engagements of 1852', Napier to Russell, 25 May 1864. P.R.O. 30/22, vol. 84, k. 211.
373. *Ibid.* k. 202-4.
374. After Bluhme came to power he tried unsuccessfully, through Dircking-Holmfeldt, to persuade Brunnow to act to help the conservative government in Denmark. P.R.O. 30/22, Denmark. Miscellanea, 1861-1864, vol. 52, 24 and 26 July 1864, K. 175-8.

IV
From the Resumption of Hostilities to the Treaty of Vienna

Immediately after the end of the London Conference the German allies resumed hostilities. Their capture of the island of Als on 29-30 June showed that they were capable of overcoming the barrier of the sea. The behaviour of Monrad, whose reaction to the fall of the island was to order the Danish army to fight to the last man, can only be put down to severe psychiatric illness.[375] The last hopes had vanished and, as Nicolay noted,[376] even *Dagbladet* no longer urged 'de la résistance à tout prix'. Quaade, whom the ambassador called 'un homme sensé et pratique dans ses opinions', stressed in a talk with him that Denmark had to secure a suspension of hostilities quickly on the terms 'qu'il pourrait obtenir'.[377]

The day after Monrad's resignation the King asked Charles Moltke to form a government (on 9 July) and when Moltke's efforts ended in failure he turned to Ch. Bluhme. On 11 July a new government was formed. Bluhme accounced that he wanted direct negotiations with Germany and a suspension of hostilities for an unlimited period; he regarded it as impossible to continue fighting, since the whole country would soon be captured by the German allies.[378]

According to Nicolay's report, the main idea of the new government was to save the integrity of the Danish monarchy. Basing itself on the Treaty of London, the government sincerely intended to fulfil its obligations under that treaty and to remind the German side that the obligations were reciprocal. Nicolay presumed that Bluhme would attempt to merge the German duchies with the Danish monarchy on the principle of a personal union and the division of Schleswig on a nationality basis. If that did not succeed, he would try to merge the whole of Schleswig-Holstein with Denmark by personal union. The hardest problem would be to reconcile the rights of the Danish crown with the claims of the German Confederation. But the greatest internal difficulty for Denmark would be to establish co-existence with Schleswig-Holstein. The King could be sovereign of Denmark or Schleswig-Holstein, otherwise he would risk losing them for the state.

Monrad had thought that the strength of the ties between the Kingdom and the Danes in northern Schleswig was so great that if the Germans would not agree to

---

375. *Monrads Deltagelse ...*, p. 148, J.S. Nielsen, p. 570. After his resignation Monrad behaved like a man who was not normal. He began to speak with the obstinacy of a maniac of the need to fight to the end, and in November he opposed the ratification of the provisions of the treaty concluded in Vienna. For his speech in the Rigsraad see: *Monrads Deltagelse ...*, pp 284-87, Møller, *Helstatens Fald*, vol. II, p. 191, Neergaard, *Under Junigrundloven*, vol. II, pt 2, pp. 1531-1535. R. Skovmand, in his book *D.G. Monrad, Politiker og Gejstlig* (1984) rightly argued that 'Monrad's manic-depressive temperative might have influenced the above-mentioned events'. And Nielsen explained: 'Monrad constituted a manic-depressive personality (the cyclothymic type) and suffered from mild to moderate manic-depressive state.' (pp. 370, 557, 572). See also A. Nyholm, *D.G. Monrad. Efterladte prædikanter* (1961), pp. 269ff., 295ff.
376. Nicolay, 25 June (7 July). (Lettre particulière).
377. *Ibid.*
378. Nicolay's report no. 87, of 4 (16) July.

the division of Schleswig according to nationality the Danish nation would prefer, rather than be forcibly divided from its brothers in northern Schleswig, to be merged with them and be 'Allemande à son tour'. It was strange, observed Nicolay, that the possibility of Denmark joining the German Confederation[379] was now being discussed by the very same people who not long ago were still seeking support for a move in precisely the opposite direction.[380] In Nicolay's opinion, even Bluhme had begun to incline towards the idea of Danish entry into the German Confederation in order to avoid division of Schleswig. But he had abandoned it when he received a report from Bille informing him that the British government was not keen on this solution.[381] The plan for union with the German Confederation would also have run into opposition in the Rigsraad, which preferred division of Schleswig.[382]

On 18 July a truce suspending hostilities was signed and on 21 July the Royal Council met and analysed the international situation and the state of affairs at the front. The opinion was expressed that Denmark was and would remain isolated, as no help was to be expected from the Western powers and Russia had long since yielded to the German states and agreed to the separation of the duchies from Denmark.[383] Seven-sixteenths of the country was in the hands of the enemy, and the financial situation was bad. The Council therefore decided to conclude peace.[384] On 25 July the Danish plenipotentiaries, Quaade and Col. Kauffmann, arrived in Vienna for talks with Bismarck and Rechberg, and on 30 July the Danish government accepted the conditions dictated by Prussia and Austria.[385]

The national-liberal party's departure from power and the assumption of office by the conservatives in Denmark was welcomed by Gorchakov.[386] The Vice-Chan-

---

379. The idea of Denmark joining the Confederation was rejected by all the states – Denmark, Prussia and the Confederation. See Nicolay's reports on the subject, nos. 128 and 129, 8 July 1864, in Kabinettet for utrikes brev. Depescher.
380. Nicolay, no. 88. 8 (20) July 1864.
381. Dep. England, 15 July 1864, no. 75, RA Copenhagen; Nicolay, no. 89, 9 (21) July 1864.
382. Nicolay, no. 89, 9 (21) July 1864.
383. After the meeting in Kissingen there was a general belief that there had been a further rapprochement between St Petersburg, Vienna and Berlin. The Danish ambassador in Paris, among others, reported this in reports no. 59 and 73, 14 July and 16 September. Dep. Frankrig. R.A. Copenhagen. The report from the Bavarian ambassador in St Petersburg on 17 (5) July deserves noting: L'intégrité du Danemark abandonée par les Puissances, la Russie se porte tout naturellement vers la Prusse pour obtenir par elle des advantages du nouvel ordre des choses, qui va être établi dans les Duchés, c'est son intérêt de soutenir Mr de Bismarck, et son système, qui lui est utile à cause de la Pologne ... Il y a une alliance naturelle, qui existe à présent entre la Russie et les deux grandes Puissances allemandes, une entente à l'égard de la Pologne, garantie par des intérêts commun, qu'on ne saurait contester ...
Perglas to Ludwig II, no. 81, St. Petersburg 17 (5) July 1864, in *Rusland 1852-1871. Aus den Berichten der Bayerischen Gesandtschaft in St. Petersburg.* Ed. Barbara Jelavich (Wiesbaden, 1963), p. 118.
384. *Statsraadets Forh. om Danmarks udenrigspolitik,* 1863-1879, pp. 237-45, 245-50, and *Statsraadets Forhand. 1864-1866,* vol. X, p. 37. The Ministers for War and Marine, Hansen and Lütken, argued that Russia had become very close to the German powers.
385. Neergaard, *Under ...,* vol. II, pt 2, pp. 1411-1415. Preliminaires to a peace treaty were signed on 1 August.

cellor regarded Denmark's situation as extremely serious and said that the recent rumours about Christian IX wanting to join the German Confederation had dealt a severe blow to his authority.[387] Gorchakov wished the Danish government to make every effort to conclude peace.

Je prie V E d'être persuadé que mon plus vif désir est de me rendre utile autant que possible au Gouvernement du Roi et que tous mes efforts sont dirigés vers ce but.
On regrette – Gorchakov telegraphed to Nicolay – la vague quant aux conditions de la paix. La cause qui traverse le Danemark ne peut-être conjurée que par l'attitude nette et la promtitude d'action. Le salut du Danemark est dans la paix.
La levée immédiatement du blocus paraît indispensible comme une induce de la sincérité des intentions du Gouvernement Danois.
Télégraphiez sous quelle date le Rigsraad pourrait être renvoyé.[388]

According to Vind's and Wedel-Jarlsberg's reports, Gorchakov had expressed to the German states his wish that they should be moderate in their demands, and he had, he said, urged this most categorically.[389] But the claim that he intended to intervene personally in connection with the signing of peace preliminaries in Vienna was not taken seriously.[390]

Meanwhile, disturbing news arrived from Berlin about the unprecedented growth of Bismarck's ambitions. This, as Wedel-Jarlsberg reported, intensified Gorchakov's interest in seeing peace concluded as quickly as possible.[391] Gorchakov was also disturbed by the fact that France had been defending the national rights of the Danes in northern Schleswig.[392] Bismarck, on the other hand, according to influential information, was trying to neutralise Russia, thanking her for the position she had taken in the Danish-German conflict and the disinterestedness she had displayed in putting forward Prince Oldenburg as a candidate for the duchies.[393] Bismarck was also promising to establish the best possible relations with Denmark, as the balance of power in Europe required this.[394] Russia, Wedel-Jarlsberg reported, was in a difficult situation, for neither the collapse of Denmark, nor the rise of a Scandinavian union, nor of a strong Germany, were in her interest.

At Bluhme's request, Plessen asked the Vice-Chancellor if the Russian government, which was on such such friendly terms with the German powers, particularly Prussia, would persuade the German states to agree that Denmark should receive the most favourable territorial settlement in northern Schleswig and that territory inhabited exclusively by a Danish population should not pass into the hands of the

---

386. See Vind's report, no. 29, 5 August (24 July) and Wedel-Jarlsberg's report, no. 74, 25 (13) July.
387. Dotézac to Drouyn de Lhuys, 24 and 27 July *Origines,* vol. III. pp. 353-4, 361-2.
388. 17 July (old style), A.M.I.D., vol. 68.
389. Vind, no. 29, 5 August (24 July) and Wedel-Jarlsberg, no. 74, 25 (13) July.
390. See Dotézac's letter to Drouyn de Lhuys, 5 August 1864, *Origines,* vol. IV, p. 17.
391. Wedel-Jarlsberg, no. 75, 1 August (20 July) 1864.
392. Wedel-Jarlsberg, no. 80, 22 (10) July.
393. See also Plessen, no. 30, 24 (12) August.
394. *Ibid.*

German states. Plessen's intervention, however, had no effect.

Le Gouvt. Russe entretient des relations si amicales avec les puissances alliées et surtout avec la Prusse que je suis convaincu qu'un appui prêté à nous demandes modérées de la part du Cabinet de St Pétersbourg ne manquerait pas d'exercer une très grande et très heureuse influence sur les déterminations de M de Bismarck,[395]

wrote Bluhme.

In reply to this request, Gorchakov said Russian policy did not go beyond a general appeal to the German states to exercise moderation. In this spirit he had sent letters to Oubril and Knorring on 7 September (old style) instructing them to urge Berlin and Vienna to come to a compromise with Denmark on matters of finance and the frontier.[396]

Gorchakov dit not want to intervene on specific questions and referred to the fact that in the current situation neither Britain nor France intended to involve themselves in more direct questions either.[397] As Plessen noted,[398] relations between Russia and Prussia had become so close that, in spite of immense financial difficulties, the Russian government had decided to pay Prussia 322,000 thalers compensation for losses sustained by Prussia on the Bydgoszcz-Warsaw railway during the Polish uprising.

On 22 September[399] Bluhme again asked Plessen to intervene with the Russian government, as the German claims were still completely contrary to the principles of maritime law. It was not just a question of Denmark's interests, Bluhme argued, but of the interests of all maritime countries which did not want to see the existing principles overthrown. No country, Bluhme explained, could be interested in paying compensation because of a blockade of ports. Both Gorchakov and the acting minister, Maltsev, to whom Vind next turned, refused to intervene against the excessive demands of the German states for compensation for losses sustained as a result of the interception of their ships during Denmark's blockade of German ports. Russia, said Maltsev, did not consider the peace terms or the demands of the German states contrary to the principles of international law. The vanquished had to accept, or could reject, the terms set by the victor. This, replied Vind, meant that might was right.[400]

Wedel-Jarlsberg also tried fruitlessly to persuade Russia, as one of the neutral countries, to intervene in Vienna and Berlin jointly with the other powers to ease Denmark's burden.[401] The position adopted by the Russian ministry of foreign

---

395. Bluhme to Plessen, 2 September 1864. P.A. Registratur – Udenrigsm. Tag. A, 798. R.A. Copenhagen, 1863-64.
396. Møller, vol. II, p. 178.
397. Plessen, no. 34, 31 (19) August; Møller, vol. II, p. 179.
398. Plessen, report no. 30, 24 (12) August 1864.
399. A.M.I.D., vol. 68.
400. Vind's report, no. 43, 16 (4) October 1864. For Gorchakov's refusal, Gorchakov to Nicolay, 7 October (old style). Rus. Films. RA. Copenhagen. Cf. also Dotézac's report to Drouyn de Lhuys, no. 213, 29 October 1864. A.M.A.E. Corresp. Danemark, vol. 248.
401. Wedel-Jarlsberg, no. 44, 28 (16) October. The Swedish ambassador expressed the fear that if Manderström made a move in isolation it would have little effect on Berlin, ('mediocre' was the word he used).

affairs was of course fully supported by the Tsar. Alexander II said there was a difference between supporting Denmark and calling for moderation, on the one hand, and formal involvement by a neutral country in the negotiations, on the other. Such support would mean taking one side against the other, which no neutral country did.

There was no reply either to the request in the form of a personal letter to Alexander II from Princess Dagmar, the fiancée of Grand Duke Nicholas, heir to the throne. On 29 October, before the signing of the unprecedentedly onerous treaty of Vienna which the German states imposed on Denmark, she sent a letter to the Tsar, whom she addressed as 'Mon Cher Papa!', imploring him to help her poor father, her country and nation, which were under such an unjust yoke. She asked him for help and protection, if possible, against their monstrous foes.

J'espère, Cher Papa, que Vous ne trouverez pas Votre future belle fille trop indiscrète, mais la triste situation de ma chère patrie, me tennant très à cœur m'a suggéré l'idée de m'adresser à Vous ...

This letter went unheeded. In any case it reached St Petersburg too late. On 30 October 1864, the Treaty of Vienna was signed.[402]

In a talk with Revertera, Alexander II expressed the wish that peace should be quickly concluded and conservative governments in Copenhagen strengthened. He praised Austria for her moderation, but expressed regret at Bismarck's impetuous character and his quest for victories, and said that he intended to ask the Prussian King to be understanding towards Denmark. Bismarck's statements that he would like nothing better than a war with Britain were strange, thought the Tsar, and he expressed disquiet on that account. He appealed for a union of conservative forces in the face of Bonapartism and regretted that the war with Denmark had obstructed the creation of a four-power alliance.[403]

Plessen was not surprised by the attitude of Alexander II and Gorchakov. He

---

402. See Danica R.A. Czarfamiliens Papirer, Russiske Films. Dagmar til Kejser Aleksander II og Kejserinde Maria Alexandrovna, 1864-79, and A. Friis, *Den Danske Regering og Nordslesvigs Genforening med Danmark,* vol. II, (Copenhagen, 1939) pp. 13-15.
   On 27 September the heir to the throne, Grand Duke Nicholas, arrived in Copenhagen from Kiel, via Korsør. (A.M.A.E. no. 194, Corr, Danemark, vol. 248). On 28 September it was offocially announced that Dagmar and Nicholas were to be married. (*Ibid.,* no. 196). The King and Queen had satisfied their ambitions, but the country did not share these ambitions. 'Ce n'est pas du côté de la Russie que les Danois portent leurs symphathies...' (Dotézac's report of 29 September, and also Meroux de Valois from Kiel, 1 Oktober, to Drouyn de Lhuys. *Origines,* vol. IV, p. 213) 'Les fiançailles de la Princesse Dagmar avec le Prince héritier de Russie n'ont point flatté l'orgueil des Danois. Ils ne veulent voir dans cette alliance qu'une ménace pour leur liberté. (Meroux de Valois, 8 October 1864, *Origines,* vol. IV, p. 229).
403. A-B P.A.X Karl. 55 H.H.S.A. no. 1, from St Petersburg 3 September (22 August) 1864). Austria's attitude in the conflict was also praised by Gorchakov. (*Ibid.* no. 8 B. 23 (11) November 1864). Russia timidly criticised Bismarck, but in essence she supported his policy, because, as Revertera later reported to Mansdorff, 'in general Prussia is the inevitable connecting link between us and Russia', and Gorchakov 'continue à me prêcher l'entente avec la Prusse'. (Reports of 19 November and no. 12C, 12 December (30 November) 1864). As Clark said, 'the Schleswig-Holstein problem had ceased to be a purely German one'. (pp. 95-96).

knew, after all, from the moment Gorchakov assumed office, that while he had continually emphasised his positive attitude towards Denmark, he had never concealed the fact that in his opinion Denmark was pursuing an erroneous policy. For seven years Gorchakov's attitude had been consistent, even if disagreeable. He had continually given Denmark advice and regretted the way she behaved. When the conflict broke out openly he had informed Denmark what role Russia intended to play in it. Russia put her own vital interests first. Her principal motto was solidarity with the two German powers because of the Polish question. Russia, Plessen concluded, would not alter her friendly attitude towards the Vienna and Berlin cabinets during the negotiations currently taking place between Denmark and the German states.[404]

The behaviour of Alexander II was similar to Gorchakov's. 'Nous ferons ce que nous pourrons', the Tsar said to Plessen during an audience at Tsarskoe Selo, 'mais ne Vous attendrez pas à ce que nous puissions effectivement améliorer Votre situation'. The Tsar had said that during his meeting with the King of Prussia he had urged on him restraint. The Tsar, wrote Plessen, hoped the King of Denmark would understand that in view of the general situation, and his personal one, Russia could adopt no other position. The Tsar had said the same thing the previous year when Plessen had presented his credentials in connection with the accession of Christian IX to the throne, Plessen recalled. Plessen said he was fully convinced that the circumstances were extremely advantageous for the victors.[405]

On the territorial question, Knorring reported from Vienna, the victors would make no concessions. Hopes that they could be persuaded to compromise over the question of indemnity were also an illusion. The financial question was the most difficult, Knorring thought.[406]

Peace was signed in Vienna on 30 October and ratifications were exchanged on 18 November 1864. Not only the German duchies of Holstein and Lauenburg but

---

404. Plessen, no. 34, 31 (19) August 1864.
405. Plessen did not change his opinion of Russia's behaviour even after the events of 1864. When Prussia and Austria concluded the convention of Gastein concerning the future of the German duchies they had seized, he wrote: 'La loyauté du Cabinet Russe à Notre égard est incontestable. La Russie voulait la conservation du Danemark dans ses limites d'autrefois. Elle le voulait parce que cette conservation répondait le mieux à ses intérêts.' And, as before, he explained Russia's behaviour by internal troubles which in his opinion looked as bad in 1865 as they had two years before, and being fully involved in internal problems she had decided to keep her distance from other matters which did not directly impinge on her interests. Because of Poland, solidarity with Prussia had been 'prime dans la situation'. And in that situation Bismarck had been the dominant factor.
Looking back in retrospect at Denmark's policy and her defeat, Plessen came to the same conclusion as before, that the loss of Norway had come about because instead of sticking to her friendship with her strongest neighbour, Russia, Denmark had been faithful to the conqueror from afar (Napoleon, in 1813). The duchies, on the other hand, had been lost, in his opinion, because Denmark had failed to show restraint in taking advantage of victory over a powerful neighbour and had not abided by the beneficial agreements negotiated by Bluhme.
Finally, Plessen came to the conclusion that in the situation created by her defeat Denmark should seek rapprochement with Prussia, however difficult that might seem to be. Plessen's report to Bluhme, no. 24, 29 (17) November 1865.
406. Cf. Plessen's report no. 38, 9 September (28 August 1864).

the whole of southern Jutland were ceded to Prussia and Austria. The territory of Denmark was reduced from 58,000 sq.m to 39,000 sq.km. The day after the signing of the treaty, F. Lecomte, Lieutenant-Colonel on the General Staff in Switzerland, wrote of the tragic situation of the little country:

Son principal enseignement (from the war, which he called 'la triste guerre de Danemark en 1864') est de montrer que si des petits états indépendants se trouvent dans une position toujours fâcheuse lorsqu'ils sont liés à un puissant voisin par des convention constituant en définitive le contrôle suprême de celui-ci, la bravoure et l'energie ne suffisent pas toujours à compenser le désavantage du nombre, ni le bon droit à procurer des alliés.[407]

A natural outcome of the defeat in Denmark was a feeling of deep bitterness and despair.

'Le sentiment national – M. Harald Nielsen wrote – a été malade et désespéré; une angoisse de mort nous a saisis et nous avons failli finir en sommeil. Nous nous sommes demandé si nous pouvions rester une nation'.[408]

And J.H. Birch wrote:

There were many who doubted whether the country would emerge from this disaster to her pride and integrity with the courage and will to face a new world. But time was to show that the Danish national spirit – Birch concluded – had not been broken by the afflictions of 1864.[409]

Another Danish historian drew this conclusion from Denmark's rich history:

Denmark is a cat that always lands on its feet.[410] Russia's policy 'd'abstention'[411] might seem to have been successful, in the sense that peace in Europe was maintained and the conservative states emerged victorious from the Danish-German conflict. But in reality, as was soon to become clear, Russian policy was short-sighted and brought several consequences for Russia herself.[412]

---

407. F. Lecomte, *Guerre du Danemark en 1864,* p. 436.
408. J. Coussange, *La Scandinavie,* (Paris, 1914), p. 56.
409. J.H. Birch, *Denmark in History,* p. 369. Cf. also Peter Ilsøe and Johs. Lomholt-Thomsen, *Nordens Historie,* vol. 1 (Copenhagen, 1964), p. 249.
410. P. Lauring, *A History of Denmark,* (Copenhagen, 1981), p. 259).
411. See Plessen's report of 29 (17) November 1865 and Wedel-Jarlsberg's of 7 January 1865 (25 December 1864).
412. Cf. Revertera's reports Nos. 8B and 8C of 23 (11) November 1864. In his report No. 12B of 12 December (30 November) 1864 Revertera argued: 'D'ailleurs, Monsieur le Comte nous chercherions vainement dans la conduite de la Cour de Russie par rapport aux Duchés une logique solidement assise sur la conscience du droit ... Il veut que la dynastie du Glücksburg continue à régner au Danemarc, mais il ne veut pas moins obtenir dans la personne du Grand Duc D'Oldenbourg la reconnaissance des anciens titres de la maison Gottorp. Ce double but étant posé comme un intérêt russe, et cela prouve suffisament que la politique, ou autrement l'intérêt russe est le seul mobile caché sous l'apparence du droit ... Dans aucune des conversations que j'ai eu [F.R.] avec M. le Prince Gortchacov au sujet des Duchés de l'Elbe, ce Ministre m'a manifesté le moindre intérêt pour les droits de la Diète de Francfort. Il semblait toujours reconnaître que l'Autriche et la Prusse pouvaient faire valoir leur droit de conquête en faveur du candidat qui, à leurs yeux, sera muni des meilleures titres, et offrirait les plus grandes garanties personnelles. Il va de soi, que c'est le Grand Duc D'Oldenbourg qui, selon le Cabinet russe, réunirait en sa personne ces précieuses qualités'.

9. The Semi-Official *Le Nord - Journal International* and the Danish-Russian Conflict

It is not surprising that the seventeenth-century Muscovite state employed such propaganda techniques as 'utilisation of the natural hatred of the Orthodox population subjugated by the Turks' in its conflicts with Turkey, or that Muscovy undertook a struggle to put an end to foreign press propaganda against Russia, including demands for the destruction of anti-Russian books abroad. Russian diplomacy had wide experience of use of both the spoken and the written word, going back to the reigns of Catherine II and Peter the Great. Peter had organised 'a literary struggle abroad against political attitudes harmful to Russia' and Catherine II improved these methods and personally participated in this propaganda through the correspondence she conducted with some of the most prominent thinkers of eighteenth-century Europe - Voltaire, Diderot and Grimm.[1] The French liberal historian Jules Michelet similarly stressed the danger of subversive Russian propaganda.

He believed that the Russian danger did not stem primarily from a threat of aggresion, from 800.000 bayonets, but from Russian propaganda which disseminated doubt and confusion in Europe by perverting Western concepts of help to the oppressed and concern for liberty. Russian propaganda aimed at paralysing the intellectual and moral understanding of the potential victims. 'Cette force dissolvante, ce froid poison, qu'elle fait circuler peu à peu, qui détend le nerf de la vie, démoralise ses futures victimes, les livre sans défense,' is of an infinite variety. 'Yesterday it (Russian propaganda) told us: I am Christianity; tomorrow it will tell us: I am socialism'.

... 'La Russie n'admet rien de nous que le mal. Elle absorbe, attire à elle tout le poison de l'Europe. Elle le rend augmenté et plus dangereux'.[2]

A similar point of view on Russian policy was formulated by Marquis A. Custine in his fascinating work *La Russie en 1839,* published in Bruxelles in 1843.[3]

'La Russie - he wrote - voit dans l'Europe une proie qui lui sera livrée tôt ou tard par nos dissensions; elle fomente chez nous l'anarchie dans l'espoir de profiter

---

1. P. Potemkin, ed. *Istoriya diplomatii,* (Moscow, 1941), pp. 247-8; Frederick G. Barghoorn, Instruments of Policy. Propaganda: Tsarist and Soviet, in *Russian Foreign Policy,* pp. 280-2; E. Halicz, *'Le Nord* o konflikcie rosyjsko-polskim i o jego perspektywach', *Zeszyty Historyczne,* no. 74, (Paris, 1985), pp. 58 ff.
2. Hans Kohn, *Russian Imperialism,* Introduction, pp. 8-9, and *Prophets and Peoples,* (N.Y., 1946), pp. 43-76. Cf. also *Panslavism,* (Notre Dame, Indiana, 1953), pp. 89 ff.
3. Cf. The English edition entitled *The Empire of the Czar* came out in London, 1843.

d'une corruption favorisée par elle parce qu'elle est favorable à ses vues: c'est l'histoire de la Pologne recommencée en grand. Depuis longues années Paris lit des journaux révolutionnaires payés par la Russie. 'L'Europe, dit-on à Pétersbourg, prend le chemin qu'a suivi la Pologne; elle s'enerve par un libéralisme vain, tandis que nous restons puissants, précisément parce que nous ne sommes pas libres: patientons sous le joug, nous ferons payer aux autres notre honte.' (Vol. IV. Lettre Trente-Sixième. Des eaux d'Ems, le 22 octobre 1839, p. 421).

Marx and Engels considered Russia shrewd and skilled in this field and accused the tsars of using their agents to manipulate public opinion in Europe and the USA by means of blackmail and bribery. In his article 'Traditional Russian Policy', published in the *New York Tribune* on 12 August 1853, Marx cites as an example of Russian propaganda activity the establishment of a consulate on Serbian territory in Orsov, a small place in which there were no Russian inhabitants at all.[4] One victim of this subversive activity was Alexander Hertzen, who was the object of a propaganda campaign organised through Baron Feodor Fircks, an attaché at the Russian embassy in Brussells, who wrote under the pseudonym D.K. Schedo-Ferroti.[5]

The great importance attached to public opinion by certain circles close to the court is also shown by a memorandum from an unknown author to Alexander II and Nesselrode in March 1856.[6] The writer of the memorandum concluded that Russia had lost the recent war not only on the battlefield but also in the moral sphere. Russia lost because opinion among the powers of Europe turned against her, which led to her total isolation. She would only be able to win in future if there were a fundamental change in the moral sphere and public opinion switched to Russia's side. Catherine II had been able to accomplish so much partly because she knew how to win public opinion. Alexander I had become the arbiter of Europe, and could do so because he was likewise supported by public opinion. Nicholas I had been successful in the war of 1829 because public opinion was prepared for this and wanted it. The press must be employed to win over public opinion and gain recognition for the Tsar as the arbiter of Europe. It would be necessary, he advised, to engage journalists and establish newspapers which would mould opinion in favour of Russia, although obviously reliance on this means alone would not be sufficient to achieve the aim.[7]

Gorchakov was alive to the question of propaganda and understood what an important role it could play, particularly in influencing public opinion in Western Europe. Consequently he maintained close contact with many Russian periodicals,

---

4. Paul W. Blackstock and Bert F. Hoselitz, *The Russian Menace to Europe,* (Glencoe, Ill. 1952), p. 166.
5. A.I. Hertzen, *Polnoe sobranie sochinenii i pisem,* ed. M.K. Lemke, Vol. 5, (Petrograd, 1919), p. 303, vol. 15, (1920), pp. 83-90, vol. 17, (1920), pp. 347-62. Cf. Rafal Gerber, 'Z dziejów prowokacji wsród emigracji polskiej w XIX wieku', in Albert Potocki, ed. *Raporty szpiega,* vol. 1, (Warsaw, 1973).
6. 'K istorii paryskogo mira 1856g. O politicheskom polozhenii Rossii posle zaklyucheniya mira', *Krasnyi Arkhiv* 1936, No. 2 (75), pp. 45-51.
7. *Ibid,* pp. 49-50.

especially in St. Petersburg, made use of the press, particularly the *Journal de St. Pétersbourg*, for the purpose of propagating the political line he had laid down, and took an active part in the discussions of the censorship. He was very concerned about his reputation in the international arena: 'Que dira l'Europe'[8] and 'Il faut bien poser la Russie dans l'opinion liberale de l'Europe' became Gorchakov's slogans.[9] To this end he decided to use *Le Nord-Journal International,* which was edited and published in Brussels[10] but was founded in 1855 on Russian initiative and enjoyed Russian material support. The editor of the paper was J.N. de Poggenpohl, who gathered around him many able publicists who were well versed in international politics, and its principal task, as Theophile Franceschi, one of its staff, explained many years later, was the promotion of Russian policy, especially in France, where the Russian nation was unknown and knowledge of Russia was distorted, mainly as a result of the Polish question.[11]

The paper did not succeed in hiding the fact that it was the mouthpiece of Gorchakov and a semi-official organ of the Russian ministry of foreign affairs. The articles on its pages were not only inspired by Gorchakov but were often written by his staff or even perhaps dictated by Gorchakov himself and sometimes contained formulations identical to those used by the minister in his discussions with diplomats.[12] The paper's editorial line thus coincided with the line authorised by Gorchakov. Furthermore, he could use its pages not only to publish his propaganda but also to sound out European opinion and even gain an impression of how certain moves, which he planned but had not yet implemented, could be received by Western governments, particularly the French government, to which Gorchakov attached so much importance.

For these reasons reading *Le Nord* is a valuable additional source for a fuller understanding of Russian policy during these years. Some problems which are not reflected in the official foreign correspondence can be studied on the basis of *Le Nord*.[13] Hence I decided to examine the position taken by *Le Nord* on the Danish-German conflict, particularly during the period from November 1863 to the conclusion of the peace treaty in Vienna.

In the years 1856-63 the paper pronounced many times on the Danish-German conflict. Its view was expressed broadly in articles such as 'La question des Duchés' (18 November 1857, 12 January 1858) and 'La politique de la Russie dans le différend Dano-allemand' (28, 29 and 30 July 1858). It expatiated on this theme in

---

8. Meshchersky, Moi vospominaniya, vol. 1, 1850-1865, (St. Petersburg, 1897), p. 305.
9. K. Schlözer, *Petersburger Briefe,* 9.X(28.IX)1859 (Berlin and Stuttgart, 1922), p. 143; K. Stählin, 'Russland und Europa'. *Historische Zeitschrift,* vol. 132, p. 212.
10. From January 1863 in Paris.
11. 'Notre Programme', *Le Nord,* 2 July 1864.
12. Thun to Rechberg, no. 6A-E, 28/16 January 1861, P.A. Russland, Karton 50, H.H.S.A. Vienna; *Bismarcks Briefwechsel mit Schleinitz 1858-1861,* (Berlin, 1905), p. 151; Halicz, *Le Nord* o konflikcie .. *Ibid.* pp. 58-66, *Fœdrelandet* called *Le Nord* the Russian organ (No. 2, 4 January 1858).
13. Danish diplomats were also well aware of the role of the Brussels paper; the diaries of Krieger and his private archive, to be found in Copenhagen (Rigsarkivet, n. 5810) are sufficient evidence of this.

1861 and 1862, especially in connection with the Gotha telegram. From November 1863 to the autumn of 1864 the Danish problem featured continually in the columns of *Le Nord,* which provided systematic information about the course of the conflict and an analysis of events. The point of departure of its analysis was the events connected with the situation resulting from the death of Frederick VII.

Informing its readers on 16 and 17 November 1863 of the death of the Danish King, the paper stated that in view of the qualities which distinguished the deceased monarch, this sad event acquired especial gravity owing to the situation in Denmark. The discussions in the Rigsraad of a new, common constitution for the monarchy and Schleswig had exacerbated the conflict with Germany. In the opinion of *Le Nord* the incorporation of Schleswig, which would be the inevitable consequence of this constitution, would encounter a vigorous reaction in certain parts of Schleswig and in the German duchies. Must one not fear, the paper asked, that in this situation there would be a repetition of the attempts in 1848, on the occasion of the death of Christian VII, to throw off Danish rule and create an independent Schleswig-Holstein? In addition - the author observed - the German Confederation had not yet expressed its agreement to the method of conducting the succession introduced by the Treaty of London of 1852 and in fact almost throughout Germany public opinion was using the occasion to speak out loudly in favour of the creation of the old [! - E.H.] state of Schleswig-Holstein. Would the German governments [of Austria and Prussia] be in a position to resist public opinion and prevent events similar to those of 1848?

In conclusion we read: The serious complications were a threat to the Elbe Duchies' affairs. These complications would be indisputably in the sphere of international affairs 'du domaine international' and the grievous prospect 'la fâcheuse perspective' would give an opportunity for convening a congress which by itself would be able to bring the conflict to a peaceful 'pacifique' solution. Whilst it was true that the Danish government maintained a conciliatory position in the Frankfurt Diet and declared that it was ready to recognise all the rights vested in the Estates of Holstein, and that in this way the complaints lodged by the German Confederation had been refuted, there remained the problem of the incorporation of Schleswig (as the paper had said many times, the writer noted) which was the real crux ('la véritable nœud') of the conflict and in respect of which the Danish government had no intention of yielding. This was demonstrated by the Hall government's acceptance of the concept of a new and common constitution for the monarchy and Schleswig, which was the prelude to definitive incorporation ('prélude d'une incorporation définitive').

As we can see from these passages, the appropriate emphasis had already been made. Disapproval of Hall's policy was expressed without any consideration of the motives which guided him in introducing the new constitution, while at the same time, in contrast to liberal-nationalist elements in Germany, there was sympathy for the difficult situation in which the larger German states found themselves. From the beginning *Le Nord* was firmly opposed to the claims of Prince Augustenburg. 'Une grande fermentation règne dans le Holstein', said the paper when Frederick of Schleswig-Holstein-Augustenburg officially claimed the rights to the Elbe duchies for himself and his family (20 November), and 'the affairs of Denmark, as we predicted, are taking yet another turn for the worse'.

This line of thought was developed in the issue of the paper on 1 December. Seeing, on the one hand, the vigour with which Germany opposed the incorporation of Schleswig into the Kingdom of Denmark in the narrow sense of the word, and, on the other, the growth of tension in the duchies, which could lead to uprising despite the presence of Danish troops there and the military measures taken by the authorities, the writer doubted whether the mounting difficulties could be successfully overcome, although both the larger German states were exercising moderation and the Danish government was adopting a conciliatory tone. It was significant that, following the *Gazette de l'Allemagne,* published in Berlin (the issue of 28 November), *Le Nord* cited Russell's opinion on the Schleswig question, expressed in 1861, and also quoted Gorchakov's memorandum of 24 May 1862 on the matter, in which the Russian minister adopted the following position:

Jusqu'à présent les Allemands qui habitent le Schleswig n'ont pas eu une autorité tutélaire spéciale ou un organe au moyen duquel ils puissent légalement faire parvenir leurs vœux et leurs plaintes aux pieds du trône, le droit de pétition n'y existe pas. Il est donc naturel que le gouvernement danois ne puisse être informé toujours avec exactitude et avec une parfaite impartialité de leurs vrais besoins et de l'esprit dans lesquels ses intentions sont remplies chez eux. Ni le Danemark ni la Confédération ne sauraient se prévaloir du fait que le Schleswig n'est pas membre de la Confédération germanique. Il existe entre eux, relativement à ce duché des engagements réciproques, dont l'exécution impartiale jusqu'à présent du côté du Danmark réclame le concours des deux parties qui ont contracté en 1851 et 1852.

'Ces paroles sont assez claires pour l'Allemagne contre le traité de Londres, dont les conséquences désastreuses se manifestent de plus en plus. Heureusement que la Diète germanique ne l'a pas reconnu'. The quotation of this last sentence from the *Gazette de l'Allemagne du Nord* without any comment on the part of *Le Nord* told its own story.

Le Nord shared the opinion expressed by the Berlin newspaper, and added that the contrast between the democratic conditions prevailing in Denmark itself, where there was freedom of the press, the right to lodge petitions and freedom of assembly, and the absence of freedom in Schleswig-Holstein, which was treated as a conquered province ('une province conquise'), was symptomatic. In this situation the duchies were not in a position to present their demands and wishes. *Le Nord,* like Russian diplomacy, regarded the Danish government's withdrawal at the beginning of December (on 4 December) of the decree of 30 March 1863 concerning Holstein as a meaningless step and quite insufficient in the new situation which arose after the King had signed the November Constitution. This decree had played a negative role and its withdrawal at the appropriate time could have diminished the hopes of the ultra-Danish party and the suspicions of the Germans. The fact that neither Prussia nor Austria would submit to being outvoted by the German Assembly in Frankfurt, on the other hand, was greeted with approval. (*Le Nord,* 8 December).

Le Nord came to the conclusion that no Danish government, neither under Hall nor under Monrad, nor even under General Oxholm (that is, a conservative one – E.H.), would be in a position to take measures which could end the crisis unless the constitution were withdrawn. But a quick decision was essential as Prussia and Austria were under growing pressure from the lesser German states and were outnumbered by them in the German Union.

The paper considered the behaviour of the major European powers when German troops occupied Schleswig; would they remain calm 'à une occupation du Schlesvig par des troupes allemandes, ou bien s'opposeront-elles à ce que la Prusse et l'Autriche prennent les mesures nécessaires pour faire respecter un acte international auquel elles viennent de sacrifier dans une certaine mesure leurs devoirs fédéraux, en se constituant à Francfort les défenseurs des intérêts allemands? Le débat prend ainsi dès à présent un caractère européen.' (Résumé, Paris, 30 Décember 1863).

The debate in Frankfurt thus acquired a European character. The need to convene a conference for the purpose of settling the conflict, which was threatening to assume considerable proportions, was beyond discussion. But there was no hiding the fact that it was hard to establish the competences of such a diplomatic assembly ('les attributions de cette réunion diplomatique'); it was also hard to distinguish what were European and what narrowly German questions. (Le Nord, 31 December).

It is characteristic that the paper, following the *Journal de St. Pétersbourg* and the Prussian conservative *La Gazette de la Croix,* twice reprinted the text of the Warsaw protocol of 1851, on 18 and 23 January 1864, as proof that in 1851 Russia had indeed renounced her rights to the duchy of Gottorp-Holstein, but not in favour of Prince Augustenburg. It added that the St. Petersburg cabinet had declared to many German courts that it would take up the question of its rights to Gottorp-Holstein again if the provisions of the Treaty of London were annulled.

From the beginning of February the question of the crossing of the Eider by Prussian and Austrian troops occupied a central place in Le Nord. Characteristically, it defended the moves made by Bismarck and the position he then adopted towards Schleswig. As we know, Bismarck argued that the two German states intended to occupy Schleswig in defence of the provisions of the Treaty of London and regarded the fact of the occupation as a pledge designed to compel Denmark to comply with the provisions of that treaty. This encountered a categorical refusal on the part of Copenhagen. Le Nord criticised the position taken by the Danish government, blaming Copenhagen rather than Berlin for the possible outbreak of war.

M. Monrad ne vient-il pas de déclarer en plein *Folkthing* que le meilleur indice de la politique de la Prusse se trouve dans les paroles même de M. Bismarck; que, tandis que ce ministre dit au Danemark que la Prusse prend Schleswig comme un gage, afin de forcer le Cabinet de Copenhague à remplir les engagements de 1851 it 1852, il déclare à la Chambre prusienne qu'en prenant ce gage, son but est de détruire ces mêmes engagements? Nous craignons fort – replied *Le Nord* – que M. Monrad ne se trompe; M. de Bismarck ne s'est pas rendu coupable de la contradiction qu'il lui reproche; le président du cabinet de Berlin a toujours déclaré, aussi bien dans ces actes diplomatiques que devant les Chambres prusiennes, que la Prusse saisirait le Schleswig à titre de gage seulement, et pour rappeler le Danemark a l'observation des traités, par lesquels elle se croyait elle-même engagée. L'erreur du ministre danois est d'autant plus déplorable, argues *Le Nord* cynically - - qu'en jetant un jour complétement faux sur la politique des grandes puissances allemandes et en éveillant sur celles-ci les soupçons injustes des Danois, elle diminue sensiblement les chances que cette politique offrait au maintien de la paix et de l'intégrité de la monarchie danoise.

Si la question du Schleswig-Holstein, si difficile pour elle-même, qui touche à tant d'intérêts, à tant de susceptibilités, doit se compliquer encore de ces malentendus par lesquels la presse anglaise aime tant à embrouiller toutes les affaires et dont M. Monrad ne se garde peut-être pas assez alors, il n'y a plus de doute, la guerre est inévitable – concluded *Le Nord* on 1 February 1864.

The chief publicist on the paper, Max Guttenstein, in an article published on 5 February under the title 'L'entrée de l'armée austro-prusienne dans le Schleswig', undertook a fundamental defence of the policy of the larger German states, particularly Prussia. In his view, in the immensely complicated situation which was the result of Denmark's policy over many years and of her attitude to the just and well-founded German demands, Prussia and Austria faced an unprecedentedly difficult task; how to reconcile their positions as both German and European states:

Chercher à concilier leur position de puissances allemandes avec leur position de puissances européennes, et à faire triompher les doits de l'Allemagne dans les duchés, sans compromettre la paix européenne en provoquant des modifications dans l'état territorial de l'Europe, telle était la tâche qui s'imposait à l'Autriche et à la Prusse.[14]

This task presented them with extremely difficult and numerous obstacles especially in the shape of public opinion in Germany, which was generally in favour of an extremist solution – demanding the establishment of an independent state of Schleswig-Holstein, which should be included in the German Confederation, and the transfer of this newly created state to Prince Augustenburg, thus refusing to recognise the King of Denmark as the ruler of the duchies, which was equivalent to annulment of the Treaty of London.

It was not the purpose of his article, wrote Guttenstein, to describe the course of Austria's and Prussia's struggles with the German Confederation. It was sufficient to recall that their achievement was that the entry into Holstein took place in the framework of a military distraint, rather than occupation, and that by this means the question of the succession was merely placed in suspension. Unfortunately, the blame for the resulting state of affairs, namely that the Prussian and Austrian armies had entered Schleswig, and that this was not done in a peaceful manner, lay with Copenhagen. It would not listen to the advice of 'many countries' [essentially only Russia – E.H.] and events had moved with unbelievable speed. Prince Fre-

---

14. The same problem was broached by *Revue des Deux Mondes* in 'Revue de la semaine', *Revue ...,* Vol. 49, 31 January 1864, pp. 762-3.

derick had been proclaimed ruler of Holstein and bands of volunteers had invaded Schleswig in order to throw off Danish rule. This had been greeted with applause in Germany.

Faced with this difficult situation, Prussia and Austria had decided to propose the occupation of Schleswig to the German Assembly, if Denmark did not revoke the November Constitution. The fate of that proposal was well known – it was rejected. But the German states had not abandoned their plan. The aggressive actions of the people of Holstein and part of Germany, directed against Denmark, had to be restrained, and time was pressing, said the author, thus justifying the behaviour of Austria and Prussia. Was the step taken by Vienna and Berlin, he asked, a threat to Denmark? Had their armies entered Schleswig in order to incite a revolt against Denmark in the province?

To answer these questions in the affirmative one had to be either blind or ignorant. Had the Prussian and Austrian proposals at Frankfurt not clearly stated that the occupation of Schleswig was to be solely for the purpose of making Denmark carry out the obligations it had undertaken in 1851-52? Would not the provisions of the treaty and the integrity of Denmark be upheld if Denmark carried out the obligations it had undertaken? The aim of Prussia and Austria, and the purpose of their action on the Eider – here the cynicism of the author, or rather of his principals, or paymasters, reached a peak – was 'seulement de sauver et non de démembrer la monarchie danoise'. But Denmark (his peroration continued) would not make the concessions which would have prevented the invasion by Austrian and Prussian troops. In view of the difficulties they had encountered in Frankfurt, Austria and Prussia had to act with great openness and vigour and could not give Denmark any period of grace. The moment the Eider was crossed the military action had begun.

It was a matter for some comfort that although the reverberations of the affair had been going on for three days there was nothing to indicate that the great powers would become involved in the conflict and no word of protest had been heard except from Sweden. Was it possible that Europe would calmly watch the course of a war which could result in the break-up of the Danish monarchy and disturb the balance of power in Europe? Obviously not. The signatories of the Treaty of London saw nothing in the action of Austria and Prussia which conflicted with the integrity of Denmark.

If the aims of the war were to change, that would be sad and a matter for regret. But it was to be hoped that it would not come to the point where one match would start a fire in Europe.

S'il en était, ainsi – et il serait infiniment désirable que nous ne nous trompassions pas, – si la lutte engagée en ce moment dans le Schlesvig ne portait que sur une question de constitution et excluait toute idée de modification territoriale, elle serait encore bien regrettable et bien douloureuse, il est vrai, mais du moins pourrait-on nourrir l'espoir de la voir se terminer rapidement et de voir rater, pour cette fois, "l'allumette qui devait allumer l'Europe". (*Le Nord*, 5 February 1864).[15]

15. By Max Guttenstein.

Another writer for the paper, Camille Guinhut,[16] attacked the *Morning Post* – the semi-official organ of Palmerston – on 6 February and expressed his disbelief in the effectiveness of action in defence of Denmark. 'L'Angleterre, que nous sachions, n'a jamais fait la guerre pour une idée. A plus forte raison ne le ferait-elle pas pour un sentiment. Est-ce la crainte de voir éventuellement se former une marine allemande assez forte pour lui disputer la domination de la mer du Nord'?[17] If Britain were really concerned about anything it was Helgoland – a very important naval base.

Certes, la cause de l'integrité du Danmark vaut la peine qu'on fasse preuve en sa faveur de résolution et d'énergie, et nous ne trouvons rien que très – louable à ce que le gouvernement britannique se montrât décidé à s'en faire le champion, si elle était réellement en danger. Mais en voyant jusqu'ici la Russie et la France demeurer calmes, nous ésperons – argued Guinhut – que cet intérêt majeur n'est pas encore sérieusement compromis, et nous craignons que les démonstrations anglaises, en donnant au Danemark l'espoir d'être soutenu, et en engageant le point d'honneur de la Prusse et de l'Autriche, n'aient contribué plutôt à précipiter les hostilités, et ne risquent d'éloigner la solution désirable.

The Danes should not be deluded by memories of 1849, we read in *Le Nord* on 12 February. At that time Prussia was preoccupied and had many problems. Germany was in disarray and Denmark could count on successful resistance. Now conditions were different. France and Russia were passive, and as for Britain's theoretical encouragement, no one would be deceived. The defeat of Denmark was inevitable and any attempt to avert it would only prolong this ruinous struggle ('une lutte ruineuse'). This was understood by General Meza, who had preserved the army unscathed by withdrawing it to Dannewirke.

War could have fatal consequences. 'Ce serait peut-être beaucoup demander à l'Autriche et la Prusse victorieuses de se contenter du rétablissement pur et simple de *status quo ante bellum.* (emphasis in the original) Le Danemark vaincu subira la loi du plus fort?' [! E.H.] Being in no doubt about the course of the action and the final outcome, the writer listed the demands which the victors would probably put forward: 'Une indemnité de guerre, compensation des dépenses d'hommes et d'argent faites pour le réduire, sera peut-être réclamée, des garanties plus solides, plus onéreuses, relativement la constitution des duchés seront sans doute exigées; mais l'integrité de la monarchie danoise, qui n'est pas seulement un intérêt danois, à ce titre, n'est pas en cause dans la lutte actuelle et ne dois pas en subir les conséquences'. (*Le Nord,* 13 February 1864) Thus as early as February 1864 a journalist under the wing of Gorchakov had publicly formulated the programme of demands which Prussia and Austria would make from Denmark. This could only encourage Bismarck to more vigorous action.

Le Nord also repudiated rumours that France was preparing to attack Prussia: 'il est bien entendu que nous n'acceptons que sous toute reserve la mention d'une

---

16. Executive Editor.
17. 'L'Angleterre fasse jamais la guerre pour une question d'honneur,' were Gorchakov's words to Napier at the beginning of February 1864. Lord Redesdale, *Memories,* vol. 1 p. 245.

nouvelle aussi *grave* (emphasis added) qui, en tout état de cause, nous paraît pour le moins prématurée', we read on 14 February. 'Si nous la relevons, c'est qu'elle est, au main l'état de bruit, dans les limites de la situation actuelle, et qu'elle peut être considerée comme un echo naturel des velléités d'annexion que l'on prête au gouvernement prussien'.

Le Nord concentrated on attacking the uncompromising position adopted by the Monrad government. The Danish government's refusal to take part in the London Conference seemed to it regrettable. ('La réponse du Danemark', 28 February)

Le peuple danois – wrote *Le Nord* – sous la pression duquel le gouvernement a évidemment agi, a perdu de vue les exigences de la situation. Il a trop oublié que ce qui fait l'unique force du Danemark dans le conflit actuel, c'est la sauvegarde de l'Europe, gardienne de son intégrité dans un intérêt d'équilibre.

En répudiant le patronage du concert européen, en rompant la chaîne diplomatique qui le relie par le traité de Londres à l'édifice du droit international, le Danemark, commet un acte encore plus imprudent qu'héroïque. En risquant de donner au conflit dano-allemand les proportions d'une guerre générale, et peut-être en spéculant en cette éventualité, le Danemark reconnaît mal la sollicitude que lui a toujours temoignée l'Europe et se conduit à l'égard de celle-ci d'une façon répréhensible. ... Les nations faibles – warned Th. Franceschi – sont tenues à plus de sagesse encore que les fortes. Ce qui peut-être pour celles-ci que le sacrifice des forces et de la prospérité d'une génération à l'honneur national, peut équivaloir pour les premières à un véritable suicide, et un peuple n'a jamais le droit de se suicider. (*Le Nord,* 28 February).

The paper's sympathies, like those of the St. Petersburg cabinet, lay with Christian IX. In an article with the title 'Christian IX et le peuple danois',[18] we find this passage: 'Christian IX est placé littéralement entre "l'enclume et le marteau", entre les exigences armées de l'Allemagne et l'exaspération patriotique de son peuple'. The Danes presented their King with a choice which was as difficult as it was dangerous – abdication or a coup d'état. Abdication would be equivalent to the collapse of the monarchy. A coup d'état carried out with the help of the army, among which the King was becoming more and more popular, from the military point of view would be equivalent to the desertion of Schleswig – from the moral point of view an act 'de salut publique' for which the responsibility would fall on Christian IX alone, 'une responsibilité bien lourde dans des circonstances extrêmes auxquelles l'union intime du peuple danois et de son souverain suffirait à peine pour parer'.

A call to Denmark to change its position and agree to participate in the conference, which enjoyed the support of both Russell and Gorchakov, was the principal line of an article on 29 February. *Le Nord* expected Denmark to change its attitude to the peace proposals owing to the impossibility of forcing the German powers to evacuate Schleswig before they had achieved the aims for which they had entered it. Despite bravery and heroism, Denmark was, after all, in no position to drive the German troops out of Schleswig.

18. By Th. Franceschi.

The political situation in Europe at the end of February and the beginning of March was described by the editor-in-chief of the paper[19] as '*l'imbroglio* diplomatique'. (*Le Nord,* 2 March) It was the result of the transitional state of Europe at the time. Europe had changed and was no longer as it had been in 1815, but was not yet the new Europe. This situation was the consequence of the weakness of statesmen who saw the danger ('ce malaise général' referred to by Napoleon III in his November appeal), but few of whom had the boldness to understand and avert it. In some cases the reason was that they lacked the energy, others lacked the power and yet others lacked the intelligence, and almost all were too old. Hence they were incapable of adapting to the new situation together with the fears, changes of opinion, hesitations and contractions which it brought ('ces réticences, ces craintes, ces revirements, ces hésitations, ces flagrantes contradictions'), in its wake, new evidence of which was provided by European diplomacy every day.

Although he pointed to Napoleon III as an example, the writer of the article seems to have been thinking principally of Palmerston and Russell when he spoke of helmsmen of European diplomacy who were too old and unable to adapt to the new situation. But did he really not appreciate that his remarks could apply equally well to the ageing Gorchakov?

In an article under the title 'Les anomalies de la situation' on 4 March, Poggenpohl, referring to the article of 2 March, tried to explain in what way the international situation was abnormal. It was because relations were not at their best either between Britain and France or within the German Confederation. Austria and Prussia had drawn closer together, but their interests were in conflict as far as the duchies were concerned. Russia had moved closer to Prussia and Austria, but the reason for this was the Polish question, and this rapprochement was neutralised by the attitude of France and Austria to the same issue.

Following the official Russian view, Poggenpohl expressed his fears that the war in Denmark could spread and envelop the whole of northern Europe, leading to the development of a revolutionary movement in the province of Poznań, in Hungary, and possible in Venice too, and causing a ministerial crisis in Britain.

Thus at the beginning of spring the political horizon in Europe was darkening. The lack of agreement among states made it more difficult to achieve consolidation and peace. Hence the eagerness to convene a conference in which the interested states would participate. But could one be sure that it would also serve to prevent war? To this question the answer was 'qu'il est vrai de dire qu'il ne faut jurer de rien ...'.

In this uncertain and increasingly entangled international situation in northern Europe there was a possibility that the idea of Scandinavianism would gain prominence in the Scandinavian countries, and that a defeated and truncated Denmark might join them in a Scandinavian union. This problem featured more and more frequently in the pages of *Le Nord,* which took an identical position on the matter to that of Russian diplomacy, firmly attacking any manifestations of Scandina-

---

19. Poggenpohl.

vianism as a threat to the political balance in northern Europe. Basically it was a question of Russian interests. *Le Nord* conducted a campaign against the French press, and principally *Revue des Deux Mondes,* on this matter and also against the Swedish press's advocacy of the necessity of political rapprochement between Denmark and Sweden-Norway.

Camille Guinhut expressed disquiet at the growth of the Scandinavian idea in Denmark and Sweden. However, if Schleswig were detached from Denmark, he reasoned, then there would be the problem of the loss of Jutland and the natural capital for these parts of Denmark would be Hamburg rather than Copenhagen. ('L'idée Scandinave, En Danemark et en Suède',[20] *Le Nord,* (8 March) But intellectually Denmark was closely connected with Germany and the sympathies of the upper classes were pro-German rather than pro-Swedish. Only the bourgeoisie and the intelligentsia, a considerable part of which was of German origin, was opposed to the German incursion.

If Denmark were given the right to choose between absorption by Germany or by Sweden, the majority of the population would probably incline towards the former, at least in the continental part of the Kingdom. To a large extent this was a result of the policy currently being pursued by Sweden. Basically, however, it was not this but the territorial integrity of Denmark which was predominant, with France, Britain and Russia seemingly in agreement on this principle, since none of these powers wanted any threat to peace in Europe. It depended on Prussia and Austria, however, as to whether the war remained localised or became a general conflict, wrote *Le Nord* on 10 March.

Like Gorchakov, *Le Nord* (14 March) strove to make light of the entry of German troops into Jutland, regarding it as a purely military problem. It also made light of London's attacks and the accusations directed against Austria and Prussia concerning outrages committed by the German troops, which in the paper's opinion were counterbalanced by the goodwill ('la complaisance') which they had displayed. They had expressed their wish to join in the conference and had given assurances that they supported the integrity of Denmark. The paper perceived signs of caution in all this and a policy consistent with the interest of Europe, since the Austro-Prussian alliance was directed both against the excessive aspirations of the German national party and of the diametrically opposite tendencies represented by the Scandinavian party. Both of these, although they cherished different aims, sough the break-up of Denmark, which was contrary to the maintenance of equilibrium in Europe.

Although, as *Le Nord* recognised, confidence in the disinterestedness of the Austro-Prussian coalition had been somewhat shaken, the paper regarded its policy as within reasonable limits and designed to maintain the balance of power (14 March). Disturbance of this balance, as was explained in articles on 26 March and

20. 'Tant que le Schleswig reste uni au Danemark, ce royaume peut à la vigueur continuer à exister seul, mais la séparation du Schleswig entraînerait infailliblement la perte du Jutland, dont la capitale naturelle serrait plutôt Hambourg que Copenhague.' (By C. Guinhut).

2 and 12 April, would mainly serve the interests of France. Following correspondence from St. Petersburg on 7 March, *Le Nord* criticised *Revue des Deux Mondes* for its attacks on Russia's attitude towards the Danish-German war.[21] In its reply *Le Nord* asserted that the aim of the *Revue* was the division of Denmark and the subsequent fusion and unity of Scandinavia.[22] Russia could not be interested in seeing the history of the Black Sea repeated and the Baltic come under the control of a single relatively strong state which at an appropriate time would be able to close the Baltic. It was not a question of trade in peace-time, of course, but of the serious consequences in time of war if a Scandinavian union took the opposite side to Russia. Therefore the conception of Scandinavian union advocated by the *Revue* was unacceptable to Russia. In any case, added *Le Nord,* the whole problem would not have existed if Denmark had fulfilled its legal obligations towards Germany as she had been advised.

Mais le gouvernement danoise s'est laissé dominer par l'école révolutionnaire qui n'écoute que la passion, ne respecte aucun droit, ne ménage rien ni personne. Une crise était donc inévitable. Lorsqu'elle a éclaté, le gouvernement russe a tout fait pour l'apaiser ou la restreindre, dans la conviction que le plus médiocre arrangement vaut mieux que la meilleure guerre, parce que celle-ci impose des sacrifices, déchaîne des passions, perpétue des haînes, amène des représsailles qui ouvrent la porte à des calamités sans fin. (*Le Nord,* 26 March).[23]

This was a defence of the policy and conduct of Prussia and the conservative camp, and demonstrated firm opposition to France's thoughts of possible joint action with Sweden against Prussia, but it was also a sharp attack on the democratic government of Denmark for its refusal to capitulate to Germany. This anti-Danish campaign was continued in the article headed 'Le Danemark et le principe des nationalités' in which the paper criticised articles in the Swedish press, especially in the Stockholm, *Nya Dagligt Allehanda,* defending Denmark. *Le Nord* accused the national-liberal party in Denmark and Sweden of changing its tactics and implied that it supported a national uprising, in the expectation of similar outbreaks in Hungary, Poland and Italy. Analogous phrases, and fears of the development of a revolutionary movement in Europe, were also contained in the secret memoranda from Gorchakov to the Russian ambassadors in European capitals during these months. Furthermore, the paper enquired captiously whether the Scandinavianists' plans did not also include aims such as making Finland the Schleswig of

---

21. See *Revue ...,* vol. 49, pp. 252, 1008, 1018; *Chronique de la quinzaine,* 31 December 1863 and 14 February 1864.
22. See *Revue* about the union the Scandinavian countries: '... l'union scandinave ne peut se former un jour, elle ne peut subsister, pour le bien de l'Europe et du Nord, qu'à la condition que chacun des trois peuples destinés à la composer soit intact et respecté. Nul d'entre eux n'entend chercher un joug au milieu de ses frères et de choisir parmi eux un maître, et c'est sur la base d'une dévouement commun, non sur celle d'un calcul égoiste, qu'une telle union, pour être conforme aux vœux et aux intérêts de notre temps, peut se contracter et devenir féconde'. Vol. 51, p. 756; Chronique ..., 31 May 1864.
23. By C. Guinhut.

Scandinavia. This threat, which, as it were, hung over Scandinavia, is also taken up in another part of the article 'Le Danemark et le principe des nationalités'. (*Le Nord,* 2 April) But in essence *Le Nord* did not believe in this, as it was convinced that the Danish nation, like the other Scandinavian nations, were nations of peasants and sailors, deeply conservative and moderate. Denmark, it said, was a country in which there were no social problems which could be exploited by utopians.

In its article 'La Solution du suffrage universel dans la question danoise' (2 April), *Le Nord* took a similar attitude towards the French plan for a referendum in Schleswig as the Russian government. In the paper's opinion, quite apart from serious reservations of principle, this solution could not be put into effect for practical reasons. 'Comment concilier d'abord la sincérité de l'expression des vœux populaires avec l'état actuel des esprits dans les duchés? Comment faire fond sur les suffrages émis dans les circonstances présentes?' Did not Gorchakov and Brunnow use just the same arguments in relation to the French proposals? Moreover, we read in *Le Nord* on 12 April in the article 'Le suffrage universel dans la question dano-allemande', if the population had to choose between Denmark and Prince Augustenburg, it would create a dangerous precedent.

Le Nord recognised that after the Prussians captured Düppel Denmark's situation had become more difficult:

Ainsi la destruction de l'armée danoise est désormais imminente. Il faut – the paper appealled – que la Conférence intervienne, et cela sans perdre une minute. En Europe, qui ne veut pas que la monarchie danoise perisse, ne peut pas vouloir davantage que l'unique armée danoise soit anéantie. Laisser celle-ci avec son matériel devenir la proie de ses ennemis, équivaut à supprimer le Danemark comme puissance européenne. Il ne se remettrait jamais d'une pareille atteinte, et serait pour toujours livré à la merci du prémier assaillant. Si donc on veut réellement sauver le Danemark, il faut aviser sans délai. L'établissement d'un armitrice est le premier point que doive régler la Conférence; le reste doit passer après, sous peine de devenir complètement inutile. ('La Prise de Duppel', 20 April.)[24]

... Il faut reconnaître que cet échec a bien plus d'importance que l'abandon du Danevirke ... C. Guinhut wrote. (28 April).

La force de résistance du Danemark – sinon entièrement détruite, du moins paralysée pour longtemps, le Jutland entier à la merci des Allemands, une grande humiliation nationale infligée aux Danois, – car l'impuissance est toujours humiliante, quelque supérieure que soit la force de l'adversaire, – voilà les résultats dont il semble que la Prusse devrait se contenter ...

... En attentant, à Copenhague on espère contre tout espoir. Les journaux qui encouragent à la résistance font toujours entrevoir au public la possibilité de commotions prochaines en Europe ... Toute cette politique ressemble un peu à celle de l'insurrection polonaise. Espérons qu'elle n'aura pas des conséquences trop fatales pour le pays qu'on veut sauver ... Les Danois ont-ils placé leur espoir dans la Révolution? Bien des signes paraissent l'indiquer ... Evidemment les Danois ne se rendent pas assez compte de la différence radicale qui existe entre le libéralisme incolore des boureois de Copenhague et les aspirations de la *schliachta* polonaise ou des volontaires garibaldiens ... ('La situation morale et militaire du Danemark', 28 April).

24. By A. Luçon.

But the only way out of the situation, in view of the impossibility of resisting the Germans and, as events demonstrated, the indifference of Europe to the Danes' national theories, was a peaceful solution. ('Les alternatives de la politique danoise', 29 April). The setbacks which the Danes suffered during the course of the London Conference *Le Nord* blamed mainly, if not wholly on the Danish government and the national-liberal party, which it described as doctrinaire.

Le Nord published a series of articles discussing the course of the conference; 'Le parti doctrinaire en Danemark' (8 May), 'La crise ministérielle à Copenhague' (13 May) 'Le Danemark à la conférence de Londres' (18 May), 'Le démembrement du Danemark' (30 May), 'La conférence de Londres et le Danemark' (9 June), 'La Situation' (18 June). Reflecting on the reason for the reverses sustained at the conference, the writer came to the conclusion that the blame lay with the Danish government and the 'doctrinaire' national-liberal party. Twelve years of experience, we read on 8 May, had taught the party nothing. The conduct of the representatives of the Monrad government at the conference furnished new and indisputable evidence that the government could see that the methods of conciliation and compromise which it had employed over the past twelve years had satisfied neither the Danes nor the Germans. The aim of the Danish national party was the incorporation of Schleswig into Denmark, while the Schleswig-Holstein party sought to merge Schleswig into Germany. A partition on the basis of nationality would have been more logical, because it would have sanctioned the division which already existed. But there was no knowing how such an attempt at a solution of the problem would be received by either side.

It seemed, said *Le Nord,* that Monrad preferred to leave the problem unsettled until more favourable conditions would allow the national party to carry out its programme in respect of Schleswig. Monrad was not regarded as a fanatical advocate of Helstat, but both he and many members of his government shared the national party's belief in palliatives and he undoubtedly wanted to retain Schleswig for Denmark. But both he and the majority of Danish statesmen combined these clear nationalistic tendencies with great uncertainty as to the means of implementing their plans.

This was characteristic of the class which the revolution of 1848 had brought to power in Copenhagen.[25] The Danish bourgeoisie had come into being during the reigns of Frederick VI and Christian VII, the paper explained, and had immediately become a very active force. Lawyers and professors at the University of Copenhagen had quickly gained influence[26] and had come to the conclusion that their direct influence on political life was not commensurate with their place in the intellectual life of the country. According to them, the old bureaucracy in the duchies did not sufficiently understand the separatist tendencies in the duchies, although it came mainly from urban circles and its views conformed to the semi-German

25. See: 'Le Parti Doctrinaire en Danemark', 8 May. By C. Guinhut.
26. The writer was surely thinking of politicians like C.C. Hall, P. Vedel, C.E. Fenger and A.F. Krieger.

ideals of the court. Patriotism and fear of the break-up of the monarchy were characteristic of the liberal press. Poets and enthusiasts proclaimed Scandinavianism as an effective defence against their neighbours to the east and the south.

More practical people supported the idea of a frontier on the Eider, a constitutional system and a common parliament. Their guiding principle was a similar ideal to that of the national party in Germany, the Nationalverein. And there was nothing surprising about this, explained *Le Nord:* the majority of the Danish intelligentsia was closely connected with Germany 'malgré la haîne un peu factice des Danois contre cette nationalité. Les noms de la plupart des chefs du parti ultranational trahissent leur origine allemande'. German liberal theories had found a fertile breeding ground in the liberal party in Denmark and in 1848 many politicians in the party had shared German liberal ideas. Berlin University had exerted an influence on Copenhagen for many years. The doctrinaire party thought that it was enough to introduce a constitution and merge Schleswig with the Danish monarchy in the narrow meaning of the word, and that then national unity would be achieved. History showed that parliamentarianism had never meant national unity and unity was not built with its help – a characteristic generalisation which accorded with the practice of Russian absolutism.

First of all, Schleswig had to be assimilated. A constitution could be introduced afterwards, as a result of this unity. The liberals had followed the opposite course and this was the source of the difficulties. Ministers from the Helstat party had temporarily saved Denmark by sacrificing the fundamental idea of the constitution of 5 June 1848, which remained in force only in Denmark proper ('le Danemark proprement dit'). But this government had fallen under pressure from the national party.

Basically, the article argued, the Danish doctrinaire politicians wer not really revolutionaries, they were 'd'une nature inoffensive'. They admired John Hampden[27] and George Washington.[28] They wanted only a frontier on the Eider. They were opposed by many Danish diplomats. The party had brought about the conflict with Germany, and what had finally exasperated the Germans was the adoption of the Constitution of 18 November 1863. As *Le Nord* pointed on 8 and 18 May:

L'exaspération les Allemands était au comble, lorsque le ministère, sous la pression du parti national, proposa en fit voter la Constitution du 18 Novembre 1863. On pouvait donc considérer le principe du "Helstat" comme définitivement abandonné des deux côtés ...

Aujourd'hui, il paraît que le parti doctrinaire, en désespoir de cause, ne demande pas mieux que de revenir aux essais stériles du "Helstat" qu'il a lui-même combattus pendant de longues années, mais on peut, sans être pessimiste, affirmer que toute proposition dans ce sens, surtout venue de la part de M. Monrad et consorts, sera repoussée avec la plus grande unanimité par les habitants des duchés et par l'Allemagne entière. (18 May).[29]

27. 1595-1643. One on the leaders of the republican party in England during the civil war.
28. 1732-1799. General and first President of the USA.
29. By O. Gunlogsen.

Le Nord welcomed the departure of A.L. Casse, the Minister of Justice, and C.L.V.R. Nutzhorn, the Minister of Internal Affairs, from the government, [they resigned on 10 May 1864 – E.H.] describing them as advocates of 'résistance à outrance', but in view of their relatively minor role in the government it noted with regret that those with doctrinaire views were still predominant. The author of the article 'La crise ministérielle à Copenhague' (13 May) did not believe in the possibility of reaching an agreement in London, as long as power in Denmark remained in the hands of the same government. Agreement with the Germans would be extremely difficult if not impossible to achieve. Was Vedel, Hall's right-hand man, not in reality acting minister in place of Quaade (who of course was leading the Danish delegation at the London Conference), asked *Le Nord*. This question, set against the assertion that the government in Copenhagen was not capable of bringing the negotiations to a favourable outcome, told its own story.

Although *Le Nord* called itself a liberal and impartial paper ('Notre programme', 2 July), essentially it was not so and, being dependent on the Russian cabinet, could not be so. It fully approved the policy of the conservative German powers, disapproved of the policy of German liberal circles and vehemently opposed the candidature of Prince Augustenburg. It subjected the policy of the Danish government to crushing criticism, much sharper than, for tactical reasons, Gorchakov could allow himself personally.

In this context the articles 'Le démembrement du Danemark' (30 May) and 'La conférence de Londres et le Danemark' (9 June) are illuminating. The first contains a shattering criticism of what had occured in the duchies, namely that the sovereign – the King of Denmark recognised throughout Europe – had been deposed by military intervention. The people of Schleswig and Holstein had not done this. Europe, assuming that the break-up of Denmark was a *fait accompli,* had adopted the principle of non-intervention. Earlier there would have been intervention against the people in support of rulers whom they no longer wanted. But would the annexation of Schleswig-Holstein by Germany not sanctify a new kind of intervention directed not against populations but sovereigns? Did this have fewer negative features than the previous kind, was it not no less of a threat to the general peace?

The article was concerned both with attacking Prince Augustenburg and German liberal circles and with defending the idea of personal union of the duchies with Denmark and the establishment of the Danish King, Christian IX, as ruler of the duchies.

The paper spoke out against widespread rumours in the European press on the subject of a possible neutralisation of Denmark under a protectorate guaranteed by Europe, or on conferment of a statute such as Belgium enjoyed after it gained its independence and status of neutrality in 1831. In criticised the argument put forward in the Paris *Constitutionnel* that after Denmark had lost the duchies, Kiel and Rendborg, it should be declared a neutral state in order to guarantee its security and protect it against possible aggression on the part of Germany. *Le Nord* scoffed at the so-called guarantee from Europe and asked if it was not generally known that such guarantees meant nothing, citing as an example the infringement by A. Cuza of the treaties guaranteed in 1858. There was no way, said the author, of giving Denmark a guarantee against German attack. 'Est-il étonnant, après cela, que le Danemark veuille continuer la guerre?' (1 June).[30]

After the annulment of the Treaty of London, the question of determining the frontier between the Danish and the German parts of Schleswig definitely became the principal problem under discussion at the London Conference. *Le Nord* could not afford an objective view on this matter either. It criticised Copenhagen for being unwilling to accept the German plan for the division of Schleswig, and because (owing to the impossibility of reaching an agreement with Germany) calls for the continuation of the war were multiplying in Copenhagen. Some, according to the article 'La conférence de Londres et le Danemark', (9 June), wanted war in order to maintain the integrity of the monarchy and union ('séculaire') between Denmark and the duchies; others wanted a frontier on the Eider; whilst for some the starting point was the treaty of London, and for others the 18 November Constitution. Special indignation was reserved for the Danish publicist M. Hansen, who criticised the idea of the division of Schleswig sharply in the pages of *La France*. *Le Nord* quoted Hansen; (9 June)

Si mon pays a fait et s'il veut faire encore les plus douloureuses sacrifices dans cette lutte si inégale contre toute l'Allemagne, ce n'est pas pour disputer quelques lieues carrées de territoire, ce n'est pas par un point d'honneur exagéré, insensé. Non, il sent qu'il agit aussi de son existence même, et quelle est compromise *dès qu'il perd un pouce de cette province de Schleswig, qui lui a appartenu de temps immémorial;*

and added that in its view this was an 'ultra-national' programme. In the opinion of *Le Nord* the Danish government only harmed its own cause by putting the matter in such terms. 'Il ne s'agit pas de ce que le Schleswig était ou n'était pas à l'époque de Charlemagne, mais de ce qu'il est actuellement'. Schleswig was a mixed country in the strictest sense of the word and at the same time homogeneous in its community of material interests. In the upper classes the German element was predominant and was the major force, but it was hard to find a part of the duchy where the population was not varied in respect of nationality.

By placing the emphasis on the principle of the will of the people ('sur le terrain de la volonté nationale') and basing themselves on historical considerations, the more or less devoted supporters of Denmark were doing her the worst possible service. The population of the country, the paper further informed its readers (although Germans predominated in the south and the Danes in the north) was completely intermixed, as was demonstrated by the fact that there had been pro-German demonstrations in Haderslev in the north and pro-Danish ones in Hutten in the south. Their customs were similar despite the difference in dialects – Jutland, Friesian and low German *(platt-deutsch)* – and there was no way of establishing a

30. By Max Guttenstein.

nationality frontier. A German resident in Schleswig was as remote from Berlin as was a Danish-speaking one from Copenhagen. 'De fait, un habitant du Schleswig, qu'il parle danois ou allemand, est également étranger à Copenhague et à Berlin'.

This was the argument of those in Copenhagen who were in favour of 'Helstat', and therefore of the integrity of Denmark, but against the incorporation of Schleswig. If the Danish state organisation based on the principles evolved in 1851-52 had to be dismantled, either through the separation of Holstein alone, or the division of Schleswig, this was of no importance for Europe, nor for the ultimate fate of Denmark; nor did it matter whether the amputation stopped with a slightly smaller or larger number of people, whether a few thousand souls more or less were incorporated into Germany.

Despite some effort at an objective presentation of this complicated problem, one cannot fail to detect the real editorial position of the paper. It rejected *a priori* all solutions proposed by liberal elements, above all in Denmark, but also in Germany. It was anxious to torpedo any French proposals which followed the aspirations of national liberal forces in Germany and sought to transfer Schleswig and Holstein to Prince Augustenburg. This of course would have strengthened the national liberal front in Germany and would not have been in the interests of either Bismarck or Gorchakov. Russia countered this idea with that of a personal union of Schleswig-Holstein and Denmark under the aegis of Christian IX, whom she supported.

Russia pushed this solution more and more strongly as it became clear that the conference would end in a fiasco because of fundamental differences not only between the warring parties, but also between the neutral states, and between the major German powers and the smaller German states, although in the final account this last was certainly of less practical significance. Russia remained true to her guiding principle, not to let the conflict spread and develop into a European war, for fear of France's attitude and the possibility of an agreement between France and Britain on joint action against Austria and Prussia. She supported Prussia throughout the duration of the conflict from the autumn of 1863, despite certain reservations and anxieties about Bismarck's true plans and intentions, and launched the idea of a personal union, seeking supporters for it both in the international arena and in Denmark among Danish conservatives. *Le Nord* promoted this line, and returned to it in the article 'La situation morale et politique en Danemark' (25 June)[31] in which the policy of the Hall and Monrad governments was once again criticised, the paper declaring itself in support of the 'Helstat' party and the leaders of the Conservative party in Holstein. *'La paix par le congrès* ou *la guerre malgré les conférences.* Telle est la situation',[32] we read in the article 'La situation' (18 June). And the moment when it was settled whether there would be peace or war was only a few hours away. The great powers, seeking to withdraw from the

---

31. By. J. Vossen.
32. By Poggenpohl.

Treaty of London, a treaty which they had previously regarded as inviolable, agreed on the partial division of Denmark. They were afraid to sacrifice Denmark, as they were afraid of the responsibility, since they were afraid of war. The decision hung on them – war or congress.

If France, Russia and Britain began to intervene actively, war would break out the next day. But Britain, which was encouraging Denmark to resist, did not want that. She could attack Germany by sea via the Baltic and the Adriatic. But would other states remain indifferent to this? Sweden would be the first to take Britain's side. Russia, which did not have a direct interest in the matter – let us accept that – would not hesitate to join in the action ('à une résolution énergique'), but only on condition that it was a joint ('collective') action, and in order to ensure that it was so, demanded that France should take part as well. The latter, however, repeated that she would like to stand aside.

We can see from this that *Le Nord* did not trust Britain and, like Gorchakov, did not believe that Britain would become actively involved; even if she did, the action would be ineffective if France did not participate. The key therefore lay in the hands of Napoleon III.

'Le désir de la paix est général', *Le Nord* commented on the Kissingen meeting, in 'L'entrevue de Kissingen' (26 June). 'On désire l'éviter une conflagration dangereuse. Voilà la position. L'Autriche est moins engagée que la Prusse dans des questions qui se débattent au nord de l'Europe, la Russie est très intéressée à la conservation de la paix; les deux Empéreurs ont dû se rencontrer facilement sur ce terrain'. It is not hard to see from these words that Russia was disturbed by Bismarck's growing appetite and, as we know, by the possibility of an agreement between Britain and France. Seeing the difficulty of restraining Bismarck's endeavours, Russia sought an agreement with Austria, which throughout the conflict with Denmark displayed restraint and moderation. Austria's conciliatory policy corresponded more closely to Gorchakov's political principles.

All aspects of Scandinavianism were followed with care by J. Vossen, the *Le Nord* correspondent in Copenhagen. At the beginning of June (5) in his reportage 'Les démonstrations scandinaves en Norvège' (*Le Nord* 18 June) he called into question the formation of the Scandinavian Union. There was much to be said against the union. Both the historical experiences (he reminded readers of the fate of the Kalmar Union)[33] and the negative attitude of the Norwegians and the Danes towards the Swedish hegemony. If – as Vossen argued – Denmark were to be incorporated into Sweden, the Copenhagen 'doctrinaires' would furiously start fighting against Sweden, as they did against Germany.

'L'expérience du passé fait présumer que, plutôt que de consentir à l'incorporation à la Suède, les Norvégiens prendraient les résolutions les plus radicales. D'un autre côté, en ajoutant à l'union le Danemark comme troisième royaume indépendant, la Suède se créerait une position intolérable. Dans toutes les questions de politique générale, le Danemark et la

---

33. The Union of the three crowns established in Kalmar in 1397 came to a final end in 1523.

Norvège s'uniraient contre elle et rendrait complément illusoire cette hégémonie qu'elle ambitionne.

Toutes les rancunes nationales, aujourd'hui apaisées, ne tarderaient pas à se réveiller, et les dernières conséquences seraient probablement analogues à celles de l'union de Calmar.

Si, au contraire, le Danemark était simplement incorporé à la Suède, nous verrons bientôt le parti doctrinaire à Copenhague se tourner contre ses frères suédois avec la même fureur qu'il a jusqu'à présent deployée contre les Allemands. Pour ce parti – he concluded – le scandinavisme n'a jamais été qu'un moyen de tenir la première place sur un champ plus vaste, et si cette attente venait à être trompée, comme tout le porte à croire, on verrait sous peu combien ce sentiment d'unité dont on a fait aujourd'hui tant de bruit a des racines peu profondes à Copenhague'.

Only three weeks later, J. Vossen, influenced by the intensifying activities of the Scandinavianists in Sweden and Norway, changed to some extent his mind and verified his point of view about the possibilities of this political movement.

'Le démonstrations du parti scandinaviste continuent, et nous apprenons qu'il se prépare à Stockholm la formation d'une association scandinave, analogue à celle de Christiania' (25 June).

As rumours of the possibility of Denmark joining the Scandinavian union increased during the summer months, the anti-Scandinavian campaign in the pages of *Le Nord* intensified. It saw it as disturbance of the balance in the north and a threat to Russian hegemony in the Baltic. It feared that co-operation between Sweden and the western states, especially France, would revive the question of Sweden's claim for the return of Finland, seized by Russia in 1809, which was a fundamental problem for Russian policy.

Scandinavianism, said the paper, was a brake on the development of the Finnish language and culture: 'Le Finlandais craint la civilisation et l'influence suédois qui le dominent encore malgré lui, et auxquelles il veut s'arracher à tout prix', we learn from 'Le Scandinavism et le droit nouveau' (6 July).[34]

Il est vrai que, par une contradiction singulière, l'agitation *fennomanese* fait encore en grande partie en suédois et que la littérature finnoise est encore a créer. Mais les Finlandais savent qu'ils n'ont rien à redouter du côté de la Russie, elle leur permettra sans difficulté de chanter *"Vart land"*[35] et de s'enivrer des souvenirs du *"Kalevala"*,[36] tandis que les Suédois et les Scandinaves pourraient bien trouver que *Wainemoinen* ferait une concurrence dangereuse à Thor et à Odin...[37]

Ce qui est juste sur les bords de l'Eider ne saurait être injuste au Cap Nord.

This was the kind of comment directed at Swedish policy in Finland. This particular article opened a series of polemics against the Scandinavian idea, the pretext for which was some articles by M. Nefftzer,[38] the chief editor of the liberal *Le Temps*,

---

34. By C. Guinhut.
35. Finnish national athem by J.L. Runeberg.
36. Finnish national epic compiled by Elias Lönnrot from old ballads, lyrical songs and incantations in two editions 1835, 1849.
37. Principal gods in Norse mythology.
38. August Nefftzer, liberal journalist, a writer for *La Presse* in 1861, founded *Le Temps*, which was said to be 'plus ouverte que le *Débats*, plus serieux que *La Presse*'. *Histoire générale de la Presse Française*, vol. II (Paris, 1969), p. 319.

in which the main idea was that a Scandinavian union would be a 'Solution du litige dano-allemande et comme combinaison cœrcitive à l'égard de la Russie, de gêner la Russe', as *Le Nord* described it in its answer to Nefftzer in its issues of 11 July and 13 July, 'La vieille politique et les hommes nouveaux' and 'L'union Scandinave et le journal *Le Temps*'. The division of Denmark, *Le Nord* argued, had the fatal effect of strengthening the quest for a Scandinavian union. Russia's attitude towards this quest was firmly negative, and here were the reasons:

La Russie – nous en jugeons par les donnés qui sont à la portée de tout le monde – n'aurait que deux motifs de prendre ombrage de la formation de l'union scandinave: elle pourrait s'alarmer, d'abord, si les frontières s'étaient inquiétées par l'accroissement subit et menaçant d'un Etat limitrophe; en second lieu, si les communications de la mer Baltique avec la mer du Nord se trouvaient sous le coup d'une interruption. En général, la transformation d'un Etat faible en Etat du premier ordre est un phénomène dont se préoccupent les puissances voisines.

This was a general phenomenon and was best illustrated by the attitude of the French government to the question of the unity of Italy. Without doubt, *Le Nord* recognised, to have a Kingdom embracing the whole of Scandinavia as her neighbour could be inconvenient ('incommode') for Russia, since it was always unpleasant to have a centre of internal quarrels ('un foyer de dissensions intestines') on one's doorstep. (13 July).

It is perhaps intriguing that, immediately after the London Conference broke off, articles appeared in the paper's columns casting a broader light on Russia's foreign policy and its special importance. It is significant that just at this moment the article 'Notre programme' appeared (2 July), emphasising that the purpose of the paper, which had been established in 1855, was the dissemination of the idea of peace in Europe. In this context it stressed above all the role of Franco-Russian understanding after the Crimean War and the role of the paper, the principal task of which was to strengthen that understanding by acquainting the French nation with the customs, organisation, history and real trends of development prevailing in Russia, which were too little known, or even totally unknown, in France. This article could have been inspired by Gorchakov personally, as he never abandoned the idea of a return to the policy of the previous period, and it could have been in the nature of a sounding.

This is the context in which we should see the two articles in *Le Nord* on 16 and 17 July which attacked the arguments put forward by Nefftzer, the editor of *Le Temps*. The editor of this liberal paper accused Russia of excessive expansionism in Europe at the expense of her neighbours, Poland and Sweden in particular. In two articles under the title 'Les aggrandissements de la Russie' Th. Franceschi attacked Nefftzer, arguing that it was not Russia that was responsible for the conflicts with Poland. These conflicts had grown out of the objective geopolitical situation and out of cultural and religious differences. In essence, there was not room for two powers in that part of Europe.

As far as relations between Russia and Sweden were concerned, on the other hand, the acquisition of a gateway to the Baltic through the intuitive genius of Peter the Great had been a necessity for Russia, cut off as she was from the rest of Europe and wanting links with civilisation. The provinces which Russia had acquired in the Baltic, whose people were equally foreign to the Scandinavian as they were to the Slav races, did not feel any more connection with Sweden that with Russia, and as a result naturally felt closer to the latter. (He was talking about Estonia and Latvia.) As for Finland, possession of which had given Sweden access to the gates of St. Petersburg and made the capital of the empire a border town, it would be hard today to lament this loss since a few years later, in 1813, Sweden had been compensated by the transfer of Norway from Denmark and Norway was very pleased to be liberated from the 'Danish yoke', even if it was far from satisfied with its connection with Sweden, although the links were nothing more than union.

So much for *Le Nord* on the reasons for Russian expansionism. It is doubtful whether these arguments could have been convincing to the French reader.[39] If we add that at the same time *Le Nord* firmly rejected all talk of renewal of the Holy Alliance, which had appeared in the *Morning Post,* in 'La Sainte Alliance du Morning Post' (9 July), we may wonder whether the whole thing was not a feeler put out by Gorchakov, using *Le Nord,* to try to find out what French diplomacy thought of the possibility of renewal of a friendly dialogue between Russia and France at a time when the European horizon was once again darkening.

The resumption of military action after the break-up of the London Conference, the defeat of Denmark on the field of battle, the fall of the Monrad government, Moltke-Nutschau's unsuccessful attempt to form a government and the appointment of the Bluhme government, were matters to which *Le Nord* devoted a great deal of space in the second half of July. In the Bluhme government the paper saw new hopes of settling the Danish-German dispute ('Le nouveau ministère danoise' (14 July) and 'Les chances de paix dans la question danoise' (23 July)). The new government was immediately labelled as peaceful, even though, as the paper noted, it was not known in which way it intended to act or how it planned to settle the dispute with Germany.[40] Theoretically there were many possibilities: the duchies could simply be abandoned and handed over to the German Confederation or to Prussia, the frontier could be fixed on the Schlei, Denmark could become a mem-

---

39. Cf. Halicz, *'Le Nord* o konflikcie ...', pp. 58-66.
40. '... héritiers du système funeste de MM. Hall et Monrad, ils auront de plus à redresser toutes les fautes diplomatiques commises dans les derniers temps, ce qui parait dépasser les forces humaines ... Le programme du cabinet actuel', wrote *Le Nord* when Moltke was still attempting to form a government (this attempt was unsuccessful and Bluhme then followed) - 'est donc beaucoup plus simple que ne l'ont prétendu bien des journaux étrangers. Le nouveau ministère ne représente ni une réaction violente a l'intérieur ni la haîne absolue des principes constitutionnels; il veut simplement obtenir des ennemis du Danemark les meilleures conditions de paix possibles, et sauver ce qui peut encore être sauvé de la monarchie danoise, avec le concours de la représentation nationale, et au besoin sans elle, en faisant appel au bons sens du pays. La conservation de la monarchie sera naturellement le but principal ...'
'La politique du parti conservateur à Copenhague', Copenhagen, 11 July, *Le Nord,* 17 July 1864. The idea of appointing a conservative government was thus received very positively by *Le Nord.*

495

ber of the German Confederation, or there was the concept of personal union. In the paper's opinion, the latter option seemed the most probable and was commended as in accordance with the wishes of Christian IX and, of course, of Russia.

Le Nord displayed very cautious optimism at the suspension of operations, as it was not yet a truce which opened the door to negotiations and peace. The King had taken the correct decision in appointing to the government people who appeared to guarantee that Danish policy was taking the right course. A personal union, division of the monarchy into two parts, Denmark and the duchies connected only by the dynasty, seemed both to meet German aspirations and to be consistent with the principle of the integrity of the Danish monarchy. The entry of Schleswig into the German Confederation would merely strengthen the ideas which were at the root of the conflict. The only question which arose, said *Le Nord,* was which combination was more appropriate: Denmark, Schleswig and Holstein, or Denmark and Schleswig-Holstein. There remained the problem, however, of the attitude of the larger German states, Prussia and Austria. Austria was in favour of a quick peace, but did Bismarck take the same view? Prussia's position, said *Le Nord,* was crucial since she had played such an important role, both militarily and politically, in the war. 'En Allemagne, l'opinion le plus généralement accréditée sur la nature des propositions de paix du gouvernement danoise est celle que nous avons exprimée nous-mêmes: le retour à l'union personelle'. But, judging by articles which had appeared in Berlin periodicals, wrote *Le Nord* on 16 July, this solution did not seem to have been favourably received by the Prussian government.

La Prusse demande plus que jamais la séparation complète de Schleswig-Holstein entier de la couronne danoise, et comme il n'est pas probable que les ministres du roi Christian IX, pas plus ceux d'aujourd'hui que les précédents, veuillent souscrire à de pareilles conditions, la conclusion de la paix pourra bien être reculée à une échéance encore assez éloignée. ('Partie politique. Résumé, Paris 15 July 1864', *Le Nord,* 16 July).

Russia, it was emphasised, was playing an important part in the peaceful settlement of the dispute. The paper criticised those who made pessimistic predictions about the Kissingen meeting and who maintained that Russia had not performed a useful role there. Following what Gorchakov said on the subject of the Kissingen meeting, *Le Nord* promoted the view that Russia had played a useful role there. 'Les idées échangées à cette occasion ne joueraient pas sans doute une rôle inutile dans ce travail persistant de pacification'. And again, 'Ne semble t-il pas naturel de rapprocher ces indications du changement favorable qui viennent de s'opérer dans la situation des affaires danoises?' asked *Le Nord* in 'Les chances de paix dans la question danoise'. (23 July).

On 31 July J. Vossen was writing indignantly, on the basis of reports from Copenhagen dated 24 July, about the growth of anti-Russian feeling there in connection with the arrival of O. Plessen from St. Petersburg and his proposals. It was rumoured, despite denials, that Plessen was the bearer of certain proposals from the Russian government and as a result there had been a storm of public protest and a ministerial crisis. But what was all the fuss about, asked the author of the reports. What were these terrible proposals which were attributed to Russia? Personal union, claimed *Dagbladet,* unable to gloss over ('embellir') the proposals, as though the whole of Schleswig and Holstein were to be included in the union, and not only the southern part of Schleswig up to Gelting or Flensborg.

Would they prefer Prussian annexation or Prince Augustenburg? The Danish government, lamented Vossen, had rejected a personal union, which in his estimation, was 'la seule ancre de salut de la monarchie et les conseils sympathiques de la seule puissance vraiment désintéressé dans la question' [i.e. Russia. – E.H.] Anyone who held a different opinion *Le Nord* recommended to read the minutes of the London Conference to see for themselves the position taken by Brunnow, who had spoken there in defence of Denmark 'avec une verve et une lucidité étonnantes et soutint la cause du Danemark avec énergie et élévation'. He concluded then that 'rien n'est plus naturel pour le Danemark que de se tourner vers la Russie. La Russie ne nous a jamais menacés ni opprimés, ni trompés par de fausses promesses, mais elle nous a donné de bons et utiles conseils, que nous avons eu le tort de ne pas suivre'. (24 July).

It was true, wrote the author of the report, that Russia was the only power which could help Denmark in its dangerous situation, not only because she was powerful and could make the larger German States keep to a moderate line, using arguments of a moral nature. Russia had always favoured the preservation of the Danish monarchy.

The role she had played in 1848 had been forgotten owing to national prejudices ('superstitions nationales').

Ainsi, l'idée qui désigne le grand-duc d'Oldenbourg pour le trône du Holstein, idée qui d'abord a été pour nous – wrote the Copenhagen correspondent – une diversion très utile et qui serait peut-être la solution la plus convenable, ils s'y opposent en criant à l'influence russe, comme si cette influence, si elle existait dans le Holstein, ne serait beaucoup moins aggressive et remuante que celle de la Prusse![41]

The advocates of Scandinavianism were working to undermine the efforts intended to preserve the Danish state. But whatever acts of political subversion might be committed, it was indisputable that many thinking people in Copenhagen were aware that Russia had always helped Denmark in moments of crisis. Such people, who would have liked a return to a pro-Russian policy, were known in Copenhagen as russophiles.

Par malheur, – lamented Vossen – ce sera peut-être trop tard. Il est triste de penser que tout un peuple bon et brave soit puni dans son honneur et ses intérêts, parce que quelques chefs inhabiles ont manqué régulièrement toutes chances favourables qui se sont présentées depuis la naissance de la crise.

The old monarchy of Canute and Waldemar, which had once dominated the Baltic and reigned from the Eider to Finland and Greenland, had fallen to the rank of

---

41. Cf. also 'La candidature du Grand-Duc d'Oldenbourg', *Le Nord,* 18 July, which defended the moves made by Alexander II.

Switzerland and Belgium and ceased to play a role in Europe. The Copenhagen dynasty had been raped by bandits. But it was clear from the tone of *Le Nord* ('Le démembrement du Danemark', 10 August) that the bandits it had in mind were not the German states.

Only Russia was in favour of integration of the monarchy and maintenance of the provisions of the Treaty of London. Denmark now really faced two alternatives, neither of which would guarantee her territory ('le bien') on account of which she had gone to war and which she valued above all, or the preservation of her national life. If she relied on Germany it would not be long before Denmark completely lost her national identity. If on the contrary she sought salvation in a Scandinavian union she would soon see that Sweden was just as powerless to defend the Jutland peninsula and prevent its gradual incorporation into Germany.

In this complicated situation, when there was so much obscurity concerning the future of Denmark, doctrinaire voices were raised more and more loudly, to the indignation of *Le Nord,* which luckily could treat them as not serious. ('Les ennemis réels et imaginaires du Danemark', 12 September, and 'Le Danemark et la révolution', 31 October) 'Les déclamations anti-russes sont un moyen de se mettre bien avec la révolution et de se faire pardonner leur tiédeur pour la cause polonaise'. Fortunately the majority of the population of Sweden and Norway would not lightly be drawn into a fight against its own interests, that was to say, into a war against Russia. In Denmark the population, *Le Nord* observed, 'ne compte plus au point de vue militant'.

Russia, after all, had always been a friend of Denmark and had pointed out the danger which threatened her because of the Eider party, and the illusory nature of its programme. Apart from Prussia, the Eider party had attacked Russian policy since the time of Peter I, criticised Peter III for his planned war against Denmark, accused Russia of causing Denmark to lose Norway and criticised Russian policy towards Denmark right up to the Treaty of London.

This Treaty [signed in 1852 – E.H.] was not worth more than the paper it was written on, as the doctrinaire party argued. They also criticised Russia for the idea of a personal union with the duchies, which in the Eider party's opinion had frustrated the implementation of the Scandinavian idea. In reality, concluded *Le Nord,*

'Les sentiments de la Russie à l'egard du Danemark ne sauraient être autres que ceux de toutes les puissances européennes désintéressées dans la question; sympathie pour les faibles, sollicitude pour la paix et l'équilibre.

Que les Danois, qui jusqu'ici ont trouvé leurs plus grands ennemis dans leur propre sein, emploient leur temps et leur volonté à restaurer de leur organisation nationale ce qui peut encore être relevé, au lieu de s'égarer dans des illusions pessimistes après s'être bercés dans des rêves optimistes.'[42]

The best evidence of Russia's conciliatory and amicable attitude ('le meilleur indice du rôle concilliateur et sympathique') towards Denmark during the Danish-

42. By C. Guinhut.

German conflict was the forthcoming betrothal of Princess Dagmar to the heir to the Russian throne, Nicholas. ('Report from Copenhagen', 7 September). Amid the general agitation about the Vienna negotiations, which had been so fatal for Denmark, it was hard to tell what exasperated public opinion most or to predict what new difficulties awaited Denmark on top of those which it faced already. ('La situation intérieure du Danemark', 12 August and 23 August).

The close links which Austria and Prussia maintained with each other where the settlement of the dispute with Denmark was concerned aroused serious fears among supporters of the national party, in the opinion of *Le Nord*. *Fædrelandet* and *Dagbladet* accused Bluhme of launching the idea of a personal union in order to save Christian IX and his dynasty and argued that if this union were put into effect, Denmark would become a vassal of Prussia and her army and navy would be at Germany's disposal. Such were the misfortunes which could befall the Danish nation, in the national party's view.

It was hard, *Le Nord* confessed, to believe in the existence of such a conspiracy directed at Danish democracy. But the danger of Danish subordination to Prussia did exist. Scandinavianism, on the other hand, had been pushed into the background. As early as 25 June, in the article 'Situation morale et politique en Danemark', the paper maintained that because of her economic difficulties Sweden was disinclined to take any action.

'Nous verrons bientôt si ces considérations économiques suffiront pour détourner la Suède de la voie dans laquelle l'agitation scandinave, appuyée sur les sympathies personelles du roi, tend à l'engager, et où entraînerait assurément l'intervention beaucoup moins improbable aujourd'hui de l'Angleterre'[43]

And on August 12 C. Guinhut summarized the Danish situation as follows:

En somme, – he wrote – si l'on examinait les tendances générales du gouvernement suédois, on trouverait peut-être au fond de ses sympathies pour le Danemark la politique scandinave de Charles et Gustav, qui se contenterait de l'incorporation pure et simple des îles suédoises.

Le sort du Jutland ne serait alors plus douteux.

Il est toutefois peu probable que des considérations tirées de l'analogie historique aient quelque poids aux yeux du parti scandinave à Copenhague.

L'orgueil national humilié et le patriotisme au désespoir sont des mobiles trop puissants pour qu'on puisse encore pendant longtemps compter sur son inactivité. Les dernières événements lui ont préparé la voie car à ses yeux l'Europe, en abandonnant le Danemark, a implicitement consacré tous les changements territoriaux qui pourraient résulter du partage actuel. ('La situation intérieure du Danemark').

Anti-German feeling had grown rapidly (23 August). It was being said in Denmark that everything German should be eradicated, that political ideas and notions of civilisation originating in Germany should be abandoned, and instead close connections should be maintained with the Scandinavian countries. This was being said by the same party which had failed to understand the situation before the outbreak of the war. But the mass of the people in both Copenhagen and Denmark as a whole were living normally, just as before, asserted *Le Nord*.

43. By J. Vossen.

Despite the despondency prevailing in Denmark, *Le Nord* did not believe that in essence the loss of Schleswig meant the beginning of the end,[44] nor that the talk of a link between Denmark and the Scandinavian countries, and with the revolutionary movements in Europe, would be put into effect. ('Les espérances du parti conservateur du Danemark', 7 October). The paper explained why it regarded it as unlikely that Denmark would join the revolutionary current in Europe: ('Danemark et la révolution', 31 October).

Le Nord attacked the Frankfort and Paris press (*L'Europe* and *L'Opinion National*) and used arguments which I find useful to quote *in extenso* because they were so characteristic of the opinion about Denmark at that time in most European countries.

À Copenhague de pareilles assertions (Denmark as an 'auxiliaire de la révolution, a côté des Principautés danubiennes') seraient trop ridicules pour avoir besoin d'être réfutées – *Le Nord* argued. Le peuple danois d'aujourd'hui est loin d'avoir des tendances aventureuses et cosmopolites; sa véritable force est plutôt une certaine *vis inertiae* qui a résisté victorieusement à des grandes calamités nationales et qui ne s'est pas démentie dans cette dernière épreuve, la plus terrible de toutes ... L'idée de rechercher l'appui de la révolution, même pour reconquérir le Schleswig, froisserait le sentiment monarchique encore très fort chez la masse du peuple, et la perspective d'une nouvelle guerre alarmerait la propriété foncière, dont la situation matérielle a besoin de se remettre après le régime de M. de Falkenstein ... Il existe bien à Copenhague un petit groupe d'hommes politiques qui ont franchement envisagé les conséquences d'une alliance avec la révolution, et qui ont compris la nécessité de mettre en pratique leur dogme de la solidarité des peuples. C'est dans ce sens qu'il faut comprendre les manifestations universitaires au commencement de l'insurrection polonaise, mais la réponse évasive de Mgr. Monrad aux propositions de M. Demontowicz et la tiédeur générale de la nation, ont suffisamment prouvé que le Danemark ne contient pas des éléments qui pourraient en faire un allié de quelque valeur pour la révolution ....

Toute révolution qui éclaterait en Europe porterait nécessairement sur des réformes sociales dont le Danemark n'a aucun besoin. De plus, les hommes d'Etat danois qui probablement arriveraient au pouvoir pour le cas d'un bouleversement européen, seraient encore pour longtemps de l'école doctrinaire et bourgeoise qui, en Danemark comme partout, est la plus antipathique aux véritable radicaux. L'alliance avec la révolution serait l'alliance avec l'inconnu, et ce ne sont pas les hommes de la trempe de M. Hall qui pourraient espérer réussir dans un jeu aussi dangereux – Guinhut maintained. (31 October).

Espérons – we read in the article 'Danemark' on 26 October – cependant que la paix une fois conclue et le litige convenablement reglé, le Danemark, quoique diminué, reprendra la marche libérale vers laquelle il tendait avant la guerre et que, grâce à elle, il accroîtra son importance commerciale et profitera de ses ressources si abandontes pour consolider son bien-être et sa richesse.[45]

The news of the conclusion of the Treaty of Vienna between Denmark and Austria and Prussia on 30 October, and its text, were published by *Le Nord* without comment on 9 November. It preferred to confine itself to reproducing the commen-

---

44. This was the pessimistic opinion expressed by Tscherning in the Rigsraad; cf. also letter from Brøchner to the poet Chr. K.F. Molbeck, 2 June 1864, in T. Fink, *Geschichte des Schleswigschen Grenzlandes,* (Copenhagen, 1958), p. 155 and the opinion of D.G. Monrads *Deltagelse i begivnehederne 1864,* (Copenhagen, 1914) p. 287.
45. By Louis Tavernier.

taries on the document which had appeared in the French and British press. ('Les insignes du traité de paix dano-allemand', 29 November).

Thereafter the Danish problem receded into the background. On 13 November there appeared a denial that Russia had recommended Prince Oldenburg to withdraw as a candidate in the Schleswig-Holstein affair. This, *Le Nord* said, was a manœuvre by the Augustenburg party designed to compromise Russia and her policy in 1864. Finally, in a report on 1 December, *Le Nord* dealt with the rumours concerning Bismarck's plans for the unity of Germany and the future of the duchies, which, the story went, Bismarck would like to annex. *Le Nord* neither corrected these rumours nor expressed surprise at them, since, 'M. de Bismarck a déjà tant étonné le monde, qu'il n'y aurait rien d'extraordinaire à ce qu'il lui ménageât de nouvelles surprises'.

The future would show whether the rumours were right or wrong. The paper confined itself to telling its readers what journalists were writing and what its correspondents in Germany were reporting.

This concern about the plans of Bismarck was shared then by both Gorchakov and Alexander II.

10. Russian Public Opinion and the Danish-German Conflict

I

To examine Russia's attitude to the Danish-German conflict exclusively from the point of view of so-called official policy would be to take too narrow a view. The policy represented by Gorchakov was, as we have seen, essentially conservative and pro-Prussian, or, more accurately, pro-Bismarck, and thus in practice anti-Danish and certainly firmly anti-Scandinavian. At the same time, Gorchakov had no sympathy with German national aspirations. Formally, Russia took a neutral stance in the conflict and aimed to prevent it spreading, and on no account to let herself be drawn into it. But policy was only one side of the matter. Of course, we must not oversimplify the problem and interpret it as if Gorchakov did only what Bismarck wanted. Gorchakov was certainly not a tool in Bismarck's hands. Nor did he act in accordance with Bismarck's dictates; on the contrary, he frequently criticised him and flinched at the news of new moves by Bismarck. But, on the other hand, throughout the conflict he did nothing which could in fact have thwarted the Prussian minister's plans.

Both Alexander II and even Gorchakov, who was well-versed in matters of foreign policy, lacked political imagination and the capacity for long-term thinking, and they thought their pro-Prussian policy conformed to the basic principles of Russian policy; namely to seek to support conservative forces in Germany and Europe and to aim to preserve peace in Europe, from which Russia would be the chief beneficiary. In reality this was only a short-term policy. What the Russian cabinet failed to see was seen by a significant sector of public opinion in Russia, which from the start of the Danish-German conflict expressed a different view and took a position on many matters which was by no means identical to that of the government, and in some instances was directly opposite to it.

In the title of this chapter I have used the term 'public opinion'. Is this appropriate in the situation which existed in nineteenth-century Russia? Was there any such thing in the absolutist empire of the tsars? There are many definitions of public opinion to be found, but if we take the simplest, 'that public opinion is an aggregate of the individual views, attitudes and beliefs about a particular topic, expressed by a significant proportion of a community';[1] I think we can answer this question in the affirmative.

---

1. *Encyclopaedia Britannica,* (1974 ed.) vol. VIII, p. 285, vol. XV, p. 210.

Nearly all scholars of public opinion, regardless of the way they may define it, agree that at least four factors are involved in public opinion: there must be an issue, there must be a significant number of individuals who express their opinion on the issue, there must be some kind of a consensus among them, at least of some of these opinions, and this consensus must directly or indirectly exert influence.[2]

These factors, as we shall try to demonstrate below, did exist to a greater or lesser extent in Russia in the years in which we are interested.

On the other hand, we must note from the outset that the circle of people which our study will cover is extremely narrow. It takes in only the circles close to the court, persons connected with the army, the small number of representatives of the scientific world, and the handful of people engaged in the literary world with an interest in politics and the opportunity to express their views, as a rule in the press. Apart from them Russia was silent, particularly on matters of foreign policy, which was the domain of a narrow group of experts. The sources on which we can draw, originating from diplomatic circles, as a rule written by diplomats accredited to the court of the Tsar, and the information derived from the few memoirs left by contemporaries, are fragmentary and modest. We are greatly helped, however, by the press, which was relatively rich and displayed a broad range of interest and views.

Public opinion, which had formed an element in the public life of Russia, particularly during the first part of the reign of Alexander I, had been stifled by Nicholas I at the time when the Decembrist movement was suppressed. From then on, as M. Raeff correctly observes:

Toute solution pratique serait proposée et appliquée exclusivement par la bureaucratie, sans participation de l'opinion publique ni de la société.[3]

But public opinion once again took an active part in the process of transformation which took place in Russia during the post-Sebastopol Spring and, in fact, played a vital role in the transformation of Russia from a traditional to a modern society based on an economic system founded on industrialisation and modern principles of state administration.[4]

There can be no question, in the light of the sources at our disposal, that the Danish-German conflict aroused interest among various circles in Russia, particularly in 1864, and became the subject of a lively discussion, especially in the Moscow and St Petersburg press. There was no lack of disagreement with and criticism of official policy, although they were sometimes expressed publicly in a camouflaged form. It is another question whether these views had, or could have, any influence on official policy in a despotically ruled country.[5]

---

2. *Ibid.* vol. XV, p. 211.
3. M. Raeff, *Comprendre l'Ancien Régime Russe*, p. 152.
4. *Ibid.* pp. 174-6.
5. Research on this topic advanced considerably after the Second World War. See J.N. Rosenau, *Public Opinion and Foreign Policy: An Operational Formulation* (New York, 1961); P. Renouvin and J.B. Duroselle, *Introduction to the Territory of International Relations* (New York, 1967); R. Tucker, 'Autocrats and Oligarchs', in I.J. Lederer ed. *Russian Foreign Policy* (New Haven and London,

It must be said at the outset that in the period from 1856 to 1863 attitudes towards Russia's pro-French policy in the circles close to the ministry of foreign affairs and the court were not uniform either. Throughout the whole period the so-called 'Deutsche Strömmungen' or German tendency existed and spoke out against the rapprochement with France. In 1859 it supported a policy of backing Austria in her fight with France and Italy, arguing mainly that it was essential to maintain solidarity with Vienna on account of the Polish question. This line was supported by, among others, Peter Meyendorff and his wife (the sister of the Austrian minister, Buol), the war minister, Sukhozanet, and other ministers – Chevkin, Panin and V.A. Dolgorukov.[6]

These circles changed their attitude to Gorchakov's policy in 1863 when the Polish uprising caused the collapse of the policy of rapprochement with France and Prussia became Russia's principal ally, and when towards the end of 1863 Austria became an object of special concern to Gorchakov. At the turn of the year 1863-64 these circles supported Gorchakov's pro-German line in the Danish-German conflict. But even they had doubts about how far the policy being pursued by Bismarck should be supported, particularly when the German states went on the offensive in Schleswig and Jutland. Even among Gorchakov's closest collaborators there were those who said the most natural and advantageous policy for Russia was one designed to divide the western states, rather than concentrating on an alliance with any one state. Only if divided would the western states cease to be a threat to Russia.[7] 'Ne dobrozhelalel'nyi neutralitet' but 'usobit'sya na zapade – vot nash luchshii politicheskii soyuz',[8] Tyutchev observed in a letter to J. Aksakov on 2 October 1867.[9] The same idea was expressed by Danilevsky in his catechism 'Russia and Europe', first published as an article in *Zarya* in 1869.[10]

The predominant opinion was that in the specific situation where a process of transformation was going on, and neither the Polish question nor the question of Scandinavian union had yet been removed from the agenda of European politics, Russia must continue to support the two conservative German states. But there were not many enthusiasts for closer co-operation with the German states, and both among ministers and persons close to the court there was no shortage of voices expressing fear that Denmark had been deserted, and of the possible consequences for Russia in the event of the complete destruction of Denmark and the establishment of German power in the Baltic.

1962); Melvin Small, ed. *Public Opinion and Historians: Interdisciplinary Perspectives* (Detroit, 1970); Niels Thomsen, *Opinion og udenrigspolitik belyst ved et oprør fra midten i 1861* (Copenhagen, 1980); Gordon A. Craig and Alexander L. George, *Force and Statecraft: Diplomatic Problems of our Time* (New York and Oxford, 1983).

6. K. Pigarev, 'F.I. Tyutchev i problemy vneshnei politiki tsarskoi Rossii', *Literaturnoe nasledstvo*, 19/21 (Moscow, 1935), p. 221: A.F. Tyutchev, *Pri dvore dvukh imperatorov*, pt II (Moscow, 1928), p. 193.
7. See for example Tyutchev's opinion on 26 June 1864, Pigarev, 'F.I. Tyutchev ...', pp. 205-6.
8. Not benevolent neutrality, but intestine war in the West is our political ally.
9. *Ibid.* p. 206.
10. N. Danilovsky, 'Rossiya i Evropa', *Zarya*, (1869), p. 493.

The views of these circles seem to me well represented by the memorandum 'La politique du présent', probably written by some diplomat whose name we do not know, and handed to the Tsar in May 1864.[11] The author of the memorandum was against Russia involving herself in European affairs in order to preserve peace, but he thought that as a continental power Russia should not isolate herself completely. His ideal would have been a return to the policy of Catherine II's time, and in view of the central place occupied by the Polish question he favoured alliance with the larger German conservative states, Prussia and Austria. He thus distanced himself from the pro-French policy Gorchakov had pursued in the recent past. The second crucial problem for Russia was Scandinavianism, which he saw as a potential threat to Russia, especially in the event of war in that part of Europe. And, although Russia had no interest in the partitioning of Denmark, he supported the policy pursued by the larger German powers, the more so since he had lost sympathy for the democratic government in Copenhagen, which had backed the Polish uprising in 1863. Behind Denmark lurked Scandinavianism, and behind Germany, Germanism. In Germany itself there was a difference of opinion on the question of the duchies. Many matters were unclear, and diplomats had to reckon with this.

The author of the memorandum took the view that it was not in Russia's interest for Denmark to be driven back into Jutland and the islands, as violation of the integrity of the Danish monarchy could mean disturbing the balance of power in the north, and events might then lead to Denmark throwing herself into the embrace of Scandinavianism.

Nonetheless, in view of the complicated situation in Europe – and here he listed the Polish question; the growth of the democratic movement in Germany and the possibility of French interference in European affairs; the situation in Italy, Hungary, the Danube principalities and among the south Slavs, and the difficult situation of Russia herself, especially financially – the author favoured support for the German powers' policy in their conflict with Denmark. He stressed the need to strengthen ties with Prussia, as she was a buffer against France, and he saw it as being in Russia's interest to strengthen Austria too, on account of the situation in Poland. In other words, although the author of the memorandum was critical of Gorchakov's former policy, during the 1864 war he took a similar although not identical position to the Vice-Chancellor on the key question.

Diplomatic reports show that in the early months of 1864 certain nuances were to be detected between the attitude of the Tsar and his minister of foreign affairs towards Denmark. On 4 February Napier reported to Russell: 'The Emperor, the Court, the Government and the public are more Danish than Prince Gortchakof. Their influences, with an example, might gradually move the Minister onwards'.[12]

11. 'La politique du présent' was published in J.W.A. Eckhardt, *Von Nicolaus I zu Alexander III: St Petersburger Beiträge zur Neuesten Russischen Geschichte* (Leipzig, 1881), pp. 199-240. The memorandum was headed 'Eine russische geheime Denkschrift von 1864'. The document was discussed at length by Herman Robolsky, *Bismarck und Russland: Enthüllungen über die Beziehungen Deutschlands und Russlands von 1859 bis heute* (Berlin, n.d. [-1887?]) pp. 55-69.
12. P.R.O., 30/22, vol. 84, Private, k. 187-9 and 199 (13 April 1864).

The Tsarina and the heir to the throne, Grand Duke Nicholas, who was about to marry the daughter of King Christian IX, Dagmar, showed especial sympathy for the royal court in Copenhagen.

In Russia – Lord Redesdale wrote in his *Memories* – there was certainly no desire for war ... but a marriage had recently been arranged between the Tsarevitch and the Princess Dagmar, the second daughter of the King of Denmark, so the Court (which at that time was still Russia), with Prince Gortchakoff, eager for an English alliance, and a great number of ministers and nobles, were strong partisans of the Danes; and the whole chivalry of the country would have donned its armour to do battle for the father of their future Empress.[13]

There was particular satisfaction that the Danish troops were successfully resisting the attacks of the German armies which had invaded Schleswig.

L'impression est immence ici – reported Wedel-Jarlsberg – et plus que jamais l'opinion publique se prononce en faveur du Danemark.[14]

Le rejet des trois assauts prussiens entre les fortifications de Düppel a généralement fait grande plaisir ici.[15]

L'Empereur même parait plus sympatique à la cause Danoise que son Ministre. Il en est général de même de la cour et de la société qui applaudit hautement à la vaillante résistance des Danois et fait des vœux pour que les agresseurs soient rejetés.[16]

Fournier, basing himself on Wedel-Jarlsberg's reports, informed Paris

... que les premiers succès des Danois avaient reçu dans la société russe, et même très haut, un accueil fort sympathique. La Russie n'aime guère en effet les Allemands que quand elle ne peut pas faire autrement et pour les faire servir à ses fins.[17]

Redern reported that, apart from the government, which was displaying great caution towards Prussia, public opinion was firmly anti-Prussian, anti-Austrian, and in support of Denmark.[18] Thun was of a similar opinion, and reported to Vienna on 30 (18) March 1864:

La nouvelle de l'attaque infructueuse de la position de Düppel nous est arrivée hier par Copenhague, elle a de nouveau ranimé ici les sympathies danois que les succès des troupes Impériales en Schlesvig avaient déjà considérablement diminuées.

Supposant que la Prusse ne voudra pas rester sous le coup d'un échec et croyant que ce succès, aussi petit qu'il soit, ne manquera pas de confirmer le Danemark dans sa résistance, on considère ce fait comme une entrave à l'œuvre de la paix de laquelle la conférence de Londres doit s'occuper.[19]

The pro-Danish feeling in St Petersburg, and especially the great sympathy for Denmark among a large part of the senior officer corps, was reported by Col. von

---

13. Redesdale, *Memories,* vol. I, p. 238.
14. Wedel-Jarlsberg, no. 21, 7 February (26 January) 1864.
15. Wedel-Jarlsberg, no. 39, 30 (18) March 1864.
16. Wedel-Jarlsberg, no. 20, 6 February (25 January) 1864.
17. Stockholm, 16 February 1864. A.M.A.E. Suède, 334, no. 58. *Origines,* vol. I, p. 320.
18. Redern to Bismarck, 12 February 1864. APP IV, p. 534, Heinze, *Bismarck u. Russland,* pp. 57-8, 101.
19. H.H.S.A. P.A.X. Kart. 55, no. 6A-B.

Loën. The officers recognised Prussia's military glory, but sympathised with the weaker side, the Danes, who had to suffer so much.[20]

As a matter of fact this spontaneous reaction had not had any influence on the events, nor on Russian policies.

I would like to draw attention to this last report concerning the attitude of the officer corps to the Danish-German conflict. The officer corps, and in particular the war minister, D.A. Milyutin, took a different position on the Danish-German problem from the Tsar and the minister of foreign affairs, although it is doubtful whether they showed this during the 1863-64 war. In his memoirs Milyutin expressed his disapproval of the official pro-German policy, which was really pro-Prussian, and also took a negative view of Prussian plans for the unification of Germany.

While the Tsar was enjoying the splendid victories won by his uncle und friend, the majority of thinking people in Russian society recognised the danger threatening Russia in the future. Whereas the Tsar firmly trusted the traditional friendship and alliance between Russia and Prussia and saw it as a sound foundation for peace in Europe, public opinion did not trust the durability of this alliance, based more on personal sympathy between monarchs than on interests shared between the two states. With the exception of people close to the Tsar and his family, and the Baltic Germans, all the rest of Russia condemned the Tsar's inclination towards the Prussians and his open declarations and expressions of sympathy for the victories of Prussian arms ... It was completely nonsensical to bestow the Russian order of St George so generously;[21] German generals and officers were showered with them as if they had fought for the interests of Russia.[22]

Milyutin's anti-German attitude was a result of the fact that, as a Russian patriot, he viewed the reaction of the Germans in Russia to the German victories with disquiet.[23] He saw it as all the more dangerous because Germans occupied key positions in the Russian state administration. In some departments and ministries in St. Petersburg this was indeed the case: for example in the ministry of foreign affairs the proportion of Germans amounted to 57%; in the war ministry it was 46%; in the navy ministry 39%, and in the ministry of posts and telegraphs a record 62%.[24] Also, in the higher military command the percentage of Germans was 41%.[25] He was also worried about the problem of the Baltic Germans, their aristocratic attitude towards the population of the Baltic provinces, and the strong

---

20. APP V. 22 May 1864, p. 150. See also Redesdale, *Memories,* vol. I, p. 238.
21. During the Tsar's visit to Berlin in June 1864.
22. The differences of view between Milyutin and Gorchakov also concerned policy in Asia and the Balkans, as well as military affairs. Gorchakov was against the universal military service introduced by the war minister.
23. *Dnevnik D.A. Milyutina,* vol. I (Moscow, 1947), p. 46; P. Zaenchkovsky, *D.A. Milyutin: Biograficheskii ocherk.* Cf. Fond D. Milyutina, m. 7851, pp. 109-10. Lenin Library, Moscow. Milyutin did not hide his feelings about the Germans, and Bismarck was right when he wrote to Wilhelm I about Milyutin: 'Dieser ist für den Hass bekannt, den er gegen die Deutschen im Herz trägt'. *Dnevnik ...,* vol. I, pp. 52-3.
24. T.G. Masaryk, *The Spirit of Russia,* vol. I (London, 1968), p. 158.
25. *Ibid.*

separatist and nationalist tendencies which were revealed there during the 1864 Schleswig war.[26]

The attitude in military circles was presented by V. Chudovsky, a captain on the general staff, in *Voina za Shlezvig-Golshtein 1864 goda,* which came out in St Petersburg as early as 1866 and certainly must have been sanctioned by the minister himself. In the introduction the author said that when the whole of Russia's attention was on the Western Territory, where the final acts of the Polish uprising were being played out, western and central Europe were occupied with a no less vital question, namely the Schleswig-Holstein problem. The Federal Execution in Holstein and the capture of the Dannewirke, Düppel, Fredericia and Alsen were of little interest to Russia and not many Russians knew anything about them. Yet this war was of no little importance, both from the political and the military point of view. The two great states' invasion of little Denmark, behind a screen of defence of treaties and a persecuted nationality, which in fact concealed egotistical aims, the passive attitude of states which claimed to be the defenders of justice and used threatening words but did nothing, and the lamentable role of the German Confederation in all this, on the one hand, and, on the other, the appearance of the Prussian and Austrian armies in action in the military arena after over fifty years of peace, and the fact that the Prussian army was superbly armed, too, as well as the tactics of this army – all this taken together should be of interest both to military and non-military readers.

Chudovsky's sympathies were with Denmark. Outlining the history of the conflict over Schleswig-Holstein he came to the conclusion that Denmark, guided by the peaceful policy of Britain and Russia, had initially met a considerable portion of the German demands. These concessions, however, had aroused more and more protests from the Danes themselves, since they did not satisfy the arrogant Germans, who put forward new demands which were harder to meet.[27]

Chudovsky stressed particularly the perfidious role which Bismarck and Prussia had played. By presenting the problem in this way he was criticising Russia's pro-Prussian and anti-Danish policy. An even sharper critic of Gorchakov's cynicism and his policy in 1864 was Senator K.N. Lebedev; he maintained that Gorchakov's actions had been contrary to Russia's interest,[28] and that his attitude had been in-

26. Cf. A.M.A.E. Mémoires et documents. Russie 1863-1873. vol. 46. 'Les Russes en Russie et la Russie en Europe', written by Ch. de Saint-Robert and appended to report no. 36, 6 January 1864. This discusses the question of the separatist tendencies of the Baltic Germans, which were appearing there as absolutism was declining, just as had occurred in Schleswig-Holstein in relation to Denmark. It also discusses the overwhelming influence of Germans in Russian political and economic life and foresees a conflict between German and Russian nationalism, also as had happened in Denmark. Cf. also A.V. Nikitenko, *Zapiski i dnevnik (1822-1877),* vol. II, pp. 448-9 and Ya. Zutis, 'K istorii ostzeiskogo voprosa v 60-ykh godakh XIX veka', in *Iz istorii obshchestvennykh dvizhenii v mezhdunarodnykh otnosheniyakh* (Moscow, 1957) pp. 475-93.
27. See N. Ya. Danilevsky, *Rossiya i Evropa,* 4th edition (St. Petersburg, 1889), the chapter '1864 i 1854 gody! Vmesto vvedeniya'.
28. 'Iz zapisok senatora K.N. Lebedeva 1865 god', *Russkii Arkhiv,* vol. 6, (Moscow, 1911) pp. 243-4.

compatible with Russian national pride. 'Kakoe zhalkoe polozhenie zanimaem my v Shlezvig-Golshteinskom voprose!',[29] the Senator lamented. He regarded the separation of the duchies from Denmark as contrary to both the law and the practice by which Russia was guided. As a Russian he felt insulted. In his opinion Bismarck did not ask Russia about anything and paid no attention to her. It was true, the Senator said, that the internal changes taking place in Russia required restraint and a concentration of effort, but they did not relieve her of the need to defend her rights and to pursue a fitting policy in the diplomatic field. He was angered by the way Prussia had usurped the right to Schleswig, which had never belonged to the German Confederation, and ignored the fact that the Russian Emperor possessed the right to the house of Holstein-Gottorp.

The duchies, Lebedev thought, would regret that they had left Denmark, which had given them democratic institutions. They were against military administration and the rule of the Prussian junkers, as it was in practice irreconcilable with the desire to maintain the constitution in the duchies. The German National Verein was raising its head, creating a navy and stepping up its propaganda. Prussia was making things difficult for the secondary German states, which were seeking help from Napoleon III as their neighbour on the Rhine and Alexander II as their blood relative. To demonstrate the growth of Prussian influence Lebedev cited a quip which was circulating in St Petersburg. When Olga Nikolaevna, Queen of Württemberg, was asked if she would prolong her stay in St Petersburg, she replied laughing: 'Je ne sais pas, cela dépend de Bismarck'.[30]

B.N. Chicherin was also critical of Gorchakov's policy in his memoirs.[31] The well-known lawyer, historian, philosopher and professor at Moscow University criticised Gorchakov for his refusal to join the planned Anglo-French show of naval force in the spring of 1864. As a result of this fatal step Denmark had been delivered up to hostile states. The vain and impressionable Gorchakov, whose policy was not based on well thought-out aims and who did not understand Russia's real interests, was incapable of foreseeing anything. Russia had paid dearly for Prussian diplomatic support in 1863, which had cost the latter nothing.[32]

Peter Vladimirovich Dolgorukov[33] also thought Gorchakov's policy in 1864 was wrong.

From fear of Prussia, which sooner or later would put forward a claim to the Baltic provinces, the Vice-Chancellor allowed Denmark to be devoured, not foreseeing that two years later Denmark would give Russia a future Tsarina.

Prince V.V. Meshchersky, who was close to the court, criticised Gorchakov sharply for his pro-Prussian policy in 1864, and tried to explain it as follows:

29. *Ibid.*
30. *Ibid.* 1866 god, vol. 7, pp. 365-6.
31. B.N. Chicherin, *Vospominaniya,* vol. I.
32. V.D. Zorkin, *Chicherin B.N. 1828-1904.* Monografiya o vidnom russkom uchenom yuriste, filozofe, istorike. (Moscow, 1984) says not a word about Chicherin's views on Russian policy in the 1860s.
33. *Peterburgskie ocherki, 1860-67* (Moscow, 1934), p. 281.

1. The root of the puzzle was Bismarck's policy. He had succeeded in intoxicating Gorchakov, persuading him that he was the best diplomat in Europe and really controlled European diplomacy. This, wrote Meshchersky, was like the music of the Aeolian harp to Gorchakov's ears, and he succumbed to Bismarck's influence.
2. Gorchakov's colleagues also had an essential influence in causing him to pursue such a pro-German policy. If they had been more Russian and had been masters of their jobs, as had been the case in 1863, they would not have allowed Bismarck to dispose of Denmark as he did, with consequences of immense importance.

If, Meshchersky concluded, Gorchakov had had different, not pro-German colleagues, they would have led the way to a Franco-Russian rapprochement, which would have been a colossal advantage to Russian interests and would have frustrated Bismarck's design. So much for Meshchersky.[34] His reasoning is undoubtedly over-simplified, but it casts light on the personality of the minister of foreign affairs and reflects the feeling prevailing in certain circles of the Russian aristocracy close to the court.

Of all the contemporary accounts really only one, by Dzunkovsky, defends Russian diplomacy.[35] In his opinion Russia had made concessions and renounced her historical rights with one aim only, namely to preserve peace in Europe and maintain the integrity of the Danish monarchy. The fact that her disinterested behaviour had not brought the desired results was not Russia's fault.

Characteristically, Dzunkovsky thought that Prussian diplomatic behaviour in relation to Denmark had been open, though at the same time skillful, and that was why it had been successful. But it was impossible to say whether it would have been so without the vacillations and mistakes of French diplomacy and the complete recklessness of Austrian diplomacy.[36]

II.

Up to this point we have discussed the views of a narrow group, represented mainly by circles close to the court, or the war ministry, using diplomatic sources which,

---

34. V.V. Meshchersky, *Moi vospominaniya,* vol. I, pp. 300-1, 306.
35. S.S. Dzunkovsky, 'Politika Danii pri Friderike VII. Z Zapisok ochevidtsa 1855-61', *Vestnik Evropy,* December 1866.
36. Speaking of Dzunkovsky, it must be mentioned that this cleric, who carried out missionary work in all the Scandinavian countries, including Iceland, on behalf of the Apostolic See, converted to Orthodoxy after his return to Russia, and the possibility that from the start of his missionary activity he was connected with the Russian secret service cannot be excluded. In the archives in Vienna I found documents relating to his activities in Sweden which indicate that missionary work was not his only interest. See H.H.S.A. P.A. XXVI Sweden, No. 34, 3 November 1856. That he was a suspicious figure is shown by the fact that during his stay in Copenhagen the Danish police conducted a search of his hotel room. I am grateful to Professor Troels Dahlerup for this last piece of information.

incidentally, are not very plentiful on this matter, and some personal accounts and memoirs. The fullest source, however, for studying how opinion in educated Russian circles reacted to government policy, and what views they expressed, is undoubtedly the press, both that published abroad beyond the reach of censorship and that appearing in Russia itself. What we are interested in is how it reacted to current events in the international arena, how it saw Russia's place in them, and whether it approved of Gorchakov's policy or took a critical view of it.

A partial analysis of the contents of the Russian press in these years was carried out by Narochnitskaya,[37] but she was only interested in one aspect, namely how the problem of the unification of Germany by Bismarck, the unification, as she puts it, 'from above', was reflected in the Russian press. If she touched on the Danish question she did so only fragmentarily and only to the extent that it was connected with her central problem – the unification of Germany.

I use the term 'press' here to mean dailies, bi-weeklies and monthlies.[38] The number of periodicals published in Russia increased from 104 in 1855 to 230 in 1860. These figures include the provincial newspapers, and also periodicals published by government departments.[39] Our analysis is confined to the press published in St Petersburg and Moscow, but we could not overlook *Kolokol,* published by A.J. Hertzen and N.P. Ogarev in London, or the semi-official *Le Nord,* published in Brussels. In view of the specific character of the latter, however, we devote a separate chapter to it. Before we proceed, we must remember that, apart from *Kolokol* and *Le Nord,* these periodicals were appearing in Russia, a country where censorship was in operation. It is true that it was relaxed a little during the post-Sebastopol Spring, but it still existed, and its limits were not established until 1865, when a new statute on the censorship was issued.[40]

In a country in which there were still no forms of representation, with a narrow group of aristocrats holding a monopoly of power, only the press, even though limited in scope and subject to censorship, could exercise some degree of influence on relations between government and society. It could also show an autocrat, as the Tsar was, the mood of society and point to some burning problems or dissatisfaction felt really by all classes of society, from the peasants to the intelligentsia and the gentry. This is why the press was listened to. This is why, among other things, not only Russian dignitaries but the Emperor himself, too, according to contemporaries' reports, was frequently interested in reading the opposition *Kolokol.*

37. L.I. Narochnitskaya, *Rossiya i voiny Prusii v 60-ykh godakh XIXv,* (Moscow 1960). See also Ya. Gerasimova, *Iz istorii russkoi pechati v period revolyutsionnoi situatsii kontsa 1850-ykh – nachala 1860-ykh godov,* (Moscow, 1974); Lemke, *Ocherki* ...; Z. Dietrich Geyer, *Der Russische Imperialismus* (Studien, Göttingen, 1977), pp. 28-29.
38. *Istochnikovedenie istorii SSSR,* ed. I.D. Kovalchenko (Moscow, 1973), pp. 266-73. G. Brandes, *Indtryk fra Rusland,* (Copenhagen, 1888), pp. 185 ff.
39. Daniel Balmuth, 'Origins of the Russian Press Reform of 1865' *Slavonic and East European Review,* (London, July 1969) pp. 369ff. See also Charles Ruud, 'The Russian Empire's New Censorship Law of 1865', *Canadian Slavic Studies,* vol. III, no. 2 (Summer 1969). pp. 233-45. Cf. *Istoriya SSSR,* vol. 6 (Moscow, 1968) p. 736, which gives a figure of 220 periodicals in 1859.
40. Von Schweinitz, *Denkwürdigkeiten,* vol. I, p. 189.

On the other hand, the government, which had a monopoly of policy, was afraid of controversial discussion in the press. The government's opposition to an independent press was shown by Valuev's diary.[41] We know there were complaints that, for example, *Moskovskie Vedomosti*[42] played the role of 'supreme court' and that 'as A.E. Timashev complained, it put itself above the central authority of the state'. The uncertainty of the reform process, fear for the government's prestige, fear that its monopoly of policy would be broken by the appearance of different political trends (conservatives, liberals, slavophils), and the fact that the press had gained greater and greater authority among the educated part of Russian society may have disturbed both the government and the Tsar. In the case of rivalry between the court and ministries, or between coteries in the court, the importance of the press could be not insignificant.[43] For this reason, too, the government was unwilling to give up the use of censorship, and the battle over censorship absorbed almost the entire government and important social groups for years.[44]

'Censorship is the most delicate and sensitive nerve in our social life, this problem must be approached very cautiously', wrote A.V. Nikitenko, a member of the censorship committee during the post-Sebastopol Spring years.[45] But the conviction of the need for a change in the censorship law grew, not only in liberal circles but in those close to the government, too. F.I. Tyutchev convinced Gorchakov in 1857 that a change in the censorship law was essential. The change in attitude towards the press in Prussia, which in 1848 had hated it but now sought backing for the government in it, showed the direction in which Russia should move, said Tyutchev.[46]

On various occasions when the Danish and French ambassadors had protested about items in the press, Gorchakov emphasised that it was not directly inspired by the government. In a talk with the French ambassador he explained the place of the press in Russia and offered the following interpretation of the freedom of the press:

La presse russe, par le seul motif qu'elle était soumise à la censure préalable, ne saurait être regardée comme inspirée plus ou moins directement par le Gouvernement Impérial. Le Prince a ajouté qu'en ouvrant en Russie une voie plus large à la presse le Gouvernement avait entendu dégager sa propre responsabilité sauf les obligations qui découlaient des principes sociaux et internationaux respectés par tous les états civilisés, que la censure préalable à laquelle les journaux restaient toujours soumis, n'avait pas d'autre objet et que la mission principale des censeurs était de veiller à ce que rien dans les opinions livrées à la publicité ne soit contraire à la réligion, à la morale, à l'ordre social ni aux égards dûs aux Souverains et aux Gouvernements; que du reste toute opinion honnête pouvait se produire en Russie et que la presse, qui y était parfaitement autorisée à discuter dans une juste mesure les ques-

---

41. *Dnevnik Valueva*, vol. II, pp. 496ff, 503ff.
42. '... welche damals Orakel war', as von Schweinitz described it. Vol. I, p. 190.
43. Geyer, pp. 29-30. Vind asked Hall for permission to contact the *Journal de St. Pétersburg* because the information concerning the budget for Holstein might influence Russian opinion in the direction opposite to the Danish interests. Dep. Rus. 25 (13) April 1863.
44. Ruud, *Ibid*.
45. A.V. Nikitenko, *Dnevnik*, vol. I 1826-57 (Moscow, 1955), pp. 410-11.
46. Pigarev, 'F.I. Tyutchev ...', p. 200.

tions intérieures, jouissait de la même faculté quant à celles de la politique étrangère; que les journaux ne pouvaient représenter que leurs propres opinions et que, par conséquent, le Gouvernement n'était dans le cas ni de les approuver ni de les désapprouver, bien moins encore dans celui d'en accepter la solidarité à quelque titre que ce soit.[47]

Up to a point this was the truth.

Die Zensur besteht zwar annoch, ist aber bei der stets anwachsenden Masse von Zeitungen, Broschüren und anderweitigen Druckschriften nicht mehr im Stande, deren Inhalt mit hinlänglicher Genauigkeit zu prüfen, als dass nicht häufig Aufsätze veröffentlicht würden, welche die Propositionen oder Handlungen der Regierung, ebenso die Lebensweise der höchstgestellten Beamten des Reiches mit der einschneidesten Schärfe besprechen.

Die Freiheit womit seitens der Redaktoren wenigstens der Versuch nicht nur hierzu, sondern selbst zur Kritisierung des Benehmens der Allerhöchsten Personen gemacht wird, übersteigt alle Grenzen der Schicklichkeit.[48]

An analysis of the Russian press's attitude towards Gorchakov's policy is interesting because the press reflects different tendencies and trends and points of view on Russian policy in these years. With the exception of the emigré Hertzen's *Kolokol*, none of the Russian papers published in the country attacked Gorchakov and his policy directly. This would have been impossible anyway in the conditions of Russian absolutism, and instead they raised certain postulates, desiderata and questions, wondering whether the line taken was the most suitable and advantageous for Russia. The basic policy line adopted by the minister was supported by the press, which argued that Russia was primarily interested in maintaining peace in Europe. There was no question of active Russian involvement in the Danish-German conflict. In this respect there was no difference between the firmly pro-German *Petersburger Zeitung*, the conservative *Vest'*, and the liberal *Otechestvennye zapiski*, the scientific and literary periodical edited by A.A. Kraevsky and S.S. Dudyshkin, which had been published in St Petersburg since 1839.

The differences concerned matters such as the origin of the Danish-German dispute and the direction of Russian policy towards the conflict. There was also discussion whether Russia should support Prussia, and to what extent, on account of the Polish problem, or whether she should back Denmark in view of the need to preserve the balance of power in the north and protect Russia's interest in the Baltic. The tactics to be adopted during the London Conference were also discussed. After there had been a fundamental change in the north as a result of Denmark's shattering defeat, the press wondered how Bismarck's ever-growing demands would affect the maintenance of a balance there, and also whether the separatist demands of the Germans in the Elbe duchies would influence the attitude of the Baltic Germans towards St Petersburg.

47. L. Montgelas to Maximillian II, no. 98/XXIII, St. Petersburg, 15 September 1859. Rusland 1852-71. *Aus den Berichten der Bayerischen Gesandschaft in St. Petersburg*, p. 85. See also Dashkov's opinion on the subject of the censorship, report by W. Scheel-Plessen, no. 16, 14. April 1858. R.A. Sverige Depecher 1856-61.
48. Montgelas, no. 49, 4 April 1860, p. 85.

On the margin of the Danish-German conflict a discussion was also going on about the central strategic question of Russian foreign policy, which direction was more important for Russia, Western Europe or the East. Only *Kolokol,* published in London, really launched a frontal attack on Gorchakov's policy. From the start it took a consistent position in defence of Denmark and attacked the pro-German policy, which it saw as a continuation of the conservative Russian policy inaugurated by the Holy Alliance of 1815. The article 'Die heilige tripel Allianz', which appeared in *Kolokol* on 15 June 1864,[49] was typical. In the paper's opinion Gorchakov's policy favoured Germany's interests exclusively. If reflected the anti-Polish and anti-Scandinavian, and ultimately anti-Slav, policy of Russia. This new alliance was more cynical than that of 1815 since not even a pretext for it had been given. The purpose of Russia's alliance with Germany was the destruction of a weak state fighting to preserve its modest territory, an unfortunate nation fighting for its existence, which after all was no threat to Potsdam. *Kolokol* blamed Gorchakov for this policy, which was so contrary to Russia'a interests.

And you, Prince Gorchakov – cried Hertzen – were the creator of this ... Why did you not resign, why do you dislike Russia so much? The nationality[50] which you adopted in former years has been destroyed because of Bismarck's preening.

In his article 'And What Next', published on 1 December 1864, Hertzen vehemently attacked the Russian empire, which was a mixture of western military despotism in its most brutal and ruthless form with a dash of oriental despotism. He attacked it for the suppression of Poland and the defeat of Denmark. At this moment, he wrote, the three-headed German eagle is satisfied after pecking Denmark to death and is living in friendship with its Byzantine comrade. The Polish question and the Danish war are the two biggest steps on the way to the precipice towards which the old world is heading. As the Crimea destroyed the empire of Nicholas I, so Denmark and Poland dispelled fear of the western powers. History abhors nothing – just as nature does not choose paths and when it cannot pass with dry feet, goes through the swamp – so when history cannot pass with the help of Britain and France it uses Prussia and Austria.

The West's inconsistent policy had allowed Russia to stifle Poland and stand face to face with Germany. By frustrating each other Britain and France had enabled Germany to take on a role for which she was unsuited, allowed her to mutilate Denmark and, with blood on her mouth, to stand face to face with Russia hanging Poland. The rest would happen by itself, thanks to the savage instincts of nations, the passions aroused and the rapacity of governments.

This may exasperate and preoccupy for a while, but this is not the real point. The real point is that Catilina[51] has approached the gates, since the gates moved from

---

49. A.I. Hertzen, *Polnoe sobranie sochinenii i pisem,* edited by M.K. Lemke, vol. XVII, (Petersburg, 1922), pp. 293, 302-4. Brandes, *ibid.* pp. 159-60.
50. The National Politics.
51. S.L. Catilina's conspiracy (63 B.C.) was supressed by M.T. Cicero.

the Thames and the Seine to the Danube and the Vistula ... If the western world does not have the strength to regenerate itself, it will be better if a new American or Russian Attila[52] appears ... If, on the contrary, the West has the strength, then either there will not be a fight or it will defeat the Russian empire. In either case the Russian nation will lose nothing.

These were the far-reaching conclusions Hertzen came to in connection with the two closely related problems, the overthrow of Poland and the defeat of Denmark.

Bakunin came out with an equally violent attack on Gorchakov's firmly anti-Danish and pro-German policy somewhat later.[53] His agreement to the plundering of the Danish monarchy and to Prussia's seizure of Holstein and Schleswig meant the undoing of what Peter I had achieved and opened the way to hegemony in the Baltic for Bismarck's Prussia, wrote Bakunin. Prince Gorchakov, he said, should have realised what the consequences would be when he agreed to the division of the Danish Kingdom and the incorporation of Holstein and Schleswig into Prussia. This presented a dilemma – whether he had betrayed Russia or whether, by agreeing to sacrifice the pre-eminence Russia had in the north-west, he had obtained Bismarck's formal agreement to support Russia in her plans for new conquests in the south-east. Even the smallest show of force by Russia, such as a movement of troops towards the Prussian border, would have been sufficient to restrain further advances by the Prussian war machine, both in Prussia's war against Denmark and in the later one against Austria. But Bismarck was not afraid, as he was evidently certain that Russia would not be unfaithful to him.

But let us return to the press published in Russia. The official organ of the government was *Severnaya pochta*, founded in 1809, which became the government organ during the years 1825-64, something like *Moniteur Universel*,[54] while the *Journal de St Pétersbourg* was the semi-official organ of the ministry of foreign affairs.[55] From the political point of view the press was varied. The leading conservative papers were *Vest'* and *Petersburger Zeitung*. The best known and most influential was *Moskovskie Vedomosti*, founded in 1756 and edited by the former liberal and prominent publicist M.N. Katkov. During the Polish uprising Katkov became one of the most popular people in Russia. He set the tone of the anti-Polish policy and created Gorchakov's reputation as a great patriot and made him the second most popular man in Russia after the Tsar.[56]

The organ of the Russian liberals was *Golos*, edited by A.A. Kraevsky. This paper was connected with the well-known railway building entrepreneur Polyakov and with some ministers, among them the minister of internal affairs, P.A. Valuev

52. Attila (406?-453) the Scourge of God, King of Huns.
53. M. Bakunin, *Izbrannye sochineniya*, vol. I. 'Gosudarstvennost i anarkhiya', 1873 (Petersburg and Moscow, 1922), pp. 144-5. Cf. W. Laqueur, *Russia and Germany*, (Boston and Toronto, 1965), pp. 13, 28, 41.
54. Meshchersky, vol. I, p. 294; *Istochnikovedenie*, ... p. 272.
55. Cf. 40. Szechenyi to Rechberg, 21 (9) October 1859. H.H.S.A. P.A. X. Berichte, 1859, Karton 49, no. 40 A-B; Schweinitz, p. 189.
56. F.I. Tyutchev, Letters to Gorchakov, *Literaturnoe nasledstvo*, 19-21 (Moscow, 1935) pp. 203-6, 223-6.

(who was an enemy of Katkov and protected *Golos*)[57] and the minister of education, A.V. Golovnin. *St Peterburgskie Vedomosti,* founded in 1728, was edited by V.F. Korsh in a spirit of moderate liberalism, and the *Journal de St Pétersbourg,* being close to Gorchakov, devoted relatively great attention to Russia's foreign policy. *Den'* (1861-65), edited by I.S. Aksakov, was the Slavophil organ. *Russkii invalid,* founded in 1813, edited by E.M. Feoktistov, was close to the war minister, D.M. Milyutin.[58] This paper followed a different line from the official policy on many matters, especially the problem of the Baltic Germans, which incidentally was a by-product of Milyutin's attitude to the German question in general and which incurred the displeasure of Alexander II.[59]

Russian democratic opinion in the 1860s was represented by *Otechestvennye Zapiski,* and particularly *Sovremennik,* edited by N.A. Nekrasov and I.I. Panaev, as well as *Russkoe slovo,* edited by G.A. Kushelev-Bezborodko and from 1860 by G.E. Blagosvetlov, and also *Iskra,* the satirical paper published since 1859 by V.S. Kurochkin and N.A. Stepanov.[60]

After the defeat in the Crimean war, and even more so after the suppression of the Polish uprising, peace became the chief motto of Russian policy and the primacy of internal affairs was axiomatic. Any war in Europe might not only disturb the *status quo* and interrupt the work which had been started on domestic reforms, it might also put the Polish question, which by universal agreement was the most important, politically and strategically, for Russia, back on the agenda.[61] But neither the conservatives nor the liberals, following this axiom, were entirely opposed to further conquests in Central Asia and colonisation of the Caucasus, and both *St Peterburgskie vedomosti*[62] and *Otechestvennye zapiski*[63] considered this more important for Russia's future than adventures in the west.

Discussing the problems of European politics and considering what should be done to maintain the *status quo,* particularly in the Polish lands, the press in the majority of cases put forward the view that the best guarantee of this was to strengthen co-operation not only between Russia and Prussia but also with Austria. There was, however, disagreement about the scope of such co-operation and how far it should go. The representatives of the liberal camp, not to mention the radicals, had serious reservations about Prussian policy and practices, and the latter thought that, despite the disappointment of 1863, Russia's interests required a rapprochement with France rather than Prussia.

How did the Danish-German dispute fit into this background? We shall begin with explanations of the roots of the conflict. The most thorough analysis of the

---

57. Meshchersky, vol. I, p. 293.
58. Schweinitz, vol. I. p. 190.
59. The chief of police, V.A. Dolgorukov, on the instructions of the Tsar, demanded that Milyutin cease 'attacking the Germans', F.M. Feoktistov, *Za kulisamy politiki i literatury,* pp. 314-5.
60. *Istochnikovedenie ...,* p. 273.
61. *Golos,* 6 May 1864; *Moskovskie vedomosti,* no. 84, 1864.
62. No. 213, 1865.
63. No. 6, 1864, p. 946.

history of the conflict over Schleswig-Holstein is to be found in *Russkoe slovo, Otechestvennnye zapiski* and *Sovremennik.*

In the opinion of *Russkoe slovo* the Danish-German conflict had deep historical roots and was being played out on many levels. On the one hand, Germany was frustrated because it was playing a secondary role in Europe, arousing less interest than even Italy recently, and wanted to draw Europe's attention to itself. On the other hand, there was an age-old antagonism between the two sister races – the Germans and the Scandinavians. There was a dispute about which of them had made the greater contribution to the development of culture in the past, and there was a continuing battle for hegemony in northern Europe. Over the course of time the Germans had come to dominate Denmark, introducing feudalism, serfdom, bureaucratic absolutism and other arrangements such as the *Rangverordnung,* the system of division into different hierarchical groups in civilian, military and spiritual life. The German language had gained a privileged position in Denmark and Danish had become merely the language used by the lower classes. The slow rebirth of the Danish language had not begun until the XVIII century. Reflecting on the origin of the conflict with the duchies, *Russkoe slovo* came to the conclusion that the dispute would not have arisen but for the fact that in 1848 Denmark had taken the road of constitutional development, and the German barons who owned estates in the duchies and exploited the peasants there felt their possessions and their privileged position threatened.

These, in the paper's opinion, were the causes of the conflict with Denmark which had flared up in 1848 and led to the war between Denmark and Germany. 'Was ist des Deutschen Vaterland!', the Germans cried in Frankfurt, and a verse by E.M. Arndt ran: 'Schleswig-Holstein Meer umschlungen!'[64]

Otechestvennye zapiski published an article in 1863[65] with the title 'The Schleswig-Holstein-Zonderburg-Glücksburg Puzzle' *(putanitsa),* which gave a historical outline of Schleswig and Holstein in the context of the history of the Baltic over the past 700 years. In the author's opinion historical reason indicated that Schleswig was more closely connected with Denmark than with Holstein. In spite of what the Germans said, the majority of the population of Schleswig was Danish; there were only five Germans to every eight Danes, and if the principle of nationality were to be decisive eight-thirteenths of Schleswig should belong to Denmark and five-thirteenths to Holstein. But the Germans would hear nothing of this. The problem was complicated by the question of the succession to the throne in Denmark.

Because the German language was very widely used in Europe, whereas Danish was unknown, only the German arguments in this bitter political battle were familiar. But they were not correct, and this applied not only to the essence of the conflict but also to what the Germans said about the Danes themselves. The Ger-

---

64. *Russkoe slovo,* 1864, no. 1, pp. 1-6.
65. Vol. CL.

mans portrayed them unjustly as enemies of civilization, savages who imagined themselves to be Europeans. The Germans said the Danes were cannibals, whereas in fact Denmark had abolished the slave trade before other nations had. [NB This was mainly for economic reasons – E H]. The very word Danicisation had become hateful for the Germans. The Congress of Vienna had confirmed Denmark's right to Schleswig, in which the Danes were the majority. Only Holstein belonged to the German Confederation.

In the opinion of *Otechestvennye zapiski* Denmark had shown good will in the dispute with Germany, particularly when she made concessions in 1858; but she could not accept the 1862 Gotha programme. Holstein had always opposed Denmark and had answered all her proposals with one word, no. For that reason the King had been forced to issue the decree of 30 March 1863. Holstein had then received complete freedom and remained thereafter exclusively in personal union with Denmark. Denmark and the liberal party in power in Copenhagen aimed to merge Schleswig with the Danish monarchy in the narrow sense of the word, to establish the frontier on the Eider and to stop Germany interfering in the affairs of Schleswig.

The author compared the Holstein problem with the Polish question – only, in his opinion, the Polish question had been blown up to enormous proportions. But at least there was no problem of religious difference between Holstein and Denmark. In contrast to the Russians, whom he described as gentle and conciliatory, the behaviour of the Danes was distinguished by the inflexibility typical of Scandinavians. Denmark's hard line might be the result of the influence of a free press and free discussion in both legislative chambers, the Folketing and the Landtag. Unlike Russia, which had resisted European diplomacy over the Polish question, Denmark, as a small country faced with a strong enemy, was not in a position to do this.

In the event of a war the German land forces would easily deal with the small Danish army. Denmark could only offer resistance at sea, by blockading German ports, which would impose great losses on Germany. Austria had no interest in Holstein, but wanted to fulfil her obligations to Germany. Prussia had aspirations to the duchies and also wanted to meet her obligations to Germany.

The personality of Prince Augustenburg himself, said *Ostechestvennye zapiski* at the end of 1864,[66] played a minor part in the whole affair. The crux of the matter was the separation of the duchies from Denmark and their merger with Germany. There was not a single state in the whole of Germany which enjoyed such institutions of freedom as Denmark possessed, and which she would willingly give to Holstein. But Holstein hated Denmark and preferred to remain under the old type of administration rather than receive liberal institutions from Denmark.

The essence of the problem was the desire to bring all the German lands together in a single entity. This was not a new aim. The *amour propre* of the German nation

---

66. 'Politicheskaya Khronika Evropy', *Otechestvennye zapiski,* 1864, no. 1.

had long been suffering because the political system pertaining in Germany deprived it of a part in European affairs. This had come about as a result of the provisions of the treaty of Vienna, which had succeeded in making a great nation powerless by shrewdly giving it only a defensive organ, without aggressive strength and without a voice in the concert of the great powers. The Frankfurt Diet did not conceal the fact that the aim of the great movement which had seized Germany was the abolition of the provisions of the Congress of Vienna.

By invading Schleswig, Prussia and Austria had disturbed and shattered the unity of Germany, which was split into two camps with different interests, because south and north Germany had varying interests. There were also differences between Catholics and Protestants in Germany. In this way the German aspiration for unity had been hampered by the two great German powers and Germany had been divided into two different streams, southern and northern, in anticipation of the moment when the fence erected by the two larger German powers would collapse and the barrier to unity would disappear.

A similarly objective position on the essence and history of the conflict between Denmark and Germany was taken by the liberal *Golos*. In its issue on 9 November 1863, *Golos* outlined the history of Denmark's relations with the duchies and Germany from the beginning of the nineteenth century up to 1852. The German Diet, the paper informed its readers, had not recognised the succession of Christian IX, despite the provisions of the Treaty of London, nor did Germany recognise the Danish constitution, the aim of which was to link Schleswig with the remaining parts of the Danish monarchy. Germany regarded this move as an infringement of the sacred rights of the German nation.

Prince Augustenburg, without waiting for the decision of the German Diet, had proclaimed himself Duke of Schleswig-Holstein, and Prussia had placed her army on the alert, ready to give him military support. It was no accident that Bismarck was following in the footsteps of Napoleon III. He too found it advantageous to divert his country's attention from domestic affairs and concentrate all its interest on matters abroad . The situation, in the judgement of *Golos,* was tense and if a flame flared up in this hitherto unnoticed corner of Europe, the fire could turn into something threatening for the whole of Europe. France would want to take advantage of the difficulties experienced by Denmark and Germany on account of the conflict. Britain had a strong interest in the problem and would be allied with Denmark because of family connections. The current difficulties could seriously complicate relations between Russia and Europe and even change them, only it was hard to predict whether it would be for the better or the worse.

Since 1848 Russia had continually helped Denmark and in 1848 there had almost been a conflict with Russia's old and powerful ally, Prussia, in this connection. During the London negotiations Russia had defended the integrity of the Danish monarchy. The paper had no doubt that the Germans were not concerned about principles in the conflict over Schleswig-Holstein. The German Confederation simply wanted to detach the duchies from Denmark. But the nature of the affair had changed when Prussia became involved in the conflict.

Britain, in the opinion of *Golos,* would never agree to the partitioning of Denmark. France would be pleased that Prussia was involved in the question because this would provide a pretext for Napoleon III to occupy the left bank of the Rhine. But although Prussia and the German Diet were preparing for war, and although the threats from the lesser German states would not cease, the whole storm would blow over and would not extend beyond diplomatic notes.

Some days later, however, this optimistic tone changed. Forty million Germans, the paper said in alarm, were shouting 'now or never'. New developments had occurred, like the mobilisation of volunteers and the severing of relations between Austria and Denmark.[67] Because Denmark was weak, Germany could say to her peremptorily: 'fulfil your obligations immediately'. The Schleswig-Holstein question, the paper opined, had aroused the whole of Europe, and the Polish question had faded into the background. The congress proposed by Napoleon III had been forgotten and Germany had stopped fighting Bismarck. Written law, historical law and the interests of the whole of Europe apart from Germany were on Denmark's side. The majority of the population of Schleswig and educated opinion in Europe backed Denmark because she was a country governed in the spirit of enlightenment and liberalism.

Germany wanted not only Holstein but Schleswig too, and was using the idea of nationality as a pretext. If it succeeded in obtaining what it was demanding, Denmark would lose one of her richest provinces and would decline to the ranks of the poorest countries in Europe. Germany itself was not united nationally and on this account had no right to seize foreign lands. The national character which Germany was attributing to this venture was a very artificial thing. Why did Germany want to occupy Schleswig and Holstein but not Luxemburg, for instance? Why did it not think about Alsace – there were far more Germans there than in Holstein? The answer was that Denmark was small and weak. Germany wanted access to the sea, as she wanted to have a fleet in the Baltic and the North Sea. The German national character was exceptionally envious, covetous and greedy. All the great nations had fleets and Germany did not. These were the motives which drove her to seek to free her brothers in Holstein from the hateful Danes. As far as Russia was concerned, it was to her advantage to maintain the Danish monarchy intact and independent. Russian and British interests coincided in this.[68]

In the next issue[69] *Golos* emphasised another feature, namely that Russia, which had signed the Treaty of London, did not recognise Prince Augustenburg's claims, as they were without foundation, and could not deny King Christian IX the right to the whole Danish monarchy. For Russia, he was not only the sole legal King of Denmark, but also Duke of Schleswig, Holstein and Lauenburg. Germany's claims were unjustified, illegal and synthetic. Denmark was necessary to Russia to ensure the freedom of the Baltic. The emergence of a strong German navy was not in Russia's

---

67. *Golos,* no. 318, 30 Novembre 1863.
68. *Ibid.*
69. No. 319. 1. december 1863.

interest. It was contrary to both her political and her trade interests. 'We must support Denmark', *Golos* proclaimed.

Furthermore, Denmark was the guardian of the Sound. If Denmark possessed only Jutland and the islands she would be an insignificant state which would not survive for long in the face of a strong and hostile Germany. Circumstances would force her into a Scandinavian union, something, in the nature of the union of Kalmar, and then the guardian of the Sound would be a Scandinavian state comprising Sweden, Norway and Denmark. 'Can we really wish this?', asked *Golos*. The Sound in the hands of a powerful state would be the same thing as the Dardanelles and the Bosphorus. A Scandinavian union in control of the Sound could mean the closure of the Baltic to trade. Could this be allowed? Russia's interest, *Golos* concluded, lay in Denmark remaining an independent but second-rank state. Britain wanted this too. Hence Russia's interests required her to act with Britain to support Denmark.

As the dispute between Denmark and Germany became more serious and Germany took more and more drastic steps against Denmark, *Golos* became more and more sensitive about the methods used by Germany.[70] It maintained that the reason for Germany's increasingly violent attacks was, among other things, that she was worried by the democratic system of government in Denmark. There was nothing Germany did not accuse the Danes of being: barbarians and enemies of civilization were the kind of epithets Germany used to emphasise that she was guided by the highest considerations of civilization in seeking to occupy the duchies. Her motto was 'Nur immer langsam vorwärts', but in fact she aimed to use the Federal Execution to achieve her purpose quickly. The first shot on the Eider, *Golos* argued, would be the signal for important events, which Europe would watch with disquiet.

Golos believed[71] that Russia was being cautious in the current circumstances and was just waiting for a suitable moment to cast her veto. On the basis of information just received, the paper expressed the opinion that Germany's cause was lost, as long as the Emperor of the French, who liked surprises, did not act as a *deus ex machina*. In time, the Holstein question would fade into the background and the conscientious Germans, sated with bravado *(nakhrabrivshis' v volyu)*, would continue the peaceful work which was their reason for fame unsullied by blood, and humanity would admire their manufactures as before and praise the name of Germany.

There were differences between the political line taken by *Golos* and the official government line on Germany's policy and the question of Denmark's 'guilt'. The paper did not trust Bismarck's explanation of the reasons why Austria and Prussia intended to enter Schleswig. 'We shall see', the paper commented on the larger German states' plans,[72] but it did not exclude the possibility that if they really did not want to detach Schleswig from Denmark, but only to guarantee their rights arising from previous agreements, Denmark would presumably agree to this and the affair would be ended by a diplomatic solution.

70. *Ibid.,* no. 342, 24 December 1863.
71. *Ibid.,* no. 343, 27 December 1863.
72. *Ibid.,* no. 16, 16 (28) January 1864.

The basic arguments propounded in *Golos* during the period from October to December concerning Germany's policy and attitude towards Denmark were countered by polemics from *Peterburgskie Vedomosti*. It attacked the opinion put forward by *Golos* that Germany's behaviour towards Denmark was dishonourable, that Holstein had been seized by deceit, and that the whole blame for the conflict lay exclusively with the behaviour of the German states.[73]

Germany could not be accused of a lack of openness over the Holstein-Schleswig question. She had concealed nothing. Her aim was to separate Holstein from Denmark, and if she had been against Federal Execution it was because she regarded it as an inadequate method. Execution had been demanded by a small majority in the Diet, the minority had favoured military occupation of the duchies. The revolution, *Peterburgskie Vedomosti* argued, had been brought about not by the Federal Execution but by the Holsteiners themselves. Could troops resist a national upsurge, were they supposed to disperse the meeting at Elmshorn, tear down the Schleswig-Holstein flags and fire on the masses? The truth was that the appearance of the execution armies had accelerated the revolution and contributed to the change of regime. An attempt to remove Prince Augustenburg could lead to a fight with the execution armies.

As far as the Execution in Schleswig was concerned, on the other hand, it was a question of compelling Denmark to fulfil her obligations to the German Confederation. If these demands were just, then the decision to occupy Schleswig was just, in so far as means of coercion could be just. It was up to Denmark whether she regarded the occupation of Schleswig as equivalent to a declaration of war, and whether she wanted to teach Germany a lesson, as *Golos* put it. 'The least desirable thing', *Peterburgskie Vedomosti* ended, 'would be for diplomacy to muzzle Germany, for that would mean putting off a decision on a conflict which is equally hard for both sides and is fully ripe for a final solution'.

Peterburgskie Vedomosti, which was close to Gorchakov's political line, represented (like the liberal papers, incidentally) an anti-Scandinavian policy and received the Havas agency report from Copenhagen that Denmark had not yet signed a defensive pact with Sweden with satisfaction.[74] It concluded from this that after the death of Frederick VII neither party would express its readiness to sign such a convention in advance, which it thougt could influence the decisions of the Frankfurt Diet. *Peterburgskie Vedomosti* saw the crux of the whole problem as early as the turn of the year 1863-64, namely that Germany was concerned with something more than seizing the Elbe duchies. 'Germany's quest for unity has not achieved great success hitherto, but there are reasons for thinking that the Schleswig-Holstein affair will be more profitable in this respect than debates among a gathering of delegates would be'.[75] (The reference of course was to the Frankfurt Diet).

73. *Peterburgskie Vedomosti*, 28 December 1863 (9 January 1864).
74. *Ibid.*, no. 246, 6 (18) November 1863.
75. *Ibid.* no. 3, 4 January 1864.

Russkii invalid was more critical of Germany than the semi-official organ. On 19 November (1 December) 1863 it submitted, following *The Times,* that the German movement was not a sudden impulse but a desire for annexations, a desire to transform Schleswig into a German province and to capture Kiel, which, as a German port on the Baltic, would form the essential base for the future creation of a fleet and the development of Germany as a naval power. Britain understood how extensive such a fleet would become if Germany succeeded in obtaining Holstein and Schleswig, and what a great military power Germany could become in the future. The paper was inclined to the view that Germany wanted a war with Denmark and would not give up any of the demands she had put forward.

Russki invalid had serious reservations about whether Schleswig would share the same fate as Holstein, and whether Prussia and Austria could be trusted when they said they wanted to occupy Schleswig as a pledge to compel Denmark to fulfil the obligations she had undertaken. 'Who can guarantee that after they have seized their booty German greed will be willing to let it go? Do we not know that Germany sees Holstein as an inseparable part of its German Vaterland from now on?'[76] As this passage shows, this paper, which was close to the war ministry, had no illusions about how events would develop if Germany were successful in carrying out her plans. Gorchakov, as we know, preferred to ignore this question and afterwards consoled himself and others that the process of creating a naval power must take a long time.

It was in the interests of both Austria and Prussia, said *Russkii invalid,* to take the Schleswig-Holstein question into their own hands, so as to eliminate the revolutionary party and keep the lesser German states out of the decisions on the matter, in order to prevent a European war. The German states were counting on the support of the European powers, which were also interested in preserving peace, and on their influencing Denmark to make concessions. On this point – the question of peace – the interests of Russia and Britain were the same as those of Austria and Prussia. At any rate, it seemed, the rapprochement between Austria and Prussia in connection with the Schleswig-Holstein problem was a lasting development which could not fail to influence other European matters. In the event of France proceeding with some of her ideas, Austria would not be so isolated as she had been in 1859, and if France made an attempt on the Rhineland, Prussia would not be without allies either.[77]

Only, really, the extremely conservative *Vest',* like the firmly pro-German *Petersburger Zeitung,* welcomed the fact that, thanks to the attitude of Austria and Prussia, the Schleswig-Holstein question had been considerably simplified, since they were opposed to the aspirations of the German national party, whose aim was to free Germany of the obligations entered into in London in 1852. Austria and Prussia, on the other hand, were faithful to the Treaty of London, and their aim was to compel the Danish king by means of military execution to fulfil his obligations to Schleswig, Holstein and Lauenburg. *Vest'* saw the whole problem in a rather

76. *Russkii invalid,* no. 2, 3 (15) January 1864.
77. *Ibid.,* no. 6, 9 (21) January 1864.

optimistic light, as Austria and Prussia were acting in solidarity with each other and Britain had no intention of going to war in defence of Denmark.[78]

Even *Vest',* however, said that in no circumstances could Russia want a German victory over Denmark. That would mean a victory for the rule of force, for the medieval law of the fist *(Faustrecht),* and a radical upheaval in international law. Russia was not interested in territorial changes, since that could weaken her own position. In Germany, as in France, a medieval thirst for booty prevailed, the only difference being that in the nineteenth-century custom required that it be hidden behind the mask of voting, or done on the pretext of execution led by an offended party. Germany wanted to capture Kiel, in order to create the fleet of which she dreamt. To fulfil this plan she was ready to do anything. The German democrats, and Bavaria and Saxony and Württemberg all wanted this; hence their support for Prince Augustenburg, who had no right to the duchies. But thanks to the larger German states, Germany would not succeed in plundering and partitioning Denmark.[79]

A similar tone was also to be found in Katkov's *Moskovskie vedomosti* which had been, as it were, the leading organ of the Russian nationalists since the time of the Polish uprising and exerted a strong influence in shaping public opinion.[80] Katkov's paper launched its main attack against France and her idea of convening a conference, which it saw as a design on the part of Napoleon III to escape from isolation.[81] It spoke out firmly against the intentions of the liberal camp in Germany, Augustenburg's designs, and the plan outlined by the Triad states in respect of the Schleswig-Holstein question.[82] In the paper's view the Triad meant the subordination of the lesser German states to France. Katkov saw the hand of France behind what was happening at the stormy sessions of the Frankfurt Diet in December 1863. France was helping the liberals because it was in her interest if they punished Austria and Prussia for the latter's efforts to strengthen German unity. Only the reassurance of German patriots and the restoration of their rightful role to the second-rank German states, in Katkov's opinion, could help to mitigate the Danish-German conflict.[83]

A mature presentation of the essence of the Danish-German problem was to be found in *Sovremennik,* published by the democratic camp, in volume XCIC, which came out at the turn of the year 1863-64. The editors had no illusions about the behaviour of Germany, that at least half the European powers would take an irresolute attitude towards the conflict, and that it would be resolved not by diplomatic means but by force.

The article started with a discussion of the fashionable idea of nationality and its advantages. It could be an ally for governments (Napoleon III, Victor Emanuel),

78. *Vest',* no. 16 (47), 24 November 1863 (old style).
79. *Ibid.,* no. 21 (52), 31 December 1863.
80. On the role of Katkov see *Vospominaniya B.N. Chicherina,* vol I. p. 92 and vol. II. pp. 173 ff. See also: Brandes, *ibid.* p. 167 ff.
81. *Moskovskie vedomosti,* no. 243, 7 November 1863.
82. *Ibid.,* no. 245, 9 November 1863.
83. *Ibid.,* no. 274, 18 December 1863.

but in the opinion of *Sovremennik* the idea would not help to improve the situation of the masses. It made sense when it was combined with improvement of the civic and national situation, if the working masses really received these rights. But in the case of Germany, 'das deutsche Vaterland' was just a matter of seizing lands belonging to a weaker neighbour.

Germany wanted a language used by one-fifth of the population to be obligatory in the whole of Denmark. It was the Junker bureaucracy opposition in Holstein that had launched the first attack against Denmark. The reactionary Holstein aristocracy had stirred up anti-Danish agitation and the more concessions the Danes made the more aggressive the German demands became. Prussian liberals regarded the anti-Danish policy as meaning the abandonment of Olomunc and a switch from Manteuffel's conservative policy to the nationalist line of the Nationalverein. The Gotha party wanted to make Schleswig-Holstein the cradle for a German fleet, and the German democrats were misled by a false concept of nationality.

The Danes, hard pressed by Germany and urged by Russia to respect the national and constitutional rights of the Germans in the duchies, had made concessions (1858), but they could not accept Russell's Gotha programme unless they wanted to kill the Danish monarchy with their own hands and make it a German province. The March 1863 patent, which was in the nature of an interim act, and, even more so, the 18 November 1863 Constitution, were regarded by Germany and other states as acts joining Schleswig with Denmark in violation of international treaties, and the death of Frederick VII had complicated an already difficult situation.

Sovremennik was very critical of the position taken by the great powers. It did not believe that any of them really intended to come to Denmark's aid, not even Sweden. And since the forces involved in the conflict were so uneven it anticipated that the outcome would be the partitioning of Denmark and the sacrifice of basic political institutions to the feudal and false national demands of Germany, unless the European states reconsidered their attitude to the question. But up till then (the end of 1863) there seemed no likelihood of that. Right was on Denmark's side, and injustice and force on Germany's. The Monrad government, which had replaced Hall's, was unwilling to change the constitution, convinced that concessions would achieve nothing, but would only lead to new and even more unjust demands from Germany. Denmark's military strength, however, was small in comparison with Austria, Prussia and Germany.

The entire press displayed great interest in the conflict, with the single exception of *Den'*, the organ of the Slavophils edited by I.S. Aksakov. This was a product of their ideological principles; they were interested in the problems of the Southern Slavs and saw Russia's missionary role in liberating them from Turkey, but they often had a contemptuous attitude to problems fermenting in Western Europe. *Den'* considered that Russia's political interests lay on the Danube and in the East, and that a shift in the centre of gravity of Russian policy to Germany would be a mistake. Was it not all the same to Russia, the paper asked, if Prince Augustenburg or Prince Oldenburg ruled Schleswig and Holstein? It saw no reason why Russia had to become involved in the Schleswig-Holstein 'muddle'. How could it be a danger to Russia if the German Union seized the duchies and Kiel?[84]

Let Germany settle German problems; the most important thing for us is not to be infected by the German spirit and not to let German interests become Russian interests,

declared Aksakov.[85]

In his opinion, the threat was not from Germany, but Germanism, not the German states but German statecraft *(deutsche Staatskunst)*. In order to demonstrate its indifference to the affairs of Western Europe *Den'* enquired whether it was not all the same to Russia if Napoleon ruled the Rhineland.[86] Russia's interests were not on the Rhine but on the Danube, and especially in the East.

For reasons of principle the paper opposed the policy of solidarity with Austria, both because of her attitude to the Polish question in 1863 and in view of Russia's and Austria's conflicting interests in the East, on the Danube.[87] *Den'* also had a negative attitude to Prussia. While it was true that Prussia had not abandoned Russia during the Crimean War, she had not co-operated with her either. Currently it was not hard to imagine a Russo-Prussian conflict on account of the situation in the Balkans and in Germany itself.[88]

The negative attitude which *Den'* took to Russia's links with the German states was a result of the Slavophils' ideology. In their opinion the German-Latin world hated Slavonic and Orthodox Russia. This hatred was the consequence of their two different styles of spiritual life. But peace would be impossible in Europe if Russia renounced her Slavonic origin and her Orthodox faith.[89]

As the reader can see from the above excerpts, Russian papers and periodicals understood the connection between the Schleswig-Holstein question and the battle for the unification of Germany right from the start. They doubted whether Germany needed unification purely for the purposes of defence against France.[90]

The conservative papers[91] feared the revolutionary movement and a revolutionary united Germany and therefore welcomed the fact that Austria and Prussia had

---

84. *Den'*, 30 May 1864.
85. See *Otechestvennye zapiski*, vol. 6, (1864), pp. 944-6.
86. *Den'*, 30 May 1864.
87. *Ibid.*, 28 March 1864.
88. *Ibid.*, 7 November 1864.
89. See *Sochineniya I.S. Aksakova*, 'Pribaltiiskii vopros, 1860-1886', vol. VI (Moscow, 1887), 'Kak ponimaet Ostzeiskii Nemets ideal Rossii', *Den'*, 2 June 1862, *Ibid.*, pp. 3-9 and 27 October 1865, pp. 9-16. I.S. Aksakov, *Sochineniya*, vol. I, 'Slavyanskii vopros, 1860-1886', (Moscow, 1886), pp. 24-34; N.Ya. Danilevsky, *Rossiya i Evropa*, (1st ed. 1871); Ya. Zitis, 'K. Istorii..', E. Kattner, *Preussens Beruf im Osten* (Berlin 1868); E.M. Feoktistov, *Vospominaniya*, pp. 108-9, recalls that as early as 1856 the minister of internal affairs, A.E. Timashev, summmoned the editors of the newspapers and criticised Katkov's ultra-patriotism in connection with the question of the Baltic Germans. *Moskovskie vedomosti* expressed the opinion that the unification of Germany could threaten the territorial rights of Russia in the Baltic lands. Timashev called on the editors not to inflame relations with a friendly country, i.e. Prussia, Cf. Nikitenko, *Dnevnik*, vol. II, 3 July 1864, p. 448, vol. III, p. 41; D. Beyrau, *Russische Orientpolitik und die Entstehung des deutschen Kaiserreiches 1866-1870/71*, (Wiesbaden, 1974), pp. 17-20.
90. *Golos*, nos. 16, 150, 1864; *Peterburgskie Vedomosti*, no. 140, 1864.
91. For example *Vest'*, no. 37, 1864.

taken the Schleswig-Holstein question into their own hands. Initially even Katkov was inclined to argue that Germany unified under the aegis of Prussia was not a threat,[92] among other things because it would help to block claims to new lands by Napoleon III.[93] But when it transpired that Prussia sought to conquer the Elbe duchies he sounded the alarm, as this was contrary to Russia's interests. 'Europe must not allow Prussia to annex Schleswig and Holstein', he wrote.[94]

The democratic press, and to some extent the liberal press, too, from the start took a critical and distrustful attitude to Bismarck's policy, particularly his manœuvres over Schleswig, and *Golos* thought that a unified Germany of forty million inhabitants was against the interests of both Europe and Russia.[95] The press saw the events connected with the conflict over the duchies from the point of view of Russian interests in the Baltic. It regarded any change in this part of Europe as undesirable because it would mean disturbing the balance of power in the north and weakening Russia's position. Irrespective of political direction it warned against letting the Sound become a second Dardanelles and Bosphorus. Hence it unequivocally rejected the idea of a Scandinavian union as unacceptable to Russia. It would also be a threat to Russia if Prussia established herself in the duchies, built up a German fleet in Kiel and created a naval power in the Baltic and North Sea. Besides this, any territorial changes in this part of Europe could prompt Napoleon's France to conquer Belgium and the Rhineland.[96]

The entire press was against any military involvement in the conflict by Russia, and all the papers apart from the democratic press supported the conservative forces in Germany, represented by Austria and Prussia, and the policy of co-operation with Britain, which took a similar position to Russia in the conflict at the turn of the year 1863-1864.

News of the Austrian and Prussian troops' invasion of Schleswig was received unfavourably by public opinion in Russia. After the fall of the Dannewirke, sympathy was expressed for little Denmark under attack from the two larger German powers. *Golos* expressed surprise that Britain, which had issued so many threats, did not move and that Sweden was silent. There was no longer any doubt that Prussia and Austria wanted something considerably more than just Denmark's fulfilment of the obligations she had undertaken in 1852.[97] If the great powers seriously wanted peace they would use strong and realistic means to that end and could exert such strong moral pressure on Germany that she would not have dared to touch Denmark.[98] The German forces' crossing of the Eider was regarded as yet one more crying injustice at which Europe made no protest. Germany did not even conceal the fact that now the first shots had been fired she wanted the duchies, and

92. *Moskovskie vedomosti*, no. 36, 1864.
93. *Ibid.*, nos. 86, 144, 1864.
94. *Ibid.*, 12 March 1864; see Narochnitskaya, p. 43.
95. *Golos*, no. 140, 22 May (3 June) 1864.
96. *Ibid.*, nos. 42, 126, 171, 1864; *Moskovskie vedomosti*, nos. 37, 42, 1864.
97. *Golos*, no. 25, 25 January (6 February) 1864.
98. *Ibid.* no. 25, 1864.

Austria and Prussia were the executants of German demands. It was not hard to foresee that Denmark could lose the duchies to Germany. Europe, which had threatened Germany if she started a war, was now silently admiring her firmness and prowess. 'Podlinno smelomu i sil'nomu sud'ba pomagaet',[99] wrote *Golos*.[100] The Prussians knew that Prince Augustenburg's role would be merely nominal and their influence would be strong enough to ensure their interests, though they were hiding this from Austria. Nor did they want to begin negotiations before they had conquered Schleswig.[101]

Golos thus had no illusions about Prussia's aims and expounded them clearly. In its opinion the policy of Palmerston and Russell (it did not dare to criticise Russian policy) had led to bankruptcy. If things went so far, *Golos* asked, what would happen to small states. How could their existence be guaranteed. Today Germany was plundering Denmark, tomorrow France would find a pretext to occupy Belgium, Spain would seize Portugal and Austria part of Turkey. The great nations would permit lawlessness in the pursuit of their material interests.[102]

Golos defended Denmark and attacked *Moskovskie vedomosti*, which had argued in its 13 February issue that Danish demagogues and democrats were the reason for Denmark's misfortune and had caused the outbreak of war.[103] At the same time *Golos* defended Russian policy and rejected the *Morning Post*'s accusations about the creation of a new Holy Alliance.[104] To back this up it quoted the statement on this matter published in the *Journal de St Pétersbourg*, in which the minister of foreign affairs categorically denied the widespread rumours on the subject in Western Europe. *Golos* also quoted the opinion of the *Journal de St Pétersbourg* that the Holy Alliance was a memory of another age. Russia wanted peace, not a league of states against the freedom of nations, and was opposed to a European coalition directed against any state. The only alliance, *Golos* quoted the *Journal*, was an alliance for peace, progress and the general good.[105]

The *Golos* commentary was not very original, as *Otechestvennye zapiski* also quoted the denial in the *Journal de St Pétersbourg* and used the same wording in its comment, that the only possible alliance was a union of peace, progress and welfare. This was the course Russia was following, and she needed peace to complete the reform process.[106] But *Golos* did not deny that some problem or other (it was probably thinking of the Polish question) could draw Russia close to Austria and Prussia, but a situation could also arise in which there would be a rapprochement between Russia and Britain.[107]

99. Fate helps the truly brave and strong. (Who dares, wins).
100. *Golos*, no. 28. 28 January (9 February) 1864.
101. *Ibid.*, no. 38, 7 (19 February) 1864.
102. *Ibid.*, no. 32, 1 (13) February 1864.
103. *Ibid.*, no. 46, 15 (27) February 1864.
104. *Ibid.*, no. 57, 26 February (9 March) 1864.
105. *Ibid.*, no. 65, 5 (17) March 1864.
106. *Otechestvennye zapiski*, vol. 3, 1864, p. 48.
107. *Golos*, no. 57, 26 February (9 March) 1864.

On the other hand, this liberal paper was firmly against Scandinavianism and a union of the Scandinavian states. A new discussion on this topic was prompted by articles in the British press arguing that the Swedes wanted Denmark driven to extreme measures so that she would agree to a merger with Sweden. Sweden, said *Golos*,[108] had encouraged Denmark to resist Germany and promised her support, but had not kept this promise. Such behaviour could not fail to engender suspicions about Sweden's intentions in respect of Denmark. *Golos* consoled itself that these matters were not easy. Neither the Swedes nor the Danes liked each other. For a true *(istiinnogo)* Swede a Dane was what an Irishman was for John Bull. The Danish language was something comical for him and the Swedes were convinced of their national superiority. Trade and naval rivalry augmented these antipathies, but that might not be an obstacle to a merger between Sweden and Denmark.

Neither Russia nor Prussia would agree to this, and it was doubtful if Britain would either, as she, too, did not want to see a powerful state in the Baltic. Russia, *Golos* considered, would not agree to the rise of a strong Sweden, which would attack Russia at the first opportunity in order to occupy Finland. Sweden would be able to make the Baltic into a Swedish lake and obstruct Russia's trade. The Swedes were deluding themselves about Britain's attitude to a union of the Scandinavian states. Britain wanted to weaken Russia, but not to such an extent that the Baltic passed into the hands of a single powerful state, even if it was close to Britain and hostile to Russia.

The press presented the course of events at the front in a light favourable to Denmark, and emphasised the heroism and valour of the Danes in the face of a powerful and much better equipped enemy.[109] Much was written too about the brutal behaviour of the Austro-Prussian troops towards the population of Schleswig.[110] The papers reported that the Prussian and Austrian officials were governing Schleswig like a conquered country and, at the same time as overthrowing the 18 November Constitution, had taken a series of measures such as introducing the German language in schools.[111] *Peterburgskie Vedomosti* had no illusions that if Schleswig came entirely under German rule life would be as hard for the Danes in northern Schleswig as it had previously been for the Germans in the south.[112]

At the same time the papers criticised the Danish government's refusal to participate in a conference, despite many weeks of effort by Britain and Russia. Denmark, said *Russkii invalid*,[113] and especially the government of Christian IX, answered all suggestions and attempts to persuade her to enter into negotiations with an unchanging *non possumus,* like Pius IX, counting on her allies finally deciding to defend her, however difficult their own position.

---

108. *Ibid.,* no. 42, 11 (23) February 1864.
109. *Ibid.,* no. 181, 3 (15) July 1864.
110. *Russkii invalid,* no. 97, 2 (14) May 1864; *Otechestvennye zapiski,* vols. 1-2, 3-4, 1864.
111. *Peterburgskie Vedomosti,* no. 36, 13 (25) February 1864.
112. *Ibid.,* no. 24, 30 January 1864.
113. *Russkii invalid,* 4 (16) March 1864.

The Russian papers deluded themselves that Britain would not allow Denmark to be defeated. They thought Britain was no less interested than Russia in the Danish-German dispute, and they therefore favoured diplomatic and political co-operation with the cabinet of St. James.[114] But if on the one hand they lamented Britain's passivity, on the other hand they were afraid she might push Russia into war. Such a war would expose her to the double risk of having to fight the whole of Germany. In a situation where Britain stood on the side lines while Russia and Sweden were both involved, Napoleon III might come together with Germany.[115]

The illusion that Britain would join in the conflict persisted right up to the opening of the London Conference. The press expected that Russia and Britain would co-operate at the conference in order to settle the conflict.[116] After the German armies had occupied Kolding, the press ceased to believe that Austria and Prussia would agree to peace on the previous terms, that is to say, the conditions existing before the outbreak of the war. They would demand concessions from Denmark, but in the situation existing in Denmark she could hardly expect a compromise. The press was convinced that the Danish government would continue the fight and then a European war might prove unavoidable, because the countries which had signed the Treaty of London could not look on with indifference while their guarantees of the integrity of the whole of Denmark were so unceremoniously violated.[117]

Otechestvennye zapiski[118] regretted that a peacefully and constitutional country, in which the population enjoyed civil freedoms, where education was growing in an unprecedented manner, society was developing peacefullly and the political and social system were approaching the ideal, should be sacrificed to Germany. The paper did not agree that from the national point of view Germany was right. The national principle had been abused. Blood was being shed in the name of the national principle, which was supposed to increase the welfare of nations and be an instrument of freedom. Now the anomaly had arisen that under the feudal rule of Frederick Augustenburg and his pro-consuls in Holstein, the situation of his subjects would be ten times worse than under the rule of the Danish Rigsraad, 'Khot' khuzhe, da edinoplemyannoe, khot' khoroshee, da inozemnoe',[119] the paper sneered about Germany's attitude.

The liberal opposition in Prussia, which had seemed to be strong and hated Bismarck, ceased to attack him after he announced that Prussia no longer recognised the Treaty of London. Bismarck knew well that their words would not be followed by deeds. The idea of nationalism had triumphed over the quest for civil freedoms. As the price for duchies becoming German (and perhaps Prussian) pro-

---

114. *Moskovskie vedomosti*, no. 42; *Golos*, nos. 42, 43; *Otechestvennye zapiski*, no. 3, 1864, p. 43.
115. *Moskovskie vedomosti*, no. 42; *Golos*, nos. 170, 171, 1864.
116. *Moskovskie vedomosti*, no. 174; *Golos*, nos. 25, 32, 42, 116, 117, 1864.
117. *Otechestvennye zapiski*, vol. 3-4, 1864, p. 42.
118. *Ibid.*, pp. 40-42.
119. Better worse but of our own kind than better but foreign.

vinces, the liberals had reconciled themselves to a regime without a budget and with a feudal ministry. It was sufficient to look through the German liberal newspapers to be convinced that if the liberals attacked Bismarck they did so without malice. As the price for seeing the red, gold and black banner hanging over the town hall in every town where a handful of Germans lived they were ready to renounce civil rights. Europe had taken a different view of the German liberals until then. Now it could see that F.H. Schulze-Delitzsch and his comrades lacked the civil courage to oppose an unjust cause. Europe had been mistaken; in future it would be more careful.

The attitude of the German liberals was criticised fundamentally in *Zagranichnyi vestnik,* no. 1, 1864, in an article, 'Po datskomu voprosu',[120] which advanced similar arguments to those put forward by *Otechestvennye zapiski.* If Schleswig and Holstein left Denmark they would present a sickening spectacle of prejudiced Junker rule like Mecklenburg. Was that what the German liberals wanted? Should Germany not first work out the same freedoms for itself as the Danish constitution gave its citizens, before worrying about the extension of national rights. The editor of the paper. A. Afanasiev Chuzhbinsky, in a review of Rudolf Usinger's book *Dänisch-deutsche Geschichte 1189-1227,* pointed out how misleadingly and tendentiously the German author had outlined the history of the dispute over Schleswig seven centuries before in order 'albeit indirectly, to show that Germany had rights to the lands which were currently the subject of dispute'.[121] In order to prove this, the author of the book had presented Waldemar[122] as a warlike and treacherous Danish ruler who had taken advantage of the fact that Frederick I was so preoccupied with other matters that he was forced to cede the lands on the Elbe and the Weser to Denmark.

Zagranichnyi vestnik, vol. II, part 4, in a comment on the fine thoughts of Victor Hugo about a new era, when peace would flourish, reason and enlightenment triumph, and thinkers, philosophers and scholars hold sway, pointed out what a very different picture was presented today by the ruined towns, thousand of families deprived of the basic means of life, countries destroyed by the ravages of war, burdened by levies and ruled by military regimes. This was how it expressed its protest against the results of the German armies' invasion of Schleswig and Jutland.[123].

The sharpest criticism of Germany's behaviour towards Denmark is to be found in the organs of the democratic movement in Russia, *Russkoe slovo, Iskra,* edited by V.S. Kurochkin, and *Sovremennik.*[124] *Russkoe slovo* approached the Schleswig-Holstein question in the context of the political and social struggle in Germany. It saw that the problem was connected with the fight for changes in Germany itself,

---

120. On the Danish Question.
121. *Zagranichnyi vestnik,* vol. I, pt. 3, 1864, p. 154.
122. Waldemar (Valdemar) the Victorious (1202-1241).
123. *Ibid.,* vol. II, part 4, p. 201.
124. V.S. Kurochkin, *Sobranie stikhotvorenii,* vol. I (St Petersburg, 1869), p. 340, vol. II, pp. 214-24; N.P. Ogarev, *Izbrannye proizvedeniya,* (Moscow, 1956), vol. II, p. 11.

both political (the question of the Frankfurt Diet, abolition of the German Confederation) and social.[125] Right from the beginning of the war between Denmark and Germany the paper made the essential point of Bismarck's policy clear. The aim of this policy, it said, was to subordinate the whole of Germany to Prussia, and drawing Austria into co-operation over the Schleswig-Holstein question was only a skillful manœuvre on Bismarck's part. The paper exposed Prussia's plans to become a great power, her aspiration to be a naval power and acquire ports on the Baltic and the North Sea.[126] It supported solution of the Schleswig-Holstein question according to the will of the population rather than the conquerors. It criticised German liberals who supported Prussia's predatory plans, expressed joy at Prussian victories and identified the interests of feudal landowners with the interests of the nation.[127]

It perceived that with the successive military victories by Austria and Prussia the German liberal and democratic parties, the *National* and the *Reform Verein,* were slowly coming to agree with Prussia's way of solving the problem, and after the German army crossed the Slie the army general, Wrangel, whose group had until recently incurred the liberals' hatred, became an object of general admiration and a national hero. The paper continually exposed the perfidious policy of Bismarck, who resorted to lies at every step in order to explain the Prussian army's moves. After the capture of Kolding, for example, Bismarck tried to assure Europe that Wrangel had acted contrary to his instructions in taking this step and that the town had been captured for strategic reasons. If Prussia and Austria occupied Schleswig, Bismarck claimed, they did so in order to guarantee the integrity of the Danish monarchy; if they occupied Jutland, it was in order to recover the costs connected with the occupation of Schleswig. It was true, *Russkoe slovo* commented ironically, that if they did not occupy Copenhagen in order to recover the costs associated with occupying Jutland, and Sweden, to recompense themselves for the losses involved in occupying Denmark, it was evidently not because they lacked good will but merely because they lacked the resources.

In fairness it had to be recognised, however, said *Russkoe slovo,* in connection with the later discussions in London, that Bismarck knew how to play on that tricky instrument known as a popular vote as skillfully as Prince Cuza and Louis Napoleon.

As far as the great powers' attitudes were concerned, *Russkoe slovo* devoted most attention to British, and particularly Palmerston's, policy towards the Danish-German conflict. It saw signs of weakness in this policy. Britain was aware, however, that if, with such a splendid fleet, she did not play an active part, she would lose prestige and influence in Europe. The paper considered that Britain's position had wavered, especially when she received a hint from Gorchakov, and Palmerston's inconsistency during the London Conference was shown by the fact

---

125. *Russkoe slovo,* no. 3, 1864, pp. 18, 19.
126. *Ibid.,* no. 1, 1864, p. 12; no. 1, 1865, pp. 14-15; no. 4, 1865, p. 79.
127. *Ibid.,* nos. 2, and 7, 1864.

that on the one hand he spoke in support of the integrity of Denmark, and on the other in favour of its division.[128]

Sovremennik, no. 6, June 1864, said that all Europe's opinion was focused on the Danish question. It called Germany's behaviour towards Denmark an injustice; the use of force by the strong against the weak, and the national question, which Germany bandied around, a monstrous fraud intended to plunder Denmark. *Sovremennik* exposed the lies, deception and coercion employed by Prussia and her ally, Austria. It reported the methods being used by Germany – violence, arrests, removal of Danish officials, Germanisation of schools, offices and churches. These abuses were occuring in the territory of Schleswig in the wake of the invading German armies. In Jutland military requisitions and arrests were taking place.

If we spoke of greed, punctilliousness, violence and injustice on Germany's part, said *Sovremennik,* that did not mean that the Danes had a greater right to rule the duchies than did the Germans. The point was simply that the Germans' claims were irrelevant; they wanted to conquer the duchies and were using some theoretical ideas about a German fatherland as a pretext. But far be it from us, the paper said, to argue that the Danes should rule the duchies if the population does not want that. The whole question boiled down to whether the inhabitants wanted Prince Frederick, or whether they wanted to be part of the German Confederation, or a Danish province. Meanwhile they were being compelled to be Germans and a ruler was being imposed on them. Although there was no doubt that the situation of the population under the rule of Prince Frederick would be worse than it had been under Denmark, even if there had been shortcomings in her rule, if, despite this, the population really did earnestly want to exchange Danish rule for German, it would be folly to keep them under Denmark by force. But the paper was against the kind of comedy of marionettes which Napoleon III had used in the plebiscites in Savoy and Nice, or conducting a plebiscite under the bayonets in occupied Schleswig.

III.

From the moment the London Conference was convened, and particularly after the Prussian army's capture of Dybøl, the tone of the Russian press, from *Moskovskie vedomosti* to *Sovremennik,* underwent a further change. The failures of European diplomacy, including Russian diplomacy, at the conference, and the increasingly aggressive attitude of the German, and especially Prussian, diplomats, led the majority of the Russian press to attack Prussia more and more sharply for her aggressive statements and intentions concerning the future of the duchies. *Russkii invalid,* no. 97, 2 (14) May 1864, following the *Journal de St Pétersbourg,* criticised the Prussian press' intoxication with victories over the Danish army. At the same time the Russian press took up the defence of Russian policy. In *Golos*[129] we read that Russia

---

128. *Ibid.* no. 2, pp. 1-11, no. 3, pp. 14-22, no. 4, p. 17, no. 6, pp. 72 ff. 1864.
129. *Golos,* no. 126, 8 (20) May 1864.

had adopted a conciliatory position in the Danish-German dispute and that it was fundamentally important for her to preserve the Danish monarchy in its entirety and prevent changes in the Baltic. It was in Russia's interest that Denmark's possessions should not be reduced, nor Germany's increased. Russia had signed treaties on the integrity of Denmark and wanted to adhere to them, for Russian policy was distinguished by the fact that she was always scrupulously faithful to her treaties and obligations.

On the other hand, *Golos* recognised, Russia had no basis for breaking off her friendly relations with the German states. When the Danish-German war began Russia's relations with the German states were more friendly than before. Relations with Austria had improved. This placed Russia under special obligations to Germany. While disapproving of Germany's territorial acqusitions and defending the integrity of Denmark, Russia could influence Germany only by persuasion and advice, playing the part of mediator between the two sides.

This was the role which, in Gorchakov's opinion, Russian diplomacy had to play at the London Conference. Like Britain, Russia was seeking a solution which would take account of the fair and justified demands of Germany while being compatible with the rights of the Danes in respect of Holstein. Germany's position was not clear, however, nor was it known what she ultimately wanted. Prussia wanted to annex the duchies, but others said they did not want to go so far and would agree to the duchies being given to Prince Augustenburg, but under the control of Prussia. There were also those who said that Prussia favoured a personal union of the duchies with Denmark, but with Rendsborg becoming a federal fortress with a Prussian garrison and Kiel a federal port with a Prussian fleet. Austria would not seek anything other than what Prussia wanted. Interpreting the words of Wilhelm I, that Prussia would not agree to any solution from which she did not gain, *Golos* thought these were not careless words and behind them lay real threats.[130]

Southern Jutland would be in German hands, and this would reinforce the strenth of the nation of forty million: at the same time the naval position would change to its advantage, and Russia and Europe could not be indifferent to that. The future of Schleswig-Holstein could be viewed with equanimity if a completely separate state came into being, unconnected with the German Confederation. But the reality was different. Germany would quickly turn Kiel into a naval base ranking with Kronstadt, Portsmouth, Brest or Cherbourg. Furthermore, Prussia, with her army and fleet, would control Prince Augustenburg. So this promised to be an advantageous solution for Prussia. Knowing the history of Prussia's rapacious policy, said *Golos*,[131] it was to be expected that, in view of the weakness and transitoriness of German democracy, Prussia would sooner or later acquire hegemony over Germany, for only Prussia was capable of unifying Germany.

Golos observed the struggle between Britain and Russia at the London Conference. Russia put forward Prince Oldenburg as a candidate and then supported

130. *Ibid.,* no. 132, 14 (26) May and no. 140, 22 May (3 June) 1864.
131. *Ibid.,* no. 159, 11 (23) June 1864.

Britain's proposal for a frontier on the Slie. It was clear from this[132] that the first proposal was conditional on part of the lands really being detached from Denmark. This fact, in the opinion of *Golos,* showed that at the conference Russia had acted as a great European power, not pursuing any unilateral aims and concerned principally and solely with preserving the balance of power in northern Europe.

Russia had no interest in unleashing a new war, said *Russkii invalid,* 14 (26) June 1864, following the *Journal de St Pétersbourg* of 15 June. The duty of rulers was to stand above passing emotions, even when they were especially strongly felt.

Is there really no way – the paper asked – to end the dispute between Denmark and Germany through a court of conciliation? Will there really be damage to national pride, or someone's interests, if the warring parties agree to submit to an independent court appointed by themselves?

It was not in Russia's interest to support Germany's uncontrollable thirst for power, said *Russkii invalid,* 4 (16) June 1864, in connection with the recurrent rumours about the conclusion of a new Holy Alliance after the meeting of the three northern rulers in Kissingen. There was also a divergence of interests between Russia and Austria. The rumours of an *entente* between Russia, Austria and Prussia had no other purpose than to frighten the countries of Western Europe and induce them to come together in common defence against the alleged danger.[133] This paper's stronger anti-German trend was connected with its beliefs that the German barons in the Baltic lands were a potential danger to Russian interests.[134]

Katkov lamented the decline in Russia's authority during the Danish-German conflict. In a series of articles in *Moskovskie vedomosti* on 13, 16, 18 and 27 May 1864 he analysed in detail the situation in Europe in connection with the new elements introduced by the defeat of Denmark. Speaking of the perpetrators of the troubles which had afflicted Denmark, the conservative Katkov stressed the infamous role played, in his opinion, by 'demagogues and democrats in Copenhagen', whom he called thoughtless individuals, and regretted that by adopting a 'paper' constitution drawn up by chance they had brought such great misfortune to their country. In Katkov's view they had helped the German democrats and their representative, Prince Augustenburg, to achieve their aims.

The friends of peace should regret such an epilogue, but they could not take offence at the Western states because they preferred the collapse of the monarchy to artificial maintenance of it by means of a personal union under the rule of a single monarch. If it was impossible to maintain the Danish monarchy in its entirety, Schleswig-Holstein should certainly not become a province of Prussia, but an independent state, not under the Hohenzollerns but Prince Augustenburg. Europe

---

132. *Ibid.,* no. 172, 23 June (5 July) 1864.
133. *Russkii invalid,* 4 (16) June 1864.
134. See the article 'Spravedlivy li tolki o separatisticheskikh stremleniyakh ostzeiskogo kraya?' *Russkii invalid,* 26 September (6 October) 1864. (Are the rumours about separatist tendencies in the Baltic lands justified?).

could not tolerate annexations. If this happened, the example of Savoy and Nice would once again make its painful mark on European politics. Annexation of Schleswig and Holstein would cause France to demand recompense, and then Britain and Austria would want to better their positions in order to maintain the balance of power in Europe. Would that not cause a war in Europe? Did Europe really want to go back to another Thirty Years War?

Katkov was reluctant to believe that Europe would allow Prussia to annex the duchies. Germany itself would oppose this and not even Prussia herself was planning it seriously. But Bismarck was a skillful political player and he was unwilling to let the booty slip from his grasp and was sure to have thought up something intermediate between annexation of the duchies and complete independence for them. What was important for Prussia was a form of protectorate which would serve as a model for further conquests in Germany itself, and she would create a status whereby Prince Augustenburg was dependent on her. This was where Katkov saw the danger for Russia and the house of Oldenburg. The Prussians in Kiel would mean the development of a German fleet there. It would mean a Scandinavian union and ultimately strong German and Scandinavian fleets in the Baltic.

God knows whether Peter the Great would have built St Petersburg if he had foreseen that something of the kind could happen; or perhaps Russia's fate will compel her to shift her centre of gravity to the south, where the cradle of *Rus* lay, still not debarred from Europe and facing towards Constantinople.[135]

The next cause of dissatisfaction and fear was the problem of the Germans in Livonia and Courland.[136] The events of 1863 had damaged Russia's authority, but in 1863 she had emerged from the difficulties with honour; the coalition had collapsed and the danger of war had passed. In 1864 Russia faced new dangers. The Germans had crossed the Eider, a Scandinavian union was a possibility, and Russia's position in the Baltic was in danger. As national feeling grew in Germany, it diminished in Russia. Russia had not benefited from the events of 1863, whereas Prussia had. The tense relations between France and Britain had allowed Prussia to act before the European powers took any vigorous action or understood the crux of the Danish question.

Prussia, in alliance with Austria, had conducted a campaign against Denmark. Now almost the whole of Jutland was in her hands. Britain took a dim view of this, but how important was it to her in comparison with her accomplishments in the East? Russia, on the other hand, was losing influence in the North and might lose in the East too. The changes in Europe, warned Katkov, were occurring at Russia's expense. In this situation Russia should build up her strength in the south of Europe and thus increase her influence.

Europe's interest required that a new state on the Eider should be independent, and that Europe should be recompensed for what was happening in southern

---

135. *Moskovskie vedomosti,* 13 May 1864.
136. *Ibid.,* 16 and 27. May, pp. 399-406, 427-33, and 15 July, pp. 562-70.

Schleswig by taking Holstein out of the German Confederation and making the newly created state neutral and independent of both Denmark and the German Confederation. This neutrality would fully safeguard Germany's just interests and would allow Denmark to retain her independence and not join a Scandinavian union.[137]

When a discussion began in the pages of the Russian press in the middle of 1864, particularly after the Kissingen meeting, on the subject of Russian foreign policy, really the whole of the press apart from *Vest'*[138] came out against the idea of a new Holy Alliance as a bankrupt proposition, a relic of the outmoded Vienna system.[139] *Golos* allowed that there was just a possibility of rapprochement with Austria and Prussia on account of the Polish question,[140] but Katkov stressed the drawbacks for Russia of an *entente* with Prussia and Austria, especially the latter, in view of the differences between her and Russia over the Eastern Question.

Even less acceptable, it seemed to Katkov, was an *entente* with France, mainly although not only because of the Polish question. With Britain, too, no real alliance seemed possible because of their differences in the East, Central Asia and the Caucasus. Consequently, like *Russkii invalid,* he was against Russia concluding any alliances, at least for the time being.[141] The unification of Germany under Prussia's aegis was not in Russia's interest. Although Russia and Prussia shared a common anti-Polish interest, Prussian annexation of the duchies was too high a price to pay for Prussia's help. Russia could not support Prussian claims just because of common interests in the Polish question.[142] But in no case could this mean that Russia had to intervene militarily in the Danish-German conflict. Katkov also suggested that Russia should support Austria and the lesser German states in order to counteract Prussian designs.[143]

It can be seen from this that, from the course of the war, Katkov drew the general conclusion that Russia must be very wary of the growth of Prussian power. A similar conclusion was reached by *Golos*.[144] Europe had seen peace come. But at what price? The power of Prussia had increased enormously, Bismarck had shown himself to be a highly talented politician who had concluded a war (which could have ended in catastrophe) with unprecedented good fortune. This victory was immensely important for Germany in that her fate would now depend on Prussian arms. Prussia's strength had increased so much that from then on she would quickly settle the fate of the European continent. The future of the German nation looked darker than that of Denmark, which, despite her sufferings, had maintained her resistance to the end. Although she had lost her German lands, this did

---

137. *Ibid.,* 19 May 1864.
138. *Vest',* nos. 42, 48, 1864.
139. *Golos,* no. 173; *Moskovskie vedomosti,* nos. 144, 149, 156, 159.
140. *Golos,* nos. 57, 63.
141. *Moskovskie vedomosti,* nos. 149, 156, 177, 185; *Russkii invalid,* no. 144, 1864.
142. *Moskovskie vedomosti,* nos. 241, 256, 276, 1864.
143. *Ibid.,* nos. 241, 247, 256, 1864.
144. *Golos,* no. 213, 4 (16) July and no. 228, 19 (31) August 1864.

not mean she was doomed, and her fate would turn on the energy and ability of the Danish nation. The paper expressed its sympathy for the Danes and its recognition of the heroism they had displayed in the war. Since co-operation with Britain had proved possible over Schleswig-Holstein, the liberals saw a need for co-operation with her in other areas too – and for finding ways to delimit their respective spheres of influence in Asia.[145]

Peterburgskie Vedomosti took a different view of the situation, however. It thought Prussia's policy was not contrary to Russia's interests and her growing strength in the Baltic was not a threat to Russia; on the contrary, a strong Prussian fleet could only help to counterbalance Britain and France.[146] It did see a certain danger if German and Scandinavian unity were to come about simultaneously and this coincided with the appearance of a strong German fleet. But this was a possibility which need not be taken seriously.[147]

The conservative paper *Vest'* fully approved of Prussian policy.[148] It supported her policy towards Denmark and towards the conservative plan for the unification of Germany in which it saw many positive features, such as the diversion of European attention from the Polish question, the victory of conservative ideas, and the possibility of restraining Napoleon III, thanks to the alliance between Austria and Prussia. The paper did not believe in the Prussian 'Drang nach Osten'. If this were to happen, Russia and Britain would be able to deal with it. In contrast, the Slavophil organ, *Den'*, which had hitherto devoted little space to the Schleswig-Holstein question, saw the growth of Prussia's power as possibly leading to a conflict between Prussia and Russia, both in the Baltic and in Germany itself.[149]

Sovremennik offered a penetrating analysis of the new situation created after the final suppression of Denmark by the German states.[150] The leading problem it singled out was the aggressiveness of Prussia. The conditions she had laid down during the peace talks did not actually fully suit German patriots, but were nevertheless excessively hard for the defeated Denmark to fulfil. The victors' aggressiveness was also shown by their unceremonious behaviour in Jutland. In truth, both the German countries and Austria were against the duchies falling into Prussia's hands, as this would increase her military and naval power, but the countries of the federation would not decide the future of the duchies. In Schleswig, Germanisation was being carried out by force, enormous and unjustified contributions were

---

145. *Ibid.,* nos. 57, 126, 262, 1864.
146. *Peterburgskie Vedomosti,* nos. 25, 193, 1864.
147. *Ibid.,* no. 193, 1864.
148. *Vest',* nos. 32, 37, 1864.
149. *Den',* no. 45, 7 November 1864. The articles by the leading Slavophil N. Ya. Danilevsky published in *Zarya* in 1869 show the change in the Slavophils' view of the war in 1864. Danilevsky placed all the blame for the Danish-German conflict on the German states, particularly Prussia, and expressed great unease about her establishment in the Baltic, and its consequences for Russia. See *Rossiya i Evropa,* p. 483.
150. 'Politika. Okonchanie datsko-germanskoi raspravy. Prussiya i Germanskii soyuz'. (Politics, the end of the Danish-German discord. Prussia and the German Union). *Sovremennik,* vol. IX, 1864.

being levied, and huge fiscal demands made against Denmark. The German states, i.e. Prussia and Austria, were demanding these huge sums on the alleged grounds that they had been wrongly collected by Denmark in the duchies over the previous 12-13 years. And their army of 40,000 deployed in occupied Jutland was being used to put new pressure on the Bluhme government. Bismarck had pushed the allied troops from Hannover out of Altona, Kiel and Rendsborg and was himself, with Austria, unceremoniously conducting the negotiations with Denmark, in which representatives of the German Confederation were playing no part. Prussia had taken complete control of the duchies and could do just what she wanted with them and would give them to whomsoever she chose. The whole affair demonstrated that Germany was a political nonentity.

The result of the war, said *Otechestvennye zapiski*,[151] showed that by paying no attention to anyone or anything, apart from the general dissatisfaction of the Germans, and sticking firmly to a clear-cut course in the Danish-German dispute while being confident of her own strength, Prussia had enjoyed complete success in her enterprise. The outcome of the war had demonstrated that the small and second-rank states could only be the losers, and that only Austria and Prussia could make decisions about the political life of Germany.

What conclusions did Russia draw from the war over the duchies? An article with the title, 'Kakoi smysl' imeet datskaya voina dlya Rossii?',[152] appeared in *Otechestvennye zapiski*, vol. 6.[153] Public opinion in Russia, it said, took a keen interest in the Danish-German war and followed what was happening in this sector of European diplomacy. The Slavophil Aksakov said he was not concerned about Schleswig-Holstein, or Germany, and Germany's interests were not Russia's. Russia's road led to the East – that was where, in his opinion, altars to the Orthodox church should be built. Katkov was opposed to Russian involvement in German affairs. Initially he seemed to take the Prussian side and sharply criticised Denmark on account of her democratic system and the behaviour of her government. But his animosity soon shifted to Prussia as he saw that she sought to rule the Baltic. In Katkov's view, said *Otechestvennye zapiski,* Russia must keep her colours flying as a first rank European state. But, said the paper, 'to keep her colours flying' could mean many different things. In its opinion, Russia should not get entangled in wars for fifty years; her mission should be to settle the Crimean and southern lands, raise the level of agriculture and industry, and build up Russia's strength internally. As her influence grew in the East, the Caucasus and Central Asia, as her strength within the country increased, so her influence in the international arena would grow too. Summing up, *Otechestvennye zapiski* concluded that Russia should not intervene in German affairs, not because they were alien to Russia – as Aksakov argued – but because this was required by Russia's own vital interests.

151. *Otechestvennye zapiski,* vol. 156, 1864, pp. 961 ff.
152. What is the full implication of the Danish war for Russia.
153. *Ibid.,* vol. 6, pp. 944-6.
154. *Ibid.,* no. 4, 1864.

It would not be an oversimplification to say that the Prussian victories did not arouse enthusiasm but rather concern about the possible consequences for Russia. The Baltic Germans were a cause of concern too. There was a fear that the German barons in the Baltic lands might be emboldened by the example of the Germans in Holstein and Schleswig and follow them in demanding union with their Vaterland. Could Russia, it was asked, tolerate their negative attitude towards the reforms she was introducing, could she afford to tolerate the barons' abuses of authority over the peasants living in the Baltic lands?

A new factor was now added as well, namely dissatisfaction among the Russian *bourgeoisie* at the Russian government's policy, which gave privileges to Prussian industry. Since the Crimean War imports of goods from Western Europe to Russia had also gone via Prussia and formed an extra source of income for her.[154] Prussia had made it harder for Russia to establish direct contacts with the countries of Western Europe, and Russian merchants' discontent at the country's growing economic dependence on Prussia was increasing. Industrial circles in Russia were against the plan for a new customs agreement with Prussia, as the further reduction in tariffs which Bismarck was demanding would operate to the disadvantage of Russia.[155]

Despite this, however, there were those who said 'Russia and Prussia are mutually necessary to, and dependent, on each other, but Prussia's need is greater and this should always be remembered'. And there were even some who said 'if Russia were to regain her place on the Black Sea she would be able, at no cost to herself, to give Prussia more space *(prostor)* in the Baltic'.[156] Even the liberal *Golos* cherished illusions about Prussia's future policy.

Military circles, however, had no illusions about Prussian policy and the consequences which could follow if she established a German fleet in the Baltic.[157] These circles saw no difference and drew no artificial distinction between the interests of Prussia and Germany.

On one matter only was there no disagreement. All political orientations were united in a solid anti-Scandinavian front and a universal conviction prevailed that a union of the Scandinavian states would be the greatest danger for Russia, much more so than the establishment of a strong Prussian fleet in the Baltic. Russia saw a united Scandinavia as a mortal enemy who would not only put the fate of Finland in question but would cancel out the whole of Russia's achievements since the time of Peter I. It was seen as a threat to the capital in St Petersburg and a barrier between Russia and Western Europe. Once again the claustrophobia which had been a feature of Russian policies and rulers from the beginning reared its head. The possibility of a united Scandinavian state under the aegis of Sweden being estab-

---

155. Narochnitskaya, p. 194.
156. Danilevsky, pp. 497-8.
157. See the report from Meroux de Valois, French consul in Kiel, to Dotézac on 30 August 1864. *Origines,* vol. IV, pp. 67-8, and 'Mémoires sur les événements des Duchés de l'Elbe (de 1863 à 1866)', A.M.A.E. Mémoires et Documents, Danemark 1864-1866. Question des Duchés, III, Vol. 14.

lished on the Sound was regarded as something far more threatening for Russia than closure of the Bosphorous and the Dardanelles.

This thesis cannot be shaken despite the fact that during his sojourn in Sweden in the spring of 1863 Bakunin tried to gain a reputation as an advocate of Scandinavianism and at the banquet given in his honour at Vesterås declared:

Au nom de cette société *(Zemlya i Volya)*, au nom de cette nouvelle Russie qui doit triompher et apporta à tout le Nord de l'Europe la promesse d'un paix féconde et fraternelle, je tends la main aux nobles Suédois, et à la prospérité de la grande Union fédérale Scandinave.

Even Dashkov had not the slightest doubt that Bakunin's purpose in saying this was pure propaganda.

In his dispatch to Gorchakov he commented as follows:

il (Bakunin) a réproduit dans son discours les mêmes théories et les mêmes vœux, pour l'édification de ses auditeurs de province, qui, dans l'innocence de leur cœur, l'acclaimèrent comme un ami de l'humanité.[158]

IV

It remains to be considered whether the public discussion of Russian foreign policy actively influenced the course of that policy. To this question the answer must be in the negative. As early as 1869, Danilevsky tried to explain why public opinion in Europe, which, outside Germany, in principle disapproved of the behaviour of Austria and Prussia and was almost entirely in Denmark's side, could not accomplish anything. The reason was public opinion had remained cold and torpid and had lacked the passion which causes governments to heed it; consequently they remained free to act in accordance with their own judgement and discretion. Beside this, he added, the papers and the numerous meetings had all been against involvement in the war.[159]

Richard Pipes, influenced by the work of B. Nolde, wrote:[160]

This domestic political pressure (in the 1860s), however, never materially affected Russia's foreign policy for two reasons: (i) there were no institutional means to make such pressure effective; and (ii) Russian public opinion focused its attention almost entirely on problems of domestic politics ... the only internal factor that could have effectively influenced Tsarism's foreign policy would have been a sense of national interest. But this too was hardly developed. The country was inner-oriented in every way.[161]

In conclusion he said:

The student of both Tsarist and Soviet history is struck by the insignificant influence that public opinion and the pressures of domestic politics have exercised on the conduct of Russian foreign policy.[162]

158. Dashkov to Gorchakov No. 60, 4/16 June 1863. "Discours de Bacounine" was enclosed. Central Archive, Moscow, A.V.P.R. Microfilm in R.A. Stockholm.
159. Danilevsky, *Rossiya i Evropa*, p. 19.
160. B. Nolde, *L'alliance Franco-Russe*, (Paris, 1936), pp. 166-8.
161. R. Pipes, 'Domestic Politics and Foreign Affairs', in *Russian Foreign Policy* ..., pp. 148-9.
162. *Ibid.*, p. 168.

This fits with what Gorchakov said to the British Ambassador, Buchanan, that he paid no attention to the Russian press's support for France during the Franco-German war, 'for it had no power whatever, and the policy of the Government was entirely dependent upon the will of the Emperor'.[163] Thus public opinion in Russia, and the press in particular, had no influence on the decisions which were taken predominantly by a single individual. It is hard however, to imagine that Gorchakov and his closest colleagues were indifferent to the opinions enunciated by such famous and distinguished writers as Katkov, Aksakov or Samarin. Yet it should be pointed out that the role of public opinion in the foreign policy decisions taken by governments in Europe in the nineteenth century was not much greater either.

It was the first time [during the Crimean War – E.H.] that the new force of the middle-classes' interest in politics, as expressed in public meetings and the press, had diverted the foreign policy of government', wrote Butler.[164] In general, Metternich's view that 'foreign affairs is not for the plebs' seemed to be reasonably sound and foreign ministers did not concern themselves overmuch about what might be in tomorrow's headlines'.[165]

Even the British government only paid lip-service to the principle of popular sovereignty in the realm of foreign affairs, as was clearly seen in Disraeli's speech in the House of Commons in August 1880.

He told the House of Commons that 'what we call public opinion is generally public sentiment,' and it was clear that in his view, public expressions of opinion about foreign affairs were generally emotional and ill-formed, and hence unworthy of attention. Salisbury, Landsdowne, and Grey tended to agree'.[166]

Indeed, one of the most striking characteristics of the men who moulded British policy in the fateful days before the outbreak of war in 1914 was their lack of interest in what the public might be thinking about the drift of affairs and their irritated contempt for press views. Sir Arthur Nicolson, the permanent under-secretary for foreign affairs, complained that the public are as a rule supremely indifferent to and very ignorant of foreign affairs.[167]

Equally ominous was the self-abasement of the liberals and the middle class before the Junker aristocracy and the military experts in Germany. Denying the general ability of himself and his class to understand, even less to direct, national policy, the well known historian Hermann Baumgarten in 1866 in his essay 'Der Deutsche Liberalismus. Eine Selbstkritik' concluded that 'the citizen is born to work, but not to be a statesman'. The citizen simply lacked the knowledge necessary to understand politics. 'It is one of the most ruinous errors to believe that a good scholar, lawyer, merchant, or civil servant, who is interested in public affairs and reads the newspapers assiduously, is able to participate actually in political life'.[168]

163. Buchanan to Granville, 30 September 1870, FO 65/804 no. 374. See Mosse, *The European Powers and the German Question,* p. 394.
164. J. Butler, *A History of England 1815-1939,* (London, 1963), p. 125.
165. G.A. Craig, A.L. George, *Force and Statecraft,* p. 33.
166. *Ibid.,* pp. 60-61.
167. *Ibid.,* p. 61.
168. H. Kohn, *The Mind of Germany,* (London, 1961), pp. 157-9.

A whole class of learned and well-meaning men in Germany professed their immaturity in political affairs. These passages written with so much sincerity must be pondered if we are to understand the role of the press and public opinion in 19th century autocratic Russia.

The age of the masses had not yet dawned even in Western Europe.

Conclusion

West European and Soviet historians are agreed that the relations between Russia and the Scandinavian countries in the nineteenth century, and particularly in the years 1856-1864, have yet to be thoroughly examined.[1] But there are many works which touch on the attitude of Russia to the Northern countries in one form or another, and it is worth emphasizing that on some questions there is almost complete conformity of view in these works. Practically all historians, both in the nineteenth century and nowadays, and both Russian and Scandinavian, despite methodological differences in their approach to the matter, agree that Russia always took a negative attitude towards Scandinavianism, that is, a union or confederation of Scandinavian countries irrespective of the form in which it was expressed. Nor are there any major differences in Scandinavian and West European historiography on the assessment of the motives which led Russia to revise her attitude towards Finland in 1863. Primary importance is attributed to military-strategic considerations and the fear that Finland might in some way join in Poland's struggle for freedom.

As far as Russian-Danish relations in 1856-1864 are concerned, however, there are major differences in assessment of Russian policy, both among Soviet historians (compare the views of A.S. Eruzalimsky and L.I. Narochnitskaya) and among Danish historians (for instance P. Linstow's attack on E. Møller's views).[2] French historiography differs fundamentally from the position taken by contemporary Soviet historians (see Narochnitskaya's attack on the views of F. Charles-Roux and A. Debidour.)[3] German and Danish historians' assessments of Russian policy, especially in 1863-1864, have been diametrically opposed from the start to the present day, which of course is connected with their fundamentally different approaches to the German-Danish conflict (compare the views put forward by J.H. Voigt and A. Scharff on the German side and T. Fink on the Danish).[4]

---

1. Halvdan Koht, *Die Darstellung Norwegens und Schwedens im Deutsch-Dänischen Konflikt, zumal während der Jahre 1863 und 1864,* (Kristiania, 1908), pp. VIII, IX, Ranghild Marie Hatton, Russia and the Baltic, in *Russian Imperialism,* ed. Taras Hunczak, (New Brunswick, 1974), p. 334, A.L. Narochnitsky, ed. *Itogi i zadachi izuchenya vneshnei politiki Rossii,* (Moscow, 1981), p. 280.
2. P. Linstow, Bismarck, Europa og Slesvig-Holstein 1862-1866, *Historisk Tidsskrift,* vol. II (1978), p. 476, has argued that current criticism of Russia for deserting Denmark in 1864 as it was expressed by E. Møller must be repudiated.
3. L.I. Narochnitskaya, *Rossiya i voiny Prussii v 60-tykh godakh XIX v. za ob'edinenie Germanii sverkhu,* (Moscow, 1960).
4. Johannes H. Voigt, Englands Aussenpolitik während des deutsch-dänischen Konflikts 1862-1864, *Zeitschrift der Geselschaft für Schleswig-Holsteinische Geschichte,* vol. LXXXIX, (1964), pp. 61 ff. Alexander S. Scharff, *Schleswig-Holstein in der deutschen und nordeuropäischen Geschichte,* (Stuttgart, 1969), Troels Fink, *Geschichte des schleswigschen Grenzlandes,* (Copenhagen, 1958).

The dispute among historians centers on the character of Russian neutrality during the war of 1864, the motives and reasons for this neutrality, the attitude of Tsar Alexander II and his Minister of Foreign Affairs, Alexander Gorchakov, towards Prussia and the policy of Bismarck, and, finally, the effects of Russian policy. The basic issue might be formulated briefly: did Russia play an independent role during the 1864 War or were her policies dependent on Bismarck's politics? If dependent, to what extent?

The fundamental diversity which emerges in evaluation of these questions has its roots in a nationalistic approach to the matter and in methodological differences in approach in both Danish and German, and especially Soviet historiography. Many of the problems are hard to disentangle due to the fact that, both before the 1917 Revolution in Russia and since, access to Russian souces has been difficult and often impossible. This lack of access to Soviet archives has seriously affected the ability of historians to understand Russian policy during 1856-1864. This problem is illustrated in the classic work by L.D. Steefel, as well as in work by W.E. Mosse and by the Estonian historian L. Roots.[5]

II

Analysis of Russia's foreign policy after her defeat in the Crimean War and during the years of humiliation as a result of the imposition on her of the provisions of the Treaty of Paris of 1856 confirms that, even in those years of difficulty, in which she concentrated on domestic reforms, Russia did not abandon the pursuit of her expansionist aims. Her tactics nevertheless, did undergo a fundamental change in comparison with the years preceding the outbreak of the Crimean War.

In her weakened state Russia for some time no longer actively engaged in European affairs as she had done before, confining herself to expansion in Asia. But she did not abandon her primacy in and maintenance of control of the Baltic – *Dominium Maris Baltici* – which was a part of the balance of power established in 1815 and which essentially survived untouched after the Crimean War.[6] She was not, however, in a position to use the methods of the Nesselrode period in her Baltic policy because she was weakened and the constellation of forces in Europe had changed. Russia was isolated, could not count on co-operation with Great Britain as in 1848-1852, and had to reckon more and more with Prussia.[7] Her co-operation with France was in its initial stage and subject to many questions, and espe-

---

5. Lawrence D. Steefel, *The Schleswig-Holstein Question*, (London, 1932), W.E. Mosse, *The European Powers and the German Question, 1848-71 with Special Reference to England and Russia*, (Cambridge, 1958), L. Roots *Schleswig-Golshtinski vopros i politika evropeiskikh derzhav v 1863-1864 godakh*, (Talinn, 1957).
6. By this balance is to be understood such a disposition so, that no one rule or state shall be able to dominate and prescribe to others. Emmerich V. Vattel, *Law of Nations*, (London, 1758).
7. In the nineteenth century Great Britain was the holder of the balance. See Gordon A. Craig, Alexander L. George, *Force and Statecraft*, chapter 3, Balance of Power, 1815-1914, (New York, Oxford, 1983).

cially the question of what attitude Napoleon III would take to the problems of the Baltic, since he felt sympathy both for Sweden and for the ideas of Scandinavianism.

Analysis of Russia's policy supports the thesis of its continuity, through continuity in strategy and expansionism must be considered in dialectical connection with the problem of flexibility in mode of behavior and in choice of tactics. The external manifestation of this flexibility is found in the variety of mottos pressed on Russian diplomacy by Gorchakov and by a more individualized approach on the part of the St. Petersburg cabinet to each of the Scandinavian countries.

The reason for this varied approach derived from the geopolitical position of the Scandinavian countries and the different relations between them and Russia in the past. 'L'indépendance de sa position nous est nécessaire autant que celle des points les plus essentiels de notre Empire,' wrote Chr. Pozzo di Borgo[8] about Denmark in his memorandum of 21 January/2 February 1826. 'Le Danemarc est pour nous, pour ainsi dire une partie de nous-mêmes', he stated. Many years later Nesselrode repeated the same idea in his letter of 21 April 1848 to P. Meyendorff, arguing that ''il n'est pas de notre intérêt de laisser détruire le monarchie danoise à nos portes.'[9] On Sweden, Pozzo di Borgo wrote in his memorandum to the Tsar:

La Suède, faible par son position relative avec la Russie, l'est encore par l'origine de la familie [Bernadotte – E.H.] qui en occupe le trône. Nous n'avons pas de raison de montrer aucun empressement d'y causer des altérations, mais si nous avions à craindre ou à venger des torts, les points vulnerables de cette monarchie ne seraient pas difficiles à saisir.

The difference in tone compared with the attitude towards Denmark is clear.

In addition to this there were other factors. For example, in the struggle between Russia and Sweden for *Dominium Maris Baltici,* Denmark had as a rule been on Russia's side. It is sufficient to recall B.H. Sumner's words, that from the sixteenth century to the eithteenth century 'Russians and Swedes were pitted in war against each other for the Baltic lands nine times: five times the Danes were in alliance, ineffectually, with the Russians.'[10] As Karl Marx wrote in 1863, 'Die Zertrümmerung Schwedens als europäischer Grossmacht [war] der erste Schritt zur Gründung der russischen Hegemonie'.[11] And the Danish historian Feldbaek, in his work on the Danish policy of neutrality during the wars of 1778-1783, praises the role of Russia in upholding the national security of Denmark towards the end of the eighteenth century.[12] Only in the final period of the Napoleonic wars did the state of relations between Russia and the Scandinavian countries alter, when Sweden found herself in the same camp as Russia and Denmark was in the pro-French camp.

8. F. Martens, *Recueil des Traités et Conventions conclus par la Russie avec les Puissances Etrangères,* vol. XV, *Traités avec La France, 1802-1906,* (St. Petersburg, 1909), p. 49).
9. *Lettres et papiers du Chancelier de Nesselrode 1760-1850,* vol. IX, (Paris, n.d.), p. 88).
10. B.H. Sumner, *Survey of Russian History,* (London, 1961), p. 233.
11. K. Marx, *Beitrage zur Geschichte der polnischen Frage. Manuskripte aus den Jahren 1863-1864,* (Warsaw, 1971), pp. 90-92.
12. Ole Feldbaek, *Dansk neutralitetspolitik under krigen 1778-1783,* (Copenhagen, 1971).

The improvement in relations between Russia and Sweden in the first half of the nineteenth century did not lead to any fundamental change in attitudes between the two countries. The state of mistrust persisted and, as the Swedish poet and bishop E. Tegner accurately described it in 1841, 'they are divided by a sacred inheritance.'[13] Russia also distrusted Sweden in view of her aspiration to recover Finland, which Russia had seized in 1809. On the importance of Finland to Russia, as M. Borodkin put it, there was no need to convince anybody in Russia. 'Elle assure la position de la fenêtre que Pierre le Grand ouvrit sur l'Europe: Pétersbourg'. Borodkin also quoted Prince Shuvalov's words to Napoleon I, 'La Finlande était necessaire à la Russie, et tel était le projet de Pierre, qui sans cela n'aurait pas fondé la capitale là où elle existe maintenant.'[14] The strategic importance of Finland for Russia was demonstrated by the Baltic campaign in 1854 and 1855.[15]

The degree of mistrust between St. Petersburg and Stockholm was intensified after Sweden concluded the treaty with Britain and France on 21 Novembre 1855.

This 'work of injurious mistrust towards Russia' was followed by the much more serious 'servitude' imposed on her at the end of the war in the Treaty of Paris (1856), whereby she was forbidden to maintain any bases or fortifications on the Åland islands. This 'servitude', coupled with the public guarantee of Sweden against Russia, rankled deeply and was of serious practical inconvenience.[16]

Russia felt herself injured by Sweden's behaviour and for many years thereafter both Gorchakov and Alexander II returned to this matter in conversations with the Swedish ambassador in St. Petersburg.

In December 1858, during a talk with the newly appointed ambassador Wedel-Jarlsberg, Alexander said that if Sweden had concluded the November Treaty because Russia closed the border and passage to Lapland, then he would like to make clear that both Nesselrode and Armfeld had since adopted a conciliatory attitude towards Sweden, even though Nicholas I had inclined to the position represented by Menshikov on this matter.[17]

In contrast, Russo-Danish relations in the first half of the nineteenth century were at their best. In the years 1848-1852 Russia co-operated with Britain in her concern to maintain the balance of power in the Baltic and the North Sea and spoke out on Denmark's side and supported Denmark in the latter's conflict with Germany. Despite certain reservations, she approved of Denmark's policy of neutrality during the Crimean War and showed understanding for Denmark's moves, even if certain of her practival steps favoured the Western powers.[18]

13. Ingvar Andersson, *Sveriges Historia,* (Stockholm, 1969), pp. 350-361.
14. M. Borodkine, *La Finlande comme partie intégrante de l'Empire Russe,* (Paris, 1912), p. 7, K. Arsieniev, *Statisticheskie ocherki Rossii,* (St. Petersburg, 1848), pp. 4, 25, 50.
15. *Revue des Deux Mondes,* 1854-1855, *L'indépendance Belge,* 24 February 1903, W. Pokchlebkin, *SSSR- Finlandiya 260 let otnoshenii 1713-1975,* (Moscow, 1975), pp. 63-68, E. Halicz, *Danish Neutrality during the Crimean War (1853-1855),* (Odense, 1977).
16. Sumner, *Survey,* p. 243. A copy of the Treaty of Paris of 18/30 March, 1856 will be found in *Sbornik dogovorov Rossii s drugimi gosudarstvami 1856-1917 gg.* (Moscow, 1952), pp. 23-41.
17. F.H.F. Wedel-Jarlsberg's dispatch of 15 December 1858, no. 118, Depescher från besk. i Petersburg, 1858, Riksarkivet Stockholm. A. Jansson, *Den svenska utrikes politikens historia,* vol. III:3, 1844-1872, (Stockholm, 1961), pp. 68-75.

III

Russia's Baltic policy was initially dominated by two problems: Scandinavianism and the new phase in 1855 of the Danish-German conflict over the Elbe duchies. This was soon joined by a third problem – that of Finland. All these problems were interconnected and also affected the interests of the major Western powers in this part of Europe. The central political problem was Scandinavianism. But the most threatening was the Danish-German conflict, which always contained the seeds of renewed turmoil of war.

Analysis of the documents and of Russian policy shows that Russia was interested in maintenance of the *status quo* in the Baltic, and particularly in maintaining the integrity of Denmark, mainly because of the risk that Denmark, if deprived of the Elbe duchies, might throw in its lot with the Scandinavian Union. But after 1856 this aim was equalled and even exceeded in importance by other considerations.

After 1856 Russo-German, and above all Russo-Prussian, relations were of much greater importance than maintenance of the integrity of Denmark, and Russia could not allow herself to take the same position towards the Danish-German dispute as Nicholas I and Nesselrode had during the first Schleswig-Holstein war. In the new situation Russia was concerned not only to preserve her friendship with Prussia but also to build up the latter's strength and prestige, at the expense, of course, of Austria. Russia also preferred Prussia, with its conservative regime and family links with the Tsar, to Denmark, where a democratic system predominated, the government was in the hands of the national-liberal party and, after, 1855, there was a revival of the idea of Scandinavianism.[19] During the Crimean War the significance of Prussia for Russian trade also increased, and after 1856 Prussia became more and more important as a trading partner for Russia. But despite this, in the immediate aftermath of the Treaty of Paris, Russia tried to maintain a position of neutrality in relation to the conflict over the duchies. She reacted very sharply, on the other hand, to any signs of Scandinavianism, especially political Scandinavianism.

This unequivocal attitude towards Scandinavianism on the part of Russia was based on both military-strategic and psychological considerations. The former – the fear that Russia might encounter a similar situation in the Baltic as had arisen in the Black Sea after 1856 – was connected with a complex of other problems, namely Russia's views on the role of Germany and Scandinavia in Russian policy.

---

18. Arkhiv vneshnyei politiki Rossii, Moscow, Kantselariya, 1856, Halicz, *Danish Neutrality,* pp. 184-185.
19. Julian Klaczko, *Deux Chanceliers, Le Prince Gortchakof et le Prince de Bismarck,* (Paris, 1876), Ch. Friese, *Russland und Preussen vom Krimkrieg bis zum polnischen Aufstand,* (Berlin u. Königsberg), 1933, Hans-Werner Rautenburg, *Der polnische Aufstand von 1863 und die europäische Politik,* (Wiesbaden, 1979), Arnold Oskar Meyer, *O. Bismarck, der Man und der Staatsmann,* (Stuttgart, 1949), Walter Laquer, *Russia and Germany: A Century of Conflict,* (Boston-Toronto, 1965).

Further, Russia was afraid that she might lose the influence on Danish policy which she had recently gained thanks to the provisions of the Treaty of London of 1852. The Provision that, on the death of Frederick VII, the throne in Copenhagen should pass to Prince Christian of Glücksburg gave Russia the opportunity for even greater influence on the government of Denmark than before, owing to the Prince's Russophile views.

If Scandinavia became united and were allied with the Western powers, Russia could be deprived of passage through the Sound in time of war. Russia's contact with Western Europe and free passage through the straits were a matter of life and death for her. This was realized by Peter the Great, who had accordingly fought for supremacy in the Baltic, since without it there was no way to carry out his and his successors' plans to bring Russia out of the backwardness which they believed dated from the Mongol conquest. Peter's understanding of this was testimony to his political genius, according to an article entitled 'Les agrandissements de la Russie' in the semi-official organ of Gorchakov, *Le Nord,* on 16 July, 1864.

The land-locked country complex weighed heavily on the Russian mentality and owed much of its vitality to earlier wars with Sweden, especially the Great Northern War. It was revived in 1853-1856 by the policy of Oscar I during the Crimean War and the demilitarization of the Åland Islands to which Russia was obliged to agree under the provisions of the Treaty of Paris. A coherent and united Scandinavia, with the prospect of alliance with France in the background, would have been contrary to the Russian view of Russia's interests of state. Germany, divided into smaller and larger states, was not perceived as a danger although its population was five times as great as the whole of Scandinavia. 'L'Allemagne n'est pas une nation, c'est un peuple composé de races dont chacune a son histoire, sa physiognomonie et ces nécessités distances.' This view was expressed by King Wilhelm I of Württemberg to the Russian ambassador, Titov, on 30 November/12 December 1859. The ambassador reported these words to Gorchakov without comment.[20]

It is not impossible that Gorchakov himself may have partially shared this opinion too, since it was consistent with traditional Russian policy of seeking to keep Germany divided. This overestimation of the danger of Scandinavianism and disregard for the possible German threat was a feature of Russian policy after the Crimean War, although it did not overlook the fact that, while the conservative states were dominant in Germany, there also existed a liberal-democratic movement which had made itself felt not long before and represented a tendency towards a democratic united Germany.

This attitude of regarding Germany as a Russian sphere of influence, especially from the Congress of Vienna to Olomunc and 1853, was attributable partly to factors like the dynastic links between the Romanovs and Prussia and many of the smaller German states (Württemberg, Oldenburg, and Hesse-Darmstadt) and to

---

20. A.V.P.R., Kantselariya, 1859. d. 177.
21. T.G. Masaryk, *The Spirit of Russia,* vol. I, (London, 1955), Laquer, *Russia and Germany.*

the fact that Russia itself, at the highest levels of the state administration, was teeming with Germans who had a feeling of belonging to their *Vaterland*. There was no shortage of Germans in the Ministry of Foreign Affairs, some of whom were close associates of Gorchakov, and many Germans held key positions in the Russian diplomatic service.[21] The Cossacks had been cordially received in Berlin in 1813, and when Tsar Nicholas I died in 1855 the Berlin *Kreuzzeitung* wrote, 'Our Emperor is dead.'[22]

Russia's negative attitude towards any signs of Scandinavianism was a constant factor in Russia foreign policy. Russia saw it, first, as a liberal and constitutional movement reminiscent of the national movements in Western Europe, and thus with an anti-Russian flavour, and, second, as a threat to the predominance in the Baltic she had gained in the eighteenth century. The fear of closure of the Sound by the united Scandinavian states underlay the firm attitude of Nicholas I to any form of rapprochement between Denmark and Sweden.[23]

Russia displayed special hostility to the activities of the Scandinavianists, as can be seen from the tone of the notes addressed by Nesselrode to Denmark in 1837 and 1843. Russia also tried to influence the stepping up of repressive action against the Scandinavianists by Christian VIII, because of Scandinavianist activities directed against royal absolutism in Denmark. In the period 1830-1848 Scandinavianism was seen in Denmark as a seditious movement just as dangerous as Schleswig-Holsteinism. Denmark's political dependence on Russia, which exercised its influence on the Danish cabinet's hard line, increased as Scandinavianism in Denmark became a serious problem for Danish foreign policy. Russian pressure aimed at arresting the development of the Scandinavian movement was also visible in Sweden in the 1840s.[24]

Russia's anti-Scandinavianism and hostility to the growth of any Scandinavianist tendencies did not weaken after the Crimean War. Russia was disturbed by any outward signs of the movement, like the meetings of students from the Scandinavian countries held in 1856 in Uppsala, Stockholm, Copenhagen and (which was much more sensitive for Russia) Helsinki, the capital of Finland. She was equally disturbed by meetings of the monarchs of Denmark and Sweden, political declarations by the leaders of Scandinavianism, rumors of union between the two countries and demands for the annulment of the Treaty of London, and particularly of its provision that the Copenhagen throne should pass to Christian of Glücksburg on the death of Frederick VII.[25]

---

22. Laquer, *op.cit*. p. 29.
23. 'Prenez bien garde que les Danois et les Suédois ne deviennent trop bon amis' wrote Nicholas I to General V.T. Oxholm in 1848.
24. Henrik Becker-Christensen, *Skandinaviske drømme og politiske realiteter 1830-1850*, (Århus, 1980).
25. P.E. Ungern-Sternberg's and Ch. S. Loringshoven de Freytag's dispatches from Copenhagen (Håndskriftsamlinger XVI, vol. 46-52, in Rigsarkivet Copenhagen). Dashkov's dispatches in R.A. Stockholm, Mikrofilms, Handlingar berörande svensk-ryska forhällanden, rulle 69-74 (212-232), 1855-1864.

Russia was further worried by (i) the international aspects of Scandinavianism and the associated Franco-Swedish rapprochement; (ii) reports that Napoleon III took a positive attitude to the idea of rapprochement of the Scandinavian peoples; (iii) Prince Napoleon Plon-Plon's activities in this direction; and (iv) the presence in his entourage of Polish emigrés who, during a visit to Stockholm did not conceal their belief that the unification of Scandinavia could be favorable for Poland. Finally, there was the possibility of co-operation between the Scandinavianists and the German liberals (if only the Danish-German conflict could be successfully resolved and the frontier between the two countries established on the Eider, as Sweden saw it), or of a Scandinavian union (with Holstein and the German part of Schleswig going to Germany, as Bernstorff maintained).[26]

Gorchakov overestimated the factors in the international arena favouring the Scandinavian idea. He appeared not to see the lack of a firm line on the part of Napoleon III, nor that the latter was not so much interested in supporting the idea of Scandinavian union as in maintaining good relations with Russia. Nor did Gorchakov perceive that in Britain only a narrow group of liberals favoured the Scandinavian idea.

He also underestimated the opposition to the idea of unification of Scandinavia in the Scandinavian countries themselves. The Danish government, in the well-known circular from the Minister of Foreign Affairs, N. Scheel, in February 1857 had referred ironically to this 'poetic' idea, because among other things, it clashed with the Helstat idea.[27] In Sweden, too, there was a strong anti-Scandinavian opposition among conservative groups. L. Manderström, who was appointed Minister of Foreign Affairs at the beginning of 1858, distanced himself from the Scandinavian idea from the start, although he was not against the notion of a Danish-Swedish alliance. Nor, expect for a short period (1856-57), did the reports sent to St. Petersburg by the embassies in Copenhagen and Stockholm give cause for any great alarm. I. Dashkov, the Russian ambassador in Stockholm, and even P.E. Ungern-Sternberg, the Russian ambassador in Copenhagen, who was initially more sensitive than Dashkov to any signs of a Swedish-Danish rapprochement, and his successor, N. Nikolay, all reported that the dreams of the idealistic adherents of Scandinavianism need not be taken seriously.[28] Dashkov reported that Sweden had troubled with Norway and that the latter would have no interest at all in further strengthening Sweden or in a Scandinavian union. It is beside the point that Dashkov's reports on this subject were superficial and that he was never able to give a penetrating analysis of the mood in Sweden itself, or to point out the political, economic and structural contradiction which existed between Sweden and Den-

---

26. Jansson, *Den svenska,* pp. 131-133, A. Bernstorff's Denkschrift, August and October, 1861, in *Im Kampfe für Preussens Ehre. Aus dem Nachlass des Grafen Albrecht v. Bernstorff,* ed. Karl Ringhoffer, (Berlin, 1906), pp. 424, 434-435, 488-489.
27. N. Neergaard, *Under Junigrundloven,* vol. II, pt. 1, (Copenhagen, 1916), pp. 146-149, Erik Møller, *Helstatens Fald,* vol. I, *1856-63,* (Copenhagen, 1958), pp. 212-214.
28. Dashkov's dispatch no. 15, 25 August/6 September 1861, R.A. Stockholm, N. Nicolay's dispatches of 30 November 1861, 16 June and 20 July 1863, R.A. Copenhagen.

mark, including their different development, cultural differences and the still living tradition of Swedish-Danish wars which had been revived by the comparatively recent incorporation of Danish Norway into Sweden in 1814.[29]

Dashkov also failed to analyze the current political situation and to draw the conclusions from the fact that Denmark saw Germany as its main enemy. Sweden saw Russia as its main enemy although some government circles were flirting with Germany, particularly Prussia. In Sweden there were plenty of voices saying that personal union with Denmark would be a disaster for the country, while in democratic Denmark there was no confidence that aristocratic Sweden would defend Denmark against Germany.

Disturbed by reports of the progress and demonstrations in support of Scandinavianism, Gorchakov, on the instructions of the Tsar, advised his ambassadors in Copenhagen and Stockholm to use not only diplomatic means in the fight against Scandinavianism but police-type measures too, including investigation of activists connected with Scandinavianism, their plans, resources and prospects. He also recommended observation of agitators in Sweden who sought to spread their ideas to the territory of Finland, and additional efforts to influence conservative politicians and people sympathetic to Russia, particularly in Denmark, and to suggest to them that they should strive for a change of government in Copenhagen. The Russian ambassador in Denmark acted zealously in the spirit of these instructions and gained himself a reputation like those of Repnin and Stackelberg, the notorious ambassadors of Catherine II in Warsaw on the eve of the partitions of Poland.[30]

IV

Towards Denmark and its dispute with Germany, Gorchakov initially adopted different and more flexible tactics. Where Prussia's direct interests were not involved, as with the question of the Sound, Russia supported Denmark. This was sparked off by the United States' demand in 1855 for the abolition of the charges for passage through the Sound, which in American opinion were a medieval relic and contrary to the idea of freedom of the seas. As soon as the conflict arose, Russia, in contrast to many other countries, supported the Danish demands for compensation for the abolition of the charges. And although large sums were involved, in view of Russia's major share of the trade being carried through the Sound, and despite the fact that Russia was herself in a deep financial crisis, she stuck firmly to this position.[31] This demonstrated the primacy of politics over economics and once

---

29. Møller, *Skandinavisk stræben og Svensk politik omkring 1860,* (Copenhagen, 1947).
30. Halicz, *op.cit.* p. 136.
31. Traité Général du 14 mars 1857 concernant le rachat du péage du Sund et des Belts. Convention avec la Russie, Art. I. In Hof-Haus-u. Staatsarchiv Wien, Politisches Archiv, Dänemark, XXIV, Kart. 20, 1858-1860.

again confirmed the thesis that the primacy of politics had been axiomatic in Russia's behavior since the rise of the Russian empire. There can be no question that this position was motivated by the desire to draw Denmark away from France and not to let her follow the path of Sweden.[32]

Where the question of the Elbe duchies was concerned, on the other hand, Gorchakov, in the guise of objectivity, supported the German rather than the Danish point of view and laid the blame for causing the crisis on Denmark since, without the duchies' agreement, it had replaced their constitution with a new one, signed by the Danish King on 2 October 1855. Gorchakov called on Denmark to make concessions, but he did not encourage Prussia and Austria to take immediate action; on the contrary, he urged them towards reason and reconciliation, fearing lest they should invite intervention on the part of France, Britain and Sweden, who had spoken out in support of Denmark.

In conversations in 1856 with O. Plessen, the Danish ambassador, Gorchakov continually repeated that Russia would not take the same position towards Denmark's dispute with Germany as she had previously.[33] Thus Russia's balancing policy sought to localize the conflict and to torpedo Danish and French plans, denying them the opportunity to raise the dispute to the level of a European problem. This could have led to the calling of a conference of the signatories of the Treaty of London, at which Russia, in he weakened state, would not have had much say. The dispute lay within the competence of the German Confederation. In view of the strong liberal influence in that body, however, Gorchakov preferred that the dispute over the duchies be settled by an agreement between Denmark and the large German states (i.e., Austria and Prussia).

The position taken by Russia played a prominent part in the policy of her ally France, who, under Russian pressure during a meeting in Stuttgart in September 1857, abandoned the idea of convoking a European conference for the purpose of settling the dispute over the duchies. She adopted Gorchakov's point of view, reckoning that Russia would support her should war break out between herself and Austria as a result of Napoleon III's Italian plans.[34]

Russia's attitude contributed to an easing of the conflict between Denmark and the German Confederation at the moment when Denmark was threatened with action in February 1858. This same attitude also contributed to the temporary

---

32. Ungern-Sternberg's dispatches of 1/13 April, 18, 21, 28 June 1855, Handskr. XVI, vol. 47, Central Arhkiv (Arkhiv Ministerstva Inostrannykh Del, Moscow, vol. II (1856), nos. 88, 94, 99, 100, 8/20 June, 14/26, 18/30 June 1856, Russiske Films, R.A. Copenhagen. A. Gorchakov to Ungern-Sternberg, 2 June 1856, Rus. Films, Gorchakov to Dashkov, 4 July 1856, R.A. Stockholm.
33. O. Plessen's dispatches nos. 53 and 63, 18/30 July and 24 August/5 September 1856 and also 1/13 April 1861, Depecher Russland, R.A. Copenhagen.
34. Ernst Schüle, *Russland und Frankreich vom Ausgang des Krimkrieges bis zum italienischen Krieg 1856-1859,* (Königsberg u. Berlin, 1935), p. 92, G. Rothan, Souvenirs diplomatique, *Revue des Deux Mondes,* vol. LXXXI, 1899, pp. 72-73, 76. F. Charles-Roux, *Alexander II, Gortchakoff et Napoléon III,* (Paris, 1913), p. 210.

suspension of the conflict following the November decrees issued by the Hall government, under which the Danish constitution of 1855 was recognized as illegal and annulled in respect of the two duchies of Holstein and Lauenburg. This conciliatory move by the Danish government was a departure from the 'Helstat' idea, which was supported by conservative groups in Denmark and Russia, and represented a step in the direction of implementation of the 'Eider state' policy.

When the Danish-German conflict flared up again in 1861 as a result of the publication by the Danish government of a budget for the duchies without prior consultation with the Estates of Holstein, Gorchakov addressed Copenhagen in more sharply critical terms, as did the Western powers. With the co-operation of the other powers, Gorchakov brought about a reversal of the decision by the Danish government. Like Britain, he was opposed to the neutralization of Holstein,[35] although his reasoning was different from Britain's. He concentrated his attention on the problem of Schleswig, treating it as the central one in the whole conflict and demanding concessions from Denmark to the German population of Schleswig, particularly in the field of language and cultural rights. 'Les mauvaises passions couvrent plus que jamais sous les cendres. C'est la question du Schleswig, que va les éveiller, si vous n'y prenez garde,' Gorchakov warned Denmark in one of his conversations with O. Plessen.[36] He agreed that the Schleswig question was an international matter but, as he put it, in order not to undermine the values and principles accepted in the Treaty of London, he was opposed to the proposals from the cabinet of St. James intended to reaffirm the guarantee of the integrity of the Danish monarchy since such a move might be interpreted as meaning that even the signatories of the treaty had some reservations concerning its provisions.[37]

Despite the fact that Schleswig did not belong to the German Confederation, Gorchakov considered the German grievances justified. He maintained that Denmark had not discharged her 1851-1852 obligations with respect to Schleswig and he supported Prussia's position in particular, although he was aware that Prussia's concern in the whole affair was more with popularity in Germany than with a solution of the problem of the German population of Schleswig.[38] Although Gorchakov also had reservations about Prussia's goodwill, he had no intention of exerting pressure on her or doing anything which might alienate her from Russia.[39] The Prussian ambassador in St. Petersburg, O. Bismarck, concluded that Prussia had nothing to fear from st. Petersburg.[40] This great increase in Prussia's authority

---

35. Steefel, *op.cit.* p. 37.
36. Dep. Rusland, 29 September/11 October 1860, R.A. Copenhagen: 'Le mot de la nationalité est de nos jours et dans presque tous les pays de l'Europe un appel aux mauvaises passions, et il serait digne de la sagesse du Roi de ne pas laisser prédominer cet élément révolutionnaire dans ces discussions avec l'Allemagne' (Gorchakov). See also Gorchakov to Ungern-Sternberg, 16/28 November 1860, Rus. Films, R.A. Copenhagen.
37. A.F. Krieger, *Dagbøger,* (Copenhagen-Kristiania, 1920-1921), 20 May 1861, vol. II, pp. 210-211.
38. Dep. Rusland, 1861-1865. Compare: *Le Nord,* no. 18, 1861.
39. Dep. Rusland, no. 40, 26 June/8 July 1861.
40. *Die politischen Berichte des Fürstens Bismarck aus Petersburg und Paris, 1859-1862,* vol. II, ed. Ludwig Raschdau, (Berlin, 1920), pp. 103, 108, 195, B.E. Nolde, *Petersburgskaya missiya Bismarka, 1859-1862,* (Prague, 1925), pp. 268-269.

with Russia was connected with the vicissitudes of Russia in the Kingdom of Poland in 1861-1862 and the chill in relations along the St. Petersburg-Paris axis.

Unlike Britain, Gorchakov was unwilling to recognize that Germany was concerned not just with concessions but with the implementation of the Schleswig-Holstein program and would not rest until that program was fulfilled.[41] Thus, in the continuing dispute between the historic rights of Denmark, guaranteed in numerous international agreements going back to the first quarter of the eighteenth century and confirmed in the treaty of 8 June 1852 - which the Danish government continually cited - and the national aspirations of Germany, Gorchakov supported Germany on account of Prussia. The paradox of the situation was that, in its notes to the democratic government of Denmark, the despotic government of Russia argued on behalf of the national cause while in its conflicts with Germany, Hall's government was inclined to argue on the basis of legal interpretation since to accept national criteria would have been to put Denmark in an infinitely more difficult position.

Gorchakov, however, for fear of international complications, sough to restrain German aspirations and would not agree to their more outrageous stipulations, such as those addressed to the Danish government in August 1862, whereby Denmark was to suspend the constitution with respect to Schleswig, as it had done in the case of Holstein and Lauenburg in 1858. He also warned the German Confederation against intervention in Holstein, as such a move would arouse alarm in Paris and London,' ... Lui [Gorchakov] semblait ménager la chèvre et le chou,' was the opinion of Gorchakov's policy expressed by Manderström in a conversation with the Danish ambassador in Stockholm, W. Scheel-Plessen.[42]

When Britain lost patience with the long drawn out Danish-German dispute, and was worried about becoming isolated in Europe owing to the deterioration of her relations with France, she began to incline towards satisfaction of the German demands, judging that this would improve her relations with Prussia and the other German states. With this in mind, the Foreign Secretary, Lord J. Russell, put forward the so-called Gotha program in September 1862. It declared invalid for the Kingdom and Schleswig the constitution of 1855 and proposed the introduction of a new constitution which, after the conception of Holstein, gave equal rights to all the four provinces.[43]

Gorchakov immediately supported this program, which followed the wishes of the German states, and called on the Danish government to accept the British proposal.[44] Despite foreign pressure, particularly from Russia, this program was

---

41. A.B. Paget to J. Russell, 27 March 1860, in *The Cambridge History of Britain Foreign Policy,* vol. II, (Cambridge, 1923), p. 543.
42. W. Schell-Plessen to C.C. Hall, no. 18, 14 May 1862, Udenrigsmin. Sverige, Dep. 1862-1865, R.A. Copenhagen.
43. Keith A.P. Sandiford, *Great Britain and the Schleswig-Holstein Question, 1848-64: A Study in Diplomacy, Politics, and Public Opinion,* (Toronto, 1975), p. 53 ff, J.H.S. Birch, *Denmark in History,* (Westport, Conn., 1975), pp. 352-353.
44. Gorchakov's dispatch to the Russian envoys of 29 September/11 October 1862, in P. Vedel Privatarkiv, 6498, pk. 28, R.A. Copenhagen.

rejected by Copenhagen, mainly because it was contrary to the only policy which both the Danish government and the majority of society wanted to pursue:

The Eider as the national frontier, the June Constitution [of 1854] for the country's flag and the brotherly nations of the north as allies.[45]

Besides, from a practical point of view, as Copenhagen argued, if the plan were accepted it would mean the break-up of the Danish monarchy into four autonomous units and would paralyze both government and state. The prevailing mood in Denmark was faithfully portrayed by Charles A. Gosch in his work *Denmark and Germany Since 1815*, published in London in 1862. He ends with the conclusion:

The struggle between Germany and Denmark is, as far as the latter is concerned, one of life and death, which can only be prolonged, but not terminated, by a compromise. Justice must be done – neither more nor less; but the least that Denmark has a right to demand, is the complete vindication of the old verse – *Eidera Teutonicum terminat Imperium*.[46]

V

The year 1863 was a turning point in Russo-Scandinavian relations.[47] There can be no question that the reasons for this are to be found in the new situation created in Russia by the Polish uprising of 1863 and its consequences both for Russia itself and the new constellation of political forces in Europe forged in the aftermath of the uprising. On the one hand, the uprising compelled Russia to mobilize her internal forces and intensify her military efforts, but, on the other hand, it led to the political isolation of Russia as a result of the breaching of co-operation between her and France and of Austria's move into the Western powers' camp. But thanks to Prussia, which was no less interest than Russia in stifling the Polish uprising, and then to the collapse of co-operation between the Western states and the growing co-operation between the two larger German powers, Russia's situation improved and it was not Russia but France that found herself isolated in the autumn of 1863.

In historical perspective it is clear how the fates of Russia and Prussia were objectively linked (although Prussia rejected the Tsar's proposal for an alliance with Russia)[48] and how significant the defeat of the uprising in Poland and that event's political consequences were for the future of all the Scandinavian countries – though not to the same extent in every case. True, Russo-Danish relations did not

---

45. Birch, *op.cit.* p. 352.
46. Ch.A. Gosch, *Denmark and Germany Since 1815*, (London, 1862), p. 300.
47. Albert Olsen, Danmark og den polske opstand 1863. *Festskrift til Erik Arup*, (Copenhagen, 1946), pp. 304-316, Møller, *Helstatens Fald*, vol. I, pp. 513-515, Halicz, *The 1863 Polish Uprising and Scandinavia. The Year 1863, the Turning-Point in Russo-Scandinavian Relations*, (Copenhagen, 1988).
48. *Im Kampfe für Preussens Ehre*, pp. 554-555, Friese, *op.cit.* Halicz, *The 1863 Polish Uprising*, pp. 84-86.

undergo any fundamental deterioration in 1863, but the very fact that Denmark, although not without vacillation, had supported the Western powers' initiative and eventually decided to send a note to St. Petersburg concerning the Polish uprising meant that Denmark had, as St. Petersburg put it, joined the 'diplomatic campaign by the powers against Russia.'[49] The text of the Danish note, which was devoid of offensive features and really amounted to approval of the policy of Alexander II and reaffirmed the Danish government's confidence in his government, was of no great concern. But the fact that it was sent, like the demonstrations and meetings in support of the uprising, contrasted vividly with the position of Prussia, which actively supported Russia's policy. In the words of Debidour,

En secondant la politique dans le premier (la Pologne) de ces deux pays, la cour de Berlin s'était prémanie contre toute opposition de la Russie à ses project contre le second (le Danemark).[50]

In this context we can understand the extremely critical tone in which Gorchakov addressed Copenhagen from the moment the Danish government issued the decrees of 30 March 1863. It heralded a further step in the direction of separation of Holstein and Lauenburg from the Danish monarchy in the true meaning of the word, and the victory of the Eider state idea, until the publication of the new November Constitution.

The deterioration of relations on the St. Petersburg-Copenhagen axis was undoubtedly hastened by the personal contacts between Frederick VII and King Charles XI and between Danish and Swedish politicians, who held intensive discussions during the summer on the subject of a military alliance between Denmark and Sweden-Norway – which, it should be noted, was never concluded. The increased activity by Swedish Scandinavianists in connection with the celebrations in 1862 commemorating the battle of Poltava, the attitude of Charles XV, who did not hide his sympathy with the Scandinavian idea, his personal contacts with Polish politicians and extension of protection to Finnish Scandinavianists were all observed with disquiet by Russian diplomats.

Russia's concern increased during the Polish uprising in view of the wide-ranging pro-Polish demonstrations throughout Sweden, the pro-Polish attitude of the King who was in contact with Napoleon III and emissaries of the Polish National Government, and rumors of joint French-Swedish military action to defend Poland and recover Finland from Russia. In particular, Russia was very sensitive about the ideas openly proclaimed by the Scandinavianists concerning the need the co-operation by all the Scandinavian countries in defense of Poland and for the reconstruction of an independent Poland to form a barrier with Scandinavia against Russian despotism.[51]

49. Udenrigsministeriet, Polen, A 334, R.A. Copenhagen, Nicolay's dispatch of 16/18 and 17/29 April 1863, in A.V.P.R., vol. LXV, R.A. Copenhagen, Rus. Films.
50. A. Debidour, *Histoire diplomatique de l'Europe 1814-1878.* (Paris, 1891), vol II, pp. 273-274, *D.G. Monrads Deltagelse i begivenhederne 1864,* (Copenhagen, 1914), p. 25).
51. 'The liberation and restauration of Poland will contribute to secure the safety of our country and

It was believed that the rise of Poland would push Russia eastward and force it to switch to a defensive policy towards the European states. This would be important for Denmark, too, since the revival of a strong, free Poland could draw German attention away from Denmark.

These ideas, proclaimed officially in the Scandinavianist-influenced press in both Sweden and Denmark, and sporadically in Norway too, were a cause of displeasure in the cabinet in St. Petersburg, although at the same time, in all the Scandinavian countries, numerous voices were raised calling for restraint and non-involvement in Polish affairs. In Norway in particular, both in government circles and in society, there was great skepticism and the view was frequently expressed that Norway had no interest in Sweden's recovery of Finland, or in strengthening Sweden generally. Liberal circles supported the Polish nation's struggle for liberation chiefly out of fear of states that trampled on the rights of nations to political independence and freedom.

Despite official assurance by Manderström that the Swedish government cherished the best of intentions towards Alexander II, St. Petersburg did not trust Sweden and was afraid that she might join with the Western powers against Russia. Perhaps in order not to antagonize his northern neighbor, Gorchakov displayed no particular disapproval of the suggestions addressed to him in connection with the Polish uprising in the Swedish notes in April.[52]

Towards Finland the Tsar's government adopted different tactics. The minor reforms initiated there in 1856, to some extent forming part of the reform in the empire, began to move forward in 1863. An outward sign of the change in course in relation to Finns loyal to the Tsar was the convocation of the Finnish Sejm for the first time in many decades. It was opened in Helsinki on 6/18 September 1863 by Alexander II personally, accompanied by his closest advisers and ministers, including Gorchakov, who was an advocate of autonomy for Finland.[53] The Tsar's reforms covered a broad range of matters, starting with a law that was intended to lead to full equality of rights for the Finnish language with Swedish, through reforms in the economic and currency fields, to a military reform applying to the territory of the Grand Duchy of Finland.[54]

These changes were motivated by political and military considerations, 'la position exceptionelle du Grand-Duché', as the Tsar put it to Wedel-Jarlsberg. Russia, facing a difficult situation, wanted to reward the Finns for their loyal, although not servile, attitude towards her. But her main concern was to strike a decisive blow against Scandinavianism and once and for all to undermine Swedish influence in

---

the future at the Scandinavian North'. The Scandinavian Proclamation. 13 May 1863, in *Danmark*, 19. May 1863. See also Halicz, *The 1863 Polish Uprising*, pp. 97-101.

52. The Swedish Notes of 7 and 29 April 1863. Skrivelser från Stockholm til Petersburg, R.A. Stockholm.
53. M.M. Borodkin, *Istoriya Finlandii, Vremiya Imperatora Aleksandra II*, (St. Petersburg, 1908), pp. 170, 181, Pokchlebkin, *op.cit.* pp. 87-88, Lolo Krusius-Ahrenberg, *Der Durbruch des Nationalismus und Liberalismus im politischen Leben Finlands 1856-1863*, (Helsinki, 1934), pp. 430 ff.
54. L.A. Puntila, *Histoire politique de la Finlande de 1809 à 1955*, (Neutchâtel, 1964). J. Paasivirta, *Finland and Europe*. (Minneapolis, 1981), pp. 119-137.

Finland. She wanted, in the event of a decision by Napoleon III to intervene in the Baltic, to make it impossible for him to create a platform for operations on the territory of Finland. France, however, was in no hurry to help the Polish uprising and there was nothing to indicate that the Finns would be willing to join any such action. But even the fact that the idea of neutrality in case of war between Russia and a coalition of Western states and Sweden had been aired in Finland, despite censorship, caused the tsar disquiet. Russia regarded this as a hostile act and dangerous from a strategic point of view.[55]

By introducing reforms Russia sought to show the West that suspecting her of attempts of Russification of non-Russian peoples was nothing but defamation, and that Russia had no such intentions towards Finland. On the contrary, Russia was moving to meet Finnish demands because Finns were loyal to St. Petersburg.[56] Furthermore, Russia pretended to be the champion of Finnish culture against the threat of Scandinavianism. In the words of *Le Nord,* Gorchakov's mouthpiece, in an article entitled 'Le Scandinavisme et le droit nouveau' on 6 July 1864.

Le Finlandais craint la civilisation et l'influence suédois qui le dominent encore malgré lui, et auxquelles il veut s'arracher à tout prix ... les Finlandais savent qu'ils n'ont rien à redouter à côté de la Russie, elle leur permettra sans difficulté de chanter *Vart land* et de s'enivrer des souvenirs du *Kalevala,* tandis que les Suédois et les Scandinaves pourraient bien trouvez que *Wainemoinen* ferait une concurrence dangereuse à Thor et à Odin.

In Russia itself the reforms carried out in Finland met with a mixed reception. The Slavophile semi-official organ *Severnaya Pchela,* no. 305, 1863, and the democratic *Otechestvennye Zapiski,* no. 9, 1863, welcome them. But the editor of *Moskovskie vedomosti,* M. Katkov, criticized them sharply as a step towards the creation of a Russian federation and thus a dangerous precedent, 'a model for dismembering of the organic Russian state', as he described it in a letter to the minister, P.A. Valuev, on 2 December 1863.[57] Russia's conduct towards Finland, although brought about mainly by the situation in which she found herself because of the January Uprising, was nevertheless proof that in a difficult position Russia played a flexible and sophisticated political game.

---

55. Wedel-Jarlsberg to Manderström, no. 67, 21 May/2 June 1863, R.A. Stockholm.
56. I.A. Aksakov's point of view in Borodkin, *Istoriya Finlandii,* p. 170. In Pokhlebkin's book there are discrepancies concerning the interpretation of the problem of neutrality expressed by the *Helsingfors Dagblad,* 15 April 1863. See also his chapter titled 'The Myth of Russification'.
57. M. Katkov to P. Valuev, *Correspondence,* pp. 346-247, See Martin Katz, *Mikhail N. Katkov: A Political Biography, 1818-1887,* (The Hague-Paris, 1966), p. 134.

VI

In the autumn of 1863 Russia warned Copenhagen of the consequences of adopting a new constitution which would be a further step towards implementation of the Eider policy. This pressure was intensified because of the death of Frederick VII. Gorchakov's telegram evincing displeasure reached Copenhagen[58] after Christian IX had signed the constitution but it is doubtful whether the King would have been prepared to defer it even if the telegram had been received earlier, in view of the attitude of the government and society in the capital. Russia firmly condemned the proclamation of the constitution – 'Vous tendrez trop la corde,' Gorchakov declared to Plessen[59] – and supported without reservation any steps taken by the conservative German states to bring about the withdrawal of the constitution of 18 November 1863 with respect to Schleswig. He regarded intervention by the Confederation in Holstein as a legal move. Afraid lest liberal German forces, supported by Napoleon III, should take firm action towards Denmark, Gorchakov called on both of the large German states to co-operate despite their differences concerning the future of Germany. 'Il n'y a pas d'Allemagne forte ni de Souverains Allemands indépendants en dehors de cette union', Gorchakov wrote in a letter to Olga, daughter of Nicholas I and later Queen of Württemberg.[60] 'Séparer la question de succession de celle de la constitution commune déja sanctionnée', as the Swedish ambassador in St. Petersburg, Wedel-Jarlsberg, reported on 25 November 1863, became Gorchakov's principal aim when the Danish-German conflict reached its culmination.

But there was no doubt either, as the same ambassador reported on 21 November/3 December, that Gorchakov would give Denmark moral support where the integrity of the Danish monarchy and the question of succession to the throne were concerned, but would not help her 'ni par un soldat, ni par un vaisseau, ni par un écu.' In Wedel-Jarlsberg's opinion this policy was founded above all on the aim of 'self-preservation' in connection with a possible 'counter coup' in Poland and Russia's consequent interest in maintaining the best of relations with Prussia. Beside this, in the ambassador's opinion, the financial difficulties which Russia was experiencing played an important role, as they had repercussions on her capacity to equip her army.[61]

Gorchakov tried to persuade the Danish government to enter discussions with the German states, which in practice would have meant accepting their demands. The initiative took the form of the Ewers mission (December 1863 – January 1864), which was joined by Wodehouse, but which brought no result. Ewers essentially defended Bismarck's interests. The only 'reward' was the fall of the Hall govern-

---

58. Gorchakov to Nicolay, 7/19 November 1863. A.V.P.R., Fond Kantselariya, delo 34.
59. Dep. Rusland, no. 68, 12/24 November 1863.
60. Gorchakov's letter of 13 March (O.S.) 1864. Hauptstaatsarchiv Stuttgart, G.314, Bü7, no. 84.
61. Aage Friis, Einar Hedin, eds., *Henning Hamilton anteckningar rörande förhållandet mellan Sverige och Danmark 1863-1864,* (Copenhagen, 1936), p. 113.

ment, but the new government under Monrad proved no less unyielding in the face of foreign pressure.[62]

The subsequent entry of Prussian and Austrian troops into Schleswig, which was flagrant aggresion, was treated by Russia, as Bismarck intended, as a move in defense of the integrity of Denmark and the provisions of the Treaty of London. Furthermore, Gorchakov urged Denmark to forbear from resistance, as the best way out of the situation for her, almost as though it were for her benefit.[63] This cynical attitude met with incomprehension and distaste even among some of Gorchakov's close associates.[64]

What Russia really feared was reaction against the anti-Danish action of the German states, particularly on the part of Britain, perhaps accompanied by France. Gorchakov therefore sought co-operation from Britain, arguing that by not intervening militarily and refraining from a show of naval strength Britain would contribute to the preservation of peace in Europe.[65] And after the German forces had entered Schleswig, Russia urged them to issue declarations that they still, as always, supported the integrity of the Danish monarchy, in order to placate British opinion. However, Russia was satisfied with a declaration composed by the two largest German states stating only that they adhered to the content of the 1851-1852 agreements. The declaration did not mention the provisions of the Treaty of London, which was of course a deliberate dodge by Bismarck.

While the military action lasted, Russia took a neutral position. This was 'the legal status arising from the abstention of a state from all participation in a war between other states.' According to the Paris declaration of 1856, neutrality was to consist of 'the maintenance of an attitude of impartiality towards the belligerents, and the recognition by the belligerents of this abstention and impartiality.'

But the Paris declaration did not mean maintaining an equally impartial attitude towards both sides in a state of war. In this specific case, Russia urged both German states to act in such a way as to keep control of the conflict with Denmark in their own hands and not to let the democratic forces in Germany become involved. From the beginning she supported the action of the large German states in both the diplomatic and the military fields. To the German states it was 'a favourable neutrality'.[66] Without actively involving herself in the conflict, and formally maintaining good relations both with the German states and with Denmark and declaring herself in favour of the integrity of Denmark, Russia supported German actions and did not even verbally condemm the blatant aggression towards Denmark when German troops crossed the Eider. On the contrary, she justified this move as undertaken in defense of the treaty of 8 May 1852. She neutralized all British diplomatic initiatives, particularly attempts to organize a show of military strength in

62. A.V.P.R., delo 65, Russ. Films.
63. F. Napier to Russell, 4 February 1864, Public Record Office, London, 30/22, vol. 84, pp. 187-189.
64. P. Oubril to Gorchakov, 19/31 January 1864, *Krasnyi Arkhiv*, no. 2 (1939), p. 72 ff.
65. Mosse, *European Powers*.
66. Iz zapisnoi knigi arkhivista, *Krasnyi Arkhiv*, vol. LXXIV, (1936).

the Baltic, by continually declaring herself only in favour of diplomatic initiatives designed to induce both parties to agree to the calling of a peace conference. Gorchakov soberly warned Britain that, though always willing to co-operate on behalf of peace, Russia did not wish to see Denmark build-up false illusion about such collective action. (The naval demonstration initiated by the British cabinet). When the London Conference finally went into session in April, Russia did not play a constructive role, and it would be no great exaggeration to compare her role with that played by the comparatively insignificant Sweden. Brunnow, the Russian representative, was perfectly well aware of his country's weakness.[67] But nevertheless Gorchakov, true to his peacock character, strove to persuade others that he held the position of special arbiter in the Danish-German dispute and that it was mainly thanks to him that a local war had not developed into a European war.[68] Furthermore, he laid the responsibility for the course of events not on Germany but on the Western states, continually emphasizing that they, both Britain and France, had contributed to the growth of the situation in which the German-Danish dispute developed into a military clash by their attitude towards Russia during the Polish uprising.

Gorchakov's conception of an understanding between the four powers, that is the Northern states and Britain, for the purpose of preserving peace in Europe and frustrating the actions of revolutionary groups in both Germany and other countries was essentially a screen designed to hide Russia's weakness and passivity in the face of events. Behind this idea was a plan to neutralize any anti-German moves. As far as Britain was concerned, he had no difficulty owing to the division of opinion within the cabinet itself over Britain's attitude to the Danish-German conflict and the invariably pro-German position adopted by Queen Victoria.[69] The plan represented a return to the old idea of Nesselrode that as long as Russia acted in concert with Austria and Prussia this would not only avert danger from Poland but ensure that France was not in a position to subordinate the lesser German states and create something like the Union of the Rhine. At last Russia would have a secure western border and could quietly continue expansion in Asia.

The Danish question, to Russia, was in fact a secondary issue.

Central to Gorchakov's whole conception was Russia's attitude to Prussia and the future of Germany. Gorchakov had spent many years in Germany and must have realized that the dispute with Denmark about the duchies was really about something much bigger. Although we find no trace of the subject in the official diplomatic correspondence of 1863-1864, the question of the future of Germany seems sure to have been considered in St. Petersburg. Gorchakov certainly faced a dilemma over what was better for Russia – the *status quo,* that is to say the con-

---

67. A.F. Krieger to C.C. Andrae, London 17 and 26 April 1864. *Historisk Tidsskrift,* vol. IV, (Copenhagen, 1894-95), pp. 132-135 and Wedel-Jarlsberg's dispatch no. 61, 6 Juni/25 May 1864, R.A. Stockholm.
68. Gorchakov's Memorial of 5 February 1864. Arkhiv Ministerstwa Inostrannykh Del, Moscow, 1864, vol. 68.
69. Sandiford, *Great Britain,* p. 148.

tinuation of the German Confederation, or a united Germany, but only under the aegis of Prussia.

Although the federal structure of Germany was regarded in Russia as an important element of security and a condition of equilibrium in Europa, on the other hand, as the events of 1812 and 1853 had shown, Germany fragmented was in no position to protect Russia against France. It may have been this experience that inclined Gorchakov to the view, especially after the events of 1863 in Poland and the Crimean War, that backing conservative Prussia in its struggle to unite Germany could be more advantageous and serve Russia's interests better. Hence, he drew his conclusion concerning the German-Danish problem in 1864.

Fears about the attitude of Britain and France as Bismarck's rapacity increased were never overcome in St. Petersburg while the war lasted. Aware of the consequences if the Western states entered the war on Denmark's side, Gorchakov, not wanting to antagonize Bismarck and fearing that his warnings would have no effect – he already had evidence of this – decided to urge Austria to restrain Bismarck's aspirations. This was not a hard task as Austria was less involved in the dispute over the duchies than Prussia[70] and in her political and economic situation, as it was said, 'la paix est presque indispensable.'[71] Austria too entertained great reluctance about Bismarck's new initiatives designed to escalate the military action and carry it into the heart of Jutland. Her fears of the rise of an Anglo-French coalition also increased. 'It is most desirable to strengthen the influence of the cabinet of Vienna with that of Berlin', said the British ambassador in St. Petersburg, Lord Napier, who was in close contact with Gorchakov at this time.[72] Gorchakov believed that he would achieve his aim, since in a letter to Olga Nikolaevna on 13 March (O.S.) he wrote:

Si la Prusse a des convoitises, elles seront contenues par l'attitude de l'Autriche. Cette dernière veut de l'influence, mais certes aucune idée d'absorption n'entre dans ses prévisions.[73]

As the French *chargé d'affaires* Massignac reported, Gorchakov feared that Prussia's policy might cause the growth of national feelings in Germany itself, which could have repercussions in the Polish lands.[74] However, while urging Austria to restrain Prussia, Gorchakov did so in a circumspect manner, so as not to affect relations between the German states and, more important, between St. Petersburg and Berlin.

---

70. Annaliese Klein-Wuttig, *Politik und Kriegsführung in den deutschen Einigungskriegen 1864, 1866 und 1870/71,* (Berlin, 1934), pp. 14-18, A. Gramont to E. Drouyn Lhuys, 18 February 1864, in *Origines diplomatiques de la guerre 1870-71,* (Paris, 1910), pp. 322 ff, Heinrich S. Srbik, Die Bismarckkontraverse, in *Das Bismarck-Problem in der Geschichtsschreibung nach 1945,* ed. Lothar Gall, (Cologne-Berlin, 1971). p. 139.
71. F. Thun to B. Rechberg, 23 January/4 February and 19 February/2 March 1864, P.A. Rusland, X. K. 55, H.H.S.A. Wien.
72. Napier to Russell, no. 201, 13 April 1864, P.R.O. F.O. 65/659.
73. See Gorchakov's letters, H.S.A. Stuttgart.
74. No. 213, 16 February 1864, *Origines,* vol. I, p. 316.

At difficult moments for Prussia during the London Conference, St. Petersburg hastened to Bismarck's aid. An instance of this was when Brunnow put forward Prince Oldenburg as a candidate for ruler of the Elbe duchies. This posed a dilemma for Austria since, wishing to endear herself to the German Confederation, she had accepted its candidate, Prince Augustenburg,[75] but it followed the line of Bismarck's policy. If Gorchakov had reservations about the steps taken by Bismarck, they were mainly connected with the fear of complications in Europe. In essence Russian policy from start to finish was an important factor conducive to Bismarck's policy.

Gorchakov cleared the way for Bismarck, who quickly realized that despite certain reservations on her part he had nothing to fear from Russia.[76] He knew that this was of fundamental importance, for the key to the situation was in Russia's hands. Consequently, he behaved ruthlessly towards Denmark, ignored criticism from German liberal circles, and spoke with irony of the policy of the cabinet of St. James, but took care to maintain good relations with Russia. Knowing Gorchakov's weaknesses well, Bismarck preferred to give the impression that he valued his opinion highly and would strive to act in the spirit of his recommendations. At difficult moments, after the start of the war, not yet knowing how the situation would develop, he advised Redern to express 'our trust and gratitude for the continued friendly attitude of the Imperial Cabinet.'

In order to dispel any doubts which Gorchakov might harbor concerning Prussia's policy and real intentions, in April 1864 he sent F. Pirch to St. Petersburg as a special envoy, instructing him precisely what arguments to deploy in conversation with Gorchakov.[77]

Bismarck himself marshalled his argument in a masterly fashion in conversations with Alexander II and Gorchakov during their visit to Germany in June 1864, convincing them of the correctness of his policy and the baselessness of the arguments used by the Russian side.[78] Acting with the help of *faits accomplis,* he ultimately achieved a situation in which, during conversations in Berlin and Kissingen in June and July, Gorchakov was no longer an equal partner with Bismarck but rather a petitioner.

But knowing well Gorchakov's vanity Bismarck wrote to him to July 5, 1864. 'From the point of view of German interests it is not important whether the duchies are ruled by one prince or another. From the European point of view everything depends on whether Russia throws her weight into the balance on the Grand Duke [Oldenburg – E.H.] or confines herself to standing aside from the dispute.'[79]

---

75. *Monrads Deltagelse,* pp. 126, 140.
76. 2. February 1864. *Die Gesammelten Werke,* (Berlin, 1924-35), vol. IV, p. 298. *Im Kampfe für Preussens Ehre,* p. 571.
77. *Die auswärtige Politik Preussens, 1858-1871,* ed. Rudolf Ibbeken, (Oldenburg, 1933-35), vol. IV, pp. 752 ff, vol. V. pp. 75 ff.
78. APP, vol. V, pp. 208-211, *Die Tagebücher des Freiherrn Reinhard v. Dalwigk* (Deutsche Geschichtsquellen des 19. Jahrhunderts), (Osnabrück, 1967), pp. 139-140.
79. *Krasnyi Arkhiv,* LXI, (1933), p. 14.

VII

Gorchakov's position in 1864 was not the result of the special regard for Bismarck. It was the result of the opportunistic policy of Gorchakov, who lacked the ability to take a long-term view of problems and underestimated both Bismarck's skill and the capacity of Prussia in comparison with the Austrian forces. On the other hand, he overestimated the role of the revolutionary movement and the capacity of Napoleon's France. Gorchakov explained Russia's passive attitude during the war of 1864 mainly by the fact that, being in a state of internal transformation, Russia was in no position to operate actively in the international area. He also argued that Russia's passivity was caused by the situation prevailing in the Polish lands.

There can be no question that use of the Polish argument in this context in discussions with Western diplomats was mere prevarication. The Polish uprising had petered out months before. While there is no denying that the internal reforms in Russia demanded a concentration of effort and that the country was undergoing financial difficulties, there is no ignoring the fact that in 1864 Russia possessed large military forces on her western border, which would have been sufficiently strong to check Bismarck.

Even D. Milyutin, the War Minister, who would naturally be cautious in his estimate of Russia's military capacity since he had an interest in presenting the least favorable picture of the army's state of readiness for war, in order to secure the funds necessary for modernization, stated that in the course of 1863, because of the Polish uprising and the threat of intervenion by the Western states, Russia had made great efforts at reconstruction of her army. During 1863 it had increased in number by 350,000 and reached 1,137,000 at the beginning of 1864, not counting 117,000 irregular troops. An immense army was concentrated along the western border of the empire. In the north-west there were 70,000 troops, in the region of Petersburg and the Baltic there were over 100,000, and in the western provinces and the Kingdom of Poland there were 360,000. Despite shortcomings in the field of armaments, organization and system of mobilization, this was a formidable force, with which every state had to reckon.[80]

Discussion of whether Russia was or was not in a position to intervene during the 1864 war is pointless, since a show of military strength in support of Denmark never featured in the plans of Alexander II and his cabinet, although according to diplomats accredited to the Russian court, such a move would have been feasible and would have had a signal effect on the preservation of the *status quo* in the

---

80. Vospominaniya Mityutina, vol. XIII, p. 277, vol. XIV, p. 306, P.A. Zaionchkovskii, D.A. Milyutin, Biograficheskii ocherk, in *Dnevnik Milyutina*, vol. I, *1873-1875*, (Moscow, 1947), pp. 25-26, Peter von Wahlde, Dmitrii Milyutin, Appraisals, *Canadian Slavic Studies,* vol. III, no. 2 (1969), pp. 400-401, P. Zaionchkovskii, *Voennye reformy 1860-1870 godov* v Rossii, (Moscow, 1952), A. Strokov, *Istoriya voennovo iskusstva,* (Moscow, 1965), D. Beyrau, *Militär und Gessellschaft im Vorrevolutionären Russland,* (Köln, Wien, 1984), pp. 254-262. See also Wedel-Jarlsberg's report on the Russia's military situation, 27 February/10 March 1864, R.A. Stockholm.

Baltic. 'To march upon Berlin would have been a mere holiday task for the Russian army, like our march upon Magdala,' wrote Lord Redesdale, perhaps with a certain degree of exaggeration.[81] This capacity and willingness Russia lacked. Russia, in fact, was less able to intervene than any other neutral great power, owing to her political conception far more than to her continuing military weakness. This policy was perfectly described by A. Krausse:

> For the great principle of Russian policy in the East, as in the West, is the attainment of the desirable as cheaply as possible... Its opportunism has long since taugh the lesson that possibilities recur at frequent intervals, and if these prove somewhat risky, the lack of scruple, so typical of Russian reasoning, comes to the diplomatist's aid, and renders what might, without it, be considered impossible, easy ... She [Russia] formulates her aims; and attains them as opportunity serves.[82]

The claim by the Russian diplomat Rosen that 'Prince Gortschakoff was willing to protest, the other two [France and Great Britain] for various reasons holding aloof'[83] is wrong. Furthermore, both the Tsar and his minister assured Wilhelm and Bismarck that in no circumstances would Russia act against Prussia.

In order to justify his policy towards Denmark and clear himself of blame, Gorchakov continually argued that Russia had abided by the Treaty of London longest, even when the other powers had abandoned it. But we must note that this adherence to the treaty slightly longer than Britain, for example, was exclusively for propaganda purposes. Gorchakov did not intend to defend it and had long since realized that it was worthless. As early as 13 March 1864 he wrote, 'Certes, nous ne demandons pas que l'Allemange verse son sang pour conserver au Danemark les Duchés de l'Elbe.'[84] Russia formally abided by the treaty in order to show that even when others infringed an international document Russia complied with her signature.[85] Russia's true attitude to her international obligations was to be revealed in 1870 when, taking advantage of an opportune moment, she unilaterally renounced the Treaty of Paris of 1856.

In 1864 Prussia was not yet a country of the first rank and no one yet anticipated that she would soon come to the fore as a major power. It was universally thought then that she was in every respect weaker than Austria. Not until Königrätz was it realized what Prussia had become in such a short time. Thus the argument that Gorchakov supported Prussia because he already saw in her a power which would help Russia to secure the annulment of the unfavourable provisions of the Treaty of Paris is devoid of logic. Such reasoning is like saying that because of the mistakes

---

81. Lord Redesdale, *Further Memories,* (London, 1917), p. 65.
82. Alexis Krausse, *Russia in Asia: A Record and a Study, 1588-1899,* (London, New York, 1973), pp. 272-273.
83. Rosen, *Forty Years of Diplomacy,* (London, 1922), vol. II, p. 65.
84. Gorchakov to Olga Nikolayevna, H.S.A. Stuttgart.
85. 'Russia is divided between her wish to save Denmark, and her unwillingness to break with the Conservative Monarchies of Austria and Prussia', Russell wrote in his Memorandum of 5 May 1864.

he made in the 1860s Gorchakov should bear the responsibility for the events which took place in 1914.[86]

In 1864 it looked less likely that Prussia would soon be a power dictating terms to Europe and that Germany would create a formidable German naval fleet in Kiel to threaten the Baltic and the North Sea. But the helmsman of Russian policy disregarded this possibility although there was no lack of warning voices.[87]

It was not only Russian policy which showed a failure to understand the militaristic essence of Bismarck's policy. The British government, and Napoleon III, also misjudged the situation in northern Europe in 1864. In supporting Prussia, however, Palmerston was guided by a specific political idea. He chose to see a strong Prussia as a bastion against the aggressive plans of Russia and France.[88] Gorchakov, on the other hand, basically drifted with the current of events, agreed to *faits accomplis* and was used as a kind of parachute by Bismarck.[89]

In Russian policy towards the Danish-German conflict there were no fundamental differences between the positions of the Tsar and Gorchakov, or, despite the insistence of German historians to the contrary (H. Sybel, F. Cierpinski), between Gorchakov and the Russian representative at the London Conference, P. Brunnow, who had earned himself the name *amicus Daniae* for his contribution to the signing of the Treaty of London in 1852. There were certain differences of nuance between the Tsar's approach and that of his minister, although even to Bismarck's eyes it looked as if Alexander II personally was friendly to Prussia while official Russian policy was not.

As far as the positions of Gorchakov and Brunnow are concerned, there is nothing to suggest that Brunnow was perceptibly closer to Denmark than his superior. During the conference he observed the instructions he received from st. Petersburg strictly and took no step which exceeded them by one iota. Outwardly his tactics were somewhat different, and his words were more pro-Danish, but mainly when he was opposing schemes put forward by Beust, the representative of the German Confederation. He was cautious, on the other hand, about disagreeing with the position taken by Prussia.[90] He tried to make use of the reputation he had gained as

---

86. N.R. Rich and M.N. Fischer eds. *The Holstein Papers,* (London, 1955-1963), vol. I, p. 124, George O. Kent, *O. Bismarck and His Times,* (Carbondale, 1976), p. 108, Erick Eyck, *Bismarck,* vol. I, (Zurich, 1941), p. 627.
87. Lord Redesdale, *Memories,* (London, 1915), vol. I, pp. 306-308, Gorchakov's Memorial to Alexander II of 3 September 1865, in *Krasnyi Arkhiv,* no. 2, (1939).
88. H.J. Palmerston to Russell, 13 September 1865, in *Foundation of British Policy from Pitt to Salisbury* eds. H. Temperly and L.M. Penson, (Cambridge, 1938), p. 280.
89. Dubainess, a high-ranking personage at Quai d'Orsay, to J.L.R. Koefoed 9 July 1864, in Efterladte optegnelser m.m. Vedel, pk. 2, 1848-1897, R.A. Copenhagen. K.M. Schach in her unpublished dissertation *'Russian Foreign Policy under Prince Alexander M. Gorchakov: The Diplomatic Game Plan versus Austria, 1856-1873,* (Ann Arbor, 1974), pp. 279-280 wrote: 'Though Gorchakov thus favored the German position over that of Denmark instead of taking an impartial stance, he did not go to the extreme of supporting every whim or demand og Prussia ... Gorchakov found himself at times almost walking a tightrope, balancing precariously between his desire to conciliate Prussia without encouraging her to make more extreme demands.'
90. *Protokoller over Londonerconferences moder fra den 20de april til den 25de juni 1864. Aktstykker*

a friend of Denmark in conversations with the Danish delegation, exerting pressure on them to persuade them to make concessions to the German demands.

Certainly the feeling of Alexander II and Gorchakov towards Prussia were different. But neither ever imagined anything other than a pro-Prussian policy. And in the summer of 1864 when, following the defeat of Denmark, European political circles were discussing schemes for the future of the country, both the Tsar and his minister were inclined to see Denmark as becoming a member of the German Confederation, if only to frustrate any idea that might lead to the creation of a Scandinavian Union. It was beside the point that Gorchakov did, not foresee that not only the Copenhagen government but Bismarck too would immediately reject any such suggestion and would not hear of Denmark joining the German Confederation.[91]

The Tsar easily agreed to the idea that the country of his future daughter-in-law should be the booty of German invaders. St. Petersburg systematically rejected all appeals, both the official appeals in August and September from the new head of the government in Copenhagen, Ch.C. Bluhme, a representative of conservative circles, and letters from Princess Dagmar to Alexander II as her future father-in-law. They asked the Tsar to help Denmark and to restrain Bismarck's continually growing appetite during the Vienna negotiations. Russia would not hear of any help or diplomatic intervention and the Tsar did not react to Dagmar's entreaties.[92] Relations between St. Petersburg and Berlin, on the other hand, became even closer.

A significant portion of public opinion in Russia spoke out on Denmark's side and warned Gorchakov of the consequences which might result from his support of Bismarck. During the war of 1864 critical voices were also addressed to Gorchakov from circles close to the court (V.M. Meshchersky, B.N. Chicherin, K.N. Lebedev) as well as from opposition circles (A. Hertzen, M. Bakunin). M. Katkov warned against supporting Prussia. The Slavophiles warned against supporting Germany. The officer corps and the Minister of War, D. Milyutin, watched the course of events on the Danish-German front with disquiet.[93]

vedkommende den dansk-tyske strid, II, (Copenhagen, 1866). A.G. Mazour, Russia and Prussia during the Schleswig-Holstein Crisis in 1863. *Journal of Central European Affairs,* vol. I, no. 3. 1941.
91. Eyck, *Bismarck,* Kabinettet for utrikes brev, Dep. från beskickningen i Kopenhamn, nos. 128 and 129, 7 and 8 July 1864. A great number of documents on this problems are included in *Origines,* vol. III. See also Heinrich Sybel, *Die Begründung des Deutsches Reiches durch Wilhelm I,* (Munich-Leipzig, 1890), vol. III, p. 363, about Bismarck's attitude.
92. C. Vind to C. Bluhme, 4/16 October 1864, Bluhme to O. Plessen, 22 September 1864, in A.M.I.D., vol. LXVIII, R.A. Copenhagen, Czarfamiliens papirer, Rus. Films, R.A. Copenhagen, A. Friis, *Den danske regering og Nordslesvigs genforening med Danmark,* (Copenhagen, 1939), vol. II, pp. 13-15. Gorchakov to Nicolay, 7 October 1864 (O.S.), Rus. Films, Danica, R.A. Copenhagen.
93. Meshchersky, V.M. *Moi vospominaniya,* (St. Petersburg, 1897), vol. I, pp. 300-301, B.N. Chicherin, *Vospominaniya,* (Moscow, 1929), K.N. Lebedev, Iz zapisok senatora, *Russkii Arkhiv,* vol. VI, (1911), M. Katkov, *Moskovskie Vedomosti,* 13 May 1864, D. Milyutin, *Dnevnik,* vol. I, p. 46, W. Chudovski, *Voina za Slesvig-Golshtein 1864 goda,* (St Petersburg, 1864). See also *Den,* 28 March, 2 June, 7 September 1864, (O.S.), *Golos,* nos. 28, 32, 38, 127, 171, 1864, *Otechestvennye Zapiski* vol. LIII-IV, 1864, *Zagranichnyi Vestnik,* no. I, 1864, esp. *Sovremennik,* vol. 6, 1864.

At Gorchakov's instigation, Professor Chicherin asserted, Bismarck had seized the Elbe duchies, and by co-operating with Bismarck Gorchakov had helped to strengthen Germany so greatly that it was contrary to Russia's interests.[94] By supporting Prussia he contributed to the humiliation of Russia, clamored Lebedev.[95] He dissipated the fortune of Peter the Great, wrote Bakunin.[96] He had betrayed the interests of Russia, inveighed Hertzen.[97] 'It was, then, at St. Petersburg that the fate of Denmark was sealed and the first triumph of Bismarck's policy secured,' said Redesdale.[98] This accords with Engels' judgement that Bismarck's attitude during the Polish uprising 'secured for him the defection of the Tsar from his usual policy on the Schleswig-Holstein question: in 1864 the Duchy was wrested from Denmark with tsarist permission.'[99]

There can be no question that as essential part in Russia's entire policy towards Denmark, particularly in 1863-1864, was played by the fact that Russia looked upon Denmark as a small country no longer very important in Europe. This point was made many times during Gorchakov's conversations with O. Plessen. 'Vous n'êtes pas soixante-dix millions comme nous',[100] was the argument the Vice-Chancellor used to indicate that different norms of behavior prevailed in policies towards the great powers than in the case of small countries like Denmark.[101]

What is striking about the mentality of the Russians is the importance they attach to what is small or, to put it more precisely, to the distinction between small and large. It angered the Russian magnate that little Denmark was not obedient and did not act in accordance with the recommendation of friendly Russia, as Gorchakov repeatedly stressed, ignoring his advice to accept the German, and particularly Prussia, demands. Gorchakov thus behaved in accordance with the principle enunciated by Krylov in his fable of the wolf and the lamb: 'the weak are always guilty in the eyes of the strong.' Gorchakov could not agree that the small powers are more than pawns on a chessboard, or that 'they are not without some scope in the gamle of politics,' as Trygve Mathisen put it in the preface to his book *The Functions of Small States in the Strategies of the Great Powers* (Oslo, Bergen, Tromsø, 1971).

94. Chicherin, *op.cit.* p. 130.
95. Lebedev, *op.cit.* pp. 243-244.
96. Michail Bakunin, *Izbrannye sochineiya,* (Petrograd-Moscow, 1922), pp. 144-145.
97. Alexander Hertzen, *Polnoe sobranie sochinenii i pisem,* ed. M.K. Lemke, (Petrograd, 1922), vol. XVIII, pp. 302-304, *Kolokol,* 15 June 1864.
98. Lord Redesdale, *Further Memories,* p. 308.
99. The Foreign Policy of Russian Czarism, in K. Marx, F. Engels, *The Russian Menace to Europe,* (Glencoe, III), 1952, p. 48.
100. Dep. Rusland, 24 July/5 August 1863. R.A. Copenhagen.
101. See also Palmerston to the Danish envoy in London, Torben Bille: 'Qu'un grand pays comme la Russie pouvait à la rigeur se conduire en Pologne, comme bon lui semblait, mais qu'un petit pays devait respecter ses engagements, et que le Danemark, en manquant aux siens, s'exposait à soulever la réprobation de l'Europe et à attirer sur lui les plus grands dangers'. H. la Tour d'Auvergne to Drouyn-Lhuys, no. 14, 25 January 1864, A.M.A.E., Paris, Angleterre, vol. 728, *Origines,* vol. I, p. 196, *Monrads Deltagelse,* pp. 43, 282-283, F. Lecomte, *Guerre du Danemark au 1864,* (Paris, 1864), pp. 5-7. See also: *Denkwürdigkeiten des Botschafters General v. Schweinitz,* vol. I, (Berlin, 1927), p. 161, Steefel, *op.cit.* pp. 229, 242-243, 253, John Nielsen, *1864 Da Europa gik af lave,* (Odense, 1987), p. 213, A. Taylor, *Bismarck,* (London, 1974), p. 58.

Criticism of the conduct of the Danish government was accompanied by brutal pressure and calls for the acceptance of German demands by cynical insistence that 'in its own interest' Denmark should not resist the German armies' invasion of Schleswig, and by attempts to bring down the legitimate Danish government. And while the latter was impossible, Gorchakov tried to drive a wedge between the government and King Christian IX,[102] who was favourable to Russia and her ideas, especially the concept of a personal union of Denmark and the German duchies. This behavior by Russia led to a peculiar dualism in Danish policy at the most tragic moments in the summer of 1864.

However, it must be emphasized that the inflexible policy of the Danish government made it easier for Bismarck to carry out his plans. We see this particularly in the Danish rejection in December 1863 of the proposal to suspend the November Constitution (which action Hall was convinced would not guarantee Denmark peace), in categorical opposition to a personal union of the German duchies and Denmark, and in an uncompromising position on the idea of partitioning Schleswig during the London Conference.

The Danes overplayed their hand. Left to themselves, they were again defeated. Denmark paid a very high price for the failure of her diplomacy.

VIII

The period from the Treaty of Paris in 1856 to the conclusion of the Treaty of Vienna in 1864 forms an important stage in the history of the Scandinavian peoples and Russo-Scandinavian relations.[103] But the years 1863-1864 were decisive, especially as regards the events connected with the defeat of Denmark in the war with the German states. The policy which Gorchakov laid down during the war and the objectives he set himself were in the formal sense realized. European peace, at which he aimed above all else, was achieved and the Danish-German war remained localized and confined to the territory of the duchies and Jutland. The two German states kept control of the dispute with Denmark in their hands and the liberal forces in Germany were pushed completely aside. The second-rank German states did not become something like 'préfectures françaises.'[104]

The 1864 war did not lead to a growth of revolutionary feelings, as Alexander

---

102. Plessen's dispatches nos. 22, 26, 27, May, June 1864. Dep. Rusland, Letters of the Queen Louise to Plessen, May, June, 1864 in Familien v. Plessen, 6128, A. 12, R.A. Copenhagen, Gorchakov to Brunnow, 28 May 1864, vol. LXVIII, R.A. Copenhagen.
103. T.K. Derry, *A History of Scandinavia*, (London, 1979), p. 248 critized the attitude of the Scandinavian countries towards Denmark in 1863-1864. See also Johan Vogt, *Rusland og Norden*, (Copenhagen, 1947). p. 64. Vogt's criticism is very biased.
104. Russia backed Germany, above all Prussia, but, as the Bavarian diplomat Perglas reported, 'ohne Sympathie für die deutsche national Erhebung und seine legitime Ansprüche'. Perglas to Ludwig II, 22/10 April 1865. In *Rusland 1852 1871. Aus den Berichten der Bayerischen Gesandschaft in St Petersburg.* Ed. B. Jelavich. (Wiesbaden, 1963), pp. 117-118.

II and his minister feared in the spring of 1864. Denmark, defeated and deprived of the duchies and Schleswig, did not enter into a Scandinavian Union and political Scandinavianism sustained a crushing defeat, Russia, wrote R.M. Hatton.

was relieved at the collapse of the Scandinavian Union movement and the setback for Charles XV of 1863 and 1864, since both the liberal and the dynastic aspects of the movement had been seen as a threat to Russian interests.... Charles XV failed also in his own plans to conquer Finland by co-operation with Napoleon III over Poland in 1863.[105]

Furthermore, immediately after the defeat of Denmark Sweden altered its foreign policy fundamentally, withdrawing from active European politics and adopting a policy of neutrality. Denmark, and in particular the royal court, tightened its links with the house of Romanov on account of the approaching marriage of Princess Dagmar to the heir to the throne of Russia, Crown Prince Nicholas.

However, this result, with which Gorchakov could be momentarily satisfied, and which he regarded as evidence of the correctness of his policy, proved only outwardly favourable for Russia. In reality, as it soon transpired, the result of the war was very unfavourable for Russia.[106] Gorchakov abandoned the traditional Russian policy towards Denmark and sacrificed her to Prussia. The equilibrium in the Baltic was disturbed and dominion over the North Sea and the Baltic quickly passed into German hands. The idea that in certain circumstances Russia could sacrifice Denmark on account of Prussia was not new and had appeared in some political circles in Berlin[107] and even St. Petersburg as early as 1858. Gorchakov was warned against pursuing this policy and the consequences it could have. As it turned out in 1864 these voices went unheeded. Extreme caution and utmost restraint were the characteristics of Russian foreign policy during these years.

Gorchakov turned a deaf ear to the warnings that in the long run his pro-Prussian policy could become a menace to Russian domination in the Baltic.[108]

---

105. Hatton, op.cit. p. 127, Cecilia Bååth-Holmberg, *Carl XV som enskild man, konung och konstnär*, (Stockholm, 1891), pp. 444-449.
106. See considerations about the politics as 'die Kunst des Möglichen' in Dieter Hillerbrand, *Bismarck and Gorchakov: A Study in Bismarck's Russian Policy, 1852-1871*, (Standford, 1968), Chapter 8, Hajo Holborn, Bismarcks Realpolitik, Henry A. Kissinger, Der weisse Revolutionär: Reflexionen über Bismarck, in *Bismarck-Problem in Geschichtsschreibung nach 1945*, pp. 249, 410-413, Barbara W. Tuchman, *The March of Folly, From Troy to Vietnam*, (New York, 1984).
107. *Sendschreiben an den Politiker der Zukunft vom preussischen Standpunkte*, (Berlin, 1858).
108. 'L'equilibre européen est intéressé, comme en 1852, à empêcher que, sous prétexte qu'il y a des Allemands dans le Sleswig, l'Allemagne s'empare de la Baltique. C'est ce qui aura lieu si on la laissait s'y asseoir dans les ports qu'elle convoitise. Après Kiel, elle voudrait d'autres points. La race germanique est insatiable' (*Siècle*, 24 December 1863). 'La Prusse est en bonne voie. Elle veut étendre sa domination sur le Holstein; elle revendique le Sleswig; elle convoite le Jutland pour devenir puissance maritime sur la Baltique; mais c'est trop peu et voici qu'elle manifeste le désir de s'emparer du Hanovre pour s'ouvrir une large débouché sur le mer du Nord' (*Opinion nationale*, 25 June 1864). 'Quoi qu'il en soit, la politique de M. de Bismarck et l'influence prusienne triomphent, grâce à elles, l'Allemagne va pouvoir réaliser son idée fixe, 'idée de devenir une puissance maritime'. (*Siècle*, 22 July 1864). K. Malettke, *Die Beurteilung des Aussen- und Innenpolitik Bismarcks von 1862-1866 in den grossen Pariser Zeitungen*, (Lubeck a. Hamburg, 1966) pp. 141, 166, 171.

No doubt there was a link between Gorchakov's personal shortcomings and his policy. But the most telling charge against him is that he lacked vision.

Being deeply involved in the traditional anti-Polish and anti-Scandinavian policy, Gorchakov was unable to work out a new strategy and cope with the complicated situation which emerged during the 1864 War. Russian policy in 1864 demonstrated a point well understood since Thucydides' days – that governments often act against their own interests. In this instance the words spoken by Edmund Burke on 22 March 1775, 'a great Empire and little minds go ill together,' would seem to have been confirmed once again.[109]

'If Denmark prevailed – argued N. Danilevsky – all Prussia's plans for Kiel bay, her fleet, control of the Baltic and hegemony over Germany would collapse – in a word, all the German interests of which Prussia regarded and regards herself as the spokesman and, to be fair, the principal if not the only representative, would be lost'. (*Zariya* 1869), *Rossiya i Evropa,* St. Petersburg, 1889, p. 5).

109. Magnanimity in Politics, Speech on Conciliation, 22 March 1775, *Hansard,* vol. XVIII.

Appendices

A. The London Treaty of 8 May 1852

TRAITÉ DE LONDRES DU 8 MAI 1852.

Au nom de la Très Sainte et Indivisible Trinité.

S. M. l'Empereur d'Autriche, Roi de Hongrie et de Bohême, le Prince Président de la République française, S. M. la Reine du Royaume-Uni de la Grande-Bretagne et d'Irlande, S. M. le Roi de Prusse, S. M. l'Empereur de toutes les Russies, et S. M. le Roi de Suède et de Norvège,

Considérant que le maintien de l'intégrité de la Monarchie danoise, lié aux intérêts généraux de l'équilibre européen, est d'une haute importance pour la conservation de la paix, et qu'une combinaison, qui appellerait à succéder à la totalité des États actuellement réunis sous le sceptre de S. M. le Roi de Danemark la descendance mâle, à l'exclusion des femmes, serait le meilleur moyen d'assurer l'intégrité de cette Monarchie, ont résolu, à l'invitation de Sa Majesté Danoise, de conclure un traité, afin de donner aux arrangements relatifs à cet ordre de succession un gage additionnel de stabilité par un acte de reconnaissance européenne.

En conséquence, les Hautes Parties contractantes ont nommé pour leurs Plénipotentiaires, savoir :

[Suit l'énumération des Plénipotentiaires avec leurs titres.]

Lesquels, après s'être communiqué leurs pleins pouvoirs respectifs, trouvés en bonne et due forme, sont convenus des articles suivants :

ARTICLE PREMIER. Après avoir pris en sérieuse considération les intérêts de sa Monarchie, S. M. le Roi de Danemark, de l'assentiment de S. A. R. le Prince héréditaire et de ses plus proches Cognats, appelés à la succession par la loi royale de Danemark, ainsi que de concert avec S. M. l'Empereur de toutes les Russies, chef de la branche aînée de la Maison de Holstein-Gottorp, ayant déclaré vouloir régler l'ordre de succession dans ses États, de manière à ce qu'à défaut de descendance mâle en ligne directe du Roi Frédéric III de Danemark, sa couronne soit transmise à S. A. le Prince Christian de Sleswig-Holstein-Sonderbourg-Glucksbourg, et aux descendants issus du mariage de ce Prince avec

S. A. la Princesse Louise de Sleswig-Holstein-Sonderbourg-Glucksbourg, née Princesse de Hesse, par ordre de primogéniture, de mâle en mâle; les Hautes Parties contractantes, appréciant la sagesse des vues qui ont déterminé l'adoption éventuelle de cette combinaison, s'engagent d'un commun accord, dans le cas où l'éventualité prévue viendrait à se réaliser, à reconnaître à S. A. le Prince Christian de Sleswig-Holstein-Sonderbourg-Glucksbourg, et aux descendants mâles, issus en ligne directe de son mariage avec ladite Princesse, le droit de succéder à la totalité des États actuellement réunis sous le sceptre de S. M. le Roi de Danemark.

Art. 2. Les Hautes Parties contractantes, reconnaissant comme permanent le principe de l'intégrité de la Monarchie danoise, s'engagent à prendre en considération les ouvertures ultérieures que S. M. le Roi de Danemark jugerait à propos de leur adresser, si, ce qu'à Dieu ne plaise, l'extinction de la descendance mâle, en ligne directe, de S. A. le Prince Christian de Sleswig-Holstein-Sonderbourg-Glucksbourg, issue de son mariage avec S. A. la Princesse Louise de Sleswig-Holstein-Sonderbourg-Glucksbourg, née Princesse de Hesse, devenait imminente.

Art. 3. Il est expressément entendu que les droits et les obligations réciproques de S. M. le Roi de Danemark et de la Confédération germanique, concernant les Duchés de Holstein et de Lauenbourg, droits et obligations établis par l'Acte fédéral de 1815 et par le droit fédéral existant, ne seront pas altérés par le présent traité.

Art. 4. Les Hautes Parties contractantes se réservent de porter le présent traité à la connaissance des autres Puissances, en les invitant à y accéder.

Art. 5. Le présent traité sera ratifié, et les ratifications en seront échangées à Londres, dans le délai de six semaines, ou plus tôt si faire se peut [1].

[1] Les ratifications de ce traité ont été échangées à Londres le 19 juin 1852 entre le Danemark, d'une part, et l'Autriche, la France, la Grande-Bretagne, la Prusse et la Suède et la Norvège de l'autre, et entre le Danemark et la Russie le 2 juillet 1852. Les actes de ratification ont été signés par S. M. le Roi de Danemark le 18 mai 1852, par S. M. l'Empereur d'Autriche le 24 mai, par le Prince-Président de la République française le 10 mai, par S. M. la Reine du Royaume-Uni de la Grande-Bretagne et d'Irlande le 31 mai, par S. M. le Roi de Prusse le 27 mai, par S. M. l'Empereur de toutes les Russies le 5 juin, et par S. M. le Roi de Suède et de Norvège le 27 mai.

En foi de quoi, les Plénipotentiaires respectifs l'ont signé, et y ont apposé le cachet de leurs armes.

Fait à Londres, le huit mai, l'an de grâce mil huit cent cinquante-deux.

(L. S.) Signé : Bille.

(L. S.) Signé : Kubeck.
(L. S.) Signé : A. Walewski.
(L. S.) Signé : Malmesbury.
(L. S.) Signé : Bunsen.
(L. S.) Signé : Brunnow.
(L. S.) Signé : Rehausen.

B. The Vienna Treaty of 30 October 1864

SIGNÉ LE 30 OCTOBRE 1864,
ENTRE LE DANEMARK, LA PRUSSE ET L'AUTRICHE.

Au nom de la très sainte et indivisible Trinité.

S. M. le Roi de Prusse, S. M. l'Empereur d'Autriche et S. M. le Roi de Danemark ont résolu de convertir les préliminaires signés le 1ᵉʳ août dernier en traité de paix définitif. A cet effet, Leurs Majestés ont nommé pour leurs Plénipotentiaires, savoir :

[Suit l'énumération des Plénipotentiaires, avec leurs titres.]

Lesquels se sont réunis en conférence à Vienne, et, après avoir échangé leurs pleins pouvoirs, trouvés en bonne et due forme, sont convenus des articles suivants :

ARTICLE PREMIER. Il y aura à l'avenir paix et amitié entre LL. MM. le Roi de Prusse et l'Empereur d'Autriche et S. M. le Roi de Danemark, ainsi qu'entre leurs héritiers et successeurs, leurs États et sujets respectifs à perpétuité.

ART. 2. Tous les traités et conventions conclus avant la guerre entre les Hautes Parties contractantes sont rétablis dans leur vigueur en tant qu'ils ne se trouvent pas abrogés ou modifiés par la teneur du présent traité. .

Art. 3. S. M. le Roi de Danemark renonce à tous ses droits sur les Duchés de Sleswig, Holstein et Lauenbourg en faveur de LL. MM. le Roi de Prusse et l'Empereur d'Autriche, en s'engageant à reconnaître les dispositions que Leursdites Majestés prendront à l'égard de ces Duchés.

Art. 4. La cession du Duché de Sleswig comprend toutes les îles appartenant à ce Duché aussi bien que le territoire situé sur la terre ferme. Pour simplifier la délimitation et pour faire cesser les inconvénients qui résultent de la situation des territoires jutlandais enclavés dans le territoire du Sleswig, S. M. le Roi de Danemark cède à LL. MM. le Roi de Prusse et l'Empereur d'Autriche les possessions jutlandaises situées au sud de la ligne de frontière méridionale du district de Ripen, telles que le territoire jutlandais de Moegeltondern, l'île d'Amrom, les parties jutlandaises des îles de Foehr, Sylt et Romoe, etc. Par contre LL. MM. le Roi de Prusse et l'Empereur d'Autriche consentent à ce qu'une portion équivalente du Sleswig et comprenant, outre l'île d'Aaroe, des territoires servant à former la contiguité du district susmentionné de Ripen avec le reste du Jutland et à corriger la ligne de frontière entre le Jutland et le Sleswig du côté de Kolding, soit détachée du Duché de Sleswig et incorporée dans le Royaume de Danemark.

Art. 5. La nouvelle frontière entre le Royaume de Danemark et le Duché de Sleswig partira du milieu de l'embouchure de la baie de Hejlsminde, sur le petit Belt, et, après avoir traversé cette baie, suivra la frontière méridionale actuelle des paroisses de Hejls, Vejstrup et Taps, cette dernière jusqu'au cours d'eau qui se trouve au sud de Gejlbjerg et Branöre, elle suivra ensuite ce cours d'eau à partir de son embouchure dans la Fovs-Aa, le long de la frontière méridionale des paroisses d'Opis et Vandrup et de la frontière occidentale de cette dernière jusqu'à la Königs-Au (Konge-Aa) au nord de Holte. De ce point le thalweg de la Königs-Au (Konge-Aa) formera la frontière jusqu'à la limite orientale de la paroisse de Hjortlund. A partir de ce point, le tracé suivra cette même limite et son prolongement jusqu'à l'angle saillant au nord du village d'Obekjär, et ensuite la frontière orientale de ce village jusqu'à la Gjels-Aa. De là la limite orientale de la paroisse de Seem et les limites méridionales des paroisses de Seem, Ripen de Vester-Vedsted formeront la nouvelle frontière qui, dans la Mer du Nord, passera à distance égale entre les îles de Manoe et Romoe. Par suite de cette nouvelle délimitation, sont déclarés éteints, de part et d'autre, tous les titres de droits mixtes, tant au séculier qu'au spirituel, qui ont existé jusqu'ici dans les enclaves, dans les îles et dans les paroisses mixtes. En conséquence, le nouveau pouvoir souverain, dans chacun des territoires séparés par la nouvelle frontière, jouira à cet égard de la plénitude de ses droits.

Art. 6. Une commission internationale, composée de Représentants des Hautes Parties contractantes, sera chargée, immédiatement après l'échange des ratifications du présent traité, d'opérer sur le terrain le tracé de la nouvelle frontière, conformément aux stipulations du précédent article. Cette commission aura aussi à répartir entre le Royaume de Danemark et le Duché de Sleswig les frais de construction de la nouvelle chaussée de Ripen à Tondern proportionnellement à l'étendue du territoire respectif qu'elle parcourt. Enfin la même commission présidera au partage des biens-fonds et capitaux qui jusqu'ici ont appartenu en commun à des districts ou des communes séparés par la nouvelle frontière.

Art. 7. Les dispositions des articles 20, 21 et 22 du traité conclu entre l'Autriche et la Russie, le 3 mai 1815, qui fait partie intégrante de l'acte général du Congrès de Vienne, dispositions relatives aux propriétaires mixtes, aux droits qu'ils exerceront et aux rapports de voisinage dans les propriétés coupées par les frontières, seront appliquées aux propriétaires, ainsi qu'aux propriétés qui, en Sleswig et en Jutland, se trouveront dans les cas prévus par les susdites dispositions des actes du Congrès de Vienne.

Art. 8. Pour atteindre une répartition équitable de la dette publique de la Monarchie danoise en proportion des populations respectives du Royaume et des Duchés, et pour obvier en même temps aux difficultés insurmontables que présenterait une liquidation détaillée des droits et prétentions réciproques, les Hautes Parties contractantes ont fixé la quote-part de la dette publique de la Monarchie danoise qui sera mise à la charge des Duchés, à la somme ronde de vingt-neuf millions de thalers (monnaie danoise).

Art. 9. La partie de la dette publique de la Monarchie danoise qui, conformément à l'article précédent, tombera à la charge des Duchés, sera acquittée, sous la garantie de LL. MM. le Roi de Prusse et l'Empereur d'Autriche, comme dette des trois Duchés susmentionnés envers le royaume de Danemark, dans le terme d'une année, ou plus tôt si faire se pourra, à partir de l'organisation définitive des Duchés. Pour l'acquittement de cette dette les Duchés pourront se servir, au total ou en partie, de l'une ou de l'autre des manières suivantes : 1° payement en argent comptant (75 thalers de Prusse = 100 thalers monnaie danoise);

2° remise au trésor danois d'obligations non remboursables portant intérêt de 4 p. 100 et appartenant à la dette intérieure de la Monarchie danoise; 3° remise au trésor danois de nouvelles obligations d'État à émettre par les Duchés, dont la valeur sera énoncée en thalers de Prusse (au taux de 30 la livre) ou en mark de banque de Hambourg, et qui seront liquidées moyennant une annuité semestrielle de 3 p. 100 du montant primitif de la dette, dont 2 p. 100 représenteront l'intérêt de la dette dû à chaque terme, tandis que le reste sera payé à titre d'amortissement. Le payement susmentionné de l'annuité semestrielle de 3 p. 100 se fera tant par les caisses publiques des Duchés que par des maisons de banque à Berlin et à Hambourg. Les obligations mentionnées sous 2 et 3 seront reçues par le trésor danois à leur taux nominal.

Art. 10. Jusqu'à l'époque où les Duchés se seront définitivement chargés de la somme qu'ils auront à verser conformément à l'article 8 du présent traité au lieu de leur quote-part de la dette commune de la Monarchie danoise, ils paieront par semestre 2 p. 100 de ladite somme, c'est-à-dire 580,000 thalers (monnaie danoise). Ce payement sera effectué de manière que les intérêts et les acomptes de la dette danoise qui ont été assignés jusqu'ici sur les caisses publiques des Duchés seront aussi dorénavant acquittés par ces mêmes caisses. Ces payements seront liquidés chaque semestre, et, pour le cas où ils n'atteindraient pas la somme susmentionnée, les Duchés auront à rembourser le restant aux finances danoises en argent comptant; au cas contraire, il leur sera remboursé l'excédent de même en argent comptant. La liquidation se fera entre le Danemark et les autorités chargées de l'administration supérieure des Duchés d'après le mode stipulé dans le présent article, ou tous les trimestres en tant que de part et d'autre cela serait jugé nécessaire. La première liquidation aura spécialement pour objet tous les intérêts et acomptes de la dette commune de la Monarchie danoise payés après le 23 décembre 1863.

Art. 11. Les sommes représentant l'équivalent dit de Holstein-Ploen, le restant de l'indemnité pour les ci-devant possessions du Duc d'Augustenbourg, y compris la dette de priorité dont elles sont grevées, et les obligations domaniales du Sleswig et du Holstein, seront mises exclusivement à la charge des Duchés.

Art. 12. Les Gouvernements de Prusse et d'Autriche se feront rembourser par les Duchés les frais de la guerre.

Art. 13. S. M. le Roi de Danemark s'engage à rendre immédiatement après l'échange des ratifications du présent traité, avec leurs cargaisons, tous les navires de commerce prussiens, autrichiens et allemands capturés pendant la guerre, ainsi que les cargaisons appartenant à des sujets prussiens, autrichiens et allemands, saisies sur des bâtiments neutres; enfin tous les bâtiments saisis par le Danemark pour un motif militaire dans les Duchés cédés. Les objets précités seront rendus dans l'état où ils se trouvent, *bona fide*, à l'époque de leur restitution. Pour le cas où les objets à rendre n'existeraient plus, on en restituera la valeur, et, s'ils ont subi depuis leur saisie une diminution notable de valeur, les propriétaires en seront dédommagés en proportion. De même, il est reconnu comme obligatoire d'indemniser les frêteurs et l'équipage des navires et les propriétaires des cargaisons de toutes les dépenses et pertes directes qui seront prouvées avoir été causées par la saisie des bâtiments, telles que droits de port ou de rade (Liegegelder), frais de justice et frais encourus pour l'entretien ou le renvoi à domicile des navires et des équipages. Quant aux bâtiments qui ne peuvent pas être rendus en nature, on prendra pour base des indemnités à accorder la valeur que ces bâtiments avaient à l'époque de leur saisie. En ce qui concerne les cargaisons avariées ou qui n'existent plus, on en fixera l'indemnité d'après la valeur qu'elles auraient eue au lieu de leur destination à l'époque où le bâtiment y serait arrivé, d'après un calcul de probabilité. LL. MM. le Roi de Prusse et l'Empereur d'Autriche feront également restituer les navires de commerce pris par leurs troupes ou leurs bâtiments de guerre ainsi que les cargaisons, en tant que celles-ci appartenaient à des particuliers. Si la restitution ne peut pas se faire en nature, l'indemnité sera fixée d'après les principes susindiqués. Leursdites Majestés s'engagent en même temps à faire entrer en ligne de compte le montant des contributions de guerre prélevées en argent comptant par leurs troupes dans le Jutland. Cette somme sera déduite des indemnités à payer par le Danemark d'après les principes établis par le présent article. LL. MM. le Roi de Prusse, l'Empereur d'Autriche et le Roi de Danemark nommeront une commission spéciale qui aura à fixer le montant des indemnités respectives et qui se réunira à Copenhague au plus tard six semaines après l'échange des ratifications du présent traité. Cette commission s'efforcera d'accomplir sa tâche dans l'espace de trois mois. Si, après ce terme, elle n'a pu se mettre d'accord sur toutes les réclamations qui lui auront été présentées, celles qui n'auront pas encore été réglées seront soumises à une décision arbitrale. A cet effet, LL. MM. le Roi de Prusse, l'Empereur d'Autriche et S. M. le Roi de Danemark s'entendront sur le choix d'un arbitre. Les indemnités seront payées au plus tard quatre semaines après avoir été définitivement fixées.

Art. 14. Le Gouvernement danois restera chargé du remboursement de toutes les sommes versées par les sujets des Duchés, par les communes, établissements publics et corporations dans les caisses publiques danoises à titre de cautionnements, dépôts ou consignations. En outre, seront remis aux Duchés : 1° Le dépôt affecté à l'amortissement des bons du trésor (Kassenscheine) holsteinois; 2° le fonds destiné à la construction de prisons; 3° les fonds des assurances contre l'incendie; 4° la caisse des dépôts; 5° les capitaux provenant de legs appartenant à des communes ou des institutions publiques dans les Duchés; 6° les fonds de caisse (Kassenbehalte) provenant des recettes spéciales des Duchés et qui se trouvaient, *bona fide,* dans leurs caisses publiques à l'époque de l'exécution fédérale et de l'occupation de ces pays. Une commission internationale sera chargée de liquider le montant des sommes susmentionnées en déduisant les dépenses inhérentes à l'administration spéciale des Duchés. La collection d'antiquités de Flensbourg qui se rattachait à l'histoire du Sleswig, mais qui a été en grande partie dispersée lors des derniers événements, y sera de nouveau réunie avec le concours du Gouvernement danois. De même les sujets danois, communes, établissements publics et corporations qui auront versé des sommes à titre de cautionnements, dépôts ou consignations, dans les caisses publiques des Duchés, seront exactement remboursés par le nouveau Gouvernement.

Art. 15. Les pensions portées sur les budgets spéciaux soit du Royaume de Danemark, soit des Duchés, continueront d'être payées par les pays respectifs. Les titulaires pourront librement choisir leur domicile soit dans le Royaume, soit dans les Duchés. Toutes les autres pensions tant civiles que militaires [y compris les pensions des employés de la liste civile de feu S. M. le Roi Frédéric VII, de feu S. A. R. Mgr. le Prince Ferdinand et de feu S. A. R. Mme la Landgrave Charlotte de Hesse, née Princesse de Danemark, et les pensions qui ont été payées jusqu'ici par le Secrétariat des Grâces (Naades-Secretariat)] seront réparties entre le Royaume et les Duchés d'après la proportion des populations respectives. A cet effet, on est convenu de faire dresser une liste de toutes ces pensions, de convertir leur valeur de rente viagère en capital et d'inviter tous les titulaires à déclarer si, à l'avenir, ils désirent toucher leurs pensions dans le Royaume ou dans les Duchés. Dans le cas où, par suite de ces options, la proportion entre les deux quote-parts, c'est-à-dire entre celle tombant à la charge des Duchés et celle restant à la charge du Royaume, ne serait pas conforme au principe proportionnel des populations respectives, la différence sera acquittée par la partie que cela regarde. Les pensions assignées sur la caisse générale des veuves et sur le fonds des pensions des militaires subalternes continueront d'être payées comme par le passé en tant que ces fonds y suffisent. Quant aux sommes supplémentaires que l'État aura à payer à ces fonds, les Duchés se chargeront d'une quote-part de ces suppléments d'après la proportion des populations respectives. La part à l'institut de rentes viagères et d'assurances pour la vie, fondé en 1842 à Copenhague, à laquelle les individus originaires des Duchés ont des droits acquis, leur est expressément conservée. Une commission internationale, composée des Représentants des deux Parties, se réunira à Copenhague immédiatement après l'échange des ratifications du présent traité pour régler en détail les stipulations de cet article.

Art. 16. Le Gouvernement royal de Danemark se chargera du payement des apanages suivants : de S. M. la Reine douairière Caroline-Amélie, de S. A. R. Mme la Princesse héréditaire Caroline, de S. A. R. Mme la Duchesse Wilhelmine-Marie de Glücksbourg, de S. A. Mme la Duchesse Caroline-Charlotte-Marianne de Mecklembourg-Strelitz, de S. A. Mme la Duchesse douairière Louise-Caroline de Glücksbourg, de S. A. Mgr. le Prince Frédéric de Hesse, de LL. AA. Mmes les Princesses Charlotte, Victoire et Amélie de Sleswig-Holstein-Sonderbourg-Augustenbourg. La quote-part de ce payement tombant à la charge des Duchés d'après la proportion de leurs populations sera remboursée au Gouvernement danois par celui des Duchés. La commission mentionnée dans l'article précédent sera également chargée de fixer les arrangements nécessaires à l'exécution du présent article.

Art. 17. Le nouveau Gouvernement des Duchés succède aux droits et obligations résultant de contrats régulièrement stipulés par l'administration de S. M. le Roi de Danemark pour des objets d'intérêt public concernant spécialement les pays cédés. Il est entendu que toutes les obligations résultant de contrats stipulés par le Gouvernement danois par rapport à la guerre et à l'exécution fédérale ne sont pas comprises dans la précédente stipulation. Le nouveau Gouvernement des Duchés respectera tout droit légalement acquis par les individus et les personnes civiles dans les Duchés. En cas de contestation, les tribunaux connaîtront des affaires de cette catégorie.

Art. 18. Les sujets originaires des territoires cédés, faisant partie de l'armée ou de la marine danoises, auront le droit d'être immédiatement libérés du service militaire et de rentrer dans leurs foyers. Il est entendu que ceux d'entre eux qui resteront au service de S. M. le Roi de Danemark ne seront point inquiétés pour ce fait, soit dans leurs personnes, soit dans leurs propriétés. Les mêmes droits et garanties sont assurés de part et d'autre aux employés civils originaires du Danemark ou des Duchés qui manifesteront l'intention de quitter les fonctions qu'ils occupent respectivement au service soit du Danemark, soit des Duchés, ou qui préféreront conserver ces fonctions.

Art. 19. Les sujets domiciliés sur les territoires cédés par le présent traité jouiront pendant l'espace de six ans, à partir du jour de l'échange des ratifications et moyennant une déclaration préalable à l'autorité compétente, de la faculté pleine et entière d'exporter leurs biens meubles en franchise de droits et de se retirer avec leurs familles dans les États de S. M. Danoise, auquel cas la qualité de sujets danois leur sera maintenue. Ils seront libres de conserver leurs immeubles situés sur les territoires cédés. La même faculté est accordée réciproquement aux sujets danois et aux individus originaires des territoires cédés et établis dans les États de S. M. le Roi de Danemark. Les sujets qui profiteront des présentes dispositions ne pourront, du fait de leur option, être inquiétés de part ni d'autre dans leurs personnes ou dans leurs propriétés situées dans les États respectifs. Le délai susdit de six ans s'applique aussi aux sujets originaires soit du Royaume de Danemark, soit des territoires cédés qui, à l'époque de l'échange des ratifications du présent traité, se trouveront hors du territoire du Royaume de Danemark ou des Duchés. Leur déclaration pourra être reçue par la mission danoise la plus voisine, ou par l'autorité supérieure d'une province quelconque du Royaume ou des Duchés. Le droit d'indigénat, tant dans le Royaume de Danemark que dans les Duchés, est conservé à tous les individus qui le possèdent à l'époque de l'échange des ratifications du présent traité.

Art. 20. Les titres de propriété, documents administratifs, et de justice civile, concernant les territoires cédés qui se trouvent dans les archives du Royaume de Danemark, seront remis aux commissaires du nouveau Gouvernement des Duchés aussitôt que faire se pourra. De même toutes les parties des archives de Copenhague qui ont appartenu aux Duchés cédés et ont été tirées de leurs archives, leur seront délivrées avec les listes et registres y relatifs. Le Gouvernement danois et le nouveau Gouvernement des Duchés s'engagent à se communiquer réciproquement, sur la demande des autorités administratives supérieures, tous les documents et informations relatifs à des affaires concernant à la fois le Danemark et les Duchés.

Art. 21. Le commerce et la navigation du Danemark et des Duchés cédés jouiront réciproquement dans les deux pays des droits et privilèges de la nation la plus favorisée, en attendant que des traités spéciaux règlent cette matière. Les exemptions et facilités à l'égard des droits de transit, qui en vertu de l'article II du traité du 14 mars 1857, ont été accordées aux marchandises passant par les routes et les canaux qui relient ou relieront la Mer du Nord à la Mer Baltique, seront applicables aux marchandises traversant le Royaume et les Duchés par quelque voie de communication que ce soit.

Art. 22. L'évacuation du Jutland par les troupes alliées sera effectuée dans le plus bref délai possible, au plus tard dans l'espace de trois semaines après l'échange des ratifications du présent traité. Les dispositions spéciales relatives à cette évacuation sont fixées dans un protocole annexé au présent traité.

Art. 23. Pour contribuer de tous leurs efforts à la pacification des esprits, les Hautes Parties contractantes déclarent et promettent qu'aucun individu compromis à l'occasion des derniers événements, de quelque classe ou condition qu'il soit, ne pourra être poursuivi, inquiété ou troublé dans sa personne ou dans sa propriété à raison de sa conduite ou de ses opinions politiques.

Art. 24. Le présent traité sera ratifié, et les ratifications en seront échangées à Vienne dans l'espace de trois semaines, ou plus tôt si faire se peut. En foi de quoi les Plénipotentiaires respectifs l'ont signé et y ont apposé le sceau de leurs armes.

Fait à Vienne, le trentième jour du mois d'octobre de l'an de grâce mil huit cent soixante-quatre.

(L. S.) *Signé* : Werther, Balan.   (L. S.) *Signé* : Quaade,
        Rechberg, Brenner.   Kauffmann.

C. Table of the Staff of the Russian Ministry of Foreign Affairs*

Foreign Minister	A. Gorchakov
Vice Minister	I. Tolstoy (15.IV.1856-30.VIII.1861) N. Mukhanov (30.VIII.1861-28.X.1866)
Interim Minister	I. Malcov (5.VI.-25.VII.1857, 16.VIII.-3.X.1857, 22.VIII.-24.X.1864) I. Tolstoy (16.V.-12.VII.1856, 8.VIII.-22.IX.1858, 28.IX.-19.X.1859, 28.IX.-20.X.1860).
Senior Councellors	R. Osten-Sacken (19.I.1835-30.IV.1863) A. Jomini (5.I.1856-5.XII.1888) O. Ewers (30.IV.1863-6.III.1871)
Department for Asiatic Affairs	N. Lubimov (26.II.1852-20.IX.1856 E. Kovalevsky (2.X.1856-30.VIII.1861) M. Ignatiev (21.VIII.1861-14.VII.1864)
Department for Internal Affairs	A. Hilferding (8.XI.1849-17.X.1858) D. Filosofov (25.X.1856-20.XII.1862) D. Loginov (1.XI.1863-1.III.1875)

The Russian Representatives

Austria	A. Budberg (7.VII.1856-8.II.1858) V. Balabin (22.VII.1860-12.VIII.1864, from 5.VIII.1858 charged with a special mission). E. Stackelberg (3.VIII.1864-25.IV.1868)
France	P. Brunnow (6.V.1856-29.I.1857) P. Kiselev (11.VII.1856-15.IX.1862) A. Budberg (3.XI-1862-10.IV.1868)
German Confederation	P. Brunnow (8.VI.1855-6.V.1856) F. Fonton (5.I.1857-20.IX.1860) E. Ungern-Sternberg (7.XI.1860-7.IX.1866)
Great Britain	M. Khreptovich (30.VI-1856-8.II.1858) P. Brunnow (8.II.1858-21.V.1870 and 28.XI.1870-22.VII.1874)
Italy	E. Stackelberg (11.VIII.1862-3.VIII.1864) N. Kiselev (2.VIII.1864-26.XI.1869)

* (*Ocherk Istorii Ministerstva Inostrannykh Del 1802-1902*, (St. Petersburg, 1902)

Prussia	A. Budberg (6.XII.1851-7.VII.1856)
	P. Brunnow (7.VII.1856-8.II.1858)
	A. Budberg (8.II.1858-3.XI.1862)
	P. Oubril (3.XI.1862-22.XII.1879)
Sweden-Norway	I. Dashkov (26.II.1852-28.II.1872)
USA	E. Stekl (1.I.1857-20.IV.1869)

D. Table of the Staff of the Danish Ministry of Foreign Affairs*

Ministers

Ludwig Nicolaus Scheele ad interim 12.XII.1854-17.IV.1857
Ove Wilhelm Michelsen ad interim 17.IV.1857-10.VII.1858
Carl Christian Hall ad interim 10.VII.1858-2.XII.1859
Carl Axel Bror Blixen-Finecke 2.XII.1859-24.2.1860
Carl Christian Hall 24.II.1860-31.XII.1863
Ditlev Gothard Monrad 31.XII.1863-8.I.1864
Georg Joachim Quaade ad interum 8.I.1864-11.VII.1864
Christian Albrecht Bluhme 10.VII.1864-6.II.1865

Adolf Skrike	Director of the First Department from 1.IV.1854-1.X.1858 and of the Third Department from 1.X.1858-1.I.1860.
George Joachim Quaade	Director of the Second Department from 1.IV.1856-1.IV.1860
Peter August Frederic Stand Vedel	Director of the First Department from 1.X.1858-1.IV.1860 and also of the Second Department from 1.IV.1862. From 10.IV.1864-31.VIII. 1899 Director of the Political Department.

* (*Den Dansk Udenrigstjeneste 1770-1970,* vol. I, (Copenhagen, 1970), ed. K. Kjølsen a V. Sjøqvist)

Danish Prime Ministers
Peter Georg Bang 12.XII.1854-18.X.1856
Carl Christopher Andrae 18.X.1856-13.V.1857
Carl Christian Hall 13.V.1857-2.XII.1859 and 24.II.1860-31.XII.1863
Carl Edvard Rottwitt 2.XII.1859-24.II.1860
Ditlev Gothard Monrad 31.XII.1863-11.VII.1864
Christian Albrecht Bluhme 11.VII.1864-6.XI.1865

E. Table of Ministries of the Great Powers and of Sweden-Norway (Signatories of the Treaty of London of May 8, 1852)

Austria	K.F. Buol-Schauenstein 1852-IV-1859	Minister of Foreign Affairs
	J.B. Rechberg-Rothenloeven V. 1859-X.1864	Minister of Foreign Affairs
	A. Mensdorff-Pouilly X.1864-X.1866	Minister of Foreign Affairs
France	A.F.J.C. Walewski V.1855-I.1860	Minister of Foreign Affairs
	A.E. Thouvenel I.1860-X.1862	Minister of Foreign Affairs
	E. Drouyn de Lhuys X.1862-IX.1866	Minister of Foreign Affairs
Great Britain	H.J.T. Palmerston I.1855-II.1858 and VI.1859-1865	Prime Min.
	E.S. Earl of Derby II.1858-VI.1859	Prime Min.
	G.W.V. Clarendon 1853-II.1858	Foreign Secretary
	J.H.H. Malmesbury II.1858-VI.1859	Foreign Secretary
	J. Russell VI.1859-1865	Foreign Secretary
Prussia	O.T. Manteuffel 1850-XI.1858	Minister President a. Foreign Minister
	A. Schleinitz XI.1858-IX.1861	Minister President a. Foreign Minister
	A. Bernstorff IX.1861-X.1862	Minister President a. Foreign Minister
	O. Bismarck-Schoenhausen IX.1862	Minister President a. Foreign Minister
Russia	IV.1856 A. Gorchakov Minister of Foreign Affairs from IV.1862 Vice-Chancellor	
Sweden-Norway	E. Lagerheim V. 1856-III.1858	Minister of Foreign Affairs
	L. Manderström III.1858-1868	Minister of Foreign Affairs

F. Foreign Representatives in Copenhagen*

Austria	Aloys Karolyi Nagy-Karoly (17.I./17.II.-27.VII.1859) Adolph Maria Brenner Felsack (19.X./28.XI.1860-XI.1863)
Belgium	Napoléon Alcindor Bealieu (1.V.1849-10.IV.1858) Henri Bosch-Spencer (18.IV.1859-7.VIII.1867)
France	André Vincent Adolphe Dotézac (12.VII./28.VII.1848-28.VII./8.XI.1869
Great Britain	Andrew Buchanan (9.II.1853-31.III./19.IV.1858) Henry George Elliot (2.IV./19.IV.1858-3.VII./18.VII.1859) Augustus Berkeley Paget (6.VI./18/VII.1859.-8.VI./14.VII.1866)
Holland	Carl Malcolm Ernst Georg Byland (22.II.1855-XI.1856) Charles Henri Bois from 11.XI.1856 Willem Frederic Rochussen from 20.I./15.V.1863
Italy	Jean Antoine Migliorati (28.XII.1859/16.I.1860-3.XI.1863) Rodriguez Doira Préda (13.XII.1863/9.I.1864-18.I./III.1866)
Prussia	Alphons Heinrich Oriolla (26.VI./I.VIII.1854-15.IV./8.V.1859) Hermann Ludvig Balan (16.IV./11.V.1859-XI.1863)
Russia	Ernst Wilhelm Rembert Ungern-Sternberg a. Pyrkel (31.VIII.1847-7.XI.1860). Nicolaus Nicolay (7.XI./20.XII.1860-31.XII.1867)
Sweden-Norway	Elias Lagerheim (13.VII.1836-26.VIII./4.IX.1856) Christian Adolf Virgin (5.XII.1856-16.XII.1858/1.III.1859) Carl Wachmeister (26.V./6.VI.1859-20.VII.1861) Henning Ludvig Hugo Hamilton (20.VII.1861-20.II./1.III.1864) Oscar Magnus Fredrik Björnstjerna (1./12.III.1864-31.X./23.XII.1865)
USA	Henry Bedinger (30.VI.1853-24.V./9.VIII.1858) James M. Buchanan (26.VI./10.VIII.1858-10.IV./10.VI.1861) Bradford R. Wood (10.IV./1.VIII.1861-28.IX./15.XI.1865)

*) (*A.F. Kriegers Dagbøger 1848-1880,* vol. 8. pt. 2, (Copenhagen, 1943), pp. 78-86).

G. The Danish Representatives*

Austria   Henrik Bille-Brahe (25.XI.1847-4.VI.1862)
              Carl Ernst Johan Bülow (4.VI.1862-18.I.1864)

Belgium and   Julius Frederic Sick (6.XII.1853-17.IV.1857)
Holland   Torben Bille (4.VIII.1857-24.I.1860)
              George Joachim Quaade (31.III-19.X.1860)
              Frantz Preben Bille-Brahe (30.X.1860-19.X.1867)

France   Ehrenreich Christopher Ludwig Moltke (18.XII.1846-25.IX.1856)
              Johan Carl Daniel Ulysses Dirckinck-Holmfeld (28.IX.1856-9.I.1860)
              Gebhard Leon Moltke-Hvitfeldt (9.I.1860-28.XI.1896)

Geman Con-   Bernhard Ernst Bülow (23.XI.1849-20.X.1862)
federation   Johan Carl Daniel Ulysses Dirckinck-Holmfeld (20.X.1862-28.XI.1863)

Great   Waldemar Tully Oxholm (22.I.1854-31.XII.1856)
Britain   Charles Edouard Van Dockum (14.XII.1857-24.I.1860)
              Torben Bille (24.I.1860-1.XII.1864)

Italy   Iver Holger Rosenkrantz (21.VI-1863-28.III.1866)

Prussia   Ludvig Ulrich Hans Brockdorff (19.V.1854-15.IX.1860)
              Georg Joachim Quaade (19.X.1860-26.I.1864)

Russia   Otto Plessen (3.XI.1846-1.XII.1866)

Sweden-   Wulf Heinrich Bernhard Scheel-Plessen (3.XII.1851-19.VI.1872)
Norway
USA   Torben Bille (26.V.1852-4.VIII.1857).
              Waldemar Rudolph Raasløff (19.VIII.1857-1866)

* (*Kongelig Dansk Hof og Statscalender. Statshaandbog for det Danske Monarchie for aaret 1856-1864. A.F. Kriegers Dagbøger 1848-1880,* vol. 8, pt. 2, (Copenhagen, 1943), pp. 63-77).

Bibliography

Archives

No attempt has been made to list all the collections consulted. The purchase of the entries is limited to acquanting the reader in general way with the scope and nature of the archival materials used in this study.

A. Rigsarkivet (Public Record Office), Copenhagen

I. Udenrigsministeriet (Ministry of Foreign Affairs)
 1. Russland, Depecher 1854-1860, 1861-1865
 2. Russland, Ordrer 1856-1857, 1858-1863
 3. Preussen, Depecher 1857-1860, 1860-1866
 4. Preussen, Ordrer 1857-1861, 1862-1867
 5. Østrig, Depecher 1856-1857, 1858-1862, 1863-1867
 6. Frankrig, Depecher 1856-1860, 1861-1864
 7. Frankrig, Ordrer 1856-1858
 8. England, Depecher 1856-1860, 1861-1863, 1864
 9. England, Ordrer 1857-1860, 1861-1863, 1864
 10. Sverige, Depecher 1856-.1861, 1862-1865
 11. Sverige, Ordrer 1854-1860, 1861-1868
 12. Det Tyske Forbund, Depecher 1856-1858, 1858.1860, 1860-1862, 1862-1863, 1863-1864
 13. Ges. Arkiver, Russland II Depechekoncepter 1855-1859, 1860-1864
 14. Ges. Arkiver, London, Samlingspakke 28 og 29. Sager vedr. Fredskonferencen i London. I. Korrespondance mellem U.Min. og de Delegerede. II. Diverse 1864.

II. Samlede Sager
1. Den Holstenske Forfatningssag v. 210-219, 1856-1864
2. Registratur, 1859-1909
3. Krigen, Den dansk-tyske strid v. 447
4. Underhandlingerne i Wien om våbenstilstand. Fredsforhandlingerne i Wien. v. 448, 449
5. Journal A. 3332

6. Den polske opstand, Polen 1863, A 3354
7. Kongehuset, Frederic VII breve til kongen, 1861-1863, A 2938
8. R.A. Registratur til archivjournalen 1856-1864
9. R.A. Registratur 1863, 1864 Tag A. 798
10. Sleswig og Holstein politiske forhold, Tryksagen 1857-1864.
11. Håndskriftsamlingen XVI. Proveniensordnet del Rusland Staatsarkiver i Moskva. Afskrifter af indberetninger fra det russiske gesandtskab i København til regeringen i St. Petersborg, 1848-1864, vol. 40-54.

III. Private og personalarkiver
1. 5167, Bluhme, Ch. A. politiker, 1789-1865
2. 5522, Hall, C. Ch. auditør, politiker, d. 1888
3. 5982, Monrad, D.G. politiker, biskop, 1811-1887
4. 6138, Ploug, Carl Parmo, forfatter, journalist, politiker, d. 1894
5. 6089, Oxholm, Waldemar, Tully, overhofmarshal, 1848-1872.
6. 6171, Quaade, George Joachim, diplomat, minister, 1858-1888
   A.I.4. Brevskriverliste
   A.III.C. Diverse sager. Quaades notater om stormagternes syn på Danmarks politik 1848-1864
7. 6128, Familien v. Plessen, Otto Plessen (1816-1897) Arkiv 1841-81. 1.pk. VI,1
8. 5810, Krieger, Andreas Frederik, politiker, d. 1893
9. 6498, P. Vedel, direktør
   VI. Breve fra udenlandske diplomater
   X. Diverse rapporter
   Korrespondancesager ved de forskellige politiske spørgsmål
   XI. Samlinger og sager ved historiske begivenheder (manuskripter m.m. ved Monrad, fremstilling af de diplomatiske forhandlinger (1858-1862)
   XI. Samlinger og sager ved de historiske begivenheder (P. Vedels fremstilling af Danmarks udenrigspolitik 1856-1864, bilag til Vedels fremstilling af Danmark udenrigspolitik 1858-1864)
   XI. Notitser, uddrag af depecher m.m. Vedels egenhandige uddrag af depecher fra de danske gesandter og notater om begivenhederne
   XII. Privatarkiver, udskilte af P. Vedels papirer
   1863, P. Vedels erindringer
   1864-1867, P. Vedels privatpapirer
   Politiske notater og afskrifter 1854, 1861-1864, 1875
   Breve fra og om kongelige til Vedel
   Tillæg Afskrifter
   I-II Professor Aage Friis' samlinger og korrespondance ved P. Vedel
10. 5427, Privatarkiver Historikeren Aage Friis
    Håndskriftsamlinger
    II. Afskrifter og fotokopier fra udenlandske arkiver ved dansk udenrigspolitik pk. 7-12

*IV. Russiske Films. Det russiske Udenrigsministerium Akter.
(Arkhiv Vneyshnyei Politiki Rossii. C.A. Moscow.*
1. København - St. Petersburg, 1856-1857, 1858-1860, 1860-1864.
2. St. Petersburg - København 1856-1864.
3. Ordrer til Ungern-Sternberg i København, supplement, 1858
4. Danica-Filmene 485/65 - 485/68, 1863-1864.

V. Public Record Office, London, Arkhiv, n. 60.
Signatur F.P. (Foreign Office) 22
291 1862 To Mr. Paget, Mr. Manley
292-294 1862 From Mr. Paget, Mr. Manley
298 1862 Mr. Labouchere, Foreign Various, Domestic Various
299 1863 To Sir A. Paget, Mr. Lytton

VI. Deutsches Zentral-Archiv, Merseburg, Arkiv, n. 301
I. Akta der Gesandschaft zu Kopenhagen, I. Rep. 81. Signatur n. 165-172, 1856-66
VI. Österreichisches Staatsarchiv, Kriegsarchiv, Wien, Arkiv, n. 592
Signatur 45, 1864-66, Krieg gegen Dänemark, 1864
Feldakten, Fasz. 407, Operationsjournal des 6 Armee Korps, 16-1-30.XI.1864
Operationansjournal verschiedener Abteilung des 6 Armee Korps, Armeebefehle anf. 16.1.1864

B. Riksarkivet (Public Record Office), Stockholm
1. Kabinettet for utrikes brevväxlingen. Depecher från beskickningen i Petersburg. 1856-1863.
2. Beskickningens i Petersburg archiv. Mottagna skrivelser. 1856-1864
3. Kabinettet for utrikes brevväxlingen. Depescher från beskickningen i Köpenhamn. 1863-1864.
4. Beskickningens i Köpenhamn arkiv. Ankomna skrivelser. 1863 I, II, 1864, I, II
6. Beskickningens i Köpenhamn arkiv. Handlingar (dossierer). B. VIII. Question des Duchés. 1848-1864.
7. Skrivelser från Petersburg til Stockholm, 1856-1863. Centralarkivet i Moskva.
8. Depescher från Stockholm til Petersburg. 1856-1864. Centralarkivet i Moskva.
9. Film från Centralarkivet i Moskva. Handlingar beröranda svensk-ryska forhällanden, rulle 69-74 (212-232). 1855-1864.

C. Archives du Ministère des Affaires Étrangères, Paris
1. Correspondance politique.
   Allemagne 825 (1853)-840 (1864)
   Angleterre 707 (1857)-731 (1864)
   Autriche 466 (1857)-487 (1864)
   Danemark 229 (1856)-248 (1864)
   Prusse 329 (1857)-350 (1864)
   Russie 212 (1856)-233 (1864)
   Suède et Norvège 318 (1857-58)-325 (1864)
2. Correspondance consulaire et commerciale, Copenhague, vol. 13-15 (1855-1869)
3. Memoires et documents. Russie, vol. 44-46 (1850-1873)
   Memoires et documents. Danmark. Question des Duchés, vol. 13-16.

D. Public Record Office (P.R.O.), London
The Russell Papers
30/22 vol. 53-60 Lord Cowley, Paris, 1859-1864
      vol. 51, 52, 78, 102, Denmark, 1859-1864
      vol. 22, 78, 84, 102, 114, Russia, 1859-1865
      vol. 99, Austria, Embassy Vienna, 1863-1865
      Russia/Sweden 1859-1865
      Sweden/Denmark 1859-1865
      vol. 14G, 15 A,B,C, Russia 1863-1864, Repairing Department
      vol. 27, Memoranda, Cabinet Opinions, 1859-1865
      Correspondence Cabinet, Viscount Palmerston, 1861-1865

E. Hof-, Haus- u. Staatsarchiv, Vienna
I. Politisches Archiv
1. Politisches Archiv (P.A.) III Preussen
   K. 4-9 Protokoll 1856-1864
   K. 57-87 Berichte, Weisungen, Varia 1856-1864
2. P.A. VIII England
   K. 4-8 Protokoll 1856-1864
   K. 43-65 Berichte, Weisungen, Varia 1856-1864
3. P.A. IX Frankreich
   K. 5-11 Protokoll 1856-1864
4. P.A. X Rusland
   K. 5-8 Protokoll 1856-1870
   K. 43-55 Berichte, Weisungen, Varia 1856-1864

5. P.A. XXIV Dänemark
   K. 1-2 Protokoll 1856-1865
   K. 18-24 Berichte, Weisungen, Varia 1856-1864
6. P.A. XXVI Schweden- und Norwegen
   K. 2 Protokoll 1856-1865
   K. 13-16 Berichte, Weisungen, Varia 1856-1865
II. P.A. Nachlass Bernhard Graf Rechberg, 1859-1864
1. Schriftennachlass des Grafen Rechberg
   533 a-e IV. Briefe 1859-1864 und später
   V. Korrespondenz mit Kaiser und Erzherzogen, Manteuffel, Bismarck i.a. Schönbrunn 1864
III. 528. 4. Schleswig-Holsteinische Frage (Kriege 1864, 1866)

F. Hauptstaatsarchiv, Stuttgart

G. 314 Bü 1851-1871 A.M. Gorchakov letters to Olga Nicolaevna
E. 73 Gesandschaftsakten, Württembergische Gesandschaft, St. Petersburg, Fas. 85-86 (1856-1865)

G. Ministerio Degli Affari Esteri, Arkivio Storico-Diplomatico, Roma

I. Serie Politica 1861-1868
1. Rapporti Della Legazione in Copenaghen e Stoccolma Anni 1861 a 1864. Pacco nos. 170 (808), 171 (809)
2. Rapporti Della Legazione in Pietroburgo Anni 1862 a 1865. Pacco nos. 204 (842), 205 (843)

H. Arkhivum Glóvne Akt Davnykh (AGAD), Warsaw

1. Zhurnal Vojennykh Dejstvii (1863-1864)

I. Kongelige Biblioteket (Royal Library), Stockholm

Ep.M.I. Brev til Ludwig Manderström
Ep.Q.I. Brev til och från Emil von Quanten
Ep.S. 42 August Sohlmans politiska korrespondens
D. 1102 C.R.L. Manderströms diplomatiska arkiv, koncept, original och avskrifter

J. Lund Universitetsbibliotek, (LUB)

Henning Hamiltons samling

K. Bibliotèque Polonaise, Paris

Rkp. 531, 39.2, Robert Sienkiewicz, Powstanie 1863: Listy rodziny.

Newspapers and periodicals (1856-1864)

Berlingske Tidende
Dagbladet
Danmark
Dansk Maanedsskrift
Flyveposten
Fædrelandet
Illustreret Tidende
Kjøbenhavnsposten
Kronen
Morgenposten
Aftonbladet (Stockholm)
Dagbladet (Christiania)
Helsingfors Dagblad
Constitutionnel
Journal des Débats
Moniteur
Revue des Deux Mondes
Morning Post
The Times
Glos Wolny
Der Weisse Adler
Le Nord
Den'
Golos
Journal de St. Pétersbourg
Kolokol
Moskovskie Vedomosti
Otechestvennye Zapiski
Petersburger Zeitung
Ruskii Invalid
Russkoe Slovo
Severnaya Pchela
Sovremennik
St. Peterburgskie Vedomosti
Vest'
Vestnik Evropy
Zagranichnyi Vestnik

Printed Sources

The author is unable to give a full list of books and articles relating to the problem reviewed by him, as this would require a special volume. He confined himself to stating those sources on which he mostly relied and to which a special reference was made in the text.

Airas, P. *Die Geschichtlichen Wertungen Krieg und Friede von Friedrich dem Grossen bis Engels.* (Rovaniemi, 1978).
Aksakov, I.S. *Sochineniya.* vol. I. Slavyanskii vopros (Moscow, 1886).
Aktstykker vedkommende den dansk-tydske strid. Aktstykker, der belyser den svensk-norske Regjerings Stilling til Sagen (1858-1864). (Copenhagen, 1865).
Aktstykker vedkommende Londonerconferencen. (Copenhagen, 1866).
Aktstykker vedkommende Fredslutningen i Wien, Gasteineroverenskomsten og Pragerfrieden. (Copenhagen, n.d.).
Aldemingen, E.M. *The Emperor Alexander II.* A. Study. (London, 1962).
Andersson, I. *Sveriges Historia.* (Stockholm, 1969).
Andersson, I. (Ed.). *Svensk historia i rysk version.* (Stockholm, 1952).
Andræ, P. (Ed.) En brevveksling mellem Andræ og Krieger under Londonerkonferencen 1864. *Historisk Tidsskrift.* 6.R.5, (Copenhagen, 1894-95).
Arsenev, K. *Statisticheskie ocherki.* (St. Petersburg, 1848).
Arup, E. David og Hall. Krisen i Danmarks historie 1863. *Scandia.* vol. I. 1928.

Bajer, F. *Nordens særlig Danmarks nevtralitet under Krimkrigen.* (Copenhagen, 1914).
Bakunin, M. *Izbrannye sochineniya.* Vol. I. Gosudarstvennost' i anarkhiya. (Petersburg, Moscow, 1922),
Balmuth, D. *Censorship in Russia 1865-1905. (Washington D.C., 1979).*
Balmuth, D. Origins of the Russian Press Reform of 1865. *Slavonic and East European Review.* (London, 1969, Juli).
Barsukov, N. *Zhizn i trudy M.P. Pogodina.* (St. Petersburg, 1901).
Barzini, L. *The Europeans.* (N.Y., 1983).
Baumgart, W. *Der Friede von Paris 1856.* Studien zum Verhältnis von Kriegsführung, Politik und Friedensbewahrung. (Münich, Wien, 1972).
Bazarov, A.I. Svyatleishii Kniaz' A.M. Gorchakov. Iz vospominanii o nem ego dukhovnika. *Russkii Arkhiv.* 1896. vol I.
Bazylow, L. *Dzieje Rosji, 1801-1917.* (Warsaw, 1970).
Becker-Christensen, H. *Skandinaviske drømme og politiske realiteter 1830-1850.* (Århus, 1980).
Bell, H.F.C. *Lord Palmerston.* (London, N.Y., 1936).
Berti, G. *Russia e stati italiani nel Risorgimento.* (Rome, 1957).

599

Bessmertnaya, M.J. K istorii parizhskogo mira 1856 g. *Krasnyi Arkhiv,* 2 (75), (Moscow, 1936).
Beust, F.F. *Aus Drei Viertel-Jahrhunderten. Erinnerungen und Aufzeichnungen.* Vol. I. 1809-1866, vol. II. 1866-1885. (Stuttgart, 1887).
Beyrau, D. *Russische Orientalpolitik und die Enstehung des Deutschen Kaiserreiches 1866-1870/71.* (Wiesbaden, 1974).
Beyrau, D. *Militär und Gesselschaft im Vorrevolutionären Russland,* (Köln, Wien, 1984).
Birch, J.H.S. *Denmark in History.* (Westport, Connecticut, 1975).
Birke, E. *Frankreich und Ostmitteleuropa im 19. Jahrhundert. Beitrage zur Politik und Geistgeschichte.* (Köln, Graz, 1960).
Bismarcks Briefwechsel mit dem Minister Freiherrn von Schleinitz 1858-1861. (Berlin, 1905).
Bismarck, O. *Die gesammelten Werke.* Vol. II-VI. (Berlin, 1924-1925).
Bloch, I.S. *Finansy Rossii XIX stoletiya.* (St. Petersburg, 1882).
Blum, J. *Lord and Peasant in Russia from the Ninth to the Nineteenth Century.* (Princeton, N.J., 1972).
Bolsover, G.H. Aspects of Russian Foreign Policy, 1815-1914. *Essays presented to Sir Lewis Namier.* (London, 1956).
Böhme, H. *Die Reichsgründung.* (München, 1967).
Böhme, H. *The Foundation of the German Empire.* (Oxford. U.P., 1971).
Böhme, H. *Deutschlands Weg zur Grossmacht. Studien zum Verhältnis von Wirtschaft und Staat während der Reichsgründungszeit 1848-1881.* (Köln, Berlin, 1966).
Borejsza, J.W. *Piekny wiek XIX.* (Warsaw, 1984).
Borodkin, M. *Kratkaya istoriya Finlandii.* (St. Petersburg, 1911).
Borodkine, M. *La Finlande comme partie intégrante de l'Empire Russe.* (Paris, 1912).
Borries, K. *Preussen im Krimkrieg.* (Stuttgart, 1930).
Borykin, V.I. The Franco-Russian Alliance. *History,* vol. 64. 1979.
Boysen, C. Beitrage zu Bismarcks Politik in der Schleswig-Holsteinischen Frage. *Z.d.G.f.S.H.G.* vol. 64. 1936.
Bóbr-Tylingo, S. O niedoszlych sojuszach Francji r. 1863. *Teki Historyczne.* VII. (London, 1955).
Bóbr-Tylingo, S. Do tajnej dyplomacji Napoleona III (1863). *Teki Historyczne.* XI. (London, 1960-61).
Bóbr-Tylingo, S. *Napoléon III, l'Europe et la Pologne 1863-4. Antemurale 1863-1963.* (Rome, 1963).
Bradford, S. *Disraeli.* (London, 1982).
Brandenburg, E. *Die Reichsgründung.* Vols. I-II. (Leipzig, 1922).
Brandenburg, E. (Ed.). *Die auswärtige Politik Preussens 1857-1871.* (Oldenburg, 1932 sqq.)
Brandes, G. *Indtryk fra Polen.* (Copenhagen, 1888).
Brandes, G. *Indtryk fra Rusland.* (Copenhagen, 1888).
Bridge, F.R. and Roger Bullen. *The Great Powers and the European States System 1815-1914.* (London, N.Y., 1980).
Brzezinski, Z. *Game Plan – How to Conduct the U.S.-Soviet Contest.* (Boston, N.Y., 1986).
Bunsen, F. *Memoirs of Baron Bunsen.* Vol. II. (London, 1869).
Burckhardt, H. *Deutschland, England, Frankreich. Die politischen Beziehungen Deutschlands zu den beiden Westeuropäischen Grossmächten 1864-1866.* (München, 1970).
Bushuev, S.K. *A. Gorchakov.* (Moscow, 1961).

Butler, J. *A History of England. 1815-1939.* (London, 1963).
Bååth-Holmberg, C. *Carl XV som enskild man, konung och konstnär.* (Stockholm, 1891).

Callières, F. *De la manière de négocier avec les souverains.* Vols. I-II. (Paris, 1816).
The Cambridge History of British Foreign Policy 1783-1919. Vol. II. (Eds.) Ward, A.W. and Gooch, P.G. (Cambridge, 1923).
The New Cambridge Modern History, vol. X. The Zenith of European Powers 1830-70. (Ed.) Bury, J.P.T. (Cambridge, 1960).
Camneron Rondo, E. *France and the Economic Development of Europe 1800-1914,* (Princeton, 1961).
Carr, W. *Schleswig-Holstein 1815-1848. A Study in National Conflict.* (Manchester, 1963).
Charles-Roux, F. *Alexandre II, Gortchakoff et Napoléon III.* (Paris, 1913).
Chicherin, B.N. *Vospominaniya. Moskovskii Universitet.* (Moscow, 1929).
Chudovski, V. *Voyna za Slesvig-Golshtein 1864 goda.* (St. Petersburg, 1864).
Cierpinski, F. Die Politik England in der schleswig-holsteinischen Frage von 1861 bis Anfang Januar 1864. *Z.d.G.f.S.H.G.* vol. 44. 1914.
Cierpinski, F. Die Politik Englands in der schleswig-holsteinischen Frage im Anfange des Jahres 1864. *Z.d.G.f.S.H.G.* vol. 45. 1915.
Cieślak, T. *Polska-Skandynawia w XIX i XX wieku.* (Warsaw, 1973).
Cieślak, T. *Zarys historii najnowszej krajów skandynawskich.* (Warsaw, 1978).
Clark, C.W. *Franz Joseph and Bismarck. The Diplomacy of Austria before the War of 1866.* (Cambridge, Mass., 1934).
Clausen, J. *Skandinavismen. Historisk Fremstillet.* Copenhagen, 1900).
Cohen, B.C. *The Public's Impact on Foreign Policy.* (Boston, 1973).
Cohn, E. *Økonomi og politik i Danmark 1849-1879.* (Copenhagen, 1967).
Correspondence respecting the Affairs of Denmark 1850-53, Presented to both Houses of Parliament by Command of Her Majesty, 1864. (London, 1864).
Correspondence between Austria, Prussia and Denmark 1851-52. (London, 1864).
Cöster, F.B. *Historisk återblick i anledning af senast timade händelser uti Polen.* (Norrköping, 1863).
Coussange, J. *La Scandinavie: Le nationalisme scandinave.* (Paris, 1914).
Craig, Gordon, A. Totalitarian Approaches to Diplomatic Negotiation. *War, Politics and Diplomacy.* (N.Y., London, 1966).
Craig, Gordon, A. Techniques of Negotiation. *Foreign Policy* (Ed.) I.J. Lederer. (New Haven and London, 1967).
Crankshaw, E. *The Fall of the House of Habsburg.* (N.Y., 1963).
Crusenstolpe, M.J. *Ett sekel och ett år af Polska frågan 1762-1863. Historisk-kronologisk handbok.* (Stockholm, 1863).
Custine, A. *La Russie en 1839.* (Brussels, 1843).
Czapliński, W., Górski, K. *Historia Danii.* (Wroclaw, 1965).
Czapliński, W. *Dzieje Danii nowożytnej 1500-1975.* (Warsaw, 1982).
Czartoryski, W. *Pamietnik 1860-1864.* (Warsaw, 1960).

Daebel, J. *Die Schleswig-Holstein Bewegung in Deutschland 1863/4.* (Köln, 1969).
Dalwigh zu Lichtenfels. F. *Fie Tagebücher des Freiherrn Reinhard v. Dalwigk zu Lichtenfels aus den Jahren 1860-71.* (Ed.) Schüssler, W. (Osnabrück, 1967).

Danilov, N.A. *Istoricheskii ocherk razvitiya voennogo upravleniya v Rossii.* (St. Petersburg, 1902).
Danilevsky, N. Ya. *Rossiya i Evropa.* (St. Petersburg, 1889).
Dansk Biografisk Leksikon, II and III ed. (1979-1984).
David, Ch.G.N. Optegnelser om aarene 1863-1865. *Historisk Tidsskrift.* 8 R.V. (1914).
Danske Tractater 1751-1800, vol. I. (Copenhagen, 1882).
Danske Tractater efter 1800. Politiske Tractater 1800-1863. (Copenhagen, 1877).
Debidour, A. *Histoire diplomatique de l'Europe, 1814-1878.* Vol. II. La Révolution. (Paris, 1891).
Den danske udenrigstjeneste 1710-1970. Vol. I 1770-1919. Eds. Kjølsen K. and Sjøqvist V. (Copenhagen, 1970).
Delessert, E. *Le Prince Gortchakoff Ambassadeur Russe à Vienne. Souvenirs intimes 1853-54.* (Paris, 1856).
Denmark and Germany. Correspondence respecting the Affairs of the Duchies of Holstein, Lauenburg and Schleswig, 1858. (London, 1864).
Denmark and Germany. Reports from Mr. Ward and Vice-Consul Rainals respecting the Duchies of Schleswig and Holstein. Dated respectively May 28, 1857 and February 15, 1861. (London, 1864).
Denmark and Germany. Nos. I-VII. *Correspondence respecting the Maintenance of the Integrity of the Danish Monarchy.* (London, 1864).
Derry, T.K. *A History of Modern Norway 1814-1972.* (Oxford U.P. 1973).
Derry, T.K. *A History of Scandinavia.* (London, 1979).
Dietrich, R. (Ed.) *Das Jahr 1866 und das Dritte Deutschland.* (Berlin, 1968).
Dipl. Aktstykker vedrørende det Dansk-Tydske Spørgsmaal fra tidsrummet juni-august 1864. (Copenhagen, 1864).
Documenti Diplomatici Italiani. Prima Serie: 1861-1870. Vols. III-V. (Rome, 1965, 1973, 1977).
Döhler, K. K. *Napoleon III und die deutsch-dänische Frage, under besondere Berücksichtigung des französischen Politik während des Konfliktes von 1863-64.* (Halle, 1913).
Dolgorukov, P.V. *Peterburgskie ocherki. Pamflety emigranta 1860-64.* (Moscow, 1934).
Driault, E. La diplomatie française pendant la guerre de Danemark. *Revue Historique,* vol. CVII. 1911.
Dzhanshev, G.A. *Epokha velikich reform.* (St. Petersburg, 1905).
Dzhunkovsky, S.S. Politika Danii pri Friderike VII.Iz zapisok ochevidtsa 1855-1861. *Vestnik Evropy,* 1866, dekabr'.

Eckhardt, J.W.A. *Von Nicolaus I zu Alexander III. Eine russische geheime Denkschrift von 1864.* (Leipzig, 1881).
Eimer, B. *Cavour and Swedish Politics.* (Lund, 1978).
Engberg, J. *Det slesvigske spørgsmål.* (Copenhagen, 1968).
Engelberg, E. *Bismarck. Urpreusse und Reichsbegründer.* (Berlin, 1985).
Engels, F. The Foreign Policy of Russian Tsarism. I ed. in German. *Die Neue Zeit,* vol. VIII. 1890.
Engels, F. The Role of Force in History. *Marx, Engels, Selected Works.* Vol. III. (Moscow, 1973).
Entsiklopedicheskii slovar, vols IV, IX. (St. Petersburg, 1891, 1893).

Erbeling, E. *Histoire de l'idée d'un partage de Slesvig. Manuel historique de la question du Slesvig.* (Copenhagen, 1906).
Ericksson, S. *Carl XV.* (Stockholm, 1954).
Ericksson, S. *Svensk diplomati och tidningspress under Krimkriget.* (Stockholm, 1939).
Eruzalimsky, A.S. Pisma O. Bismarka A.M. Gorchakovu. *Krasnyi Arkhiv,* 1933, vol. 61.
Eruzalimsky, A.S. Iz zapisnoi knizhki arkhivista. Bismark o polozhenii v Evrope v 1868 g. *Krasnyi Arkhiv,* 1936, vol. 74.
Eruzalimsky, A.S. *Bismarka diplomatiya i militarizm.* (Moscow, 1968).
Estlander, B. *Elva Årtionden ur Finlands historia.* Vol. I. *1808-1878.* (Helsingfors, 1949).
Eyck, E. *Bismarck: Leben und Werk.* Vols. I-III. (Zurich, 1941-44).

Feldman, J. *Sprawa polska w roku 1848.* (Cracow, 1933).
Feldman, W. *Bismarck a Polska.* (Warsaw, 1947).
Fellenius, K.G. *Polska frågan i Sverige år 1863. Anteckningar ur Polsk-Svenska paper.* (Stockholm, 1936).
Fellenius, K.G. Sprawa polska w szwedzkim Riksdagu. *Przeglad Wspólczesny,* n. 10, 1938.
Feoktisov, E.M. *Za kulisami politiki i literatury, 1848-96.* (Leningrad, 1929).
Filipowicz, T. *Confidential Correspondence of the British Government respecting the Insurrection in Poland 1863.* (Paris, 1914).
Fink, T. *Geschichte des Schleswigschen Grenzlandes.* (Copenhagen, 1958).
Fink, T. *Otte foredrag om Danmarks krise 1863-64.* (Aarhus, 1964).
Fleischhauer, E. *Bismarcks Russlandspolitik im Jahrzehnt von der Reichsgründung und ihre Darstellung in der sowjetischen Historiographie.* (Köln, Wien, 1976).
Fleury, E.F. *Souvenirs du Général C-te Fleury.* Vol. II. *1859-67.* (Paris, 1898).
Florinsky, M.T. *A History and Interpretation.* Vol. II. (N.Y. 1953).
Foundation of British Foreign Policy from Pitt (1792) to Salisbury (1902). Eds. Temperly H. and Penson, L.M. (Cambridge, 1938).
Franz, E. *Der Entscheidungskampf um die wirtschaftspolitische Führung Deutschlands (1856-1867).* (München, 1933). (Reprint Aalen, 1973).
Friese, Ch. *Rusland und Preussen vom Krimkrieg bis zum polnischen Aufstand.* (Berlin, Königsberg, 1931).
Friis, A. (Ed.) *D.G. Monrads Deltagelse i Begivenhederne. 1864.* (1914).
Friis, A. C.N. David, Christian IX og Sir Augustus Paget i November 1863. *Historisk Tidsskrift.* 9.R.VI.
Friis, A. *Skandinavismens Kulmination. Ministeriet Halls planer om en Nordisk Union forud for udstedelsen af Martskundgørelsen 1863.* (Copenhagen, 1936).
Friis, A. and Heinar, E. (Eds.). *Henning Hamilton. Anteckninger rörande förhallandet mellem Sverige och Danmark 1863-1864.* (Stockholm, Copenhagen, 1936).
Friis, A. Kong Oscar II's breve til Henning Hamilton. *Danske Magazin,* 1940.
Friis, A. and Just Rahbek. (Eds). A.F. Kriegers, D.G. Monrads og P. Vedels indbyrdes brevveksling 1846-1888. *Danske Magazin,* VII.R.3. 1940.
Friis, A. *Den Danske Regering og Nordsleswigs Genforening med Danmark.* Vol. II. (Copenhagen, 1939).

Gall, L. *Bismarck. Der weisse Revolutionär.* (Frankfurt/M., Berlin, Wien, 1980).
Gall, L. *Das Bismarck-Problem in der Gesichtsschreibung nach 1945.* (Köln, Berlin, 1971).
Gerasimova, Ya. *Iz istorii russkoi pechati v period revolyutsionnoi situatsii kontsa 1850-ykh i nachala 1860-ykh godov.* (Moscow, 1974).
Geer, L. *Minnen upptecknade.* (Stockholm, 1892).
Gerber, R. *Z dziejów prowokacji wsród emigracji polskiej w XIX wieku. A. Potocki. Raporty szpiega.* vol. I. (Warsaw, 1973).
Geyer, D. *Der russische Imperialismus. Studien über den Zusammenhang von innerer und auswärtiger Politik 1860-1914.* (Göttingen, 1977).
Geyl, P. *Napoleon: For and Against.* (Harmondsworth, 1965).
Geyl, P. *Debates with Historians.* (Glasgow, 1977).
Gille, B. *Histoire de la maison Rotschild.* Vols. I-II. (Geneva, 1967).
Gindin, I.F. *I.F. Gosudarstvennyi bank i ekonomicheskaya politika tsarskogo pravitelstva 1861-1892.* (Moscow, 1960).
Gorce de, P. *Histoire du Second Empire.* Vols. I-IX. (Paris, 1894-1911).
Gordon, A. Craig A.L. George, *Force and Statecraft. Diplomatic Problems of Our Time.* (N.Y., Oxford, 1983).
Goriainov, Les etapes de l'alliance franco-russe (1853-1861). *Revue de Paris,* 1912.
Goriainov, *Le Bospore et les Dardanelles.* (Paris, 1910).
Gosch, Ch. A. *Denmark and Germany since 1815.* (London, 1862).
Grot, Z. *Pruska polityka narodowościowa w Szleswigu 1864-1920.* (Poznań, 1967).
Graef, 1864 Schleswig-Holstein und das Ausland. *Z.d.G.f.S.H.G.* vol. 45 (1915).
Grunwald, C. *Trois siècles de diplomatie russe.* (Paris, 1945).
Grunwald, C. *Le Tzar Alexandre II et son temps.* (Paris, 1963).
Guichen E. *Les grandes questions Européennes et la diplomatie des puissances sous la seconde République Française.* Vols. I-II. (Paris, 1925, 1929).
Gullberg, E. *Tyskland i svensk opinion 1856-1871.* (Lund, 1952).
Gustafsson, R. *Polen blöder.* (Stockholm, 1863).

Haffner, S. *Preussen ohne Legende.* (Hamburg, 1980).
Halicz, E. *Rosyjska ruch rewolucyjny a sprawa polska 1856-1862.* (Cracow, 1947).
Halicz, E. *Kwestia chlopska w Królestwie Polskim w dobie powstania styczniowego.* (Warsaw, 1955).
Halicz, E. *Danish Neutrality during the Crimean War 1853-1856. Denmark between the Hammer and the Anvil.* (Odense U.P., 1977).
Halicz, E. The Scandinavian Countries and the January Insurrection. *War and Society in East Central Europe.* vol. XIV. *The Crucial Decade.* (N.Y. 1984).
Halicz, E. *Polish National Liberation Struggles and the Genesis of the Modern Nation.* (Odense U.P., 1982).
Halicz, E. Le Nord o konflikcie rosyjsko-polskim i jego perspektywach. *Zeszyty Historyczne.* Paris, 1985 (74).
Halicz, E. Kraje Skandynawskie wobec powstania styczniowego. *Zeszyty Historyczne.* Paris, 1987 (81).
Halicz, E. *The 1863 Polish Uprising and Scandinavia. The Year 1863, the Turning-Point in Russo-Scandinavian Relations.* (Copenhagen U.P., 1988).
Halicz, E. Russian attitude towards the Conflict between Denmark and Germany, A.M. Gorchakov's letters to Olga Nicolayevna. *East European Quarterly,* XXIII. No. I, March 1989, pp. 63-70.

Hallendorff, C. *Konung Oscar I:s politik under Krimkriget.* (Stockholm, 1930).
Hallendorff, C. *Illusioner och verklighet. Studier öfver den skandinaviska krisen 1864.* (Stockholm, 1914).
Hamilton, H. *Anteckningar rörande förhållandet mellan Sverige og Danmark 1863-1864.* (Stockholm a. Copenhagen. 1936).
Hansen, J. *Les coulisses de la diplomatie. Quinze ans à l'ètranger. 1864-1879.* (Paris, 1880).
Hansard Parliamentary Debates. Third Series. vols. 169-170. *Poland, 1863.* Vols. 172-176. *Schleswig.Holstein, 1863-1864.*
Hatton, R.M. Rusia and the Baltic. *Russian Imperialism.* (Rutgers U.P. New Brunswick, N.J. 1974).
Hearder, H.A. *General History of Europe in the Nineteenth Century 1830-1880.* (London, 1974).
Hedin, E. Sveriges stållning i förhållande till Ryssland och våstmakterna år 1863. *Historisk Tidskrift.* Stockholm, 1922 (42.I).
Hedin, E. *Den Skandinaviske allians frågan 1857-1863 untill Ulriksdalskonferencen.* Vittehets akademiens handlingar. Vol. 81. (Stockholm, 1953).
Heinze, G. *Bismarck und Russland bis zum Reichsgründung.* (Würzburg, 1939).
Henderson, G.B. *Crimean War Diplomacy and Other Historical Essays.* (Glasgow, 1947).
Hertzen, A.I. *Polnoe sobranie sochinenii i pisem.* Ed. M.K. Lemke. Vols. V, XV, XVII. (Petrograd, 1919, 1920).
Hill, Ch. E. *The Danish Sound Dues and the Command of the Baltic. A Study of International Relations.* (Duke U.P. Durham, North Carolina, 1926).
Hillerbrand, D. *Bismarck and Gortchakov. A Study in Bismarck's Russian Policy 1852-1871.* (Unpubl. dissert. Ann Arbor, Michigan, 1968).
Hillgruber, A. *Bismarck Aussenpolitik.* (Freiburg, 1972).
Hingley, R. *The Russian Mind.* (London, Sydney, Toronto, 1977).
Histoire générale de la Presse Française publié sous la direction de C. Bellanger, J. Godechot, P. Guiral et F. Terrou, vol. II. De 1815 à 1871. (Paris, 1969).
Hjelhold, H. *British Mediation in the Danish German Conflict 1848-1850.* Vol. I. (Copenhagen, 1965).
Holmberg, Å. *Skandinavismen i Sverige vid 1800-tallets mitt.* (Göteborg, 1946).
Huber, E.R. *Deutsche Verfassungsgeschichte seit 1789.* Vol. III. *Bismarck und das Reich.* (Stuttgart, Berlin, Köln, Mainz, 1970).
Huber, E.R. *Dokumente zur deutschen Verfassungsgeschichte.* Vol. I. (Stuttgart, 1961).

Ibbeken, R. (Ed.) *Die auswärtige Politik Preussens 1858-1871.* Vol. III-V. (Oldenburg, 1933-1935).
Illsøe, P. Lomholt-Thomsen, J. *Nordens Historie.* vol. I. (Copenhagen, 1964).
Istoriya russkoi zhurnalistiki XVIII-XIX v. A.M. Zapadov. (Ed.) (Moscow, 1966).
Istoriya SSSR. vol. II. (Moscow, 1949).
Istoriya SSSR. vol. VI. (Moscow, 1968).

Jansen, K. Samwer, K. *Schleswig-Holsteins Befreiung.* (Wiesbaden, 1897).
Jansen, K. Grossherzog Peter von Oldenburg und die Schleswig-Holst. Frage. *Deutsche Revue,* 27 Jhrg. vol. IV.
Jansson, A. *Den Svenska utrikespolitikens historia III:3, 1844-1872.* (Stockholm, 1961).

Jarzebowski, J. *Wegierska polityka Traugutta.* (Warsaw, 1939).
Jelavich, B. *A Century of Russian Foreign Policy 1814-1914.* (Philadelphia, N.Y., 1964).
Jelavich, B. *Russia and the Rumanian National Cause 1858-59.* (Indiana U.P., 1959).
Jelavich, Ch. and B. *The Establishment of the Balkan National States, 1804-1920. A History of East Central Europe.* Vol. VIII. (Washington U.P. 1977).
Jelavich, B. Russland und die Einigung Deutschlands unter preussischen Führung. *Geschichte in Wissenschaft und Unterricht.* Vol. 9.
Jelavich B. (Ed.) *Rusland 1852-1871. Aus den Berichten der Bayerischen Gesandschaft in St. Petersburg.* (Wiesbaden, 1963).
Johansen, H. Ch. *Dansk Historisk Statistik 1814-1980.* (Copenhagen, 1985).
Jorgenson, T. *Norway's Relations to Scandinavian Unionism 1815-1871.* (Northfield, Minn., 1935).
Jutikalla, E. with Pirinen K. *A History of Finland.* (N.Y., 1962).
Jørgensen, T.G. Andreas Frederic Krieger, Juristen-politikeren-borgeren. (Copenhagen, 1956).

Kabanov, P.I. *Amurskii vopros.* (Blagoveshchensk, 1959).
Kan, A.S. *Istoriya Shvetsii.* (Moscow, 1974).
Kan, A.S. *Istoriya Skandinavskikh stran.* (Moscow, 1980).
Kartsev, J.S. Za kulisami diplomatii. *Russkaya Starina,* vol. I..1908.
Katz, M. *Mikhail N. Katkov. A Political Biography 1818-1887.* (The Hague, Paris, 1966).
Keep, J.E.H. *Soldiers of the Tsar. Army and Society in Russia 1492-1874.* (Oxford, 1985).
Kent, G.O. *Bismarck and His Times.* (Southern Illinois U.P., 1978).
Kersten, A. *Historia Szwecji.* (Wroclaw, Warsaw, Cracow, Gdańsk, 1973).
Khromov, P.A. *Ekonomicheskoe razvitie Rossii v XIX iXX v. 1800-1917.* (Moscow, 1950).
Kieniewicz, S. *Powstanie styczniowe.* (Warsaw, 1972).
Kinyapina, N.S. *Vneshnyaya politika Rossii vtoroi poloviny XIX veka.* (Moscow, 1974).
Kinyapina, N.S. Bor'ba Rossii za otmenu ogranichitel'nykh uslovii Parizhskogo dogovora 1856 goda. *Voprosy istorii,* 1972. No. 8.
Klaczko, J. *Études de diplomatie contemporaine. Les cabinets de l'Europe en 1863-1864.* (Paris, 1866).
Klaczko, J. *Deux Chanceliers. Le Prince Gortchakof et le Prince de Bismarck.* (Paris, 1876).
Klein-Wuttig, A. *Politik und Kriegsführung in den deutschen Einigungskriegen 1864, 1866 und 1870/71.* (Berlin, 1934).
Kobylinski, H. and Møller, E. (Eds.) Aktstykker og breve m.m. vedrørende kammerherre Bernards Bülows særlige mission til Berlin og Wien 1856 og 1857. *Danske Magazin,* 7.R,VI. 1954-1957.
Kohn, H. *Prophets and Peoples.* (N.Y., 1946).
Kohn, H. *Pan-Slavism. Its History and Ideology.* (Notre Dame, Indiana, 1953).
Kohn, H. *The Mind of Germany. The Education of a Nation.* (London, 1961).
Kohl, H. (Ed.) *Bismarck O. Gedanken und Erinnerungen.* vols. I-II. (Stuttgart, Berlin, 1922).
Koht, H. *Die Stellung Norwegens und Schwedens im deutsch dänischen Konflikt zumal während der Jahre 1863 und 1864.* (Christiania, 1908).
Kongelig Dansk Hof- og Statskalender. Statshaandbog for det danske monarchie for aaret 1856-1868.

Kolb, E. Russland und die Gründung des Norddeutschen Bundes. *Europa und der Norddeutsche Bund.* (Ed.) Dietrich, R. (Berlin, 1968).

Konopczyński, W. Le problem Baltique dans l'histoire moderne. *Revue Historique,* vol. 162, 1929.

Konopczyński, W. *Kwestia baltycka do XX w.* (Gdańsk, Bydgoszcz, Szczecin, 1947).

Kovalchenko, I.D. Istochnikovedenie istorii SSSR. (Moscow, 1973).

Kowalska-Posten, L. *De polska emigranternas agentverksamhet i Sverige 1862-1863.* (Lund, 1975).

Kowalska-Posten, L. Norwegowie a sprawa polska w roku 1863. *Komunikaty Instytutu Baltyckiego,* Gdańsk, 1979).

Kowalska-Posten, L. Stosunek sejmu, prasy i opinii publicznej w Szwecji do sprawy polskiej w 1863 r. *Przeglad Historyczny,* 1977, vol. 68.

Krausse, A. *Russia in Asia. A Record and Study. 1558-1899.* (London, 1973).

Kriegers A.F. *Dagbøger 1848-1880.* Vols. I-III. (Copenhagen, Kristiania, 1920-21).

Krusius-Ahrenberg, L. *Der Durchbruch des Nationalismus und Liberalismus im politischen Leben Finnlands 1856-1863.* (Helsinki, 1934).

Krusius-Ahrenberg, L. *Skandinavismus inställning till den schlesvig-holsteinska frågan och Rysslands hällning till bägge vid det danske tyska kriget utbrott.* 1942.

Kucharzewski, J. *The Origin of Modern Russia.* (N.Y., 1948).

Laquer, W. *Russia and Germany. A Century of Conflict.* (Boston, Toronto, 1965).

Larsen, K. *A History of Norway.* (Princeton, U.P., 1974).

Laue, T. *The Transformation of Russian Soeciety.* (Cambridge, 1960).

Lauring, P. *A History of Denmark.* (Copenhagen, 1981).

Lebedev, K.N. Iz zapisok senatora, 1865 god. *Russkii Arkhiv,* 1911.

Lecomte F. *Guerre du Danemark en 1864. Esquisse politique et militaire.* (Paris, 1864).

Lederer, I.J. (Ed.) *Russian Foreign Policy. Essays in Historical Perspective.* (New Haven, London, Yale, U.P. 1962).

Lesnik, S. Rossiya i Prussiya v Slesvig-Golshtinskom voprose. *(Krasnyi Arkhiv* 1939). No. 2.

Liewellyn, Woodward, F.B.A. *The Age of Reform 1815-1870.* (Oxford, 1962).

Lemke, M. *Ocherki po istorii russkoi tsensury i zhurnalistiki, XIX veka.* (St. Petersburg, 1904).

Lenz, M. *Geschichte Bismarcks.* (München, Leipzig, 1913).

Les Origines diplomatiques de la guerre de 1870-1871. Recuil de documents. Vols. I-IV. (Paris, 1910-1911).

Lewak, A. *Polska dzialalność dyplomatyczna r. 1863-1864.* Vols. I-II. (Warsaw, 1937, 1963).

Lindemann, M. *Die Heiraten der Romanows und der deutschen Fürstenhäuser.* (Berlin, 1935).

Linstow, P. Bismarck, Europa og Slesvig-Holstein 1862-1866. *Historisk Tidsskrift.* Vol. II.1978.

Lively, J.K. *Life and Career of Prince A.M. Gorchakov: a Political Biography.* (Georgetown, U.P., 1956).

Lobanov-Rostovsky, A. *Russia and Europe 1825-1878.* (Ann Arbor, 1954).

Lord, R.H. Bismarck and Russia. *American Historical Review,* 29, 1923.

Lundström, D. Manderström och emigranterna i Sverige. *Historisk Tidskrift.* 1953.

Lukaszewski, J. *Zabór pruski w czasie powstania styczniowego.* (Jassy, 1870).

607

Mackenzie, D. Expansion in Central Asia: St. Petersburg vs. Turkestan Generals 1863-66. *Canadian Slavic Studies,* vol. III. no. 2. 1969.

Malettke, K. *Die Beurteilung der Aussen und Innenpolitik Bismarcks von 1862-1866 in den grossen Pariser Zeitungen.* Historische Studien, vol. 39 (Lübeck, Hamburg, 1966).

Manuel historique de la question du Slesvig. Publié sous la direction de Franz de Jessen. Vols. I-II. (Copenhagen, 1906, Copenhagen, Paris, 1939).

Marcks, E. *Kaiser Wilhelm I.* (Leipzig, 1910).

Marquard, E. *Danske gesandter og gesandtskabspersonale indtil 1914.* (Copenhagen, 1952).

Martens, F. *Recuil des traités et conventions conclus par la Russie avec les Puissances Étrangères.* Vols. V, VIII, XII, XV. (St. Petersburg, 1888, 1898, 1909).

Martenson, S. *Württemberg und Russland in Zeitalter der deutschen Einigung 1856-1870. Die diplomatischen und dynastischen Beziehungen eines deutschen Mittelstaates.* (Göppingen, 1970).

Martin, W. *Switzerland from Roman Times to the Present.* (London, 1971).

Masaryk, T.G. *The Spirit of Russia.* Vol. I (London, 1968).

Mathisen, T. *Research in International Relations.* (Oslo, 1963).

Mathisen, T. *The Functions of Smale States in the Strategies of the Great Powers.* (Oslo, Bergen, Tromsö, 1971).

Mazour, A.G. Russia and Prussia during the Schleswig-Holstein Crisis in 1863. *Journal of Central European Affairs.* Vol. I. No. 3. 1941, October.

Marx, Engels, *The Russian Menace to Europa.* (Eds, Blackstock, P.W. and Hoselitz, B.P. (Glencoe III, 1952).

Marx, *Beiträge zur Geschichte der polnischen Frage. Manuskripte aus den Jahren 1863-1864.* (Warsaw, 1971).

Medlicott, W.N. and Coveney, D.K. *Bismarck and Europe.* (London, 1971).

Menor, A. *L'Allemagne nouvelle 1863-1867.* (Paris, 1879).

Meshchersky, V.M. *Moi vospominaniya, 1850-1865.* Vols. I-II, (St. Petersburg, 1897-98).

Meyendorff, P. *Ein russischer Diplomat an den Höfen von Berlin und Wien. Politischer und privater Briefwechsel 1826-1863.* (Ed.) Hoetzsch, O. (Leipzig, 1923).

Meyer, A. *O. Bismarck, Der Mensch und der Staatsmann.* (Stuttgart, 1949).

Michel, B. *La mémoire de Prague.* (Paris, 1986).

Milyutin, D.A. *Dnevnik.* Vols. I-IV. (Moscow, 1947-1950).

Moltke, H. *Militärische Werke.* Vol. I. Militärische Korrespondenz. Krieg 1864. (Berlin, 1892).

Morny, Ch. *Une ambassade en Russie, 1856.* (Paris, 1892).

Mosse, W.E. *The European Powers and the German Question 1848-71 with Special Reference to England and Russia.* (Cambridge, 1958).

Mosse, W.E. *The Rise and Fall of the Crimean System 1855-71.* (London, 1963).

Mosse, W.E. *Liberal Europe 1848-1875.* (London, 1974).

Münich, H.W. *Polska frihetskampen.* Stockholm, 1863).

Møller, E. London-Konferencens hovedproblem. *Festskrift til Kristian Erslev.* (Copenhagen, 1927).

Møller, E. Den engelske kabinet og den dansk-tydske strid. *Historisk Tidsskrift,* II.R. vol. 4. 1953-56.

Møller, E. *Skandinavisk stræben og svensk politik omkring 1860.* (Copenhagen, 1948).

Møller, E. Karl XV's og Napoleon III's personlige allianceforhandlinger 1863. *Historisk Tidskrift,* 1954.

Møller. E. *Helstatens Fald.* Vols. I-II. (Copenhagen, 1958).

Namier, L. *Vanished Supremacies. Essays on European History 1812-1918.* (London, 1962).
Narochnitskaya, L.I. *Rossiya i voiny Prussii v. 60-tykh godakh XIX v. za ob'edinenie Germanii sverkhu.* (Moscow, 1960).
Narochnitsky, E.L. (Ed.) *Itogi i zadachi izucheniya vneshnei politiki Rossii.* (Moscow, 1981).
Nechkina, M. *Revolyutsionnaya situatsiya v Rossii v seredine XIX veka 1859-61* gg. (Moscow, 1962, n. ed. 1979).
Neergaard, N. *Under Junigrundloven. En fremstilling af det danske folks politiske historie fra 1848 til 1866.* Vol. I-II. (Copenhagen, 1892, Copenhagen, Kristiania, 1916).
Nesselrode, Ch. *Lettres et papiers du Chancelier Comte de Nesselrode, 1760-1856.* Par le Comte A. Nesselrode. Vols. IX-XI. (Paris, 1910-12).
Nielsen, A. *Dänische Wirtschaftsgeschichte.* (Jena, 1933).
Nielsen, J.S *D.G. Monrad. En patografi.* (Odense U.P., 1983).
Nielsen, John. *1864 Da Europa gik af lave.* (Odense U.P., 1987).
Nielsen, John. Europæisk storpolitik omkring krigen 1864. *Historie.* Ny R.17,I, 1987.
Nikitenko. A.V. *Zapiski i dnevnik. (1822-1877).* (St. Petersburg, 1893).
Nikitenko, A.V. *Dnevnik.* Vols. I-II. (Leningrad, 1955-56).
Nolde, B.E. *Vneshnyaya politika. Istoricheskie ocherki.* (Petrograd, 1915).
Nolde, B.E. *Ryssland, Preussen och Polen 1861-1863.* (Stockholm, 1916).
Nolde, B.E. *Rossiya i Evropa v nachale tsarstvovaniya Aleksandra II.* (Prague, 1925).
Nolde, B.E. *Peterburgskaya missiya Bismarka 1859-1862.* (Prague, 1925).
Norge og den polske frihetskamp. Ed. and introduction by R. Hammering-Bang, preface by prof. dr. F. Bull. (Oslo, 1937).
Nyström, A. Resningen i Polen och sympatierna i Sverige. *Polonica.* (Stockholm, 1917).
Nørregård, G. *Danmark mellem ost og vest 1824-1839.* (Copenhagen, 1969).

Ocherki istorii ministerstva innostrannykh del 1801-1902. (St. Petersburg, 1902).
Ogarev, N.P. *Izbrannye proizvedeniya.* (Moscow, 1956).
Ollivier, E. *L'Empire libéral.* Vols. III, VII. (Paris, 1903, 1911).
Olsen, S. Danmark og den polske opstand 1863. *Festskrift til Erik Arup.* (Copenhagen, 1946).
Oncken, H. Grossherzog Peter von Oldenburg. *Preussische Jahrbücher.* Vol. 102. (1900).
Oncken, H. (Ed.) *Die Rheinpolitik Kaiser Napoleon III. von 1863 bis 1870 und der Ursprung des Krieges von 1870/71.* Vol. I. (Osnabrück, 1967).

Paasivirta, J. *Finland and Europe. International Crises in the Period of Autonomy 1808-1914.* (Minneapolis, 1981).
Palmstierna, C.F. *Sverige, Ryssland och England 1833-1855.* (Stockholm, 1932).
Pares, B. *A History of Russia.* (N.Y., 1937).
Petersen, E.L. Martsministeriets fredsbasisforhandlinger. *Historisk Tidsskrift.* II.R. Vol. IV.
Pigarev, F.I. Tyutchev i problemy vneshnei politiki tsarskoi Rossii. *Literaturnoe nasledstvo* 19/21. (Moscow, 1935).
Pipes, R. Domestic Politics and Foreign Affairs. *Russian Foreign Politics.* (New Haven, London, 1962).
Pipping, H.E. Finlands ställing till Skandinavismen. *Skrifter utgivna av Svenska Litteratursälskapet i Finland,* vol. CLVII. (Helsingfors, 1921).

Ploug, P.C. *Digte.* Vols. I-II. (Copenhagen, 1901).
Pokhlebkin, V.V. *SSSR-Finlandiya: 260 let otnoshenii 1713-1973.* (Moscow, 1975).
Pokhelebkin, V.V. Skandinavskii region. *Voprosy Istorii.* 1980, No. 2.
Pokrovsky, M.N. *Vneshnyaya polityka.* Sbornik statei. 1914-1917. (Moscow, 1917).
Pokrovsky, M.N. *Diplomatiya i voiny tsarskoi Rossii v XIX stoletii.* (Moscow, 1923).
Pokrovsky, M.N. *Brief History of Russia.* (London, 1933).
Pokrovsky, M.N. *Izbrannye proizvedeniya.* Vol. II. (Moscow, 1965).
Pokrovsky, S.A. *Vneshnyaya torgovlya i vneshnyaya torgovaya politika* Rossii. (Moscow, 1947).
Polnoe sobranie zakonov Rossiiskoi Imperii. (St. Petersburg, 1863).
Polovtsev, A.A. *Dnevnik gosudarstvennogo sekretarya.* Vol. I. *1883-1886.* (Moscow, 1966).
Polska XIX wieku. Państwo-społeczeństwo-kultura. (Ed.) Kieniewicz, S. (Warsaw, 1986).
Popov, A.L. Iz istorii zavoevanii Srednei Azii. *Istoricheskie zapiski.* Vol IX. (1940).
Potemkin, V.P. (Ed.) *Istoriya diplomatii.* Vol. I. (Moscow, 1941).
Poschinger, *Preussens auswärtige Politik, 1850 bis 1858.* (Berlin, 1902).
Preussen im Bundestag 1851-1859. (Ed.) Poschinger, H. Vols. I-IV. (Leipzig, 1882-1885).
Protokoller over Londoner Conferences Møder. (Copenhagen, 1864).
Protocols of Conferences held in London relative to the Affairs of Denmark. (London, 1864).
Copiers of Letters from the Prussian and German Plenipontiares respecting the Summary of the Proceedings of the Conferences of Danish Affairs, annexed to the 12th Protocol. (London, 1864).
Puntilla, L.A. Das Zustandekommen der öffenlichen Meinung in Finnland in den sechziger Jahren des 19 Jahrhunderts. *Historiallinen Arkivisto,* vol. 52. (Helsinki, 1947).
Puntilla, L.A. *Histoire politique de la Finlande de 1809 à 1955.* (Neuchâtel, 1966).

Quested, R.K.I. *The Expansion of Russia in East Asia, 1857-1860.* (Singapore, 1968).

Raeff, M. *Comprendre l'ancien régime. Etat et société en Russie impériale* (Paris, 1982).
Raschdau, L. (Ed.) *Die politischen Berichte des Fürsten Bismarck aus Petersburg und Paris (1859-1862).* Vols. I-II. (Berlin, 1920).
Rauch, G. *Russland im Zeitalter der Nationalismus und Imperialismus.* (München, 1961).
Rautenberg, H.W. *Der polnische Aufstand von 1863 und die europäische Politik.* (Wiesbaden, 1979).
Redesdale, Lord, *Memories.* Vols. I-II. (London, 1915).
Renouvin, P. *Histoire des relations internationales.* Vol. V. *De 1815 à 1871. L'Europe des nationalités et l'éveil de nouveaux mondes.* (Paris, 1954).
Revertera, F. Rechberg und Bismarck 1863 bis 1864. *Deutsche Revue,* vol. IV. 1903.
Revunienkov, V.G. *Pol'skoe vosstan'e 1863 g. i evropeiskaya diplomatiya.* (Leningrad, 1957).
Riasanovsky, N.V. *A History of Russia.* (N.Y., 1963).
Richter, W. *Bismarck.* (Frankfurt/M., 1977).
Ridley, J. *Lord Palmerston.* (London, 1972).
Rieber, A. (Ed.) *The Politics of Autocracy. Letters of Alexander II to Prince A.I. Bariatinskii, 1857-1864.* (Paris, The Hague, 1966).

Ringhoffer, K. *Im Kampfe für Preussens Ehre. Aus dem Nachlass des Grafen Albrecht v. Bernstorff.* (Berlin, 1906).
Ritter, G. *Europa und die deutsche Frage.* (Münich, 1848).
Robolsky, H. *Bismarck und Russland. Enthüllungen über die Beziehungen Deutschlands und Russlands vom 1859 bis heute.* (Berlin, 1887).
Roloff, G. *Deutschland und Russland im Widerstreit seit 200 Jahren.* (Stuttgart, Berlin, 1914).
Roots, L. *Slesvig-Golshinskii vopros i politika evropeiskikh derzhav v 1863-1864 godakh.* (Talinn, 1957).
Rosen, *Forty Years of Diplomacy.* Vols. I-II. (London, 1922).
Rosenau, J.N. *Opinion and Foreign Policy. An operational Formulation.* (N.Y., 1961).
Rothan, G. Souvenirs diplomatiques. L'Entrevue de Stuttgart. *Revue des Deux Mondes.* Vols. 90-91. (1888, 1889).
Rothstein, F. K istorii franko-russkogo soglasheniya 1859 g. *Krasnyi Arkhiv.* vol. 3 (88). 1938.
Rothstein, F. *Iz istorii prussko-germanskoi imperii.* (Moscow, 1948).
Rouse, F. *Populær skildring af Polens historie.* (Copenhagen, 1864).
Rubin, M. Sundtoldens afløsning. *Historisk Tidsskrift.* 7.R.vol. II.
Rudnitskaya, E.L. *Russkaya revolyutsionnaya mysl'. Demokraticheskaya pechat' 1864-1873 gg.* (Moscow, 1984).
Ruud, Ch. The Russian Empire's New Censorship Law of 1865. *Canadian Slavic Studies,* vol. III, no. 2. 1969.
Rusell, J. *The Later Correspondence of Lord John Russell, 1840-1878.* Vols. I-II. (Ed.) G.P. Gooch. (London, 1925).
Raasløff, H.I.A. *Den Hallske politik.* (Copenhagen, 1864).

Sandiford, K.A. *Great Britain and the Schleswig-Holstein Question 1848-1864. A Study in Diplomacy, Politics and Public Opinion.* (Toronto, Buffalo, 1975).
Sbornik dogovorov Rossii s drugimi gosudarstvami 1856-1917. (Moscow, 1952).
Sbornik izdanyi v pamyat dvadtsyatipyatiletiya upravleniya ministerstvom innostrannykh del gosudarstvennogo kantslera svyatkeishego knyazya Aleksandra Mikhailovicha Gorchakova 1856-1881. (St. Petersburg, 1881).
Schach, K.M. *Russian Foreign Policy under Prince Alexander M. Gorchakov. The Diplomatic Game Plan versus Austria, 1856-1873.* (Unpubl. dissert. Ann Arbor, Michigan, 1974).
Schiemann, T. *Geschichte Russlands unter Kaiser Nicolaus I.* Vols. I-IV (Berlin, 1904-19).
Scharff, A. *Schleswig-Holsteinische Geschichte. Ein Überblick.* (Würzburg, 1960).
Scharff, A. *Schleswig-Holstein in der deutschen under nordeuropäischen Geschichte.* (Stuttgart, 1969).
Schlözer, K. *Petersburger Briefe, 1857-1862.* (Stuttgart, Berlin, Leipzig, 1923).
Scheel, O. *Dannewerk und Düppel aus politischen und strategischen Hintergrund.* (Flensburg, 1940).
Schoeps, H.J. *Preussen. Geschichte eines Staates.* (Berlin, 1966).
Schultz's Danmarks historie. Vols. IV-VI. (Copenhagen, 1942).
Schüle, E. *Russland und Frankreich vom Ausgang des Krimkrieges bis zum italienischen Krieg, 1856-1859.* (Königsberg, Berlin, 1935).

Schybergson, M.G. *Finlands politiska historia 1809-1919.* (Helsingfors, 1923).
Schweinitz, H.L. *Denkwürdigkeiten des Botschafters General v. Schweinitz.* Vols. I-II. (Berlin, 1927).
Semanov, S. *A. Gorchakov, russkii diplomat XIX v.* (Moscow, 1962).
Seton-Watson, R.W. *The Russian Empire, 1801-1917.* (Oxford, 1967).
Seton-Watson, R.W. *Britain in Europe, 1789-1914).* (Cambridge, 1937).
Shelgunov, N.V. *Vospominaniya.* Vols. I-II. (Petrograd, 1923).
Sjøqvist, V. *Peter Vedel.* Vol. I. 1823-1864. (Aarhus, 1957).
Sjøqvist, V. (Ed.) Peter Vedels beretning om Danmarks udenrigspolitik fra sommeren 1863 til foraaret 1863. *Jyske Samlinger,* 1952-1954.
Ślaski, T. *Tysiaclecie polsko-skandynawskich stosunków kulturalnych.* (Gdańsk, 1977).
Smit, C. *Diplomatieke Geschiedenis van Nederland inzonderheid sedert de Vestiging van het Koninkrijk.* (S. Gravenhage, 1956).
Srbik, H. *Deutsche Einheit. Idee und Wirklichkeit vom Heiligen Reich bis Königgrätz.* Vols. I-IV. (Münich, 1936-1942).
Quellen zur deutschen Politik Österreichs 1859-1866. Vols III-IV. (Ed.) Srbik, H. (Osnabrück, 1967).
Stang, F. Sibbern, G. *Den politiske korrespondance mellem Frederich Stang og Georg Sibbern 1862-1872.* Vol. I. (Ed.) Kaartvedt A. (Oslo, 1956).
Statistisk Tabelværk. 1856-1863. (Copenhagen).
Staatsraadets Forhandlinger 1856-1866. Vols. V-X. (Ed.) Jørgensen, H. (Copenhagen, 1966-1972).
Statsraadets Forhandlinger om Danmarks Udenrigspolitik 1863-1879. Uddrag af Statsraadsprotokollerne. (Ed.) Friis, A. (Copenhagen, 1936).
Stählin, K. Russland und Europa. *Historische Zeitschrift,* vol. 132, no. 2. 1925.
Steefel, L.D. *The Schleswig-Holstein Question.* (Cambridge, Harvard, U.P., London, 1932).
Stevens, J.K. *Franco-Russian Relations, 1856-1863.* (Unpubl. dissert. Ann-Arbor, Michigan, 1980).
Sumner, B.H. *Russia and the Balkans 1870-1880.* (Osford, 1937).
Sumner, B.H. *Survey of Russian History.* (London, 1961).
Sybel, H. *Die Begründung des Deutsches Reiches durch Wilhelm I.* Vols. I-III. (München, Leipzig, 1980).

Tarnowski, S. *Z doświadczeń i rozmyślań.* (Cracow, 1891).
Tatishchev, S.S. *Vneshnyaya politika imperatora Nikolaya Pervogo.* (St. Petersburg, 1887).
Tatishchev, S.S. *Imperator Aleksandr II. Ego zhizn' i tsarstvovanie.* Vols. I-II. (St. Petersburg, 1903).
Taylor, A.J.P. *Bismarck.* (London, 1974).
Taylor, A.J.P. *The Struggle for Mastery in Europe, 1848-1918.* (Oxford, 1974).
Thomsen, N. Opinion og udenrigspolitik belyst ved et oprør fra midten i 1861. Nær og fjern. Samspillet mellem indre og ydre politik. *Studier tilegnet prof. dr. Sven Henningsen.* (Copenhagen, 1980).
Thorsen, S. *De danske ministerier, 1848-1901.* (Copenhagen, 1967).
Thorsøe, A. *Kong Frederic den Syvendes regering.* Vols. I-II. (Copenhagen, 1884, 1889).
Thurston, G.J. *The Franco-Russian Entente, 1856-1863. P.D. Kiselev's Paris Embassy.* (Unpubl. dissert. Ann Arbor, Michigan, 1973).

Toyne, S.M. *The Scandinavians in History.* (London, 1948).
Treitschke, H. *Deutsche Geschichte im Neunzehnten Jahrhundert.* Vols. I-V. (Leipzig, 1894).
Tuchmann, B.W. *The March of Folly. From Troy to Vietnam.* (N.Y., 1984).
Tyutchev i problemy vneshnei politiki Rossii. *Literaturnoe nasledstvo.* 19/21. (Moscow, 1921).
Tyutcheva, A.F. *Pri dvore dvukh imperatorov. Vospominaniya-dnevnik.* (Moscow, 1928).

Valentin, V. *Bismarcks Reichsgründung im Urteil englischen Diplomaten.* (Amsterdam, 1937).
Vandebosch, A. *Dutch Foreign Policy since 1815. A Study in Small Power Politics.* (The Hague, 1959).
Vernadsky, G. (Senior Ed.). *A Source Book for Russian History from Early Times to 1917.* Vol. III. *Alexander II to the February Revolution.* (New Haven, London, Yale U.P., 1972).
Vilbort, J. *L'oeuvre de M. de Bismarck 1863-1866.* (Paris, 1869).
Vitzthum, C.F. *St. Petersburg und London in den Jahren 1852-1864.* Vols. I-II. (Stuttgart, 1866).
Vneshnyaya polityka Rossii XIX i nachala XX veka. Vols. I.IV.V.VI.XIV. (Moscow, 1962, 1965, 1985).
Vogt, J. *Rusland og Norden,* (Copenhagen, 1947).
Voigt, H.J. Englands Aussenpolitik während des deutsch-dänischen Konflikts 1862-1864, *Z.d.G.f.S.H.G.* Vol. 89, 1964.

Ward, A.W. Wilkinson, S. *Germany.* Vol. II. *1852-1871.* (Cambridge, 1923).
Ward, A.W. *The Schleswig-Holstein Question 1852-66. The Cambridge History of British Foreign Policy.* Vol. II. 1922.
Weil, H. *European Diplomatic History, 1815-1914. Documents and Interpretation* (N.Y., 1972).
Wereszycki, H. *Austria a powstanie styczniowe.* (Lvov, 1930).
Wedkiewicz, S. *La Suède et la Pologne. Essai d'une bibliographie des publications suèdois concernant la Pologne.* (Stockholm, 1918).
Wieczynski, L.J. *The Modern Encyklopedia of Russian and Soviet History.* International Academic Press.
Wildner, H. *Die Technik der Diplomatie. L'Art de négocier.* (Wien, 1959).
Wittram, R. *Bismarck und Rusland. Deutsch-Russische Beziehungen von Bismarck bis zur Gegenwart.* (Stuttgart, 1964).
Wolowski, L. Les finances de la Russie. *Revue des Deux Mondes.* vol. 49, 1864.
Wuorinen, J.H. *A History of Finland,* (N.Y., London, 1965).

Zablotsky-Desyatovsky, A.P. *Graf P.D. Kiselev i ego vremya.* Vols. III-IV. (St. Petersburg, 1882).
Zaenchkovsky, P.A. *D.A. Milyutin. Biograficheskii ocherk. Dnevnik Milyutina.* (Moscow, 1947).
Zaitsev, V. Morskaya povstancheskaya ekspeditsiya k beregam Litvy v 1863 g. *K stoletiyu geroicheskoi bor'by za nashu i vashu svobodu.* (Moscow, 1964).

Zaluska-Stromberg, A. Odzwierciedlenie problemów mickiewiczowskich w Szwecji. *Pamietnik Literacki.* Vol. XLIX. No. 1. 1958.

Zechlin, E. *Bismarck und die Grundlegung der deutschen Grossmacht.* (Berlin, 1931, Darmstadt, 1960).

Zorkin, V.D. *B.N. Chicherin 1828-1904.* (Moscow, 1984).

Zutis, Ya. *K istorii ostzeiskogo voprosa v 60-tykh godakh XIX v.* (Moscow, 1957).

Addendum

Halicz, E. Russian Policy Towards the Scandinavian Countries, 1856-1864. *Imperial Power and Development: Papers on Pre-Revolutionary Russian History,* pp. 68-100. Selected Papers of the Third World Congress for Soviet and East European Studies. Ed. by Don Karl Rowney, Slavica Publishers, Inc. Columbus, Ohio, 1990.

Københavns Universitets
Institut for Slavistik og Øststatsforskning.
Skrifter.
The University of Copenhagen.
Institute of Slavonic and East European Studies.
Publications.

Studier 1	Knud Rasmussen: Die livländische Krise 1554-1561. 1973.
Studier 2	Ole Vesterholt: Tradition and Individuality. A Study in Slavonic Oral Epic Poetry. 1973.
Studier 3	William Thorndal: Studier over genitivens og lokativens -u/-ju-endelser i russiske middelaldertekster. 1974.
Studier 4	Hans Bagger: Ruslands alliancepolitik efter freden i Nystad. En studie i det slevigske Restitutionsspørgsmål. 1974.
Studier 5	Niels Erik Rosenfeldt: Knowledge and Power. The Role of Stalin's Secret Chancellery in the Soviet System of Government. 1978.
Studier 6	Peter Alberg Jensen: Nature as Code. The Achievement of Boris Pilniak 1915-1924. 1979.
Studier 7	Niels Rossing, Birgit Rønne: Apocryphal – not Apocryphal? A Critical Analysis of the Discussion Concerning the Correspondence Between Tsar Ivan IV Groznyj and Prince Andrej Kurbskij. 1980.
Studier 8	Christian Mailand-Hansen: Mejerchol'ds Theaterästhetik ind den 1920er Jahren – ihr theaterpolitischer und kulturideologischer Kontext. 1980.
Studier 9	The Slavic Verb. An Anthology presented to H. Chr. Sørensen. 1981.
Studier 10	Michal Mirski: The Mixed Economy – NEP and its Lot. 1984.
Studier 11	We and They. National Identity as a Theme in Slavic Cultures. Donum Stiefanum. 1984.
Studier 12	Anmartin Mihal Brojde: Aleksandr Vasil'evič Družinin. Žizn' i tvorčestvo. (A. V. Druzhinin. Life and Letters. 1824-1864). 1986.
Studier 13	Bronisław Swiderski: Myth and Scholarship. University Students and Political Development in XIX Century Poland. 1987.
Materialer 1	Pis'ma A. M. Remizova i V. Ja. Brjusova k O. Madelungu. Publikacija P. Al'berga Jensena i P. U. Mëllera. 1976.
Materialer 2	Knud Rasmussen og Niels Erik Rosenfeldt: Introduktion til studiet af Ruslands og Sovjetunionens historie og samfundsforhold. 1978.
Materialer 3	55 russiske digte. Udvalgt og gloseret af Mette Dalsgaard og Peter Ulf Møller. Med en kort verslære af Peter Ulf Møller. 1985.
Materialer 4	Rudolf Edward Kudera: Tjekkoslovakisk bibliografi 1804-1983. 1985.
Materialer 5	Paul Flandrup og Peter Ulf Møller: Ind i den russiske litteratur. 1987.

Materialer 6	Per Jacobsen: Litteraturen i Jugoslavien I. Kroatisk Litteratur 1800-1945. 1988.
Materialer 7.	Per Jacobsen: Litteraturen i Jugoslavien II. Serbisk litteratur 1770-1945. 1989.
Rapporter 1	Per Jacobsen, Narcisa V. Pedersen, Anne Ulv: Kvantitativna Analiza Balada Petrice Kerempuha. 1980.
Rapporter 2	Niels Erik Rosenfeldt: Stalinstyrets nervecenter. Nye studier i kilderne til det sovjetiske kommunistpartis hemmelige kancelli. 1980.
Rapporter 3	Bronisław Swiderski: Revolutionen som dialog. De polske konspiratører imod Rusland 1861-1864. 1981.
Rapporter 4	Christian Hougaard: Dansk overfor russisk. En kontrastiv analyse med særligt henblik på verbet. 1983.
Rapporter 5	Helen Liesl Krag: Sovjetunionens mange sprog. Mål og midler i sovjetisk sprogpolitik. 1982.
Rapporter 6	Karsten Kromann: Partitiv Genitiv i russisk sammenlignet med tilsvarende semantiske funktioner i dansk. 1989.
Rapporter 7	Kirsten Barker Hansen, Birgit Olsen, Niels Erik Rosenfeldt: Sovjet og Østeuropa: Udenrigs- og sikkerhedspolitik. En bibliografi baseret på samlingerne på Københavns Universitets Slaviske Institut. 1983.
Rapporter 8	Birthe Sørensen: Den fjernøstlige Republik. Strategi og konflikt i Sovjetunionens tilblivelsesproces. 1983.
Rapporter 9	Bronisław Swiderski: Polen efter 1945. En bibliografi over informationsmidler. 1984.
Rapporter 10	Per Jacobsen: A Concordance to Milan Rakić's Poems. 1984.
Rapporter 11	Per Jacobsen: Kompjuterska Obrad "Preobraženja" A. B. Šimića. 1984.
Rapporter 12	Niels Erik Rosenfeldt, Peter Søndergaard (red.): Information og kommunikation i Øst-Vest sammenhæng. 1985.
Rapporter 13	Eigil Steffensen (red.): Kampen mod kønnet. Omkring Tolstojs ægteskabsfortælling "Kreutzersonaten". 1985.
Rapporter 14	Kirsten Barker Hansen, Jan Koot, Niels Erik Rosenfeldt (red.): Sovjetunionen og Østeuropa i 1980erne. 1986.
Rapporter 15	Per Jacobsen og Marina Hribar: Konkordancija Proklete avlije. 1987.
Rapporter 16	Jan Hansen: Landsbyprosaen i den russiske sovjetlitteratur i 1960rne og 1980rne. 1987.
Rapporter 17	Emanuel Halicz: The 1863 Polish Uprising and Scandinavia. The Year 1863, The Turning-Point in Russo-Scandinavian Relations. 1988.
Rapporter 18	Peter Dahlgreen: Hovedlinjer i Østeuropas økonomiske og sociale historie fra folkevandringerne til Napoleonskrigene. 1988.
Rapporter 19	Tim Toftekær: Katyn affæren og den polske eksilregering. 1989.
Rapporter 20	Niels Erik Rosenfeldt: Stalin's Special Departments. A Comparative Analysis of Key Sources. 1989.